ENCYCLOPEDIA
of AMERICAN
FOREIGN POLICY

ADVISORY BOARD

ENCYCLOPEDIA
of AMERICAN
FOREIGN POLICY
Second Edition

VOLUME 1
Chronology
A – D

Alexander DeConde, Richard Dean Burns,
and Fredrik Logevall, Editors in Chief

Louise B. Ketz, Executive Editor

CHARLES SCRIBNER'S SONS

GALE GROUP

THOMSON LEARNING

New York • Detroit • San Diego • San Francisco
Boston • New Haven, Conn. • Waterville, Maine
London • Munich

Charles Scribner's Sons
An imprint of the Gale Group
300 Park Avenue South
New York, NY 10010

1 3 5 7 9 11 13 15 17 19 20 18 16 14 12 10 8 6 4 2

Printed in the United States of America

Library of Congress Cataloging-in-Publication Data

Encyclopedia of American Foreign Policy : studies of the principal movements and ideas / editors, Alexander DeConde ... [et al.]--2nd ed.
    p. cm.
Includes bibliographical references and index.
ISBN 0-684-80657-6 (set : alk. paper) -- ISBN 0-684-80658-4 (v. 1) -- ISBN 0-684-80659-2 (v. 2) -- ISBN 0-684-80660-6 (v. 3)
    1. United States--Foreign relations--Encyclopedias. 2. United States--Foreign relations--Philosophy--Encyclopedias. I. DeConde, Alexander.

E183.7 .E52 2002
327.73'003--dc21

2001049800

The paper used in this publication meets the requirements of ANSI/NISO Z3948-1992 (Permanence of Paper)

EDITORIAL AND PRODUCTION STAFF

This Book Was Produced by the Louise B. Ketz Agency

Manuscript Editors
Nancy Belanger   Michael Levine   Linda Sanders
Elizabeth I. Wilson

Bibliographic Researcher
Alison C. Kero

Proofreaders
Janet Byrne   Carol Holmes   Evangeline Legones
Laura Patchkofsky

Composition Manager
Evi Seoud

Designer
Pamela A. E. Galbreath

Typesetter
LM Design

Senior Editor
John Fitzpatrick

Associate Publisher
Timothy J. DeWerff

Publisher
Frank Menchaca

CONTENTS

CONTENTS

CONTENTS

VOLUME 2

Contents

CONTENTS

VOLUME 3

PREFACE

As in the first edition of the *Encyclopedia of American Foreign Policy* (1978), this second edition differs markedly from other works of reference dealing with the history of American foreign policy. Instead of bringing together small batches of information on many topics, it offers in-depth, original, interpretive essays commissioned from distinguished scholars who are experts in their field. Using both narrative and topical structure, the authors explain concepts, themes, large ideas, significant movements, and distinctive policies in the history of American foreign relations. Unlike textbook writers, they do not attempt to cover the full narrative history of those relations, or even to recount in detail major episodes. These essays may be used to supplement, and certainly to enrich, the traditional accounts available in history textbooks, special monographs, or other encyclopedias.

Taken as a group, the essays offer a unique approach to the study of America's international connections. Most entries are longer than articles in journals but shorter than monographs. Their length has allowed authors sufficient space to probe their topics deeply without including the usual scholarly paraphernalia. This methodology benefits students in universities, colleges, and high schools because they can quickly find and read authoritative accounts written in clear, straightforward prose in three easily available volumes rather than search through many books and academic journals, often scattered in distant libraries. Readers wishing to probe a topic in greater depth can use the carefully constructed bibliographies for more information and for leads to other sources.

In addition, the authors assess the pertinent scholarship on the topics they discuss and offer differing perspectives on viewing the past. Frequently they challenge previously established wisdom on a topic because perspectives in historical writing have always been subject to revision and change. We have encouraged this kind of investigation and debate because they make clear to the reader that research and writing in history and the social sciences are not monolithic. As with most all higher learning, these disciplines are vibrant and constantly growing. As new information becomes available and analyzed, the findings of scholars working within these disciplines are subject to assessment, modification, and even considerable alteration. This kind of probing and review by peers, like most other scholarly endeavors, enriches our understanding of the past while advancing the frontiers of knowledge.

In addition to scholarly practice, considerable changes in the conduct and theory of American foreign policy in the twenty-three years since publication of the first edition demanded revising and updating the encyclopedia's essays and supplementing them with new ones. Institutions such as the National Security Council, the Department of Defense, and the Central Intelligence Agency have expanded the government's decision-making structure and at times even eclipsed the Department of State as the main organization for making and carrying out foreign policy.

The mounting diversity of the nation's population as it has swelled over the past two decades, primarily as the consequence of new immigration laws, also has altered foreign policy considerations. While ethnic, racial, religious, cultural, and other political pressures have long been part of the foreign policy-making process, special-interest lobbies have proliferated since the 1980s. Along with their added numbers and greater prominence, these lobbies have acquired more sophistication and clout than in the past in influencing American relations with other countries and peoples. The stepped-up internationalization of finance, the international mobility of industries lured by cheap labor, the proliferation of multinational corporations, and the mushrooming of electronic systems across national boundaries also have contributed to a transformation in Washington's timing and means of reacting to international crises, and hence to its shaping of both short- and long-term foreign policies.

These developments, plus the changing demographics of the nation's student population, the growth of new educational institutions, and the remodeling of old ones, have contributed to an expansion of topics that traditionally came under the heading of foreign policy. At the same time, we have seen a marked increase in the numbers of those who teach and study the history of American foreign relations in colleges and universities, both in the United States and abroad. Equally important, a new generation of historians who write the books and the articles in academic journals on the subject has risen to prominence.

These teachers, researchers, and writers have brought fresh perspectives to the discipline of diplomatic history. They frequently view its historiography differently than had their predecessors. For example, scholars of the previous generation wrote extensively on nineteenth-century foreign policy, devoting considerable attention to topics such as continental expansion, Anglophobia and Anglophilia, and isolationism, a topic about which they felt deeply and debated at length as to its impact on policymaking. When dealing with the twentieth century, they focused mostly on the diplomatic problems of the two world wars, communism, New Left historiography, and atomic diplomacy. Although the present generation does not ignore these topics—and it should not—its field of vision also includes the problems of international terrorism, "ethnic cleansing," the end of the Cold War, post–Cold War issues, the environment as an international concern, and the role of the United States as the world's sole superpower.

The extent of this new scholarship contrasts so strikingly with that of the entries of the first edition, as readers may readily discern, that this edition deserves consideration as a new project rather than strictly an updating and revision of the old. We have increased the entries by more than 25 percent and the new authors by a larger margin. Of the initial contributions, only one has remained untouched and only a few have survived with modest updating and revision. We are fortunate that a number of the senior scholars who wrote for the first edition more than a quarter of a century ago agreed to rework their essays and offer their wisdom for this new work.

The topics investigated and depth of analysis applied to them in this edition are also more extensive than in the first and compare favorably with similar writings on American diplomacy and related subjects in books and monographs. Of the present 121 essays, 44 are new topics to this edition. They reflect our expanded coverage and the breadth of the nation's view of topics that fall within the range of foreign policy concerns or activities that influence policymaking. For example, in the first edition we had one entry that covered the Cold War. Now, as a consequence of the end of the Cold War in 1991, we have five entries that deal with that topic: "Cold War Origins,"

"Cold War Evolution and Interpretations," "Cold War Termination," "Cold Warriors," and "Post–Cold War Policy," in addition to several other Cold War–centered essays such as "Containment." Other new essays include "African Americans," "Covert Operations," "Cultural Imperialism," "Development Doctrine and Modernization Theory," "Exceptionalism," "Gender," "Globalization," "Immigration," "Narcotics Policy," "Organized Labor," "Religion," and "Science and Technology."

More than in the past, we have sought to avoid snippets of information by combining some of the smaller essays of the first edition into longer pieces. We have, for instance, combined the essays on the Monroe and Eisenhower Doctrines in a longer piece that discusses and analyzes all doctrines connected with foreign policy. To give flavor, often from primary sources, and to provoke thought, we have included sidebars with most of the essays. To help readers when they have the need to place topics in a broad chronological context, we have added a chronology that highlights the significant events in America's foreign relations from the colonial era to the present. We have continued to offer with each essay an up-to-date selected bibliography with annotations, as well as extensive cross-references at the end of each essay.

We have not devoted separate essays, as has been conventional in studies of American foreign relations, to accounts of major subjects such as the diplomacy of the American Revolution, the Louisiana Purchase, the War of 1812, the War with Mexico, the Spanish-American War, World War II, the Marshall Plan, or the Korean War. We have omitted extended commentary on these topics because we chose not to focus at length on negotiations that produced specific treaties or that led to individual conflicts, other than the Civil War and the Vietnam War. We examine the Vietnam War in depth because it was the longest in the nation's history and because of its continuing prominence in twenty-first-century American foreign policy scholarship. We have not, however, ignored other wars or downplayed the importance of traditional topics. Various authors discuss or scrutinize these matters within the context of the subjects they survey and analyze. The cross-references and a detailed subject-and-concepts index provide easy access to the standard topics.

Again, as in the first edition, we believe the encyclopedia's topical framework, as well as the quality of the essays, will appeal to the growing segment of the public interested in history, as well as to students, academicians, journalists, and others who may wish to use this work for reference or for intellectual stimulation and insight on the significant international aspects of the American experience. Since the authors have written with free rein, readers may note conflicting views of the same topic or event. These differences reflect the flexibility, complexities, and nuances of historical interpretation. They show also that while historians and social scientists cannot escape agreement on hard facts such as dates or contents of treaties when known, even experts can, and often do, clash in their evaluations of the significance of the data they use and the theories they fashion. This diversity, as the essays illustrate, enriches our understanding of the history of U.S. foreign policy.

Diversity also influenced our choice of topics. From the start, we realized that even experts would differ on which topics merited selection. Our criteria for selecting some topics while excluding others of seemingly comparable worth evolved out of decisions to bring the subject matter up to date, to avoid the usual narratives of extended diplomatic negotiations, and to explain in depth new aspects of foreign relationships as well as the significance of the old. In doing this, we canvassed various scholars for their views. Ultimately, though, we had to choose from their recommendations and from our own experiences what topics we would cover that would be of most value to potential readers. We subjected each essay to careful review and editing to make sure each fitted our objective. In both selection and editing, we balanced our own judgments with the recommendations we received from other scholars. We believe we have been fortunate in attracting to this project some of the finest scholars on the subject of America's foreign policies, past and present.

—*Alexander DeConde, for the Editors*

CHRONOLOGY OF AMERICAN FOREIGN POLICY, 1607–2001

Richard Dean Burns and Louise B. Ketz

1607 On 24 May, 105 English settlers establish a village at Jamestown, Virginia, England's first permanent American settlement.

1689 King William's War (War of the League of Augsburg) begins 12 May and inaugurates a series of hostile engagements between England and France. The war ends on 20 September 1697.

1702 Queen Anne's War (War of the Spanish Succession) begins on 4 May and ends 11 April 1713.

1739 After twenty-six years of peace, British conflict begins again, with Spain in the War of Jenkins' Ear on 19 October, and enlarged when France joins Spain in King George's War, which ends on 11 October 1748.

1754 The French and Indian War (Seven Years' War) begins in the Ohio River Valley when British and colonial troops fight French forces and their Indian allies, beginning on 17 April. The war spreads to Europe on 15 May 1756. The Albany Congress meets 19 June to 10 July, at which Benjamin Franklin's Plan of Union is rejected.

1763 British hegemony in North America is confirmed in the Treaty of Paris (10 February), which ends the French and Indian War.

1764 The Sugar Act (5 April) passes Parliament, the first parliamentary law designed specifically to raise money in the colonies.

1765 The Stamp Act Congress convenes (7 October) in an effort to unite the American colonies in protesting the Stamp Act (passed by Parliament on 22 March), the first direct tax levied by Parliament on the American colonies.

1767 The Townshend Acts are passed by Parliament requiring import duties on tea, oil, glass, lead, and paper.

1773 The Boston Tea Party on 16 December protests the Tea Act, which Parliament had approved on 10 May.

1774 On 31 March, Parliament passes the first of the Coercive Acts (called Intolerable Acts by colonial radicals). The First Continental Congress convenes in Philadelphia on 5 September, providing a forum for all of the American colonies to protest jointly British policy.

1775 The American Revolution begins on 19 April, when shots are exchanged between British troops and colonial militia at Lexington and Concord, Massachusetts. The Second Continental Congress convenes on 10 May in Philadelphia and forwards the Olive Branch Petition to the king (5 July) to seek compromise. On 23 August, King George III proclaims the colonists are in rebellion. The Continental Congress on 19 September appoints a secret committee to buy foreign arms and ammunition. Congress creates (29 November) the Committee of Secret Correspondence to Conduct Foreign Relations, which sends agents to Europe to seek loans, alliances, and the purchase of military supplies. On 23 December a royal proclamation closes the American colonies to all foreign commerce.

1776 Thomas Paine's *Common Sense* is published on 10 January. Paine's proposal that America should pursue peaceful commerce with all nations while making political alliances with none becomes the essence of American political isolationism for over a century. On 3 March, Silas Deane is sent to France to seek aid for the American cause. Congress on 6 April opens American seaports to all nations but Britain. Louis XVI of France on 2 May provides for one million livres to secretly supply the American army. On 4 July, Congress approves the Declaration of Independence. The Model Treaty of 1776 (Plan of 1776) is approved; on 26 September a diplomatic commission to France is appointed.

1777 On 17 April the Committee of Secret Correspondence is reconstituted as the Committee for Foreign Affairs. The Articles of Confederation are adopted by Congress on 15 November.

1778 The Franco-American Treaty of Alliance and the Treaty of Amity and Commerce are signed on 6 February.

1779 Spain declares war on England but refuses to recognize American independence or to join the Franco-American alliance.

1780 Catherine II of Russia on 28 February proclaims the League of Armed Neutrality. Indirectly the league helps America by placing most of Europe against Great Britain. On 5 October, Congress approves the principles of the league.

1781 On 1 March the Articles of Confederation are ratified, granting Congress the power to make decisions about peace and war and to conduct foreign relations. The British defeat at the Battle of Yorktown on 20 August leads the British government to seek peace. On 20 October, Robert R. Livingston is appointed the first secretary for foreign affairs.

1782 English-American peace talks begin informally on 12 April in Paris between Benjamin Franklin and Richard Oswald. On 23 June, John Jay joins Franklin's discussions. John Adams signs a Treaty of Friendship and Commerce with the Netherlands on 8 October and on 26 October joins Jay and Franklin in Paris to finalize a peace treaty with the British. A preliminary peace agreement with Britain is signed on 30 November.

1783 On 20 January, Great Britain concludes peace terms with France, Spain, and the United States. The Definitive Treaty of Paris is formally signed on 3 September.

1784 The first U.S. merchant ship, the *Empress of China,* sails to China from New York on 22 February. Based on the Model Treaty of 1776, on 7 May Congress approves new guidelines for commercial treaties with other nations. On 26 June, Spain closes the Mississippi River to American navigation. On 21 September, John Jay becomes secretary for foreign affairs.

1785 On 24 February, John Adams is appointed minister to Great Britain. Thomas Jefferson replaces Franklin as minister to France on 10 March. On 20 July, Congress authorizes Jay's discussions with Don Diego de Gardoqui to resolve disputes with Spain regarding the southwest boundary and navigation of the Mississippi River. On 10 September, Prussia and the United States sign a commercial treaty.

1786 Samuel Shaw is informed on 30 January that he is to be the first U.S. consul at Canton. On 17 July, Congress approves a treaty with Morocco, under which vessels of each nation would be protected from seizure by passes of safe conduct and commerce would be based on most-favored-nation principles. On 29 August the Jay-Gardoqui negotiations end when Congress does not yield on the Mississippi navigation issue.

1787 On 25 May the Constitutional Convention convenes at Philadelphia, and on 17 September the Constitution is approved. On 27 October the first of the *Federalist Papers* to promote ratification of the Constitution is published.

1789 George Washington is inaugurated the first president of the United States on 30 April. The Department of Foreign Affairs is renamed the Department of State on 15 September. Thomas Jefferson is appointed secretary of state on 26 September and takes office on 22 March 1790.

1791 On 9 November, George Hammond, the first British minister to the United States, presents his credentials to Secretary of State Jefferson, just after Thomas Pinckney is nominated as U.S. minister to England.

1792 Gouverneur Morris is appointed minister to France and received at the French court on 3 June.

1793 Following the arrival on 8 April of Edmond Genet, the new French minister to the United States, the U.S. cabinet members agree unanimously that neutrality in France's disputes with other European nations should be maintained. On 19 April,

President Washington prepares the Proclamation of Neutrality, issued on 22 April, which asserts that the United States is at peace with all nations. On 31 December, Jefferson resigns as secretary of state.

1794 On 2 January, Edmund Randolph becomes secretary of state. Legislation passed on 26 March calls for a thirty-day embargo of British ships, extended on 25 April for another month. On 19 April the Senate confirms John Jay's appointment as a special envoy to London to negotiate disputes about trade and the Northwest posts. Congress approves the Neutrality Act on 5 June, prohibiting the recruitment of soldiers or sailors within the U.S. territory by a belligerent agent. James Monroe is appointed the new minister to France on 10 June. On 19 November, Jay's Treaty between the United States and Great Britain is signed. The treaty causes controversy in America because it does not gain U.S. principles of neutral rights.

1795 The U.S. Senate ratifies Jay's Treaty on 24 June. On 19 August, Edmund Randolph resigns as secretary of state, and Timothy Pickering is appointed to the office. On 27 October, Spain and the United States sign the Treaty of San Lorenzo (or Pinckney's Treaty). Spain acknowledges that both Spanish and American citizens should have the free navigation of the Mississippi River.

1796 On 2 March the Senate ratifies a treaty with Algeria to protect U.S. commerce. On 2 July a French decree announces France will no longer treat American ships as neutral, complaining that the United States renounced its neutral rights in the Jay Treaty. On 19 September, President Washington issues his Farewell Address, urging the nation to keep free of subservience to any foreign power. On 7 December the presidential election is won by John Adams; Thomas Jefferson becomes vice president.

1797 On 31 May President Adams appoints a special commission (Charles C. Pinckney, John Marshall, and Elbridge Gerry) to France to seek a treaty of amity and commerce.

1798 On 3 April President Adams releases copies of dispatches from Pinckney, Marshall, and Gerry to Congress, revealing that French agents suggested that an American loan and bribe would permit official talks to begin. Believing any war with France would involve naval engagements, Adams on 27 April signs a law creating the Department of the Navy; Congress authorizes the construction of twelve ships. On 7 July the treaties with France are abrogated and the undeclared Quasi-War begins.

1800 As first consul Napoleon on 7 March receives the American peace commissioners in a formal audience. On 30 September the final signing of the Convention of Mortfontaine (Convention of 1800) restores friendly relations between France and the United States.

1801 Because of an electoral tie the House of Representatives selects Thomas Jefferson on 17 February as president of the United States. On 5 March, James Madison becomes secretary of state, remaining in office throughout Jefferson's eight years as president. On 14 May the pasha of Tripoli declares war on the United States.

1802 Spain, on 16 October, announces suspension of America's right of deposit at New Orleans, contravening Pinckney's Treaty of 1795.

1803 On 30 April, France cedes the Louisiana Territory to the United States, which takes possession on 20 December.

1805 The *Essex* decision by the British Admiralty on 22 May destroys the principle of "broken voyage," causing a rapid increase of U.S. shipping losses and renewed friction between England and America. On 10 June peace is established with Tripoli, and on 30 August a new treaty is made with the bey of Tunis.

1806 Napoleon establishes his continental system with proclamation of the Berlin Decree on 21 November, a (paper) blockade of Great Britain that closes all continental trade with the British. On 31 December, James Monroe and William Pinckney sign a treaty with Great Britain on neutral rights. President Jefferson and Secretary of State James Madison immediately reject it.

1807 On 2 July, President Jefferson orders all ports closed to British ships, and on 22 December signs the Embargo Act of 1807, prohibiting U.S. ships from leaving for foreign ports.

1808 James Madison is elected president on 7 December.

1809 On 1 March Jefferson signs the Nonintercourse Act, which ends the embargo on 4 March but still forbids trade with England and France. After negotiations between Britain's minister and Secretary of State Robert Smith, on 19 April President Madison proclaims the renewal of trade with Great Britain. British foreign minister George Canning disavows the Erskine Agreement on 30 May, and on 9 August Madison revives the Nonintercourse Act.

1810 Congress on 1 May passes Macon's Bill No. 2, designed to coerce England and France into ending their restrictions on neutral trade. On 27 October, West Florida, territory disputed with Spain, is annexed to the United States.

1811 James Monroe becomes secretary of state on 6 April, serving until March 1817.

1812 On 1 June President Madison asks for a declaration of war on Great Britain, and Congress does so on 18 June. On 23 June, aware the United States has declared war, British prime minister Castelreagh announces repeal of British restrictions on the trade of neutral nations.

1813 On 7 December, Congress embargoes all trade with the enemy, and on 30 December, Castlereagh's offer for direct peace negotiations is accepted by President Madison.

1814 Peace talks began at Ghent, Belgium, on 8 August. On 24–25 August the British capture and burn Washington, D.C., then withdraw. The Hartford Convention meets in secret sessions on 15 December to protest dissent against the War of 1812. The Peace Treaty of Ghent is signed on 24 December; the treaty basically restores the status quo ante bellum.

1815 On 2 March Congress declares war on Algeria, which accepts peace terms on 30 June, ending the Barbary Wars.

1816 James Monroe is elected to the first of two terms as president.

1817 In March, John Quincy Adams is appointed secretary of state, serving throughout Monroe's presidency, until 3 March 1825. The Rush-Bagot Agreement of 28–29 April provides for the demilitarization of the Great Lakes.

1818 The Neutrality Act of 1818 codifies existing neutrality laws and favors the independence movement in Latin America. The Convention of 1818 with Great Britain resolves issues on the Northeast fisheries, deported slaves, the Northwest boundaries, and transatlantic commerce.

1819 The Adams-Onis (Transcontinental) Treaty is signed on 22 February and resolves boundary disputes that had embroiled Spain and America in quarrels since 1803.

1822 Starting with Colombia on 19 June, President Monroe begins recognition of the Latin American republics and Congress appropriates $100,000 to establish diplomatic missions.

1823 On 2 December, President Monroe enunciates the Monroe Doctrine in his State of the Union message.

1825 In March, Henry Clay becomes secretary of state, serving until the end of John Quincy Adams's presidency in 1829.

1828 On 12 January a treaty is signed with Mexico recognizing the Sabine River as the U.S.–Mexico boundary. Congress approves the Tariff of Abominations on 19 May. On 3 December, Andrew Jackson is elected president.

1829 On 6 March, Martin Van Buren is appointed secretary of state.

1831 On 7 December, President Jackson and the Senate reject an arbitrated decision on the Northeast boundary.

1832 A commercial treaty is signed with Russia on 18 December.

1835 On 6 November, U.S.–French relations are severed, caused by internal politics in Washington and Paris and spoliation claims.

1836 France agrees on 5 February to pay the U.S. spoliation claims. The Alamo in Texas falls to Mexican forces on 6 March, but after victory at the Battle of San Jacinto on 21 April, Texans proclaim their independence.

1837 On 29 December the *Caroline* incident, providing military supplies to Canadian rebels, causes antagonism between Americans and Canadians.

1839 Spain demands the release of the ship *Amistad* on 6 September and the return of its cargo of slave mutineers to Cuba; the case would not be resolved until 9 March 1841.

1842 The Webster-Ashburton Treaty is signed on 9 August, settling the Northeast Boundary Dispute. On 29 August federal courts are given jurisdiction over illegal acts committed under orders of a foreign government. In a message to Congress on 30 December, President Tyler implies a "Monroe Doctrine" for Hawaii.

1843 On 30 September the State Department learns that China will grant the United States most-favored-nation status.

1844 On 12 April Secretary of State Calhoun signs a treaty to annex Texas to the union, but on 8 June the Senate rejects the treaty. On 3 July the Treaty of Wanghia is signed with China, giving the United States trading rights equal to those of Britain. James K. Polk is elected president on 4 December.

1845 On 1 March, Texas is annexed to the United States by a joint resolution of Congress. James Buchanan is appointed secretary of state on 6 March, serving throughout Polk's presidency. On 2 July the British reject Polk's offer to settle the Oregon boundary dispute. John Slidell is sent on a mission to Mexico on 10 November to settle Mexican-American disputes and purchase territory to the Pacific Ocean. President Polk on 2 December asks Congress to annex the Oregon territory and keep Britain out of California. Newspaper editor John O'Sullivan coins the term "manifest destiny" in an editorial on 27 December.

1846 On 26 February, President Polk indicates a willingness to settle the Oregon boundary question with England at the forty-ninth parallel. The Mexican War begins on 25 April with a clash of U.S. and Mexican forces on disputed territory. President Polk asks Congress for and gets a declaration of war on 13 May. Great Britain and the United States sign a treaty to settle the Oregon boundary on 15 June. On 12 December the United States and New Granada (Colombia) sign the Treaty of New Granada, giving America the right of way across Panama.

1847 On 13 January the Treaty of Cahuenga ends fighting in California and Mexican forces surrender. The independent Republic of Liberia is established on 27 July.

1848 The Treaty of Guadalupe Hidalgo is signed on 2 February ending the Mexican War.

1850 On 19 April the Clayton-Bulwer Treaty provides an Anglo-American agreement on a Central American canal.

1851 Americans greet Hungarian patriot and exiled leader Lajos Kossuth on 5 December.

1853 The Convention of 1853 with Britain, signed 8 February, settles all outstanding claims. William Learned Marcy is appointed secretary of state on 7 March. The Gadsden Treaty between Mexico and the United States is signed on 30 December, adjusting the southern boundary of the United States, which acquires nearly 30,000 square miles of new territory.

1854 On 31 March, Commodore Matthew Perry and Japanese officials sign the Treaty of Kanagawa, opening Japanese ports and granting most-favored-nation status. The Marcy-Elgin Treaty with Britain is signed on 5 June, resolving Anglo-American reciprocity and fishing rights. The Ostend Manifesto of 18 October, drawn up by U.S. ministers to Spain, France, and Great Britain, favors U.S. purchase or annexation of Cuba from Spain.

1855 On 1 March an act of Congress for the first time provides for diplomatic ranks and prescribes duties of American consular offices. William Walker, an American adventurer, conquers Grenada on 15 October and takes control of Nicaraguan government.

1856 A U.S. court ruling is accepted on 13 February giving a consular treaty precedence over the U.S. Constitution.

1857 On 1 May, William Walker's regime in Nicaragua is overthrown at the hands of a coalition Central American army assisted by Great Britain. Walker is executed on 12 September 1860, ending his filibustering adventures.

1858 The Treaty of Tientsin is signed on 18 June with China, one of the "open door" treaties. A commercial treaty is signed with Japan on 29 July, a model treaty that will regulate relations with Japan for more than forty years.

1859 On 7 April the United States recognizes the liberal, constitutional Mexican government of Benito Juarez.

1860 On 6 November, Abraham Lincoln is elected president.

1861 The Morrill Act approved on 2 March levies high tariffs to protect American manufacturing. On 5 March, William Henry Seward becomes Lincoln's secretary of state, and on 1 April he proposes a "foreign war panacea" to stimulate national unity and avoid civil war. Fort Sumter in South Carolina falls to Confederate forces on 13 April and the American Civil War begins. On 19 April, President Lincoln proclaims a blockade of the South, forbidding trade with the seceded states. The United States on 21 May insists that Great Britain's neutrality requires it to stop all intercourse with "domestic enemies" of the United States. On 17 December, Veracruz, Mexico, is occupied by French, British, and Spanish forces.

1862 The Confederate warship *Alabama* leaves England on 31 July, the ship built despite Great Britain's claimed neutrality in the American Civil War. President Lincoln on 23 September issues the preliminary Emancipation Proclamation as a means of preventing foreign recognition of the Confederate government.

1863 President Lincoln issues the Emancipation Proclamation on 1 January, formally liberating all slaves in areas still in rebellion, winning wide public support in England and France. On 7 June, French troops occupy Mexico City to establish a monarchical government. On 24 September two Russian warships arrive in New York, but Americans incorrectly believe the Russian ships are there to support the United States against British and French intervention in the Civil War.

1864 Confederate agents violate the neutrality of the U.S.–Canadian border on 19 October by an attack on St. Albans, Vermont. Lincoln is reelected president on 8 November.

1865 The Confederate Army surrenders on 9 April. On 14 April, President Lincoln is assassinated.

1866 On 17 March the United States terminates the reciprocity Marcy-Elgin Treaty of 1854 with Canada. Americans learn on 5 April from Paris newspapers that Napoleon II will withdraw French troops from Mexico. The Irish Fenian Brotherhood unsuccessfully attacks Canada from the United States, a campaign for Irish independence from Great Britain. The transatlantic cable goes into operation on 27 July.

1867 On 12 March the last French troops withdraw from Mexico. Russia sells Alaska to the United States on 30 March.

1868 The Burlingame Treaty with China is signed on 28 July, recognizing the right of unrestricted immigration of Chinese.

1869 On 13 April the Senate rejects the Clarendon-Johnson Treaty to settle indemnity claims with Great Britain.

1871 On 8 May the Treaty of Washington creates an arbitration tribunal to settle the *Alabama* claims with Britain; the tribunal's report is issued on 14 September 1872 and accepted.

1873 On 29 November, Spain agrees to indemnify the United States for the *Virginius* incident in Cuba, when on 7 and 8 November fifty-three crew members and passengers were executed by Cuban officials.

1875 A reciprocity treaty is signed on 30 January with Hawaii, giving the United States a virtual protectorship over the islands.

1878 A U.S.–Samoan treaty is signed on 17 January, providing for an American naval and coaling station at Pago Pago. On 23 March the Diaz regime in Mexico is recognized.

1880 The Treaty of 1880 with China, signed 17 November, permits restriction of Chinese immigration.

1881 President James Garfield is assassinated on 2 July.

1882 A congressional act of 6 May suspends Chinese laborers from immigration for ten years. On 22 May a commercial treaty is signed with Korea.

1883 Passage on 3 March of the Tariff of 1883 retains U.S. protectionist principles; the same day Congress authorizes the building of a modern "steel" navy.

1884 On 6 December the United States secures a naval base at Pearl Harbor, Hawaii.

1885 The United States participates in the Berlin Conference on the Congo, which adjourns on 26 February and gains U.S. commercial privileges in the region.

1887 The fur seal controversy begins on 9 January when the British protest seizure of Canadian pelagic sealing ships. Congress on 3 March empowers the president to bar Canadian ships, fish, and other products from U.S. ports.

1888 On 15 February the Bayard-Chamberlain Treaty on fishing rights with Great Britain is signed. A treaty with China on 12 March excludes Chinese laborers from immigration for twenty years. On 10 May a Pan-American conference is authorized by Congress.

1889 On 14 June the General Act of Berlin is signed, forming a German-British-U.S. protectorate over Samoa. The first Pan-American Conference is held in Washington on 2 October.

1891 On 15 June, Britain signs a modus vivendi on the Bering fur sealing dispute. Seamen from the USS *Baltimore* are attacked by a mob in Chile on 16 October; Chile makes reparations on 25 January 1892 and talk of war ends.

1893 On 30 March, Thomas F. Bayard becomes the first American to hold the rank of ambassador with his appointment as ambassador to Great Britain. An arbitration commission on 15 August rules against the United States in the sealing dispute with Britain and Canada.

1894 On 28 August the Wilson-Gorman Tariff is approved, providing for duty-free raw materials for U.S. industry.

1895 American neutrality laws are applied on 12 June in the Cuban rebellion against Spain. On 20 July the United States intervenes in the British-Venezuelan boundary dispute as a "duty" under the Monroe Doctrine.

1896 On 4 April assistance is offered to Spain to mediate with the Cuban rebels. On 12 November an arbitration treaty between Venezuela and England is established.

1897 A treaty of annexation is signed on 16 June with Hawaii. The Dingley Tariff on 7 July raises rates to a new high in U.S. history.

1898 On 12 January the USS *Maine* is sent to Havana, Cuba, and destroyed in the harbor on 15 February. Congress approves a joint resolution authorizing force to assure Cuban independence from Spain on 19–20 April. On 1 May the navy defeats the Spanish fleet in Manila Bay in the Philippines. Guam is captured from the Spanish on 20 June. The Spanish fleet in Cuba is destroyed on 3 July. Congress annexes Hawaii on 6 July. John Hay is appointed secretary of state on 20 September. On 19 November an anti-imperialist league is founded in Boston. On 10 December the Treaty of Paris is signed by Spain, formally ending the Spanish-American War.

1899 On 4 February fighting breaks out in Manila between U.S. and Filipino troops. The First Hague Conference adjourns on 29 July and the United States agrees to join the Permanent Court of International Arbitration. On 6 September, Secretary of State Hay asks six other powers to join America in the Open Door policy. An Anglo-German-American Treaty of 2 December partitions the Samoan Islands.

1900 On 3 July Secretary Hay issues the second Open Door Note. An international force lifts the Boxer rebels' siege of the Peking diplomatic legation on 14 August. On 20 December the Hay-Pauncefote Treaty for a Central American canal is ratified.

1901 Congress on 2 March approves the Platt Amendment to regulate future relations with Cuba. On 4 July, William Howard Taft becomes first civil governor in the Philippines. President William McKinley is shot on 6 September and dies on the 14th. On 22 October the second Pan-American Conference opens in Mexico City. Senate approves on 16 December the revised Hay-Pauncefote Treaty to build and control a Central American canal.

1902 Congress approves construction of a Panama canal on 26 June. The Philippine Government Act (Organic Act) is proclaimed by President Roosevelt on 4 July, ending the Philippine Insurrection. The

Drago Doctrine on 29 December proposes that European nations cannot intervene in the Latin American countries to collect debt payments.

1903 On 20 October the Alaskan boundary dispute is resolved. American rights to construct and control a Panama canal are granted by the Hay–Bunau-Varilla Treaty on 18 November.

1904 The Roosevelt Corollary to the Monroe Doctrine is declared in President Theodore Roosevelt's annual message to Congress on 6 December.

1905 Elihu Root is named secretary of state on 7 July. On 29 July the Taft-Katsura Agreement is signed, recognizing Japan's rights in Korea and maintaining the Open Door policy in Korea and Manchuria. The Russo-Japanese Peace Conference convenes at Portsmouth, New Hampshire, on 9 August with President Roosevelt serving as an intermediary.

1906 The Royal Navy launches the *Dreadnought,* first all-big-gun battleship, on 10 February. On 7 April the Algeciras Conference ends, settling French and German disputes over Morocco. The Third Inter-American (Pan-American) Conference is held at Rio de Janeiro beginning on 31 July.

1907 In a note known as the "Gentleman's Agreement" on 24 February, Secretary of State Root resolves disputes with Japan about immigration. On 18 October the Second Hague Peace Conference adjourns. The U.S. Navy by 12 December is the second largest in the world and begins an around-the-world cruise to demonstrate its power.

1908 The Root-Takahira Agreement of 30 November with Japan acknowledges the new balance of power in East Asia. On 4 December ten major naval powers meet at the London Naval Conference to clarify rules of naval warfare.

1909 On 27 January, Great Britain agrees to take the Northeast fisheries dispute to arbitration. The Payne-Aldrich Tariff of 9 April continues protectionism. Dollar diplomacy is extended to China when America seeks admission on 24 May to the banking consortium constructing a Chinese railway. On

16 December the United States assists a rebellion in Nicaragua.

1911 On 11 February the commercial treaty of 1894 with Japan is renewed, including the Gentleman's Agreement to regulate emigration of laborers. The Knox-Castrillo Convention of 6 June with Nicaragua establishes control of that nation's finances. On July 7 the pelagic sealing issue is settled with Britain, Russia, and Japan.

1912 The United States joins a six-power consortium on 20 June to offer loans to China. On 2 August the Lodge Corollary extends the Monroe Doctrine to Japan and to foreign companies. U.S. marines land in Nicaragua on 14 August to protect American property and interests. Woodrow Wilson is elected president on 5 November.

1913 General Victoriano Huerta overthrows the Mexican government on 9 February, beginning a new series of revolutions. On 5 March, William Jennings Bryan is named secretary of state. President Wilson withdraws U.S. participation in the Chinese loan consortium on 18 March. On 27 August, Wilson informs Congress of a "watchful waiting" policy toward Mexico. The Underwood Tariff is passed on 3 October lowering tariffs.

1914 U.S. forces occupy and blockade Veracruz, Mexico, on 21 April, and on 24 April, Wilson accepts mediation of the Mexican dispute. On 28 July, Austria declares war on Serbia and World War I begins. Wilson issues on 4 August the first of ten U.S. proclamations of neutrality. On 6 August, Secretary of State Bryan asks European belligerents to accept the naval rules of the Declaration of London of 1908. American loans to any European belligerent are forbidden on 15 August, the same day the Panama Canal officially opens. In the Declaration of London of 5 September, England, France, and Russia agree not to make a separate peace. On 15 October, Wilson approves "credits" to foreign belligerents by private U.S. bankers. The following day Herbert Hoover's Food Relief Program is launched.

1915 Japan submits the Twenty-one Demands on 18 January to gain predominance in China.

On 4 February, Germany declares a war zone around Great Britain, which the United States protests on 10 February. The *Lusitania*, a British passenger ship, is sunk by a German submarine on 7 May. On 11 May, President Wilson refuses to accept any Sino-Japanese agreement that impairs the Open Door policy. Secretary of State Bryan resigns on 8 June, believing Wilson's protests against German policy could lead to war. U.S. marines occupy Haiti on 29 July.

1916 The House-Grey Peace Plan is signed on 22 February to obtain a negotiated peace with Germany. Mexican bandit Pancho Villa raids Columbus, New Mexico, on 9 March, and on 15 March, General John Pershing leads an expeditionary force against Villa. On 4 May the *Sussex* Pledge is issued in which Germany agrees not to permit submarines to attack any ships without warning. On 27 May, President Wilson proposes "a new world order" at a session of the League to Enforce Peace. Denmark cedes the Virgin Islands to the United States on 4 August for $25 million. Full military occupation of Santo Domingo begins on 29 November. On 12 December the German chancellor asks President Wilson to transmit Germany's peace offer to the belligerent powers. On 18 December, Wilson asks all belligerents to state their peace objectives.

1917 On 22 January, President Wilson delivers his "peace without victory" speech. Germany announces renewal of unrestricted submarine warfare to begin on 1 February; two days later Wilson breaks diplomatic relations with Germany. The Zimmerman Telegram is revealed on 24 February, in which Germany proposed an alliance with Mexico against the United States. Wilson calls for a declaration of war against Germany on 2 April; it is granted four days later. The Trading with the Enemy Act becomes law on 6 October, prohibiting commerce with enemy nations and permitting takeover of alien property in the United States. On 2 November the Lansing-Ishii Agreement is signed, recognizing Japan's special interests in China, and Japan declares respect for the Open Door policy. The Bolshevik Revolution on 7 November overthrows the provisional government in Russia.

1918 In a speech to Congress on 8 January, President Wilson outlines his peace objectives, the Fourteen Points. On 3 March, Russia and Germany sign the Treaty of Brest-Litovsk to end their war. Germany seeks peace on the basis of the Fourteen Points on 6 October. On 11 November, Germany signs an armistice to end World War I.

1919 The Paris Peace Conference opens on 18 January; on 14 February, President Wilson develops the Covenant of the League of Nations at the conference. Senator Henry Cabot Lodge presents on 4 March to President Wilson a petition signed by thirty-nine U.S. senators opposing the League of Nations. Germany signs the Treaty of Versailles on 23 June. On 25 September, President Wilson suffers a physical breakdown during a nationwide tour seeking public support for the League of Nations. The Palmer Raids, ordered by Attorney General A. Mitchell Palmer, begin on 7 November against American socialists and communists. On 19 November the Senate rejects the Treaty of Versailles.

1920 The Red Scare raids continue on 2 January with 4,000 suspected radicals rounded up in twenty-three states. On 19 March a final vote in the Senate again defeats the Treaty of Versailles. Trade restrictions on Russia are removed on 7 July but the communist regime is not recognized. The Washington Naval Conference opens on 12 November and ends on 6 February 1922 with limits on capital shipbuilding

1921 Congress approves the Emergency Quota Act on 19 May restricting immigration. A joint resolution is passed on 2 July declaring that hostilities with the Central Powers have ceased.

1923 The Fifth Pan-American Conference adjourns in Santiago, Chile, on 3 May. Great Britain on 19 June accepts a plan to repay its U.S. war debts, a model for agreements with other Allies.

1924 On 24 May the Rogers Act unites the U.S. Consular Service and Diplomatic Service into one branch of the State Department, creating the Foreign Service. Secretary of State Charles Evans Hughes on 1 July reaffirms America's refusal to recognize the USSR. The Dawes Plan of 1 September seeks to solve the German reparations problem.

1925 The Geneva Protocol is signed on 27 June, prohibiting the use of poisonous gas and bacteriological weapons of war; only Japan and the United States do not ratify the pact. U.S. marines leave Nicaragua on 4 August.

1926 The Senate approves membership, with amendments, in the World Court on 26 January, but the Court does not accept the amendments and the United States drops its membership application.

1927 The Geneva Naval Limitations Conference convenes on 20 June but Anglo-American disputes lead to no achievements.

1928 Chiang Kai-shek's Nationalist government of China is recognized on 25 July. On 27 August fourteen nations sign the Kellogg-Briand Pact to outlaw war.

1929 The Hague Economic Conference completes agreements on 31 August ratifying the Young Plan on German reparations.

1930 On 22 April the London Naval Conference delegates agree on a three-power (United States, Britain, Japan) treaty to limit cruisers, destroyers, and submarines.

1931 The Smoot-Hawley Tariff, continuing protectionist policy, is approved on 17 June. On 20 June, President Herbert Hoover offers a moratorium on all debt payments owed America if Europeans postpone payments on debts due them.

1932 The Hoover-Stimson Nonrecognition Doctrine is announced on 7 January, protesting Japan's aggression in Manchuria.

1933 Cordell Hull becomes secretary of state on 4 March and serves until November 1944. President Franklin Roosevelt on 3 July disrupts the London Economic Conference by repudiating all temporary currency stabilization proposals. Fulgencio Batista comes to power in Cuba on 5 September but Roosevelt refuses to recognize the regime. On 17 November, Roosevelt signs an agreement to normalize relations with the USSR. A nonintervention pact is signed on 26 December at the Seventh Pan-American Conference in Montevideo, Uruguay.

1934 President Roosevelt establishes the Export-Import Bank on 2 February to encourage overseas commerce. The Tydings-McDuffie Act of 24 March grants the Philippines independence, to begin in 1936. The Nye Committee is established to investigate the arms and munitions industry as a cause of war on 12 April. The Platt Amendment is abrogated on 29 May, ending limits on Cuban sovereignty but retaining a naval base on the island. Japan gives necessary two-year notice on 29 December that it will terminate the Washington Naval Limitation Treaty of 1922.

1935 On 16 March, Adolf Hitler denounces the disarmament clauses of the Treaty of Versailles and plans to increase the German army by thirty-six divisions. The Neutrality Act of 31 August authorizes the president to embargo arms to belligerents and to forbid citizens to travel on belligerent ships except at their own risk.

1936 On 15 January, Japan withdraws from the London Naval Conference. A treaty is signed with Panama on 2 March abolishing the American protectorate over Panama. On 7 March Germany moves soldiers into the Rhineland. The Spanish Civil War begins on 17 July with insurgents led by General Francisco Franco. Secretary of State Cordell Hull announces a "moral embargo" against both belligerents in the Spanish Civil War. Germany and Japan sign an anti-Comintern Pact on 25 November.

1937 On 8 January, President Roosevelt signs legislation applying an impartial neutrality embargo to the Spanish Civil War. Another Neutrality Act is passed on 1 May, with cash-and-carry provisions on exports. On 7 July an incident near Peking leads to the undeclared Sino-Japanese War; on the 16th, Secretary of State Hull issues a peace circular to all nations urging them to adopt the "American principles of international good conduct." President Roosevelt delivers his "quarantine speech" on 5 October, urging against isolationism. On 12 December the U.S. gunboat *Panay* is sunk by Japanese airplanes; Japan's apology is accepted on 24 December.

1938 Germany invades and annexes Austria on 13 March. The Senate Foreign Relations Committee blocks a resolution for cash-and-carry provisions for arms to Spain's Loyalist government on 13 May. On 29 September at the Munich Conference, France, Italy, and Britain "appease" Hitler by transferring the Sudetenland in Czechoslovakia to Germany. President Roosevelt on 14 December announces a $25 million loan to China. The Lima Declaration of 24 December asserts that the twenty-one nations at the Inter-Americas Conference will defend against all foreign intervention.

1939 On 14 March, Hitler conquers all of Czechoslovakia, and two days later Secretary Hull announces the United States will not recognize the conquest. The Spanish Civil War ends on 28 March when Madrid surrenders to Franco's forces. The British and French pledge on 31 March to aid Poland in the event of aggression, ending their appeasement policy. Franco's government in Spain is recognized on 3 April. President Roosevelt on 15 April appeals to Hitler and Mussolini to guarantee peace by not attacking thirty-one listed nations for ten years. On 23 August a Nazi-Soviet pact is signed in which they agree not to attack each other. German armies launch an invasion of Poland on 1 September. Britain and France declare war on Germany on 3 September; Roosevelt announces U.S. neutrality on 5 September. Scientists on 11 October inform Roosevelt that an atomic bomb can be developed. Roosevelt signs a revised neutrality act on 4 November ending the arms embargo and permitting cash-and-carry sale of arms.

1940 On 26 January the 1911 commercial treaty with Japan is ended. Winston Churchill becomes Britain's prime minister on 10 May. Congress approves legislation on 28 May permitting the president to release military supplies to Latin American countries for Western Hemisphere defense. On 3 June aid is extended to Britain and France via "surplus" U.S. arms and ammunition. France surrenders to Germany on 17 June; on 19 June, Henry Stimson becomes secretary of war and Frank Knox secretary of the navy. A naval construction bill is signed by President Roosevelt on 20 July to create a two-ocean navy. On 18 August the Ogdensburg Agreement is signed with Canada for a permanent joint board of defense. The destroyers-for-bases deal with Great Britain is announced on 3 September. On 27 September, Japan signs a tripartite pact with Italy and Germany. The "Germany first" war strategy is recommended on 12 November by Chief of Naval Operations Harold Stark. President Roosevelt's radio "fireside chat" of 29 December urges a buildup of a "great arsenal of democracy."

1941 In his State of the Union Address on 6 February, President Roosevelt announces his proposal for a lend-lease program and enunciates his Four Freedoms; Congress approves the Lend-Lease Act on 11 March. On 9 April, Denmark agrees to provide rights for U.S. defense bases in Greenland. Roosevelt on 11 April informs Churchill that the U.S. Navy will patrol areas in what would become the Battle of the Atlantic. Japan and Russia sign a mutual nonaggression pact on 13 April. President Roosevelt orders all German and Italian consulates closed on 16 June. On 22 June Germany launches an invasion of the Soviet Union. On 7 July U.S. marines land on and occupy Iceland. Japanese assets are frozen on 26 July. Roosevelt and Churchill meet secretly off Newfoundland on 12 August and prepare the Atlantic Charter, a joint declaration of principles. On 9 November a settlement is reached with Mexico for an oil and agrarian expropriation compensation agreement. On 6 December, President Roosevelt appeals to Japan to maintain peace by withdrawing Japanese troops from Southeast Asia; the following day Japanese planes attack Pearl Harbor. On 8 December, Congress declares war on Japan; on December 11, Germany and Italy declare war on the United States.

1942 On 1 January the United Nations Declaration is signed by twenty-six nations, affirming the Atlantic Charter, to fight the Axis powers. Twenty-one American republics recommend breaking relations with the Axis powers on 28 January. Japanese Americans living on the West Coast are ordered relocated on 19 February. President Roosevelt on 1 June promises Russia a second front in Europe by the end of 1942. On 13 August, General Leslie R. Groves is appointed to command of the Manhattan Project to develop the atomic bomb.

1943 The Casablanca Conference results on 24 January with plans to invade Sicily and Italy and the requirement that the Axis powers must surrender unconditionally. Roosevelt,

Churchill, and military advisers finalize military decisions at the Trident Conference in Washington on 25 May and the Quebec Conference on 24 August. On 30 October the Moscow Conference of Foreign Ministers (Hull, Anthony Eden, and V. M. Molotov) ends. The United Nations Relief and Rehabilitation Administration is established by forty-four nations on 9 November. The first Cairo Conference on 26 November results in British and U.S. agreements on China and the Far East. On 1 December the Big Three Conference ends at Tehran, Iran; on 6 December the second Cairo Conference concludes.

1944 On 6 June, D-Day, an Allied invasion begins along the Normandy coast of France. Diplomatic relations are severed with Argentina on 22 June because of pro-fascist sympathies. The Bretton Woods Conference ends on 22 July, establishing the International Monetary Fund and the World Bank. At the Quebec Conference of 16 September, Roosevelt and Churchill make final plans for victory over Germany and Japan. The Dumbarton Oaks Conference on 7 October prepares a draft for the United Nations organization. The Moscow Conference of 18 October ends, during which Churchill and Stalin decide on East European "spheres of influence"; Roosevelt later concurs.

1945 The Yalta Conference between Churchill, Roosevelt, and Stalin concludes on 11 February and defines the shape of postwar Europe. Roosevelt dies on 12 April and Harry S. Truman becomes president. On 21 April the Soviet Union and Poland sign a twenty-year mutual assistance pact. The San Francisco Conference on the United Nations convenes on 25 April. Germany's unconditional surrender is signed on 7 May, and the end of the war in Europe is declared on 8 May. On 5 June the European Advisory Commission decides on the division of Germany and Berlin. The United Nations Charter is signed by delegates of fifty nations on 26 June. Truman, Churchill, and Stalin begin discussions at Potsdam on 16 July. On 26 July an ultimatum is issued to Japan for an unconditional surrender. Atomic bombs are dropped on Japan at Hiroshima, 6 August, and Nagasaki, 9 August. On 15 August Japan surrenders "unconditionally."

Lend-lease aid is terminated on 21 August. Ho Chi Minh on 2 September proclaims the independence of Vietnam. Canada, Britain, and the United States agree on 15 November to provide for international control of atomic energy; on 20 December legislation is backed by the Truman administration for civilian control of America's atomic energy.

1946 George Kennan sends his "Long Telegram" on 22 February, outlining the policy of "containment." Winston Churchill on 5 March delivers his "Iron Curtain" speech at Fulton, Missouri. On 3 June, Japanese war crime trials begin under U.S. jurisdiction. Bernard Baruch presents the American plan (Baruch Plan) for the international control of atomic energy on 14 June; the UN Security Council accepts the plan on 31 December. The Fulbright Act is passed on 1 August to finance foreign study. On 15 August, President Truman approves a memo stating Soviet aggression against Turkey would be resisted. The Nuremberg war crimes tribunal announces its decisions on 1 October.

1947 On 29 January mediation efforts between the Communists and Nationalists in China are abandoned. The Truman Doctrine is enunciated on 12 March in a request for aid to Greece and Turkey to combat communism. On 5 May the State Department Policy Planning Staff is established with George Kennan as director. Secretary of State George C. Marshall proposes a plan on 5 June for economic aid to European nations to rehabilitate their economies. The National Security Act of 26 July establishes the Department of Defense, National Security Council, and Central Intelligence Agency. The Rio Pact is signed on 2 September, a mutual assistance treaty for Western Hemisphere nations. Twenty-three nations sign the General Agreement on Tariffs and Trade (GATT) at Geneva on 30 October.

1948 On 14 May the State of Israel is proclaimed. The Vandenberg Resolution, affirming U.S. support for regional security pacts, is approved on 11 June. The Berlin blockade begins on 24 June, followed by a U.S. airlift for more than a year. On 9–10 December the United Nations adopts the Universal Declaration of Human Rights and the Genocide Convention.

1949 President Truman in his inaugural address on 20 January proposes the Point Four program; Dean Acheson becomes secretary of state on 21 January. On 4 April the North Atlantic Treaty Organization is chartered by twelve nations. The Berlin blockade ends on 11 May with a four-power accord on Berlin. On 5 August the State Department issues a "White Paper" relating to Chang Kai-shek's loss of China. A White House press release of 23 September announces that the Soviet Union has detonated an atomic bomb. Mao Zedong proclaims the creation of the People's Republic of China on 1 October. On 7 October the Soviet zone of Germany is established as the German Democratic Republic.

1950 On 12 January, Secretary of State Dean Acheson describes a "perimeter strategy" for East Asia to prevent the spread of communism. Senator Joseph McCarthy charges on 9 February that communist spies have infiltrated the State Department. NSC 68, drafted by Paul H. Nitze, a document depicting the Soviets as aggressors seeking to conquer the world, is presented to the National Security Council on 14 April. On 5 June, President Truman signs a foreign aid bill, granting nearly $3 billion for the European Recovery Plan (Marshall Plan) and the Point Four Program. North Korean forces attack South Korea on 25 June. On 23 September, Congress adopts the McCarran Internal Security Bill over President Truman's veto. Chinese communist troops launch a counteroffensive on 26 November to Korea against UN troops, forcing their retreat to the thirty-eighth parallel. On 23 December a mutual defense agreement with France and the Associated States of Indochina is signed to combat communist forces in Vietnam under Ho Chi Minh.

1951 The UN General Assembly approves an arms embargo against Communist China on 18 May. Truce negotiations begin on 8 July in Korea. A mutual defense treaty is signed with the Philippines on 30 August. On 1 September the ANZUS Tripartite Security Treaty with Australia and New Zealand is signed. A mutual security agreement is signed with Japan on 8 September. Marshall Plan aid ends on 31 December.

1952 Britain, France, and the United States agree to West Germany's internal independence on 26 May. The McCarran-Walter Immigration and Nationality Act is passed on 26 June, setting a quota for Asian immigration.

1953 Joseph Stalin dies on 5 March. An armistice agreement is signed and becomes effective 26–27 July in Korea. A coup in Iran on 19 August restores Shah Reza Pahlavi with CIA help. On 26 September, Spain agrees to creation of U.S. air and naval stations in exchange for $250 million in aid. President Dwight D. Eisenhower's "New Look" policy emphasizing massive retaliation is described on 30 October. The Atoms-for-Peace Plan is proposed by Eisenhower on 8 December.

1954 The Bricker Amendment to limit the president's executive agreement and treaty-making powers is narrowly defeated in the Senate on 25–26 February. Vietminh forces on 14 March attack French troops at Dien Bien Phu; on 4–5 April, President Eisenhower decides to send only limited assistance to the French. On 8 June the CIA assists in overthrowing the left-wing government of Jacobo Arbenz Guzman in Guatemala. The Geneva Conference of 1954 on 20 July divides Vietnam into two parts. The Southeast Asia Treaty Organization (SEATO) is formed on 8 September. On 23 October, President Eisenhower offers aid to South Vietnam. A mutual defense pact is signed on 2 December with Nationalist China.

1955 Congress on 25 January authorizes use of armed forces to defend Nationalist China and the Pescadores. The U.S. Army on 12 February agrees to take charge of training the army of South Vietnam. West Germany joins NATO on 9 May. The Warsaw Pact defense alliance is formed on 14 May by European communist nations. The Big Four Summit Conference is held 18–23 July in Geneva, where Eisenhower gains favorable world reaction to his "Open Skies" proposal, permitting aerial reconnaissance. On 26 October, Ngo Dinh Diem gains control of South Vietnam; he proclaims a republic and himself as the first president.

1956 Secretary of State Dulles refuses on 9 May to supply arms to Israel to avoid a Middle East confrontation with the Soviet Union. On 19 July, Dulles cancels U.S. offer to aid Egypt in construction of the Aswan Dam. Egypt nationalizes the Suez Canal on 26 July. On 6 November the Suez Crisis is resolved, when President Eisenhower applies pressure on Britain, Israel, and France after their attack on Egypt beginning on 29 October.

1957 The Eisenhower Doctrine, to check communist aggression in the Middle East, is presented in an address to Congress on 5 January. The Senate approves the Atoms-for-Peace Treaty on 18 June. The Soviet Union launches *Sputnik,* the first artificial Earth satellite, on 5 October.

1958 A cultural exchange agreement is signed with the Soviet Union on 27 January. On 31 January the first U.S. Earth satellite, *Explorer I,* is placed in orbit. Vice President Richard Nixon experiences intense anti-American feeling on a tour of Latin America 28 April–14 May. U.S. marines land in Lebanon on 15 July to halt aggression of the United Arab Republic. On 23 August, Chinese communists bombard the islands of Quemoy and Matsu in the Formosa Strait.

1959 Cuban president Fulgencio Batista flees Cuba after Fidel Castro's forces march into Havana on 3 January. Bilateral defense pacts are signed with Iran, Pakistan, and Turkey on 5 March. The United States supports but does not join the Central Treaty Organization (CENTO), a defensive alliance formed on 19 August by Turkey, Iran, Pakistan, and Britain. Twelve nations approve a treaty to reserve the Antarctic for scientific and peaceful purposes on 1 December.

1960 On 19 January the Japanese mutual security treaty of 1952 is renewed. The Soviet Union announces on 5 May that an American U-2 spy plane was shot down over Soviet territory; President Eisenhower accepts responsibility for the incident. On 6 July, Congress approves and Eisenhower levies cuts in Cuba's sugar quota; Castro retaliates by nationalizing all U.S. property in Cuba. The San José Declaration of 28 August of the Organization of American States condemns intervention "by any extracontinental power," a warning against Russian interference in Cuba. On 19 September the Organization of Petroleum Exporting Countries (OPEC) is formed in Baghdad. Twenty nations on 19 November form the Organi-

zation for Economic Cooperation and Development (OECD).

1961 On 20 January, President John F. Kennedy in his inaugural address calls on the nation to renew its commitment to extend freedom throughout the world. Dean Rusk is appointed secretary of state the following day. On 13 March, President Kennedy announces the Alliance for Progress program to aid Latin America. Twelve hundred Cuban exiles, trained and supported by the United States, land at the Bay of Pigs in Cuba in a failed attempt to overthrow Castro on 17 April. A "moon race" is announced on 25 May to beat the Soviet Union to the moon. On 13 August the Soviets begin construction of the Berlin Wall, dividing East and West Berlin to prevent the flow of exiles to West Germany. On 22 November, President Kennedy approves the "first phase of a Vietnam program," broadening U.S. commitment in Vietnam with U.S. troops.

1962 On 22 October, Kennedy informs the nation there are Russian-built missile sites in Cuba and imposes on 24 October a naval quarantine on all missile equipment being shipped to Cuba; after a U.S. pledge not to invade Cuba and to remove missiles from Turkey, on 28 October the Soviets agree to remove the missiles.

1963 On 20 June the Soviet Union agrees to a communications "hot line" to reduce the risk of accidental war. On 5 August, Britain, the United States, and the Soviet Union sign the Limited Nuclear Test Ban Treaty; by 10 October more than one hundred nations agree to it. On 1–2 November, Ngo Dinh Diem is assassinated in Vietnam. President Kennedy is assassinated on 22 November.

1964 The Tonkin Gulf Resolution is passed on 7 August, authorizing President Johnson to take "all necessary measures" to repel any armed attack in Southeast Asia.

1965 Claiming a threat of communism, U.S. marines land in the Dominican Republic on 28 April. The Immigration Act of 3 October 1965 replaces the quota system of 1921.

1966 The Fulbright Hearings on Vietnam open on 28 January. On 6 February, France withdraws from NATO. The Food for Peace Act is signed on 12 November.

1967 On 26 January, Secretary of Defense Robert McNamara announces the "mutual assured destruction" (MAD) nuclear strategy. Sixty nations on 27 January sign the Outer Space Treaty.

1968 On 23 January the spy ship USS *Pueblo* is seized in international waters by North Korea; the crew is released on 22 December. The Tet Offensive is launched by communist forces on 30 January in South Vietnam. On 31 March, President Lyndon Johnson announces a bombing halt in Vietnam and withdraws as a 1968 presidential candidate. On 1 July sixty-two nations sign the nuclear nonproliferation treaty. Soviet armed forces on 20 August employ the Brezhnev Doctrine to overthrow the Czech government of Alexander Dubcek. On 31 October the United States and North Vietnam agree to conduct formal negotiations for peace.

1969 On 18 March the first secret bombing of Cambodia is ordered by President Richard Nixon. The U.S. Vietnamization program is announced on 8 June and the initial withdrawal of U.S. troops from South Vietnam begins. In a speech in Guam on 25 July the president announces the Nixon Doctrine, to let countries develop in their own fashion. Strategic Arms Limitation Talks (SALT) begin on 17 November. On 25 November, Nixon announces the United States will ratify the Geneva Protocol of 1925 outlawing biological and chemical weapons.

1970 On 22 June the Senate terminates the Tonkin Gulf Resolution of 1964.

1971 On 11 February eighty nations sign the Seabed Arms Treaty prohibiting nuclear weapons on the ocean floor. The *New York Times* publishes the Pentagon Papers, a compilation from 1967–1968 of how the United States became involved in Vietnam. The People's Republic of China is admitted to the United Nations on 25 October; the Nationalist government of Taiwan is expelled.

1972 President Nixon visits China on 17 February and issues the Shanghai Communique on U.S.–China relations. Nixon orders renewed B-52 bombing raids on North Vietnam on 4 April. On 22–30 May, Nixon becomes the first U.S. president to visit Moscow and signs the ABM (antiballistic missile) Treaty and the SALT I Agreement.

1973 A military coup in Chile on 11 September overthrows President Salvador Allende with CIA assistance. Henry Kissinger is confirmed as secretary of state on 21 September. The Arab states begin a political oil embargo on 16 October when Israel invades Egypt. On 7 November, Congress overrides Nixon's veto of the War Powers Act.

1974 On 3 July in Moscow, Nixon signs an amendment of the ABM Treaty of 1972 and the Threshold Ban Treaty. President Nixon resigns on 9 August. President Gerald R. Ford meets with Soviet leader Brezhnev in Vladivostok on 24 November and a ceiling is placed on offensive nuclear weapons. On 16 December the Senate ratifies the Geneva Protocol of 1925 and the 1972 Biological Convention. Congress on 20 December refuses to grant the Soviet Union most-favored-nation status pending Jewish emigration policy.

1975 The United States finally ratifies the Geneval Protocol of 1925 on 22 January. On 29 April the last U.S. helicopter leaves Saigon and South Vietnam falls to the communists. Thirty-five nations sign the Helsinki Accords on 1 August, legitimizing the Soviet Union's territorial gains in Europe since 1940. On 29 August, Venezuela nationalizes its oil industry, largely controlled by American companies. The United Nations issues a resolution on 10 November condemning Zionism as a form of racism.

1976 The United States extends its exclusive fishing zone to 200 miles offshore on 13 April. On 30 June, Europe's communist parties declare that each national party is independent but equal to the other parties ("Eurocommunism"). Mao Zedong dies on 9 September.

1977 On 18 May thirty-two nations sign a UN agreement banning environmental warfare. On 7 September it is agreed that Panamanians will assume full jurisdiction over the Panama Canal in the year 2000.

1978 Carter persuades Egypt and Israel to sign the Camp David Accords on 17 September after twelve days of negotiations for peace in the Middle East. On 15 December agreement is made for the establishment of diplomatic relations with the People's Republic of China, to take effect on 1 January 1979, and the termination of the U.S. Defense Treaty with Taiwan.

1979 On 16 January the shah of Iran leaves Tehran; the Ayatollah Khomeini arrives in Iran from exile on 1 February and forms his own provisional government. Egypt and Israel sign a peace treaty on 26 March; a military-economic aid package is approved by Congress in May. On 18 June, President Carter and Soviet leader Brezhnev sign SALT II, a five-year treaty limiting maximum numbers of intercontinental missiles and long-range bombers. Congress passes legislation on 29 September asking for the State Department to compose a list of nations that support terrorism. On 4 November the U.S. embassy in Iran is stormed and sixty hostages are taken; President Carter then freezes Iranian assets in the United States. On 28 December, after the Soviet invasion of Afghanistan, Carter warns Brezhnev of "serious consequences if the Soviets do not withdraw."

1980 On 23 January, President Carter enunciates the Carter Doctrine, declaring that the Persian Gulf area is a "vital American interest." He also withdraws from SALT II and orders a boycott of the Olympic Games scheduled for Moscow.

1981 The American hostages in Iran are freed on 20 January, minutes after Ronald Reagan is sworn in as president. Reagan on 23 November issues National Security Decision Directive 17, giving the CIA authority to fund the contra movement against the government of Nicaragua.

1982 Strategic Arms Reduction Talks (START) begin on 29 June in Geneva with the Soviet Union. On 8 July the UN Law of the Sea Treaty is rejected. On 16 August the People's Republic of China signs an agreement to use only peaceful means to regain Taiwan, while the United States agrees to reduce its level of arms aid to Taiwan. U.S. marines arrive in Beirut on 27 September for peacekeeping activities.

1983 On 8 March, at a convention of evangelical Christians, President Ronald Reagan calls the Soviet Union an "evil empire." On 10 March

the United States claims exclusive economic zones out to 200 miles. President Reagan on 23 March announces the Strategic Defense Initiative (SDI), derisively called "Star Wars," a defense system against Soviet intercontinental ballistic missiles. On 23 October a suicide truck-bomb explodes at a U.S. marine barracks in Beirut, Lebanon. U.S. forces invade Grenada on 25 October to prevent a communist coup with Soviet and Cuban support.

1984 President Reagan concludes a five-day visit to China on 1 May, signing accords on nuclear cooperation and cultural relations. On 26 November the World Court rules that it has jurisdiction over Nicaragua's suit against the United States.

1985 On 24 April the House of Representatives rejects President Reagan's request for aid for the Nicaraguan contras. On 8 July, Reagan claims that world terrorism is sponsored by Iran, Libya, North Korea, Cuba, and Nicaragua.

1986 Meetings on 13–14 January with Canada's Prime Minister Brian Mulroney renew the long-lived North American Aerospace Defense Command System (NORAD). On 14 April, U.S. aircraft bomb five Libyan targets in retaliation for support of terrorists. The World Court on 27 June rules that the United States violated international law and Nicaragua's sovereignty, a ruling the United States ignores. Congress approves military aid to the Nicaraguan contras on 13 August. Congress on 2 October overrides President Reagan's veto of sanctions against South Africa. Reagan and Gorbachev meet on 11–12 October in Reykjavik, Iceland, about arms control; Reagan walks out of the last session.

1987 On 5 May joint congressional hearings begin on the Iran-Contra affair. Reagan and Gorbachev sign the INF Treaty on 8 December, eliminating intermediate-range missiles.

1988 On 4 February a U.S. court indicts Panama's General Noriega for racketeering and drug trafficking. The United States, Soviet Union, Pakistan, and Afghanistan sign agreements on 14 April for the withdrawal of Soviet forces from Afghanistan. With the INF Treaty of 1987 in effect as of 1 June, the United States and Soviet Union begin destruction of nuclear weaponry in September. The Montreal Protocol on depletion of the ozone layer becomes effective on 16 December after ratification by twenty nations.

1989 President George H. W. Bush and Canada's Prime Minister Brian Mulroney on 10 February agree to reduce acid rain pollution. A U.S. federal court on 4 May finds Oliver North guilty of obstructing Congress in the investigation into the Iran-Contra scandal. On May 11 U.S. troops are sent to Panama after a "fraudulent" election renews the power of Panama's military leader General Manuel Antonio Noriega. NATO on 29–30 May accepts U.S. proposals to reduce Europe's short-range missiles and U.S.–USSR conventional forces. Chinese troops kill hundreds of protestors on 3–4 June in the Tiananmen Square massacre; in response, on 5 June, President Bush suspends military sales and high-level contacts and asks the IMF and World Bank to postpone Chinese loan applications. On 14 July, President Bush attends the G-7 Summit. Aid is provided on 25 August to Colombia to combat drug trafficking. On 18 October, South Korea asks that U.S. troop strength not be reduced. The Berlin Wall falls on 9 November. An invasion of Panama by U.S. forces on 20 December overthrows Noriega.

1990 On 15 February, President Bush and the presidents of Columbia, Bolivia, and Peru sign agreements to work together in combating drug traffickers. On 29 June ninety-three nations offer aid to Third World countries in reducing ozone-depleting gases. On 2 August, Iraq invades Kuwait; on 6 August, President Bush orders U.S. forces to protect Saudi Arabia in Operation Desert Shield. On 12 September talks lead to a final treaty for German reunification on the 20th. On 17 November the Treaty on Conventional Forces in Europe (CFE) is signed.

1991 On 16 January, under U.S. direction, multinational UN forces launch the Gulf War against Iraq; by 28 February, in a 100-hour ground war, Iraq's forces are evicted from Kuwait. The Warsaw Pact's military and economic organizations are disbanded on 25 February. On 6 March, President Bush heralds a "new world order." On 7 May, UN peacekeepers arrive in Kuwait to oversee

peace between Kuwait and Iraq. On 25 June, Slovenia and Croatia declare independence from Yugoslavia. Economic sanctions against South Africa are lifted on 11 July. President Bush's Enterprise for the Americas Initiative takes its first step on 22 July to develop a hemispheric free market by signing a trade accord with thirteen English-speaking Caribbean countries. On 31 July, Bush and Gorbachev sign the Strategic Arms Reduction Treaty (START I). On 20 August the Republics of Estonia, Latvia, and Lithuania affirm their national independence from the Soviet Union. On 2 September, the United States and the European Union recognize the Baltic nations' independence. After Haiti's democratically elected president is overthrown in a military coup, on 29 October economic sanctions are imposed on the Haitian dictators. Twenty-four nations on 4 October extend the 1959 Antarctic Treaty by levying a fifty-year moratorium to ban mining and military activity and set guidelines for scientific research. On 8 November U.S. nuclear weapons are removed from South Korea and the two Koreas move toward reconciliation. Three former Soviet republics, Russia, Belarus, and Ukraine, form the Commonwealth of Independent States on 8 December.

1992 On 24 February the Supreme Court upholds President Bush's decision to forcibly repatriate Haitian refugees. An American court on 9 April convicts Noriega of drug trafficking and sentences him to forty years in prison. On 23 May the United States and the four Commonwealth of Independent States countries with nuclear arms sign the Lisbon Protocol to comply with the 1991 START I treaty negotiated with the Soviet Union. The Pentagon issues a defense guidance program for the post–Cold War era on 24 May, emphasizing a commitment to collective military action. President Bush extends most-favored-nation status on 2 June to China. On 14 June delegates of 178 countries to the Rio de Janeiro Conference on Environment and Development (Earth Summit) agree to promote economic development that would protect the earth's nonrenewable resources and sign a treaty to reduce emissions of carbon dioxide and greenhouse gases. On 17 June Bush and

Russian president Boris Yeltsin agree to draft a second strategic arms reduction treaty. Mexico, Canada, and the United States on 17 December sign the final North American Free Trade Agreement (NAFTA).

1993 On 3 January, Presidents Bush and Yeltsin sign START II to sharply reduce their nuclear arsenals. Radical Muslims bomb New York's World Trade Center on 27 February. On 4 April financial aid is provided for Russia. The Oslo Accords are signed on 13 September between Israel's Yitzhak Rabin and Palestinian Liberation Organization chairman Yassir Arafat, the first Israel–PLO peace agreement. On 20 November, Congress approves NAFTA. Sanctions on South Africa are repealed on 23 November. The Uruguay Round of GATT is completed on 14 December with tariffs reduced 50 percent by the United States and the European Economic Community.

1994 The embargo on trade with Vietnam ends on 3 February. North Korea on 15 February avoids U.S. economic sanctions by approving inspection of nuclear sites. On 28 February, NATO aircraft shoot down four Bosnian Serb aircraft violating the UN no-fly zone, NATO's first combat attack in its forty-five-year history. President Clinton renews China's most-favored-nation status on 26 May. On 8 June, President Clinton agrees to help the UN humanitarian effort in Rwanda, where warfare has killed 200,000 people and caused thousands of refugees to flee. The UN Security Council on 31 July approves a resolution for U.S.–led forces to intervene in Haiti; Haiti's President Aristide returns to Haiti on 15 October. The Senate ratifies on 1 December the GATT world trade treaty, which also creates the World Trade Organization (WTO).

1995 On 17 April, President Clinton signs an order to declassify all twenty-five-year-old records declassified after 1999, unless a special panel exempts certain sensitive materials. For assisting terrorist groups, on 1 May a trade embargo is placed on Iran. President Clinton and Fidel Castro amend their 1994 agreement on refugees on 2 May for the United States to admit 21,000 Cuban refugees being held in Guantanamo Bay. On 11 May the United Nations makes the

Nuclear Nonproliferation Treaty permanent. President Clinton on 11 July extends full diplomatic recognition to Vietnam. That same day Bosnian Serb atrocities at Srebrenica lead to U.S. involvement, and the CIA and National Security Agency release secret files on Soviet documents from the 1940s. NATO air raids on 28 August on Bosnian Serbs lead to a peace conference. A U.S. court on 1 October finds ten Islamic fundamentalists guilty of conspiracy in the World Trade Center bombing in 1993. On 2 October, Congress opposes a law to fight terrorism in America. The Dayton Accords of 21 November provide for peace in Bosnia-Herzegovina; they are signed on 14 December. Israel and Syria on 28 December renew peace talks at the Wye Conference Center near Washington.

1996 On 1 March, Colombia is declared no longer a certified country committed to the war on drugs. On 12 March, President Clinton signs the Helms-Burton Act to restrict trade of other nations with Cuba. On 24 April, Clinton signs antiterrorism legislation, providing $1.1 billion. Economic sanctions are levied on countries doing business with Libya and Iran on 5 August. On 27 September, Afghan Taliban rebels capture Kabul, imposing strict Islamic law.

1997 On 3 January, President Clinton delays enforcement of the Helms-Burton Act on Cuban trade. American George Soros on 7 September closes his foundation in Belarus. On 11 December 150 nations, but not the United States, sign the treaty banning the use of land mines. On 11 December, 150 nations prepare a treaty to limit greenhouse gases (the Kyoto Protocol). President Clinton indicates on 18 December that U.S. troops will remain in Bosnia indefinitely.

1998 Serb attacks on Kosovo lead President Clinton on 5 March to impose sanctions on Yugoslavia. On 19 April thirty-four Western Hemisphere nations agree to negotiate a free trade zone. Sanctions are imposed on 28 May on Pakistan and India because of their nuclear weapons tests; sanctions are eased on 14 July. On 20 August, President Clinton retaliates against terrorists who bombed the U.S embassy at Nairobi, Kenya, and Dar-es-Salaam, Tanzania, on 7 August.

1999 On 10 June, after seventy-eight days of bombing, Serbia's Slobodan Milosevic accepts NATO's cease-fire and peace terms. On 17 September, President Clinton lifts sanctions on North Korea after it stops missile tests. The Senate on 13 October refuses to ratify the treaty calling for ending all nuclear testing. Terms are accepted on 15 November for China to join the World Trade Organization.

2000 On 1 January, Panama gains full control of the Panama Canal from the United States. Congress approves on 24 May permanent trade relations with China. The United Nations Millennium Summit ends on 8 September. On 12 October the U.S. destroyer *Cole* is hit by a bomb in Yemen harbor, the work of suicide terrorists. A summit meeting on 16 October in Egypt with leaders of the United States, Egypt, Israel, Palestine, and Jordan, along with UN Secretary General Kofi Annan, seeks to end violence between Israel and Palestine. On 24 November the global warming treaty (Kyoto Protocol) reaches an impasse because of U.S. and European differences on best methods to reduce greenhouse gases. On 31 December, President Clinton signs a treaty for a permanent international war crimes tribunal.

2001 On 18 January secretary of state–designate Colin Powell during hearings indicates that he favors deployment of the national missile defense system (NMDS). On 11 September terrorists hijack commercial airliners and crash them into the two towers of the World Trade Center in New York City and the Pentagon outside Washington, D.C. The United States initiates military action against Taliban-supported terrorists in Afghanistan with bombing raids on 6 October.

ENCYCLOPEDIA
of AMERICAN
FOREIGN POLICY

AFRICAN AMERICANS

Brenda Gayle Plummer

Race and foreign affairs have intersected at numerous points in U.S. history. Officials in the eighteenth and nineteenth centuries were not always explicitly aware of the impact of race on foreign relations or on their own decision making, but its impact on historical events is demonstrable. Beginning with the American Revolution and continuing through the twentieth century, race influenced what the United States did and how it pursued its interests abroad.

THE AMERICAN REVOLUTION

Black volunteers, detesting slavery and wanting liberty, fought on both sides of the revolutionary war. The activities of African-American revolutionaries were matched by those of black loyalists, some of whom were deliberately recruited into military service by British commanders eager to destabilize the plantation economy, especially in tidewater Virginia. This British policy was bitterly resented by slaveholders. Many of these soldiers retreated to Canada with the British after 1783. Freedom proved elusive for black protagonists on both sides. The U.S. flirtation with freedom for blacks proved ephemeral. Slavery persisted as a national institution and free people of color increasingly faced racial discrimination during the course of the antebellum period. Some loyalists who evacuated with the British were sold into slavery in the West Indies. Others found barriers to civil equality in their new Canadian homes.

RACE, IMPRESSMENTS, AND MARITIME ISSUES

Race was a factor in the maritime trades and in navies during the age of sail. Black men from North America, the Caribbean, and Africa, slave and free, were among the thousands employed in a range of industries and at war. They served on slavers, whalers, packet boats, warships, and were represented as sailors in almost all sectors of maritime activity. Rules governing the movements of both enslaved sailors and free men of color affected relations among states. In the antebellum South during periods of slave unrest, authorities enforced regulations that restricted the portside activities of West Indian seamen. Violators were threatened with enslavement. Abuse of foreign black sailors in U.S. ports sometimes brought protests from consuls or influential persons to whom they turned for support. The seamen's papers given black American sailors in 1796 did not afford them substantial protection from infringements on their rights, and until 1823, when civil equality was extended to black sailors in the British navy, black seamen of all nationalities were readily exploited, and those who were free faced the risk of illegal enslavement.

Impressment was a danger for all U.S. seamen, regardless of race, before and during the War of 1812. Those recruited into the British navy could expect harsher treatment than that experienced aboard U.S. ships. The fate of black loyalists enslaved in the West Indies during the American Revolution contributed to anti-British feeling among some African Americans in the early nineteenth century and helped preserve their loyalty to the United States during those years. The United States, however, was reluctant to recruit blacks into any armed forces except the navy. As a result, there were few black combatants except for those enlisted as volunteers in state units. The United States and Britain ultimately employed the same tactic that had been used in the revolutionary war in promising manumission to those who fought or served as military laborers. Those who allied themselves with Britain were taken to Canada at the end of the war and settled on plots of land. While many of the manumission promises made by U.S. authorities were honored, African Americans had no guarantee of civil equality.

SLAVERY AND ABOLITION

In Western countries, efforts to limit slavery began with the prohibition of the African slave trade and attempts to enforce an international ban on this traffic. Britain outlawed the slave trade in its possessions in 1807, and the United States soon followed suit, effective as of 1 January 1808. While the U.S. law curtailed the international supply of slaves, American traders continued to retail slaves through a domestic market. The abolitionist movement then focused on eradicating slavery itself. Antislavery activists created cooperative networks where they proselytized against slavery and abetted the escape of fugitives. Some antislavery activities had an international character. One campaign, noted in the cities of the northeastern United States and in Great Britain, focused on encouraging consumers to buy products grown without slave labor. The effort met with indifferent success but provided small ephemeral markets for imports from Haiti—a country that had gained its independence through slave rebellion—and after 1833, the British West Indies. The promotion of free labor produce coincided with a growing conviction in the northern United States and Britain that wage labor was the most rational, just, and efficient method of work, and with the social and political evolution of industrial society in those areas.

The British Parliament in 1833 enacted a gradual abolition program that ended slavery in British dominions by 1838. Between 1830 and 1860 a small African-American community had gathered in Britain. As most American universities barred black students, some were attending universities of far higher caliber than those in the United States. Others were fugitives who had made their way to a country where slavery was prohibited. Such prominent U.S. abolitionists as Frederick Douglass and Charles Lenox Remond and his sister Sarah Remond visited Britain to enlist both the working classes and the bourgeoisie in the American antislavery cause. Black abolitionists gave public lectures and sold copies of slave narratives written by themselves and others. They succeeded in thwarting many of the fund-raising efforts of the American Colonization Society, established in 1816–1817 to resettle blacks on the west coast of Africa. In Ireland, the Irish nationalist Daniel O'Connell, an outspoken foe of slavery, embraced Frederick Douglass. Douglass spent nineteen months lecturing in the British Isles between 1845 and 1847. British

Quakers raised the money to buy Douglass's freedom from his Maryland owner.

Antislavery activists hoped that pressure applied by Britain, then the world's most powerful nation, would persuade the United States to deal forthrightly with the slavery question. Abolitionists did not succeed in capturing all Britons. They faced the opposition of those manufacturers and workers most dependent on imports of U.S. cotton, but benefited from a widespread revulsion among all classes against slavery. The groundwork that Douglass, the Remonds, and others laid helped neutralize British sympathies for southern slaveholders. This was a critical issue during the 1850s, when sectional animosity reached a crisis point in the United States. If Britain, despite its own antislavery stand within its realms, allied with the Confederacy during the U.S. Civil War, the United States would likely be defeated. While American abolitionists often avoided direct discussions of class conflict because of their frequent reliance on elite patronage in Britain and their desire to keep the focus on slavery, the zenith of their activity coincided with the Chartist movement, which sought to improve conditions for the industrial working class, and debates over the status of labor.

American slavery was also drawn into the international arena as a result of the activities of fugitive slaves. In the course of the nineteenth century some thirty thousand black persons from the United States entered Canada. Periods of domestic crisis, such as the passage of the Fugitive Slave Act of 1850 and the Dred Scott decision, accelerated this immigration. The Fugitive Slave Act made it easy for slaveholders and bounty hunters to threaten the liberty of free people of color. In an explicitly racist finding, the Supreme Court, in the 1857 case *Scott* v. *Sandford,* ruled that blacks could not be citizens and had no civil rights. The decision effectively ended the prospects of free people of color in the United States until after the Civil War. Many who were able left the country. In addition to the relatively familiar escapes to Canada by slaves and free people alike, blacks from Texas crossed the border into Mexico, where slavery was illegal. During the early years of the Republic, when Spain loosely administered Florida, fugitives in combination with the Seminole nation engaged the United States in wars in 1817–1818 and 1835–1842. In the aftermath of the first Seminole war, Spain, unable and unwilling to guarantee the security of U.S. real and chattel property along its Florida borders, and wishing to avoid armed conflict with Americans, ceded the rebellious territory to the United States.

Fugitives also included those whose anti-slavery activities put them in jeopardy of the law. Frederick Douglass in 1859 was a suspect in John Brown's conspiracy to seize the federal armory in Harpers Ferry, Virginia. Douglass fled to England to avoid arrest. Once there, he contacted the U.S. minister to the Court of St. James's hoping to secure a passport to visit France. The passport was denied on grounds that Douglass, according to Supreme Court dicta, was not a U.S. citizen. Douglass was an early victim of passport denial, a practice that would be used in the twentieth century to restrict the movements of blacks who were known critics of racial discrimination.

COLONIZATION AND EMIGRATION

Opinion leaders on both sides of the slavery question during the antebellum period expressed fears about the consequences of emancipation. Some abolitionists believed that slavery was morally wrong but did not think that freed slaves could be assimilated into American society for racial reasons. Certain proslavery advocates used these doubts about assimilation to argue that slavery could not be eradicated. A third alternative to slavery or abolition was the removal of freed slaves from the United States. The option appealed to blacks who wished a homeland of their own, and to proslavery and antislavery advocates alike who thought blacks could not be assimilated into American life. Paul Cuffe, a black New England shipowner, was committed to civil rights for African Americans and an outspoken opponent of slavery. He nevertheless employed his own resources in a back-to-Africa project in the early 1810s. After correspondence with prominent British abolitionists, including the parliamentarian William Wilberforce, Cuffe sought to repatriate selected emigrants to the British African colony of Sierra Leone. His plans were interrupted by the War of 1812 and by his own death not long thereafter, but he did succeed in settling some thirty-eight persons in Africa.

In 1821 the American Colonization Society resumed Cuffe's work. Members of the organization included such figures as Henry Clay, Francis Scott Key, and other prominent white Americans for whom the United States had to remain a white man's country. The society purchased African land

from local rulers, and in 1847 the settlement, called Liberia, became an independent republic. Many antislavery activists opposed the American Colonization Society, believing that it was simply a stratagem to solidify slavery by removing from the United States the only blacks in a position to contest it. Others endorsed colonization and emigration in principle, reserving their objections for the society per se. There were, accordingly, other colonization ventures. In the 1820s and 1850s, two emigration movements to Haiti were organized with the cooperation of the Haitian government. A project in the 1830s involved the removal of American blacks to the island of Trinidad. President Abraham Lincoln, who endorsed colonization as a strategy to prevent a civil war over the slavery question, researched the possibility of a black homeland on the isthmus of Central America. These schemes involved negotiations with heads of state for land grants and concessions. Foreign leaders had their own reasons for endorsing these programs. Haiti had traditionally offered itself as an asylum for blacks in the Western Hemisphere and in the 1820s wanted to create a buffer on its frontier with Santo Domingo (now the Dominican Republic) by settling African Americans there. Great Britain in the 1830s sought labor to work on the Trinidad plantations abandoned by the beneficiaries of its own emancipation laws, a need for which it later recruited workers from India.

CIVIL WAR AND RECOGNITION OF BLACK COUNTRIES

During the nineteenth century, slavery and its accompanying racist ideology prevented the United States from conducting full diplomatic relations with Haiti and Liberia, states modeled on modern republics that were populated and governed by blacks. Many U.S. diplomats did not believe it possible to consort with black counterparts on an equal basis and receive them into the polite society of the period. Proslavery southerners saw Haiti as anathema on social and political grounds and as a security problem. Some southern states passed laws that forbade the entry of sailors and other free people of color from Haiti. Before the Civil War, the U.S. government did not recognize Haiti and was represented there only by consuls. Southern secession removed the obstacles to recognition, which occurred on 12 July 1862 when the State Department appointed a chief of mission, Benjamin Whidden. In 1869, U.S. representation was raised to the ministerial level with the appointment of the first African American in such a post, Ebenezer Don Carlos Bassett. The defeat of the Confederacy and the abolition of slavery meant improvement in Haitian-American relations, ending the threat of slavery expansionism and filibustering raids on Haitian coasts. Beginning with Bassett's appointment, diplomatic and consular posts to Haiti and Liberia became patronage posts for loyal black Republicans, a pattern that persisted until well into the mid-twentieth century.

In the late nineteenth century, American activists sought to bring international attention to the lynching problem in the "Jim Crow" South. Hampered by lack of access to sources of state power, activists such as the anti-lynching advocate Ida B. Wells-Barnett searched for unconventional and less restrictive venues for international contact. Just as American activists had sought British support for abolition during the slavery era, Wells-Barnett toured the United Kingdom in 1893 and 1894 to publicize the lynching problem and bring the weight of British public opinion to bear on the issue. She devised another way to focus international attention on U.S. domestic affairs when, in 1893, Chicago hosted the Columbian Exposition, which brought visitors from all over the world. Through the mediation of Frederick Douglass, the government of Haiti selected Wells-Barnett to manage its exhibit and provided her with a table in the Haitian pavilion. There she sold copies of a book she had written to document lynching and the context in which it occurred. Wells-Barnett was thereby able to reach a wide audience in one of the first efforts to employ an international cultural festival to air concerns about U.S. race relations.

THE LEAGUE OF NATIONS AND THE PAN-AFRICAN CONGRESS

World War I shattered the balance of power in Europe and destroyed the Russian, German, Ottoman, and Austro-Hungarian empires. These state systems lost control of the diverse ethnic groups previously under their control. Subject nations and national minorities began demanding language rights, sovereignty, and democratic governments. When the Allies met in the Paris suburb of Versailles in 1919 to rebuild the world order, their agenda included the construction of nations in eastern Europe and the revitalization of

JIM CROW AND THE COLD WAR

"A vast literature has explored the major American cold war initiatives of the late 1940s and early 1950s. The decision-making processes and ramifications of the Truman Doctrine, the European Recovery Plan (Marshall Plan), the North Atlantic Treaty Organization (NATO), and National Security Council document 68 (NSC 68) have received painstaking analysis from a variety of political perspectives. But there has been only occasional attention paid either to the ways in which these policy initiatives emerged from a racially hierarchical domestic and international landscape or to their racial meanings and ramifications. Yet, people of color at the time were well aware of this other context. Winston Churchill's 'Iron Curtain' speech of February 1946 represented a declaration of cold war, but it also served as a call for Anglo-American racial and cultural unity. The Truman Doctrine of March 1947 opposed potential 'armed minorities' of the left but not those of the right who actually ruled much of the world: European colonialists. The Marshall Plan (1948) and NATO (1949) bolstered anticommunist governments west of the Elbe River but also indirectly funded their efforts at preserving white rule in Asia and Africa. NSC 68 laid out an offensive strategy of diminishing Soviet influence abroad, but it also revealed American anxieties about a broader 'absence of order among nations' that was 'becoming less and less tolerable' when the largest change in the international system was coming not from communist revolutions but from the decolonization of nonwhite peoples."

— From Thomas Borstelmann,
"Jim Crow's Coming Out: Race Relations
and American Foreign Policy in the
Truman Years," Presidential Studies
Quarterly 29, no. 3 (1999): 549–569 —

the empires that remained. European debates on political autonomy and territoriality were the model for Asians and Africans seeking to bring their own interests to world attention.

The Pan-African Congress was an important vehicle for formulating and disseminating such demands. The association emerged from a 1900 London conference. Organized by a Trinidadian attorney resident in London and an African-

American bishop, the congress brought together blacks from Britain and its colonies, the United States, and South Africa. The purpose was to discuss colonialism and racism and suggest strategies for reform. The association made little headway in its first twenty years, the zenith of European colonial domination of Africa. World War I provided an opportunity to renew its goals, however, and it planned a Paris conference that would convene simultaneously with the Versailles peace conference.

African-American leaders sought representation as observers at the peace conference and began discussing it before the war ended. Those most interested included the intellectual activist W. E. B. Du Bois, entrepreneur C. J. Walker, National Equal Rights League founder William Monroe Trotter, and activist Wells-Barnett. The Universal Negro Improvement Association, an international organization founded by Marcus Garvey, named delegates to the congress, including the labor leader A. Philip Randolph. Other interested organizations included the National Association for the Advancement of Colored People (NAACP) and the National Race Congress. The thinking was that if representatives of black organizations were denied admission to the proceedings or audiences with principals, they could use the Pan-African Congress and their proximity to the peace talks to bring their issues to public attention.

President Woodrow Wilson led the U.S. delegation at Versailles. Wilson believed in international organization and saw the peace conference as an opportunity to put the United States permanently at the center of power in the global community. Like other Allied leaders, Wilson wished to maintain control over national minorities. He was, additionally, a committed segregationist who as president of Princeton University had excluded African-American students from dormitories, and as president of the United States had separated federal civil servants by race, placing black employees behind partitions.

The Wilson administration did not want minority observers or protesters in Europe. The State Department accordingly refused passports to most of the black Americans wishing to go to France. Those who managed to cross the Atlantic attended a Pan-African Congress composed of fifty-seven delegates who discussed, under the careful scrutiny of the French government, such issues as the status of defeated Germany's colonies and colonial reform. The more militant civil rights activists and nationalists were less inter-ested in the Pan African Congress than in addressing the peace conference, the forum where decisions affecting the world's national minorities and subject peoples would be made. President Wilson was determined to prevent such initiatives. He refused to see either Trotter or a young Vietnamese leader, Nguyen That Thanh, later known as Ho Chi Minh. Wilson and British Prime Minister David Lloyd George prohibited the presence of delegates of colonized peoples and racial minorities at Versailles, but Du Bois succeeded in representing the NAACP at the first conference of the League of Nations in 1921.

THE ITALO-ETHIOPIAN WAR

In October 1935, Benito Mussolini's fascist Italy invaded Ethiopia. The war there occurred at the height of isolationist sentiment in the U.S. Congress and the nation at large. While public sympathy for Ethiopia was considerable, so was the disinclination to intervene. The minority that pressed for a more forthright stand included African Americans and Irish Catholics who broke with the Catholic majority on the issue. The administration of Franklin D. Roosevelt showed concern about Italian aggression, but domestic opposition to even rhetorical intervention discouraged firm action. When Secretary of State Cordell Hull and President Roosevelt sent Mussolini a note suggesting that the United States would not necessarily remain indifferent to what his government did in Africa, the message was so subdued that Mussolini readily dismissed it. A neutrality act banned the sale of finished war products to belligerents, but it did not deny them access to strategic materials, which could be purchased proportionately to the rate of prewar consumption. Italy, a growing industrial power, bought large quantities of American oil. Ethiopia, still feudal, bought none. The neutrality act thus helped ensure that Italy would be well equipped to defeat its decrepit adversary.

Administration officials shrank from the prospect of ventilating an issue that would bring down isolationist wrath. For actors at the policy center, domestic considerations and the ultimate collapse of Ethiopian resistance tabled the question for the duration of World War II. At the periphery, however, the Ethiopian issue enabled the development of linkages that remained timely. Ethiopia was a ready-made issue for black nationalists and permitted liberals and leftists to focus their general opposition to fascism. The Ethiopian government-in-exile played a leading role itself in keeping public interest alive through publicity campaigns and appeals for funds. It also made explicit appeals to African Americans as a usable pressure group. Ethiopia's experience with fascist conquest facilitated a sharper critique of racism and imperialism and focused postwar attention on the disposition of colonies in northeast Africa and colonialism in general.

GERMAN RECONSTRUCTION AND RACIAL SEGREGATION

In 1945 the Allies claimed victory over a German state that had taken racism to its logical extreme in the pursuit of eugenic purity and the destruction of millions of lives. African-American troops were part of the force that occupied Germany from 1945 to 1955, when efforts were made on all fronts to reform its institutions and reconstruct it physically. From the beginning of the occupation, U.S. racial practices in the military contradicted the essence of its mission in Germany and led to confusion and resentment among the conquered.

In the American zone of occupation, commanding officers could approve soldiers' marriages as they saw fit. Many of those holding conventional American ideas about race often prohibited mixed marriages even when children were involved. When individual soldiers appealed these prohibitions, military judges relied on the laws of the various U.S. states to determine whether a proposed union could be approved and compiled the relevant statutes for their own use. If a soldier resided in a state where interracial marriages were illegal, his application to marry outside his race would be turned down. Racial record keeping on marriages began in 1947. German courts followed this example. The Allies, having struck down the racist Nuremberg laws, oddly found themselves reapplying them in the American zone of occupation, where the German courts followed suit.

Military opposition to mixed marriages gradually declined, but in the interim approximately three thousand biracial children were born in Germany between 1945 and 1951, almost all the offspring of African-American servicemen. As a result of the continuing ambivalence among all parties about the children's prospects for adoption in the United States, the West German state, autonomous in 1955, was charged with the responsibility for absorbing them into German society. Germans witnessed the contradictions between U.S. opposition to nazi racism and policies governing intermarriage. The first cohort of biracial children reached their teens as violence associated with segregation in the United States made international headlines. While some Germans continued to believe that homes in the United States should be sought for those who were not already adopted, the prevailing opinion was that the orphans should not be sent into a society characterized by racial violence. If the United States' goal had been to transform Germany into a democracy characterized by tolerance, the biracial orphans provided them a paradoxical opportunity to show the world they had shed Hitlerism.

THE UNITED NATIONS PETITION

At the Dumbarton Oaks Conference in the autumn of 1944, delegates planned the foundations of a postwar international organization that would reprise the work of the League of Nations. Conferees rejected a racial and national equality clause that the Chinese government had put forward but failed to energetically defend. In the early years of the United Nations, efforts were made to insert ethnic and linguistic rights into the UN Charter and other central documents. Cold War tensions entered the deliberations of the Sub-Commission on Prevention of Discrimination and Protection of Minorities in the late 1940s, as many sovereign states proved reluctant to permit international oversight of their treatment of national minorities.

For African Americans in particular the era reflected a rising interest in social science and world affairs and the secularization of black protest that moved it away from philanthropic church control. Black opinion widely supported a pluralist United Nations that would counter the "Anglo-American" conception of a postwar peace elaborated by Winston Churchill in his Fulton, Missouri, "Iron Curtain" speech. While no blacks attended the 1945 United Nations Conference on International Organization in San Francisco, Walter White, secretary of the NAACP; W. E. B. Du Bois, the NAACP's director of special research; and Mary McLeod Bethune, of the National Council of Negro Women, were present as observers. Their attendance resulted from extensive organizing activities by black nongovernmental organizations to formulate an agenda for international activism. The black Republican Perry Howard urged blacks to send telegrams to their congressional representatives to demand that the UN Charter protect minority rights. Despite setbacks, the UN continued to be seen as a potentially useful instrument in checking Western abuses of national minorities and colonial subjects. In 1948 the chair of the Baltimore chapter of the NAACP urged UN Secretary-General Trygve Lie to reject the University of Maryland's offer to house the Food and Agricultural Organization (FAO). Segregation at the institution, including its college of agriculture, would inconvenience FAO personnel from non-European countries.

Attempts in 1945 to influence the United Nations to protect minority rights were among the first of several efforts. Backed by labor, professional, fraternal, and veterans' associations, the National Negro Congress drafted a petition to the United Nations in mid-1946. It was formulated at the same time that similar petitions were being presented by Indonesians and the Jewish diaspora, and shortly before the General Assembly voted to censure South Africa for its treatment of its East Indian resident population. Encouraged by parallel international events, the NAACP followed suit with its own petition in 1947. The NAACP asked the UN Commission on Human Rights to investigate racial discrimination in the United States. Supported by hundreds of black organizations across the political spectrum, and by African and Caribbean nationalists and labor federations overseas, the appeal was also viewed favorably by India, Pakistan, Egypt, Ethiopia, Belgium, Haiti, Norway, China (Formosa), and the USSR, which introduced the petition in October 1947. Despite its popularity with the black public in the United States and international endorsement, the petition died in the Sub-Commission on Prevention of Discrimination and Protection of Minorities. Pressure applied on the United Nations by the United States, the influence of Eleanor Roosevelt, then a UNESCO commissioner, and misgivings among certain NAACP officials about Soviet support of the appeal, led to its demise.

RACIAL REFORM AND COLD WAR IDEOLOGY

The U.S. rivalry with the Soviet Union and its Cold War partners involved political as well as military competition. President Harry S. Truman articulated the need to improve U.S. race relations not only because the Soviets were exploiting the race issue but also because U.S. credibility was at stake. Truman and his successor, Dwight D. Eisenhower, articulated a need for reform and coupled this with the same repression of black communists and other radical black critics of America that generally characterized the early Cold War period in U.S. society. Such activists as Du Bois and Paul Robeson were refused passports. U.S. representatives abroad interfered with American-born dancer Josephine Baker, a French citizen and an outspoken critic of U.S. racial mores. The Eisenhower administration, committed to the reduction of military spending but putting greater emphasis on promoting the economic and cultural superiority of American life, had come to associate winning the Cold War with improving the civil rights climate for black Americans. While Eisenhower was not enthusiastic about desegregation, he was committed enough to the principle of civil equality to support a modest civil rights bill in 1957.

The belief that America's ability to champion democracy depended on its success at practicing it at home continued during the Kennedy years. The Cold War rationale for racial reform was strengthened by evidence that hostile countries utilized negative news about race relations to discredit the United States. In an increasingly decolonized world, where Africans and Asians now headed sovereign states, racial discrimination could no longer be endorsed or accepted. Technological change meant that journalists could record instances of racial violence and broadcast them to the world. The Soviet Union and its allies were not the only critics. Disapproval emanated from non-aligned countries, especially India, and from such conventional Western states as Denmark. In contrast to the world press, pro-apartheid South African journalists played up racial incidents in the United States, especially the exploits of white supremacists. This also constituted part of the embarrassment that necessitated a significant propaganda effort to neutralize damaging racial news stories about segregation.

Members of the intelligentsia and business communities also employed arguments that linked foreign and domestic affairs. In September 1950, for example, the NAACP convened the Breakneck Hill Conference, where senators, UN officials, journalists and broadcast executives, State Department representatives, educators, and activists considered the impact of racial discrimination on the nation's foreign policy objectives. Civil rights proponents, including participants in sit-ins and other demonstrations in the 1960s, also used Cold War arguments to rationalize their challenge to discriminatory statutes. Segregation tainted the U.S. reputation abroad, they claimed, and the limited opportunities for minorities that resulted from it meant fewer human resources available to defend the nation and extend its interests.

U.S. government efforts to counter the bad publicity involved activities sponsored by the State Department and the United States Information Agency (USIA). These included providing news to international readers, stocking U.S. libraries abroad with what was perceived as balanced information about black life in the United States, and enlisting African-American lecturers and entertainers to travel abroad and entertain or provide information to interested foreigners. Some individuals who toured foreign countries for this purpose sometimes exaggerated the amount of progress made in race relations. The State Department and USIA, for their part, did not deny the existence of racism but rather emphasized what they portrayed as a national commitment to effect change through nonviolent means. The appointment in 1964 of the African-American journalist Carl Rowan as USIA director was intended to emphasize the latter. Rowan had previously served as deputy assistant secretary of state for public affairs and as ambassador to Finland.

AFRICAN AMERICANS AND THE DIPLOMATIC CORPS

The civil rights movement presented the State Department and other government branches not only with the problem of trying to counter America's racist image abroad but also that of dealing with discrimination within their own ranks. Since Reconstruction, most African-American consuls, ministers, and ambassadors had been political appointees posted to black countries. The number of career black foreign service officers and consular officials remained minuscule until the second half of the twentieth century. The State Department, an executive department in a staunchly segregated capital, steadfastly resisted integration. In addition to racial segregation, its institutional culture traditionally relied on eastern elites. The democratization of the State Department through geographic and demo-

graphic diversification evolved only gradually. Its racial desegregation occurred chiefly at the initiative of presidential administrations and informal pressure from black leadership.

Civil rights organizations had expressed dissatisfaction with the unrepresentative character of the State Department since the 1940s, but changes were desultory until the early 1960s. The Kennedy White House, seeking to consolidate its gains with the African-American electorate while maintaining a moderate posture on civil rights, looked to Africa for the solution. Well-publicized visits from African heads of state and the appointment of African Americans to diplomatic posts provided the symbolic politics the situation required. The United States would also realize the additional benefit of encouraging ostensibly nonaligned African states to view the West more favorably and limit their contacts with Warsaw Pact states. The State Department remained slow to change, however, and only after criticism of the pace and scope of reform accelerated were significant numbers of African-American diplomatic representatives named to countries outside Africa and the Caribbean.

In line with the perceived need to court newly independent African states and encourage them to maintain close ties with the West, U.S. officials tried to insulate U.S. foreign relations from the repercussions of domestic racism by assisting diplomats from Africa, the Caribbean, and other regions who encountered discrimination while living and traveling in the United States. In the 1950s and early 1960s, negative experiences of foreign envoys chiefly involved the refusal of service to Africans (as well as South Asians and others) in states where segregation was official, the relegation of nonwhites to Jim Crow sections of public facilities, and housing discrimination in states ranging from New York to Virginia.

Initially, the State Department dealt with the problem by attempting to isolate foreign blacks from African Americans, a task facilitated by the nature of diplomatic relations. Nonwhite envoys could, for example, simply be exempted from segregation laws by virtue of their status. Federal officials could intervene in particular cases, but they were not always present when visitors experienced embarrassments. When the Ghanaian finance minister was denied service at a Delaware restaurant in 1957, Eisenhower invited him to breakfast at the White House, and Vice President Richard Nixon sent him a formal apology. The

State Department discussed the matter with the restaurant's franchisee. The most serious incident was the beating of a Guinean foreign service officer by New York City police officers following a traffic accident. The presence of nonwhite envoys also forced adjustments in the elite social life of Washington. State Department chief of protocol Angier Biddle Duke resigned in 1961 from the prestigious Metropolitan Club because of its refusal to continue extending what had previously been automatic membership to foreign diplomats and its absence of black members.

To be sure, another consideration that drove reform within the diplomatic corps was the awareness that segregation as a whole made a bad impression on foreigners regardless of race. As early as June 1951, the solicitor general of the United States, Philip Perlman, filed an amicus curiae brief in a U.S. Court of Appeals case that involved a Washington, D.C., restaurant's refusal of service to a U.S. citizen on racial grounds. Perlman argued that foreigners judge the United States by their experiences in its capital and that segregation marred the image of American democracy. The solicitor general thus linked the reform of racial policies in the United States to the nation's best interests abroad.

In August 1961 the Kennedy administration created a task force composed of representatives from the White House, State Department, and local state governments to address the problem of racial discrimination. Because of local entrepreneurs' inability to distinguish between Africans and African Americans and favor the former, public facilities along the Washington-Maryland corridor ultimately had to be desegregated for everyone.

THE VIETNAM WAR

African-American opposition to the war in Vietnam, the overriding U.S. foreign policy concern of the 1960s and early 1970s, reflected perceptions of self-interest. During the 1950s the major civil rights organizations had stopped taking action on foreign policy questions. As the war escalated, civil rights leaders feared both the loss of organizational revenues if prowar advocates withdrew their support and the prospect of internal friction among organizations over the peace issue. Anxiety about possible accusations of subversion, and concern lest the civil rights focus be dissipated, were other causes of apprehension. The immediacy of

civil rights insurgency in the South provided a powerful pretext for channeling organizational energies to domestic questions only.

Moreover, by the mid-1960s the reluctance of black leaders to engage in issues apart from domestic civil rights was reinforced by an increasingly beleaguered presidential administration fighting to maintain a "one voice" approach for U.S. foreign policy around the globe. President Lyndon B. Johnson, for whom Africa was a low priority, particularly opposed the consolidation of an African-American foreign policy constituency. Johnson did not want to multiply the number of players in international affairs and perceived such a constituency as contradicting the goal of fully integrating blacks into American life. Johnson believed that racially and ethnically based interest groups generally fragmented what should be a unitary national position on foreign affairs as government experts defined them.

In 1965, however, the Mississippi Freedom Democratic Party, at the center of some of the most sweeping changes in American society, publicly advocated draft resistance. The Student Nonviolent Coordinating Committee became the first national body to oppose the war. While antiwar sentiment did not overtake the black majority until 1969, activist organizations mounted pressure on Martin Luther King, Jr., to take a stand. Vietnamese Buddhists who sent him an "open letter" joined with domestic war critics in urging action. In 1967, King formally reiterated his inability to square the war with his conscience, his belief that the war was sapping the economic and spiritual vigor of the country, and his conviction that the national mission needed redefinition. In an April speech at the Riverside Church in New York City, King delivered a radical critique of U.S. foreign policy.

Ultimately, Vietnam was a broad enough issue to absorb many of the questions that had long preoccupied African Americans. Critiques of the war called into question the integrity of the political process and opened the door to large-scale insurgency. On this issue black foreign policy audiences entered the controversy late, had dwindling access to increasingly less responsive policymakers, and were considerably alienated from "normal politics." Their efforts to influence the conduct of the war were also hampered by strategies that were based on addressing legislatures and courts rather than executive officials.

The spirit of insurgency in the late 1960s combined with new global media to afford

African-American activists new forums for international exposure to U.S. domestic problems. One of the most prominent examples was the 1968 Olympic Games in Mexico City, from which South Africa had been excluded owing to worldwide opposition to that country's apartheid policy. Certain African-American athletes had contemplated a boycott of the games because of their dissatisfaction with racial conditions in the United States, but they ultimately decided to participate. African-American medalists Tommie Smith and John Carlos, feeling the need to make at least a symbolic gesture, raised their fists in protest at U.S. racial injustice as the "Star-Spangled Banner" was being played. Both athletes were widely criticized and their careers were destroyed. In an ironic twist in 1980, the U.S. government asked African-American boxing champion Muhammad Ali to persuade various countries to boycott the 1980 Olympics in Moscow.

the 1980s to an international protest movement against apartheid. Anti-apartheid activists set out to discourage artist exchanges in the belief that they had no effect on apartheid, degraded the artist involved, and lent credibility to the South African regime. Through adverse publicity and boycott, many U.S. entertainers were pressured into avoiding South Africa. Similar actions were mounted when the South African government sent African troupes to the United States if they apologized for conditions in their homeland.

Pressure from advocacy groups was a crucial factor in leading the United States to impose economic sanctions against South Africa in the 1980s. Thus, in February 1990, South African President F. W. de Klerk released the African National Congress leader Nelson Mandela from his twenty-seven-year imprisonment, and in March 1992 white South Africans passed a referendum that would end white minority rule.

SOUTH AFRICA

By the mid-1950s, only in South Africa could U.S. diplomats be committed and outspoken racists. The State Department sent envoys to South Africa whose own outlook aligned closely with that of their hosts. In light of U.S. reliance on South African raw materials, mutual anticommunism, and interest in free trade, policymakers acquiesced to South African segregation laws that paralleled those that were still current in the United States. As civil rights insurgency and changing views toward race worldwide eroded segregation at home, U.S. official acceptance of South African racial practices could no longer be direct. Washington attempted to distance itself rhetorically from apartheid while continuing harmonious relations with South Africa.

As noted, the State Department and USIA often sponsored goodwill tours of African-American entertainers to foreign countries, and these included South Africa. U.S. authorities may have believed that exposure to the diversity of U.S. society would give proponents of apartheid pause. Visits to South Africa by American performers were not limited to government-sponsored ventures. South African promoters signed U.S. artists to lucrative contracts, but they were often required to perform before segregated audiences.

The gap between U.S. democratic beliefs on one hand, and government and private sector ties to the South African regime on the other, led in

BIBLIOGRAPHY

Ahrari, Mohammed E., ed. *Ethnic Groups and U.S. Foreign Policy.* New York, 1987.

Blackett, R. J. M. *Building an Antislavery Wall: Black Americans in the Atlantic Abolitionist Movement, 1830–1860.* Baton Rouge, La., 1983.

Borstelmann, Thomas. *Apartheid's Reluctant Uncle.* New York, 1993.

Collum, Danny Duncan, ed. *African Americans in the Spanish Civil War: "This Ain't Ethiopia, but It'll Do."* New York, 1992.

DeConde, Alexander. *Ethnicity, Race, and American Foreign Policy: A History.* Boston, 1992.

Du Bois, W. E. B. "Inter-Racial Implications of the Ethiopian Crisis: A Negro View." *Foreign Affairs* 14 (October 1935): 82–92.

Dudziak, Mary L. "Desegregation as a Cold War Imperative." *Stanford Law Review* 41 (November 1988): 61–120.

———. *Cold War Civil Rights.* Princeton, N.J., 2000.

Fairclough, Adam. "Martin Luther King Jr. and the War in Vietnam." *Phylon* 45, no. 1 (1984): 19–39.

Füredi, Frank. *The Silent War: Imperialism and the Changing Perception of Race.* New Brunswick, N.J., 1998.

Gatewood, Willard B. *Black Americans and the White Man's Burden, 1898–1903.* Urbana, Ill., 1975.

Hannaford, Ivan. *Race: The History of an Idea in the West.* Washington, D.C., 1996.

Harris, Robert L., Jr. "Racial Equality and the United Nations Charter." In Armstead L. Robinson and Patricia Sullivan, eds. *New Directions in Civil Rights Studies.* Charlottesville, Va., 1991.

Horne, Gerald. *Black and Red: W. E. B. Du Bois and the Afro-American Response to the Cold War, 1944–1963.* Albany, N.Y., 1986.

Hunt, Michael H. *Ideology and U.S. Foreign Policy.* New Haven, Conn., 1987.

Isaacs, Harold Robert. *The New World of Negro Americans.* New York, 1964.

Krenn, Michael L. *Black Diplomacy: African Americans and the State Department, 1945–1969.* Armonk, N.Y., 1999.

Krenn, Michael L., ed. *The Impact of Race on U.S. Foreign Policy: A Reader.* New York, 1999.

Lauren, Paul Gordon. *Power and Prejudice: The Politics and Diplomacy of Racial Discrimination.* 2d ed. Boulder, Colo., 1996.

Lockwood, Bert, Jr. "The UN Charter and U.S. Civil Rights Litigation: 1946–1955." *Iowa Law Review* 5 (1984): 901–956.

Noer, Thomas J. *Cold War and Black Liberation: The United States and White Rule in Africa, 1948–1968.* Columbia, Mo., 1985.

Plummer, Brenda G. *Rising Wind: Black Americans and U.S. Foreign Affairs, 1935–1960.* Chapel Hill, N.C., 1996.

Smith, Tony. *Foreign Attachments: The Power of Ethnic Groups in the Making of American Foreign Policy.* Cambridge, Mass., 2000.

Weston, Rubin Francis. *Racism in U.S. Imperialism: The Influence of Racial Assumptions on American Foreign Policy, 1893–1946.* Columbia, S.C., 1972.

See also CIVIL WAR DIPLOMACY; PEACE MOVEMENTS; RACE AND ETHNICITY.

ALLIANCES, COALITIONS, AND ENTENTES

Warren F. Kimball

During the end of the 1990s, globalism for most Americans meant an exhilarating combination of political security and economic prosperity. The Cold War had dissipated, while wages and profits seemed on an endless uptick. Intervention in a new outbreak of the Balkan wars came in association with some of the major western European states and partly under the aegis of NATO, but the reaction against the U.S. bombing of Belgrade illustrated just how tenuous alliance policy really was. For the administration of President Bill Clinton and most Americans, globalism did not mean becoming the world's police officer, or even joining a police force with worldwide responsibilities. The United Nations was not an alliance.

But on 11 September 2001, globalism took on a new meaning. The suicide attacks by nineteen Muslim terrorists on the World Trade Center in New York City and the Pentagon in the District of Columbia demonstrated that America's comfort zone, that sense of political security originally fostered by time and distance across oceans, no longer existed—not even as wishful thinking. The long-held belief in American invulnerability, enhanced by modern technology and dreams of Star War–like defenses that could not be breached, collapsed along with the twin towers of the World Trade Center.

The initial response by the administration of George W. Bush was to seek revenge under the guise of "infinite justice." But that quickly gave way to the realities of identifying, locating, and either capturing or executing those who planned the hijacking of the commercial aircraft that flew into the towers and the Pentagon and their use as fuel-laden missiles. The implications of what could appear to be a "crusade" against Islam, particularly for U.S. oil policy in the Middle East, had a chastening influence, and American opinion seemed to move slowly but firmly against rash action. The administration acknowledged the difficulties and began the process of preparing the public for a long-term "war against terrorism."

Diplomats, led by Secretary of State Colin Powell, fanned out around the globe in an attempt to persuade, cajole, and even bribe (with foreign aid) other states to join the war effort as allies. Two old Cold War alliances, NATO and ANZUS, each formally declared the terrorist actions an attack on the entire alliance—invoking for the first time the "an attack on one is an attack on all" clause in each treaty. Even France, seen so often as hypercritical of the United States, praised President Bush for acting in a measured, responsible fashion. The Russian Federation, with its own history of concern about Islamic political influence (Afghanistan, Chechnya), led the way for new partners in the alliance against terrorism. And the United Nations Security Council passed an emergency resolution mandating that all members assist in the international effort against such terrorist attacks. Even China agreed. Islamic nations likewise condemned the attacks but backed away from allowing the United States to launch military operations from their territory against terrorists, while in Indonesia and Pakistan there were organized public demonstrations against the United States. Clearly, nearly all states recognized that terrorism posed a deep and frightening threat to the nation-state. The immediate aftermath of the World Trade Center and Pentagon attacks was history's most remarkable example of global cooperation. But for how long? During World War II, President Franklin D. Roosevelt understood that the Soviet Union was indispensable to victory, but that alliance did not survive the end of the common crisis. How the United States came to the point of making its twenty-first-century decision on globalism is buried, but not hidden, in the past.

THE TRADITIONAL VIEW

American reluctance to participate in alliances, coalitions, and ententes was traditional until

World War II. According to the conventional wisdom, in 1778, out of sheer necessity, but remembering the colonial experience of being dragged into European wars, the revolutionary leaders unhappily agreed to sign a political alliance with France. Some twenty years later, when that treaty seemingly forced the young American nation to choose between the two great antagonists in the Anglo-French conflict in Europe, the United States repudiated that alliance, fought a brief and undeclared war to make that repudiation stick, and then, embittered by the brief experience with "European-style" alliances, swore off such political activity forever. In his Farewell Address, George Washington warned against "permanent alliances," and in an inaugural address Thomas Jefferson provided the slogan that Americans seem always to need for a policy—"entangling alliances with none."

For a hundred and fifteen years, until World War I, the American nation refused to indulge in the kind of international alliance politics that characterized European diplomacy. Even then, once propelled into the Great War, the United States took the moral high ground and refused to accept full membership as an ally in the coalition against the Central Powers, opting instead for the label "associated power." Disillusioned and angered by the selfishness that the European powers exhibited during the 1919 Paris Peace Conference, the United States attempted to withdraw from the international arena during the interwar period, only to be forced by Japanese and German aggression to come again to the rescue of the civilized world. The events of World War II forced the United States into what became a long-term alliance with Great Britain and a very short-term one with the Soviet Union. Then, as Cold War tensions mounted, the U.S. government negotiated a series of defensive mutual security alliances aimed at protecting the "free" world against Russian (communist) aggression.

Reluctant participation is clearly the tone of the entire story. Perhaps the thrust of generally accepted interpretations was best summarized by Thomas A. Bailey in his extraordinarily popular text *A Diplomatic History of the American People*: "The United States cannot afford to leave the world alone because the world will not leave it alone." In other words, historians have treated coalition and alliance diplomacy as part and parcel of the story of America's traditional isolationism.

TERMINOLOGY

Although the American public has never drawn sharp distinctions between alliances, coalitions, and ententes, its leaders have frequently acted in a way that indicated that they understood the differences. Alliances are properly formal agreements between nations that call for specific joint action and responses to given political situations. They can be outlined verbally, but they are normally committed to paper and are, therefore, recognized in international law. Although alliances relate to wartime situations, they are usually concluded in times of peace and last for significant periods of time.

Coalitions bring to mind the various European joint efforts against France in the late eighteenth and early nineteenth centuries. Those wars saw various nations unite in military action against France frequently only after the fighting had actually begun. Short term and often not defined by written agreements, coalitions aim simply at the military defeat of a common enemy and do not relate to postwar considerations. Although the term is rarely applied, Russo-American cooperation during World War II against Nazi Germany was a coalition rather than an alliance. The only common ground was military victory over the enemy, and attempts by both nations to expand that limited relationship met with failure.

Entente, properly used, describes a far deeper relationship between nations than either alliance or coalition. An entente becomes possible only when two or more nations share a set of political goals and perceptions. The most obvious entente in American history has been the one that began to develop between Great Britain and the United States after the War of 1812. Frequently subjected to great strains, that entente was formalized as an alliance during World War II and the Cold War era. Such an entente is more a friendship than an alliance or coalition stimulated by sheer power politics, although the realities of international relations are never completely ignored.

REVOLUTIONARY DIPLOMACY: THE NECESSARY ALLIANCE

Historians have frequently argued that America's antipathy to political involvement with Europe originated with the colonial experiences, when

European wars spread to the Western Hemisphere. Yet even a cursory glance at colonial newspapers indicates that the English settlers in America viewed the wars with France and Spain as their own. Historians agree that the colonials considered themselves Englishmen right up until the American Revolution began, and there is no evidence to show that this feeling did not extend to England's wars as well. Reluctance to pay war taxes proves nothing; taxes are generally unpopular at any time. The peace settlements negotiated by the English may have angered the colonists, but only because the treaties seemed to give more benefits to the French or Spanish than the American colonists thought necessary. Even after the revolutionary war had begun in earnest, many American leaders could not bring themselves to negotiate any sort of alliance with their traditional enemy—France.

What American leaders sought was not isolation but rather situations that clearly benefited national interests. Born into a world of traditional alliances and coalitions, the new American nation chose to avoid such associations not out of any moral or philosophical judgments, although such rhetoric abounded, but because, at least temporarily, an independent policy seemed to promise greater rewards. Thomas Paine, often misinterpreted as recommending isolation, made his point clear in the pamphlet *Common Sense* (1776):

> Any submission to, or dependence on Great Britain, tends directly to involve this Continent in European wars and quarrels, and set us at variance with nations who would otherwise seek our friendship, and against whom we have neither anger nor complaint. As Europe is our market for trade, we ought to form no partial connection with any part of it. It is the true interest of America to steer clear of European contentions, which she can never do, while, by her dependence on Britain, she is made the make-weight in the scale of British politics.

Paine, who soon became impatient with the Revolution's conservatism, argued not for isolation but for a policy of impartiality designed to open all of Europe's markets to American trade. That policy, which soon stimulated America's strong support of neutral rights, hardly represented a new departure in foreign policy. The smaller nations of the world have always attempted to avoid choosing sides in struggles between the greater powers, although sheer geographic gravity made that rarely possible in Europe's history.

The debates among the revolutionary leaders over broad guidelines for American diplomats, discussions that culminated in the Model Treaty of 1776, illustrate the distinctions made by Paine. Despite the precarious military situation, some argued for only a commercial connection with France. Led by John Adams, these men obviously feared that the presence of French troops in America would mean merely swapping one imperial master for another. Although Adams's statements were couched in the broad, sweeping terms so popular with Enlightenment thinkers, his objections stemmed from two factors: his practical appraisal of America's political weakness and economic needs and his intense distrust of French motives—a distrust he held in common with his fellow New Englanders. Despite Americans' claims that they stood for a new approach to world politics—a *novus ordo seculorum*—they had adopted policies that were merely variations of the realistic power politics of the Europe they professed to scorn. When military necessity forced the Continental Congress to seek a military alliance with France in 1778, the terms of that treaty were not fundamentally different from alliances negotiated by European nations. The French intended the United States to become a permanent client-state of His Christian Majesty, a sentiment embodied in a clause stating that the alliance would last "from the present time and forever." A plea from the United States to Spain for a similar treaty of alliance was ignored.

Nor did the United States go about alliance diplomacy any differently than its European predecessors. The peace negotiations aimed at ending the revolutionary war found the Americans as deceptive as France. Interpreting the alliance with France as selectively binding, Benjamin Franklin, John Adams, and John Jay negotiated an effective and separate treaty of peace with the British—a violation of their agreement with France. Although they justified their actions by pointing out that France had intended to betray the United States, their argument contrasts sharply with the self-righteous claims that America would practice a new diplomacy in which, to quote Adams, "the dignity of North America . . . consists solely in reason, justice, truth, the rights of mankind, and the interests of the nations of Europe." Ironically, Franklin—a man with long experience in the world of eighteenth-century diplomacy—opposed such a violation of treaty obligations, while Adams demanded that they open negotiations with the British.

Although the treaties of alliance and commerce with France represented no breakthrough into some sort of new diplomacy, American leaders, particularly the New Englanders, viewed the new nation's diplomacy as somehow flowing from values and purposes different from those of Europe. Distracted by the social implications that went with their repudiation of an aristocratic class, many Americans confused diplomatic forms with substance. Refusal to dress like European diplomats became equated with a refusal to indulge in European-style power politics.

That image proved to be longer lasting than the alliance with France. The rhetoric of America's uniqueness and exceptionalism, something common among young, intensely nationalistic nations, meshed neatly with the notion that the United States practiced a new form of diplomacy. In reality, the only thing new about America's diplomacy was that geography permitted it to remain aloof from the constantly shifting balance of power in Europe. Hence, the decision not to join the League of Armed Neutrality was made because it was thought that the league offered no benefits to America, not because of any ideological opposition to taking sides.

By the mid-1790s, the French Alliance had become a detriment to the young republic. With the outbreak of the wars of the French Revolution, soon to merge into the Napoleonic wars, Presidents George Washington and John Adams feared that the United States would be drawn into a conflict in which it had no interest. Again myth overtook reality. French restrictions on American naval freedom appeared to be a direct retaliation for the refusal of the United States to live up to its treaty obligations, whereas the reality was that the French Directory believed that the recently negotiated commercial treaty between Britain and America (Jay's Treaty) contained secret clauses that amounted to a political alliance. The treaty contained no such political commitments, but the French argument struck home. When great powers go to war, neutrals can maintain their trade only at the risk of losing any claim to impartial economic policies. Although the United States did not sign Jay's Treaty as part of an anti-French policy, the French quite logically believed the opposite. Historians have argued that Washington's famous Farewell Address sprang primarily from domestic political considerations, but it was the awkward confrontation with France—including attempts by the French directly to influence American elections—that clearly stimulated his

warning against alliances. Washington included a caveat that Americans soon forgot; he warned only against "artificial" connections with Europe, not ones that were natural and in the national interest. Since the Quasi-War with France followed soon after Washington's warning, Americans tended to view the address as an accurate prediction of the outcome of U.S. involvement in European alliances. The economic consequences that might have followed any American attempt to maintain real impartiality—something that would have required economic isolation—were forgotten.

JEFFERSONIAN REALISM

Thomas Jefferson obviously understood the difference between artificial and natural connections with Europe. His condemnation of "entangling" alliances referred to involvements in European politics, not to the defense of American interests. When, in 1802, France seemed about to occupy the Louisiana Territory, striking a wedge between the United States and land that many Americans assumed was destined to become part of the United States, Jefferson's thoughts turned to plans of alliance with Great Britain. The Louisiana Purchase made that unnecessary, and Jefferson then followed policies that subtly favored France in its conflict with the British. His reasoning was simple and logical: only the English had a fleet large enough to pose a military threat to the United States, and, hence, they were America's only potential enemy of substance. But none of his talk of alliance or his attempts to play at a timid and small form of alliance politics came to public attention. With "no entangling alliances" already a tradition, domestic political considerations made Jefferson keep such thoughts to himself and his closest advisers.

After a brief period of peace beginning with the Treaty of Amiens (1802), the Napoleonic wars started anew in 1803. Again the United States found itself caught between two great powers. As both England and France turned increasingly to economic warfare, American attempts to maintain business as usual were less and less successful. Frustrated in his attempts to negotiate arrangements that would permit American foreign trade to continue without harassment, Jefferson overestimated the value of that trade to the European powers and also turned to economic coercion. An embargo prevented all American ships from sailing to foreign destinations but drove home the lesson of America's economic dependence upon trade with Europe—a lesson statesmen have never forgotten.

IN ENGLAND'S WAKE: THE NINETEENTH CENTURY

The United States eventually became involved in the Napoleonic wars. Logic demanded that the nation choose one side or the other, but tradition, past experience, and the intense national division over the foreign policies of Jefferson and his successor, James Madison, made the decision difficult. George Washington had already become the nation's father figure, and no leader could ignore such pronouncements as the Farewell Address with impunity. Moreover, the unhappy experience with the French alliance made both politicians and the public cautious. More important, however, was the domestic political tug-of-war regarding foreign policy. Although President Madison and his supporters had strong sympathies for France, to have suggested an alliance with Napoleon would have confirmed the accusations of the Federalists, who claimed that the president had called for war to aid France, not to defend American interests. Since French violations of neutral rights had been as flagrant as those committed by England, that argument seemed plausible. So the United States entered the war against Britain, but without any alliance with France—a technique that the nation followed again in World War I a hundred years later.

The combination of luck and domestic politics that kept the United States out of a formal alliance with France in 1812 also made it possible for war-weary England to extend remarkably generous peace terms to the Americans. Despite an almost unbroken string of military defeats, the American public viewed the war as a great victory, thus adding to the tradition and myth that the United States need not and should not enter into alliances.

In the years immediately after the Treaty of Ghent (1815), the United States followed a foreign policy that took advantage of the European political situation. Designed and implemented primarily by Secretary of State John Quincy Adams, the policy took shrewd advantage of Europe's economic and psychological exhaustion following the defeat of Napoleon, of the Latin American revolts against Spain, of geography, and

of the British desire to keep European power politics restricted to Europe. When the Latin American colonies revolted against Spain, the threat of intervention by the Holy Alliance (Russia, Prussia, Austria, and France) made Adams reconsider his earlier rejection of a British offer of an alliance. Nevertheless, Adams finally concluded, correctly, that England would act to keep other European countries out of the Western Hemisphere with or without an alliance with the United States, and he again spurned the offer. The British obtained a commitment from the French that they would not permit their fleet to be used for any transfer of Holy Alliance troops to Latin America. Once again American leaders had examined the possibility of entering into an alliance but had rejected that move; not because of tradition, but because a careful appraisal of the situation convinced them that such an alliance was simply unnecessary.

But it is out of such stuff that traditions are made. President James Monroe's Doctrine for the Western Hemisphere (1823) made British policy appear to be a function of American diplomacy. John Quincy Adams knew full well the emptiness of any threat from the Holy Alliance, but the American public treated the entire episode as proof of their nation's ability to solve its international problems without help. And so the United States proceeded through the nineteenth century armed with Washington's advice and a conviction that there was no need to play balance-of-power politics with the European nations.

British foreign policy continued to make such beliefs come true. Great Britain, busy in Europe and Asia, hoped to see the United States restricted in size and power, but never did the potential gains of such desires warrant the use of military force to ensure that they materialized. British leaders encouraged the Texans to remain independent after 1836, tried to hold onto the Oregon country, and hoped for a Confederate victory during the American Civil War, but whenever the U.S. government threatened to respond with force, the British backed away from the confrontation. Unwilling to fight the Americans, British statesmen repeatedly, if reluctantly, chose policies designed to make a friend of the United States.

At the same time two events served to fortify America's opposition to alliance diplomacy. The bloody and inconclusive Crimean War during the late 1850s seemed to demonstrate the bankruptcy of the European alliances, and the withdrawal of French troops from Mexico in 1867 indicated once again that the United States could itself deal with the "untrustworthy" European powers. The alliance system developed after 1871 by German Chancellor Otto von Bismarck only led American statesmen to condemn further such power politics.

THEODORE ROOSEVELT AND AMERICA'S DESTINY

By the end of the nineteenth century, American policymakers and political writers were convinced that alliances, coalitions, and ententes were all part of a dangerous concept of international relations. Convinced that alliances caused wars rather than prevented them, Americans looked upon the European political scene with contempt. Yet, at the same time, a small group of statesmen-politicians led by such ultranationalists as Henry Cabot Lodge, Albert Beveridge, and Theodore Roosevelt concluded that its size and economic power made it necessary for the United States to play an active role in international politics. As Theodore Roosevelt put it: "We have no choice, we the people of the United States, as to whether or not we shall play a great part in the world. That has been decided for us by fate, by the march of events. We have to play that part. All that we can decide is whether we shall play it well or ill."

With Roosevelt as president from 1901 through 1909, the United States had, for the first time as chief executive, a man who saw the nation's mission as much more than merely an example to others. Roosevelt—taking his cue from the social Darwinists, but adding an optimism based on the American experience—saw America's role in the world as unique and tinged with messianic destiny. He not only believed the United States was a nation with international responsibilities, he also unquestioningly embraced the idea that the fate of mankind depended upon America's willingness to accept those responsibilities. Roosevelt saw no need for anything less than American superiority in the Western Hemisphere, but he sought to avoid antagonizing Great Britain in the process. The community of Anglo-American interests had been growing since 1815, but not until Roosevelt's presidency did the government establish a strong, if unofficial, entente with Great Britain. Roosevelt's prejudice in favor of Anglo-Saxon "civilization" as well as his realistic appraisal of America's economic and military interests resulted in American influence invariably but-

tressing British goals in Europe. Roosevelt was not alone, as can be seen by such editorials as appeared in *Harper's Weekly* openly advocating American participation in the Anglo-French entente. Although Roosevelt, largely because of domestic politics, did not heed such advice, he supported various British attempts to dominate the European balance of power, the best example being his secret diplomacy during the Moroccan crisis of 1905–1906.

The political situation in Asia concerned Roosevelt deeply. Convinced that the United States had to act like a Pacific Ocean power, he even expressed a vague desire for America to join the Anglo-Japanese alliance, which was designed to delineate British and Japanese interests in China and to halt Russian expansion in the area. Although such active participation in an alliance seemed politically impossible, Roosevelt attained that goal in part without any domestic struggle. His role as peacemaker during the Russo-Japanese War found him privately applying diplomatic pressure; yet the American public, still committed to nonentanglement, approved what appeared to be a role of disinterested and uninvolved organizer of a successful peace conference. From 1905 through 1908, American and Japanese representatives held almost continuous talks about other mutual problems. Although the discussions were frequently unpleasant, a special relationship developed between the two nations. Roosevelt firmly believed that Japanese-American cooperation—the beginnings of entente—would bring peace, order, and stability to East Asia; and, as part of that policy, he recognized Japanese spheres of influence in Korea and northern China.

Roosevelt committed the United States to an active role in international affairs—a commitment that had been growing out of American power as well as his actions—and put the nation on a path that could not be reversed regardless of the rhetoric of isolation and the natural desire to avoid the responsibilities that accompanied the thrill of world power. His successors, William Howard Taft and Woodrow Wilson, reversed his policies toward Japan (with dire consequences), but the commitment to an active international role remained.

THE TRAUMA OF WORLD WAR I

On 6 April 1917 the United States formally joined a wartime coalition for the first time in its history. In refusing actually to join the Anglo-French-Russian alliance, President Woodrow Wilson hoped to avoid even an implied commitment to the many secret treaties that provided for the division of the spoils among the Allied Powers, although he also realized that American public opinion would support the idea of continuing some measure of aloofness from European political systems.

American entry into World War I supported Theodore Roosevelt's contention. Whether the cause was German submarine warfare, American national security, business investments in Europe, or a desire to control events, the United States obviously if unknowingly had accepted his argument that it had to "play a great part in the world." Inspired by Wilson's rhetoric about a world safe for democracy, Americans set out upon their own "Great Crusade." After the defeat of Germany and its allies, the United States hoped to reform Europe and establish a permanent peace. Frustrated by the slow pace of reform at home, many Progressive Era reformers looked to Europe and the world for new opportunities. Coalition diplomacy during the war reflected American distrust of Europe. It took the pressure of a German offensive to get U.S. generals to coordinate their actions with a newly created Allied commander in chief, and even then the United States refused to permit its troops to come under foreign command.

Woodrow Wilson's historic proposal for the League of Nations has rightfully dominated the history of the postwar period. Wilson's concept of collective security, however incompletely developed, clearly represents one of the few attempts by a major world statesman to find a workable substitute for the diplomacy of power politics—alliance, coalition, and entente. Wilson's proposal had a fatal flaw: it rested upon the creation of a homogeneous world economic-political system. The collective security approach required a remarkable degree of cooperation and trust among the major world powers, but such trust could develop only when they shared similar political and economic creeds, and that was not to be.

Instead, the peace settlements that followed World War I created a system of alliances and ententes by which the victors hoped to preserve the status quo. Although the United States refused a role in Europe when it rejected membership in the League of Nations, a proposed alliance with France against Germany might well have received Senate approval, but the Wilson administration lost interest in it following the rejection of the Treaty of Versailles. It soon became "traditional"

again for Americans to speak disdainfully of Europe's power politics, never realizing that their government continued to display a strong interest in European events. In fact, American "observers" at the league's meetings frequently attempted to influence the deliberations, and throughout the 1920s and 1930s American policy paralleled that of Britain and France.

The peacekeeping system in Europe operated without overt American support, but the system for Asia sprang primarily from the efforts of the United States. The Washington Naval Conference of 1921–1922, called by Secretary of State Charles Evans Hughes, resulted in a series of treaties, each of which involved the United States in Asian power politics. The Five-Power Naval Disarmament Treaty was aimed directly at ending the naval arms race between Japan, Britain, and the United States. The Four-Power Treaty between Britain, Japan, France, and the United States replaced the old Anglo-Japanese alliance with one that promised only consultations. Both agreements clearly implied American support for the status quo in the Pacific. The Nine-Power Treaty, which merely endorsed the Open Door in China, served to distract critics from the realities of the power relationships being established. American participation in this informal system had one limitation: there could be no prior commitments (entangling alliances?) requiring the use of either economic or military coercion.

The onset of the Great Depression in 1929 eliminated whatever slim chance there might have been of that system developing into a meaningful and long-term entente. Moreover, Germany, China, and the Soviet Union, all excluded from the power structure, soon mounted challenges that spelled the demise of the informal system that had spurned them. The 1930s saw most nations withdraw into themselves, but none more so than the United States. Embittered and cynical about their experience in Europe and the international community following the Great Crusade, Americans indulged in self-recrimination and vowed never again to try to "save" Europe from itself.

Despite the rising tension caused by Nazi Germany during the early and mid-1930s, Americans opposed any participation by their government in European politics. President Franklin D. Roosevelt, although concerned about the actions of Adolf Hitler, chose to follow the lead of Britain and France. Those nations, eager to avoid a military confrontation, repeatedly asked the United

States for firm commitments. The pattern held for all of Hitler's and Benito Mussolini's aggressive moves right up until war began. The remilitarization of the Rhineland in 1935, the Italian invasion of Ethiopia in 1936, the intervention in the Spanish Civil War beginning in 1936, German *Anschluss* with Austria in 1938, and the takeover of Czechoslovakia in 1939, all saw the United States draw away from Anglo-French requests for some sort of alliance. Inaction resulted as each blamed the other for a lack of leadership. Whether an alliance would have prevented a conflict with Germany is questionable; so is the claim that American support would have made the British and the French more courageous in their diplomacy. What is not questionable was the American attitude toward an alliance. The general public, Congress, and most public leaders believed that alliances caused wars instead of preventing them, and they opposed any such arrangements for the United States.

THE RUDE AWAKENING: WORLD WAR II

Hitler's violation of the Munich Pact of 1938 opened the eyes of French and British leaders, and the outbreak of World War II in September 1939, following Germany's invasion of Poland, forced Americans to reconsider. Still, while they supported the Roosevelt administration's decision to permit the Allies to buy military supplies in the United States, few seriously considered an alliance and intervention. Memories of World War I were too strong. Despite later claims that public opinion had limited his freedom of action, Roosevelt apparently agreed with the majority of Americans. He understood that Britain and France were fighting America's war but saw no need for the United States to be anything except what he later labeled "the arsenal of democracy." The collapse of French resistance in June 1940 made the president willing to lend money, equipment, and technical aid to Britain (which culminated in the Lend-Lease Act of March 1941), but he remained convinced, even until early 1941, that a military alliance, and the shedding of American blood, might be avoided.

Hitler's invasion of the Soviet Union made Roosevelt less optimistic, for it raised the specter of a level of German strength that would necessitate U.S. armed intervention, and by the fall of 1941 he had concluded that American intervention was necessary. But it took the Japanese attack on Pearl Harbor to bring the United States into the war. Only then did Americans begin to understand the degree to which an Anglo-American alliance—based upon firm entente—already existed. During 1941 the United States and Great Britain developed a remarkably close relationship at the level of military and logistical planning, based on the probability of an alliance.

Even with such close cooperation, the Anglo-American entente, like almost all other ententes and alliances, was not an equal partnership. The British found themselves repeatedly in the position of the pleader, while the United States, with its vast economic strength, soon began to act like a senior partner. Only during the early stages of the war, when the overriding concern was the prevention of a defeat at the hands of Germany and Japan, did the two nations meet on equal ground. After it had become clear that victory was certain—roughly about the time of the Tehran Conference in December 1943—the United States more and more frequently forced the British to accept American decisions, particularly with regard to matters affecting the postwar situation.

Problems with what Winston Churchill called the Grand Alliance fell into three categories: military strategy, politics, and economics. Disputes over military strategy found the Americans stubborn and rarely willing to compromise. Exhibiting a strong distaste for consistent British attempts to make war serve politics, particularly the preservation of the empire, American military leaders refused to consider any alternatives that did not combine the quickest and least costly path to victory. Except for the invasion of North Africa, Roosevelt refused to overrule his military chiefs of staff, and that one exception came more from his desire to get American troops into action than because he accepted Churchill's grand strategy. The Normandy invasion, the daylight bombing of Germany, and the invasion of southern France are only the most striking examples of America's insistence upon implementing its own military strategy.

As ever, economics and politics interacted. Economic diplomacy between Britain and the United States, at least as it related to the critically important questions of the structure of the postwar world, found the Americans rigid in their views. That rigidity was modified by the American desire for a postwar political alliance with Britain. Thus, the United States could and did demand that Britain eliminate the imperial preference system, which gave special trading benefits to members of the British Empire. The British realized that the system itself had outlived its usefulness; but when the Americans pressed Britain to give up its colonies, the Churchill government dug in its heels. Faced with that response, Roosevelt backed off, partly in order to preserve the wartime alliance, but more and more in the later stages of the war because of his commitment to an Anglo-American political alliance in the postwar world.

A good example of this interplay between economic and political desires is in the case of atomic energy. Early in the war, the United States and Great Britain had agreed to work together to develop an atomic bomb. Initially, that cooperation was stimulated by fears that the Germans would develop the bomb first. But midway through the war, once the British had no more to offer, Roosevelt, at the instigation of his advisers, cut off the flow of information on atomic energy to England. They argued that Britain wanted to be privy to the secret in order to use atomic energy for commercial purposes after the war and that sharing nuclear knowledge would tie the United States to England politically—a reference to Britain's colonial problems. When Churchill protested vigorously, Roosevelt changed his mind. Not only had the president begun to worry about Britain's economic problems following the war, but he had come to assume Anglo-American alliance—and their atomic monopoly after the war.

The Anglo-American entente was the deepest commitment made by the United States during World War II, but the coalition with the Union of Soviet Socialist Republics proved the most important—and the most difficult. Even during the early 1930s, Franklin Roosevelt's attitude toward the Soviet Union had been one of practicality and persuasion, and once Hitler had invaded the Soviet Union, the president's nonideological stance made it easy to welcome the Russians as a military partner. Although Roosevelt has frequently been criticized as a political "fixer" rather than a man with an organized grand strategy, he clearly recognized the cardinal fact of the Russo-American coalition: if it defeated Germany and Japan (a certainty after the battles of Kursk, Stalingrad, El Alamein, and Midway—all by mid-1943), the Soviet Union would pose the major barrier to Anglo-American predominance in the postwar world. That left Roosevelt three simple but critical alternatives. First, he could include the Russians in the postwar power structure, hoping they would moderate their political and economic demands. Second, he could begin to confront Soviet power during the war by shaping

military planning to meet postwar political needs. Third, he could firmly confront Soviet power late in the war, but only after military victory over Germany and Japan had been assured.

Despite advice from many, including Churchill, Roosevelt based his policy on the principle that the United States was not fighting one war in order to lay the groundwork for the next. Roosevelt refused to follow the path of confrontation; but cooperation, during and after the war, did not mean simple compliance with every Russian political demand nor did it mean that Roosevelt expected postwar Soviet-American relations to be without serious tensions. He merely emphasized the positive approach in the hope that it would engender a similar response. Nor was the dire warning given Roosevelt about Soviet intentions timely, for most came late in the war and well after most of the basic military strategies had been carried out.

Roosevelt's strategy failed to take into account the magnitude of the Soviet Union's distrust of the capitalist nations as well as his own advisers' intense fear of communism. He was by inclination a believer in personal diplomacy, and the general lack of enthusiasm within the U.S. State Department for a cooperative policy toward the Soviet Union forced Roosevelt to rely even more heavily on his own power and ability to shape events. More significantly, his conciliatory policies were not faithfully reflected by the American bureaucracy. Major changes in foreign policy can occur only when they generate the kind of national support that ensures that subordinates in the executive branch are actually thinking like the leadership. American policy toward the Soviet Union prior to World War II and the anticommunism of the Cold War show that Franklin Roosevelt's cooperative approach—a policy that foreshadowed the idea of "peaceful coexistence"—deviated from the norm of American foreign policy.

How the Soviet leaders, given their own ideological commitments and revolutionary experiences, would have responded to a totally candid and open Anglo-American policy during the war is uncertain. What is clear is that whenever Roosevelt hedged his bets—on the opening of a Second Front, on the Russian role in the occupation of Italy, on aid to left-wing partisan groups in Europe—Soviet leaders invariably accused the Anglo-Americans of playing political games. Although American policy toward Great Britain was frequently characterized by the same level of distrust as with the Russians, for example on the question of the imperial preference system, Soviet-American relations did not possess that community of interests that made it possible to transcend the differences. That, in essence, sums up the difference between an entente and a coalition.

The lesser partners in the Grand Alliance of World War II varied from such potential giants as China, to the small Central American states, to latecomers such as the newly constituted Provisional Government of the French Republic, which signed the Declaration of the United Nations in 1945. Intentionally vague, the declaration called only for mutual aid against the Axis nations and promised that no signatory would agree to a separate peace. Convinced that postwar questions were best left to personal diplomacy, Roosevelt refused to consider anything more substantial. American diplomacy during the war centered on the military defeat of the Axis, and relations with the less-important members of the United Nations were largely reserved to integrating their economic resources into the overall war production effort. Individual bureaucrats occasionally initiated and implemented policies that concerned America's postwar economic and political interests, particularly in Latin America, but such actions reflected traditional American attitudes, not any overall plan approved by the president.

Although Roosevelt's conception of a global balance of power—the Soviet Union, the Anglo-American alliance, an Anglo-French association in western Europe, and eventually China—seems reflected in the Cold War power structure that soon developed, the president's vague ideas possessed a crucial difference: they emphasized cooperation, not distrust.

By the end of World War II the United States seemed on the verge of a radical departure from past policies. With Harry S. Truman replacing Roosevelt in the White House, alliance diplomacy aimed increasingly at containing and defeating what appeared to be the new enemy, the Soviet Union. The nature of that Cold War determined part of the structure of America's alliance system, but other aspects of alliance diplomacy stemmed from traditional American attitudes.

THE AMERICAN ALLIANCE SYSTEM: AN UNAMERICAN TRADITION

Much has been made of the shift in 1945 and 1946 of some key Republicans, particularly Senator Arthur H. Vandenberg, from apparent isola-

tionism to internationalism. Their approach toward alliance diplomacy demonstrates why that shift was really a logical progression. Isolationism had never argued against alliances per se, only against "entangling" ones. The atomic bomb, when added to America's conventional military strength and to the nation's demonstrable economic might, seemed to guarantee that any participation in alliances would be on American terms. Only the other nations would be entangled. Even the British, rhetorically an equal partner because of the sharing of nuclear weapons, quickly found that economics put them in a secondary role. Participation in the United Nations organization posed no problems, since pro-American states could dominate all voting. Moreover, the United Nations made internationalism appear somehow different from and more moral than balance-of-power politics. Alliances, however, appeared unnecessary until 1947, when clumsy Soviet attempts to influence domestic developments in Greece and Turkey caused the president to announce the Truman Doctrine. A unilateral pronouncement rather than a negotiated alliance, the results were the same. The United States had committed itself to defend two distant nations— and by implication many more.

Those implications became fact in September 1947, when the Inter-American Treaty of Reciprocal Assistance, the first of many so-called mutual security agreements, came into being. The very label given such treaties—mutual security agreements—testifies to the long-lasting antipathy to the very word "alliance," although it was also a means of making such arrangements seem to fit the United Nations Charter. Although such a Western Hemisphere arrangement, dominated by the power of the United States, was part and parcel of the historic Monroe Doctrine, this particular treaty aimed primarily at preventing internal communist subversion—a concern that related directly to the Cold War.

At the same time that formal alliances became part of American foreign policy, the United States used its entente with Great Britain to retain and expand the invaluable security assets of the British Empire. Reading the British a lesson in "informal" empire, the Americans continued to argue for independence for British colonies but then quietly provided financial and military incentives that would allow Britain to hang on to its military bases in those same colonies. Those bases would allow the United States to project its power and influence throughout the world.

As Cold War tensions increased, the United States resorted more and more to traditional balance-of-power politics in an attempt to maintain complete control. President Dwight Eisenhower and his secretary of state, John Foster Dulles, have usually been pictured as the architects of the American alliance system, but the bulk of those alliances came into being during the administration of Harry Truman and his secretary of state, Dean Acheson. Following the Berlin airlift and the establishment of Russian hegemony in Czechoslovakia, the keystone of what was to become a worldwide structure of alliances came in April 1949, when, at the instigation of the United States, eleven other nations in the North Atlantic area joined the United States in signing the North Atlantic Treaty. The role played by that treaty in the Cold War is told elsewhere in this volume; but much of America's conception of its own role within that treaty structure existed separately from Soviet-American tension. From the inception of the treaty, the United States used the North Atlantic alliance to pursue two frequently contradictory goals. The treaty was primarily aimed at the military and political containment of the Soviet Union, a function in which the United States, by virtue of its overwhelming military power, dominated all strategic planning. Since the conventional and small nuclear forces of western Europe depended upon American nuclear weapons to act as the ultimate deterrent against any Russian aggression, the crucial decisions always lay with American leaders. Accordingly, the major NATO commands fell to Americans.

Yet that role as the military leader of the alliance became increasingly offset by American insistence upon western European unity. At the time that the United States initiated the North Atlantic Treaty it had already begun implementing the Marshall Plan. Although ostensibly designed to promote European economic recovery, the Marshall Plan also added an economic facet to NATO. The long-term program supported by the United States called for economic and political unity among the western European nations. In a transparent attempt to transfer their own federal system to Europe, Americans consistently demanded that western Europe work together; first at the economic level and then, it was hoped, at the political level. American leaders spoke jejunely of a "United States of Europe" and frequently seemed to assume that, once European unification had occurred, the United States could pull back into the Western Hemisphere. This new reform movement—reminiscent of the Grand Crusade of three decades earlier—frequently clashed with American images of an evil and fanatical Soviet Russia, so powerful that only American military strength could defend the "free world." Just as an economically stable western Europe would eventually be able to compete with American business interests on an even basis, so the political and military strengthening of those nations inevitably meant that the United States would lose the total control of the North Atlantic Alliance that characterized the late 1940s and 1950s.

Initially, the North Atlantic Alliance exhibited great unity and strength under America's leadership, but only when the crisis was in Europe. As long as the Europeans feared Soviet expansion, either by force or subversion, they found NATO useful. But the Korean War, and American attempts to involve all its allies, found the western Europeans reluctant to translate a regional defense agreement into a worldwide crusade against communism. Despite a UN resolution that sanctified America's "police action" in Korea, the contribution made by the other members of the North Atlantic Alliance was a token one.

Asia posed special problems for the United States. The victory of the communist forces in China in 1949 stimulated an immediate attempt by the Truman administration to contain communism in Asia. In 1951 the United States signed a peace treaty with Japan that provided bases and similar methods of integrating that nation into the American alliance system, even if the Japanese constitution—written by the U.S. government—prohibited the development of any large-scale military forces. Less hypocritical were the mutual defense treaties the United States signed with its ex-colony, the Philippines, and with Australia and New Zealand (the Pacific Security Treaty or, more usually, the ANZUS Pact). Yet those alliances too were a disappointment during the Korean War. Japan had no choice but to provide bases and similar logistical support, but the ANZUS Pact brought little in the way of concrete assistance to American forces.

By 1952 it should have been clear to American leaders that their conception of alliances against worldwide communism differed significantly from that of most of their allies. But the Eisenhower administration refused to reexamine the alliance system, choosing instead to expand it in two areas where the collapse of the European and Japanese colonial empires had left political chaos behind—Southeast Asia and the Middle East. Although specific events frequently stimulated the negotiation of specific alliances, the overarching purpose of the system was geographically obvious. The North Atlantic Treaty, which included Canada, Greece, and Turkey in addition to the United States and western Europe, blocked any Soviet expansion to the west, southwest, or north. The Southeast Asia Collective Defense Treaty, prompted by the collapse of French rule in Indochina and fear of the People's Republic of China, completed another portion of the cordon sanitaire, which also included Japan, South Korea, and the Republic of China on Taiwan (the last two each signed bilateral alliances with the United States shortly after the Korean Armistice of 1953). The containment ring around Russia and its supposed satellite, China, was nearly completed with the Baghdad Pact of 1955, which brought Iran, Iraq, Pakistan, Turkey, and Great Britain into alliance together. The United States never formally joined the alliance (renamed the Central Treaty Organization, or CENTO, after Iraq dropped out in 1959 following a coup d'état against the pro-British Hashimite monarchy). But Congress and the president publicly committed America to aid the members in the event of aggression or externally supported subversion. There were large gaps in the geographic encirclement; India and Afghanistan, for example, refused all blandishments from the United States. Nevertheless, American schoolchildren during the 1950s and 1960s, their teachers, and their leaders all reveled in the illusory security of world maps, which imitated the ones that so delighted the English in the nineteenth century.

The enormous disparity in economic and military power between the United States and its Southeast Asian and Middle Eastern allies meant that their relationship was that of patron and client. Although Americans claimed to prefer liberal democracies as allies, they did not become involved in the domestic affairs of their clients unless there was communist subversion or aggression. The only criterion for an alliance with the United States became anticommunism. The liberal community in America justified actual or inferred alliances with dictatorships such as those in South Korea, Taiwan, Iran, and Spain because of the greater danger posed by militant, expansionist communism. Such nations had little choice but to accept American leadership, since American military and economic aid provided important props for their regimes.

THE SYSTEM CHANGES

Two events and two long-term developments in the late 1950s and in the 1960s forced major changes in America's alliance system. The events were the Suez crisis of 1956 and the Vietnam War; the developments were the steady relaxation of European fears of Russian aggression and the rise of mainland China as an effective world power.

The Suez crisis of 1956 found Great Britain and France, with Israel joining in for its own reasons, invading Egypt following that nation's nationalization of the Suez Canal. Ostensibly a fight to protect property, the Anglo-French action aimed at the restoration of their influence in the Middle East—influence that had begun to diminish rapidly in the face of rising Arab nationalism. Since the Middle East had not yet become a zone of confrontation between the United States and the Soviet Union, American leaders and the public viewed the Anglo-French action through their traditional prism of anticolonialism. Secretary of State Dulles publicly condemned the two European countries, and, in an ironically cooperative move, joined the Russians in applying intense pressure to force Britain and France to withdraw. Faced with such superpower unity, the two western European nations had little choice; but the diplomatic defeat at the hands of their longtime ally rankled. British conservatives had nowhere else to go, but a few years later, under the leadership of newly elected president Charles de Gaulle, the French redefined their relationship to the North Atlantic Treaty Organization. Arguing that Korea and Suez had proven that the United States cared only about its own interests and could never be counted on to defend western Europe (or anyone else), De Gaulle eventually pulled France out of virtually all the political aspects of NATO and withdrew French forces from the NATO military pool. Although the French promised to consider reintegrating their military forces if the need arose, the North Atlantic Alliance had obviously begun to deteriorate.

Still, the NATO alliance would have survived Suez and similar crises intact had the western European nations continued to fear either massive subversion or outright military attack by the Soviet Union. But those fears, at their height between 1948 and the end of the Korean War, had steadily subsided. Russian-instigated subversion seemed less likely in the wake of the remarkable economic redevelopment of western Europe, and all the members of the alliance simply assumed that the United

States would retaliate with all necessary force in the unlikely event of open aggression. In short, the NATO alliance, like others, possessed a strength directly proportional to the size and immediacy of the jointly perceived threat to its members.

Another foundation of the North Atlantic Alliance, the Anglo-American entente, also changed drastically in the twenty years following the end of World War II. The outward signs of that change came in such episodes as the Skybolt missile debacle. The United States forced the British to accept an American missile system over strong protests from the British military establishment and then failed to put the system into production. But the real problem was the increasing American contempt for the deterioration of the British economy. Although Americans and the English continued to view the world through the same spectacles, the United States no longer looked for Britain to carry its share of the burden. Indeed, Britain appeared to be on the verge of economic and political collapse. Although fears of Britain's complete collapse were exaggerated, the United States refused to treat Britain as even a major partner, equal partnership having disappeared during World War II. Even the Conservative Party in the United Kingdom was thus forced to rethink its relationship with Europe. The result—and the apparent end of the Anglo-American entente—was Britain's decision, reaffirmed in 1975, to join the European Common Market. But that decision, however clear-cut it seemed in the mid-1970s, did not eliminate the Anglo-American entente. Despite De Gaulle's insistence that Britain had to choose between Europe and the United States, as the twenty-first century dawned, British policymakers still assumed that they were best suited to act as the honest broker between the United States and Europe.

THE 1970S AND AFTER

The North Atlantic Alliance had, by the 1970s, changed significantly from what it had begun as in 1949, but it still remained an important part of international power politics. The curious combination of historical experience, liberal political institutions, and varying but compatible combinations of capitalism, socialism, and the welfare state that characterize western Europe, Canada, and the United States provided a vague sort of entente—even though many rejected the proposition that Russia and world communism posed a military threat.

In Asia the situation was far different. Although American leaders tended to believe, at least until the late 1960s, that the People's Republic of China took instructions from Moscow, U.S. policy still had to react to the reality of increasing Chinese power. Fears of another confrontation with China such as had occurred during the Korean War directed American efforts toward alliances that would guarantee that only Asians would confront Asians. Supporters and opponents both likened such policies to that of the Roman Empire, which relied upon mercenaries to guard its frontiers. American troops remained in South Korea, but a massive military aid program made the Republic of Korea forces the first line of defense. The Japanese had proven surprisingly reluctant to rearm themselves, and the United States retained military bases in Japan.

The Southeast Asia Treaty Organization of 1954 (SEATO) represented an attempt by the United States to stabilize the political situation in that area by bringing Britain, France, Australia, New Zealand, Thailand, Pakistan, the Philippines, and the United States together after the collapse of French rule in Indochina. With Malaysia, the Philippines, and the nations of Indochina all struggling against communist-led guerrillas, America's alliance diplomacy sought to bolster the existing governments with military and economic aid. Although such aid helped maintain the status quo in Malaysia and the Philippines, the situation in Vietnam seemed to leave the United States no choice between direct military intervention and a communist victory. Working on the assumption that the entire alliance structure in Southeast Asia would collapse one country at a time—like "dominoes"—if Indochina came under communist domination, the United States guaranteed that very result by intervening unsuccessfully. Although the Southeast Asia Treaty remained in force, by the mid-1970s it had lost its effectiveness. Moreover, American requests to the SEATO and NATO nations for military or diplomatic support in Vietnam had met with even less success than during the Korean War. Clearly western Europe saw no connection between their security and the spread of communism in Asia, particularly since they no longer had colonies to protect.

By 1976 the American system of alliances so painstakingly constructed after World War II lay in disarray. Arab nationalism, focused on the problems of the Palestinian refugees and the existence of the state of Israel, had effectively destroyed the Middle East treaty. Although the ANZUS Pact remained, the defeat of American efforts in Vietnam and the rise of the People's Republic of China brought about American recognition of the communist Chinese government and a scramble by nations from Australia to Japan to establish friendly relations with the Chinese. Latin America, once so obediently pro–United States in international affairs outside the hemisphere, now shifted to an increasingly anti–United States position as both the political left and right vied for public support. Outside of NATO, America's most entangling alliances were with the kinds of governments that the United States had condemned during World War II. Totalitarian regimes in Nationalist China, South Korea, Spain, and Greece all offered bases and staunch anticommunism in return for American economic and military aid. The key alliance, the North Atlantic Treaty Organization, still functioned, but the integration of Britain into Europe, the development of détente between the Soviet Union and the United States, the rise to prominence in many western European countries of seemingly moderate and democratic communist parties, and the reestablishment of the West German army as the most powerful in Europe outside the Soviet Union promised to force major alterations in the North Atlantic alliance as well.

On paper the Cold War alliance system appeared to be a radical departure from the early American proscription against entangling alliances. Actually those alliances had never "entangled" the United States. Rather, such agreements, whether explicit or implicit, had supposedly served American interests. George Washington might have disputed the argument that America's national interest demanded the worldwide containment of communism, but he would not have rejected on principle a system of alliances as the best way to achieve that goal. Like most American presidents, he was at home in the world of alliance diplomacy and power politics.

America's feeling of comfort with its post–World War II alliance system allowed that structure to survive the demise of its putative rationale—the Cold War. But the Cold War had only been the front man, so to speak, for a deeper, more fundamental motive. Because the Western alliance system was so dependent on U.S. economic and military strength, it served as a vehicle for a unilateral globalism that allowed America to extend its hegemony—its influence and power—throughout the world. But because that globalism was largely on American terms, it did not break the traditional rule against "entangling" alliances.

When the Soviet Union disintegrated in the early 1990s and NATO lost its enemy, the United States led the movement to preserve and expand the NATO Alliance. The western Europeans, their historical memories sharply focused on recent history, sought to prevent another German problem by perpetuating Franco-German collaboration (entanglement?). But for U.S. policymakers NATO expansion offered an opportunity to extend their nation's influence by fostering "democracy," both political and economic. Expanding the free marketplace for commerce and ideas replaced the "containment" of communism and the Soviet Union as the justification for retaining and expanding the NATO alliance and its extensive infrastructure. This was no new idea—it had been a basic element in the rhetoric of Ronald Reagan and his administration during the 1980s. But once the Soviet threat disappeared, a debate ensued over whether or not the United States should continue to play the same extensive leadership role it had assumed during the Cold War. Was NATO even needed?

The administration of William Jefferson Clinton, fearful of losing its leverage in Europe, effectively ended the debate when it supported NATO expansion and then sent American military forces to the former Yugoslavia in an attempt to help end the bloodletting that had broken out along ethnic and religious lines. Democratic Party rhetoric may have referred more to political democracy than to the free market, but that was a matter of emphasis, not design. The epithet "isolationist" came to be applied to those who advocated anything but global involvement on American terms—not a new use of the term, but one that demonstrated the persistence of the desire, and ability, of the United States to follow a unilateral, my-way-or-the-highway style in foreign policy. By the beginning of the twenty-first century, the Republican administration of George W. Bush had confirmed U.S. involvement in the southern Balkans and expanded the American commitment in Macedonia.

American policymakers managed to square the circle, making a holy pretense of noninvolvement in the world while trying to shape that world in their own interests. Convinced that their nation offered a *novus ordo seclorum*—a new and better world order—they used alliances, coalitions, and ententes to extend the nation's reach. In 1776 that reach was limited by the practicalities of distance, wealth, and population. Two hundred twenty-five years later, those practicalities had disappeared, but the reach had not.

BIBLIOGRAPHY

Barnet, Richard J., and Marcus G. Raskin. *After 20 Years.* New York, 1965. Argues that the alliance has outlived its usefulness and was, by the mid-1960s, contributing to increased world tension.

Beale, Howard K. *Theodore Roosevelt and the Rise of America to World Power.* Baltimore, 1956.

Coolidge, Archibald C. *The United States as a World Power.* New York, 1912.

DeConde, Alexander. *Entangling Alliance.* Durham, N.C., 1958. Investigates the French Alliance and its role in both foreign and domestic American politics during the 1790s.

———. *The Quasi-War.* New York, 1966.

Esthus, Raymond A. *Theodore Roosevelt and Japan.* Seattle, 1966.

———. *Theodore Roosevelt and the International Rivalries.* Waltham, Mass., 1970. Both Esthus works amply illustrate the president's search for closer relationships with the other world powers.

Gilbert, Felix. *To the Farewell Address: Ideas of Early American Foreign Policy.* Princeton, N.J., 1961. Stimulating group of essays that emphasize the intellectual and ideological attitudes of the Founders.

Goetzmann, William H. *When the Eagle Screamed: The Romantic Horizon in American Expansionism, 1800–1860.* New York, 2000. Short but stimulating essay dealing with nineteenth-century Anglo-American relations.

Goldgeier, James. *Not Whether But When: The U.S. Decision to Enlarge NATO.* Washington, D.C., 1999.

Graebner, Norman. "Northern Diplomacy and European Neutrality." In David Herbert Donald, ed. *Why the North Won the Civil War.* Baton Rouge, La., 1960.

Hinton, Harold C. *Three and a Half Powers: The New Balance in Asia.* Bloomington, Ind., 1975. Studies the Sino-Soviet rift as it relates to American foreign policy.

Iriye, Akira. *After Imperialism: The Search for a New Order in the Far East, 1921–1931.* Cambridge, Mass., 1965. Puts forth the concept of an informal system.

Kaplan, Lawrence S. *Jefferson and France.* New Haven, Conn., 1967. Imaginative discussion of Thomas Jefferson's willingness to consider alliances as well as his overall efforts to work within a world dominated by European power politics.

Kimball, Warren F. *Roosevelt, Churchill, and the Second World War.* New York and London, 1997. Examines the wartime Anglo-American alliance.

Kissinger, Henry. *The Troubled Partnership: A Reappraisal of the Atlantic Alliance.* New York, 1965. Defends the continued utility of a revamped NATO and is helpful for understanding the later policies of the Nixon and Ford administrations.

Louis, William Roger, and Ronald Robinson. "The Imperialism of Decolonization." *Journal of Imperial and Commonwealth History* 22 (September 1994): 462–511. Discusses U.S. support for British military bases.

McNeill, William H. *America, Britain, and Russia: Their Cooperation and Conflict, 1941–1946.* London, 1953; New York, 1970. A remarkably perceptive study of the anti-Hitler coalition, only slightly outdated by the vast amount of documentation that has become available since it first appeared.

Neustadt, Richard E. *Alliance Politics.* New York, 1970.

Osgood, Robert E. *NATO: The Entangling Alliance.* Chicago, 1962. The standard historical study of the North Atlantic Treaty Organization, although it must be supplemented by more recent studies.

Perkins, Bradford. *Prologue to War: England and the United States, 1805–1812.* Berkeley, Calif., 1961. Explains how the United States managed to enter the Napoleonic wars without joining either side.

Sherwood, Robert E. *Roosevelt and Hopkins.* New York, 1950. Perhaps the best study of Anglo-American relations during World War II.

Wolfers, Arnold, ed. *Alliance Policy in the Cold War.* Baltimore, 1959. Essays examining the broad sweep of alliance diplomacy.

See also ARMED NEUTRALITIES; BALANCE OF POWER; CIVIL WAR DIPLOMACY; COLLECTIVE SECURITY; CONSORTIA; CONTAINMENT; DOMINO THEORY; FOREIGN AID; INTERNATIONALISM; INTERNATIONAL ORGANIZATION; ISOLATIONISM; NORTH ATLANTIC TREATY ORGANIZATION; POST–COLD WAR POLICY; TREATIES.

AMBASSADORS, EXECUTIVE AGENTS, AND SPECIAL REPRESENTATIVES

Kenneth J. Grieb

International relations involve negotiations between the governments of nation-states, which are conducted by their executive branches under the auspices of their heads of government. Since each state is sovereign, agreement is reached only when the parties involved in an issue reach unanimous agreement among themselves. Those nations that do not agree with the consensus among the participants do not sign the resulting agreement and hence are not bound by its provisions. Diplomatic negotiations are difficult and time-consuming, since all those involved must agree on every aspect and word of the agreement. When the General Assembly of the United Nations (UN) adopted the Universal Declaration on Human Rights in 1948 amid the tensions following the Second World War, over 1,400 separate votes were required before the full declaration was adopted.

Achieving unanimous consensus requires extensive, constant, and precise communications between the heads of government of the nations involved. Such communications are conducted through a variety of representatives. The number and types of such representatives have proliferated throughout history and in particular during the twentieth century, when rapid communications increased the need for speedy and ongoing contacts. The end of colonialism during the second half of the twentieth century meant that many more nations and peoples were involved in global and regional issues.

These trends increased the need for representatives abroad as the United States became a global power and then a superpower during the twentieth century, and then the sole global superpower in the last decade of that century. During this period the United States found itself involved in virtually every major issue in international affairs, regardless of the part of the world in which it occurred. Not surprisingly, the increasing complexity of American foreign relations necessitated increased numbers of envoys and new forms of representation.

Ambassadors, executive agents, and special representatives are different categories of envoys conducting the constant negotiations between the governments of the world's nations. The type of envoy that is appropriate varies with the circumstances of each issue and the parties involved. Use of each type has evolved through modifications since the founding of the United States. Technically, each of these types of envoys serves as the representative of the president to foreign governments.

AMBASSADORS

Ambassadors (the official title is ambassador extraordinary and plenipotentiary) have been utilized since the beginning of international relations as the principal representative of one government to another. Ambassadors normally reside in the state to which they are accredited, and serve as the head of the resident mission, called an embassy if it is headed by an ambassador. Technically, an ambassador reports to the president, though in fact he or she does so through the secretary of state. Ambassadors are accredited as representatives from one head of government to another. Consequently, they are part of a system designed to deal with bilateral relations between the governments of two nations.

The widespread use of ambassadors is also a phenomenon of the second half of the twentieth century, with most nations employing that rank extensively only from the era of World War II. In the early days of the republic, the title of ambassador was rarely used. Even the European nations posted individuals with the exalted title of ambassador only to the capitals of the most important nations, which in the eighteenth and nineteenth centuries meant the principal European powers.

Most of the diplomatic missions throughout the world were headed by ministers and were referred to as legations. (Minister is a standard rank that is one level below ambassador; a legation is one level below an embassy.) Indeed, it was not unusual for the chief representative in any given nation to hold a lesser title such as consul or to be designated as the temporary chief of mission, known as a chargé d'affaires, while holding a rank below that of minister. The United States frequently followed this pattern from its early existence well into the nineteenth century since throughout most of this period, it was involved in only a limited range of interchange with other nations.

It was nearly the end of the nineteenth century before the United States began to bestow the title of ambassador on envoys, and then only in European capitals. Only in 1893 was the status of U.S. representatives in such pivotal nations as England, France, Italy, and Germany raised to the level of ambassador. Gradually, additional European posts were raised to embassies during the years prior to World War I, but even by the start of that conflict, ambassadors were posted to fewer than ten European capitals. Prior to World War I, the only nations outside Europe in which the United States was represented by an ambassador were Japan and Mexico. This pattern followed the then-prevailing diplomatic practice. Indeed, the U.S. envoy to Mexico was the only representative of ambassadorial rank in that capital, making the U.S. ambassador automatically the dean of the diplomatic corps no matter how new he was, since he outranked all other envoys. The sending of an envoy with the rank of ambassador was regarded as a sign that the government regarded relations with the host nation as of particular importance.

While the president may select any individual as an ambassador, the United States has developed a formal system and a standing diplomatic corps from which most ambassadors are drawn. This system was not formalized until the twentieth century. In the early days of the nation, Congress adopted legislation establishing separate diplomatic and consular services, in 1790 and 1792 respectively. Yet there were few precise criteria for envoys, and presidents were free to appoint individuals of their choosing to either.

In the twentieth century it became evident that, since the United States was becoming increasingly involved in world affairs, the nation needed a corps of highly skilled negotiators to represent it abroad so it could effectively reach agreement with other governments. The Rogers Act of

1924, later amended in 1963, established set ranks and provided for selection based on merit through competitive exams. This legislation, and the Foreign Service Act of 1946, combined the diplomatic and consular services, although full integration of the personnel involved into a single corps of professionals that comprise the Department of State and the Diplomatic Corps was accomplished only in the mid-1950s. As a result, the formal establishment of a diplomatic corps is a relatively recent development.

Since the establishment of the U.S. Foreign Service, presidents have been able to draw on a body of specialists, selected on the basis of merit and apart from politics. The overwhelming majority of ambassadors are selected from the skilled professionals of the Foreign Service who serve all administrations. Usually, ambassadors are experienced envoys who have come through the diplomatic ranks, giving them considerable expertise and familiarity with several different nations and cultures. This is especially important in multilateral negotiations, which require skilled and detailed negotiations to achieve the necessary consensus among all the nations concerned with a particular question.

The president, however, may also select individuals from private life with sufficient expertise. These are called political appointees, since they normally serve only for a single presidency. While such appointments include political contributors, they also include distinguished former senators, representatives, governors, cabinet members, and military officers, as well as prominent industrialists and businessmen, cultural figures, and journalists. For example, the U.S. ambassadors to the UN have included a past presidential candidate, a chief justice of the U.S. Supreme Court, a former secretary of state, a former senator, and distinguished individuals from private life, in addition to a number of career diplomats. The existence of a pool of career diplomats makes it possible for the president to utilize experts both within the administration and as special representatives. A significant number of ambassadors have served as presidential advisers and as assistant and under secretaries of state.

Political appointees are used regularly in certain posts by all administrations, especially at embassies in Europe. This is necessitated by the very limited funding provided for American diplomatic missions by Congress, which renders it virtually impossible to appoint regular foreign service officers to U.S. missions in European capitals where the cost of living, including the cost of receptions that are mandatory for national holidays and diplomatic occasions, is extremely high. The entire annual entertainment allowance for most U.S. embassies would not pay the cost of the single reception or party. Therefore, presidents appoint independently wealthy individuals to European posts, since only individuals with the wherewithal and willingness to spend large amounts of their own funds can entertain in the style expected. For this reason, U.S. embassies in Europe are invariably staffed with wealthy presidential supporters and contributors to presidential campaigns, regardless of the administration in power.

The appointment of ambassadors requires confirmation by the Senate, and ambassadors serve at the pleasure of the president. The head of any mission normally holds the rank of ambassador for protocol purposes, regardless of whether or not he or she has been appointed as a permanent envoy and confirmed by the Senate.

Ambassadors head a regular diplomatic mission residing in the country to which they are accredited, and are expected to report regularly on all aspects of the governance and life of that country, to assist the president and his cabinet in understanding the concerns of that nation and the factors that influence its government. Daily and other periodic reports are expected to deal with all facets of activity in the host country, including its political and economic circumstances. Ambassadors are also expected to assist American citizens and protect their interests. The embassy staff, finally, is counted upon to provide routine information to American citizens, investors, and businessmen working in the country.

Accordingly, the ambassador and the staff he heads serve as the official observers and sources of information about the nation to which they are accredited, and maintain a wide range of contacts with the host government, opposition political figures, and private citizens of that nation. An embassy staff includes specialists in a number of areas in which the two governments are cooperating, including investigative, security, scientific, artistic, and cultural liaison. The embassy staff also invariably includes specialists in trade, agriculture, political affairs, law, administration, and finance, as well as military representatives and consular officers. The ambassador thus serves as the normal channel of communication and information between the two governments. Ambassadors are also expected to conduct negotiations regarding pending matters with the host government. In addition, the ambassador and the embassy staff are responsible for helping the government and citizens of the host nation understand the United States and its concerns. To do this they provide information regarding the United States and promote cultural events and official visits by American citizens from many walks of life.

In addition to reporting, ambassadors are expected to recommend policy actions, and their recommendations are often very influential in the determination of American foreign policy. This reflects the fact that resident ambassadors are often in the best position to understand the outlook of the government and nation to which they are accredited. Often, helping policymakers in Washington understand the domestic situation in the host nation is one of the ambassador's most important duties. Because ambassadors provide Washington with their host nation's perspective, they are often accused of identifying with that nation and adopting its viewpoint. Yet in fact they are simply performing their duty to be sure that the views and concerns of the country in which they are stationed be taken into consideration prior to action. Career ambassadors acquire a broad viewpoint through service in many nations. For example, from 1974 to 1996 Ambassador Thomas R. Pickering served as United States ambassador in Jordan, Nigeria, El Salvador, Israel, India, and Russia and to the UN.

During the second half of the twentieth century, when the United States emerged as a global superpower, the United States maintained embassies in virtually every nation of the world. This reflected the involvement of the United States in a wide range of issues, particularly economic and security issues, in every region of the world. This engagement widened even further after the end of the Cold War, when the United States emerged as the sole global superpower. Less than 10 percent of the nations of the world maintain as extensive a representation in all nations as the United States. The governments that do so are primarily the industrialized nations. Most countries can afford to maintain only a limited number of diplomatic posts abroad, and conduct most of their relations with a small number of neighbors and trading partners or through global organizations where all nations are represented.

The twentieth century has also witnessed an increase in the number of independent nations, especially with the virtual end of colonialism during the 1960s. The increasing number of nations resulted in a corresponding increase of multilateral issues—that is, issues involving or of concern to a number of nations, and sometimes even of interest to all nations. Throughout the twentieth century multilateral negotiations have become increasingly frequent. This, in turn, has resulted in the need for new types of representation to supplement the permanent system of embassies, which was designed to facilitate bilateral rather than multilateral negotiations.

Throughout its history the United States has been served by a dedicated corps of diplomatic representatives. Many exercised considerable influence in policymaking, though a large number served prior to the extensive use of the title of ambassador. Since the appointment of ambassadors initially served to enhance the importance of missions to those nations with which diplomatic interaction was most frequent, the list of influential envoys includes many ambassadors.

Mexico has provided several instances of influential ambassadors playing key roles in settling troublesome questions peacefully. For example, ambassador to Mexico Josephus Daniels was one of the ambassadors who were instrumental in resolving disputes that averted conflict and launched a new era of friendship at a crucial moment. Franklin D. Roosevelt appointed Daniels in 1933, a time when relations with Mexico were extremely sensitive as a result of the role of the United States during the turmoil of the civil war that had characterized the Mexican Revolution some twenty years earlier. The subsequent revolutionary policies that led to expropriations of large landholdings impacted foreign landowners. These included many prominent Americans, including some who were influential in politics. More important, the expropriations affected the operations of several large mineral extracting corporations, which demanded intervention by the United States government to protect their property.

Daniels proved to be just the right person to represent the United States in Mexico during the regime of General Lázaro Cárdenas, when tensions reached their highest. In 1937, after a prolonged dispute with the oil companies operating in Mexico, Cárdenas nationalized the oil fields in an immensely popular move in Mexico. This immediately created a new crisis with the United States and Britain, whose oil companies were involved, while the delicate negotiations regarding the land claims continued. The nationalization of the oil fields and the land redistribution, which constituted the defining moments of the Mexican Revolution, nearly brought Mexico and the United States to war.

Ambassador Daniels, who had worked diligently to dispel the ill feeling toward the United States remaining from the intervention in Mexico during its Revolution, redoubled his efforts to explain each nation's viewpoint to the other. He carried on an extensive personal correspondence with President Roosevelt throughout his tenure in Mexico. At one point, Washington sent a harshly worded note to Daniels for transmission to the Mexican government, a note that would surely have led to deadlock. Daniels, however, saved the situation by simply refusing to deliver the note. Only his close friendship with President Franklin D. Roosevelt enabled him to do this. His action made it possible for negotiations to continue, and despite domestic outcries in both countries, they contributed significantly to the eventual settlement. The importance of a settlement with Mexico became clear when, just a few months later, Pearl Harbor plunged the United States into World War II; then Mexico's support was essential to enable the United States to focus on the war effort. Daniels's actions played a major role in restoring friendly relations between the United States and Mexico, and dissipating the mutual mistrust. His efforts made him genuinely popular in Mexico by the time his tenure ended in 1941.

Another influential ambassador to Mexico who prevented a break in relations and helped settle pressing disputes in the aftermath of the revolutionary turmoil was Dwight W. Morrow, who served in the post from 1927 to 1930. A Wall Street banker, Morrow was an unlikely envoy in the midst of disputes regarding land seizures that raised compensation issues and angered the business community in the United States. Yet he proved the perfect individual for the job. Like Daniels, Morrow genuinely liked Mexico and understood Mexican sensitivities and nationalism. He began the process of overcoming the unfavorable image of the United States in Mexico by befriending its leaders, particularly Plutarco Elias Calles, the former president who headed the governing party. Morrow worked to find solutions that were acceptable to Mexican sensitivities. It was his efforts in working with Calles that produced the solution to the initial stage of the land and oil issues. Morrow suggested that the Mexican government's interpretation of the provisions of the Mexican Constitution regarding those issues be submitted to the Mexican Supreme Court. Since at that time Calles controlled the court, this suggestion made it possible for Mexico to alter its stance without offending Mexican nationalism or appearing to bow to United States pressure, while retaining its position. Since the government would be responding to a decision of its own Supreme Court, nationalism was satisfied and the United States protest eliminated without any Mexican concession, because the court remained free to reconsider its decision, which it did several years later, enabling the government to revive the issues at a more propitious time when relations with the United States were more cordial. This was precisely the formula needed to alleviate a crisis.

Given the importance of relations with the Soviet Union and later Russia, it is scarcely surprising that several ambassadors serving there played pivotal roles in developing U.S. policy towards Moscow. Policymakers in Washington often found it necessary to rely heavily on the recommendations and judgments of envoys in Moscow, since they provided necessary insights into a closed society. Among the influential ambassadors in Moscow, Charles E. Bohlen during the 1950s and Jack F. Matlock during the late 1980s and early 1990s stand out. Both were specialists in Russia and Eastern Europe, having completed many tours of duty in Moscow as junior officers before heading the embassy. This meant that they had detailed knowledge of the obscure functioning of the Soviet and Russian governments and good Russian language skills. Other ambassadors are particularly influential because of their previous political service and their relationship with presidents. Notable among these was Ambassador Michael J. (Mike) Mansfield, a former Senate majority leader, who served as ambassador to Japan from 1977 to 1988.

Ambassador Joseph C. Grew, who served as ambassador to Japan from 1932 until the start of World War II in 1941, had the thankless and ultimately impossible task of attempting to prevent war between two mutually suspicious nations during the period of Japanese military expansion. Grew devoted considerable effort to building a basis of understanding between the United States and Japan, a difficult task at a time when few in Washington understood Japanese ambitions. United States communications to Japan were often written for domestic consumption, which exacerbated disagreements. Although Grew repeatedly managed to stave off conflict by insisting on rewording notes in a more diplomatic manner that would be acceptable to the Japanese,

eventually his efforts proved futile despite the accuracy of his warnings and explanations of the Japanese outlook. His efforts delayed war at a time when the United States was not yet prepared for conflict, although the divergent ambitions of the two nations and the fact that all eyes in Washington were focused on Europe ultimately prevented further negotiations.

Ambassador Grew was disappointed when the United States abandoned neutrality in the Far East by adopting the Stimson Doctrine, named after Secretary of State Henry L. Stimson, which announced that the United States would not recognize the Japanese conquest of Manchuria. While this stance seemed inevitable to most Americans in view of the Japanese actions, Grew recognized that it placed the United States on a collision course with Japan without having any real effect on the situation in Manchuria. In actuality, the Stimson Doctrine and its ultimate adoption by the League of Nations led to Japanese withdrawal from the League, removing an important channel of diplomatic negotiations with Japan. In addition, the fact that nonrecognition changed nothing on the ground, leaving the Japanese in control of Manchuria, caused the Japanese to view this as an indication that the powers of the world would not act meaningfully to contest military expansion in Asia. Throughout the years leading up to the war, Grew worked tirelessly to promote a negotiated settlement, and even proved willing to risk a summit conference in an effort to seek a solution. But the viewpoints of the two nations were simply incompatible, and eventually Japan made the decision to attack the United States. Given the circumstances, it is doubtful if any efforts at a negotiated settlement would have succeeded.

While ambassadors and the embassies they head have remained the principle instruments through which American foreign relations with other nations are conducted, other categories of representatives have also been employed throughout the history of the United States. The use of these alternative channels increased as the nation's role on the world stage grew larger. Delicate situations and the need to be constantly involved in multiple, simultaneous negotiations, particularly those regarding sensitive security matters, led increasingly to the practice of employing types of representatives outside the normal channels provided by embassies to address special matters and separate them from routine negotiations. This practice is utilized to indicate the importance of particular questions, to separate negotiations regarding particular matters from other issues, and to enable the appointment of specialists or individuals particularly close to the president to handle specific questions. Such an approach provides additional flexibility to the president and to the conduct of American foreign relations. These alternate forms of representations include executive agents and special representatives.

EXECUTIVE AGENTS

Executive agents have been employed in the conduct of American foreign policy throughout the history of the nation. The term "executive agent" denotes an individual appointed by the president, acting without legislative consultation or sanction, for the purpose of carrying out some specific function, often of limited duration. In some instances, executive agents have received instructions from and were directly responsible to the chief executive—that is, they reported directly to the president rather than through the secretary of state. The use of executive agents derives indirectly from the constitutional stipulation that the appointment of heads of regular diplomatic missions requires Senate approval, a procedure that frequently proves cumbersome and time-consuming and is especially inconvenient when politically sensitive issues are involved. As a result, even delegations including members of the Senate are routinely appointed without Senate confirmation, particularly for missions of short duration. This approach can be particularly valuable when the Senate is controlled by the opposition party. Distinct procedures are required for special missions responding to temporary situations, such as conferences, that necessitate prompt action. Congress recognized this fact by providing the president with a contingent fund for special expenses, and salaries of agents are normally drawn from this fund.

In practice, such individuals are sometimes considered to be the personal representatives of the president, as distinct from regularly accredited diplomats who are responsible to the secretary of state (though theoretically to the president through the secretary) and are regarded as representatives of the government of the United States. This may be a fine distinction that appears somewhat technical to the layperson, but it is an important differentiation in terms of function and operation, and one to which diplomats and governments are closely attuned.

That executive agents are employed for a wide variety of purposes, sometimes to make contacts possible outside regular diplomatic channels, reflects the flexibility of the office. In the strictest sense, the use of an executive agent rather than a regular ambassador is a pragmatic device available to the chief executive whenever expediency requires some fresh or supplemental channels. Consequently, the functions of agents and the nature of their office vary with circumstances and with presidents.

Given the flexible nature of the instrument and its dependence on presidential initiative, it is scarcely surprising that executive agents tend to be employed most extensively by strong chiefs of state. Presidential dynamics is thus a key element in the use of agents and their powers, for chief executives who prefer to act independently and conduct their office in a vigorous manner utilize this device to assume some degree of personal control of foreign policy. Consequently, the greatest use of such envoys has occurred under Presidents Woodrow Wilson and Franklin D. Roosevelt, both rated as strong executives by historians. Whether the agents supplement or supersede regularly accredited diplomats depends upon the president, and is generally indicative of his vigor and the nature of his relations with the State Department.

It is no accident that the two presidents making the most extensive use of agents, Wilson and Roosevelt, sought to conduct personal diplomacy, attempted to circumvent relatively weak secretaries of state appointed because of domestic political considerations, and mistrusted the personnel of the regular Foreign Service. Both employed executive agents as a means of placing the conduct of key aspects of foreign policy directly in presidential hands, effectively circumventing the regular diplomatic corps and the State Department. Since there is obviously a limit to the number of situations to which a president can effectively devote personal attention, the appointment of this class of envoys can also provide an indication of the importance attached to a particular problem, nation, or region.

The type of individuals presidents appoint and the basis of their selection affect not only the operation of the institution, but also the degree of controversy surrounding its use. Since the very nature of the position renders it a dependency of the president, the chief executive is free to select the individuals according to any criteria he chooses. Full congressional debates regarding the constitutional powers involved have been rare, although a notable exception occurred in the Senate in 1831. Even in this discussion, the question was not whether the president had the right to appoint such agents, but rather what functions they could perform and their relation to regular diplomatic representatives. If the president seeks simply to secure the temporary services of an individual with recognized expertise in a given realm, whose talents would not otherwise be at the disposal of the government and whose abilities are especially suited to a specific task, little dispute will ensue. Similarly, agents assigned to discrete or minor tasks seldom breed controversy.

It is a different matter, however, when the chief of state sends a personal representative to supersede a regularly accredited head of mission. In such instances, the agent clearly displaces an individual appointed with the consent of the legislature, allowing more direct control by the executive. If the agent is dispatched to an important theater of foreign policy on a highly visible or sensitive mission, the likelihood that such an action will arouse the ire of Congress is increased. A president also assumes a greater risk of controversy when relying upon agents because of suspicion about the objectives of the regular diplomatic personnel or as a means of placing the matter in the hands of an individual more ideologically compatible with his own views. This is particularly true if the individuals employed as agents are political figures associated with the chief executive or political contributors. These agents are likely to be controversial figures whose employment can be expected to antagonize the opposition party. Although the resultant disputes often focus on the agents, the basic issue involves the policies pursued by the president.

The controversy regarding the activities of Wilson's surrogates in Mexico provides an example of such a situation. The issue was not the use of agents per se, but rather the uses to which they were put. Wilson was clearly employing executive agents to circumvent the regular diplomatic officers, who disagreed with his policy. This was particularly evident in the type of individuals he dispatched on such missions, for they were invariably "deserving Democrats" who were politically associated with the president or Secretary of State William Jennings Bryan. Wilson felt that the most important qualifications for a prospective appointee were loyalty and similarity of outlook, which he considered more significant than knowledge of the area involved or the possession of any diplomatic skills. It is scarcely surprising that the appointment of partisans to carry out partisan policies provoked political controversy. Franklin D. Roosevelt, by contrast, although he also employed executive agents extensively and was himself scarcely less of a storm center than Wilson, managed to minimize such disputes through the selection of men of stature and experience who were clearly well qualified, and by employing them only on missions that obviously required special procedures.

Early Examples   One of the most common uses of executive agents has been in dealing with nations or governments with which the United States did not at the time maintain normal diplomatic relations. In these circumstances, recourse to some special type of temporary representative is plainly necessary for the transaction of any business, including the inauguration of formal diplomatic contact. Inevitably, such agents were common during the early days of the Republic, when the United States had not yet been accorded recognition by many of the world's nations, and during the nineteenth century when the United States maintained regular diplomatic missions in only a small portion of the world's capitals. Indeed, the first representatives of the United States in the immediate aftermath of independence had the status of simple diplomatic agents. Technically, the initial representatives were congressional rather than executive agents, since they were dispatched during the days of the Continental Congress and the Articles of Confederation, prior to the existence of a separate executive branch. These individuals were appointed by the Committee of Secret Correspondence and later the Committee for Foreign Affairs, and only appointments to regular diplomatic missions were considered by the full Congress. Thus, the use of agents whose designation was not subject to confirmation by Congress actually predated the existence of the executive branch.

Four of the nation's first five chief executives—George Washington, John Adams, James Madison, and James Monroe—found it necessary to employ executive agents extensively. Among the earliest agents was Colonel David Humphrys, whom President Washington dispatched in 1790 to conduct negotiations leading to the establishment of diplomatic relations with Portugal. A series of similar emissaries was employed during the 1820s to arrange the nation's first treaty with Turkey. Executive agents were also utilized extensively in the intermittent negotiations with the Barbary states of North Africa from the 1790s to the 1820s, an instance where piracy in the Mediterranean required negotiations prior to the establishment of formal diplomatic relations. Similar appointees were also employed during the early nineteenth century in establishing initial contact with the newly independent former Spanish colonies in the Western Hemisphere. In Latin America, individuals such as Joel R. Poinsett—an appointee of President James Madison—conducted reconnaissance missions and represented U.S. interests during the period when the ability of the new republics to maintain themselves was still in doubt and when formal recognition was delayed by negotiations with Spain regarding the purchase of Florida. Temporary representatives proved convenient for this type of mission and have served as the instrument of this class of exchanges throughout the existence of the United States. In the 1970s Henry A. Kissinger played a pivotal role in establishing relations with the People's Republic of China while serving as President Richard M. Nixon's national security adviser.

Purposes and Functions Agents are often employed as a means of dealing with nations or governments with which formal diplomatic contacts have been severed or temporarily suspended. This is another situation in which agents are well suited to a particular need, for preliminary negotiations are often a necessary prelude to the renewal of formal ties. When used in this manner, agents can serve as a vehicle to conduct negotiations regarding the legitimacy of the new government and the conditions attached to formal recognition. Such exchanges are obviously of temporary character and must be handled through some vehicle other than a regularly accredited representative, for the appointment of an individual with the latter status would in itself constitute de facto recognition of the government in question. This also applies in instances when it proves necessary to negotiate with the leaders of rebel movements. Talks with rebel leaders must take place outside normal diplomatic channels, since diplomatic relations with a rebel movement would constitute an unfriendly act toward the government of the nation involved.

This last circumstance became common in the latter quarter of the twentieth century when the United States, and indeed all the principal powers of the world, increasingly found it necessary to deal with civil wars in order to prevent

conflicts from spreading and becoming full-scale international wars. The distinction between internal affairs and the maintenance of international peace and security became blurred in the twentieth century, and especially since the end of the Cold War. That is because modern conflicts, which involve weapons that are far more destructive than those employed in earlier centuries, often start as internal rebellions and then spread across borders to affect neighboring nations.

Missions of this type have included efforts to protect American citizens and their rights in areas controlled by unrecognized governments or rebel factions, simple negotiations regarding the procedures for the renewal of regular relations with new governments resulting from internal uprisings, and attempts to impose preconditions as a price for full recognition. In cases involving new governments resulting from civil war or revolution, if the break in relations is of recent origin and short duration, the appointment of a special agent is often unnecessary, since members of the regular diplomatic service still on the scene can serve as the vehicle for such exchanges. In instances where the use of such individuals proves inconvenient or where they have been withdrawn as part of the break, the appointment of an executive agent is essential.

Agents of this nature also date from the initial days of the nation, when President George Washington dispatched Gouverneur Morris to England in 1790 in a futile effort to open negotiations seeking a commercial treaty and the establishment of regular diplomatic relations. Since at this time there was no foreign service, the designation of agent was a matter of title and indicated a less formal status and a temporary mission. In the twentieth century, executive agents were most often employed in dealing with the newly emerging nations of the so-called Third World, where governmental instability and internal turmoil is more frequent. This is particularly true in the Western Hemisphere, where the United States is more likely to attempt to exact concessions as a precondition for recognition. Such efforts have frequently included attempts to secure pledges of elections or the resignation of a government that has recently seized power. Wilson's dispatch of John Lind—a former Democratic governor of Minnesota and a political associate of Bryan—to Mexico in 1913 was one example of this type of mission. Lind, who had no prior diplomatic experience and no previous contact with Mexico, was appointed "adviser to the American Embassy in

Mexico City," but in reality served as the personal representative of the president of the United States. In this manner he superseded the regularly accredited diplomats in that country. Acting as Wilson's spokesman and "confidential agent," Lind conducted negotiations with the incumbent government of General Victoriano Huerta, which included the presentation of demands that stipulated Huerta's surrendering his office. This is an instance in which Wilson, who was suspicious of the regular foreign service personnel, chose to employ his own representative because he preferred an adherent of his policies as his instrument. While controversial at the time, such situations have become far more common in the post–Cold War era.

In some instances more formal negotiations are employed prior to recognition. One such cased was the so-called Bucareli Conference in 1923, when executive agents designated as commissioners representing the United States and Mexico held an extended "exchange of impressions" whose "sole object" was "to report afterwards to their respective high officials." The use of the title "commissioners" served to allow negotiations with a government that had seized power through a coup d'état and had not yet been recognized officially by the United States. Because the conferees were executive agents, the sessions did not technically constitute recognition of the Mexican government of General Álvaro Obregón, but they did prove to be the vehicle for eventual recognition through a resulting memorandum of understanding that enabled the satisfactory settlement of the questions regarding damage claims and oil land. Executive agents are frequently used in comparable situations, but it must be noted that although they are a useful vehicle for this type of negotiations, such envoys are but one mechanism for completing the necessary arrangements.

At times, executive agents have even been employed to conduct negotiations for an early peace with nations with which the United States was at war. Executive agents are the only appropriate vehicle for such delicate discussions. The outstanding example of this type of mission was that of Nicholas P. Trist, chief clerk of the State Department. He was dispatched by President James K. Polk to Veracruz in 1847 to accompany the military expedition of General Winfield Scott, which had landed at that port and was advancing toward the Mexican capital. Since the United States had entered the war for limited and clearly delineated objectives and had already established

effective control of the territory it desired, Polk hoped that Trist's presence would enable negotiations to be conducted simultaneously with the military campaign and possibly render the completion of the latter unnecessary. The use of an executive agent was essential because Mexican reaction was uncertain and because it was necessary to maintain secrecy as a means of circumventing a mounting domestic sentiment to extend the original war aims. Trist's mission resulted in an incongruous combination of intermittent combat and negotiations that failed to produce results until after the military expedition had fought its way into Mexico City.

During the early twentieth century, executive agents were frequently employed as the instruments of intervention in the domestic affairs of Latin American nations, a practice extended to other regions of the world during and after the Cold War. In numerous instances this constituted a conscious attempt to avoid military intervention through mediation between internal factions or the imposition of a political settlement. Admittedly this entailed political intervention, but such action was far less controversial than the landing of troops to terminate an internal conflict or to protect American citizens. Such roles were particularly prominent in the Caribbean and Central American regions, with which the United States was especially concerned because of their significance for the security of the nation and because of the necessity of protecting the approaches to the Panama Canal.

The mission of Henry L. Stimson to Nicaragua in 1927 illustrates the use of an agent to mediate between internal factions. Civil war broke out in that Central American republic within a few months of the withdrawal of a U.S. Marine detachment that had kept the peace while serving officially as a legation guard. The United States considered it necessary to act to preserve peace in Nicaragua, owing to the potential in that country for an alternative canal route. Stimson went to Nicaragua as the personal representative of President Calvin Coolidge to mediate between the Liberal and Conservative Party forces in an effort to secure an agreement providing for a cessation of hostilities and the transfer of the dispute from the battlefield to the ballot box. The special envoy negotiated with the leaders of both factions, notwithstanding the fact that this entailed dealing with both the rebels and the incumbent government, which had been installed with the support of the United States and was still recognized.

The mission of General Enoch H. Crowder to Cuba from 1921 to 1923 constituted a similar effort to substitute political intervention for military action. Crowder was dispatched to Cuba in 1921 by the Wilson administration in an effort to forestall hostilities over a disputed election when Liberal ex-president José Miguel Gómez challenged the reported victory of his former vice-president, Alfredo Zayas y Alfonso, who now had the support of the Conservative Party. Crowder was continued in his position as the president's personal representative by Warren G. Harding. Crowder's open intervention and the implied threat of force prevented a civil war but failed to satisfy the opposition. When a compromise agreement proved impossible, Crowder remained in Cuba as a virtual viceroy, in effect an American governor of Cuba, overseeing and dictating to that nation's government. Such methods prevented an insurrection but constituted forceful intervention. It is interesting to note that Crowder's position became far less imposing when in 1923 his title was changed from the "president's personal representative" to ambassador to Cuba.

In addition to mediation and political intervention, executive agents have been employed as a means of establishing and maintaining contact with rebel movements during times of turmoil, when it is apparent that such factions have established effective control of substantial territory. Although such agents often participate in mediation efforts, in some instances the primary purposes are to protect American lives and property within rebel-controlled territory, exert some influence upon the policies of the insurrectionist leaders, and gather and report to Washington information regarding the revolution and its leaders. The most notable example of this practice occurred in Mexico during the Wilson administration. While Mexico was torn by civil war, Wilson dispatched numerous personal representatives and confidential agents to that country, usually stationing such individuals at the headquarters of two or three of the factions simultaneously. This practice resulted in a confusing welter of overlapping jurisdictions, with agents at times reporting on each other's activities, yet it also served to promote contacts between the rebel factions for the purpose of ending the conflict. It was necessary to utilize executive appointments because only in this manner could Wilson maintain representatives in more than one of the camps and attempt to influence the factions without technically conferring recognition upon them.

Other agents have been employed on similar missions. For example, William M. Churchwell was dispatched late in 1858 to confer with Mexican leader Benito Juárez in the midst of civil war. He arrived early in 1859, at a point when several factions claimed control of the nation and Juárez had been driven from the capital. Churchwell's mission paved the way for formal U.S. recognition of the Juárez regime.

In conducting negotiations or investigations of special delicacy it may be inexpedient for the president to inform Congress and the public in advance by requesting confirmation of a formal appointment. In such cases, presidents have found executive agents a convenient device. The mission of Robert D. Murphy to French North Africa during World War II is an example. Although ostensibly an American consul, Murphy was in fact dispatched as Roosevelt's personal representative to determine whether French officials in North Africa were loyal to the German-dominated Vichy government, and to conduct negotiations to arrange for their cooperation with an Anglo-American invasion of North Africa. Clearly, the success of a mission of this character depended on secrecy, which could not be maintained through a congressional confirmation proceeding.

Executive agents are also useful to the president when a disagreement with Congress precludes a request for advance approval. President Grover Cleveland's dispatch of former Representative James H. Blount on an investigatory mission to Hawaii in 1893 was such an instance. A revolution had led to the installation of a new government, dominated by American landowners and settlers, that promptly negotiated a treaty of annexation with the United States. Despite considerable sentiment for approval of the treaty, Cleveland withdrew it from the Senate and dispatched Blount, whose report confirmed that U.S. naval forces had aided the rebellion. The knowledge that the United States had been implicated in the revolt led to rejection of the annexation accord.

President Ulysses S. Grant's use of his private secretary, General Orville E. Babcock, as his personal representative and special agent in Santo Domingo in 1869 constituted one of the first instances of the executive employing a member of his personal staff to conduct confidential negotiations in the face of congressional disapproval. Grant was convinced of the advisability of acquiring Samaná Bay as a naval base, and dispatched Babcock ostensibly on a mission of investigation. Babcock negotiated a series of protocols providing for a lease on the bay and a virtual protectorate over the Dominican Republic, even though this action exceeded his instructions. The accords meticulously stipulated that they constituted merely the "basis" for a "definitive treaty" to be negotiated subsequently by a duly accredited envoy. Consequently, the accords had the character of an agreement between the two presidents acting personally, rather than between their respective governments. Grant later sent his secretary back to Santo Domingo to sit in on the formal treaty negotiations as an unofficial observer who was "fully possessed of the President's views." Despite the fact that the negotiating powers were technically vested in the regularly accredited American minister in Santo Domingo, Babcock conducted the negotiations while the minister merely signed the accord. The effort proved futile, as the resulting treaty was rejected by the Senate.

Executive agents also serve as channels of direct communication with other heads of state in instances when particular circumstances require the bypassing of normal diplomatic channels, either as a matter of expediency or as a means of emphasizing the special importance of the talks. Usually, this involves the dispatch of a prominent individual of considerable stature who is closely associated with the chief executive. Frequently, the envoy is one of the president's principal advisers. This indicates that the emissary is speaking for the president; consequently, his or her mere appearance as a negotiator demonstrates the importance attached to the matter at hand.

Woodrow Wilson resorted to this type of agent to bypass normal diplomatic channels when he sent Colonel Edward M. House to Europe in 1916. House's mission was to offer a plan designed to terminate World War I or, failing in that, to bring the United States into active participation in the war. The dispatch of House made possible direct negotiations with the British secretary of state for foreign affairs, Sir Edward Grey, while also ensuring that only the two executives and the emissary were aware of the precise contents of the proposal until the completion of the negotiations. This was vital, because had the Germans learned of the talks, the result would have been immediate United States involvement in the war at a time when it was not yet ready to enter the conflict. Since House was a close ally of Wilson, his dispatch on a mission automatically endowed it with considerable importance, for in this instance the president's personal representative was indeed an individual who could be presumed to speak fully for him.

President Franklin D. Roosevelt also employed a close personal associate as a special envoy when he sent Harry Hopkins to Moscow to initiate discussions regarding Lend-Lease aid to the Soviet Union shortly after Nazi Germany invaded Russia in 1941. The president chose to use a separate channel both to ensure confidentiality and to demonstrate, through the selection of an individual so closely associated with him, his desire that the envoy's mere appearance on the mission be regarded as a symbolic commitment. This approach succeeded in assuaging the suspicions of Soviet premier Joseph Stalin.

Roosevelt used a similar method in dealing with Generalissimo Chiang Kai-shek of China, who proved highly resistant to pressures exerted through normal diplomatic channels. Roosevelt resorted to a number of special officials in addition to the regular ambassador, ranging from Owen Lattimore, a political adviser to Chiang, to General Patrick J. Hurley, a personal representative. Hurley later became ambassador to China, although his influence as special representative was greater. President Harry S. Truman resorted to similar tactics when he dispatched former chief of staff General George C. Marshall to China during 1945 in an unsuccessful effort to convince the nationalist and communist factions to negotiate an agreement to terminate their civil war. President Richard M. Nixon sent his personal foreign policy adviser and head of the National Security Council staff, Henry A. Kissinger, on several missions, in particular in 1969 for negotiations in Moscow regarding the Strategic Arms Limitation Treaty. President James Earl Carter employed a special envoy, Sol Linowitz, to deal with the negotiations regarding the future of the Panama Canal.

Executive agents have also been utilized in dealing with international organizations, where they function as unofficial observers rather than as full delegates. Harding employed such individuals to establish contact with some agencies of the League of Nations and several other European conferences as a means of circumventing the isolationist sentiment in the United States. This procedure was necessary since—as a consequence of isolationism—the United States was not officially a member of the League and therefore could not appoint an ambassador to it. Such unofficial observers are usually members of the regular diplomatic service who are stationed at nearby posts, and function in a dual role.

The principal variables in the institution of executive agents are the type of mission, the particular individual involved, and the method of reporting to the chief executive. Of necessity, the purpose of the mission is one of the primary determinants of the activities of the agent and the importance of the effort. The personality and prominence of the agent are other significant factors. Dispatch of a prominent individual who also functions within the government, particularly if he is closely associated with the chief executive, endows the mission with significance. It is scarcely surprising that such individuals are most frequently employed in missions to the heads of governments of important powers or allies. The use of members of the regular Foreign Service can also affect the institution. Although such individuals come to their missions with greater diplomatic expertise, their appointment has less dramatic force, and consequently less impact, than the dispatch of a prominent individual or political figure. Accordingly, regular diplomatic officers tend to be employed as executive agents principally on missions requiring some degree of secrecy, as their movements are less conspicuous.

The channels through which executive agents file their reports and receive their instructions are also significant determinants of their activities. Some agents are of such stature, or are so closely associated with the chief executive, that they report directly to him, bypassing the Department of State. Such individuals obviously have greater latitude, and acquire the stature of spokespersons for the chief executive. Yet the impact of their labors is somewhat limited by this very fact, since the Department of State and its diplomats in the field are often unaware of the details of the mission until after the fact. In some instances this lack of communication has caused serious difficulties. At the least, it prevents the regular diplomatic officers from providing assistance or advice, and it can also delay the implementation of the resulting agreements. On the other hand many agents, usually those from the regular diplomatic corps or those not closely associated with the president, file their reports through the Department of State. Indeed, some of these individuals, although executive agents, are not in fact the president's personal representatives, but rather officials on special mission under the control of the Department of State, just as regular diplomats are.

During the second half of the twentieth century, the employment of executive agents has become increasingly institutionalized, reflecting a trend throughout the government. The growth of the Washington bureaucracy, which has expanded rapidly as the government assumes more extensive functions, has necessitated a formal and complex structure that has affected even so flexible an institution as that of executive agents. The formalization of a White House staff with distinct foreign policy advisers has been a gradual development occurring primarily after World War II. Many presidents have employed their own advisers since Woodrow Wilson's use of Colonel Edward House, but these were ad hoc arrangements until World War II. Then, their use was formalized so that foreign policy advisers became an ongoing presence in the White House in all administrations.

PRESIDENTIAL FOREIGN POLICY STAFF

The use of specific presidential foreign policy consultants and personal envoys expanded during World War II and the postwar years. Franklin Roosevelt's use of Harry Hopkins and a "brain trust" of advisers contributed to the development of a separate White House office distinct from the existing cabinet departments such as the Department of State, although in large measure its emergence merely reflected the growth of the government that came with the increasing complexity of its functions in the modern world. It was Roosevelt, regarded as a strong chief executive, who initiated the development of the Executive Office of the president. By the 1950s there was an entirely separate White House staff of considerable size. Although only a small portion of it dealt with foreign policy, this portion was expanded under later presidents, eventually evolving into a sizable National Security Council (NSC).

The NSC, originally established as a small office in 1947, grew to importance during the administration of Richard M. Nixon. It has continued throughout all subsequent administrations as part of the White House staff, becoming virtually an alternate State Department functioning wholly under the president's control. While officially functioning as a coordinating body to assemble the recommendations of different agencies involved in foreign relations, it has provided the chief executive with a separate foreign affairs staff and enabled him to act independently in foreign affairs. Its power derives from proximity to the president and the ability to set agendas by providing the chief executive with daily morning security briefings that cover important international events. The NSC proved especially important during the height of the Cold War, when security and national defense matters assumed precedence over other aspects of foreign policy. The prominence of the NSC, however, has continued beyond the end of the Cold War.

The existence of White House foreign policy advisers, and the creation of the National Security Council within the Executive Office as a separate body, provides the president with a staff of specialists of his own, distinct from the State Department and the regular Foreign Service. This has strengthened the hand of the president in foreign affairs, enabling him to conduct his own policy through what virtually amounts to an alternate foreign office. That it is housed in the building formerly occupied by the State Department is symbolic both of the increased size of the two institutions (the State Department moved to larger quarters) and of the change in the relationship between the chief executive and the State Department.

The process of utilizing special representatives in the conduct of foreign affairs accelerated in the years after World War II, reflecting the increasing complexity of world affairs; the increasing interconnectedness of the world, known as globalization; and the larger involvement of the United States in international affairs. Security cooperation on global and regional scales expanded, and economic interchange between nations and across borders accelerated greatly. In the 1960s the demise of colonialism doubled the number of independent nations in the world and the number continued to increase afterward. In addition, more rapid communications and transportation links enabled rapid movement of goods, business, and citizens, which meant that governments needed to remain in much closer contact. It also meant that individual citizens and organizations interacted constantly with their counterparts in other nations, in addition to the interaction between their governments. Issues formerly regarded as exclusively domestic were now considered part of the international system, and many previously domestic concerns extended beyond borders and were regarded as global or regional problems to be addressed jointly and cooperatively by many nations. Many problems had to be addressed at the global level, since they affect peoples in many nations, regardless of borders.

MULTILATERAL ORGANIZATIONS

After World War II, a new range of multilateral international institutions developed, leading to increased interaction between nations and a consequent need for new types of representatives beyond those in traditional embassies. The emergence of the United Nations, a series of specialized agencies associated with it, and other international organizations—ranging from regional security groups to free trade areas to military alliances—resulted in an extensive series of regularly scheduled meetings at which the United States needed to be represented. The increasing multilateralism of world affairs and the increasing importance of global issues necessitated dealing with groups of nations rather than addressing issues bilaterally with individual governments, which is the function of embassies.

Reflecting the fact that the UN system required a different level of representation than do individual nations, the U.S. representative to the UN was usually given cabinet rank to make possible his or her participation in policymaking. Hence, although the UN representative received instructions from the Department of State, she or he also ranked well above other ambassadors. While representatives from all nations at the UN held the rank of ambassador, their responsibilities were far more extensive than those of traditional ambassadors, since they dealt with envoys from all other governments in the world. In recognition of this fact, each nation's head of mission at the United Nations was called a permanent representative.

Individuals with the rank of ambassador, often drawn from the regular Foreign Service ranks, were assigned to represent the United States at a number of other permanent regional multilateral organizations. These included intergovernmental organizations such as the European Union and the North Atlantic Treaty Organization. Other individuals with ambassadorial rank were sent to observe the meetings of regional organizations.

An increasing number and range of issues were addressed as global questions during the last quarter of the twentieth century. This required U.S. representation at many organizations, conferences, and meetings dealing with topics on a worldwide, multilateral basis. These sessions cover a wide range of vital subjects. Specialized agencies, commissions, and programs of the United Nations dealt with human rights, the environment, trade, drug trafficking, crime, corruption, food, agriculture, health, air and maritime trade, postal and telegraph linkages between nations, intellectual property rights and protections, refugees, population, and many additional issues. All were problems that spanned national boundaries, and hence required international cooperation, which necessitated negotiations and agreements by national governments. In addition, the UN convened a series of world conferences to deal with topical issues, particularly the various aspects of development. The annual meetings of organizations formed by treaties to enforce or monitor the enforcement of treaty provisions often dealt with vital issues of international peace and security, such as arms proliferation; weapons of mass destruction including nuclear, chemical and biological weapons; and the rights of civilians in wartime.

These meetings and conferences required representatives with particular expertise regarding the particular issues under discussion. The representatives involved came from a range of governmental agencies, in addition to the diplomatic corps. Such meetings were often covered by special representatives. Even when the delegation was headed by the Foreign Service officer, the members of the delegation included specialists and even members of Congress. These representatives were appointed on a short-term basis by the president, without confirmation by the Senate.

SPECIAL REPRESENTATIVES

Many of these international issues achieved such importance that regular offices dealing globally with these matters have been established, usually within the Department of State. The United States now had—in addition to the regular regional geographic bureaus—special officers, or assistant secretaries of state, dealing with various topical themes. These included drug control, human rights, the environment, scientific affairs, and communications and information policy. The administration of President George H. W. Bush established such a special representative for religious freedom. Such offices proliferated in response to domestic lobbying, and many citizens have come to believe that an issue is not receiving high priority unless a special office is established to deal with it. These offices served to provide the necessary expertise and monitoring for negotiations and conferences, just as such separate organizations as the Central Intelligence Agency

and the Arms Control and Disarmament Agency do in their fields.

Economics and trade grew in importance, resulting in the development of a series of international organizations to establish rules to regulate and facilitate the exchange of goods and services between nations, and to settle disputes regarding the internationally accepted rules. These organizations required not only special representatives, but the establishment of new governmental offices to deal with these economic and trade issues. The organizations, all of which have regular meetings, included the International Monetary Fund; the World Bank; the Group of Seven (which became the Group of Eight in the 1990s), the nations with the largest economies in the world; and the Organization for Economic Cooperation and Development. The meetings of these groups usually involved representatives of the Treasury and Commerce Departments as well as the State Department. Some were held at the summit level.

Trade and international economic matters became so vital that it proved necessary to establish a separate office to deal with these matters. The Office of the United States Trade Representative within the Executive Office of the president was established in 1962 and given broader status by the Omnibus Trade Competitiveness Act of 1988. The trade representative's office was responsible for the negotiation of agreements relating to international trade; it conducted all global, multilateral, and bilateral trade discussions, both for the establishment of global and bilateral accords and for the effective implementation of such agreements. Its responsibilities encompassed the World Trade Organization (WTO)—which evolved from the General Agreement on Trade and Tariffs—the North American Free Trade Agreement (NAFTA), and all bilateral trade disputes and agreements. Globalization increased the importance of these economic matters, and the Office of the Trade Representative played an increasingly central role in U.S. foreign relations from the time it was established.

The use of executive agents and special representatives greatly increased in the late twentieth century as new issues emerged and as all of them became more global in their impact. The result was a proliferation of offices that often created confusion as to which had ultimate responsibility; this resulted in rivalry between agencies. So many issues came to involve multiple offices and departments that the making of foreign policy increasingly involved interagency task forces to coordinate the efforts of the many agencies involved. These groups gained considerable importance under the administrations of Presidents Jimmy Carter and the senior George Bush. This created new problems, but also assured that experts with the appropriate knowledge are consulted regarding all issues.

CONFLICT MEDIATION AND MIGRATION

The use of special representatives also expanded, during the 1980s and 1990s, in dealing with regional crises involving international peace and security. Increasingly, it became normal for all presidents to appoint so-called special envoys to deal with crises regarded as important to the preservation of peace.

For example, the United States had a special envoy on a continuing basis to deal with the disputes between Israelis and the Palestinians. In this way, a single individual was placed in charge, making it possible for shuttle diplomacy to replace separate negotiations with the parties. This approach was particularly important since the United States did not officially recognize Palestine as a state, and consequently had no ambassador to Palestine, despite the fact that reaching any settlement required the inclusion of the Palestinians in the negotiations. Recognizing Israel's sensitivity to an extension of American recognition prior to a final peace agreement, the United States withheld recognition of Palestine until implementation of such an agreement, using recognition as a means of pressuring the Palestinians.

Yet the volatile situation between Israel and Palestine constituted one of the situations in the world most likely to lead to full-scale war. Because of the lack of trust between the two parties, it was essential that the United States continue to pursue actively a settlement in order to avert conflict, and hence, the appointment of a special U.S. envoy. Only an envoy accredited to both sides could engage in the necessary shuttle diplomacy, negotiating separately with both parties to the conflict. The service of Dennis Ross in such a capacity during the administration of President William Jefferson Clinton played a key role in the Madrid peace process during the 1990s. The existence of a special envoy became so common that both sides protested if none was appointed, since they viewed the absence of such a representative as an indication that the United

States was not devoting appropriate attention to the conflict. Usually, the official appointed was a regular Foreign Service officer, often also serving as assistant secretary of state for Middle Eastern affairs or as ambassador to a state in the region. In other instances, the special representative came from another of the Washington bureaucracies. Indeed, on two occasions the director of the Central Intelligence Agency mediated arrangements for temporary cease-fire agreements between Israel and the Palestinians.

This approach was also used in the Balkans during the 1990s after the collapse of Yugoslavia. The United States needed the ability to talk to all parties involved in the conflict that followed the collapse, even before the new states were recognized, and to continue discussions with ethnic factions within these states. Even after ambassadors were designated, a "super envoy" able to engage in shuttle diplomacy was essential to convince the parties, and NATO allies as well, that the United States regarded the situation as particularly critical. The Dayton Peace Accords of 1995 that ended the conflict between Serbia and Croatia in Bosnia-Herzegovina and at least temporarily stabilized the internal situation in the latter nation were negotiated in advance and then pressed upon the parties to the dispute by the special representative, Ambassador Richard C. Holbrooke. African civil wars were also often addressed through such envoys. Under the Reagan administration, Assistant Secretary of State for African Affairs Chester Crocker developed a reputation for facilitating the settlements that ended long-standing conflicts on the continent, particularly in Mozambique.

The appointment of a special envoy to deal with conflict situations made it possible to separate the negotiations to settle disputes from all other aspects of ongoing relations between the United States and the countries involved in the conflict. Consequently, such envoys proliferated. By the turn of the century, they were constantly appointed to deal with particular conflicts in Africa and with the situation in the Korean peninsula. Such appointments reflected worldwide trends, since crises throughout the world came to be often addressed by the principle powers working with global and regional organizations. United States special representatives invariably found themselves working in cooperation with a special representative of the UN secretary general, and often with similar envoys representing regional organizations such as the European Union or the

Organization of African Unity. These practices reflected what globally is referred to as conflict prevention or preventive diplomacy, through which disputes and conflicts anywhere are addressed in their early stages by the international community to prevent them from spreading into a regional war involving several nations. In previous eras of slower communications, less interdependent economies, and less destructive weapons, civil wars were regarded as the internal affairs of states, and were addressed by the international community only after other nations had become involved. In the late twentieth century, however, localized conflicts were addressed before they spread. Once other nations and organizations dispatched special envoys, the appointment of a U.S. special representative was both expected and necessary. In this sense, the expanded use of such envoys in conflict situations was merely part of a global trend reflecting the greater interdependence of the era.

Use of the power to appoint executive agents and special representatives without the approval of the Senate, in addition to regular ambassadorial appointments, increased greatly during the latter decades of the twentieth century, though such appointments were employed by many presidents since the beginning of the nation. The extent to which this power was utilized varied with each chief executive. While the appointment of agents and representatives outside the regular diplomatic corps inevitably led to rivalry and controversy with the State Department, when combined with the emergence of a White House staff, it provided the president with a body of specialists at his disposal to serve as personal envoys who could speak for him in the conduct of negotiations and the direct execution of policy. During the twentieth century executive agents dispatched abroad were frequently drawn from the presidential staff.

The late-twentieth-century trend toward summitry, or personal negotiations between heads of state, rendered the use of executive agents to conduct direct negotiations not only convenient but highly desirable in dealing with key allies or important questions. The dispatch of such an agent in itself constituted an indication that the matter had been brought to the personal attention of the president, and hence assumed a certain symbolism of its own. Inevitably, the use of executive agents tended to downgrade the importance of regularly accredited diplomats, who were considered representatives of the government—that is, the bureaucracy as represented by the State Department—rather than of the president himself.

This development was obviously fraught with difficulties, particularly since instant communications enabled regular envoys to be in constant touch with Washington. As the complexity and size of the Washington bureaucracy increased, the issue of whether communications to the Department of State reached the president became important in the perception of other governments. Many governments preferred to be dealing with envoys who reported directly to the White House staff rather than the State Department, since they believed that his views would be more likely to reach the president. This perception has endowed the special agent with a status as a demonstration of concern by the chief executive. In some respects, this pattern is an inevitable result of the burgeoning of bureaucracy caused by the complexities of the modern world. President Nixon's use of Kissinger to conduct important negotiations during his service as national security adviser constituted a clear example of other governments preferring to negotiate with what they considered a direct presidential envoy. Since heads of state felt neglected if approached by someone other than the person with the president's ear, the mere appearance of a special envoy tended to facilitate serious exchanges and promote accord. This is one of the reasons why the use of executive agents gradually expanded.

The institution was adapted to serve yet another purpose, that of signaling that a situation was regarded as particularly important and was receiving the direct attention of the president. Such appointments also made more rapid action possible by circumventing the necessarily complex channels of modern governmental bureaucracy.

The increasing use of executive agents and special representatives caused considerable controversy regarding their role in enlarging presidential control of foreign policy. Some commentators contended that reliance upon such agents led to the bypassing of the State Department and Congress, thereby contributing to the expansion of presidential power at the expense of the legislature. Although the Constitution clearly vests authority and responsibility for the conduct of foreign affairs in the president, it also provides for congressional controls by placing the sole war-making power in the hands of the legislature and the requirement of Senate "advice and consent" to treaties. Also, Senate approval is needed to confirm the appointment of the ambassadors and ministers who represent the nation abroad, as well as for the selection of the secretary of state. Hence, while the State Department is clearly part of the executive branch, the legislature has a greater say in its functioning than in the case of presidential advisers and agents.

The expanded use of agents other than regular ambassadors occurred at a time when Foreign Service officers felt that their role was being considerably diminished. During the early days of the nation, all relations with a given country were conducted through the ambassador, whose advice played a significant role in the determination of policy. Ambassadors were sent out with broad instructions that allowed for considerable discretion. They were expected to report only occasionally, and hence were able to focus on crises and issues of overriding importance. In the new age of instant communications, however, ambassadors were required to report constantly, sending many communications each day dealing with a wide range of items, and required as well to clear virtually all actions with Washington in advance. Many former ambassadors and Foreign Service officers felt that diplomats and ambassadors had consequently lost considerable authority and influence. Envoys of all types often felt that they were being micromanaged. They believed the requirement that all actions be authorized in advance reduced their role and authority, placing more power in the hands of the president's political aides and handlers. Retired Foreign Service officers complained about this situation for many years. They invariably commented that instant communications enabled domestic politics to interfere with foreign policy decisions.

Presidents have expressed concern regarding the diminishing role of professional diplomats in the making and conduct of foreign policy. President John F. Kennedy attempted to alleviate the difficulty by appointing the veteran diplomat Averell Harriman as a permanent executive agent, or roving troubleshooter, with the title ambassador-at-large. The selection of a diplomat closely attuned to the State Department as the president's personal envoy provided a link between the two foreign affairs staffs. Yet the mere institutionalization of the position made it part of the bureaucracy, and this arrangement proved functional only because of the stature of Ambassador Harriman.

The use of such ambassadors continued under subsequent presidents, and became so institutionalized that at any given moment the United States had several individuals designated as ambassadors-at-large whose appointments were designed to deal—separately from the regular interchanges involved in bilateral relations between governments—with particularly important topics or with global issues. Individuals holding this rank were invariably drawn from experienced career ambassadors. President Nixon's concern about the resulting dichotomy between the White House foreign affairs staff and the State Department was evident when he shifted Henry Kissinger from the White House to the State Department, though such a step was unusual.

The use of such special appointments originally reflected the proclivities of individual presidents to conduct their own foreign policy and assume personal management of certain questions. At the turn of the twenty-first century, the accelerating expansion of such appointments merely reflected the expanding role of the United States in world affairs, and also the need to deal with emerging issues resulting from increasing globalization and global interdependence. Also contributing to this trend were disputes with Congress and delays in Senate confirmations of ambassadorial nominees, which often resulted from opposition party control of the Senate. Congressional problems increased as a result of close elections and the razor-thin legislative majorities that resulted.

Clearly, the use of executive agents and special representatives greatly expanded and changed during the twentieth century, particularly during its latter half. Originally they were utilized as an ad hoc arrangement to enable strong presidents to bypass the regular State Department bureaucracy on a temporary basis. As the Executive Office evolved in the post–World War II era, the president effectively had his own foreign policy advisers to oversee the bureaucracy. As that bureaucracy grew more complex, presidents found it even more necessary to utilize such agents to deal with situations requiring special attention. Increasingly, such agents and representatives were drawn from the regular bureaucracy; with growing frequency, they already held positions in either the State Department or on the White House staff. Thus, executive agents and specialized agents became part of the normal spectrum of representatives employed by presidents to deal with the increasingly complex international scene.

If such agents were employed to supplement normal diplomatic interchange and execute a policy upon which a broad national consensus existed, they aroused little concern. The institution became far more debatable, however, when a particular chief executive employed it on a large scale in an effort to concentrate control of foreign policy exclusively in his own hands or to bypass objections to a controversial policy. The result has been a decline in the morale of the State Department and its Foreign Service officers as their functions were partially usurped, leaving them with largely routine duties.

It is significant that as the use of special representatives and executive agents increased, at times becoming the seeming norm in multilateral situations, such representatives were increasingly drawn from the professional diplomatic corps. This reflects the fact that expert negotiating skills were especially important in multilateral meetings. The increasing use of assistant secretaries of state to deal with particular issues and the appointment of ambassadors-at-large within the State Department reflected this trend. It was particularly evident in the tendency during the 1990s to appoint as a special representative the ambassador to one of the countries involved in the conflict with which the representative was to deal. This was done both in the Middle East and in the Balkans. Hence, while professional diplomats often complained that ambassadors were now often limited to bilateral issues, and found themselves sharing responsibilities with others in multilateral matters, increasingly both were drawn from the same pool of expertise. It can be argued that despite the proliferation of special representatives, the centrality of ambassadors was gradually increasing because of the need to draw on the relatively limited pool of foreign relations specialists represented by the Foreign Service. In an era of multilateral diplomacy, it was necessary simply to supplement the position of ambassador with a new type of ambassador whose mandate extended beyond traditional bilateral relations.

Whatever the result of this continuing evolution, it is clear that executive agents have played and will continue to play an important role in American foreign relations. The institution has proven sufficiently flexible to adapt to a wide variety of uses and functions, and this has rendered it valuable. It remains primarily a supplement to normal diplomatic channels, to be employed in critical circumstances requiring special attention, or to make it possible to focus attention upon the multilateral issues that characterize diplomacy at the turn of the twenty-first century.

BIBLIOGRAPHY

Bemis, Samuel Flagg. *The Latin-American Policy of the United States.* New York, 1943. A general survey, useful since agents were frequently employed in Latin America.

Bemis, Samuel Flagg, and Robert H. Ferrell, eds. *The American Secretaries of State and Their Diplomacy.* New York, 1928– . An extensive, ongoing series containing a volume on each of the individuals who served as secretary of state throughout American history. Offers some comments on the relationship of special agents to the regular diplomatic establishment and brief descriptions of some of the missions.

Brzezinski, Zbigniew. *Power and Principle: Memoirs of the National Security Adviser: 1977–1981.* New York, 1983.

Destler, I. M., Leslie H. Gelb, and Anthony Lake. *Our Own Worst Enemy: The Unmaking of American Foreign Policy.* New York, 1984. Devotes special attention to the role of the National Security Council, while also providing an overall analysis of the delicate balance of powers and the offices involved in the making and conduct of American foreign policy.

George, Alexander L. *Presidential Decisionmaking in Foreign Policy: The Effective Use of Information and Advice.* Boulder, Colo., 1980.

Graebner, Norman A. *An Uncertain Tradition: American Secretaries of States in the Twentieth Century.* New York, 1961.

Grieb, Kenneth J. "Reginald Del Valle: A California Diplomat's Sojourn in Mexico." *California Historical Society Quarterly* 47 (1968). A full discussion of the mission to Mexico of an agent sent by Woodrow Wilson.

——. *The United States and Huerta.* Lincoln, Nebr., 1969. Includes a detailed examination of an era during which Woodrow Wilson employed numerous agents in Mexico, with full discussions of the various missions.

Halperin, Morton H. *Bureaucratic Politics and Foreign Policy.* Washington, D.C., 1974.

Harriman, W. Averell, and Ellie Abel. *Special Envoy to Churchill and Stalin: 1941–1946.* New York, 1975.

Hastedt, Glen P. *American Foreign Policy: Past, Present, and Future.* 4th ed. Upper Saddle River, N.J., 2000. Offers a concise discussion of the various branches and offices of the government involved in the making of U.S. foreign policy.

Henkin, Louis. "Foreign Affairs and the Constitution." *Foreign Affairs* 66 (winter 1987–1988). Updates his earlier monograph.

———. *Foreign Affairs and the United States Constitution.* 2d ed. New York, 1996. Provides a detailed examination of the constitutional provisions and the roles of the executive and the legislature.

Hill, Larry D. *Emissaries to a Revolution.* Baton Rouge, La., 1973. Examines Woodrow Wilson's use of agents in Mexico throughout his administration.

Inderfurth, Karl F., and Lock K. Johnson, eds. *Decisions of the Highest Order: Perspectives on the National Security Council.* Pacific Grove, Calif., 1988.

Kissinger, Henry. *Diplomacy.* New York, 1994.

Munro, Dana G. *Intervention and Dollar Diplomacy in the Caribbean, 1900–1921.* Princeton, N.J., 1964. Includes a brief consideration of some missions in this area.

———. *The United States and the Caribbean Republics: 1921–1933.* Princeton, N.J., 1974.

Ripley, Randall B., and James M. Lindsay, eds. *U.S. Foreign Policy after the Cold War: Processes, Structures, and Decisions.* Pittsburgh, Pa., 1997.

Rosati, Jerel A. "United States Leadership into the Next Millennium: A Question of Politics." *International Journal* (spring 1997).

———. *The Politics of United States Foreign Policy.* 2d ed. Fort Worth, Tex., 1999. Provides an effective overview of the evolution of foreign policy instruments and offices.

Rubin, Barry. *Secrets of State: The State Department and the Struggle over U.S. Foreign Policy.* New York, 1985. Gives an overview of the functioning of the Department of State, the role of political appointees, and the tensions between the Department and the National Security Council.

Schlesinger, Arthur M., Jr. *The Imperial Presidency.* New York, 1989. Contains a detailed history of the evolution of the role of the president and Congress in foreign policy.

Scott, James M., ed. *After the End: Making U.S. Foreign Policy in the Post–Cold War Era.* Durham, N.C., 1998.

Seymour, Charles, ed. *The Intimate Papers of Colonel House.* 3 vols. Boston, New York, 1926. Provides the personal records of House's missions.

Sherwood, Robert E. *Roosevelt and Hopkins: An Intimate History.* 2d ed. New York, 1950. Details the relationship between the two title figures and contains chapters referring to Hopkins's service as an executive agent.

Smith, Jean E. *The Constitution and American Foreign Policy.* St. Paul, Minn., 1989.

Wriston, Henry M. *Executive Agents in American Foreign Relations.* Baltimore, Md., 1929; Gloucester, Mass., 1967. The most extensive study available, deals mainly with the nineteenth and early twentieth centuries. A rather cumbersome discussion because of a broad interpretation of the term, but useful for consideration of the reasons for agents, early precedents, and congressional debates.

See also ARBITRATION, MEDIATION, AND CONCILIATION; DEPARTMENT OF STATE; INTELLIGENCE AND COUNTERINTELLIGENCE; INTERVENTION AND NONINTERVENTION; NATIONAL SECURITY COUNCIL; PRESIDENTIAL ADVISERS; PRESIDENTIAL POWER; RECOGNITION.

ANTI-IMPERIALISM

Robert Buzzanco

"America goes not abroad in search of monsters to destroy," Secretary of State John Quincy Adams told his audience during a Fourth of July oration in 1821. "She is the well-wisher of the freedom and independence of all. She is the champion and vindicator only of her own." Should the United States adventure into other lands, Adams warned, "she might become the dictatress of the world. She would no longer be the ruler of her own spirit." It is a great irony that such words, which would constitute a foundation of anti-imperialist thought for future generations, were uttered by the man who acquired Florida, crafted the Monroe Doctrine, and was a principal architect and defender of America's continental empire.

But then, any examination of anti-imperialism in the United States is replete with irony, ambiguity, and complexity. Whereas in other lands anti-imperialism was often closely identified with the political left and followed socialist or even Leninist models, and criticized the occupation and control of less-developed countries, American critiques of empire necessarily evolved differently because the United States did not have as strong a radical tradition and did not possess a formal empire in the European sense. Thus, anti-imperial ideas and actions have to be seen in a broader construction in which individuals or groups challenged the expansion of state hegemony, but did so based on the objective conditions of a particular time rather than on a doctrinaire or sustained ideology. Even more, anti-imperialists in the United States developed a broad comprehension of America's imperial mission, and so might oppose not just the political or military control of other lands, but also an aggressive foreign policy, supporting dictatorships abroad, the establishment of international organizations and compacts, or the excessive accumulation of executive power at home, all of which were perceived as antithetical to national values.

America's imperialism certainly could be coercive and militarized, but it was conceptually a grand strategy of economic penetration, a substitution of dollars in trade and investment for the armies and bullets of wars and occupations. As part of the imperialist pursuit for areas in which to invest, manufacture cheaply, find consumers, or trade, American military forces did in fact frequently intervene abroad, but usually pulled out after those lands were made secure for American political and economic objectives, often leaving proxy armies and puppet governments in their stead. Without a tradition of conquest and occupation, and believing in an ideology of republicanism, Adams and others therefore could champion both unrestrained expansion and anti-imperialism with plausible claims that they were not contradictory. By developing the historical sense, or myth, that the United States was not an imperialist power, the national elite—political leaders, business interests, media—could attempt to counter and delegitimize its anti-imperial critics. Making matters more complex, groups often critical of the state in domestic matters, such as farmers or workers, could be advocates of imperial growth out of self-interest because they needed foreign markets for their crops and manufactures.

Nonetheless, since the earliest days of the Republic, there have been significant opponents of American aggrandizement into new lands. Because U.S. imperialism had many justifications—economics, security, a sense of national purpose, racial identification, and so forth—critics offered an analysis and condemnation of empire based on different factors at different times and to varying degrees. American anti-imperialists could oppose foreign interventions because of a moral repulsion at the consequences of such involvement, the betrayal of self-government in other areas, a sense of geographic insularity or security, the contradictions of empire with democracy, or a rejection of the capitalist economic system. It was, then, a varied line of thought that had economic, political, and moral roots, and was real, effective, and significant, though at times elusive and not part of a sustained and comprehensive historical process. At the same time, however, the words of John Quincy Adams and others with similar views would be invoked a century and a half later as the United States waged war in Indochina and intervened in various Third World areas, so there is indeed a salience to American anti-imperialism that must be recognized.

THE ROOTS OF AMERICAN ANTI-IMPERIALISM

Expansion and empire building were concerns for American leaders as soon as national independence became a reality, and issues of growth and hegemony grew more important into the first half of the nineteenth century. The United States expanded rapidly and significantly across the continent. By purchase and conquest, national leaders gained lands in the Northwest Territory, the Louisiana Territory, Florida, the Pacific Northwest, and the Southwest, while attempting to bring Canada and Caribbean areas such as Cuba under American sway, too, though without success. While it would be difficult to observe a consistent anti-imperial ideology in this period, there was criticism of and actions directed against territorial acquisition, Indian removal, and manifest destiny. Often, such opposition served the interests of political expediency or power—as with northeasterners or Federalists voting against the Louisiana Purchase or the War of 1812. Critics, however, also objected on moral grounds or, presaging an argument that would become especially powerful in the Cold War era, the excessive, or imperial, use of executive power in foreign affairs.

The United States was born out of a war of national liberation against the world's greatest empire at the time, and thus tended to deny its imperial ambitions or to describe them benignly. Benjamin Franklin and Thomas Paine, for instance, popularized the idea that America could establish a "benevolent" empire while they condemned the British for policies of the "extermination of mankind," rather than just conquest, in their colonies. Indeed, the founding generation was conflicted despite the apparent consensus on expansion. While there was a compelling political will to develop an "empire of liberty"—to use

President Thomas Jefferson's words—there was also a continuing republican ideal that was distrustful of empire and its needs for standing armies, heavy taxes, large bureaucracies, and centralized decision making.

At the same time, there were strong isolationist tendencies among the ruling class. Not anti-imperialist per se, these isolationists did warn against American "entanglements" in other lands. Indeed, in his farewell address President George Washington, like John Quincy Adams an ardent expansionist using anti-imperial rhetoric, suggested that "harmony, liberal intercourse with all nations are recommended by policy, humanity, and interest. But even our commercial policy should hold an equal and impartial hand, neither seeking nor granting exclusive favors or preferences; consulting the natural course of things; diffusing and diversifying by gentle means the streams of commerce, but forcing nothing." Rooted in the fresh memories of the war against British imperialism, ambivalent views on state power, and an attachment to republican values, this isolationism had real meaning to many Americans and was practiced in their political affairs.

Thus, when President Jefferson purchased the Louisiana Territory from France, effectively doubling the size of the United States, critics attacked his actions as unconstitutional and imperial. Federalists, ironically using arguments that had been advanced against them by their political foes during the debate over the Constitution, contended that the purchase of trans-Mississippi lands was unnecessary and dangerous, for emigration into the new areas would "be attended with all the injuries of a too widely dispersed population, but by adding to the great weight of the western part of our territory, must hasten the dismemberment of a large portion of our country, or a dissolution of the Government." Such disputes notwithstanding, the Senate approved the acquisition of Louisiana, although the Constitution did not explicitly grant executive power for territorial expansion; subsequently, it authorized commercial restrictions and military engagements against Britain and accelerated a national program of Indian removal.

While the growth of a continental empire in the early nineteenth century may have been inexorable, it did not always proceed smoothly, for diverse voices were raised in protest against American expansion during the major episodes of territorial aggrandizement in the period. Representative John Randolph of Virginia was wary of imperial designs. "What! Shall this great mammoth of the

American forest leave his native element," he asked, "and plunge into the water in a mad contest with the shark?" Federalists stung by a swing in political influence and sectional growth toward the south and west opposed the War of 1812, with some beginning to develop a critique of expansion and even to consider the secession of New England states at the Hartford Convention (1814–1815). The defeat of Indians in the Creek War and the Battle of Tippecanoe, followed by General Andrew Jackson's invasion and eventual seizure of Florida in 1818, however, made anti-imperial critiques more difficult. Still, many questioned what they saw as the contradiction of maintaining republican virtues within a growing empire with an expanding military and a willingness to use force in the pursuit of national interests. Although the enthusiasm for new lands might have seemed frenzied, many Americans were concerned about unrestrained growth and especially lamented the destruction of Indian society.

After the War of 1812, the federal and state governments intensified their efforts to oust Native Americans from their lands, with General (later President) Andrew Jackson the leading figure in the era, attacking the Seminole in Florida and the Cherokee and other tribes in the southeast with particular ferocity. By the 1820s and 1830s, there was significant division over Indian removal and continental expansion. In 1831, when Georgia, relying on a Supreme Court decision that Indians were neither U.S. citizens nor a foreign nation, and with the support of President Jackson, expelled the Cherokee from their indigenous lands despite their treaty rights to it, evangelical Christians organized mass protests and condemned removal, comparing it to a crime against humanity.

Questions of morality and constitutionality—not unlike those raised in the late twentieth-century debates over the Vietnam War or intervention in Central America—were common throughout the Cherokee crisis as critics scored the national and state governments for violating the Constitution by rejecting Indian treaties. Writing under the pseudonym William Penn, Jeremiah Evarts, the chief administrator of the American Board of Commissions for Foreign Missions, an interdenominational missionary organization, exposed and denounced the U.S. attack on Indian sovereignty on the bases of morality, history, and the Constitution. Throughout the colonial period and under the Articles of Confederation and the Constitution, Evarts pointed out, various authorities had, by treaty, guaranteed the territorial integrity of Indian

lands; the Cherokee and other tribes, which had never surrendered such title, still held "a perfect right to the continued and undisturbed possession of these lands." The Indians, he added, did not hold lands *in* Georgia or any other state, but were sovereign, "separate communities, or nations." Removal was, in the minds of Evarts and many other critics of aggressive expansion, "an instance of gross and cruel oppression." While such views held great currency—the vote in Congress to approve Jackson's removal program was quite close in fact—they were not those of the majority, and Indians embarked on their infamous "Trail of Tears" while many millions of acres of Native American lands in the southeast were soon opened to agricultural exploitation.

The appropriation of Indian territory occurred in a period of great expansion, because Americans believed it was their "manifest destiny" to acquire new lands. Advocates of this ideology believed that the United States had a providential right and obligation to assume control over less-developed areas in the name of republicanism, Christianity, and white supremacy. Expansionists even had a quasi-legal justification for building a continental empire, the Monroe Doctrine. Crafted by Secretary of State John Quincy Adams and announced by President James Monroe in 1823, the doctrine was a statement of Pan-American influence in which the United States warned European powers to keep their "hands off" newly independent states in Latin America. Unspoken but just as compelling was the idea that the United States had a natural hegemony over the region and would expand control over all the Americas in time.

Again, however, John Quincy Adams seemed to be of two minds, refusing diplomatic or material aid to revolutionaries in South America and Greece because it would jeopardize the national interest by entangling the United States in the affairs of other countries and delivering his "America goes not abroad" oration, but also penning the Monroe Doctrine as part of his vision of a continental empire. To some critics, Adams's ideas were in fact endangering the national interest, with one member of Congress describing the Monroe Doctrine as "assuming an unwarrantable power; violating the spirit of the Constitution; assuming grounds and an attitude toward European Powers, calculated to involve us in the strife which there existed, and in which we had no interest; and indirectly leading to war, which Congress alone had the right to declare."

In addition to such continuing constitutional questions and insular concerns, critiques of expansion and empire invariably became intertwined in the intensifying slavery controversy, and almost always included attacks on the southern political and planter aristocracy, which had designs not only on the continental west but also on areas in the Caribbean, such as Nicaragua and Cuba, in which to extend their slave system. By the mid-1840s, these conflicting forces of southern expansionism and antislavery sentiment would lead to a national antiwar-cum-anti-imperialist movement.

The effective cause of the acute division of the era was the American war against Mexico, begun in 1846 but the culmination of a generation of U.S. attempts to absorb Texas into the Union. While there were strong sentiments north and south for bringing Texas and other southwest lands into the United States, the inevitable expansion of slave states gave rise to often fierce condemnations of expansion. John Quincy Adams, now an independent representative in Congress and a leader of antislavery, anti-imperialist political forces, feared that the annexation of Texas would turn the United States into a "conquering and warlike nation." Ultimately, "aggrandizement will be its passion and its policy. A military government, a large army, a costly navy, distant colonies, and associate islands in every sea will follow in rapid succession." Senator Thomas Corwin of Ohio echoed Adams's views, describing President James Polk as a "monarch" and his cabinet as a "court," and considering justifications for the war as a "feculent mass of misrepresentation." The "desire to augment our territory," Corwin lamented, "has depraved our moral sense." Ralph Waldo Emerson, noted essayist and earlier advocate of taking Texas, now predicted that the United States would gobble up new lands "as the man swallows arsenic, which brings him down in turn," and his fellow Transcendentalist Henry David Thoreau refused to pay poll taxes, received a jail sentence, and wrote his famous essay "Civil Disobedience" in protest of the Mexican War.

Such critiques held great popular and political appeal in the 1840s as pacifists, abolitionists, religious leaders, and literary figures pressed an anti-imperial agenda while 90 percent of Whig Party members in Congress voted against the war. Following the acquisition of Texas, California, and other Mexican lands in the southwest, anti-imperialists may have been on the defensive, but they were not quiescent. When, in the 1840s and 1850s, southern planters began to create and subsidize filibusters, military adventurers who tried to invade and secure Latin American lands for new plantations and slavery, abolitionist anti-imperialists protested vigorously. Whig politicians and an emerging political movement of Free Soilers, opponents of the extension of slavery into new territories, especially attacked the deeds of soldiers of fortune such as Narcisco López, who sought to invade Cuba in 1849, 1850, and 1851, and William Walker, the "grey-eyed man of destiny," who briefly conquered and ruled Nicaragua in the late 1850s. Indeed, the firm opposition of the Whigs and Free Soilers, as well as abolitionists and some evangelical elements, effectively thwarted southern dreams of a Caribbean empire in the antebellum period. They could not, however, suppress the intensifying sectional crisis, and civil war had become unavoidable by 1860 when Abraham Lincoln, who as a Whig representative opposed the Mexican War, was elected president. Within a half-decade, the conflict between the Union and the breakaway states of the Confederacy was over, and the United States was about to embark on its greatest imperial efforts yet, but not without protest and opposition at all points along the way.

THE NEW EMPIRE AND ITS DISCONTENTS

The Civil War not only ended slavery and the southern plantation system but marked the conclusive triumph of industrial capitalism as well. Within a few decades the United States emerged as a global economic power, with the opportunities and problems attendant to such status, including the acquisition of an extracontinental empire. Indeed, as soon as the Civil War ended, Secretary of State William Henry Seward embarked on a campaign to augment American territory by acquiring Santo Domingo (the Dominican Republic) and Haiti, Cuba, the Virgin Islands, Hawaii, and Alaska. Seward's plans, however, met heavy opposition from anti-imperialists like the noted author and social critic Mark Twain (later president of the Anti-Imperialist League), Senator Justin Morrill, and editor of *The Nation* magazine E. L. Godkin, who collectively called on American leaders to settle domestic issues and create a showcase society that others could emulate instead of seizing or otherwise taking on new territories. Subsequently, Seward's ambitions, except for buying Alaska, were shelved, though expansion and empire building would remain a priority in U.S. foreign policy.

By the end of the nineteenth century the American economy, producing more goods and agricultural commodities than the home market was consuming, seemed in deep peril, and government, corporate, and intellectual leaders urged that new markets abroad for trade and investment be found and acquired. Such economic pressures—along with calls for new coaling stations and a larger navy, the popularity of social Darwinist ideas calling on America to "civilize" the less-developed and nonwhite world, Christian ideology seeking to convert adherents of "pagan" religions, and the sense that America needed to extend its frontiers as a form of national renewal—led to a rush for new lands to control in the 1890s and set the stage for new levels of imperialism in the twentieth century.

In the 1890s the United States colonized or at least forcibly established hegemony over Hawaii, Cuba, the Philippines, Puerto Rico, and Guam, while Secretary of State John Hay was insisting that an "open door" for American products and capital be recognized by other nations. Because the European powers and Japan had colonial footholds—with administrators, collaborating elites, and occupying armies—in various areas, especially China, the United States would have to use its economic strength to develop a new world system based on a free and open door for trade and investment. The 1890s, then, marked the establishment of a "new empire" not only because the United States forcibly took territory outside the continent but also because it was announcing a different form of imperialism, one based on equal access to the markets and investment houses of other lands rather than on administrative control and military occupation.

American hegemony over Hawaii, Cuba, and the Philippines prompted significant and striking opposition. Politicians, commentators, Christians, and intellectuals spoke out against the new aggrandizement and presented a comprehensive analysis of the new empire that foreshadowed later anti-imperial arguments and movements. The war against Spain and intervention in the Philippines, critics charged, gave "militarists" too much power; the United States could acquire coaling stations or new trading opportunities without war or empire, they explained. Liberal Republicans known as "mugwumps," who had been drawn to the party by its stand against slavery, equated anti-imperialism with abolitionism. Many dissenters contended that the United States had no right or need to "civilize" other peoples, especially considering its own treatment of blacks at home. Conversely, some did not want America to assume control over and responsibility for nonwhite, and thus inferior, peoples. Labor leaders, such as the Socialist Eugene Debs and the conservative Samuel Gompers, agreed that conquest and empire were dangerous, in large measure because they feared the loss of American jobs to foreign workers who would accept lower wages, a charge echoed in the late twentieth century by antiglobalization activists.

Perhaps most pointedly, anti-imperialists argued that territorial annexation would pervert American principles. William Jennings Bryan, titular leader of the Democratic Party and agrarian spokesman, anticipated that the "just resistance" of the United States to Spanish rule in Cuba and the Philippines would "degenerate into a war of conquest," giving others the right to charge America with "having added hypocrisy to greed." Senator George Hoar lamented "the danger that we are to be transformed from a Republic, founded on the Declaration of Independence . . . into a vulgar, commonplace empire, founded upon physical force." The Anti-Imperialist League, tormented by the specter of Filipino blood on American hands, even "more deeply resent[ed] the betrayal of American institutions" such as representative government at home, international law, and self-government for others. Mark Twain used his biting wit to condemn the new imperialism, offering new lyrics to the "Battle Hymn of the Republic": "Mine eyes have seen the orgy of the launching of the sword / He is searching out the hoardings where the strangers' wealth is stored / He has loosed his fateful lightning, and with woe and death has scored / His lust is marching on." He was particularly outraged by the occupation of and ongoing war against the forces of liberation in the Philippines, reporting from Manila and comparing the nationalist leader Emiliano Aguinaldo to Joan of Arc and George Washington. Twain was also quite vitriolic about missionaries who justified imperialism as an extension of the religious duty. "I bring you the stately matron named Christendom," he wrote angrily, "returning bedraggled, besmirched, and dishonored from pirate raids in Kiao-chou [Tsingtao, China], Manchuria, South Africa, and the Philippines, with her soul full of meanness, her pocket full of boodle, and her mouth full of pious hypocrisies." Notwithstanding their impassioned opposition, the anti-imperialists were fighting rearguard actions against faits accompli in the Philippines and elsewhere, leading Theodore Roosevelt, assistant secretary of the navy, strong expansionist, and later president, to deride them

MARK TWAIN AND THE IMPERIAL APOLOGISTS

Not only was Mark Twain the author of some of the greatest works in American literature, such as *The Adventures of Huckleberry Finn* and *Tom Sawyer,* but he was also, less known, an acerbic critic of U.S. politics, challenging the idea that so-called captains of industry were creating a better society in the Gilded Age, and, more intensely, railing against American imperialism, the wars of 1898 in particular. In one of his more notable essays, "To the Person Sitting in Darkness," Twain both rages against the U.S. intervention in the Philippines and mocks apologists, such as the "person sitting in darkness," for supporting the actions of the "Blessings-of-Civilization Trust," the imperialists:

> Having now laid all the historical facts before the Person Sitting in Darkness, we should bring him to again, and explain them to him. We should say to him: They look doubtful, but in reality they are not. There have been lies; yes, but they were told in a good cause. We have been treacherous; but that was only in order that real good might come out of apparent evil. True, we have crushed a deceived and confiding people; we have turned against the weak and the friendless who trusted us. We have stamped out a just and intelligent and well-ordered republic; we have stabbed an ally in the back and slapped the face of a guest; we have bought a Shadow from an enemy that hadn't it to sell; we have robbed a trusting friend of his land and his liberty; we have invited our clean young men to shoulder a discredited musket and do bandit's work . . . but each detail was for the best. We know this. The Head of every State and Sovereignty in Christendom, including our Congress and our fifty State Legislatures, are members not only of the church, but also of the Blessings-of-Civilization Trust. This world-girdling accumulation of trained morals, high principles, and justice, cannot do an unright thing, an unfair thing, an ungenerous thing, an unclean thing. It knows what it is about. Give yourself no uneasiness; it is all right.

— *"To the Person Sitting in Darkness,"* North American Review, *February 1901*—

as "men of a by-gone age having to deal with the facts of the present."

Roosevelt's observations probably represented the views of most Americans, who appreciated the extension of American power and influence in 1898 and subsequently. Still, critics of the new empire persisted into the twentieth century, and American anti-imperialism was part of a broader, global attack on colonialism, but one that developed quite differently than elsewhere. Liberals like the Briton J. A. Hobson were offering a pointed economic analysis of empire, tying the European reach into new lands to underconsumption in the home market. More powerfully, the Russian theorists and revolutionists Nikolai Bukharin and Vladimir Lenin, writing during World War I, put forth a new socialist critique of empire that would find great currency in the coming years, though not so much in the United States as in Europe or the less-developed world. The great industrial powers, Lenin explained, were matched in a global contest for markets, and would increasingly come into conflict in areas yet to be exploited—later termed the "third world"—where they would vie with each other to establish colonies for consumers, raw materials, and invest-

ment. Although there were, to be sure, left, labor, and progressive political forces in the United States using such a radical model, anti-imperialism also continued to be an American ideology, unique to the nation's history and perceived values.

Anti-imperialists of the Leninist, liberal, or American variety found proof for their theses in the years after the Spanish-American-Philippine War and especially with the outbreak of World War I in August 1914. Struggles for materials and colonies in Africa, Asia, the Balkans, and elsewhere had led to the widespread carnage, principally, many critics held, for the benefit of state elites and corporations who needed expanded economic opportunities. In Europe, Bolshevik, socialist, labor, and other left parties, after initially supporting the entry of their various states into the war, emerged with this critique of empire. In the United States, similar analyses were current, though usually without the Leninist twist. The war, many American critics believed, was a product of great power, sphere-of-influence rivalries, not necessarily the inevitable consequence of economic expansion.

Henry Adams, grandson of John Quincy Adams, often debated the issue of American imperialism with Theodore Roosevelt and other expansionists after 1898. "I incline now to anti-imperialism, and very strongly to anti-militarism," Adams observed. "If we try to rule politically, we take the chances against us." Any U.S. attempt to establish hegemony comparable to the British empire, Adams and others maintained, was dangerous, futile, and un-American. Many socialists and other radicals unleashed their wrath on "dollar diplomacy"—the American policy of sending bankers, rather than armies, to foreign lands to gain influence and power—as another form of imperialism, just as nefarious and effective, albeit more subtle, as traditional colonialism. Walter Lippmann, a young but influential journalist, spoke for many progressives in 1914 when he observed that "the arena where the European powers really measure their strength against each other is in the Balkans, in Africa, in Asia. [T]he accumulated irritations of it have produced the great war." Between 1914 and the April 1917 U.S. entry into the war, Americans pressed their government to stay out of hostilities, effectively enough for President Woodrow Wilson's 1916 campaign slogan to be "He kept us out of war." Senator Robert La Follette, House of Representatives Majority Leader Claude Kitchin, William Jennings Bryan, and activists such as Jane Addams, Lillian Wald, Oswald Garrison Villard of *The Nation,* and others invoked American antimilitarist traditions to oppose entry into the war, contending that intervention would dampen reform at home, provoke a curtailing of civil liberties, and increase political repression, lead to war profiteering by big business, and otherwise sully American values. One group, the American Union Against Militarism, even had a mascot, a dinosaur named "Jingo," with the motto "All armor plate—no brains."

Despite such public dissent, Wilson asked Congress for a declaration of war shortly after his reelection was secured, thus alienating progressives, liberals, and anti-imperialists who had supported him in 1916 on the basis of his claims of neutrality, noninvolvement, and anti-imperialism. Wilson did in fact advocate self-determination, believing that empires would collapse if their colonies had the right to rule themselves, but his vision was limited, essentially covering the states of Europe that had been constituents of the Ottoman and Hapsburg empires, not the underdeveloped and nonwhite world. More to the point, Wilson's anti-imperialism was, like John Hay's earlier, a means to promote the Open Door; by breaking down existing empires, the United States could use its economic strength to gain a foothold in new markets.

After American entry into the war, many of Wilson's previous supporters began to comprehend his version of anti-imperialism and were part of a large and diverse antiwar movement, which, though not exclusively an anti-imperialist movement as well, did create a broader critique to challenge the decision to go to war as a dangerous departure from American traditions. Progressives and future isolationists like senators La Follette, Hiram Johnson, and William Borah and others, and radicals like Eugene V. Debs, Elizabeth Gurley Flynn, John Reed, Kate Richards O'Hare, Emma Goldman, "Big Bill" Haywood, Scott Nearing, and various socialist and labor organizations condemned the war and the imperialist frenzy attending it. Randolph Bourne charged that war, with its opportunities for profits and new territories, was "the health of the state." Woodrow Wilson, anti-imperial critics charged, had never been neutral but was always pro-England because of American economic ties to the British empire. Businessmen and their media propagandists, they added, had pushed the government into the war for their own self-interest and were hoping to use intervention to expand the Open Door. The war, critics concluded, served the interests of corporations and imperialists, not the national interest.

CHALLENGING A NEW WORLD ORDER

Such ideas became even more prevalent in the aftermath of the war as Wilson sought to develop a new global system, based on the Open Door rather than traditional colonialism. The keystone of the president's new program was to be the League of Nations, a body of the world's governments that would ensure "collective security" by taking action against aggressor states, militarily if necessary. Immediately a large and diverse coalition of critics came forth to condemn this departure from America's isolationist ideology, as they saw it. Some politicians, led by Senator Henry Cabot Lodge, an old-line Republican from Massachusetts who represented northeastern commercial interests, feared that the league would damage U.S. sovereignty, forcing America to participate in collective action at the behest of other members of the new organization. "Are you willing to put your soldiers and your sailors," he asked, "at the disposition of other nations?" Missouri Senator James Reed invoked a sense of racial superiority, charging that "black, brown, yellow and red races," ranking low in "civilization" and high in "barbarism," would be on equal footing with the great, white United States.

Lodge and Reed, however, were not specifically opposed to the extension and use of American power, but many others were, and saw danger in the league. La Follette believed that it would become an "imperialist club" that would maintain the status quo and keep colonies such as Ireland and India in bondage because the new body was not likely to sanction action against the great powers that held sway over the less-developed world. Like La Follette, others such as senators Borah, Hiram Johnson, and George Norris were so-called irreconcilables, who were progressive on domestic matters and believed that the league not only would limit American autonomy but also would deny autonomy to poor nations, and was not consistent with traditional national virtues of self-determination and isolation from the intrigues and squabbles of Europe and elsewhere. Further, a broad consensus was emerging to question America's involvement in and future after World War I; it was feared that the United States was embarking on a path of global behavior, with entanglements and interests abroad, which would resemble that of the existing empires. Indeed, in the years during and just after the war, a number of anti-imperialist and antimilitarist groups—including the Fellowship of Reconciliation, the American Friends Service Committee, the War Resisters League, and the Women's International League for Peace and Freedom—emerged to lobby for a more insular and less aggressive foreign policy. In the face of such widespread criticism, Wilson held his ground and refused to negotiate or compromise with his detractors, and the Senate accordingly rejected the treaty to join the League of Nations. While the war had marked America's debut as a great world power, the United States would not don the trappings of empire.

That is not to say, however, that the United States retreated from world affairs. Although the period between World Wars I and II is usually referred to as one of isolationism, the 1920s, as the historian and anti-imperialist Charles Austin Beard remarked, saw a "return to the more aggressive ways . . . to protect and advance the claims of American business enterprise." Trade and investments, and intervention, abroad increased between the wars as a corporative alliance of government offices and business institutions sought to create order and stability at home as well as to establish such conditions outside of national boundaries. In addition to reestablishing and aug-

menting economic ties to a rebuilding Europe and pressing for a greater opening of Asian markets, U.S. officials and corporations continued to move into Latin America in pursuit of expanded business opportunities.

Such circumstances led to another wave of anti-imperialism in the 1920s and 1930s but, once more, in complicated and seemingly contradictory ways. American officials such as secretaries of state Charles Evans Hughes and Frank Kellogg, concerned about exorbitant military spending and the potential for another outbreak of hostilities, brokered international agreements on disarmament and to outlaw war as an instrument of national policy. They and their successor Cordell Hull believed that free trade would promote peace, whereas empire led to conflict. Isolationists in public life and the media also believed that Europe was still trapped in the type of rivalries that had caused war in 1914, and warned that the United States should stay clear of foreign engagements until that continent stabilized. Such critics, however, were often internationalists who did not question America's right or need to expand abroad, but saw contemporary conditions as a deterrent to foreign involvements at that time.

Others offered a more pointed analysis. Critics of the war and the League of Nations treaty, such as La Follette and Borah, continued to warn against American imperialism and militarism, and spoke out against U.S. attempts to crush nationalist liberation movements in Nicaragua and El Salvador. Marine General Smedley Butler became something of a folk hero and offered a compelling critique of American imperialism when he called himself a "racketeer, a gangster for capitalism." During his thirty-three years in the Marine Corps, Butler boasted, he had

> helped make Mexico and especially Tampico safe for American oil interests in 1914. I helped make Haiti and Cuba a decent place for the National City Bank boys to collect revenues in. I helped in the raping of half a dozen Central American republics for the benefit of Wall Street. The record of racketeering is long. I helped purify Nicaragua for the international banking house of Brown Brothers 1909–12. I brought light to the Dominican Republic for American sugar interests in 1916. I helped make Honduras "right" for American fruit companies in 1903. In China in 1927 I helped see to it that Standard Oil went its way unmolested. . . . Looking back on it, I feel that I could have given Al Capone a few hints. The best he could do was to operate his racket in three districts. I operated on three continents.

Butler's views gained widespread acceptance. Huey Long, governor of Louisiana and putative presidential candidate when assassinated in 1935, agreed with the general and promised to nominate him to be secretary of (anti)war if elected in 1936. In fact, throughout the 1930s, disillusioned with World War I and alarmed by revelations and charges from the senate's Nye Committee that corporations, particularly in the munitions industry, had lobbied, if not conspired, for entry into the Great War, a majority of Americans held isolationist positions. Decrying what Senator Gerald Nye had termed the "rotten commercialism" of American businesses during the war years, Congress, with public support, passed a series of neutrality acts and other measures to prohibit President Franklin Roosevelt from becoming involved in conflicts in China, Ethiopia, and Spain.

The continuing aggression of Nazi Germany and imperial Japan, culminating in the attack on Pearl Harbor on 7 December 1941, however, undercut the anti-intervention, anti-imperial consensus and set the United States onto a path of apparently irreversible global empire. By war's end in 1945 the United States stood as the world's only great power: as a condition for aiding Britain during the war, the United States had insisted on the opening up of the markets of the empire and the beginning of a process of decolonization; Germany and Japan were in ruin as a result of the fighting that laid waste to Europe and Asia; and the principal rival to American hegemony, the Soviet Union, had lost more than 20 million people and millions of farms and factories during the war. The United States controlled half the world's trade and had established an economic order, the Bretton Woods system, and a political institution, the United Nations, as means to wield its power and influence. The so-called American century was in full bloom but, U.S. leaders warned, without a permanent military establishment and arms buildup it would be in constant peril. Accordingly, the United States embarked on its greatest military expansion, began to establish a global network of bases, sought an international Open Door, and established a national security state at home.

FIGHTING FOR AMERICA'S SOUL

Such measures attracted opposition. Henry Wallace, Roosevelt's vice president from 1941 to 1945 and presidential candidate in 1948, challenged the emerging "cold war" against the Soviet Union, charging that the United States was using "a predominance of force to intimidate the rest of mankind." Atomic scientists such as Albert Einstein and Leo Szilard eloquently warned of the perils of a nuclear arms race and established organizations and journals to challenge the political status quo. Journalists like Walter Lippmann and the radical I. F. Stone expressed their concern over the extensions of American power and responsibility into all parts of the world. Senators as diverse as the liberal Claude Pepper and "Mr. Conservative" Robert Taft feared the establishment of a military government. Vito Marcantonio, a Labor Party member of the House of Representatives, attacked business and military influences in Washington and the expansion of American capitalism into the developing world. Many liberals feared that the United States was abandoning its republican virtues, especially as the political repression associated with Senator Joseph McCarthy consumed the nation's political affairs in the 1950s.

African-American critics in particular challenged the intensified imperialism, as they saw it. Black leaders like W. E. B. Du Bois, Paul Robeson, and Harry Haywood believed it was dangerous, not to mention hypocritical, for the United States to spread its values and institutions abroad while maintaining a system of apartheid in its southern states. In particular, black spokespersons began to point out the common struggles of Africans trying to gain their national independence from colonial powers and of blacks in the United States seeking civil rights. Americans could hardly lead the "free world" by example, they argued, while maintaining legal segregation at home and endorsing continued colonization in Africa and other parts of the Third World. Although many mainstream black leaders supported the Cold War, hoping to parlay their loyalty to foreign policies into a commitment to act against racism at home, Du Bois, Robeson and others offered a more critical analysis, even invoking a Leninist critique of capitalist expansion and looking to the Soviet Union as an anti-imperialist model and champion of the rights of nonwhite peoples. Paul Robeson condemned Winston Churchill's "Iron Curtain" speech as a scheme for "Anglo-Saxon domination" of the world, and called for "united action of all democratic forces to achieve freedom for all colonial and subject peoples."

Views such as Robeson's, however, were not conventional wisdom, even in the black community, and most Americans accepted the new global role ushered in by the Cold War. Throughout the 1950s, then, the United States, without much dissent, intervened in a civil war in Korea, overthrew governments in Iran and Guatemala, offered economic and military support to military dictatorships throughout the globe, and continued to expand the Open Door. By the end of the decade, however, some Americans were uneasy with such hegemony, and various figures emerged to again challenge the U.S. empire. Cultural figures such as the beatniks condemned the conformity of Cold War life, the arms race, and the American denial of self-determination in other lands. More powerfully, and perhaps surprisingly, President Dwight Eisenhower, as he was leaving office in 1961, warned against "the acquisition of unwarranted influence . . . by the military-industrial complex. The potential for the disastrous rise of misplaced power still exists." Such thoughts may have remained a novelty in the 1960s, but U.S. intervention in Vietnam, still limited as Eisenhower left office, would mushroom in the coming years and give rise to a mass antiwar movement that would also question what critics saw as America's imperial behavior overseas and the military-industrial complex at home.

As in the 1840s and 1890s, many Americans in the 1960s opposed U.S. intervention in a foreign war and developed a larger anti-imperialist critique as a result of their challenge to the conflict at hand. Even before the major decisions to commit advisers, airpower, and combat forces, and essentially "Americanize" the Vietnam War, there was evident concern over the growing U.S. role in the world. Movements calling for an end to the arms race, peace with the Soviet Union, normal relations with Cuba, and recognition of the People's Republic of China, for instance, were in existence during the presidency of John F. Kennedy, and the Cold War consensus on an aggressive foreign policy, though still noticeable, was being questioned in some quarters. Vietnam accelerated that process, however, and brought about the greatest domestic challenge to American involvement abroad in the twentieth century.

By 1964, as the United States began to conduct air attacks against the National Liberation Front in Vietnam, peace activists, professors, and students were beginning to challenge the growing American role in Indochina and the larger foreign policy context of the cold war. Scholars such as the linguist Noam Chomsky, the historian William Appleman Williams, and the political scientist Hans Morgenthau participated in "teach-ins" on

Vietnam, giving rise to a national movement on college campuses and serving as a foundation for the antiwar movement. The Students for a Democratic Society, the largest radical student group of the period, held the first antiwar rally in 1964, and its adherents not only scored intervention in Vietnam but also offered a comprehensive analysis of the leaders of the American "empire," which, they charged, denied self-determination to Third World nations, intervened on behalf of corporate interests, and betrayed American principles. African Americans, engaged in an epic struggle for civil rights, added, as had Du Bois and Robeson earlier, that the United States had assumed the position of a white imperial power suppressing the yearnings for freedom of nonwhite peoples, whether in Indochina or below the Mason-Dixon Line. Martin Luther King, Jr., Nobel Peace Prize winner and civil rights leader, went so far as to call the United States "the greatest purveyor of violence in the world today," while the militant Black Panther Party called on African Americans to refuse to join the military or support U.S. intervention and openly sympathized with Third World revolutionary and anti-imperialist movements.

Politicians entered the debate as well, as they had during the League of Nations fight after World War I. Senators J. William Fulbright, George McGovern, Ernest Gruening, Wayne Morse, Mark Hatfield, Frank Church, and others were, like the progressives of the 1920s, anti-imperialist and internationalist. Fulbright, like Borah, chaired the Senate Committee on Foreign Relations and opposed the policies of the president of his own party. The senator from Arkansas believed that America had "betrayed its own past and its own promise . . . of free men building an example for the world. Now . . . it sees a nation that seemed to represent something new and hopeful reverting to the vanity of past empires."

Similar opinions were held by a significant number of Americans, including religious leaders, businessmen, and even military officials. Following in the tradition of Smedley Butler, former Marine Commandant David Shoup blasted not only the war but also the foundations of U.S. foreign policy. "I believe that if we had and would keep our dirty, bloody, dollar-crooked fingers out of the business of these nations so full of depressed, exploited people," he said in 1966, "they will arrive at a solution of their own. That they design and want. That they fight and work for. [Not one] crammed down their throats by Americans." Shoup's views, bluntly expressed, were shared by a significant number of Americans by the late 1960s and 1970s. Millions demonstrated publicly against the war and also called for a new, noninterventionist foreign policy. "Dove" senators tried to pass legislation to limit the war and, after U.S. withdrawal from Vietnam in 1973, enacted the War Powers Act to restrict the power of the president to commit U.S. forces abroad, a measure that was principally a response to the "imperial" presidency of Richard Nixon, who had waged war without authorization in Cambodia and Laos and was responsible for the Watergate crisis at home. By the mid-1970s, the United States seemed less prone to intervene in world affairs, a condition derided as the "Vietnam syndrome" by conservative critics but hailed as an anti-imperialist triumph by progressive and internationalist forces.

Such restraint, however, was short-lived; the Carter and Reagan administrations began to ratchet up the Cold War, increasing military spending, taking a more bellicose approach to the Soviet Union after the détente of the 1970s, and asserting American imperium in Central America and elsewhere. Millions of citizens, often invoking the legacy of Vietnam, challenged such policies as violations of national and international laws and of American values. Amid the Iran-contra scandal, they pointed out the similarities between the imperial presidencies of Richard Nixon and Ronald Reagan. Still, the 1980s and early 1990s were not periods of great anti-imperial activity. That would change dramatically, however, by the later 1990s as Americans had a vital role in a global coalition that was challenging the world's economic structure. In some measure, conservatives such as Pat Buchanan and Ross Perot, maverick presidential candidates in 1992 and 1996, used anti-imperial and nativist themes to sound the alarms about the new global economy. Sounding like progressives in the 1890s or isolationists after World War I, they believed that transnational corporations were moving abroad to find cheaper labor, thus causing American workers to lose jobs, and that the government and business elite was more interested in extending its interests abroad than in taking care of its citizens at home. Ironically, they even called for an end to U.S. sanctions against enemy states such as Iraq and Cuba, governments for which they held little love, because such economic warfare was damaging the people of those lands and not helping to oust Saddam Hussein and Fidel Castro. The United States was "a republic, not an empire," Buchanan often reminded Americans throughout the 1990s.

By the later part of that decade—with many major powers establishing regional and world economic groups such as the European Union, signatories of the North American Free Trade Agreement, and the World Trade Organization—anti-imperialists went on the offensive. Although such institutions had usually existed with little fanfare or opposition, critics such as Chomsky, the longtime consumer advocate Ralph Nader, and the anti-globalization activist Kevin Danaher emerged to attack what they considered a new form of global empire, with the United States as hegemon. From 1999 to 2001, when environmentalists, union members, student activists, anarchists, and other forces disrupted meetings of the World Trade Organization in Seattle, of the World Bank in Washington, D.C., and of the Free Trade Area of the Americas in Quebec, the lines were drawn in this new round in the global contest between the great powers and the forces of anti-imperialism.

As critics of American power, expansion, or empire entered the twenty-first century, they were using many of the same arguments that George Washington, John Quincy Adams, Mark Twain, William Borah, and J. William Fulbright put forth in earlier periods. Broadly defined to mean the aggressive use of power, the denial of self-determination abroad, militarism, or actions inconsistent with a republican form of government, American imperialism has a long tradition, but so does its anti-imperial counterpoint. Clearly, anti-imperialists, isolationists, doves, and others opposed to the excessive use of power or the extension of U.S. influence have been on the defensive as American leaders have tallied up an impressive array of territorial holdings, military interventions, proxy governments, and economic opportunities. One can ponder, however, how much more expansive the reach of American power or the extent of American militarism would have been without critics at home challenging the establishment and augmentation of "empire" at all steps along the way.

"The price of empire," J. William Fulbright remarked during the Vietnam War, "is America's soul, and that price is too high." Those words could just as easily have been uttered by John Quincy Adams at the turn of the nineteenth century. As America goes abroad in the future, in search of markets, bases, or even monsters to slay, one can be reasonably certain that there will be significant forces at home questioning and protesting against such extension of U.S. power, as there have been for more than two centuries.

BIBLIOGRAPHY

Beisner, Robert L. *Twelve Against Empire: The Anti-Imperialists, 1898-1900.* Chicago, 1992.

Buchanan, Patrick J. *The Great Betrayal: How American Sovereignty and Social Justice Are Being Sacrificed to the Gods of the Global Economy.* Boston, 1998.

———. *A Republic, Not an Empire: Reclaiming America's Destiny.* Washington, D.C., 1999.

Buhle, Paul M., and Edward Rice-Maximin. *William Appleman Williams and the Tragedy of Empire.* New York, 1995.

Bukharin, Nikolai. *Imperialism and World Economy.* New York, 1925.

Chilcote, Ronald H., ed. *Imperialism: Theoretical Directions.* Amherst, N.Y., 2000.

Cole, Wayne S. *Roosevelt and the Isolationists, 1932–1945.* Lincoln, Neb., 1983.

Danaher, Kevin, ed. *50 Years Is Enough: The Case Against the World Bank and the International Monetary Fund.* Boston, 1994.

Danaher, Kevin, and Roger Burbach, eds. *Globalize This! The Battle Against the World Trade Organization and Corporate Rule.* Monroe, Me., 2000.

Feuer, Lewis. *Imperialism and the Anti-Imperialist Mind.* Buffalo, N.Y., 1986.

Fulbright, J. William. *The Arrogance of Power.* New York, 1966.

———. *The Crippled Giant: American Foreign Policy and Its Domestic Consequences.* New York, 1972.

Fulbright, J. William, and Seth Tillman. *The Price of Empire.* New York, 1989.

Healy, David. *U.S. Expansionism: The Imperialist Urge in the 1890s.* Madison, Wis., 1970.

Hobson, J. A. *Imperialism: A Study.* New York, 1902.

Horne, Gerald. *Black & Red: W. E. B. Du Bois and the Afro-American Response to the Cold War, 1944–1963.* Albany, N.Y., 1986.

Johnson, Robert David. *The Peace Progressives and American Foreign Relations.* Cambridge, Mass., 1995.

LaFeber, Walter. *The New Empire: An Interpretation of American Imperialism, 1860–1898.* Ithaca, N.Y., 1963.

Lenin, Vladimir Ilyich. *Imperialism, the Highest Stage of Capitalism.* Peking, 1975.

Louis, William Roger. *Imperialism at Bay: The United States and the Decolonization of the British Empire, 1941–1945.* New York, 1978.

Magdoff, Harry. *The Age of Imperialism: The Economics of U.S. Foreign Policy.* New York, 1969.

———. *Imperialism: From the Colonial Age to the Present.* New York, 1978.

Mander, Jerry, and Edward Goldsmith, eds. *The Case Against the Global Economy and for a Turn Toward the Local.* San Francisco, 1996.

Miller, James. *Democracy Is in the Streets: From Port Huron to the Siege of Chicago.* New York, 1987.

Mommsen, Wolfgang. *Theories of Imperialism.* New York, 1980.

Ninkovich, Frank. *The United States and Imperialism.* Malden, Mass., 2001.

Parenti, Michael. *Against Empire.* San Francisco, 1995.

Paterson, Thomas G., ed. *Cold War Critics: Alternatives to American Foreign Policy in the Truman Years.* Chicago, 1971.

Salisbury, Richard V. *Anti-Imperialism and International Competition in Central America, 1920–1929.* Wilmington, Del., 1989.

Schirmer, Daniel. *Republic or Empire: American Resistance to the Philippine War.* Cambridge, Mass., 1972.

Schroeder, John H. *Mr. Polk's War: American Opposition and Dissent, 1846–1848.* Madison, Wis., 1973.

Tompkins, E. Berkeley. *Anti-Imperialism in the United States: The Great Debate, 1890–1920.* Philadelphia, 1970.

Twain, Mark. *Following the Equator and Anti-imperialist Essays.* New York, 1996.

Von Eschen, Penny M. *Race Against Empire: Black Americans and Anticolonialism, 1937–1957.* Ithaca, N.Y., 1997.

Williams, William Appleman. *The Tragedy of American Diplomacy.* Cleveland, Ohio, 1959.

———. *Empire as a Way of Life: An Essay on the Causes and Character of America's Present Predicament Along with a Few Thoughts About an Alternative.* New York, 1980.

See also CONTINENTAL EXPANSION; DOLLAR DIPLOMACY; ELITISM; IMPERIALISM; INTERVENTION AND NONINTERVENTION; ISOLATIONISM; THE NATIONAL INTEREST; PAN-AMERICANISM.

ARBITRATION, MEDIATION, AND CONCILIATION

Calvin D. Davis

American statesmen learned early that the discussions of diplomats and the conclusion of treaties are not always sufficient to settle international disputes peacefully. Their search for other methods of peaceful settlement began during the administration of George Washington and has been a continuing concern in the conduct of the foreign relations of the Republic since that time. In fact, it was a major aspect of American foreign policy before World War I and was of profound influence upon American thinking about international organization before that war.

HISTORICAL BACKGROUND OF THE ARBITRATION CONCEPT

International arbitration may be defined as the settlement of a difference between states through the decision of one or more individuals or a tribunal or court chosen by the parties to the dispute. An arbitrator may be the chief of state of a nation not concerned with the dispute; an ambassador, minister, or other official; or even a private individual. When a monarch or a president is an arbitrator he usually does not act personally; indeed, he delegates most responsibilities to the appropriate legal authorities of his government. When the parties to an arbitration decide to establish a tribunal, they may choose judges from their own nationals and then agree upon another individual to act as umpire. Sometimes they ask the head of another government to choose an umpire or leave the choice of umpire to the arbitrators already appointed. In several nineteenth-century cases no individuals were designated as umpires. Arbitrations may be concerned with questions of international law or facts. When arbitrations are primarily concerned with facts, as in pecuniary claims or boundary cases, the group of arbitrators is generally called a commission, but no precise distinction can be

drawn between commissions and tribunals. An arbitral decision is called an award, and it may be set aside if there are reasons to believe that it was not given in good faith or was not in accord with international law or the preliminary special agreement, usually called a *compromis,* concluded by the parties to the arbitration.

Historians and anthropologists have discovered arbitral customs and institutions in many cultures. The city-states of ancient Greece developed fairly elaborate arbitral procedure; on occasion they organized groups of arbitrators similar to modern international tribunals. During the Middle Ages, popes, princes, jurisconsults, and even city governments acted as arbitrators. Arbitration was less important during late medieval and early modern times, but it never disappeared altogether from international relations. Occasionally, European governments made use of it when trying to resolve American questions. In fact, some aspects of the first problem in the diplomatic history of the European conquest of the Western Hemisphere—the location of the dividing line between Spanish and Portuguese interests—suggest later arbitral practices. When Portugal challenged Spain's rights in the lands Columbus had discovered, King Ferdinand asked Pope Alexander VI to confirm the Spanish title. The pontiff obliged, issuing in 1493 a series of bulls in which he drew a line between the imperial claims of the two countries. The Portuguese protested the papal decision, and in 1494, Spain and Portugal, in the Treaty of Tordesillas, moved the line westward and agreed that a commission of surveyors and mariners should locate the line. While the two governments never set up the commission, the provisions of the treaty calling for such a body are evidence that commissions were of some importance in international relations at that time.

Commissions appeared occasionally in connection with England's colonial problems during the seventeenth and eighteenth centuries. The Treaty of Westminster, which Oliver Cromwell concluded with the Dutch at the end of the First Anglo-Dutch War in 1654, referred claims concerning the East Indies and the Americas to a commission. Apparently this commission met but failed to arrive at a decision. England and France in 1686 referred disputes over American matters to a commission, but it disbanded after outbreak of the War of the League of Augsburg. The Anglo-French treaties of Ryswick in 1697 and Utrecht in 1713 and the Treaty of Seville concluded by Great Britain, France, and Spain in 1729 provided for commissions to deal with American problems. All failed. After the War of the Austrian Succession, Britain and France established a commission for American questions. Again, failure. Certainly, the performances of commissions during the colonial era should have encouraged no one to believe that arbitration would be of large importance in later American history, yet that series of failures kept the idea alive. After the United States won independence, there were many problems that American and British diplomats found difficult to settle through negotiation, and they turned to commissions almost as a matter of course.

JAY'S TREATY AND THE TREATY OF GHENT

The United States and Great Britain for the first time agreed to use arbitration in their relations with each other when they concluded their first commercial treaty, usually called Jay's Treaty, in 1794. That treaty provided for three joint commissions to deal with disputes over boundaries, compensation due British creditors for obligations incurred by Americans before the Revolution, and questions arising from Britain's treatment of American shipping in the war with revolutionary France then in progress. The commission for maritime matters decided several questions, and the boundary commission also attained some success. It identified the Schoodiac River as the St. Croix, the river which was supposed to be part of the boundary between Maine and British territory according to the treaty of independence. But the debt commission broke up in an angry exchange, and it was necessary for the two governments to resume negotiations. According to a treaty concluded in 1802, the United States paid Britain a lump sum and the controversy came to an end.

The Treaty of Ghent, signed 24 December 1814, like Jay's Treaty, provided for three joint commissions. Only one commission completed its assignment—determination of the ownership of islands in the Passamaquoddy Bay. One commission tried to determine boundaries between British territory and the United States from the St. Lawrence River to the Lake of the Woods; it agreed upon a boundary through the Great Lakes but failed to determine the line from Lake Superior to the Lake of the Woods. The third commission was supposed to decide the boundary from the St. Croix to the St. Lawrence, but it failed to reach accord. The two governments thereupon referred the dispute to William I of the Netherlands. That monarch failed to find a clear basis for a decision but in 1831 made an award anyway, giving the United States and Britain what he believed to be equitable shares of a wilderness. The United States refused to accept this award, protesting that the king had not acted in accord with the agreement referring the controversy to him. While arbitration had failed in this instance, the case was of considerable importance, for it clearly established the principle that arbitrators should abide by the terms of a *compromis* or other preliminary agreements. (The U.S. government probably erred in refusing to accept the award, for the Webster-Ashburton Treaty in 1842 gave the United States less territory than it would have received according to the king's decision.)

The United States and Britain meanwhile had one other arbitration in connection with the Treaty of Ghent. The two powers were supposed to restore all property, both public and private, that they had seized from each other during the War of 1812. The treaty specifically mentioned slaves, but the British failed to return all American slaves under their jurisdiction at the close of hostilities. After many protests from Washington, British leaders agreed that an arbitrator should deal with the matter, and the two governments referred their dispute to Alexander I of Russia. The czar decided that Britain had failed to meet its obligations and should pay an indemnity. Upon his recommendation the United States and Britain concluded a convention setting up a commission to decide the amount due the United States. After elaborate proceedings, the commissioners decided that the indemnity should be $1,204,960, and, in a convention concluded 13 November 1826, the British government accepted this decision.

ANGLO-AMERICAN RELATIONS AND THE GENEVA TRIBUNAL

During the last half of the nineteenth century, the United States and Britain both made increasing use of arbitration. The United States had arbitrations with Brazil, Chile, Colombia, Costa Rica, Ecuador, Haiti, Mexico, Paraguay, Peru, Denmark, France, Portugal, and Spain. Britain, too, entered into many arbitrations with Latin American and European states, but the two English-speaking countries continued to have more arbitrations with each other than with other powers. Several minor but difficult Anglo-American controversies were settled by arbitration during the 1850s and 1860s; after the Civil War, arbitration became a major feature of relations between Washington and London.

The nineteenth century's most important arbitral decisions concerned Anglo-American controversies arising from the Civil War. British shipbuilders had built warships for the Confederacy, a practice stopped by London only after vehement protests from Washington. But British authorities acted too late to prevent the sailing of several ships, among them the *Alabama,* the most notorious commerce raider of the war. When the *Alabama* and its sister ships began destroying Union merchant ships, many American shipowners transferred their ships to foreign registry, Britain receiving the largest number of registrations. The American merchant marine almost disappeared. As the war closed, influential Americans fulminated against British misdeeds. Senator Charles Sumner of Massachusetts charged that Britain was really responsible for prolonging the war for two years and demanded a large indemnity. Britain, too, had grievances, for British shipping had sustained considerable damages at the hands of the Union. As charges and counter-charges were exchanged by intemperate speakers on both sides of the Atlantic, diplomats found negotiation of a settlement extremely difficult. Finally, in a treaty signed at Washington on 8 May 1871, the two governments agreed to arbitration of their Civil War claims and two other difficult matters, the boundary through the San Juan waterway between Vancouver Island and the United States and the compensation due Britain for recent concessions to the United States in the fisheries off Newfoundland and Canada.

The two governments used all the best-known forms of arbitration to resolve their four disputes. They made their most elaborate preparations for claims concerning the *Alabama* and the other commerce raiders, establishing a tribunal of five members in Geneva, Switzerland. Each of the two parties appointed an arbitrator, as did Brazil, Italy, and Switzerland. Presenting its case, the United States demanded payment of indirect claims, that is, damages sustained as a result of the prolonging of the war through actions of the raiders. The tribunal denied this demand, but in a decision announced 14 September 1872, it awarded the United States $15.5 million for actual destruction of ships and cargoes. Other American maritime claims against Britain and British claims against the United States were referred to a commission of three members, appointed by the United States, Britain, and Spain. Meeting in Washington, the commission soon decided against American claims but, in a decision announced 25 September 1873, awarded the British $1,929,819. Meanwhile, the United States and Britain had referred the San Juan waterway boundary dispute to German Emperor William I, who announced his decision on 21 October 1872, an award essentially in accord with American contentions. A commission of three members—an American, a Briton, and a Belgian—handled the fisheries case in sessions at Halifax. The commission announced on 23 November 1877 that the United States should pay Britain $5.5 million.

Of the four arbitrations, that of the *Alabama* claims was by far the most important. No other arbitration has so stimulated imaginations. While it is no doubt true, as Woodrow Wilson wrote, that the award "ended, not a controversy but a judicial process at the end of a controversy," many individuals convinced themselves that in this instance arbitration may have been a substitute for war. Long before the Civil War, arbitration had attracted the attention of people anxious to find ways of ridding mankind of the curse of war, and to such people the decisions of the Geneva tribunal seemed proof of what arbitration could accomplish. The spokesmen and journals of the American Peace Society, the Universal Peace Union, and many other peace organizations found in the Geneva arbitration topics for countless lectures and articles. Even before the Geneva tribunal announced its award, there were earnest recommendations that Britain and America negotiate treaties between themselves and with other nations in which they would recognize an obligation to resort to arbitration rather than war. Charles Sumner, on 31 May 1872, introduced a resolution in the Senate declaring that "in the determination of international differences Arbitration should become a substitute for war in reality as well as in name, and therefore coextensive with war in jurisdiction, so that any question or grievance which might be the occasion of war or of misunderstanding between nations should be considered by this tribunal."

A British peace leader, Henry Richard, on 8 July 1873 secured passage of a similar resolution in the House of Commons, and Sumner on 1 December of that year introduced another resolution urging arbitration in the Senate. While the two governments took no actions in response to these resolutions, the idea of treaties of obligatory arbitration continued to gain adherents. American and British peace advocates were probably unaware that Latin American governments almost as a matter of course included promises of arbitration in many of their treaties, and most Americans had probably forgotten that the Treaty of Guadalupe Hidalgo (1848), which ended the Mexican War, contained an article by which the United States and Mexico agreed to arbitration of differences in connection with the treaty. The peace movement in the United States and Britain gave little attention to developments in Latin America; it focused attention upon Anglo-American relations. If the United States and Britain were to conclude a permanent arbitration treaty, they would set an example for the rest of the world, peace leaders reasoned.

THE HAGUE PEACE CONFERENCES

It was not until the 1890s that there came many new opportunities to advance the ideas of arbitration enthusiasts. During that decade, marked as it was by naval building, imperial rivalries, and war, arbitration nonetheless seemed to emerge as a major feature of international relations, and the U.S. government was at the forefront of this development. As the period began, President Benjamin Harrison's secretary of state, James G. Blaine, brought together in Washington during late 1889 and early 1890 the First International Conference of American States. This conference recommended a number of proposals to promote hemispheric unity, among them a plan by which the American republics would have referred to arbitration all disputes that diplomacy could not settle, excepting questions of independence. Blaine called this agreement "the first and great

fruit" of the conference, but he rejoiced too soon. No government ratified the agreement.

Even before it was apparent that the Pan-American arbitral plan would fail, the United States was concluding an agreement with Britain for arbitration of an acrimonious dispute. Endeavoring to stop the indiscriminate killing of fur seals in the Bering Sea by both British subjects and American citizens, State Department officials grasped at mistaken translations and interpretations of Russian documents which seemed to prove that sovereignty over the sea had passed to the United States with the acquisition of Alaska. The Coast Guard seized Canadian ships and arrested their crews. Britain protested vigorously. Blaine's successor, John Watson Foster, negotiated an agreement by which the two powers established a tribunal in Paris to hear the case. In an award announced in 1895 the tribunal upheld Britain's contention that the Bering Sea was part of the high seas and thus not subject to the police actions of any government in time of peace. It became necessary for the State Department to resume negotiations to save the seals.

The Bering Sea tribunal had barely completed its labors when a serious Anglo-American quarrel arose over arbitration in another matter. The United States had long urged arbitration of the border dispute between Venezuela and British Guiana, but the British government, fearing that such an arbitration would encourage demands for changes in boundaries of other British colonies, repeatedly rejected American suggestions. Late in 1895, President Grover Cleveland's new secretary of state, Richard Olney, convinced himself and the president that Britain was very possibly claiming territory without real justification and was, therefore, about to violate the Monroe Doctrine. The secretary sent stern messages to London. Lord Salisbury, who was both prime minister and foreign minister, responded with a statement that sounded much like a schoolmaster explaining a few simple facts to a student with little intelligence. The Monroe Doctrine was not "public law," as Olney claimed, it was simply a statement made by a distinguished American statesman. Salisbury was accurate enough, but Americans insisted that the Monroe Doctrine had a larger meaning that other nations should recognize. Cleveland sent Congress a special message that resounded with appeals to honor and patriotic duty. In both the United States and Britain there were calls for war. After a few days calmer counsel prevailed. The British government decided that arbitration, after all, was the best way out of the crisis and concluded a treaty with Venezuela by which the two countries established a tribunal in Paris to determine the boundary. To the irritation of many Americans, the tribunal, in an award announced in 1899, largely upheld the British position.

In addition to the proceedings at Paris, the boundary controversy had another important result for arbitration. Shocked by the emotional excesses of the recent crisis, British and American leaders at last yielded to the pleas of peace spokesmen for a treaty of arbitration. Secretary Olney and the British ambassador, Sir Julian Pauncefote, negotiated a treaty according to which their governments were to agree that for a five-year period they would settle territorial and pecuniary claims through arbitration. The treaty made no exception for national honor, but it provided an elaborate procedure for setting up tribunals and handling appeals that should have been adequate safeguards for the interests of both parties. Optimists believed the treaty could be a first step toward a permanent world tribunal. Olney and Pauncefote signed the treaty on 11 January 1897, and Cleveland and his successor, William McKinley, both urged ratification. Unfortunately, partisan politics, dislike for Britain, and fear of a departure from the traditional policy of avoiding entangling alliances influenced many senators. After approving amendments that would have deprived the treaty of any real force, the Senate on 5 May 1897 declined consent for ratification. Great was the disappointment of arbitration enthusiasts, but there soon came another opportunity for their cause.

The Russian foreign ministry, on 24 August 1898, sent a circular note to all governments with diplomatic representation in St. Petersburg. Czar Nicholas II proposed a conference to consider limitation of armaments. The United States was quick to accept, although there was no interest in Washington in limiting or reducing armaments, and some influential people suspected a connection between the Russian proposal and the recent American victory in the war with Spain. When the Russians added improvements in the laws of war and arbitration to the agenda, American officials became more interested. Secretary of State John Hay instructed the American delegates to work for agreement on these subjects, and he told them to present a plan for a permanent international tribunal modeled on the Supreme Court of the United States.

Upon request of Nicholas II, Queen Wilhelmina of the Netherlands provided the conference with a meeting place at The Hague. Representatives of twenty-six governments were present for the opening session on 18 May 1899 at one of the Dutch royal palaces, the House in the Wood. In addition to the delegates, peace workers gathered at The Hague, anxious to encourage the "Peace Conference," as they called it, to make large initiatives for peace. To many people, the term "Peace Conference" soon seemed a misnomer, for the conference spent much of its time discussing war. It failed to agree to any reduction in armies and navies or their budgets but did adopt declarations against poison gas, needlessly cruel bullets, and the throwing of projectiles or explosives from balloons or similar devices. It was more successful in its work with the laws of war. It framed two conventions about this subject, one of which was a codification of the laws of land warfare and the other a convention extending the Geneva Convention of 1864 (popularly known as the Red Cross Convention) to naval warfare. While humanitarians hailed these conventions, another document, the Convention for the Pacific Settlement of International Disputes, was more interesting to peace workers. This convention summarized experience with arbitration, mediation, and commissions of inquiry and made several significant innovations in the application of these methods to the resolution of international differences.

No part of the conference's work required more diplomacy than Title IV of the Pacific Settlement Convention, "On International Arbitration." The American delegates soon discovered that there was little chance for adoption of their plan for a permanent tribunal, and they decided not to press for its acceptance. Instead, they supported a plan offered by Pauncefote, the chairman of the British delegation. The British proposed that each signatory power name two jurists to a list and that parties to an arbitration should choose judges from that list. The Russians also advanced a plan, proposing that five powers be given authority to name one judge each and that these judges should always be ready to act as arbitrators. Both plans called for an administrative bureau at The Hague. The chairman of the U.S. delegation, Andrew D. White, and the delegation secretary, Frederick W. Holls, worked closely with the British and Russians to secure an acceptable compromise. For a time German objections threatened to defeat their efforts; and it required much persuasion before the German government agreed to support a plan believed somewhat weaker than the original British and Russian proposals. The conference then agreed that each signatory power should select "four persons at the most, of known competency in international law, of the highest moral reputation, and disposed to accept the duties of Arbitrator." These people were to be members of a permanent international institution, the Permanent Court of Arbitration. A bureau at The Hague would maintain their names on a list and carry out all administrative responsibilities. Powers wishing to enter into arbitrations could choose arbitrators from the list, but there was no requirement that they do so.

Efforts at incorporating obligatory features into the convention largely failed. The Germans, in particular, opposed obligatory arbitration, and without their support little was possible. The completed convention included, however, a statement that the signatory powers recognized arbitration "as the most effective, and at the same time the most equitable, means of settling disputes which diplomacy has failed to settle," and article 27 declared that the signatory powers would "consider it their duty, if a serious dispute threatens to break out between two or more of them, to remind these latter that the Permanent Court is open to them." This provision, based on a French proposal that Holls had warmly supported, was the subject of serious disagreement within the American delegation. The naval delegate, Captain Alfred T. Mahan, the famed historian of sea power, argued that the article could lead to conflict between the Hague Convention and the Monroe Doctrine. Debate within the delegation ceased only when White read a statement to the conference that in signing the convention the United States was in no way departing from its traditional policies toward Europe or the Americas.

Many of the framers of the Peaceful Settlement Convention were as concerned with good offices and mediation as with arbitration. When a government extends an offer of good offices to powers in controversy or at war, it makes its diplomatic services and facilities available to them. When a power acts as a mediator, it takes an active part in negotiations, acting much as a middleman. In actual practice, it is difficult to distinguish between good offices and mediation, and the First Hague Conference did not make such a distinction, but it did recognize the need to guarantee their benevolent character. Too often such offers had been viewed as unfriendly interventions, sometimes for good reasons. Americans remem-

bered how the imperial French government during the Civil War had been unsympathetic to the Union cause and had, at an inconvenient moment, offered mediation. The Peace Conference sought to prevent such problems in the future by including in the convention a declaration that powers that were strangers to a dispute had the right to offer good offices and mediation even during hostilities and that the exercise of this right could "never be regarded by either of the parties at variance as an unfriendly act." The convention was as careful in its treatment of recipients of offers of good offices and mediation. Article 6 declared that offers of good offices and mediation "have exclusively the character of advice, and never have binding force," while article 7 stated that mediation could not interrupt, delay, or hinder mobilization or other preparations for war.

Article 8 of the mediation section was in a class by itself. The result of a proposal by Holls—other delegates referred to it as *La Proposition Holls*—it provided for what was called "special mediation." According to its terms, each party to a conflict could choose another power to act in its place. For thirty days the disputing powers would cease all communication about their controversy and let their seconds make an effort at settlement.

In addition to the articles on mediation and arbitration, the conference included provisions in the convention for commissions of inquiry. It was already an accepted practice to promote international conciliation by appointing commissions to ascertain facts. Such commissions were not expected to make recommendations for settlement, but they were expected to make reports that could aid quarreling governments to work out their differences. There was, however, no generally accepted procedure for establishing commissions. Cleveland had appointed a commission to gather evidence during the Venezuelan boundary controversy, and while the commission did much good work, the fact that it was constituted by only one party to the dispute was lost on no one. Obviously, such one-sided arrangements should be avoided in the future. The Hague Convention provided that commissions should be organized according to a procedure similar to that by which arbitral bodies could be constituted from the list of the Permanent Court of Arbitration and that the commissions should confine their activities to the determination of facts. They would present reports to the conflicting powers but those powers would retain full freedom to interpret the findings of the commissions.

During the fifteen years following the Peace Conference of 1899, the Convention for the Pacific Settlement of International Disputes was of considerable importance in international relations, and no country displayed more interest in the convention and the Hague Court than the United States. American statesmen made promotion of the court an important part of foreign policy. Upon the suggestion of President Theodore Roosevelt, the United States and Mexico gave the court its first case, a dispute over whether the cession of California to the United States had ended Mexico's obligation to give financial support to an ancient fund for the conversion of the California Indians—the Pious Fund of the Californias. The court carefully examined a large quantity of historical evidence and, on 14 October 1902, rendered an award stating that Mexico was still obligated to support the fund.

Roosevelt's initiative in the Pious Fund case won approval from American and European peace movement leaders, but soon he made clear the limits of his confidence in the Hague Court. He refused to submit the controversy over the Alaska Panhandle's boundary with Canada to the court. A joint commission had failed to settle the matter, a problem since the Klondike gold rush in 1896, but Roosevelt agreed to what was essentially another commission, although called a tribunal. The president and the British monarch were each to appoint three "impartial jurists of repute." Roosevelt appointed his secretary of war, Elihu Root; his close friend Senator Henry Cabot Lodge of Massachusetts; and former senator George Turner of Washington, who was well acquainted with commercial relations between his state and the Alaskan gold-rush ports. King Edward VII appointed the lieutenant-governor of Quebec, Sir Louise A. Jetté; a Toronto lawyer, A. B. Aylesworth; and the lord chief justice of England, Lord Alverstone, who had a prominent role in the Bering Sea arbitration. Alverstone voted with the Americans for a decision favorable to American contentions. Great was the anger of Canadians who charged that no one could have expected the American jurists to be impartial, despite reasons for believing that the impartiality of the British Empire jurists was also suspect. Roosevelt told people who believed he had risked a sound claim to arbitration that a tie was the worst that could have happened, and he insisted that the London proceedings had not been an arbitration. History does not support what the president was saying, but his interpretation has, nonetheless, been widely accepted.

With regard to a more serious controversy, the Venezuelan debt affair, Roosevelt was as pleased to make use of the Permanent Court of Arbitration as he had been determined to avoid it in the Alaska boundary dispute. After Britain, Germany, and Italy blockaded Venezuelan ports in late 1902 and early 1903 to force Venezuela to honor financial obligations due their nationals in that country, other governments asked that the claims of their nationals in Venezuela also be paid. The question then arose as to whether the blockading powers should have preference when the payments began. Roosevelt saw an opportunity for the Hague Court. Upon his suggestion a court was again constituted from its list of arbitrators, and the interested powers began a long and complicated arbitration. The court finally announced, on 22 February 1904, an award stating that the blockading powers should have preference, a disappointing decision to many of the warmest friends of the court, for it seemed to reward violence.

Before World War I broke out, the Hague Court rendered awards in twelve other cases, two of them involving the United States. The Treaty of Washington of 1871 and the Halifax commission had failed to put to rest all difficulties over the North Atlantic fisheries, and the American and British governments referred their controversy to the Permanent Court in 1909. The court, on 10 September 1910, announced an award that upheld most British contentions but which was so carefully stated that the Americans as well as the British believed justice had been done. A few weeks after making this award, the court, on 25 October, made an award in another case involving the United States, the Orinoco Steamship Company case, a dispute between a company owned by U.S. citizens and the Venezuelan government. The award was substantially in accord with the position of the United States government.

The provisions of the Pacific Settlement Convention for commissions of inquiry and good offices and mediation were not used as often as the arbitration sections from 1899 to 1914, but they were of importance in connection with the most serious armed conflict of the era, the Russo-Japanese War. When Russia's Baltic fleet, en route to the Far East, fired into a British fishing fleet off Dogger Bank on the night of 21–22 October 1904, having mistaken the fishing boats for Japanese torpedo boats, there was a furor in Britain, and high officials in London talked of using force to stop the Russian fleet. Anger subsided when the

Russian government suggested establishment of a commission of inquiry under terms of the Hague Convention. Four admirals—one each from Russia, Britain, France, and the United States—were appointed to a commission that carefully investigated the matter. Upon receiving the commission's report, the Russian government paid damages and the matter was closed.

As the war passed its decisive stages, peace movement spokesmen hoped that powers signatory to the Hague Convention would remember its provisions for good offices and mediation, and they were elated when President Roosevelt mediated a settlement, the Peace of Portsmouth of 1905. The American president made no use of the language of the Hague Convention, but it is probable that that document influenced him, for at one time he suggested that the Russians and Japanese hold peace negotiations at The Hague.

Many peace spokesmen in the United States and Europe believed Roosevelt's efforts to improve the Hague system would prove as important in the long run as his mediation of the Russo-Japanese conflict. The president in 1904 promised the visiting Interparliamentary Union that he would call another Hague peace conference, and in October of that year Secretary of State Hay sent out a circular suggesting a new conference. Later, Roosevelt stepped aside in response to a Russian request that Nicholas II have the honor of calling the conference officially, but the United States took an active role in the conference.

The Second Hague Peace Conference, which met in 1907, was much larger than the 1899 conference, for it included delegates from most Latin American countries. The Latin Americans were present because the United States asked for their inclusion. Indeed, Latin American policy was one of the most important considerations of the United States at the conference, but Secretary of State Elihu Root and the president did not forget the old dream of a world court. The chairman of the U.S. delegation, Joseph Hodges Choate, and another American member, James Brown Scott, struggled valiantly to secure establishment of a new tribunal, the Court of Arbitral Justice, which would have stood alongside the Permanent Court of Arbitration but would have been a truly permanent court, always in existence and ready to hear cases. Unfortunately, it proved impossible to agree upon a system of appointing judges without offending smaller powers that could not have continuous representation. As the conference closed, the Court of Arbitral Justice was only a project attached to a

voeu (formal wish) that the powers signatory to the Final Act bring the court into existence as soon as they agreed upon the selection of judges and several details of the court's constitution.

The negotiation of arbitration treaties and treaties of conciliation were other important aspects of the diplomacy of peace from 1899 to 1914. Britain and France in 1903 negotiated a treaty of arbitration, and peace movement leaders then urged the United States to follow this example. Roosevelt and Hay yielded to their pleas, and Hay, in 1904 and 1905, negotiated treaties with France, Switzerland, Germany, Portugal, Great Britain, Italy, Spain, Austria-Hungary, Mexico, and Sweden and Norway. To the anger of Roosevelt and Hay, the Senate in advising ratification insisted that the preliminary arbitration agreements be actual treaties and therefore subject to the ratifying process. Roosevelt thereupon refused to proceed further, but Hay's successor, Root, was convinced that treaties amended so as to meet the Senate's requirements would be better than none. He prevailed upon the president to consent to negotiation in 1908 of a new set of treaties. The Senate found these treaties more to its liking and approved ratification.

It would have been well if President William Howard Taft and his secretary of state, Philander C. Knox, had been as cautious as Root in dealing with the Senate, for they would have been spared a large disappointment. Knox negotiated arbitration treaties with Britain and France in 1911 that made no exceptions for such considerations as national honor. The treaties merely stated that any matter that was justiciable would be arbitrated. Since whether or not a dispute was justiciable was subject to varying interpretations, it seemed that the treaties contained adequate safeguards for the interests of the governments concerned, but the Senate saw the matter in a different light. Believing that the treaties could limit the nation's freedom of action, the Senate refused consent for ratification.

President Woodrow Wilson's first secretary of state, William Jennings Bryan, was less interested in arbitration than his immediate predecessors, although he negotiated renewal of the Root treaties. He was more impressed with the conciliatory effects of commissions of inquiry and believed that their development could be carried much farther than the Pacific Settlement Convention had done. He hoped for treaties of conciliation incorporating new ideas about investigating commissions. Soon after the Wilson administration took office, he advanced what he called the president's peace plan. He urged nations to agree to refer their disputes to investigating commissions for six months or a year. While awaiting the reports of the commissions, they would refrain from going to war or increasing their armaments. The signatories of the treaties would be free to accept or reject conclusions of the commissions or to go to war, but Bryan was confident that the period of waiting could have a cooling-off effect and help avert war. He negotiated twenty-nine treaties according to this plan, and twenty of them were ratified. Sadly, this initiative for peace was interrupted by the outbreak of World War I.

The declarations of war in 1914 also interrupted American efforts to bring the Court of Arbitral Justice into existence and to ensure the meeting of a third Hague peace conference. Since the conference of 1907, American diplomats had been conducting quiet negotiations with the British, French, and Germans to establish the Court of Arbitral Justice without waiting for the consent of all powers that had participated in that conference. While these negotiations had reached no definite conclusion, in 1914 there were some reasons to hope for success. Negotiations for a third Hague peace conference were even more promising. The 1907 conference had recommended that another conference meet after an eight-year interval, the same as between the first two conferences. To many peace spokesmen and theorists, the conference seemed to be developing into a permanent institution. A periodic world conference and a world court with judges always ready to hold sessions—these were the institutions necessary for a viable world organization, they believed. In the United States the peace societies and the new Carnegie Endowment for International Peace brought pressure to bear upon Wilson and Bryan to use their influence to bring about the meeting of the conference, and this the president and the secretary of state agreed to do. Planning for the conference had made considerable progress when war began in 1914.

THE LEAGUE OF NATIONS AND THE WORLD COURT

The Hague period of modern internationalism ended abruptly with the declarations of war. The Pacific Settlement Convention and the treaties of arbitration and conciliation were brushed aside as the armies of the warring nations hastened to secure strategic positions. Four years later, as the war moved toward its close, European nations and the United States advocated a world organization. Occasionally there were recommendations that the new world system be founded on the work of the Hague conferences, but at Paris, in 1919, Wilson and other internationalists sought to break with the Hague traditions as they planned the League of Nations.

Fundamental in Wilson's thinking was the famous pledge in Article X of the League of Nations Covenant "to respect and preserve as against external aggression the territorial integrity and existing political independence" of the league's members. Wilson's small respect for the work of the Hague conferences notwithstanding, other members of the drafting committee incorporated into the covenant the prewar experience with arbitration and conciliation. Members of the league were to refer disputes that threatened rupture to arbitration, judicial settlement, or inquiry by the League Council. Parties to a dispute were not to go to war for three months after arbitral awards, judicial decisions, or reports from the council. The league convened a conference of experts at The Hague in 1920 to draft a statute for a new international court. The conference took the 1907 draft Hague convention for a Court of Arbitral Justice as the basis of its work and quickly produced the draft Statute for the Permanent International Court of Justice. The older Permanent Court of Arbitration was to have a special role in the new judicial system: its judges were to meet in national groups to make nominations for the new court. The Permanent Court of International Justice met for the first time in the Peace Palace at The Hague in 1922. The creation of the Permanent Court, usually called the World Court, was a special challenge to the United States. Elihu Root and James Brown Scott were among the experts who drafted the World Court Statute. Despite the failure of the United States to ratify the Treaty of Versailles and the attached Covenant of the League of Nations, adherence to the statute was possible. The isolationism resulting from the league struggle was, however, so strong that even the court aroused senatorial opposition. Presidents and secretaries of state during the 1920s and 1930s made several attempts to secure American entry into the World Court system. All failed. Secretaries of state, nevertheless, pursued arbitration policies like those of Elihu Root, renewing Root's treaties and negotiating entirely new arbitration agreements. The United States was one of sixteen republics at a Pan-American conference in Santiago, Chile, in 1923 that signed a treaty providing for commissions of inquiry to investigate disputes neither diplomacy nor arbitration could settle. At the Conference on Conciliation and Arbitration in Washington on 5 January 1929, the United States was one of twenty American republics signing a general arbitration treaty and conciliation convention.

The European experience with peaceful settlement between the world wars was no more promising than that of the United States. The World Court decided several cases, and governments continued to make use of arbitration. The Geneva Protocol was an important proposal to strengthen the covenant's arbitration provisions, but it failed in 1925 when a new Conservative government in London withdrew support. Later that year, at the Locarno conference, the German government concluded treaties with Belgium and France recognizing their boundaries with Germany and concluded arbitration treaties with those two countries and Poland and Czechoslovakia. All such initiatives for peace were swept aside when World War II began.

THE UNITED NATIONS

As World War II neared its conclusion, Allied statesmen reasoned that a new beginning for world organization was necessary, so at conferences at Dumbarton Oaks in Washington, D.C., and at San Francisco, they wrote the Charter of the United Nations. The charter included even more peaceful settlement procedures than the League Covenant. Parties to disputes were first of all to seek solutions "by negotiation, enquiry, mediation, conciliation, arbitration, judicial settlement, resort to regional agencies or arrangements, or other peaceful means of their own choice." The charter provided for a new World Court and declared that all UN members would be ipso facto parties to its statute. The new World Court Statute was a revision of that of 1920. When the International Court of Justice held its first meeting at The Hague on 3 April 1946, the most noticeable change was the dropping of "Permanent" from its official name.

The United Nations has been a major factor in world affairs since its founding. Decisions of the General Assembly and the Security Council have repeatedly tried to maintain order and peace.

Intervention in Korea and many peacekeeping operations have often given the impression of a military alliance, but the quieter means of settling disputes peacefully have, nonetheless, been of importance. The International Court of Justice has made decisions in numerous disputes, and governments have continued to make use of the Permanent Court of Arbitration and ad hoc arbitration tribunals. Such tribunals make possible preservation of greater secrecy and, at the same time, allow each party to a dispute to name some of the jurists who will hear the case. The UN secretary-general, Kofi A. Annan, in 1998 noted that the Permanent Court of Arbitration and the International Court of Justice were neighbors in the Peace Palace and were "complementary institutions offering the international community a comprehensive range of options for the peaceful resolution of disputes."

When one reflects upon American initiatives to promote arbitration and a world tribunal before World War I and the consistency with which U.S. presidents during the 1920s and 1930s recommended adherence to the World Court Statute, American support since 1945 for the World Court and other means for pacific settlement has often seemed tepid. The memoirs and biographies of presidents and secretaries of state since 1945 include many references to the United Nations, but it is rare that they mention the International Court of Justice, arbitration, or other means for pacific settlement. As a former U.S. ambassador to the United Nations, Daniel Patrick Moynihan, has pointed out, American diplomacy has often appeared to be unaware of the resources offered by international law. Yet, a century after the Pious Fund case, arbitration again was of importance in some aspects of American foreign relations. Problems resulting from the Iranian Revolution led to establishment at The Hague of the Iran–United States Claims Tribunal in 1981. It was reported in April 2000 that the tribunal had settled 3,700 claims cases involving hundreds of billions of dollars. Certainly Iranian–United States relations continued to be unsatisfactory, but the tribunal demonstrated that through arbitration, progress toward a better relationship could be made.

BIBLIOGRAPHY

Blake, Nelson M. "The Olney-Pauncefote Treaty of 1897." *American Historical Review* 50

(1945). A study of the Senate's rejection of the treaty.

Brower, Charles M., and Jason D. Bruesche. *The Iran–United States Claims Tribunal*. The Hague, 1998. A comprehensive study.

Campbell, John P. "Taft, Roosevelt, and the Arbitration Treaties of 1911." *Journal of American History* 53 (1966). The failure of the last important American effort to conclude obligatory arbitration treaties before World War I.

Cook, Adrian. *The Alabama Claims: American Politics and Anglo-American Relations, 1865–1872*. Ithaca, N.Y., 1975. Careful discussion of the Washington Treaty and the Geneva arbitration.

Corbett, Percy Ellwood. *Law in Diplomacy*. Princeton, N.J., 1959. Chapter 5. Fine survey of the history of arbitration.

Cory, Helen May. *Compulsory Arbitration of International Disputes*. New York, 1932. Describes development of its special topic from 1820 to 1931.

Crackanthorpe, Montague H. "Arbitration, International." *Encyclopaedia Britannica*. Vol. 2. Cambridge, 1910. The basic concepts and terminology of arbitration, mediation, and conciliation as they were understood early in the twentieth century.

Curti, Merle. *Peace or War: The American Struggle, 1636–1936*. New York, 1936. Discusses the promotion of arbitration by the peace movement.

Davis, Calvin DeArmond. *The United States and the First Hague Peace Conference*. Ithaca, N.Y., 1962. A detailed account of the negotiation of the Convention for the Pacific Settlement of International Disputes.

———. *The United States and the Second Hague Peace Conference: American Diplomacy and International Organization, 1899–1914*. Durham, N.C., 1976. Describes the establishment and development of the Permanent Court of Arbitration, the attempt of the Second Hague Peace Conference to establish a stronger world tribunal, and the efforts of American diplomacy to further development of the Hague Conferences and Court into a permanent world system.

Duberman, Martin B. *Charles Francis Adams, 1807–1886*. Boston, 1961. Excellent accounts of the Washington Treaty and the Geneva arbitration.

Ferrell, Robert H. *Peace in Their Time: The Origins of the Kellogg-Briand Pact*. New Haven, Conn., 1952. Arbitration in the period between the world wars.

Gray, Christine, and Benedict Kingsbury. "Developments in Dispute Settlement: Inter-state Settlement Since 1945." *British Year Book of International Law 1992*. Oxford, 1993. One of the most important studies of the subject since 1945.

Herman, Sondra R. *Eleven Against War: Studies in American Internationalist Thought, 1898–1921*. Stanford, Calif., 1969. Analyzes important peace ideas.

Kuehl, Warren F. *Seeking World Order: The United States and International Organization to 1920*. Nashville, Tenn., 1969. Discusses proposals for organization of the world and its regions.

Mashkour, Mashkan. "Building a Friendly Environment for International Arbitration in Iran." *Journal of International Arbitration* 17 (2000). The latest information about Iran–United States arbitration.

Moore, John Bassett. "International Arbitration: Historical Notes and Projects." *Collected Papers of John Bassett Moore*. New Haven, Conn., and London, 1944. One of the best general surveys.

Moynihan, Daniel Patrick. *On the Law of Nations*. Cambridge, Mass., 1990. A searching commentary on international law since 1945.

Oppenheim, Lassa. *International Law: A Treatise*. Vol. 2. London, 1906. Explains arbitration, mediation, and conciliation as international lawyers understood them early in the twentieth century.

Patterson, David S. *Toward a Warless World: The Travail of the American Peace Movement, 1887–1914*. Bloomington, Ind., 1976. An outstanding history.

Reisman, W. Michael. "The Multifaceted Phenomenon of International Arbitration." *Arbitration Journal* 24 (1969). Modern legal scholarship.

Sanders, Pieter, ed. *International Arbitration: Liber Amicorum for Martin Domke*. The Hague, 1967. Essays by leading scholars.

Savelle, Max. *The Origins of American Diplomacy: The International History of Angloamerica, 1492–1763*. New York, 1967. Important background for the later interest of the United States in arbitration, mediation, and conciliation.

Stuyt, A. M. *Survey of International Arbitrations, 1794–1989*. The Hague, 1990. A basic reference.

United Nations Secretary-General and International Bureau of the Permanent Court of Arbitration. *Permanent Court of Arbitration.* The Hague, 1998. Contains primary sources for the arbitral court's history.

See also AMBASSADORS, EXECUTIVE AGENTS, AND SPECIAL REPRESENTATIVES; INTERNATIONALISM; INTERNATIONAL LAW; PEACEMAKING; TREATIES.

ARMED NEUTRALITIES

Ian Mugridge

One of the more difficult problems attached to all wars is that of relations between belligerents and neutrals. In land wars the question is not of such magnitude, although Switzerland is probably the only nation to have arrived at a satisfactory solution. In naval wars, however, in situations where maritime commerce and other activities are involved, the question of the relationship between belligerents and neutrals, that is, of neutral rights, has long been debated, almost always with inconclusive results.

The question of neutral rights in wartime is almost always discussed, especially by neutrals, within the context of international law. It is usually claimed that such international law is supported by principles established either by earlier treaties or by practice or both, that it is an expression of some accepted view of maritime conduct in wartime, which should therefore govern relations between belligerents and neutrals.

The problem is that international law has no validity beyond that accorded it in particular situations by particular nations. It only exists either when nations agree that it does or when they can uphold their interpretation of it by whatever means are appropriate. In a narrower context, the problem with stating and attempting to uphold neutral rights at sea is that, in the end, neutrals have no rights except those that they can maintain by their own actions, in which case they often cease to be neutrals, as the Dutch discovered in the American Revolution. Again, the example of the Swiss is instructive. They have preserved their neutrality inviolate for hundreds of years by the simple but effective expedient of placing themselves in such a position that challenging their neutrality would not be worth the cost.

The introduction of principles to regulate relations between belligerents and neutrals has never been motivated by anything other than self-interest. Since at least the seventeenth century, declarations, opinions, judgments, and conventions on neutral rights in seaborne commerce have been common. But if one strips away the philosophical disguises, legal circumlocutions, and endless casuistry, what remains is really very simple: neutrals have constantly been trying to trade with some or all of the belligerents in a given war while some or all of the same belligerents have been trying to stop neutral trade with their enemies. For example, the cause of most of the problems concerning the West Indies, particularly the French islands, during the American Revolution was the clear and avowed intent of the French to assist the Americans and the equally firm intent of the British to stop this. What mattered in this situation was not declarations of neutral rights or expressions of principle but the possession of the force required to carry out national policy.

There has, nevertheless, developed during the last three hundred years a great body of pronouncements on neutral rights as both neutrals and belligerents have sought to regulate their relations and to justify their self-interested conduct by appeals to principle and to precedent. No nation has been absolutely consistent in the principles and doctrines to which it has appealed and on which it has acted, and this has been as true of the United States as of any other nation.

In *The Diplomacy of the American Revolution* (1935), still a valuable work on the topic, Samuel Flagg Bemis noted that, in espousing unequivocally the principles of the Armed Neutrality of 1780 and in embodying some of these principles in the Treaty of Paris, the United States established what he called "the American doctrine of freedom of the seas." This doctrine, which he recognized as being rooted in practice, was by no means American nor has it been one to which the United States has consistently adhered. During the Civil War, the British in particular tried, unusually for them, to uphold the principle of free ships, free goods; but the government of

Abraham Lincoln refused to do anything but cling to maritime doctrines more usually espoused by the British. In the two major wars of the twentieth century, the neutral rights of American shipping were one of the causes of contention between the United States and Germany, but in neither case was the real neutrality of the nation clearly established. In the 1960s, it might be maintained that one of the ingredients of the Cuban missile crisis was the unwillingness of the United States to uphold the principle of freedom of the seas when such an action would seriously have threatened its security. This is not to criticize particularly the actions of the United States in successive crises, merely to point out that its governments, like those of other major and minor powers over the years, have been motivated by self-interest rather than by continuous adherence to principle.

An examination of the conduct of the maritime powers in time of war, however, indicates that the body of international maritime law, ephemeral and even illusory as it may be, has yet had considerable influence on their actions.

INTERNATIONAL MARITIME LAW IN THE EIGHTEENTH CENTURY

In his *Colonial Blockade and Neutral Rights, 1739–1763* (1938), Richard Pares noted that the classic age in the struggle between land power and sea power occurred in the middle years of the eighteenth century and that one of the results of this was that the same period became the classic age in the development of international maritime law. During the two great colonial wars, the War of the Austrian Succession and the Seven Years' War, important doctrines on contraband, blockade, and colonial trade, advanced by theorists like the Dane Martin Hupner, were defined by English and Continental jurists in a long series of opinions in prize cases and the like. These definitions were in turn embodied in government pronouncements and treaties to build up reference points for the future. As Pares noted at the close of his work, "for Admirals, for Foreign Ministers, and for judges, [these wars] were the dress rehearsals for greater struggles to come." By implication at least, this view was taken up much later by Max Savelle in his *The Origins of American Diplomacy* (1967), in which he examined the international history of the European and particularly the British colonies in America from 1492 to the end of the Seven Years' War in 1763.

At the beginning of this war, as both Pares and Savelle noted, the neutral powers assumed that free ships made free goods and that they would be able to continue their lucrative trade with the belligerents as if nothing had happened. This was not, however, the British view. In response to the neutral position, the British developed what came to be known as the Rule of the War of 1756, which drew a distinction between trading *with* the enemy and trading *for* the enemy. The former was to be regarded as permissible so that trade that would have been carried on in peacetime remained free and uninterrupted during war. The latter, however, was not permissible and the British reserved the right to interfere with any trade in war matériel that would not have been carried on in peacetime. During 1757 and 1758, however, it became obvious to the British that even this rather strict rule was being continuously evaded by transferring contraband from one ship to another. The response to this problem was to promulgate a supplementary order that became known as the doctrine of continuous voyage. This rule laid down the principle that for a confiscatable cargo to begin a voyage in one ship and then to continue "in the ship of a friend" made no difference, for the British government would regard such a voyage as a continuous one. In other words, it was the cargo and not the ship that mattered.

These principles governed the actions of the British government and their navy throughout the Seven Years' War. From their point of view, it was a simple problem: in Pares's words, "English trade had nothing to gain from the vindication of neutral rights." In addition, the British war effort might be placed in considerable jeopardy by adherence to the principles being espoused by the French foreign minister, Etienne François, duc de Choiseul, in his attempts to win over the neutral powers. These powers did not take the same view of the problem as the British. Although Choiseul and his agents discovered that the neutral position was by no means a united one, there was yet sufficient feeling of grievance against Great Britain among all the neutral powers in Europe to make the construction of a maritime league of neutrals a serious proposition. The British desired to establish overwhelming power at sea and were not altogether unsuccessful in their attempts to do so.

It was to the creation of such a league that the French government, posing as the champion of the neutrals, bent its energies in the early years of the war. It was a difficult and ultimately fruitless task, but in many ways it provided the model for the League of the Armed Neutrality of 1780.

There were precedents for a league of neutrals, especially in northern Europe where, as early as 1690, Denmark and Sweden had combined to try to enforce their concept of neutral rights in the Baltic, the area where a league of neutrals stood the greatest chance of success. It could easily be closed to the shipping of nations refusing to respect neutral rights, much to the disadvantage of, in particular, the British, who at this time were beginning to rely increasingly on Baltic naval stores. The Danes, however, also relied heavily on the income they gained from dues collected on the Sound, and the Baltic trading nations as a group were growing more dependent on their naval stores industries. Nevertheless, the French concentrated on this area, especially in view of the agreement on neutral rights signed by Denmark and Sweden shortly before hostilities began.

William Pitt the Elder, the British prime minister, was forced to make some concessions to neutral protests lest these powers respond favorably to French efforts to form a maritime league. But the French were to fail through the weakness of the neutral position, the unwillingness of the British to recognize claims not already granted by treaty, and the resultant reluctance of the neutrals to make a firm commitment to a maritime league. Not only was the Baltic project doomed almost from the beginning—the Danes, for example, would never actually say that free ships made free goods—but attempts to put together a wider league met with equal reluctance to participate. Whatever their long-term interests might have appeared to dictate, whatever blandishments the French used on them, the neutrals, and particularly the Danes and the Dutch, always lacked sufficient confidence in their own ability or that of the French to uphold the principles with which they were flirting. They were always too reliant on British friendship, or at least noninterference, in maintaining their overseas trade to give unequivocal assent and support to a league that might oblige them to sacrifice concrete gain for abstract principles. By the spring of 1759, Choiseul had essentially given up the attempt, despite a rather half-hearted effort a few months later.

In many ways, as Pares noted, the events of the Seven Years' War were a rehearsal for later wars. In the War of American Independence and later struggles, both neutrals and belligerents appealed to the body of maritime law developed in the years up to 1763. As in the past, efforts to set up a maritime league of neutrals, a concept that became a reality in only a limited sense, foundered, like later attempts, on the rock of national self-interest. In one important respect, however, the league of 1780 differed from attempts made by Choiseul and the French to bring together a group of neutral powers in the 1750s. It may be this difference that goes a long way toward explaining its success, if not in limiting the belligerents' interference with neutral shipping then at least in providing mediation aimed at bringing the American war to a close.

LEAGUE OF THE ARMED NEUTRALITY

Formed in the spring and summer of 1780, the League of the Armed Neutrality was the first genuine league of neutrals formed because of complaints of the neutral powers against the major belligerents—with the possible exception of the United States. Although, in this respect as in others, the United States was of rather limited importance to anyone except Great Britain, France, and Spain, there is some evidence that the activities of American privateers were partly responsible for the movement to form a league of neutrals.

From the beginning of the war, Great Britain, still supremely, though as it turned out misguidedly, confident in the ability of its navy to hold the world at bay, had reverted to the maritime doctrines it had espoused in the past; and its actions had provided a constant source of complaint for the Danes and the Swedes as well as the Dutch and, later, the Russians. After the entry of France and Spain into the war in 1778, France made attempts to conciliate the neutrals as it had done in the Seven Years' War. Spanish policy hovered somewhere between the two. Whatever the avowed policies of the belligerent powers, however, they all, in varying degrees, offended the neutrals and produced a growing sense among them that some kind of joint expression of disapproval and firm resolve to take action was necessary to protect their interests.

Ultimately, leadership in this project was provided by Catherine II of Russia, who, under pressure from Great Britain on the one hand to enter an alliance and from the northern powers on the other to help protect their neutrality, found her own shipping becoming more subject to interference from the belligerents. The result was the declaration of 1780, identifying the principles by which Catherine proposed to act and the means—commissioning a substantial portion of her fleet to go "wherever honour, interest, and necessity compelled"—by which she proposed to enforce those principles. Broadly, these principles were that neutral shipping might navigate freely from port to port and on the coasts of nations at war; that the property of subjects of belligerent states on neutral ships should be free except when it was classed as contraband within the meaning of the Anglo-Russian Treaty of 1766; and that a port was assumed to be blockaded only when the attacking power had rendered its ships stationary and made entry a clear danger.

Through the summer of 1780, other neutral powers issued similar declarations, and the belligerents protested that they had always treated and always intended to treat Russian shipping according to these principles. By August, Denmark and Sweden, by almost identical agreements, had joined Russia in conventions establishing an armed neutrality, and, beginning with the Dutch United Provinces in January of the following year, most of the major neutrals of Europe acceded to the league before the end of the war. Of these powers, only the Dutch were obliged, at least partly because of their joining the league, to go to war with Great Britain. In this case, Catherine and her allies agreed to regard the Dutch as neutrals in their dealings with France and Spain to mitigate the effects on them of war with the British. Even so, the Dutch suffered severely from the war which, despite repeated attempts at mediation by Catherine and other members of the league, dragged on into the early summer of 1784 before Great Britain and the United Provinces finally signed a treaty of peace.

What, in the end, did the league achieve? Its existence made little, if any, difference in the attitude of the British navy in dealing with neutral shipping. Indeed, in the case of the United Provinces, adherence to the league was at least partly responsible for a far more serious situation than that nation might otherwise have faced. Any slackening in British depredations on the neutrals in general was perhaps due more to the declining effectiveness of the British navy, to the ineptitude of those running the war effort, and to the appearance of France and Spain on the rebel side than to the unity and effectiveness of the league. Nevertheless, resentment against the Rule of the War of 1756 was still strong among the Continental powers, and when, after 1778, the British escalated their actions against neutral commerce, they reacted in a way that, strengthened by Catherine's firm support, resulted increasingly in British isolation. As Paul Kennedy notes, in 1783 even Portu-

gal and the Two Sicilies joined Russia, Prussia, Austria, Sweden, and Denmark in the league, leaving Britain completely isolated, a situation that led the scholar G. S. Graham to comment that it was the principal factor in the British defeat. It is at least clear that the mediation of Catherine and Joseph II of Austria was partly responsible for the treaties that ended the war in the fall of 1783.

This was probably the limit of the achievements of the first armed neutrality. It had little or no influence on American affairs and diplomacy in general, beyond the threat it imposed on the British. For the United States, as for other nations, it provided a set of principles of maritime law that were useful when they became convenient or necessary but that were to be discarded when neither of these conditions existed. At the end of the war, Charles James Fox, the British foreign secretary, proposed drawing up a treaty embodying the principles of armed neutrality, but his plan came to nothing. Ten years later, with Europe once again at war, Sweden and Denmark signed a convention renewing the provisions of the Armed Neutrality; but Catherine had already concluded an alliance with Great Britain, which, by virtue of the fact that one of its objects was to destroy French commerce, deliberately ignored the principles of the league.

THE SECOND LEAGUE

In the words of Isabel de Madariaga, the idea of a league of neutrals "flickered into brief life again in 1800" before it was finally abandoned. At that point, Napoleon Bonaparte, first consul of the French Republic, was anxious to construct a continental alliance against Great Britain, whose opposition to his designs was proving intransigent. He was attempting to use against the British a league of neutral powers, particularly those of northern Europe, who were angered by British refusal to recognize the rights of neutral commerce.

Paul I of Russia had withdrawn from the Second Coalition against Napoleon early in 1800, believing that his interests lay more in the Baltic than in Italy and Germany and vexed by British refusal to surrender Malta to him as the new Grand Master of the Order of St. John of Jerusalem. As a result of his diplomacy, the 1780 Declaration of Armed Neutrality was renewed. Beginning with the Prussians and Danes, Paul recreated the league, and by mid-December 1800, Norway, Denmark, Sweden, and Russia had also signed separate conventions with France to further their "disinterested desire to maintain the inalienable rights of neutral nations." Napoleon had earlier declared that he would not make peace with the British while they refused to respect the neutral rights not only of these powers, but also of the United States. He hoped to attach the Americans to the league, particularly after Thomas Jefferson's accession to the presidency early in 1801.

Late in 1800, John Adams, on the advice of his son, John Quincy Adams, minister to Prussia, sent an embassy to Paris that signed a convention reaffirming the principles of the 1780 declaration. This was ratified by the Senate early in 1801, but both Jefferson and his secretary of state, James Madison, were cautious about entering into a firm attachment with a league in which, in the words of one of the American envoys in Europe, "the silly powers of the north" had responded to "this interested and politic cry of France against Great Britain." They recognized too that the situation could be turned to their advantage if the Baltic trade were denied to the British, and they were suspicious of Napoleon's designs in the Western Hemisphere and fearful of the seriousness with which the British government clearly took the league.

So they hung back, and while they did the league collapsed. In the spring of 1801, two events destroyed it. Late in March, Paul I, the main prop of the league, was assassinated. Up to and past this point, the league worked: no British ships passed through the Denmark Strait in the first four months of 1801. But now decisive and ruthless action in the form of Horatio Nelson's destruction of the Danish fleet in Copenhagen Harbor hit the league at its weakest point. The league was finished, because the new czar, Alexander I, refused to maintain the policies of his father. The League of the Armed Neutrality of 1780 had, because of the temporary concurrence of a number of factors, some effect on the course of the American Revolution and, more particularly, on the European policies that surrounded it. A weakened Great Britain, faced with rebellious colonies and declarations of war by the major European powers, was in no position to resist effectively a league that eventually contained all the other major European powers. For once, an unusual show of neutral strength and unity had an effect on European politics, although even this did not extend fully to all the members and particularly to the Dutch.

The effectiveness of the league, however, had nothing to do with the principles it had espoused, with their justice or their strength. It had to do with the strength of the league's members and the comparative weakness of the major object of its existence. In 1800, when such a situation did not exist, this fact was illustrated graphically by the collapse of the second League of the Armed Neutrality. On this occasion, helped by a fortunate accident of Russian politics, the British, strong and confident, led by a resolute and able prime minister and served by a brilliant and fearless admiral, struck hard at the league's weakest link and destroyed it. Unable to maintain the rights they claimed, the neutrals returned to conciliation of Great Britain. They had learned a severe lesson—and so, watching them, had the government of the United States.

BIBLIOGRAPHY

Alexander, John T. *Catherine the Great: Life and Legend.* New York, 1989.

Bolkhovitinov, Nikolai N. *The Beginnings of Russian-American Relations, 1775–1815.* Translated by Elena Levin. Cambridge, Mass., 1975. Discusses American influence on the first Armed Neutrality.

Carnegie Endowment for International Peace. *Extracts from American and Foreign Works on International Law Concerning the Armed Neutrality of 1780 and 1800.* Washington, D.C., 1917.

———. *Official Documents Bearing on the Armed Neutralities of 1780 and 1800.* Washington, D.C., 1917.

———. *The Armed Neutralities of 1780 and 1800.* Washington, D.C., 1918.

DeConde, Alexander. *The Quasi-War: The Politics and Diplomacy of the Undeclared War with France, 1797–1801.* New York, 1966. Gives the U.S. perspective of the second League of Armed Neutrality.

De Madariaga, Isabel. *Britain, Russia, and the Armed Neutrality of 1780: Sir James Harris' Mission to St. Petersburg During the American Revolution.* New Haven, Conn., 1962. The most comprehensive treatment of the establishment and working of the first League of Armed Neutrality.

———. *Russia in the Age of Catherine the Great.* New Haven, Conn., 1981. Supplements her *Britain, Russia, and the Armed Neutrality of 1780.*

Feldbaek, Ole. *Denmark and the Armed Neutrality, 1800–1801: Small Power Policy in a World War.* Copenhagen, 1980. The second League of Armed Neutrality from the viewpoint of a small power.

Griffiths, David M. "An American Contribution to the Armed Neutrality of 1780." *Russian Review* 30, no. 2 (April 1971).

Kennedy, Paul M. *The Rise and Fall of British Naval Mastery.* London, 1976. A good though brief account of the first League of Armed Neutrality.

LeDonne, John P. *The Russian Empire and the World, 1700–1917: The Geopolitics of Expansion and Containment.* New York, 1997.

Pares, Richard. *Colonial Blockade and Neutral Rights, 1739–1763.* Oxford, 1938. Best treatment of neutral rights in the eighteenth century.

Piggott, Sir Francis, and G. W. T. Ormond, eds. *Documentary History of the Armed Neutralities of 1780 and 1800.* London, 1919. Contains a useful introduction and chronological account of the events surrounding the Armed Neutralities.

Saul, Norman E. *Distant Friends: The United States and Russia, 1763–1867.* Lawrence, Kans., 1991. Contains a brief discussion of the United States and the first Armed Neutrality as well as a short section on the second league.

Savelle, Max. *The Origins of American Diplomacy: The International History of Anglo-America, 1492–1763.* New York, 1967. Contains a good account of international issues affecting the colonies in the prerevolutionary period.

Tucker, Robert W., and David C. Hendrickson. *Empire of Liberty: The Statecraft of Thomas Jefferson.* New York, 1990. An interesting discussion of the United States and neutrality.

See also BLOCKADES; FREEDOM OF THE SEAS; INTERNATIONAL LAW; NAVAL DIPLOMACY; NEUTRALISM; NEUTRALITY.

ARMS CONTROL AND DISARMAMENT

Richard Dean Burns

Historians have been slow to grasp the significant, occasionally dominating, role that arms control negotiations played in Cold War diplomacy—a situation undoubtedly the result of the often mind-numbing technical aspects of these lengthy deliberations. In the prenuclear era, political disputes might spark threatening military buildups, but political dimensions remained the focus of subsequent negotiations. This changed after 1950 as weapons systems themselves took on a political character. "The arms race . . . was both a result of the Cold War and a cause," as the former Soviet President Mikhail Gorbachev emphasized, "as it constantly provided new stimuli for continued rivalry." The arms control pacts that gradually emerged from various multilateral and bilateral negotiations helped neutralize the insecurities brought on by the constant arrival of new weapons systems. "The decision to reduce arms," Gorbachev concluded, "became an important step on the road to ending confrontation and creating healthier relations between East and West."

Arms control and disarmament agreements were traditionally designed to accomplish two essential purposes: to stabilize the military climate and to diminish the military violence in any subsequent hostilities. The various arrangements, which reduced, limited, and regulated armaments, provided a more stable international environment; but could not themselves resolve other threatening, contentious issues. Controlling armaments had to be coupled with diplomatic resolve so that in an atmosphere temporarily cleared of insecurities inspired by unregulated weaponry, statesmen might deal with critical political, social, and economic differences.

DEFINING ARMS CONTROL AND DISARMAMENT TECHNIQUES

Although the terms "disarmament" and "arms control" have been widely used, there often has

been, and still is, considerable confusion over their meanings. "Disarmament" became the fashionable term during the nineteenth century, particularly during and after the Hague Conference of 1899, to describe all efforts to limit, reduce, or control the implements of war. While some individuals may employ disarmament in the literal sense—the total elimination of armaments—most diplomats and commentators do not. The United Nations and its subsidiary agencies use it as a generic term covering all measures, "from small steps to reduce tensions or build confidence, through regulation of armaments or arms control, up to general and complete disarmament."

In the early 1950s, academic specialists linking the technology of nuclear weaponry to the strategies of the Cold War began substituting the term "arms control." For them "disarmament" not only lacked semantic precision but carried utopian expectations, whereas "arms control" involved any cooperation between potential enemies designed to reduce the likelihood of conflict or, should it occur, its scope and violence. Most arms controllers sought to enhance the nuclear deterrence system, and only occasionally sought force reductions, while literal "disarmers" dismissed arms control as a chimera and supported proposals seeking general and complete disarmament.

From a historical perspective the basic techniques that comprise arms control and disarmament undertakings may be divided into six general categories:

1. Limitation and Reduction of Armaments. These pacts put specified limits on the mobilization, possession, or construction of military forces and equipment, and may result in reductions. The restrictions may be qualitative, regulating weapons design, as well as quantitative, limiting numbers of specific weapons.
2. Demilitarization, Denuclearization, and Neutralization. Demilitarization and denu-

clearization involve removing or placing restrictions on military forces, weapons, and fortifications within a prescribed area of land, water, or airspace. Neutralization is a special status that guarantees political independence and territorial integrity, subject to a pledge that the neutralized state will not engage in war except in defense. The essential feature of all three is the emphasis on geographical areas.

3. Regulating or Outlawing Specific Weapons. These agreements regulate the military use or the possession of specific weapons. Their rationale is that the unrestricted use, or any use, of a particular weapon exceeds recognized "just use of force."

4. Controlling Arms Manufacture and Traffic. This approach involves restrictions, including embargoes, on the sale or transfer of weapons and munitions. It may prohibit the manufacture of specific weapons.

5. Laws of War. These efforts seek to lessen the violence and damage of war. The principles underlying the rules of war (or laws of war) are (a) the prohibition of weapons that cause unnecessary or disproportionate suffering; (b) the distinction between combatants and noncombatants; and (c) the realization that the demands of humanity should prevail over the perceived necessities of combat.

6. Stabilizing the International Environment. This technique seeks to lower international tensions through lessening the possibility of an uncontrollable cause célèbre provoking an unwanted war. In addition, it seeks to protect the environment from lasting damage due to the testing or use of military weapons.

Obviously, the six categories are not exclusive. The outlawing of weapons has the same effect as limiting them. Thus, a treaty that prohibits placing weapons of mass destruction in outer space (1967) is also an example of geographic demilitarization. In addition, a treaty may incorporate several arms control techniques: the Treaty of Versailles (1919), for example, limited the number of German troops, demilitarized specific zones, and outlawed German manufacture of military aircraft, submarines, and tanks.

The methods of achieving arms control and disarmament objectives may be classified into three broad categories—retributive measures, unilateral measures, and reciprocal measures—which can be subdivided into six general methods:

1. Extermination. A retributive measure, extermination is an ancient and drastic means of ensuring no future warlike response from one's opponent, dramatized by Rome's destruction of Carthage or the elimination of some American Indian tribes.

2. Imposition. Also a retributive measure, imposition results when victors force arms limitation measures on the vanquished, such as the terms imposed upon Germany and other enemy states in 1919 and 1945.

3. Unilateral Neglect. Often confused with unilateral decisions, unilateral neglect refers to a nation's decision not spend for defense, as in the U.S. unilateral reduction of army and naval forces after the Civil War (1866) or the British and U.S. self-imposed arms reductions between the world wars.

4. Unilateral Decision. A consciously decided policy of self-imposed military restrictions or limitations, as in Japan's post–World War II constitution and the Austrian Peace Treaty (1955), both restricting armaments to defensive purposes.

5. Bilateral Negotiation. A reciprocal measure, bilateral negotiation is a traditional method by which two nations seek mutually acceptable solutions to tensions heightened by armaments, as with the Rush-Bagot Agreement (1817) and the SALT, START, and INF treaties.

6. Multilateral Negotiation. Another reciprocal measure, multilateral negotiation is a common twentieth-century approach to regional and global military-political problems that involve the interests of several nations. The Hague treaties (1899, 1907) and the Nuclear Non-Proliferation Treaty (1968) are multilateral agreements. The Latin American denuclearization treaty of 1967 is a regionally negotiated pact.

ARMS CONTROL AND DISARMAMENT TO WORLD WAR II

Most American leaders, at one time or another, have defined the United States as a "peace-loving nation" that deplores the existence of large military forces and believes that their reduction will lead to a more peaceful world. Yet while American diplomats have frequently supported arms control objectives, they also have opposed them. For example, they rejected the idea of naval reductions at the 1899 Hague Conference and refused to consider political-military "guarantees" that might have brought about arms reductions during the League of Nations negotiations. Thus, early U.S. involvement in the efforts to limit weapons and warfare has been mixed.

Apart from early efforts to halt the trading in arms with various Indian tribes, the United States pursued three major undertakings during this period: demilitarizing the Great Lakes; formulating "rules of war" to govern the actions of its armed forces; and participating in the two Hague peace conferences.

Rush-Bagot Agreement   The War of 1812 demonstrated that the Great Lakes were of strategic importance to the United States and Britain's eastern Canadian provinces. At war's end, the British flagship on the lakes was a three-decker more powerful than Admiral Horatio Nelson's *Victory,* and two even larger vessels were being built at Kingston, Ontario. The Americans responded by beginning construction of two vessels that would be the world's largest warships.

These undertakings conflicted with the U.S. Congress's economy drive, so, on 27 February 1815, President James Madison was authorized "to cause all armed vessels of the United States on the lakes to be sold or laid up, except such as he may deem necessary to enforce proper execution of revenue laws." Economies also led Great Britain to curtail construction and dismantling of warships.

Despite these unilateral actions, many in Washington were concerned that minor border incidents between Canadians and Americans might lead to a renewed naval race. In November 1815, President Madison endorsed efforts to negotiate with the British to limit the number of armed ships on the lakes. If the building of warships began again, he feared, a "vast expence will be incurred" that might lead to "the danger of [a] collision" between the two countries. In London, Lord Castlereagh agreed that such a naval race was "ridiculous and absurd."

The 29 April 1817 bilateral agreement limited the naval forces of each party "on Lake Ontario, to one vessel, not exceeding one hundred tons burden, and armed with one eighteen pound cannon. On the upper lakes, to two vessels, not exceeding like burden each, and armed with like force," and "on the waters of Lake Champlain, to one vessel not exceeding like burden, and armed with like force." However, the

pact did not end competitive armaments in the Great Lakes region. Fortifications continued to be built, and there were violations of the naval terms, and during the Civil War, the U.S. Senate voted to terminate the agreement. Despite these obstacles, the Rush-Bagot Agreement remains one of the most successful U.S. arms control undertakings—and certainly its most enduring, for it enhanced the security of both parties and saved them a great deal of money. Also, it paved the way for the Treaty of Washington (1871), which resolved remaining political issues between the parties and led to the "unguarded frontier" between Canada and the United States.

Rules of War   In 1863 a Columbia University professor, Francis Lieber, submitted his *Code for the Government of Armies of the United States in the Field* to the War Department. The Lieber Code, as it became known, was drawn from medieval jurists and was incorporated into the Union army's General Order No. 100. Among other things, it recognized the status of noncombatants, regulated treatment of prisoners of war, prohibited the use of poison, forbade the seizure of private property without compensation, and ordered that cultural treasures not be willfully destroyed. Lieber's contribution later influenced the Declaration of Brussels (1874) on the rules and customs of war.

Hague Conferences   Peace advocates everywhere welcomed Czar Nicholas II's 1899 invitation for a meeting of the great powers at The Hague to deal with the threatening international arms race. The Americans were optimistic about the conference's prospects for peace even though their own government had recently concluded a war against Spain and was committed to a naval buildup and army modernization.

President William McKinley took the position that "it behooves us as a nation to lend countenance and aid to the beneficent project." Yet the active military force of the United States "in time of peace [is] so conspicuously less than that of the armed powers of Europe," he said, "that the question of limitations had little practical importance for the United States." Thus, while the U.S. peace movement collected petitions registering popular support for reducing armaments, at The Hague, Captain Alfred T. Mahan, the U.S. delegate, joined Admiral John A. Fisher, the British naval delegate, to prevent any limitation of naval forces. Other proposals sought to restrict military budgets, prohibit the use of new types of firearms and explosives, restrict the use of certain munitions, prohibit the dropping of projectiles or explosives, prohibit the use of submarines or similar engines of destruction, and revise and codify the laws and rules of war, especially those from the Conference of Brussels that were still unratified.

Secretary of State John Hay stated that the first four restrictions "seem lacking in practicability, and the discussion of these propositions would probably prove provocative. . . . But it is doubtful if wars are to be diminished by rendering them less destructive, for it is the plain lesson of history that the periods of peace have been longer as the cost and destructiveness of war have increased." Despite Washington's lack of interest, declarations prohibiting the use of asphyxiating gas and expanding (dum-dum) bullets and the throwing of projectiles from balloons were approved. With the U.S. delegation's support, rules of war aimed at preventing armies from committing excesses—such as those at the expense of noncombatants and prisoners of war—also were endorsed by the conferees.

At the Second Hague Conference of 1907, some thirteen new declarations clarifying and codifying the law of war were agreed upon. These were revised in 1929 and 1949. The conventions relating to prisoners of war and noncombatants were the basis of considerable diplomatic activity during World War II, the Korean War, and the Vietnam War.

Prior to the Second Hague conference, President Theodore Roosevelt indicated that the United States might support naval limitations; however, none of the major European powers would consider reducing or limiting their military forces. In June 1910 both houses of Congress unanimously endorsed naval limitations, a decision sparked by the British launching of the dreadnoughts, a new class of battleship, which promised another round of expensive ship construction. The proposal failed to gain support abroad, but it pointed to new efforts a decade later.

BETWEEN THE WORLD WARS, 1919–1939

The enormity of death and destruction wrought by World War I focused the attention of the American public and its government on ways of preventing future war. America's role in these interwar undertakings included the introduction of disarmament in the League of Nations Covenant, sponsorship of the Washington naval limitation system, 1922–1935, endorsement of the Kellogg-Briand Pact aimed at "outlawing" war, and belated, ambivalent support of the League of Nation's disarmament efforts.

League Covenant and Disarmament   In January 1918, President Woodrow Wilson emphasized disarmament in Point Four of his Fourteen Points (a statement of the Allies' war aims) and in his endorsement of it as Article Eight of the League of Nations Covenant. Point Four called for "adequate guarantees given and taken that national armaments will be reduced to the lowest point consistent with domestic safety." Wilson did not consider arms reduction a high priority, but he clearly saw it as in the U.S. interest. A commitment to general disarmament, no matter how ambiguous, would justify the imposition of arms restrictions on Germany and its allies.

At the Paris Peace Conference Wilson reduced his emphasis on arms reductions because of considerations of national sovereignty, the threat of Bolshevism, and demands of economic nationalism. He even threatened a new naval race by urging Congress to fund the construction of 156 warships, including ten super-dreadnoughts and six high-speed battle cruisers, called for in the Naval Appropriation Act of 1916, in order to obtain political concessions. British Prime Minister David Lloyd George was unwilling to accept U.S. naval parity, nor did he agree with Wilson's desire to append the Monroe Doctrine to the League Covenant. Unwilling to undertake a costly naval race, Lloyd George relented on the latter point and agreed to future negotiations on the former.

Wilson tried the same strategy during the Senate's ratification hearings (May 1919–March 1920), insisting there were only two alternatives: the League of Nations and disarmament, or increased naval construction and higher taxes. The Senate rejected league membership on the grounds it impinged upon the nation's sovereignty and left the naval problems for the Harding administration.

The Washington Naval System   In the spring of 1921, President Warren G. Harding and Secretary of State Charles Evans Hughes confronted a burgeoning naval race—before the year was out, more than 200 warships were under construction. Hughes invited the other major naval powers—Great Britain, Japan, France, and Italy—to meet at Washington, D.C., on 12 November 1921. Overruling his admirals, Hughes developed a detailed plan grounded on two themes: an immediate halt of all capital ship construction and the defining of national strategies in terms of "relative security." By presenting his proposal for capital ship reductions and limitations in his opening speech, Hughes seized the diplomatic initiative and gained widespread public support.

The Washington Conference produced seven treaties and twelve resolutions, two of which contained arms control provisions. The most significant was the Five Power Naval Treaty of 6 February 1922, which established a reduction in battleships, quantitative limits (or ratios—United States 5:Britain 5:Japan 3) on capital ships and aircraft carriers, qualitative restrictions on future naval construction, and restrictions on fortifications and naval bases in the central Pacific. The ratios established battleship parity between the United States and Britain and acknowledged Japan's de facto preeminence in the western Pacific. Naval limitation was realized because the United States, Britain, and Japan had temporarily resolved their political differences, especially regarding China, and desired to reduce naval expenditures.

Attempts to abolish or restrict submarines failed, and the agreement to prohibit the "use in war of asphyxiations, poisonous or other gases" was not ratified, but the two concepts did reappear—the former in the London Naval Treaty of 1930, and the latter in the Geneva Protocol of 1925.

Since a formula for limiting smaller warships was not found, a new naval race appeared as admirals rushed to build cruisers that would fall just below the 10,000-ton limit that defined capital ships. Facing an expensive naval building program, Congress urged President Calvin Coolidge to negotiate limits on cruisers, destroyers, and submarines. At the Geneva Naval Conference (1927), the administration wanted to extend the Washington Treaty's Big Three capital ship ratios (5:5:3) to auxiliary categories. However, the U.S. delegation abandoned Hughes's earlier approach of considering naval armaments as one thread in existing political relationships, and instead focused on technical issues.

With Japanese negotiators on the sidelines, American and British naval experts agreed on the idea of parity, but could not define it because the British and U.S. fleets were structured quite differently. Whereas the British sought strategic equality that acknowledged commercial and imperial obligations, the Americans demanded mathematical parity. The U.S. insistence on fewer large

cruisers with eight-inch guns and Britain's determination to have more, smaller cruisers with six-inch guns deadlocked negotiations.

The failed Geneva effort paved the way for the London Naval Conference of 1930. Herbert Hoover's election in 1928 coincided with that of British Prime Minister Ramsay MacDonald, who, like Hoover, believed that the reduction of armaments could contribute to world peace. Secretary of State Henry L. Stimson indicated that he and the president, employing naval experts as advisers, would seek a "yardstick" to bridge the difficulties that had plagued the 1927 Geneva Conference—but no yardstick was forthcoming. The yardstick episode emphasized a recurring dilemma that plagued U.S. arms control efforts well into the Cold War era: arms control requires a perspective beyond technical considerations, for by concentrating on mathematical or other engineering factors, U.S. policymakers often tended to obscure or avoid basic political problems.

The 1930 London Naval Treaty refined the Washington naval system by applying a 10:10:7 ratio to capital ships and aircraft carriers. All five powers agreed not to build their authorized capital ship replacements between 1931 and 1936, and to scrap a total of nine capital ships. By 1936 the United States would have eighteen battleships (462,400 tons), Britain eighteen battleships (474,750 tons), and Japan nine battleships (266,070 tons). Aircraft carrier tonnage remained unchanged, despite attempts to lower it.

While the United States and Britain ultimately reached an agreement on naval "equality," many senior Japanese naval officers believed that applying the "battleship ratio" to all classes of warships would be disastrous for their nation's security. Reluctantly, however, the Japanese government accepted negotiated ratios for cruisers, destroyers, and submarines.

Naval arms control pleased most American politicians and their constituents, and President Herbert Hoover estimated that the United States saved $1 billion. However, the limits outraged professional naval officers in all three countries. The Japanese lamented that they must stop cruiser construction; the British complained that fifty cruisers did not provide protection for long sea-lanes; and the Americans felt that Japan's higher cruiser ratio reduced the chance of a U.S. victory in a western Pacific war.

The years following the signing of the London Naval Treaty saw increased political tensions in the Mediterranean and undeclared wars in

Ethiopia and Asia. Japan demanded naval parity, but Britain and the United States refused. Subsequently, Japan withdrew from the Second London Naval Conference (1935) and abrogated the Washington naval system. On 31 December 1936, the quantitative and qualitative limitations on naval armaments ended.

Naval arms control had rested on the assumption that Japan was satisfied with its world position. However, Japanese expansionists, both military and civilian, who dominated policy by 1934 believed that the United States and Britain were hindering Japan's economic expansion, and thus keeping that nation's industries depressed. Consequently, Japan's admirals argued that, if freed from treaty restrictions, they could build a strong fleet, dominate China and Southeast Asia, and become the leading power in Asia.

Throughout the interwar negotiations over naval limitations, U.S. policies were clearly motivated by a desire to reduce military expenditures and, at the same time, gain whatever strategic advantages were possible. The desire for the former drove most civilian policymakers, while efforts to achieve the latter were foremost in the minds of senior naval officers. Only the most single-minded analyst would suggest that U.S. negotiating positions involved any significant measure of altruism.

Outlawing War   The Kellogg-Briand Pact, also known as the Pact of Paris for the Renunciation of War (1928), renounced offensive war as "an instrument" of national policy. It called on nations to settle their differences by pacific means. The idea originated with a Chicago lawyer, Salmon O. Levinson, who argued that international law should declare war a criminal act. While this idea appeared to be utopian, many opponents to the League of Nation's concept of collective security saw an alternative in the movement to outlaw war.

The Kellogg-Briand Pact emerged as an attempt by the Coolidge administration to induce Paris authorities to alter their position that France's security needed to be enhanced by British or U.S. political-military commitments before they agreed to arms limitations. Secretary of State Frank B. Kellogg's offer to French Foreign Minister Aristide Briand acknowledged the virtue of a world tribunal to enforce the outlawry of war, but he was realistic enough to know that the Senate and the American people (and those of most other nations) were not ready for such a commitment.

Most historians have criticized the pact for its failure to provide for enforcement. Only a few believe it influenced international law, even though after World War II major war criminals were found guilty of violating the treaty. Any reappraisal of the Kellogg-Briand Pact should take into consideration that it did not abolish "defensive" war and that the United States and other nations made various reservations upon signing.

The League of Nations and Disarmament

After several early committees failed to come up with a disarmament proposal, the League of Nations created an "independent" preparatory commission in 1926 to prepare a draft treaty. President Calvin Coolidge accepted the league's invitation to send a representative. In a message to Congress on 26 January 1926, he declared that "the general policy of this Government in favor of disarmament and limitation of armaments cannot be emphasized too frequently or too strongly. In accordance with that policy, any measure having a reasonable tendency to bring about these results should receive our sympathy and support."

The American delegation, headed by Hugh Gibson, U.S. minister to Switzerland, maintained a fairly consistent policy between 1926 and 1930. He emphasized that the U.S. Army had been unilaterally reduced after World War I from some 4 million men to 118,000, which he acknowledged America's geographical situation made possible. Gibson also emphasized—pointing to the Washington naval system—that his government favored the limitation of naval forces by categories and approved qualitative restrictions only when accompanied by quantitative limitations. Still, the United States opposed budgetary limitations and any regulation that might restrict industrial potential.

The Conference for the Reduction and Limitation of Armaments—also known as the World Disarmament Conference—convened in Geneva on 2 February 1932 and began negotiations on the preparatory commission's draft convention. Secretary of State Stimson declared that President Hoover would not authorize discussions involving political arrangements to facilitate arms control measures. Nevertheless, on 9 February 1932, Gibson assured the gathered diplomats that the United States wished to cooperate with them to achieve arms limitations. As the disarmament conference bogged down, President Hoover and, later, President Franklin D. Roosevelt attempted to stimulate negotiations. Citing the Kellogg-

Briand Pact's outlawing of aggressive war, Hoover on 22 June 1932 proposed a one-third reduction in all armies and battle fleets. Additionally, he urged the abolition of tanks, large mobile guns, and chemical weapons and the prohibition of aerial bombardment.

When the French argued that his plan must be anchored to some kind of verification, Hoover reversed the earlier U.S. position. President Wilson initially rejected permanent supervision of German disarmament at Versailles because this precedent might run counter to America's future interests. "The United States," he declared, "will not tolerate the supervision of any outside body in [disarmament], nor be subjected to inspection or supervision by foreign agencies or individuals." Secretary of State Frank Kellogg restated this policy in January 1926. "The United States will not be a party to any sanctions of any kind for the enforcement of a treaty for the limitation of armaments," he asserted, "nor will it agree that such treaties to which it may be a party shall come under the supervision of any international body—whether the League of Nations or otherwise." Arms limitation measures, he insisted, "so far as we are concerned, must depend upon the good faith of nations." On 30 June 1932, Stimson announced that the United States was prepared "to accept the right of inspection" if there was any likelihood of concluding "a treaty of real reduction." This belated change of policy was insufficient because the French now also demanded a guarantee of military assistance in case of attack.

On 16 May 1933, President Roosevelt proposed abolition of modern offensive weapons. He also announced America's willingness to consult with other states in the event of threatened conflict, but since the Senate showed little interest in abandoning neutrality for international cooperation, this initiative failed. Confronted by French intransigence and German aggressiveness, the World Disarmament Conference slowly dissolved without any accomplishments.

EVALUATING INTERWAR EXPERIENCES

At the beginning of the Cold War, some American leaders were wary of entrusting any element of national security to arms control and disarmament, even if the agreements were linked to functioning international organizations. Harking back to the U.S. lack of military preparedness on the eve of World War II, these individuals believed that interwar disarmament activities had compromised national security. Bernard M. Baruch, who presented the initial U.S. proposal for international control of atomic weaponry, recalled that in preparing the plan "the [interwar] record of meaningless disarmament agreements and renunciations of war" was "very much in my mind."

Other policymakers believed that Japan's decision to challenge the United States was the result of naval limitation treaties that had left the United States with an inferior navy. After World War II, James Byrnes, President Harry Truman's secretary of state, recalled that as a young congressman he had approved of the Washington Naval Treaty and that "what happened thereafter influences my thinking today." Byrnes felt that "while America scrapped battleships, Japan scrapped blueprints. America will not again make that mistake." Secretary of State Dean Acheson, who assisted in developing the Baruch Plan, reportedly saw in international efforts to control atomic energy "a parallel with the Washington Disarmament Conference of 1921–1922. The idea of heading off a naval race had been a good one, but the content of the treaties was wrong. Worse, the United States did not build all the ships allowed by the treaty limits and the Japanese fortified their island bases."

"Policymakers ordinarily use history badly," Ernest R. May points out in *"Lessons" of the Past* (1973), because there is more assumption than analysis in their retrospective views. Even a brief analysis would have shown that at the Washington conference it was the United States that scrapped the most blueprints and uncompleted hulls. Congressional and public opposition to the expenditure necessary to complete the building program had made the treaty a virtue out of necessity. Later, Coolidge and Hoover were more interested in balancing the budget than in building ships, and their actions went unchallenged by legislators with little enthusiasm for increasing naval expenditures. While the notion that Japan secretly violated its pledge not to fortify the league-mandated Pacific islands has long persisted, historical investigations have revealed very little evidence to support such a conclusion.

Even more significantly, these critics and others failed to consider the relationship between naval limitation and its political setting. President Harding and the Republican Party oversold the system as one that would, by itself, bring about a new era of peace and considerable savings. Few leaders were willing to face the fact that the naval treaties were only first steps toward a more stable, mutually beneficial international system for the western Pacific region, and that additional political arrangements to resolve new issues were required to maintain that stability. Consequently, when extremists—isolationists in the United States and military expansionists in Japan—thwarted political accommodation, it was impossible for the naval limitation treaties, by themselves, to prevent the oncoming conflict.

THE COLD WAR

After World War II, as the new weapons technology threatened the very survival of American society and its people, its policymakers continued to pursue traditional objectives. They sought to enhance the nation's (and its allies') security through deterrence, to reduce military expenditures, to influence international public opinion, and to gain domestic partisan political advantage. Politics became more important when arms issues became embroiled in election campaigns.

American public opinion during the Cold War reflected an ambiguity regarding arms control and disarmament treaties, especially with the Soviet Union. Opinion polls invariably showed that a majority of Americans favored arms control agreements with the Soviets, but at the same time a majority also said that they expected the communists to cheat if given an opportunity. Many politicians sought to follow the polls: they claimed to favor arms limitations, yet they never hesitated to demonstrate to their constituents that they were "tougher on communists" than their opponents. Thus, as the Cold War lengthened, the politicians' desire to be seen as strong on national defense often resulted in misleading, even derogatory, appraisals of arms limitations.

The unstable political-military environment with increasingly accurate nuclear weapons systems capable of obliterating cities, equally worrisome to leaders and to the public, persuaded the United States to engage in talks with the Soviet Union. Each successive administration after 1945 found itself—despite certain individual misgivings—engaged in protracted arms control negotiations. Washington's desire to sustain its influence in the United Nations and to maintain relations with its allies, especially in western Europe, often spurred arms control efforts.

The Arms Control and Disarmament Agency, nourished by Hubert Humphrey and sponsored by John F. Kennedy, was established on 26 September 1961 to facilitate these negotiations. Its director was to be the principal adviser to the president on arms control and to act under the direction of the president and the secretary of state—a unique and often strained administrative arrangement. Despite limited staff and resources, the agency was instrumental in negotiating the Limited Nuclear Test Ban, the Comprehensive Nuclear Test Ban, the Nuclear Non-Proliferation Treaty, and the treaties banning chemical and biological weapons. Perhaps because of its global approach, the agency was sacrificed to the new unilateralists—led by Senator Jesse Helms—in 1997; its transfer to the State Department was completed in March 1999.

The United Nations, United States, and Disarmament Government leaders, peace reformers, and the general public hoped that the new United Nations, with active U.S. participation, might provide the venue for controlling tensions and reducing the prospects of a nuclear war. The Atlantic Charter, issued by President Franklin D. Roosevelt and Prime Minister Winston Churchill on 14 August 1941, declared that "all nations of the world, for realistic as well as spiritual reasons must come to the abandonment of the use of force." It further envisaged the creation of "a permanent system of general security" as well as practicable measures to "lighten for peace-loving peoples the crushing burden of armaments." The United Nations Charter emphasized the maintenance of peace and security. The General Assembly was to consider the principles governing "disarmament and the regulation of armaments" (Article 11, paragraph 1), while the Security Council was responsible for developing plans for the establishment of a system for "the regulation of armaments" (Article 26).

Bernard Baruch presented the U.S. proposal dealing with atomic weapons at the initial meeting of the UN Atomic Energy Committee on 14 June 1946. Although he regarded his remarks as a basis for discussion, they came to be known as the Baruch Plan—the definitive statement of U.S. policy. The plan called for the creation of the International Atomic Development Authority (IADA), which would control or own all activities associated with atomic energy, from raw materials to military applications, and would control, license, and inspect all other uses. In addition, it would foster peaceful uses of atomic energy by conducting research and development.

When the IADA was established, the manufacturing of atomic bombs would cease and all existing weapons were to be destroyed. Baruch declared that sanctions must be imposed on nations possessing or building an atomic device without a license. Finally, he insisted that "there must be no veto to protect those who violate their solemn agreement not to develop or use atomic energy for destructive purposes."

From the outset, American and Soviet diplomats were at odds. The United States viewed the atomic bomb as an important source of its military power and insisted on extensive safeguards before destroying its atomic weapons or releasing information on their manufacture. The Soviets and others argued that the Americans were insincere, because they would not relinquish their atomic arsenal while expecting others to forgo developing their own atomic energy programs. And they were not far off target. "America can get what she wants if she insists on it," Baruch asserted in December 1946. "After all, we've got it and they haven't, and won't for a long time to come."

While some writers blame Washington for the failure of the negotiations, the historian Barton J. Bernstein suggests a more realistic perspective: "Neither the United States nor the Soviet Union was prepared in 1945 or 1946 to take the risks that the other power required for agreement. In this sense, the stalemate on atomic energy was a symbol of the mutual distrust in Soviet-American relations." Not until the ill-fated UN discussions focusing on general and complete disarmament in the 1960s were such broad-gauged approaches again examined.

In a September 1961 address to the General Assembly, President John F. Kennedy responded to Soviet Premier Nikita Khrushchev's 1959 proposal for "general and complete disarmament" by offering one of his own. Both plans primarily sought to influence international and domestic opinion, since neither leader had any reason to expect their plan would gain approval. Extended discussions of the plans by the Eighteen Nation Disarmament Committee (ENDC) revealed that a major point of contention continued to be that of verification. The United States insisted that verification must not only ensure that agreed limitations and reductions had taken place, but also that retained forces and weapons never exceed established limits. The Soviet Union countered that continued verification of retained forces and weapons constituted espionage.

While a few arms control agreements have emerged from the General Assembly and its subordinate bodies, their debates have been more valuable for the discussion of practically every aspect of disarmament. Arthur H. Dean, who represented the United States at the ENDC, wrote: "The discussions—at Geneva, at the United Nations, and in confidential diplomatic conversations—were a necessary means whereby the nations of the world could become educated on disarmament questions and the ground could be broken for concrete agreements."

Nuclear Test Bans and Nonproliferation

The nonnuclear states' search for a comprehensive test ban was closely linked to the major nuclear powers' desire to restrict the spread of nuclear weapons through a nonproliferation treaty. The inability to achieve a comprehensive test ban was a source of friction between the two groups for five decades, especially during the periodic nonproliferation treaty review conferences. Beginning with President Dwight Eisenhower, successive administrations declared that a comprehensive test ban was their goal although they varied greatly in efforts for its accomplishment.

Limited Test Ban

The spread of radioactive fallout resulting from atmospheric nuclear tests aroused public protests in the 1950s—led by Albert Schweitzer, Linus Pauling, and a host of "peace" groups—and put pressure upon President Eisenhower to halt the testing. When a 1957 Gallup Poll revealed that 63 percent of the American people favored banning tests, compared with 20 percent three years earlier, the president initiated the tripartite (U.S.–British–Soviet) test ban negotiations. Eisenhower turned to technical experts to develop a verification system, a move that was to have unexpected long-term results. With the advent of the nuclear age, even greater use was made of experts—including military officers, scientists, and technical specialists. Unquestionably, these experts were vital to the proper shaping of negotiating positions; however, they often complicated issues to a point where they become technically, and therefore politically, insoluble. A case in point is that during early test ban negotiations, seismologists sought a verification system that could distinguish between earthquakes and small underground nuclear explosions. After techniques acceptable to most were developed, technical experts kept searching for more and more refinements to reduce the already low error rate. As a result, it was impossible to negotiate a comprehensive test ban because critics would argue that one could not be absolutely certain that no cheating was going on.

While Eisenhower's efforts resulted only in obtaining an informal test moratorium, John F. Kennedy came to the presidency committed to obtaining a comprehensive ban on tests. His sobering encounter with Khrushchev at Vienna in 1961 and the subsequent Berlin crisis, however, derailed his plans. The October 1962 Cuban missile crisis, paradoxically, brought Kennedy and Khrushchev closer and led to the signing on 5 August 1963 of the Limited (or Partial) Nuclear Test Ban (LNTB).

The 1963 Moscow experience again suggests that successful arms control negotiations cannot be structured as an engineering or technical exercise; they must be essentially a political undertaking. When ambassador-at-large W. Averell Harriman was sent to Moscow to finalize the test ban, he took scientific advisers with him but deliberately excluded them from the negotiating team. He later explained, "The expert is to point out all the difficulties and dangers . . . but it is for the political leaders to decide whether the political, psychological and other advantages offset such risks as there may be."

The Kennedy administration's inability to provide absolute guarantees of Soviet compliance resulted in the LNTB's banning all tests except those conducted underground. This provided the Department of Defense and its nuclear scientists with a "safeguard" or guarantee that the United States would continue underground testing, as they put it, to ensure the safety and reliability of nuclear weapons. From 1964 to 1998, the United States conducted 683 announced tests, compared with 494 for the Soviet Union. Washington's emphasis on the "safeguard" continued to be used to justify testing after the Cold War ended.

The Non-Proliferation Treaty

The People's Republic of China's first nuclear test on 16 October 1964, focused President Lyndon B. Johnson's attention on the dangers of nuclear proliferation. In 1965 both the United States and Soviet Union responded to the UN call to prevent the proliferation of nuclear weapons by submitting their own draft treaties to ENDC, and, after resolving a few differences, became identical by 1967. The committee's nonaligned members argued that a nonproliferation treaty must not simply divide the world into nuclear "haves" and "have nots," but

must balance mutual obligations. Thus, to stop states from engaging in "horizontal" proliferation (the acquisition of nuclear weapons), the nuclear powers should agree to end their "vertical" proliferation (increasing the quantity and quality of their weapons). The nonaligned nations specified the necessary steps, in order of priority: (1) signing a comprehensive test ban; (2) halting the production of fissionable materials designed for weapons; (3) freezing, and gradually reducing, nuclear weapons and delivery systems; (4) banning the use of nuclear weapons; and (5) assuring the security of nonnuclear states.

The Non-Proliferation Treaty was signed on 1 July 1968, after the United States and Soviet Union reluctantly agreed "to pursue negotiations in good faith" to halt the nuclear arms race "at the earliest possible date" (the fig leaf they tried to hide behind), and to seek "a treaty on general and complete disarmament under strict and effective international control." The dubious adherence to this pledge has been a point of serious contention at each subsequent review conference.

The Non-Proliferation Treaty is the cornerstone of a carefully structured regime that emphasizes the banning of nuclear tests and several other elements. The Vienna-based International Atomic Energy Agency was created in 1957—as the coordinating body for Eisenhower's Atoms for Peace project—to promote and safeguard peaceful uses of atomic energy. It has established a system of international safeguards aimed at preventing nuclear materials from being diverted to military uses. During 1974 and 1975, the Nuclear Suppliers Group was established in London to further ensure that nuclear materials, equipment, and technology would not be used in weapons production. Finally, nuclear-weapons-free zones further extended the nonproliferation effort.

Comprehensive Test Ban

The comprehensive test ban issue was dormant during the early years of Richard Nixon's presidency, largely so it would not interfere with U.S.–Soviet negotiations on strategic arms limitations. At a Moscow summit meeting with Premier Leonid Brezhnev in July 1974, the two leaders resurrected the bilateral Threshold Test Ban Treaty, under which they agreed to hold underground tests to less than 150 kilotons, restrict the number of tests to a minimum, not interfere with the other's efforts at verification, and exchange detailed data on all tests and test sites. The Peaceful Nuclear Explosions Treaty, signed by Brezhnev and President Gerald

Ford in May 1976, allowed nuclear explosives under 150 kilotons to be used in a peaceful manner—such as "digging" canals. The pact provided, for the first time, on-site inspections under certain circumstances.

President Jimmy Carter shifted his focus from the unratified threshold test ban back to a comprehensive test ban. In 1977 the Soviet Union indicated that it was willing to accept a verification system based on national technical means (each nation's intelligence-gathering system), supplemented by voluntary challenge inspections and automatic, tamperproof seismic monitoring stations known as "black boxes." When signs pointed to an agreement on a comprehensive ban, major opponents—including the weapons laboratories, the Joint Chiefs of Staff, and the Secretary of Energy James Schlesinger—killed the effort by emphasizing America's need for periodic tests to assure the reliability of the nuclear weapons stockpile.

In July 1982, President Ronald Reagan ended U.S. participation in the comprehensive test ban talks, arguing that the Soviet Union might be testing over the 150-kiloton threshold. He insisted that verification aspects of both the threshold ban and peaceful explosions treaties must be renegotiated before a comprehensive accord could be considered. Critics pointed out that proving a test had taken place was much easier than verifying a specific magnitude; therefore, the administration had things backward. When Premier Mikhail Gorbachev informed Reagan in December 1985 that he would accept on-site inspections as part of a comprehensive ban, Reagan's refusal to consider the offer made it clear that the administration's concern about verification was a sham and that it had been used to avoid any agreement.

President George H. W. Bush issued a policy statement in January 1990 that his administration had "not identified any further limitations on nuclear testing . . . that would be in the United States' national security interest." Negotiations proceeded on verification protocols for the 1974 threshold treaty and the 1976 peaceful explosions pact; in June 1990, Bush and Gorbachev signed the new protocols clearing the way for their ratification.

The UN General Assembly, supported by the United States, overwhelmingly adopted a Comprehensive Nuclear Test-Ban Treaty on 10 September 1996. President William Jefferson Clinton signed the agreement and announced that its entry into force would be of the highest priority. The Senate Foreign Relations Committee's Republican chairman, Jesse Helms, a longtime opponent of the test ban, blocked its consideration until late in 1999, when Senate Majority Leader Trent Lott unexpectedly scheduled a ratification vote. After a bitter partisan battle, the Senate by a vote of 51–48 on 13 October 1999 refused to ratify the treaty. Apart from political partisanship, opposition to the treaty centered on two old issues: whether the treaty's "zero-yield" test ban could be adequately verified; and the potential long-term impact of a permanent halt on America's nuclear arsenal.

Critics refused to place much confidence in the Clinton administration's plans for a U.S. nuclear weapon custodianship, which was to ensure the safety and reliability of aging nuclear weapons. The directors of the three national laboratories (Sandia, Lawrence Livermore, and Los Alamos) testified—not at all surprisingly, since they are in the testing business—that there was no guarantee the custodianship program would work, and it would take five to ten years to prove its effectiveness.

LIMITING NUCLEAR WEAPONS SYSTEMS

Bargaining between the United States and the Soviet Union (later Russia) began in the late 1960s, and eventually these efforts resulted in a series of bilateral agreements: the two SALT I pacts of 1972 (the Anti-Ballistic Missile Treaty and the Interim Agreement on Strategic Offensive Weapons); the SALT II Treaty of 1979; the INF agreement of 1987; the START I Treaty of 1991; and the START II Treaty of 1993.

SALT I and II Negotiations   In late 1966, President Lyndon Johnson notified Soviet leaders that he wanted to limit strategic nuclear arms. The explosion of China's first thermonuclear device on 17 June 1967 persuaded Soviet Premier Aleksey Kosygin to meet with Johnson a short time later at Glassboro, New Jersey. When Secretary of Defense Robert McNamara lectured Kosygin on the need to restrict antiballistic missiles (ABMs) because they lessened the deterrent effect of their strategic nuclear systems, the Soviet leader angrily pounded the table and exclaimed: "Defense is moral, offense is immoral!"

After failing to get his message across at Glassboro, McNamara bowed to demands for the

ARMS CONTROL AND COMPLIANCE

"Most public attention in the area of arms control and disarmament has focused on the process of agreement negotiation. The news media emphasize the meetings of official delegations, the proposals and counterproposals, the compromises each side makes, and the debates over ratification that occur once an agreement has been reached. The negotiating process draws so much attention because it is dramatic, and because the personalities of national leaders and their prominent representatives are involved. In a negotiation, a clear objective is identified, and dramatic tension surrounds the question of whether the objective will be reached and what the terms of the deal will be.

"But the negotiating phase of an arms control agreement is only a prelude. The purpose of arms control pacts is to change or constrain the behavior of the parties in the realm of military security. While the terms of an agreement are important, the real substance of arms control lies in whether or not the parties are successful in accomplishing the objectives set out by the agreement; that is, whether they uphold the agreement over time. Arms control compliance is the actual implementation of the agreements that are concluded with such public fascination and dramatic flair. Compliance does not attract as much public attention as the process of negotiation,

but it is arguably the most substantial and significant aspect of the arms control process.

"Arms control compliance has been surrounded by a considerable amount of controversy. Questions about compliance have often stirred states' deepest fears and insecurities about the intentions and military behavior of their adversaries, especially when tensions have been high and when international conflict or war has been imminent. Leaders are extremely uncomfortable with adherence to an arms control agreement when it is suspected that an adversary is gaining unfair advantage by violating the agreement.

"Charges of 'cheating' on arms control agreements have frequently been made, sometime on the basis of dubious evidence or arguments. The issue of arms control compliance was particularly politically charged in the 1930s and again in the 1980s. In an atmosphere of high political tension, the distinction can be lost between legitimate obligations that are sanctioned by international agreements, and expectations, promises, or verbal statements."

— *From Gloria C. Duffy, "Arms Control Treaty Compliance,"* Encyclopedia of Arms Control and Disarmament, *vol. 1, New York, 1993* —

---

construction of an ABM system in September 1967. Three months later he announced that the United States also had decided to develop a new multiple, independently targetable, reentry vehicle (MIRV), which, after being carried aloft on a single missile, was capable of delivering two or more warheads to different targets. In late June 1968, Soviet Foreign Minister Andrey Gromyko asked that discussions on limiting both offensive and defensive weapons begin on 30 September; unfortunately, Soviet and Warsaw Pact forces intervened in Czechoslovakia in August, causing Johnson to postpone the talks.

Shortly after his inauguration, President Richard Nixon announced that his administration would seek strategic nuclear "sufficiency." On 17 November 1969 delegates initiated the strategic arms limitation talks (SALT). But the two nuclear arsenals differed significantly. The United States had developed technologically sophisticated, accurate missiles with relatively small warheads

of one to two megatons, while the Soviets had deployed a number of different types of weapons. Some were similar to American weapons, but others were larger and had a greater throw weight—the maximum weight that a missile is capable of lifting into a trajectory—a difference that caused difficulties in negotiations for more than thirty years.

Nixon's national security adviser, Henry Kissinger, often met secretly with the Soviet ambassador to Washington, Anatoly Dobrynin, in late 1970 when the talks stalled. These "back-channel negotiations," carried on without informing the U.S. delegation, assisted in formulating a compromise—negotiations would focus on limitations of both defensive and offensive systems—which permitted the formal delegations to reach two distinct agreements.

At the Moscow summit, 18–22 May 1972, terms were agreed to on the Antiballistic Missile

(ABM) Treaty and an Interim Agreement. Each side would deploy no more than 100 ABM launchers at each of two sites, one at the capital and the other at least 1,300 kilometers from the capital. The treaty called for verification by national technical means (satellite reconnaissance, electronic monitoring) without interference, and established a U.S.–Soviet Standing Consultative Commission to considering questions about such issues as compliance and interference. The Interim Agreement established, among other restrictions, a quantitative limit on both intercontinental ballistic missiles (ICBMs)—1,054 for the United States, 1,618 for the Soviets—and submarine-launched ballistic missiles (SLBMs), but no limits on warheads. Using a formula that exchanged dismantled ICBMs for SLBMs, the United States could have up to 710 SLBMs on 44 submarines, and the Soviets 950 SLBMs on 62 submarines. The Interim Agreement's limits on strategic systems for each side were actually higher than what was currently possessed; but it did set ceilings on future deployments. The pact was to last five years (1972–1977), during which time both sides would work for a permanent treaty.

Nixon and Kissinger viewed the pacts as significant accomplishments. However, the Defense Department and Joint Chiefs of Staff had insisted on pursuing new strategic weapons systems—including the Trident submarine, an ABM site, a submarine-launched cruise missile, and multiple, independently targeted warheads—before giving their approval. Senator Henry Jackson, along with a former delegate to the talks, Paul Nitze, was concerned about Soviet retention of 308 heavy ICBMs, which conceivably might be fitted to carry forty warheads each. Jackson introduced an amendment that any future treaty would "not limit the U.S. to levels of intercontinental strategic forces inferior to the limits for the Soviet Union"—thereby launching a search for a new "yardstick" that had a dampening effect on subsequent negotiations.

After ratification of SALT I, the second phase focused on "quantitative" limits, with delegates meeting at Geneva to seek "qualitative" restrictions on the capabilities of weapons systems, a very difficult assignment. After Nixon's resignation, President Gerald Ford and Soviet Premier Leonid Brezhnev met at Vladivostok in November 1974, to sign an "agreement in principle" that listed agreed-to objectives—each side should be limited to 2,400 ICBMs, SLBMs, and long-range bombers, of which 1,320 could have multiple warheads. Both sides of the strategic weapons debate in America were unhappy with the terms: some Americans complained about the lack of reductions; others were critical because the Soviets could still protect their heavy ICBMs. Meanwhile, to improve the accuracy of its missiles, the United States developed a larger ICBM known as the MX and introduced a more sophisticated warhead, MARV (maneuverable reentry vehicle), which greatly multiplied the challenges facing any missile defense system.

Jimmy Carter entered the White House hoping to quickly conclude a SALT II treaty that included deeper cuts in nuclear weapons than previously endorsed by the Vladivostok Accord. The Soviets rejected his March 1977 proposal because it took them by surprise, and because Carter had publicly announced his plan before presenting it to them. Finally signed in Vienna on 18 June 1979, the SALT II Treaty initially limited each side to a total of 2,400 strategic nuclear launch vehicles within this ceiling no more than 1,320 ICBMs, SLBMs, and long-range bombers could carry MIRVs or air-to-surface cruise missiles; and within this sublimit no more than 1,200 ICBMs, SLBMs, and air-to-surface cruise missiles could be MIRVed; and within that sublimit no more than 820 ICBMs could be MIRVed. The seventy-eight-page treaty did require both parties to dismantle some systems to make room for new deployments, and it also included an extensive list of qualitative restrictions.

The SALT II agreement was a mix of an engineering document and a lawyer's brief—the text was extraordinarily complex, and extensive definitions and elaborate "counting rules" were appended. As a result, opponents could employ the "fine print" to justify their claims that Backfire bombers were not properly counted or that the allowed "heavy" missiles gave the Soviets an unacceptable advantage. Despite these problems, Carter might have obtained sufficient support for ratification but for two problems: the "discovery" of Soviet combat troops in Cuba and the Iranian seizure of U.S. embassy personnel in Tehran.

INF Proposals Early in his administration, President Ronald Reagan was primarily concerned with expanding and modernizing U.S. military forces and actively avoiding serious arms control negotiations. Under pressure in late 1981 from antinuclear protesters in NATO countries and the "nuclear freeze" movement at home, he opened the intermediate nuclear forces (INF) negotiations. These discussions were triggered by a NATO decision, late in the Carter presidency, to deploy 108 Pershing II and 464 ground-launched cruise missiles to West Germany, Belgium, Britain, the Netherlands, and Italy to offset the Soviet Union's superior intermediate nuclear force, especially the new SS-20 with its three warheads. Not wanting to bow to "pacifist" demonstrators, the Reagan administration offered its "zero option" concept—the United States would cancel its scheduled deployment in the unlikely event the Soviets withdrew their intermediate-range missiles with 1,100 warheads. Moscow rejected the proposal, and U.S.–Soviet relations deteriorated under the Reagan administration's abusive rhetoric.

After Secretary-General Mikhail Gorbachev assumed power in 1985, the two sides examined a variety of INF proposals until in 1987 he stunned NATO and Washington leaders by accepting the U.S. zero option with its disproportionate reductions and, ultimately, the removal of Soviet intermediate-range missiles from Asia. Gorbachev also agreed to America's extensive 1986 verification demands, and on 8 December 1987 he and Reagan signed the INF Treaty in Washington, D.C. To carry out the on-site inspections that would verify compliance with treaty provisions, the United States created a new umbrella organization, the On-Site Inspection Agency. Despite a few minor controversies, the verification process functioned successfully, and on 1 June 2001 inspections ended as both sides announced that all intermediate missiles had been removed and destroyed.

START I and II Negotiations   During the 1980 presidential campaign, Ronald Reagan denounced SALT II as "fatally flawed" and claimed it allowed a "window of vulnerability" during which the Soviet Union could easily overwhelm U.S. land-based nuclear forces. On 9 May 1982, Reagan outlined his plan for the "practical, phased reduction" of strategic nuclear weapons in two-stages. In phase I, warheads would be reduced by a third, with significant cuts in ballistic missiles; in phase II, a ceiling would be put on ballistic missile throw weights and other elements. While the public response was enthusiastic, analysts found the proposal, like the zero option, so one-sided that they considered it nonnegotiable. In phase I the Soviets would have to dismantle nearly all of their best strategic weapons, while the United States would be able to keep most of its Minutemen and proceed with its planned

deployment of 100 heavier MX missiles. In addition, the United States would be allowed to go ahead with cruise missile deployments and the modernization of its submarine and bomber fleets. In phase II, the Soviets were to reduce the total aggregate throw weight of their strategic missiles by almost two-thirds, while the United States made no cuts at all.

Not until 1985, when Gorbachev got the START talks back on track, was there any progress in the on-and-off negotiations. In their first summit meeting in November, Reagan and Gorbachev shared a belief that "a nuclear war cannot be won and must never be fought," but Reagan's insistence on pursuing a ballistic missile defense system became a major sticking point. In March 1983 he had announced his Strategic Defense Initiative (SDI) proposal, which was to render nuclear weapons "impotent and obsolete." The Soviets, and many NATO allies, opposed SDI (also dubbed "Star Wars") because it threatened the existing mutual nuclear deterrent system. Although the Geneva summit made little progress, both men agreed to work for a 50 percent reduction in strategic forces.

The spring of 1986 found the Reagan administration embroiled in a fierce struggle over whether or not to ignore the SALT II limits. Secretary of Defense Caspar Weinberger and Central Intelligence Agency chief William Casey insisted that alleged Soviet noncompliance demanded a response; while State Department officials and Admiral William Crowe, the new chairman of the Joint Chiefs of Staff, argued that there was no operational reason for going over SALT limits. On 27 May, Reagan announced that the United States would no longer be bound by the unratified SALT II ceilings, a decision that caused a loud outcry in Congress, dismay among allied leaders, and a public uproar. Gorbachev was unperturbed because he was readying a new arms control package.

At the Reykjavik summit, on 10–11 October 1986, Reagan suggested the elimination of all ballistic missiles within ten years. Gorbachev immediately countered with the elimination of all Soviet and U.S. strategic nuclear weapons within ten years and limits on SDI. Since Reagan refused to accept any limitations on his Star Wars system, these radical arms reduction proposals were dropped—much to the relief of U.S. military leaders and the NATO allies, and undoubtedly to senior Soviet generals. In mid-1987 START negotiations began anew on reductions in strategic nuclear launch vehicles and ceilings on intercontinental ballistic missiles, submarine-launched ballistic missiles, and air-launched cruise missile warheads.

When George Bush entered the White House in January 1989, the basic framework of START existed except for several unresolved details. While Moscow favored on-site inspections to determine whether ships were carrying sea-launched cruise missiles, the U.S. Navy rebelled at the idea of the Soviets snooping about its newest nuclear submarines. The United States now proposed that each side declare the number of submarine-launched cruise missiles it planned to deploy. At every meeting with Soviet leaders, Reagan had repeated the Russian proverb "Trust, but verify"; now, however, the United States wanted only trust.

The Soviets pressed for complex verification arrangements. Even though the basic procedures had been established in the INF treaty, verification continued to pose special problems. Congressional Cold War hawks still demanded intrusive inspections, but the Department of Defense and intelligence agencies did not want the Soviets prowling American defense plants. Secretary of Defense Frank Carlucci admitted, "Verification has proven to be more complex than we thought it would be. The flip side of the coin is its application to us. The more we think about it, the more difficult it becomes."

After eight and a half frustrating years, President Bush and Soviet President Gorbachev signed the complex 750-page START I treaty on 31 July 1991. Basically, it limited each side to the deployment of 1,600 ballistic missiles and long-range bombers, carrying 6,000 "accountable" warheads by 5 December 2001, and established further sublimits. This was the first agreement that called upon each side to make significant cuts in its strategic arsenal. Almost 50 percent of the nuclear warheads carried on ballistic missiles were eliminated. The Lisbon Protocol, signed on 23 May 1992, created a five-state START I regime joining Belarus, Kazakhstan, Russia, Ukraine, and the United States. However, Belarus, Kazakhstan, and Ukraine agreed to turn over the strategic nuclear weapons based on their territories to Russia. The verification regime under START I was complex and intrusive, with a Joint Compliance and Inspection Commission that served as a forum to facilitate implementation and to resolve compliance questions and ambiguities.

As the realization settled in that the Cold War was over, the START II treaty was quickly put in place on 3 January 1993 (although ratification was delayed—the United States took three years and Russia nearly seven years). This agreement further reduced the number of strategic nuclear warheads to be held by each party on 1 January 2003 to no more than 3,500. To persuade the Russian Duma to ratify SALT II, Presidents Bill Clinton and Boris Yeltsin met in Helsinki during March 1997 and drew up the so-called Helsinki Initiatives (Protocol to START II), which reassured Russia about the addition of former Warsaw Pact members to NATO and enhanced the prospects of further bilateral nuclear arms cooperation. These initiatives included a package of amendments to various SALT I terms designed to alleviate some the Duma's fears that since the Soviets could not afford to replace all their aging missiles, they would lose parity with U.S. forces. Most significant was that now the core of SALT II would be a ban on all land-based strategic ballistic missiles carrying MIRVs. The removal of the MIRVs eliminated what most experts considered to be the most destabilizing weapons in their mutual arsenals. They also reached agreement in principle on an outline for START III that would stipulate even deeper cuts. The United States and Russia were ahead of schedule in reducing their strategic nuclear arsenal in 1997, when the outline for a START III pact would reduce the aggregate levels of strategic nuclear warheads to between 2,000 and 2,500 for each side by 31 December 2007.

The demise of the Soviet Union and the chaos that followed led to the sometimes controversial 1991 Cooperative Threat Reduction Program (often called the Nunn-Lugar Program), which provided U.S. funds to aid in consolidating the former Soviet arsenal and ensuring its custodial safety. Belatedly, the program was expanded to provide financial and technical assistance in disposal of chemical weapons and of fissile material extracted from nuclear warheads. The cost of disarming proved to be considerably more than expected.

CONVENTIONAL AND OTHER ARMS CONTROL AGREEMENTS

In addition to the major agreements dealing with nuclear weapons, several other arms control activities were undertaken in the post-1945 era, including a multilateral treaty limiting the conventional forces in Europe, agreements on chemical and biological weapons, pacts creating nuclear-weapons-free zones, and protocols aimed at preventing accidental war.

Limiting Conventional Forces   Immediately after World War II, the victors dismantled Germany's military forces and divided the nation. With the onset of the Cold War, however, the Western allies authorized controlled rearmament of (West) Germany and integration into NATO. In Japan the U.S. authorities endorsed, perhaps initiated, Article 9 in the 1946 constitution, which renounced war as an instrument of national policy and prohibited offensive military forces. Later, during and after the Korean War, the United States urged the development of Japanese "self-defense forces."

Negotiations seeking to limit conventional military forces in Europe began in the early 1970s and went on for nearly twenty years. The imbalance between the much greater Soviet and Warsaw Pact forces and U.S. and NATO forces meant that Moscow was reluctant to offer concessions. Under these circumstances, the Conference on Security and Cooperation in Europe (CSCE) measure adopted in the Helsinki Final Act of 1975—which called for regulating major military exercises—was more easily achieved than arms limitations. Several critics belittled the CSCE or "Stockholm" conventional arms control accord; yet the reduced size of these exercises, force concentrations, and armaments involved—along with the advance notice—realistically reduced concerns that "maneuvers" might become a surprise attack.

Negotiations in 1989–1990 finally resulted in the Conventional Forces in Europe (CFE) Agreement. Several factors contributed to their success: France joined the talks; Gorbachev unilaterally withdrew troops and equipment from forward areas; the Warsaw Pact disintegrated; and a reunited Germany agreed to troop limitations. The 11 November 1990 agreement limited five categories of conventional armed forces stationed in Europe from the Atlantic Ocean to the Ural Mountains. These included three categories of ground equipment (tanks, artillery, and armored combat vehicles), aircraft, and helicopters. The process included a full of sharing conventional arms information among all parties and a joint consultative group to iron out differences. By 1998 more than 3,000 on-site inspections had been carried out, and the dismantling of 58,000 units of weapons and equipment had been verified.

Negotiations soon began to establish troop limits and to resolve or clarify other issues. A CFE 1A treaty signed on 10 July 1992 at Helsinki, Finland, spelled out national personnel limits, including restricting the United States to 250,000 personnel in Europe. Another parallel agreement was the "Open Skies" Accord, signed at the Conference on Security and Cooperation in Europe ministerial meeting in Helsinki on 24 March 1992. In July 1955, President Eisenhower had proposed aerial reconnaissance to eliminate "the possibility of great surprise attack, thus lessening danger and relaxing tensions," and to "make more easily attainable a comprehensive and effective system of inspection and disarmament." The Soviets rejected the idea as an espionage plot. After it had lain dormant for three decades, President George H. W. Bush gave the Open Skies concept new life in 1989 because he needed a new arms control proposal; because aircraft, cheap and more flexible, complemented reconnaissance satellites; and because NATO could directly observe Soviet-bloc nations without relying on U.S. satellites.

Banning Land Mines   The "humanitarian" approach won out in the efforts to negotiate a ban on the use of land mines—which in 1997 were estimated to kill or maim 2,000 people each month, some 80 percent of whom were civilians. The ban's origins may be traced back to the little-known 1981 "inhumane weapons" convention that sought to prohibit the use of "mines, booby-traps and other devices." From the convention's 1995–1996 Review Conference emerged support from worldwide nongovernmental organizations.

The United States rejected the original Inhumane Weapons Pact because the Defense Department was reluctant to give up its stockpile of high-technology mines. According to Pentagon estimates, the use of these "smart mines" (with self-destruction or self-deactivation mechanisms) could reduce American casualties on the Korean Peninsula by one-third by limiting the mobility of enemy troops and provide an early warning of attack. Military officials argued that U.S. policy ought to focus on eliminating "dumb" mines and postpone negotiations on other antipersonnel mines.

In October 1996 the Canadian government launched an initiative (the Ottawa Process) aimed at banning antipersonnel mines. Washington announced on 17 January 1997 that it would permanently ban the export and transfer of land mines and would cap its own inventory at current levels. U.S. Senator Patrick Leahy led the American campaign to ban land mines, against opposition from the Joint Chiefs of Staff, and found a growing number of military officers, both retired generals and those holding commands, questioning the utility of battlefield antipersonnel mines. In June, fifty-six senators signed a resolution calling for a ban on the use of land mines by U.S. forces after 2000.

At the Oslo conference in the fall of 1997, the Clinton administration introduced "improvements" in the draft text in line with Pentagon wishes; however, this endeavor drew the unanimous response "no exceptions, no reservations and no loopholes." On 17 September 1997 the administration decided not to sign the final text; later, however, it decided to unilaterally cease using land mines outside of South Korea by 2003 and to sign the Anti-Personnel Mines Convention by 2006 if alternative mines and mixed antitank systems could be developed. Moreover, the Clinton administration promised to raise $1 billion to carry out a U.S.-led "Demining 2010 Initiative" to remove all land mines from more than sixty-four countries by the year 2010. Between 1993 and 1997, the United States spent $153 million and planned to spend $68 million in 1998 to assist in mine removal in seventeen countries.

Banning Chemical and Biological Weapons

Although the United States had signed the Geneva Protocol of 1925, which prohibited the use of "asphyxiating, poisonous or other gases," the Army Chemical Warfare Service and the chemical industry prevented its ratification. Ignoring his Chemical Warfare Service's recommendations, President Franklin Roosevelt in June 1943 unilaterally announced a "no-first-use" policy: "I state categorically that we shall under no circumstances resort to the use of such weapons unless they are first used by our enemies."

During the first two decades of the Cold War, the United States and the Soviet Union accumulated large stocks of chemical weapons and integrated them into their military planning. When a resolution to augment the 1925 Geneva Protocol was introduced in the UN General Assembly in 1966, the United States immediately objected to the addition of herbicides and riot-control agents. The Senate ratified the Geneva Protocol in January 1975—fifty years after signing—with reservations: it did not apply to riot-control agents or herbicides (widely used by the United States in Vietnam), and the United States reserved the right to retaliate in kind should a foe violate the protocol.

On 25 November 1969, President Nixon reaffirmed the chemical warfare "no-first-use" policy. At the same time, he unilaterally renounced U.S. use of bacteriological or biological weapons, closed all facilities producing these offensive weapons, and ordered existing stockpiles of biological weapons and agents destroyed. At Geneva the Conference of the Committee on Disarmament had been preparing a convention that would ban production, acquisition, or stockpiling of biological weapons and would require destruction of stocks. Because of the complexities involved, there were no formal verification procedures. On 10 April 1972 the Biological Convention was signed; however, U.S. ratification was delayed until the Geneva Protocol was approved in 1975.

In 1989 a Soviet defector revealed that Moscow had possessed an extensive biological weapons program in violation of its treaty obligations. The 1979 accidental release of anthrax spores at Sverdlovsk, apparently leading to many deaths, had prompted U.S. officials to ask privately for an explanation. The Soviets were less than candid until President Yeltsin acknowledged in April 1992 that an illicit program had existed but had been terminated. While Iraq's biological weapons efforts were known, their surprising size and scope became known only in 1995 with Saddam Hussein's son-in-law's defection.

The threat of Iraq's biological arsenal during the Gulf War prompted the 1991 Biological Weapons Review Convention to search for a means of verification. The United States took the position that the convention was not verifiable, but other nations were not satisfied. The conference created the Group of Verification Experts, which began a protracted scientific and technical examination of potential measures, and was reviewing the verification techniques employed by the chemical weapons convention at the end of the twentieth century.

Following inconclusive bilateral negotiations from 1977 to 1980 for a chemical weapons convention, the United States and Soviet Union reluctantly agreed to let the UN Conference on Disarmament wrestle with the problems. As finally signed, on 13 January 1993, the Convention on Chemical Weapons eliminated an entire class of weapons and established the most elaborate verification regime in history. The Organization for the Prohibition of Chemical Weapons would collect declarations as to nations' stockpiles and oversee their destruction. In April 1997 the Senate finally granted its approval.

Nuclear-Weapons-Free Zones   There is no authoritative definition of nuclear-weapons-free zones, but there are certain accepted elements implicit in the term. These include no manufacture or production of nuclear weapons within the zone, no importation of nuclear weapons by nations within the zone, no stationing or storing of nuclear weapons within the borders of nations within the zone, and preferably a pledge by nuclear weapons states not to use or threaten to use nuclear weapons against nonnuclear nations within the zone. Although early proposals were caught up in the Cold War rivalry, the United States agreed to three multilateral agreements that prohibited nuclear weapons in specific, nonpopulated areas—Antarctica, outer space, and the seabed.

The Antarctic agreement (1959) has been acknowledged as the forerunner of nuclear-weapons-free zone treaties because of its demilitarizing provisions. An innovative verification system was established whereby the treaty parties might conduct aerial inspections and, at all times, have complete access to all areas and installations. Ten years of UN-sponsored, multilateral disarmament sessions resulted in the Outer Space Treaty (1967), in which the parties agree "not to place in orbit around the Earth any objects carrying nuclear weapons or any other kinds of weapons of mass destruction" or establish "military bases, installations and fortifications, the testing of any type of weapons and the conduct of military maneuvers on celestial bodies." The nuclear test ban accords and the ABM treaty (1972) also have constraints on testing or deploying various weapons in outer space, and the SALT and START treaties prohibit interference with the monitoring of space vehicles. The objective of the Seabed Treaty (1971) is to prevent the placing of nuclear weapons on the ocean floor beyond national territorial waters.

The Treaty of Tlatelolco (1967) pledged its Latin American signatories to keep their territories free of nuclear weapons; not to test, develop, or import such weapons; to prevent the establishment of foreign-controlled nuclear weapon bases in the region; and to negotiate International Atomic Energy Agency safeguards. The United States ratified the protocols asking nations having territorial interests in the region "to apply the status of denuclearization in respect to warlike purposes" to these territories, and "not to use or threaten to use, nuclear weapons against" treaty signatories. Signatories of the Treaty of Rarotonga (1985), including Australia and New Zealand, along with other nearby island states, modeled their pact after the Tlatelolco Treaty. The motivation for creating this nuclear-weapons-free zone was the desire to pressure France to stop underground nuclear tests on Mururoa Atoll in the Tuamoto Archipelago and to prevent disposal of radioactive waste in the region. Many in Washington feared that Rarotonga might encourage additional nuclear-weapons-free zones in the South Pacific that would restrict the navy's freedom of movement; consequently, the United States signed but, as of 2001, had not ratified the agreement. The Reagan administration's talk of winnable nuclear wars aroused intense opposition in New Zealand and Australia. In February 1985, New Zealand's government banned a U.S. destroyer from its ports, because the United States refused to say whether or not it carried nuclear weapons. The episode caused a serious rift between New Zealand and Washington for nearly two decades.

In the mid-1990s, two post–Cold War nuclear-weapons-free zones emerged—the Southeast Asia Nuclear Weapons-Free Zone (Treaty of Bangkok, 1995) and African Nuclear-Weapon-Free Zone (Treaty of Pelindaba, 1996). Protocol I to both treaties states that the nuclear weapons states, including the United States, are "not to use or threaten to use nuclear weapons" within these zones or against any treaty parties. The United States has argued that, regarding the innocent passage of its warships and aircraft, the Bangkok Treaty is "too restrictive" and has insisted on modifications before signing. The Treaty of Pelindaba apparently met with Washington's criteria and, although the United States signed it, as of 2001 ratification was still pending.

PROTOCOLS AIMED AT PREVENTING ACCIDENTAL WAR

History may hold few examples of accidental wars, but the advent of nuclear weapons—and the premium placed on striking first—gave rise to concerns that miscalculation, misperception, and pressures for haste might bring about an "unintended" nuclear conflict. The desire to provide each side the opportunity to consider a situation fully before taking irreversible action led to diplomatic, usually bilateral, negotiations seeking to improve rapid, direct communication in times of high tension.

Hot-Line Systems   The Washington-Moscow "hot line," established in 1963, consists of a group of machines—IBM terminals, encryption machines, and teleprinters. Informally known as Molink, it came into being because the Cuban missile crisis had pointed up the inadequate means of communication between Washington and Moscow. The initial hot-line system consisted of one cable routed across Europe and a backup circuit routed through North Africa. During the 1971 SALT talks it was agreed that two other links be added to the original cable by using an American commercial satellite (INTELSAT) and a Soviet government satellite (MOLNIYA). In 1984 the hot-line technology was further modernized when the system was upgraded for high-speed fax transmission. An urgent message from a Russian leader to the president's ear takes well under five minutes—including translation.

Although the actual number of times Molink has been used is not known, the Defense Department indicates that it is used sparingly "but has proved invaluable in major crises." These include the June 1967 Israeli preemptive strike against Arab forces during the Six-Day War; in 1971 during the India-Pakistan War; during the 1973–1974 Arab-Israeli war; during the 1974 Turkish invasion of Cyprus; in 1979–1980 during the Soviet invasion of Afghanistan; and in 1982–1984 when the Soviets needed to discuss Lebanon and the United States used it regarding Poland. Not surprisingly, other nations adopted the idea of direct communication systems. The British and French have their own direct links with Moscow; and Israel and Egypt have direct lines, North and South Korea are linked, and India and Pakistan have been connected since the 1971 war.

Preventing Untoward Incidents   The Americans and Soviets were particularly active during the 1970s in seeking measures designed to prevent an isolated clash from sparking a much wider conflict. The Accidents Measures Agreement (1971) hoped to reduce the likelihood of nuclear accidents and to minimize the chance of war should such an accident occur. It urged both sides to undertake measures to improve the safety and security of their nuclear activities, and to notify one another immediately of unauthorized or accidental nuclear weapons detonations. Among other provisions, the agreement provided for advance notice of missile test launches in the direction of the other party.

The significance that Soviet diplomats placed on broad statements of principle is reflected in the Agreement on Prevention of Nuclear War (1973), which found the United States refusing to give a nonuse of nuclear weapons pledge or to renounce the option of "first use" of nuclear weapons. Consequently, the two nations agreed to consult with one another in crisis situations that posed a risk of nuclear war.

In contrast, the American emphasis on technical details may be found in the Agreement on the Prevention of Incidents at Sea (1972), which updated the existing international guidelines to prevent collisions at sea. During the 1960s and early 1970s, Soviet and American naval commanders engaged in various forms of harassment. These included an occasional game of "chicken" in which two rival warships threatened to ram one another, each waiting for the other to turn away; buzzing an enemy ship with aircraft; aiming one's large guns at an opponent's ship; and nudging or "shouldering" hostile ships. Both sides recognized the obvious need to expand the traditional "rules of the road" to reduce these incidents and prevent an actual military engagement. The 1989 Agreement on the Prevention of Dangerous Military Activities consisted of measures to improve military-to-military communication in times of crisis. It also created areas of "special caution," where U.S. and Soviet forces were operating in close proximity; outlawed the dangerous use of lasers; prohibited interfering with command and control communication networks by jamming; and agreed to treat minor territorial incursions as accidental rather than automatically threatening greater consequences.

EVALUATING THE COLD WAR EXPERIENCES

The protracted Cold War arms control negotiations did result in a number of accords—for example, the nonproliferation treaty system, the strategic arms pacts, and the hot lines—that stabilized the military climate and provided an avenue for easing political tensions. Although these were significant accomplishments, the tendency in American political circles and in the public mind during the Cold War era was to emphasize—even dramatize—the military dimensions of national security while playing down the contributions of arms control agreements.

The headlines featured those individuals who frequently exaggerated the U.S. vulnerability to Soviet nuclear weaponry. "For more than four decades," Strobe Talbott concluded, "Western policy has been based on a grotesque exaggeration of what the USSR could do if it wanted, therefore what it might do, therefore what the West must be prepared to do in response. . . . Worst-case assumptions about Soviet intentions have fed, and fed upon, worst-case assumptions about Soviet capabilities." Some Cold War hawks defended their frightening scenarios as a patriotic duty. "Democracies will not sacrifice to protect their security in the absence of a sense of danger," Richard Perle, a Reagan Defense Department official, explained in a *Newsweek* article (18 February 1983), "and every time we create the impression that we and the Soviets are cooperating and moderating the competition, we diminish the sense of apprehension."

Despite public pronouncements that America's continually growing nuclear arsenal would provide diplomatic "bargaining chips" or allow "negotiating from strength," U.S. leaders who were so inclined found it extremely difficult to put forth mutually negotiable proposals that could diminish the unthinkable threat posed by nuclear weapons. The interminable bickering between government agencies—especially, the Defense Department, State Department, Arms Control Agency, and intelligence agencies—often stymied presidents and diplomats. Such squabbling prompted a senior member of the National Security Council staff to declare, "Even if the Soviets did not exist, we might not get a START treaty because of disagreements on our side." Another high-ranking U.S. official complained that if the Soviets "came to us and said, 'You write it, we'll sign it,' we still couldn't do it."

America's proclivity to seek security almost exclusively through an ever-expanding nuclear arsenal allowed Defense Department officials, along with the cold warriors in Congress, to dominate arms control policies. Their frequent short-sighted objections to halting or placing limits on emerging weapons systems—such as MIRVs, cruise missiles, and nuclear testing—when the United States held a temporary technological lead often prevented agreements that could have forestalled another surge in the arms race. Not surprisingly, the SALT treaties, while establishing limitations, actually provided for both sides to expand their strategic nuclear forces. It was only with the INF accord and the START agreements that actual reduction of nuclear-armed weapons

systems occurred, and these came about largely as a result of Gorbachev's initiative as he was terminating the Cold War.

During the pre-Gorbachev decades, hardy cold warriors argued that the authoritarian nature of the Soviet Union would most likely lead it to secretly violate arms control agreements in order to gain political or military advantage. Not surprisingly, the Reagan administration spent an extraordinary amount of time and energy in a persistent search for Soviet arms control violations. Three White House reports implied an accelerated pattern of Soviet noncompliance—seven alleged violations in 1984, thirteen in 1985, and eighteen in 1986. All but one of the allegations were found to be "inaccurate, ambiguous, or no longer relevant" by a 1988 report titled *Compliance and the Future of Arms Control* (Gloria Duffy, project director). "The overall pattern on the part of both the United States and the Soviet Union," the report declared, "has been one in which compliance with agreements has clearly far out-weighted noncompliance." But the report observed:

> Through this politicization of the compliance issue in the United States, the Reagan administration has at times behaved as if it desired to withdraw from all existing strategic arms control agreements with the Soviet Union. The United States has acted in a fashion that undercuts the essential process of resolving disagreements that arise with regard to treaty compliance, rather than seeking to make the process work. This, combined with Soviet stretching of the terms of agreements and stubbornness in dealing with many of the compliance issues, has caused the arms control process to lose its give-and-take.

Dynamic changes in arms control and disarmament activities came about unexpectedly when in 1985 Mikhail Gorbachev began essentially unilateral steps to wind down the Cold War by accepting the political democratization of Soviet and Soviet bloc societies, and by seeking ways to end the nuclear arms race. There have been many claimants seeking credit for the demise of the Cold War. The "peace through strength" perspective of containment and confrontation has been cited as prompting Gorbachev's actions. However, this view, as Daniel Deudney and G. John Ikenberry noted in *Foreign Affairs* (1992), obscures "the nature of these momentous changes. Engagement and interdependence, rather than containment, are the ruling trends of the age. Mutual vulnerability, not strength, drives security politics. Accommodation and integration, not confrontation, are

ARMS CONTROL AND DISARMAMENT

the motors of change." Recognition of mutual vulnerability, accommodation, and integration were, and are, the essence of the arms control process.

The old cold warriors were replaced in the 1990s by unilateralists who disdained accommodation, distrusted arms control and feared mutual vulnerability. Their doomsday scenarios featured North Korea, Iraq, and other "radical terrorists" as threatening adversaries against whom the United States must build a missileproof umbrella regardless of how detrimental it might be to its relations with China, Russia, or its friends. Those most ardently pushing in 2001 for a strategic defense system of doubtful reliability—a Pentagon searching for missions, "defense" contractors, former cold warriors unwilling to recognize the changed world, and a woefully inexperienced President George W. Bush—appeared to be little concerned with its impact on existing arms control agreements. Any treaty, including arms control pacts, must be kept in line with changing international realities; however, in this process mutuality of interests must be a significant consideration.

CONCLUSION

During the twentieth century arms control and disarmament issues, spurred by developments in weapons technology, emerged as fundamental political and policy considerations. Concerns with modern weaponry led to the Hague Conferences of 1899 and 1907, which updated the laws of war and sought to focus attention on the dangers of poison gas and aerial bombardment. The decades between the two world wars saw the unilateral disarmament of Germany in 1919, the controversial naval limitation treaties, and the inability of the League of Nations to deal with a rearming world. And, with the emergence of the nuclear era after World War II, debates over arms control and disarmament occupied much of the United Nations' attention and stimulated bilateral superpower negotiations.

The process of negotiating arms control and disarmament agreements became increasingly complex. As policymakers prepared for negotiations, they wrestled with the objectives they wished to achieve and the risks they were willing to accept. Utopian aspirations or broadly gauged disarmament proposals rarely figured prominently in arms control objectives even when peace groups aroused public sentiment in support of such negotiations—such as at the first Hague Conference and with the nuclear-freeze movement of the 1970s and 1980s.

While the bargaining was usually strenuous between teams of competing diplomats, it was often even more intense between competing bureaucracies at home. Indeed, chiefs of state frequently discovered that their latitude in negotiating specific issues had been sharply curtailed in the process of getting all major players at home to agree. In Washington, this was often referred to as the Battle of the Potomac, and a similar struggle usually took place in Moscow.

As weapon systems became more complicated, it was necessary to call upon experts for advice. At the unsuccessful Geneva Naval Conference of 1927, naval delegates completely bewildered the conferees with elaborate formulas comparing the relative merits of eight-inch versus six-inch guns and heavy versus light cruisers. The senior British diplomat returned home arguing that from then on, experts "should be on tap, but not on top." With the advent of the nuclear age, it was often the case that specialists could complicate issues to a point where they became technically, and hence politically, insoluble. During the early test ban negotiations, seismologists developed verification techniques that appeared to be acceptable to many scientists and diplomats; however, these experts kept refining the already low error rate so it would be even smaller. It took a long time to develop a comprehensive test ban because critics—who often had a vested interest in continuing underground testing—argued that one could not be absolutely certain that there was no cheating. From all of this, there is one obvious lesson. To be successful, the negotiation of an arms control and disarmament agreement cannot be an engineering or technical exercise; it must be essentially a political undertaking.

Initial risks involved in arms control and disarmament agreements are sometimes difficult to perceive. Treaties that are termed controversial (that is, they involve some obvious risk) inevitably stimulate contemporary observers to judge the agreements consistent with their personal beliefs and values. The optimistic, enthusiastic supporters of the agreement usually tend to minimize the risks, whereas the pessimistic, suspicious opponents generally overestimate the risks.

Not all contemporary critics have been military officers, as some opponents of the London Naval Limitation Treaty of 1930 illustrate. As Fredrick Hale stated before the U.S. Senate: "The British by the terms of this treaty have us hamstrung and hog-tied and there will keep us as long as limitations of armaments are the order of the day." Winston Churchill stated before the House of Commons: "I am astonished that any Admiralty board of naval officers could have been found to accept responsibility for such a hamstringing stipulation." T Inukai, speaking before the Japanese Diet, stated that the government had "betrayed the country by entering into an agreement at the London Conference inadequate for Japan's defense needs."

These were three civilian statesmen from the three principal signatory nations each insisting that his country's security had been impaired by the treaty. Each was, of course, assessing the risks incurred in the naval treaty based on his own personal convictions and assumptions about the nature of a nation's security.

During the Cold War it was obvious that most American policymakers disregarded the admonishment of Truman's Secretary of State, General George C. Marshall, that if you define a political problem in military terms, it will soon become a military problem. As the cold warriors emphasized the military dimension of national security and scorned arms control and disarmament policies, their mantra was the old Roman precept—if you desire peace (security), prepare for war. A little historical insight might have given them pause, for the more Romans prepared for war, the more war they waged, until, in the end, Rome was conquered.

Clearly, national security cannot be defined simply in amounts of weaponry. Few in Washington reflected on the fact that during the nineteenth century the United States felt quite secure with its policy of political isolationism and its meager armed forces while, conversely, never had the United States felt so insecure as it did during the Cold War years when it possessed a vast peacetime nuclear arsenal, substantial military forces, and allies around the world. A nation's security, then, may rest as much on a sense of national well-being—a psychological state—as it does on the size of its military forces. It would appear, as H. A. L. Fisher wrote during the interwar years, that "in reality, security is a state of mind; so is insecurity."

Whether or not an arms control agreement might be violated was a matter of special concern in the nuclear era. Consequently, the search for effective means of verifying or supervising the compliance with arms control and disarmament agreements has been far more intense since 1945

than in earlier years. The verification or supervision process employs several methods of monitoring compliance that may be classified as "national means" and "cooperative/intrusive means."

The traditional method used to verify treaty compliance has been national means, in which human observers—including military attachés assigned to foreign capitals; national intelligence agencies (for example, the CIA); international businessmen and tourists; and clandestine or undercover sources, including spies—have served as important sources of information. The naval limitation treaties of the 1920s and 1930s, as well as agreements dealing with the outlawing of weapons and demilitarization, used these methods. Prior to World War II, the reports of military attachés were considered to be particularly valuable because of the expertise of the observers; indeed, most of the treaty evasions reported were initially noted by the attachés. Equally important has been the analysis of foreign publications, especially commercial and industrial reports. In such documents, sharp-eyed readers could detect significant changes taking place in the allocation of resources and the establishment or conversion of factories. In this undramatic fashion, the allies learned in the mid-1920s of Germany's evasion of the Versailles Treaty clause forbidding a "general staff" by examining the telephone book of the German military headquarters, which listed the various offices and their functions.

With the advent of modern electronics, photography, space vehicles, and other devices, a new dimension called "national technical means" was added. Such devices have been employed to verify both the quantitative and the qualitative features of strategic weaponry, particularly the numbers and characteristics of ballistic missiles, information that was vital to negotiation of the SALT and START accords. The restrictions on nuclear testing have been monitored—quite effectively, according to private scientific groups—by specially devised seismic devices.

An obvious example of cooperative/intrusive supervision is on-site inspection employed to verify compliance. Such inspection has been used in the efforts to ensure that terms of, for example, the Treaty of Versailles, the Antarctic Treaty, the INF agreement, and the Iraqi armistice were carried out. They also have been used regularly by the International Atomic Energy Agency to ensure that matériel employed in the peaceful use of nuclear energy is not illegally shifted to the manufacture of nuclear weapons.

The Antarctic and INF treaties and the International Atomic Energy Agency inspections have been carried out in cooperation with various treaty members because of the perceived mutual advantages. With the Treaty of Versailles and the Iraqi armistice, on the contrary, inspection teams attempting to verify that all imposed terms were carried out were unwelcome in countries whose governments viewed the terms as unfair and the inspection teams as intrusive.

The historical record of compliance is somewhat mixed, but on the whole, agreements in which a sense of mutuality was established have been honored. Often, evasions or violations that occurred were unintended and marginal—with the possible exception of the Soviet violation of the biological weapons pact. There is no evidence of any unknown treaty violation having had a significant impact on the outcome of a military engagement. Few, if any, governments have negotiated and signed an arms control agreement while deliberately planning to evade the terms of the agreement.

Finally, people in general, even quite sophisticated individuals, usually expect too much from arms control agreements. These techniques are designed to accomplish essentially two basic purposes: to reduce the feasibility of electing war as a means of resolving disputes by reducing the armaments available; and, if that should fail, to diminish the military violence in any subsequent hostilities. These agreements, which usually have been rather specific and technical, focused on armaments or the employment of weapons. The arms control process requires a minimum level of political cooperation and, even then, progress can be slow where suspicions and hatreds must be mitigated. Often the first steps to break down the wall of suspicion are measures that provide for exchanging verified information concerning each side's military forces—confidence- and security-building measures. Rarely have arms control and disarmament accords sought to address the basic political, economic, social, and moral issues that are at the heart of the international disputes that have prompted nations to go to war.

BIBLIOGRAPHY

Adams, Valerie. *Chemical Warfare, Chemical Disarmament*. Bloomington, Ind., 1990.

Adelman, Kenneth L. *The Great Universal Embrace: Arms Summitry—A Skeptic's Account*. New York, 1989. Written by a director of the Arms Control and Disarmament Agency during the Reagan administration.

Almond, Harry A. "Demilitarization and Arms Control: Antarctica." *Case Western Reserve Journal of International Law* 17, no. 2 (1985): 229–284.

Atwater, Elton. *American Regulation of Arms Exports*. Buffalo, N.Y., 2000.

Barnaby, Frank, ed. *A Handbook of Verification Procedures*. New York, 1990.

Barnhart, Michael, ed. *Congress and United States Foreign Policy: Controlling the Use of Force in the Nuclear Age*. Albany, N.Y., 1987.

Blechman, Barry, and Janine Nolan. *The U.S.–Soviet Conventional Arms Transfer Negotiations*. Washington, D.C., 1987.

Borawski, John. *From the Atlantic to the Urals—Negotiating Arms Control at the Stockholm Conference*. Washington, D.C., 1988. Confidence- and security-building process.

Borawski, John, ed. *Avoiding War in the Nuclear Age*. Boulder, Colo., 1986. Useful essays dealing with measures to prevent accidental war.

Brown, Frederic J. *Chemical Warfare: A Study in Restraints*. Princeton, N.J., 1968.

Bunn, George. *Arms Control by Committee: Managing Negotiations with the Soviets*. Stanford, Calif., 1992.

Burns, Richard Dean, comp. *Arms Control and Disarmament: A Bibliography*. Santa Barbara, Calif., 1977.

Burns, Richard Dean, ed. *Encyclopedia of Arms Control and Disarmament*. 3 vols. New York, 1993.

Burns, Richard Dean, and Donald Urquidi. *Disarmament in Perspective: An Analysis of Selected Arms Control and Disarmament Agreements Between the World Wars, 1919–1939*. 4 vols. Washington, D.C., 1968. Surveys most treaties of the interwar years.

Caldwell, Dan. *The Dynamics of Domestic Politics and Arms Control: The SALT II Treaty Ratification Debate*. Columbia, S.C., 1991.

Carnesale, Albert, and Richard N. Haass, eds. *Superpower Arms Control: Setting the Record Straight*. Cambridge, Mass., 1987. Looks at compliance.

Chatfield, Charles, with Robert Kleidman. *The American Peace Movement: Ideals and Activism*. New York, 1992.

Clarke, Duncan L. *Politics of Arms Control: The Role and Effectiveness of the U.S. Arms Control and Disarmament Agency*. New York, 1979.

Daadler, Ivo H. *The CFE Treaty: An Overview and an Assessment*. Washington, D.C., 1991.

Dean, Arthur H. *Test Ban and Disarmament: The Path of Negotiation.* New York, 1966.

Debenedetti, Charles. *The Peace Reform in American History.* Bloomington, Ind., 1980.

Dingman, Roger. *Power in the Pacific: The Origins of Naval Arms Limitation, 1914–1922.* Chicago, 1976. Explores the decision-making process.

Divine, Robert A. *Blowing on the Wind: The Nuclear Test Ban Debate, 1954–1960.* New York, 1978.

Duffy, Gloria. *Compliance and the Future of Arms Control.* Cambridge, Mass., 1988. Report of a project directed by Duffy and sponsored by the Center for International Security and Arms Control, Stanford University, and Global Outlook.

Dunn, Lewis A., and Amy E. Gordon, eds. *Arms Control Verification and the New Role of On-Site Inspection: Challenges, Issues and Realities.* Lexington, Mass., 1990.

Dyson, Freeman. *Weapons and Hope.* New York, 1984. Insight into the science and politics of Cold War arms control.

Fischer, David, and Paul Szasz. *Safeguarding the Atom: A Critical Appraisal.* Edited by Jozef Goldblat. Philadelphia, 1985. A study of the IAEA safeguards system.

Fitzgerald, Frances. *Way Out There in the Blue: Reagan, Star Wars, and the End of the Cold War.* New York, 2000.

Flowerree, Charles C., and Ricki Aberle. *Multilaterial Negotiations for Chemical Weapons Ban.* Washington, D.C., 1993.

Friedman, Leon, ed. *The Law of War: A Documentary History.* 2 vols. New York, 1972. Contains relevant documents.

Fry, Michael P., Patrick Keatinge, and Joseph Rotblat, eds. *Nuclear Non-Proliferation and the Non-Proliferation Treaty.* New York, 1990.

Garthoff, Raymond L. *Policy Versus the Law: The Reinterpretation of the ABM Treaty.* Washington, D.C., 1987.

——. *Détente and Confrontation: Soviet-American Relations from Nixon to Reagan.* Rev. ed. Washington, D.C., 1994.

Graybeal, Sidney N., and Michael Krepon. "Making Better Use of the Standing Consultative Commission." *International Security* 10 (fall 1985): 183–199. The commission deals with SALT and START problems.

Hall, Christopher G. L. *Britain, America, and Arms Control, 1921–1937.* New York, 1987.

Hirschfeld, Thomas J., ed. *Intelligence and Arms Control: A Marriage of Convenience.* Austin, Tex., 1987.

Katz, Milton S. *Ban the Bomb: A History of SANE, the Committee for a Sane Nuclear Policy, 1957–1985.* Westport, Conn., 1986.

Kaufman, Robert G. *Arms Control During the Pre-Nuclear Era: The United States and Naval Limitations Between the Two World Wars.* New York, 1990.

Kelleher, Catherine M., and Joseph E. Naftzinger, eds. *Intelligence in the Arms Control Process: Lessons from "INF."* College Park, Md., 1990.

Kelleher, Catherine M., Jane M. O. Sharp, and Lawrence Freeman. *The Treaty on Conventional Armed Forces in Europe.* The Hague, 1996.

Krass, Allan S. *The Verification Revolution.* Cambridge, Mass., 1989.

Krepon, Michael, and Dan Caldwell, eds. *The Politics of Arms Control Treaty Ratification.* New York, 1991. Reviews problems associated with achieving ratification of selected treaties negotiated from World War I to the end of the Cold War.

Krepon, Michael, and Mary Umberger, eds. *Verification and Compliance: A Problem-Solving Approach.* Cambridge, Mass., 1988.

Mandelbaum, Michael, ed. *The Other Side of the Table: The Soviet Approach to Arms Control.* New York, 1990.

May, Ernest R. *"Lessons" of the Past: The Use and Misuse of History in American Foreign Policy.* New York, 1973.

Meyer, David S. *A Winter of Discontent: The Nuclear Freeze and American Politics.* New York, 1990.

Newhouse, John. *Cold Dawn: The Story of SALT.* New York, 1973. Negotiating SALT I.

Noel-Baker, Philip J. *The First World Disarmament Conference, 1932–1933 and Why It Failed.* Oxford and New York, 1979.

O'Connor, Raymond G. *Perilous Equilibrium: The United States and the London Naval Conference of 1930.* Lawrence, Kans., 1962.

Pelz, Steven E. *Race to Pearl Harbor: The Failure of the Second London Naval Conference and the Onset of World War II.* Cambridge, Mass., 1974. Examines the final phase of naval limitation efforts.

Ramberg, Bennett. *The Seabed Arms Control Negotiation: A Study of Multilateral Arms Control Conference Diplomacy.* Denver, Colo., 1978.

Roberts, Brad, ed. *Chemical Disarmament and U.S. Security.* Boulder, Colo., 1992.

Rose, William. *U.S. Unilateral Arms Control Initiatives: When Do They Work?* New York, 1988.

Royse, Morton W. *Aerial Bombardment and the International Regulation of Warfare.* London, 1928.

Scheer, Robert. *With Enough Shovels: Reagan, Bush, and Nuclear War.* New York, 1983. Insight into their attitudes toward arms control.

Seaborg, Glenn T., with Benjamin S. Loeb. *Kennedy, Khrushchev and the Test Ban.* Berkeley, Calif., 1981.

———. *Stemming the Tide: Arms Control in the Johnson Years.* Lexington, Mass., 1987.

Sims, Nicholas Roger Alan. *The Diplomacy of Biological Disarmament: Vicissitudes of a Treaty in Force.* London, 1988.

Smith, Gerard. *Doubletalk: The Story of the First Strategic Arms Limitation Talks.* Garden City, N.Y., 1980. Written by the delegation head for SALT I.

Stares, Paul B. *The Militarization of Space: U.S. Policy, 1945–1984.* Ithaca, N.Y., 1985.

Stockholm International Peace Research Institute. *SIPRI Yearbook: World Armaments and Disarmament.* Stockholm, 1968–1969. An excellent resource with worldwide coverage.

Talbott, Strobe. *Endgame: The Inside Story of SALT II.* New York, 1979.

———. *Deadly Gambits: The Reagan Administration and the Stalemate in Nuclear Arms Control.* New York, 1984.

———. *The Master of the Game: Paul Nitze and the Nuclear Peace.* New York, 1988. Survey of policymaking during the Reagan presidency.

Tate, Merze. *The Disarmament Illusion: The Movement for a Limitation of Armaments to 1907.* New York, 1942. Covers the Hague Conferences.

Tower, John G., James Brown, and William K. Cheek, eds. *Verification: The Key to Arms Control in the 1990s.* Washington, D.C., 1997.

Tsipis, Kosta, David W. Hafemeister, and Penny Janeway, eds. *Arms Control Verification: The Technologies That Made It Possible.* Washington, D.C., 1986.

United Nations. *The United Nations Disarmament Yearbook, 1976–.* New York, 1977–.

———. *The United Nations and Disarmament, 1945–1985.* 2 vols. New York, 1985. These two volumes are surprisingly comprehensive accounts.

———. *The United Nations and Disarmament: A Short History.* New York, 1988.

United States Arms Control and Disarmament Agency. *Arms Control and Disarmament Agreements.* Washington, D.C., 1990.

Westing, Arthur H., ed. *Environmental Warfare: A Technical, Legal and Policy Appraisal.* London and Philadelphia, 1984.

Wheeler-Bennett, John W. *Disarmament and Security Since Locarno, 1925–1931.* London, 1932.

Wunsch, Charles R. "Environmental Modification Treaty." *A.S.I.L.S. International Law Journal* 4 (1980): 113–131. Also known as the Enmod Convention.

York, Herbert F. *Race to Oblivion: A Participant's View of the Arms Race.* New York, 1970. Interesting for its particular insights into science and politics.

See also ARMED NEUTRALITIES; ARMS TRANSFERS AND TRADE; BALANCE OF POWER; COLD WAR EVOLUTION AND INTERPRETATIONS; COLD WAR ORIGINS; COLD WAR TERMINATION; DETERRENCE; NORTH ATLANTIC TREATY ORGANIZATION; NUCLEAR STRATEGY AND DIPLOMACY; OUTER SPACE; POST–COLD WAR POLICY; SCIENCE AND TECHNOLOGY; SUPERPOWER DIPLOMACY; TREATIES.

ARMS TRANSFERS AND TRADE

Michael T. Klare

Arms transfers and trade—both imports and exports—have been a significant issue in American foreign policy since the revolutionary war. During the Revolution and in the decades immediately following, the United States was primarily concerned with the import of arms, in order to equip its nascent military forces. Following the Industrial Revolution, however, the United States became a major producer of arms, and since then the principal question facing American policymakers has been when and under what circumstances to permit the export of arms. The latter question has gained in significance over time as the United States emerged as the world's leading producer and exporter of conventional weapons (weapons that do not incorporate nuclear, chemical, or biological munitions).

Arms transfers are an important question for foreign policy because they bear on the military capability of the United States and on those states to which the United States chooses to provide (or to deny) instruments of war. When the United States was relatively weak and lacked the ability to manufacture weapons for itself, it needed to obtain arms from foreign sources in order to enhance the capacity of its military forces to overcome both foreign and internal enemies. Since the United States has emerged as a major military power, and acquired the ability to manufacture weapons of all types, its decisions on when and to whom to export arms have had a direct impact on the relative strength of other, less powerful nations.

This capacity to affect the military power of other states became a major factor in American foreign policy before and during World War II, when the United States chose to mobilize its immense arms-making capacity to help defeat the Axis powers, and again during the Cold War, when Washington sought to construct a global network of anti-Soviet states. In both cases, decisions on arms transfers were viewed by American policymakers as issues critical to U.S. national security, requiring assessment and approval at the very highest (usually presidential) level.

Although the end of the Cold War alleviated some of the urgency once associated with decisions regarding arms transfers, such transactions remained a significant factor in U.S. foreign policy. In the mid-1990s, for example, the United States arranged major new arms deliveries to Saudi Arabia, Kuwait, and the United Arab Emirates in order to enhance their capacity to resist attack by Iran or Iraq. And as China proceeded with a substantial buildup of its forces, the United States supplied Taiwan with increasingly sophisticated weapons.

At various times the question of when and under what circumstances to export arms has also been seen as a moral issue facing the United States. This is so because weapons are, by definition, instruments of violence, and so their transfer to another party is thought by many to entail some degree of responsibility for any uses to which they are put by their recipients. After World War I, for example, many Americans opposed the export of arms on the grounds that their sale contributed to the likelihood of war and also provided obscene profits to the "merchants of death." Similarly, during the Cold War some people objected to the sale or transfer of arms to pro-American dictators such as Anastasio Somoza of Nicaragua and Mobutu Sese Seko of Zaire (now the Democratic Republic of the Congo) who had been accused of egregious human rights violations.

For both security-related and moral reasons, arms transfers have become an important subject for international arms control negotiations. During the Cold War, for example, the United States conducted intermittent talks with the Soviet Union over proposals to restrict the flow of conventional arms to areas of conflict, such as the Middle East. And after the Persian Gulf War of 1990–1991, the United States and the Soviet

Union held similar talks with the other permanent members of the United Nations Security Council (the P-5 negotiations).

Finally, it is important to note that arms exports are viewed by U.S. weapons manufacturers—and their supporters in Congress, the military, and the business community—as a legitimate source of revenue. Although such considerations have always been viewed as being subordinate to matters of national security, several presidential administrations (most notably those of Richard Nixon, Ronald Reagan, and Bill Clinton) have embraced arms export promotion as a valid concern of American foreign policy. The purely economic dimensions of arms export policy have been accorded particular attention since the end of the Cold War, when the United States found itself in a less threatening international environment.

For all of these reasons, arms transfers and trade have been an important—and sometimes contentious—issue in U.S. foreign policy. Every American president since Franklin D. Roosevelt has had to direct considerable attention to this issue at one time or another, and it is likely that this will remain the case for all future presidents. As long as there are discrepancies in the military capabilities of states, and as long as nations continue to go to war with one another, arms transfer considerations will figure prominently in the security planning of the U.S. government.

FROM THE REVOLUTION TO WORLD WAR I

The original European settlers in what became the United States brought firearms with them for hunting and self-defense. Weapons were also imported from Europe to equip the militias formed in the English colonies in the seventeenth and eighteenth centuries to fight hostile Indian tribes and to resist incursions by the French and the Spanish. Later, many of these weapons were used by revolutionary forces to fight the British. There were never enough weapons to go around, however, and so the importation of arms from friendly European governments became a major priority for the Continental Congress and its overseas representatives, including Benjamin Franklin. Only when France agreed in 1778 to aid the American rebels with arms and troops was the success of the Revolution assured.

After the Revolution the infant Republic continued to rely on imported weapons for many of its military requirements. To reduce this reliance, Congress voted in 1794 to establish government-owned facilities for the manufacture of firearms. These installations, most notably the army arsenals in Springfield, Massachusetts, and Harpers Ferry, Virginia (now West Virginia), gradually acquired expertise in the mass production of rifles and carbines.

Although these facilities were largely able to satisfy government requirements during periods of relative calm, they could not produce sufficient weapons in times of war—as during the War of 1812 and the Mexican War of 1846–1848. To supplement production at Springfield and Harpers Ferry, the War Department contracted with private gunmakers such as Robbins and Lawrence of Windsor, Vermont, and Remington Arms of Ilion, New York—thus giving a significant boost to the development of a commercial arms industry in the United States. Many of these firms failed or were absorbed by others when government contracts disappeared, but others survived by embracing new technologies and finding foreign customers for their innovative products.

When the Civil War broke out in 1861, the United States possessed a significant arms-making capacity. Together the various army arsenals and their civilian counterparts were capable of manufacturing hundreds of thousands of firearms per year. But even this impressive capacity was insufficient to satisfy the prodigious demands of war, and so both sides were forced to procure additional arms from abroad. Although both the Union and the Confederacy turned to foreign suppliers for a certain percentage of their military equipment, the need for imports was especially acute in the South. Because most of America's arms-making capacity was located in the North, the Union could satisfy a larger share of its military requirements from domestic factories than could the South. As a result, the Confederacy placed a greater emphasis on military imports than did the North, and both sides became engaged in an elaborate diplomatic struggle over arms transfers—with the South seeking to procure weapons from sympathetic powers in Europe and the North seeking to persuade these states to deny arms to the rebels. In the end the Northerners prevailed in this contest, as the major European powers—whatever their political sympathies—chose to eschew involvement in the conflict. This did not, however, deter the North from declaring a naval blockade of the South and deploying hundreds of ships in a determined effort to prevent the smuggling of arms to Confederate forces.

The Civil War, like the wars that preceded it, proved to be an enormous boon to the private arms industry. Once the war ended, however, the U.S. government sharply reduced its procurement of commercially manufactured weapons. To survive in this new environment, private arms companies such as Remington, Winchester, and Colt looked to the civilian market and to foreign customers for the orders needed to survive. This in turn spurred the introduction of new gun designs and manufacturing processes. As a result, American gun firms became adept at the mass production of cheap, reliable, and highly effective firearms.

Although the U.S. government did not always take advantage of this burgeoning capability, other governments were less inhibited. Samuel Remington, the president of Remington Arms Company, opened a sales office in Paris and secured lucrative contracts for the sale of rifles and ammunition to several European countries. Other U.S. firms, including Winchester, also obtained significant contracts from European governments. During the Franco-Prussian War of 1870–1871, for example, the French army ordered 100,000 rifles and 18 million rounds of ammunition from the Union Metallic Cartridge Company of Bridgeport, Connecticut (later a division of Remington Arms).

The capacity of American military firms to produce large quantities of weaponry in a relatively short amount of time was next tested in 1914, when World War I broke out in Europe. Although the U.S. government initially adopted a policy of neutrality in the conflict, President Woodrow Wilson allowed American firms to sell arms and ammunition to the Allied powers. Desperate to supplement their own manufacturing capabilities, Britain, France, and Russia then contracted with American companies to produce large numbers of guns and cartridges. The British, for example, ordered one million Enfield rifles from Remington. As one such order followed another, American military exports jumped from $40 million in 1914 to $1.3 billion in 1916 and $2.3 billion in the final nineteen months of war. This marked the first time that U.S. arms manufacturers played a truly significant role in the international weapons trade.

THE INTERWAR PERIOD AND WORLD WAR II

At first America's emergence as a major arms supplier was lauded as a significant contribution to the Allied war effort. Once the war ended, however, many Americans became fearful of U.S. participation in future European conflicts, and therefore opposed any activities—including arms transfers—that conceivably might increase the risk of such involvement. The most significant expression of this stance, known as isolationism, was the Senate's 1920 rejection of the Treaty of Versailles, which established the League of Nations. The United States also refused to participate in other arrangements associated with the league, including the St. Germain Convention for the Control of the Trade in Arms and Ammunition (1919) and the Geneva Convention for the Supervision of the International Trade in Arms and Ammunition and in Implements of War (1925).

Although leery of international arrangements like the League of Nations, the United States was prepared to support disarmament efforts aimed at the prevention of great-power conflict. Most notable in this regard was U.S. participation in the Washington Naval Conference of 1921–1922, which aimed at setting limits on the naval capabilities of the major powers. Under the resulting Washington Naval Arms Limitation Treaty, ceilings were set on the total allowable tonnage of battleships and aircraft carriers in the fleets of the United States, Great Britain, Japan, France, and Italy. A follow-on treaty, signed at London in 1930, extended the tonnage restrictions to the cruisers, destroyers, and submarines of the United States, Great Britain, and Japan. Although not bearing directly on the issue of arms transfers, these measures represented a significant effort to reduce the risk of war by constraining the arms procurement policies of the major powers.

The American public's antipathy to involvement in overseas conflicts was also reflected in calls for prosecution of U.S. arms firms for their alleged role in fomenting World War I. Antiwar crusaders like Dorothy Detzer of the Women's International League for Peace and Freedom traveled the country, demanding a congressional investigation of the domestic weapons industry. Critical books and articles—most notably *The Merchants of Death* (1934) by Helmuth Engelbrecht and Frank Hanighen—further aroused public opinion. "Arms makers engineer 'war scares,'" Engelbrecht and Hanighen wrote in their widely popular exposé. "They excite governments and peoples to fear their neighbors and rivals, so that they may sell more armaments." In addition, "bribery is frequently associated with war scares" of this sort.

In response to these and other such charges, the U.S. Senate voted to establish the Special Committee Investigating the Munitions Industry in 1934. This body, headed by Senator Gerald P. Nye of North Dakota, was empowered to pursue allegations that American and European weapons producers had conspired to instigate World War I and other conflicts in order to stimulate the demand for weapons. The Nye Committee (as it was called) was also authorized to investigate other charges of wrongdoing by the international arms industry.

After conducting numerous hearings, the Nye Committee concluded that U.S. arms firms had, in fact, employed bribery to clinch overseas sales and had spread tales of imminent hostilities in order to play one prospective buyer off another; it did not, however, find that they had conspired to ignite World War I. In the end, the Senate investigation did not result in any legal action against American arms companies. It did, however, lead to the establishment of the U.S. Munitions Control Board, the first governmental agency charged with regulating the arms traffic. It also sustained the national mood of isolationism and helped ensure passage of the Neutrality Act of 1935, which compelled the president to impose an arms embargo on nations at war.

The Neutrality Act of 1935 was followed by the adoption of similar measures in 1936, 1937, and 1939. The 1936 statute banned U.S. loans to belligerents, and the 1937 measure extended the provisions of the two earlier statutes to civil wars—a step that effectively precluded the sale of arms to the Republican government in Spain, then under attack from right-wing forces led by General Francisco Franco (and backed by the fascist governments in Germany and Italy). The 1939 act, passed at a time of growing tension in Europe, banned U.S. ships from carrying goods or passengers to belligerent ports, but allowed the United States to sell arms to friendly powers on a cash-and-carry basis.

Although they enjoyed strong support from Congress and the American public, the Neutrality Acts and related expressions of isolationism appeared increasingly constrictive to President Franklin D. Roosevelt at a time when the Hitler regime in Germany was accelerating its rearmament effort and pursuing a strategy of regional domination. While Roosevelt argued against repeal of the ban on arms transfers to belligerents in March 1939, when Hitler's armies overran Czechoslovakia, he changed his stance in September of that year, when Germany invaded Poland. Two months later, after Congress finally repealed the Neutrality Acts, Roosevelt authorized a series of cash-and-carry sales of U.S. arms to the European democracies.

A year later, following the fall of France, Roosevelt proposed a much more ambitious program of arms transfers, under which the U.S. government would lend, lease, or donate military equipment to the nations fighting Adolf Hitler. The new U.S. goal, Roosevelt told the nation on 29 December 1940, was to convert the United States into the "great arsenal of democracy," and thereby provide America's allies with the arms needed to defeat Hitler's armies. To fulfill this pledge, Roosevelt asked Congress to approve the Lend-Lease Act, which allowed the transfer of U.S. arms to friendly powers that lacked the funds to pay for them.

Although opposed by isolationists in Congress, the Lend-Lease Act was finally passed by a vote of 60 to 31 in the Senate and 317 to 71 in the House. Signed into law on 11 March 1941, it empowered the president to "sell, transfer title to, exchange, lease, lend, or otherwise dispose of" military articles to "any country whose defense the President deems vital to the defense of the United States." Congress initially appropriated $7 billion for this purpose, and later authorized total expenditures (by war's end) of more than $50 billion—the largest amount ever committed for arms aid until that time. The lion's share of this bounty, totaling $31.6 billion, went to Great Britain; the second largest share, worth some $11 billion, to the Soviet Union.

Ultimately, it was the direct involvement of U.S. soldiers and sailors, rather than the delivery of American weapons, that turned the tide in Europe and the Pacific. But U.S. arms transfers under the lend-lease program enabled America's allies—especially Great Britain and the Soviet Union—to hold out through two years of unrelenting warfare until the full weight of American combat strength could be brought to bear. The lend-lease program also established the principle—adhered to by all American presidents since World War II—that arms transfers can play a significant role in enhancing U.S. national security.

THE COLD WAR

Following World War II many of the factories that had been devoted to military production during the fighting were converted back to their prewar, civilian uses. However, the cessation of fighting in Europe and Asia was not greeted—as the end of World War I had been—with a wave of revulsion against American arms makers. Instead, the nation's military industries were widely viewed as a major pillar of American military strength and an important source of technological innovation. Thus, when the Cold War began in earnest, most members of Congress were prepared to support a new round of arms transfers along the lines of the lend-lease program.

The resumption of U.S. arms aid to friendly powers abroad did not occur without prodding from the White House, however. With World War II barely concluded, many in Congress were at first reluctant to authorize significant military aid to the European powers—fearing, as had their counterparts in the 1920s and 1930s, that this would eventually lead to U.S. military involvement in overseas conflicts. To overcome this resistance, President Harry S. Truman and his close advisers, including Secretaries of State Dean Acheson and George C. Marshall, sought to portray the expansion of Soviet power in eastern Europe and the Mediterranean as a vital threat to the Western democracies and, by extension, to U.S. national security.

The first significant test of U.S. attitudes on this issue came in early 1947, when Great Britain announced that it could no longer afford to support the royalist government in Greece—which at that time was under attack from a communist-backed insurgency. Fearing that the loss of Greece to the communists would invite Soviet aggression in neighboring countries, including Turkey, President Truman concluded that it was essential for the United States to provide arms and military training to the Greek military. On 12 March 1947, Truman appeared before a joint session of Congress to request funding for this purpose. In what became known as the Truman Doctrine, the president articulated a new guiding principle for American foreign policy: "I believe that it must be the policy of the United States to support free peoples who are resisting attempted subjugation by armed minorities or by outside pressures."

As noted by many historians since then, this speech shaped U.S. security doctrine for the next several decades. Henceforth it would be the unquestionable obligation of the United States to provide economic, political, and especially military assistance to any nation threatened by Soviet (or Soviet-backed) forces. As the first expression of this principle, Congress voted $400 million in military assistance for Greece and Turkey on 15 May 1947; this was soon followed by the appropriation of even larger amounts for these two countries and for many others in Europe and Asia.

In time the transfer of arms to anticommunist governments abroad came to be seen in Washington as a critical component of "containment," the strategy that governed American foreign and military policy throughout the Cold War. As articulated by its original architects, containment held that the totalitarian Soviet system was forced by its very nature to seek domination over the rest of the world, and thus, in response, the United States had no choice but to join with other nations in resisting Soviet aggression. And because many of the nations on the periphery of the Soviet empire were too poor to provide for their own defense, it was up to Washington to supply the necessary arms and equipment.

This principle was given formal expression in the Mutual Defense Assistance Act (MDAA) of 1949. Signed into law by President Truman on 6 October of that year, the MDAA (later incorporated into the Mutual Security Act of 1950) gave the president broad authority to conclude mutual defense assistance agreements with friendly powers and to provide these countries with a wide range of military goods and services. In its initial authorization Congress awarded $1 billion to members of the newly formed North Atlantic Treaty Organization (NATO); $211 million to Greece and Turkey; $28 million to Iran, the Philippines, and South Korea; and $75 million for the "general area" of China. These appropriations were increased in subsequent years, reaching a peak of $5.2 billion after the outbreak of the Korean War.

These arms aid endeavors were accompanied, of course, by U.S. efforts to strengthen its own military capabilities. If a full-scale war were to break out, it was believed, the United States would have to provide the bulk of the required forces. But the initial tests of strength were assumed to take place in the border zones between East and West. As a result, much of U.S. diplomacy during the Cold War was directed at the establishment of military alliances with friendly states in these areas and at bolstering the defensive capabilities of their armies. The linkage between military aid programs and U.S. national security was formally articulated in National Security Council policy document number 68 (NSC 68) of April 1950. Described by Representative (later Senator) Henry Jackson as "the first comprehensive statement of national strategy," NSC 68 called on Washington to aid any nation that might conceivably fall under Soviet influence.

At first U.S. arms aid was given primarily to the NATO countries and to other friendly powers on the periphery of the Soviet Union and China, including Iran, South Korea, Turkey, and the Nationalist government on Taiwan. In later years such assistance was also supplied to friendly nations in Africa and Latin America. Between 1950 and 1967 the United States provided its allies with a total of $33.4 billion in arms and services under the Military Assistance Program (MAP), plus another $3.3 billion worth of surplus weaponry under the Excess Defense Articles program. The United States also sold weapons to those of its allies that were sufficiently recovered from World War II to finance their own arms acquisitions; between 1950 and 1967 Washington exported $11.3 billion worth of arms and equipment through its Foreign Military Sales program. (All of these figures are in uninflated "current" dollars, meaning that their value in contemporary dollars would be significantly greater.)

Although the basic premise of American arms transfers—to strengthen the defenses of U.S. allies facing a military threat from the Soviet Union—did not change over the years, many aspects of these programs underwent significant transformation. Thus, while the bulk of U.S. weaponry was originally funneled to the industrialized powers of Europe and Asia, by the late 1950s an increasing portion of these arms was being provided to friendly nations in what was then called the Third World. The primary impetus for this shift was Moscow's apparent success in using arms transfers to establish military links with Egypt (beginning in 1954), Syria (in 1955), Iraq (in 1958), and Cuba (in 1961). In order to combat the growing Soviet presence in the Middle East, Africa, and Latin America, Washington began supplying vast quantities of arms and ammunition to its own allies in these regions—thereby triggering fresh Soviet arms transfers to its Third World clients, in what was to become an ongoing pattern of U.S.–Soviet arms competition.

Although the primary objective of U.S. arms transfer policy during this period was to bolster the defensive capabilities of key allies, American leaders did on occasion emphasize other priorities. In the early 1950s, for example, the United States joined with Great Britain and France in restricting arms deliveries to the Middle East. As noted in the 1950 Tripartite Declaration, the aim of this effort was to prevent the outbreak of an uncontrolled and destabilizing arms race in the region. (This effort collapsed in 1954, when the Soviet bloc began selling arms to Egypt and the United States responded by increasing its arms deliveries to Israel and other friendly powers in the area.)

In another attempt at restraint, the Kennedy administration attempted in the early 1960s to dissuade Latin American countries from acquiring expensive, "big-ticket" weapons such as jet fighters and armored vehicles. Believing that persistent underdevelopment—rather than the distant threat of Soviet power—represented the greatest threat to these states' long-term stability, President John F. Kennedy suggested that any funds saved by reducing arms imports be devoted to economic and social development. When supplying U.S. arms to these countries under the MAP program, moreover, Kennedy favored the transfer of "counterinsurgency" gear—small arms, light vehicles, helicopters, and so on.

For the most part, however, U.S. policymakers favored a liberal approach to arms transfers, permitting the flow of increasingly costly and sophisticated arms to American allies in Europe, Asia, and the Middle East. This policy was strongly backed by U.S. military leaders, who saw arms transfers (and their accompanying training and advising operations) as a valuable instrument for establishing and nurturing ties with the military elites of friendly countries. It also enjoyed strong support from the domestic arms industry, which consistently opposed any restrictions on the sales of weapons to friendly powers abroad.

THE VIETNAM WAR AND THE NIXON DOCTRINE

Although the principal recipients of U.S. arms aid in the 1950s were the NATO countries and other friendly powers on the periphery of the Soviet Union, in the early 1960s, Washington began to direct considerable attention to Southeast Asia, where communist insurgents had become increasingly active. In line with the Truman Doctrine and NSC 68—which viewed a gain by communist forces in any part of the world as a strategic defeat for the West—the Kennedy administration established major military aid programs in Cambodia, South Vietnam, and Thailand. By 1975 U.S. military aid to these countries came to an estimated $18 billion.

As the fighting between insurgents and government forces in South Vietnam intensified, the United States sent ever-increasing quantities of military equipment to the South Vietnamese army, along with large numbers of U.S. military advisers. By doing so, Washington hoped to avert direct U.S. military involvement in the conflict. As the insurgents—backed by increasingly powerful forces sent from North Vietnam—gained in strength, however, U.S. leaders determined that it would be necessary to deploy American combat forces to prevent the collapse of the South Vietnamese government. At the peak of the conflict in the late 1960s, some 550,000 U.S. soldiers were serving in Vietnam. But when U.S. intervention failed to produce a quick and decisive victory, the American public turned against the war and U.S. forces were eventually withdrawn.

The American failure in Vietnam had a profound impact on U.S. foreign and military policy. Probably its longest-lasting consequence was to engender a deep-seated antipathy on the part of the American people to the long-term commitment of U.S. ground troops to ambiguous conflicts in the developing world—a reluctance that shaped U.S. strategy in the Gulf War of 1990–1991 and the Kosovo conflict of 1999. Congress also grew leery of major arms-supply arrangements with unpopular Third World regimes. In 1968, for example, the Foreign Assistance Act was amended to require a reduction in U.S. military aid to any underdeveloped country that diverted excessive funds to the acquisition of sophisticated military hardware. Subsequent amendments also prohibited the provision of military assistance to governments cited for egregious human rights violations.

But while Congress was reluctant to approve any increase in U.S. military assistance to repressive Third World countries, it also sought to prevent the deployment of U.S. combat forces in these areas—and so could be persuaded in some cases to sacrifice one goal for the other. This was the genesis of the Nixon Doctrine, which called for the substitution of U.S. arms aid for American troops in unstable areas deemed essential to U.S. security.

As articulated by President Richard Nixon in 1970, this policy held that the United States

"shall furnish military and economic assistance when requested and as appropriate" to friendly nations that come under attack in remote areas of the world. But, at the same time, the United States would "look to the nation directly threatened to assume the primary responsibility of providing the manpower for its defense."

Initially, the Nixon Doctrine was said to apply to the nations of Southeast Asia and the surrounding region. Before long, however, the main focus of this policy was shifted to the Persian Gulf, where Great Britain had long served as the regional hegemon. When Prime Minister Harold Wilson announced that London would withdraw its forces from the Gulf by the end of 1971, the Nixon administration undertook an immediate review of American strategy in the area. Believing that the U.S. public—still in the throes of the Vietnam debate—would not tolerate the deployment of American forces in the Persian Gulf, the White House concluded that U.S. strategy would have to rest on the supply of weapons to friendly powers.

The administration's new policy toward the Gulf was spelled out in National Security Council Decision Memorandum number 92 (NSDM-92). Although the text of this document was never made public, its basic thrust was later articulated in congressional testimony by Undersecretary of State Joseph J. Sisco. "What we decided," Sisco told the House Committee on Foreign Affairs in 1973, "is that we would try to stimulate and be helpful to the two key countries in this area—namely, Iran and Saudi Arabia—that, to the degree to which we could stimulate cooperation between these two countries, they could become the major elements of stability as the British were getting out."

As suggested by Sisco, this policy was aimed at both Iran and Saudi Arabia. In practice, however, the greater emphasis was placed on Iran. This was so because Iran's armed forces were considered far more capable than those of Saudi Arabia, and because its leader, Shah Mohammad Reza Pahlavi, was more attuned to U.S. policy objectives. Eager to enhance his nation's status as a regional power and to attract the support of Washington, the shah ordered $20 billion worth of American arms between 1970 and 1978—at that time a record for weapons acquisitions by a developing country. Indeed, Representative Gerry E. Studds of Massachusetts went so far as to state that these transfers constituted "the most rapid buildup of military power under peacetime conditions of any nation in the history of the world."

Although U.S. sales to Iran were motivated primarily by national security considerations, as spelled out in NSDM-92, the Nixon administration was not unmindful of the economic dimensions of arms exports. Facing a significant balance-of-payments crisis as a result of Vietnam War expenditures and the OPEC oil price increase of 1973, the White House saw in military sales a practical means for recouping some of the massive dollar outflows. Accordingly, U.S. arms firms were given a green light by Nixon to provide the shah with some of America's most advanced and sophisticated weapons, including F-4, F-5, and F-14 aircraft.

So massive were U.S. arms transfers to Iran at this time that many members of Congress became alarmed at the scale of the sales program and its potential for abuse. These concerns were increased by reports that U.S. weapons firms had employed bribery to solicit major orders from Iran—recalling the sort of charges made by Engelbrecht and Hanighen in 1934—and that U.S. officials had failed to impose any limits on the sophistication of the arms that could be supplied to that country. After investigating these charges, the Senate Foreign Relations Committee concluded in 1976 that U.S. arms sales to Iran were "out of control."

This report, and others like it, led Congress—for the first time since the 1930s—to adopt significant legislative restraints on U.S. military sales abroad. Under the Arms Export Control Act (AECA) of 1976, Congress gave itself veto power over all individual arms transfers worth $14 million or more and over all munitions packages worth $50 million or more. The AECA also required the White House to provide Congress with advance notice of pending arms agreements, and placed restrictions on the "re-transfer" of U.S. arms from their intended recipient to another country.

CARTER AND REAGAN

The issue of profligate arms sales to Third World countries arose in the presidential campaign of 1976. "I am particularly concerned by our nation's role as the world's leading arms salesman," then-governor Jimmy Carter told the Foreign Policy Association in New York. Arguing that "the United States cannot be both the world's leading champion of peace and the world's leading supplier of the weapons of war," he promised that, if elected president, he would work to "increase the emphasis on peace and to reduce the commerce in arms."

Once elected, Carter renewed his promise to reduce U.S. weapons sales. In his first interview as president, he told reporters that the National Security Council had reached agreement on the need to place "very tight restrictions on future commitments" of U.S. arms to overseas recipients. These restrictions were contained in Presidential Directive 13 (PD-13), adopted on 13 May 1977. In announcing the provisions of PD-13 on 19 May 1977, President Carter affirmed that "the United States will henceforth view arms transfers as an exceptional foreign policy instrument, to be used only in instances where it can be clearly demonstrated that the transfer contributes to our national security interests."

To implement this "policy of arms restraint," as he termed it, Carter imposed a ceiling on the total dollar value of U.S. arms transfers (set at the sales level for 1977) to all but a few traditional allies, and pledged that the United States would not be the first supplier to introduce into Third World areas "newly developed, advanced weapons systems which could create a new or significantly higher combat capability." Moreover, to dampen the overseas demand for U.S. weapons, Carter ordered American diplomats to refrain from assisting U.S. arms firms in their efforts to secure foreign buyers. (This instruction was incorporated in the "leprosy letter" of 31 August 1977, sent to all U.S. embassies and military missions abroad.)

For the next three years Carter struggled to preserve his self-imposed ceiling on the dollar value of U.S. arms exports to nonexempt countries and to fulfill the other aspects of his policy. In Latin America, for example, he reintroduced the ban on sales of high-technology weaponry first instituted by President John F. Kennedy. He also succeeded in reducing total U.S. sales to non-NATO countries from $9.3 billion in fiscal year (FY) 1977 to $8.6 billion in FY 1978 and $8.4 billion in FY 1979.

From the beginning, however, Carter came under intense pressure from both domestic and international forces to abandon his arms restraint policy. At home he was besieged by supporters of Israel, who sought to exempt that country from any of the restrictions on high-technology arms exports. The domestic arms industry also campaigned strenuously against the restrictive provisions of PD-13. Overseas the president's determination to adhere to these provisions was undermined by growing Soviet assertiveness in the Third World, most notably in Afghanistan. Buffeted on both sides by antagonistic forces, Carter decided to abandon the arms ceiling in 1979.

Even before announcing this decision, Carter had made a virtual about-face on the arms export issue. In February 1978 he authorized the transfer of two hundred advanced combat aircraft to three countries in the Middle East—supplying sixty F-15s to Saudi Arabia, fifty F-5Es to Egypt, and a combination of ninety F-15s and F-16s to Israel. Six months later he gave preliminary approval to the sale of another $12 billion worth of high-tech weaponry to Iran. Other major sales of this sort were announced in the final months of his administration.

The changing international environment doomed another key aspect of the Carter policy: a determined U.S. effort to persuade the Soviet Union to agree to mutual restraint on arms exports to the developing areas. Between December 1977 and September 1978, the United States and the Soviet Union held four meetings to consider restrictions of this sort. Known as the Conventional Arms Trade Talks (CATT), these negotiations produced consensus on certain matters of principle and terminology, but never resulted in agreement on specific control measures. With superpower tensions rising in the Middle East and elsewhere, the two sides discontinued the talks at the end of 1978.

Ronald Reagan, who became president in 1981, repudiated what little survived of the Carter arms policy and promised to expand U.S. military aid to threatened allies abroad. His administration's revised, pro-sales stance was initially spelled out in a speech by Undersecretary of State James L. Buckley before the Aerospace Industries Association on 21 May 1981. Rejecting the notion that arms sales are "inherently evil or morally reprehensible," Buckley affirmed that "this administration believes that arms transfers, judiciously applied, can complement and supplement our own defense efforts." These views were incorporated into a new presidential directive on arms transfers, signed by Reagan on 8 July 1981.

In contrast to the Carter directive on arms transfers, the Reagan policy did not portray the global arms flow as a potential threat to international peace and stability. Rather, U.S. arms exports were described as a vital adjunct to America's efforts to counter (what was seen as) the growing power and assertiveness of the Soviet Union. As Undersecretary Buckley explained on

21 May, "We are faced not only with the need to rebuild and modernize our own military forces, but also to help other nations in the free world to rebuild theirs."

In line with this outlook, Reagan repudiated the arms-export ceiling set by President Carter and abolished the ban on sales of high-tech weapons to friendly Third World nations. The new administration also eased the repayment terms for any U.S. arms purchased by developing countries with credits supplied through the Foreign Military Sales (FMS) program. And, in a move that was eagerly sought by American arms manufacturers, Reagan rescinded the "leprosy letter" of 31 August 1977, and instructed U.S. diplomatic personnel to assist American military firms in securing contracts abroad.

As a result of these and similar initiatives, U.S. arms exports soared during the Reagan era. According to the Department of Defense, military sales under the FMS program jumped from $8.2 billion in FY 1981 (the last year affected by the Carter policy) to $20.9 billion in FY 1982—a one-year increase of 155 percent. In addition to condoning a dollar increase in military exports, the Reagan administration approved the sale of some of America's most sophisticated aircraft, missiles, and tanks to Israel, Saudi Arabia, and other favored clients in the developing areas. All told, the United States exported approximately $92 billion worth of arms and military equipment during the Reagan era.

For the most part, President Reagan enjoyed strong congressional support for his efforts to boost U.S. arms sales abroad. He did, however, encounter significant opposition to a number of specific transactions. Most notable in this regard was his 1981 plan to sell five Advanced Warning and Control Systems (AWACS) aircraft, along with other sophisticated weapons, to Saudi Arabia for $8.5 billion—the largest single U.S. arms package until that date. Many members of Congress, including a substantial number of Republicans, announced their intention to block the AWACS sale in accordance with the veto provisions of the Arms Export Control Act, on the grounds that it would pose a potential threat to the security of Israel. Only after a major lobbying campaign by the president was the White House able to defeat the veto effort in the Senate by the narrow vote of 52–48.

Aside from the AWACS sales to Saudi Arabia, the arms transactions of the Reagan era that provoked the most controversy involved the covert delivery of weapons to anticommunist insurgents in countries ruled by allies of Moscow. As part of his drive to combat Soviet influence in the developing areas, President Reagan authorized the transfer of arms and ammunition to the Islamic *mujahideen* in Afghanistan, the rebel forces of Jonas Savimbi in Angola, and the anti-Sandinista contras in Nicaragua. Although these efforts were supported by some in Congress, the covert arms program provoked a major national crisis when it was discovered in 1986 that the National Security Council staff had sold U.S. anti-tank missiles to archenemy Iran, then ruled by the Ayatollah Khomeini, in order to finance arms deliveries to the contras. In what became known as the Iran-Contra affair, the administration's covert arms program came under intense congressional scrutiny and was subjected to a number of severe constraints.

THE GULF WAR AND BEYOND

Until 1990 U.S. arms exports were largely governed by Cold War priorities and a desire to reap the economic benefits of military sales. During all the years in which the United States and the Soviet Union competed for political influence in Third World areas, arms transfers were viewed in Washington as an indispensable tool of foreign policy—thus making reductions of the sort envisioned by President Carter nearly impossible to implement. With the end of the Cold War, however, the national security justification for arms transfers lost some of its persuasiveness, and greater emphasis was placed on the economic justification for export sales. This, however, exposed U.S. arms sales to objections of a moral nature, like those articulated after World War I. And, indeed, international events were to lend fresh vigor to these sorts of concerns.

The Cold War was still winding down in August 1990 when Iraqi forces commenced their invasion of Kuwait. Observers were initially struck by the speed and brazenness of the invasion, which could only be viewed as a willful violation of international law. But another aspect of the invasion also sparked international attention: the fact that Iraqi forces were equipped with very large numbers of sophisticated weapons that had been obtained from foreign suppliers. During the previous eight years Iraq had spent an estimated $43 billion on imported weapons, giving it the most modern and powerful arsenal of any nation

in the developing world. Many of these arms were supplied by the Soviet Union (long Iraq's major supplier), but others were acquired from France and other Western countries. This led to widespread charges that the major suppliers bore some degree of responsibility for Iraq's aggressive behavior, in that they had provided the means for mounting the 1990 invasion. Thus, when the Gulf War concluded in late February 1991, many international figures called for the adoption of new multilateral restraints on the transfer of arms to areas of conflict.

In response to these pressures, representatives of the five permanent members of the UN Security Council (the P-5 powers) met in Paris in July 1991 to address the problem of conventional arms transfers—the first multilateral discussions of this sort since the failed CATT negotiations of the 1970s. At the end of the meeting, the P-5 delegates issued a communiqué in which they pledged to develop new controls on the arms trade. For the first time these countries acknowledged that "indiscriminate transfers of military weapons and technology contribute to regional instability," and that, as the world's leading suppliers of such items, they bore "special responsibilities" to practice restraint. With this in mind they promised to develop a set of "agreed guidelines" for a regime of mutual restraint.

At a second meeting of the P-5 nations, held in London on 17–18 October 1991, the delegates adopted a formal set of guidelines for conventional arms restraint. While reserving the right to provide arms to established states for the purpose of legitimate self-defense, they agreed to avoid transfers that would be likely to "(a) prolong or aggravate an existing armed conflict; (b) increase tension in a region or contribute to regional instability; (c) introduce destabilizing military capabilities in a region." But, although they were united on these basic points, the P-5 states still had to establish formal criteria and procedures for their effective implementation. This task was left to subsequent meetings, to be held in 1992.

Before the P-5 states could meet again, however, domestic politics in the United States intruded into the process. As the November 1992 presidential election approached, President George H. W. Bush (then trailing in the national polls) agreed to sell 150 F-16 fighter planes to Taiwan, thus providing a significant economic boon to Texas (where the planes would be built). Although of dubious political benefit to Bush (who subsequently lost the election), the F-16 sale to Taiwan greatly angered China, which immediately withdrew from the P-5 negotiations. With China out of the picture, the other participating states saw no reason to proceed on their own, and the talks were suspended—never to be revived.

In his final months in office, Bush approved a number of major military sales abroad, claiming they served to enhance U.S. security by bolstering the forces of friendly nations in strategic areas, especially the Middle East. Arguing that the United States would need to rely on the support of Kuwait, Saudi Arabia, and the United Arab Emirates (UAE) in any future encounter with Iraq, he authorized the sale of billions of dollars' worth of advanced aircraft, missiles, and armored vehicles to these three countries. In justifying these sales, Bush was not inhibited about touting the economic advantages of such transactions; at the same time, however, he sought to breathe new life into the national security arguments of the Cold War period by emphasizing their application to the new realities of the post–Cold War era.

Many of these sales were announced during the 1992 presidential campaign, and so it is hardly surprising that Democratic candidate Bill Clinton expressed concern over the magnitude of U.S. arms exports. Moreover, after winning the election, Clinton indicated that he would take a fresh look at American arms transfer policies. This suggested to some that he would resurrect some of the restrictive policies of the Carter administration. Once in office, however, Clinton followed essentially the same path as his predecessor—approving major sales that benefited American arms manufacturers while supporting U.S. security objectives in vital areas, such as the Middle East and the Pacific Rim.

To provide greater coherence to U.S. policy in this area, Clinton appointed a special commission on conventional arms exports. On the basis of this review, he announced a new conventional arms transfer policy on 17 February 1995. Reiterating many of the arguments made by previous administrations, the Clinton policy embraced both the security and the economic justifications for military sales. With respect to the latter, the policy specifically mandated that "the impact on U.S. industry" of pending sales was to be taken into account when deciding on future transactions.

In line with this policy, Clinton approved a series of major arms sales to friendly nations in the Persian Gulf area. Arguing that the United States had vital security interests in this region—notably the free flow of oil—and that these countries would be called on to assist U.S. forces in the event of an attack by Iran or Iraq, Clinton authorized the transfer of $46.5 billion worth of military hardware to the Middle East in 1993–2000—an amount that represented about three-fourths of the total value of all U.S. military transfers to the developing world. Saudi Arabia was the principal beneficiary of this largess, obtaining 72 advanced F-15XP Eagle jet fighters, 150 M-1A2 Abrams tanks, 12 Patriot air-defense missile batteries, and thousands of missiles of various types; Kuwait obtained 6 Patriot missile units, 256 M-1A2 Abrams tanks, and 16 AH-64 Apache attack helicopters; and the UAE obtained 10 AH-64s and 80 F-16 fighters.

By the time Clinton left office in early 2001, arms transfers had come to be seen in Washington as a normal, legitimate aspect of U.S. foreign policy. The United States completely dominated the international market, providing about two-fifths of all weapons transferred to developing countries in the 1992–1999 period (measured in dollar terms). Although Clinton encountered opposition to a number of specific transactions in Congress—for example, the sale of advanced jet fighters to Latin American countries—most lawmakers endorsed the basic premises of U.S. arms export policy.

Little change in this picture was expected when George W. Bush entered the White House in 2001. Even more than Clinton, the younger Bush emphasized the centrality of national security considerations in the shaping of U.S. foreign policy—a stance that typically has entailed a predisposition to provide favored allies with large quantities of sophisticated weaponry. Indeed, Bush signaled his support for this approach in April 2001, when he approved the sale of four missile-armed warships and eight diesel-powered submarines to Taiwan.

But while most senior U.S. policymakers generally harbor a relaxed attitude toward arms transfers, the historic concern over the moral implications of such exports has not disappeared altogether. Many peace, human rights, and religious organizations continue to argue that foreign military sales undermine American values and interests by enhancing the repressive capabilities of authoritarian governments, by fueling local arms races in areas of tension, and by encouraging states to seek military rather than negotiated solutions to their disputes with others. These concerns have surfaced in a number of legislative proposals introduced by sympathetic members of Congress, and in occasional newspaper editorials.

Whether they will have any impact on future policy remains to be seen, but such efforts are likely to remain an important feature of the national debate over U.S. foreign policy.

BIBLIOGRAPHY

Grimmett, Richard F. *Conventional Arms Transfers to Developing Nations, 1993–2000.* Congressional Research Service Report to Congress. Washington, D.C., 2001. See also earlier editions of this annual publication.

Hammond, Paul Y., David J. Louscher, Michael D. Salomon, and Norman A. Graham. *The Reluctant Supplier: U.S. Decisionmaking for Arms Sales.* Cambridge, Mass., 1983.

Harkavy, Robert E. *The Arms Trade and International Systems.* Cambridge, Mass., 1975.

Hartung, William D. *And Weapons for All.* New York, 1994.

Klare, Michael T. *American Arms Supermarket.* New York, 1984.

Krause, Keith. *Arms and the State: Patterns of Military Production and Trade.* Cambridge, U.K., 1992.

Laurance, Edward J. *The International Arms Trade.* New York, 1992.

Neuman, Stephanie G., and Robert E. Harkavy, eds. *Arms Transfers in the Modern World.* New York, 1979.

Pierre, Andrew J. *The Global Politics of Arms Sales.* Princeton, N.J., 1982.

Stockholm International Peace Research Institute. *SIPRI Yearbook 2000: Armaments, Disarmament and International Security.* London, 2000. See also earlier editions of this annual publication.

Thayer, George. *The War Business.* New York, 1969.

Zwoll, Wayne van. *America's Great Gunmakers.* South Hackensack, N.J., 1992.

See also ARMS CONTROL AND DISARMAMENT; BALANCE OF POWER; CONTAINMENT; COVERT OPERATIONS; FOREIGN AID; MILITARISM; TERRORISM AND COUNTERTERRORISM.

ASYLUM

Michael Dunne

John Bassett Moore, the greatest American international lawyer of his age, wrote in his monumental *Digest of International Law* (1906): "No legal term in common use is perhaps so lacking in uniformity and accuracy of definition as the 'right of asylum.'" A century later, the same can still be said. Asylum, originally conceived as a right claimed by an individual fugitive, is now more readily regarded as a privilege abused by hordes of foreigners, self-styled refugees seeking to avoid the immigration restrictions of beneficent countries. The twentieth century, which began at the high point of intercontinental and peaceful migration, ended as intracontinental migration became increasingly salient and more and more contentious politically. Western and northern Europeans worried about "economic migrants" from the Balkans and the former Soviet bloc. From the Horn of Africa through the Great Lakes to the mouth of the Congo millions of people have been displaced through war and famine; South and Southeast Asia have seen comparable human exoduses. In the Western Hemisphere the debate has concerned the movement of migrants, overwhelmingly Spanish-speaking people, into the United States from the Caribbean and Central America. Thus to understand "asylum" in an American context we need to look at the historical evolution of the term as it has become entangled with the twin issues of immigration and refugee policy, both of which are themselves part of the larger pattern of domestic and foreign policymaking in the United States.

THE EVOLUTION OF ASYLUM

The practice of asylum (like the word itself) can be traced to ancient Greece, where particular altars and similar holy places offered sanctuary to fugitives, especially ill-used slaves. In the early Roman Republic the comparable custom protected aliens fleeing from other states, and though the practice was weakened during the first centuries of the Roman Empire, losing what little legality it originally possessed, the tradition that fugitives might seek at least temporary protection against those with greater physical power or apparent right reemerged with the establishment of Christianity. Churches were now designated as places of sanctuary, and the rights and duties of both fugitive and pursuer became formulated in increasing detail through imperial promulgations (such as the fifth-century *Codex Theodosianus,* books 9 and 16) and customary law. So it was for a thousand years in Europe until the Reformation began eroding such religious privileges—a process of abatement that continued until the late eighteenth century and the advent of the American and French revolutions.

As the authority of Rome and the Catholic Church declined, so conversely grew the power of the secular though usually Protestant state. For many centuries asylum had been understood as the granting of a privileged and protected area within a wider jurisdiction (the precincts of a church within the territory of a feudal lord). Since the seventeenth century, however, asylum has been understood as the creation by one jurisdiction (a "sovereign" state) of a privileged status for an individual from the reach of an opposing claimant, invariably another sovereign state whose "subject" the fugitive was. Thus, the common theme that links present-day notions and practices of asylum to those of the classical and premodern world is the special or "privileged" status of the would-be asylum-seeker vis-à-vis the state of original jurisdiction and the sought-after haven or sanctuary within a state of refuge.

Against this element of continuity, which emphasizes the individual's pursuit of safety from the executive and judicial power of one authority, has to be set the distinctive feature of asylum as it developed in the twentieth century, especially in the years since World War II. Now when the term "asylum" is used, attention focuses upon the mass movement of people. The involuntary migration of people, of minorities expelled or fleeing from a hostile majority, is nothing new: so it was for the Jews and Muslims after the Reconquista in Spain in the late fifteenth century and for the Huguenots in France following the revocation of the Edict of Nantes in 1685. In the twentieth century similar enforced population movements met the barriers created by the immigration policies of host countries. Thus, in the discourse of the early twentieth-first century, asylum became a term connoting mass migration, the laws and practices of host states in dealing with would-be immigrants, and the formal responsibilities of such states in the face of the legal rights and humanitarian demands of such alien refugees. The putative rights of a single individual are now overshadowed by the vision of those self-same rights exercised by thousands, even millions, of prospective incomers.

Given that the United States was rhetorically created partly as a haven for the oppressed; given the historical fact that the United States is a country of immigration ("a nation of nations"); and given the range of responsibilities that positive and customary international law now places upon the United States and all other sovereign states toward refugees, the issue of asylum has unsurprisingly become intensely debated and highly controversial. Even so, one element may be briefly—and relatively uncontentiously—explicated. Paradoxically, it is the topic that was once regarded as synonymous with asylum *tout cour*, namely diplomatic asylum.

DIPLOMATIC ASYLUM

In the course of the rise of the modern state system, diplomats became invested with various privileges and immunities, part and parcel of the convenient but necessary fiction that ambassadors and their entourage occupied within their country of posting (the "territorial" sovereign) an enclave of their own sovereign power. Thus persons and property of the "sending state" enjoyed within the protected zone customary (so-called extraterritorial) rights and were exempt from the normal reach of the executive and judicial power of the host or "receiving state," to cite the language of the two Vienna conventions of 1961 and 1963 governing diplomatic and consular practice,

respectively. Accordingly, an embassy could by custom extend the protection of its premises to fugitives from the summary justice or even lynch law of the host country. (Warships and merchant vessels were treated similarly.)

This tradition of diplomatic asylum became particularly strong in Latin America during the nineteenth century—a reflection of the political violence that frequently accompanied regime changes within the continent. By custom such asylum was not extended to ordinary criminals ("persons accused of or condemned for common crimes") but rather to "political offenders," those refugees whose only offense, it was asserted, lay in their beliefs. To regulate this tradition, in the first half of the twentieth century the Latin American republics negotiated a series of conventions (Havana in 1928, Montevideo in 1933, Caracas in 1954), though not all the countries ratified the results. The Caracas convention followed a bitterly fought dispute between Peru and Colombia before the International Court of Justice at The Hague. In two connected decisions, the Asylum and Haya de la Torre cases, 1950–1951, the court held that the right of diplomatic asylum did not exist through customary international law but, if at all, only by virtue of explicit bilateral or multilateral treaties, or through the established and reciprocal action of both countries. (Ironically, in the absence of a legal solution, the court urged the parties to resolve their dispute by negotiations and compromise, in other words, through what in lay terms would be called diplomacy.) Surveying the history and jurisprudence of diplomatic asylum, *sub voce* the scholar and advocate Ian Brownlie writes that, despite the examples drawn from "Latin American regional custom, . . . it is very doubtful if a right of asylum for either political or other offenders is recognized by general international law."

The United States, like other major powers, has generally disapproved of the invocation of diplomatic immunity for fugitives. But not long after the eventual resolution of the Colombian-Peruvian case, the U.S. embassy in Budapest granted diplomatic asylum to the Roman Catholic primate of Hungary, Joseph Cardinal Mindszenty, as the Americans registered their profound opposition to the Soviet repression of the Hungarian uprising in October–November 1956. This episode—an exception to normal U.S. policy—was a deliberate Cold War tactic and has to be seen as part of a larger pattern of American diplomatic and legal responses to the political and ideological challenges of communism. At the end of the Korean War (1950–1953), for example, the U.S.–led United Nations negotiators offered asylum en masse to North Korean and mainland Chinese prisoners of war who did not wish to be repatriated to their home countries.

INTERNATIONAL EXTRADITION AND INTERSTATE RENDITION

Diplomatic asylum, understood as a particular form of sheltering fugitives, may be seen as the correlative to extradition, the mainly executive but also partly judicial process whereby an escapee is denied asylum (whether territorial or extraterritorial) and surrendered by one sovereign power to another for trial and punishment of criminal offenses. The usual protections for political offenders have been part of the custom and treaty law governing such rendition since the 1830s, the pioneering work of French, Belgian, and Dutch jurisconsults and legislators who reversed the pre-French Revolution tradition of surrendering political opponents and harboring ordinary criminals. In the United States, the paradigmatic act of 1848, "for the apprehension and delivering up of certain offenders," limited U.S. extradition practice not by category of alleged offense but through reciprocal international treaty. (The United States in 2001 had extradition treaties with more than one hundred other states.) As for multilateral extradition treaties, once again the republics of the Western Hemisphere led the way, beginning with the somewhat abortive treaties of 1889 and 1902, the distant precursors of the 1981 Inter-American Convention on Extradition, which explicitly protects "the right of asylum when its exercise is appropriate." There the burden of the proviso is to protect "political" fugitives specifically, though not exclusively. But, as the U.S. Departments of Justice and State both glossed apropos a typical extradition treaty with Jordan, "political offense" is a category frequently used but never defined in such treaties.

Until the post–World War II period the most controversial example of the political exemption for asylum-seekers was the refusal of the Dutch authorities to surrender Wilhelm II of Hohenzollern to the victorious Allies for trial as a war criminal under the terms of the Treaty of Versailles (article 227), which had arraigned the former kaiser for his "supreme offence against international morality and the sanctity of treaties." Since World War II and particularly the establishment of the ad hoc Nuremberg and Tokyo International Military Tribunals for the trial of war criminals (1945–1948), various multilateral instruments have diminished such residual protections, allusively so in the exhortatory Universal Declaration of Human Rights and specifically in the Convention on the Prevention and Punishment of the Crime of Genocide, both adopted by the UN General Assembly in December 1948. Controversies that have remained have usually been not for substantive reasons but rather on procedural grounds, for example grants of domestic immunity, the forceful seizure (kidnapping) of the accused, and unfitness to plead, the latter being argued in the high-profile case in 1998–2000 of the former president of Chile, General Augusto Pinochet, whose case was taken on appeal against extradition to the highest court in England, the House of Lords. (In this instance the executive rather than the judicial branch—an uncertain distinction in the British constitutional system—released Pinochet from extradition to Spain.)

Here again, American and European attitudes have been similar: "forcible abduction" is permissible, provided the terms of any extradition treaty are applicable; such was the decision in *United States* v. *Verdugo-Urquidez* (1992). Undoubtedly the most famous modern case in which kidnapping was ruled to be inconsequential to the prosecution of inter alia "war crimes" and "crimes against humanity" was that of the German Nazi leader Adolf Eichmann, which was decided on appeal before the Israeli Supreme Court in 1962. In this case the judges, as they put it, "rel[ied] on a long array of local, British, American and Continental precedents" to deny the appellant "asylum" in his former refuge of Argentina.

In the federal system of the United States extradition between states rests upon article 4, section 2, of the Constitution, requiring that "A Person charged in any State with Treason, Felony, or other Crime . . . shall . . . be delivered up" on demand by the applicant state. Significantly, the following paragraph implicitly invalidates the competence of any state to offer asylum and hence possible freedom to a fugitive slave—an interpretation borne out by the provisions of the contemporaneous Northwest Ordinance. (Congress passed a combined fugitive slave and extradition act in 1793.) This conjunction of principles in the federal Constitution acts as a valuable reminder of the intimate relationship between law and politics in American history, the permeability of the so-called domestic and foreign spheres, and that general and particularly universal statements of rights —what we would today call "human rights"— must always be seen in their historical and specific context. The defense of slavery by the signatories of the Declaration of Independence is the locus classicus of this discordant interplay, and the invocation of this same Declaration by the delegates to the Convention of Seneca Falls in 1848 likewise confirms the general rule, with this latter meeting on American women's rights itself deriving from the worldwide antislavery campaign.

Slavery and particularly the slave trade were a constant irritant in Anglo-American relations from Jay's Treaty of 1794 (which provided for limited extradition for certain felonies—hence conditional denial of "asylum"—between the two countries) through the War of 1812 and the abolition of slavery within the British empire in 1833 until the time of the Civil War. In the case of the slave mutiny upon the brig *Creole* in 1841, law officers in England ruled that the colonial authorities in the West Indies could not surrender the fugitives to the U.S. government without specific parliamentary approval. (There was also the separate though weighty matter of the slaves' gaining freedom by virtue of their arrival within the jurisdiction of the English courts—an issue that had pre-independence roots in the groundbreaking *Sommersett* case of 1772.) Extradition, in other words, though an executive function of government, required in this case statutory authority—a process of legitimation that came most notably through the first (British) Extradition Act of 1870, with its protections for political refugees.

The negotiation of the Webster-Ashburton Treaty of 1842 between Britain and the United States helped to resolve the legacy of the *Creole* dispute while agreeing on the terms of nonpolitical extradition. But the difficulties between American and British jurisdictions and jurisprudence over the definition of political as distinct from criminal ("terrorist") offenses reemerged with the resumption of the Irish Troubles in the late 1960s. Yet the two countries are not unique in their differences. As Guy Goodwin-Gill authoritatively observed: "International law provides no guidance on the substance of the concept [political offence exception], other than its outermost limits." Inside the United States, the early federal legislation on interstate rendition was interpreted by the U.S. Supreme Court in *Kentucky* v. *Dennison* (1861) as merely declaratory and thus discretionary. It remained until long after the

abolition of slavery for the Supreme Court (*Puerto Rico* v. *Branstad,* 1987) to rule that state authorities had no discretion on rendition. Interstate asylum, in other words, did not exist.

PRE–WORLD WAR II BARRIERS TO ASYLUM AND REFUGE

Diplomatic and territorial asylum (the latter term employable even in an interstate context) are concepts with a largely nineteenth-century resonance, privileges understood as benefiting individuals. Since the early part of the twentieth century, however, asylum has become linked with the fate of groups. Thus, to understand U.S. asylum law as currently practiced and debated, three different chronologies or narratives must be brought together. The first is the pattern of formal U.S. immigration legislation and executive action since the 1870s, the second is the contemporaneous and related history of international migration, and the third is the development of an international regime governing refugees and asylum-seekers, particularly in the years since World War II.

Whatever the proper interpretation of the discretionary power or mandatory obligations of the individual states in interstate rendition, the exclusive power of Congress over the admission and deportation of aliens is beyond dispute. Such was the import of two groups of cases the Supreme Court adjudicated in line with article 1, section 8, of the Constitution: the so-called Passenger Cases of 1849 and 1876, followed by the notorious half dozen Chinese Exclusion Cases from 1884 to 1893. This was the jurisprudential context in which Congress drafted immigration policy along explicitly racial lines and thus set in place for eight decades one of the three basic categories of inclusion and exclusion of aliens (and ultimately their safe refuge and asylum). In the first phase, from the Chinese Exclusion Act of 1882 until the Immigration Act of 1917, Asian immigration was severely restricted. Meanwhile, as increasing numbers of immigrants came from southern and eastern Europe, Congress reacted in the 1920s with two laws, the (Temporary) Quota Act of 1921 and the (Johnson-Reed) Immigration Act of 1924. Together these two laws placed for the first time a descending ceiling over the annual number of immigrants, so that the aggregate of permitted immigrants dropped from a pre–World War I average of just under one million down first to approximately 360,000 and then to 150,000.

Within this shrinking total the ratio of new to old immigrants was also drastically reduced, with the countries of the old immigration being eventually awarded more than four-fifths of the final quotas: Germany, for example, was allocated some 26,000 visas, versus Italy's 6,000. The unprecedented "national-origins" or "quota" system, which required entry visas to be issued in the country of application, came fully into operation in 1929. These basic formulas set American immigration policy until the 1960s, not least in excluding from the calculations those born in the Western Hemisphere, mainly Mexico and Canada, who would form a growing number relatively and absolutely of the "non-quota" immigrants.

As immigration into the United States from Europe was severely limited under the legislation of the 1920s, migration within Europe and Asia Minor took on a new importance during and immediately after World War I. Hundreds of thousands of Armenians, Bulgarians, Greeks, Russians, and Turks were displaced as so-called nation-states succeeded former multinational empires in eastern Europe and the Near East. Under the new League of Nations regime, negotiated population transfers (notably between Greece and Turkey), the protection of remaining minorities (in Poland and Romania), and the relief of indigent refugees (Bulgaria, Czechoslovakia, and Yugoslavia) became international responsibilities, with League of Nations bodies such as the High Commission for Refugees and the International Labor Office (predecessors of today's Office of the United Nations High Commissioner for Refugees and the International Labor Organization, respectively), individual countries (France particularly), and nongovernmental agencies such as the Red Cross supplying various kinds of help. The legacy of these different responses would be most clearly seen during and shortly after World War II, when the United Nations, with the United States in the leading role, assumed a comparable role in meeting the needs of the latest generation of refugees.

If the 1920s was the decade of a new international responsibility for displaced persons, then the 1930s and the first half of the 1940s produced forced migrations and displacement on a scale not seen for centuries in Europe and Asia. (Events in China had no effect upon U.S. refugee policy; but experts calculate that the onset of all-out war by the Japanese in 1937 led to the flight of tens of millions of Chinese inland from the coastal regions toward the north and west.) Figures cap-ture the horror rather than express precisely the enormity of the human suffering: an estimated minimum of 40 million Europeans were displaced in two main stages, first under the Nazis and their allies until the failure of Operation Barbarossa, the German invasion of the Soviet Union, in 1942–1943. The war was followed by a decade of "ethnic Germans" (*Volksdeutsche*) removing to the defeated fatherland and Slavs migrating mainly eastward and within the enlarged Soviet Union and its satellites (especially the Ukraine and Poland). Despite calling an intergovernmental conference at Evian, France, in July 1938 on the refugee crisis, President Franklin D. Roosevelt provided no leadership at home to effect changes in immigration policy to permit extra-quota places for victims of Nazi persecution.

After the net emigration that characterized the first (Great Depression) half of the 1930s came a net immigration in the second half of the decade and early war years that saw a maximum of 250,000 refugees enter the United States within quota. The end result was the lowest absolute decennial total admission of immigrants into the country since the census period 1820–1830, when 143,000 persons had arrived on U.S. shores. (The period 1831–1840 saw 600,000 immigrants, while in 1931–1940 it was just 528,000.) Thus, despite the arrival of some famous asylum-seekers (Hannah Arendt, Albert Einstein, Thomas Mann) into the United States from the Europe of the impending Holocaust, numerically the impact of such refugees was minimal. Indeed, Eichmann argued in his own defense that the "final solution to the Jewish question" was facilitated by the general resistance to Jewish immigration—a claim corroborated by contemporary American opinion polls.

THE POST–WORLD WAR II YEARS

The interwar years had shown no sign of the adaptation of the immigration laws to cope with asylum-seekers en masse: such is the message authoritatively recorded in the 1945 analysis by Charles Cheney Hyde, *International Law Chiefly as Interpreted and Applied by the United States*. The legacy of national quotas in U.S. immigration law lasted beyond the weakening of the anti-Asian nativism that had been at work since the 1880s, the latter hostility mitigated and overlapping in the short term with more overtly political criteria for exclusion.

The Immigration and Nationality (McCarran-Walter) Act of 1952 exemplified this more recent mixture in a tense Cold War context, as did the earlier Internal Security (McCarran) Act of 1950, which also dealt, inter alia, with alien exclusion. Yet there was a wartime hint of the remaking of U.S. immigration policy by different criteria from the national-origins ideals of the 1920s, when in 1943 the total prohibition against Chinese immigration was minutely but significantly eased as part of the American conciliation of Nationalist China, one of the Big Five in the wartime anti-Axis alliance. Two years later President Truman by executive order gave priority to "displaced persons" in the allocation of European quotas—though within the existing national totals. Only with such measures as the Displaced Persons Acts of 1948 and 1951 and the Refugee Relief Act of 1953 were the annual quotas actually increased, at first simply by amortizing initial excesses against correspondingly reduced later totals. (An exception was made for the entry of non-quota wives, husbands, and orphans.) From 1945 until 1960 some 700,000 people were admitted to the United States under various "refugee-escapee" exemptions and programs—the beneficiaries of a deliberate Cold War policy directed against the Soviet bloc and communism in general by encouraging disaffected emigrants.

It required the more liberal, 1960s civil rights atmosphere to eliminate (via the landmark 1965 Hart-Celler Immigration Act) the ethnically coded national-origins system as the basis for the selection of immigrants. Yet quotas remained under the 1965 act, as they had under McCarran-Walter. But now they were absolute, limited to 20,000 for any one country, while for the first time immigration from within the Western Hemisphere was restricted to 120,000, effective in mid-1968, within a global maximum set initially at 290,000. (The 20,000 per country limit was extended to the Americas in 1976, and in 1978 the hemispheric subtotals were aggregated to 290,000 worldwide.) Within this changing ideological and numerical framework exceptions would be made for refugees, who under the new seven-category "preference" system of the Hart-Celler Act would technically occupy the last and smallest category at a maximum of 6 percent of the total for extrahemispheric entrants: an estimated 10,200, who would also include victims of natural disasters. (The refugees were expected to come from the Soviet bloc and the Middle East.) Finally, an unspecified number of refugees could be "paroled" into the

United States by the attorney general—in other words, given a conditional right to reside despite their irregular status. This latter provision gave statutory form to the situation after the Hungarian uprising, when the great majority of the 38,000 refugees were initially admitted through the attorney general's parole power.

Edward P. Hutchinson, concluding his classic account *Legislative History of American Immigration Policy* with an analysis of the Hart-Celler Act, emphasizes the interconnection of legislation since the formative post–Civil War Immigration Act of 1875 with both the older tradition of political and religious asylum and the development of a post–World War II refugee regime by the U.S. government. He then blends all these factors together under the rubric "refugee asylum" as an "element of immigration law and policy." Indeed, at least half a dozen legal instruments between 1875 and the consolidating Immigration Act of 1917 contained provisions protecting political and religious freedoms—what we would call offering "political asylum"—while simultaneously barring racial undesirables. Thus, like other authorities Hutchinson endorses the argument that "asylum" in its more technical sense has to be understood within the wider context of the roads and obstacles to would-be migrants to the United States. As Colin Harvey perceptively writes, "Law is Janus-faced, it both coerces and enables. Refugee law . . . both excludes and includes."

The mutation of the quota system from its 1920s ethnic bias and the introduction of an allotment for refugees were two innovations in the Hart-Celler Act. (For all its ideological importance, the law was technically an amendment to the 1952 Immigration and Nationality Act.) Conversely, a more recent tradition was continued outside the provisions of Hart-Celler, with asylum privileges extended ad hoc sometimes by formal legislation and at other times by presidential action. This twin-track approach has characterized federal policy since the 1940s, despite at least six major general laws passed by Congress in the succeeding decades. Yet other factors have also been involved, the practical force of which is difficult to quantify but which have been important at a rhetorical, symbolic level.

One example is the role of the United States as the most powerful country within the United Nations and, therefore, inescapably identified with exhortatory UN pronouncements, even when the United States has either opposed or not signed the relevant multilateral treaties, later failed to ratify such binding instruments, or qualified ratification with terms seriously limiting the resultant obligations—a three-way method of American conduct traced by scholars such as David Forsythe, Louis Henkin, and Natalie Kaufman. (The Genocide Convention, which provided for extradition and voided pleas of "political crimes," was signed by the U.S. government in 1948, submitted to the Senate in June 1949, and finally received conditional consent from the Senate almost four decades later, in 1986.) Thus, the years since World War II show a pattern of complicated adjustments to U.S. immigration policy (which ultimately determines the legal entry for refugees and asylum-seekers) alongside an international rhetoric and the growth of a legal regime governing refugees and asylum-seekers, both of which are significantly shaped by the United States but not necessarily put into practice within its own borders.

THE UN ASYLUM AND REFUGEE REGIME

The Hart-Celler Act became fully operational in 1968, by coincidence the Human Rights Year celebrated by the United Nations to mark the twentieth anniversary of the Universal Declaration of Human Rights (UDHR). Endorsed by the UN General Assembly in December 1948, the UDHR echoed those provisions of the 1945 UN Charter that explicitly "reaffirm faith in fundamental human rights," stating, in the precise formulation of the UDHR article 14: (1) Everyone has the right to seek and to enjoy in other countries asylum from persecution; (2) This right may not be invoked in the case of prosecutions genuinely arising from non-political crimes or from acts contrary to the purposes and principles of the United Nations.

Given the crucial role of the United States in the establishment in 1945 of the United Nations Organization—the multifaceted structure that gave institutional and eponymous form to the U.S.-led wartime alliance initially created by twenty-six states in January 1942 "to preserve human rights and justice in their own lands as well as in other lands"—there might seem no possible exception to an American obligation to provide asylum to asylum-seekers. Yet a number of factors show the weakness of this deduction. At the most general level the UN Charter (chapter 1, article 2) forbade any UN "interven[tion] in matters which are essentially within the domestic

jurisdiction of any state." The government of the United States, both the Congress and the executive, had traditionally regarded immigration (under the broader heading of the admission of aliens) as a matter determinable solely by the United States itself—a claim of national prerogative amply demonstrated in the senatorial and wider public debate in 1945–1946 over the conditions for American adherence to the UN Charter and Statute of the International Court of Justice. Furthermore and specifically, even the terms of the nonbinding UDHR simply expressed traditional legal practice: the right of an individual to seek asylum was not disputed, but it remained for the host state or sovereign to grant asylum so that it might then be enjoyed—a qualification repeated passim in the Declaration on Territorial Asylum adopted by the UN General Assembly on 14 December 1967. Moreover, even the granting and enjoyment of so-called diplomatic asylum was not unconditional. Such considerations must be borne in mind when we read the later resolution of the General Assembly (24 October 1970) that the UN Charter precepts "constitute basic principles of international law."

As for refugees and would-be asylees, here the UN formulated two documents detailing international obligations toward those in need of such "social and humanitarian" protection: the 1951 Convention Relating to the Status of Refugees and the 1967 Protocol Relating to the Status of Refugees. Although "asylum" is a term absent from the body of both texts, the respective preambles and the context of the documents make the identification clear. The United States became a party to both instruments by signing and ratifying the later protocol, the purpose of which was to remove the temporal and geographical limits of the convention. Aside from the shift of UN (and American) concern from postwar Europe to Cold War Africa and Asia, the accession of the United States to the Refugee Protocol was yet another sign, paralleling the Hart-Celler Act, of the erosion of overt racialism in foreign policymaking. In refugee law, the convention and later protocol established an important textual commitment. In the formula of the convention, article 33 (subsumed in the protocol, article 1): "No Contracting State shall expel or return ('refouler') a refugee in any manner whatsoever to the frontiers of territories where his life or freedom would be threatened on account of his race, religion, nationality, membership of a particular social group or political opinion."

This paragraph gave multilateral treaty form to the principle of nonrefoulement (from the French *refouler,* to turn back, expel)—the obligation of a state not to expose a refugee within its territorial limits or under its jurisdiction to expulsion into the hands of former or likely persecutors. To this particular commitment two rather different qualifications can be made here. First, the convention's governing condition was the "well-founded fear of being persecuted" in the mind of the refugee, phrasing that would allow judges and officials of the host state to consider a mixture of subjective and objective factors in determining entitlement to asylum for the supplicant. Second (as noted by Hannes Tretter in *International Human Rights*), the wording left unanswered the question "how human rights standards and principles of humanitarian law could be guaranteed to war-refugees or refugees fleeing on economic and social grounds, considering . . . that neither the Convention nor its Protocol offers protection for them." While the United States would become a (conditional) signatory to a number of other human rights treaties—though not, perhaps paradoxically, the 1969 American Convention on Human Rights within an inter-American juridical regime—these parameters of nonrefoulement and the selective extension and denial of asylum to economic, social, and political mass-migrants would constitute part of the framework of U.S. immigration policy in the last third of the twentieth century. (The American Convention on Human Rights must be distinguished from the American Declaration of the Rights and Duties of Man, in which article 27 speaks of the right "to seek and receive asylum," adopted at the Ninth International Conference of American States at Bogotá in 1948, where the Charter of the Organization of American States was approved.)

THE DEVELOPMENT OF CONTEMPORARY ASYLUM LAW AND POLICY

Since the passage of the Hart-Celler Act in 1965, four major U.S. laws have been written regulating immigration, and each has contained provisions governing the treatment of refugees and asylum-seekers. In chronological and substantive precedence was the Refugee Act of 1980, the first omnibus refugee law ever passed by Congress. Prompted by the acute refugee crisis following the Vietnam War and the atrocities of the Khmer Rouge in Cambodia as well as the long-term problems of Cuban emigration, the legislation enlarged the annual permitted total of refugees (defined along the lines of the 1967 UN protocol) from 17,400 to 50,000, within an overall raising of the immigration ceiling from 290,000 up to 320,000. This figure of 50,000 would be reviewed after three years. Meanwhile, increases for "grave humanitarian" reasons would be possible—if agreed to by the president and Congress, who would also determine the initial annual per-country allocation. (Refugee admissions during the 1980s averaged twice this rate.) Five thousand places within the refugee total were assigned specifically for asylum-seekers, but within a very short time the applications ran at ten times this number. (In later years acceptances for asylum status would move toward 10,000 per year.) Individual states would be reimbursed for the costs of both the future refugee and past asylum programs. Those arriving with refugee status, which is accorded outside the United States, would be permitted to convert to "permanent resident alien" status within one year and thus embark on the road to citizenship.

Three specific features of the act were politically significant: the twenty-year-old Cuban refugee program would be phased out, the previous requirement (a legacy of the 1950s) that refugees hail either from the Middle East or communist regimes was ended, and a proviso was added that, in following the UN definition of refugees, future policy would be guided by the victims' "special humanitarian concern to the United States"—a qualification for selective U.S. engagement. Thus the 1980s would show far more admissions from unfavored regimes in eastern Europe than from favored regimes in Latin America—prima facie evidence of the political definition of refugees and the political selectivity of asylum grants. As a result of the 1980 act, total immigration under the refugee and asylee categories rose to an exceptional peak of 140,000 in fiscal year 1991 (including 23,000 asylees). The figure dropped back to 54,000 in 1998 from 112,000 in 1997, the latter aggregate figure being more representative of the 1990s as a whole.

The next law, the Immigration Reform and Control Act of 1986 (IRCA), was primarily designed to regularize undocumented Hispanic aliens ("illegals" who lacked or had abused appropriate entry visas) by a double tactic of penalizing employers and offering amnesty to those who had evaded existing immigration regulations. While these aspects of the IRCA harked back to the labor-control elements of earlier immigration legislation (notably the *bracero* program for migrant Mexicans, 1942–1964), other sections of the law eased the plight of Cuban and Haitian "illegals" who were regarded as political rather than economic victims. Legislators and commentators agreed that the IRCA was designed as the first in a two-stage revision of existing procedures, and four years later Congress more systematically revised the Hart-Celler Act. Under the Immigration Act of 1990, visas for specified labor skills were increased almost threefold (to 140,000) at the relative cost of family-reunification within a larger aggregate of immigrants (up from 500,000 to 700,000, then dropping to 675,000). Asylum-seekers and refugees, if qualified, were to be admitted outside of quota limits: an estimated 131,000 in the first year with an allocation of 10,000 for asylees. Furthermore, the attorney general was given powers to widen the categories (and thus the potential numbers) of aliens in need of "temporary protected status," such as victims of natural disasters and civil wars.

The fourth law in this important quartet was the Illegal Immigration Reform and Immigrant Responsibility Act of 1996. Beginning its legislative life in the Senate and House as bills to reduce legal immigration as well as to police illegal immigration, the final product in an all-purpose appropriations measure was eventually designed mainly to minimize the numbers, penalize the presence, and expedite the expulsion of "illegals" in general. The annual number of legal immigrants approached pre–World War I highs—against a host population almost three times larger. Fiscal year 1993 was the decade's peak for "new arrivals." Even so, the 1996 act treated asylum-seekers somewhat ambivalently. The grounds for claiming persecution were enlarged to include state-enforced family planning (most obviously in the People's Republic of China), yet the numbers so protected were arbitrarily limited to one thousand per annum.

An authorized speed-up in processing and a later actual increase in rejecting asylum claims, together with limitations on the judicial review of rejections, were part of a growing general hostility to such claimants. (There were comparable immigrant increases and legislative and bureaucratic responses in the European Union.) Asylum applications were running at an annual average of 140,000, with almost four times that number unresolved. This huge figure was mainly due to

the acceptance by the INS of an out-of-court settlement of a lawsuit, *American Baptist Churches* v. *Thornburgh* (1991), in which the churches charged that INS asylum policy toward Central American appellants during the 1980s had been driven by political priorities (hostility to the left-wing Sandinistas in Nicaragua and opponents of the U.S.–supported Salvadoran and Guatemalan governments) rather than disinterested application of the refugee criteria. More generally, under the new law the discretion of the executive to parole fugitives en masse would be inhibited by the offset of these parolees against the permitted totals for legal, "documented" immigrants. This particular provision was less the legacy of the Reagan administration in Central America than the particular case of "boat-people" from Cuba and Haiti.

U.S. ASYLUM AND REFUGEE PRACTICE: CUBA AND HAITI

From the early 1960s Cuba has played a peculiar role in the making and conduct of U.S. refugee policy. Since Havana and Washington have periodically agreed to limit Cuban emigration and immigration, both governments have conspired to deny asylum to actual and would-be refugees. Nowhere does the interplay between the domestic and foreign spheres, or the practical limitations of multilateral commitments, appear more starkly than in the control of exit and entry between the two countries. (Article 13, section 2, of the Universal Declaration of Human Rights, for example, defines the right to leave and return to one's country as fundamental; but Cuba is not a party to the Refugee Convention or Protocol.) Given the level of official U.S. rhetoric about the denial of human rights in Cuba, the implementation of selective admission for Cuban refugees must be seen as politically inspired.

There have been three notable stages in the pattern of U.S. immigration policy toward Cuba. For two decades following Fidel Castro's assumption of power in 1959, Cuban émigrés in the United States enjoyed a privileged position as refugees not subject to the prevailing immigration regulations. The legislative pinnacle was the Cuban Adjustment of Status Act of 1966 (CASA), which permitted some 130,000 Cubans living mainly in Florida and New Jersey to become "permanent resident aliens . . . lawfully admitted for immigration" and thus start on the road to citizen-

ELIÁN GONZÁLEZ

On Thanksgiving Day 1999 a five-year-old Cuban boy, Elián González, was found floating on a tire tube in the sea off Florida. His mother, stepfather, and ten others had drowned when their small boat had capsized during the hazardous voyage. The rescue was *un milagro* (a miracle) in the eyes of many Cuban Americans, especially the powerful Cuban American National Foundation. For the next seven months the fate of Elián filled the media and involved at least four different courts, all three branches of the federal government, and lobbyists nationwide, as family members in Greater Miami and in Cárdenas near Varadero in Cuba struggled over the well-being of the *Cubanito*. Human interest aside, Elián's story showed the workings of the immigration and asylum system in dramatic form.

Initially, as an undocumented alien and a minor, Elián was paroled formally by the attorney general into the care of Miami relatives, who unsuccessfully used the Florida courts to gain long-term legal custody. The state court determined that the matter was properly within the federal remit of the Immigration and Naturalization Service, to which the local family applied for asylum status for Elián, and was not a matter of state family law. (In Cuba, Elián's father, Juan Miguel González, opposed these actions, later coming to the United States to plead for the return of his son.) The INS meanwhile refused an asylum application, filed both by Elián and on his behalf by a great-uncle, Lázaro González, adjudging that Elián did not qualify under any statutory provisions, specifically the likelihood of persecution and torture if returned to Cuba. This executive decision, supported by Attorney General Janet Reno, was upheld first at the local level by a U.S. district judge and then by the U.S. Court of Appeals for the Eleventh Circuit sitting in Atlanta.

In the several judicial decisions it was reiterated that the discretionary though delegated powers of the executive over immigration are virtually plenary; and even a paroled alien does not enjoy the constitutional protections of a U.S. citizen. (Bills were introduced in Congress to confer citizenship upon Elián.) The Eleventh Circuit also emphasized that if there was an issue about Elián's age (born 6 December 1993), then this made the role and wishes of his father, Juan, that much more important—rather than the counterclaims of Lázaro and his cosuitors. (For jurisprudential guidance the INS had examined even the Cuban Family Code as well as the 1989 UN Convention on the Rights of the Child, though the United States is not a party to the CRC.) Furthermore, the Eleventh Circuit accepted the appropriateness of the INS's considering the foreign policy aspects of any decision. Thus, by late June 2000 state and federal courts had moved to retain the jurisdiction of Elián's status within the INS under the higher authority of the Department of Justice—a sequence confirmed on 28 June, when the U.S. Supreme Court announced it would not take cognizance of the controversies. Later that same day, Elián was flown back to Cuba in the company of his father, having been seized nine weeks earlier—by armed federal agents—from his Miami relatives, whose temporary guardianship had been revoked by the INS. The federal operation, technically authorized or not, shocked even supporters of Elián's reunion with his father.

ship (and, in some states, register their professional qualifications to obtain appropriate employment). Having come as refugees, these beneficiaries of CASA had originally entered under visa waivers or as parolees (at the ultimate discretion of the attorney general), and the Hart-Celler Act had just outlawed such change of status.

The second significant chapter in the Cuban refugee story began in 1980, when as many Cubans left the island in five months as had benefited under CASA. More dramatically—and with much greater political effect—these fugitives, many encouraged by Castro himself in the Mariel boat lift episode, were joined by some 35,000 fugitives from nearby Haiti in a common armada of fragile and tiny boats sailing toward Florida. The 1980 Refugee Act had just been passed; but neither group of *bolseros* had been formally classified as refugees, which meant that neither they nor the host communities (Dade County and Greater Miami) would be eligible for earmarked federal funds such as Medicaid and Aid to Families with Dependent Children for individuals and a support program for school districts.

As in 1966, Congress and the president agreed on a solution, in this case to accord refugee status to the fugitives—thus repeating the process that had brought almost a million Indochinese refugees into the United States. Through the 1980s the numbers of fugitives from Cuba fell back to the hundreds, then in the early 1990s, as a consequence of the deep economic crisis following the collapse of the Soviet Union, the numbers rose to thousands, with almost 40,000 intercepted by the Coast Guard and other agents in 1994 alone. Such numbers (all potential beneficiaries of CASA) led to the 1994–1995 U.S.–Cuban compromise, whereby Washington agreed to accept 20,000 refugees while Havana would seek to discourage emigration. Those Cubans denied entry (even after an appeal along the terms of the Refugee Act of 1980) were to be repatriated without reprisals. Complicated in its details (which included using the U.S. naval base at Guantánamo Bay on Cuba as a transit camp, operating the parole provisions of CASA to increase the numbers of legal permanent residents, and instituting a "visa lottery" to bridge the gap between applicants and available places), Washington's Cuban immigration policy of the 1990s confirms the general point that asylum, despite the formidable bureaucratic and judicial framework in which it operates, has been employed in practice as a means of promoting broader foreign policy goals while responding to domestic lobbies.

A similar lesson may be drawn from U.S. policy toward Haitian refugees. During the 1980s more than 20,000 Haitian boat people were interdicted (arrested) by U.S. officials at sea—and only one in a thousand was permitted to make an application for asylum. Although the UN High Commissioner for Refugees and the Organization of American States Inter-American Commission on Human Rights demurred, the U.S. Supreme Court in 1993 (*Sale* v. *Haitian Centers Council Inc., et al.*) upheld 8 to 1 the authority of the executive effectively to refoul such migrants despite the explicit commitments of the 1951 Refugee Convention and 1967 Protocol and the provisions of the 1980 Refugee Act. Supporters of the interdiction policy, begun in earnest by President Ronald Reagan and continued through Bill Clinton's presidency, argued that the Haitians were "economic migrants" instead of political refugees, while some critics, particularly from the Congressional Black Caucus, detected racism at work. (The 1980 post-Mariel settlement had been less favorable to the Haitian refugees.) But there was another echo of the Cuban saga: in 1998 the Haitian Refugee Immigration Fairness Act, modeled on CASA, was passed by Congress to allow more than 40,000 Haitian asylum claimants or parolees to adjust to "legal permanent residence"—while the policy of interdiction continued.

CONCLUSION

Tracing the pattern of executive and congressional actions in the twentieth century bears out the general point made by Joyce Vialet, an authority on the law and history of U.S. immigration, that "the distinction between immigrants and refugees, unheard of during the mass migrations of the 19th century, . . . developed in the wake of World War II, primarily as a means of reconciling our traditional ideal of asylum with restrictions in the immigration law." With the designation of the "Asiatic barred zone" in the 1917 act, tightened by the Johnson-Reed Act of 1924, the barriers to immigration from Asia and the Pacific were made virtually impregnable. In the 1920s the former "open door" was almost closed to Mediterranean Europe, the Balkans, Asia Minor, and the Black Sea region, where the "push" of poverty, often associated with the minority status and religious and ethnic persecution of disadvantaged groups (notably pogroms against Jews in czarist Russia), drove increasing millions toward the attractive "pull" of the United States during the three decades preceding World War I. (The Catholic Irish immigration of the 1840s–1850s was an earlier microcosm of similar economic, religious, and ethnic factors driving exiles to the United States.) This was the "new immigration" so distasteful to the older, established immigrant groups who in the 1960s would be dubbed the WASPS: White Anglo-Saxon Protestants.

After World War II, which had brought no real opening of the immigration door, those who once would have come to the United States as ordinary immigrants now could come in any numbers only as refugees. Likewise in the 1980s and 1990s, many poor, frightened, persecuted migrants—and the simply ambitious—came from Central America and the Caribbean to the United States seeking a better life, economically, politically, and socially. The great majority came legally as admitted immigrants, and others came as technical refugees; the "illegals" arrived surreptitiously without documentation, and the desperate appealed for formal asylum. Where once "Asian" race and then European "ethnicity" had been categories of exclusion, now family unification, employment skills, and even levels of social and personal threats and violence became the criteria for admission. Such has been the recent history of asylum in the much longer history of American immigration—a history of inclusion and exclusion that was encapsulated in the exhortation of Thomas Paine's *Common Sense* on the eve of American independence:

> O ye that love mankind! Ye that dare oppose, not only the tyranny, but the tyrant, stand forth! Every spot of the old world is overrun with oppression. Freedom hath been hunted round the globe. Asia, and Africa, have long expelled her—Europe regards her like a stranger, and England hath given her warning to depart. O! receive the fugitive, and prepare in time an asylum for mankind.

BIBLIOGRAPHY

Anker, Deborah E. *Law of Asylum in the United States.* 3d ed. Boston, 1999. The standard work written for lawyers; very detailed text and heavily footnoted.

Bessiouni, M. Cherif. *International Extradition: United States Law and Practice.* 3d ed. Dobbs Ferry, N.Y., 1996. A substantial work that, like Vialet, makes the argument that asylum and refugee regimes must be seen in the context of reducing immigration.

Bolesta-Koziebrodzki, Léopold. *Le Droit d'Asile.* Leiden, 1962. An older work, useful for a non-U.S. perspective and valuable for Latin America.

Brownlie, Ian. *Principles of Public International Law.* 5th ed. Oxford, 1998. A manageable introduction by an authoritative scholar and practitioner before the bar of the International Court of Justice.

Columbey, Jean-Pierre, ed. *Collection of International Instruments and Other Legal Texts Concerning Refugees and Displaced Persons.* 2 vols. Geneva, 1995. A publication of Office of the UN High Commissioner for Refugees, Division of International Protection; volume 1 contains "Universal Instruments"; volume 2 deals inter alia with Latin America.

Dunne, Michael. "American Judicial Internationalism in the Twentieth Century." *Proceedings of the American Society of International Law* 90 (December 1996): 148–155. Discusses the work of David Forsythe, Louis Henkin, and Natalie Kaufman.

Ermacora, Felix, Manfred Nowak, and Hannes Tretter, eds. *International Human Rights: Documents and Introductory Notes.* Vienna, 1993. The comparative materials are intelligently contextualized with excellent references.

Frey, Linda S., and Marsha L Frey. *The History of Diplomatic Immunity.* Columbus, Ohio, 1999. Set to become the standard account.

Goodwin-Gill, Guy S. *The Refugee in International Law.* 2d ed. Oxford, 1996. The detailed and authoritative starting point for the subject, written by a former member of the UNHCR. The text is wide-ranging and fully referenced; indispensable for the world picture.

Grahl-Madsen, Atle. *Territorial Asylum.* London, Rome, and New York, 1980. Half this book, by a contemporary leader in the field, is documentation pleading for a convention on asylum comparable to the 1951 Refugee Convention.

Hailbronner, Kay. *Immigration and Asylum Law and Policy of the European Union.* The Hague, London, and Boston, 2000. An exhaustive work that deals with refugees and asylum-seekers.

Hall, William Edward. *A Treatise on International Law.* 8th ed. Edited by A. Pearce Higgins. London, 1924. A classic, relatively brief work.

Harvey, Colin. *Seeking Asylum in the UK: Problems and Prospects.* London and Dublin, 2000. Contextualizes somewhat dated "critical legal theory" and useful for European developments, political and legal.

Hathaway, James C. *The Law of Refugee Status.* Toronto, 1991. Monograph on the 1951 Refugee Convention by an authority.

Hutchinson, E. P. *Legislative History of American Immigration Policy, 1798–1965.* Philadelphia, 1981. The classic and indispensable account.

Hyde, Charles Cheney. *International Law Chiefly as Interpreted and Applied by the United States.* 2d rev. ed. 3 vols. Boston, 1945. First published in 1922, this work by an eminent international lawyer reveals how little interwar crisis affected U.S. immigration policy and practice.

Jennings, Robert, and Arthur Watts, eds. *Oppenheim's International Law.* 9th ed. London and New York, 1996. In this classic work, volume 1 examines asylum and refugees from a very wide international perspective with voluminous references.

LeBlanc, Lawrence J. *The United States and the Genocide Convention.* Durham, N.C., and London, 1991. Deals in chapters 8 and 9 with the "reserving" of international treaties by the Senate.

Morgenstern, Felice. "'Extra-territorial' Asylum." *British Year Book of International Law* 25 (1948): 236–261. The first in a trio of essays discussing asylum from an international, comparative perspective. See also "The Right of Asylum," *British Year Book of International Law* 26 (1949): 327–357; and "Diplomatic Asylum," *Law Quarterly Review* 67 (July 1951): 362–382.

Nicholson, Frances, and Patrick Twomey, eds. *Refugee Rights and Realities: Evolving International Concepts and Regimes.* Cambridge, 1999.

Ronning, C. Neale. *Diplomatic Asylum: Legal Norms and Political Reality in Latin American Relations.* The Hague, 1965. The appendices and bibliography are useful in a study that puts the Columbia-Peru Asylum Case in context and also covers U.S. practice.

Skran, Claudena M. *Refugees in Inter-War Europe: The Emergence of a Regime.* Oxford, 1995. Places the Evian conference of 1938 in the larger picture of U.S. interwar policy.

United Nations High Commissioner for Refugees. *The State of the World's Refugees, 2000: Fifty Years of Humanitarian Action.* Oxford, 2000. This important serial provides the annual monitoring of the implementation of the 1951 Refugee Convention and 1967 Protocol; contains factual information and statistics together with essays by regions, periods, and topics.

U.S. Committee for Refugees. *World Refugee Survey.* This annual survey is the most outstanding of relevant unofficial publications and presents the global picture.

U.S. Immigration and Naturalization Service. *Statistical Yearbook.* Annual review that contains informative and clear essays on the published data.

Vialet, Joyce. "A Brief History of U.S. Immigration Policy." 91-141 EPW (25 Jan. 1991): 2.

See also EXTRATERRITORIALITY; HUMANITARIAN INTERVENTION AND RELIEF; HUMAN RIGHTS; IMMIGRATION; NATIVISM; RECIPROCITY; REFUGEE POLICIES.

BALANCE OF POWER

A. E. Campbell and Richard Dean Burns

The balance of power appears at first sight a simple concept. It has been defined as "a phrase in international law for such a 'just equilibrium' between the members of the family of nations as should prevent any one of them from becoming sufficiently strong to enforce its will upon the rest." Yet the phrase has always been of more use in political polemic than in political analysis. Like other phrases with a strong emotional appeal it is vague, and it would lose its appeal if it were more precise. Its obscurities are several, but the most important is that it blends the descriptive and the normative. The condition is one, the term "balance" implies, toward which international life is forever tending. That is the descriptive element. But the condition is also one that may be upset, and right-thinking statesmen should constantly be on the alert to preserve or restore it. That is the normative element. These two elements reinforce one another. Because such a balance will be established in any event, it is sensible and moral to work toward it. Because people work toward it, it will be more readily established. Difficulties arise if either element is weakened. At what point is it right to abandon an old balance and accept a new one? Can a balance exist if people are unconscious of the need to maintain it?

Behind all the interpretations of the balance of power lies the appeal to realism in the conduct of international affairs. Realism remains the best, perhaps the only persuasive, argument for restraint; and it is common ground that the doctrine of the balance of power is a device to promote restraint, whether it is argued that lack of restraint is wrong, or dangerous, or ultimately bound to fail. In that sense the balance of power in international affairs is clearly related to the idea of checks and balances within a government, which is equally a device to impose restraint on men who might otherwise, seduced by power, abandon it.

THE EIGHTEENTH CENTURY

The international balance received its classical exposition during the eighteenth century, about the time at which, largely during the struggle for independence of the American colonies, the idea of checks and balances within a government was elaborated. Although linked, the doctrines had important differences. The international balance existed, if at all, among similar entities, the recognized powers, which placed in the scale weights of the same kind—military power, actual or potential. It was the lack of any precedent and effective authority among nations that made the balance of power necessary. The threat of war maintained the balance, and sometimes war was needed to restore it. By contrast the domestic balance refined by the Founders was not among powers of the same sort, but among powers of different sorts. All these were derived from the people, who might limit, redistribute, or withdraw what they had given. And few believed that domestic society rested on the perpetual threat of strife.

It is not an accident that the doctrine of the balance of power—alike in international and in domestic politics—received its classic and most rigorous statements at a time when foreign policy was largely a matter for rulers who could use the war potential of their states for their own aggrandizement. It was because a ruler had to be able to wage effective war that he had to be allowed the armed force that contributed to his domestic control. British reliance on a navy rather than on a standing army was, and was known to be, important to the growth of British liberties—and later to American liberty. In a sense, therefore, the international balance of power was needed to check the pretensions of rulers who lacked any effective domestic check.

Many of the early American leaders, however, held the belief that in their new world a more just—a more perfect—society than that of Europe could be formed. Historians may differ about the degree to which that implied a regard for democracy. The tyrant people was hardly less to be feared than the tyrant king. But that sensible, rational men—men of property and standing—could cooperate for the common good, few doubted. To balance the servants of the public against each other was both a political safeguard and a political convenience, rendering excess less likely and vigilance less demanding. It was not a political necessity of the same order as the international balance of power. Americans quickly came to believe, and continued to believe through most of their history, that sound domestic institutions must bring sound foreign policies with them.

The balance of power, however, although it may act to restrain the actions of those who believe in the doctrine, is in the first instance a device to restrain others. Should not Americans, very conscious that other states were not founded on their own good principles, have been ready to consider contributing to the maintenance of an international balance when appropriate, more rather than less because their own domestic principles were sound? There is little evidence that they did consider doing so, and that fact may throw light on the limitations of the doctrine.

The revolutionary war itself provides an example of the balance of power in operation. A desire not to be involved in the European balance, not to be a weight in the British scale, had played an important part in the American demand for independence. It was the readiness of the allies in the coalition against Britain to abandon each other, and the readiness of Britain to calculate relative gains and losses, that made the outcome possible. Behind the behavior of all the parties in the American war lay a tacit agreement that American independence was acceptable—the Americans wanted to be removed from the British scale, the French and Spaniards wanted the colonies removed from the British scale, and on their side the British were finally convinced that that removal would not have disadvantages only. Such calculations may imply a large element of uncertainty as to how the independent United States would behave—Why should their independence weaken Britain more than their continued existence as disaffected colonies?—but in the event few of the negotiators had any doubt as to the only possible conclusion of the war.

For a short time after independence, Americans remembered that the European balance of power had played some part in their victory.

George Washington's famous injunction against "excessive partiality for one foreign nation and excessive dislike of another" would hardly have been necessary had there been no Americans who wanted to align themselves either with Britain or with France. It would not have been uttered had American interests clearly required an alignment with either side. Yet in the political debates at the end of the eighteenth century there was already a large ideological element. Washington was not merely arguing that a due regard for the balance of power requires powers to hold themselves aloof until it is clear that the balance is about to tip, and then to place in the scale only such weight as is needed to adjust it. He was urging his countrymen not to take sides in European quarrels whose outcome could not affect the United States.

THE NINETEENTH CENTURY

So well did Americans learn their lesson and follow Washington's injunction that during the Napoleonic Wars (1803–1815) Americans seemed to have little or no interest in the issues. Neutral rights, and no doubt a free hand in the Americas, were what concerned them. Neither the possibility that Napoleon might come to dominate the world, which loomed so large to many Britons, nor the possibility that he might overthrow the archaic monarchies of Europe and bring in a new order, which seemed to others an exciting prospect, affected Americans to any great extent.

By that time the doctrine of the balance of power had ceased to interest Americans, and so it remained for a full century. Most students would contend that a balance of power existed in the nineteenth century and perhaps worked more effectively than ever before or since, and that whether they chose to recognize the balance or not, Americans were beneficiaries of it. Americans then gave little weight to that proposition, and they were right. They quickly discovered a doctrine, or a practice, that served their needs better than any contribution to a balance of power. This was the American withdrawal from the affairs of Europe—in certain matters only—enshrined in the Monroe Doctrine of 1823. Attacking the international system, the British radical Richard Cobden could use as one of his chief arguments the fact that *"America, with infinite wisdom, refuses to be a party to the 'balance of power'"* (Cobden's emphasis).

If Americans could so largely ignore the existence of the balance on which their security finally rested, it follows that the balance was more stable than it has often been. This is, clearly, a balance in one sense, and perhaps in the most obvious sense—forces resting in equilibrium without perpetual adjustment and still more without fundamental readjustment. When the balance of power is most noticed, it is because it must be maintained—that is, because it is in perpetual danger of tipping too far to one side or the other. What, then, is the condition of stability such that it can even be neglected? American experience suggests that it is the introduction of what might be called an element of friction into the balance, something that operates on neither side, but inhibits movement or makes it more difficult.

It was this friction that the geographical distance of the United States from the power center of Europe introduced, so that for Americans the balance of power was always less delicate. Until the era of modern communications, this distance clearly made it more difficult for the United States to intervene in a European quarrel. Both more resources and more time were needed to sustain effective intervention. On the other hand, the converse was equally true. While it might be arguable that the complete overthrow of the European balance, and the dominance of Europe by one power or group of powers, would endanger the security of the United States, it was also arguable that that dominance would have to be more complete than it was ever likely in practice to be. The balance in Europe would have to be tipped far past the point at which the security of some European states was endangered before there could be any threat to the security of the United States. As Abraham Lincoln put it, rhetorically enough, in an address before the Young Men's Lyceum of Springfield, Illinois, on 27 January 1838: "All the armies of Europe, Asia and Africa combined, with all the treasure of the earth (our own excepted) in their military chest; with a Bonaparte for a commander, could not by force, take a drink from the Ohio, or make a track on the Blue Ridge, in a trial of a thousand years."

This meant that American reluctance to be drawn into the quarrels of Europe was for long a realistic one. Americans could benefit from the balance of power without being fully conscious of it. The European states made little effort to involve the United States in their concerns. The well-known claim made in 1826 by George Canning, then British foreign secretary, to have "called the New World into existence, to redress the balance of the Old," was confined in practice to denying France "Spain with the Indies." With that accomplished, there was an agreement (so general that it could be ignored) that there was no effective and inexpensive way of using American support in a European quarrel; nor, per contra, of using European support in an American quarrel. For most of the nineteenth century Britain was the only major power that had serious differences with the United States. Difficulties arose over Canada, over Britain's remaining Caribbean possessions, and over trade, but the British always concluded that such differences should be settled—if need be, even by British surrender—without attempting to involve other powers. They were not prepared to call in the Old World to redress the balance of the New.

Perhaps this became most obvious at times when it looked as if the United States might not continue to dominate North America. In 1842 and 1843 it was widely supposed that Britain would guarantee the independence of Texas in return for the abolition of slavery there—as a preliminary to attacking slavery in the United States. "The present attempt upon Texas is the beginning of her operations upon us," wrote Secretary of State Abel P. Upshur. It came to nothing. Still more obviously, during the Civil War the Confederacy hoped for European recognition and even intervention. The hope rested on several grounds, but clearly implicit was the belief that a restored American union could not be in the interest of Europe. Nor was it. But none of the European powers—among which Britain was the key—had sufficient interest in creating an American balance to justify the European risks that the effort would entail. The relative remoteness of America meant that the effort would have had to be greater than the rewards justified, and great enough to entail unacceptable risks nearer home. It remained possible, and it was easier and safer, to exclude the United States from a European balance than to draw the Americas into an enlarged world balance.

Social change in the nineteenth century, however, was to reveal certain limitations in the doctrine of the balance of power. Some advocates of the balance have defended it on the ground that it maintains peace, or, at all events, sets limits to wars—a proposition supported to some extent by the American revolutionary war. Others have contended, with Edmund Burke, that the balance "has been the original [origin] of innumerable and fruitless wars" and "ever has been, and it is to be feared always will continue a cause of infinite contention and bloodshed." To such critics the purpose, or at any rate the desirable result, of the balance was the maintenance not of peace but of liberty. As many have pointed out, there is something inconsistent about the notion of going to war to preserve peace. One must calculate that continuing peace will result in some undesirable consequence, before war is justified. Loss of freedom is the most persuasive such consequence.

The nineteenth century saw the growth of romantic nationalism and democracy, and with it the demand of peoples for some voice in policy. In some areas rulers could behave as before, but increasingly the aggrandizement of princes was felt to have natural limits and was overshadowed by other forms of state activity. Within Europe, transfers of territory were found to cause more trouble than they were worth unless they were accompanied by wholesale transfers of population, a resource more acceptable in the twentieth century than in the nineteenth. The great revolution in nineteenth-century Europe, the unification of Germany—the unification of Italy had no equal consequences—was tolerated partly because its effect on the balance of power was not immediately foreseen, and partly because it was held to be an expression of nationalism that could not justly be opposed, rather than mere Prussian aggrandizement—so that it would increase stability rather than lessen it. In a war of the ordinary sort, by contrast, there were natural limits to what the victor could gain, and the destruction of a rival nation lay outside them. As that was accepted, it became possible to argue that defense itself, the most traditional and urgent duty of the nation-state, might have unacceptable consequences for the quality of life within the state. There seemed better ways than conquest to increase wealth and power. With the modern revolution in technology, and with the ever-increasing role of government in the lives of citizens, discussions of the balance of power took on a new dimension.

1914–1945

Thus, when World War I broke out, although all parties made some play with the need to maintain or protect the balance of power (which, of course, they interpreted variously), none of them could argue that governments, or princes, were behaving in the way that one would expect. German apologists had to contend that Germany was surrounded by malevolent foes and that the survival of Germany was at stake. The allies had to contend not merely that Germany was too powerful for comfort, but that German militarism threatened a European civilization that would otherwise be peaceable. The argument, in short, could not be cast in terms of the balance of power.

Americans were presented with a dilemma. It was not, in the first instance, a dilemma of policy. Clearly the United States was not immediately threatened. The great growth of American power during the nineteenth century, if it made the policy of fortress America less necessary, made it no less appealing. It was hard to argue that the victor in the European war, whatever the outcome, would turn on the United States. Americans were therefore forced toward moral judgments about the merits of the war. Some indeed argued that what was going on was an old-fashioned struggle for the balance of power, of a sort that revealed how politically backward even the most advanced European states were, and of a sort with which the United States had no concern. Others accepted the argument that German militarism was the root of the trouble. Historians will long continue to debate the causes that finally brought the United States into the war, and their merits, but it is clear that no balance of power argument would have sufficed. A balance of power argument would have kept the United States neutral. (With the advantage of hindsight it might be argued that since the United States was the beneficiary of a balance of power in Europe likely to be upset, the proper American course was to intervene delicately to tip the balance back to the point at which it had been—and no more. Yet because the balance was bound to shift, war or no war, as the whole history of Europe in the 1920s and 1930s was to show, that kind of intervention could not have been temporary and would have required a degree of anxious vigilance over the long term, which could have been neither sustained nor justified.) Neutrality, defended on grounds of self-interest and its morality, or intervention, defended on moral grounds, were the only serious alternatives and the only alternatives debated.

The decision for war was President Woodrow Wilson's, and in taking it he was much moved by the realization that if the United States did not participate in the war, it would have no voice in the settlement that followed it. As part of the settlement Wilson was determined to establish an international concert—the League of Nations—which would bring about a better world order. Wilson's hostility to the balance of power was intense, and it was widely shared by Americans of his day. In an address at the Guildhall, London, on 29 December 1918, Wilson stated that

> the center and characteristic of the old order was that unstable thing which we used to call the "balance of power"—a thing in which the balance was determined by the sword which was thrown in the one side or the other; a balance which was determined by the unstable equilibrium of competitive interests; a balance which was maintained by jealous watchfulness and an antagonism of interests which, though it was generally latent, was always deep-seated.

Wilson made an automatic connection between the balance of power and spheres of influence, to which he was equally opposed. That connection is characteristic of much American thinking on the subject; its consistency with adherence to the Monroe Doctrine is clearer to Americans than to others.

The approach of World War II presented Americans with a dilemma of a different sort. The Great Depression diverted attention from international affairs, but increasingly Americans could not avoid being drawn into efforts to mitigate both the depression itself and the political consequences that seemed to follow. The whole structure of reparations and war debts set up at Versailles would alone have required American involvement. The rise of aggressive regimes in Italy, Germany, and Japan, together with the long-cherished hope that they might be rendered more moderate by well-calculated economic concessions, or by democratic strength and solidarity, or a combination of these, ensured it. By contrast with the years before World War I, few Americans doubted on which side their sympathies lay. Whatever their fears of communism, the Soviet Union was quiescent, and the actions of the Nazis deprived their claim to be a bulwark against communism of all appeal. Secretary of State Cordell Hull (1933–1944) shared Wilson's dislike of the balance of power, and had learned it in the same school; but such views, although they became influential again later, were irrelevant in the 1930s, when it became ever clearer—certainly to President Franklin D. Roosevelt—that the important contest was not among rival states but between dictatorship and democracy.

Paradoxically, the desire of Europeans, especially the British, that the United States should become part of the balance of power—that the New World should be called in to redress the balance of the Old—and the fact that Americans had little doubt on which side their sympathies lay, did almost nothing to make policy decisions easier. The arguments, both within the American government and between Americans and British, are a fascinating and complex field, on which much work remains to be done. But in essence a dispute developed among the allies—even before the alliance was formed—over who should contribute how much to the common cause. The residue of American security, which was very great, together with well-founded doubts as to whether the interests of the United States might not be better served if some accommodation were reached in Europe without American intervention—doubts shared by some European statesmen, such as Neville Chamberlain—meant that American activity was diplomatically ineffective. A slow process of economic support for the Western democracies did begin, and might in time have drawn the United States into the war, but Hitler had the good sense to avoid the mistakes of his predecessors, and he was at great pains to avoid giving the United States an occasion for belligerency. That occasion was, of course, provided by Japan.

Some exponents of balance of power theory have argued that the theory requires that nations should match, if need be by war, any increase in a rival's power, actual or foreseen, even in the absence of any aggressive act. But all the evidence suggests that even when nations have adequate cause for war, they do not go to war unless they also have an occasion for war. The occasion, the indicator that the right moment for war has arrived, is vital. Of course, occasions for war can be manufactured when they are needed; but they are hard to manufacture, or even to identify, for a nation that disposes of such great reserves of security as the United States. One important argument is missing—the argument that if the nation does not fight now, it will be too late to fight tomorrow. It is that argument—with its corollary that opponents must be supposed to know how sensitive one's position is, and that therefore their threats are not accidental but evidence of real intention—which identifies most clearly the occasion for war. At Pearl Harbor, in 1941, the Japanese faced the United States with an affront such as no nation could possibly let pass. The Germans had been most careful to avoid an affront. (In World War I, on the other hand, when by reviving their unrestricted submarine campaign they

135

deliberately took the risk of American intervention, a good many Americans could still be found to argue that the affront was not great enough to justify war in the absence of a real threat. The cause of neutral rights and of democracy had to be invoked.)

Just as a nation needs a signal to begin a war, so it needs a signal to stop, and that signal is often even harder to give or to detect. Because statesmen in the modern world are seldom wholly cynical, they commonly feel that war has been forced on them. As a war continues, they begin to raise their demands to include compensation for losses incurred. It is therefore hard to identify the point at which agreement for a truce can be reached, short of the final defeat of one side. Every success by either side leads it to think that final victory may be possible; every defeat, that this is not the moment to negotiate. It is the intellectual difficulty of translating the theory of the balance of power into a workable policy in a specific situation that, more than anything else, ensures that this theory is seldom of use when the time comes for negotiation.

These generalizations are supported by American practice in two world wars, yet American practice was not different from that of any other nation. Neither Britain nor France paid any special heed to the balance of power during either war. No way could be found of ending either war without the complete defeat of one side. After each war the recourse was not to some restored balance, but to a congress system. The experience of the League of Nations suggested to the allies in 1945 that no security structure was worth anything unless the great powers agreed, and that the right of veto might as well be formally accepted. If the five powers were not in agreement, the hope was at best for stalemate, by the agreed inactivity of four if one stood out. As always at the end of a war, what was in people's minds was peace, rather than either liberty or justice.

BALANCE OF POWER SINCE 1945

In neither world war, then, did the United States enter for considerations of the balance of power. In both, the entry of the United States so quickly and completely tilted the balance of power in favor of the side it joined, that had the United States been regarded as an element in the balance, the wars in the form they took would never have broken out. After World War I, the United States withdrew in disillusionment. After World War II that recourse was not open, although many in the Truman administration feared it and worked to prevent it. It took time before it became apparent, either to Americans or to any others, that the balance had been shifted permanently during, and to some extent as a result of, the war. It took time before it was realized that Britain would not recover, that France was not a world power, and that noncommunist China would not become the guardian of the Far East. Yet, paradoxically, while the postwar hope of a concert gave way, just as it did after the Congress of Vienna (1814–1815), to an ideological confrontation, the balance of power was being restored.

It has often been argued that the balance of power is really an imbalance of power. If the balance is to work at all, there must be at least three parties, such that any two can overpower the third, should its activities become too threatening. More than three is better; but three is the minimum. The idea of balance as implying some sort of equality gives way readily to the idea of balance as superiority of force on the side of the existing order. The balance between two powers or groups—sometimes called the "simple" balance—is altogether too unstable. It requires a degree of vigilance, of preparedness, of national concentration on defense, which is ultimately intolerable. The Cold War implied just such a balance, of course, and it should come as no surprise that the rhetoric of the Cold War, on both sides (although recent attention has been given to that of the West), did not speak of balance at all, but looked to victory. That is a characteristic of the simple balance.

It was well recognized that the United States and the Soviet Union were in direct and unique competition. The appalling consequences of nuclear war introduced a new kind of stability. The so-called balance of terror or balance of deterrence ensured that each nuclear power was anxious not to give the other power any sort of signal that would justify an attack, and was also anxious not to identify such a signal. This caution was compatible with, and even required, an arms race. It was not by accident that for a time the chief danger to stability was thought to arise in an area—western Europe—where nuclear power could not be used with any advantage, yet which was regarded as vital. Talk of tactical nuclear weapons showed more wishful ingenuity than realism, and much of the American emphasis on strategic nuclear superiority derived from the knowledge that only such superiority could counter Soviet geographical advantages in Europe.

If it was compatible with an arms race, the American-Soviet balance was also compatible with an ideological struggle waged with vigor on both sides. It is false to claim, as some revisionist historians now do, that the Cold War was started and maintained only by the United States; and that the Soviet Union, much weakened by the world war, was merely pursuing the traditional aims of Russian policy. (Those aims had been opposed by Great Britain for a century, and it is odd to find the Left arguing that a policy of old-fashioned imperialism is acceptable and, in essence, advancing the doctrine, if not of the balance of power, at least of spheres of influence.) The ideological struggle reflected the knowledge of both great powers that they contended in a fast-changing world; and the Cold War began to lose intensity, not when the protagonists decided to abandon it but when world circumstances changed and new elements began to contribute to the balance—lacking nuclear capacity, it is true, but disposing of real force. It became almost conventional to speak in terms of a world of five poles—the United States, the Soviet Union, Europe, China, and Japan—to which perhaps the oil-producing states should be added. These poles differ from the great powers of old in that they are not of the same sort. Only two are nuclear in any serious sense. Other differences readily suggest themselves. It is as a consequence of this development that serious discussion of the balance of power is again taking place.

Secretary of State Henry Kissinger, a student of Clemens von Metternich and Otto von Bismarck, naturally introduced the concept of balance into his discussions of foreign policy; he would not have done so if the preconditions had not been there. Yet, while he spoke of Soviet policy as "heavily influenced by the Soviet conception of the balance of forces" and as "never determined in isolation from the prevailing military balance," he was more apt to speak of American policy as seeking a "balance of mutual interests" with the Soviet Union and as moving toward détente through a "balance of risks and incentives." Such language was chosen with an American audience, and with the preconceptions that Kissinger believed Americans have, in mind. Nevertheless it shows two elements almost wholly lacking in classic balance of power theory: the recognition that nations may now offer domestic rewards and suffer domestic penalties in

the conduct of international relations, and the conviction that the domestic penalties will be too great without an agreement on restraint—deliberate if tacit—by the opponents. The balance of power is seen not as replacing cooperation, but rather as requiring it.

The Cold War ended with a whimper, not the civilization-ending "bang" some analysts predicted. The Soviet Union simply chose to withdraw from the superpower competition. With the subsequent disintegration of the Soviet Union, the United States became incontrovertibly the world's dominant economic-military power (a title it had actually had for much of the Cold War). Without an apparent foe to challenge its security, the major question confronting U.S. foreign policy was what would succeed the Cold War's bipolar balance of power. The issue among academics and political commentators was whether the United States should (1) emphasize its dominant position as a "unipolar" global power, or (2) seek a leading role in a tripolar or multipolar system.

The conservative commentator Charles Krauthammer advocated the former. Krauthammer defined "unipolar" as meaning the United States should act unilaterally in resolving international matters that threatened its national interests. Acknowledging that the United States had lost the dominant economic position it had held during the early Cold War years, he nevertheless asserted that America remained the principal center of the world's economic production. An aggressive, determined U.S. foreign policy, backed by the world's greatest military prowess, Krauthammer argued, could dominate world politics. Perhaps in the future the United States might become the largest partner in a multipolar world; until then, however, he wanted Washington leaders to continue acting unilaterally. He concluded that "Our best hope for safety is in American strength and will, the strength and will to lead a unipolar world, unashamedly laying down the rules of world order and being prepared to enforce them." It would be a Pax Americana in which the world would acquiesce in a benign American hegemony.

Other analysts envisioned a multipolar post–Cold War world, probably comprised of three or four power centers, in which the United States would remain the most affluent and powerful but would not be hegemonic. Joseph Nye, for example, suggested that a U.S. long-term unilateral hegemony was "unlikely because of the diffusion of power through transnational interdependence."

Preferring the term "multilevels of power," Nye endorsed preserving a strong military but predicted that the United States would not be able to dominate or direct the economic and political centers in an interdependent world. Thus, Washington should cooperate with like-minded nations in meeting such international concerns as conflicts between world markets, the acquisition by small nations of unconventional but destructive weapons, the international drug trade, environmental dangers of technological society, and diseases that can spread across continents.

Lawrence Freedman, who shared Nye's basic conception, focused on America's successful strengthening of democracy in Asia and western Europe after 1945. This, he argued, had created valuable political-military allies who rebuilt the world's economic foundations, promoted political democracy, and played the crucial role in halting communist expansion. In due course, these nations began competing with American business for world trade and investments because the United States had encouraged European economic unity and a prosperous Asia-Pacific rimland. Freedman foresaw that these European and Asian allies would press for a greater post–Cold War role in international affairs and, if Washington accommodated their expectations, all parties would benefit. If, however, the United States chose to deal unilaterally with economic and trade issues, there could be greatly increased tensions or even military conflict.

Both Freedman and Nye anticipated that states outside the American-European-Japanese centers would likely pose the gravest threat to global stability. During the Cold War the superpowers had been able to dampen most conflicts in Third World regions; it proved more difficult thereafter. The demise of bipolar constraints made violent confrontations stemming from festering ethnic, tribal, nationalist, religious, and territorial disputes more likely. And indeed, as John Lewis Gaddis reminded us, the first post–Cold War year "saw, in addition to the occupation of Kuwait, the near-outbreak of war between India and Pakistan, an intensification of tension between Israel and its Arab neighbors, a renewed Syrian drive to impose its control on Lebanon, and a violent civil war in Liberia." It seemed a harbinger of things to come.

In Nye's view, attempting to deal unilaterally with these and other looming upheavals would place a heavy burden on the American treasury and national will. Far better, he argued, to seek multilateral cooperation to control the peripheral troubles. Failure to contain regional conflicts could put global stability in jeopardy.

President George H. W. Bush's formation and direction of an international coalition to drive Iraq out of Kuwait in 1990 and 1991 had the trappings of both unilateral determination and multilateral cooperation. In his victory speech of 6 March 1991, Bush called for a "new world order" that would enable the United Nations to fulfill its obligation to provide for the collective security of the weaker nations, and for a U.S. program that would assist in stabilizing the Middle East.

Bush's visionary statement generated much discussion in the months thereafter, but skeptical voices were quickly heard. Henry Kissinger, now a political commentator, lauded President Bush's building of a coalition to defeat the Iraqi aggression, but he derided the notion of a new world order. "The problem with such an approach is that it assumes that every nation perceives every challenge to the international order in the same way," he wrote, "and is prepared to run the same risks to preserve it. In fact, the new international order will see many centers of power, both within regions and among them. The power centers reflect different histories and perceptions." In Kissinger's view, the essential thrust of the new American approach should be the recognition of regional balances of power to establish order. "History so far has shown us only two roads to international stability: domination or equilibrium. We do not have the resources for domination, nor is such a course compatible with our values. So we are brought back to a concept maligned in much of America's intellectual history—the balance of power."

Kissinger was correct to point to Americans' complicated relationship with the balance of power, but it was also true that the nation's leaders had often—and especially after 1945—consciously sought the equilibrium he so valued. The 1990s witnessed numerous regional, ethnic, and nationalistic struggles; U.S. officials, finding few of these conflicts fundamentally threatening to the global equilibrium, stayed out of most of them. When they did intervene, humanitarian concerns were a key motivation—the American military and economic response to such episodes as upheavals in Somalia, Haiti, Bosnia, and Kosovo were aimed in large measure at reducing human suffering and restoring local political stability. Even then, intervention happened at least in part because Washington policymakers determined that these upheavals, if allowed to spread, could in fact upset the regional balance of power.

American decision makers understood that the military component of the global equilibrium increasingly shared center stage with other elements as the world became more interconnected. The impact of technology, most notably personal access to various forms of global communications—worldwide telephone systems and television networks, and later the Internet—was impossible to ignore, and the 1990s witnessed economic interdependence that found manufacturing, banking, and merchandising virtually ignoring national borders. In search of continued economic growth and prosperity, Americans increasingly embraced the idea of globalization. President Bill Clinton stressed the interconnectedness of global economic affairs and the necessity of U.S. leadership in this area.

Few in Washington disagreed, and the 2000 presidential campaign saw much more agreement than disagreement between the two major candidates about how the United States ought to exercise leadership in the world arena. Once in office, however, the administration of George W. Bush immediately moved to adopt a starkly unilateralist approach of the type espoused by Charles Krauthammer and others. The Bush team ignored or refused to endorse several international treaties and instruments, most notably the Kyoto agreement regarding environmental pollution standards, and insisted on pursuing a missile defense system that would involve the abrogation of the 1972 ABM treaty and, perhaps, stimulate a new arms race. Even though these policy decisions provoked serious objections from America's allies, and more strenuous protests from other nations, there seemed little concern in Washington about searching for an international consensus.

Critics of George W. Bush and of unilateralism complained that the approach indicated a failure to see the fundamental limits of American power, even in a one-superpower world. The critics achieved a measure of vindication with the terrorist attack on the United States on 11 September 2001. The assaults on the World Trade Center and the Pentagon exposed America's vulnerability to a new destabilizing force: global terrorism. The Bush administration, while not disavowing its unilateralist inclinations, appeared to recognize the desirability of a "global coalition" to meet a newly recognized challenge that largely ignored the traditional international power structure. There were differences of opinion inside and outside the

administration on how best to wage the struggle against terrorism, but on one thing all could agree: the United States could not do it alone.

The history of modern international relations, and of the American part in them, then, suggests a certain pattern. Americans, though often professing a distrust of European-style balance of power politics, have nevertheless sought precisely such a balance of power, or equilibrium, in world affairs. That preference survived the important shift from a world of very slow social change to a world of awesomely fast social change. It survived the end of the Cold War. It had not prevented wars nor served effectively to restrain any state that sought advantage from an active policy; it meant only that at the eleventh hour, coalitions formed to oppose serious attempts at world dominion. In this process the United States played an appropriate part, allowance being made for the great security provided until the mid-twentieth century by its geographical position.

The practical preference for an international balance does not always give rise to anything that can be called a theory of the balance of power, nor even to the use of the term in political discussion. At times when the balance is a "simple" balance—as during the Cold War or the years immediately preceding World War I—there is little discussion of a concept to which appeal cannot usefully be made, and what discussion there is, is apt to be critical. Equally, a period of great international complexity and uncertainty does not seem to be one that a theory of the balance of power can helpfully elucidate. Somewhere between these extremes the greater flexibility provided by a "complex" balance allows the idea of a balance, as something desirable and as a positive interest of the contending parties themselves, to be advanced. Because the balance is at its most stable when people need not consider its maintenance or even its existence, the discussion of balance is at best an indicator of strain in international affairs; but it may indicate the least amount of strain that mankind is likely to achieve.

BIBLIOGRAPHY

Allison, Graham, and Gregory F. Treverton, eds. *Rethinking America's Security: Beyond Cold War to New World Order.* New York, 1992. A stimulating collection of essays by leading thinkers.

Butterfield, Herbert. "The Balance of Power." In Herbert Butterfield and Martin Wight, eds. *Diplomatic Investigations*. London, 1966.

Cronin, Patrick M., ed. *From Globalism to Regionalism: New Perspectives on U.S. Foreign and Defense Policies*. Washington, D.C., 1993.

Dehio, Ludwig. *The Precarious Balance*. Translated by Charles Fullman. New York, 1962.

Dosch, Jöm, and Manfred Mols. *International Relations in the Asia-Pacific: New Patterns of Power, Interest, and Cooperation*. New York, 2000.

Gaddis, John Lewis. *The United States and the End of the Cold War: Implications, Reconsiderations, Provocations*. New York, 1992.

Gulick, Edward V. *Europe's Classical Balance of Power*. Ithaca, N.Y., 1955. Focuses on the struggle against Napoleon and the Congress of Vienna.

Haas, E. B. "The Balance of Power as a Guide of Policy-Making." *Journal of Politics* (1953).

Henrikson, Thomas H. *Balance-of-Power Considerations for U.S. Foreign Policy in the Post-Soviet Era*. Stanford, Calif., 1993.

Hinsley, F. H. *Power and the Pursuit of Peace*. Cambridge, 1963. Dated but still useful.

Kegley, Charles W., and Gregory Raymond. *A Multipolar Peace: Great-Power Politics in the Twenty-first Century*. New York, 1994.

Kegley, Charles W., and Eugene R. Wittkopf, eds. *The Future of American Foreign Policy*. 2d ed. New York, 1994.

Kissinger, Henry. "Balance of Power Sustained," In Graham Allison and Gregory F. Treverton, eds. *Rethinking America's Security: Beyond Cold War to New World Order*. New York, 1992.

Krauthammer, Charles. "The Unipolar Movement." In Graham Allison and Gregory F. Treverton, eds. *Rethinking America's Security: Beyond Cold War to New World Order*. New York, 1992.

Lang, Daniel G. *Foreign Policy in the Early Republic: The Law of Nations and the Balance of Power*. Baton Rouge, La., 1985.

Link, Arthur S. *Wilson the Diplomatist*. Baltimore, 1957. A small classic on the American statesman who gave most thought to this problem.

Morgenthau, Hans. *Politics Among Nations*. 5th rev. ed. New York, 1978.

Nye, Joseph S., Jr. "What New World Order?" In Charles W. Kegley and Eugene R. Wittkopf, eds. *The Future of American Foreign Policy*. 2d ed. New York, 1994.

Wight, Martin. "The Balance of Power." In Herbert Butterfield and Martin Wight, eds. *Diplomatic Investigations*. London, 1966. An elegant and perceptive essay, historical in approach.

———. "The Balance of Power and International Order." In Alan James, ed. *The Bases of International Order*. London, 1973.

Wolfers, Arnold. *Discord and Collaboration*. Baltimore, 1962. Adopts the approach of political science.

Wright, Moorhead, ed. *Theory and Practice of the Balance of Power 1486–1914*. London, 1975. A convenient short selection of European writings.

See also ALLIANCES, COALITIONS, AND ENTENTES; COLD WAR EVOLUTION AND INTERPRETATIONS; COLD WAR ORIGINS; COLD WAR TERMINATION; COLLECTIVE SECURITY; POST–COLD WAR POLICY; PROTECTORATES AND SPHERES OF INFLUENCE.

THE BEHAVIORAL APPROACH TO DIPLOMATIC HISTORY

J. David Singer

When it comes to the ability to understand and predict events of importance, students and practitioners of American diplomacy manifest a fair degree of ambivalence. On the one hand, we find many bold efforts to explain why certain events unfolded as they did, and, on the other, we find frequent statements to the effect that these phenomena are so complex as to defy comprehension. According to Henry Kissinger, one of the more celebrated practitioner-scholars, such understanding is often "in the nature of things . . . a guess." Or, as Robert Bowie put it, "The policymaker works in an uneasy world of prediction and probability." And George F. Kennan put it still another way: "I can testify from personal experience that not only can one never know, when one takes a far-reaching decision in foreign policy, precisely what the consequences are going to be, but almost never do these consequences fully coincide with what one intended or expected."

While there is truth in these statements, such uncertainty may not necessarily inhere in the phenomena we study. It may well be, rather, in the ways in which that study is conducted. At the risk, then, of suggesting that students of diplomatic history—American and otherwise—have plied their trade with less than a full bag of tools, this essay addresses a number of ways in which the behavioral approach might usefully supplement the more traditional procedures.

By behavioral approach, it is not meant to say that we should pay more attention to the *behavior* of individuals, factions, and states than to their *attributes* and *relationships* or to the regional and global environment within which such behavior occurs. If anything, diplomatic history seems to be overly attentive to behavioral phenomena, and insufficiently attentive to the background conditions and ecological constraints within which these phenomena occur. Normally, the behavioral sciences include psychology, anthropology, sociology, economics, and political science, but the range of disciplines embraced can be less interesting than the range of methods, concepts, and findings that might be borrowed from those who labor in those particular vineyards.

SOME PURPOSES OF HISTORICAL RESEARCH

One way to examine those possibilities would be in the context of the various purposes and goals that diplomatic historians might set for themselves. For some, the purpose of research is to locate and present the facts alone: What happened, in what sequence, under what conditions, and who was involved? Others go a step further and try to put those facts into graceful narrative. More typically, we seek not only to tell the story, but to do so in an interpretive fashion. This involves both a selection from among all the facts and an interpretation of them. In interpretive history, once we are persuaded as to the facts, we make certain inferences from them: causes, motives, and likely consequences, as well as missing facts.

Some historians (even some diplomatic historians) consider these missions too modest, and tend to be more ambitious. Among these, there are the "grand theorists," who offer up wide-ranging interpretations of several sets of events, telling us just what it all means, in terms reaching from the plausible to the outrageous. A growing number are, however, beginning to redefine their mission, albeit in a less pretentious direction. Instead of offering sweeping inferences from a limited and selected set of facts, these historians are moving toward the generation of knowledge that may be not only more complex, but more useful than that to which we have been accustomed.

TYPES OF KNOWLEDGE AND RELATED METHODS

The most distinctive characteristic of the behavioral approach is its emphasis on reproducible knowledge. This approach does not belittle or ignore knowledge and evidence of a more intuitive or subjective sort, but it does recognize the very real limits of such knowledge. Without insights and suspicions as to certain historical patterns, there would be no place to begin, no hypotheses to test, and no theoretical models to formulate. But in recognizing the impermanence and contestability of subjective knowledge, the behavioral approach seeks methods that might avoid some of those liabilities. These methods are of several types and are best understood in connection with the types of knowledge sought.

Historical knowledge may be distinguished by two very different sets of criteria. The first are essentially theoretical and substantive in nature: Are we indeed getting at the relevant combination of variables in our search for explanation? The second are epistemological: Assuming that we are on a promising substantive and theoretical path, what is the quality of knowledge that we think has been acquired or that we hope to acquire? Leaving the matter of the *relevance* of our knowledge aside for the moment, we can focus on the *qualitative* dimensions of our knowledge. One possible way of evaluating the quality of historical knowledge is to first reduce it to its component assertions or propositions, translate these (if need be) into clear and operational language, and then ascertain where each such proposition or cluster of propositions falls along each of three dimensions.

The first, or *accuracy,* dimension reflects the degree of confidence that the relevant scholarly community can have in the assertion at a given point in time; this confidence level is basically a function of the empirical or logical evidence in support of the proposition, but may vary appreciably both across time and among different scholars and schools of thought at any particular moment. The second qualitative dimension reflects the *generality* of the proposition, ranging from a single fact assertion (of any degree of accuracy) to an assertion embracing a great many phenomena of a given class. Third is the *existential-correlational-explanatory* dimension: Is the assertion essentially descriptive of some existential regularity, is it correlational, or is it largely explanatory? With these three dimensions, an epistemological profile of any proposition or set of propositions can be constructed and a given body of knowledge can be classified and compared with another, or with itself over time.

For many the objective is to move as rapidly as possible on all three dimensions. We seek propositions in which the most competent, skeptical, and rigorous scholars can have a high degree of confidence, although these propositions may have originally been put forth on the basis of almost no empirical evidence at all. They will be propositions that are highly "causal" in form, although they may have been built up from, and upon, a number of propositions that come close to being purely descriptive. And they will be general rather than particular, although the generalizations must ultimately be based on the observation of many particular cases. As to the accuracy dimension, a proposition that seems nearly incontrovertible for decades may be overturned in a day, one that is thought of as preposterous may be vindicated by a single study or a brilliant insight, and those that have stood at the "pinnacle of uncertainty" (that is, a subjective probability of 0.5) may slowly or quickly be confirmed or disconfirmed. Moreover, a statement may enjoy a good, bad, or mixed reputation not only because of its inherent truthfulness or accuracy, but merely because it is not in operational language and is therefore not testable.

Shifting from the degree-of-confidence dimension to that of generality, the assertion (of whose accuracy we are extremely confident) that World War I began on 29 July 1914 is less general than the assertion that more European wars of the past century began in the months of April and October than in others, and this in turn is less general than the assertion (which may or may not be true) that all wars since the Treaty of Utrecht have begun in the spring or autumn. Theory (defined here as a coherent and consistent body of interrelated propositions of fairly high confidence levels) must be fairly general, and no useful theory of any set of historical events can be built upon, or concerned only with, a single case. As Quincy Wright reminds us: "A case history, if composed without a theory indicating which of the factors surrounding a conflict are relevant and what is their relative importance, cannot be compared with other case histories, and cannot, therefore, contribute to valid and useful generalizations. On the other hand, a theory, if not applied to actual data, remains unconvincing." (In the same article, he also noted, "Comparison would be facilitated if quantifications, even though crude, are made whenever possible.")

Existential Knowledge and Data-Generating Methods When we leave the accuracy and the generality dimensions and turn to the third proposed dimension along which a piece or body of knowledge may be described, we run into greater conceptual difficulty. A useful set of distinctions are existential, correlational, and explanatory types of knowledge. Existential knowledge is essentially a data set, or string of highly comparable facts. If, for example, we are told that one army had 1,248 men killed or missing in a given battle and that the enemy had "also suffered heavily," we would have something less than data. Similarly, statements that the United States has had two separate alliances with France since 1815, running a total of forty-seven years, and that American alliances with England and Russia have been nearly the same in number and longevity as those with France, would also be something less than data. That is, data provide the basis for comparison and generalization across two or more cases, situations, nations, and so on, and permit the generation of existential knowledge.

Of course, existential knowledge would not be very useful to the diplomatic historian if restricted only to phenomena that are readily quantified. Most of the interesting phenomena of history are of the so-called qualitative, not quantitative, variety, and it is usually assumed that the world's events and conditions are naturally and ineluctably divided into those two categories. Many phenomena that are thought to be "qualitative in nature" at a given time turn out to be readily quantifiable at a later date. In the physical world, examples might range from the difference between yellow and orange to the amount of moisture in the air; these were originally believed to be qualitative concepts. In the biological world, one thinks of metabolic rate or genetic predispositions. Likewise, in the world of social phenomena a good many allegedly qualitative phenomena turn out to be quite quantitative. Some illustrations might be the "linguistic similarity" of two nations, the extent to which nations gain or lose diplomatic "importance" after war, the changing "cohesion" of work groups, or the national "product" of given economies.

It is one thing to think of a way to measure or quantify a phenomenon that has been considered nonquantifiable and quite another thing to demonstrate that the measurement is a valid one. That is, we may apply the same measuring procedure to the same phenomenon over and over, and always get the same score; that demonstrates that our measure is a reliable one. But there is no way to demonstrate that it is a valid one—that it really gets at the phenomenon we claim to be measuring. The closest we come to validation of a measure (also known as an index or indicator) is a consensus among specialists that it taps what it claims to be tapping, and that consensus will rest upon (a) the "face validity" or reasonableness of the claim; (b) the extent to which it correlates with a widely accepted alternative indicator of the same phenomenon; and (c) the extent to which it predicts some measurable outcome variable that it is—according to an accepted theoretical argument—supposed to predict.

Quantification, however, may take a second, and more familiar, form. That is, in addition to assigning a numerical value to each observation of a given phenomenon, one can quantify by merely (a) assigning each such case or observation to a given nominal or ordinal category, and then (b) counting the number of observations that fall into each such category. The nominal category pertains to a set of criteria that are used to classify events and conditions; an ordinal category refers to the criteria used to rank them. To illustrate, generalizing about the American propensity to form alliances might require distinguishing among defense, neutrality, and entente commitments. Once the coding rules have been formulated and written down in explicit language (with examples), a person with limited specific knowledge could go through the texts and contexts of all American alliances and assign each to one of those three categories.

The same could be done, for example, if one wanted to order a wide variety of foreign policy moves and countermoves, in the context of comparing the effects of different strategies upon the propensity of diplomatic conflicts to escalate toward war. The judgments of a panel of experts could be used to ascertain which types of action seem to be high, medium, or low on a conflict-exacerbating dimension. The earlier distinction between the reliability and validity of measures is quite appropriate here. There might be almost perfect agreement among experts that economic boycotts are higher on such a dimension than ultimata, since the latter are merely threats to act. But if one examined a set of diplomatic confrontations and found that those in which boycotts were used seldom ended in war, whereas those characterized by ultimata often did end in war, one might be inclined to challenge the validity of the ordinal measure.

So much, then, for existential knowledge. Whether merely acquired in ready-made form from governmental or commercial statistics, or generated by data-making procedures that are highly operational and reproducible, propositions of an existential nature are the bedrock upon which we can build correlational and explanatory knowledge.

Correlational Knowledge and Data Analysis Methods.

Although many diplomatic historians will be quite content to go no further than the acquisition of existential knowledge, there will be others who will not only want to generalize, but also to formulate and test explanations. To do so, it is necessary to begin assembling two or more data sets and to see how strongly one correlates with the other(s). Correlation or covariation may take several forms and may be calculated in several ways, depending on whether the data sets are in nominal, ordinal, or interval (that is, cardinal number) form.

In general, a correlational proposition is one that shows the extent of coincidence or covariation between two (or more) sets of numbers. If these sets of numbers are viewed as the varying or fluctuating magnitudes of each variable, the correlation between them is a reflection of the extent to which the quantitative configuration of one variable can be ascertained when the configuration of the other is known. Or, in statistical parlance, the coefficient of correlation, which usually ranges from +1.00 to −1.00, indicates how accurately one can predict the magnitudes of all the observations in one data set once one knows the magnitudes in the other set of observations. Even though the measured events or conditions occurred in the past, we still speak of "prediction," since we know only that those phenomena occurred, but do not know the strength of association until the correlation coefficient has been computed.

Another way to put it is that the correlation between two sets of data is a measure of their similarity, whether they are based on pairs of simultaneous observations or ones in which variable Y was always measured at a fixed interval of time after each observation or measurement of variable X. If they rise and fall together over time or across a number of cases, they are similar, and the correlation between them will be close to +1.00; but if Y rises every time X drops, or vice versa, they are dissimilar, giving a negative correlation of close to −1.00. Finally, if there is neither a strong similarity nor dissimilarity, but randomness, the correlation coefficient will approach zero. There are many different measures or indices of correlation, usually named after the scholar who developed and applied them, but two of them can serve as good examples. Although any correlation coefficient can be calculated with pencil and paper or a calculator, the most efficient method is the computer, which can be programmed so that it can automatically receive two or more sets of data along with instructions as to which correlation formula to use, and almost instantaneously produce coefficient scores. Looking, then, at the very simple "rank order" correlation, we note that it is used to calculate the similarity or association between two sets of ranked data. It is particularly appropriate when we can ascertain only the orderings, from high to low or top to bottom, of two data sets and cannot ascertain with much confidence the distances or intervals between those rank positions. The rank order statistic is also especially appropriate for checking the validity of two separate measures or indicators and ascertaining whether they "get at" the same phenomena.

To illustrate, if we suspect that a fairly good index of a nation's power is simply the absolute amount of money it allocates to military preparedness—regardless of its population, wealth, or industrial capability—we might investigate how strongly that index correlates with an alternative measure. And, since power is itself a vague and elusive concept, we might decide to derive the second measure by having the nations ranked by a panel of diplomatic historians. When these two listings—one based on a single, simple index and the other based on the fallible human judgments of scholarly specialists—are brought together, we then compute the rank order correlation between them. The results of any such computation can in principle, as noted earlier, range from +1.00 to −1.00, with 0.00 representing the midpoint. If there is absolutely no pattern of association between the two rankings, we say there is no correlation, and the figure would indeed be zero. Further, if each nation has exactly the same rank position in both columns, the rank order correlation between the two variables is +1.00, and if the orders are completely reversed (with the nation at the top of one column found at the bottom of the other, and so on), it would be −1.00. None of these three extreme cases is likely to occur in the real world, of course, and on a pair of variables such as these, a rank order correlation of approximately +0.80 is pretty much what we would expect to find when the computation has been done.

The above example illustrates how a rank order correlation might be used to estimate the similarity between two different rankings. While a high positive correlation would increase confidence in the validity of military expenditure levels as a measure of power, we assumed no particular theoretical or causal connection between the two data sets. Now, however, suppose that we believed (that is, suspected, but did not know with very much confidence) that the war-proneness of a nation was somehow or other a consequence of its level of industrialization. If we only know how many wars a nation has been involved in during a given number of decades, we have a rather crude indicator of its war-proneness. Such a number does not discriminate between long and short wars; wars that led to a great many or very few fatalities; and wars that engaged all of its forces or only a small fraction. Thus, we would be quite reluctant to say that a nation that fought in eight wars is four times more war-prone than one that experienced only two military conflicts in a given period. We would even be reluctant to say that the difference between two nations that participated in six and four wars respectively is the same as that between those nations that fought in seven and five wars. In sum, we might be justified in treating such a measure of war-proneness as, at best, ordinal in nature.

Suppose, further, that our measure of industrialization is almost as crude, based, for example, on the single factor of iron and steel production. Even though we might have quite accurate figures on such production, we realize that it is a rather incomplete index, underestimating some moderately powerful nations that have little coal or ore and therefore tend to import much of their iron and steel. In such a case, we would again be wise to ignore the size of the differences between the nations and settle for only a rank order listing. Depending on the magnitude of the resulting coefficient of correlation between these two rank orderings, we could make a number of different inferences about the relationship between industrialization and war-proneness. Suppose now that we were working with much better indices than those used in the two illustrations above, and that we could measure our variables with considerably greater confidence. That is, we now have a basis for believing that our indicators or measures are not only valid (and that has no bearing on the statistical tests that can be applied to a variable) but reliable and quite precise. If one variable were the amount of money spent for the operation of IGOs

(intergovernmental organizations) in the international system each half-decade, and the other were the number of nation-months of war that ended in each previous half-decade, and such interval scale data appeared to be very accurate, we could employ a more sensitive type of statistical test, such as Pearson's product moment correlation.

The reason that a product moment type of correlational analysis is more sensitive is that its computation does not—because it need not—ignore the magnitude of the differences between the rank positions on a given pair of listings. Whereas rank order data merely tell us that the nation (or year, or case, or observation) at one position is so many positions or notches above or below another, interval scale data tell us how much higher or lower it is on a particular yardstick. The magnitude of those interrank distances carries a lot of useful information, and when the data are of such a quality to give us that additional information, it is foolish to "throw it away." Thus, when the measures of the variables permit, we generally use a product moment rather than a rank order correlation. As we might expect, certain conditions regarding the normality of the distributions, independence of the observations, randomness of the sample, and so on, must be met before we can use this more sensitive measure of statistical association. Once we have computed the rank order or product moment correlation coefficient between any two sets of measures, several inferences about the relationship between the variables become possible, providing that one additional requirement is met. If the correlation score is close to zero, we can—for the moment, at least—assume that there is little or no association between the variables and tentatively conclude that (a) one measure is not a particularly good index of the other (when validation of a measure is our objective), or (b) that one variable exercises very little impact on the other (when a correlational proposition is our objective). If, however, the correlation coefficient is about 0.50 or higher, either positive (+) or negative (−), we would want to go on and ask whether the above-mentioned requirement has been met.

That requirement is that the correlation be high enough to have had a very low probability of occurring by chance alone. That is ascertained by computing (or looking up in a standard text) the statistical significance of the correlation. When we have very few pairs of observations (or cases) in our analysis, even a correlation as high as 0.90 can occur by sheer chance. And when we have a great many cases, even a figure as low as 0.30 can be statistically significant. To illustrate with what is known as the Z-test, statisticians have computed that a product moment correlation would have to be as high as 0.65 if the association between 12 sets of observations were to be thought of as having only a 1 percent probability of being mere coincidence. Conversely, if there were as many as 120 cases, they calculate that a correlation as low as 0.22 would also have only a 1 percent probability of being mere coincidence. In statistical parlance, we say that for a given number of cases, a given correlation score is "significant at the 1 percent (or 2 percent or 5 percent) level."

Once we have ascertained that the strength of a given correlation, as well as its statistical significance, is sufficiently high (and the evaluation of "sufficiently" is a complex matter, still debated by statisticians and scientists), we can then go on to make a number of inferences about the predictive or the explanatory association between the variables being examined. The nature of those inferences and the justification for them is explored in the next section. Suffice it to say here that when two variables are strongly correlated, and one of them precedes the other in time, we have a typical form of correlational knowledge but are not yet able to say very much of an explanatory nature.

Explanatory Knowledge and Causal Inference
It should now be quite clear that operational classification and enumeration, combined with statistical analysis of the resulting data sets, can eventually produce a large body of correlational knowledge. Further, it should be evident that correlational knowledge can indeed provide a rather satisfactory basis for foreign policy prediction, despite the limitations noted above. But the major limitation lies in the difference between predictions based on correlations from the past, and predictions based on theories. Without a fairly good theory (which, it will be recalled, is more than either a hunch or a model), our predictions will often be vulnerable on two counts.

First, there is the problem that has often intrigued the philosopher of science and delighted the traditional humanist. If the decision makers of nation A have a fair idea what predictions are being made about them by the officials of nation B, they can often confound B by selecting a move or a strategy other than the one they think is expected. A good theory, however, has

built into it just such contingencies, and can often cope with the "we think that they think that we think, etc." problem. Second, a good theory increases our ability to predict in cases that have no exact (or even approximate) parallel in history. That is, it permits us to first build up—via the inductive mode—a general set of propositions on the basis of the specific cases for which we do have historical evidence, and then to deduce— from the theory based on those general propositions—back down to specific cases for which we do not have historical evidence.

If theories are, then, quite important in the study of foreign policy, how do we go about building, verifying, improving, and consolidating them? To some extent, the answer depends on one's definition of a theory, and the word has, unfortunately, disparate meanings. To the layman, a theory is often nothing more than a hunch or an idea. Worse yet, some define theory as anything other than what is real or pragmatic or observable; hence the expression that such and such may be true "in theory, but not in practice." The problem here is that—and this is the second type of definition—a number of scientists also imply that same distinction by urging that a theory need not be true or accurate, as long as it is useful. To be sure, many theories do turn out to be useful (in the sense that they describe and predict reality) even though they are built upon assumptions that are not true. One example is in the field of economics, where some very useful theories rest on the assumption that most individuals act on the basis of purely materialistic, cost-versus-benefit calculations. We are fairly certain that a great many decisions are made on the basis of all sorts of noneconomic and nonrational considerations, but, somehow or other, the market or the firm nevertheless tends to behave as if individual shoppers, investors, and so on do make such calculations. The important point here is that the theory itself is not out of line with reality, but that the assumptions on which it rests may be untrue without weakening the predictive power of the theory.

This leads to the need for distinguishing between theories that are adequate for predictive purposes and those of a more comprehensive nature that seek to not only predict, but to explain. While the dividing line between them is by no means sharp and clear, we can nevertheless make a rough distinction between those theories that are supposed to tell us *what* happens, or will happen under certain conditions, and those that tell us *why* it happens. Even in economics, it is recognized that the predictive power of its major theories can be improved, and their explanatory adequacy markedly enhanced, by looking into and rectifying the psychological or other assumptions on which they rest.

Thus, even though short-run needs may be served by theories that are merely predictive, the concern here is with theories that are capable of explaining why certain regularities (and deviations therefrom) are indeed found in human affairs. To repeat the definition suggested earlier, a theory is a logically consistent body of existential and correlational propositions, most of which are in operational and testable form, and many of which have been tested and confirmed. This definition requires that all of the propositional components in the theory be, in principle at least, true; further, if the theory is to explain why things occur as they do, the propositions underlying it must also be true. Given these stringent requirements, small wonder that that there is so little in the way of explanatory theory in the social sciences.

SOME BEHAVIORAL CONCEPTS

Shifting now from some of the methods associated with the behavioral approach, one of the more serious obstacles to a richer and more subtle understanding of diplomatic history may well be the rather restricted set of concepts used in seeking to put together predictive and explanatory models. To a considerable extent, concepts are limited to those used by the practitioners, their spokesmen, and the journalists who cover diplomatic events. Are there in the behavioral science literature some concepts that might provide new insights or suggest more powerful ways of thinking about diplomatic history?

First, there are several conceptual schemes that have developed to such a degree that they might qualify under the rubric of "theories"; indeed, they are so labeled by many of those from whose disciplines they emerge. Perhaps most promising is that set of notions that are called general systems theory. Proceeding from the assumption that there are structural similarities in different fields, and correspondences in the principles that govern the behavior of entities that are intrinsically widely different, this approach seeks to identify those similarities and correspondences (as well as dissimilarities) that might be found in the universes of all the scientific disciplines. In its search for an integrated theory of behavior, the general systems approach postulates the existence of a system, its environment, and its subsystems. Some of the key concepts employed are feedback, homeostasis, network, entropy, and information, reflecting a considerable intellectual debt to cybernetics. By thinking of the states as subsystems within the international system, which in turn has a particular environment of physical and social dimensions, we are provided with a rather fruitful taxonomy that suggests, in turn, a fascinating array of hypotheses. Within the same context, the idea of homeostasis is particularly suggestive to those concerned with balance, stability, and equilibrium in the international system.

Another set of concepts that seems to offer real promise is that employed in the theory of games. The clearest model postulates two or more players (individuals, groups, states, coalitions) pursuing a set of goals according to a variety of strategies. If the goals are perceived by the players as incompatible, that is, only one player may win, we have a so-called "zero-sum" or win-lose game, with the players tending to utilize a "minimax" strategy. If, however, they perceive a possible win-win outcome, their strategies tend to deviate sharply from the conservative minimax pattern, in which they place prime emphasis on minimizing their maximum losses. The appropriateness of such a model for an enduring rivalry seems rather evident.

We now turn from these very general conceptual schemes to some of the more limited concepts found in the specific behavioral disciplines. Looking first at psychology, from learning theory, stimulus-response theory, and the concepts associated with reinforcement, a wide range of models can be adapted and modified and could ultimately shed useful light on diplomatic influence, a central aspect of international relations. For example, is a major power more likely to shape the policies of a weaker neighbor by punishment, reward, denial, threat, promise, or calculated detachment? Or, in seeking to explain the way in which public opinion in a given state ultimately influenced a certain policy decision, we might find some valuable suggestions in reference-group theory, the concepts of access and role-conflict, or some of the models of communication nets. To take another problem area, if one were concerned with the emerging attitudinal characteristics of the international environment, such notions as acculturation, internalization, relative deprivation, self-image, or consensus might prove to be highly productive.

"THE NEXT ASSIGNMENT"

"[H]istorians, having dedicated their lives to the exploration and understanding of the past, are apt to be suspicious of novelty and ill-disposed toward crystal-gazing. In the words of my distinguished predecessor, they lack the 'speculative audacity' of the natural scientists, those artisans of brave hypotheses. This tendency on the part of historians to become buried in their own conservatism strikes me as truly regrettable. What basically may be a virtue tends to become a vice, locking our intellectual faculties in the molds of the past and preventing us from opening new horizons as our cousins in the natural sciences are constantly doing. If progress is to be made we must certainly have new ideas, new points of view, and new techniques."

— *From William L. Langer,*
"The Next Assignment, American
Historical Review 63,
no. 2 (1958): 283–304 —

Or consider the discipline of sociology, from which many contemporary researchers in foreign affairs have borrowed heavily. If we seek to better understand the foreign policy of the United States or any other nation, we may want to think of the international system (regional or global) as similar to other social systems, but with national states—rather than individuals or groups—as the component units. Such systems manifest certain characteristics, and as these change, the behavior of the component units might also be expected to change. For example, certain social systems are highly stratified at certain times, in the sense that people who rank high on wealth are also high on education, prestige, and political power. Under such conditions, one might expect more conflict because the underdogs are deprived on every dimension. Might it also be that when the international system is highly stratified—with a few nations ranking at the top in wealth, resources, population, military capability, industrial output, and diplomatic status—the likelihood of sharp conflict goes up?

Remaining with sociological concepts, but shifting down from the systemic to the unit level of aggregation, certain individuals tend to be much more mobile than others, and as a result may acquire power more easily, or perhaps experience more conflict. That is, lateral mobility—by which is meant the rate at which individuals move in and out of certain cliques or associations—may also apply to nations, reflecting the rate at which they move in and out of blocs, alliances, or international organizations. Similarly, rapid vertical (upward or downward) mobility might be expected to get nations, as well as individuals, into more conflict than if they occupied a constant niche or moved up or down very gradually.

In the same vein, the concept of status inconsistency and its relationship to "deviant" behavior might merit closer examination. For example, if an individual ranks high on education or some other status-relevant dimension but low on political influence, he should—according to some sociologists—show a fair amount of deviant behavior. Do nations that rank high in certain prestige or status dimensions but low in power, manifest more odd and unpredictable behavior than those that are status-consistent?

As an example from the discipline of economics, consider the concepts of monopoly and oligopoly, reflecting the extent to which a given market is dominated by one firm or a handful of firms. The concentration of economic power may have its parallel at the international level, with a regional, functional, or global system manifesting a high degree of concentration as one or two nations enjoy most of the trade, industrial output, energy consumption, or military might in that system. The consequences of such high concentration, among firms or among nations, could be quite profound in its effects on such phenomena as conflict and cooperation, vertical mobility or stagnation, or the formation and dissolution of coalitions.

The range and variety of concepts that have been developed in the behavioral sciences is impressive indeed, as is the extent to which those concepts have often helped to differentiate, clarify, synthesize, or explain phenomena that had hitherto been quite baffling.

SOME BEHAVIORAL FINDINGS

Turning to the third possible sector in which the behavioral science approach might enhance our comprehension of diplomatic history, let us consider briefly some of the findings that emerge from these disciplines. By findings, we mean either existential or correlational propositions that seem to enjoy some standing in their home disciplines, and on the basis of which explanatory theories might be articulated.

One can hardly exaggerate the importance of these findings for diplomatic historians, and, of course, for practitioners. That is, those interested in foreign policy rest many of their interpretations, analyses, and predictions on behavioral science propositions that may or may not be accurate. First, they often extrapolate from the individual to the group or national level of aggregation, assuming that what holds for the individual will also hold for the collectivity. This is for purposes of speculation and hypothesis only. That is, in the absence of evidence to the contrary, it is probably economical to assume that if, for example, individuals tend to be more cooperative in the face of reward rather than in the face of punishment, so will corporations or nations.

On the other hand, there are some fundamental differences between individuals and collectivities. The primary difference, of course, is that individuals (or, more precisely, rational, intelligent, and informed ones) can be thought of as purposive, problem-solving entities, trying to maximize their particular values. Collectivities, on the other hand, exactly because they are made up of such individuals—each pursuing a mix of private and public goals—cannot be so conceived. The group or organization will, almost inevitably, pursue a range of goals reflecting a compromise and amalgam of the often incompatible goals of its more powerful individuals and subgroups. Thus, it is essential to be sufficiently familiar with the findings of such microsocial disciplines as psychology and the macrosocial ones of economics, sociology, and political science and to know something of the discontinuities between the individual and the collective levels of aggregation. The second way in which we rest analyses and predictions on behavioral science findings is more direct, with many models depending heavily upon the accuracy of assumptions about individual and collective behavior. This dependence is quite heavy, whether the focus is upon public opinion, elite recruitment, executive-legislative relationships, bureaucratic responsibility for policy execution, or the decision process itself. In each of these areas of activity, individuals and groups—with considerable propensities toward regular and consistent behavior—are playing key roles, and to the extent that there is an unawareness of the findings that reflect those regularities

and consistencies, the accuracy and completeness of analyses is seriously limited.

Rather than select some limited number of existential and correlational propositions from the behavioral sciences and summarize the evidence in support or contravention, we can turn for a large number of these findings to the general source *International Encyclopedia of the Social Sciences* (Sills, 1979, which replaced the 1930–1935 and 1967 editions). Each section of the encyclopedia is written by a leading authority, and virtually all topics in the field are covered. Embracing nearly a dozen disciplines, however, rather than only part of one, it runs to sixteen volumes plus an index.

In the *Encyclopedia*, one finds summaries of the existential and correlational knowledge on such concepts as acculturation, aggression, anxiety, avoidance, business cycles, charisma, coalition formation, cognitive dissonance, mass communication, cybernetics, conformity, conditioning, conflict, cultural diffusion, decision making, defense mechanisms, demography. deviant behavior, diplomacy, disarmament, dominance, dreams, ecology, economic equilibrium, elites, ethnology, ethology, evolution, family structure, fatigue, fertility, forgetting, frustration, geopolitics, gestalt, motivation, homeostasis, identity, ideology, imperialism, income distribution, influence, inflation, interest groups, interpersonal interaction, kinship, land tenure, language, leadership, learning, legitimacy, loyalty, migration, social mobility, monopoly, norms, national character, neurosis, oligopoly, pacifism, paranoid reactions, perception (ten separate articles), personality, persuasion, pluralism, prejudice, prestige, propaganda, psychoanalysis, public opinion, punishment, race relations, reciprocity, reference groups, response set, roles, sanctions, self-image, sex differences, social stratification, stereotypes, stress, sympathy and empathy, thinking, traits, utilitarianism, utility, voluntary associations, voting, wages, war, and worship. (One also finds in the encyclopedia articles on such methodological matters as content analysis, contingency table analysis, curve-fitting, experimental design, multivariate analysis, statistical distributions, factor analysis, field work, forecasting, game theory, historiography, hypothesis testing, index construction, statistical inference, Markov chains, observation, panel studies, probability, rank correlation, scaling, simulation, spectral analysis, statistical inference, survey analysis, time series, typologies, and validity.)

Another very general source, although seriously outdated, is *Human Behavior: An Inventory of Scientific Findings* (Berelson and Steiner, 1964). After discussing the six most frequently cited procedures for generating the findings they report, the compilers go on to summarize what they consider to be the more interesting propositions to have emerged from research in the behavioral sciences. The substantive topics covered are behavioral development (meaning biological, emotional, and cognitive change as individuals mature); perceiving; learning and thinking; motivation; the family; small face-to-face groups; organizations; institutions; social stratification; ethnic relations; mass communications; opinions, attitudes, and beliefs; the society; and culture.

There are also collections of articles, summarizing the correlational and explanatory knowledge in the specific disciplines or problem areas. Among the more relevant are: *Handbook of Developmental Psychology* (Wolman, 1982); *Handbook of Personality Theory and Research* (Pervin, 1999); *Handbook of Psychiatry* (Solomon and Patch, 1974); *Small Group Research: A Handbook* (Hare, 1994); *Handbook of Social Psychology* (Gilbert, Fiske, and Lindzey, 1998); *World Handbook of Political and Social Indicators* (Taylor and Jodice, 1983).

There are two other—if dated—anthologies that not only summarize a good many concepts and findings from these related disciplines, but select and organize the articles on the basis of their applicability to specific topics in international affairs—*Man and International Relations* (Zawodny, 1966) and *Human Behavior and International Politics* (Singer, 1965).

Two collections that bring together the findings of research in foreign policy and international politics are *Beyond Conjecture in International Politics: Abstracts of Data-Based Research* (Jones and Singer, 1972) and *Empirical Knowledge on World Politics* (Gibbs and Singer, 1993). In these, the compilers attend only to published articles in English that generate, or rest upon, reproducible evidence. No effort is made to interpret, integrate, or evaluate the 300 or so studies that are covered, but they are very systematically arranged. Further, each is abstracted in accordance with a checklist that includes the following: query, spatial-temporal domain, outcome variable, predictor variable(s), data sources, data-making operations, data preparation and manipulation, data analysis procedure, findings, and related research. In addition, there is a recent compilation that brings together the ideas and research findings of both the behavioral scientists and the diplomatic historians in the very useful three-volume collection *Encyclopedia of Violence, Peace, and Conflict* (Kurtz, 1999).

When the first edition of the *Encyclopedia of American Foreign Policy* was published in 1978, the behavioral movement was just getting under way in the foreign policy and world politics fields. There were relatively few data-based findings to report. Since then, the number of scholars working in the behavioral science mode has risen from a mere dozen or so to about two hundred worldwide; these scholars have written perhaps four hundred articles and books, almost exclusively in English and largely designed to help account for war. Most of these have been summarized, and modestly integrated, in *Nations at War: A Scientific Study of International Conflict* by Daniel S. Geller and J. David Singer (1998).

World War I and the Iraq-Iran War of 1980–1988 are two examples to be used to ascertain and illustrate the extent to which such examples conform to the patterns that emerge from the many studies that have looked at the effects of only two or three variables at a time across many historical cases since 1916. In the case of the Iran-Iraq War (1980–1990), there are the following specific instances of the more general patterns found in the larger literature: geographical contiguity, the absence of joint democratic regimes, the absence of joint advanced economies, a rapid shift in the joint relative capabilities, and, finally, the existence of an enduring rivalry characterized by seventeen militarized disputes during the half century run-up to war. Similarly, the case of World War I is marked by quite a few of the more general statistical findings: major powers on both sides, contiguity, shifting capabilities and an unstable balance, highly autocratic regimes on both sides, and, again, the longstanding rivalries.

CONCLUSION

There are several ways in which one might react to the foregoing information and suggestions. One might, for example, paraphrase that observer who told us that "history is bunk" and assert that "social science is bunk." Less frivolously, one might see little value in trying to apply the behavioral sciences to the study of diplomatic history, concluding that the investment will far exceed the likely gain. For those who conclude otherwise, it may nevertheless appear to represent a radical break with traditional style, and thus one that should not be taken lightly.

Not only can we benefit considerably by attending to the behavioral sciences, but to do so represents only a logical expansion of practices and procedures that for decades have been the stock-in-trade of historians. First, we note that the scientific method has been utilized for centuries in the solution of all sorts of physical and biological problems. But for a variety of reasons, ranging from religious taboos and superstition to the allegedly greater complexity of social phenomena, we have shied away from (if not vigorously resisted) its application to the study of social problems. That orientation has, however, been gradually eroded, partly through the work of courageous and creative scholars and partly because of the increasingly obvious need to replace folklore with knowledge.

In addition to the fact that social science is merely an extension of a given intellectual style already well established in the study of physical and biological phenomena, it is also quite nonrevolutionary in that it is little more than an extension of certain problem-solving processes that have always been used. While it is clearly an extension, the fact is that human beings have used a combination of logic and sensory observation for centuries in coping with social problems. In trying to understand what people did under certain conditions and why they did it, philosophers, kings, merchants, and soldiers have often employed a rudimentary form of scientific method. That is, they have tried (a) to identify and classify a variety of social events and conditions; (b) to ascertain the extent to which they occurred together or in sequence; and (c) to remember those observed co-occurrences.

But since they seldom have used explicit criteria in classification, they often placed highly dissimilar events and conditions in the same category; and since they seldom used constant criteria, they often forgot which criteria they had used for earlier classifications, with the same garbled results. Moreover, because one could not put social events on a scale, or measure the length and breadth of a social condition, their basic belief that social phenomena were not tangible, and therefore not measurable, was reinforced. This failure to measure and scale further reinforced the philosophic notion that whereas physical (and later, biological) phenomena were inherently quantitative, those of a social nature were inherently qualitative. Given this widespread belief, there was little effort to develop either the instruments of observation or the tools of measurement.

For centuries, then, social phenomena could be studied in a no more reliable or accurate fashion than if physical ones were studied without yardsticks, balance scales, or telescopes. To put it another way, the primitive essentials of scientific method were used but the critical refinements were ignored. Instead of aiding and enhancing their natural capacities to observe, remember, and reason, observers made a virtue of these very frailties and inadequacies by arguing that the incomprehensibility of social phenomena was inherent in the events and conditions themselves, rather than in the grossly inadequate methods used in that effort to comprehend. Modern social science, then, is nothing more than an application of methods already found useful in the other sciences and an extension and refinement of the basic methods always used. As in the familiar cliché, we have been "speaking prose" all along, but prose of a rather poor quality.

To be sure, the study of foreign relations remains as it was in the 1970s and 1980s. But this is not necessarily good news. First, there was the lively and early interest in the behavioral sciences approach among certain scholars and practitioners. In the early days of the peace research movement, for instance, one found copies of the *Journal of Conflict Resolution* and the *Journal of Peace Research* on the desks and shelves in certain self-selected offices in the Departments of State and Defense. Further, such agencies as the Advanced Research Projects Agency or the Office of Naval Research were practically caught up in the early enthusiasm of the 1960s for computer simulation, game theory analyses, or even the wide-ranging survey research and field interview strategies, as in the U.S. Army's Project Camelot. And the years following the Cuban missile crisis also saw moderate levels of involvement between U.S. and Soviet groups around a variety of conflict resolution conferences and field studies in Washington, New York, London, Moscow, and Ann Arbor, Michigan. But worth noting is, first, the relatively limited reflection of these interests in the scholarly literature of diplomatic and military history, and, second, the impact of U.S. intervention in the Vietnam War. By the early 1970s, the behavioral science enthusiasm had pretty much disappeared from both the policy and academic scene, with almost no residue in the scholarly literature.

Worse yet, with the demise of the Cold War, the early curiosity and experimentalism of the Cold War–Cuban missile crisis–Vietnam epoch was gradually replaced with a nouveau vague interest in approaches that were not only nonscientific but explicitly and ideologically antiscientific. For reasons not yet clearly evident, the collapse of the Soviet Union in the late 1980s culminated in the flowering of a scholarly literature of remarkable vitality and intellectual vacuity. Reference, of course, is to the postmodernist movement, embracing such variations as poststructural, postpositivist, and, perhaps, postbehaviorial. These orientations are found primarily in the humanities and those of the more humanistic social sciences, including, of course, history. In addition to the appearance of a new vocabulary in which words like "discourse," "contested," and "social construction" figure prominently, it is not surprising that the discipline of history is paying less attention to diplomatic and military phenomena and more to gender, race, and social class. While such variables were admittedly underrepresented in the study of foreign affairs and world politics during the twentieth century, this radical shift in both the theoretical and the methodological hardly bodes well for the future of the discipline.

Some might suggest that none of this matters a great deal, given how modest has been the contribution of the behavioral sciences. Scholars such as John L. Gaddis (1992) have gone out of their way to remind us that with all of the modern scientific paraphernalia in their toolbox, the behaviorists utterly failed to predict either the Soviet collapse or the end of the Cold War. Three responses seem appropriate. First, the behavioral science researchers in international politics were not alone in being asleep at the switch. Second, those who should have been alert to the Soviet demise were the specialists in the Cold War, Kremlinology, and contemporary diplomacy. Third, there were some who did indeed predict the end of the Cold War (as J. David Singer did in his 1986 article "The Missiles of October—1988: Resolve, Reprieve, and Reform").

In sum, it is very difficult to quarrel with Robin G. Collingwood's early recognition (1922) of the intellectual similarity between history and science:

> The analysis of science in epistemological terms is thus identical with the analysis of history, and the distinction between them as separate kinds of knowledge is an illusion. . . . When both are regarded as actual inquiries, the difference of method and of logic wholly disappears. . . . The nineteenth century positivists were right in thinking that history could and would become more scientific.

BIBLIOGRAPHY

Barbieri, Katherine. *Trade and Conflict.* Ann Arbor, Mich., 2000. A careful and systematic examination of the historical pattern between trade and conflict.

Berelson, Bernard, and Gary A. Steiner. *Human Behavior: An Inventory of Scientific Findings.* New York, 1964. Although dated, this inventory summarizes much of the flowering research of the post–World War II period.

Brams, Steven J. *Theory of Moves.* New York and Cambridge, 1994. One of the richest and most accessible works on the game theory approach for the nonmathematical scholar.

Brecher, Michael, and Jonathon Wilkenfield. *A Study of Crisis.* Ann Arbor, Mich., 1997. An original and ambitious analysis of most diplomatic crises since 1919.

Bremer, Stuart A., and Thomas R. Cusack, eds. *The Process of War: Advancing the Scientific Study of War.* Amsterdam, 1995. Papers from a Correlates of War conference emphasizing the strengths of thinking of war as part of a process.

Bueno de Mesquita, Bruce, and David Lalman. *War and Reason: Domestic and International Imperatives.* New Haven, Conn., 1992. A strong presentation of the rational choice interpretation of the decisions for war.

Collingwood, Robin G. "Are History and Science Different Kinds of Knowledge?" *Mind* (1922). A prediction that historians would begin to embrace the procedures of scientific method.

Cusack, Thomas R., and Richard J. Stoll. *Exploring Realpolitik: Probing International Relations Theory with Computer Simulation.* Boulder, Colo., 1990. An exemplary examination of how computerized simulations of international interactions can shed light on underlying dynamics.

Diehl, Paul F., and Gary Goertz. *War and Peace in International Rivalry.* Ann Arbor, Mich., 2000. The most comprehensive investigation into the dynamics of international rivalries and the propensity to go to war.

Gaddis, John L. "International Relations Theory and the End of the Cold War." *International Security* 16 (1992): 5–58. A widely cited article that sought to understand Western failures to predict the end of the Cold War.

Geller, Daniel S., and J. David Singer. *Nations at War: A Scientific Study of International Con-*

flict. Cambridge and New York, 1998. A thorough codification of data-based findings on the correlates of international war.

Gochman, Charles S., and Alan Ned Sabrosky, eds. *Prisoners of War? Nation-States in the Modern Era.* Lexington, Mass., 1990. An anthology of papers summarizing data-based findings on war as of the late 1980s.

Goldstein, Joshua S. *Long Cycles: Prosperity and War in the Modern Age.* New Haven, Conn., 1988. Examines the concept of cycles of a half-century or longer and how war and economic cycles correlate.

Houweling, Henk, and Jan G. Siccama. *Studies of War.* Dordrecht, Netherlands, 1988. Exemplary papers testing certain correlates of war models.

Huth, Paul K. *Standing Your Ground: Territorial Disputes and International Conflict.* Ann Arbor, Mich., 1996. Models and findings on the role of territorial disputes in the onset of war.

Janis, Irving L. *Victims of Groupthink: A Psychological Study of Foreign-Policy Decisions and Fiascoes.* Boston, 1972. Applies psychological findings to foreign policy decision making and its high error rate.

King, Gary, Robert O. Keohane, and Sidney Verba. *Designing Social Inquiry: Scientific Inference in Qualitative Research.* Princeton, N.J., 1994. A broad examination of the quantitative-qualitative relationship in political science.

Lemke, Douglas, and Jacek Kugler, eds. *Parity and War: Evaluations and Extensions of the War Ledger.* Ann Arbor, Mich., 1996. Data-based studies of the impact of material capabilities of states, and rates of change therein, on the probabilities of war.

Leng, Russell J. *Bargaining and Learning in Recurring Crises: The Soviet-American, Egyptian-Israeli, and Indo-Pakistani Rivalries.* Ann Arbor, Mich., 2000. Examines which strategies make crises more or less escalation prone.

Maoz, Zeev. *Paradoxes of War: On the Art of National Self-Entrapment.* Boston, 1990. Fascinating discussion of the ways foreign policy decision makers generate outcomes quite different from those preferred.

Midlarsky, Manus I. *Handbook of War Studies II.* Ann Arbor, Mich., 2000. Excellent articles reviewing some of the central issues in the study of war and peace.

Morgan, T. Clifton. *Untying the Knot of War: A Bargaining Theory of International Crises.* Ann Arbor, Mich., 1994. Use of bargaining and game theory to understand the ways in which conflicts can lead to war.

Ray, James Lee. *Democracy and International Conflict: An Evaluation of the Democratic Peace Proposition.* Columbia, S.C., 1995. Evaluation of the evidence for and against the role of democratic regimes and reducing the incidence of war.

Russett, Bruce M. *Grasping the Democratic Peace: Principles for a Post-Cold War World.* Princeton, N.J., 1993. Systematic evaluation of the democratic peace proposition.

Singer, J. David, ed. *The Correlates of War II: Testing Some Realpolitik Models.* New York, 1980. Anthology of data-based studies of some correlates of international war.

———. "The Missiles of October—1988: Resolve, Reprieve, and Reform." *Scandinavian Journal of Development Alternatives* 5, no. 2 (1986): 5–13. A science fiction prediction that the Cold War would end in 1988.

Stam, Allan C., III. *Win, Lose, or Draw: Domestic Politics and the Crucible of War.* Ann Arbor, Mich., 1996. A suggestive, rare, valuable look into the role of domestic politics in decisions for war and peace.

Thompson, William R. *On Global War: Historical-Structural Approaches to World Politics.* Columbia, S.C., 1988. A long cycle historical interpretation of economic and strategic factors in war and the evolving hierarchy in the global system.

Vasquez, John A. *The War Puzzle.* Cambridge and New York, 1993. An influential effort to assemble and interpret data-based findings on the explanation of war.

Wayman, Frank W., and Paul F. Diehl, eds. *Reconstructing Realpolitik.* Ann Arbor, 1994. Collection of studies that scrutinized some of the more widely believed realpolitik models.

Wright, Quincy. "Design for a Research Proposal on International Conflicts." *Western Political Quarterly* 10 (1957). Some early proposed research foci by one of the pioneers of scientific research on world politics.

See also DECISION MAKING; PUBLIC OPINION.

BIPARTISANSHIP

Randall Woods

In the United States, foreign and domestic affairs are inextricably intertwined. Because they are responsible to the electorate, presidents and secretaries of state must take into account public opinion when they shape foreign policy. Under the Constitution, the legislative branch is a partner, albeit a junior one, with the executive in the conduct of foreign affairs. Treaties may not become law without the two-thirds approval of the Senate, the Senate must confirm the president's top foreign policymakers, only Congress can declare war, and only Congress can fund both the diplomatic and military establishments. Throughout their history, the American people have been represented in Congress and the White House primarily by two major parties. There have been a multitude of third parties, a few of them with the power to determine the outcome of national elections, but national and international policymaking has been dominated by the two-party system. Hence, the term "bipartisanship" to denote periods of inter-party cooperation on foreign and domestic affairs.

Not even advocates of a foreign policy based on inter-party and executive-congressional cooperation have been able to agree on a name for this phenomenon, however. Franklin D. Roosevelt's secretary of state, Cordell Hull, wanted to classify close executive-congressional cooperation as "nonpartisan," because he was determined not to share credit with the Republicans. Michigan Senator Arthur Vandenberg sought acceptance of the term "unpartisan," by which he meant policy developed above partisan purposes and for the national interest. Political scientist H. Bradford Westerfield prefers the term "extrapartisanship," which he defines as a presidential resolution "to associate in active collaboration with his Administration's conduct of foreign relations enough influential members of the opposition party to prevent its lines from solidifying against basic administrative foreign policies." Significantly, only Franklin

D. Roosevelt and John Foster Dulles preferred the term "bipartisanship," which has become the most widely accepted and used term.

Bipartisanship is a process of foreign policy formulation that presupposes presidential leadership in the establishment of the overall parameters defining the national interest. The chief executive, his advisers, and the State Department develop policy, working together closely and providing complete information to leaders in the Senate and House, especially to the chairman and members of both parties who serve on the Senate Committee on Foreign Relations. The president must be willing to consult with leaders of both parties, especially those senators who can assist the administration in gaining broad-based support. He must appoint members of both parties to serve on U.S. delegations to important international conferences. He must be amenable to modifications, amendments, revisions, and changes in treaties or legislation and administer those policies in such a way as to help win the widest support in Congress and in the body politic. Bipartisanship does not preclude differences and partisan advantage but should, as much as possible, secure general agreement on a course of action before it becomes the victim of partisan squabbling. Underlying bipartisanship is the hope that the United States can present a unified voice in international relations. Obviously, bipartisanship is especially critical to a president when he is confronted with domination of both houses of Congress by the opposite party. Close staff work among the Senate Committee on Foreign Relations, the State Department, and presidential advisers must accompany changes in policy. The cooperation between the administration and Congress must also withstand the strains of political campaigns, which recur every two years.

At its best, bipartisan foreign policy functions as part of the American democratic process. Through their representatives in Congress, both parties freely debate, and in the process issues receive the fullest possible airing. In addition, that policy must be based on generally agreed-upon principles and assumptions that are shared by the president and congressional leaders, including those of the opposition party.

Bipartisanship is usually associated with an activist, interventionist foreign policy such as that seen during World War II and the period of the Cold War through Vietnam. But throughout much of its history the dominant theme in America's approach to the world was isolationism, and it was around this theme that the first bipartisan consensus emerged. America was created out of a desire by certain Europeans to escape political and religious persecution. The wave of immigrants that began flooding across the Atlantic in the seventeenth century were hoping to escape the evils of monarchism and religious intolerance. They were fleeing a hierarchical system that denied them the opportunity for economic advancement, political power, and free religious expression. Even those who continued to regard themselves as loyal subjects of the British crown deeply appreciated the three thousand miles that separated them from the motherland.

FEDERALISTS AND REPUBLICANS IN THE EARLY REPUBLIC

The American Revolution was itself a deliberate act of separation and self-isolation. In order to secure its independence from Great Britain, the newly created United States of America was forced in 1778 to ally itself with monarchical France. But that was indeed a marriage of convenience. The United States had no desire to trade its British masters for French ones. At its inception, the United States was a fifth-rate power of some economic but no military consequence. Its first president, George Washington, perceived that it was in his country's interest to avoid the power politics of Europe. The American Revolution served as a prelude to the French Revolution and a generation of war as first revolutionary and then Napoleonic France and its allies struggled with Britain and its allies for control of the Western world. Washington perceived that it behooved his infant republic to remain aloof from this great conflict. Not all agreed, and from this disagreement, in part, came America's first party system.

The Federalist Party emerged out of the bloc in Congress that supported Secretary of the Treasury Alexander Hamilton's financial program and the commercial and business interests that benefited from it. Ideologically, most Federalists were suspicious of the judgment and wisdom of the mass of citizens who in their opinion were prone to unchecked passions and social disorder; witness the activities of the mobs in the French Revolution. Federalists in general believed in a strong central government capable of acting decisively to maintain order and to restrain the popular tendency toward anarchy. To achieve such a government, they embraced Hamilton's "broad construction" of the Constitution. They detested the French Republic and agreed with Hamilton that the British system was "the best in the world." The opposition to the Federalist program developed under the leadership of James Madison, then a U.S. representative from Virginia, and Thomas Jefferson, who from 1790 to 1793 served as secretary of state in the Washington cabinet. The Republicans articulated the widespread fear among the people of a powerful, overbearing central government wedded to the particular interests of an economic elite that was little concerned with either the rights of states or the welfare of yeomen farmers and ordinary citizens. To preserve local and states' rights, and to protect individual liberty, they advocated the "strict construction" of the Constitution. Republicans accused Federalists of wanting to shape the American government to resemble the British monarchy. Republicans initially expressed admiration for the French and sought to portray the French Revolution as the natural playing out of the American Revolution.

In February 1793, France declared war on England, Spain, and the Netherlands, and in so doing set off a debate in the United States over what its policy should be if the government in Paris invoked the treaties of 1778. Hamilton argued that treaty obligations followed governments and because Louis XVI had been beheaded and the monarchy replaced by a republic, the United States was released from the terms of the treaty and free to declare neutrality as its national interest dictated. Jefferson countered that Louis had only been the agent of the sovereign nation of France and that that sovereignty remained intact. Nonetheless, he concluded, the United States should not come to France's aid if asked because it should not become involved in Europe's wars. Thus did the president proclaim and enforce neutrality with the support of both Federalist and Republican leaders. George Washington's Farewell

Address, published in September 1796, was a paean to isolationism and nonpartisanship. Europe's interests, he declared, were different from those of the United States, and thus Americans should permit only "temporary alliances for extraordinary emergencies." The president also warned that party division "opens the door to foreign influence and corruption," because it meant that "the policy and the will of one country, are subjected to the policy and will of another."

John Adams defeated Thomas Jefferson for the presidency in 1796. Although himself a Federalist, Adams resisted the blandishments of Hamilton and other Anglophile members of his own party and refused to align the nation with Britain against France in the ongoing wars of the French Revolution. So angry were the extreme (High) Federalists that they conspired against Adams in the election of 1800 in an attempt to throw the contest to one of their own. As a result, Thomas Jefferson was elected, and the so-called Republican revolution was launched.

By the time Jefferson ascended to the presidency, the principal of neutrality had become the cornerstone of American foreign policy. As the Napoleonic wars unfolded, the Jefferson administration struggled to preserve its asserted right to trade with both sides. Anglophiles in the Federalist Party agitated for a tilt toward Britain, while Anglophobes in the Republican Party advocated a neutrality that, if not pro-French, was strict. Jefferson and his Republican colleagues looked forward to an America inhabited permanently by independent yeoman farmers. Land ownership, they asserted, was the primary guarantor of an independent electorate and thus of democracy. Consequently, when the opportunity to purchase from France the vast territory between the Mississippi River and the Rocky Mountains arose in 1803, Jefferson leaped at it. Federalists mobilized to fight the resulting treaty with France, insisting that it authorized too much money for land that the country did not need. They pointed out that nowhere in the Constitution was the president authorized to purchase real estate or convert the inhabitants of territories into citizens. These were but masks, however, for their concerns were that the new western states would ally with the South to further damage New England and the Federalist Party's position in the Union. Only John Quincy Adams, son of the former president and then a senator from Massachusetts, voted with the Republicans. But that was enough. The Louisiana Purchase Treaty was approved 24 to 7.

Great Britain's efforts to cut off trade with Napoleonic France and its allies led it to seize hundreds of American ships, and its unquenchable thirst for able-bodied seamen prompted it to impress American sailors. Although it worked assiduously to avoid the conflict then raging in Europe and on the oceans of the world, the Republican administration of James Madison, who had taken office in 1809, led the nation into war against Great Britain in 1812. While High Federalists proclaimed the conflict to be a Republican plot to align the nation with Napoleonic France, the decision to declare hostilities was bipartisan. Republican nationalists, angered by Britain's refusal to abandon the Northwest posts and to stop inciting American Indians against white settlers, joined with New England merchants and shipowners to push a declaration of war through Congress. When a plot by High Federalists to lead New England out of the Union was uncovered in 1814 and peace ensued with Great Britain later that year, the Federalist Party was effectively undone.

What ensued from 1816 to 1824 was a period in American politics known as the Era of Good Feelings. It was, in effect, a time of one-party Republican rule. In 1816, James Monroe defeated the Federalist presidential candidate by winning 183 of 217 possible electoral votes. He was elected four years later with only one symbolic electoral vote cast against him. Firmly committed to the view of a nonpartisan chief executive first articulated by President Washington, Monroe regularly condemned the "party spirit" as destructive to republican institutions. In an effort to create and sustain a national consensus, Monroe and Republican leaders touted a program that called for high tariffs to protect infant American industries, federal appropriations to fund internal improvements such as roads and canals, and ongoing efforts to solidify and extend the nation's burgeoning western empire. The ultimate manifestation and statement of Republican nationalism was the Monroe Doctrine.

In 1823 it appeared that in the wake of the Napoleonic wars, Spain, with the help of France's newly restored Bourbon monarchy, was preparing to resubjugate the republics of Latin America, which had taken advantage of Spain's involvement in the great European conflict to rebel and declare their independence. The Monroe administration, led by Secretary of State John Quincy Adams, was determined to prevent the restoration of Spanish power in the Americas. In the knowledge that whatever it did, the British Navy would prevent the departure of a Spanish-French armada for the New World, Monroe enunciated a doctrine that was simultaneously expansionist and isolationist. Posing as a defender of republicanism against monarchism, the United States declared that henceforward the Western Hemisphere was off limits to further European colonization. It posited the existence of two spheres, each with a separate set of interests, warned Europe to stay out of the affairs of the Americas, and promised not to interfere in European politics. Unspoken but generally recognized was that the United States did not include itself in the restrictions; indeed, the nation's generally agreed objectives were territorial and commercial expansion, and, ultimately, domination of the Western Hemisphere.

JACKSONIAN DEMOCRACY AND CONTINENTAL EXPANSION

By the 1840s the prevailing theme in American diplomatic history was continental expansion. In an 1845 editorial, New York newspaperman John L. O'Sullivan captured the mood of the country when he asserted that it was "the right of our manifest destiny to overspread and to possess the whole of the continent which Providence has given us for the development of the great experiment of Liberty and federated self-government entrusted to us." Meanwhile, a new two-party system had emerged in America. In 1832 the war hero Andrew Jackson rode into the presidency claiming to be heir to the Jeffersonian Republican tradition. At the heart of Jackson's new National Republican Party was an ideology that assumed the inherent conflict between "producing" and "nonproducing" classes, an assumption that enabled it to turn to its advantage the fears and aspirations of those voters in the throes of adjusting to the market revolution and simultaneously to those largely untouched by the revolution. Jackson had special appeal to the hundreds of thousands of newly enfranchised voters of the expanding West. It proved impossible for Jackson, as it would have for anyone, to maintain a national consensus in the face of changes wrought by the market economy and westward expansion. Small farmers in the West clamored for greater access to public lands, while those in the South pressed for a greater share of political power. In the Northeast and the Northwest, urban labor mobilized first in local workingmen's parties

and later in unions, and the evangelized middle class took up the cause of various moral and social reforms. At the same time, southern slaveholders enacted increasingly repressive slave codes in response to abolitionism and continually pushed the cotton kingdom and its slave labor system into the trans-Mississippi West. Inevitably, during the middle of Jackson's second administration anti-Jacksonians galvanized to form the Whig Party (the National Republicans had by now renamed themselves Democrats). The new organization was a conglomeration of National Republicans, southern proslavery states righters, anti-Masons, high-tariff advocates, and various evangelical reformers from the Northeast.

Andrew Jackson was in favor of continued westward expansion, but he equivocated for fear of alienating northern antislavery elements who saw manifest destiny as a massive conspiracy by slaveholding interests to spread their nefarious institution to the Pacific. James K. Polk, the Democratic presidential candidate in 1844 who had outpolled Henry Clay, shared no such qualms. Under his leadership, the United States established clear title to the Oregon territory and set in motion a series of events that led to the annexation of Texas in 1845. The latter development in turn led to the Mexican War of 1846–1848 and ended the period of increasingly troubled bipartisanship that had characterized American foreign policy since the Era of Good Feelings. Even though the commanding general of U.S. forces in the Mexican War was a Whig, members of that party, including Representative Abraham Lincoln, became increasingly vocal in their criticism of the conflict. Aside from the opportunity the war presented to charge the Democrats with being mindless, unfeeling imperialists, the Whigs were concerned that the conflict with Mexico would add more western territory to the union. The ability of the party to remain national depended in no small part on its ability to finesse the question of whether slavery should be extended into the territories. House Democrat David Wilmot of Pennsylvania introduced a proviso to the appropriations bill of August 1846 that would bar slavery from areas taken from Mexico during the war. Northern support was not sufficient to override the opposition of southern Whigs and Polk Democrats, but California and the New Mexico territory were added to the union as a result of the peace treaty with Mexico (the Treaty of Guadalupe Hidalgo, 1848). The increasingly rancorous debate whether slavery in the territories was or should be legitimate would come to dominate national politics.

With the coming of the Civil War, bipartisanship became largely a moot issue because the strength of the Democratic Party lay in the South. When the southern states seceded, Democratic senators and representatives were reduced to a handful. The Lincoln administration's efforts to prevent European intervention on the side of the Confederacy and to interdict trade between Great Britain and France on the one hand and the rebels on the other enjoyed overwhelming support among Republicans and loyalist Democrats.

THE AGE OF IMPERIALISM

The foreign affairs issue that dominated the late nineteenth century was overseas expansion. With the acquisition of the New Mexico territory and California, the United States had rounded out its continental boundaries, but the notion that America had a mission to spread its institutions and mores to the less fortunate peoples of the world remained a powerful part of the American psyche. The Industrial Revolution initially diverted the nation's attention from foreign affairs, but by the 1890s it had become a powerful force for overseas expansion. As the United States advanced from fourth to first among the manufacturing nations of the world, industrialists became convinced that under truly competitive conditions they could outsell their foreign rivals anywhere in the world. As the century came to a close, industrialists and financiers began pressuring various administrations and their State Departments to help them secure markets abroad that would absorb surplus capital and products. Especially attractive were the underdeveloped areas of Asia and Latin America. And finally, Americans were extremely conscious of the fact that they had reached the status of a great power in terms of population, agricultural output, and industrial production. In the late nineteenth century, colonies were the badge of great power status.

There were many obstacles to American expansion. Anti-imperialist groups, led by Senator Carl Schurz, writer Mark Twain, and newspaper editor E. L. Godkin, argued that the nation ought to concentrate on improving its own institutions and social conditions rather than acquiring overseas territories. Some Americans simply opposed the addition of dark-skinned peoples to the United States. Others argued that the estab-lishment of colonies necessarily ruled out self-government and led to competition that caused wars. Up until the 1890s, the Democratic Party generally remained the party of expansion with the Republicans exhibiting reservations or outright opposition. There were exceptions. Lincoln's secretary of state, William H. Seward, was an ardent expansionist who brought Alaska into the Union.

That began to change in the 1890s, as the Republican Party (founded in the 1850s when the Whigs disintegrated as the party of economic nationalism and free soil) became increasingly the party of big business. The social Darwinists and naval expansionists found a receptive audience in a group of young, ambitious Republican politicians who decided to use overseas expansion as a vehicle to carry them to national prominence. Theodore Roosevelt, soon to accede to the presidency, and Senators Henry Cabot Lodge and Albert Beveridge worked energetically and successfully to sell the Republican Party and the American people on the idea of using naval power to build an empire. Meanwhile, the Democratic Party continued to draw its strength primarily from farmers, large and small; its supporters were concentrated in the South and rural Midwest. The economic calamities of the 1890s spawned the Populist Party, which railed against a conspiracy by Republicans, Wall Street, and the federal government to oppress and exploit farmers and workers. Racism was a strong component of both the Democratic and Populist parties, with the latter strongly supporting immigration restriction and the former racial segregation. Grover Cleveland, the only Democrat to sit in the White House between 1861 and 1914, was not an expansionist; indeed, he and the Democratic Party fought against the annexation of Samoa and Hawaii during the late 1880s and 1890s. The Populists saw overseas empire as just an extension of the exploitive polices of the GOP-business coalition, policies that held no advantage for farmers and working people. In 1896, with the nomination of William Jennings Bryan on both the Democratic and Populist tickets, the former effectively swallowed the latter. In the national debate over the treaty with Spain ending the Spanish-American War, in which the United States would annex the Philippines and Guam and supervise Cuba as a protectorate, Bryan led the anti-imperialist opposition. He did so in vain, however, as Roosevelt, Lodge, and influential manufacturers rallied behind the McKinley administration and ratification. In matters of tariff and trade, however, the Republicans were the nationalists, favoring high protective tariffs, and the Democrats the internationalists. Farmers, who depended upon world as well as domestic markets, and business owners, who depended upon trade with developed nations, favored low tariffs. Imperialism, then, was hardly the same as internationalism.

THE PROGRESSIVE ERA AND WORLD WAR I

Each of the Progressive Era presidents—Republicans Theodore Roosevelt and William Howard Taft and Democrat Woodrow Wilson—was committed to protecting America's empire in the Pacific and to solidifying the nation's economic and strategic position in the Western Hemisphere. All were determined to guard the strategic approaches to the Panama Canal (acquired in 1903 and completed in 1914), expand U.S. trade with the Americas and China, and pursue balance-of-power policies in Europe and East Asia to ensure that no one power emerged to dominate those respective areas. Although they differed in techniques and rationales, the goals of the Progressive Era presidents were essentially the same, and they evoked little significant partisan opposition. Their approaches did: Democrats were particularly critical of Taft's dollar diplomacy and Republicans of Wilson's missionary diplomacy.

Woodrow Wilson led the United States into World War I to "make the world safe for democracy" and to safeguard American interests on the high seas. He and most of his countrymen regarded German submarine warfare as a threat to the nation's seafarers and to its economic health. They regarded Germany and its allies as totalitarian, expansionist powers who posed a threat to democratic societies everywhere. The majority of Democrats and Republicans enthusiastically supported the Wilson administration's decision to go to war. Indeed, Theodore Roosevelt had blasted the president for not coming to the Allies' aid earlier. The principal figure opposing the administration's preparedness policies and aggressive diplomacy was William Jennings Bryan, Wilson's first secretary of state. In the aftermath of the war, however, bipartisanship crumbled as Wilson sought to push his controversial peace program through Congress.

Wilson was an internationalist who envisioned a League of Nations that would act collectively to prevent aggression and war. His creation called for member nations to surrender a degree of their selfish national interests for the good of the community. When he and the Democrats in the Senate organized to push the Treaty of Versailles, which contained the charter of the League of Nations, through Congress, they found themselves opposed by two groups, both predominantly Republican. First were the so-called Lodge Republicans, who were determined to modify the covenant of the league. Personally, Lodge hated Wilson, but, in addition, the president had made no attempt to involve the Republican Party in the peacemaking process. The American delegation to the Paris Peace Conference of 1919 included neither a prominent Republican nor a member of the Senate. Finally, the Lodge Republicans were nationalists. They saw no reason why the United States should surrender its freedom of action and be committed by a majority of the league members to a course that was not necessarily in its interests. The other faction opposing the treaty was a group of isolationists, dubbed "irreconcilables" by the press, who were opposed to membership in an international organization under any conditions. Led by Senator William Borah of Idaho, the fourteen Republicans and one Democrat insisted that the United States ought to focus on domestic problems of poverty, ignorance, corporate wrongdoing, and political corruption. Many were midwestern Progressives who had more in common with Bryan and the Populists than they did with the eastern, business-dominated wing of the Republican Party. When Wilson refused to compromise with Lodge and his followers, the Senate rejected the treaty and with it membership in the League of Nations.

INTERWAR ISOLATIONISM

Isolationism was the byword of American foreign policy in the 1920s and 1930s. During the buildup to U.S. entry into World War I, a major shift in the two major parties' posture toward foreign affairs had taken place. Before 1916 Democrats had generally followed Bryan's lead in opposing a more assertive, interventionist role in world affairs. Under Wilson's leadership, however, the party gradually embraced a more active role for the United States in world affairs in which it identified its economic and strategic well-being with that of other democracies and in which it would be willing to use force in behalf of world peace. A similar change was taking place in the Republican Party. Its support of the Spanish-American War and acquisition of the Philippines, together with the activism of Roosevelt, Lodge, and other prominent Republicans, had earned the party a reputation for favoring a larger role for the United States in world affairs. But in 1916 the Republicans refused to seriously consider nominating Roosevelt for the presidency. In the debate over the Versailles treaty, the party identified itself with nationalism and isolationism against Wilsonian internationalism. In truth, the rank and file of the Republican Party, especially outside the East, identified more with Borah and his followers than with Lodge and his. In the 1930s, influenced by the Great Depression and the gathering war clouds in Europe, the Republican Party, as well as a majority of Americans, would invoke the concept of Fortress America and insist that the rise of the fascist powers in Europe and Asia posed no threat to the United States.

During the height of the Great Depression, the Democratic administration of Franklin Roosevelt chose not to challenge the Republican consensus. But as the 1930s progressed with Hitler gobbling up Austria and Czechoslovakia and Japan's invasion of China, Roosevelt began inching the country toward nonbelligerent alliance with Great Britain, China, and the other nations standing against the Axis. With the outbreak of World War II in 1939 and the fall of France in 1940, the debate over America's proper role in world affairs escalated, with the Democrats generally opting for interventionist policies and the Republicans clinging to isolation. In 1940 isolationists formed the America First Committee. The organization was Midwest-centered and made up largely of business-oriented opponents of the New Deal, although it included former Progressives and elements of the extreme left who espoused the "merchants of death" thesis. Opposing them were the Committee to Defend America by Aiding the Allies. Ideologically, interventionists tended to be liberal New Dealers and politically they were generally Democratic, although members of the eastern, liberal wing of the Republican Party supported all-out aid to the Allies. In the spring of 1941, the Roosevelt administration went head-to-head with the isolationists in Congress and secured passage of the Lend-Lease Act. With that measure the United States became a non-fighting ally of Great Britain and the Soviet Union. With the attack on Pearl Harbor on 7 December 1941, the United States became a full-fledged belligerent, and partisan opposition to intervention effectively ended.

WORLD WAR II AND ITS AFTERMATH

What changed dramatically during World War II, a shift neither understood nor appreciated by President Roosevelt and Secretary of State Cordell Hull, was the attitude of the American people. They were willing, as they had not been earlier, to assume their country's burden of responsibility in world affairs. Americans were guilty over their refusal to participate in the League of Nations. If only the most powerful nation in the world had thrown its weight behind a collective security system, the Holocaust and World War II might have been prevented. The war experience had been so painful and after 1945 the prospect of nuclear war so horrible that Americans were willing to make sacrifices in the form of economic aid for the rebuilding of Europe and to provide funds for defense against the looming threat of Soviet expansion. Reflecting these changed attitudes, Congress, on 21 September 1943, passed the Fulbright-Connally Resolution, which pledged U.S. participation in an international organization to keep the peace. Even before the passage of this measure, the leadership of the Republican Party had gathered on Mackinac Island, Michigan, to hammer out a position on the postwar order. Under the tutelage of Senator Arthur H. Vandenberg of Michigan and Governor Thomas E. Dewey of New York, the conferees devised a compromise resolution acceptable to most Republicans, which favored the formation of an international organization after the war.

The realization that positive measures would be needed to prevent a third world war convinced them that their leaders, regardless of party, must cooperate to best serve the national interests abroad. In order that the United States have a full and constructive impact on world events, Americans demanded that partisan politics be removed from foreign policy so that the United States could speak with a single voice in foreign affairs. Politicians, presidents, senators, and the members of the House of Representatives were to work to develop policies that would receive broad-based support.

Franklin D. Roosevelt, who was never fully committed to State Department planning for a postwar international organization, held a fuzzy conception of what the postwar world should look like. Roosevelt, however, did believe in cooperation among the great powers and summit diplomacy to maintain the peace. He was convinced that such cooperation had won the war and that major-power agreement would prevent another conflict. He never thought that the American people would support the stationing of U.S. troops abroad and the rebuilding of Western Europe. Moreover, to the president, bipartisanship meant total congressional acquiescence in the executive branch's conduct of foreign policy. In brief, he wanted to run foreign policy himself without congressional interference.

Into the breach stepped Senator Arthur Vandenberg. In an address to the Senate on 10 January 1945, marking another step in the establishment of bipartisan foreign policy, he rejected isolationism and pledged cooperation if the administration would state its plans for the postwar world with candor. Vandenberg announced that he would support the evolving United Nations. To further guarantee the peace and allay Russian distrust of the West, he called for a four-power military alliance to prevent another war and to ensure that Germany would not rearm. More important, he suggested maximum consultation and cooperation between the administration and the Senate in charting the course of American diplomacy in the postwar world.

The succession of Harry S. Truman to the presidency portended well for bipartisanship. Truman knew the senators as friends and had respect for their abilities. As a former member of the Senate establishment, he well understood the benefits of working closely with Senate and House committees, and as a new president, he needed all the support and advice he could garner. In the summer of 1945, the U.S. Senate ratified the charter of the United Nations by a vote of 89 to 2.

THE COLD WAR

From 1946 to 1949, with bipartisan support, the Truman administration gradually took a more confrontational stance toward Soviet expansion into Eastern Europe. With bipartisan support, Congress in March 1947 approved the Truman Doctrine, which appropriated funds to aid the Greek and Turkish governments as they combated communist-led revolution and external Soviet pressure, respectively. More important, Congress and the executive, Republicans and Democrats,

joined together to declare that it would be the policy of the United States "to support free peoples who are resisting attempted subjugation by armed minorities or by outside pressures." Later that year, the Marshall Plan, devised to fund the reconstruction of Western Europe, passed Congress with bipartisan support. Over the next four years, the United States poured more than $13 billion into areas ravaged by World War II, in part out of a belief that communism thrived in areas where economic deprivation and social instability prevailed. In 1949, by a wide bipartisan margin, Congress approved U.S. participation in the North Atlantic Treaty Organization (NATO), which committed its members to view an attack on one as an attack on all.

By 1950 anticommunism had become perhaps the most important theme in American politics, but it was no longer a rallying point for bipartisanship. The Republicans were deeply frustrated by their inability to win a presidential election. Truman's upset victory over Thomas E. Dewey in 1948 was particularly galling. The New Deal and the permanence of the emerging welfare state in America had left the Republicans without a compelling domestic issue. In the aftermath of Truman's victory, the party leadership decided that it could no longer afford a me-too position on American foreign policy. With Wisconsin Senator Joseph R. McCarthy charging that the administration had permitted infiltration of the federal government by Soviet espionage agents, and Senators Robert Taft and Everett Dirksen indicting Roosevelt and Truman for selling out Eastern Europe to the Kremlin, the Republicans launched a relentless campaign to portray the Democrats as soft on communism.

The effect of this campaign was to create an anticommunist consensus in the United States of monumental proportions. In late January 1950, President Truman directed the State and Defense departments "to make an overall review and reassessment of American foreign and defense policy" in light of the fall of China to the communists and the detonation of an atomic bomb by the Soviet Union (both in 1949). The result was National Security Council Document 68 (NSC 68), a policy paper committing the United States to combating the forces of international communism "on every front," to use the historian Thomas G. Paterson's phrase. This paper led to a fourfold increase in defense budgets and committed the United States to defending democracy against communism on the global stage. It paved the way for the transformation of the United States into a national security state and institutionalized a Cold War between the United States and its allies on the one hand and the Soviet Union and its allies on the other that would last until 1989. It led to U.S. intervention into the Korean War and provoked a series of brushfire conflicts throughout the developing world with the Soviets or Communist Chinese backing one side and the United States the other.

Meanwhile, the Republicans continued to hammer the Democrats with the soft-on-communism issue. In 1950, with General of the Army Douglas MacArthur in command, United Nations forces drove invading North Korean troops out of South Korea and pushed toward the Yalu River, the boundary between communist North Korea and Communist China. In November, 180,000 Chinese communist troops crossed the river and smashed MacArthur's troops. They retreated below the Thirty-eighth Parallel separating the two Koreas, but MacArthur soon halted the advance and mounted a counteroffensive. When the general regained the Thirty-eighth Parallel in March 1951, he asked permission of the Truman administration to once again proceed north. This time the president and his advisers refused. Undaunted, MacArthur wrote a letter to the leading Republican in the House of Representatives, Joseph Martin, in which he asserted that "there is no substitute for victory." When Truman subsequently relieved MacArthur of his command, the Republican leadership decided that they had the perfect presidential candidate for 1952. In May and June, Republican senators ostentatiously held hearings on MacArthur's firing. His demise and the refusal of the Truman administration to reunify Korea under a noncommunist government was clear proof that Democrats were either appeasers or soft-headed. When it became clear subsequently that MacArthur was defying not only Truman but also the Joint Chiefs of Staff, who took the position that an all-out war with Communist China would make it impossible for the United States to defend Western Europe, MacArthur's popularity faded, and the Republicans had to look for another war hero to run for president.

During the 1950s, many Democrats suspected that Dwight D. Eisenhower's frequent appeals to bipartisanship were merely attempts to trick the Democratic Party into sharing the blame if policies already decided upon failed. Senate Democratic Majority Leader Lyndon B. Johnson continued to act as a partner with President Eisenhower and his secretary of state, John Foster Dulles, in pursuing a policy of combating communism through a policy of cooperation with allies and economic and military aid to noncommunist developing nations. The Eisenhower administration actually received more support in Congress from Democrats than from the conservative wing of his own party. Indeed, led by Senator Robert Taft and former President Herbert Hoover, conservative Republicans espoused a form of neo-isolationism. They insisted that America's resources were limited and that it ought to concentrate on perfecting its own institutions and guaranteeing its own prosperity. They were particularly adamant about the need to balance the budget. The neo-isolationists opposed the stationing of U.S. troops in Europe as part of a NATO armed force, and they somewhat paradoxically warned about the perils of being drawn into a land war in Asia. The Eisenhower-Johnson axis prevailed, however, and in December 1954 Congress approved a pact between the United States and Chiang Kai-shek's Nationalist government on Formosa that committed the United States to stationing troops "in and about" the island. In 1957 bipartisan support led to congressional approval of the Eisenhower Doctrine, empowering the president to use military force if any government in the Middle East requested protection against "overt armed aggression from any nation controlled by International Communism."

It was with Democratic help that the Eisenhower administration fended off a proposed constitutional amendment authored by the conservative Republican senator John Bricker of Ohio, which would effectively have given Congress veto power over executive agreements with foreign powers.

During the presidential campaign of 1960, Democrat John F. Kennedy, running against Vice President Richard M. Nixon, criticized the Eisenhower administration for being passive and unimaginative in dealing with the forces of international communism. He promised a more active policy in which the United States would fund and participate in "counterinsurgencies" against communist guerrillas, augment America's nuclear stockpile, and continue to furnish military and economic aid to developing nations. Kennedy and his advisers also promised to open dialogue with noncommunist leftist elements fighting for social and economic justice. Kennedy won, but his pragmatic intentions were soon dashed on the rocks of Fidel Castro and communist Cuba. When the new president failed to press home the abortive Bay of Pigs invasion in 1961, which was intended to rally popular opposition to Castro and lead to his overthrow, Republicans once again raised the "soft on communism" cry. From that point on, the president tended to base his assessment of nearly every hot spot in the Cold War upon his bitter experience with Cuba.

VIETNAM: CONFLICT AT HOME AND ABROAD

By the 1960s the salient features of American foreign policy were the domino theory, the Munich analogy, and the notion of a monolithic communist threat. American strategists believed that, in a world characterized by a life-and-death struggle between the forces of totalitarian communism and democratic capitalism, the fall of one nation to communism would inevitably lead to the fall of its neighbors. Moreover, to acquiesce in appeasement would only lead to further appeasement. Thus did the administrations of Democrats John F. Kennedy and Lyndon B. Johnson and the Republican administration of Richard M. Nixon feel it necessary to involve America in the burgeoning conflict between communist North Vietnam and noncommunist South Vietnam. At first there was strong bipartisan support for making Vietnam a testing ground for America's will to combat communism. In August 1964, after reports that North Vietnamese torpedo boats had attacked U.S. destroyers on the high seas in the Gulf of Tonkin, the Johnson administration secured Senate passage (with only two dissenting votes) of the Tonkin Gulf Resolution. In it Congress empowered the president to "take all necessary measures to repel any armed attacks against the forces of the United States and to prevent further aggression." The State Department subsequently called the resolution "the functional equivalent of a declaration of war." President Johnson did not reveal at the time that the U.S. vessels had been engaged in secret espionage and raiding activities directed against North Vietnam.

As the war progressed, opposition to it mounted in Congress. The activist foreign policies of the post–World War II era that produced the war in Southeast Asia were a product of the melding of conservative anticommunists who defined national security in terms of bases and alliances and who were basically xenophobic

(many of them former Republican neo-isolationists), and liberal reformers who were determined to safeguard the national interest by exporting democracy and facilitating overseas economic prosperity. By 1966 a coalition of moderate-to-liberal senators, led by the powerful chairman of the Senate Foreign Relations Committee, J. William Fulbright, began to express doubts not only about the war in Vietnam but about the assumptions that underlay it. To them, nationalism was more important than the Cold War in precipitating Third World conflicts. The communist world, especially given the emerging Sino-Soviet split, seemed hardly monolithic. In addition, there was no convincing proof that if South Vietnam fell under the rule of communists, Thailand, Indonesia, and the Philippines would follow. Finally, and most important, congressional dissidents pointed out that most of the regimes the United States was defending in the name of democracy, including the governments of South Vietnam, were either authoritarian or totalitarian.

Lyndon Johnson had doubts about the war in Southeast Asia, but in order to get his domestic Great Society programs through Congress he perceived that he would have to appease the so-called conservative coalition—Southern Democrats and Republicans who had allied to battle the growth of the welfare state and federally mandated civil rights since the late 1940s—who were ardent in their anticommunism and hence supported the war in Vietnam. Johnson was obsessed with consensus and not just because of his desire to achieve domestic reform. He truly believed in the efficacy of bipartisanship in foreign policymaking. The contradictions inherent in the Cold War proved too much for the Texan, however. In 1968, facing opposition from the liberal and moderate wings of his own party, Johnson opted not to run for reelection, paving the way for the presidency of Republican Richard Nixon.

Nixon and his national security adviser and secretary of state, Henry Kissinger, were determined to create a new international order that would simultaneously contain communism and restore America's freedom of action. The new president could use his strong anticommunist credentials as a cover to build bridges to the communist superpowers. Once disarmed, the Soviet Union and Communist China could be persuaded to take their places as responsible members of the international community. Then, the great powers could act to control revolutions that threatened international stability. Unfortunately, such a pol-

J. WILLIAM FULBRIGHT

James William Fulbright, educator, senator, and Vietnam-era dissenter, was born in Sumner, Missouri, on 9 April 1905, and was raised in Fayetteville, Arkansas. In 1942 he ran successfully for Congress, where he made a name for himself by cosponsoring the Fulbright-Connally Resolution, which placed Congress on record as favoring membership in a postwar collective security organization. In 1944 he captured a Senate seat, and two years later introduced legislation creating the international exchange program that bears his name. In 1950 he became chair of the Senate Foreign Relations Committee and served in that capacity until his departure from the Senate in 1975. In 1993, President William Jefferson Clinton, one of Fulbright's protégés, presented him with the Medal of Freedom. Fulbright died on 9 February 1995 following a massive stroke suffered two years earlier.

The themes that dominated the public life and work of Fulbright were cultural tolerance and international cooperation. During his thirty-two years in Congress, he appealed to the people of the world but particularly Americans to appreciate and tolerate other cultures and political systems without condoning armed aggression or human rights violations. His dedication to internationalism generally and the United Nations specifically and his passionate support of the Fulbright Exchange Program followed logically. He was convinced that the exchange of students and scholars would increase understanding and breed political elites capable of pursuing enlightened foreign policies.

Frightened by the resurgence of the radical right and greatly impressed by Soviet Premier Nikita Khrushchev's conciliatory visit to the United States in 1959, Fulbright moved beyond competitive coexistence to embrace the concept of détente. He was pleased with the Kennedy administration's flexible response to the communist threat and, following the Cuban missile crisis in 1963, with its willingness to make a fresh start with the Soviet Union. During the 1964 presidential election, Democrat Fulbright took the point in the foreign policy debate with Republican Senator Barry Goldwater and the "true believers." He was a devoted advocate of the liberal internationalism espoused by the Kennedy-Johnson administrations, that is, he believed that the United States ought to deter Sino-Soviet aggression through military preparedness and combat communist wars of liberation through foreign aid and counterinsurgency, but at the same time, he was committed to peaceful existence. The communist world, he argued, would eventually collapse of its own internal contradictions.

Fulbright parted company with Lyndon Johnson because he believed that his longtime political comrade-in-arms had sold out to the very forces that Johnson had defeated in 1964. The decision to intervene in the Dominican Republic and to escalate the war in Vietnam signaled to the senator the triumph of the nationalist, xenophobic, imperialist tendencies that had always lurked beneath the surface of American society. Fulbright came to the conclusion that the war was not a case of North Vietnam aggression against South Vietnam. Rather, the north's Ho Chi Minh represented the forces of authentic Vietnamese nationalism and the war in the south pitted an American-supported puppet government against indigenous revolutionaries who were seeking social justice and national self-determination.

In February 1966, the Senate Foreign Relations Committee held televised hearings on Vietnam. The misgivings expressed began the national debate on the wisdom of U.S. policy toward Southeast Asia. From then until Johnson's departure from the presidency, Fulbright labored to undermine the consensus that supported the war in Vietnam. In 1967 he published *The Arrogance of Power,* a best-selling and sweeping critique of American foreign policy.

Concerning the executive-legislative prerogatives, Fulbright's concern was not with a particular interpretation of the Constitution. In the aftermath of World War II, with the tide of isolationism still running strong, an assertive, active executive was needed to advance the cause of internationalism and keep the peace. But over the years, the stresses and strains of fighting the Cold War under the shadow of a nuclear holocaust had taken their toll. Its actions sometimes circumscribed and sometimes dictated by a fanatical anticommunism, the executive had embarked on an imperial foreign policy that had involved America in its longest war and created a maze of international commitments and overseas bases not seen since the British empire was in full bloom. The only way to check this trend, Fulbright believed, was to restore congressional prerogatives in foreign policymaking.

icy was profoundly insensitive to the social and economic injustice and intense nationalism that characterized most Third World societies and that fueled the revolutions that the U.S. government hoped to contain. Although he quickly became disillusioned with Nixon, primarily because of the continuation of the war in Vietnam, Senator Fulbright was enamored of Henry Kissinger and his vision of a peaceful world based on rationality and a concert of interests. The administration's openings to China and Russia and its efforts to negotiate an end to the war in Vietnam generally enjoyed Democratic support—sometimes more so than from conservative Republicans.

Nixon had promised "peace with honor" in Vietnam. The president had no intention of surrendering South Vietnam to the communists; he merely wanted to turn the ground war over to the army of the Republic of Vietnam while continuing to furnish all-out military aid and to bomb communist positions throughout Southeast Asia. Congress, especially the Senate, had different ideas. A bipartisan coalition spearheaded by Fulbright and Republicans John Sherman Cooper of Kentucky and Jacob Javits of New York moved to limit the executive branch's power to make war. That effort culminated in passage of the War Powers Act by Congress in the fall of 1973 over President Nixon's veto. The measure obligated the president to inform Congress within forty-eight hours of the deployment of U.S. military forces abroad and bound him to withdraw them in sixty days in the absence of explicit congressional endorsement. The following week the House and Senate endorsed an amendment to the Military Procurement Authorization Act banning the funding of any U.S. military action in any part of Indochina.

America's ignominious withdrawal from Vietnam and the Watergate scandal created a crisis of confidence in national politics unknown since the Great Depression. The war in Vietnam brought home to Americans the truth that there were severe limitations to their nation's ability to determine the course of global events. Not only did it appear that the forces of international communism had scored a clear victory, but also that in the process of defending its perceived interests, the United States had transgressed many of the values and principles for which it claimed to be fighting. Moreover, Americans' sense that they had been lied to and deliberately deceived during crucial periods in the Vietnam War created an attitude of deep cynicism toward government at all levels, particularly the federal government.

THE CARTER YEARS

In an effort to restore integrity to the presidency, Americans elected Jimmy Carter in 1976. A nuclear engineer and devout Southern Baptist, Carter promised to continue the struggle against the forces of international communism but to insist on respect for human rights whether from Cold War foe or Cold War friend. During the campaign, he condemned Henry Kissinger for his secrecy and his penchant for power politics. Carter promised open covenants openly arrived at, recalling memories of Woodrow Wilson. The president's belief that he could make morality the basis of American foreign policy and simultaneously safeguard its strategic and economic interests was flawed. His emphasis on human rights alienated friend and foe alike and led to renewed charges of Yankee imperialism.

There was some bipartisan cooperation during the Carter years. Democrats led by Senator Robert Byrd of West Virginia and moderate Republicans led by Senator Howard Baker of Tennessee banded together in Congress to ratify a new set of Panama Canal treaties that provided for the gradual transfer of sovereignty over the Canal Zone to Panama. The treaty was approved by a narrow margin of 68 to 32. If support for the pact was bipartisan, so was opposition. Nationalists led by Republican Governor Ronald Reagan of California and former Alabama Governor George C. Wallace argued that the treaty was just one more instance of America acting through weakness, surrendering part of its sovereignty, and opening the door to the communists. Despite Senate ratification of the Canal treaties, as well as the Camp David Accords, in which Carter persuaded the governments of Israel and Egypt to agree to "a framework for peace," the president quickly earned a reputation for ineptness that alienated both Republicans and Democrats. The Iran hostage crisis, deteriorating relations with the Soviet Union over human rights and the war in Afghanistan, and the Arab boycott and resulting oil shortage reduced support in Congress for Carter's foreign policy almost to zero.

NEOCONSERVATISM AND THE REAGAN YEARS

In the election of 1980, in which one out of every four voters settled on a candidate during the last week of the election, Ronald Reagan scored a landslide victory, outpolling Carter in the electoral college 489 to 49. Unlike Richard Nixon's landslide victory in 1972, Reagan's thumping of Jimmy Carter seemed to signal a sea change in American politics, a major shift from a liberal to a conservative majority. Whereas the Republicans made virtually no gains in Congress in 1972, they gained twelve seats in the Senate four years later (defeating such liberal Democratic heavyweights as Gaylord Nelson of Wisconsin, George McGovern of North Dakota, and Frank Church of Idaho) and thirty-three places in the House of Representatives. In fact, Reagan's victory coincided with and was in part made possible by the continuing growth and political activism of the New Right.

Neoconservatism was a blend of both old and new. It encompassed traditional positions such as anticommunism, opposition to government intervention and bureaucracy, and support for free enterprise and a balanced budget. At the same time, the New Right included Americans, many of them working-class Democrats, who were outraged at social issues that they believed attacked and undermined conventional morality, the nuclear family, and religious faith. Thus did they mobilize in anger over school busing, bans on prayer in public schools, the 1973 *Roe* v. *Wade* Supreme Court decision legalizing abortion, the extension of the First Amendment to cover pornography, the ongoing campaign to have Congress pass the Equal Rights Amendment (ERA), and the extension of antidiscrimination laws to cover homosexuals. Demographic patterns continued to favor the Republicans. The 1980 census indicated a shift of seventeen seats in the House of Representatives from the Northeast and Midwest to the South and West. The so-called Sun Belt was relatively white, relatively nonunion, and overwhelmingly conservative on fiscal matters and many social issues.

But, in fact, a closer look at the election statistics for 1980 reveals that massive voter apathy had as much to do with Reagan's election and GOP successes in Congress as the "conservative revolution." Reagan was elected by 28 percent of the voting population. In 1980 the largest voting bloc (47 percent) was comprised of those who did not vote. Between the 1960s and 1970s, the number of people believing that the government was run for the wealthy and influential few grew from 28 percent to 65 percent. Those who were convinced that the people governing them were basically intelligent and competent fell from 69 percent to 29 percent. Ironically, the disaffected

middle and upper classes continued to vote Republican or switched parties, while the disaffected working classes and poor stopped voting, making their view that the government was controlled by a wealthy and powerful elite a self-fulfilling prophecy.

Reagan's view of Soviet communism seemed frozen in the mid-1950s. The Kremlin, Reagan was convinced, was at the head of a worldwide conspiracy to export totalitarianism to all parts of the world. For the new president, as for members of the Moral Majority, Soviet communism represented all the negative forces abroad in the world: atheism, state socialism, and immorality. Likewise, anticommunism was a crucial component of the struggle to resurrect the hallowed principles of liberty, free enterprise, patriotism, and family values. To overcome the Soviet Union's alleged "margin of superiority," the administration committed to a series of new weapons systems including the MX missile system, the B-1 bomber, and the Strategic Defense Initiative (SDI), a network of lasers and particle beams projected from ground stations and satellites in space. These "death rays" would allegedly destroy incoming enemy missiles before they entered the earth's atmosphere. Shamelessly invoking the domino theory and the image of a monolithic communist threat, the Reagan administration began funneling massive amounts of arms and money to the government of El Salvador in its battle against leftist guerrillas and to the contras, right-wing rebels battling the Marxist Sandinista regime in Nicaragua.

Congress took issue not so much with the aims of the Reagan administration's foreign policy but with its methods. Concerned over charges of U.S. intervention into Nicaraguan internal affairs and stories of atrocities committed by the contras, in 1982 Congress passed the Boland Amendment, sponsored by Representative Edward P. Boland of Massachusetts, limiting Central Intelligence Agency aid to the contras to $24 million and stipulating that none of the funds be used to overthrow the Sandinistas. Reagan, who shared Nixon and Kissinger's views on executive control of foreign policy, directed his subordinates to circumvent the law. The Pentagon began donating "surplus" equipment to the contras while CIA agents trained the rebels in assassination techniques and coordinated attacks on transportation and port facilities. In 1984, an angry Congress passed an updated version of the Boland Amendment that barred the CIA or any other agency involved in intelligence activities from aiding the contras. Meanwhile, a bloody life-and-death struggle between Iran and Iraq had erupted in 1980. Iraq, ruled by the secular military strongman Saddam Hussein, and Iran, controlled by a group of extreme Islamic clerics headed by the Ayatollah Khomeini, were age-old rivals. This new chapter in their ongoing struggle was the product of an intense competition for regional leadership and control of petroleum resources, refining facilities, and strategic ports. The State Department feared both and attempted to keep either from winning a decisive victory. From 1981 to 1986, the Reagan administration secretly funneled aid to Iran but from 1987 on tilted toward Iraq. The second Boland Amendment only strengthened the White House's determination to aid the "freedom fighters" in Nicaragua. With Reagan's approval, a team of National Security Council and CIA officials began raising money from abroad from anticommunist governments and from wealthy conservatives at home. In 1985 the president approved a scheme whereby the United States would secretly sell large numbers of antitank missiles to Iran with the proceeds going to aid the contras in Nicaragua. Revelations concerning the deal touched off a year of congressional investigations, administration stonewalling, document shredding, and lying. It became clear that Reagan had been fully informed throughout the Iran-Contra deal; Congress settled for indicting several of his lieutenants. That body was unwilling to press the matter further for fear of incurring the public's wrath at its bringing down a second president in a decade.

The making of American foreign policy in the 1980s and into the next decade was not characterized either by conspicuous bipartisan strife or by conspicuous bipartisanship. Both parties wanted to stem the tide of communism in Latin America, to prevent the Soviet Union from profiting from the Arab-Israeli crisis, and to maintain superiority in nuclear weapons. Democrats tended to be less supportive of large defense budgets and more critical of authoritarian regimes that used anticommunism to elicit aid and support from the U.S. government than Republicans. Democrats tended to be less confrontational toward the Soviet Union and Communist China than Republicans and more willing to countenance peaceful coexistence. There were notable exceptions, however; Senator Henry "Scoop" Jackson of Washington, for example, was a liberal on domestic issues and a hard-line cold warrior. Reagan's campaign to prevent the spread of Marx-

ism-Leninism in the developing world and his determination to spend the Soviet Union into oblivion garnered less support among Democrats than Republicans. Both parties, of course, rejoiced in the end of the Cold War.

BIPARTISANSHIP IN THE 1990S

President George H. W. Bush's decision to go to war in 1990–1991 to evict Iraq from Kuwait captured widespread bipartisan support. Because the Defense Department carefully controlled the media and because the United States achieved its stated, limited objectives there was no repeat of the deep divisions that had accompanied the Vietnam War. With the end of the Cold War, a new set of issues emerged to dominate the Clinton years: terrorism, ethnic cleansing, sectarian violence, free trade, environmentalism. Although Democrats and Republicans fought bitterly over domestic social and economic issues, they were not clearly divided over foreign policy matters. Like the Clinton administration itself, the two major parties were more reactive than proscriptive, more pragmatic than ideological.

William Jefferson Clinton's election to the presidency in 1992 hardly represented a sea change in American politics. It certainly had nothing to do with foreign affairs. Clinton won because of George Bush's mishandling of the economy and because the Arkansan was able to keep traditional Democratic constituencies in place—among them African Americans, labor unionists, and intellectuals—and attract moderate conservatives by promising to reduce the bureaucracy and cut the budget. In foreign affairs, Bill Clinton had promised, in rather vague terms, to address the problems of the post–Cold War era. The United States, he said, should provide aid to the former Soviet Union to help it down the road to democracy and free enterprise. Indeed, there were Wilsonian overtones to his foreign policy statements. Advancing democracy should be the object of "a long-term Western strategy," he said. At the same time, the president emphasized that the focus of future foreign policy would be the global economy. America would have to learn how to compete peacefully with Japan and the German-led European community. Finally, Clinton seemed to echo former President Carter in calling for an American-led campaign to ensure respect for human rights. In the years that followed, the Clinton administration placed peacekeeping troops in Bosnia and Kosovo to keep ethnic and religious conflicts in the former Yugoslavia from embroiling the Balkans and perhaps all of Europe in war. The administration intervened in Haiti in 1994 under a UN resolution, helping to bring down the military dictatorship of General Raul Cedras, and pushed through Congress the North American Free Trade Agreement (NAFTA), which provided for the gradual elimination of tariffs and other trade barriers between the United States on the one hand and Canada and Mexico on the other.

In 1994 the Republicans captured both houses of Congress, but conflicts over foreign policy did not split along party lines. Indeed, far more Democrats, representing organized labor, were opposed to NAFTA than Republicans. There were certainly congressional opponents of American participation in Balkan peacekeeping operations, but that opposition, like the support for the initiative, was bipartisan. Republican antipathy toward Clinton was intense, but that animosity had only a marginal impact on foreign policy. As the turn of the century approached, the terms "liberal" and "conservative" were in transition, and, as a result, so were the major parties. Bipartisanship in foreign policy reigned, even if by default.

BIBLIOGRAPHY

Ambrosius, Lloyd E. *Woodrow Wilson and the American Diplomatic Tradition: The Treaty Fight in Perspective.* New York and Cambridge, Mass., 1987. The best study of the conflict between Wilson and opponents of the treaty.

Atkinson, Rick. *Crusade: The Untold Story of the Persian Gulf War.* Boston, 1993. A balanced, accurate, if necessarily incomplete account.

Beale, Howard K. *Theodore Roosevelt and the Rise of America to World Power.* Baltimore, 1956. Still a masterpiece, surveying Roosevelt's internal and external world.

Beisner, Robert L. *From the Old Diplomacy to the New, 1865–1900.* 2d ed. Arlington Heights, Ill., 1986. A survey of the new imperialism by a leading authority on the period.

Bemis, Samuel Flagg. *John Quincy Adams and the Foundations of American Foreign Policy.* New York, 1949. Still a must-read for students of American Foreign Policy.

Berman, Larry. *Lyndon Johnson's War: The Road to Stalemate in Vietnam.* New York, 1989. A concise analysis of Johnson's decisions to escalate the war.

Beschloss, Michael R. *The Crisis Years: Kennedy and Khrushchev, 1960–1963.* New York, 1991.

Brown, Roger Hamilton. *The Republic in Peril: 1812.* New York, 1964. A classic analysis of politics and public opinion before and during the War of 1812.

Campbell, Charles S. *The Transformation of American Foreign Relations, 1865–1900.* New York, 1976. A classic example of the "open door" approach.

Carothers, Thomas. *In the Name of Democracy: U.S. Policy Toward Latin America in the Reagan Years.* Berkeley, Calif., 1991. The only credible treatment.

Charles, Joseph. *The Origins of the American Party System: Three Essays.* Williamsburg, Va., 1956. Three provocative essays.

Cherny, Robert W. *American Politics in the Gilded Age, 1868–1900.* Wheeling, Ill., 1997. The most balanced treatment.

Cole, Donald B. *The Presidency of Andrew Jackson.* Lawrence, Kans., 1993. An excellent overview.

Cole, Wayne S. *Roosevelt and the Isolationists, 1932–1945.* Lincoln, Neb., 1983. The definitive work on the subject.

Combs, Jerald A. *The Jay Treaty: Political Battleground of the Founding Fathers.* Berkeley, Calif., 1970. Combs remains the leading authority on Jay's Treaty.

Cooper, John Milton, Jr. *The Warrior and the Priest: Woodrow Wilson and Theodore Roosevelt.* Cambridge, Mass., 1983. A comparative study by a leading Progressive Era historian.

Elkins, Stanley, and Eric McKitrick. *The Age of Federalism: The Early American Republic, 1788–1800.* New York, 1993.

Ferguson, Thomas, and Joel Rogers. *Right Turn: The Decline of the Democrats and the Future of American Politics.* New York, 1986. An insightful analysis of contemporary politics.

Freeland, Richard M. *The Truman Doctrine and the Origins of McCarthyism: Foreign Policy, Domestic Politics, and Internal Security, 1946–1948.* New York, 1985.

Gaddis, John Lewis. *Strategies of Containment: A Critical Appraisal of Post War American National Security Policy.* Oxford and New York, 1982. The authoritative survey of American Cold War foreign policy.

———. *The United States and the End of the Cold War: Implications, Reconsiderations, Provocations*. New York, 1992. A provocative essay on the end of the Cold War.

Gienapp, William E. *The Origins of the Republican Party, 1852–1856*. New York, 1987. The best treatment of this complex phenomenon.

Gilbert, Felix. *To the Farewell Address: Ideas of Early American Foreign Policy*. Princeton, N.J., 1961.

Hamby, Alonzo L. *Man of the People: A Life of Harry S. Truman*. New York, 1995. The best biography of one of liberalism's founders.

Hersh, Seymour M. *The Price of Power: Kissinger in the Nixon White House*. New York, 1983.

Horsman, Reginald. *Race and Manifest Destiny: The Origins of American Racial Anglo-Saxonism*. Cambridge, Mass., 1981. A classic treatment of a key element in U.S. expansionism.

Immerman, Richard H., ed. *John Foster Dulles and the Diplomacy of the Cold War*. Princeton, N.J., 1990.

Isserman, Maurice. *If I Had a Hammer: The Death of the Old Left and the Birth of the New Left*. New York, 1987.

Jones, Howard. *To the Webster-Ashburton Treaty: A Study in Anglo-American Relations, 1783–1843*. Chapel Hill, 1977. The enduring work on Anglo-American relations during the Republic's first century.

Kaplan, Lawrence S. *Jefferson and France: An Essay on Politics and Political Ideas*. New Haven, Conn., 1967.

Kaufman, Burton I. *The Presidency of James Earl Carter, Jr.* Lawrence, Kans., 1993. An excellent survey.

McQuaid, Kim. *The Anxious Years: America in the Vietnam-Watergate Era*. New York, 1989. The best overview of the period.

Osborne, Thomas J. *"Empire Can Wait": American Opposition to Hawaiian Annexation, 1893–1898*. Kent, Ohio, 1981.

Pletcher, David M. *The Diplomacy of Annexation: Texas, Oregon, and the Mexican War*. Columbia, Mo., 1973. The definitive study.

Sellers, Charles. *The Market Revolution: Jacksonian America, 1815–1846*. New York, 1991.

Sharp, James Roger. *American Politics in the Early Republic: The New Nation in Crisis*. New Haven, Conn., 1993.

Spanier, John. *The Truman-MacArthur Controversy and the Korean War*. Cambridge, Mass., 1959. The best treatment of this crucial episode.

Varg, Paul A. *New England and Foreign Relations, 1789–1850*. Hanover, N.H., 1983.

Watson, Harry L. *Liberty and Power: The Politics of Jacksonian America*. New York, 1990.

Watts, Steven. *The Republic Reborn: War and the Making of Liberal America, 1790–1820*. Baltimore, 1987. An excellent study of the roots of American liberalism.

Widenor, William C. *Henry Cabot Lodge and the Search for an American Foreign Policy*. Berkeley, Calif., 1980. A classic political/foreign affairs biography.

Woods, Randall B. *J. William Fulbright, Vietnam, and the Search for a Cold War Foreign Policy*. Cambridge, Mass., and New York, 1998.

Woods, Randall B., and Howard Jones. *Dawning of the Cold War: The United States Quest for Order*. Athens, Ga., 1991.

See also CONGRESSIONAL POWER; DEPARTMENT OF STATE; ISOLATIONISM; THE NATIONAL INTEREST; PARTY POLITICS; PRESIDENTIAL POWER; PUBLIC OPINION.

BLOCKADES

Frank J. Merli and Robert H. Ferrell

Blockade, historically speaking, has been a maritime measure, to restrict entrance to a harbor or its environs. The word has been stretched to include entire countries. Sometimes "blockade" has meant enforcement or threat of enforcement by land rather than by sea, along the borders of an opposing nation or nations. The blockade has always been an attractive concept to the American people and government, for it has been seen as a way of restricting war and even of preserving peace. In time of war, a narrowly drawn blockade might ward off a conflict and allow a neutral nation, perhaps the United States, to carry on its trade much as before. In time of peace, a blockade might prove sufficient to discourage a quarreling nation from employing military force. According to international law there can be pacific as well as belligerent blockades, but most, of course, have been instituted in wartime. Although other terms—"quarantine," "interdiction," "interception"—have gained currency over the years, the basic concept of blockade has remained an important component of American diplomatic and military policy.

DEVELOPMENT OF THE LAW

The law of blockade, that is, the rules governing proper legal practice, originated in the early struggles for supremacy among the maritime nations of Europe in the fifteenth and sixteenth centuries. During that time, belligerents hacked and hewed, by sea as by land, and neutrals constantly found themselves involved in quarrels, whether they wished to be or not. Early in the seventeenth century a compromise of sorts emerged between neutrals and belligerents, in which the latter undertook to define carefully the list of items that were contraband and subject to capture. They also agreed that blockades could not merely be proclaimed: acceptable practice required that a port be cordoned off by the sta-

tioning of naval vessels at its entrance. As originally conceived, a blockade was a maritime equivalent of a land siege. When a port was properly blockaded, an investing belligerent could prohibit all trade with that port, including that of neutral nations. The idea apparently appeared first in a 1614 treaty between the Netherlands and Sweden. A refinement of the concept of effective blockade appeared in a Dutch announcement or *Placaart* of 1630, issued after consultation with private jurists and judges of the courts of admiralty. Its first article declared: "Neutral ships and goods passing in or out of the ports of the enemy in Flanders; or being so near them, that there can be no doubt but they will go into them, shall be confiscated: Because their High Mightinesses continually beset those ports with ships of war, in order to hinder any commerce with the enemy." Interestingly enough, the drafters of this rule justified it as "an ancient custom, warranted by the example of all princes"—a useful, if not entirely accurate, assessment of prior practice. The "law" of blockade, however, unlike other branches of international law, owed less to statutory enactments and more to the customs and precedents of naval officers and admiralty lawyers as they sought to bend the definitions of blockade to accommodate national interests, especially the need for victory in war.

In the early modern period of European history, with its frequent maritime wars, new rules of blockade rapidly evolved, and as they grew they acquired increasing importance as effective instruments of naval coercion. But those rules never remained static. They required frequent adjustment to new circumstances, technological innovation, and modified strategic concepts. More importantly, over the centuries, blockades had to be adapted to the exigencies created by new definitions of the nature of war.

From the mid-seventeenth century onward, new concepts of blockade were developed, and soon the nations of Europe agreed on some basic rules governing their use. Hugo Grotius, the father of international law, set out a rule that foodstuffs, so-called provisions, should be treated as contraband only when an attempt was made to introduce them into a blockaded port in extremis, and this humane refinement received general approval from naval authorities. For their part, legal theorists such as Cornelis van Bynkershoek generally agreed that international law recognized no right of access to ports effectively closed by naval squadrons. When the United States drew up a model treaty of commerce in 1776 for submission to foreign nations, it overlooked an article defining blockades, but soon remedied that omission. American statesmen took inspiration from the attempted Armed Neutrality of 1780. Catherine the Great sought to bring together some of the European neutrals in the general war then raging, to unite them in a pact of armed neutrality that would enforce an expanded definition of neutral rights in wartime. Russia proposed that "the denomination of a blockaded port is to be given only to one which has the enemy vessels stationed sufficiently near to cause an evident danger to the attempt to enter." Although little came of Catherine's initiative, the government of the United States incorporated this proviso into its Treaty Plan of 1784, and it sought international recognition of this principle.

In the seventeenth and eighteenth centuries, the practices of nations vis-à-vis blockade tended to follow their treaty obligations, and those treaties spelled out a wide variety of reciprocal rights and duties that would become operative in time of war. Naturally, a good many of the arrangements concerned the proper implementation of the rules of blockade, for nations that were neutral had no wish to become embroiled in the quarrels of their neighbors. It might be said that no branch of international relations received more attention than the search for a viable definition of blockade, one that would protect the rights of neutrals without too seriously impeding the war efforts of belligerents. Part of the reason for a certain tolerance on the subject stemmed from necessity: the naval powers of that day, Britain and Holland, depended upon Scandinavian sources of naval stores. Prudence dictated a circumspect policy toward the northern neutrals of Europe, while the conditions of warfare made such a policy easier to pursue.

In that time of limited war, full-scale blockades were rarely imposed, for men-of-war and privateers usually found it more profitable to waylay merchantmen that might be subject to seizure and condemnation in a prize court (with consequent enrichment of the captors). In prize law, problems of blockade violation remained largely a subdivision of the law of contraband until the era of the wars of the French Revolution. In the 1790s, British Admiralty officials began to pay closer attention to the problems posed by blockade. The altered circumstances of the time required new approaches, and all concessions toward neutrals had to be reevaluated.

The struggle that engulfed Europe from 1793 to 1815 ushered in a new era of international relations. Changed conditions of warfare required the belligerents to impose heavy restrictions on trade with the enemy. Almost at once, Great Britain and France narrowed their definitions of neutral rights; and as the struggle between them intensified, both nations demonstrated that they would take whatever measures seemed necessary to defeat the enemy. At one point the French proclaimed that there were no neutrals, and the British echoed that sentiment. According to one commentator, international law, if it existed at all, had been known only "through the declamations of publicists and its violation by governments." Whatever the cynicism of that mot, it accurately reflected the views of an age caught up in revolutionary upheaval.

When the wars of the French Revolution led Britain to an assault on America's presumed right of unfettered trade with all the nations of the world, belligerent as well as neutral, Secretary of State Thomas Jefferson drew up a strong protest. The provision order of 1793 had instructed British naval commanders to bring in for preemptive purchase all neutral ships en route to French ports with cargoes of corn, flour, or meal. By this arbitrary redefinition of contraband, by an order that would keep American grain out of French markets in Europe and in the West Indies, by a decree that arrogantly restricted American produce to the ports of Britain or its allies, the infamous provision order threatened the new nation's honor and interests. The threat led Jefferson to a spirited defense of America's canons of commerce and international law. After denouncing the British order as contrary to the law of nations and asserting that food could never be classified as contraband, he acknowledged a "single restriction" on the right of neutrals to use the seas freely: "that of not furnishing to either party implements merely of war . . . nor anything whatever to a place blockaded by its enemy." Jefferson thus put his finger on an important point, for if food could be classified as contraband, as an implement of war, British cruisers could legally seize it on American ships. If an order in council could declare entire islands of the West Indies or the entire coast of France blockaded, then Americans could carry nothing whatever to those places.

In the practice of the times, a legal blockade "entitled the blockading power to intercept all commerce with the blockaded port and to confiscate ships and cargoes of whatever description attempting to breach the blockade." As a nation that lived largely by export of foodstuffs, America had a vested interest in the outcome of arguments on the fine points of international law.

But Jefferson could not bring the British around to his view. Nor could John Jay when, in 1794, he went to London to draw up a commercial treaty and to resolve a number of simmering disputes, including claims for damages that had grown out of the British attacks on American commerce. In part, Jay sought to bring the British around to Jefferson's definition of neutral rights, to get them to agree that foodstuffs could never be classified as contraband (although they might be captured on ships attempting to enter a blockaded port). In these negotiations the Americans also desired British assent to the definition of effective blockade incorporated in the Armed Neutrality of 1780. Unable to obtain these arrangements, Jay had to be satisfied with a British promise to indemnify American citizens for captured articles "not generally regarded as contraband," and for assurances that vessels approaching a blockaded port would be turned away rather than captured, if the captain had no knowledge of such blockade. Beyond these innocuous concessions the British refused to go.

Meanwhile, on the French side during the 1790s, matters became so trying for the United States that a quasi-war broke out in 1798, largely because of French interference with American commerce. Lasting two years, the war ended with the Treaty of Mortefontaine (better known as the Convention of 1800), which contained a Napoleonic affirmation of neutral rights, including a narrow definition of blockade. No altruism dictated such a concession; in all probability Napoleon sought to embarrass the British for their provision order and for other executive acts of the British cabinet that both interfered with his supplies and irritated neutrals by their arbitrary nature. Or he may have sought to lure the United States into another league of armed neutrals that was then forming in Europe.

The Treaty of Amiens (1802) momentarily brought peace to Europe, but when war resumed barely a year later, the concept of neutral rights and the definition of blockade again came in for heavy pummeling by both belligerents. Horatio Nelson's victory at Trafalgar in October 1805 and Napoleon's at Austerlitz in December of that year made England supreme on the sea and France supreme on land. As Napoleon moved from triumph to triumph thereafter and consolidated his hegemony over the Continent, the British sought to bring him down with ever more restrictive maritime regulations. The military stalemate required full-scale economic war, which spelled trouble for the neutrals. The British had already tightened up on neutral trade with French colonial possessions by invoking the Rule of 1756—a diktat that forbade in wartime trade not allowed in peacetime—to cut neutrals out of the profitable French carrying trade.

During the wars of Napoleon, blockade proved the most potent weapon in the arsenals of both belligerents, although sometimes its bark was worse than its bite. Upon becoming prime minister in 1806, Charles James Fox sponsored an order in council that declared the coast of Europe, from Brest to the Elbe, in a state of blockade (although its prohibitions were absolute only between the Seine and Ostend). It amounted to a paper blockade, unsupported by ships stationed off the ports in blockade. Even the mistress of the seas did not have sufficient ships to cordon off so extensive a portion of seacoast.

The French responded with the Berlin (1806) and Milan (1807) decrees. These imperial enactments placed the British Isles in a state of blockade, and any ship submitting to search by British cruisers or complying with regulations requiring a stop at a British port the French considered denationalized and a lawful prize. Essentially a set of domestic French regulations, Napoleon's continental system remained legal in territories under French control, in the dominions of its allies, or in consenting neutral countries. The system amounted to "a fantastic blockade in reverse." Its main purpose was not blockade but the ruin of British commerce, as Napoleon himself admitted. "It is by dominating all the coasts of Europe that we shall succeed in bringing Pitt [the Younger, then prime minister] to an honorable peace," he had written in 1800, but "if the seas escape us, there is not a port, not the mouth of a river, that is not within reach of our sword." By denying his adversary access to continental markets, the emperor hoped to destroy British power.

Faced with competing blockades (the British, for their part, desired only to push their own goods onto the Continent, contrary to Napoleon's desire), confronted with ever more restrictive practices on the part of the European belligerents, the neutral United States twisted and turned, without finding a satisfactory resolution of its dilemma. On one occasion President Jefferson told the French minister in Washington that "we have principles from which we shall never depart. Our people have commerce everywhere, and everywhere our neutrality should be respected. On the other hand we do not want war, and all this is very embarrassing." The situation called for action, but action risked war. Under such circumstances, and given the peaceful proclivities of the Jeffersonians, it was tempting to resort to ingenuity; the more so because Napoleon had cunningly remarked in the Milan Decree that its provisions would not be enforced against neutrals who compelled Britain to respect their flag. The president sponsored a series of legislative enactments, including the embargo of 1807–1809, which, through unfortunate timing, coincided with the apogee of Napoleonic power. The baleful effects of the embargo helped convince some Federalists in Boston and elsewhere that the president was in league with the emperor. Nothing could be further from the truth. The European situation remained beyond the influence of American stratagems, no matter how ingenious, as Jefferson and his successor James Madison learned.

The British openly violated their own blockade of Europe by a system of licenses encouraging neutrals to carry both British and colonial goods through the French self-blockade, albeit after those goods had passed through British hands at a profit. In 1807 some 1,600 such licenses were granted; and by 1810 the number had reached 18,000. By that time Russia had deserted the continental system, opening the Baltic to neutral and British trade.

The result of all these twists and turns, taken under the name of blockade, was an extension of the war that soon involved the United States. Unable to control the periphery of his system, in Spain, Portugal, and Russia, Napoleon took his Grande Armée to Moscow and disaster. The object of that campaign, of course, was to force the Russians back into the system and to

reconstruct his continental blockade. Shortly before this great effort commenced, the United States, with its sixteen assorted ships of war, entered the conflict against England. Soon the British blockaded ports in the American South and West, although they carefully refrained from blockading New England, where there was much disaffection with Mr. Madison's war. Merchants who carried foodstuffs for British troops received passes through British squadrons. For two months after the declaration of war, the British consul in Boston licensed cargoes.

The wars of 1793–1815 clearly demonstrated the irreconcilable difference between belligerents and neutrals over use of the flexible doctrines of blockade. For the belligerents, especially the naval powers, blockade was a weapon that, if used imaginatively, could do much to bring the enemy to its knees; for the neutrals, blockade constituted a danger to trade and a means of involvement in the war. To the extent that a neutral acquiesced in "unlawful" definitions, that nation decreased its impartiality by actions that gave sustenance to one side while denying it to the other. Conversely, a too vigorous assertion of neutral rights might involve the nation in war. Still, the imprecisions inherent in formulations satisfactory to all, hence to none, provided loopholes that required no great legal legerdemain to stretch meanings to fit the exigencies of a particular war. By selecting from an assortment of precedents and practices, a belligerent could easily define the rules of blockade so as to make neutral commerce a victim of the drive for victory.

When the British sought to close the Continent to neutral trade or to control that trade in their own interest by whatever arbitrary or quasi-legal means they might devise, their higher objective, the destruction of Napoleon's warmaking capacity, took precedence over abstract, poorly defined, and largely unrecognized neutral rights and theoretical definitions of how the Royal Navy might or might not use one of its most powerful weapons. In like manner, when Napoleon's continental system came into conflict with American views of proper conduct, the emperor proved no less ingenious or heavy-handed in bending practice to fit his military or economic objectives. Between the infringements of the British and French, Americans had little to choose. Caught between implacable forces in the war that raged over Europe for nearly a generation, Americans struggled to define and defend principles for which the world, at that dangerous time, could find no use. When war threatened the safety of the state, right gave way to might. In its life-or-death struggle for national existence, Britain could not countenance interpretations of blockade that interfered with the pursuit of victory. Failure to understand that fact of international life did much to embroil the United States in a war it did not really want.

A WARLESS ERA

With the close of the Napoleonic wars in 1815, attendant upon Waterloo and the emperor's banishment to St. Helena, there followed almost a century when, with the possible exception of the American Civil War, no major conflict involving neutral rights took place. The important wars of the nineteenth century, from 1815 to 1914, were either civil conflicts such as the Taiping rebellion in China (1850–1864) and the American Civil War, or land wars of relatively short duration such as the Franco-Prussian War (1870–1871). Commentators on the law of war therefore had ample opportunity to refine their concepts and to sharpen their definitions. Statesmen of the time, especially American leaders, stressed the need for a new, more reasonable international order. As secretary of state, Madison had set the lines of this litany when he denied the legality of a British blockade of the entire islands of Martinique and Guadeloupe. In 1805 he told the British chargé d'affaires in Washington that international law required the presence of sufficient force to render "access to the prohibited place manifestly difficult and dangerous." In defense of this doctrine—and for the sake of American exports of food and naval stores—he added: "It can never be admitted that the trade of a neutral nation in articles not contraband, can be legally obstructed to any place, not actually blockaded." In 1824, Secretary of State John Quincy Adams ventured a new definition of a legal blockade, one that required "ships stationary or sufficiently near" the place prohibited, so that there was "evident danger" in attempting an entry. Then, during the Mexican War (1846–1848), the United States again affirmed its opposition to nominal blockades by telling the neutral British that according to American rules, "no Mexican port was considered blockaded unless a force was stationed sufficiently near to make trade with that port dangerous."

The United States refused to adopt the 1856 Declaration of Paris by which the major European powers at the end of the Crimean War attempted to promulgate a new code of neutral rights. That set of rules included a revised definition of blockade: "Blockades, in order to be binding, must be effective—that is to say, maintained by a force sufficient really to prevent access to the coast of the enemy." That article coincided with traditional American views. Other portions of the declaration did not measure up to Washington's expectations of what a proper code of conduct should be. During the war, with the fighting mainly on land and hardly touching neutral commerce, the maritime powers, France and Britain (then allied against Russia), realized that privateers, that is, legalized private ships of war, might prove attractive to the Russians in some future war. Having renounced use of such vessels during the war, the victorious allies sought in peace a formal international prohibition against their use. Part of the price for such an abolition was adoption of a more liberal view of neutral rights, and the powers of Europe, including Britain, subscribed to the rules set out at Paris. Hence, the ideal statement about blockade. But the American government, like the Russian, found fault with the new code. With its small navy, the United States might find future utility in use of private vessels of war and was therefore reluctant to surrender their use. Until belligerents were willing to afford a total immunity to all private property at sea, the Americans did not want to abolish privateering. They sought, rather, to trade off American acceptance of the article abolishing privateers for European recognition of the principle of immunity for private property at sea during wartime.

Failure to sign the Declaration of Paris did not enhance America's status as a champion of expanded neutral rights or as a proponent of the need for clear limits to blockades. Nor was the American position advanced by the circumstances of the Civil War, a conflict that became so heated—the need to contain the rebellious South being so pressing—that Washington officials proved willing to abridge the national record on the rights of neutrals, particularly in the use of blockade theory and practice, if only such abridgment would bring victory. Indeed, some observers and later historians have argued that the United States had been a champion of neutral rights when it had a small navy and little military power, but when it marshaled the most effective army and largest navy in the world, it jettisoned the principles of an earlier generation in favor of a more expedient approach.

In retrospect, the Civil War seems to have been so large an anomaly in American national life that no easy judgment can be made on whether President Abraham Lincoln and his aides forsook the principles of the Founders to save the Union. For the president and his secretary of state, William H. Seward, the fundamental international problem during the war was to preserve the neutrality and if possible the goodwill of Britain. Blockade measures against the South therefore had to be arranged so as to put maximum pressure on the Confederacy without provoking British reprisals. To be sure, other European neutrals occasionally encountered difficulties—Spain, for example, because of ownership of Cuba, from whence blockade-runners sometimes passed, and Denmark because of the proximity of the Virgin Islands to the Confederate coast—but their involvement never reached crisis proportions. The Mexican government frequently complained about actions by Union captains off Matamoros, contrary to the Treaty of Guadalupe Hidalgo (1848), which forbade any blockade of the Rio Grande. But the British response to problems generated by the war always concerned Union leaders most, for they realized that Britain's international position, its merchant fleet and naval strength, gave Her Majesty's government a vital interest in transatlantic affairs. For example, when the British almost from the outset of the war failed to push any blockade cases with the American government, that forbearance provided Lincoln's administration with a helpful leeway in manhandling aid for the South coming in by sea, or any effort by Southerners to ship cotton abroad in order to import the arms and supplies needed to prosecute the war. Britain's lack of militancy on issues concerning blockade became so marked by the second year of the war that the federal government in Washington enjoyed virtual carte blanche in its measures to seal off the South from supplies.

At the outbreak of war the Lincoln administration made a slip, when on 19 April 1861 it proclaimed a blockade of Southern ports from South Carolina to Texas and then eight days later of the ports of North Carolina and Virginia. The president should have declared the ports closed. Proclamation of a blockade was a presumption that the South enjoyed belligerent status and might merit international recognition as an independent nation. Officials in London felt that, in any event, they could not look upon 5 million people as pirates or as engaged in unlawful combination, and on 13 May they issued a neutrality proclamation, which included a warning to British subjects against the violation of any blockade established by either belligerent. Months later, in July, President Lincoln tried to amend the legal faux pas by saying that the blockade was "in pursuance of the law of nations" against a domestic insurrection: "A proclamation was issued for closing the ports of the insurrectionary districts by proceedings in the nature of blockade." These changes in legal terminology did not result in European withdrawal of recognition of Confederate belligerent status.

Later, debate would focus on the effectiveness of the Union blockade or on the "proceedings in the nature of blockade." Writers have contended that Union efforts were effective, but one twentieth-century southern historian argued that the blockade was a sieve. He calculated that blockade-runners made 8,000 trips to the South. He further points out that, in the early stages, the Union did not have sufficient ships to give even a semblance of effectiveness to its declaration. The porous nature of the blockade invited attempts to run into Southern ports with profitable cargo. Many of the adventurers who tried their hand at the business were "retired" British naval officers and other subjects of Her Majesty, the Queen. So many Britons took part in blockade-running that Lord John Russell, the foreign secretary, offhandedly quipped that his countrymen would, "if money were to be made by it, send supplies even to hell at the risk of burning their sails." Throughout the war, profits remained high; a return of 1,000 percent upon investment was not uncommon. Even in 1864, a captain who ordinarily made $150 per month might earn $5,000. A popular toast celebrated the blockade-runners' thankfulness to everyone: "The Confederates that produce the cotton; the Yankees that maintain the blockade and keep up the price of cotton; the Britishers that buy the cotton and pay the high price for it. Here's to all three, and a long continuance of the war, and success to blockade-runners." Still, the blockade was effective enough for the British government, despite considerable pressure against the move, to recognize its existence. Lord Russell, who can hardly be described as pro-North in outlook, eventually concluded that the Union blockade had to be considered "generally effective against foreign trade." His minister in Washington, Lord Lyons, regarded it as more than a mere paper blockade, noting that if it were "as ineffective as Mr. Jefferson Davis says . . . he would not be so very anxious to get rid of it." From reports of the commander of their North American station, the British carefully monitored the performance of Union blockading squadrons, and not until early 1862 did they formally accept the blockade. In February of that year, Russell told Lyons that there were enough Union vessels on blockade duty to prevent access to Southern ports or "to create an evident danger" to ships seeking to enter them.

Another Southern wartime hope—that the need for cotton would force European powers to press Lincoln's government to relax its blockade—also proved illusory. As it turned out, King Cotton proved a weak champion and an inept diplomat. By chance, the crop of 1860, one of the largest on record, had been shipped to Europe before the war started, and by the time a shortage developed, in the winter of 1862–1863, the South's military position was too precarious to warrant European intervention in American affairs.

One additional facet of the Civil War blockade deserves mention. Four captures of ships made during the first months of the war raised questions about the right of the federal government under international law to establish a blockade of its own ports during an insurrection, and of the right of the president to do so in the absence of a congressional declaration of war. Attorney General Edward Bates was advised to delay the cases until the president could appoint more politically reliable justices to the Supreme Court. After three Lincoln appointees joined the court, the government's position on the utility of the blockade was barely upheld in 1863, by a vote of five to four. The five cooperative justices made up in ardor what they lacked in support from their less certain brethren; and the dissenters no doubt blanched to hear that they had taken the "wrong" side of an issue involving "the greatest civil war known in the history of the human race," and that their negative arguments had threatened to "cripple the arm of the government and paralyze its power by subtle definitions and ingenious sophisms."

In one of the prize cases, that of the *Springbok*, the court ruled that any cargo ultimately intended for a blockaded port could be captured whenever it left the territorial waters of its port of origin. This rule applied, the court said, "even if the cargo was to be transshipped at an intermediate port, and the vessel in which it was found when captured was not the one which was to carry it to a blockaded port." In this case the court assigned a penalty for a breach of blockade "to a guilty cargo in an innocent ship." The court, in

effect, ruled that the cargo was on a continuous voyage from its port of origin to a blockaded port. Acceptance of this definition increased the power of the Union navy in intercepting supplies en route to the South. Such rulings went far toward making a blockade of Confederate ports almost unnecessary by substituting what amounted to a paper blockade of neutral ports in the Caribbean and Mexico. The case of the *Peterhoff* raised a question of the shipment of contraband overland, from Matamoros, Mexico, across the Rio Grande to Brownsville, Texas. The Union navy found itself with a perplexing problem in Matamoros, which before the war had had scarcely half a dozen visiting vessels a year. This hardly vibrant entrepôt welcomed 200 ships by 1864. Union captains hesitated to move against a neutral port, but they took ships en route to it, the *Peterhoff* being one of their more famous captures. After the war the case of the *Peterhoff* came before the Supreme Court; Chief Justice Salmon P. Chase roundly affirmed America's traditional record of respecting neutral ports and internationalized rivers such as the Rio Grande; he also asserted that the nation did not favor paper blockades. Release of the ship seemed a reasonable price for so many reassuring affirmations.

In another ploy to increase the efficacy of the blockade, Union officials even refused clearances to suspicious cargoes from their own ports or required the posting of heavy bonds to assure that such cargoes were intended for peaceful purposes. (During the war, suspiciously large amounts of clean-burning anthracite coal, a key component of successful blockade-running, were being shipped to British ports in Canada and the Caribbean.) The British chargé d'affaires complained about these export restrictions, remarking that the congressional enactment that sanctioned them was "a cheap and easy substitute for an effectual blockade." These practices so irritated British merchants that in 1864 Lord Lyons threatened that Her Majesty's government might have to reconsider its recognition of the legality of the Union blockade. Secretary of State Seward knew that, so late in the war, such an action could not serve British interests, so he ignored the minister's protest. For the remainder of the war the Union continued to use all the legal and economic weapons that it possessed to defeat the South.

During the half-century from the close of the Civil War to the opening of World War I, there were only one or two refinements in the concept of blockade. As noted, the Franco-Prussian War provided no opportunities for the expansion of old definitions or the creation of new ones. The Boer War and the Spanish-American War were local conflicts—the one a civil war, the other a splendid little affair. In the course of operations before Manila, prior to the capture of that city in 1898, Admiral George Dewey came to dislike the pretensions of a German admiral who happened to be in the harbor, and there is some evidence that Dewey told his German opposite that he wanted to "damn the Dutch." But that was hardly a refinement of blockade; nor did anything of a novel nature accompany use of blockades in the Caribbean, although the closing off of Santiago de Cuba was one of the last pre-submarine, close-in blockades, while the one at Havana, which began on 22 April 1898, had a closer connection with strategic considerations than with economic ones. The Americans believed that they could not capture Havana Harbor without risking heavy losses.

More important developments took place in a contretemps before the ports of Venezuela in 1902, when Britain, Germany, and Italy instituted a blockade to collect the debts owed by Venezuela to European creditors. The United States served notice that there was no right to interfere with ships of third parties, that is, American ships; whereupon the blockading powers announced that their blockade "created ipso facto a state of war" and gave themselves belligerent rights. When the issue went to the Permanent Court of Arbitration, the tribunal carefully skirted questions about the legality of the blockade, but in adjudicating the claims of the creditors decided in favor of the blockading powers. Shortly thereafter the nations of the world made another illustrious, if inconsequential, pronouncement about blockade. The second Hague Peace Conference (1907) had sought to establish an International Prize Court, but the delegates could not agree on the rules of prize law. To fill this gap a conference met in December 1908 in London, and after two months the delegates signed the London Declaration. Its provisions on blockade demonstrated once again the great difficulty in arriving at a satisfactory definition; indeed, these men of the twentieth century did little better than their nineteenth-century counterparts at Paris in 1856. Unable to agree upon a definition that would be acceptable to all, and recognizing the need for a "certain imprecision," the delegates reaffirmed the illegality of paper blockades and said that for a blockade to be binding it had to be maintained by an "adequate" naval force. No government ratified the London Declaration, even though during World War I the United States pressed the British to accept its principles. The resultant refusal highlighted a basic ambiguity of international life. Despite the best intentions, a power at war will retain loopholes in commitments to other nations so as to permit maximum use of offensive and defensive weapons.

WORLD WAR I AND AFTER

The theory and practice of blockade entered a third stage (following the formative period in the seventeenth and eighteenth centuries and the somnolent period dating from 1815) when the major nations of Europe joined in the Great War in 1914 and the United States entered the conflict in 1917. In the opening campaign along the Marne, the French army and a small British force slowed the German army, and the war turned from movement to position. By this time, the narrow definitions of the Paris and London declarations were all but obsolete—inoperable except in the most unimportant situations. Those formulations could not serve the needs of twentieth-century war. Transportation networks had grown up across all modern countries—rivers and canals, railroads, macadamized roads and highways for motor travel. New navies of steel and steam plied the seas, epitomized by the launching of the British battleship *Dreadnought* in 1906, and the conversion of merchant shipping from sail to steam was virtually complete. The new network of transportation made enemy ports of less consequence as goods could be shipped in and out via nearby neutrals. The conversion to steam made it unnecessary for warships to catch the wind before they moved out against blockade-runners or illicit neutral traders. Merchant shipping could operate apart from trade routes and prevailing winds, quite literally turning up anywhere. Then, too, the industrialization of much of Western Europe, especially of Germany, the principal antagonist of the Allies, gave a new dimension to blockade—the right sort of blockade might destroy German industry, or at least severely cripple it. And, as if blockade in the sense of Grotius and Bynkershoek would have had much chance at all, practical submarines and highly reliable mines were invented just prior to the outbreak of the war. Small wonder that World War I virtually ended blockade as it had been known.

In several instances, the old, traditional blockade of close-in surveillance of enemy ports was practiced during World War I, but these operations, carried out in reasonable conformity to the strictures of the London Declaration, occurred in secondary theaters of naval activity—the Mediterranean, Africa, and China. Where things really mattered—the blockade off the European coast and in the North Sea—the British government at least made a formal effort to maintain that the old rules still roughly applied. Its foreign secretary, Sir Edward Grey, indulged in frequent long explanations to the American ambassador in London and to the secretary of state in Washington. He assured them and reassured them that any changes in traditional rules of blockade stemmed not from a spirit of innovation but from the need to adjust old definitions to new circumstances. He implied that nothing really had changed.

In fact, the purposes of a blockade during the war were assisted by other measures not given that name, and the belligerents were usually careful in avoiding use of that term to describe their actions. The outstanding examples of such measures were the German declarations of war zones and the British designations of mine areas, military areas, and danger zones. It was a piquantly interesting fact that every one of the belligerent resorts to what might be described as measures of quasi-blockade was adopted via the principle of international law known as the law of retaliation.

It is hardly necessary to explain in detail how the British and German blockades operated during World War I. The Germans first used mines, giving notice of their intent to do so in August 1914; the British countered in November by closing the entire North Sea because of minefields. In a proclamation of 4 February 1915, the Germans announced unrestricted submarine and mine warfare, and the following month the British and French retaliated by declaring their intent to detain and take into port all ships "carrying goods of presumed enemy destination, ownership, or origin." To the Americans, Grey described that move as a blockade, and the U.S. government took his note as a formal notice of the establishment of a blockade and sought to get the Allies to respect neutral ports and vessels according to traditional standards of international law. In responding to the strictures of Washington officials, Grey took the stand that the March order amounted to "no more than an adaptation of the old principles of blockade." A decade later in his memoirs he wrote more candidly: "The Navy acted and the Foreign Office had to find the argument to support the action; it was anxious work."

And well done. The order in council of 11 March 1915 was one of the most powerful weapons in the British system of economic warfare against Germany. With the order the Allies gained all the advantages that would have come from a formal declaration of blockade of German ports—and without the inconvenience of stationing "adequate" naval forces off the ports. Also, when the Royal Navy acted under that mandate it succeeded in reducing the flow of supplies to the enemy via neutral ports, while at the same time cutting down on Germany's overseas trade. If the Allied pursuit of victory impinged too closely upon the interests of neutrals, if American shippers complained about innovations or illegalities, the lawyers at the Foreign Office had little trouble finding arguments.

Ironically, the British government found quite a few in the practices of the Union navy during the Civil War. One of the more interesting adjuncts to the British system of blockade closely paralleled a technique used by the North in its efforts to subdue the South, although there is no evidence that the British borrowed the idea from the Americans. From 1861 to 1865, Union officials sought to cut off supplies to the Confederacy by requiring exporters to obtain licenses, which, of course, could only be procured upon evidence that the cargoes in question had a bona fide neutral use. During World War I the British played a variation of this theme in order to make their restrictions more acceptable to neutrals. Their system, called navicerting, worked thusly: A neutral exporter, say an American interested in perfectly legal, noncontraband trade with a Scandinavian country, applied to British authorities (usually a consul) for permission to send his ship through naval cordons guarding approaches to European coasts. If he convinced the consul of the innocence of his venture, he received a navicert, a sort of commercial passport, which in most cases assured noninterference with his ship and cargo. The innovation conferred enormous advantage on the British, for in effect it transferred control of a large measure of neutral trade "from the deck to the dock."

The Allies introduced other refinements in their practice of blockade. They censored neutral mail to discover firms trading with the enemy and then blacklisted them and subjected them to harassment, such as depriving them of coal or denying them facilities for repairs. In the case of the *Kim* a British prize-court judge accepted statistical evidence to establish a presumption that American goods consigned to a Danish port were actually on a continuous voyage to Germany. Prize courts also made a slight but significant alteration in procedure when they transferred the burden of proving the innocence of a cargo to the claimant. With such pressures the British secured neutral cooperation with their system of economic control. The alternative, to be sure, was not to cooperate, but the Allied supremacy at sea meant that noncooperation had unpleasant consequences: detention of cargo, expensive and time-consuming legal proceedings, confiscation of goods, and the denial of facilities needed to conduct business. All the while the German blockade of Britain moved back and forth from observance of rules of cruiser warfare (meaning that submarines would not sink on sight but instead would visit and search and if necessary make provision for the safety of passengers and crew) to the waging of unrestricted submarine warfare, with its barbaric killing of noncombatants.

With a poor harvest in the United States in 1916 it appeared possible to prevent grain from other neutrals entering the British Isles, and in that hope the German government at the end of January 1917 announced unrestricted submarine warfare and knowingly brought the United States into the war, believing that their submarine blockade would bring victory before the Americans could raise and transport an army to Europe.

That the Allied long-range blockade of Germany was effective in helping the Allies win the war must admit of little doubt. Its effect upon the enemy, however, took far longer than expected. During the great German offensives in the spring and early summer of 1918, the troops were astonished at the quality of the equipment of the routed British Fifth Army, and also at the relative luxury in which French civilians were living. In the last weeks of the war the German home front virtually caved in. The military forces had been defeated first—there may be no doubt about that. But the civilians had been standing in line for years, and the word *Ersatz* had become a commonplace. When the prospect of peace emerged during the diplomatic exchanges of October 1918, the German civilians came to believe that they had suffered too long. The British blockade at last had placed an impossible burden. Continuation of the war into 1919, which otherwise might have been possible, was too harrowing to contemplate.

In examining the operation of the blockade during World War I, there remains the practice of

the United States once it entered the war. Popular wisdom at the time and later had it that the Americans turned the principles of neutral rights around as soon as they became a belligerent. Such was not the case. There appear to have been only two clear-cut and rather minor violations of international law by the U.S. government. Use of embargoes, bunker control, and the blacklist were all unquestionably legal, involving only domestic jurisdiction and municipal law. The task of enforcing the blockade remained in British hands; the U.S. Navy took no prizes. It is true that it laid a great barrier of 70,000 mines from Scotland to Norway. During the period of neutrality, the United States had reserved its rights on British and German mining of the seas, and so, technically at least, did nothing startlingly novel by constructing a huge mine barrier in 1918. Fear of German use of Norwegian territorial waters disappeared when Norway closed the gap in the barrage by mining its own waters. In the pre-armistice negotiations with the British about their insistence upon reserving freedom of the seas from discussion at the peace conference (because they feared it might restrict the right of blockade) President Woodrow Wilson stated that blockade was "one of the many things which will require immediate redefinition in view of the many new circumstances of warfare developed by this war." But there was, he said, "no danger of its being abolished."

In the decades to come, "blockade" as a term would give way to terms such as "quarantine," "interdiction," and "interception." The belief was that the new world organizations, the League of Nations and, later, the United Nations—not to mention the Kellogg-Briand Pact (1928), by which almost all the nations of the world renounced and outlawed war—ensured that neutrality in the old sense was gone, perhaps replaced by collective security.

The record of the League of Nations in this regard was probably too short to be conclusive. Article 16 of the Covenant of the League of Nations provided for sanctions, and the first assembly of that organization created an International Blockade Committee, which issued a cautious report in 1921. The committee felt that "to pronounce an opinion in regard to the naval blockade and the right of search" was outside the scope of its work because more study was needed on those subjects. It noted that three great exporting countries (the Soviet Union, United States, and Germany) remained outside the league, and in a curious bit of logic concluded that its name was a misnomer, since application of Article 16 did not involve imposition of blockades in the traditional sense.

In the 1930s there was talk, in and out of the league, about quarantining aggressors. Membership in the league did not seem to make much difference in the results of the talk, for there were virtually no results. League members hesitated to include an oil embargo among the measures invoked against Mussolini's adventure in Ethiopia in 1935–1936, for the Duce said that he would consider an oil embargo an act of war. In 1937, President Franklin D. Roosevelt spoke in Chicago about quarantining aggressors, but he gingerly withdrew the idea when it aroused a storm of protest from his fellow citizens. In that troubled decade before the outbreak of World War II, there was plain evidence that neutral thoughts had not disappeared. In 1932 the United States ratified a Pan-American Convention that reaffirmed the belligerent right of visit and search. The neutrality acts (1935–1941), passed by Congress to keep the country out of war, went into great detail about neutral rights and duties, including those that involved blockades. The acts implied that for the United States the league's new order would not function. Nor did it.

During World War II the United States again was forced to confront the problems of blockade, both as a neutral and as a belligerent. While neutral, it took an indulgent stand in regard to British blockade measures and sought to avoid repetition of the arguments during World War I. The United States reserved its rights under international law but in practice reached a cozy accommodation with British restrictions, including a much expanded version of the navicert system. Then, as a belligerent, the United States found frequent occasion to expand the use of blockade as a weapon of victory. When the U.S. Navy achieved dominance in the Pacific, it instituted a tight cordon around the Japanese home islands to cut off imports and enforced that cordon with the chilling efficiency of its submarine fleet. Clearly, the demands of total war imposed a need for permutations of what international lawyers describe as the latent law of blockade—the belligerent that possesses command of the sea is entitled to deprive an opponent of use of it. Drafters of the Dutch *Placaart* of 1630 would have understood that need.

But what had been appropriate to the period of total war proved inappropriate to the era of limited wars that plagued the world after 1945. Once more the United States devised modifications in its use of blockade. These variations have been called "special function blockades" and had a wide use in the Korean and Vietnam wars, during the Cuban missile crisis of 1962, and in conflicts with unfriendly regimes in Iraq, Haiti, and the former Yugoslavia in the 1990s.

Because of its predominant naval power during the Korean conflict, the United States imposed a close-in blockade of all Korean ports and coasts that was reminiscent of the practice of earlier eras. In Vietnam, other tactics were used to interdict the flow of supplies to enemy contingents operating in South Vietnam. To prevent introduction of war matériel by sea, the South Vietnamese, with the aid of U.S. naval craft, conducted what might be described as a self-blockade. During this time they practiced all the traditional techniques of visit and search off their own coasts and in their own territorial waters. Perhaps a more interesting case was the mining of Haiphong Harbor and the internal waterways and coastal waters of North Vietnam by American aircraft in the spring of 1972. By this process of air interdiction of seaborne supplies the United States hoped to carry out the purposes of a blockade, and took extreme care to minimize the danger to neutral commerce. The U.S. Navy even observed the ancient custom of allowing a grace period for neutral vessels to leave the coast and harbors before activating the mines.

The most important invocation of a special function blockade occurred in the Caribbean during the missile crisis in October 1962. Thus, the United States relied on one of the oldest weapons in its arsenal to avoid resorting to more deadly ones. In a speech to the nation, President John F. Kennedy announced "a strict quarantine of all offensive military equipment under shipment to Cuba" and a turning back of all ships found to be carrying offensive weapons "from whatever nation or port." The subsequent proclamation ordered U.S. forces to interdict delivery of such matériel, and the navy set up a quarantine line around the eastern and southern approaches to the island. The president carefully coordinated his naval maneuvers so as to leave room for compliance by the Russians with these restrictions on their freedom of the seas. Successful resolution of the missile crisis again demonstrated the protean possibilities of concepts of blockade or "proceedings in the nature of a blockade," that is, as flexible instruments of national policy.

KENNEDY AND THE CUBAN MISSILE CRISIS

"Good evening, my fellow citizens. The government, as promised, has maintained the closest surveillance of the Soviet military buildup on the island of Cuba. Within the past week unmistakable evidence has established the fact that a series of offensive missile sites is now in preparation on that imprisoned island. The purpose of these bases can be none other than to provide a nuclear strike capability against the Western Hemisphere. . . .

"Acting, therefore, in the defense of our own security and of the entire Western Hemisphere, and under the authority entrusted to me by the Constitution as endorsed by the resolution of the Congress, I have directed that the following initial steps be taken immediately: First: To halt this offensive buildup, a strict quarantine on all offensive military equipment under shipment to Cuba is being initiated. All ships of any kind bound for Cuba from whatever nation or port will, if found to contain cargoes of offensive weapons, be turned back. This quarantine will be extended, if needed, to other types of cargo and carriers."

—From a radio and television address by President John F. Kennedy, 22 October 1962—

"Now, therefore, I, John F. Kennedy, president of the United States of America, acting under and in virtue of the authority conferred upon me by the Constitution and statutes of the United States, in accordance with the aforementioned resolutions of the United States Congress and of the Organ of Consultation of the American Republics, and to defend the security of the United States, do hereby proclaim that the forces under my command are ordered, beginning at 2:00 Greenwich time October 24, 1962, to interdict, subject to the instructions herein contained, the delivery of offensive weapons and associated material to Cuba.

"For the purposes of this Proclamation the following are declared to be offensive material: Surface-to-surface missiles, bomber aircraft, bombs, air-to-surface rockets and guided missiles, warheads for any of the above weapons, mechanical or electronic equipment to support or operate the above items, and any other classes of material hereafter designated by the Secretary of Defense for the purpose of effectuating this Proclamation."

—Proclamation signed by President Kennedy, 23 October 1962—

In the case of blockading—such in reality was the word behind the other words—of Iraq that began in August 1990, the action against Iraqi trade divided into phases I and II. Phase I came at the outset of Operation Desert Shield, the effort by the United States together with a large number of other members of the United Nations to persuade Iraq to give up its occupation of Kuwait, which it had just accomplished. The lead in this effort to make Iraq move its military forces back behind its own borders was necessarily taken by President George H. W. Bush, for it was mostly U.S. Navy forces that would have to handle restrictions on ocean-borne trade; 95 percent of Iraq's exports were oil. The president skirted mention to blockade, at first referring to interdiction, then to interception. His effort to avoid a possible act of war was due to the sensibilities of UN members, some of which—notably France and Russia—were not in favor of strong measures. The president also hesitated because of lack of full support by Con-

gress. But diplomacy abroad and at home gradually resolved the fears of the president's critics. Only two pipelines exited Iraq, one to Turkey and the other to Saudi Arabia. The former nation was cooperative, as was the latter, with a border to Kuwait. The only local supporter of the Iraqi dictator, Saddam Hussein, was Jordan, the monarch of which, King Hussein, might have been expected to oppose Iraq, where Saddam's political party, the Baath, had murdered Hussein's cousin, King Faisal, years before. Jordan's trade with Iraq also was at stake. President Bush managed to persuade Hussein to support a naval interception. As the months passed, with U.S. forces and those of its allies gathering in preparation for Operation Desert Storm, Saddam managed to alienate even more UN members by defying, if only in words, the interception of tankers by the U.S. Navy. To no avail the Iraqi representative in the UN denounced what he described as a U.S.-dominated action, asserting it was naught but a blockade.

Phase II of interception of Iraqi trade commenced after the triumphant few weeks of Desert Storm, and, to the confusion of U.S. and UN officials, continued into the twenty-first century. The basic problem during Phase II was to get the Iraqi regime to change its ways, for they were intolerable—a total disregard for human rights, support of international terrorism, hegemonic ambitions in the area, and development of weapons of mass destruction and missile delivery systems, not to mention refusal of reparations for its invasion of Kuwait. But how to force a reformation? Claims by Iraq that children suffered from lack of food were difficult to resist, and the UN was tempted to allow oil for food if only to pay Kuwait and nations such as Jordan, which had to house and feed refugees during Desert Shield and Desert Storm, as well as nations whose nationals had been trapped in Iraq during that time. Meanwhile, the U.S. Navy's interceptions were difficult to enforce. Ships bringing cargoes into the country, particularly container ships, had to make space for inspectors, and the loss of cargo thereby led to complaints. Ships destined for Jordan's port of Aqaba required inspection at sea or at the port prior to land transshipment. Sentiment arose, encouraged by Iraq, to hold inspections at a designated point on the Jordan-Iraq border, so that the Iraqis could boast about doing everything properly, while goods could come in at other border points illegally and without notice. (The borders in the area had no passes or notable roads; they were lines drawn in the sand after World War I.) In 1997 the commander of the U.S. Fifth Fleet accused Iran of complicity for smuggling oil through Iranian territorial waters. As late as March 2001 a notable breach in the interception was occurring by land transit of oil into Turkey, with the oil duly taxed by the Turkish government. Both the United States and United Nations informally accepted the traffic, amounting annually to hundreds of millions of dollars, for it benefited the weak Turkish economy.

Meanwhile, between 1991 and 1994 actions leading to interdiction were taken in Haiti, to force out a military regime that had deposed an elected president, and against Serbia for attacking Slovenia and Croatia, which had declared independence from Serbia. At the beginning in Haiti the international opposition was marshaled by the Organization of American States and was voluntary. At last, in 1993, the United Nations took over from the OAS and imposed mandatory prohibition on entry of oil, arms, police equipment,

and "spare parts for the aforementioned." There nonetheless was trouble over border smuggling from the Dominican Republic, the government of which reluctantly allowed policing by U.S. military helicopters. On 19 September 1994, without any clear evidence that a limited embargo had had any effect, a small invasion force landed and the military regime came to an end.

In regard to Serbia, a situation developed not unlike that of the American Civil War, in which the Yugoslav federal government, dominated by Serbia, sought to bring back its independence-minded provinces. Two international squadrons stationed in the Adriatic undertook to enforce an embargo. But the government in Belgrade needed no arms support, unlike its seceding provinces. And other supplies to Serbia were easily available via the Danube or neighboring states. As in Haiti, naval measures of interception ultimately failed, and led to employment of air power and land-based peacekeeping forces.

CONCLUSION

And so the meaning of "blockade" has shifted over the years—perhaps it is more correct to say that it has been "jostled." Everything has depended upon the nation with available power, whether that nation wished to employ it for its own benefit or that of the international community. At the time when international law was a novelty, the time of Grotius, there was no such thing as an international community. In the seventeenth, eighteenth, and nineteenth centuries, blockade was a point of argument governed by power and, for the United States, by hope—trust that trading nations could make their ways without interference. After World War I the word "blockade" tended to go out of style. The international organizations created after the world wars anticipated the prevention of conflicts through the cordoning off of "aggressor" nations by multilateral action and not by the traditional bilateral maneuvers involving blockade. Then, too, other words—"quarantine," "interdiction," "interception"—have seemed less provocative than "blockade" and also would not automatically involve inconvenient rules and practices of the not-too-distant past.

As to the future of blockade, it may not have one. New words from the late twentieth century give indication that it is a concept of the past.

BIBLIOGRAPHY

Behrens, C. B. A. *Merchant Shipping and the Demands of War.* London, 1955.

Bernath, Stuart. *Squall Across the Atlantic: American Civil War Prize Cases.* Berkeley and Los Angeles, Calif., 1970. Makes international law not only intelligible but interesting to the general reader.

Blair, Clay. *Silent Victory: The U.S. Submarine War against Japan.* Philadelphia and New York, 1975.

Burt, A. L. *The United States, Great Britain, and British North America: From the Revolution to the Establishment of Peace After the War of 1812.* New Haven, Conn., 1940.

Chayes, Abram. *The Cuban Missile Crisis.* New York, 1974.

Deak, Francis, ed. *Neutrality in History, Economics, and Law.* 4 vols. New York, 1935–1936. Treatment of the evolution of a key portion of international law.

Field, James. *America and the Mediterranean World: 1776–1882.* Princeton, N.J., 1969.

Gilbert, Felix. *To the Farewell Address: Ideas of Early American Foreign Policy.* Princeton, N.J., 1961.

Lurabaghi, Raimonndo. *A History of the Confederate Navy.* Annapolis, Md., 1996. Translated by Paolo Coletta.

Mallison, W. T. *Studies in the Law of Naval Warfare: Submarines in General and Limited Wars.* Washington, D.C., 1968. Legal problems raised by submarine war.

Medlicott, W. N. *The Economic Blockade.* 2 vols. London, 1952.

Merli, Frank J. *Great Britain and the Confederate Navy.* Bloomington, Ind., 1970. A portion deals with keeping blockade-runners out of the South.

Moore, John B. *Digest of International Law.* 8 vols. Washington, D.C., 1906. Old but useful.

Morison, Samuel Eliot. *History of the United States Naval Operations in World War II.* Boston, 1947–1962.

Savage, Carlton. *Policy of the United States Toward Maritime Commerce in War.* 2 vols. Washington, D.C., 1934. Handy compilation of documentary material.

Savelle, Max. *The Origins of American Diplomacy: The International History of Anglo-America, 1492–1763.* New York, 1967. Although there is no index entry for blockade, there is the important chapter "The Impact of the New World of the Colonies upon the Evolution of the Theory and Practice of International Law."

Siney, Marion C. *The Allied Blockade of Germany: 1914–1916.* Ann Arbor, Mich., 1957.

Tracy, Nicholas. *Attack on Maritime Trade.* Toronto, 1991. The perspective is from naval strategy rather than economics or international law.

Trask, David. *Captains and Cabinets: Anglo-American Naval Relations, 1917–1918.* Columbia, Mo., 1972.

Varg, Paul. *Foreign Policies of the Founding Fathers.* East Lansing, Mich., 1963.

Wise, Stephen. *Lifeline of the Confederacy: Blockade Running During the Civil War.* Columbia, S.C., 1988.

See also ARMED NEUTRALITIES; ARMS TRANSFERS AND TRADE; CONTINENTAL SYSTEM; ECONOMIC POLICY AND THEORY; EMBARGOES AND SANCTIONS; FREEDOM OF THE SEAS; INTERNATIONAL LAW; NAVAL DIPLOMACY; NEUTRALITY.

THE CHINA LOBBY

Warren I. Cohen

"China lobby" is a pejorative phrase first applied in the 1940s to a disparate collection of Chinese and Americans who tried to influence the people and government of the United States on behalf of the Nationalist regime of Chiang Kai-shek (Jiang Jie-shī;) and in opposition to the Chinese communists. Opponents of aid to the Nationalists commonly used the term to imply that Chiang's American supporters were paid and that their activities were coordinated by Chiang and other officials of his government or members of his family. A second usage implied the existence of an organization of Chinese Nationalist officials and American rightists joined to stimulate anticommunism in the United States. Americans most commonly associated with the China lobby were the noted publisher Henry R. Luce; Alfred Kohlberg, a retired New York importer; Frederick C. McKee, a wealthy Pittsburgh manufacturer and philanthropist; Republican Representative Walter H. Judd of Minnesota; and the Republican senators William F. Knowland of California and Joseph R. McCarthy of Wisconsin. The lobby was presumed to have tremendous influence in American politics by contemporaries. It has been credited with forcing a reluctant Truman administration to continue aid to Chiang during the Chinese civil war, preventing recognition of the People's Republic of China and barring it from the United Nations, and blocking the distribution of a book exposing the operations of the China lobby.

Although the Chinese Nationalist regime employed American lobbyists and public relations operatives and had the support of the American right in the struggle against communism in China, support for Chiang's China cannot be written off as either hired or right wing. In the United States popular support for Chiang—or, more precisely, opposition to communist control of China—was broadly based, including liberals and conservatives, Democrats and Republicans, and southerners, northerners, easterners, and westerners. Popular antipathy toward the Chinese communists derived from a widespread and profound distaste for communism and from traditional sympathies for the heathen Chinese. But it was the Korean War—especially the intervention of the People's Republic of China in the war—that brought about the results for which Chiang's supporters worked in the late 1940s and early 1950s. Without the Korean War, the limited public interest in Asian affairs and the reality of the communist victory in China might well have led to an early accommodation between the United States and the regime of Mao Tse-tung (Mao Zedong), despite the efforts of the friends of Nationalist China.

LOBBYING EFFORTS FROM THE 1920S THROUGH WORLD WAR II

Pressure group activity on behalf of the Nationalist regime dates back to the Nationalist revolution (1925–1928), when Chiang Kai-shek was struggling to unite China with Soviet and Chinese communist assistance. Fearing intervention by the United States and other governments, a group of American missionaries and educators, led by individuals like A. L. Warnshuis, secretary of the International Missionary Council; J. Leighton Stuart, president of Yenching University (Beijing); and Roger S. Greene of the China Medical Board of the Rockefeller Foundation, worked to alert policymakers, members of Congress, and the public to the need for an accommodation with Chinese nationalism. Links between Chiang's government and American missionaries and reformers continued into the 1930s as Madame Chiang Kai-shek and other American-educated Chinese leaders sporadically attempted to gain American assistance in the modernization of China. Major lobbying activities did not begin, however, until after the outbreak of the Second Sino-Japanese War in 1937.

Of the various groups that were organized to influence U.S. policy on behalf of China between 1937 and 1941 the most important was the American Committee for Non-Participation in Japanese Aggression, also known as the Price Committee. In 1938, appalled by the inaction of the U.S. government in the face of Japanese aggression in China, Frank and Harry Price, sons of the famous missionary P. Frank Price, called together a small group of men, including an American employed as a propagandist for the Chinese government. To campaign against the flow of American supplies to Japan, they created an organization that soon received financial support from the Chinese government. There is no evidence that the formation of the committee was inspired by Chinese authorities, but given the relations between the two, especially during the early stages, this possibility cannot be ignored. Furthermore, the Chinese government considered itself entitled to reports.

Despite the initial role of the Chinese, the Price Committee subsequently attempted to restrict contributors to Americans and to sever potentially embarrassing ties to Chinese officials. One member who was employed by the Chinese government and required to register as the agent of a foreign principal resigned from the committee. Roger Greene and Henry L. Stimson served respectively as chairman and honorary chairman; Harry Price, as executive secretary; and Walter Judd, a former medical missionary, proved to be its most effective speaker. Frederick McKee and Geraldine Fitch, wife of the well-known missionary George A. Fitch, were also important members of the organization.

The central program of the Price Committee called for an embargo on supplies of military value to Japan. Beginning in 1939, it worked closely with key figures in the U.S. government, especially with Stanley K. Hornbeck of the Department of State and with Stimson, who became secretary of war in 1940. Individual members, like Greene and McKee, were also active and influential in the most important of the pressure groups espousing collective security. The activities of these friends of China may have been responsible for President Franklin D. Roosevelt's decision in July 1939 to notify Japan of the intention of the United States to terminate the commercial treaty between the two nations, thus facilitating economic sanctions. With access to Roosevelt and other top administration officials, Greene and Price may have shaped a number of important government actions, such as credits to

China for the purchase of trucks and the National Defense Act of 1940, which gave Roosevelt authority to control exports. Similarly, these lobbyists on behalf of China utilizing the most sophisticated public relations methods then available—mass mailings, press releases, speaker tours, petition drives—mobilized opinion leaders in the colleges, churches and civic organizations across the country behind administration efforts to help China. Indeed, they generated pressures designed to push Roosevelt faster than he wanted to move. In the autumn of 1941, their warning against a Far Eastern Munich made a modus vivendi with Japan extremely difficult.

After the United States entered World War II, many groups emerged to raise money for China, enlisting men and women who had participated in the Price Committee's efforts. Most of these groups were brought together under United China Relief, a kind of holding company that attempted to coordinate private aid to China. Typical of the new groups that were organized during the war was the American Bureau for Medical Aid to China (ABMAC), with which Greene was involved and in which Kohlberg played a major role. All of these organizations reminded the American people of the long suffering of their Chinese allies, filled the country with stories of Chinese resistance and heroism, and, to simplify their story, personified China in the figures of Generalissimo and Madame Chiang Kai-shek. From the Weekly Reader to the newsreels and the public prints, these glamorous figures appeared as the spirit of Free China, with greatly exaggerated references to their dedication to democracy and to the Four Freedoms that Roosevelt had offered as symbols of the ideals for which Americans fought.

From 1937 on, as Americans who believed China to be worthy of American support exercised their right to attempt to influence the policies of their government, various Chinese officials worked toward the same end. The Chinese ambassador, Hu Shih, made strenuous efforts to obtain aid for his country; and he was supported by a host of other officials, most prominent among them Madame Chiang's brother, T. V. Soong. Madame Chiang was herself probably the most effective propagandist for her country: an attractive, American-educated Christian who made marvelous copy for the mass media. Lin Yutang, a well-known popularizer of Chinese culture, also spent the war years in the United States on a diplomatic passport, advertising the virtues of Chiang's regime to the American people. These and similar Chinese activities were sometimes irritating to U.S. officials who resented pressures to do more for China, but the Chinese were not known to be violating any laws and were engaged in practices whose legitimacy was sanctioned by custom in the United States.

Chinese officials and American friends of China naturally came together frequently to discuss China's needs and strategy for various campaigns. Again, there was nothing improper about this sort of cooperation. Most of the American participants were not acting as agents for the Chinese government and those who were did so openly and legally. They shared a concern for China, and their countries were allies in war, sharing an interest in the effort to defeat Japan. Problems developed only as questions arose as to whether Chinese and American interests remained congruous, and whether Chiang's regime represented the best interests of the Chinese people.

In 1943 the cohesiveness that Japanese aggression had produced among Americans interested in China began to wear away. The initial friction between the Chinese and U.S. governments had come about because of the limited Chinese share of lend-lease material, and American friends of China generally shared Chinese dissatisfaction. But in 1943 the focus was shifting to the Chinese war effort and to tensions between Chiang's regime and the Chinese Communists—tensions that threatened to erupt into civil war and already prevented Chinese forces from devoting their full attention to the Japanese invader. More and more criticism of Chiang was heard in U.S. government circles and leaked to the press. A few knowledgeable Americans began to argue in favor of sending aid to the Chinese communists, who seemed more willing to fight against Japan and more committed to democratic principles than were Chiang's Nationalists. Among China's American friends a growing number despaired of Chiang's repressive tendencies, brooded over corruption in his regime and, although apprehensive of the Chinese communists, wondered if the U.S. government might find an alternative to its total support of Chiang.

On a trip to China in 1943, Kohlberg was troubled by criticisms he heard of Chiang's regime—criticisms that did not appear to him to be justified. Increasingly he brooded about the source of these charges. Increasingly the Chinese government became fearful of the effects on American support if a corrupt and repressive image prevailed. Lin Yu-tang and Hu Shih pub-

licly and privately contended that communist agents were responsible for the attacks on Chiang. Hu Shih maintained that American scholars affiliated with the Institute of Pacific Relations (IPR) depended on Chinese researchers who were in fact communists. Greene was troubled by the publication of articles that appeared to substantiate Hu Shih's argument. Kohlberg gradually became convinced of a communist conspiracy to deceive the American people, convinced that the IPR, the center of East Asian studies in the United States, was an instrument of this conspiracy.

As Chiang's regime and some of its staunchest American friends, such as Judd and Fitch, tried to preserve the idealized image of the early war years, Kohlberg attacked the IPR. A man of great energy and considerable wealth, Kohlberg conducted a one-man campaign to purge the IPR of alleged communist domination. His initial charges in 1944 were ignored, but he persisted tirelessly, gaining support from professional ex-communists and Red-baiters who helped him to formulate charges and to obtain broader publicity for his effort. In particular, George E. Sokolsky, a widely syndicated Hearst columnist with strong ties to the House Un-American Activities Committee, helped Kohlberg with contacts and provided a public platform for his accusations.

COLD WAR AND THE "TWO CHINAS"

At the end of World War II, China faced civil war, and U.S. efforts to mediate failed. The few Americans interested in East Asian affairs fell into two main categories. One group argued that American interests would be served best by a scrupulous neutrality, allowing Chiang and his communist enemies to work toward their own resolution of China's problems. Another group contended that the interests of the United States would be served best by providing whatever aid short of troops was necessary to maintain Chiang in power. Members of the former group generally warned that the communists enjoyed greater support among the Chinese people and would ultimately triumph. They contended that U.S. aid to Chiang left him unwilling to compromise while peace was possible and would prolong the war and the agony of the Chinese people once the conflict began. The latter group generally mistrusted the Chinese communists, fearing they would serve Soviet rather than Chinese interests and bring misery to the Chinese people. They argued that a communist-controlled China would be a negation of the ends for which the United States had fought in the Pacific. As fear of the Soviet Union increased in the United States in the late 1940s, anticommunist sentiment grew apace, and more and more Americans became receptive to the arguments of Chiang's supporters—that is, to the China lobby.

In the late 1940s the two major organizations calling for American aid to Nationalist China were the American China Policy Association and the Committee to Defend America by Aiding Anti-Communist China. The American China Policy Association was founded by Kohlberg; John B. Powell, one of the best-known American journalists in China during the 1920s and 1930s; and Christopher Emmett, a writer with decidedly liberal pretensions. The members worked to reveal what they considered the insidious nature of the Chinese communist movement, and, within the matrix of intense anticommunist feeling, the association began on a moderate note. Soon, however, it was dominated by Kohlberg, who was himself becoming increasingly irresponsible in his charges against diplomats and scholars critical of Chiang Kai-shek.

The Committee to Defend America by Aiding Anti-Communist China was run by Frederick McKee, who had long contributed to liberal causes and to the collective security wing of the peace movement. Since the late 1930s, he had contributed both time and money in China's behalf, joining existing groups and organizing his own. Unlike Kohlberg, McKee did not become involved in extremist activities. Restrained and responsible, McKee was easily overshadowed. Membership in the Kohlberg and McKee organizations overlapped, but McKee was able to muster the support of several prominent men not identified with Chinese affairs, such as the former Democratic National Committee chairman James A. Farley and the labor leader David Dubinsky.

If the Kohlberg and McKee operations could claim some degree of respectability, there were other operations that could not. The Chinese embassy in Washington, D.C., and a variety of more or less independent entrepreneurs like T. V. Soong and his brother-in-law, H. H. Kung, lobbied frenetically for aid. Although their operations appear to have remained within the law, there is evidence of some sleight of hand within the embassy, resulting in the disappearance of large sums of money, the disappearance of senior Chi-

nese military officers attached to the mission who presumably had the money, and the appearance of Chinese documents revealing some of their operations and including extravagant claims of success with U.S. congressmen. These activities had no discernible effect on American policy, and only the Chinese government seems to have been swindled.

Another unsavory but legal Chinese activity was the employment of William J. Goodwin as a lobbyist. In the 1930s, Goodwin had distinguished himself by his affiliation with the Christian Front and with the American fascists Gerald L. K. Smith and the Reverend Charles E. Coughlin. Like the Chinese operatives in the embassy, Goodwin was probably most effective at obtaining money from the Chinese government while claiming to be influencing American politicians.

A majority of congressmen in both houses were sympathetic to the Chinese Nationalist cause and willing to vote for aid to Chiang in his fight against the communists. There is no evidence that any of these congressmen had been bought by the Chinese government or by Kohlberg or McKee. Virtually all of these people equated the Chinese communist movement with Soviet totalitarianism and looked with regret upon the likelihood of such oppression being levied upon their erstwhile Chinese allies. Most of these congressional supporters of the Chinese Nationalists were not committed to Chiang or his regime but rather to what they saw as a worldwide struggle against international communism. Furthermore, if the administration asked for funds to protect endangered Greeks and Turks against communist subversion, why not aid the Chinese as well? Having once conjured up fears of an international communist conspiracy for world domination, the Truman administration failed to convince Congress or the American people that China could be or had to be written off. When providing aid for a beleaguered Europe, Congress forced the administration to continue aid to Chiang Kai-shek and anticommunist China.

Despite congressional and public sympathy for Chiang, and the intimidating efforts of Kohlberg and his allies in the Hearst press, when the communists drove Chiang from mainland China, the Truman administration was prepared to recognize the People's Republic of China and to allow it to take the Chinese seat in the United Nations. Even in early 1950, when Kohlberg and Sokolsky found an ally in Senator Joseph R. McCarthy, the Truman administration proceeded with plans to thwart them and to come to terms with reality. The outbreak of war in Korea and the subsequent confrontation between troops from the United States and troops from the People's Republic of China accomplished what Kohlberg and his friends and the Chinese embassy could not have accomplished by themselves. It created a climate of opinion in the United States in which Kohlberg's charges of treason in high places could be taken seriously and in which an accommodation with the People's Republic of China proved impossible.

Ironically, it was the Democratic senator Pat McCarran of Nevada, an archconservative whose reelection McKee had earlier tried to prevent, who chaired the congressional committee that investigated the Kohlberg-McCarthy charges against the Institute of Pacific Relations. The 1952 hearings were used to discredit and intimidate American critics of Chiang Kai-shek. But from 1951 to 1953 it was McCarthy—advised by Kohlberg, Sokolsky, and Roy Cohn—who succeeded in driving some of the State Department's ablest men from Chinese affairs and from the foreign service. Whether from McCarran or McCarthy, Kohlberg or Sokolsky, the story was always the same: China had been lost to the communists because disloyal Americans had prevented Chiang from receiving the aid with which he could have won; and American boys died in Korea because they had been betrayed by disloyal and stupid liberals who had turned China over to the communists. It was not until the marked change in the climate of opinion that came with revulsion against the war in Vietnam that some of the men vilified during the McCarthy era were vindicated.

By 1952, the legitimate concern some Americans had for the future of China had been transformed into an instrument with which the extreme right tried to destroy liberalism in the United States. Sokolsky, whose earlier writings showed him to be unusually well informed about the history of the Chinese communist movement, consistently misled his readers, in keeping with his assumed role as a spokesperson for the extreme right. The success that he and his colleagues enjoyed in discrediting Dean Acheson, George C. Marshall, John S. Service, and Owen Lattimore demonstrated the validity of George Washington's warning about the consequences of "excessive partiality" for a foreign nation. In the 1950s, when criticism of Chiang Kai-shek invited charges of disloyalty to the United States, foreign service officers and scholars were intimidated, with a consequent crippling of both national policy and scholarship.

There were reactions against the work of Chiang's friends even at the height of their power, but to no avail. The Truman administration tried to neutralize them in 1951, promising friendly senators that it would cooperate in an investigation of the China lobby. In Congress, however, there was little interest in the investigation and the administration's own effort could turn up nothing to stimulate interest on Capitol Hill or in the press. In April 1952, the *Reporter* published two long articles that named some of the participants (Kohlberg, McKee, and Goodwin), implied more shady dealings than could be proven, and provided less than a model example of investigative reporting. Nonetheless, the articles contributed to the notoriety of the China lobby, and there were reports that mysterious Chinese were buying enormous quantities of the issues of the *Reporter,* in which the articles appeared. In April 1952, the Republican senator Wayne L. Morse of Oregon introduced into the Senate Chinese documents outlining the plans of the Nationalist regime to influence American policy. Some of the documents referred to cooperation with Goodwin, Judd, and Knowland, who was sometimes referred to as the senator from Formosa. Although the authenticity of the documents was never proven, the Chinese embassy admitted that they were cables sent from its offices, but denied that the counselor of the embassy had sent them, as alleged by Morse. There was little to be learned from the documents, which contained merely evidence of the deceits the embassy was practicing on its principal—and its agents were practicing on it.

As a result of the Korean War, American determination to keep the People's Republic of China out of the United Nations intensified, and a powerful new pressure group was created to retain the seat for Chiang's rump regime. Beginning with a petition drive, a Committee of One Million Against the Admission of Communist China to the United Nations emerged in 1953. After collecting the requisite million signatures, including those of prominent Democrats and Republicans, the organizers disbanded in 1954, only to reorganize as the Committee of One Million in 1955. Liberal Democratic and Republican senators lent their names to the new committee, including the Democrats Paul Douglas of Illinois, William Proxmire of Wisconsin, and Hubert H. Humphrey of Minnesota, and Republican Thomas

H. Kuchel of California. As with earlier organizations, anticommunism rather than approval of Chiang's regime explains the widespread support for the Committee of One Million, run by Marvin Liebman, an ex-communist.

In 1960, Ross Y. Koen, a young professor in California, prepared to publish his dissertation, *The China Lobby in American Politics,* but the book was not distributed. The Chinese embassy reportedly threatened legal action against the publishers for defamatory statements in the book, and it was widely assumed that the power of the China lobby had succeeded in frightening them. That power continued to seem impressive as President John F. Kennedy shied away from a rapprochement with the People's Republic, secretly promising Chiang that the United States would veto any effort to seat the communist regime in the United Nations. Lyndon Johnson's presidency brought no hope of change, although McCarthy, Kohlberg, and Sokolsky were dead, Judd and Knowland had lost their national offices, and the reality of the Sino-Soviet split had finally penetrated the American consciousness.

RECOGNITION OF THE BEIJING GOVERNMENT AND DEMISE OF THE CHINA LOBBY

The election of Richard M. Nixon in 1968 provided no expectation of new directions in American policy toward China. Nixon, the personification of the cold warrior, had been close to many of Chiang's staunchest supporters and had repeated many of the same inflammatory and unsubstantiated accusations that Kohlberg had levied. But, slowly and cautiously, the Nixon administration moved to improve relations with the People's Republic, and in July 1971 presidential adviser Henry Kissinger suddenly turned up in Beijing. A few months later a stunned world watched Richard Nixon and Mao Zedong exchanging pleasantries in Mao's study. In 1972 the United States facilitated the admission of the People's Republic to the United Nations and acquiesced in the expulsion of Chiang's government. There was hardly a whimper of opposition— and that from a few supporters of the president who felt they had been betrayed. The day of the China lobby had passed.

American recognition of the People's Republic of China in 1979 did not end lobbying activities aimed at influencing American policy toward China and Taiwan. The governments in Beijing and Taipei remained intensely active and found support across the political spectrum in the United States. The Republic of China, headquartered in Taipei, and led by Chiang Kai-shek's son, Chiang Ching-kuo, was not abandoned.

The Carter administration had won agreement from Deng Xiaoping to allow the United States to maintain "unofficial" relations with Taiwan and to permit continued arms sales to Taipei. Taiwan's diplomats quickly rallied their friends in the U.S. Congress and won a much stronger Taiwan Relations Act (TRA) than the administration had intended. The TRA explicitly stated that the use of force against Taiwan would be a matter of "grave concern" to the United States and committed the United States to provide such arms as Taiwan required to defend itself.

In the 1980s and 1990s, as Taiwan evolved into a democratic society, and especially after the Tiananmen massacres in Beijing in 1989, support for Taiwan increased dramatically among the American people and their elected representatives. The island's economic success allowed it to spend vast sums to woo the American media as well as American officials. Taiwan's lobbying activities, considered by specialists in foreign policy second only to those of Israel in effectiveness, frequently forced administration officials to take actions they considered undesirable. Most notable among these was the decision to issue Taiwan's president, Lee Teng-hui, a visa to visit the United States in 1995, precipitating a crisis in relations between Beijing and Washington and generating serious tensions in the Taiwan Strait.

Less effectively, the People's Republic also lobbied for support in Washington. Hampered by its human rights record and American admiration for democratic Taiwan, Beijing was fortunate to win powerful friends within the American business community. The U.S.–China Business Council, the Emergency Committee for American Trade, and major corporations, most prominently Boeing, labored assiduously to persuade Congress of the congruity of Chinese and American interests. In the 1990s, they succeeded in protecting China's most-favored-nation trade relations with the United States against attacks from human rights and labor organizations, ultimately winning passage of the Permanent Normal Trade Relations Act. China was thus assured that increased tariffs on its goods would not be used as a weapon by its adversaries in the United States.

In the early twenty-first century, lobbying by both Beijing and Taipei continued, with most of the public criticism directed against presumably pro-China groups who were accused by some conservatives of sacrificing U.S. security interests. Complaints against Taiwan's activities came primarily from within the executive branch of the U.S. government, where those responsible for policy toward China feared being pushed into an unnecessary and dangerous confrontation with Beijing. But the notorious China lobby of the Cold War era was gone.

BIBLIOGRAPHY

Bachrack, Stanley D. *The Committee of One Million: "China Lobby" Politics, 1953–1971.* New York, 1976.

Borg, Dorothy. *American Policy and the Chinese Revolution, 1925–1928.* New York, 1947. Includes references to the activities of Americans sympathetic to the Chinese Nationalist cause during the 1920s.

Cohen, Warren I. "The Role of Private Groups in the United States." In Dorothy Borg and Shumpei Okamoto, eds. *Pearl Harbor as History: Japanese-American Relations, 1931–1941.* New York, 1973. Discusses the lobbying activities of a number of groups and individuals between 1931 and 1941.

Friedman, Donald J. *The Road from Isolation: The Campaign of the American Committee for Non-participation in Japanese Aggression, 1938–1941.* Cambridge, Mass., 1968. A useful study of the organization and its work.

Keeley, Joseph. *The China Lobby Man: The Story of Alfred Kohlberg.* New Rochelle, N.Y., 1969. A biography that epitomizes Kohlberg's exploitation by the American right.

Koen, Ross Y. *The China Lobby in American Politics.* New York, 1974. A comprehensive account of Chinese Nationalist and pro-Nationalist activities in the United States during Truman's term as president. Koen is better at describing the impact of these activities than at explaining how the Chinese and their American friends functioned.

Liebman, Marvin. *Coming Out Conservative: An Autobiography.* San Francisco, 1992. A first-person account of the origin and activities of most of the right-wing fronts of the Cold War era, including the Committee of One Million.

Sutter, Robert G. *U.S. Policy Toward China: An Introduction to the Role of Interest Groups.* Lanham, Md., 1998. Focuses on lobbying activities on behalf of China and Taiwan in the post–Cold War era.

Thomas, John N. *The Institute of Pacific Relations: Asian Scholars and American Politics.* Seattle, Wash., 1974. An unsympathetic study of the organization with a useful chapter on Kohlberg.

See also CONGRESSIONAL POWER; ECONOMIC POLICY AND THEORY; FOREIGN AID; PUBLIC OPINION; RECOGNITION.

CIVIL WAR DIPLOMACY

Kinley Brauer

The importance of diplomacy during the American Civil War has long been underestimated. Both Northerners, who were committed to the preservation of the Union, and Southerners, determined to create a new nation, understood that without support from Europe, the secession movement in the United States was doomed. Thus, the foreign policy of the Union, in the able hands of Secretary of State William Henry Seward, was directed toward preventing the Confederacy from securing diplomatic recognition, military supplies, and any kind of encouragement from abroad. Toward that end, Seward conducted a vigorous foreign policy composed of bluff, bluster, and ultimately cautious moderation. The Confederates, on the other hand, were confident that the reliance of Britain and other industrialized nations of Europe on Southern cotton for their economic health and well-being and their desire for free trade guaranteed full support. Confederate foreign policy, therefore, was largely passive and dependent on King Cotton. Britain and France were indeed dependent on Southern cotton, and their leaders were convinced that the United States was irrevocably divided. All that was needed, they thought, was for the Union to recognize that fact. That conviction, a broad hostility toward slavery, an ample supply of cotton already in British warehouses, and a highly profitable wartime trade with the Union led to a uniform European policy of neutrality. That policy, however, which helped the North but hurt the South, was never carved in stone. Union blunders, British impatience, the actual and feared depletion of cotton stocks, and European horror at the bloodshed and destruction in America all threatened to move Europe from neutrality to intervention and Confederate success. Diplomacy, as much as military leadership, strategy and tactics, and Northern economic dominance, provided an essential key to the ultimate triumph of the Union and preservation of the United States as a single nation.

Because of the phenomenal development of the American economy and the expansion of the United States during the first half of the nineteenth century, Europe and Latin America closely watched the American crisis unfold. The health of the economies of Britain and France depended greatly upon the import of American raw materials, primarily cotton, and access to the prosperous American market. Early on it was recognized that peace in North America best served European interests and therefore European leaders hoped that Americans would not engage in hostilities. They were convinced that restoration of the Union was impossible. When hostilities began, they decided that neutrality best served their interests.

The Confederate States of America also hoped for a peaceful separation. Shortly after his appointment as provisional president, Jefferson Davis and his secretary of state, Robert Toombs of Georgia, dispatched a mission to Washington to secure recognition and the transfer of all federal property to Confederate authorities. Davis and Toombs also dispatched three commissioners to Europe to explain the reasons for the creation of the Confederacy and to secure recognition and treaties of amity and commerce. Support from Europe, Southerners understood, was critical, for without a navy or industry of its own, the Confederacy had to have foreign backing. They placed primary reliance on European, and particularly British, dependence on their cotton, believing this ensured a favorable response.

Northern leaders, particularly Abraham Lincoln and Seward, were absolutely committed to the preservation of the Union and also understood that the European reaction to the American crisis was critical. Seward, especially, believed that secession lacked majority support in the South and that Southern Unionists would rise and end the secession movement by the spring of 1861. It was essential that the Southern extremists receive no encouragement from abroad, without which expectation, Seward believed, the Confederacy would be short-lived.

SEWARD AND EARLY UNION POLICY

Seward was the driving force behind American Civil War diplomacy, and much of his diplomacy was shaped by his imperial vision. For more than thirty-five years, Seward had extolled the promise, potential, and perpetuity of the American empire, and much of his Civil War diplomacy aimed at preserving, expanding, and ensuring the successful completion of that empire. Well before "manifest destiny" became the slogan of expansionists, Seward envisioned the expansion of the United States to include all of North America and quite likely South America and the islands of the Caribbean as well. He also spoke eloquently about the certain growth of the American economy and American overseas commerce and predicted that U.S. merchants, commercial agents, and diplomats would spread the principles and ideology of the American System around the world.

Seward's program required the centralization of American political power and the containment and eventual abolition of slavery in the United States. He promoted legislation to attract, Americanize, and assimilate immigrants, liberalize land policies, centralize banking and monetary programs, and fund internal improvements and federal money. He also believed that the gradual end of slavery and its replacement by free labor were essential for peaceful American expansion and the full growth of the American economy. Without the stain of slavery, he thought, Canada and Mexico would eagerly seek admission to the American commonwealth.

Slavery also gave excessive power to reactionary agrarian interests in the South. Containment of slavery to the states where it presently existed, gradual emancipation, and the reduction of Southern power in Congress, Seward believed, were made possible by the Republican victory of 1860, as was the restructuring of the American political economy and the expansion of the American territorial, commercial, and ideological empire. During the war years these programs were subordinated to the preservation of the Union, an end that Seward never questioned and a goal from which he never wavered.

Throughout the secession winter of 1860–1861 that followed Lincoln's election, Seward worked tirelessly to find a compromise or modus vivendi with those Southern leaders whose states had not left the Union. While Lincoln remained in Springfield, Illinois, preparing for his inauguration, Seward made a number of public speeches emphasizing the dangers, impracticality, and fruitlessness of secession. He opposed all actions that would close the door to the return of the disaffected states and tried to ensure that the Confederates received no encouragement, prospect of support, or tangible aid from overseas.

Although Seward did not assume office until Lincoln's inauguration on 4 March, he engaged European diplomats in Washington in private conversations that aimed, first, at assuring them that the secession effort would shortly collapse, and, second, warning Europe that the United States would not tolerate any foreign intervention in American or hemispheric affairs. Seward had predicted that if the United States became divided, European nations would sweep down upon the Americas to reestablish or expand their authority and influence. During the last weeks of March, these concerns appeared justified. Rumors were rife that Britain, France, and Spain were planning to intervene in Mexico, that Spain was about to recolonize the Dominican Republic, and that France was about to move back into Haiti. The first two had a basis in fact. The three European powers were discussing an intervention limited to collecting debts for their nationals who had invested in Mexican bonds, and the Dominican Republic, engaged in civil war, had asked Spain to return. Spain had agreed and dispatched a force from Cuba to reestablish a colonial government in Santo Domingo. The information that France was contemplating recolonizing Haiti was groundless. Seward chose to use this information both to reassert his waning authority in the cabinet and perhaps to take effective control of the Lincoln administration and generate an issue calculated to reunite the fractured nation.

On 1 April 1861, Seward sent Lincoln an extraordinary memo entitled "Some Thoughts for the President's Consideration." In the memo, Seward complained that the government lacked both a domestic and a foreign policy and was adrift. He recommended that Lincoln change the thrust of the American dispute from the question of slavery to that of union, and proposed that the United States seek "explanations" from France, Spain, Britain, and Russia for their plans and actions. (The Russian minister, Edouard de Stoeckl, had met with one of Davis's Confederate commissioners, and

Northern newspapers reported that Russia was about to recognize the Confederacy.) If, Seward continued, France and Spain could not satisfactorily explain their intentions and their recent actions, Lincoln should convene Congress and ask for a declaration of war. In addition, Seward recommended sending agents to Canada and Latin America to promote independence and opposition to European interference in the New World. Finally, he suggested that this policy required energetic and constant attention and implied that if Lincoln was unwilling to provide leadership, Seward was willing to assume it himself.

Lincoln responded to Seward immediately, pointing out that he had already made it clear that his administration would not interfere with slavery in the states where it already existed and that the fundamental issue in the crisis was indeed the question of union. He also noted that recent dispatches which Seward had sent to American agents abroad clearly stated his administration's foreign policy. Finally, Lincoln said that he would continue to determine policy with the help of his entire cabinet.

Seward's chief purpose, aside from taking control of the administration, had been to create a crisis that was calculated to restore unity. It is most unlikely that he either expected or wanted war with Europe—a foreign crisis only, not war, would have served his purpose. It was a dangerous strategy, however, and it is just as well that Lincoln rejected it. Although the memo remained confidential, Seward's foreign war panacea was well known among diplomats and merely confirmed their view that Seward would be a difficult person with whom to deal.

Seward's memo stemmed partly from his disagreement with his fellow cabinet members over the question of maintaining federal control of Fort Sumter in the harbor of Charleston, South Carolina. The fort, well within the range of shore batteries, could not be defended, and when President James Buchanan had attempted to send provisions to the fort early in January, Confederate gunners opened fire on the supply ship *Star of the West*, forcing it to retreat. Buchanan left the question of reprovisioning the fort or evacuating it to his successor, and shortly after Seward took office, he recommended the evacuation of Fort Sumter. Initially, Seward had majority support in the cabinet. He argued that attempting to resupply the fort would be regarded as a hostile act against the Confederate States of America and would not only strengthen the separatists' hands

"SOME THOUGHTS FOR THE PRESIDENT'S CONSIDERATION"

On 1 April 1861, less than two weeks before the outbreak of hostilities between the Union and the Confederacy, Secretary of State William Henry Seward sent a memo to President Abraham Lincoln criticizing the president for not developing either a domestic or foreign policy and urging him to "change the question before the Public from one upon Slavery for a question upon Union or Disunion." The most extraordinary part of the memo dealt with foreign policy. Spain was in the process of reestablishing colonial authority in the Dominican Republic at the invitation of the Dominicans, France was rumored to be considering the recolonization of Haiti, Britain had objected to the impending interference with its trade in Southern ports, and there were rumors that Russia was about to recognize the Confederacy. Seward thus wrote Lincoln:

> I would demand explanations from Spain and France categorically at once. I would seek explanations from Great Britain and Russia, and send agents into Canada, Mexico, and Central America, to rouse a vigorous continental spirit of independence on this continent against European intervention, and if satisfactory explanations are not received from Spain and France, would convene Congress, and declare war against them.

Lincoln responded to Seward privately the same day, pointing out that his domestic policy was clear and explicit. His foreign policy, he reminded Seward, had been expressed in circulars and instructions to American ministers abroad that the two of them had framed, "all in perfect harmony." Finally, referring to Seward's proposals and offer to take over its administration, Lincoln informed Seward, "If this must be done, I must do it." So ended one of the most extraordinary proposals ever submitted by a cabinet member to a president.

but also cause critical border states, such as Virginia, to secede from the Union. Lincoln, however, did not agree. He had pledged that he would yield no federal property to the Confederate government and decided to let events help him decide on a course of action. Over the following few weeks, public sentiment for holding the fort strengthened, and by the end of March, a majority of the cabinet came to the same position. This isolated Seward, who still counseled delaying any confrontation and who now feared that attempting to reprovision the fort would lead to war. His memo was his last effort to dissuade Lincoln from sending fresh supplies to the fort.

On 6 April, Lincoln notified South Carolina authorities that he had dispatched a supply force to Fort Sumter. Four days later, South Carolina demanded that the commandant of the fort, Major Robert J. Anderson, immediately surrender. When Anderson offered to surrender only after a few days when his supplies ran out, the Confederates, aware that fresh supplies were in transit, rejected Anderson's offer. On 12 April, Confederate General Pierre G. T. Beauregard opened fire on Fort Sumter. As Seward had feared, the decision to hold on to the fort had provoked the Confederates. The Civil War had begun.

Following the outbreak of hostilities and Jefferson Davis's announcement on 17 April that the Confederacy would issue letters of marque and reprisal, creating privateers for action against Union shipping, Union policy changed. Lincoln responded to Davis on 19 April by announcing that the Union would treat privateers as pirates and proclaiming a blockade of Southern ports. Seward attempted to open negotiations with the British foreign minister, Lord John Russell, for American adherence to the Declaration of Paris of 1856, an international agreement that, among other things, outlawed privateering. The United States had declined to participate earlier because, as a small-navy nation, it wanted to hold on to the privateering option. Seward hoped that the negotiation would cause Britain to postpone recognition of the Confederate belligerency and that an Anglo-American convention committing the United States to the Declaration of Paris would require Britain and other nations to treat Confederate privateers as pirates. Negotiations, however, began on 18 May, four days after Britain had recognized Confederate belligerency and collapsed in July, when Russell announced that if negotiations with the Union were successful, Britain would neither hold the Confederacy to the agreement nor treat Confederate privateers as pirates.

Lincoln's blockade proclamation had an important effect on British policy. A blockade was universally regarded as an act of war and therefore an implicit recognition that a state of belligerency existed. Therefore, Lincoln's proclamation opened the door to a British proclamation of neutrality and recognition of Confederate belligerency, which (except when in violation of neutrality laws) gave the Confederate States the right to, among other things, solicit loans, buy arms, engage in recruiting, and put cruisers on the high seas with the rights of search and seizure. Because British commerce with the United States and reliance on Southern cotton was so heavy, Russell had to respond to Lincoln's proclamation. The British proclamation became public on 14 May 1861, and as Seward had feared, the other nations of Europe immediately followed with their own proclamations of neutrality. The way was now clear for Confederate agents to scour Europe for money and material to conduct their war.

The Union blockade was a double-edged sword. If effective, or even moderately effective, it would reduce the ability of the Confederates to import war material. But it would also interfere with foreign commerce and deprive Britain, France, and other industrialized nations of vital supplies of cotton. Reducing the export of cotton to Europe could increase pressure in Europe for involvement in American affairs in support of the Confederacy, which the Confederates hoped and expected would be the case.

CONFEDERATE AGENTS IN WASHINGTON AND EUROPE

While Seward was meeting regularly with diplomats in Washington and, after Lincoln's inauguration on 4 March 1861, sending elaborate instructions to American ministers abroad, Confederate leaders—confident that foreign support would be forthcoming with little or no effort on their part—had a casual attitude toward foreign affairs. Thus, Jefferson Davis chose Robert Toombs of Georgia as his first secretary of state, despite the fact that Toombs had no experience and little interest in foreign affairs. After six months Toombs resigned to become a general in the Confederate army. Davis then replaced Toombs with Robert M. T. Hunter of Virginia, who also lacked experience and had previously declined appointment as secretary of state when it was offered by Franklin Pierce and James Buchanan. Hunter remained in office only seven months. Finally, on 17 March 1862, Davis appointed his close personal friend, former attorney general, and current secretary of war Judah P. Benjamin of Louisiana to the post. Benjamin, who had had limited experience dealing with international legal disputes regarding slavery, served ably until the end of the Confederacy. Neither Davis nor any of these secretaries of state, however, ever attempted to develop a cohesive or imaginative foreign policy program.

Confederate officials did not develop a foreign policy program chiefly because they were confident they did not need one. Committed to the notion that "cotton is king," they were certain that Britain, France, and the other industrial nations of Europe could not tolerate a destructive civil war in the United States that would weaken or destroy the cotton culture. Neither, Confederates believed, would Europeans tolerate interference in their North American commerce. Furthermore, for decades Southerners had demanded free trade and had resisted the high, protective tariffs favored by Northern manufacturing interests. Confederates reasoned that the prospect of free trade with the Confederacy would also win British approval and ensure support. And surrounding these economic considerations, Confederate leaders were certain that the European elite felt a special affinity to the planter class. All that was needed, therefore, was to explain why the Southern states had seceded, to convince European governments that the Confederacy had an effective government, and to assure European governments that the Confederates were determined to preserve their independence.

On 25 February 1861, Davis and Toombs dispatched A .B. Roman, Martin J. Crawford, and John Forsyth to Washington to negotiate a peaceful separation and the evacuation of all federal property in the Confederacy. Two days later, Toombs sent William Lowndes Yancey, Pierre A. Rost, and Ambrose Dudley Mann to Europe to secure de jure recognition of the Confederate States of America and treaties of amity and commerce. No thought was given to establishing permanent missions in Washington or any European capital.

Not surprisingly, Roman, Forsyth, and Crawford—who arrived in Washington in early March—had no success there. Seward refused to meet with the commissioners or to arrange a meeting with Lincoln, which they had requested. Unwilling, however, to antagonize the agents, Seward maintained contact through a third party. He assured the Confederates that the Union would not attempt to coerce the seceded states into returning to the Union and still hoped that a peaceful reunion was possible. On 8 April, after a month of waiting impatiently and distrusting Seward's assurance of Lincoln's commitment to the maintenance of peace, Crawford informed Davis of rumors that Lincoln was committed to war. A few days later the three Confederates returned home.

The Confederate mission to Europe began with considerably more promise than the mission to Washington. Russell and French foreign minister Edouard Thouvenel both received Yancey, Rost, and Mann unofficially, as was common practice in dealing with nonaccredited agents. Toombs had instructed the Confederate agents to visit Britain first, and then continue on to France, Russia, and Belgium. They were to explain that the secession of Southern states was provided for by the U.S. Constitution, and was necessary to prevent Northern social, political, and economic domination of the Southern states. Toombs had instructed the commissioners to avoid mention of slavery and emphasize the economic benefits to Europe of an independent Confederacy.

Meeting with the British and French foreign ministers was all that the commissioners accomplished. Russell expressed sympathy for the Confederacy but refused either to discuss treaty negotiations or to grant de jure recognition without a treaty. The British neutrality proclamation was already forthcoming when he spoke with the Confederate commissioners on May 3 and May 9. Russell had also reached an agreement with France that the two nations would act jointly on American affairs and instructed his minister in Washington, Lord Lyons, to coordinate policy and work closely with his French counterpart, Henri Mercier. In France, Thouvenel also expressed sympathy for the Confederacy but would go no further than Britain.

Britain's proclamation of neutrality did not address the question of whether the Union blockade was effective and therefore legal. Confederate agents understood that access to Southern ports was essential for the import of war material legitimized by belligerent status, and that the ability of the small Union navy to blockade all Southern ports and the extensive Southern coast was implausible at the least. Britain was divided on the issue. Commercial interests, legal purists, Southern sympathizers, and Confederate propagandists insisted the blockade was ineffective and demanded that Britain, with its powerful navy, confront the United States; the Admiralty and several in the government, however, understood that a loose interpretation of effectiveness could be most useful to the British navy sometime in the future.

The consequence of this division was that Russell never challenged the legality of the Union blockade, which became more effective as the war continued. Initially, the appearance of effectiveness was inadvertently enhanced by the decision of Southerners to impose a voluntary cotton embargo of their own. The Confederates reasoned that the sooner Britain and France felt the effects of the loss of fresh supplies of cotton, the more rapidly the former would demand the end of the Union blockade and come to the aid of the South. Southerners stated that no cotton would leave the Confederacy until the Northern blockade ended and Europe provided recognition and support. Their policy created the illusion that the blockade was more effective than it was, which Union agents and propagandists abroad used to their advantage; it also opened the Confederacy to charges of blackmail and hypocrisy.

Yancey, Rost, and Mann, having failed to secure de jure recognition from either Britain or France, saw no reason to continue their mission on to Russia and Belgium. They returned to Britain and began an intensive propaganda campaign in association with a number of other Southerners whose goal was to strengthen and expand support for the Confederacy among sympathetic members of Parliament and the upper classes, journalists, and conservatives generally. Yancey was confident that the upper classes and those in power in both Britain and France supported the Confederacy, but he understood that positive sentiment was not enough. Only a decisive Confederate military victory and a deprivation of fresh cotton would move both nations to act.

LATIN AMERICAN DEVELOPMENTS

After Lincoln squelched Seward's call for an aggressive program to meet European interference on 1 April, the secretary's policy changed. The secretary of state followed a surprisingly mild policy toward Spain, toward British, French, and Spanish intervention in Mexico, and toward the subsequent French occupation of Mexico City and establishment of Archduke Maximilian of Austria as emperor of Mexico. For example, he officially protested the Spanish occupation of Santo Domingo to the Spanish minister to the United States, Gabriel García y Tassara, and to the Spanish Ministry of Foreign Affairs in Madrid through the American chargé in Madrid. Tassara dismissed Seward's note as being meant primarily for the American public and not to be taken seriously. When Spanish officials explained that Spain had returned to Santo Domingo by invita-

tion and asked Seward to explain his note further, Seward retreated, noting to Tassara that Congress would consider sometime later on whether war was justified.

With regard to the impending tripartite intervention in Mexico, Britain had been firm in insisting that the three powers invite the United States to participate. Seward declined the offer, and since foreign intervention for the purpose of collecting debts was allowed under international law, he had no justification to oppose the three nations. Seward did propose lending Mexico funds to pay off its creditors with Baja California and other Mexican territory as collateral if the European nations would agree not to intervene. The plan failed when Britain, France, and Spain responded unenthusiastically and the U.S. Senate rejected the proposal. In October 1861 the three European nations signed the Tripartite Treaty of London and in December they jointly landed troops in Vera Cruz.

It soon became apparent that the French emperor, Louis Napoléon, had more ambitious schemes in mind, and Britain and Spain withdrew their forces. Seward warned France that the United States would not "view with indifference" the establishment of a European monarchy in the New World, especially so close to the United States, but Napoléon was undeterred. In June 1863, French troops seized Mexico City. Napoléon, with the support of Mexican conservatives in the capital, offered Maximilian an imperial throne. Maximilian accepted and set up his government in the following year. Benito Juárez fled to the countryside and initiated a guerrilla war against Maximilian and the French army that protected him. Seward was unhappy with this turn of events, but did nothing to oppose either Napoléon or Maximilian. War with France or even a threat of war, he decided, would not serve Union interests. Mexican affairs, like Caribbean matters, could wait until after peace had returned to the United States.

Confederate involvement in Mexico began in May 1861, when Toombs sent John T. Pickett to Mexico City to open a permanent embassy, secure recognition, and negotiate a treaty of amity and commerce. Astonishingly, Toombs also instructed Pickett to point out to the reformist Juárez the similarity of the Confederate and Mexican economies and the resemblance between slavery and peonage. Pickett's career as a filibusterer in Cuba and his record as consul in Vera Cruz did not inspire confidence among Mexicans, and Juárez was not impressed.

Pickett's mission was a disaster. He was unable to overcome Mexican fears of Southern expansionism or hostility toward slavery, both emphasized by the Union minister, Thomas Corwin. When Pickett suggested that the Confederacy might return some of the territory taken in the Mexican War in exchange for recognition, Mexican officials were skeptical. By the fall of 1861 Pickett had alienated all of those with whom he had dealt, chiefly by exposing his contempt for Mexico and his racism. When he became involved in a public brawl with a Union sympathizer in November, the Mexican authorities arrested him as a common criminal. When Davis and his cabinet learned of Pickett's behavior and arrest, they did not defend him but, rather, recalled their diplomat in disgrace and repudiated his actions. The damage, however, had been done. Juárez had no interest in supporting the Confederacy and maintained a strict neutrality throughout the Civil War.

In Mexico, the Confederates had greater success in negotiations with Santiago Vidaurri, the governor of Nuevo León and Coahuilla, who had long had separatist inclinations and conducted his affairs autonomously. The Confederate agent, Juan A. Quintero, had solid relations with Vidaurri. Quintero secured an important commercial agreement and a promise from Vidaurri that he would block any requests for the transit of Union troops across territory under his authority. The Confederate government instructed Quintero to discourage Vidaurri from separating from Mexico and asking for annexation to the Confederacy. President Davis doubted the Confederate Congress would welcome the addition of a Mexican province to their nation and he wished to avoid the embarrassment of a rejection. For all their efforts, Mexico was a low priority for the Confederates. They understood that the key to a successful foreign policy remained in Europe.

PRESSURE AND COUNTERPRESSURE ON BRITAIN AND FRANCE

Seward understood that British policy would be decisive in Europe, and he was pleased that in the patronage battles, he had succeeded in having Charles Francis Adams, the son and grandson of former American ministers to the Court of St. James, appointed to Britain. Lincoln's choice, William Dayton of New Jersey—John C. Frémont's running mate on the Republican ticket in 1856—went to France instead. Adams had his first interview with Russell on 18 May. Seward had been outraged by the British neutrality proclamation and the granting of belligerent rights to the Confederacy, and Adams complained to Russell. Russell only assured Adams that Britain had no intention at that time to move to the next step of recognizing Confederate independence.

Seward also reacted harshly to the willingness of Russell to meet, even informally, with the Confederate agents. He sent Adams his notorious Dispatch No. 10, dated 21 May 1861, instructing Adams to break off all relations with the British government if Russell continued to meet with the Confederate commissioners. Seward had wanted Adams to read the message to Russell, but Lincoln wisely insisted that Seward change the instructions so that Adams had discretion in his discussion with Russell and was to use the document only for his own guidance. Adams had the good sense to soften the dispatch by presenting only noninflammatory parts to Russell. Russell, as it happened, had already decided to have no further discussions with the Confederate commissioners.

By late summer Yancey, Rost, Mann, and their colleagues had had enough success in arousing British and French support to alarm both Adams and Dayton. Hunter, who had replaced Toombs as Confederate secretary of state, saw great potential in the use of propaganda and decided to formalize the propaganda effort by appointing journalists Henry Hotze and Edwin De Leon to promote the Confederate cause in London and Paris, respectively. Hotze established a weekly journal, the *Index,* that was highly successful. After De Leon ran into difficulties, Hotze took over the French propaganda operation as well.

Whatever success these agents had in shaping opinion, however, Britain and France refused to move from their neutral policies. Yancey remained confident that a military victory and lack of cotton would bring about British support, and he was relieved when Lincoln emphasized that the Union had no intention to abolish slavery. All of the elements he believed necessary for tangible British support were in place by midsummer 1861. The Confederates scored a stunning military success on 21 July at Bull Run, Virginia, and distress was already apparent in the cotton manufacturing areas. When, however, the Confederate agents requested an unofficial meeting with Russell, he put them off and informed them that Britain would remain neutral. Both British public opinion and the cabinet remained divided, and whatever Lincoln's position on slavery, British abolitionists and Union sympathizers emphasized that the Confederacy was based on slavery and its expansion. Neither Prime Minister Lord Palmerston nor Foreign Minister Russell were willing to appear as champions of a slave nation or to contribute to its perpetuation and expansion.

Shortly after Russell's response, Davis and Hunter decided to take a more aggressive approach and establish formal diplomatic missions in Britain, France, Spain, and Belgium. The previous passive policy was clearly not working; Yancey submitted his resignation to Davis and prepared to return to Alabama. Davis ordered Mann to open a diplomatic mission in Belgium, and he sent Rost to Spain. More significantly, Davis selected James Murray Mason of Virginia to establish a mission in London and John Slidell of Louisiana, a highly experienced and able diplomat, to go to Paris.

Following Adams's assumption of his duties in London, Anglo-American relations proceeded smoothly until the end of the year. Adams deftly handled Seward's Dispatch No. 10, and Russell's decision to have no further meetings with the Confederates resolved the matter raised by the dispatch. For the most part, Adams attempted to counter the increasingly effective Confederate propaganda campaign and to gather information on the activities of Confederate agents. The only major diplomatic issue was the unsuccessful negotiation on the Declaration of Paris.

THE *TRENT* AFFAIR AND ITS AFTERMATH

A much more serious dispute in Anglo-American relations arose over the Union capture of Mason and Slidell in November. The two Confederate diplomats ran the blockade on 12 October 1861, sailing from Charleston to Nassau and thence to Cuba. On 7 November they boarded the *Trent*, a British mail packet, for the remaining leg of their voyage to England. On the next day the USS *San Jacinto*, under the command of Captain Charles Wilkes, stopped the *Trent* on the high seas, boarded the vessel, and after a minor skirmish removed Mason and Slidell and their secretaries. Wilkes carried his prisoners to Boston where they were imprisoned in Fort Warren in Boston harbor. Wilkes had acted without instructions and the seizure raised a number of questions of international law that resembled the issue of impressment that had so aroused Americans before 1812.

While feigning outrage, the Confederates were delighted with Wilkes's action. They were certain that the Union would never give up the prisoners and that the resulting Anglo-American hostility could only help the Confederate cause overseas. Wilkes was widely applauded in the North, and the seizure of Confederate "traitors" from a British ship struck many as just and a proper response to Britain's assumed partiality toward the Confederacy. The crisis intensified during November and December as Secretary of the Navy Gideon Welles, the House of Representatives, and the Northern press extolled Wilkes's heroism. Meanwhile, the British developed an extensive case for the illegality of his action and made it clear that they regarded the seizure as an affront to Britain's national honor. Prime Minister Palmerston was furious. Britain prepared for war, and sent more than eleven thousand troops to Canada. Russell charged that Wilkes had violated international law and instructed Lyons to demand the immediate release of Mason and Slidell and an apology. At Queen Victoria's request, Prince Albert, although mortally ill, softened Russell's dispatch and provided an out for the Americans by allowing Seward to deny that Wilkes had acted under instruction.

Seward may have initially been pleased by Wilkes's action, but he very quickly adopted a moderate tone in a dispatch to Adams that the latter presented to Russell. Seward's note did much to defuse the crisis at the highest level. Lyons also presented Russell's demands in such a way to make a favorable American response more likely. Finally, on 25 December Seward responded by informing the British that Wilkes had indeed acted on his own and, while not violating international law, had made certain technical errors. The two diplomats would be "cheerfully liberated" and turned over to Lord Lyons. Seward had convinced Lincoln, others in the cabinet, and a number of prominent senators that retaining the Confederates was decidedly not in the Union's interest.

The furor generated by the *Trent* affair dissipated quickly. Support for Wilkes disappeared as American attention turned to the war at home and journals published calculations of the costs of a war with Britain. Seward had demonstrated genuine statesmanship that Russell and others recognized. For the first time, British officials began to reconsider their early estimation of the secretary of state. Seward perhaps understood better than before that threatening war was, indeed, a dangerous policy. Seward's reputation among influential associates, however, did not improve. A number of prominent Radical Republicans, never supportive, renewed efforts to remove him from office. By this time Lincoln had come to regard Seward as an effective secretary and as a valuable ally in his opposition to the Radical Republicans and was determined to keep him in the cabinet.

Seward meanwhile sought to capitalize on the relief felt in Britain and the Union over the peaceful resolution of the issue. Although the details remain vague, there is evidence that he facilitated the deployment of British troops in Canada—they had arrived after the St. Lawrence River froze over. Whatever the case, Seward skillfully used the story that he had granted permission to Her Majesty's troops to cross American territory to emphasize that he held no animosity nor aggressive intent toward Britain. Seward also resisted suggestions that the United States abrogate or let expire the Marcy-Elgin Reciprocity Treaty of 1854. The treaty, set to expire in 1864, eliminated duties in trade between the United States and Canada, opened the St. Lawrence to the United States, and regulated fishing off the Canadian coast. Seward saw Canadian-American free trade as a means of integrating the Canadian economy into America's as a prelude to annexation.

Seward also concluded negotiations with Lyons in April 1862 for the suppression of the African slave trade. The agreement extended the reciprocal right to search and detain merchant ships off the coasts of Africa and Cuba and established prize courts in Sierra Leone, the Cape of Good Hope, and New York. In February 1863, Seward and Lyons expanded the agreement to include the coasts of Madagascar, Puerto Rico, and Santo Domingo. These treaties completed efforts to end the Atlantic slave trade that had begun a half century earlier. (In the absence of Southern senators, Seward also recognized Liberia and Haiti in 1862 and treaties of amity and commerce with Liberia on 21 October 1862 and Haiti on 3 November 1864.) These agreements with Britain after the *Trent* crisis contributed to the restoration of friendlier relations. This was especially important at a time when pressure for mediation was increasing in Britain and France because of a developing crisis in cotton textile manufacturing centers.

COTTON DIPLOMACY

Confederates were disheartened by the peaceful settlement of the *Trent* affair, and by 1862 had realized that their best hope for British and European support would come from a cotton famine in England. Distress in the cotton manufacturing districts increased greatly during the spring and summer of 1862. The jobs of an estimated 900,000 workers in the textile industry, centered in Lancashire, were in jeopardy. The British welfare system was severely strained, and Southern sympathizers increased their demands for intervention to relieve the cotton shortage. Although Seward made available cotton that came into Union hands, and imports of non-American cotton increased, the distress in Lancashire did not diminish, and Confederate reliance on cotton diplomacy seemed to be working.

In fact, although less American cotton was reaching Britain, British manufacturers, unlike their workers, were not in dire straits. In 1859 and 1860 the South had produced bumper crops that had glutted the market and driven down world prices. British warehouses were thus filled with huge stocks of cheap cotton fiber, and manufacturers were producing cloth at unprecedented levels, which also depressed textile prices. The Union blockade and Southern embargo were a blessing for these manufacturers as well as financiers dealing in cotton securities and futures. The prospect of a shortage of fiber and cloth immediately caused the value of both raw and finished cotton to rise dramatically. Merchants and manufacturers hoarded their goods, reduced their output, and made fortunes in the process. Those who had been promoting the development of alternate sources in Egypt and India appeared vindicated as planters in those regions also reaped huge profits. Only the workers suffered.

Outside of the cotton districts, other British industries prospered from the war. Both the Union and the Confederacy purchased war materials in increasing quantities, and producers of woolen cloth benefited from the reduced production of cotton cloth and inflated textile prices. Finally, Confederate raiders had enormous success in attacking Northern commercial vessels. American merchantmen were driven from the seas or forced to pay enormous premiums for maritime insurance. British merchants replaced American merchants in direct trade and strengthened their domination of other markets.

Despite the new wealth generated by the American war and continued national prosperity, by the fall of 1862 the distress in Lancashire was real and the news of bloodshed and destruction from America was shocking. It also seemed that the

201

Union would never be able to subdue the South and that continuing the war was pointless. With the approval of Palmerston and Chancellor of the Exchequer William E. Gladstone and the prior agreement of Napoléon, Russell therefore brought the question of mediation to the cabinet. The discussion was extensive, and the cabinet was divided. Russell and Gladstone urged their colleagues to support an offer of mediation to both sides. However, after an impassioned argument against offering mediation by Minister of War George Cornewall Lewis—who pointed out that neither Lincoln nor Seward would accept the offer and that Britain could be forced into supporting the slaveholding Confederacy—news arrived that the Battle of Antietam had ended without a clear victory by either side. Palmerston decided to continue waiting until the war took "a more decided turn." Napoléon then proposed offering the Americans a six-month armistice if both Britain and Russia agreed to act jointly with him. Russia declined first, and on 13 November the British also declined. Confederate confidence in King Cotton was shaken, and the Confederate government sought support from Europe along other avenues.

DECLINING CONFEDERATE PROSPECTS

In May 1861 Confederate secretary of the navy Stephen Mallory sent James Dunwoody Bulloch, a retired naval officer, to Britain to build or purchase six steamships to serve as commerce raiders and James H. North to purchase two ironclads for use against the Union blockade. By August, Bulloch had begun the construction of two ships, later christened the *Florida* and the *Alabama,* and in 1862 the North contracted for the construction of an ironclad ram.

Union agents learned of Bulloch's plans and Adams attempted to prevent the sailing of the *Alabama.* Russell refused to seize the ship for lack of evidence that its construction violated British neutrality laws. When Adams amassed evidence and a legal opinion to the contrary, Russell sought legal opinion himself and ultimately became convinced that the ship should be detained, but his order to that effect arrived too late to prevent the launching of the *Alabama* in early August 1862. Captained by Raphael Semmes, the ship wreaked havoc on Union shipping, which after the war became the basis of demands by the United States for massive compensation. After the departure of the *Alabama* from Britain, Adams and Russell

engaged in a rancorous exchange of notes. Adams was determined to prevent future Confederate cruisers from leaving British ports.

Russell ultimately decided that it would better serve British interests if other ships being constructed for the Confederacy did not put to sea. In April 1863 he ordered seizure of the *Alexandria,* then under construction. Later in the year, following strong protests from Adams and the threat of privateering by the Union, Russell decided to detain rams that Bulloch was having constructed. By 1863 the Confederates had given up hope for recognition and substantial support from Britain. British consuls, whom the Confederate government had allowed to remain at their posts and who initially had written home about Confederate invincibility, had antagonized Confederate officials by their protests on behalf of British subjects being conscripted into the Confederate army. (Seward had gone out of his way to appease British consuls in the North over the same problem.) In October 1863, President Davis expelled all British consuls still at their posts. Two months earlier, on 4 August 1863, Judah Benjamin ordered Mason to close his London mission and to join Slidell in Paris.

Confederate officials had come to the conclusion that their best hope for support lay in Napoléon and France rather than in Palmerston and Britain. Napoléon had taken the initiative, following the failure of the Anglo-French mediation discussions in 1862, in proposing an armistice. In January 1863 he unilaterally proposed mediation, which Seward summarily rejected. During the previous September and October, Slidell successfully concluded a loan of $14.5 million with the French firm Emile Erlanger and Company that allowed Confederate agents used to purchase war materials.

Also, Mallory honored Bulloch's request that he shift operations to Paris, and in April and June 1863 the latter contracted for four commerce raiders and two ironclad rams. Unfortunately for the Confederates, France proved little more hospitable than Britain. Napoléon clearly sympathized with the Confederates, but pressure from Seward and Dayton forced him to prevent the ships from sailing. Napoléon, about to embark on his imperial program in Mexico, had no wish to become embroiled with the Union.

The construction of Confederate naval vessels in Britain and France was not the only issue that created difficulties on the high seas. As the demand for goods rose in both Britain and the Confederacy, success in running the Union blockade became ever more profitable. Similarly, the owners of Union vessels that captured blockade runners could take the ships to prize courts and receive a substantial proportion of the value of condemned prizes. The system led to a number of questionable seizures of not only British ships but also of vessels flying French and Spanish colors. Charles Wilkes continued to create problems after the *Trent* affair by using neutral ports as bases of operation against ships suspected of intentions to run the blockade. These possibly illegal seizures and violations of international law led to continual protests, legal battles, and ill will. Palmerston, however, saw value in the continual stretching of international law by Americans. They were setting precedents that could be useful to Britain in subsequent conflicts. None of these issues rose above the level of annoyances.

THE SLAVERY ISSUE AND THE END OF CONFEDERATE DIPLOMACY

Until 1863 the slavery issue lingered in the background of the American crisis. For domestic reasons, Lincoln and Seward had attempted to make it clear that the conflict in the United States had little to do with slavery and everything to do with preserving the Union. The North, they argued, had no intention of interfering with slavery in the states, and even after hostilities began they suggested that no assault would be made on the institution. Confederate agents abroad did their best to avoid discussion of slavery altogether, and when pressed argued that the war was not about slavery but rather over the right of states to preserve their social and economic institutions. British supporters of the Confederacy took Lincoln at his word, and Palmerston, firmly hostile to slavery, was relieved that it was not an issue, since otherwise Britain would have had less flexibility in developing policies toward the American war. Nevertheless, the Confederates could not disguise the fact that their nation was committed to the preservation of the slave system, and the British could never forget that to aid the Confederacy was to aid a slave nation. Furthermore, whatever the wishes of Lincoln and Seward, Radical Republicans at home and abroad, abolitionists on both sides of the Atlantic, and Union propagandists called for a change in Union policy toward slavery and kept the issue alive in public discourse. The question of the future of American slavery never disappeared from view.

Following the Battle of Antietam in September 1862, Lincoln decided to confront slavery directly. On 22 September he issued his Preliminary Emancipation Proclamation freeing all slaves in areas that were still in rebellion in January 1863. Lincoln had presented the plan to his cabinet on 22 July, but Seward and others persuaded him to wait until the Union had a military success lest the policy be regarded as an act of desperation. Seward strenuously objected to the proclamation because he feared it would antagonize slaveholders who had remained loyal; strengthen Confederate morale and determination; and, worst of all, encourage blacks in the South to rise in "servile insurrection." He also doubted that emancipation was constitutional and feared that the sudden end of slavery would permanently weaken the American economy and either delay or destroy altogether the rise and completion of the American empire. Seward remained committed to the containment of slavery and its gradual abolition and replacement by free labor.

European diplomats in Washington were uniformly critical of the Preliminary Emancipation Proclamation. They regarded it, indeed, as an act of desperation following the Union failure to score a major victory at Antietam; some saw it as signifying the triumph of the Radical Republicans and abolitionists in the North. All worried that its enunciation would trigger a slave insurrection, extend race war, and then lead to the thorough destruction of the cotton culture in the United States. The European home offices were also critical of this turn in Union policy, especially since Seward had continually warned Britain and France that it was their policies of neutrality and support for the Confederacy that had extended the war and increased the danger of a slave uprising.

Nevertheless, by 1 January 1863, when the Emancipation Proclamation was issued, Europeans had reconciled themselves to the impending end of slavery in the United States should the Union win the war. (It was expected that slavery could not long survive in areas not in rebellion.) This understanding made it appear that the outcome of the war would determine the future of slavery, which changed the character of European-American relations for the remainder of the conflict by making it even more difficult for Europe to adopt policies in support of the Confederacy. When the Union armies scored major victories in July at Gettysburg and Vicksburg, European ministries began to regard a full Union military victory as more likely, and the continued successes of Generals Ulysses S. Grant and William Sherman convinced them that victory was certain. As the British and French discarded their working assumption that the division of the United States was irreversible, their foreign policies changed accordingly. Confederate appeals for support were now largely ignored.

Jefferson Davis and Judah Benjamin understood that survival depended on European support and that this support would not be forthcoming without altering the Confederate position on slavery. In November 1864, Davis presented to the Confederate Congress a plan to employ forty thousand slaves in noncombatant military service to be followed by their emancipation. While this proposal was being considered, he dispatched Duncan F. Kenner of Louisiana to Europe on a secret mission with instructions to offer European governments a promise of emancipation of the slaves in exchange for recognition. Napoléon, then deeply involved in his Mexican policy, declined the offer and replied that France could not act without British concurrence. When Kenner made the same proposal to the British government, Palmerston rejected it out of hand, informing Kenner that Britain would never recognize the Confederate States of America. Confederate diplomacy in Europe had come to a dead end.

The final episode in the diplomacy of the American Civil War occurred in February 1865, when Lincoln and Seward agreed to meet with a delegation of Confederate leaders at Hampton Roads, Virginia. Francis P. Blair, Sr., had arranged the meeting at Davis's request, and Davis had selected Confederate Vice President Alexander H. Stephens, former Confederate secretary of state Robert M. T. Hunter, and former U.S. Supreme Court justice and Confederate assistant secretary of war John A. Campbell to conduct the negotiations. Both Lincoln and Davis hoped to arrange a return of peace, but their terms were incompatible. Lincoln demanded reunion, acceptance of emancipation, and the disbanding of all Confederate military forces. He was prepared to offer the South generous terms on a number of issues, including compensation to slaveholders. Davis had wanted an armistice, to be followed by discussion of all these and other issues. When Lincoln would not yield in his demands for reunion and the breakup of Confederate military force first, the meeting collapsed.

Military action resumed fully after the Hampton Roads conference, and within four months the last of the Confederate armies had surrendered to Union forces. Jefferson Davis, who refused to admit defeat and promoted guerrilla war to the end, was captured by Union troops in Irwinsville, Georgia, on 10 May. He was imprisoned and indicted for treason, but was paroled two years later.

CONCLUSION

It is doubtful that the Confederacy could ever have achieved the support that it expected during the Civil War. It never was in the interest of the nations of Europe to become entangled in the American conflict. Rather, they profited by a neutral policy. Confederates relied on sympathy and the pressure from cotton textile manufacturers to force Britain, and then other nations in Europe, to their support and defense. They believed that time was on their side. As a consequence, the Confederate government delayed in adopting a bold diplomatic strategy until it was far too late. At the same time, William Henry Seward, with the significant aid of Charles Francis Adams in London and a number of other superb diplomats, developed an aggressive and consistent program that did not always win friends but was effective. Seward began his term of office with a reputation for recklessness and hostility toward the British, and his initial maneuvers seemed to confirm, as Lyons wrote home, that he would be a "dangerous foreign minister." Seward's erratic behavior had the positive effect of making European foreign ministers more cautious. During the critical first year of the war, Palmerston and Russell worried that Seward had little understanding of the limits to which he could go in his threats and bluster against British policy, and so as not to arouse him and precipitate a crisis, the British leaders adopted a largely passive policy, ended official contacts with Confederate officials, and resisted attempts by pro-Confederate members of Parliament to support the Southern cause. After Seward's first year in office, his reputation improved, and by the end of the war, he and Adams were highly regarded overseas.

It is clear that international relations during the war years were largely determined by the interests of all the nations involved directly and indirectly in the struggle. It is difficult to see how the Confederacy could have acquired the support it needed or how the Union could have done better. It is also clear that the Confederacy's weak policy did not help its cause and that the strong and clearsighted Union policy, conducted by able hands, made a profound difference and was essential to a Union victory in 1865.

BIBLIOGRAPHY

Adams, Ephraim D. *Great Britain and the American Civil War.* 2 vols. New York, 1925. The classic study.

Bernath, Stuart L. *Squall Across the Atlantic: American Civil War Prize Cases and Diplomacy.* Berkeley, Calif., 1970. A superb analysis.

Blackburn, George M. *French Newspaper Opinion on the American Civil War.* Westport, Conn., 1997.

Blackett, R. J. M. *Divided Hearts: Britain and the American Civil War.* Baton Rouge, La., 2001. A thorough and sophisticated analysis.

Blumenthal, Henry. "Confederate Diplomacy: Popular Notions and International Realities." *Journal of Southern History* 32 (1966): 151–171. An important essay.

Brauer, Kinley. "Gabriel Garcia y Tassara and the American Civil War: A Spanish Perspective." *Civil War History* 21 (1975): 5–27.

———. "The Slavery Problem in the Diplomacy of the American Civil War." *Pacific Historical Review* 46 (1977): 439–469.

Carroll, Daniel B. *Henry Mercier and the American Civil War.* Princeton, N.J., 1971. An excellent examination of the diplomacy of the French minister to the United States.

Case, Lynn Marshall, and Warren F. Spencer. *The United States and France: Civil War Diplomacy.* Philadelphia, 1970. A thorough and judicious examination.

Clapp, Margaret. *Forgotten First Citizen: John Bigelow.* Boston, 1947. A biography of the American consul in Paris.

Cortada, James W. "Spain and the American Civil War Relations at Mid-Century, 1855–1868." *Transactions of the American Philosophical Society* 70, no. 4 (1980).

Crook, D. P. *The North, The South, and the Powers, 1861–1865.* New York, 1974. An able synthesis that emphasizes British and Canadian relations with the Union and Confederacy.

Cullop, Charles P. *Confederate Propaganda in Europe, 1861–1865.* Coral Gables, Fla., 1969.

Duberman, Martin B. *Charles Francis Adams, 1807–1866.* New York, 1961. Excellent biography of the U.S. Minister to Great Britain.

Ellison, Mary. *Support for Secession: Lancashire and the American Civil War.* Chicago, 1972. Excellent study of the effects of the cotton famine on British opinion in the Lancashire cotton district.

Evans, Eli N. *Judah P. Benjamin: The Jewish Confederate.* New York, 1988. Especially strong on Benjamin's relations with Jefferson Davis.

Ferris, Norman B. "Diplomacy." In Allan Nevins et al., eds. *Civil War Books: A Critical Bibliography.* Vol. 1. Baton Rouge, La., 1967. An excellent starting point for books published before 1967.

———. *Desperate Diplomacy: William H. Seward's Foreign Policy, 1861.* Knoxville, Tenn., 1976. A study of the difficult first year of the war.

———. *The Trent Affair: A Diplomatic Crisis.* Knoxville, Tenn., 1977. Best detailed study of the crisis.

Hanna, Alfred J., and Kathryn Abbey Hanna. *Napoleon III and Mexico: American Triumph over Monarchy.* Chapel Hill, N.C., 1971.

Hyman, Harold, ed. *Heard Round the World: The Impact Abroad of the Civil War.* New York, 1968. Looks at the influence of the Civil War primarily on Europe.

Jenkins, Brian A. *Britain and the War for the Union.* 2 vols. Montreal, 1974, 1980. More recent and useful treatment than the Adams work.

Jones, Howard. *Union in Peril: The Crisis over British Intervention in the Civil War.* Chapel Hill, N.C., 1992. Excellent study of the mediation crisis of 1862.

———. *Abraham Lincoln and a New Birth of Freedom: The Union and Slavery in the Diplomacy of the Civil War.* Lincoln, Nebr., 1999.

Mahoney, Harry T., and Marjorie Locke Mahoney. *Mexico and the Confederacy, 1860–1867.* San Francisco, 1998. Good narrative survey.

May, Robert E., ed. *The Union, the Confederacy, and the Atlantic Rim.* West Lafayette, Ind., 1995. Information on the impact of the Civil War on Europe, European colonies, and Latin America and examines the role of African Americans in influencing British opinion.

Meade, Robert D. *Judah P. Benjamin, Confederate Statesman.* New York, 1943. A good treatment of Benjamin's diplomacy.

Merli, Frank. *Great Britain and the Confederate Navy, 1861–1965.* Bloomington, Ind., 1970. Best study of the subject.

Monaghan, Jay. *Diplomat in Carpet Slippers: Abraham Lincoln Deals with Foreign Affairs.* New York, 1945. A popular study that overemphasizes Lincoln's role and is oversimplified.

Owsley, Frank L. *King Cotton Diplomacy: Foreign Relations of the Confederate States of America.* 2d ed. Chicago, 1959. A full examination of Confederate diplomacy but somewhat dated.

Richardson, H. Edward. *Cassius Marcellus Clay: Firebrand of Freedom.* Lexington, Ky., 1976. Covers Union diplomacy with Russia.

Saul, Norman E. *Distant Friends: The United States and Russia, 1763–1867.* Lawrence, Kans., 1991. Based on research in both Russian and American materials.

Schoonover, Thomas D. *Dollars over Dominion: The Triumph of Liberalism in Mexican–United States Relations, 1861–1867.* Baton Rouge, 1978.

Smiley, David L. *Lion of Whitehall: The Life of Cassius M. Clay.* Madison, Wis., 1962. On Union diplomacy with Russia.

Spencer, Warren F. *The Confederate Navy in Europe.* University, Ala., 1983. Deals with Bulloch and Confederate naval warfare.

Stern, Philip Van Doren. *When the Guns Roared: World Aspects of the American Civil War.* Garden City, N.Y., 1965. A popular study.

Taylor, John M. *William Henry Seward: Lincoln's Right Hand.* New York, 1991. A readable popular account.

Tyler, Ronnie C. *Santiago Vidaurri and the Southern Confederacy.* Austin, Tex., 1973. On Mexican-American relations.

Van Deusen, Glyndon G. *William Henry Seward.* New York, 1967. A scholarly biography.

Warren, Gordon H. *Fountain of Discontent: The Trent Affair and Freedom of the Seas.* Boston, 1981. A study of the first year of the war.

Willson, Beckles. *John Slidell and the Confederates in Paris, 1862–1865.* New York, 1932.

Winks, Robin. *Canada and the United States: The Civil War Years.* Baltimore, 1960. An able treatment of Canadian-American relations.

Woldman, Albert A. *Lincoln and the Russians.* Cleveland, Ohio, 1952. A narrative based on diplomatic correspondence from the United States.

See also AMBASSADORS, EXECUTIVE AGENTS, AND SPECIAL REPRESENTATIVES; BLOCKADES; EMBARGOES AND SANCTIONS; REALISM AND IDEALISM.

COLD WAR EVOLUTION AND INTERPRETATIONS

Walter L. Hixson

Interpreting the history of the Cold War has been a notoriously controversial pursuit. New evidence, unearthed in recent years from archives on both sides of the Atlantic and the Pacific, has not resolved old debates, but it has added immensely to our collective knowledge. Much remains to be learned and understood about the history of the global power struggle, the impact of which on the latter half of the twentieth century can scarcely be exaggerated. As it recedes into history, the passions of presentism (interpreting history on the basis of contemporary prejudices) have receded as well. These developments open up new possibilities for stimulating discussion of the evolution and interpretations of the Cold War.

Five key interpretive themes can be employed to explain the evolution of the Cold War and to interpret the history of the conflict: ideology, national expansionism, economic hegemony, militarization, and patriotic culture. These forces help explain the origins, evolution, and end of the Cold War. Despite the primary focus on Soviet-American relations, no one questions that the Cold War became a *global* phenomenon enveloping the fates of scores of nations, some modern and industrial, others premodern and developing. Nations such as Great Britain and China played key roles in the evolution of the Cold War, but so did smaller states as diverse as Angola, Cuba, Egypt, Greece, India, Israel, Japan, Korea, South Africa, Vietnam, and many more. As this list suggests, the Cold War encompasses a vast and complex history, overshadowing the latter half of the twentieth century.

IDEOLOGICAL DIVIDE

Ideology is a central element in coming to grips with the Cold War. In this respect, the Cold War actually began in 1917, with the triumph of the Bolshevik communist revolutionaries in Russia.

The Bolsheviks, led by Vladimir Ilich Lenin, a committed Marxist revolutionary, denounced capitalism as an exploitative and moribund social system. Lenin's contribution to Marxism was his theory that imperialism was the last gasp of capitalism. The Bolsheviks believed that the bloodletting then under way in World War I reflected the penultimate crisis of modern capitalism. Lenin and other communists sought to build socialism in Russia while doing what they could to facilitate expansion of Marxism-Leninism abroad.

The West greeted the Bolshevik Revolution with implacable hostility, including an ill-fated Allied intervention against the Bolsheviks in the Russian civil war, which the Marxists eventually won. The Western worldview was capably represented in the rhetoric of President Woodrow Wilson, who had called for U.S. intervention in World War I to make the world "safe for democracy." Wilson spoke not just for constitutional government but also for free-trade capitalism as well. Bolshevism, with its emphasis on state economic planning, was anathema to the deep-seated faith in free enterprise, a cornerstone of American ideology. Moreover, Wilson, like millions of Americans deeply religious, found Marxist atheism, which had condemned religion as the "opiate of the masses," profoundly offensive.

Hence, an ideological gulf between the Soviet Union and the United States, between communism and capitalism, emerged from World War I and divided East and West throughout the interwar period. Beginning in 1929 the Soviet Union came under the iron authority of Joseph Stalin, a pitiless autocrat responsible for the deaths of millions of his own countrymen in purges, forced agricultural collectivization, and breakneck industrialization. Washington declined to accord formal diplomatic recognition of the Soviet Union until 1933. Among other consequences, East-West hostility ensured that efforts to forge an antifascist alliance against Nazi Germany during the late 1930s would come to grief. When the Western powers rejected Soviet overtures for an alliance against the Nazis, Stalin negotiated his own pact with Adolf Hitler in 1939, paving the way for World War II. After sacking much of Europe, Hitler turned on the Soviets, long his primary target, in an invasion of Russia launched on 22 June 1941. The West quickly embraced the Soviet cause as its own in a mutual conflict against Nazi aggression.

Clearly the wartime Grand Alliance, forged by the Nazi bid to dominate Europe, was little more than a marriage of convenience. Indeed, nothing less than Hitler's bid to dominate Europe could have brought Stalin and the Soviet Union into alliance with Great Britain and the United States. Winston Churchill's memorable comment that he would ally with "the devil himself" against the Nazi regime was no mere quip; Churchill was explaining just how extraordinary the prime minister himself considered the unlikely alliance between East and West. Equally cosmopolitan, but markedly less anti-Soviet than Churchill, President Franklin D. Roosevelt saw the war as an opportunity not only to defeat Nazi aggression but to create a framework through Soviet-American cooperation for something like the world order Wilson had envisioned all too prematurely during the previous European war.

Roosevelt came to understand, however, in the weeks before his death on 12 April 1945, that his vision might not stand up to the hard realities embodied in a renascent Stalinist Russia. Once seemingly on the brink of destruction, the Soviet Union had turned the battle at Stalingrad in the winter of 1942–1943 and never looked back. Despite the unparalleled destruction of the Soviet state, including some 27 million dead in the war, the Red Army found itself ensconced in the heart of Europe, all with the blessing of its wartime allies. The onetime pariah state now stood poised to exert unprecedented influence on the postwar world.

NATIONAL EXPANSION

World War II redrew the map of the world, creating vast power vacuums from the defeat of Nazi Germany in Europe and imperial Japan in Asia. Given his own ruthlessness and the lens of Marxist historicism, Stalin could only interpret the Soviet victory as an opportunity both to ensure his nation's security and to promote the inevitable expansion of the communist system. None of the

new archival evidence that began emerging in the 1990s has contradicted Stalin's explanation to a group of comrades in 1945 that to the victors would go the spoils; that is, whichever power occupied a liberated European country could be expected to impose his own social system on that state. Stalin heard his allies' pleas for him to pay lip service to a postwar democratic order, best embodied in the Declaration of Liberated Europe issued at the Yalta Conference in February 1945, but at the end of the day this was "algebra," as far as the Soviet dictator was concerned, and he averred a preference for simple math.

Presiding over a vast global empire—though one verging on dissolution rather than expansion—Winston Churchill understood simple math as well. He and Stalin had engaged in just such an exercise in coming to the so-called percentages agreement during a tête-à-tête in Moscow in 1944. Running down the nations of East-Central Europe one by one, the two Allied leaders came to agreement as to which powers would call the shots in the states then being liberated from the Nazis. In effect, Churchill went a long way toward acquiescing in the very division of Europe that he later bitterly decried in his 5 March 1946 "Iron Curtain" address in Fulton, Missouri. Churchill hoped to temper Soviet ambitions, but when it came to the fates of neighboring states such as Poland and Romania, Stalin understood only one language—domination.

U.S.–Soviet relations, vastly improved during the war under Roosevelt, began to deteriorate. Within less than a year after the end of the European war, Cold War declarations emanated from both capitals. In a February 1946 address, Stalin offered up a plateful of Marxist verities, including the warning that conflict between communism and Western imperialism was inevitable and would continue. George F. Kennan, America's foremost Soviet expert, dispatched the "long telegram" from Moscow that same month warning of an unstable, xenophobic, and expansionist regime. The policy Kennan urged in response— "containment" of Russia's "expansive tendencies"—soon became the watchword of American foreign policy. Churchill's address in Fulton, delivered in Truman's presence in his home state, followed on the heels of Kennan's landmark 8,000-word telegram. Stalin responded to Churchill's speech by labeling Britain's wartime leader a "convinced reactionary" and accusing the Western powers of planning a new cordon sanitaire against the Soviet Union.

Rising Cold War tensions focused next on the Near East. Only a showdown in the new United Nations prompted Stalin's grudging withdrawal from neighboring Iran, where the Red Army had remained past an agreed-upon March 1946 deadline. By the spring of 1947, the threat of a leftist triumph in Greece, fear of Soviet influence in Turkey, and the decline of British power in the Mediterranean region combined to give rise to the Truman Doctrine. In a speech that has long been interpreted as an American declaration of cold war, Truman averred in April 1947 that the world had become divided between "alternative ways of life" and that "it must be the policy of the United States to support free peoples who are resisting attempted subjugation by armed minorities or by outside pressures."

Despite its own history of often bellicose national expansion (such as the Mexican War or annexation of the Philippines), the United States would not accommodate itself to postwar Soviet expansion. Washington dominated postwar Japan and western Europe, both of which were reoriented along Western lines, and established a system of military bases across the world. The United States built and controlled the Panama Canal and backed British and French control of the Suez Canal, yet it rejected Soviet efforts to extend influence over the Black Sea straits. In addition to resenting these double standards, Stalin and his comrades feared America's ability to wield its unprecedented economic clout.

AMERICAN FINANCIAL HEGEMONY

In addition to the ideological divide and issues of national expansion, U.S. economic hegemony fueled the Cold War. The Soviets—who had suffered far more devastation, both human and material, in World War II than the United States (or any other country)—sought loans, grants, and reparations to rebuild. Washington had contributed immeasurably to the Soviet war effort through lend-lease and other forms of aid. The United States also promised a postwar loan but delayed the matter and then linked economic assistance with political issues, notably the fates of postwar governments in East-Central Europe. No loan was ever made.

In striking contrast to the devastation of Russia's economy, World War II had been phenomenally good for American business. Government-fueled war production ended the Great Depression and brought full employment and rapid economic growth to the United States. Unscathed by war and prosperous at home, the United States emerged as the unquestioned economic powerhouse of the postwar world. The dollar dwarfed all other currencies and New York displaced London as the world's financial center. At the 1944 Bretton Woods (New Hampshire) Conference, the United States established the World Bank and the International Monetary Fund, agencies that would issue loans and assistance to anchor postwar economic recovery. Such assistance came with strings attached. In order to be eligible, countries would have to meet certain criteria compatible with free-market capitalism. After attending the conference, the Soviet Union never joined the Washington-based and U.S.-dominated international financial agencies.

If there was any hope of heading off the Cold War, it ended with the Marshall Plan. The European Recovery Program, launched by the U.S. Army general turned secretary of state George C. Marshall, laid the foundation for decades of American and western European economic and political integration. The program of loans, assistance, and psychological recovery from the destitution of war succeeded brilliantly in effecting the economic and political recovery of western Europe, especially in France and Italy, where communist parties backed by Moscow had been poised to bid for power. The Marshall Plan exemplified "empire by invitation," an interpretive framework that emphasized that American economic assistance and political influence were welcomed by the western European governments and the majority of public opinion. U.S. propaganda and covert operations, especially in Italy, played a significant role in the process, however. Nevertheless, there is little doubt that western Europeans welcomed American power and influence far more than Eastern Europeans welcomed Soviet power. This single reality carries a great deal of explanatory power as to both the origins and the eventual end of the Cold War.

By the late 1940s, the Marshall Plan had begun to achieve its aims of fostering western European economic recovery and political confidence building. It gave rise to a postwar order in which the United States emerged as the unquestioned world leader. It advanced an American campaign of global financial hegemony. As successful as the Marshall Plan was in advancing Western political and economic integration, the economic recovery program also cemented the division of Europe. Although the Soviets had attended the initial discussions in Paris, Stalin and his foreign minister, V. I. Molotov, understood all too clearly that they would be left, by design, on the outside looking in. With American economic clout dwarfing that of the devastated Soviet Union, Stalin and Molotov understood that the Marshall Plan posed a grave threat to the budding "people's democracies" of East-Central Europe. After Molotov strode out of the Paris discussions, Stalin ordered out the Czech delegation as well. Within months the Kremlin orchestrated a coup, brutally ousting Czech liberals in tactics that revived vivid memories of Hitler. "Moral God-fearing peoples," Truman declared, "must save the world from Atheism and totalitarianism."

THE DIVISION OF GERMANY

There was, of course, no precise moment when the Cold War can be said to have begun, yet there is no question that it was in place by 1948, the same year in which the term itself was popularized. The breakdown of Allied cooperation in Germany brought the division of the postwar world into the capital of the vanquished former common enemy. American, British, and French forces colluded in floating a new German currency without notifying the Soviets. The Kremlin and its German comrades cut off road, rail, and canal links to Berlin in an effort to force the Western powers out of the former Reich capital, which reposed in the heart of Soviet-occupied eastern Germany. The subsequent American airlift broke the back of the Kremlin blockade, which Stalin abandoned after eleven months in May 1949. The emergence of two rival German states, and years of bitter propaganda and covert operations, followed in the wake of the Berlin blockade and airlift.

The United States and its west European allies accepted the division of Germany under a strategy of "dual containment." The larger, more productive western Germany—soon to become the Federal Republic of Germany—would anchor the postwar European economy under U.S. occupation and supervision. This approach would not only fuel recovery but would reassure France and other past victims of aggression that Germany was now contained within the Western alliance. The Soviets incorporated into their sphere the smaller eastern rump Germany—which became the German Democratic Republic—and which the West subjected to unremitting psychological warfare in

the form of radio propaganda, covert operations, and various forms of subversion. In any case, the division of Germany cemented, in both real and symbolic terms, the division of Europe.

MILITARIZATION

One of the most significant outcomes of World War II was the enormous momentum of militarization. Four years of global conflict—indeed, two world wars in a single generation—had left a powerful imprint. Neither the Soviet Union nor the United States ever fully demobilized. Troops from both nations remained encamped in the heart of Europe, while U.S. air and naval bases spread throughout the world. Although the Soviet Red Army was the world's largest ground force, the United States possessed a formidable two-ocean navy and the most powerful air force the world had ever seen. As the Soviet economy and society struggled to rebuild from the ruins of war, U.S. economic might laid the foundation for the emergence of an awesome military power.

Sole possession of the atomic bomb offered both real and symbolic evidence of U.S. military superiority. Some historians have argued that the United States dropped the two bombs on Japan as much to make an impression on the Soviets as to end the Pacific war. "Atomic diplomacy" did not work, however, as Stalin adopted a nonchalant stance toward the bomb and refused to adjust Soviet political aims in deference to the U.S. monopoly. While Washington had shared atomic information with Great Britain during the war, the Soviets were kept in the dark—or so Americans thought. In actuality, Soviet spies had penetrated the atomic research program and stolen the secrets of the atom. Talks on international control of atomic weapons quickly foundered and became another casualty of the Cold War.

Both sides cultivated their military prowess and vowed to defend their territory and spheres of influence. While the Soviets trumpeted the heroic defense of the motherland against the Nazis, the Americans reorganized their defense establishment, now housed in the sprawling new Pentagon building. Under the National Security Act (1947), Washington created a new Department of Defense and departments of Air Force and Marines to join the Army and the Navy, all four branches coordinated by a new phalanx of generals, the Joint Chiefs of Staff. The legislation also created the National Security Council to advise the president on global foreign policy and the Central Intelligence Agency to gather information and carry out covert operations.

The West took the lead in dividing Europe into hostile military alliances. In 1949, acting under a UN provision for collective security arrangements, the West promulgated the North Atlantic Treaty Organization (NATO), a military alliance aimed squarely at the Soviet Union. The actual threat of a Soviet military attack on western Europe was remote, yet memories of Nazi blitzkrieg and Pearl Harbor remained vivid. More to the point, however, NATO furthered the course of Western economic and political integration and created a market for perpetuating the profitable wartime collusion between science, government, and the defense industry. The successful Soviet atomic test in 1949 fueled the nuclear arms race, as both powers pushed ahead with development of hydrogen, or thermonuclear, weapons. From this point forward, the two superpowers each cultivated the power to destroy one another in an all-out war.

THE COLD WAR IN ASIA

Tumultuous developments in Asia ensured that the Cold War would become global. U.S. policy appeared well in hand in the early postwar years, as the occupation of Japan provided an unprecedented opportunity to further Washington's economic and political agenda in Asia. Establishing Japan as the focal point of an economic program across the "great crescent" of Asia, Washington sought to ensure an anticommunist order friendly to the supremacy of the dollar and U.S. ideology. The Japanese proved largely compliant, but the triumph of the communists in the Chinese civil war promptly shattered the American quest for a noncommunist Asian postwar order.

The rise to power of the Chinese Communist Party in October 1949 was a stunning blow to Americans, who had long waxed sentimental about the prospects of expanding Western influence in "the Orient." Roosevelt had given rise to false hopes during the war by floating the ill-fated concept that China would serve as one of the "four policemen" of the postwar world. In reality, the democratic China was a chimera. And while Stalin had repeatedly shown himself willing to sell out the Chinese communists during the war, now that they had come to power, he entered into an alliance with Mao Zedong's regime in 1950. Inexperienced in foreign affairs, and plagued by

demagogues and opportunists in Congress, millions of Americans believed the leaders who told them that only domestic subversion could account for the dastardly turn of affairs in East Asia. Still adjusting to the burdens of world power, Americans became resentful when events did not unfold as they expected.

KOREA AND NSC 68

With capitalist and communist regimes ensconced in Japan and China, respectively, Korean communists led by Kim Il Sung sought to "liberate" their peninsula through armed aggression. Archival evidence found in the 1990s revealed that Kim practically pleaded with Stalin, on numerous occasions, before gaining the Kremlin autocrat's assent to an attack against southern forces backed by the American-educated Syngman Rhee. The outbreak of war in Korea in June 1950 stunned the Truman administration and an American public already reeling from a series of Cold War setbacks. Unaware and unwilling to consider that Kim, and not Stalin, had fomented the war in Korea, the Truman administration decided immediately to respond with force to what it was sure was a deliberate *Soviet* provocation. Within months, U.S. and UN forces reversed the battle, prompting a massive Chinese intervention that turned the Korean War into a bloody three-year stalemate. Korea would remain a divided nation for at least the rest of the century, yet another casualty of the Cold War.

The outbreak of war in Korea, punctuated by the approval of the historic U.S. foreign policy document National Security Council Document 68 (NSC 68) marked the end of the first phase of the Cold War. The apocalyptic policy paper envisioned a fight to the finish with Soviet-sponsored world communism. The document, approved by Truman, literally envisioned spending whatever was necessary in the name of national security. During the course of the Korean War, defense spending more than tripled, ensuring the predominance of military Keynesianism for the remainder of the century. Military Keynesianism encompassed stimulation of the economy through federal investment and expenditure on defense.

Among other significant repercussions of the Korean bloodletting was the establishment of U.S. military bases in Asia; lasting involvement in the dispute between Taiwan and mainland China; assignment of U.S. troops to Europe on a permanent basis; and West German rearmament. Approval of NSC 68 culminated the first phase of the Cold War. The Korean War cemented militarization and the adoption of worst case scenarios of "enemy" behavior on both sides. Sometimes referred to as the "forgotten war," insofar as it was sandwiched between World War II and the Vietnam War, the Korean War was one of most significant conflicts in modern world history.

PATRIOTIC CULTURE IN THE UNITED STATES

Cold War anxiety reached new heights, or depths, during the Korean War and had a profound effect on American society. Conservatism outpaced reform. The process began early in World War II, when Roosevelt himself announced that "Dr. New Deal" had been replaced by "Dr. Win the War." The reform era was over, replaced by the inevitable conservative reaction of war, mirroring the World War I experience. War and Cold War provided an opportunity that conservative elites, alarmed by the specter of creeping socialism in the New Deal, would not let pass. The profitable matrix revolving around science, business, government, and defense cemented military Keynesianism over government spending on domestic concerns. While federal dollars fueled Cold War militarization, spending on social programs, deemed socialistic by many conservatives, would be contained at home. An inveterate New Dealer, Henry Wallace, launched a last-gasp campaign against the new order but was thoroughly repudiated in the 1948 election. Truman's stunning upset victory over Thomas Dewey underscored that containment, anticommunism, and militarization would illuminate the path to electoral triumph.

Hysteria over domestic communism brought repression and exercised a lasting chilling effect on left-wing sentiment. Beginning with the "Hollywood Ten" in 1946, former communists and left-wing sympathizers were harassed, purged, and put on notice. In 1950 the Alger Hiss case, in which a former high-level State Department diplomat was convicted of perjury for lying about being a communist agent, put liberals and former New Dealers on the defensive while giving rise to a new breed of politician, best embodied by Richard Nixon, for whom the Cold War provided the core of their identity. Federal Bureau of Investigation director J. Edgar Hoover—accountable to no one and since World War I obsessed with

destroying radicalism—launched a campaign against thousands of Americans who had harbored left-wing sentiments. Despite the extraordinarily crude and reckless tactics of Joseph McCarthy, the junior senator from Wisconsin conducted a four-year campaign against thousands of alleged subversives. The victims of the postwar hysteria were not only the tens of thousands of men and women harassed by McCarthy and the FBI, but the basic constitutional rights of freedom of thought and association as well.

THE FAILED QUEST FOR "LIBERATION"

While U.S. national security elites still hoped to force the Soviet Union to allow political independence throughout Eastern Europe, the State Department grasped the possibilities inherent in the independent communist course being pursued in Yugoslavia since the open breach in 1948 between Stalin and Josip Broz Tito. Both Truman and his successor, Dwight D. Eisenhower, sought to promote "Titoism" in Eastern Europe, but the confrontational quest for "liberation" of the "captive nations" undermined this effort. Right-wing critics insisted that containment was a fatalistic and unmanly (even "pantywaist," to some critics) policy, which supposedly acquiesced in Soviet hegemony over Eastern Europe. In reality, Kennan's conceptualization of containment, embraced as U.S. Cold War policy, had always encompassed liberation, or rollback, of communist power in Eastern Europe.

Eisenhower intensified a campaign of "psychological warfare" that had begun under Truman in an effort to destabilize Soviet hegemony. A variety of strategies, focused especially on radio propaganda, did indeed help shake the foundations of Communist Party authority in Eastern Europe. When necessary, however, as in East Germany in 1953 and Hungary in 1956, the Soviet Union simply resorted to direct military intervention to maintain its hard sphere of influence over East-Central Europe. Nothing the United States and its NATO allies could have done, short of initiating World War III, would have altered this fundamental geopolitical reality flowing from the World War II settlement and the postwar ideological clash.

A more subtle Western approach might have enhanced the possibility of the post-Stalinist leadership loosening the bonds of authority over the East-Central European Communist Party regimes. However, by confronting the Soviet Union with both NATO and aggressive psychological warfare, Washington gave the Kremlin no opportunity to allow for liberalization, or Titoism, in the region. It was all too clear to Soviet leaders that if the "satellites" were allowed to go their own way they would end up ultimately—as in fact occurred decades later after the end of the Cold War—being transferred directly into the hostile NATO orbit. The Kremlin had no choice, short of capitulation to the West, but to protect its sphere at all costs. With psychological warfare having failed to deliver the ultimate prize of liberation, the Eisenhower administration was compelled to adopt an evolutionary approach emphasizing toned-down radio propaganda, exchanges of film, trade fairs, exhibitions, and people-to-people contacts.

Following the death of Stalin in 1953, Nikita S. Khrushchev eventually emerged as the new Kremlin leader. In 1956, Khrushchev stunned communists throughout the world by denouncing Stalin for his many "crimes" against the people. A dedicated Marxist-Leninist known for his thundering denunciations of the West, Khrushchev also took concrete steps, including meaningful cuts in Soviet defenses, toward achieving "peaceful coexistence" with the West. Khrushchev's brash style, however, combined with deeply ingrained American Cold War anxieties, continued to plague any progress toward a genuine détente. A hysterical American reaction to the Soviet launch of *Sputnik*, the first Earth satellite, in 1957 complicated Eisenhower's hopes for a breakthrough in the Cold War. The president's own decision to authorize a campaign of aerial spying over Soviet airspace doomed the Eisenhower-Khrushchev "thaw" in the Cold War. Hopes for achieving what would later be called détente came crashing down with Gary Powers's U-2 spy plane in May 1960. Eisenhower limped out of office decrying the "unwarranted influence" of the military-industrial complex, a phenomenon that, ironically, had gained substantial momentum on his own watch.

KENNEDY AND CRISES

The essential forces that fueled the Cold War—ideology, geopolitics, economics, militarization, and patriotic culture—persisted throughout the conflict. The Cold War manifested itself in waves, or cycles, of varying intensity. After the brief thaw of the mid-1950s, another intense wave of conflict emerged during the presidency of John F. Kennedy. Bitter confrontation over the anomalous western enclave in Berlin, deep inside East Germany, ended with construction of the Berlin Wall in August 1961. The wall brought a pernicious settlement to the German problem, but the concrete and barbed wire divide gave substance to Churchill's metaphor of an Iron Curtain. Despite scores of bold and often successful escapes by East Germans, the wall was an effective physical barrier, though ultimately a devastating propaganda liability and harbinger of the West's eventual triumph in the Cold War.

The 1962 Cuban missile crisis marked the apogee of Cold War confrontation, including a palpable threat of nuclear annihilation. Already livid over the loss of Cuba to communism under Fidel Castro, Americans were angered even further by Khrushchev's decision to place medium-range nuclear warheads ninety miles off U.S. shores. From the Cuban and Soviet perspective—a perspective rarely considered under a monolithic U.S. patriotic culture—the action might have been seen as an understandable response to blatant American efforts to topple Castro, which had failed once in the Bay of Pigs invasion in April 1961 but would continue in no fewer than eight assassination plots against the Cuban leader. Moreover, as Khrushchev pointed out, nuclear missiles in Cuba would confront the United States with an analogous situation to that faced by the Soviet Union, which had nuclear weapons targeting its cities and defense sites from a variety of hostile NATO states.

Kennedy ultimately rejected the most hawkish advice he received—unilateral bombing of Cuba—but the president opted for a national television address rather than private diplomacy to demand that Khrushchev dismantle the missile sites. Kennedy then confronted the Soviets with a naval blockade, an act of war that the administration tried to soften by employing the euphemism of a "quarantine." Khrushchev backed down, but only after Kennedy renounced intervention in Cuba and pledged privately to dismantle U.S. missile sites in Turkey.

The last months of Kennedy's abortive presidency marked a turning point in the history of the Cold War. Following the crises in Berlin and Cuba, a sobered Kennedy and Khrushchev began to usher in a new thaw by establishing a "hotline" for instant communication and signing the 1963 Limited Test Ban Treaty, terminating aboveground nuclear test blasts. Cultural exchange picked up throughout the 1960s as well. Cold

War rivalry continued on a global scale, but after 1963 the shadow of Armageddon began to recede, particularly as the Soviets achieved a rough parity in the nuclear arms race by the end of the decade.

THE THIRD WORLD

While both sides accepted the status quo in Europe and embraced mutual deterrence through MAD (mutually assured destruction), the Cold War continued to rage in the so-called Third World of developing nations. From 1946 to 1960, thirty-seven new nations emerged from under a history of colonial domination to gain independent status. Both the United States and the Soviet Union, backed by their respective allies, competed intensively for influence over the new nations of Africa, Asia, Latin America, and the Middle East. Strategists in both camps believed that ultimate victory or defeat in the Cold War depended on the outcome of Third World conflicts. Moreover, many of these areas harbored vital natural resources, such as oil in the Middle East, upon which the developed world had become dependent. With American and allied automobiles, industry, and consumerism dependent on ready access to vast supplies of crude oil, maintaining access to foreign energy sources emerged as a key element of U.S. foreign policy.

Both the United States and the Soviet Union abhorred neutralism, that is, they demanded that their allies and Third World nations side with them against their Cold War rival. Both powers equated neutralism with appeasement and sought to punish not just states that sided against them but those that attempted to remain equivocal. Both the United States and the Soviet Union worked tirelessly in Asia, Africa, Latin America, and the Middle East to convince Third World leaders that their ideology was on the right side of history and held out the best hope for those nations to grapple with their pressing social problems, including poverty, disease, and rampant population growth. The Soviets had less money and a weaker economy than their Western rivals, but they did have the advantage of arguing that communist ideology offered liberation from the legacy of colonialism.

Adopting a much harsher line toward the West than Khrushchev, China's leader, Mao Zedong, called on Third World revolutionaries to launch "wars of national liberation" against the capitalist world. The message had resonance since

the overwhelming majority of Third World states had been under the control of foreign powers, including Belgium, Britain, France, Germany, Holland, and the United States, for much of the previous century. Washington sought desperately to counteract the Soviet message and to contain revolutionary movements in the Third World. U.S. leaders went to great lengths to stave off defeat in even the most obscure and strategically insignificant corners of the globe out of fear of a bandwagon or domino effect. They insisted that a communist victory anywhere would encourage other revolutionaries and thus precipitate the much-feared red avalanche.

While the United States was most sensitive to revolutionary movements in neighboring Latin America, Cold War intervention was a global phenomenon. For years Washington coveted as a strategic partner South Africa, at the time a racist white minority regime that attempted to isolate and contain black radical movements in southern Africa. In North Africa and the Middle East, Washington backed Egypt and Israel against more radical regimes, some of which, such as Syria, became close Soviet allies. The United States and the Soviet Union supported different sides in the Middle East Arab-Israeli conflict. The United States backed the Zionist state, a policy supported by most American Jews—the largest population in the world in any one country—but also by a majority of overall public opinion. While Washington became Israel's chief diplomatic benefactor and weapons supplier, the Soviet Union embraced the cause of Arab nationalism and Palestinian statehood. When wars erupted in 1956, 1967, and 1973, however, Washington and Moscow ultimately found the common language to work together to prevent the conflicts from escalating into longer wars.

While the Soviets and Chinese appealed to the Third World on the basis of Lenin's theory of imperialism, Washington offered its democratic ideology as well as its advanced economy to woo Third World nations. Through its supervision of the World Bank and the International Monetary Fund, the United States offered aid and loans on the condition that the recipients join the capitalist camp in the Cold War struggle. The United States confronted serious obstacles, however, in its efforts to win over the Third World. First of all, most of the Third World consisted of populations of people of color. The leaders and peoples of those nations condemned America's history of slavery, racism, and support for imperialism based on a racial hierarchy. Many scholars believe, in fact, that the Cold War played a significant role in the slow emergence of federal government support for the civil rights movement, which culminated in the United States in the mid-1960s. U.S. leaders recognized that they could not hope to appeal successfully to the Third World while sanctioning segregation, denial of voting rights, and other forms of racial discrimination in the United States itself.

CIA COVERT OPERATIONS

When economic, ideological, and cultural appeals failed, the United States, like the Soviet Union, employed spies and covert operations in an effort to achieve its aims in the developing world. Both employed a variety of tactics, including bribes, intimidation, propaganda, and violence. As a Communist Party dictatorship, the Soviets were less accountable to their public than the Americans were to theirs. Anxious to avoid public scrutiny, the Central Intelligence Agency and other covert branches of the national security state conducted their operations in secret. U.S. covert operations included extralegal coups against revolutionary regimes in Africa, Asia, Latin America, and the Middle East. In 1953, for example, a CIA operation, approved directly by Eisenhower, led to the overthrow of the elected leader of Iran, Mohammad Mosaddeq. The Iranian leader had moved to assert national control over his nation's oil supplies, an action that menaced the interest of U.S. and British oil conglomerates and smacked of socialism. The coup succeeded, as the CIA paved the way for Shah Reza Pahlavi to assume power and keep Iran open to the West. The foreign policy of intervention proved shortsighted a quarter-century later, however, as Iranian fundamentalists overthrew the shah, condemned the United States as the "Great Satan" in world affairs, and held fifty-three American hostages for more than a year.

In 1954 another CIA coup overthrew Jacobo Arbenz Guzmán, the legitimate ruler of the Central American nation of Guatemala. Arbenz had engaged in land redistribution, threatening the interest of the United Fruit Company, a U.S. corporation. Moreover, Washington was determined to curb such socialist-style behavior out of fear that it would inspire similar actions by other nations of the region. The coup replaced Arbenz with a more compliant leader but ultimately led to more than a

quarter-century of factionalism, poverty, and state terror in Guatemala. In part it was the success of the Guatemalan coup that led the Eisenhower and Kennedy administrations to confidently approve plans for a takeover in Cuba, an initiative that failed spectacularly at the Bay of Pigs. Castro's fully prepared forces destroyed the U.S.-backed Cuban exile guerillas shortly after their landing at Cochinos Bay. Lack of air support and widespread publicity on the eve of a putatively "covert" operation doomed the invasion and left a humiliated Kennedy administration even more determined to contain communism. An even more disastrous intervention subsequently unfolded in Asia.

THE VIETNAM WAR

While securing Japan as the centerpiece of the "great crescent" strategy, Washington successfully fended off a leftist insurgency in the Philippines after granting independence to the archipelago in 1946. U.S. economic and strategic influence (weapons sales, for example) helped contain radical movements in the new nations of Indonesia and Malaysia. Taiwan depended heavily on the United States to maintain its defensive posture and separation from mainland China.

In 1954, just a year after the Korean armistice, a new Cold War crisis arose in Indochina (Cambodia, Laos, and Vietnam) as France suffered a humiliating defeat following an eight-year campaign to reassert imperial authority. The Viet Minh, a nationalist group led by a communist, Ho Chi Minh, won the battle of Dien Bien Phu, forcing France to capitulate. Determined to prevent Vietnam from falling to communism, the United States helped sabotage an international agreement that elections would be held in 1956 to unify the Southeast Asian nation. The problem with the elections, as the Eisenhower administration well understood, was that Ho Chi Minh would have won them. Washington threw its support behind Ngo Dinh Diem, who proclaimed the existence of a separate Republic of Vietnam (South Vietnam) in opposition to Ho's regime in the northern half of the country. The United States thus began a commitment that would eventually cost billions of dollars and more than 58,000 American lives while bringing unparalleled death and destruction to Indochina.

Despite occupying the country with more than half a million ground troops and pummeling the region with the most intensive bombing campaign in world history, Washington could neither subdue the Vietnamese opposition nor create a viable government in Saigon. By the time President Richard M. Nixon pulled out in January 1973, the United States itself had become deeply divided over the war. Saigon fell to the communists two years later. The much-feared domino effect never transpired in Southeast Asia. Laos and Cambodia did "go communist," but well before the end of the Indochina war, the Soviet Union and China had become enemies. In 1979, Communist Party governments of the region were at war with one another, as China briefly invaded Vietnam, a Soviet ally, for its attack on the bloodthirsty regime of the Khmer Rouge in Cambodia, a Chinese ally.

The consensus interpretation is that the Vietnam War was a tragic foreign policy blunder. Some diehard elements of the patriotic culture insisted that Washington could have won the war with a divergent strategy, but this argument ignores the decisive political aspects of the struggle as well as the very real possibility that an unlimited assault on North Vietnam in the mid-1960s would have brought China into the war, much as events had transpired in Korea. The nation as a whole struggled for decades to recover from a foreign policy debacle that, however tragic, had flowed logically from U.S. Cold War ideology and perceptions.

DÉTENTE

Despite the aggressive U.S. militarism in Southeast Asia, and a brutal Soviet invasion of Czechoslovakia in 1968, a new thaw in East-West relations emerged in the 1960s and 1970s. Détente (relaxation of tensions) emerged as part of the cyclical pattern of Cold War history in which periods of relative calm followed periods of bitter great-power conflict. Kennedy and Khrushchev started the process in the wake of the missile crisis, but both were removed from the scene with Kennedy's assassination in Dallas and Khrushchev's ouster in a 1964 Kremlin power shift. The new, hard-line regime of Leonid Brezhnev aggressively pursued Soviet aims, including sending the Red Army into Czechoslovakia to repress the "Prague Spring." Although the Czechs had not rejected the Warsaw Pact alliance with the Soviet Union, the Brezhnev Doctrine proclaimed that none of the East European states would be allowed to vacate the communist camp.

Preoccupied with his foreign policy debacle in Vietnam, Lyndon Johnson made little progress toward détente, but his successor, Nixon, was keenly interested in improved East-West relations. Nixon's support for détente was ironic, since he had made his reputation in politics as a fervent anticommunist, yet he would achieve a breakthrough in the Cold War. The impetus for détente, however, actually came from European leaders Charles de Gaulle, president of France, and Willy Brandt, the West German chancellor. Bitterly opposed to the U.S. war in the former French colony of Indochina, De Gaulle excoriated U.S. foreign policy, withdrew France from NATO's integrated military command, and met with Brezhnev in Moscow in 1966. Brandt, a former mayor of West Berlin, pursued a diplomacy of *Ostpolitik* (Eastern policy), improving relations with neighboring East Germany.

Nixon and Henry A. Kissinger, a refugee from Nazi Germany and a former Harvard professor turned national security adviser, pursued détente in part to prevent the Europeans from undermining Washington's leadership. Nixon and Kissinger also hoped to use improved relations to gain the assistance of Moscow and Beijing in bringing an end to the Vietnam War without the United States suffering a humiliating defeat. Nixon and Kissinger exploited the Sino-Soviet rift with a "triangular diplomacy" that sought to play off the great communist powers against one another to the betterment of U.S. national interests. After Kissinger traveled secretly to Beijing for talks in 1969, the momentum toward rapprochement (reconciliation) was irreversible. During a dramatic state visit in 1971, Nixon clinked cocktail glasses with Mao Zedong in Beijing and posed for photographers atop the Great Wall of China. The next year the two powers issued the Shanghai Communique, a joint statement that China and the United States would strive to improve their relations and to contain "hegemony," a euphemism for the Soviet Union.

The dramatic "Nixinger" summit diplomacy with the onetime archenemy "Red" China wowed the American public and created anxiety in Moscow. The Kremlin warned the Americans against playing the "China card" but also received Nixon in Moscow in 1972 despite the American mining of Haiphong Harbor in North Vietnam, where Soviet supply ships regularly anchored. The high point of the U.S.–Soviet détente was the signing of the 1972 Strategic Arms Limitation Agreement, known as SALT I. The treaty established ceilings on offensive missiles and sharply limited destabilizing defensive weapons systems, but it was more important as a political vehicle for improved relations than for its actual achievements in limiting the weapons of mass destruction. Nixon and Kissinger failed completely in their quest to go through China and the Soviets to prevail upon North Vietnam to accept an independent South Vietnam, which instead fell in April 1975.

The momentum of détente began to wane in the mid-1970s. Nixon, its chief architect, met his political demise in the Watergate scandal. With the Soviet Union maintaining its hegemony over Eastern Europe, sponsoring revolutionary movements in the Third World, and denying human rights to many of its own citizens, American critics began to equate détente with appeasement. In the southwest African nation of Angola, the two superpowers backed competing forces in a raging civil war. Cuban troops, viewed as Soviet "proxies," fought in behalf of leftist rebels in Angola while the United States and China supported the opposition. A Cold War battle also emerged in Ethiopia and throughout the horn of Africa. Soviet and Cuban influence was confined mainly to those two countries, as U.S. trade and diplomacy proved advantageous in several other key African states.

Critics of détente advocated "linkage"— linking trade, arms control, and improved relations with Soviet behavior in world affairs and in the regime's human rights policies. The Soviets bitterly resented this approach and any effort to influence their internal affairs. They had left themselves vulnerable to such criticism, however, not only by denying freedom of intellectual and religious expression in Russia but by violating pledges to respect human rights embodied in the 1975 Helsinki Accords. Under this agreement, the United States, Soviet Union, and governments throughout Europe recognized current borders as permanent, thus in effect renouncing the old U.S. Cold War depiction of Eastern Europe as a set of "captive nations."

Jimmy Carter, elected president in 1976, advocated arms control but made human rights the centerpiece of his diplomacy and criticized the Soviets for their violations. U.S. relations with China continued to improve, however, a process that culminated in 1979 with formal recognition of Beijing at the expense of the longtime U.S. ally on Taiwan. The Japanese, too, expressed dismay at not being consulted about the dramatic shift in U.S. East Asian policy. Détente deteriorated under Carter, who adopted conflicting policies that reflected the conflicting advice he received from Secretary of State Cyrus Vance, an advocate of détente, and national security adviser Zbigniew Brzezinski, a Polish emigré who adopted a harder line toward the Soviets. Carter himself allowed the SALT process to break down. Although a SALT II treaty was negotiated, Carter never took it before the U.S. Senate, where it faced rejection.

Two climactic events in 1979 destroyed détente and ensured Carter's defeat in the 1980 presidential election. First, in November a militant fundamentalist regime in Iran took over the U.S. embassy in Tehran, holding fifty-three Americans hostage. Carter began painstaking negotiations aimed at securing their release, which would not come for more than year. Meanwhile, the United States appeared helpless as Iranian radicals burned the U.S. flag and shouted "Death to Carter" in daily rituals outside the embassy. In December the Soviet Union launched an invasion of neighboring Afghanistan, where the pro-Soviet government in Kabul had come under siege. The Soviet assault seemed to confirm critics' charges that détente had been a form of appeasement. Carter declared that Brezhnev had lied to him and instituted a variety of sanctions, including a U.S. boycott of the 1980 Olympic games in Moscow.

REAGAN'S COLD WAR

Yet another cycle of Cold War confrontation followed in the wake of the collapse of détente and the foreign policy disasters in Iran and Afghanistan. Like the previous similar waves, this one featured hostile rhetoric, military escalation, little or no diplomacy, and fear of a superpower conflict. What distinguished the new cycle of conflict was the dynamic personality of President Ronald W. Reagan, an inveterate cold warrior who labeled the Soviet Union an "evil empire." A former Hollywood actor and two-term California governor, Reagan declared that the country had grown weak but soon would once again "stand tall" in world affairs. The new president embarked on an enormous campaign of militarization reminiscent of similar spurts following NSC 68 (1950) and in the wake of the "missile gap" controversy in the late 1950s and early 1960s.

U.S.–Soviet relations deteriorated sharply in Reagan's first term. Diplomacy virtually ceased. In March 1983 Reagan stunned the Soviets, and threatened to destabilize the nuclear arms race, by announcing his support for a space-based defensive shield. The president glibly declared that nuclear weapons could be rendered "impotent and obsolete" by developing a perfect defense against incoming ballistic missiles. The program, known as the Strategic Defense Initiative (SDI), was both costly and a violation of the 1972 treaty limiting defensive systems. The Kremlin feared, however, that the initiative would force the Soviets, already suffering from a badly flagging economy, into a costly new arena of superpower competition. The Kremlin bitterly criticized SDI, launched an offensive missile buildup of its own, and accused the United States of enhancing the threat of another world war.

On 1 September 1983, U.S.–Soviet relations reached their nadir when a Soviet pilot carried out an order to shoot down Korean Airlines Flight 007 en route from Anchorage, Alaska, to Seoul, Korea. The passenger jumbo jet had deviated from its course and flown hundreds of miles into Soviet territory. The Soviet pilot could not distinguish the Boeing aircraft from U.S. reconnaissance jets, which routinely played "chicken" with Soviet forces along their vast border. The Reagan administration claimed that the Kremlin had deliberately destroyed the civilian airliner, which had gone off course as a result of a computer programming error. The Soviets, after remaining silent for days, insisted, apparently truthfully, that they had not recognized the plane as a civilian airliner. The Kremlin charged that the civilian jet clearly had been on a U.S.– and South Korean–backed intelligence mission.

While Reagan unnerved the Soviets, most of the American public supported his policies. Even foreign policy disasters did not undermine the president's appeal. In one such incident in 1983, Reagan dispatched U.S. forces to Lebanon on an uncertain mission to combat "terrorism" and contain Syrian "aggression." The action brought little more than the deaths of 241 U.S. marines from a radical suicide assault on their position. Reagan also overthrew a leftist government in Grenada by direct invasion and conducted a series of raids against the Libyan dictator Muammar Qaddafi. The most intense arena of the revived Cold War, however, was Central America. In Nicaragua, the Sandinista rebels, named for a martyred reform leader from the 1930s, came to power in 1979 and launched a socialist government. In neighboring El Salvador, leftist rebels battled a murderous U.S.-backed military regime. Although Carter had

initiated the move to contain the perceived threat, it was Reagan who embarked on an all-out campaign to destroy the left in America's "backyard." While employing every possible means to isolate and economically weaken Castro's Cuba, Reagan sharply increased aid to the Salvadoran military, which allied with "death squads" responsible for executing not only leftist leaders but liberal critics of the government, students, citizens, Catholic priests, and even American churchwomen. The CIA authorized funding for the contras, rebels whose aim was to overthrow the government in Managua. Funded, armed, and trained on U.S. bases in Florida as well as in Honduras, the contras began to fight their way through the Nicaraguan jungles.

Although the United Nations, the Organization of American States, and the World Court condemned the United States for actions such as the illegal mining of Nicaragua's harbors in 1982, Reagan ignored the world community. Reagan's campaign against the left led to the Iran-Contra scandal, which tarnished his presidency. The president either authorized illegal actions or failed to exercise supervision over his subordinates—he was not sure himself which had been the case. What became clear was that the administration had secretly sold arms to Iran—officially a terrorist nation with which Washington had refused to conduct diplomacy—as part of a scheme to gain the release of hostages being held in Lebanon as well as to circumvent congressional restrictions on funding for the contra rebels in Nicaragua.

While Reagan remained a popular president, the damage done by the Iran-Contra scandal as well as changes in the Soviet Union prompted him to reconsider his hard-line Cold War policies. Throughout the 1980s, antinuclear protesters in the United States and Europe, as well as liberal and moderate critics, also brought pressure to bear on the White House to pursue an arms-control agreement and a renewal of East-West diplomacy. Some of the president's advisers, including his wife, Nancy, urged him to leave a legacy of peace rather than one simply of zealotry and confrontation.

THE GORBACHEV PHENOMENON

A dynamic new Soviet leader, Mikhail S. Gorbachev, prompted Reagan's turn to moderation. Following the death of Brezhnev in 1982, two more

Soviet leaders assumed the helm but died within a short period. Born in 1931, well after the Bolshevik Revolution, Gorbachev represented a new generation of Communist Party leadership in Moscow. Assuming power in 1985, Gorbachev sought to revitalize Soviet society through a series of dramatic reforms. He called the program *perestroika,* or restructuring, a concept that included sweeping economic and social reforms. The Soviet government authorized joint ventures with foreign companies, allowing some free enterprise to emerge in the socialist economy, and lifted restrictions on free speech and intellectual expression. Gorbachev called that reform *glasnost,* or openness.

Decrying the Cold War as dangerous and wasteful, Gorbachev unilaterally reduced Soviet investment in the great-power struggle. Declaring that intervention in Afghanistan had been a mistake, he pulled out Soviet troops in 1989. Gorbachev implemented sharp cuts in Soviet defense spending, including the withdrawal of tens of thousands of Red Army troops occupying Eastern Europe. Reagan and his advisers reacted with skepticism to Gorbachev's initiatives in world affairs, but the sweeping changes promoted by the charismatic new Russian leader soon became impossible to ignore. Gorbachev pressed Reagan to join him in bold new diplomatic ventures, and the U.S. president nearly responded at the Reykjavik summit in Iceland in 1986. There the two world leaders flirted with the "zero option"—an agreement to eliminate all nuclear weapons by the year 2000. This breathtaking proposal collapsed, however, over Reagan's refusal to sacrifice research and development of his Strategic Defense Initiative. Despite the summit breakdown, Reagan and Gorbachev had formed a bond, one that led the next year to a successful nuclear arms summit in Washington, D.C. Under the INF Treaty, both sides agreed to dismantle all intermediate range nuclear forces throughout the world. The Soviets agreed to on-site verification of their missile installations, a concession that would not have been possible in the pre-Gorbachev era.

By the time Reagan left office in 1989, the warlike atmosphere he had fostered in the early 1980s was but a distant memory. Both the U.S. and Soviet presidents were calling for an end to the Cold War, but no one envisioned just how sudden, dramatic, and complete that end would be. *Perestroika* and *glasnost* could not help but reverberate beyond Russia's borders. The sweeping economic reforms and loosening of restrictions on freedom of speech, the press, and artistic and intellectual life unleashed powerful forces that proved impossible to contain. Before they had run their course, the Communist Party regimes would topple throughout Europe and the Soviet Union and the Cold War would come to an end.

Skeptics assumed Gorbachev would inevitably respond in the fashion of the Chinese Communist Party, which conducted a bloody crackdown on student demonstrators in June 1989 at Beijing's mammoth Tiananmen Square. The United States condemned the repression at Tiananmen but maintained trade, diplomatic, and cultural ties with the People's Republic of China. U.S. national security elites concluded that continuing dialogue with China was too important to make an issue of the regime's repressive action. Rejecting the Chinese model, Gorbachev concluded that the costs—militarily and politically, and in world opinion—were too high to forcefully maintain Soviet hegemony over Eastern Europe. The Soviet leader stunned Western national security experts by renouncing the Brezhnev Doctrine, which held that the Kremlin would use force to maintain communist regimes.

THE END OF THE COLD WAR

Once Soviet intervention had been renounced, the people of Eastern Europe took matters into their own hands. Poland had assumed the lead, well before Gorbachev's time, under Lech Walesa and the Solidarity trade-union movement. Similar pro-democracy reform movements emerged in Czechoslovakia and throughout Eastern Europe. The movement climaxed in 1989 with the sudden dissolution of the Soviet empire. A leader of Solidarity became prime minister of Poland, where a year later the first free elections in sixty-eight years were held to turn out the communists. Soviet troops departed from Hungary, where a new government unearthed the remains of the martyred reform leader Imre Nagy, executed by the Soviets after the 1956 rebellion, in order to give him a burial ceremony with full honors. The poet and playwright Vaclav Havel led the "velvet revolution" in Czechoslovakia. In November 1989 security forces bludgeoned hundreds of protesters in Wenceslas Square in Prague, but even more massive crowds returned on successive days, shouting for an end to communism. The regime came tumbling down.

The most dramatic change came in Berlin, the heart of the nation that had been divided by the

Cold War. After the East German authorities announced under pressure that citizens would no longer be prevented from traveling to the western sector of the city, the Berlin Wall, the ultimate symbol of the Cold War, literally crumbled in the hands of crowds of jubilant, hammer-wielding Germans. German reunification soon followed. Contending parties agreed on free elections in Albania and Bulgaria, but the regime of Nicolae Ceausescu in Romania grimly clung to power. In December, after his security police fired into crowds murdering hundreds of protesters, the Romanian army joined forces with the street protesters to topple the regime. Ceausescu and his wife were summarily executed by firing squad on Christmas Day 1989.

Meanwhile, in the Soviet Union itself, the three Baltic states of Estonia, Latvia, and Lithuania, forcibly annexed by Stalin in the 1939 pact with Hitler, demanded independence. All across the vast Eurasian empire, ethnic republics such as Azerbaijan, Belarus, Georgia, Moldavia, Tajikistan, Ukraine, and Uzbekistan rejected the essence of Soviet political life: the central authority of the Kremlin. Gorbachev repeatedly ruled out military intervention against the breakaway republics, but violence erupted in regions throughout the Soviet Union. Finally, in August 1991, on the eve of Gorbachev's planned signing of a new union treaty that would have created a formal confederation, hard-liners effected a coup, placing Gorbachev under house arrest in the Crimea. Protests, led by renegade Russian Communist Party leader Boris Yeltsin, overwhelmed the plotters of the coup after three days of tense standoff.

The collapse of the coup left a changed world in its wake. Gorbachev attempted to return to power after the coup, but in fact—because he was the leader of the discredited Communist Party—he had no real authority left. The Soviet reformer had won the Nobel Peace Prize but had lost the real prize: state power. Yeltsin assumed the Russian presidency under a new democratic system. Russia, and most of the fifteen other republics, rejected the Soviet system, though individual communists could remain engaged in parliamentary politics. The infamous KGB security police assumed a new name and no longer hounded intellectual critics of communism but otherwise remained active. Western Europe and the United States embraced the newly independent East European regimes, even encouraging several to join NATO over the opposition of Yeltsin and many residents of the former Soviet Union.

The United States confronted a world in which the nation's preeminent adversary for almost a half century had suddenly ceased to exist. President George H. W. Bush, who had succeeded Reagan in 1989, reacted cautiously to the dramatic change before declaring the triumph of the United States in the Cold War. The Cold War had been costly and dangerous but had provided a pernicious kind of stability in world affairs. With regional conflicts raging in the former Yugoslavia, Africa, parts of Asia, and in ethnic enclaves of Russia, many wondered if the post–Cold War world might bring even greater instability and uncertainty to world affairs.

INTERPRETING THE COLD WAR

From the outset of the Cold War, the two adversaries blamed one another for the conflict. For a long time, historians, echoing the patriotic culture of their nations, followed in train. In the Soviet Union, historical interpretation adhered to the rigid Communist Party line, which held the "imperialist" United States responsible for the Cold War. The Americans had tried to strangle the Soviet Union during its infancy and had sought ever since, with the brief interlude of World War II (known there as the Great Patriotic War) to contain Russia by surrounding it with hostile states. The United States and its allies had menaced the Soviet Union with the atomic bomb and had tried to isolate and destroy the "motherland" with their economic power and trade restrictions. The Soviet Union depicted itself as a defensive outpost of progressive reform in a world dominated by ruthless but ultimately doomed capitalist imperialists.

Until a wave of revisionism emerged in the 1960s, historians in the United States interpreted the evolution of the Cold War in orthodox terms: that it was a struggle to contain an expansionist and "totalitarian" Soviet regime. The totalitarian model linked Nazi Germany and the Soviet Union as two ruthless military powers that forced their will upon neighboring states and employed terror at home against their own people. Like the Soviets, Americans insisted that their actions in the Cold War had been primarily defensive, as the term "containment" suggested. The essential argument, reflected in the language of NSC 68, was that the United States represented the "free world" in a struggle against atheist totalitarianism.

Revisionists of various shades began to emerge in the United States in the late 1950s, reaching their apogee in the wake of the disastrous U.S. intervention in Indochina. Revisionists challenged the patriotic culture with their willingness to consider the Soviet point of view. Some argued that economic necessity, specifically the need for foreign markets, determined the direction of U.S. Cold War diplomacy. Revisionists emphasized that the United States, not just the Soviet Union, had been an expansionist power throughout its history. They also underscored the willingness of U.S. national security elites to ally themselves with a host of dictators across the globe, as long as those rulers embraced anticommunism and left their nations open to U.S. economic penetration.

Orthodox interpretations returned with a vengeance with the end of the Cold War and the collapse of the Soviet Union. The triumphalist argument held that the Cold War policies of the United States and its allies had been necessary to contain communism and that they had proven spectacularly successful. Despite the violence of the era, some viewed the Cold War as a "long peace," because, in fact, the superpowers had not gone to war. One scholar went so far as to assert that the end of the Cold War marked the "end of history" insofar as democratic politics and capitalism soon would be embraced by everyone.

Others rejected the triumphalist interpretation of the history of the Cold War as well as the notion that the long struggle had been worth the effort. They argued that the Cold War had been extremely expensive, diverting resources to the respective militaries and away from economic and social development. Moreover, the superpowers typically carried out military conflicts on Third World battlefields, leaving many of those nations divided and wracked by poverty and degradation. The East-West struggle might have come to an end, but the great divide in wealth and quality of life between North and South had never been greater. Moreover, market reforms failed to revive the Russian economy. Indeed, "shock therapy" brought a sharply lower standard of living for most of the population, which had lost the guaranteed employment and safety net once provided under the Soviet system. In 1999, Yeltsin stepped down for Vladimir Putin, a little known former KGB officer, who became the new Russian president.

Interpretations of the Cold War will continue to evolve as scholars gain access to more evidence and as world events continue to unfold and illuminate fresh perspectives on the past. New archival evidence, made available by the collapse of the former Communist Party regimes, has revealed fascinating insight into Cold War conflicts such as the Korean War and the Cuban missile crisis. Scholars now argue that Third World countries, rather than being mere pawns in the Cold War, often shaped the agenda for their superpower allies. Others argue that the real significance of the Cold War was its impact on science, technology, and culture, including popular culture and consumerism.

By century's end, the Cold War may have been over but many legacies remained. Russian-American and Sino-American relations continued to be strained. Ethnic and regional conflicts simmered across the globe. The threat posed by nuclear, chemical, and biological weapons remained real, whether they might be wielded by terrorists or by so-called outlaw regimes. At the same time, information technology, rapid population growth, and environmental threats such as global warming began to establish an agenda for the new millennium. The efforts of the people of the world and their leaders to meet these challenges would determine the character of the post–Cold War world.

BIBLIOGRAPHY

Brands, H. W. *The Devil We Knew: Americans and the Cold War.* New York, 1993. A pithy overview of Cold War history.

Carroll, John M., and Herring, George C., eds. *Modern American Diplomacy.* Rev. ed. Wilmington, Del., 1996. An excellent anthology.

Chomsky, Noam. *World Orders Old and New.* New York, 1994. A radical perspective on the end of the Cold War and its implications.

Engelhardt, Tom. *The End of Victory Culture: Cold War America and the Disillusioning of a Generation.* New York, 1995. An enlightening cultural perspective.

Gaddis, John Lewis. *Strategies of Containment: A Critical Appraisal of Postwar American National Security Policy.* New York, 1982. A worthwhile read on American grand strategy.

Gardner, Lloyd C. *Spheres of Influence: The Great Powers Partition Europe, from Munich to Yalta.* Chicago, 1993.

Garthoff, Raymond L. *Détente and Confrontation: American-Soviet Relations from Nixon to Reagan.* Washington, D.C., 1985. A magisterial history.

———. *The Great Transition: American-Soviet Relations and the End of the Cold War.* Washington, D.C., 1994. The best work on the end of the Cold War.

Gorbachev, Mikhail. *Perestroika: New Thinking for Our Country and the World.* New York, 1987. The deposed Soviet leader's revolutionary ideas on society and foreign policy.

Herring, George C. *America's Longest War: The United States and Vietnam, 1950–1975.* New York, 1996. 3d ed. An excellent survey of the Indochina war.

Hixson, Walter L. *Parting the Curtain: Propaganda, Culture, and the Cold War, 1945–1961.* New York, 1997. Assesses psychological warfare and cultural perspectives.

Hogan, Michael J. *A Cross of Iron: Harry S. Truman and the Origins of the National Security State, 1945–1954.* New York and Cambridge, 1998.

Hunter, Allen, ed. *Rethinking the Cold War.* Philadelphia, 1998. The best anthology on the end of the Cold War.

LaFeber, Walter. *The American Age: United States Foreign Policy at Home and Abroad Since 1750.* 2d ed. 2 vols. New York, 1994. One of the best texts on postwar U.S. foreign policy.

Lebow, Richard Ned, and Janice Gross Stein. *We All Lost the Cold War.* Princeton, N.J., 1994. A critical perspective on the argument that the West "won" the Cold War.

Leffler, Melvyn P. *A Preponderance of Power: National Security, the Truman Administration, and the Cold War.* Stanford, Calif., 1992.

Lundestad, Geir. *East, West, North, South: Developments in International Politics Since 1945.* 4th ed. New York, 1999. The perspectives of a top Norwegian scholar.

May, Ernest R., ed. *American Cold War Strategy: Interpreting NSC 68.* New York, 1993. Multiple perspectives on perhaps the most revealing document on the American side of the Cold War.

Pessen, Edward. *Losing Our Souls: The American Experience in the Cold War.* Chicago, 1993. A historian's biting assessment of U.S. Cold War diplomacy.

Schulzinger, Robert D. *American Diplomacy Since 1900.* 4th ed. New York, 1998. One of the better texts on modern U.S. foreign policy.

Sherry, Michael S. *In the Shadow of War: The United States Since the 1930s.* New Haven, Conn., 1995. The best analysis of the role of militarism in American society.

Smith, Tony. "New Bottles for New Wine: A Pericentric Framework for the Study of the Cold War." *Diplomatic History* 24, no. 4 (fall 2000): 567–591. Emphasizes the centrality of peripheral nations in the Cold War era.

Stueck, William W. *The Korean War: An International History.* Princeton, N.J., 1997. A solid international history of a pivotal Cold War conflict.

Trachtenberg, Marc. *A Constructed Peace: The Making of the European Settlement, 1945–1963.* Princeton, N.J., 1999. An excellent analysis of the first generation of the Cold War.

Westad, Odd Arne. "The New International History of the Cold War: Three (Possible) Paradigms." *Diplomatic History* 24, no. 4 (fall 2000): 551–565. A stimulating reconceptualization based on new documentation.

White, Donald W. *The American Century: The Rise and Decline of the United States as a World Power.* New Haven and London, 1996. A mammoth study of the American empire.

Williams, William A. *The Tragedy of American Diplomacy.* 2d rev. ed. New York, 1972. A classic work on the economic imperatives underlying U.S. diplomacy.

Zubok, Vladislav, and Constantine Pleshakov. *Inside the Kremlin's Cold War: From Stalin to Khrushchev.* Cambridge, Mass., 1996. The best assessment of Soviet Cold War diplomacy by two accomplished Russian scholars.

See also ARMS CONTROL AND DISARMAMENT; ARMS TRANSFERS AND TRADE; BALANCE OF POWER; COLD WAR ORIGINS; COLD WAR TERMINATION; COLD WARRIORS; COLLECTIVE SECURITY; CONTAINMENT; COVERT OPERATIONS; DETERRENCE; DOMINO THEORY; FOREIGN AID; GLOBALIZATION; INTELLIGENCE AND COUNTERINTELLIGENCE; INTERNATIONAL ORGANIZATION; INTERVENTION AND NONINTERVENTION; THE NATIONAL INTEREST; NATIONAL SECURITY COUNCIL; NORTH ATLANTIC TREATY ORGANIZATION; NUCLEAR STRATEGY AND DIPLOMACY; OUTER SPACE; POST–COLD WAR POLICY; SCIENCE AND TECHNOLOGY; SUMMIT CONFERENCES; SUPERPOWER DIPLOMACY; THE VIETNAM WAR.

COLD WAR ORIGINS

Anders Stephanson

Since the astonishing disintegration of its empire in eastern Europe in 1989 and the subsequent collapse of the Soviet Union itself, "Cold War" has widely come to designate the entire postwar period in international relations from 1945 onward, during which the tense relationship between the United States and the Soviet Union formed the pivot of world politics. The end of one side, then, evidently ended the relationship as such and thus the period as well. This is not, however, precisely the way in which the term emerged or was always understood and used. The "end" of the Cold War was declared on a number of earlier occasions, perhaps no more emphatically so than during the height of so-called détente in the early 1970s, when the respective leaders Richard M. Nixon and Leonid Brezhnev, on partly different grounds, announced that the relationship had entered a new kind of state. While the usage today assumes, more or less explicitly, that the designation and period are essentially to be derived from the nature of the two parties themselves and their supposedly inherent antagonism, Nixon and Brezhnev considered the term to signify, simply put, a particular phase of a continuing relationship.

For the sake of transparency, let it be known that the present writer is inclined to agree with Nixon and Brezhnev. If the Cold War is coeval with the entire relationship and simply rooted in systemic difference, then, for one thing, it would seem natural to locate the beginning in the Bolshevik Revolution. This is a coherent position but immediately puts into question how one is to characterize the alliance during the Second World War. Similarly, it becomes hard to account for the peculiar shift in the U.S. posture toward the far more radical People's Republic of China during the 1960s and 1970s, a shift from utter, relentless hostility to something close to a great-power alliance.

By contrast, here the Cold War will be grasped as a state of abnormally intense conflict between the United States and the Soviet Union that resulted from the inability of the two powers to resolve the monumental political issues at the end of World War II. Beginning in 1947, the Cold War was "abnormal" in the sense that while the level of enmity resembled that of outright war, the conflict took place, according to the classical terms of international law, in conditions of peace. The Cold War was cold because it did not issue in outright war at its core. Whatever ending date (1963, 1972, or 1989–1991) one chooses, the fact remains that the United States and the Soviet Union, along with their military alliances NATO and the Warsaw Pact, never entered into military conflict. Actual war was displaced to the periphery and carried out by proxies or by independent actors whose interests, projects, and associations became entangled within the larger conflict. As a *condition* or state of affairs, the conflict can be characterized as a warlike antagonism, executed by means short of war, where the adversary's legitimacy as a regime was essentially denied, and diplomacy, understood as a process of resolving issues of mutual concerns in times of peace, withered away and was replaced by diplomacy as ideology and propaganda. The structure of international politics became, as a consequence of the projection of the conflict onto the rest of the world, increasingly bipolar in nature. The division was accompanied by an immense and escalating arms race. Finally, there was suppression of internal dissidence on both sides, vastly more brutally and extensively in the Soviet case.

Seen as a *phase* of the U.S.–Soviet relationship, the Cold War thus comes to an end when these characteristics expire or change into their opposites. The legitimacy of the other is recognized de facto and the irreconcilable ideological animosity is replaced by a general emphasis on the need for peaceful coexistence. The existing divisions and balance of power are implicitly acknowledged in the form of spheres of influence or control. It is agreed, by fact rather than formal treaty, that nuclear weapons must never be used unless in conditions of ultimate resort. From this perspective, the end can thus be located in 1963 after a series of recent events: the apparently final division of Berlin and Germany, the emergence of the Sino-Soviet conflict, the horrendous, mutual experience of the Cuban missile crisis, and the ensuing expression of cooperation in the nuclear limited test ban treaty. However the Cold War is understood, it is clear in any case that some qualitative change occurs around this moment.

A defining set of features or a typology can serve as a description of a condition and means of periodization but it says nothing much about the origins of the Cold War and its deeper meaning. The following account, indeed, takes as its starting point that the "Cold War" is more than a descriptive term or a simple metaphor: it assumes that it is a genuine concept of explanatory potential. For analytical reasons, we will thus keep distinct "origins" and causes from the problem of the Cold War as a dynamic project and projection. "Cold War," it should also be borne in mind, is not everything that happens in international politics or even in U.S.–Soviet relations during the Cold War. The significance of these differentiations will be evident once the term is situated against the background of the opposition and semantic field that originally produced it, namely, that of war and peace.

GENEALOGY OF THE TERM

It was in the United States, not accidentally, that the Cold War as a term entered popular discourse. It was there too that much of the early discussion about its nature and causes took place and where the preponderance of historiography on the subject would later appear. The Cold War was from the beginning an American concern. It has never quite been established who coined the phrase. Nor does it much matter. Bernard Baruch, the aging financier and sometime policymaker, used the term in the spring of 1947 but in passing and without any elaboration. By his own subsequent account, Baruch took it from his friend and speechwriter Herbert Bayard Swope, who claimed he had come up with it while considering the so-called Phoney War of 1939–1940, the odd and extended early phase of World War II in Europe when nothing substantial by way of military activity took place.

The person who turned it into an integrated part of the political language, however, was the powerful newspaper columnist Walter Lippmann. In the fall of 1947, he published a series of wide-ranging articles on foreign policy that took as their critical starting point an important analysis of the Soviet Union that had appeared in the July issue of *Foreign Affairs,* the authoritative journal of the foreign policy establishment in the United States. The author, George F. Kennan, was a high official in the State Department, and because the piece was controversial it appeared anonymously under the signature "X"—thus rendering it known and famous subsequently as the "X Article." At the end of the year, Lippmann collected his columns in a short book he entitled *The Cold War.* Although he nowhere used the term in the actual writings, the idea was present throughout. In the next few years it gradually became a common reference but it only achieved general usage in the early 1950s. Against the Baruch-Swope claims to authorship, Lippmann maintained later that his choice of title had been inspired by a certain French vocabulary of politics in the 1930s, where terms such as *la guerre froide* (cold war) and *la guerre blanche* (white war) designated a state of war without open war. French lexographers have disputed Lippmann's retrospective account but the matter remains open.

There are, in any case, other and earlier appearances. Two are of considerable interest. In October 1945 the English writer George Orwell had referred to a "cold war" in the context of what he saw as a new historical stage where a few "monstrous super-States" would be able to divide the world between them because of their control of the awesome new weapon, the atomic bomb. Orwell surmised that these superpowers, now essentially unassailable, would agree not to use the bomb against each other but deploy it as a means of intimidating their respective neighbors in what would constitute "a permanent 'cold war.'"

Vast conflagrations such as World War II might then be replaced by a "'peace that is no peace,' an epoch as horribly stable as the slave empires of antiquity." Three such Cold War power configurations would emerge: the United States, the Soviet Union, and, potentially, China–East Asia. Highly suggestive, Orwell's grim scenario thus reserved "cold war" for the relationship between the powerful and the weak, probably an extrapolation from fascist examples of intimidation and expansion during the 1930s. His use of the term had little effect; but the notion of three global hegemons would reappear three years later in his classic novel of dystopian drabness, *1984,* where Oceania, Eastasia, and Eurasia engage in seemingly useless wars on the periphery in the name of meaningless propagandistic slogans, language having been reduced to a political instrument of pure manipulation.

Orwell's geopolitical vision was a postwar version of an idiosyncratic work that appeared in the United States in 1941, James Burnham's *The Managerial Revolution.* Here, another tripartite division of superstates, each impossible to conquer, is envisaged (Japan, Germany, and the United States). Enduring in its fundamentals, the system would nevertheless feature a myriad of diffuse conflicts, hard to get a grip on because they would be undeclared, their origins, beginnings, and endings forever mired in obscurity. Orwell's peace that is no peace, already discernible in this account, will become more explicit once Burnham had moved from renegade Trotskyist to relentless cold warrior. By 1947 he was arguing that a sort of World War III had broken out even before the second one was over, a conflict triggered in April 1944 by the outbreak of civil war in Greece. This new and all-encompassing contest required, above all, unflinching assertion of American power in the form of a world empire: the United States, not least because of its atomic monopoly, would be able to intervene to decide all global issues vital to its national security. Should the United States fail, the Soviet Union would take its place. Burnham thought the imperial project, necessarily entailing a great deal of coercion, could be combined with democracy at home. Moreover, he suggested that, rather than calling the whole endeavor an empire, one should give it the more palatable name of a "democratic world order."

The idea of a new historical condition outside the "normal" polarity of peace and war, initially distilled from the experience of fascist aggression in the 1930s, was thus in circulation by the time Lippmann put the term on the public map. There is, however, a much older use, though not as old as sometimes alleged. It appears to originate in the early fourteenth century with a Castilian aristocrat, Don Juan Manuel, who was part of the long and continuing Christian campaign to reconquer the Iberian peninsula from Islamic power. This struggle featured a wide range of irregular engagements and changing frontiers against the backdrop of a "total" political and cultural conflict between religious ideologies. Don

Juan Manuel, reflecting deeply on the nature of the antagonism, is said to have called it a cold war. What his manuscript actually says is probably "tepid" or "lukewarm." The rendition "cold" is the accidental result of erroneous editorial transcription in the 1860s. Yet Don Juan Manuel's image of tepid war is not without relevance in the present context. Real war, he says, has real results in the form of either death or peace. Tepid war, by contrast, is not an honorable war between equal enemies and seems not to result in any real peace. The mistake of his subsequent editor in any case illustrates some of the problems with the metaphorical aspects of the term: the opposite of cold may be hot, in this case signifying open war, but a rising temperature can also indicate a "thaw," as in a warming relationship replacing a frosty, frigid, and unresponsive one. The term indicates, then, the absolute, polar enmity of real war without any real fighting: it is warlike in every sense except, paradoxically, the explicitly military.

In pondering his Muslim enemies, Don Juan Manuel was highly respectful of their qualities as warriors; but in the end his study had to do with a conflict that was doctrinally irreconcilable in nature, indeed civilizational: there was no frame in which European Christendom and Islam could understand one another as equal adversaries. "Peace" could only result from a total victory and liquidation of the enemy as an independent force. A century later, however, Europe itself was rent asunder by confessional struggles regarding the very orthodoxy of Christianity. In the long process during which these struggles were played out, the modern concept of the state emerged along with a sharply defined, dichotomous understanding of war and peace. Simply put, confessional conflicts (and war) were effectively banished from the sovereign inside of the new, inviolate state borders. To wage war from then on is, supposedly, the exclusive right of sovereigns. Understood as a legitimate political means, such warmaking can only take place externally against enemies who are essentially legitimate equals similarly engaged. These intramural, European wars, in principle, are only to be conducted for limited gains, not for the absolute end of total liquidation of the enemy as a political entity. A whole apparatus regulating these limited wars is constructed, based on the premise of an absolute distinction between inside and outside as well as between war and peace.

This is, in short, the birth of international law as we know it. It is a profoundly Eurocentric order. Although challenged severely by the French Revolution, it survived essentially down to the 1930s, when the fascist powers launched a series of aggressions that broke decisively with the earlier, sharp distinction between the states of war and peace. Thus, Japan's war against China was officially classed as an "incident"; Italy called its intervention in the Spanish Civil War "not warmaking"; and Hitler expanded his territory through successive ultimatums and threats of violence that did not become open war. A range of state actions seemed to have emerged that constituted some form of state close to but below the level of actual war. The traditional system (declaration of war, rules of conduct, rights of noncombatants, neutrality), which had been codified in the Hague Convention in 1907 and achieved a strong resurgence in the legalistic 1920s, appeared to have been set brutally aside. It was this process, then, that eventually would draw two immense new powers onto center stage, both with universalizing, quasi-confessional claims: the United States and the Soviet Union. The "origins" of the Cold War lie in this event, more particularly in the diverging ways in which the two regimes understood and dealt with the antifascist war and its aftermath.

THE SOVIET WAY

The Bolshevik Revolution in 1917 ushered in a regime that, in its initial stages, assumed that it could only be a transitory moment in a world-historical process of socialist revolution. Existing state arrangements constituted a mask, falsely legitimizing class rule. What mattered was the relations and struggle between the international working class and its counterpart, the bourgeoisie. Peace in this context was merely an appearance, a veil behind which an always present class struggle was taking place. Real peace could only arrive with the global victory of rational socialism. The premise of class relations as a systemic condition of antagonism across state borders was traditional Marxism. Lenin's Russian appropriation, however, added a strongly militarized concept of politics as a field of alliances, battles, and positions, necessarily ordered around the analysis of a complex of contradictions that served in turn to identify a "main enemy," either tactical or strategic. Everything must be arranged in relation to the all-important task of winning the struggle against that enemy. State sovereignty

as a principle, consequently, had no fundamental sanctity within this frame. Indeed, by resurrecting the moral right to revolution on a global scale, the early Soviet regime formed as formidable a challenge to the traditional European world order as one could imagine.

What followed instead was the uneven integration of the Soviet Union into the existing system. By 1923 the insurrectionary wave in the wake of the First World War had expired. In this (by definition) temporary lull, and having finally established its rule, Moscow settled down to constructing socialism at home while establishing formal diplomatic relations with the capitalist outside. Eventually but not inevitably, the anomaly of a revolutionary state in such circumstances was resolved by Lenin's successor, Joseph Stalin. In the first place, Stalin territorialized Lenin's militarized concept of politics by turning the defining "fundamental contradiction" from the vertical, deterritorialized antagonism between capital and labor to a "horizontal" one between the capitalist outside and the Soviet Union. From then on, what was in Moscow's immediate interest was by definition also in the interest of the international working class. Because this new and territorialized interest happened to be lodged on an immense Eurasian landmass, it was possible as well to freeze in part the dialectical interaction constitutive of the previously pivotal contradiction: whereas capital and labor presumably exist and act upon each other in the same space, the Soviet Union and its outside capitalist state enemies were physically separated in space. The concept of dialectical contradiction remained, but once territorialized on a horizontal plane, its two sides featured only one readily identifiable pole and actor, namely, the Soviet Union. Where "the main enemy" of the Soviet state was to be found on the capitalist outside was a matter of tactical and strategic assessment by the Kremlin. The terrain was thus open for realist statecraft of the most traditional and cynical kind.

The tendency to subjective maneuvering for Moscow's narrowly conceived objectives in foreign policy was reinforced by the manner in which Lenin's stage theory of capitalist development was applied to the novel phenomenon of fascism. Around 1900, according to Lenin's erstwhile concept, capitalism had reached its classical limits and mutated into monopoly capitalism, a qualitatively new form expressed in imperialism, presumably the final stage of the system as such. Overripe and on the verge of stagnation, the system had to find new spaces of exploitation abroad and more intense levels of exploitation at home. The propensity to resolve the periodic and intensifying crises by aggression and violence thus typified the new epoch, a feature demonstrated with the greatest clarity in the advent of the First World War.

From this perspective it was subsequently possible for the Stalinist regime initially to see fascism in the 1920s and 1930s as a sign of capitalist weakness and to locate its objective class basis narrowly in, supposedly, the most rabidly reactionary parts of monopoly capital. Not only was this a remarkably slim social foundation but the analysis left actual identification of who was "the most" reactionary up to the judgment of the Kremlin, a judgment in turn not uninfluenced by which powers and forces happened to fit its geopolitical interests at the moment. Once it became apparent that fascism, especially its Nazi variant, was an immediate threat of appalling potential, the strategic and tactical outlook was thus suitably adjusted. As this was the Great Depression, there was little reason to revise the view that fascism expressed the final, structural crisis of monopoly capitalism; but it became absolutely imperative to prevent such regimes of violence from attacking and endangering the rapid achievements of putatively rational socialism in one country. Fascism consequently became the new main enemy and mobilization against it across the board the all-consuming task. Because the class basis of fascism had been conceived so narrowly, the potential targets for that mobilization were extraordinarily wide in scope, so that they came to include, in theory, capitalist elements and regimes. Antifascism in the name of the broadest possible coalition was not, however, merely a momentary tactic ultimately designed to defend the Soviet Union. It was a strategy for the eventual achievement, again in theory, of the final victory of socialism. For if monopoly capitalism was inherently stagnating, the planned rationality of the Soviet Union was obversely destined historically to win out, provided the danger of fascist aggression could be prevented.

Hence there was, in principle, nothing in the Soviet position after the shift in the mid-1930s that rendered long-term relations of coexistence possible with capitalist powers. Far from having to do directly with capitalism and socialism, the main contradiction—and main enemy—was now located socially in the division between monopoly capital (strictly speaking, a fraction of it) and the amorphous "people." Geopolitically, the contradiction was between any given anti-Soviet powers and the Soviet Union and its assorted affiliates. Since this latter form of the contradiction was decisive, it is not surprising that Stalin abruptly changed his foreign policy in 1939 when the former strategy of antifascist alliance seemed manifestly to have failed and an opening presented itself to strike a cold-blooded deal with Hitler. Yet the geopolitical shift did not cause any correspondingly radical alteration in the basic ideological outlook, thus facilitating the desperate return to antifascist alliance politics and patriotic defense after the Nazi assault in June 1941 with the largest single military force in history.

At no point on the Soviet trajectory from Leninist internationalism to geopolitical realism did Stalin or his regime cease to be "communist." Given the ideological transmutations since 1917, Soviet foreign policy made sense (of a certain kind) both as Realpolitik and communist strategy. The two postures were eminently compatible, for there could be no contradiction, in theory or practice, between the geopolitical interests of the Soviet Union and the historical interests of communism as a movement. Defense of the regime in Moscow, securing what had been achieved in Stalin's fortress, was always paramount. It was the precondition for future victories, victories that could only be won elsewhere by a strategy of class and state alliances broadly conceived, not by any confrontational policy of socialist revolution. The merits or demerits of this posture are of no direct concern here. What should be borne in mind for future reference, however, is the fact that the doctrine featured no positive conceptual space for conducting a Cold War against capitalist powers after the defeat of fascism. Such a policy would have been theoretically nonsensical. It would also have been politically foolish in the extreme. The United States, after all, was a colossally superior power that produced half of all manufactures in the world at the time, a nation that had not only suffered no physical damage in the war but had actually seen its depressed economy brilliantly revived by the war effort, while the Soviet Union had incurred staggering losses in every domain. Short of another outright assault on the regime, such a Cold War was as nightmarish a scenario as could be imagined: a vast set of anti-Soviet alliances around the periphery led by a ferociously anti-Soviet power with unprecedented, seemingly unlimited resources.

The notion of a Cold War was indeed never contemplated before it became a fact and a system. Given the autarkic inclinations, Stalin's policy may instead be said to have envisaged distant but stable postwar relations with the capitalist ("peace-loving") democracies, based on mutually demarcated spheres of material and strategic interests. When this did not happen and the advent of full-blown Cold War had taken place in the latter part of 1947, the Soviet policy was still recognizably based on the established concept of defensive antifascist alliances: mobilizing against the "reactionary circles" that had now apparently again taken over at the helm of Western capitalism was to be carried out in the interclass name of national independence, not socialism. The U.S. thrust to world leadership was interpreted as an aggressive reaction to the achievements and advances of the Soviet Union and the "democratic" movement everywhere. An authoritative analysis in September 1947 thus found U.S. expansionism "highly reminiscent" of the fascist drive to "world supremacy." The world was divided between the "imperialist and antidemocratic camp" and its "anti-imperialist and democratic" counterpoint. Logically enough, the struggle against the former was everywhere to be based on patriotic support for peace and "national sovereignty." At the same time, the principle of "coexistence for a long period" between capitalism and socialism was reaffirmed, as was the corresponding idea of "cooperation" between the Soviet Union and capitalist powers, provided the principle of "reciprocity" and existing "obligations" were honored. This was uttered right before the Cold War became a political term; when it did, Moscow consequently saw it as a violently anticommunist policy, an aggressive U.S. attempt to prevent peaceful coexistence and indeed prepare for war against the Soviet Union. Signs of a thaw in the late 1950s would be interpreted as a victory for the (Soviet) policy of peace over the Cold War policy of anticommunism.

None of this, to reiterate earlier distinctions, is to say anything about "causes" or actual "origination." One might well argue that Stalin "caused" the Cold War unwittingly by pursuing policies likely to bring about just such an unwanted situation. Stalinism provided few analytical resources for any genuine understanding of Western politics, or for that matter the dynamics of nazism. Extreme materialist determinism reduced such "surface" Western phenomena to transparently clear economic and geostrategic interests, while Soviet society, because the economy had supposedly been socialized and classes largely abolished, was conversely subject to the pure, rational will of the regime. Such an outlook was not conducive to sophisticated evaluation of long-term interests in a highly volatile situation with immense issues at stake.

THE AMERICAN WAY

The product of a war of emancipation from one of the most powerful European states, and a nation that identified itself as the embodiment of universal right, the United States always had a problematic relationship with the reigning world order, alien, different, and European as it was. The United States was, however, able largely to escape the ill effects of that system, indeed paradoxically to profit from it by being allowed, as it happened, the luxury to develop its rapidly expanding continental space in geopolitical seclusion. This experience, wholly unlike that of the Soviet Union (and its czarist predecessors), lacked sustained dialectical interaction with powerful enemies. The United States, then, could afford to conceive of itself as a privileged place singled out by history to demonstrate the proper principles of humankind as such. Affirmation of that truth was of course continuously to be found in the phenomenal material progress visible throughout. It was really only through Woodrow Wilson's intervention in World War I and his ambitious attempt to restructure the old European order afterward that the United States was momentarily forced to reflect on what a properly "American" alternative to the given international order might look like. As it turned out, Wilson's project of law, discussion, arbitration, and self-determination in the interest of humankind was rejected at home and fared little better abroad than Lenin's contemporary counterpart. What followed instead, eventually, was the fascist challenge. Thus, in 1941 both of the two continental powers that had tried to maintain distance from the lethal center of world politics for most of the 1930s suffered fascist attacks, surprise attacks, without previous declarations of war.

A vital precondition for the Cold War was the diverging conceptions of what the ensuing, common war against fascism was ultimately about, in particular what sort of peace the colossal effort was to achieve. When the Soviet Union went from being a wartime ally of the United States to a postwar adversary (1945–1947) and then to a mortal enemy (1947–1963)—or, to put

228

it differently, when a hot war against fascism became a Cold War against communism—the quite specific way in which Franklin D. Roosevelt (and to a lesser extent his auxiliaries) had grappled with the issue of war and peace in the world and the international role of the United States was transplanted, with important modifications, to his successor. This in turn allowed the previous understanding of fascist aggression to be superimposed on its allegedly similar communist counterpart. We will pursue this changing trajectory from Roosevelt to Harry S. Truman (and his administration) by also including a reflection on the person who provided much of the raw material for the new Cold War analysis of the Soviet Union and whose writings also inspired Lippmann to name the international condition a "Cold War," namely, George F. Kennan. What will be of particular interest is the "rejectionist" aspect common, on different grounds, to Roosevelt, Truman, and Kennan alike: the notion, in short, that the enemy had no legitimacy because it in turn not only failed to recognize the legitimacy of others (especially the United States and the West) but was itself by nature bent on world conquest. This was an enemy, therefore, that had to be eradicated by a struggle to the death or (in Kennan's case) cast out of the international community so that it would eventually wither away.

Geopolitical noninvolvement was popular in the United States during the 1930s. No one was more keenly aware of this than President Roosevelt. By 1935, however, it was becoming impossible not to worry about the deteriorating international climate. Roosevelt began to take special note here of the rapid proliferation of aggression carried out, technically speaking, below the level of outright, declared war. Using the naval war of 1798 against France as historical reference, the administration introduced the term "quasi-war," which Roosevelt deployed specifically to illustrate the difficulty in maintaining the old, sharp distinction between war and peace. In his famous "Quarantine" speech of October 1937, he spoke of "times of so-called peace," and by the outbreak of the world war in September 1939, he had come to view this condition of mounting aggression quite specifically as a problem of international "lawlessness." Accordingly, he saw the advent of generalized war as a result of already existing gangsterism, enormously magnified and intensified, to be sure, but long rampant. Dealing with such a phenomenon was not war as traditionally conceived but essentially a "policing operation,"

albeit a huge one. To conduct that endeavor on traditional principles of recognizing the legitimacy of the enemy was palpably absurd. From the beginning, it was now apparent, the fascist regimes had unleashed their illegal aggression with the utmost contempt for international law and order. The distinction between war and peace, it was clear to Roosevelt, meant nothing to them. As he declared at a moment in July 1941 when the United States was still officially at peace with Germany, "the only peace possible with Hitler is the peace that comes from complete surrender."

The polarity of gangsterism and law, then, made retrospective sense of the events of the 1930s. Less obviously, it also allowed conceptually for the inclusion of the defensive Stalinist dictatorship in the camp of good, good being understood negatively here as not bad. The Nazi surprise attack on the Soviet Union in June 1941 probably confirmed for Roosevelt that the aspect of "dictatorship" did not in itself provide any precise gauge of what that regime would do in the international arena. Some dictatorships, though not perhaps proper admirers of "law," might indeed favor order, and without initial order in the sense of stability and international respect, there could be no ensuing institutionalization of civilizing law. Thus, on closer inspection Roosevelt's polarity turns out to harbor an important temporal dimension: while fascism/gangsterism could only disastrously lead to death and destruction, the powers of caution and order overall might, if nurtured in appropriate ways, evolve into something recognizably closer to home. There was, then, a civilizational potential here to be realized, given enough time and resources. The precondition was complete and utter destruction of gangsterism. It is in this light that one can understand Roosevelt's attempt to treat Stalin as a member in good standing in the association of orderly forces. This Rooseveltian posture must not be mistaken for any standard version of U.S. "legalism" or utopianism. Order, the essence of law, was always much more important to him (as it had been to his predecessor and relative Theodore) than the formal, procedural aspects. One recalls the court packing scheme of 1937, an ill-fated attempt to alter the political complexion of the Supreme Court and illustrative of Roosevelt's deeper attitude toward supposedly sacrosanct institutions of law. His explicit vision of a postwar world dominated by four great policing powers may be read in similar ways. It is not farfetched to detect in this concept of pacification and order a suitably updated Progressivism of the early 1900s, Roosevelt's own formative era.

In the event, Roosevelt's formula for all this, "unconditional surrender," performed a range of services from his viewpoint: it was an absolute precondition for the future construction of a reasonable world order; it offered the simplest possible platform for the wartime alliance; and by subordinating everything to the military objective of defeating the enemy it allowed for the postponement of sticky geopolitical issues such as territorial demands and exclusive spheres of influence. By the same token it was unclear what would follow that surrender. The underlying notion of pacification and policing entailed no vision of the political future. With a discerning eye on domestic opinion, Roosevelt chose accordingly to combine the demand for unconditional surrender with a declaration that the war was ultimately about "freedom." Both positions were absolute and general in character, but unconditional surrender was as precise as the goal of freedom was diffuse. One referred to the enemy and the only possible way the war could end in that regard. The other referred to the deeper meaning of the struggle and what would happen to the forces of good once the enemy had been defeated. The choice of "freedom" in the latter case may now seem natural, given that the idea had always been a constituent part of politics in the United States and its presence later on in Cold War language would become ubiquitous. Yet it was not always the most central referent in the political vocabulary, and Roosevelt's deployment was in fact the product of recent domestic controversies over the New Deal, which had been attacked from the right precisely as subversive of revered American values of freedom. The administration returned the salvo by appropriating the term and connecting it to "security," the notion that people have a substantial right to, among other things, a certain social and economic security in life.

The argument enjoyed, not surprisingly, considerable resonance during the Depression decade when deep "insecurity" was indeed rife among the public at large. At the end of the decade, when the insecurity of the United States itself was becoming manifest, the coupled concept was thus readily available for Roosevelt to project onto the world, above all through the Atlantic Charter and the "Four Freedoms" speech. The position entailed nothing much, again, by way of commitment to any concrete political arrangements, but because it was pro-

claimed in a language of inherent rights, a certain awkwardness was potentially attached to the procedure. Respect for the universal rights of individuals and nation-states in their capacity as autonomous, self-determining entities was not immediately apparent in British imperial rule, the brutal domestic repression of the Soviet regime, white supremacism, internment of Japanese Americans, and semicolonialism of the United States. These problems were manageable, however, since the suppression of gangsterism was always a prior condition for freedom in full-blown form. Thus, for instance, Roosevelt's support for "trusteeship" as a reasonable intermediate stage for colonial peoples deemed unready for full independence.

There the matter might have rested, but Roosevelt went on to connect unconditional surrender, order, freedom, and security into a single, neo-Wilsonian frame such that there would be and could be no real, final security for the United States and humankind until everyone everywhere had come to encompass and recognize these freedoms. Partly launched as domestic polemic against "isolationism," Roosevelt's crucial move had several related effects. It was now incumbent on policymakers, in principle, to demonstrate in every international matter that, negatively, the issues involved were irrelevant to the overall struggle for freedom, on which hinged in turn the security of the United States. This was extremely difficult to do, as the Truman administration would find out when China was being "lost" in 1948–1949. Moreover, if the world was now to be divided into two exclusive zones of freedom and un-freedom, any conceivable gain for the latter was not only a defeat for the former but also automatically an infringement on the security of the United States. During World War II this made sense because the dividing line was easily defined in straightforwardly military terms and no one could deny that the position of that front was vital for the very future of the world. The free world was for all practical purposes all areas beyond fascist control, while "liberated" ones, specifically, were those freed from such domination. Gains, then, were graphically clear in the movement of the line. Drawing the same line in the postwar world, however, where the antifascist free world was now the anticommunist free world, was a very different matter: areas of contention might technically be at peace, the demarcation vis-à-vis the enemy could not always take the form of a clear front and the issue of "freedom" might well be a good deal blurrier. The Rooseveltian matrix, then, expanded American security concerns in principle to the entire world and structured them in terms of a continuous, epic struggle for final, positive freedom everywhere.

The globalist implications were quietly reinforced by the addition, again for contingent domestic reasons, of a peculiarly American historical referent. To the image of gangsterism, never hard to grasp presumably with the Prohibition era in fresh memory, was added that of a global civil war, understood as a typological reenactment of the U.S. Civil War. Roosevelt himself liked to argue that he had taken the formula of unconditional surrender from Ulysses S. Grant, a nifty triple play on the Civil War, unconditional surrender, and the United States. Distinguished figures around him, moreover, began to talk of the struggle in the religiously flavored terms of abolitionism and slavery. Henry Stimson, the incoming (Republican) secretary of war, invoked Abraham Lincoln's biblical metaphor of a house divided which cannot stand but must turn either slave or free. Vice President Henry Wallace referred similarly to a "fight to death between the free world and the slave world" just as in the United States during the Civil War. Now a matter of the world as a whole, there could be "no compromise with Satan," as he put it. Wallace, interestingly, followed the historical analogy to its conclusion by insisting that the lethal struggle had to be followed by a phase of reconstruction, where the social and economic rights of the underprivileged, the enslaved as it were, would be secured. This aspect tended to disappear or at least be severely constricted when the trope came to provide core concepts for Cold War thought. Eradicating gangsterism, however, was for Roosevelt himself what the struggle was immediately and foremost about: the sequence began with the liquidation of the lawless and continued with policing and establishment of order, followed by the opening up of a long and winding road of progress toward freedom and final, true peace everywhere.

The end of World War II and consequent expiration of the alliance happened almost to coincide with the death of Roosevelt. His successor, Harry S. Truman, not a politician of equal world-historical ambition, inherited a deceptively simple scheme from a figure of deceptively open character who had actually kept much of his geopolitical project to himself, managing to combine in his policymaking extraordinary publicity with extraordinary privacy. Truman was far more

literal-minded. The future focus of world politics was to be the war alliance of the United Nations as transformed into a universal operation of cooperation. Pronouncements, such as the Declaration on Liberated Europe at the Yalta Conference in February 1945, meant exactly what they said, as did the agreements on democratic elections in Poland. To the subtleties and nuances of traditional geopolitics he was largely deaf. Four months later, when Truman had the satisfaction of achieving the first of Roosevelt's absolute aims, unconditional surrender (or something close enough to it), he was thus left with the open-ended commitment to the accomplishment of U.S. security through the global victory of freedom. Whereas the first goal had been clearly strategic and measurable in character, directed as it was to the total defeat and liquidation of a well-defined enemy, it was not at all clear after the final victory in early August 1945 what would follow in regard to the second aim. Crushing the enemy had eliminated the immediate strategic terrain for Roosevelt's second, more positive idea, the concept of freedom. The next two years would thus be a period of reconnaissance and reinvention of that terrain through the gradual installment of the Soviet Union as the new mortal enemy of freedom and U.S. security.

For Truman, the postwar period of 1945–1947 seemed indeed to feature nothing but a whole string of such Soviet transgressions. Moscow was staking claims in two theaters of traditional Russian interests, eastern Europe and the Near East, in ways that appeared to him not only disquieting but in explicit violation of existing agreements. Thus, Stalin imposed his own kind of regime in Poland and never allowed the free elections promised in the Yalta accords. In fact, by the fall of 1945 it seemed clear that the future of Soviet-controlled eastern Europe would not entail anything resembling the sort of "freedom" envisaged by the wartime declarations. Strikingly hard-nosed in the Council of Foreign Ministers, the forum where the peace treaties were to be hammered out, the Soviet representatives appeared little interested in anything but their own very narrowly conceived concerns. Subsequently, in 1945–1946 civil war revived in Greece, apparently instigated by communists, while Moscow itself proceeded to make a series of exceedingly hostile demands on Turkey and refuse to leave northern Iran as previously agreed. At the same time there was little or no progress on the economic rejuvenation of Germany and western Europe because of

Soviet obstruction, and the situation was clearly (or so it seemed) deteriorating fast.

Truman's response was typically hard: support for the Iranian regime in 1946, strong assumption of previous British responsibilities in the eastern Mediterranean through massive military assistance to Turkey and Greece in the spring of 1947, and, the crowning achievement, the launching of the Marshall Plan in June 1947 to restore the western European economies, followed by institutionalized military ties in the form of the North Atlantic Treaty Organization in 1949. The western and by far richest parts of Germany being under western control, the process was completed with the creation of the Bundesrepublik in 1949.

Whether or not this was an accurate understanding of Stalin's actual policies is an interesting historical question. Having faced the Nazis mostly alone for almost three epic years of monstrous war, the Stalinist regime was hardly about to jeopardize its new positions in eastern Europe for the sake of any general declarations on liberty. One wonders if the United States would have done so either had there been invasions of comparable scale and devastation through, say, Canada. Indeed, Stalin was doubtless aware that the United States had not been unwilling historically to order and arrange the domestic politics of states in its vicinity for reasons apparently of far lesser magnitude. The Soviet demands on Turkey were imprudent, as were the equivocations and obstructions in northern Iran; but in neither case were the actions beyond the traditional bounds of the czarist predecessors.

In western Europe, meanwhile, the communist parties continued a policy of class coalitions and reconstruction until the Marshall Plan divided the region from the East. The German matter, however, was the paramount one in the end. Here the Soviet Union considered itself entitled chiefly to two things: reparations and absolute guarantees that a reconstructed Germany would never again constitute a threat. In the end it got nothing close to what it had anticipated by way of reparations, and it also witnessed the emergence of the powerful anti-Soviet state in western Germany that was to join NATO. Seen as statecraft in pursuance of its interests, then, the Stalinist policies were not impressive. A more subtle and clever regime, for example, could have wrecked the Marshall Plan by appearing to accept it.

Sharp and pointed as these various actions and counteractions were, however, they do not in themselves add up to a Cold War. That would only come about when the Truman administration had cast a new, modified version of Roosevelt's wartime matrix and superimposed it on the novel condition of what seemed to be a peace that was no peace. What enabled this critical process to take place was the concept of "totalitarianism." By 1950 the "American" translation of the totalitarian theme was to be completed with the full-blown reintroduction of the wartime idea of a global civil war about freedom and slavery.

As a neologism of Italian fascism in the 1920s, totalitarianism had signified the goal of "total" confluence between state and society. At the end of World War II it had of course become an entirely pejorative word, indicating (simply put) a tyrannical regime in dictatorial control of its population by modern means of propaganda and secret police. Dormant if not irrelevant during the war because of the alliance with the Soviet Union, it reentered the Western frame after the war as a focus for the attempt to understand the emerging divergencies with the Kremlin. By the spring of 1947 the Truman administration was announcing in no uncertain terms that the Soviet camp was totalitarian and thus essentially the same as fascism. The reversal abstracted certain similarities in technologies of rule and turned the resultant concept into an explanation of what such regimes would be doing in foreign relations. Fusing two very different adversaries under the rubric of totalitarianism carried with it, then, the projection of fascist modes of aggression and ultimate objectives of world conquest onto the Soviet Union.

The idea of totalitarianism served to reactivate a certain dual lesson already painfully learned at Pearl Harbor, if not before, about the origins of the Second World War and the proper role of the United States in the world. The first part of the lesson had to do with what had actually been done. Legitimate governments in the 1930s, accordingly, had not only failed to stand up to the dictators but, when pressed, actually helped them along by obsequious negotiations and the most abject concessions, only to find the insatiable aggressors escalating their demands and finally throwing the world into generalized war. Tyrants recognized no language, it was clear, other than that of force. This historical lesson was encapsulated in the harsh references after the war to "Munich" and "appeasement," both of which became instantly recognizable signifiers of condemnation.

The second part of the lesson had to with what had not been done. For there was of course the more particular problem of the inactivity of the United States itself. The weaker democracies France and Britain had at least been in a position during the 1930s to choose whether to appease or not. The United States, though possessed of vastly greater potential power, had removed itself even from this choice. Deeply bogged down in self-imposed "isolationism," the country had eventually paid the devastating price at Pearl Harbor. Thus, the model analogy impressed on the public the indisputable imperative of global responsibility and action against threats of the totalitarian type. Given that frame and the experience of Pearl Harbor, it was only with the greatest difficulty from now on that one could find any morally and politically plausible way of opposing such a vast engagement. Perhaps the only truly "American" counterargument was that of the traditional Republican right to the effect that unlimited commitments conjured up the nightmare of an un-American Leviathan, a normalization and entrenchment of the expanded wartime state, in turn a continuation of the corruptions invented by the detested New Deal apparatus. In evoking Munich and Pearl Harbor, however, the "internationalist" response could easily insinuate that some blame for these events had to be put on the Republican stab in the Wilsonian back after the First World War.

The lesson learned, in short, was double. First, dictators could only be stopped with unequivocal force and never appeased with concessions. Second, the United States must never again retreat into "isolationism" or abdicate judgment over international events but must always play a leading role in the world. These two truths had been established unequivocally on 7 December 1941, the day of "infamy" at Pearl Harbor. The graphic clarity of the ensuing war effort, however, did not require much reiteration and elaboration of the lesson. Roosevelt's twin vision of unconditional surrender and future cooperation for order naturally dominated the proceedings. When postwar realities seemed to disappoint those expectations, when the American eye began to detect in Soviet behavior something beyond mere intransigence, when one began to see crude impositions and violations of agreements honestly and fairly concluded, when, in short, the Soviet Union became a systemic problem—it was then that "totalitarianism" became a powerful device for the Truman administration, through which it could explain Moscow's conduct in a way that reinforced and recast the twin lessons of World War II in novel circumstances. In a word, communism became identical to fascism. The development was momentous.

Once the identity had been established, some implicit differentiation could take place. For one thing, the older Rooseveltian theme of aggression as gangsterism no longer seemed pertinent. While the Kremlin was no doubt an illegitimate regime, expressive of the cruel, arbitrary will of a tyrant and willing, should the occasion arise, to engage without compunction in every illegal act, it was not on the international level a criminal regime in the sense of, say, an Al Capone. (Indeed, Stalin had been bitterly indignant at the sheer illegality of Hitler's surprise attack, and once the Cold War got going, the Soviet view began to denounce "recklessness" and gangsterism in the name of peaceful relations, now with the United States as target.) The notion, in short, of an adventuristic outfit launching massive assaults at will did not square with the Soviet Union and the communist movement. Early analytical accounts spoke instead of a fairly cautious government, proceeding by secrecy, subversion, conspiracy, proxies, and creeping takeovers, in fact avoiding hot war if possible. This was an adversary with a strong sense of power, equipped with a disciplined, patient machine of great ingenuity, "a far-flung apparatus" in George F. Kennan's phrase. It was the piecemeal, covert as opposed to overt, aspect of totalitarian aggression that appeared to mark the Kremlin.

Another difference, tacitly recognized now and then, was ideological: rather than attacking democracy along fascist lines as degenerate, communism appealed to a putatively better and fuller form of it; rather than declaring racial superiority, communism offered strong critiques of it, not least as it appeared in the United States; rather than celebrating geopolitical expansion, it mobilized against "American imperialism" in terms of national independence and colonial liberation; rather than glorifying war, it proposed a politics explicitly calling for adherence to international agreements and the promotion of peace. One could easily (and often quite rightly) disparage this as empty propaganda, but the fact remained that the ideology of totalitarian communism was not the same as the ideology of totalitarian fascism. "Cold War" was the name of that difference, the name eventually given to the new and lethal challenge of the Soviet incarnation of totalitarianism.

Much of the concrete view of the Soviet Union here stemmed from Kennan. His Soviet morphology, first conveyed in early 1946 in the so-called Long Telegram from his post at the Moscow embassy, proved extraordinarily persuasive to the Truman administration. The grand narrative of freedom and totalitarianism appeared to be amply confirmed by the particulars of the analysis: the image of a hostile, powerful state, predetermined by its very nature to expand and destroy, refusing all normal, decent relations with the West, looking for "security only in patient but deadly struggle for the total destruction of rival power, never in compacts and compromises with it." When combined with the totalitarian trope and the historical lessons of Munich and Pearl Harbor, this account became irresistible ideology.

Curiously, however, Kennan himself was not especially interested in the concept of totalitarianism, nor for that matter in the universal issue of freedom and slavery. What was inimical about the Moscow regime for him was, simply put, what he took to be its despotic, fanatically anti-Western character and inherent need to expand that rule, not the fact that it was "unfree" as such. Kennan's conservative outlook combined two partly overlapping, partly contradictory orientations or sensibilities, neither of which had any extensive anchoring in American traditions. On the one hand, he was a realist, conceiving politics purely as a matter of power, interests, and security, not of ideology or norms: the primary question for the realist is what sort of "interested" policy any given power structure might give rise to or permit. On the other hand (and more fundamentally), Kennan espoused what one might call an ideology of the cultural West. He understood this entity as a wide civilization, the central and most mature areas of which lay in western Europe but which was made up of a whole range of specific political traditions and customs, some of which quite legitimately evinced few or no similarities with U.S. democracy. Real diplomacy (or at least extensive relations) could and should take place only within this realm, a realm of "intimacy" as he liked to think of it. Contrary to his realist impulse, then, Kennan felt that cultural proximity should be the decisive criterion in determining the manner of Western diplomacy. Toward the outside, where shared meaning was limited or nonexistent, one should maintain one's natural distance with dignified reserve. In particular, there could be no proper relationship with any fanatical regime that by its very nature was defying the West.

Ever since the late 1920s, when Kennan had begun his career as one of the first experts on the Soviet Union in the State Department, he had argued that the regime did not belong to the normative community of the West and should be isolated. Accordingly, he had opposed Roosevelt's diplomatic recognition of Moscow in 1933. A few years later he had also opposed the idea of any Western collaboration with the Soviet regime against fascism. The best policy, all things being equal, toward such disagreeable regimes was really a nonpolicy of no interaction, except where absolutely necessary. This was indeed to be his chief recipe for dealing with the nationalism of what would come to be known in the 1950s as the Third World. In Kennan's view, the Stalinist regime, because it was at once the most fanatical and powerful foe, could not just be ignored, especially not now that historical accident in the form of Hitler's immense betrayal of the West had served to place the Red Army in the middle of the civilizational heartland. It could, however, be isolated, or, in Kennan's own term, contained. Thus he argued that the United States should act rapidly and vigorously to restore to health the remaining parts of the central West, while preventing the enemy by all means necessary from making any advances into those areas and any others that might be deemed strategically vital for the West. Toward the Soviet regime itself, by contrast, one ought to maintain very low relations or none until such a time that its thwarted need to consume decaying Western body parts began to result in collapse, a change into something qualitatively different or at least some "mellowing" into manageable form.

Kennan imagined this whole scenario in the language of bodies, health, and disease because societies and civilizations were for him essentially organic substances. The body whose health mattered to him and which worried him a great deal was the West, always under threat of disease from within and without. The central threat after the war was the Soviet disease, a parasitical if not cancerous regime. The first step in diagnosing and coming to terms with this threat was to study it as though it were an object under a microscope in order to lay bare its inner nature. Intelligent countermeasures might then contain it—not ignore but isolate it. Deprived of feeding grounds, this inherently expanding entity would either wither and die or become innocuous. The parasite, while maliciously alive and energetic, could be treated throughout as an object, an object of knowledge and of action. To have dealt with it as an equal other would have been unthinkable. Kennan's was a policy of rejection and isolation, of no real diplomacy.

This may be compared with Roosevelt and Truman. For Roosevelt there could be no proper relations with gangsters, whose clearly stated aim was to destroy the world of order by means of massive war. Thus they themselves had to be destroyed by similar means. For Truman there could be no proper relations with totalitarians, whose clearly stated aim was to destroy the world of freedom by means of Cold War. Thus, they, too, had to be destroyed by appropriate measures, the specifics of which were to be worked out. For Kennan there could be no proper relations with fanatical and despotic regimes antithetical to the West. Mostly one could afford to ignore them because their means of carrying out their aims were severely limited; but the Soviet foe had to be contained and neutralized by rebuilding damaged parts of the West and preventing any further advances on Moscow's part in any areas of supreme strategic value. All three outlooks begin, accordingly, by assuming a priori the existence of a mortal threat, the character of which is determined by its inner nature and which in turn generates a struggle to death, as the enemy denies others the right to exist.

Eliminating the threat was for Roosevelt and Truman a matter of acting and imposing one's will entirely upon the enemy, for Kennan (chiefly) to prevail by isolation and containment. It is readily apparent how Roosevelt could take this view, given the events of the 1930s and early 1940s: the phenomenon of fascism offered up no great analytical enigmas as far as foreign affairs were concerned, and the answer to it seemed equally obvious, all-out war to eradicate. For Truman and Kennan, the matter should have been a little more complicated. Soviet behavior, as Lippmann was to indicate, was not simply the product of some DNA structure to be delineated with iron certainty through laboratory procedures. Soviet policy was a product of what others did and what the regime expected others to do and claim. Indeed, the brutal cynicism of Stalin's foreign policy was eminently within the interactive, realist tradition of European geopolitics, and, far from never seeking any "compacts and compromises," as Kennan would have it, the Soviet regime had historically engaged in a whole string of such efforts. Given to seeing its interests and security in terms of autarky, Moscow was in fact always prepared to strike deals.

What Kennan's containment really amounted to, by contrast, was in fact precisely a refusal to strike deals. This was also the gist of Walter Lippmann's realist critique of the X Article. The columnist made two particularly incisive observations. Equating, not unnaturally, Kennan's views with Truman's, he argued first that the administration was now espousing "a disbelief in the possibility of a settlement of the issues raised by this war." Second, he found Kennan's concept of diplomacy deficient. Rather than being based on "intimacy," as Kennan seemed to think, diplomacy was in effect about the political resolution of concerns of mutual interest between states. The idea of containment was for Lippmann not only unnecessarily passive but also implied that the West should refuse to engage in the sort of deal-making that states normally do in times of peace. Whereas the Truman-Kennan position assumed that the U.S.–Soviet relationship was incommensurable because of the very character of the Kremlin regime and consequently that no agreements of a lasting nature were possible, Lippmann maintained that the systemic differences between the two powers were less important than their respective state interests. He went on in that regard to suggest that concrete negotiations on such essential questions as troop withdrawals from central Europe would be eminently doable and certainly verifiable: armed forces were either present or not present. From the U.S. standpoint it seemed most imperative to get the Red Army to return to the Soviet Union, in which case it made sense to figure out what Moscow would demand in return. Lippmann's umbrella term, meanwhile, for the existing impasse was "Cold War."

Ironically, Kennan himself would soon come to embrace this approach internally in the Truman administration, while the latter became increasingly wedded to what Lippmann had singled out as Kennan's view. By the middle of 1948 the Soviet expert had thus begun to see the solution to his paramount "culturalist" concern with the future of the intimate West in realist terms: the only way to prevent the permanent, militarized division of Europe, the anchor of the West, down the middle would be some sort of agreement with the Soviet Union on Germany, an agreement that would presuppose the principle that Moscow had legitimate security interests. Kennan would spend a very long lifetime from then on elaborating an extraordinarily trenchant critique of Cold War thinking, while the administration on its part went in the other direction, applying a simplified concept of Kennan's containment within the context of a grand narrative about totalitarianism and appeasement. One consequence was that, as of 1947–1948, there ceased to be any real need for fresh analyses of the Soviet problem: Moscow became an axiom, its essence written in stone. A crucial, contributing reason for this was that the established account solved the issue of legitimizing the permanent, peacetime presence of the United States throughout the world: it provided the essential premise of a ubiquitous, mortal threat, which could and should not be appeased by any diplomatic concessions. This is not to say there was no real threat. It is to say, however, that there was no urgency about revising the image once it had opened up for the United States to become "leader of the free world" and to initiate a formidably successful effort to restore order in the Western capitalist world. By 1949 Kennan had been marginalized, and by the end of the following year, he had effectively left the State Department. The professional background of Paul Nitze, his replacement as head of the Policy Planning Staff, was on Wall Street.

One of Nitze's early achievements is indeed indicative of another notable development. In the massive, foundational policy document known as NSC 68, written under Nitze's auspices in the spring of 1950, the totalitarian frame was thoroughly "Americanized." It is sometimes contended that NSC 68 was merely a rhetorically overcharged pitch for what was really a call for immense budgetary increases and military buildup. NSC 68 was certainly that, but its ideological content was actually remarkably telling. The document returns powerfully to the Rooseveltian subtheme of a civil war between freedom and slavery and a combat to death between entirely incompatible principles; a return to the image of a world divided, doomed to go completely one way or the other. Freedom is under constant, global threat from a monumental conspiracy, engendered by an enslaving, evil agent of epic proportions. At times, in fact, the language seems taken directly from the abolitionist movement of a century earlier. Soviet communism appears here in a guise not unlike that of the southern slave owners before the Civil War: inherently incapable of tolerating the very existence of freedom, Moscow must destroy its every last trace by any means necessary. Hence, there can be no recognition of one another as equal enemies. The opposition is not symmetrical. While freedom is conceived as the natural, independent condition of humankind, slavery is merely its perversion, a parasitical, degraded other. The former thrives on its own; the latter can exist solely as a subversive attempt to destroy freedom. This is the reason there is a relation at all. By definition, the relation begins with the attack on freedom. By definition, too, the agents of slavery can have no legitimate interests. Their whole modus operandi is in fact to invent a range of devious "designs" to liquidate the free world and its leader. The name of this enslaving attack, then, is the "Cold War." In the following "total" conflict, the free world must learn to use the Soviet techniques against the Kremlin itself, to subvert the subversive agent.

The political vocabulary of NSC 68, a sort of neo-abolitionism, gave a recognizably domestic coloration to the otherwise slightly alien notion of totalitarianism and to the narrative of Munich and World War II. That the struggle overall is irreconcilable, a struggle to death, is reinforced here by the historical evocation of the Civil War. Henry Wallace had moved on to become a Cold War critic, but his adage from the Second World War could stand for NSC 68: "no compromise with Satan." However, writing after the "loss" of China and the detonation of a Soviet atomic device in 1949, the authors of NSC 68 were not interested in maintaining the status quo, what the document in a crucial passage characterizes as the "diplomatic freeze." To settle down along existing lines would not only be to accept the morally and politically indefensible but to encourage continuing encroachments, in some sense to recognize slavery. Although containment is summoned as a legitimating principle, the argument against the "diplomatic freeze" is in fact, not surprisingly, a critique of Kennan's notion as altogether too inactive and conservative. Thus NSC 68 culminates in an exhortation to mobilize the vast, untapped resources of the United States for victorious combat against evil.

The Republican Party, in the same vein, would shortly come to declare containment as somehow un-American since it implied a stalemate as evidenced by the Korean War. Containment was just appeasement on the installment plan, as the slogan went in the campaign of 1952. The spatial metaphor of containment was thus to be replaced by another, more appropriate one: "rollback." The lines of communist power would have to be forced backward, not merely stabilized. Nothing much by way of substance, however, would happen on that front, and the irony is that the actual posture of Democrats and Republicans alike remained remarkably similar to the isolating strategy of the early Kennan. For in the end, by far the most important aspect of the entire Cold War project was not what happened to the communist camp. It was the rebuilding and securing of the West and the maintenance of some kind of order in other parts of the noncommunist world. Roosevelt's policing, in another irony, came to be a matter of ordering the free world, so that the temporal idea of progress following order could be applied to various right-wing dictatorships, eradication of domestic radicalism in the name of anticommunism being the precondition for orderly development and civilization.

If the primary aim was not really "rollback" but leading the "free world," then serious negotiations about issues of mutual concern would be doubly wrong. They would be wrong because any real settlement would remove the axiomatic divisions that permitted the whole project to be set forth in the first place. They would also be wrong because they presupposed concessions and compromises, deeds already declared morally intolerable and strategically disastrous. At the same time, negotiations as such were supposed to be a good thing in the Western idiom, and public opinion, especially overseas, might well find them politically congenial. NSC 68 grappled pensively with the issue. The authors grasped that the only politically correct negotiations, given their frame, would have to concern "a settlement which calls for a change in the Soviet system." This was obviously fatuous, and so negotiations turn into something to be done for tactical purposes in order to make the Soviet regime look bad or, alternatively, a sort of registry for presumed future successes in "the policy of gradual and calculated coercion," the phrase used in NSC 68 to encapsulate the newly invigorated essence of containment.

The problem with the act of negotiating and making concessions had an interesting echo in Roosevelt's wartime scheme. That one would not strike deals with aggressors and gangsters was of course not a problem. The problem was that the framework really did not allow much by way of deals with one's allies either. This was especially the case with the Soviet Union, whose fierce struggles against the Nazis in the East presented prospects of an order there not easily accommodated within the U.S. image of what a liberated, free world would and should look like. The temporary escape from this quandary was Roosevelt's dual set of absolutes, unconditional surrender and freedom. One was minimalistic, an easily defined, immediate goal, the other a vast and almost entirely abstract desire. "Unconditional surrender" allowed for the postponement of the nasty issues that threatened to render the meaning of freedom too concrete. Neither, in any case, provided any clear room for deals short of the U.S. ideal. The intermediate notion, order and policing, might have done so, but it largely faded with Roosevelt himself. The victory may have been absolute, but it turned out not to be total, because it produced a peace that was no peace and certainly no peace of freedom. Thus was reinstated the idea of unconditional surrender as the object of the ensuing war that was no real war.

CONCLUSION

The argument here has delineated a certain U.S. horizon of expectations that permitted the Cold War to appear as a worthy, indeed vitally necessary, project to be undertaken on a massive, global scale. Roosevelt's particular framing of World War II made possible a political reorientation afterward such that Washington was able to interpret Soviet behavior as a totalitarian, fascist-like, lethal attack on the very being of the Western states and to label this attack a Cold War. The derivation, then, began with the revealed inner nature of the Soviet regime itself, which no immediate U.S. act and no negotiation or settlement could change. The Soviet Union and the communist movement were by definition a Cold War. Indeed, the central reason there was not an outright open war on the West was that the latter happened still to be stronger than the Soviet Union. The response to this mortal challenge was first to maintain and preferably increase one's massive preponderance of strength so as to keep Moscow from launching such an open attack and, second, to fight the already existing Cold War to the lethal end, an end that, logically, could only come about when the Soviet regime ceased to be or surrendered unconditionally.

This configuration or outlook was uniquely "American." The Cold War would not have happened had Britain been the overwhelmingly superior Western power. The infamous "percentage deal" between Stalin and Winston Churchill in October 1944 about their respective future influence in eastern Europe, unthinkable in any properly American context, is enough to illustrate the difference. The Soviet view, meanwhile, was conceptually and geopolitically defensive. Launching a

Cold War made no sense whatsoever for Moscow and was never projected before it became a reality. When it did, the Soviet interpretation could only place it within the old antifascist frame and the heroic narrative about the Great Patriotic War. Thus, Moscow saw the Cold War as fascist-like aggression to destroy the progressive achievements of the Soviet Union and the progressive camp. At first sight this seems to be a mirror image of the U.S. position. The crucial difference lies in the logic of the response: defensive coalition politics for relative gains, the strategic object always being prevention of exacerbated forms of aggression, to be achieved by making it politically impossible for the other side not to come to terms. Such a process of recognition would then secure the foundations for future Soviet successes, presumably in the interest of everyone. Negotiations and deals in the traditional sense of Lippmann's diplomacy were at the center of this strategy of recognition. Détente, not surprisingly, would be its apotheosis.

If the manner in which Roosevelt's matrix was transposed in the United States after the war was the pivotal condition of possibility for the Cold War, it was not necessarily the ultimate "cause." A war, even a virtual Cold War, is not supposed to be a good thing, and so gives rise to questions of who is to blame for starting it, the perennial question of "war guilt." As there is no agreement on what the Cold War is or was and no agreement on when it started or ended, there can be no agreement on who began it. The present account has assumed that the question of war guilt is less interesting than the question of emergence. The decisive element in that regard was the shifting view of the United States as to the nature of the Soviet regime, occasioned by the string of events in 1945–1947 that undermined existing ideas of cooperation and served to confirm the new understanding of relentless, totalitarian antagonism. One might think this a justified view or one might think that the actual result was good for the United States and the interests of history, even if the analysis happened to be wrong. The Cold War was in any case a deeply "American" project.

BIBLIOGRAPHY

Adler, Les, and Thomas G. Paterson. "Red Fascism: The Merger of Nazi Germany and Soviet Russia in the American Image of Totalitarianism, 1930s–1950s." *American Historical Review* 75 (April 1970).

Alperovitz, Gar. *The Decision to Use the Atomic Bomb and the Architecture of an American Myth.* New York, 1995.

Backer, John H. *The Decision to Divide Germany: American Foreign Policy in Transition.* Durham, N.C., 1978.

Claudin, Fernando. *The Communist Movement: From Comintern to Cominform.* 2 vols. New York, 1975.

Cold War International History Project. *Bulletin.* Washington, D.C., 1992– .

Cumings, Bruce. *The Origins of the Korean War.* Vol. 1. *Liberation and the Emergence of Separate Regimes, 1945–1947.* Princeton, N.J., 1981.

Eisenberg, Carolyn. *Drawing the Line: The American Decision to Divide Germany, 1944–1949.* Cambridge and New York, 1996.

Etzold, Thomas H., and John Lewis Gaddis, eds. *Containment: Documents on American Policy and Strategy, 1945–1950.* New York, 1978.

Feis, Herbert. *From Trust to Terror: The Onset of the Cold War, 1945–1950.* New York, 1970.

Gaddis, John Lewis. *The United States and the Origins of the Cold War.* New York, 1972.

———. *Strategies of Containment: A Critical Appraisal of Postwar American National Security Policy.* New York, 1982.

———. *We Now Know: Rethinking Cold War History.* Oxford, 1997.

Gardner, Lloyd C. *Architects of Illusion: Men and Ideas in American Foreign Policy, 1941–1996.* 8th ed. New York, 1997.

Fleming, Denna F. *The Cold War and Its Origins, 1917–1960.* 2 vols. Garden City, N.J., 1961.

Halle, Louis. *The Cold War as History.* New ed. New York, 1991.

Hogan, Michael. *The Marshall Plan: America, Britain, and the Reconstruction of Western Europe, 1947–1952.* Cambridge and New York, 1987.

Kennan, George F. "The Sources of Soviet Conduct." *Foreign Affairs* 25 (July 1947).

———. *Memoirs, 1925–1950.* Boston, 1967.

Kimball, Warren. *The Juggler: Franklin Roosevelt as a Wartime Statesman.* Princeton, N.J., 1991.

Kolko, Gabriel. *The Politics of War.* Rev. ed. New York, 1990.

Kolko, Gabriel, and Joyce Kolko. *The Limits of Power: The World and United States Foreign Policy, 1945–1954.* New York, 1972.

Kuniholm, Bruce. *The Origins of the Cold War in the Near East: Great Power Conflict and Diplomacy in Iran, Turkey, and Greece.* Princeton, N.J., 1980.

Leffler, Melvyn. "The American Conception of National Security and the Beginnings of the Cold War, 1945–48." *American Historical Review* 89 (April 1984).

———. *A Preponderance of Power: National Security, the Truman Administration, and the Cold War.* Stanford, Calif., 1992.

Lippmann, Walter. *The Cold War: A Study in U.S. Foreign Policy.* New York, 1947.

Lundestad, Geir. *The American Non-Policy Towards Eastern Europe, 1943–1947.* Tromsø, Norway, and New York, 1978.

McCormick, Thomas J. *America's Half-Century: United States Foreign Policy in the Cold War.* Baltimore, 1989.

Mastny, Vojtech. *The Cold War and Soviet Insecurity: The Stalin Years.* New York, 1996.

Messer, Robert L. *The End of an Alliance: James F. Byrnes, Roosevelt, Truman, and the Origins of the Cold War.* Chapel Hill, N.C., 1982.

Naimark, Norman M. *The Russians in Germany: A History of the Soviet Zone of Occupation, 1945–1949.* Cambridge, Mass., 1995.

Milward, Alan. *The Reconstruction of Western Europe, 1945–1951.* London and Berkeley, Calif., 1984.

Reynolds, David, ed. *The Origins of the Cold War in Europe: International Perspectives.* New Haven, Conn., 1994.

Schaller, Michael. *The American Occupation of Japan: The Origins of the Cold War in Asia.* New York, 1985.

Schlesinger, Arthur M., Jr. "Origins of the Cold War." *Foreign Affairs* 46 (October 1967).

Steel, Ronald. *Walter Lippmann and the American Century.* New York, 1980.

Stephanson, Anders. "Fourteen Notes on the Very Idea of a Cold War." In Geróid O'Tuathail and Simon Dalby, eds. *Rethinking Geopolitics.* New York, 1999.

Trachtenberg, Marc. *A Constructed Peace: The Making of the European Settlement, 1945–1963.* Princeton, N.J., 1999.

Ulam, Adam B. *Expansion and Coexistence: Soviet Foreign Policy, 1917–1973.* New York, 1974.

Vogt, Timothy R. *Denazification in Soviet-Occupied Germany: Brandenburg, 1945–1948.* Cambridge, Mass., 2000.

Yergin, Daniel. *Shattered Peace: The Origins of the Cold War and the National Security State.* Boston, 1977.

Zubok, Vladimir, and Constantine Pleshakov. *Inside the Kremlin's Cold War: From Stalin to Khrushchev.* Cambridge, Mass., 1996.

See also COLD WAR EVOLUTION AND INTERPRETATIONS; COLD WARRIORS; COLD WAR TERMINATION; THE MUNICH ANALOGY; POST–COLD WAR POLICY; PRESIDENTIAL ADVISERS; PRESIDENTIAL POWER.

COLD WARRIORS

Andrew J. Rotter

Architects of the conflict that gripped the world for nearly fifty years, cold warriors were the men, and few women, who gave shape to the ongoing conflict between the United States and the Soviet Union from 1945 to 1989. They built the Cold War's institutions, forged its diplomacy, oversaw its military flare-ups and its diplomatic stand-downs, and supplied its fierce rhetoric and its silent espionage. In the West, the so-called free world, cold warriors were usually well-born and well educated. In revolutionary societies and communist countries, high class standing was no asset for a leader, so cold warriors either came from humble stock or claimed that they did. The most prominent cold warriors were men of power—commanders of great armies, of the masses, of economic might, of words and ideas. Cold warriors were frequently messianic in their convictions, believing they represented the one best political, economic, and social system. They were serious men, disinclined to joke about their work and for the most part innocent even of a sense of irony about it; with the exception perhaps of their hubris, they masked their emotions, though they could never fully erase them. Cold warriors were often pragmatic men, able to calculate their nations' interests and if necessary to negotiate with their adversaries in order to protect those interests. Still, despite their pragmatism cold warriors contained within their bodies the cells of history and ideology that compelled them to the contest, in the belief that they were defending their nations' values or in the hope of spreading their values to others beyond their borders.

Cold warriors lived most obviously in the United States and the Soviet Union, but because the Cold War enveloped the world its warriors were everywhere. They included the presidents of the United States, from Harry S. Truman to George H. W. Bush, and their secretaries of state, among them John Foster Dulles, Dean Rusk, and Henry Kissinger. Many other U.S. government officials were cold warriors: appointees such as George F. Kennan, Paul Nitze, and Jeane Kirkpatrick, and elected representatives including senators William Knowland, Joseph McCarthy, and Hubert H. Humphrey. There were members of the intelligence community (J. Edgar Hoover, Edward G. Lansdale, William Colby), prominent journalists who interpreted the Cold War to the American people (Walter Lippmann, James Reston), and theologians, among them Reinhold Niebuhr and Billy Graham, who saw the Cold War as a moral challenge to Americans. In the Soviet Union a commitment to the Cold War was necessary for the leaders who followed Joseph Stalin after 1953, from Nikita Khrushchev to Konstantin Chernenko. The ideologue Andrei Zhdanov was a cold warrior of the first magnitude. Soviet diplomats carried out their superiors' orders but contributed as well their own mite to the conflict; among them were the longtime foreign minister Vyacheslav Molotov and the ambassador to the United States Andrei Gromyko. Lavrenti Beria, head of Stalin's secret police, maintained a bloodstained vigil against all forms of Cold War heterodoxy.

Outside the United States and the Soviet Union, cold warriors fought their own battles in the shadows cast by their powerful allies. Their Cold Wars were similar to the principal superpower conflict in their ideological and geopolitical purposes, but different to the extent that they were influenced by histories that preceded the Cold War and in some ways transcended it, and also different because local concerns pressed down upon a broad Cold War foundation, reshaping it as wood construction forms mold wet concrete. There were British cold warriors, among them Winston Churchill, prime minister and influential statesman, foreign ministers Ernest Bevin and Anthony Eden, and in the last decade of the Cold War, Prime Minister Margaret Thatcher. In Canada there was Lester Pearson (prime minister, 1963–1968). France had Charles de Gaulle (whose Cold War had an overwhelmingly Gallic flavor), South Africa Hendrik Verwoerd (prime minister 1958–1966, who invoked the Soviet threat in order to defend white supremacy in his country), and the Philippines Ferdinand Marcos (president 1965–1986), who traded his support for U.S. military bases on his islands for U.S. help against his domestic enemies, communist or not. On the other side were Kim Il Sung of North Korea, Vietnam's revolutionary nationalist Ho Chi Minh, Walter Ulbricht of East Germany, and Cuban leader Fidel Castro.

There were thousands of cold warriors; the four profiled here were selected because they represented different sides of the conflict and because, taken together, their influence spanned nearly the length of the Cold War. Joseph Stalin was dictator of the Soviet Union from the late 1920s until his death in 1953. Dean Acheson was U.S. undersecretary of state from 1945 to 1947, secretary of state from 1949 to 1953, and foreign policy adviser without portfolio thereafter. Mao Zedong led the communists to victory in China in 1949 and became the nation's supreme ruler for nearly thirty years. And Ronald Reagan, U.S. president from 1981 to 1989, stoked the flickering fire beneath the Cold War cauldron. All of these men made decisions that had enormous consequences for the world in which they lived and for the world inherited by the next generation of leaders. Strenuous as it was to fight the Cold War, it proved even harder to unmake it.

JOSEPH STALIN

That Stalin came to lead the Soviet Union following Vladimir Ilych Lenin's death in 1924 was a surprise to nearly everyone. Stalin was a man people underestimated. He was short (five feet, four inches tall) and stocky, with a face pitted by smallpox and a left arm bent permanently by a childhood accident. He mumbled or talked so quietly that he was hard to hear; possibly he was embarrassed at his poor grasp of Russian, which he spoke with an accent. On the eve of the October 1917 revolution, one of Stalin's colleagues on the Executive Committee of the Petrograd Soviet wrote that he gave "the impression . . . of a grey blur which flickered obscurely and left no trace. There really is nothing more to be said about him." But some by then could see in his eyes a fixity of purpose that promised a good deal more.

"He's not an intellectual," noted the American journalist John Reed in 1920. "He's not even particularly well informed, but he knows what he wants. He's got will-power, and he's going to be on top of the pile some day."

He was born in 1879, in the Russian state of Georgia. His family name was Dzhugashvili. (Joseph would take the name Stalin, meaning "man of steel," in the early 1900s.) Possibly he was illegitimate. His father, or the man who raised him, was a cobbler, while his mother was a domestic servant. Joseph attended local schools and was a good student, though inclined to challenge the authority of his teachers. His boyhood hero was Koba, a character in a novel called *The Patricide,* who battled against the forces of injustice and rewarded the downtrodden with the spoils of his victories. Joseph identified so fully with this Russian Robin Hood that he later took "Koba" as one of his code names.

Stalin had no philosophy in the usual sense of the word. Unlike Marx or Lenin he was not much good at theorizing. He understood Russian history as a narrative of triumph and tragedy and took from it the lesson that an unguarded Russia would be ripe for exploitation or worse. Russia had saved Europe from the Mongols in the thirteenth century, had stopped Napoleon in the nineteenth, and would destroy Adolf Hitler's Reich in the 1940s. Each of these hard-won triumphs had saved civilization. Yet it seemed to Stalin that Russia's reward for its sacrifice was to be attacked yet again; the nation was surrounded by enemies who wished for its demise. Superimposed on this view of Russia's haunted history was a particular version of revolutionary communism. Stalin believed that the revolution required a long period of incubation at home, that it would not be ready for export to other nations until it had totally transformed Russia. Agriculture must be collectivized. The state must control industry, goading factory workers to new heights of production. Art, literature, and even science ought to reflect the noble purposes of the communist state, valorizing the proletariat and refusing to indulge in bourgeois fripperies. Suspicious of Russia's neighbors, suspicious of ideological deviation, suspicious, really, of almost everyone, Stalin built by the 1930s an industrial power and a state ruled by intimidation and terror.

No one knows how many Soviet citizens died as a result of Stalin's agricultural policy or by his direct order. Judging the rich peasants, or kulaks, inherently selfish and therefore incompatible with the goal of collectivization, Stalin eradicated them as a class. When grain production fell short of expectations in 1932, Stalin demanded more. The result was the starvation of perhaps five million Russians. Between 1936 and 1938 Stalin instituted the Terror, in which millions more of his political opponents real or imagined were deported to Siberia or executed following a show trial. On one December day in 1937 Stalin and Molotov signed 3,167 death warrants, then went to a movie. A cult of Stalin developed throughout the country. Poems and songs celebrated the dictator. One of his speeches was pressed onto seven sides of a gramophone record; the eighth side contained nothing but applause.

Once disclosed, the horrors of the Stalinist gulag convinced many observers that Stalin's foreign policy would proceed, by comparably brutal steps, to threaten the world with a bloodbath in the guise of revolution. There was a germ of logic to this fear. If Stalin did not hesitate to murder Russian citizens, why should he have scruples about killing foreigners? Revolutionary ideology would not respect national boundaries. The metaphors used to describe it by those who dreaded it—a conflagration, a disease, or even, in George Kennan's more measured analysis, "a fluid stream"—suggested that Stalinist communism was relentlessly expansionistic.

The reality was a good deal more complicated. Certainly Stalin was opportunistic, looking for trouble spots or turmoil to exploit. He had not abandoned hope of inspiring revolution in other countries, only shelved it temporarily in favor of consolidating control at home. Yet Stalin's first concern was always the preservation of the Soviet state from invasion or erosion from without. There was much to lose—including, of course, his own power. A shrewd foreign policy must, therefore, state the Soviet Union's claim to survival while nevertheless avoiding antagonizing neighboring countries that were capable of destroying the motherland. This meant, for example, that when Germany was restored to its military power under Hitler during the 1930s, Stalin would seek to offset German strength by finding friends among the bourgeois states that were ideologically anathema to him. When it became clear, after the Munich Pact of 1938, that the British and French had no stomach for opposing Hitler's absorption of other countries, Stalin decided to make his own arrangement with the Germans. The result was the Nazi-Soviet Pact of August 1939, in which the two nations agreed not to fight each other, and (secretly) to divide Poland and the Baltic states between them. Stalin even promised that if Germany seemed in danger of losing a war, he would send a hundred divisions to the West to defend his new ally. It turned out badly for the Soviet Union, which in June was invaded by the Germans.

Stalin was at first shocked into near paralysis. "Lenin founded our state, and we've fucked it up!" he said. He fled Moscow and failed to communicate with his generals, who were desperate for instructions. But he recovered and began issuing orders. Russia would not surrender. There would be bloody battles, and many lives would be lost—indeed, well over twenty million by the war's end. Germany would be beaten, and the Soviet Union would have a peace that would at last guarantee the protection of the nation against all outside forces.

The Soviet victory over Germany was bought with help from the United States, which provided equipment through President Franklin D. Roosevelt's Lend-Lease program. Stalin was grudgingly appreciative of this aid. Still, he believed that the Americans, along with the British, could have done much more, and he suspected that his new allies wanted Russians and Germans to kill each other in droves, leaving Roosevelt and British prime minister Winston Churchill free to dictate the peace. Stalin was especially angry at the allies' failure to open a meaningful second front against Germans in Europe before mid-1944.

It seemed to Stalin that the Russians bore the brunt of the German attack. Over time, however, Stalin found the policy could work to his advantage. Once the Nazis had been defeated at Stalingrad, in February 1943, they fell into retreat, pursued by the Red Army. By the spring of 1944, as the Americans and British were preparing at last to invade Normandy, the Russians had begun arriving at the eastern frontiers of the European nations that had made common cause with the Nazis.

Ultimately, by dint of having the largest army in the region, the Soviets gained predominant influence after the war in Romania, Bulgaria, Hungary, Czechoslovakia, Poland, and the eastern quarter of Germany. Yugoslavia was controlled by communists. To gain these prizes seemed to Stalin nothing more than a reasonable division of the postwar spoils. He did not picture the eastern European satellites as an entering wedge toward world domination but rather as recompense for

Russian suffering at Nazi hands and the logical result of occupation policies established by his allies. And he sought a buffer zone of politically compliant states along the western face of the Soviet Union.

It was not so much ideological conformity as simple cooperation that Stalin sought, in eastern Europe and elsewhere. He hoped that the Americans and British would allow him the buffer zone and a good deal of reconstruction aid as well. Churchill, after all, had in 1944 conceded major Soviet influence in several eastern European countries. Franklin Roosevelt endorsed a spheres of influence arrangement in the postwar world, to include a Soviet sphere roughly east of the Elbe River. Meeting with Stalin at Yalta in February 1945, Churchill and Roosevelt had seemed to accept a face-saving formula on the composition of the emerging Polish government. Stalin felt sure that the others would permit him to do essentially what he wanted there. "The logic of his position was simple," as one of Stalin's biographers has written. "He had won the war in order to have good next-door neighbors." He thought his allies accepted this.

Elsewhere Stalin probed in places where his predecessors had long had interests. He pressured the Turks to revise the Montreux Convention, up for renewal, and grant him joint management of the strategically vital Dardanelles strait. He dragged his feet on the matter of withdrawing Soviet troops from northern Iran in 1946, though he had previously agreed to pull out. And he demanded a share of the occupation authority in Japan, having sent his armies against Japanese forces in China in the last days of the war. When the allies remonstrated or acted firmly against him, however, Stalin backed down. The Dardanelles remained Turkish, Soviet troops left Iran without having guaranteed Moscow's access to Iranian oil, and Stalin pretty much conceded his exclusion from Japanese affairs after 1945. He did not want a confrontation with the United States. He emphatically did not want war.

But between April 1945 and March 1946 Stalin came to believe that the British and Americans sought a confrontation with him. Roosevelt's death in April 1945 deprived Stalin of a rival who had nevertheless shown flexibility in negotiations and apparent sympathy for Soviet predicaments. Roosevelt's successor, Harry S. Truman, seemed less inclined to give Stalin the benefit of the doubt. The American use of atomic bombs against Japan in August was a shock. The Russians had known

and had been receiving information that scientists in the United States were working on the bomb, but until he read reports of what had happened at Hiroshima and Nagasaki Stalin had not appreciated the power of the new weapon. He immediately authorized a major effort to build the bomb; unless the Soviets tested their own weapon, he believed, they remained subject to intimidation by the United States. The Soviet bomb was tested successfully in August 1949. Finally, as the disagreements mounted between Russia and the West—quarrels over the disposition of postwar Germany, reparations or loans or aid due the Soviet Union, and the future of atomic weapons—the United States and Great Britain seemed to conspire against the Russians. The rhetoric on both sides intensified; the Cold War had begun.

To statesmen in the West, Stalin's culpability seemed obvious. He had clamped down ruthlessly in eastern Europe, suppressing freedom throughout the region, most outrageously in Czechoslovakia in early 1948. He stripped Soviet occupation zones of their factories, refused to bargain reasonably over German reunification, and in 1948 blockaded Berlin. He reestablished the Cominform to coordinate the menacing activities of communist parties everywhere. It looked different to Stalin. He wished only for security, prosperity, and noninterference by other nations in Russia's affairs. Just five years after defeating Germany, the Soviet Union was threatened with encirclement once more.

The emergent Cold War was not confined to Europe. In China a long-simmering civil war between the Nationalist forces of Generalissimo Chiang Kai-shek and the communist peasant army of Mao Zedong came to a full boil following Japan's surrender. Stalin did not at first embrace Mao's revolutionary quest and doubted the efficacy of Mao's movement; however, Mao was able to establish the People's Republic of China on 1 October 1949. Stalin hoped to preserve Soviet influence in China, which the 1945 treaty provided, and could not afford to subsidize the People's Republic to the extent that Mao would have liked. Strains developed between the two men: Stalin was suspicious of Mao's plans, while Mao resented what he considered to be his second-class treatment in Moscow. While the two men agreed on a treaty of friendship in mid-February 1950, the differences between the communist leaders remained.

The most strenuous test of the new Sino-Soviet relationship, and the most dangerous flare-up of the Cold War to that point, was the Korean War. The North Korean leader, Kim Il Sung, visited Stalin at least twice, in April 1949 and March 1950, and corresponded with him at other times. Stalin at first splashed cold water on Kim's assertion that he could reunite Korea by military means. Stalin worried, as ever, that the United States would intervene, thus threatening Soviet security. By the early spring of 1950, though, Stalin had come around. Assured by Kim that his forces were far superior to those in the south, that the Americans were unlikely to act, and that there were 200,000 communists in South Korea who would rise up in support of the North Korean invaders, Stalin went along with Kim's plan to attack. Stalin offered increased military aid and some military advisers. At the same time, he urged Kim to ask Mao for help.

The Truman administration's decision to intervene in the Korean War, buttressed by the United Nations Security Council (from which the Soviet representative was conveniently absent), confirmed Stalin's worst fears. It was a measure of his reluctance to venture too deeply into conflicts with the United States, even those in places close to Russia's border, that he would not commit Soviet troops to the fray. He did nudge the Chinese forward, promising aid and support to Chinese brave enough to go to war, but the aid came stintingly, and Soviet air cover appeared over Korean airspace a full month after the first Chinese soldiers crossed the Yalu River into North Korea. Stalin, who had worried about a U.S.–China rapprochement, was not unhappy to see Americans and Chinese killing each other.

The Korean War became a bloody stalemate in 1951, and by then Stalin's health was failing. He continued to rule with an iron hand, arresting those of whom he contrived any reason to be suspicious, reducing more and more the size of the trusted circle around him. But his body had weakened, and his thinking was no longer clear. He had a brain hemorrhage on the night of 28 February–1 March 1953, though he managed to remain alive for another four days. Just as he died, according to his daughter, "he suddenly lifted his left hand as though he were pointing to something up above and bringing down a curse on us all. The gesture was incomprehensible and full of menace." It was a fitting end for a man who had brought so much suffering to Russian citizens, while nevertheless making the Soviet Union a nation to be respected, or feared, throughout the world.

DEAN ACHESON

When Dean Acheson became U.S. secretary of state in early 1949 he hung in his office two portraits: one of John Quincy Adams, the other of Henry Stimson. These were significant choices. Adams, perhaps the greatest secretary of state in U.S. history, had conceived the first American empire but had warned his overzealous compatriots against going "abroad in search of monsters to destroy." Stimson, who had served as secretary of state for Herbert Hoover and became secretary of war (for the second time) under Franklin Roosevelt in 1940, had preserved Adams's imperial vision. Both men were among the best and brightest of their generations: Adams the scion of the famous political family, Stimson a partner in Elihu Root's law firm. And both men were dedicated to the service of their country, had a keen sense of right and wrong, and believed that gentlemen should behave honorably—as Stimson said, they did not read one another's mail. Dean Acheson believed these things too.

Acheson was born and raised in Connecticut. His father, Edward, was an Episcopal rector; his mother, Eleanor (Gooderham), was a grande dame with a sense of humor. Both were British subjects. Eleanor spoke with a British accent, and the family celebrated the queen's birthday. Thus was Acheson's Anglophilia instilled at an early age. He went to Groton and Yale, finishing both (Groton barely) without academic distinction. His Yale classmate Archibald MacLeish recalled that Acheson was "socially snobby with qualities of arrogance and superciliousness." Seriousness arrived in his second year at Harvard Law School, when he took a class with Felix Frankfurter. The law captured him, especially for its possibilities as training for government service. Frankfurter arranged a clerkship with Supreme Court Justice Louis Brandeis.

Acheson's career in government began in 1933, when he was named Roosevelt's treasury undersecretary. The appointment was short-lived. Acheson opposed FDR's plan to buy gold to shore up prices, and he was asked to resign that fall. But he had made himself known to Roosevelt's men, and early in 1941 Secretary of State Cordell Hull brought Acheson to the State Department as assistant secretary for economic affairs. Acheson quickly made his presence felt. He helped negotiate the lend-lease agreement with the British, into which, and despite his Anglophilia, he inserted a clause demanding an end to preferential economic arrangements within the British empire. Acheson also insisted on tightening an embargo on oil shipments to Japan. And after the United States had entered the war, he became one of the American architects of the International Monetary Fund and the World Bank, both of which would do much to stabilize the economy of the capitalist nations following the war. When, in late 1944, Hull was replaced by Edward Stettinius, Acheson became assistant secretary of state for congressional relations and international conferences.

Acheson fortuitously had had a lengthy meeting with Truman two days before Roosevelt's death in April 1945. Truman made "a very good impression. He is straightforward, decisive, simple, entirely honest." He would "learn fast and inspire confidence." But Acheson was not at first moved to stay on in the government, and after seeing through to completion the drafting of the United Nations Charter, in midsummer he submitted to the president a letter of resignation. Truman and his new secretary of state, James Byrnes, refused to accept it. They wanted Acheson to stay in the administration and to promote him to undersecretary of state, second in command in the department. Acheson hesitated but finally agreed to return.

He was thrust immediately into the maelstrom. Byrnes was a clever politician but a poor administrator, and the volume of information flowing into the department, as well as the demands placed on its employees by the developing Cold War, threatened to overwhelm all of them. Acheson became the department's leading organizer and troubleshooter. Truman assigned him to the crucial task of finding a way to control atomic energy without sacrificing American security. His report, written with David Lilienthal and submitted in March 1946, was a sincere (if doomed) effort to accommodate Soviet concerns about the American nuclear monopoly by establishing an international agency to regulate the production of atomic energy. Yet Acheson found himself, along with his president, moving toward a tougher stance against the Soviet Union. If Stalin thought by early 1946 that his capitalist enemies were encircling him despite the reasonableness of his position, the view from Washington was different. U.S. policymakers came to believe that the Soviets would push and probe and stir up trouble anywhere they were not met with resistance, including potential military action. While the hallmark of American resolve

was George Kennan's 1947 essay "The Sources of Soviet Conduct," in which he called for the employment of "counterforce" against the Soviets "at a series of constantly shifting geographical and political points," the Truman administration had in fact been pursuing an ad hoc version of this containment strategy since early 1946. Acheson was its lead author. It was he who wrote Stalin a stern note, delivered by Kennan, demanding the withdrawal of Russian troops from northern Iran. And it was Acheson who wrote the Truman administration's sharp response to the Soviet demand, in August 1946, that Turkey agree to a joint Russian-Turkish defense of the Dardanelles. Acheson's note, along with arrival in the area of a U.S. naval task force, caused the Soviets to back down.

Acheson also played a vital role in shaping the political and economic institutions of Truman's Cold War. In early 1947, with Byrnes out and George Marshall in as the secretary of state, the anticommunist governments of Turkey and Greece claimed to be under severe Soviet pressure and could not guarantee their own survival. Convinced that the United States must help the Turkish and Greek governments, the administration nevertheless faced the difficult task of persuading a fiscally careful Congress to provide the aid needed to shore up these governments. On 27 February, Truman called a meeting between administration officials and a handful of leading senators and members of congress in hopes of winning over the legislators. Acheson described this encounter as "Armageddon." Marshall spoke first, emphasizing the need for the United States to act because it was the right thing to do and because no one else would help. The legislators seemed unmoved. Was it America's fight? Was the bill likely to be enormous? Acheson asked to speak. Immediately he changed the terms of the debate. The crisis in southeastern Europe, he said, was no local dustup but one that involved the two Cold War powers. The Soviets were pressuring Turkey and Greece as they had pressured Iran. At stake was a vast portion of the free world, for if Greece went communist, "like apples in a barrel infected by one rotten one, the corruption of Greece would infect Iran and all to the east. It would also carry infection to Africa through Asia Minor and Egypt, and Europe through Italy and France," which faced communist threats of their own. Only the United States stood in the way of a communist onslaught that would, if successful, snuff out freedom and destroy all hope of economic recovery in parts of three continents. The congressional leaders were impressed, and the pronouncement of the Truman Doctrine followed on 12 March, promising that the United States would fight communism everywhere.

The world's biggest problems remained economic, and the chief area of concern for Acheson, as always, was neither Iran nor Greece but western Europe. Policymakers in Washington believed that communism fed on economic distress; European nations were vulnerable to radicals promising the redistribution of wealth as a panacea for poverty. Economic aid from the United States—and in far greater magnitude than that proffered to Turkey and Greece—was essential to Europe's economic recovery, its revival as a market for U.S. exports, and its people's continued faith in democracy. Acheson said as much in a speech he gave in Cleveland, Mississippi, in early May 1947. His call for massive economic aid to Europe found its manifestation in the Marshall Plan, announced by the secretary of state at Harvard the following month. If the Truman Doctrine had made the strategic case for containment, the Marshall Plan was designed to give economic spine to American's closest friends and trading partners in western Europe. Once more, Acheson had played a crucial role in shaping the new policy.

Acheson had previously decided to leave the administration, and when he tendered his resignation effective 1 July 1947, Truman this time reluctantly let him go. He was, however, receptive when Truman, surprisingly victorious in the 1948 election, invited him to return to public life, this time as secretary of state.

The problems to which Acheson returned in January 1949 were even knottier than they had been when he had departed eighteen months earlier. Europeans and Soviets no longer doubted American resolve. But the Nationalist government of China was in the final stages of collapse; as Acheson remarked ruefully, he arrived back in service just in time to have it fall on him. There was not yet a peace treaty with Japan, and France's effort to return to power in its colony of Indochina had met with firm resistance from Vietnamese nationalists associated with communism. The Soviet Union would explode its first atomic bomb later that year. Above all, at least as far as Acheson was concerned, Europe remained dangerously unstable. The Italian and French governments turned over with distressing frequency, threatening Europe's stability and ultimately its solvency. Great Britain still depended on U.S. aid,

and a slight U.S. recession in the spring of 1949 undermined the sterling pound and forced a new round of austerity on London. Germany remained divided, with Berlin under siege in the East and with the West, its capital at Bonn, a seeming outpost of Western interests thrust provocatively into the Soviet bloc, economically infirm and utterly defenseless. Here especially, thought Acheson, something had to be done.

Acheson addressed the problems systematically, blending a staunch anticommunism, a fervent faith in liberal capitalism, and a healthy measure of pragmatism. There was not much to be done about China: Chiang Kai-shek was plainly a loser and it would be necessary to "let the dust settle" following the communists' victory. Japan would have a peace treaty in 1952. Vexed by French behavior in Indochina but unwilling to weaken France further or cede more territory to what he construed as world communism, Acheson supplied some economic and military aid to the French-backed (read "puppet") government of Bao Dai in Vietnam. What Europe and especially West Germany needed was an infusion of confidence that the United States would come to the rescue in the unlikely event that the Soviet Union attacked. Working with the Europeans, Acheson helped fashion, in the spring of 1949, the North Atlantic Treaty, which created a group of like-minded nations committed to the proposition, as article 5 of the treaty put it, that "an armed attack against one . . . shall be considered an attack against them all." For Acheson the treaty was valuable as a morale boost for U.S. allies, as well as a means to permit, someday, the military restoration of (West) Germany under multilateral aegis.

Acheson had not spent much time thinking about Korea. His State Department predecessors, and the military, had already put into motion the withdrawal of U.S. forces from South Korea. In a speech in January 1950 Acheson described a U.S. "defense perimeter" in East Asia that incorporated various islands, among them the Philippines and Okinawa. It was possible to take from Acheson's words the implication that mainland Asian nations, including South Korea, fell outside the U.S. picket, though this was a strained interpretation; Acheson did say that the United States had "direct responsibility" for Korea. Certainly Acheson was naive to assume, as he told the Foreign Relations Committee, that South Korea "could take care of any trouble started by" the North. But no cold warrior of Acheson's type would have

KONRAD ADENAUER

The United States and Soviet Union were undisputed superpowers after 1945, but the bipolarity of the postwar system did not make all other nations onlookers in the Cold War. Konrad Adenauer, formerly mayor of Cologne, became chancellor of West Germany in 1949. He wished to restore the strength, pride, and importance of Germany (even if only the western part of it) by emphasizing the culture and commerce of the Rhine, and especially by establishing a closer relationship with France, which he thought a far healthier role model for Germany than were the nations of central or eastern Europe. He was instrumental in creating the European Coal and Steel Community, the joint French-German authority for the mining of coal and the production of steel. Adenauer also exploited the Korean War to good effect for Germany. He put it about that West Germans were worried about a Soviet attack on their territory or at least that East German police might now probe the border between the Germanys. Given these worrisome possibilities it would be best, Adenauer indicated, for the Allies to end their occupation of Germany and to permit the arming of some West German troops. In this Adenauer ultimately got his way.

Adenauer, who died in 1967 at the age of ninety-one, was a cold warrior as surely as Joseph Stalin and Dean Acheson were. Adenauer accepted the premises of the conflict and believed in its necessity, he was ideologically sympathetic to the West and staunchly opposed to communism, and he never shrank from the prospect of military action to deter, defeat, or at least delay a Soviet attack on western Europe—one that would begin, inevitably, in West Germany. At the same time, Adenauer looked back to a time before the Cold War began, grasping the older and deeper forces that had shaped German political culture and European politics since the early nineteenth century. Because of this, Adenauer's principal goals preceded and transcended the Cold War: he sought the creation of a stable and economically viable Germany (or part of Germany), the end of Germany's pariah status, the attachment of Germany to the largely democratic and capitalist West, and, following on all of these, the return of Germany to its prewar position as a regional power. In his efforts to achieve these goals Adenauer found the Cold War useful. He reminded the British, the French, and above all the Americans that a strong and friendly West Germany was vital to their security. Soviet behavior in eastern Europe and Korea seemed to confirm his fears. At the end of his life he could take satisfaction in what he had done for the Cold War, and what the Cold War had done for him.

invited an attack on an ally, even one as troublesome as Syngman Rhee's South Korea. The proof of Acheson's commitment came in the last days of June, once Kim Il Sung had launched his offensive. Truman, closely advised by Acheson and the military, committed U.S. forces to the conflict, seeking UN support for this step afterward.

The Korean War would ultimately serve the ends of the containment strategy. The North Koreans, who were presumed by Acheson to be proxy soldiers for Moscow, were stopped. Still, Acheson's reputation suffered as a result of the war. Conservatives attacked him because he had not seen it coming. He would have, they argued, had he understood the implications of his do-nothing policy on China; his abandonment of Chiang had encouraged communists throughout Asia to think they could launch attacks with impunity. Republicans led by Senator Joseph McCarthy accused

Acheson of appeasement or worse. He was part of a "crimson crowd," said McCarthy. Senator Hugh Butler exclaimed: "I look at that fellow. I watch his smart-aleck manner and his British clothes, and that New Dealism in everything he says and does, and I want to shout, 'Get out, Get out. You stand for everything that has been wrong with the United States for years!'"

Truman and Acheson could not achieve a truce in Korea. An armistice was signed only in July 1953, six months after Dwight Eisenhower and John Foster Dulles had succeeded them as the nation's chief cold warriors. Out of harness Acheson drifted. He wanted badly to have influence again on U.S. diplomacy. This was not possible in the Eisenhower administration: Acheson was tainted by his association with the humiliations of the United States in East Asia. In any case he disparaged the administration's reliance on nuclear weapons, a strategy dubbed "massive retaliation," and thought Dulles sanctimonious. Nor would Democrats embrace him. Adlai Stevenson, the Democrats' presidential nominee in 1952 and 1956, thought Acheson irascible and controversial, and kept his distance. In Germany in 1957 Ambassador David Bruce, who was Acheson's friend, found the former secretary "devastating, clever, bitter and not constructive. . . . Dean is overfull of bile and it is sad."

John F. Kennedy, the Democrat who won the presidency in 1960, did consult with Acheson. Kennedy took Acheson's advice on cabinet appointments (Secretary of State Dean Rusk was Acheson's suggestion, though Acheson later regretted having made it) and the need to build NATO forces in Europe. Elsewhere Kennedy resisted Acheson's increasingly reflexive militancy. During the Cuban Missile Crisis, Acheson, a member of Kennedy's high-level ExCom, urged the president to bomb Soviet missile sites and was disgusted when JFK decided to interdict Russian ships instead, a tactic Acheson thought timid. As the war in Vietnam expanded, particularly under Kennedy's successor, Lyndon Johnson, Acheson found himself more and more in demand as an adviser. Johnson treated Acheson with deference. And Acheson's early position on Vietnam—that the United States had no choice but to fight until South Vietnam was preserved against a communist takeover—matched Johnson's.

Averell Harriman said in 1970: "Some people's minds freeze. Acheson's hasn't changed since 1952." That was unfair. While Acheson never lost his suspicion of the Soviet Union, and thus remained convinced of the necessity of containment, and while his contempt for his intellectual inferiors, especially those in Congress, remained undiminished, he came to see the Vietnam War as a waste of American power. Harriman himself, along with Undersecretary of State George Ball, made Acheson see by early 1968 that Vietnam was a peripheral Cold War theater. At a meeting of Johnson's Vietnam "wise men" on 25 March 1968, Acheson spoke bluntly and eloquently of the need for the administration to disengage from the conflict. Johnson, shaken, announced less than a week later that he would seek to negotiate with Hanoi. He added, almost as an afterthought, that he would not seek reelection in 1968 but would instead devote all his energy to finding a way out of the morass in Southeast Asia.

Acheson had come full circle. He had started his public career as a man of principle, demanding to see evidence that one policy choice was better than another, just as Felix Frankfurter and Louis Brandeis had taught him. His Cold War—like Stalin's, ironically—sprang from ideology tempered by pragmatism. There was assertiveness but no adventurism in the man who helped shape the United Nations, the Bretton Woods economic system, the Truman Doctrine, the Marshall Plan, and NATO. But the harsh criticism of conservatives inclined Acheson toward greater militancy and left him unable to resist the temptations of victory in Korea. Thereafter he grew increasingly sharp with those with whom he disagreed. That never changed. But the Vietnam War restored Acheson to his former view that the United States could not solve every world problem, especially not by military means. When Acheson died on 12 October 1971 he left a legacy worthy, in ambition and execution, of the two secretaries of state he admired most.

MAO ZEDONG

The Chinese Communist leader Mao Zedong and Dean Acheson were exact contemporaries, born in 1893. But while Acheson enjoyed a comfortable boyhood and moved rather casually through Groton and Yale, Mao left school at thirteen to help with the family farm, married at age fourteen (and was widowed at seventeen), and in 1911 joined the Republican army in its quest to unite and strengthen China. When he was twenty years old Mao, who came from the rural province of Hunan, returned to school and came under the influence of a teacher named Yang, who inspired in him a passion for reform, a strong ethical sense, and an enthusiasm for exercise, generally taken in the nude. When Yang got a job at Beijing University, Mao went north with him. It was the young farmer's first time out of Hunan.

He took a job as a clerk at the university library and came to know a corps of intellectuals who published an influential magazine called *New Youth,* which became the literary centerpiece of an inchoate but determined reformist movement that emerged following the formal end of the Qing dynasty and the establishment of a republic in 1912. Sun Yat-sen, a Japanese-educated radical from Canton, was the movement's leading political light, but his faith in republicanism was not shared by some young Chinese who sought the end of class oppression. Li Dazhao proclaimed an interest in Marxism and endorsed the Bolshevik revolution. Hu Shih, who had a degree from Cornell, was a literary critic who wrote on women's liberation. Mao was not in their intellectual circle, but the yeastiness of the Beijing scene plainly affected him.

Mao returned to Hunan and the city of Changsha in the early spring of 1919. He thus missed the great urban demonstrations of 4 May, out of which would flow reformist currents that would dominate China for the next thirty years. But Mao contributed a small tributary of his own. He taught history at local schools. And he edited a journal called the *Xiang River Review,* for which he wrote nearly all the articles. His writing heralded the forthcoming "liberation of mankind," which would arrive when people lost their fear of those who ruled them and the superstitions that held them in thrall. When the local warlord stopped publication of the *Review,* Mao shifted to another journal; when it, too, was suppressed, he wrote for Changsha's biggest newspaper.

On 23 July 1921 thirteen Chinese and two members of the Soviet-sponsored Comintern (one Dutch, one Russian), met in Shanghai for the First Congress of the Chinese Communist Party. Mao Zedong was among them. After days of discussion the Congress decided that it should devote its efforts to organizing the working class, putting off plans to mobilize the peasants and the army. The capitalists would be overthrown and "social ownership" of land and machinery would ensue. Buoyed by these resolutions, and presumably in agreement with them, Mao returned to Hunan to begin building a mass movement.

He organized workers and orchestrated strikes. Mao did not attend the Second Party Congress meeting in July 1922, but he soon after learned that the party, nudged by the Comintern agents, had decided to enter into coalition with the Nationalist, or Kuomintang, Party, then headed by Sun Yat-sen. Communists were instructed to form "a bloc within" the party. In this way, they would work alongside the bourgeois elements in China to overthrow the feudal oppressors, all the while securing their bonds to the working class and awaiting the revolutionary situation that would someday emerge in the country. Mao dutifully joined the Kuomintang. Certainly the Communist decision to create a United Front with the Kuomintang seemed reasonable at the time and was consistent with Marxist doctrine. The Kuomintang under Sun was a militant organization, sympathetic to workers and willing to help them strike for their rights. Nor were there many Communist Party members in

China, and the party was broke. The Communists could decide their ultimate course as events unfolded.

Sun Yat-sen died in 1925, and leadership of the Kuomintang, and thus the United Front, was grasped by Chiang Kai-shek, a general who was commandant of the United Front's military academy. In the spring of 1926 Chiang led his forces north out of Canton, determined to destroy the power of local warlords and unite the nation under United Front rule. Communists marched alongside Kuomintang troops, but even more important were the Chinese Communist Party (CCP) organizers, among them Mao, who were assigned to prepare the way for Chiang's soldiers. The men and women of the CCP served as agitators, turning peasants and workers against their local regimes in order to soften them up for the expedition forces. Alarmed at the success of CCP organizers in mobilizing workers, Chiang decided to purge the United Front of its Communists, thus purifying the Kuomintang ideologically and eliminating any awkwardness about power sharing in the future. Chiang's purge was bloody everywhere, but particularly so in Shanghai, where Kuomintang troops killed thousands of their recent allies in April 1927. As the ideological cleansing spread westward, Mao found himself the de facto leader of a demoralized peasant army whose ranks dwindled daily. Increasingly isolated, he moved his remaining supporters to a mountainous area on the border between Hunan and Jiangxi provinces.

His force, as he noted at the time, consisted of "ten thousand messy people." The description was not altogether disparaging. In 1927 Mao had written a report on the peasants in two Hunan counties. Contrary to the Comintern view that peasants were benighted and thus unlikely revolutionary tinder, Mao discovered that the country people were doing a remarkable job of radicalizing and organizing themselves. The Communist Party was at a crossroads: it could continue to deny the revolutionary potential of the rural masses, or it could break with Moscow-inspired orthodoxy, take its place at the revolutionary vanguard, and guide the peasants to victory. For Mao the second road seemed best; however, this decision put Mao at odds with the Comintern and Stalin.

Under pressure from Kuomintang forces, in 1930 Mao and his peasants moved to a new border base and created a government in what they called the Jiangxi Soviet. Mao's grasp of power now slipped. He fell seriously ill several times. In 1932 the national CCP leadership removed to Jiangxi, and the bosses pushed Mao to the side. It was they who decided that the Soviet had become indefensible, and that the Communists would have to leave, though exactly where they would end up was unsettled. Thus began the Long March, an event that would assume legendary status among the Communists, especially as the passage of time dimmed memories of its horrors. Some eighty-six thousand people left Jiangxi in the fall of 1934, Mao among them, though without a leading role. Harried by Kuomintang troops, exploited by the locals, frozen, hungry, and sick, the Communists lost marchers at an alarming rate. As the former Soviet leaders were blamed for the debacle, Mao's star rose. By the time the remnants of the column—only eight thousand people—reached far off Shaanxi province a full year after its departure from the Soviet, Mao was back in charge.

The Communists made their new headquarters in the town of Yan'an. Living in caves carved into the sere hillsides, they worked to create their version of a just society, to include some land redistribution and respect for the local peasantry. Mao was the acknowledged leader in these efforts. He insisted that intellectuals learn from rather than teach the masses. But he abandoned sociology in favor of political theory that he represented as unassailable.

In July 1937 the Japanese forced a clash with Chinese troops at the Marco Polo Bridge near Beijing, then used the incident as a pretext to launch a full-scale assault against China. The Japanese attacked the major eastern cities, took Shanghai, then drove Chiang's Nationalist Kuomintang out of its capital at Nanjing, committing appalling atrocities as they did so. The spreading war forced Chiang to reinstitute the United Front with the CCP. Mao welcomed this step, though he understood that it was born purely of expediency; once the Japanese were defeated, he knew, war between the parties would resume.

Nationalist and Communist troops frequently fought hard against the Japanese, but they cooperated minimally and kept a wary eye on each other. When the war ended in August 1945 Japanese troops remained on Chinese soil. The Americans, who had sent representatives to Yan'an during the war and had encouraged the maintenance of the United Front, were nevertheless determined to help Chiang regain political and military superiority. They gave weapons to the Kuomintang, ferried its troops north to accept the Japanese surrender and thus their weapons as well, and kept Japanese soldiers armed in order to prevent Communist advances. The Russians, for their part, ushered Communist troops into Manchuria in the wake of their own departure. Thus did the Cold War come implicitly to China.

Hoping to prevent the resumption of civil war, President Truman sent George Marshall to China in late 1945. Marshall wanted a coalition between the Communists and the Nationalists, a desire that was as sincere as it was unrealistic. Mao, whose postwar position seemed weaker than Chiang's, proved cooperative, agreeing to remove Communist fighters from southern China and accepting in principle Marshall's proposal for a unified Chinese army. Chiang balked at nearly every American suggestion, preferring to pursue his war against the Communists. When a discouraged Marshall left China in January 1947 he labeled Chiang "the leading obstacle to peace and reform" on the scene. Yet the Americans would not abandon Chiang. He was, the Truman administration judged, the only hope for a united, noncommunist China.

Mao may have hoped for a more genuinely balanced U.S. policy but he could not have been shocked when the Americans sided with Chiang. Never, despite his pretensions, a sophisticated political theorist, Mao soon proved his abilities as a battlefield strategist. He maintained high morale and fought relentlessly and without quarter. Within each new area seized from the Kuomintang, Mao instituted land reform, with the understanding that the beneficiaries in their gratitude would become eager recruits for the Communist army. Beginning in the fall of 1947 CCP forces won battle after battle against the Kuomintang. On 1 October 1949 Mao declared in Beijing the founding of the People's Republic of China. Chiang Kai-shek fled to Taiwan, taking with him the remnants of the Kuomintang government and vowing to reconquer the mainland.

China desperately needed help. There had been a flicker of hope of establishing a diplomatic relationship with the United States. Even after the failure of Marshall's mission, Mao had signaled that he would welcome American assistance, and Mao's compatriot Zhou Enlai, who would become premier of the People's Republic, had seemed even more willing to make overtures to Washington. But in June 1949 Mao had given a speech in which he declared the need for China to "lean to one side" in the Cold War, specifically toward the Soviet Union. Mao's pronouncement did not ensure that the Soviets would embrace the Chinese Communists. Stalin had all along treated the

Chinese revolution as an odd and ominous strain of the species, and he remained ambivalent about its prospects even after the CCP had won. Mao came to resent the widely held perception that he was Stalin's junior partner in revolution, and he was not reassured by the treatment he received when he arrived in Moscow in December, seeking a new relationship with the Kremlin and a good deal of economic aid. He got far less than he had hoped for with the Sino-Soviet Treaty of Friendship signed in February 1950.

Mao's most important goal was to consolidate the revolution at home, which required the establishment of Communist political legitimacy and economic policies that would eradicate poverty. He was also intent on liberating Taiwan from Chiang; without this step, the revolution would remain unfinished. Stalin promised no help, but when the Americans indicated their disinterest in defending the island, Mao began to concentrate his forces along China's southwest coast in preparation for an attack across the Formosa Strait. But Kim Il Sung moved faster. Having received Stalin's permission to go to war, Kim came to Beijing in May 1950, seeking Mao's blessing as well.

Mao was unenthusiastic about Kim's plans and asked him to reconsider. Kim refused. In the end Mao offered Kim a green light but promised nothing in the way of help, and Kim did not then pursue the matter, figuring he was likely to win quickly or that the Soviets would give him any assistance he needed. Mao was also surprised when the Americans intervened to halt the North Korean attack and placed their fleet in the Formosa Strait. The United States, Mao decided, was determined to destroy the People's Republic, and had taken its first step toward doing so in Korea. In response Mao began redeploying troops to northeast China near the Korean border. In September, following Douglas MacArthur's successful landing at Inchon and the subsequent rout of the North Korean army, Mao wrote to a Manchurian comrade: "Apparently, it won't do for us not to intervene in the war. You must accelerate preparations."

On 16 October Chinese units crossed the Yalu River in force. Mao professed confidence in their ultimate victory. Once the Chinese had bloodied U.S. forces in battle the American people would demand an end to the conflict. Privately Mao looked for additional help from the Soviet Union. Stalin was not at first forthcoming; he evidently wanted to test Chinese determination, and he remained wary of antagonizing the Americans. But as the Chinese routed UN forces and gave

every indication that they intended to stay the course, Stalin relented, putting Soviet warplanes into action over Korea in mid-November.

Military stalemate came in Korea by the spring of 1951. The negotiations toward ending the war then dragged on for two frustrating years. During this time Mao used the war to rally people to the CCP. He mounted campaigns aimed at rooting out "counterrevolutionaries," crypto-capitalists, and Kuomintang sympathizers. His own power grew. By 1953 he was not only chairman of the Communist Party but also chairman of the People's Republic of China itself and in charge of its armed forces. Stalin's death in March left Mao unrivaled as a source of revolutionary wisdom and experience. He became the leading symbol of the communist Cold War, dispensing advice to would-be revolutionaries throughout the world, rattling sabers at the capitalist powers and their "running dog" allies, and threatening, as always, to absorb Taiwan.

The relationship between the People's Republic of China and the Soviet Union, tense during the best of times, deteriorated rapidly following Stalin's death. Nikita Khrushchev, who ultimately succeeded Stalin and who exposed some of Stalin's crimes to the world, found Mao cruel and megalomaniacal. At a time when Khrushchev was seeking to coexist with the United States, Mao seemed always to be courting war. In Moscow in 1957 Mao, according to Khrushchev, told Communist Party delegates that they should not fear "atomic bombs and missiles." If the imperialists started a war China might "lose more than three hundred million people. So what? War is war. The years will pass, and we'll get to work producing more babies than ever before." The Russians present were appalled. The following year Mao confronted the United States (for a second time) over the status of Quemoy and Matsu, two Nationalist-held islands in the Formosa Strait. Having precipitated a crisis Mao then backed down, which suggested to Khrushchev that the Chinese leader was better at creating confrontations than he was at resolving them. (Mao would say the same thing about Khrushchev following the Cuban missile crisis in 1962.)

By then the breach between the People's Republic of China and the Soviet Union was total. The Russians found intolerable Chinese abuse of Soviet advisers sent to help China develop its oil and build an atomic bomb, and in 1960 the Soviets removed their people. Mao, meanwhile, was incredulous that the Soviets would sell advanced MIG jets to India in 1962, given the friction that existed on the border between China and India. For his sixty-ninth birthday that year, Mao wrote a poem that contained the defiant lines "Only the hero dares pursue the tiger,/ Still less does any brave fellow fear the bear." It may be presumed that Mao himself was the "hero," even more contemptuous of the Russian bear than of the paper tiger of imperialism.

As ever Mao's Cold War abroad directly affected his domestic policies. In 1958 Mao inaugurated a program of economic acceleration called the Great Leap Forward, in which all farm cooperatives would be joined into twenty thousand enormous communes and in which the nation's steel production would be increased through the efforts of workers who would erect blast furnaces in their backyards. Mao also announced a campaign to "let a hundred flowers bloom, and a hundred schools of thoughts contend." This seemed encouragement to Chinese to write or say anything, even if it was critical of their government. Both policies proved catastrophic. The Great Leap Forward resulted in a famine that killed twenty million in 1960–1961. Intellectuals and journalists who took seriously Mao's invitation to let flowers bloom quickly found themselves branded as "poisonous weeds" by an orchestrated "anti-rightist" campaign. Mao grew increasingly dictatorial and unpredictable.

He also seemed to withdraw from the battlements of the Cold War. He continued to support revolution around the world, and he was helpful in particular to the North Vietnamese in their war with the United States after 1965. China, not the contemptibly revisionist Soviet Union, would summon what Mao called "the mighty revolutionary storm" in the Third World. But Mao had never been greatly interested in affairs beyond China's borders, or he was circumspect about China's ability to control them. He did not leave China for the last twenty years of his life. It is too much to say that he mellowed, but he nevertheless came to understand that the world was changing. Seeking to offset the emerging détente between the United States and the Soviet Union, Mao invited President Richard Nixon to China. The two men met on 17 February 1972, shaking hands in front of a thicket of cameras in Mao's study. Mao apologized for his slurred speech and waved away Nixon's compliments. The policy implications of the visit were left to men other than Mao to sort out. Still, Mao enabled the meeting to take place, and he, along with Nixon, could take credit for initiating the first improvement in Sino-American relations since the establishment of the People's Republic of China.

Like other cold warriors, Mao Zedong, who died on 9 September 1976, left a mixed legacy. He was one of those responsible for introducing ideology into the realm of foreign policy, for defining opponents as enemies, for menacing others with his rhetoric, for maintaining large military forces and authorizing construction of an atomic bomb. Yet like the others, in the end Mao granted pragmatism primacy over ideology in foreign affairs. That he regarded the Americans as imperialists would not stand in the way of cultivating them if that proved necessary to preserve China's security and well-being in an increasingly complicated world.

RONALD REAGAN

By the time Mao Zedong died in the year of the U.S. bicentennial, it was clear that the Cold War had changed significantly. The Soviet Union, under Khrushchev and his successors, had thrown aside the cult of Joseph Stalin and had proved willing to consider limiting its nuclear arsenal if the United States would reciprocate.

The man who won the American presidency in 1980 and again in 1984 was instinctively suspicious of this effort for conciliation. Ronald Reagan was born (6 February 1911) and raised in small towns in Illinois. His memoir begins: "If I'd gotten the job I wanted at Montgomery Ward, I suppose I would never have left Illinois." Later in life Reagan recalled not small-town parochialism and racism, nor his father's alcoholic rages, but a life of summer days, lifeguarding at Lowell Park in Dixon, having fun at Eureka College, and after college taking a job in Des Moines in which he broadcast Chicago Cubs baseball games as if he were watching them, while in fact reconstructing them from a running telegraphic account sent from the field. He went to Hollywood in 1937 with a six-month contract from Warner Brothers studio. He became a star in B movies and took leadership of the Screen Actors Guild. He did not leave the United States during World War II, though he later claimed to have done so, even asserting that he had filmed Nazi concentration camps for the army. In fact, Reagan made war movies at home.

By the early 1950s Reagan was convinced that communists had infiltrated Hollywood and the Actors Guild, and he so told the FBI. His career in film was waning. But in 1954 the General Electric Company asked Reagan to host a weekly dramatic show on television. To promote the show Reagan went around the country talking with workers at GE plants about life in Hollywood and about the virtues of private enterprise. In 1960 Reagan switched his party affiliation from Democrat to Republican, and in 1966 he surprised nearly everyone by beating the two-term Democratic incumbent for the California governorship.

Reagan served two terms as governor, a tenure marked by incendiary rhetoric. He insisted that people who accepted government welfare were chiselers or cheats, and he threatened a "bloodbath" if students in Berkeley kept taking to the streets to protest against Vietnam War. Reagan's stature grew. In 1976 he challenged the Republican president, Gerald Ford, and nearly gained the nomination by attacking Secretary of State Kissinger's policy of détente. When Ford lost the election to Jimmy Carter, Reagan was established as the Republican frontrunner in 1980. He thrashed Carter in that election, returning to themes that had made him famous: the venality of big government, the horrors of communism, and the unique ability of Americans to overcome all their problems and secure a luminous future.

Reagan's Cold War was a product of his experience in Middle America, in Hollywood, and on the circuit for GE; his chief source of information about the Soviet Union was *Reader's Digest*. He was not much interested in foreign countries. Like Mao he traveled abroad only reluctantly. Still Reagan knew what he did not like. The Soviet Union was an "evil empire," and its agents, he said at his first presidential press conference, "reserve unto themselves the right to commit any crime, to lie, to cheat," in order to foment "world revolution." The Berlin Wall should be ripped down, free elections should be held throughout eastern Europe, and the Soviet government should stop violating the human rights of its citizens. The Vietnam War had been "a noble cause." ("We should declare war on Vietnam," Reagan had said in October 1965. "We could pave the whole country and put parking stripes on it and still be home by Christmas.") Revolutions, or even experiments in socialism, were the result of Soviet imperialism.

Reagan brought to office a set of convictions rather than a foreign policy. He delegated to his advisers the task of turning his dreams and fears into directives. This might have worked if everyone agreed on how to do a thing, but as Reagan's men and women often disagreed among themselves, the result was frequently chaos.

Again and again Reagan displayed an alarming ignorance of his own nation's foreign policy. He misstated the name given by the CIA to the Soviets' largest long-range missile, and when his error was pointed out to him he accused the Soviets of changing the name in order to fool the West. He mistook defensive weapons for offensive ones, failed to understand the strategic difference between placing missiles in silos or putting them on mobile carriers, and claimed that neither bombers nor submarines carried nuclear weapons. He prepared for his 1986 summit meeting with Soviet leader Mikhail Gorbachev, to be held in Reykjavik, Iceland, by reading the Tom Clancy thriller *Red Storm Rising*—because, he said, much of it was set in Iceland. Briefings of the president had to be short and snappy, reducible to a few small note cards or film clips. These were by definition devoid of detail or ambiguity, which tended to reinforce Reagan's black-or-white view of the world.

Yet the president was not altogether without assets as a foreign policymaker. He commanded the world's strongest economy. He put it into recession early in his first term, and ran up an enormous national debt thereafter, but the Gross Domestic Product nevertheless increased through the 1980s. Possessed of a sense of humor and an actor's charm, Reagan was liked even by those who disagreed with him. And despite his caustic characterizations of the Soviets and his resolve to build American military power until his enemies cried uncle, Reagan feared a nuclear holocaust and was determined to find a way to prevent it. Back in 1979 Reagan had visited the headquarters of the North American Aerospace Defense Command (NORAD), at Cheyenne Mountain, Colorado. At the end of his tour Reagan asked the base commander what the United States could do if the Russians launched a missile at an American city. NORAD could track the missile, the commander replied, but could do nothing to stop it.

Reagan was astonished. "We have spent all that money and have all that equipment, and there is nothing we can do to prevent a nuclear missile from hitting us," he said. To Reagan it seemed that, armed to the teeth with weapons of mass destruction, the United States and the Soviet Union had come to the brink of Armageddon.

There might be a way out. The loophole was a system of lasers or rockets, deployed in space, that could destroy or knock off course any missile launched by Russia at the United States. Proposed by Reagan at the end of a defense budget speech to the nation on 23 March 1983, the Strategic Defense Initiative (SDI), popularly known as "Star Wars," soon after became the centerpiece of the administration's strategic planning. To Reagan it was a matter of logic and simple humanity: if you can prevent something as awful as a nuclear warhead from striking your nation, it would be irresponsible not to do so. But the Soviets reacted strongly against SDI. What Reagan had not said, they pointed out—and they assumed he realized it—was that a U.S. monopoly on missile defense would tempt the Americans to launch a first strike against them, secure in the knowledge that the Russians could not effectively retaliate. They were also concerned about a new arms race. The Americans would have to spend billions to develop SDI technology, while the Russians would be forced to increase their offensive capabilities in the hope of defeating the American shield. (The possibility of bankrupting the feeble Soviet economy had occurred to Reagan, though the strategic hazards of missile defense perhaps had not.) In any case, the Soviets said, meaningful arms negotiations could not take place between the powers so long as SDI remained on the table.

Reagan was disinclined to grant the Soviets any sympathy; moreover, he had found arms control distasteful. The Soviets continued, in his judgment, to stir up trouble around the globe: in the Middle East, Africa, and in Latin America, of special concern because of its proximity to the United States. When Reagan took office in 1981 the hot spot in Latin America was Nicaragua. Convinced that the Sandinista government was not only Marxist but a hemispheric agent of world communism, Reagan sought ways to unseat it. At the urging of William Casey, the director of the CIA, Reagan authorized the creation of an anti-Sandinista army, dubbed the contras, that would train in Honduras and harass the Sandinistas across the border. The contras were constituted mostly of members of Somoza's National Guard; at their peak they numbered about 7,500.

U.S. aid to the contras, and its related efforts to overthrow the Sandinistas, proved impossible to hide. In April 1984 the *Wall Street Journal* revealed that the CIA had mined Sandino harbor, hoping to discourage Nicaragua's trade. Congress now put its foot down, refusing to allow further funding of the anti-Sandinista war. Reagan branded the Sandinista government "a Communist reign of terror," and insisted that the United States had a moral right to overthrow it. The contras were "freedom fighters" similar to the American Founders. The administration would find alternative sources of funding for its sunshine patriots.

The Israelis refused to help, but the Saudis and the sultan of Brunei agreed to back the contras financially. Then National Security Council aide Oliver North, in the company of Casey and national security adviser Robert C. "Bud" McFarlane, had what North called "a neat idea." The fundamentalist Islamic government of Iran desperately wanted weapons to continue its war against Iraq. Despite its antipathy for the United States it was willing to buy U.S. arms and might out of gratitude intervene to secure the release of several American hostages then being held in Lebanon. North saw another benefit from selling arms to Iran: the money paid by the Iranians for the weapons might then be diverted to the contras. It would work as long as it was kept secret.

Word of the arms for hostages deal leaked out of the Middle East in November 1986. The contra connection was then uncovered as well. Congressional investigators wanted to know what role the president had played in the arms for hostages scheme and the diversion of monies to the contras, but either because he was stonewalling or because he genuinely could not remember what he had authorized and when, Reagan was unhelpful. He denied that he had known about the attempted swap, but documents indicated otherwise, and Reagan confessed, almost: "A few months ago I told the American people I did not trade arms for hostages. My heart and my best intentions still tell me that's true, but the facts and the evidence tell me it's not." He continued to deny that he had known about the diversion of funds to the contras. Senator William Cohen, a member of the congressional group that investigated Iran-Contra, participated in two interviews with Reagan and concluded, "with Ronald Reagan, no one is there."

The Iran-Contra affair and the nuclear freeze movement undoubtedly made him more tractable in negotiations with the Soviet Union. Mikhail Gorbachev, who emerged as the leader of the Soviet Union, declared his intention to reform the Soviet economy and pursue greater flexibility in foreign affairs, especially to move forward with arms control. At first suspicious that Gorbachev's offer to negotiate a meaningful arms agreement was a ploy to weaken U.S. vigilance, Reagan came ultimately to accept Gorbachev's sincerity, but he would not fully grasp the opportunity provided by Gorbachev's policy.

The obstacle to a full-scale nuclear rollback was SDI. At summits with Gorbachev in 1985, 1986, and 1988, Reagan continued to insist that defense against a nuclear attack could not be wrong, especially if Armageddon loomed. When Gorbachev pointed out that a missile shield would enable the United States to launch a first strike with impunity, Reagan, who was amazed that anyone would think the United States capable of such a thing, offered to share SDI technology with the Soviets. Gorbachev thought this unlikely. He urged Reagan to agree to confine SDI to the laboratory for ten years; Reagan refused. Still, Gorbachev wanted arms reduction enough that he was willing to make cuts in the Soviet arsenal even in the absence of an agreement on SDI. The result was the Intermediate Nuclear Force (INF) treaty of 8 December 1987, by which the Americans and Russians agreed to eliminate all intermediate-range nuclear missiles from Europe. But Reagan's commitment to SDI slowed the progress of further arms negotiations.

Gorbachev then unmade the Cold War. He ended the bloody Soviet intervention in Afghanistan, released Soviet control of the eastern European satellites and the Baltic states, allowed the destruction of the Berlin Wall, wrenched the Soviet economy off its rusty statist moorings, began opening Soviet archives to scholars, and traveled the world, creating about himself an international cult far more Reaganesque than Stalinist. He brought change so quickly and with such verve that Reagan and his successors mistrusted it. George H. W. Bush, who followed Reagan to the presidency in 1989, reacted so slowly to Gorbachev's revolution that critics charged him with being "nostalgic for the Cold War." Bush finally got it and embraced what he called "the new world order," which meant that the United States would now call the shots. Meanwhile Ronald Reagan returned to California, firm in the belief that his policies had brought about the end of the Cold War but not fully understanding how. He was the last cold warrior. The Alzheimer's disease that dissolved his memory made for a sad yet fitting metaphor: a dark era had passed, and there was a world to be remade.

BIBLIOGRAPHY

Acheson, Dean. *Present at the Creation: My Years in the State Department.* New York, 1969.

Brands, H. W., Jr. *Cold Warriors: Eisenhower's Generation and the American Foreign Policy.* New York, 1988.

Brinkley, Douglas. *Dean Acheson: The Cold War Years, 1953–1971.* New Haven, Conn., 1992.

Cannon, Lou. *President Reagan: The Role of a Lifetime.* New York, 1991.

Chace, James. *Acheson: The Secretary of State Who Created the American World.* New York, 1998.

Clark, Suzanne. *Cold Warriors: Manliness on Trial in the Rhetoric of the West.* Carbondale, Ill., 2000. The subtitle suggests how much the field of Cold War studies has changed since the early 1990s.

Conquest, Robert. *Stalin: Breaker of Nations.* New York, 1991.

FitzGerald, Frances. *Way Out There in the Blue: Reagan, Star Wars, and the End of the Cold War.* New York, 2000.

Goncharov, Sergei N., John W. Lewis, and Xue Litai. *Uncertain Partners: Stalin, Mao, and the Korean War.* Stanford, Calif., 1993.

Hunt, Michael H. *The Genesis of Chinese Communist Foreign Policy.* New York, 1996.

Isaacson, Walter, and Evan Thomas. *The Wise Men: Six Friends and the World They Made: Acheson, Bohlen, Harriman, Kennan, Lovett, McCloy.* New York, 1986.

Khrushchev, Nikita. *Khrushchev Remembers: The Last Testament.* Translated and edited by Strobe Talbott. Boston, 1974.

Mastny, Vojtech. *Russia's Road to the Cold War.* New York, 1979.

McLellan, David S. *Dean Acheson: The State Department Years.* New York, 1976.

Raack, R. C. *Stalin's Drive to the West, 1938–1945: The Origins of the Cold War.* Stanford, Calif., 1995.

Radzinsky, Edvard. *Stalin.* New York, 1996.

Reagan, Ronald. *An American Life.* New York, 1990.

Schmertz, Eric J., Natalie Datlof, and Alexej Ugrinsky, eds. *President Reagan and the World.* Westport, Conn., 1997.

Schram, Stuart. *Mao Tse-tung.* New York, 1966.

Spence, Jonathan. *Mao Zedong.* New York, 1999.

Tucker, Robert C. *Stalin in Power: The Revolution from Above, 1928–1941.* New York, 1990.

Wills, Garry. *Reagan's America: Innocents at Home.* Garden City, N.Y., 1987.

Zubok, Vladislav, and Constantine Pleshakov. *Inside the Kremlin's Cold War: From Stalin to Khrushchev.* Cambridge, Mass., 1996.

See also COLD WAR EVOLUTION AND INTERPRETATIONS; COLD WAR ORIGINS; COLD WAR TERMINATION; PRESIDENTIAL ADVISERS; PRESIDENTIAL POWER; SUMMIT CONFERENCES.

COLD WAR TERMINATION

Thomas R. Maddux

Most historians and foreign policy analysts in 1981 did not anticipate that within a decade the Cold War would be over and that it would end with relatively little violence and the end of the Soviet Union. Instead, they expected, like this author, to keep teaching their courses on the Cold War with new sections such as "Renewed Containment," "Détente II," and "Cold War IV." The widespread failure to remember the fundamental historical principle that change is continuous no matter how rigid and intractable problems appear to contemporaries led most historians to view the Cold War as an evolving but never-ending reality of international relations.

Historians did debate the central issues of causation, responsibility, and consequences of the Cold War as it came to its surprising conclusion. In the leading journal in the field, *Diplomatic History,* published by the Society for Historians of American Foreign Relations, specialists reviewed many of the Cold War issues including the interaction of impersonal, structural forces such as the economic challenges faced by both sides and the relative policy contributions of major players such as President Ronald Reagan and Soviet leader Mikhail Gorbachev.

Structural forces have received considerably less attention than the players in assessments on the end of the Cold War. There is widespread recognition that a stagnating Soviet economy definitely shaped Gorbachev's policy of *perestroika* to revive a command economy dominated by the Soviet Communist Party and state. The American economy in 1981, however, also looked shaky. Reagan's predecessor, President Jimmy Carter, had battled soaring inflation and an energy crisis driven by shortages of gasoline and rising prices; Americans also lacked confidence in the face of a mounting challenge from the export-driven Japanese economy. Although Gorbachev struggled to transform the Soviet economy, the American economy revived after a severe recession in 1982 and

took off into sustained growth, offering a striking contrast to the Soviet scene. As Soviet party officials attempted to maintain restrictions on use of copiers to limit the circulation of critical writings by Russians, American technology launched the next information revolution with the increasing spread of computers, from the mainframe and minicomputer of business and scientific research to the personal computer of the 1980s.

Cultural forces had less immediate impact on Soviet and American policymakers and remain more elusive with respect to demonstrating their impact on the endgame of the Cold War. Nevertheless, they shaped the long-term competition between the United States and the Soviet Union. By 1980 the Soviet Union had fallen far behind in most significant areas, with a few exceptions such as length of time spent in space by Russian cosmonauts versus American astronauts orbiting the earth in the space shuttle. The Russians had long since lost out with respect to influence around the globe in areas such as the media, consumer products, and lifestyle. The emerging global interdependence of the late twentieth century brought increasing exposure to American television, Hollywood feature films, McDonald's, and American consumerism. As the Soviet Union and its eastern European allies struggled to keep their citizens from leaving, the United States once again became a mecca for global immigration.

The Soviet Union also had lost the ideological competition, a central feature of the Cold War since its origins. Although Gorbachev launched *glasnost* to open the door to new ideas and to reduce the remaining repression in the Soviet system as it struggled with the legacies of Stalinist totalitarianism, the Soviet leader faced a difficult challenge to overcome both the resistance inherent in the Soviet system as well as the stubborn opposition of party officials who had a vested interest in the status quo. Since Gorbachev emerged from within the party, he also had to grapple with the increasing necessity for a fundamental discarding of Marxist-Leninist doctrine in order to redirect both the economy and the political system in the direction of a European parliamentary system with respect for the rule of law and individual rights. Reagan, however, never had to make any adjustments in his vigorous articulation of America as the land of freedom, and he never passed up a chance (until near the end in 1988) to point this out to Gorbachev on issues ranging from human rights to the continuation of the Berlin Wall.

Yet these structural forces did not predetermine when the Cold War would end and how it would end. The players on both sides, as they interacted with these impersonal pressures, had the most to do with the actual historical dynamics, and the literature has emphasized the role of the players. Early American assessments written by leading U.S. officials including Secretary of Defense Caspar Weinberger, Secretary of State George P. Shultz, Attorney General Edwin Meese 3d, and White House Chief of Staff Donald T. Regan, as well as Ronald Reagan, give themselves credit for ending the Cold War. Through a peace-through-strength strategy based on increased defense spending, a shift to the new Strategic Defense Initiative (SDI) that posed a technological challenge to the Soviet Union, and a willingness to apply significant rhetorical and other pressures against the Soviet empire, Washington brought a successful resolution to the conflict.

The most thorough development of this perspective appears in Peter Schweizer's *Victory: The Reagan Administration's Secret Strategy that Hastened the Collapse of the Soviet Union.* Relying extensively on interviews with leading officials including Weinberger, National Security Advisers Robert McFarlane and John Poindexter, and other officials who supported a hard line with respect to the Soviet Union, Schweizer focuses on the development and implementation of a strategic offensive led by William Casey, the director of the Central Intelligence Agency. Casey's campaign aimed at resisting, weakening, and rolling back the Kremlin's effort to control Afghanistan, to retain a communist regime in Poland and hegemony in eastern Europe, and to increase Soviet access to Western technology and markets in order to modernize the Soviet economy and military forces. By the time Gorbachev took over as general secretary of the Soviet Communist Party in March 1985, the victory campaign had, according to Schweizer, significantly contributed to the

problems that Gorbachev faced, so that he had few alternatives but to seek an accommodation with Reagan.

A second influential perspective puts more emphasis on the contributions of Reagan and Gorbachev and their chief diplomatic advisers, Secretary of State George Schultz and Soviet foreign minister Eduard Shevardnadze, than on Schweizer's hard-liners. In *The Turn: From the Cold War to a New Era,* Don Oberdorfer, a distinguished diplomatic correspondent for the *Washington Post,* emphasizes Reagan's shift to diplomacy with respect to Moscow by 1983 and the willingness of Gorbachev and Shevardnadze to bring a fresh perspective and approach to Soviet diplomacy. Although Reagan and Gorbachev never achieved final agreements on all arms control issues, such as strategic missiles and SDI, Oberdorfer gives them credit for making considerable progress toward an end to the Cold War. He also gives credit to Reagan's successor, George H. W. Bush, and Secretary of State James Baker, despite their cautious initial response to Gorbachev, for managing the U.S. response to the collapse of the Soviet empire in eastern Europe and the Soviet Union itself. In *The Great Transition,* Raymond Garthoff, a former Department of State official, shifts more of the credit for the way the Cold War ended to Gorbachev. Garthoff believes the hard-liner offensive, including Reagan's Cold War rhetoric, contributed to the resistance of Soviet officials to Gorbachev's initiatives and reduced opportunities for earlier accommodation and agreements on strategic weapons and SDI.

A third perspective focuses more directly on Gorbachev and his efforts to reorient Soviet domestic and Cold War policies. These studies have made extensive use of Soviet memoirs, interviews, and published sources and significantly enhance understanding of Gorbachev's role. In *Russia and the Idea of the West,* Robert English focuses on the origins of new thinking in the Soviet Union that came to fruition in Gorbachev's policies. English correctly notes that most of the new thinking emerged before Reagan arrived in the White House and that Reagan's military buildup, SDI, and the hard-liner "victory" campaign may have made it more difficult for Gorbachev to gain power and, with his "new thinking" advisers, implement fundamental changes in Soviet outlook and policies. Matthew Evangelista's *Unarmed Forces* and a 2001 article in the *Journal of Cold War Studies* has also expanded our understanding by focusing on Gorbachev's political skills, which helped him persuade his Soviet critics to go along with his significantly new proposals on arms reductions, withdrawal from Afghanistan, and his goal of allowing the eastern Europeans to determine their own domestic systems.

THE SOVIET PERSPECTIVE

All three perspectives note that little opportunity existed for significant changes in the Cold War before 1985. Under Leonid Brezhnev, the Soviet Union had attempted to maintain the détente relationship established with President Richard Nixon but at the same time pursue new opportunities to aid Marxist regimes. When the Soviet Union invaded Afghanistan on 27 December 1979 to restore reliable communist control of the government, the Carter administration abandoned any remaining hopes for an accommodation with the Soviet Union, most notably the unratified Strategic Arms Limitation Talks (SALT II), and moved to aid the Afghan resistance to Soviet forces.

Moscow may have hoped that Reagan would follow in the footsteps of Richard Nixon and shift from a career of anticommunism to a strategy of détente with the Soviet Union, especially since the Kremlin had not achieved very much in its recent international activities and faced a mounting crisis with Poland in 1980–1981. Economic problems in Poland, along with the deterioration of the Polish Communist Party, had contributed to the rise of Solidarity, an independent labor union. Soviet documents published by the Cold War International History Project reveal the desire of Soviet leaders to avoid another military intervention but at the same time defeat the challenge of Solidarity and keep it from spreading into the Baltic states and the Ukraine.

Ideology blended with great-power Realpolitik and regime preservation in the Soviet deliberations. Although the politburo received very detailed reporting on the Solidarity movement and the extent of public and worker support for Solidarity, Soviet officials and their eastern European allies filtered the situation through their ideological categories and jargon. In reports to the politburo as well as meetings of Soviet officials and Warsaw bloc allies, "forces of counterrevolution," "enemies of socialism," and "petit-bourgeois ideology" served as substitutes for challenging analysis of the situation. During a Politburo meeting on 29 October 1980, Brezhnev

and Yuri Andropov worried about a "raging counterrevolution underway" in Poland with Solidarity leaders like Lech Walesa trying to "take power away from the workers." Brezhnev and other officials also frequently referred to Western capitalist forces seeking to aid counterrevolution in Poland. When Marshall Wojciech Jaruzelski finally imposed martial law in December, Soviet officials quickly stepped up their assistance to arrest Solidarity leaders. As a member of the politburo, Gorbachev participated in the many discussions on Poland in 1980–1981 but in his recorded comments never questioned the pressure policies and the traditional class struggle analysis.

REVITALIZED COLD WAR

If Soviet leaders had hoped for renewed détente with Reagan, they were quickly disappointed by the rhetoric and policies of the new administration. As part of his transition from New Deal liberal Democrat during the 1930s and World War II to conservative anticommunist by the early 1960s, Reagan had developed a strong personal distaste for communism through his bruising battles with communists in Hollywood as president of the Screen Actors Guild and a strong opposition to the Soviet Union as the source of global communism. Reagan never endorsed Richard Nixon's strategy of détente and quickly stepped up public criticism of Moscow. In his first press conference, on 29 January 1981, Reagan responded to a question by dismissing détente as "a one-way street that the Soviet Union has used to pursue its own aims," that is, the promotion of world revolution. Reagan expanded his views in an address to the British Parliament at Westminster in 1982 with a call for a crusade for freedom and democracy that would "leave Marxism-Leninism on the ash heap of history" and pointed to the communist states in eastern Europe and the Soviet Union itself as prime candidates for this fate. Finally, in March 1983, Reagan used a speech to the National Association of Evangelicals to refer to the Soviet leaders as "the focus of evil in the modern world" and to the Soviet Union as an "evil empire."

The Kremlin resented Reagan's remarks but worried more about the campaign that hard-liners initiated to step up U.S. resistance to the Soviet empire and intensify a wide range of pressures on the Kremlin. Reagan and his advisers had argued in the campaign of 1980 that the United States had fallen behind in the Cold War and needed a substantial defense buildup to catch up to the Soviet Union and its allies, most seriously with respect to a "window of vulnerability" related to strategic missile forces. Secretary of Defense Caspar Weinberger proposed a $32.6 billion increase to the defense budgets for 1981 and 1982, although Congress had already approved a 1981 budget with a 9 percent increase. Defense spending would increase from $142 billion in 1980 to $222 billion in 1982, and the Department of Defense anticipated requests for further yearly increases of 7 percent. After Congress approved the first defense budget in October, Weinberger presented a new request for a strategic modernization of U.S. forces, including plans to build a hundred MX missiles, six Trident submarines, three thousand air-launched cruise missiles, and a new Stealth B-2 bomber, and to reactivate the B-1 bomber that President Carter had canceled. Although the emerging deficit would prompt Congress to cut back the Defense Department's projected increase, Reagan's substantial increase clearly troubled Soviet officials as they attempted to ascertain the intentions of the new administration.

Hard-liners in the Reagan administration had the most influence with Reagan at the start and quickly pushed for a strategic offensive against the Soviet Union. According to Schweizer, the hard-liners, led by CIA Director Casey, the National Security Council staff under the direction of Richard V. Allen and William P. Clark, and Secretary Weinberger, with advisers such as Richard Perle and Fred Ikle, shifted their pre-1981 perception of the Soviet challenge to emphasize fundamental Soviet political and economic weaknesses. Casey frequently presented Reagan with unfiltered intelligence data on the Soviet economy that supported this assessment.

Reagan endorsed the recommendations of Casey and the NSC without much opposition from his advisers or Secretary of State Alexander Haig, who favored more negotiations with the Soviet Union than did the hard-liners. Most of the initiatives developed gradually and did not require either congressional approval or extensive publicity. Several focused specifically on economic objectives, including an effort to reduce Soviet hard currency earnings through the sale of oil and natural gas and stepped-up restrictions on the export of technology to the Soviet Union, as well as a CIA disinformation campaign to sell flawed technology and equipment to Moscow.

Along with the defense buildup, the most significant dimensions of the hard-liner campaign involved U.S. covert support for Solidarity in Poland and the Afghan mujahedin resistance to the Red Army. After the declaration of martial law in Poland and the arrest of Solidarity leaders, Reagan invoked economic sanctions against the Polish government and pursued a covert plan to aid Solidarity through financial assistance and communications equipment.

In Afghanistan the Reagan administration took over an existing Carter policy of aid to the Afghan resistance through Pakistan. Casey made numerous trips to Pakistan to bolster the government's commitment to the mujahedin. Casey also persuaded Reagan to increase the flow of arms, training, and assistance. When Moscow stepped up the war in 1985, Reagan approved an increase in high-tech weapons supplied to the mujahedin, which helped them blunt the Soviet offensive, including the delivery of Stingers, effective ground-to-air missiles that made Soviet helicopters and jets vulnerable below 15,000 feet.

THE REAGAN DOCTRINE, FREEDOM FIGHTERS, AND CENTRAL AMERICA

The hard-liner strategy certainly helped Solidarity stay viable and enhanced the mujahedin resistance. There were definite limits, however, to what the hard-liners could accomplish, especially when they attracted congressional and public attention to their aid to resistance movements against communist regimes. In October 1983, President Reagan expanded the campaign by calling for freedom against Soviet totalitarianism with aid to freedom fighters who challenged communist domination. Under this perspective, which acquired the title "Reagan Doctrine" after the 1984 election, Casey and the hard-liners pushed to extend covert assistance to a variety of movements including those in Angola, Ethiopia, Cambodia, and Central America. Central America posed the most immediate challenge to Reagan and the hard-liner strategy, especially since the Soviet Union's role appeared distant and indirect with the exception of its alliance with Fidel Castro in Cuba. Washington faced the difficult challenge of how to deal with crumbling authoritarian regimes in Central America that the United States had supported throughout the Cold War. Should security and Cold War concerns receive priority or should Washington attempt to support reform, representative government, and negotiations among the contending factions? The Carter administration had wavered on this question but ended up attempting to work with a popular coalition in Nicaragua that included the Sandinist National Liberation Front (FSLN), which had overthrown Anastasio Somoza's regime there in 1979, and to encourage reform by moderates in El Salvador, where the Farabundo Martí National Liberation Forces (FMLN) challenged the authoritarian regime but had failed to overthrow it in a January 1981 offensive.

President Reagan and the hard-liner coalition preferred to emphasize Cold War concerns and moved quickly to step up U.S. aid to the government of El Salvador. Military aid jumped from $6 million in 1980 to $82 million in 1982, and economic aid to El Salvador tripled during the same period to $189 million. Washington also supported a moderate Christian Democrat, José Duarte, against the right and left and used Duarte's victory in the 1984 election to increase military aid to $196 million. U.S. training of El Salvadoran troops expanded and U.S. Green Beret advisers increased.

Secretary Haig wanted to go after what he considered the most direct source of communist influence, Fidel Castro's Cuba, with a naval blockade to shut off the flow of arms to Central America. Reagan's chief White House advisers, Michael Deaver, Edwin Meese, and James Baker, however, opposed any foreign adventures that would disrupt achievement of the Reagan domestic agenda, and they proceeded to keep Haig, but not Casey, from meeting alone with Reagan so that they could monitor the secretary's more aggressive Cold War scenarios. Haig also underestimated public and congressional resistance to a policy of direct U.S. involvement in Central America. Public opinion polls indicated majority support for staying out of the area, especially any U.S. involvement beyond economic aid, and the media stepped up its criticism in 1981 when a news photo revived memories of Vietnam by showing U.S. military advisers in the field carrying M-16 rifles instead of the handguns allowed under policy guidelines. Congressional reaction to El Salvador also limited the White House's options as representatives cut aid requests, demanded that the junta restrain the killing by security forces and right-wing death squads, and pushed for investigations on the killing of American churchwomen and labor advisers.

Washington faced an even more difficult challenge in dealing with Nicaragua and the Sandinista regime, a coalition increasingly dominated by Daniel Ortega and the FSLN. Washington maintained diplomatic relations with Nicaragua and engaged in discussions focused on persuading the Sandinistas to stop the flow of arms to the FMLN in El Salvador. CIA Director Casey, however, persuaded Reagan and the National Security Council to approve a covert operation ostensibly to interdict arms from Nicaragua to El Salvador and to disrupt any Soviet-Cuban ties in Nicaragua. Casey turned to Argentinian military veterans to train Nicaraguans, initially veterans of Somoza's National Guard, into a 500-man force that would operate out of Honduras. House and Senate intelligence committees received some information from Casey about this operation and raised many concerns, particularly about the extent to which this force, which would be called the contras, would operate in Nicaragua.

From 1982 on, Reagan and his advisers found themselves in an escalating campaign against the Sandinistas in the face of continuing public and congressional criticism and resistance. As the number of contra forces grew, the army's Special Operations Division replaced the Argentinians and provided training, arms, and intelligence assistance. In April 1982, Washington increased its demands from the arms issue to an insistence that Managua follow through on earlier pledges to permit political pluralism and hold free elections as well as tolerate a mixed economy. Congressional concerns about contra raids into Nicaragua prompted the first of many attempted restrictions: an amendment in December 1982 by Representative Edward Boland that prohibited the CIA and the Defense Department from using funds to support anyone trying to overthrow the Nicaraguan government. Casey's CIA heightened public and congressional criticism with operations to blow up Nicaraguan fuel storage depots at Caribbean coastal cities in October 1983 and to mine Nicaraguan harbors with small C-4 explosives that wounded fishermen and seamen and hit Soviet and British ships. Congress responded with a second Boland Amendment in June 1984 that cut off all lethal aid to the contras but not $27 million in humanitarian assistance. Casey and the National Security Council, with Oliver North as the manager of the supply effort to the contras, proceeded to turn for the next two years to other sources of funding including the diversion of funds from the sale of arms to Iran. The ensuing

Iran-Contra affair drove a number of the hard-liners out of the administration and considerably weakened and distracted Reagan in his handling of not only the Central American crisis but also direct relations with the Soviet Union.

Reagan persisted in the campaign to get renewed funding for the contras in annual battles over military and nonmilitary assistance and resisted various negotiated attempts to end the conflicts in Central America. When President Oscar Arias of Costa Rica advanced a new Central American peace plan in 1987 that called for cease-fires throughout the region, an end to outside military aid, and negotiations among all of the contending forces as well as free elections, Reagan and his declining number of hard-line advisers tried without success to head off the plan. Reagan remained adamant in his denunciation of Ortega and the Sandinistas as unreliable communists who would not keep any agreements that threatened their rule.

By the time George Bush arrived in the White House in January 1989, joined by Secretary of State James Baker, the Arias peace process had moved farther beyond Washington's influence. In February, Arias and the Central American presidents persuaded Ortega to agree to reforms and an election during February 1990. Bush and Baker moved to demobilize the contra camps in Honduras and test Arias's prediction that a withdrawal of military pressure would lead to a Sandinista defeat in the election in light of the resentment toward some of their more heavy-handed policies and accumulated economic problems. Secretary Baker also followed up on earlier conversations with Gorbachev concerning a Soviet willingness to encourage the Sandinistas to negotiate, a reflection of Gorbachev's "new thinking" in international relations and his desire to reduce the drain of Soviet aid to Cuba and its allies in Central America. Gorbachev indicated a willingness to cut off arms shipments to the Sandinistas and urge them to accept the results of the election if Bush and Baker supported the Arias peace plan. When Violeta Chamorro defeated Ortega in the February election and a settlement in El Salvador brought an end to the conflict in 1992, Baker and Bush expressed both relief and satisfaction that the end of the Cold War had enabled them to achieve through negotiations what Reagan and the hard-liners had pursued unsuccessfully since 1981 through substantial aid, covert activities, and annual battles with Congress.

THE REAGAN REVERSAL?

Reagan looked, acted, and talked like an anticommunist Cold Warrior from start to finish in his doctrine about aid to freedom fighters and in his policies on El Salvador and Nicaragua. Yet Reagan did lower the rhetoric and move to meaningful negotiations with Gorbachev. Did this represent a reversal by Reagan, as Beth A. Fischer argues in *The Reagan Reversal* (1997)? Or did Reagan maintain a hard-liner perspective and accept concessions from Gorbachev as the Soviet leader moved to end the Cold War? Fischer suggests that by January 1984 Reagan was backing off of his hard-line rhetoric and rejection of negotiations because of a growing awareness that confrontation with Moscow could get out of control and lead to a nuclear Armageddon. Fischer points to three events after October 1983: the Soviet shooting down of Korean Airlines flight 007, which not only horrified Reagan but raised the danger of a series of human errors producing a disaster; the controversial television movie *The Day After*, which focused on the effects of nuclear war on Lawrence, Kansas; and, third, Able Archer 83, war games carried out by U.S. and NATO forces in Europe that raised Kremlin concerns about a nuclear first strike to such a degree that the Soviets put their forces on alert.

Reagan was more multi-sided with respect to the Soviet Union and the Cold War than Fischer suggests. Although he never gave up on aid to freedom fighters, Reagan did respond to conflicting recommendations from his advisers and exhibited some flexibility toward Moscow before Gorbachev arrived. In the spring of 1983 hard-liners and Secretary of State Shultz encouraged Reagan to move in two somewhat contradictory directions. Hard-liners led by William Clark and the National Security Council strongly endorsed Reagan's speech on 8 March with its reference to the Soviet "evil empire" and his endorsement of the Strategic Defense Initiative (SDI) on 23 March.

Shultz disliked both speeches and SDI and did not know about the "evil empire" reference. When Shultz met with Reagan on 10 March with a well-prepared rationale for a new approach to Moscow, to his dismay he found the room filled with Clark and other National Security Council officials opposed to negotiations. As Shultz later recounted, he met privately with Reagan the next day and told him that "I needed to have direction from him on Soviet relations. I went through with him again what I was trying to achieve. 'Go ahead,' he told me." Shultz noted that despite the green light from the president he had to be careful and keep checking back with Reagan on the "proposed route" to improved relations with the Kremlin. On SDI, Shultz indicated that he first heard about the strategic defense idea at a dinner with the president on 12 February and in a debate with Clark early in March. Shultz took his concerns to the president, emphasizing that Reagan was changing basic strategic doctrine without much scientific and technological basis or consultation within the administration or with Western allies. Shultz supported research and development consistent with the ABM Treaty and reliance on existing doctrine and the structure of U.S. alliances. Reagan, however, brushed aside the secretary's rationale and his offer to redraft the reference to SDI in Reagan's speech. The president pushed to announce SDI before it disappeared in the face of resistance and criticism from administration officials, Congress, allies, and public critics.

Shultz had more success when he persuaded Reagan, against the resistance of Clark and the National Security Council, to open a dialogue with Soviet officials. At the 12 February dinner with Reagan, Schultz suggested that Reagan meet with Soviet ambassador Anatoly Dobrynin. "Great," responded Reagan, although Clark and the National Security Council tried to head off a wayward president who had yet to meet with any Soviet official. For two hours Reagan and Dobrynin reviewed issues, including human rights and the Pentecostals, a small group of Christians who had been in the U.S. embassy in Moscow for five years and wanted to emigrate to practice their religion. According to Shultz, Reagan thoroughly enjoyed the discussion, wanted to be involved, and wanted to move forward. On 28 February, Moscow responded with a less than direct indication that if the Pentecostals left the embassy and went home they would eventually be able to emigrate. After the "evil empire" speech Reagan approved a response to Dobrynin, and the Kremlin began to allow the Pentecostals to leave. Dobrynin kept repeating "the less said publicly the better," and Shultz kept repeating "quiet diplomacy." From April through July, Shultz kept up the quiet diplomacy, Moscow released Pentecostals and family members, and Reagan stayed silent as promised.

REAGAN AND ARMS CONTROL

If Shultz or other advisers opened a path to negotiations with the Soviet Union, Reagan would pursue it, but he needed alternatives because the hard-liners rejected any meaningful negotiations with Moscow. Reagan always was confident that he could set aside his longtime hostility toward communism and the Soviet Union to solve problems, even the more intractable arms control issues, such as intermediate missiles (INF) and strategic missiles (START). The White House delayed resuming negotiations on either issue—both of which had been pursued by the Carter administration—until initiating the defense buildup. When public criticism, a nuclear freeze movement in western Europe, and pressure from Western allies finally prompted hard-liners, they developed negotiating positions that arms control negotiators believed were guaranteed to produce a Soviet rejection.

The hard-liner positions appealed to Reagan, and he used some of their recommendations to achieve much more than either the hard-liners or Democratic critics believed possible. On INF the Soviet Union had modernized its forces with the SS-20, a powerful missile that brought any city in western Europe within its range. The Carter administration had promised NATO allies that the United States would deploy a new generation of missiles, the Pershing II and ground-launched cruise missiles, and negotiate a reduction with the Kremlin. Weinberger's aide, Richard Perle, proceeded to develop the zero option of proposing to the Kremlin that it remove all of its missiles and that the United States cancel deployment of the Pershing. President Reagan went for the zero option because it involved meaningful arms reduction (unlike the previous SALT I and II accords, which had primarily put ceilings on the number of weapons) and because he could sell the zero option to the public.

On strategic weapons Weinberger and Perle again recommended to the president a negotiating stance that would ensure the absence of an agreement. They urged Reagan to support a dramatic reduction, particularly on the Soviet side, by insisting on a reduction in ballistic missile throw-weights that would reduce the Soviets' land-based, more powerful rockets by 60 percent but would not affect the U.S. forces. State Department specialists opposed this stance, but in order to win Reagan's endorsement they had to support a negotiating stance that would reduce launchers, cut warheads by one third, and also include Perle's throw-weight ceiling. Again Reagan approved a position that would significantly reduce strategic missiles even as his negotiators on both sides believed the Kremlin would respond with another *nyet.*

GORBACHEV AND THE COLD WAR

The Soviet response confirmed their expectations as the Kremlin struggled with a series of elderly, incapacitated leaders: Brezhnev died in November 1982, followed by Yuri Andropov, who had a reform agenda but became ill within a year, and then Konstantin Chernenko, who was also ill. Even if Reagan had pursued more quiet diplomacy, it is very unlikely that he would have accomplished much before the arrival of Gorbachev in March 1985.

Gorbachev came to power as a new-generation leader who had both practical experience in the Soviet system as a party official and substantial exposure to "new thinking" within the Soviet intellectual elite. As Robert English persuasively demonstrates in *Russia and the Idea of the West,* Gorbachev had had long-term exposure to "new thinking" at Moscow State University (which produced many of the leading reformers), in Czechoslovakia in 1968, in travel to the West in the 1970s, in the reading of restricted works on socialism and the West, and in the development of close relations with Eduard Shevardnadze in the neighboring Georgian Republic.

After his return to Moscow in 1979, Gorbachev significantly expanded his quest for new ideas with reform economists and foreign policy specialists, surprising many of them with the extent of his reading and interest in reforms of Soviet relations with the West and with eastern European socialist countries. As head of the international affairs committee in 1983, Gorbachev interacted with new thinkers in foreign policy such as Yevgeny Velikhov, Georgy Arbatov, and Alexander Yakovlev. When Andropov appointed Gorbachev to direct a plenum on economic issues, Gorbachev brought in new thinking advisers and ideas for shaping a domestic reform agenda with some veiled international implications.

Gorbachev confirmed the suspicions of the old guard in the politburo, which had tried to deny him the chairmanship of the party. His bold ideas on domestic-economic reform, military cutbacks, and foreign policy with respect to

Afghanistan and eastern Europe stimulated significant opposition. (He informed party leaders in eastern Europe, for example, that the Brezhnev Doctrine of 1968, which insisted that a state that had joined the socialist camp could not leave, was dead.) Gorbachev, however, demonstrated superior leadership skills in outmaneuvering his critics through use of the prestige of the general secretary office and the politburo tradition of consensus behind the general secretary, as well as his personal skills at manipulating the agenda, persuading his critics, and replacing his adversaries with new thinking allies. In July 1985, Gorbachev replaced longtime foreign minister Andrei Gromyko with a colleague and confidant, Eduard Shevardnadze, who shared Gorbachev's belief in the need for economic and foreign policy reform. When resistance to his policies picked up in 1986, Gorbachev promoted Yakovlev as Central Committee secretary for ideology and replaced many Brezhnev supporters with new thinking advisers such as Anatoly Chernyaev as his personal foreign policy aide.

SUMMIT DIPLOMACY: GENEVA, NOVEMBER 1985

When Secretary Shultz initiated discussions with Soviet officials for a summit conference between Gorbachev and Reagan in Geneva in November 1985, Reagan made a significant contribution to ending the Cold War by overruling hard-liner objections and by recognizing that Gorbachev provided new possibilities for at least a reduction of tensions and nuclear risks in the Cold War. Weinberger and the hard-liners opposed a summit with Gorbachev, but Shultz persuaded a wavering president to go ahead, especially since Gorbachev and Shevardnadze had indicated a significant interest in the reduction of the burden of strategic weapons to enable the Kremlin to stimulate economic reform. Shultz, however, failed in an effort to persuade Reagan to accept a trade-off between offensive missiles and defense with limits on SDI. Instead, the secretary found himself fighting something of a rearguard action against efforts by hard-liners to reinterpret the Anti-Ballistic Missile (ABM) Treaty of 1972 so that it would permit development, testing, and deployment of new space weapons.

Gorbachev also faced resistance to the Geneva summit and a significant arms control settlement, but he did start to shift Soviet positions.

Eastern European leaders and Soviet conservatives opposed any change in bloc relations and affirmed a class-struggle perspective in international relations. They pushed for an expanded offensive in Afghanistan and continued Soviet aid to anti-imperialist forces. In late August, however, Gorbachev signaled the possibility of a trade-off on offensive missiles and defense by dropping the longtime Soviet stance that called for a complete ban on SDI research, as opposed to a ban only on research outside of the laboratory. On 27 September, Shevardnadze followed up Gorbachev's comments with a proposed 50 percent reduction in strategic weapons in exchange for an agreement affirming the ABM Treaty against the development, testing, or deployment of space-based weapons. This represented the first of a significant number of concessions from Gorbachev on arms control that started to move the Soviet Union toward the U.S. position.

The summit did not produce significant movement in any of the three areas of arms control—intercontinental ballistic missiles, intermediate range missiles, and missile defense. It did establish the agenda for future summits, as the leaders agreed to hold two more meetings in Washington and Moscow, with regional issues such as Afghanistan and Central America and human rights issues receiving attention along with bilateral questions. Through substantial private exchanges during the two days, Reagan and Gorbachev initiated a personal relationship that started to break down entrenched stereotypes of the Soviet head of the evil empire and the American leader of capitalist imperialism. Shultz had finally brought Reagan into a policy of negotiation with the Soviet Union despite the continuing resistance of hard-liners, who leaked a letter by Weinberger on the day the president left for Geneva that warned the president against any agreements to restrain SDI or continue the unratified SALT II treaty.

In the aftermath of Geneva, Gorbachev faced the most serious challenges from critics who argued that he came home from Geneva without anything. The Soviet leader, however, moved the farthest to work out an accommodation with Washington. In January he proposed the elimination of all nuclear weapons by the year 2000 and a response on INF missiles that moved toward Washington's position of zero on both sides. The prospect of getting rid of all missiles clearly interested President Reagan, who brushed aside the criticism of Richard Perle, the original author of

the zero strategy, that Gorbachev was just engaging in propaganda. Gorbachev, however, had to use all of his powers of persuasion as well as the strong Soviet commitment to disarmament to persuade the Soviet military to accept his proposals.

Gorbachev went on to establish a new policy line on both the domestic and international fronts with the Twenty-seventh Party Congress in February. Before the congress, Gorbachev, Yakovlev, and Shevardnadze met to work out a new philosophy of foreign policy with input from a number of new thinkers and with much personal struggle. They ultimately moved from Lenin's basic precept of a divided world and Marxist class struggle to a concept of an interdependent world that needed cooperation on global problems rather than an arms race and Cold War with the imperialist camp.

Shevardnadze went ahead in the Foreign Ministry to implement this perspective with new officials. Under this agenda the Soviet Union would aim at the reduction of regional conflicts, the withdrawal of Soviet forces from Afghanistan, the establishment of a security system in Europe, the significant reduction of nuclear and conventional arms, respect for neighboring states with a policy of noninterference, and the end of the Cold War with the United States. In May, Gorbachev presented this perspective to the Soviet diplomatic corps, including all ambassadors. Although this new thinking effectively abandoned the traditional Soviet Marxist-Leninist framework and any ideological rationale for a Cold War, practical implementation would be more difficult with both Soviet and American hard-liners, who remained suspicious.

REYKJAVIK SUMMIT: OCTOBER 1986

Instead of new thinking in Washington, the old conflict between hard-liners and moderates persisted. Weinberger and Perle, for example, pushed to break through the SALT II restrictions that the United States still had not reached. The arms control bureaucracy also continued its usual disagreements, and Undersecretary of Defense Fred Ikle tossed a knuckleball into the field with a zero ballistic missile proposal. Shultz liked the idea as a way to get Reagan to agree to limit SDI, as less offense would reduce the need for defense. Only Paul Nitze, a veteran arms control negotiator, vigorously objected to the proposal as nonnegotiable and very disruptive to both the ongoing strategic modernization program and to the Western allies. Nevertheless, Reagan went away with the zero missile proposal in July and linked it to SDI with a proposal to not withdraw from the ABM Treaty for five years and to continue research, development, and testing as permitted by the treaty.

After the disruptive FBI arrest of a Soviet scientific attaché, followed by the KGB arrest of an American journalist in Moscow, Nicholas Daniloff, Washington announced that Reagan would meet with Gorbachev in Iceland in fifteen days for discussions to complete arrangements for the next summit in Washington. The Reykjavik meeting, however, turned into an intense two-day summit in which a prepared Gorbachev attempted to obtain a significant settlement of offensive and defensive weapons. Gorbachev presented new proposals on START and INF that significantly moved toward Washington's position, to the increasing enthusiasm of Shultz and other officials. At the same time, Gorbachev continued to link agreement on these two issues with missile defense, insisting that both sides keep the ABM Treaty for ten years and confine all research and testing to the laboratory. Gorbachev wanted the offensive reductions, but the politburo and Soviet military insisted on the maintenance of the ABM agreement to prevent space weapons that could be used for offensive and defensive purposes.

Despite the disclaimers in their memoirs, Reagan, Shultz, and the U.S. delegation had not prepared for substantial negotiations and consequently had to scramble to prepare responses and counterresponses, at one point redrafting the U.S. position in an upstairs bathroom in Hofdi House. Reagan defended SDI and indicated that the United States would share the technology when it became available so that both sides could eliminate ballistic missiles. After discussions that continued through the first night of the meeting, the negotiators made progress on START and agreed to zero missiles in Europe for the INF agreement. SDI remained the main obstacle. Reagan and his advisers and Gorbachev began to maneuver less for an agreement during the afternoon session on the second day and more for an advantageous position with respect to public perceptions on the results. Since the United States had not prepared any offers to make in response to Soviet proposals, Shultz and his advisers put the zero missile proposal on the table. Reagan wanted to leave and suggested they take it up again at the Washington summit. The negotiators, however, went off into a series of confusing exchanges in which they ended up with a proposal to get rid of all strategic weapons—missiles, bombers, cruise missiles— until a failure to get any movement on SDI prompted Reagan to stand up and say, "Let's go, George, we're leaving."

The Reykjavik discussions initially looked like a failure, but the negotiations did foreshadow the eventual INF agreement signed at the Washington summit and the START agreement that President George Bush finally concluded in 1991. The very critical reaction of the Joint Chiefs of Staff, congressional leaders, and Western allies to Reagan's willingness to give up all strategic weapons would have forced a U.S. retreat from this position if SDI had not blocked any preliminary agreement.

STAR WARS: THE STRATEGIC DEFENSE INITIATIVE

SDI could have been limited to the laboratory for ten years and the ABM Treaty affirmed as requested by Gorbachev without any real damage to meaningful research on defense technology. By the end of 1986 most of the exotic, space-based weapons such as the X-ray laser, chemical lasers, and other directed-energy programs had moved backward rather than forward toward the actual design of a weapons system. SDI research increasingly focused on kinetic-energy weapons, interceptor missiles fired from space or on the ground to destroy incoming missiles.

As Congress proceeded to cut fiscal year 1987 funding for SDI to 3 percent growth, versus the administration's request for 5 percent, or $3.5 billion, Weinberger and conservatives pushed for deployment of SDI despite the fact that the program remained a research program with nothing adequately tested for deployment. Hard-liners feared that if Reagan failed to persuade Congress to move to deployment, SDI would never make it out of the laboratory and would eventually be cashed as a bargaining chip in negotiations with Gorbachev.

During a prolonged battle with Congress over SDI in 1987 that intersected with the Iran-Contra affair and its damage to Reagan's confidence and political standing, the president refused to back off. In a push for a reinterpretation of the ABM Treaty that would permit testing, the White House succeeded in uniting Democrats and the Joint Chiefs of Staff in support of the established meaning of the treaty. The Joint Chiefs sent SDI back to the laboratory by insisting that any weapon would have to go through the standard Defense Acquisitions Board where it would have to fulfill a series of requirements starting with a statement of what the weapon could accomplish. Since SDI officials presented an initial plan that consisted mainly of theoretical components of space-based battle stations and ground-based interceptors, defense specialists strung out the review through the year and by 1988 had sent SDI back to the laboratory.

Although Reagan refused to make any deal that would limit testing and deployment of SDI, Gorbachev and Soviet leaders moved to detach the issue from an agreement on INF and START. Soviet officials had extensive experience with an ABM system around Moscow and shared the skepticism of American scientists about the Star Wars lasers and exotic technologies. They also recognized that any space-based system would be very vulnerable to attack. Yet they worried that the potential of American science and technology, combined with the expenditure of billions, could lead to a technological breakthrough and a first-strike capability. As Frances FitzGerald suggests in *Way Out There in the Blue,* information from Washington about the status of SDI research and a recommendation from Andrei Sakharov, a leading Soviet scientist recently released from internal exile, influenced Gorbachev's decision to unlink SDI from an INF agreement and START.

WASHINGTON AND MOSCOW SUMMITS: DECEMBER 1987 AND MAY 1988

Neither the Washington nor the Moscow summits achieved agreements on all of the arms control issues. At the Washington summit the leaders did sign an important INF treaty to get rid of all intermediate missiles, both in Europe and Asia. Weinberger and hard-liners joined by the Joint Chiefs of Staff, however, resisted a START accord. Since the Joint Chiefs had never expected an agreement to be concluded, they had not worked out the force reductions that would be required by START, and they worried about Soviet statements that they might suspend any treaty if the United States engaged in SDI testing that violated the traditional interpretation of the ABM Treaty. Washington lacked an agenda to negotiate with Gorbachev, who arrived with numerous interesting proposals such as a Soviet withdrawal from

Afghanistan and joint Soviet-American support for the Central American peace process led by Oscar Arias of Costa Rica.

Beyond the INF Treaty, the most significant effect of the summits was in the public impact that Reagan and Gorbachev had in one another's capitals. Reagan played the genial host in Washington and Gorbachev swept the Washington media, intelligentsia, and congressional leaders off their feet, charming audiences with his dynamic personality, quick mind, and friendly demeanor. Crowds lined the streets as Gorbachev zoomed around Washington in a black limousine, and Gorbachev reciprocated with a spontaneous American-style movement into the crowd at Connecticut and L streets. Public opinion polls taken after the summit indicated that by giving a public endorsement of Gorbachev as his friend, Mikhail, Reagan weakened the traditional Cold War view of Soviet leaders and raised public perceptions that the Soviet threat and the Cold War had declined.

Reagan's visit to Moscow had a similar impact on the Soviet public. Reagan followed a carefully designed script with fourteen presentations that emphasized visual impressions and the emotional impact of Reagan on the Russian people as he acted out the ceremonies of the summit. Sounding the trumpet of human rights, Reagan also spoke to Soviet intellectuals and students at Moscow State University about freedom and democracy. On a morning walk in Red Square, Reagan and Gorbachev jointly held a small boy, like two candidates running for office. When asked later by a reporter about the "evil empire," Reagan replied: "I was talking about another time, another era." Just as Americans warmed up to Gorbachev, the Soviet public gathered around Reagan's visit and by the end applauded him in the streets.

END OF THE COLD WAR: 1988

As Caspar Weinberger followed many hard-liners into retirement, U.S. officials found it very difficult to recognize and act upon the significant changes in Soviet domestic and foreign policies. Gorbachev stepped up the pace of change in 1987–1988 with economic reforms and a surprising push to democratize the party system, initially with internal changes for secret ballots and multiple candidates. The more Gorbachev pushed a *glasnost* opening, the more demands he encountered from domestic pressure groups of reformers to move toward a Western representative system that tolerated more than just the Communist Party and operated with a government independent of the party, an independent judiciary, a president and bicameral legislature, and respect for individual rights. Although faced with increasing conservative resistance, Gorbachev achieved politburo approval for his agenda except for a multiparty system. Gorbachev used the appearance of arms control agreements with the United States and the growing normalization of relations for additional leverage against his conservative adversaries.

Gorbachev and Reagan moved toward announcing the end of the Cold War. When exchanging the INF ratification documents in Moscow with Reagan, Gorbachev stressed that each of the four summit meetings had undermined the foundations of the Cold War. During his visit to the United Nations in New York City and his brief meeting with Reagan and president-elect George Bush, Gorbachev articulated a new international order free of Cold War competition and guided by self-determination. This further development of new thinking shaped Gorbachev's successful persuasion of the Soviet military and the politburo to agree in November to significantly reduce Soviet conventional forces and shift to a defensive strategy as well as to initiate planning for the withdrawal of Soviet forces from eastern Europe. At the end of the Moscow summit Reagan came close to agreeing that the Cold War was over in response to a reporter's question, but he hesitated and then repeated his favorite refrain on Moscow, "trust but verify." Later, as he left Washington for retirement in California, Reagan announced that the Cold War was indeed over.

BUSH, BAKER, AND THE REVOLUTION OF 1989

President George Bush and Secretary of State James Baker had participated in the evolving Soviet–U.S. relationship, but they found it difficult to keep up with the dynamic changes that Gorbachev had unleashed to end the Cold War as well as the increasing ethnic, national, and political tensions that erupted in the Soviet empire. Bush rejected Reagan's remark that the Cold War was over and initiated a strategic review that provided very little guidance when completed in mid-March 1989. Instead, the review reflected how American officials, like many of their Soviet counterparts, were finding it difficult to shift out of the Cold War paradigm of suspicion and com-

petition. Bush, Baker, and national security adviser Brent Scowcroft preferred a return to stability and deterrence rather than the high-wire negotiations at Reykjavik and the antinuclear and anti-Soviet rhetoric of the hard-liners. Gorbachev's continuing moves to cut Soviet military spending and take Soviet missiles out of eastern Europe to support a request for the elimination of all short-range nuclear weapons in Europe, however, prompted the White House to return to negotiations with Moscow in May.

Gorbachev had urged Communist Party leaders in eastern Europe to implement reforms and warned them that the Soviet Union would not bail them out with force as it had done since 1945. Poland began belated changes in the spring of 1989 when Jaruzelski opened talks with Solidarity leaders that led to an election for the new upper house in the Polish parliament with Solidarity sweeping ninety-nine of one hundred seats. Solidarity joined a coalition government in July, an action endorsed by Gorbachev, and elected a Solidarity prime minister. Bush and his advisers recognized that the United States should support Gorbachev's willingness to allow freedom in eastern Europe by avoiding giving any ammunition to Soviet hard-liners through triumphal statements on the situation or by efforts to recruit the eastern European states to join the West against Moscow.

In the fall of 1989 the pace of change intensified as Hungary opened its western border to allow East Germans to escape to the West and the Hungarian Communist Party abandoned Leninism to become the Hungarian Socialist Party. By the end of October, Hungary had become a republic with a representative government, and national elections held in 1990 voted out the old Communist-Socialist Party. In November the East German communists dumped the veteran party leader Erich Honecker, and East Germans dramatically forced open the Berlin Wall on 9 November. On the same night, the Bulgarian Communist Party discarded Todor Zhivkov, the longest-ruling party leader in eastern Europe, and within little more than a year the party joined Zhivkov on the sidelines. Demonstrations also escalated in Czechoslovakia, leading to the resignation of Gustav Husák, another veteran communist leader, and the eventual election of Václav Havel, a leader of the opposition.

By the time Bush and Baker met with Gorbachev at a summit in Malta in December, Baker and Shevardnadze had met several times and resolved most remaining arms control issues as

Gorbachev again offered to cut offensive strategic missiles without any agreement on SDI. Despite the stormy weather that kept the U.S. and Soviet leaders confined to a docked Soviet cruise liner, Bush successfully greeted Gorbachev with a series of proposals to remove Cold War economic restrictions against the Soviet Union and to step up the pace of the START negotiations.

Germany remained the most difficult challenge for Gorbachev and Bush. The collapse of eastern Europe in 1989 intensified Soviet conservative criticism of Gorbachev, with the prospect of a united Germany, raising memories of World War II, as the issue of greatest concern. With the assistance of Western allies and West German leaders, Bush and Baker successfully went to a "two plus four" negotiating approach, with the German regimes as the "two" and the World War II Allies as the "four." Despite the mounting problems that Gorbachev faced with independence movements in Lithuania and elsewhere, and increased resistance from the Red Army and Soviet hard-liners, Baker and Bush, in numerous meetings with Shevardnadze and Gorbachev including a Washington summit in May 1990, patiently achieved a favorable settlement on Germany.

Bush and Baker had less success in satisfying critics when the focus shifted to the emerging disintegration of the Soviet Union. Liberals and moderates in Congress and the media had urged the White House to back Gorbachev, but when Gorbachev fell behind the demands for change, such as the Baltic states' insistence upon independence, these critics urged Bush to shift U.S. support to Boris Yeltsin, a former Gorbachev ally who, as president of the Russian Federation in 1991, was now leading the opposition movement seeking to get rid of Gorbachev and the Soviet Union. U.S. conservatives and hard-liners, on the other hand, resisted offering any support for Gorbachev both because they remained suspicious that his ultimate loyalty was to communism and the Soviet party and because they hoped the rollback of communism in eastern Europe would reach Moscow and other communist regimes.

By moving to negotiate with Gorbachev on a growing number of issues in 1989–1991, Bush and Baker established a successful relationship with him. Although Gorbachev and his advisers wanted quicker and more U.S. support, they came to view Bush and Baker as sympathetic officials even when the latter felt compelled to criticize Gorbachev for some of the Soviet pressure used to resist independence in Lithuania. In the context of the tremendous changes that took place in eastern Europe in 1989 and the fragmentation that occurred in the Soviet empire with the independence movements in the Baltic states, Ukraine, Belarus, Georgia, and the Central Asian regimes such as Kazakhstan, U.S. officials achieved essential objectives and at the same time avoided excessive involvement in the internal turmoil and disintegration of the Soviet empire and communist system.

CONCLUSION

In his famous article in 1947 advocating a strategy of containment against the Soviet Union, the foreign service officer George F. Kennan addressed the issue of how to achieve a successful conclusion to the expanding conflict with the Soviet Union. Kennan suggested that a patient and thoughtful policy that blended pressure and negotiations would ultimately be successful when the Soviet Union found it impossible to hold on to its new empire in eastern Europe, given the powerful nationalist forces at play in the relationship, and when the Soviet leaders abandoned their Marxist-Leninist attachment to supporting revolutionary movements and accepted normal international relations with Western capitalist states.

Kennan came fairly close to anticipating the most significant forces shaping the eventual end of the Cold War, as formally announced by the Western allies and their new Soviet partner, Gorbachev, in 1990. The U.S. strategy of containment—pursued in different forms with different rhetoric by all presidents since 1945, and pursued with failure and excess in some areas—shaped the resistance that Soviet leaders faced, both to their domestic system and revolutionary-imperial foreign policies. The broader success of the American economy, technology, commitment to freedom, and cultural appeal also ultimately stood in striking contrast to what the Soviet system looked like in all of these areas.

The end result, however, was not predetermined. Although the general economic, political, and ideological decay of the Soviet system certainly shaped Soviet policy, different leaders than Gorbachev, Shevardnadze and other "new thinking" advocates could have resisted these forces. They could have held onto eastern Europe with force if necessary and circled the wagons against the Reagan hard-liner campaign, which faced its own problems with budget deficits, the SDI controversy, and public and congressional resistance that limited the most significant Reagan Doctrine campaign to aid freedom fighters in Nicaragua.

Gorbachev and his new thinking advisers, along with Reagan and Shultz and their successors, Bush and Baker, contributed the most to shaping the endgame of the Cold War. Despite his career orientation and commitment to the Soviet Communist Party, Gorbachev made revolutionary changes in Soviet foreign policy even if his efforts to reform the Soviet economy lacked similar success. Through long exposure to new thinking ideas and advocates, Gorbachev moved as skillfully as he could to win over both Soviet hardliners and Reagan and his advisers to a significant relaxation of the Cold War, the nuclear arms race, and the expensive and destructive global Cold War competition between the two countries. When faced with resistance at home and abroad from Reagan's Cold War suspicions and inflexibility on SDI, Gorbachev stepped up both campaigns, pushing the Soviet Union toward a Western parliamentary system and moving to abandon the fundamental Marxist-Leninist class and revolutionary precepts undergirding the Soviet perspective on international relations.

Washington policymakers certainly contributed significantly to both the way the Cold War ended and the fact that it ended. The support that Reagan and the hard-liners achieved for their "victory" version of containment, particularly in their aid to the Afghanistan resistance and to Solidarity in Poland, contributed to Gorbachev's successful reorientation of policy in both areas as necessary steps to wind down the Cold War. SDI and the defense buildup, on the other hand, probably increased the resistance of Soviet conservatives and the military to any arms control agreements and delayed Gorbachev's efforts to achieve significant reductions in this area. Yet Reagan did not remain just a preacher for the hard-liner campaign. In response to the persistent campaign of George Shultz and the overall impact of Gorbachev's personality and policies, Reagan warily but steadily opened up negotiations with the evil empire and, ultimately, agreed to significant changes in arms control. Although Bush and Baker initially stepped backward, they did engage in increasing meetings, visits, talks, and summits with Gorbachev in order to manage successfully the spectacular revolution of 1989 in eastern Europe, the reunification of Germany, and the U.S. effort to establish a new relationship as the Soviet Union gave way to Russia and Gorbachev exited the stage.

BIBLIOGRAPHY

Adelman, Kenneth. *The Great Universal Embrace: Arms Summitry—A Skeptic's Account.* New York, 1989.

Baker, James A., 3d. *The Politics of Diplomacy.* New York, 1995.

Beschloss, Michael R., and Strobe Talbott. *At the Highest Levels: The Inside Story of the End of the Cold War.* Boston, 1993.

Bush, George, and Brent Scowcroft. *A World Transformed.* New York, 1998.

Cannon, Lou. *President Reagan: The Role of a Lifetime.* New York, 1991.

Cold War International History Project. *Bulletin* 5 (spring 1995) and 11 (winter 1998).

Crowe, Admiral William J. *The Line of Fire: From Washington to the Gulf, the Politics and Battles of the New Military.* New York, 1993.

Dobrynin, Anatoly. *In Confidence: Moscow's Ambassador to America's Six Cold War Presidents (1962–1986).* New York, 1995.

English, Robert D. *Russia and the Idea of the West: Gorbachev, Intellectuals, and the End of the Cold War.* New York, 2000.

Evangelista, Matthew. *Unarmed Forces: The Transnational Movement to End the Cold War.* Ithaca, N.Y., 1999.

———. "Norms, Heresthetics, and the End of the Cold War." *Journal of Cold War Studies* 3 (winter 2001): 5–35.

FitzGerald, Frances. *Way Out There in the Blue: Reagan, Star Wars, and the End of the Cold War.* New York, 2000.

Garthoff, Raymond L. *The Great Transition: American-Soviet Relations and the End of the Cold War.* Washington, D.C., 1994.

Gates, Robert M. *From the Shadows: The Ultimate Insider's Story of Five Presidents and How They Won the Cold War.* New York, 1996.

Gorbachev, Mikhail. *Memoirs.* New York, 1996.

Haig, Alexander M. *Caveat: Realism, Reagan and Foreign Policy.* New York, 1984.

Hogan, Michael J., ed. *The End of the Cold War.* New York, 1992.

Matlock, Jack F. *Autopsy on an Empire: The American Ambassador's Account of the Collapse of the Soviet Union.* New York, 1995.

McFarlane, Robert C. *Special Trust.* New York, 1994.

Mendelson, Sarah E. *Changing Course: Ideas, Politics, and the Soviet Withdrawal from Afghanistan.* Princeton, N.J., 1998.

Menges, Constantine C. *Inside the National Security Council: The True Story of the Making and Unmaking of Reagan's Foreign Policy.* New York, 1988.

Oberdorfer, Don. *The Turn: From the Cold War to a New Era: The United States and the Soviet Union, 1983–1990.* New York, 1991.

Palazchenko, Pavel. *My Years with Gorbachev and Shevardnadze: The Memoir of a Soviet Interpreter.* University Park, Pa., 1997.

Reagan, Ronald. *An American Life.* New York, 1990.

Regan, Donald T. *For the Record.* New York, 1988.

Shevardnadze, Eduard. *The Future Belongs to Freedom.* New York, 1991.

Shultz, George. *Turmoil and Triumph.* New York, 1993.

Talbott, Strobe. *Master of the Game: Paul Nitze and the Nuclear Peace.* New York, 1988.

Weinberger, Caspar. *Fighting for Peace: Seven Critical Years in the Pentagon.* New York, 1990.

See also ARMS CONTROL AND DISARMAMENT; COLD WAR EVOLUTION AND INTERPRETATIONS; COLD WAR ORIGINS; COLD WARRIORS; COVERT OPERATIONS; DOCTRINES; GLOBALIZATION; POST–COLD WAR POLICY.

COLLECTIVE SECURITY

Roland N. Stromberg

Collective security may be defined as a plan for maintaining peace through an organization of sovereign states, whose members pledge themselves to defend each other against attack. The idea emerged in 1914, was extensively discussed during World War I, and took shape rather imperfectly in the 1919 Covenant of the League of Nations and again in the Charter of the United Nations after World War II. The term has subsequently been applied to less idealistic and narrower arrangements for joint defense such as the North Atlantic Treaty Organization.

The shorthand term "collective security," not used until the 1930s, is more accurately "security for individual nations by collective means," that is, by membership in an international organization made up of all or most of the states of the world pledged to defend each other from attack. "Collective security" is a handier term, and it entered deeply into the international vocabulary when—from about 1931 to 1939—many hoped, in vain, that the League of Nations through its machinery for collective action might avert war by checking the "aggression" of the revisionist powers—Germany, Italy, and Japan.

EARLY HISTORY

Although the modern idea of collective security was born in 1914, it has roots in the distant past. Elements of collective security were present in some of the leagues of ancient Greek states, and likewise in the experiment of the Holy League in Renaissance Italy (1495). China saw some unsuccessful experiments in cooperative leagues of independent states in the seventh and sixth centuries B.C. prior to a period of bitter warfare ending in the victory of one state that imposed unity. In his *De recuperatione sanctae terrae* (ca. 1306), Pierre Dubois produced a plan of this sort in Europe, and in the seventeenth century, Maximi-

lien de Béthune, duc de Sully, produced a more famous plan, which proposed keeping the peace by general pledges to defend the territorial status quo. Similar schemes flourished in the eighteenth century, when such philosophers as Immanuel Kant and Jeremy Bentham were among the authors of "plans for perpetual peace." Among the romantic utopians of the earlier nineteenth century was Comte Henri de Saint-Simon. The little world of Swiss independent cantons proved an interesting laboratory for such experiments. Although it seldom worked effectively, collective security as a "universal alliance" of all the states within a given international system (which in former times could embrace a particular area such as China, Greece, Italy, or Switzerland) is a basic, archetypal mode of international relations, lying somewhere between total state egoism (in which states may be allied with each other in hostile or "balance of power" groupings subject to alteration) and a federated or unitary superstate that has managed to absorb the lesser sovereignties.

In the nineteenth century, the classic era of nationalism, Europe found little room for collective security. The nineteenth-century "peace movement" looked mainly in other directions. Quite vigorous in the decades preceding the outbreak of war in 1914, this world peace movement put its emphasis on arbitration, disarmament, and the growth of international law by voluntary agreement. In accordance with the spirit of the times, people felt that progress toward peace would come gradually and voluntarily. The long era of European peace embracing most of the period from 1815 to 1914, and especially from 1871 to 1914, was not favorable to the consideration of drastic plans. Most people complacently assumed that the Western world had set its feet firmly on a path that led slowly but inevitably to the extinction of war. The Hague Peace Conferences of 1899 and 1907 reflected this outlook. Leading spokesmen of the pre-1914 period rejected a "league of force" as impracticable and too extreme, although in the early 1900s there was some discussion of a European "league of peace" pledged to nonaggression and arbitration of disputes. Thus, for example, the French socialist Jean Jaurès suggested such a league in 1900.

In the realm of practical statecraft, the "concert of Europe" invoked from time to time was a nebulous conception without any permanent organization or specific constitution. A general congress of all the European powers might be assembled to deal with a particular crisis, as happened in 1856 and 1878, but this was really only an extension of the methods of traditional diplomacy, in which states negotiated with each other through their appointed agents of foreign policy. Multistate conferences of a more restricted membership, including the signatories to a particular treaty or convention, might also be held on an ad hoc basis, as, for example, the Algeciras Conference of 1906 that dealt with the Moroccan crisis. In such meetings of the powers there was at most a faint foreshadowing of a permanent and regularized international league or society.

WORLD WAR I AND THE LEAGUE OF NATIONS

The shock of August 1914 forced total reconsideration. The old ways of diplomacy—rival alliances and balances of power—appeared to have failed. One could no longer believe in the path of steady progress toward international order. Bolder remedies were needed if civilization was not to be destroyed by devastating wars. Numerous schemes soon proposed basic reorganization to end the "international anarchy" that, a consensus held, had been responsible for the coming of the war. The most important of these plans, beginning with Sir James Bryce's proposals in 1914 and including the American-based League to Enforce Peace, as well as the Fabian Society plan, asked the nations of the world to join a league or association of nations, and in so doing to agree to submit their disputes to arbitration or mediation before going to war and to apply penalties or sanctions to any member state that resorted to war without so doing. As Bryce put it, "The League shall undertake to defend any one of its members who may be attacked by any other State who has refused to accept Arbitration or Conciliation."

These theorists assumed realistically that the hour was not ripe for a world state and that

sovereign states cannot be coerced, but they hoped that states would voluntarily accept and honor such a pledge in the cause of peace. Some critics thought that these collective security proposals did not go far enough, since states could still in the end resort to war; others felt they went too far, since no great power could or would bind itself in advance in any significant way.

Uncertainty also existed about who should belong to the league, especially with reference to the enemy powers in the ongoing war; about the mode of representation; and about the method of identifying aggression and responding to it. This far-ranging discussion tended to expose as many difficulties as it resolved. Underlying it was the urgent feeling that somehow the scourge of war had to be eliminated, under pain of the extinction of civilization, and that the old idea of "selfish nationalism" was bankrupt. Yet informed people also knew that nationalism was far from a spent force and that no chance then existed to set up a world superstate. Collective security hoped to establish a halfway house on the road to true world government. Its advocates frequently cited the analogy of a vigilante stage of law enforcement, one in which, prior to the arrival of formal government, settlers suppressed crime by forming a posse or voluntary citizens' organization.

During World War I, many organizations and individuals contributed to the formulation of plans for a league of nations. In the United States, the League to Enforce Peace included former president William Howard Taft, Harvard president A. Lawrence Lowell, and a host of other prominent citizens. Lord Bryce or his colleague G. Lowes Dickinson may best be given credit for initiating the entire discussion, but an extensive British debate also featured books by Leonard Woolf and H. N. Brailsford, among others; a committee headed by Sir Walter Phillimore eventually produced an official British plan. The numerous plans varied in details, but all sought to unite the major states of the world in a permanent organization, in which they would be represented as states and which would have power to deal with their disputes and prevent war. The broad concept of a "league to enforce peace" was endorsed "not only by pacifists and thinkers, but by practical statesmen." It was the great idea of the years from 1914 to 1918, although skeptical criticism was not lacking even then.

Although there was some interest in collective security in France and in the neutral countries (the Netherlands, for example), the ideas that were to be incorporated into the League of Nations came mainly from Anglo-American sources. It is a mistake to attribute these ideas preeminently to President Woodrow Wilson, as is frequently done. Wilson showed relatively little interest in any explicit plan for a league based on collective security principles until quite late. At Paris he played a part in framing the Covenant of the League of Nations but received assistance from his aide, Colonel Edward M. House, U.S. adviser David Hunter Miller, British advisers Lord Robert Cecil and Sir Cecil Hurst, and South African leader General Jan C. Smuts. Wilson did of course become an earnest and tireless advocate of the League of Nations Covenant.

This covenant, drawn up at Paris in 1919 and made part of the Treaty of Versailles imposed on a defeated Germany, was an incongruous amalgamation of the various ideas discussed during the war and was destined to have a disappointing life. Article 10, the most controversial and debated provision, seemed to demand of member states an obligation to "preserve as against external aggression the territorial integrity and existing political independence of all members of the League." But, in fact, the league, through its council (upper chamber), could only request them to act, not force them to do so. Some of the issues that were to plague collective security thus arose early: Is it possible to get binding commitments from states to suppress any future forcible alteration of the status quo? Is this even desirable, since the status quo may not be just or reasonable, at least not to everybody?

Although the French (for obvious reasons) asked for the creation of an international army under control of the League of Nations, this idea received no serious support. Frightened by the specter of American soldiers being summoned to fight on foreign soil at the behest of an alien organization, the Senate refused to ratify the Treaty of Versailles. Thus, the United States did not become a member of the league, nor was the new, outcast Russian socialist state a member. Also excluded at first were the defeated powers of World War I. The league thus began life with serious, if not fatal, handicaps. In 1924 and 1925 the security-conscious states—such as Poland and Czechoslovakia, which had profited by the peace settlement, or France, which most feared any revision of it—unsuccessfully tried to clarify and tighten the security obligations of members.

It thus became evident that the league would have to function in ways other than as an agent of collective security standing guard against revision of boundaries. In the 1920s, Geneva became instead a place of diplomacy and conciliation, along with more modest forms of functional international cooperation. Germany's entrance into the league in 1926 signaled this change of perspective. For a number of years little was heard about plans to suppress war by joint military action; much was said of the uses of the league to help cultivate habits of negotiation and peaceful settlement of disputes between nations. "Collective security" lay dormant. The events of the 1930s revived it.

American opinion in the 1920s strongly opposed any political involvement in the quarrels of Europe and was all but unanimous in rejecting an obligation to act as policeman in areas outside the Western Hemisphere. The treaties of peace executed after the war had become unpopular, and many regarded them as unjust and unlikely to last. The United States participated in most of the nonpolitical activities of the League of Nations and also played a leading part in the movement to "outlaw war" by voluntary renunciation, which culminated in the Kellogg-Briand Pact (1928), but it exhibited an almost pathological fear of any commitment that might entail the possible use of armed force in some "foreign quarrel." (Intervention in the small Caribbean countries lying at the doorstep of the United States might be another matter, although there was also a reaction against this sort of "imperialism.") This fear of repeating what a large majority of Americans now regarded as the terrible mistake of having entered World War I receded only slowly in the 1930s under the threat of a renewal of war in Europe and Asia. Initial American reaction to rumblings of conflict from 1931 on was to reaffirm vows not to be duped again by appeals to "save the world" by marching off to fight in Europe. The Great Depression intensified these feelings by intruding much more urgent questions of domestic recovery and reform. Isolationism reached its peak from 1934 to 1936, when legislation attempted to cut ties between the United States and all belligerent countries in the event of war, without discriminating between aggressor and victim.

THE 1930S AND THE FAILURE OF THE LEAGUE OF NATIONS

The international disturbances of the troubled 1930s began with the Japanese extension of military control over Manchuria in 1931. This was followed by the Italian campaign in Ethiopia in 1935 and Adolf Hitler's demands that the "fetters of Versailles" be smashed and that the German nation be allowed lebensraum (living space) for expansion. In 1936, Germany reoccupied the Rhineland (where, by the terms of the Versailles Treaty, it was not supposed to have armed forces) and in 1938 annexed Austria. Czechoslovakia followed in 1939. Faced with this determined assault on the post–World War I boundaries, diplomats in western Europe and in the Soviet Union, which joined the league in 1934, sought to make the machinery of the league an effective tool of war prevention by means of collective action against "aggression."

The attempt was not successful. Although Japan received a verbal rebuke from the league in 1933 for its behavior in Manchuria, it simply resigned from the league and did not end its forward policies in China, which may even have been stimulated by what was construed in Japan as a hypocritical insult. Following the eloquent appeal of Ethiopian emperor Haile Selassie for aid, the league, under British leadership, tried to organize economic sanctions against Italy in 1935, but that did not prevent the Italian conquest of Ethiopia and probably helped move Benito Mussolini closer to Hitler's side. The embargo was not sufficiently enforceable to be effective. This fiasco, which ended in a British-French retreat from high principles to offer Italy a compromise deal (the Hoare-Laval proposals), did much to diminish enthusiasm for collective security through the League of Nations. Direct negotiations between the major European powers during the tense crises of 1938 and 1939 bypassed the machinery of the league.

But many came to believe that a more vigorous and less selfish support of the league might have checked the aggressions of Japan, Italy, and Germany and prevented World War II. In much of the literature on the origins of the war, collective security appeared as the opposite of "appeasement," which had gambled on winning the goodwill of Germany by yielding to its demands. The lesson that one should never appease (yield to) the demands of an aggressive "criminal" nation became deeply engraved in the public mind during the grim years when Hitler's appetite only grew with eating. And the dishonor of the 1938 Munich "appeasement" did not prevent war the following year. Popular, too, was a similar thesis applied to Japan's expansion in the Pacific.

Between 1938 and 1941, American opinion shifted dramatically toward the view that isolationism, or the avoidance of American responsibility to keep the world secure from aggression, had been a fearful blunder. To this was added the widespread belief that the United States should have followed Wilson's vision, joined the League of Nations, upheld collective security, and thus prevented World War II.

Critics were to cast doubt on this interpretation insofar as it involved the assumption that the league represented anything more than the sum of its parts. The league obviously commanded no military power of its own. If Great Britain, France, the Soviet Union, and the United States could not see their way to thwarting Hitler's goals at the risk of war, as a matter of national interest, the league could not help them. If they would not help the league, it was impotent. The league might at most supply convenient machinery or a meeting place, but what really mattered was the will to resist, which was notably lacking in the democracies in these years. Some argued that the idea of collective security was even an obstacle to a firm policy, because public opinion at times, as in England in the mid-1930s, tended to look upon collective security and the league as a substitute for national power. Evidently, some people thought that if only the problem of stopping the dictators could be turned over to Geneva, nothing need be done by the separate nations. This clearly was a dangerous illusion.

THE UNITED NATIONS AND THE COLD WAR

World War II brought a surge of hope that a revised League of Nations, now supported by the United States and the Soviet Union and profiting from the lessons of the 1930s, might serve as the basis for a new international order. Because the League of Nations had become discredited, especially in the eyes of the Soviet Union, which was expelled from the league in 1940 for attacking Finland, it was necessary to create a new world organization. With strong support from American public opinion, the United Nations was officially established in 1945 after earlier conferences and discussions. It differed in some particulars from the League of Nations but reflected the same basic philosophy of collective security. In order to make it more effective, the United Nations Charter placed more power in the hands of the five major states, which were given veto powers and permanent representation in the upper chamber, the Security Council, which had exclusive jurisdiction in security matters. Initially, the Security Council also had six nonpermanent members. (This was later expanded to ten.) Based according to the charter on "the principle of the sovereign equality of all its members," all of which pledged themselves to "refrain in their international relations from the threat or use of force against the territorial integrity or political independence of any state," the United Nations endowed the Security Council with "primary responsibility for the maintenance of international peace and security," charging other members with a duty to "accept and carry out the decisions of the Security Council." Seven of the eleven votes were declared necessary to decide substantive issues, including the votes of all the permanent members—the United States, the Soviet Union, China, France, and the United Kingdom. The Security Council "shall determine the existence of any threat to the peace, breach of the peace, or act of aggression" and decide what to do, including taking "such action by air, sea or land forces as may be necessary to maintain or restore international peace and security." The idea of the "four policemen" (China, the Soviet Union, Britain, and the United States), each maintaining peace in its area of the globe, was one popular formulation of this big-power conception of collective security, which encountered some criticism from the smaller countries but appeared practicable as a continuation of the wartime alliance against the Axis.

Once the war was over, amity dissolved in quarrels between the United States and the Soviet Union. Their continued goodwill and cooperation was a condition for United Nations success. The spreading post-1945 Cold War between the Soviet (and soon Chinese) and U.S.–west European blocs ensured the failure of collective security and rendered the United Nations increasingly irrelevant except as one more arena for the power struggle between the blocs.

Critics of collective security pointed out at this time that as a plan of war prevention it suffers from the defect of assuming the problem already solved. It assumes that the great majority of the world powers are naturally peace loving, and that war is caused only by the occasional transgressions of a bad nation, led into wickedness by unusual circumstances. If this is true, the problem of war is not so great in any case. Put concretely, if the superpowers could keep on friendly terms

and cooperate for world peace, all would be reasonably well; if they could not, then no collective security plan could work. Under Cold War conditions, collective security's inclination to use force to defend peace—always something of a paradox—became a positive menace.

In 1950 the United States took the lead in persuading the United Nations Security Council to condemn the aggression of North Korea against South Korea, in a land left divided by the post-1945 Soviet-American rift. The apparently fortuitous absence from the Security Council at that time of the Soviet Union, which otherwise could have vetoed the resolution, facilitated this decision. A major war ensued in Korea, as United Nations forces, of which the great majority were American, turned back the North Korean "aggressors" and then invaded the north, only to encounter Chinese intervention. The paradox of calling war on this scale a peaceable "police action" struck home forcibly. Not everyone was then persuaded that North Korea was the aggressor, although, subsequently, clear evidence emerged that, encouraged by China and the USSR, it did launch an overt attack in 1950. Border incidents and provocations in an unnaturally divided land had been going on for several years, and the UN forces, commanded by an American general, Douglas MacArthur, seemed less those of the United Nations than of the United States. The armistice negotiated in 1953, which left the north-south border in Korea not far from where it had originally been, underscored the futility of the enterprise, if one thought of it as "punishing the aggressor." Although initially it was hailed as a successful application of collective security, and many continued to believe in resisting the expansion of communist power, the Korean War tended to discredit collective security.

THE DECLINE OF COLLECTIVE SECURITY

United Nations forces went into the Congo in some strength in 1961 under conditions of chaos and strife in that recently liberated former Belgian colony, as leaders spoke of "putting out a brush fire" before it became a major conflagration. The UN force in the Congo suffered from divided counsel, reflecting the divergent aims of the various interests involved: East, West, and Third World. The action was hardly a success and resulted in fresh disillusionment with use of the

United Nations as a military force. From this time on, "crisis management" took the form of direct negotiations between the powers concerned, or special conferences, with the United Nations usually playing a peripheral role as supplier of truce-observing teams.

The North Atlantic Treaty Organization paved the way for thinking of regional resistance to communist expansion as "collective security." Created in 1949 as an alliance between states of noncommunist Europe with Canada and the United States, it was a reaction to the Soviet threat to Europe (real or imagined). American ideologists justified it as something more than an old-fashioned military alliance based as of yore on the realities of power in a world of hostile blocs. During the 1950s, it became a means of persuading the American people that they might, against all their ancestral instincts, take part in the tangled and violent affairs of the world without sullying their innocence; they would have many allies and act jointly against the forces of evil. The Cold War converted the term into a commitment to check, "contain," if not suppress the USSR and communism. Called "collective security," it was somewhat uneasily squared with the United Nations Charter by an appeal to Articles 51 and 52, which referred to the validity of "collective self-defense" via "regional arrangements." It was argued that the paralysis of the United Nations, resulting from Soviet noncooperation, forced recourse to such arrangements. In the wake of NATO's apparent success in "containing" Soviet expansion in Europe, American policy sought, with little success, to create other regional security groupings, including the Southeast Asia Treaty Organization (SEATO) and Central Treaty Organization (CENTO) in the Middle East.

The most traumatic international conflict of the 1960s, the Vietnam War, also had an anti–collective security fallout. The motives for American entry into Indochina initially included a feeling, derived from the collective security complex of ideas, that aggression was being checked in the spirit, if not exactly the letter, of the United Nations Charter. Behind the designs of North Vietnam to unite a war-divided country under its leadership, many saw the expansion of a monolithic Asiatic communism centered in China, and they invoked the lesson of the Hitler years: Draw the line and fight rather than allow "appeasement" to erode your position. Collective security as a factor in the crucial decisions of the Cold War is often understressed if not overlooked. It is for-

gotten that in Korea, then in Vietnam, the fighting was not just to check communism but to defend world order by punishing "aggression." Leaders like Harry Truman, Dwight Eisenhower, John Kennedy, and Lyndon Johnson might not have taken their agonizingly close decisions to send U.S. troops to far places without the reassuring motive of war prevention; the naked idea of simple American self-interest was not enough.

The initially small U.S. involvement in Southeast Asia, joined by some forces from other SEATO members, swelled into the nightmare of major war as the conflict steadily escalated, creating a formidable backlash of public opinion against the war in the United States and elsewhere. Some of the key themes of collective security suffered severe damage in the revolution of opinion resulting from the Vietnam War (1957–1975). The so-called Nixon Doctrine announced an American withdrawal from unlimited commitments to serve as policeman in remote places. It may be added that during the Vietnam War, the United Nations was almost altogether excluded from important negotiations. At various times each side brought complaints of "aggression" before the Security Council—Laos in 1959 against Hanoi, Cambodia in 1964 against the United States and South Vietnam, the United States later the same year against Hanoi—but these resulted in no action and were employed chiefly for propaganda purposes. Both the Geneva Accords of 1954 and the Paris Conference peace settlement of 1973 completely ignored the United Nations. This was unquestionably a blow to the prestige of the United Nations, although optimists might point out that the admission of Communist China to the United Nations in 1971 made it a more ecumenical body. Exclusion of mainland China from the United Nations had prevented use of that organization in matters involving Chinese interests.

The assumption of the classical collective security doctrine that "aggressors" were always wicked, rogue nations that ought to be resisted and punished, was contradicted in the notable case of Israel and the Palestinian Arabs. However justified on grounds of ancient possession, redress of recent injustices elsewhere, or superior civilization, Jewish incursions into Palestine from the 1948 takeover surely constituted an aggression rarely equaled in modern history. But in the Arab-Israeli conflict the United States and most of its European allies supported the latter, making the Jewish nation virtually an ally and the recipient of lavish support, from motives of sentiment and interest. In 1956, President Eisenhower (to the amazement of the Soviet leaders) was indeed so shocked by the case of planned aggression against Egypt of France and Britain along with Israel that a rift in the NATO alliance temporarily appeared. But thereafter the United States reverted to almost uncritical support of Israel, often voting in the United Nations with a tiny minority against any condemnation of the Jewish state.

"Collective security" is still frequently used to describe the North Atlantic Treaty Organization. In this usage it merely means military cooperation between allied states or having allies for defense against a common enemy. Needless to say, "security" and "cooperation for security" are common terms. But, in its original sense, of a new plan for world peace based on a "universal alliance" and pledges to suppress war by joint action of all its members against aggression, collective security seems to have become a casualty of history. "The growing tendency for States to revert to a reliance on force as a means of resolving their international differences," as former UN Secretary General U Thant said in 1970, might be blamed on the United Nations itself or more often on the "selfishness" of powers that do not give it necessary support.

Revision of the UN charter as a means to improvement no longer arouses much enthusiasm; the roots of the problem are recognized as going deeper. Changes in the charter included enlarging the Security Council, but the five permanent members and the veto power remain the same. Paralyzed by the vetoes of the superpowers, the Security Council diminished in importance during the Cold War. Its concept of a dictatorship of a few big powers became outmoded in view of the flood of new, smaller states that has more than doubled United Nations membership since 1960. In the 1950s the General Assembly asserted its own right to recommend action in support of peace and security (the Uniting for Peace Resolution), but it can only recommend.

"Peacekeeping" is increasingly distinguished and dissociated from collective security, the stress being placed not on a large UN army capable of crushing an aggressor, but on small, noncombat units, serving only with permission of the host country and acting as observers of truces or as buffers along sensitive frontiers. Disputes and financial problems plagued even these forces, though they served useful functions in Cyprus and New Guinea, and on the Israeli-Egyptian border (intermittently). At the beginning of the twenty-first century, more than 40,000 UN peacekeepers were stationed around the world, at rather randomly chosen trouble spots such as East Timor and Sierra Leone, but—ill trained and forbidden anything but "neutral" actions—they were often pathetic. In November 2000, Indian and Moroccan soldiers of the UN force in Sierra Leone were withdrawn because they were not safe; assaulted and kidnapped, they had to be rescued by British troops (who did not plan to stay). Vows to improve this performance periodically came from UN headquarters but had little effect. Some private organizations like Oxfam, Greenpeace, and Amnesty International provided as much help. The outmoded UN membership structure allowed no place as permanent member of the Security Council for such important countries as Japan, India, and Brazil. Its own claims to internationalism were thus rather dubious.

A NEW FORM OF INTERVENTIONISM

In the last decades of the twentieth century, military interventions took a different form and were justified in different ways. Peace broke out among the major powers of Europe that had waged war against each other in the past so many times, for reasons that had little to do with collective action against aggression. The Cold War standoff between two great blocs that characterized the decades after 1945 also ended with the collapse of the Soviet communist side in the late 1980s and the beginning of the 1990s. In other parts of the world, and indeed in southeastern Europe, the problem was less about armed aggression across borders than about upholding order within collapsing states. In her *New and Old Wars* (1999), Mary Kaldor described the new kind of violence as a "mixture of war, organized crime, and massive violations of human rights." Ethnic feuds that crossed boundaries, civil wars, guerrilla movements, and private armies appeared in states that were breaking up or, as in much of Africa, not clearly defined. For example, guerrilla warfare in Colombia, anarchy in Bosnia, and ethnic massacres in Burundi did not involve repelling an invasion of one nation by another. It was even hard to find an "aggressor": though blame might be placed on Serb wickedness in Bosnia and Kosovo, or on the Hutus of Rwanda and Burundi for unleashing the latest round of genocide in 1994, in fact these were ancient feuds in which both sides had been guilty many times. This did not prevent brutal punishment of the Serbs for committing savagery in Kosovo, but this NATO action, not approved by the UN Security Council, was hardly a "collective security" success, leaving as it did the problem in Kosovo, as in Bosnia, still unresolved. When the United States and NATO decided in 1999 to condemn and then bomb Serbia for its atrocious actions in Kosovo, they chose a shocking episode of violence and genocide ("ethnic cleansing") that did not at all fit the collective security model, for here was no case of one nation assaulting another: Kosovo, like Bosnia, was a part of the Yugoslav state that Serbia headed. This was a civil war resulting from the dissolution of the Yugoslavia created in 1919.

Huge losses of life, dwarfing even those of the two great European or World Wars of the first half of the twentieth century, occurred in these new wars outside the Western world or on its fringes. A true holocaust took place in Cambodia from 1975 to 1979, barely noticed at the time, conducted by a regime that Western governments recognized and evidently approved of. No one knows quite how many millions were slain, not by nuclear bombs or even guns but hacked to pieces by knives. In Algeria, a ferocious internal war took an estimated 100,000 lives, in massacres first by terrorist rebels and then by government death squads.

There were literally millions of killings in Rwanda and Burundi. So many other instances of deadly internal conflict throughout the world came into view that the public mind became saturated with them. They were usually in places formerly remote, but now very much a part of the international society, such as Sri Lanka, Indonesia, Afghanistan, Azerbaijan, many parts of Africa from Angola and Sierra Leone to the Sudan, and so on. But they also appeared in southeastern Europe.

"Security" was not a factor in the new interventionism. Nobody thought of Serbia, much less Sierra Leone, as a threat to the security of the United States or Great Britain or the NATO powers, or indeed to anybody to any serious degree except themselves. In British Prime Minister Tony Blair's words, this was "a new internationalism where the brutal repression of whole ethnic groups will no longer be tolerated," an internationalism defined by intervention to prevent or punish "massive violation of human rights" or "crimes against humanity," committed usually by a government against its own people, or by one segment of its people against another. In the case of Bosnia, the motive for intervention was partly to limit and punish ethnic massacres, partly just to end the chaos and confusion of a region left stranded by the dissolution of Yugoslavia.

The trouble with this doctrine was that its application was selective to the point of whimsy, and thus subject to the criticism of being hypocritical, even cynical. Russia did things in Chechnya similar to what Serbia did in Kosovo, but there was no thought of intervention, and only the mildest of protests, because Russia was, well, Russia, a great power still and a nuclear one. There were worse massacres in several places in Africa but no intervention. "Why do British troops help to bring peace to Bosnia and Kosovo but not to Angola and Sudan?" asked Douglas Hurd. The other problem was that where such humanitarian interventions did take place, they did little good and had to be prolonged into something like permanent occupations. (NATO and international forces entered Bosnia in 1996 promising to stay only a year; five years later they were still there with the situation almost as bad as before. Only the continued presence of UN forces prevented more bloodbaths; no legal system was in effect, and murder and gangsterism were prevalent. The punitive bombing of Belgrade left the economy not only of Serbia but also of much of the adjoining region a shambles.) British Foreign Secretary Robin Cook argued that a few such interventions might "deter future perpetrators of crimes against humanity," but this seemed to the highest degree improbable.

The Soviet Union's massive invasion of Afghanistan in 1979 and 1980 elicited from the United States only the response of a boycott of the Olympic Games being held in Moscow, though subsequently much aid was given to the Afghan resistance. But in 1991, Iraq's attempt to seize its small neighbor Kuwait resulted in the Persian Gulf War, which repelled this invasion. Here was a classic case of aggression. The United Nations approved the response, which was overwhelmingly an American military action, although other NATO powers contributed. The Soviet Union was then in the process of dissolution, and its total disarray precluded any Russian veto. But many Middle Eastern countries remained aloof or disapproved, and the outcome was not very satisfactory. While Iraqi forces were defeated and expelled from Kuwait, the Iraqi regime that had launched the attack remained in power and the issue of how to handle Saddam Hussein became a headache and a source of divisions within the West for the next ten years.

DILEMMAS OF COLLECTIVE SECURITY

In brief, the world seemed to be back in that state of international anarchy, in which power alone counted, from which it was to have been rescued by collective security. To sum up the analysis, collective security failed to find a compromise between national and world sovereignty because sovereignty is inherently indivisible. In the last analysis, sovereign states cannot be fully bound by pledges to act in some hypothetical future case, especially where such pledges involve the risk of war. Plans for collective security demand such ironclad commitments, or the system decays into just another instrument of national policy (as the United Nations has tended to become). United Nations actions do not supersede politics among nations; they become a branch of these politics. The United Nations only mirrors the existing international society. National sovereignties remain the basis of world politics, and in the last analysis these sovereignties will agree to cooperate only so far as that serves their interests. Such cooperation may indeed accord with their interests at times, but there is no assurance that it will. The larger powers (who, after all, must bear the major burdens of enforcing peace under a collective security system) have never been willing to give an unconditional commitment to carry out the commands of the world organization; they have always reserved for themselves some escape hatch. They have never been willing to set up an international army of any significant strength, under direct control of the League of Nations or the United Nations without strings attached. This is to say that it still is a world of nationalism and national states. If a world superstate could somehow be set up, this would obviate and supersede collective security, which in theory is a hypothetical stage somewhere in between. In the terminology of the German sociologist Karl Mannheim, collective security is a "relative utopia"—one that tries to be realistic but retains elements of fantasy.

An army under the direct control of the international organization, one that could be used without asking permission of the various member states, seems necessary to collective security; otherwise, as has been the case, it must make ad hoc requests for military contingents, which the various governments may or may not choose to honor, depending on their interests. If it had its own army, the United Nations would already be a world government, possessing sovereign powers over the subordinate member units.

One of the illusions of collective security, as was observed, seems to be that conflict is relatively rare, is a product of criminality, and can readily be recognized as "aggression" and as such suppressed by the great majority of law-abiding, peace-loving peoples. But conflict is both much more endemic in the world and much less possible to categorize as good and evil than this theory concedes. Aggression has proved much more difficult to identify and to define than collective security plans foresaw. In such clashes as those between Israel and the Arab states, North and South Vietnam, North and South Korea, India and Pakistan, and perhaps most others, there is great difficulty in ascertaining who in fact struck the first blow, as well as a certain aridity in making this the crux of the matter. Does aggression include indirect attacks such as subversion and propaganda? How far back in time should one carry the feud? What states were ever at war and did not each charge the other with the aggression? Historians still debate the responsibility for World War I and most other wars. In this respect, Hitler's unashamed Realpolitik from 1936 to 1941 was a rarity in the history of wars.

Although some have argued that any "breach of the peace" ought to be a signal for a "police action" by the world organization, regardless of who is responsible, or have suggested formal tests such as willingness to submit the dispute to an arbitrator or mediator, in fact the validity of the theory seems to depend on clear criteria of aggression. But attempts to reach a satisfactory definition of aggression failed in long years of debate, first in the League of Nations and then in the United Nations. Some argued that a definition is undesirable, because it could not cover all the contingencies and would be "a signpost for the guilty and a trap for the innocent." States might find themselves in the position of having to act against a friend or defend a foe. The reality of international relations in a world of particular sovereignties thus again confuses and thwarts the ideal of a pure collective security system. (After twenty-four years of effort, the United Nations Special Committee in 1974 did finally agree on a tortuous definition of aggression, but one too full of exceptions to be very helpful.)

There is also the argument of redundancy. A workable collective security order is one in which most of the powers are in harmony, and which has enough unity to agree on basic definitions, for example, of justice and aggression. It is significant that the idea has come into play in state systems marked by considerable underlying cultural unity, as in ancient China or modern Europe. But if there is this much unity, there is hardly any need to install a system of collective security, for the problem will virtually solve itself. To create the formal institution of a League of Nations or United Nations does not alter the existing order of power and international relations.

Insofar as collective security is based on a firm defense of existing borders, it is open to criticism on the ground that this freezes the status quo. This raises the problem of justice. Many states will not accept the justice of existing boundaries, which probably reflect the results of recent war and may contain arrangements clearly unacceptable to the losers. Many groups fervently advance claims for the revision of frontiers at all times, as, for example, at the beginning of the twenty-first century with the Arabs and Pakistanis. Collective security thus was in danger of being labeled the selfish policy of satiated or victor states. (Germany consistently viewed it in that light between the world wars.) One must allow for some method of revising existing boundaries or one has condemned a dynamic world to immobility, which clearly is impossible. Proponents of collective security may urge "peaceful change," but how is this to come about? Their theory contains no specific answer. In a world without a single government possessing laws and courts that are binding on and acceptable to all, war must remain a possible last-resort remedy for injustice. Here we impinge upon arguments against pure pacifism and confront again the nonexistence of world government. It may be noted that support for wars of revolution and "liberation" runs counter to collective security's immobilism. Those who believe that there is indeed a "just war" for national independence, recovery of a region forcibly seized in the past by another state, overthrow of an oppressive government, or some other such compelling cause will defend the right to resort to it rather than submit indefinitely to an unjust peace. (In the late 1960s and early 1970s the United Nations General Assembly, with a Third World majority, voted that nations should wage war on the "racist" government of Rhodesia, not for violating any frontier, but for being unjust.)

Insofar as it is based on guaranteeing frontiers, collective security assumes not only that these frontiers are just but also that they are well-defined. Collective security was more suited to the classical European state system than to much of the world today, where boundaries are ill defined or even nonexistent, and where civil wars, wars of secession, and wars of "liberation"—sometimes with outside aid—are the most usual types of violent conflict.

Finally, the basic dilemma of collective security is—assuming its efficacy—that of waging of war to prevent war. War by any other name, including "police action," is still war. Of course, the advocates of collective security hoped that vigilant international police work performed in time would nip a potential war in the bud—stamp out the brush fire before it became a raging inferno. But experiences such as Vietnam suggest that well-intentioned interventions of this sort may result not in diminishing war but intensifying it. Intervention by outside powers, even if acting in the name of an international organization, is, after all, not usually apt to reduce a conflict. In principle, collective security abolishes neutrality; no state may stand aside and observe, all must become involved to stop a war. (The 1930s saw a considerable debate on the implications of the new doctrine for traditional neutrality.) But the venerable principle of neutrality may be valuable in confining the scope of a war. To abandon it may involve the risk of widening wars.

In this connection, "limited war" theorists and strategists advise accepting the inevitability of war while seeking to keep it as confined and limited as possible, rather than trying vainly to abolish it. Collective security has been accused of unrealistically demanding the total suppression of war, and in its anxiety to achieve that goal, blowing up every skirmish into an international crisis.

The criticisms have called seriously into question the workability of collective security, perhaps the chief idea of the twentieth century addressed to the problem of war. It was born of the shock of 1914 and nourished by the further horror of World War II. Its goal was to bring an end to the "international anarchy" of blindly competing states, acknowledging no limitations on their powers except those of brute force. Recognizing the existence of nationalism as a powerful fact not likely soon to be extinguished, followers of collective security conceded to realism that dreams of a world state are as yet wholly premature; they tried to build on the foundation of independent sovereignties a society or league of nations to which these sovereign powers would offer their voluntary cooperation, in the common interest of suppressing war. In the last analysis such a compromise between national and international sovereignty seems impossible—the gulf is unbridgeable. Those who are unprepared to accept continuing prospects of rivalry between nations and peoples, mitigated only by diplomacy and leading intermittently to war, must face the formidable task of creating a world community able to support a world government.

BIBLIOGRAPHY

Bassett, Reginald. *Democracy and Foreign Policy: A Case History, the Sino-Japanese Dispute, 1931–1933.* London and New York, 1968.

Bloomfield, Lincoln Palmer. *The United Nations and U.S. Foreign Policy.* Boston, 1960.

———. *The U.N. and Vietnam.* New York, 1968.

Bowie, Robert R., and Richard H. Immerman. *Waging Peace: How Eisenhower Shaped an Enduring Cold War Strategy.* New York, 1998.

Claude, Inis L. *The United Nations and the Use of Force.* New York, 1961.

Current, Richard N. "The United States and 'Collective Security': Notes on the History of an Idea." In Alexander DeConde, ed. *Isolation and Security: Ideas and Interests in Twentieth-Century American Foreign Policy.* Durham, N.C., 1957. Semantically helpful.

Finkelstein, Marina S., and Lawrence S. Finkelstein, comps. and eds. *Collective Security.* San Francisco, 1966. A handy collection of readings.

Gaddis, John Lewis. *Strategies of Containment: A Critical Appraisal of Postwar American National Security Policy.* New York and Oxford, 1982.

Goldstein, Avery. *Deterrence and Security in the Twenty-first Century: China, Britain, France, and the Enduring Legacy of the Nuclear Revolution.* Stanford, Calif., 2000.

Haas, Ernst B. *Collective Security and the Future International System.* Denver, Colo., 1968.

Hatton, Ragnhild, and J. S. Bromley, eds. *William III and Louis XIV: Essays 1680–1720, by and for Mark A. Thomson.* Toronto and Liverpool, 1968. A useful case study.

Hemleben, Sylvester John. *Plans for World Peace through Six Centuries.* Chicago, 1943. Early history of the idea of collective security.

Howard, Michael Eliot. *The Invention of Peace: Reflections on War and International Order.* New Haven, Conn., 2001.

James, Alan. *The Politics of Peace-keeping.* London and New York, 1969.

Kaplan, Lawrence S. *The United States and NATO: The Formative Years.* Lexington, Ky., 1984.

Kuehl, Warren F. *Seeking World Order: The United States and International Organization to 1920.* Nashville, Tenn., 1969. A history of the American approach to international organizations to 1920.

Lefever, Ernest W. *Uncertain Mandate: Politics of the U.N. Congo Operation.* Baltimore, 1967.

McNamara, Robert S., et al. *Argument without End: In Search of Answers to the Vietnam Tragedy.* New York, 1999.

Rappard, William E. *Collective Security in Swiss Experience, 1291–1948.* London, 1948. A case study of interest.

Stromberg, Roland N. *Collective Security and American Foreign Policy: From the League of Nations to NATO.* New York, 1963.

———. "Uncertainties and Obscurities about the League of Nations." *Journal of the History of Ideas.* 23 (January–March 1972): 139–154. Mixes analysis with history.

Williams, Bruce Stockton. *State Security and the League of Nations.* Baltimore, 1927.

See also ALLIANCES, COALITIONS, AND ENTENTES; ARBITRATION, MEDIATION, AND CONCILIATION; GLOBALIZATION; INTERNATIONALISM; INTERNATIONAL ORGANIZATION; INTERVENTION AND NONINTERVENTION; PEACE MOVEMENTS.

COLONIALISM AND NEOCOLONIALISM

Edward M. Bennett

Traditionally, colonialism is understood to refer to an area of the world acquired by conquering the territory or settling it with inhabitants of the nation holding it in control, thereby imposing physical control over the region and its population. There are two ways this condition may be terminated: the area may be freed of the control of the colonial power by allowing it to become an independent nation, or if the area is absorbed into the borders of the controlling nation.

The United States began its history as a colonial possession of Great Britain and confronted two other colonial powers in contiguous areas during its infancy and contested France and Spain for control of that territory. After the American Revolution, gradually the European powers were expelled, and the new United States expanded its influence by absorbing the contiguous territories until it controlled the area it occupies today. (Later, Russia was one of those powers expelled.) A debate has ensued concerning whether in this process the United States became a colonial power by its absorption of these areas. This discourse continues, but by the traditional definitions of colonialism, the American experience is quite different from that which characterized the European colonial tradition, as it was not until the late nineteenth century that the United States entered the race for noncontiguous colonies.

With the elimination of colonialism per se in the twentieth century, there emerged a new form, called neocolonialism, which may be defined as the establishment of a form of sovereignty or control without the encumbrance of physical possession or actual colonial rule. Here, the United States may be defined as a neocolonial power because it influences less powerful or Third World nations by its economic authority exercised through its control or preeminent influence on such agencies as the World Bank and the International Monetary Fund. When this new colonialism began is another debatable question, but there can be no argument with

the assertion that it was certainly in place shortly after World War II and may have begun with the Marshall Plan.

COLONIALISM AND IMPERIALISM

Colonialism began as a descriptive term and subsequently assumed a pejorative connotation. In recent times, most studies of the subject have focused attention on attacking both the idea and its practitioners but have also tended to confuse it with imperialism to such a degree as to blur the lines of distinction between the two. (Some people have argued that neocolonialism is a form of imperialism, but this is a specious argument because each has a distinct and separate existence.) It is necessary to discuss imperialism in the context of colonialism and to make the differences clear. For example, it is possible to be imperialistic without having colonies, but it is not possible to have colonies without being an empire. Thus, in the case of the Soviet Union, which exercised rigid controls over the economies of its small neighbors and forcefully absorbed within its structure Latvia, Lithuania, and Estonia, the Soviets practiced imperialism but not colonialism. If Stalin had succeeded in holding Manchuria under his control at the end of World War II, the Soviet Union would also have become a colonial power. The United States, however, must be judged a colonial power because it holds American Samoa, Guam, and the Northern Mariana Islands, the latter formerly held as part of the strategic Trust Territory of the Pacific. Some of the islands of the trust area were not inclined to move toward independence and sought instead territorial status, while one large area, Palau, sought first a compact of free association with the United States and in 1994 became completely independent. In exchange for military base rights, which have not been exercised, the United States agreed to give Palau $700 million in what was called "compact money" over a period of fifteen years.

A state possessing territories not incorporated within its borders, the native inhabitants of which are not granted the full rights or privileges of citizenship of the possessing state, is a colonial power. There is, however, a difference between colonizing an area and colonialism per se. For example, in the American experience colonialism did not exist while the United States was annexing contiguous areas on the continent of North America, for the areas being colonized were recognized as territories destined to be incorporated into the United States as an integral part of the nation.

While there were numerous efforts by various presidents and secretaries of state to make the United States a colonial power in the nineteenth century, none succeeded in permanently adding territory not destined for statehood until the United States formally annexed the Midway Islands in the Pacific Ocean on 28 August 1867, after their discovery in 1859 by the American N. C. Brooks. This was not, however, a true colonial venture, because the American purpose was to provide a way station and fueling stop en route to the Far East. The United States made no effort to develop the islands economically or politically or to populate them with colonists. Therefore, another definition of colonialism is that there must be a conscious effort on the part of the possessing power to develop or exploit the area in the interest of the possessor and to provide some form of government or control through colonial administrative machinery. This does not mean that the colonial power must necessarily neglect or abuse the interests of the native inhabitants of the territory taken as a colony, although more often than not such neglect and abuse does occur. It does mean, however, that the colonial nation has the power to impose its rule over the area and to assert its economic preeminence without resistance from the inhabitants of the area.

COLONIAL AMERICA

Probably no region under colonial administration received more considerate treatment by the mother country than Great Britain's colonies in North America, partly because they were peopled in the main by British subjects transplanted for the purpose of developing raw materials and markets for England. Where a colonial administration was imposed on an already existing and alien population, treatment of the native residents was less benign and generally considered more degrading by those thus possessed, depending on their level of civilization and organization at the time of conquest or occupation. For example, in the areas where Islamic or Asian culture, religion, and laws had existed for a thousand or more years there was often fierce resistance to being subjected to colonial status, whereas in parts of Central Africa, New Guinea, and Borneo, where the native inhabitants were less developed in an economic and material sense, the resistance was less prolonged or nonexistent.

If the American colonists were treated more as equals than most, they also resented more than most that they were not accorded exactly equal status with Englishmen who had not emigrated to the colonies. Therefore, when they rebelled and gained their independence, they had a particular dislike for the very concept of colonialism. Representatives of the new United States wrote their prejudices into the Constitution in 1789, insisting that new acquisitions must become states after securing sufficient population and complying with the laws of the land. This anticolonialism continued as the preeminent view of Americans and their government until the end of the nineteenth century when the new manifest destiny seized the popular imagination and propelled the United States into the race for colonies.

EXPANSIONISM AND MANIFEST DESTINY

When John L. O'Sullivan coined the term "manifest destiny" in 1845, it referred to the "destiny" of the United States to occupy and develop the American continent because of its superior institutions and form of government. Relative to its later counterpart, the "old" manifest destiny provided a modest program for the development and population of contiguous areas to the then existent United States. The new manifest destiny at the end of the nineteenth century bespoke a certain arrogance, since it claimed for Americans a superior system of government, a superior culture, and a superior race destined to carry mankind to the highest pinnacle of achievement. Many of the adherents of this philosophy extolled Yankee capitalism as part of the superior culture.

A man worthy of the task of educating the nation to the needs of expansion appeared in the form of Captain Alfred Thayer Mahan, whose major work, *The Influence of Sea Power Upon History, 1660–1783* (1890), extolled the virtues of a big navy as the route to national greatness—which required colonies to extend the defense perimeters of a great nation, and a merchant marine to carry trade to and from the colonies that would be defended by the navy. Mahan's great fear was a forthcoming contest with a rising China, and by means of its navy he wished to put the United States in a position that would keep China confined to the Asian continent. In numerous books, articles, speeches, and through his classes at the Naval War College in Newport, Rhode Island, Mahan bombarded Americans with his perception of the need for colonies. Ironically, while his impact was great in the United States, before World War I it was possibly even greater in Germany and Japan. Mahan was not nearly as interested in colonies for their commercial value as for their strategic value, but commerce became a selling point to attract a broad segment of the American public.

Social Darwinism added a sinister bent to the American urge for colonial expansion. American exponents of this pseudoscientific philosophy espoused by the Englishman Herbert Spencer adapted the concept of the survival of the fittest to the new manifest destiny, urging the spread of the Anglo-Saxon race and system of government to the less fortunate peoples of Asia and the Far Pacific. Such proponents of expansion for security motives as Theodore Roosevelt might stress the strategic value of port facilities in the Philippines, but they were drowned out by the more flamboyant spokesmen like Senator Albert Beveridge, who demanded annexation of the whole Philippine archipelago. Roosevelt warned President William McKinley that it was feasible to hold a military naval base to protect American interests in Asia, but possession of the whole of the Philippines would be a commitment that the American people would not support in the long run. His advice was ignored. Again in 1907, Roosevelt referred to the Philippines as an Achilles' heel, which should be given at least nominal independence at the earliest possible moment.

Various answers have been proposed for why Americans, with an anticolonial bias deeply ingrained in their political system, turned to colonialism, or, in other words, what the cause was of the development of the new manifest destiny. Obviously, social Darwinism and the hold that it established on the opinion makers in the United States provide one of the many answers. Richard Hofstadter ascribed America's outward thrust for colonies to what he called the psychic crisis. In *The Paranoid Style in American Politics and Other Essays* (1965) he argues that the severity of depressions of the period created fears about radicalism that caused the upper-middle and upper classes in the United States to look for some diversion from internal crises, and they found relief by focusing on the expansionist issue. Restless energies, which had concentrated on internal development in the first century of American history, turned in some degree to external adventures, such as Frederick Jackson Turner feared they would with the closing of the frontier in 1890. Missionary enthusiasts saw fields available for the spread of Protestant doctrine. Idealists dreamed of lifting the yoke of European monarchists from the Western Hemisphere and then also from Asia. Some proponents of the Spanish-American War hoped to reunite the North and the South through this uplifting national endeavor. A search for markets motivated some enthusiasts for annexation of the Philippines. A desire to be included among the nations of great powers, which required colonial possessions in the late nineteenth century, proved yet another component to the expansionist movement. But Hofstadter's main emphasis in the psychic crisis rests on internal stimuli for external policy, not the least of which was the contest for political position as each of the major parties struggled to become the repository of public confidence.

ASIA AND THE PACIFIC

In a perceptive study of Sino-American relations pertaining to Manchuria in the period 1895–1911, Michael H. Hunt examines the forces that worked toward American involvement in China. He stresses the misperceptions that guided both powers' views of one another and their vital interests. He sees racism or ethnocentrism along with excessive provincialism as contributing factors on both sides, keeping the Chinese and Americans from seeing their true interest. Contrary to a number of writers who attempted to discover a carefully developed imperial plan underlying American moves in Asia at the end of the nineteenth and beginning of the twentieth centuries, Hunt found American imperialism to be ill-defined or haphazard in its goals. Many policymakers dreamed of cooperation with China in preserving and developing Chinese nationalism and of profiting by trade with this emergent nation. Opportunities for such cooperation existed but foundered on mistrust and misunderstanding.

An important conclusion that emerged from this study was Hunt's observation that while imperialism was in part a motivating force for a number of Americans promoting U.S. involvement in Manchuria, with some even demanding territorial concessions, the government dragged its feet on implementing imperial plans, did not stand firm on economic penetration, laid its faith in the open door, and criticized China for the failure of American policy. The Americans asked why the Chinese did not stand up to the powers trying to carve out spheres of influence, especially when the Americans gave them the Open Door policy to use as a weapon to deny special rights, while the Chinese asked why the Americans did not help to enforce the open door with more than words. Hunt also reinforced much of Hofstadter's argument concerning the importance of the psychic crisis as an influence on American foreign policy and the impetus to "look outward" as an escape from domestic problems.

George F. Kennan, the historian-diplomat, argued cogently for the idea that the legalistic-moralistic tradition of the United States accounted for adventures in imperialism without commensurate understanding of the burdens or responsibilities of empire by most Americans and some policymakers, especially President McKinley and his third secretary of state, John Hay. Hay, who assumed office on 30 September 1898, the day before the peace commission met in Paris to determine the settlement of the Spanish-American War, spoke the language of the new manifest destiny: "No man, no party, can fight with any chance of final success against a cosmic tendency; no cleverness, no popularity avails against the spirit of the age." Hay was a determined annexationist, but more significantly he was the author of the Open Door policy, proclaiming the need and obligation of the powers involved in Asia to maintain the open door to trade in China and the maintenance of China's territorial integrity. Later historians accused Hay of fomenting through the Open Door policy a kind of imperialism, one that denied the need for territory and promoted instead economic exploitation of areas not strong enough to resist it.

Kennan said Hay did not understand the far-reaching commitments assumed under the Open Door policy. It was part of the effort to ensure U.S. participation in the external world by legalism and appeal to the moral conscience of Americans defending China against the assault of the great powers at no cost save legal definition of the obligations of the powers. This is probably true as far as it goes, but it also was intended to guarantee the entrance into the Asian world of American power and influence through a door Hay and others considered to have been opened by the acquisition of the Philippine Islands. That he became disillusioned by the inability and ineffectiveness of the United States to win support for the open door does not in any way diminish his responsibility for it. Hay opened not a door but a Pandora's box with his policy, which the United States was to pursue through a tortuous maze to participation in the Pacific phase of World War II.

Marilyn Blatt Young, in her study of U.S. China policy from 1895 to 1901, corroborates much of Kennan's viewpoint on the inefficacy of open door diplomacy, the difficulties inherent in the legalistic-moralistic perspective that permeated the Department of State, and the tendency to be more concerned with chauvinistic interests than national interests. In addition, she points out the difficulties that plagued both China and the United States because of the view each held of the other as barbarians and the attendant implications of racism stemming from the perception of social Darwinism, which gained credence in the late nineteenth century. If imperialism was the American objective, it was so poorly contrived and so reliant on rhetoric and half-baked schemes failing of genuine government support as to be ineffectual.

Kennan was one of the early and chief spokesmen for the realist perspective in assessing right conduct in America's foreign relations and ascribing colonial expansion to a lack of realism in the formulators of the policy. Hay, Beveridge, Henry Cabot Lodge, and others who promoted the idea of empire for the United States failed to take into consideration, according to Kennan, the pervasive influence of anticolonialism in the United States, and failed to advertise the cost of empire to the American people, who were unwilling to bear the expense of defending what they had won by war or annexation. Believing that the Filipinos would welcome them with open arms, Americans were flustered and embarrassed when they were greeted instead with open rebellion. As soon as the empire had been acquired, agitation began to get rid of it, with mixed results. Incorporated territories (Alaska, Hawaii, Puerto Rico) were retained without much question. Where there was a desire to adhere to American protection (for example, American Samoa), responsibility was ultimately accepted (February 1929); but the Philippines demanded independence, and by means of the Tydings-McDuffie Act (1934) were promised independence in 1944, which was postponed until 1946 because of Japanese occupation of the islands during World War II. The Virgin Islands, purchased from Denmark in 1917, became a U.S. territory, while other islands, too small for incorporation but important strategically, continued as possessions, such as Wake and Johnston islands. At the end of World War II, various Pacific Islands south of Japan—the Bonin Islands, the Volcano Islands, which included Okinawa, and the Daito Islands, which were captured from Japan during the war—were later returned, the first three groups in 1968 and the rest in 1972. But during that time span they were under American rule. The last territories considered for annexation by an incorporation agreement were part of the Trust Territory of the Pacific, under U.S. supervision as a United Nations trusteeship, including the Marshall, Caroline, Mariana, and Palau islands. Parts of the Caroline and Mariana islands asked for incorporation in 1975. It was determined in 1986 to grant the Caroline and Marshall islands sovereignty in 1986 and, as noted earlier, the Palau Islands in 1994.

HISTORICAL PERSPECTIVES ON U.S. COLONIALISM

Realist and traditionalist historians have usually judged that the United States entered the colonization business by the back door at the end of the nineteenth and beginning of the twentieth centuries and could not wait to exit by the same route because being a colonial power was embarrassing and outside the American tradition. For example, in the traditional school, Samuel Flagg Bemis, Thomas A. Bailey, and Julius W. Pratt held such views, while among the realists Norman A. Graebner and George F. Kennan agreed to the extent that colonialism was not and did not become a part of the American tradition. Another group of historians, the New Left, argued that colonialism was a conscious expression of American capitalism, which had always been the determining force in American foreign policy and merely reached a conscious level of expression in colonialism. William Appleman Williams argued

that colonialism was merely one phase of American imperialism, which became passé when it was discovered that economic imperialism that penetrated other areas by the force of dollars was superior to the actual possession of the territories that the United States wished to dominate. According to Williams and those of his persuasion, dollar diplomacy became the preeminent source of imperialism because it was easier to maintain, less embarrassing, and made it possible to eliminate the bother of colonial administration. But colonialism itself was merely an extension of the American experience and not an aberration.

One of the most respected historians associated with the New Left, Walter LaFeber, argued that there was no break in tradition. While he emphasized the economic forces behind the new manifest destiny, he recognized that other forces played a part in promoting it. He insisted that colonialism was part and parcel of the American experience, all of which was preparing the way for the surge to overseas colonial possession as a natural extension of the colonial spirit developing from the outset in America. One of the few historians normally classed in the realist tradition, Richard W. Van Alstyne, agreed with at least part of the New Left assessment that there was no break in the American pattern of expansion. According to Van Alstyne, the westward movement itself was an imperial endeavor preparing the way for further imperialism when the continent was filled or occupied.

These examples could be extended to include a number of other prominent diplomatic historians who have sided with the innocent victim-of-circumstances view of American colonial expansion versus the concept of the planned and persistent imperial thrust. Thus, the debate over how and why the United States became a colonial power at the end of the nineteenth century rages on, with definitive answers lying in neither camp.

It seems prudent to assume that like all significant events in the world's development there were many causes for American colonialism. Economic determinists assess greed or material benefits deriving from colonial possession as the determinate cause. This does not explain the correspondence of such advocates of the colonial experiment as Mahan and Theodore Roosevelt, who laid stress on the importance of prestige and great-power status for the United States resting on the needs of security, which is or should be the primary consideration underlying the motivation for formulators of foreign policy.

Realist historians tend to examine colonialism as the result of some elements of the psychic crisis, the security motives, the spread of American industry and commerce, emotional appeals to liberal humanitarian objectives, social Darwinism, nationalism, and "egoistic nationalism," a term applied by the political scientist Robert E. Osgood to explain positions taken by Lodge and Beveridge, who flamboyantly expressed American national destiny without carefully examining the consequences. The traditionalists have been more inclined to focus on the idea of the aberration of anticolonial liberal democratic ideals. In some degree they are all correct, but because the realists take into account a multiplicity of factors arguing for colonial expansion and the retreat from colonialism that followed, they would appear to provide the most complete explanation.

Of course, there are also Marxist interpretations carried to the level of prediction by Lenin, who argued that imperialism was the highest stage of capitalism, which would lead to the most flagrant exploitation of proletarians and to the ultimate collapse of capitalism as imperial rivalries led to struggles for markets terminating in enervating wars. What Lenin did not foresee was the Soviet Union's entrance into the imperial grouping through such practices as the economic exploitation of the states under its sway. While condemning the United States and other Western powers, historians of the Marxist persuasion first rationalized Soviet behavior and claimed there was not exploitation, or else dropped Russia as the exemplar of communist or Marxist principles and raised Communist China as a new model. Marxists and other economic determinists have also tended to lump together the Western colonial powers in defense of one another's interests and in support of racism, as in the case of American support of France in Algeria and Indochina, and of South Africa and Israel. This ignores Franklin D. Roosevelt's frequently expressed anticolonialism. It also overlooks such changes in position as the Department of State's shift concerning American support of South Africa until the apartheid regime was overthrown and replaced by an electoral process that allowed enfranchisement of blacks, permitting Nelson Mandela to become the first black leader of South Africa.

Ironically, while racism or ethnocentrism has undeniably played a determinant role in both colonialism and imperialism and the powers that practiced them have been justly criticized for the practice, those who were its victims have generally not illustrated a much better record in their treatment of other races or ethnic groups over whom they have been able to establish control. Fostered by the efforts to break free of colonial domination, virulent nationalism has led to extremist attitudes on the part, for example, of Arabs toward Jews, and Jews toward Arabs; of neighboring African tribes struggling to achieve preeminence over other tribes inside the borders of new states; of Chinese toward Tibetans and Indians; and of Indians toward Pakistanis and Pakistanis toward Indians. While this list is incomplete, it is still impressive of the evidence that the power to abuse is confined to no particular race. Perhaps the problem lies not in racism per se so much as in the corrupting influence of absolute power over another people. Some historians have attempted to identify racism as a phenomenon of one socioeconomic group exclusively or to whites versus other races, as though the problem would be eliminated if the world were socialist or the whites lost influence to the other races. They have not met the real challenge, which is that abuse rests with unrestrained power.

Ethnocentric behavior is a form of racism, which has permitted the Japanese to treat others of the yellow race as inferior when they held imperial control of the Chinese and the Koreans, and the Chinese to do the same when they have held similar power over Tibetans. The same phenomenon has permitted various tribal groups in Africa to persecute other tribes and the others to retaliate in kind. Ethnocentrism permitted Great Russians to maintain that their "little Slav brothers" inside and outside Russia's borders have needed special tutelage by their betters. Often ethnic bias is combined with religious bigotry, which accounts in part for the atrocities of the 1990s in Yugoslavia and the continuing contest in Ireland. What made racism identifiable with colonialism and imperialism was the unrestrained power of the colonial and imperial nations to abuse those over whom they held dominance. The decline of colonialism has not eliminated the problem, for the nationalism that grew in a virulent strain in the places formerly under colonial control has bred a similar virus.

Admittedly there are still areas that may be defined as colonial possessions, but generally, at the beginning of the twenty-first century they are headed for either incorporation within the possessing state, autonomous status within some sort of confederation like the British Commonwealth, or independence. For example, in some cases there is the fiction of independence or autonomy, as in the continued possession of Samoa by the United States; French colonial administration of Martinique, St. Pierre, and French Guiana; and British control of such places as the Falkland Islands. There are, however, very few vestiges of colonialism left.

This, however, does not mean the end of imperialism, which has taken many forms. Economic penetration of underdeveloped areas has become a competitive replacement for colonialism and is absorbing the energies of the former colonial powers. Added to this form of exploitation of resources and capital control is a new element—the oil-rich Arab states that have emerged from colonial status and exhibited all the symptoms of nationalism and desires for political power they condemned in their former imperial masters. Colonialism is virtually dead, but imperialism continues as those nations with the economic or military power to perpetuate it have refused to give up the practice.

NEOCOLONIALISM

There is one more area which must be considered and that is neocolonialism. What this is depends on who is defining it. Socialist or communist writers have defined it as the efforts of the former colonial powers to maintain colonial control by other means. This definition lacks precision, as some of the neocolonial powers were in fact previously colonies, such as the United States. A largely accepted definition of neocolonialism is as follows: it includes retention of military bases, exploitation of resources, preferential trade treaties, imposed unification of colonies, conditional aid, and defense treaties. It also includes artificially created countries or combining countries into a group or federation. However, this grouping of countries is ill-defined in terms of whether they represent neocolonialism or not, as some of the Third World countries created in such combinations contend they are not dependencies in any way, although they may retain economic ties with the metropolitan power that previously held sway there.

BIBLIOGRAPHY

Easton, Stewart Copinger. *The Rise and Fall of Western Colonialism: A Historical Survey from the Early Nineteenth Century to the Present*. New York, 1964. Examines the motives and processes of colonial expansion and development in the nineteenth century and traces the reasons for the decline of colonialism and what happened to the colonial areas through 1964.

Graebner, Norman A., ed. *Ideas and Diplomacy: Readings in the Intellectual Tradition of American Foreign Policy*. New York, 1964. Argues that the new colonialism at the end of the nineteenth century was as much motivated by a quest for prestige as for economic advantages and that strategic position for security was always a part of the American strategy.

Hunt, Michael H. *Frontier Defense and the Open Door: Manchuria in Chinese-American Relations, 1895–1911*. New Haven, Conn., 1973. Focuses on the attempts of the Chinese to use the United States to bolster defense of China's frontiers.

Kennan, George F. *American Diplomacy: 1900–1950*. Chicago, 1951. Expanded edition, Chicago, 1984. A series of lectures for the Walgreen Foundation at the University of Chicago in 1950; provides a realist viewpoint on the development of American foreign policy at the turn of the century.

Kupchan, Charles A. *The Vulnerability of Empire*. Ithaca, N.Y., 1994. Examines the structure of empires and in the case of the United States gives security motives for the foundation of American neocolonialism.

LaFeber, Walter. *The New Empire: An Interpretation of American Expansion, 1860–1898*. Ithaca, N.Y., 1963. The author is more inclined to credit motives other than economic as contributing factors to America's colonial experiment, but argues that the empire was consciously acquired as a part of the traditional role of expansionism in American history.

Morgan, Dan. *Merchants of Grain*. New York, 1979.

Obadina, Tunde. *The Myth of Neo-Colonialism* (www.afbis.com/analysis/neo-colonialism.html). Provides a very perceptive assessment of the arguments for and against colonialism in its influence on African nations.

Pratt, Julius W. *Expansionists of 1898: The Acquisition of Hawaii and the Spanish Islands*. Baltimore, 1936. The first important study that submitted the war and the imperial thrust to a multicausationist analysis.

Stuart Peter C. *Isles of Empire: The United States and Its Overseas Possessions.* Lanham, Md., 1999. Clearly defines the continuing debate over whether the United States is or has been a true colonial power and concludes it is and was but not without internal dissent over the issue.

Tompkins, E. Berkeley. *Anti-Imperialism in the United States: The Great Debate, 1890–1920.* Philadelphia, 1970. A careful tracing of the debate over whether the United States should assume an empire.

Van Alstyne, Richard Warner. *The Rising American Empire.* New York, 1960. Argues that imperial expansion was part of American historical development and disagrees with the traditionalists that it was a departure from tradition.

Verlinden, Charles. *The Beginnings of Modern Colonization: Eleven Essays with an Introduction.* Ithaca, N.Y., 1970. Translated by Yvonne Freccero, this is a good description of the beginnings of colonialism in the fifteenth century and offers some explanations for its development in Western civilization.

Williams, William Appleman. *The Roots of the Modern American Empire: A Study of the Growth and Shaping of Social Consciousness in a Marketplace Society.* New York, 1969. Presents the United States as imperialistic from its inception and the colonial expansion at the end of the nineteenth century as a further expression of the traditional posture of an economically oriented society.

Young, Marilyn Blatt. *The Rhetoric of Empire: American China Policy, 1895–1901.* Cambridge, Mass., 1968. Does not believe the Open Door policy was effective, in part because the Department of State did not limit application of the policy to the extent that the United States was willing to enforce it.

See also ANTI-IMPERIALISM; CONTINENTAL EXPANSION; IMPERIALISM; ISOLATIONISM; MANDATES AND TRUSTEESHIPS; OPEN DOOR POLICY; RACE AND ETHNICITY.

CONGRESSIONAL POWER

Robert David Johnson

Executive agents dominated the international environment into which the newly independent United States entered. Absolute monarchs ruled in Prussia, Russia, and Austria, vested with nearly absolute control of their nation's conduct in world affairs. In France, the Estates-General had no effective voice in foreign policy. And even England, despite the growth in parliamentary power following the Glorious Revolution, maintained the fiction of executive unilateralism on national security matters.

By producing a government that vested substantial foreign policy powers in an elected legislature, the American Revolution truly was revolutionary. But the complicated structure established by the Constitution provided few clear boundaries separating Congress from the president, resulting in an almost constant struggle between the two branches. Apart from this internal contest for power, a few patterns have remained constant over most of American history. First, periods of divided government (in which party or ideological gulfs separated the two branches)—the 1850s, the late 1910s, the late 1960s and 1970s—have produced the most spectacular clashes between Congress and the president. But the more substantial shifts in power, usually to the disadvantage of Congress, have come when one party, normally operating with effective presidential leadership, has firmly controlled both branches of government. Such was the case under Thomas Jefferson at the beginning of the 1800s, William McKinley at the end of the century, Franklin D. Roosevelt during World War II, and Lyndon B. Johnson during the mid-1960s. Second, because Congress has tended to feature more dissenting voices, of both the left and the right, when the legislature has exerted its influence it frequently has pushed U.S. foreign policy toward ideological extremes. Finally, the concept of congressional power has been an inherently flexible one. While the abilities to declare war and

to approve treaties are the most obvious grants of foreign policy authority the legislature received, Congress has more consistently made its presence felt on international questions through other tools, especially the appropriations power.

LEGISLATIVE POWER IN A REVOLUTIONARY ERA

The revolutionary era bequeathed an appropriately ambivalent record regarding the legislative role in foreign affairs. The new country's first government, the Articles of Confederation, granted all international authority in the Continental Congress. But this structure proved awkward, and on two occasions the Congress divested itself of the day-to-day conduct of diplomacy by appointing a secretary of state for foreign affairs. At the state level, too, executive power over militias rebounded to some degree as the revolutionary war proceeded. Finally, almost all who served as delegates to the Constitutional Convention agreed that the Articles regime could not permanently protect the weak state from national security threats.

The convening of the Constitutional Convention thus coincided with a period of intellectual ferment regarding the proper executive-legislative balance in foreign affairs. It came as little surprise that the resulting document gave neither branch clear-cut dominance on international matters, but it seemed as if Congress would have the predominant voice in the new government's foreign policy. For instance, quite beyond the power to declare war, the legislature received the commercial powers (important given the framers' belief that economic affairs would dominate post-revolutionary international relations) and the ability to issue letters of marque (the eighteenth-century equivalent of a right to wage undeclared war). Yet legal scholarship has never developed a consensus on the precise extent of Congress's warmaking power, partly because the Constitutional Convention's Committee on Style changed the Constitution's wording from giving Congress the power to "make war" to the power to "declare war."

Beyond the warmaking issue, the question of constitutional intent grows even murkier. Several framers, notably Gouverneur Morris and James Madison, described the appropriations power as the ultimate guarantee of congressional predominance in foreign affairs. But the experience of the treaty-making clause (where, at the last minute, the framers involved the executive in the process after initially planning to grant all treaty-making power to the Senate) suggests that the intended balance between the two branches changed in the president's favor as the Constitutional Convention proceeded. Memories of the chaotic and indecisive foreign policy of the Confederation period may very well have caused the framers to reconsider congressional dominance in international affairs.

The diplomacy of the early Republic, however, featured a much weaker legislative role than even the most ardent advocates of executive authority could have anticipated. In a variety of initiatives, George Washington asserted executive primacy. His handling of the nation's first treaties—with the Indian nations and then Jay's Treaty with England (1795–1796)—decreased the Senate's advisory capacity. His proclamation of neutrality in the wars of the French Revolution and his response to the revolt in Haiti strengthened the executive's hand in interpreting treaties already on the books. When Congress investigated Arthur St. Clair's disastrous military defeat by Indians on the Ohio frontier in November 1791, Washington established a precedent by invoking executive privilege so that he could withhold documents from Congress.

Although rhetorically committed to a strong foreign policy role for Congress, Thomas Jefferson also articulated a domestic agenda that aimed to forestall the corrupting effects of industrialization through territorial expansion and overseas commerce. When forced to choose between strict constructionism and his ideals, he consistently selected the latter. The most spectacular case was the Louisiana Purchase, but the most constitutionally significant came in the wars against the Barbary states—North African states whose piracy threatened Jefferson's vision of the United States carrying on an active worldwide commerce in agricultural goods. The president undertook a naval campaign without a direct declaration of war, and his policy would be cited for generations to come to justify unilateral presidential warmaking. In addition, Jefferson's effective leadership of the Republican legislative majorities allowed him to bypass a rather supine Congress on foreign policy matters. Even James Madison, who justifiably lacks a reputation as a strong president, successfully expanded executive authority. Most scholarship now downplays the significance of congressional "warhawks" such as Henry Clay and John Calhoun in forcing the president's hand to enter the War of 1812. Moreover, beyond European affairs, Madison retained primacy over policy toward the revolts in Spanish America. He consistently opposed extending diplomatic recognition to the rebellious colonies, which, because the Senate had power to confirm all ambassadors, would have involved the legislature in Latin American policy. Instead, Madison relied on private agents, unauthorized by Congress, and thus expanded executive power even further.

In contrast to such executive assertiveness, congressional attempts to establish a foothold in international affairs floundered. As Washington demonstrated, the treaty-making power did not guarantee a clear role for the Senate in making foreign policy. At the same time, the failure of House Republicans to block appropriations to implement Jay's Treaty provided the first in a series of unsuccessful attempts by the lower chamber to increase its international role. That this setback established a precedent, however, would only gradually emerge; over the next quarter century, factions within the House repeatedly challenged the constitutionality of executive predominance in foreign policy. But such initiatives, emanating from arch-Jeffersonian forces around Albert Gallatin in the 1790s, the Federalists in the early 1800s, and the small band of "Old Republicans" led by John Randolph in the 1810s, all fell well short of majority support.

IMPLEMENTING THE CONSTITUTIONAL STRUCTURE

Why, then, did what appeared to be a constitutional structure evenly divided between the two branches so quickly tip in favor of the executive? The legacy of the colonial and revolutionary eras played a key role, as did the increasing professionalization of U.S. foreign policy. So, too, did the national security threat posed by the wars of the

French Revolution. Perhaps most important was the intimate link between international issues and the first party system, which caused most contentious foreign policy questions to be debated along partisan rather than institutional lines. Not surprisingly, therefore, the presidency of John Adams, characterized by a closely divided Congress and contentious relations between the two branches, broke relatively little new ground in terms of altering the legislative-executive relationship, at least in the long term. The last Federalist president, for example, made sure to obtain congressional approval for the technically undeclared Quasi-War with France.

The War of 1812 transformed both the international and domestic environment, and in the process it altered the nature of the legislative-executive relationship. In the international arena, the Treaty of Ghent, followed closely by the Rush-Bagot agreement demilitarizing the Great Lakes and the Adams-Onís Treaty obtaining Spanish Florida, ended any credible European threat to the country's survival. Domestically, the unity between the executive branch and a majority of the legislature did not survive the 1820s schism among the Jeffersonian Republicans. In this new context, members of Congress began using foreign policy issues to obtain political advantage over the executive. One example came in 1817 and 1818, when Henry Clay attempted to force diplomatic recognition of the Spanish-American republics through direct congressional action. Clay believed that the United States, as a state founded in revolution itself, should assist other colonies attempting to win their freedom. But the speaker of the House also realized his initiative would embarrass his chief rival for the presidency, Secretary of State John Quincy Adams, and thus might work to his political benefit. Adams proved the more skillful politician, however, a trait he demonstrated again six years later when he discerned the electoral merit in a unilateral U.S. declaration opposing European recolonization in the hemisphere (the Monroe Doctrine). Partisan concerns also appeared prominently in the first major foreign policy fight between the two branches during Adams's presidency, the resolution to obtain congressional backing of his effort to send U.S. delegates to the 1826 Panama Congress. A Senate filibuster delayed the appropriations necessary to fund the delegates' mission.

These skirmishes set the stage for the period between 1844 and 1860, which featured the most clear-cut intersection of partisan, institutional,

and ideological battles matching Congress against the president. By 1860, the legislature's power on foreign policy reached, arguably, its highest point in American history. Few would have predicted this outcome when the expansionist James Polk captured the presidency in 1844. Without congressional sanction, Polk ordered U.S. troops into territory disputed between the United States and Mexico, triggering a battle between armed forces of the two nations. When Congress finally did consider a declaration of war, with fighting already under way, the administration used procedural tactics to ram the measure through both houses. Polk's conduct thus exposed him to the charge of usurping legislative prerogatives, reopening dormant debates about executive authority in foreign affairs. Meanwhile, the introduction of the 1846 Wilmot Proviso (which called for forbidding slavery in any newly acquired territories) eradicated the line between international and domestic matters by clearly linking slavery and expansion. At one pole of congressional opinion, abolitionists in the House aggressively made the case against expansionism. Led by John Quincy Adams (Whig-Massachusetts) and Joshua Giddings (Whig-Ohio), they transferred their opposition to slavery at home to an attack on imperialism abroad and used the war to indict the slave power's dominance of the nation's political structures. In the process, figures like Adams and Giddings showed how voices shut out of executive branch deliberations could make themselves heard through congressional action.

Partisan gridlock accompanied this ideological polarization, blocking any hope for Polk to retain the backing that he enjoyed in 1846, when only fourteen members of the House and no senators voted against the war declaration. The changing context of foreign policy issues splintered his electoral coalition, diluting support for the president's bid to annex all of Mexico. With Polk complaining privately about Congress having paralyzed his diplomacy, his term ended with Latin American policy immobilized by the sectionalization of manifest destiny, institutional conflict between the legislative and executive branches, intense partisan attacks, and sharp disagreement between proslavery expansionists and abolitionist anti-imperialists.

In the end, a penchant for secrecy, bypassing Congress, and allowing his domestic base to atrophy undermined Polk's freedom of action. His successors, the Whig presidents Zachary Taylor and Millard Fillmore, discovered that a foreign policy

THE U.S. SENATE AND FOREIGN POLICY

The Senate came into its own as a foreign policy force between 1850 and 1870. For most of early American history, the House of Representatives was the dominant actor on international matters. Talented politicians, like Henry Clay and Albert Gallatin, bolstered the power of the lower chamber. That the Senate conducted its debates in secret until the early 1800s decreased its public profile. And most contentious issues regarding both domestic and foreign policy—such as the War of 1812 and the Missouri Compromise—originated in the House.

In the 1830s the Senate began its golden age, peopled by the "great triumvirate" of Clay, Daniel Webster, and John Calhoun. But it was not until the end of the Mexican War that foreign policy power shifted to the Senate. The rise of the Republican Party, the institutional effects of the slavery issue, and the fact that most key initiatives in 1850s foreign policy involved powers assigned to the Senate but not the House (such as treatymaking and confirming ambassadors) facilitated the transformation.

The final factor in this process came during and after the Civil War, when Massachusetts Senator Charles Sumner assumed the chair of the Senate Foreign Relations Committee. Sumner first attracted national attention during the Mexican War, when he delivered a public speech in Boston denouncing the conflict as immoral. He became a household name after being caned—in the Senate chamber—by proslavery Representative Preston Brooks.

As Foreign Relations Committee chair, Sumner demonstrated his political skills, showing how he could use the institutional powers of the Senate to rally support even from colleagues that did not necessarily share his approach to international affairs. Sumner most made his influence felt in 1870, when he almost single-handedly blocked President Ulysses S. Grant's treaty to annex the Dominican Republic. Future Foreign Relations Committee chairs of both parties—figures such as Augustus Bacon, Henry Cabot Lodge, William Borah, Arthur Vandenberg, and J. William Fulbright—built on Sumner's precedents.

focused on limiting U.S. expansionism through treaties with other imperial powers lacked appeal in a Congress increasingly polarized over expansionism. The first attempt of the Whigs in this regard was the Clayton-Bulwer Treaty of 1850, in which the United States and England agreed that neither would unilaterally construct a trans-isthmian canal; the party's second was the Tripartite Treaty of 1852, in which the United States, England, and France agreed to respect the status quo in Cuba. Furious Senate objections, from not only southerners but northern senators such as Henry Wilson, forced Secretary of State John Clayton to interpret his 1850 handiwork restrictively; similar Senate opposition prompted President Fillmore to shelve the Tripartite Treaty altogether.

In this environment, implementing a bold international agenda could not occur without stable congressional support. In meeting this requirement, the final chief executive of the period, James Buchanan, displayed a good deal of originality. Buchanan believed that, given the domestic tumult of the preceding decade, foreign powers would take him seriously only if he could prove that, in contrast to Polk, Taylor, Fillmore,

and Pierce, Congress would not block his actions. The new president therefore attempted a variety of approaches to augment his position—at the legislature's expense. In 1858 he requested from Congress a resolution granting him discretionary authority to wage war against Paraguay, a procedure he later proposed expanding to all Latin American diplomatic issues. A year later, he sought to advance his most important goal—annexing Cuba—by urging Congress to appropriate $30 million to initiate the process. He (and his Senate critics) expected that once having spent the money, the upper chamber would not reject any future treaty bringing Cuba into the Union.

But in these and other initiatives Buchanan found himself consistently rebuffed by Senate Republicans. An ideological diverse coalition led by Republican Jacob Collamer of Vermont inflicted on the president an embarrassing defeat during initial consideration of the Paraguayan resolution. Collamer again played a leading role in attacks against the $30 million bill, and now Republicans with a higher national profile, such as New York's William Seward and New Hampshire's John Hale, joined them. This fierce opposition to the $30 million bill, for instance, attracted notice as far away as Madrid. William Preston, the minister sent by the administration to begin negotiations for the purchase of Cuba, was left to lament: "The character of the debate in Congress . . . has gone very far to revive the hopes of the Spaniards that they will be able to retain the island, and that our discord, and the distraction of party, will render the United States powerless in any struggle." The four decades following the Treaty of Ghent thus witnessed a legislature much more willing to launch (and much more effective in sustaining) ideological and legislative challenges to executive supremacy.

After 1860, however, the changing international and domestic environment caused congressional Republicans to reconsider their earlier conviction that Congress should reign supreme in U.S. foreign policy. During the Civil War, severe divisions over both military and Latin American issues split apart the GOP caucus. As Wisconsin Republican James Doolittle joked of his New Hampshire colleague John Hale, the upper chamber's most outspoken anti-imperialist, a "long habit of continued denunciation against the Administration or the party in power for fifteen or twenty years in succession has had some effect on the habits of his mind." In addition, with their party dominating the presidency throughout the period, Republicans grew less enamored (except during Andrew Johnson's presidency) with philosophical defenses of an active congressional role in foreign policy. That several leading members of the party struggled to use the congressional committee system to oversee the conduct of the Civil War undoubtedly reinforced this disinclination.

Despite these developments, Congress retained more than enough power to block aggressive international initiatives. The willingness of Gilded Age chief executives to uphold tradition and negotiate substantial agreements with foreign powers as treaties reinforced Congress's influence. The failure of the three most ambitious of these treaties—U.S. Grant's scheme to annex the Dominican Republic in 1870, the 1884 effort to establish a U.S. protectorate over Nicaragua, and Benjamin Harrison's gambit to annex Hawaii in 1892—prompted future secretary of state John Hay to compare a treaty entering the Senate with a bull going into the arena, in that neither would depart alive. Hay's comment testified to the strength of the ideologically awkward but politically potent coalition of the remaining Republican anti-imperialists, such as Carl Schurz and Charles

Sumner, and most of the body's Democrats. Once again, ideological extremes exerted a disproportionate influence in Congress. Senate Democrats cared little about anti-imperialism, but they believed that increased executive authority in international affairs would establish a precedent that presidents could later use to unilaterally advance the cause of civil rights. Congress even proved capable from time to time of acting in a more positive fashion, as in 1888, when majorities in both houses passed a resolution demanding that Grover Cleveland's administration initiate a conference of Western Hemisphere nations to address trade and other economic issues.

CONGRESS AND THE NEW CENTURY

Events at the turn of the century closed out this second era of executive-legislative relations. The political realignment generated by William McKinley's triumph in 1896 paved the way for closer partisan coordination between the executive and legislative branches (most prominently during Woodrow Wilson's presidency). As in the early years of the republic, party unity tended to dilute the strength of institutional conflicts and give the president more leeway. McKinley also employed a more active foreign policy, with the United States intervening in the Cuban-Spanish colonial war and then occupying the Philippines. The congressional response to the two conflicts provided a good demonstration of the range and limitations of the legislative role in turn-of-the-century international affairs. Regarding Cuba, consistent congressional pressure factored into McKinley's decision to declare war; at the same time, however, the Teller Amendment, which committed the United States to supporting Cuban independence, limited the president's options in 1899 and 1900. Consideration of the Treaty of Paris, under which the United States annexed the Philippines, offered a similarly ambivalent legacy. The Senate featured some of the imperialism debate's most articulate intellectual offerings. George Hoar was among the nation's most outspoken anti-imperialists, while Albert Beveridge countered that annexation would allow the United States to enter the ranks of the world's great powers. But the ultimate approval of the treaty had less to do with rhetoric than with congressional logrolling: McKinley granted Louisiana's Democratic senators control over the state's federal patronage in exchange for their votes, which allowed the administration to reach the two-thirds total required.

In addition to the political realignment, other domestic factors influenced the congressional role in early 1900s foreign policy. Political activists in the Progressive Era, convinced of the inherently corrupt and conservative nature of Congress, championed a strong presidency as a base for reform. Meanwhile, the intellectual currents of the time envisioned the United States assuming a more active, even moralizing, international presence, a mindset that guided not only McKinley's Cuban and Filipino policies but much of his successor's agenda as well. These changes shattered the nineteenth-century balance of power between the two branches. Instead, the executive undertook frequently unsanctioned, aggressive moves, as in Theodore Roosevelt's sending troops to assist the 1903 Panamanian revolution or his establishing a U.S.-sponsored customs receivership in the Dominican Republic in 1905. Use of unilateral executive actions climaxed during the Wilson presidency, during which U.S. forces were dispatched to Mexico, Russia, Haiti, and the Dominican Republic.

Although the Gilded Age system thus came to an end, Congress certainly remained a restraining influence on Progressive Era presidents. The one clear executive victory on a treaty during this period—the approval of the Treaty of Paris—occurred only because of McKinley's skillful management of Congress during both the negotiating and approval processes. McKinley's successors lacked either his political tact or luck and paid the price. In 1905, for example, Theodore Roosevelt explained that he had not submitted a treaty to implement the Dominican customs receivership lest the future Foreign Relations Committee chair Augustus Bacon, "backed by the average yahoo among the Democratic senators," block the measure to get "a little cheap reputation among ignorant people." During the presidency of William Howard Taft, the Senate not only refused to approve proposed arbitration treaties with Britain and France but also denied attempts to create protectorates over Honduras and Nicaragua. While the Senate's rejection of the Treaty of Versailles ending World War I might have served as the highest-profile example of congressional power during the Progressive Era, it was not an isolated example of the upper chamber asserting itself on international matters.

THE VERSAILLES ERA

That said, the League of Nations fight represented the most significant foreign policy confrontation between Congress and the executive in the first half of the twentieth century. It is ironic that failure to obtain Senate approval of the Treaty of Versailles plays such a role in Woodrow Wilson's historical legacy, because, in his first six years in office, Wilson had compiled a record at managing Congress unmatched by any chief executive since Thomas Jefferson. Using adept political skills, effective management of the Democratic caucus, and a keen ability to articulate his political vision to the public, Wilson had managed to push through Congress not one but two comprehensive reform packages. His record on foreign policy matters was slightly less stellar, but, nonetheless, given the complexity of the issues he confronted—not only the Great War but also the Mexican Revolution—he performed impressively.

By handing control of Congress to the Republicans, however, the 1918 midterm elections elevated Massachusetts senator Henry Cabot Lodge to the dual position of Senate majority leader and chair of the Senate Foreign Relations Committee. Personal and partisan animus shaded Lodge's response to Wilson. Before Wilson's arrival on the national scene, Lodge (who, like Wilson, held a Ph.D. degree) had been the nation's most prominent scholar in politics. Lodge, who matched Wilson's partisanship, also recognized that the treaty's unamended passage would benefit the Democrats politically. The senator confronted a problem, however: the League of Nations seemed popular, and opinion among his Republican colleagues was badly divided. A few Republican senators, such as William Borah and Robert La Follette, opposed entering the league under any circumstances, primarily because they believed that European imperialist powers would dominate the organization. "Mild reservationists," such as senators William Kenyon and Porter McCumber, supported the treaty with only minor changes. Most Republicans joined Lodge in classifying themselves as "strong reservationists," a vague designation that amounted to outright opposition to the league as constructed by Wilson.

The treaty reached the Senate in the spring of 1919. Lodge's performance between then and the first vote on the document in November 1919 provided a textbook example of how a congressional minority could use the institution's powers to alter U.S. foreign policy. Lodge began by convening lengthy hearings on the treaty, which gave the Republicans time to influence public opinion. But the hearings also exposed the many provisions in the Versailles Treaty in which diplomatic necessities had forced Wilson to compromise his ideals. As the summer progressed, criticism of the treaty escalated, from a wide variety of groups—ethnic Americans, especially of Irish ancestry, who saw the document as a sellout to the British; radicals and anti-imperialists, who viewed the treaty as a betrayal of American ideals; and nationalists, who worried that the collective security mechanism of Article X would rob Congress of its constitutional right to declare war. As a Senate critic, Lodge did not need to propose a positive alternative; he only had to ensure that one-third plus one of the members of the Senate would vote against approval. His determination, along with Wilson's equally passionate refusal to compromise and the parliamentary tactics of the Senate irreconcilables (the outright opponents of the league), paved the way for three Senate votes in which the upper chamber rejected the Treaty of Versailles and thus U.S. membership in the League of Nations.

The defeat of the Versailles Treaty confirmed the breakdown between Woodrow Wilson and the new Republican majority. But even before the 1918 elections, relations between the two branches had deteriorated. Before the U.S. entrance into World War I, the president was subjected to consistent barbs from Senate progressives for both his Mexican and his preparedness policies. Then, in 1918, Wilson confronted the dilemma of Congress exercising a prior restraint over his response to the Bolshevik Revolution: fear of a congressional investigation blocked a scheme to supply credits to Admiral Aleksandr Vasiliyevich Kolchak's antirevolutionary forces. When Wilson attempted to bypass Congress entirely by sending troops to Russia, the body employed the ultimate sanction: its power of the purse. In 1919 a resolution introduced by Senator Hiram Johnson to cut off funding for the intervention failed on a perilously close tie vote. This demonstration of the critical spirit in Congress convinced the administration that it had no choice but to withdraw the armed forces.

The intensity of the Versailles and Russian battles heightened the importance of foreign policy pressure groups of all ideological persuasions. The pattern continued during the 1920s, especially on military and Latin American issues. As would be the case later in the century as well,

such groups tended to influence Congress more than the executive. In 1926, for instance, the U.S. Army's Chemical Warfare Service waged a highly effective lobbying campaign to prevent Senate approval of the Chemical Weapons Treaty, while anti-imperialists and peace groups helped soothe the U.S.–Mexican crisis of 1926–1927. In turn, the greater public interest in foreign policy highlighted the ability of Congress, especially the Senate, to frame consideration of international questions, especially at a time when political reporters spent as much time covering events in the Senate as they did at the White House.

No figure made better use of this environment than William Borah. Combining his power as Foreign Relations Committee chair with his long-standing identification with the issue, Borah positioned himself as the chief interpreter of the 1929 Kellogg-Briand Pact to outlaw war. He also launched his own venture in private diplomacy in an attempt to prevent a military conflict with Mexico. Those executive initiatives that cleared Congress during the 1920s, such as the Washington Naval Conference treaties of 1921–1922, further confirmed the legislature's influence: the treaties overcame strong Senate opposition largely because the Harding administration appointed two prominent senators, Henry Cabot Lodge and Oscar Underwood to the U.S. negotiating team. When Secretary of State Frank Kellogg proved less willing to involve Congress in his Latin American policy—during his tenure the United States sent marines to Nicaragua without congressional sanction and nearly severed diplomatic relations with Mexico—the legislature responded in kind: in 1929 the Senate passed an amendment authored by C. C. Dill to terminate appropriations for the U.S. intervention in Nicaragua.

The Dill Amendment was the handiwork of the peace progressives, one of the most effective congressional blocs of the twentieth century. Although never more than twelve in the Senate, members of the group displayed remarkable acumen in advancing their ideological agenda. They first attracted notice in the 1910s, when senators such as Borah, La Follette, and George Norris offered an anti-imperialist, antimilitarist critique of Wilson's foreign policy. But the peace progressives made their mark in the 1920s, when they used the Senate's traditional tolerance of dissenters to influence the foreign policy of the Harding, Coolidge, and Hoover administrations. Their tactics included appropriations riders, public hearings to influence popular opinion, covert cooperation with peace groups to leak embarrassing information, and using the prestige of their positions to cement transnational alliances with like-minded groups and individuals overseas. By the end of the 1920s, U.S. policy toward Central America and the Caribbean had moved strongly in an anti-imperialist direction.

And so, as the framers anticipated, foreign policy issues remained vigorously contested between the branches. This framework continued during the first several years of Franklin Roosevelt's administration. A domestic focus made Roosevelt reluctant to spend political capital on international matters, such as the protocol for adherence to the World Court—one reason why the Senate defeated the treaty. A leading opponent of the World Court was the peace progressive senator Gerald Nye, who, like many in the group, believed that pressure from munitions makers and bankers explained Wilson's decision to bring the country into World War I. In the throes of the Great Depression, a conspiracy theory against business carried a good deal of weight, and, when Nye opened hearings on the matter in 1934–1935, the affair attracted national attention. Secretary of State Cordell Hull complained how the Nye Committee's dominance of discourse on neutrality issues strengthened isolationist sentiments. Indeed, as the secretary anticipated, the hearings resulted in Congress passing the Neutrality Acts of 1935 and 1936. Ironically, during Franklin Roosevelt's first six years as president, the most important diminution of congressional authority on foreign policy issues came with the Reciprocal Trade Agreements Act of 1934, when Congress willingly surrendered its power over foreign economic policy as part of the fallout from the Smoot-Hawley tariff.

Despite differences between eras, some common patterns emerged in the congressional approach to international relations between 1789 and 1941. The Dill and Hiram Johnson resolutions, for example, showed how powerfully military appropriations bills could influence foreign affairs. The prevalence of treaties, even though the upper chamber approved 86 percent of the 726 treaties it considered between 1789 and 1926, heightened the importance of formal roll-call votes in assuring at least some senatorial presence in the conduct of foreign policy. With the (albeit important) exception of tariffs, the House of Representatives played a minor role on international questions. (During one congressional session in the 1920s, for instance, the House Foreign Affairs Committee spent a week debating a $20,000 appropriation for an international poultry show in Tulsa, which one member recalled as the committee's most important issue of the whole session.) In the Senate, meanwhile, the Foreign Relations Committee reigned supreme. The upper chamber's considerable international powers fell under the control of a relatively small foreign policy elite, composed of Foreign Relations members and the few other senators—like the peace progressives—who exhibited intense interest in international matters.

The international threat associated with World War II altered this alignment. Perhaps no single piece of legislation highlighted the change more than the Lend-Lease Act of 1940, which passed despite knowledge that it would lessen congressional control over foreign policy. During World War II, determined to avoid the mistakes of the Wilson administration, Roosevelt hoped to place the Senate on record supporting U.S. participation in a postwar international organization. But the president did not want Congress to play an active role in forming postwar foreign policy. He strongly opposed the so-called B2H2 resolution (abbreviated for its sponsors—Senators Harold Burton, Joseph Ball, Lister Hill, and Carl Hatch), which called for the United States to join a postwar international police force. Working with Senate leaders, the administration instead championed a vaguely worded offering that praised the work of Cordell Hull at the 1943 Moscow Conference of foreign ministers. This was the first in a series of measures in which Congress was asked to provide advance authority for future executive action. Moreover, as would occur with similar postwar resolutions, the political and international conditions under which the Senate considered the substitute—after Hull had already completed his work—made it almost impossible to oppose the bill without repudiating executive commitments.

THE COLD WAR

The arrival of the Cold War further weakened the traditional levers of congressional authority. The nature of the communist threat placed the government on close to a permanent war footing, while the advent of nuclear weapons provided an immediacy lacking in any previous challenge to U.S. national security. In this new situation, a constitutional theory emerged claiming that the commander-in-chief clause bestowed an independent foreign policy power upon the executive, an argument almost never previously advanced. On the domestic front, the perceived lessons of the late 1930s bolstered the Truman administration's strategy of equating its own foreign policy principles with the concept of bipartisanship. A century and a half before, Jefferson had shown how aggressive presidential leadership and partisan unity could work to diminish congressional authority. Now, Harry Truman looked to create a party unity between executive and legislature that did not exist, with the aim of stifling congressional dissent. Faced with a Congress controlled by Republicans between 1947 and 1949, the president essentially regarded congressional attacks not as legitimate institutional challenges but as nothing more than partisanship.

Not surprisingly, then, the early Cold War is not remembered as a period of intense congressional activism in the international arena. As Arthur Vandenberg conceded during his stint as Senate Foreign Relations Committee chair in the Eightieth Congress, issues seemed to reach Capitol Hill only when they had developed to a point where congressional discretion was badly restricted. Indeed, what Truman's final secretary of state, Dean Acheson, dubbed the "Vandenberg treatment"—granting to the Michigan senator small, superficial concessions and a dose of public praise—aptly describes the common view of the congressional role in Truman's foreign policy.

In many ways, congressional power did diminish in the early stages of the Cold War, although this was partly because—as with the Reciprocal Trade Agreements Act fifteen years earlier—the legislature willingly surrendered its role. At times the body seemed eager to expand the president's foreign policy powers beyond even what Truman desired. Such sentiments explain the overwhelming approval of initiatives such as the National Security Act (1947), the North Atlantic Treaty Organization (1949), and the post-1950 expansion of the defense budget. They also affected the early congressional response to the Korean War; at the time, several senior members expressly asked Truman not to involve Congress in the decision. With the combination of NSC 68—the document that deemed the triumph of communism anywhere in the world a threat to U.S. national security—and the onset of the Korean War dramatically escalating the military budget, the beneficiaries of defense spending spread around the country. As a result, members of Congress who even considered opposing defense appropriations were vulnerable to the charge that they were not only subverting national security but also failing to protect the economic interests of their constituents. In the decade between the end of the Korean War and the end of John F. Kennedy's presidency, defense bills passed with an average of less than one negative vote in both chambers.

Until the Korean War began, however, the congressional response to the Cold War was considerably more complex. In 1947, even as the administration was uniting behind George Kennan's containment doctrine, Congress seriously considered three alternative approaches to world affairs. A small group of Democratic liberals supplied the most tenacious opposition to the Truman Doctrine, in which the president pledged to assist any government threatened by communist takeover. Led by Claude Pepper and Edwin Johnson, they charged that extending military assistance to undemocratic regimes in Greece and Turkey would contradict the internationalist ideals for which the United States fought World War II. To the administration's right, a sizable bloc of Republicans led by Senator William Knowland of California and Representative Walter Judd of Minnesota demanded that the administration reorient its foreign policy toward East Asia by aiding the Nationalists in China's civil war. Finally, nationalists ranging from the talented (Robert Taft of Ohio) to the unscrupulous (Pat McCarran of Nevada) questioned any initiative that would threaten U.S. sovereignty and argued that an activist foreign policy would dangerously strengthen the federal government. They instead advocated waging the Cold War through domestic measures that would crack down on communist sympathizers. This point of view enjoyed strong support in the House of Representatives, which was more subject to conservative pressures generated by the 1946 elections.

DOMESTIC POLITICS AND CONGRESSIONAL POWER

The unusual breakdown of Congress played a critical role in the early stages of the Cold War. With a shaky base of congressional support, Truman had little choice but to work with internationalist Republicans: more than flattery was at stake in Dean Acheson's attempts to woo Vandenberg and his ideological comrades, Henry Cabot

Lodge II and H. Alexander Smith. The temperaments, ideologies, and inclinations of the internationalist Republicans made them players on virtually every foreign policy issue of the day. Their performance set the stage for a new way for Congress to exert influence: with the foreign policy powers of the federal government expanding at an exponential rate, members of Congress could maneuver through the resulting chaos.

From a completely different ideological perspective, other domestic forces also encouraged a congressional presence in the early Cold War. Following the elections of 1946, when Republicans captured control of both houses of Congress, more than half of the House GOP caucus petitioned for membership in the House Un-American Activities Committee (HUAC). One of these freshmen, California congressman Richard Nixon, made a national name for himself with his activities on the committee, especially after he exposed perjury by the former State Department official Alger Hiss. With the committee championing the anticommunist cause in the House, Republican Joseph McCarthy took up the banner in the Senate. The Wisconsin senator was the rare member of Congress who could shape the national psyche, and both the Truman and Eisenhower administrations had to deal with the consequences of his actions. In the process, while the liberal internationalist and Asia-first alternatives that Congress considered during the early portions of Truman's years fell by the wayside, the nationalists in Congress flourished.

Even during the height of his power, McCarthy sponsored no important laws; he sought to affect the national debate on anticommunism but eschewed the hard work necessary to pass legislation. Measured by that standard, the most influential member of the postwar Congress was Nevada senator Pat McCarran, who was responsible for two critical pieces of Cold War legislation: the McCarran Internal Security Act (1950) and the McCarran-Walter Immigration Act (1952). McCarran's position as a Democrat willing to buck his party's leadership and his considerable contacts with the Federal Bureau of Investigation gave him clout on Capitol Hill. In addition, the ability of figures like McCarran to work around the traditional congressional structure to have an impact—the senator's power base was the Judiciary Committee—provided a model for future congressional initiatives that challenged executive control.

In the years following Truman's decision to commit forces to the Korean conflict, Congress's role in warmaking notably declined, while the growth of executive agreements produced a similar diminution of the Senate's treaty-making power. These developments did not escape congressional notice. During the Truman administration, a group of nationalists led by Ohio's two GOP senators, John Bricker and Robert Taft, embraced the cause of congressional power. The duo argued that Truman-style internationalism would not be possible if Congress took its appropriate place as a partner of the executive on foreign policy matters.

With the election of Republican Dwight D. Eisenhower in 1952, liberal Democrats searched for a way to use congressional power to criticize the president without being labeled soft on communism. They urged a formal, symbolic role in framing policy, with the executive conceding the principle of legislative input in exchange for Congress allowing the president freedom of action to prosecute the Cold War. Hubert Humphrey (a member of the populist Democratic-Farmer-Labor Party of Minnesota) candidly described this stance as a "limited dissent." Indeed, as practiced in the Eisenhower administration, it actually came to less than that: Eisenhower pioneered the tactic—later made famous with the Tonkin Gulf Resolution—of submitting blank-check resolutions authorizing vaguely defined overseas actions. The relationship between Eisenhower and congressional Democrats suggested that genuine collaboration interested neither side.

But in many ways, a focus on the balance of power between Congress and the president misses the most important element in the legislative response to the early Cold War. That instead came in an internal congressional development: the creation of the culture of a Cold War Congress. The position of the Senate Foreign Relations Committee weakened as the international issues (warmaking and approving treaties) over which it had clear jurisdiction fell into disuse. Within Congress, the committee came under challenge from the newly created Joint Committee on Atomic Energy and the Senate Armed Services Committee, which both proved less than zealous in challenging executive policies. With the expansion of the defense budget, influence especially shifted to the Armed Services Committee, which viewed itself less as an oversight body than as a defender of the Pentagon and as a gatherer of defense contracts for members' congressional districts. Other aspects of the national security state, especially the intelligence community, similarly stood beyond congressional control.

NEW MEANS OF
CONGRESSIONAL POWER

By the end of the 1950s, then, it seemed as if Congress had lost much of its de facto input into the making of U.S. foreign policy. But two major exceptions to this pattern existed: subcommittee government and the foreign aid program. In part because of its relative youth (it had been created only in 1947), the Armed Services Committee proved much less successful at resisting challenges to its authority than had been the Foreign Relations Committee before World War II. That inability to defend its turf helps explain the postwar explosion of subcommittees dealing with foreign policy issues. Joseph McCarthy was the most prominent senator to use a subcommittee (of the formerly low-profile Government Operations Committee) to advance his own foreign policy agenda, but his activities are best viewed more broadly, as part of the decentralization of power within Congress on national security matters. Overall, the number of Senate foreign policy subcommittees grew from seven in 1946 to thirty-one two decades later.

Eisenhower's second term witnessed the establishment of three particularly important subcommittees, each chaired by a contender for the 1960 Democratic presidential nomination. After the Soviets launched the *Sputnik* satellite, Richard Russell handed the issue over to his protégé, Lyndon Johnson of Texas, who chaired the Preparedness Investigations Subcommittee. In late 1958, Senator Henry Jackson introduced a resolution mandating a study of the National Security Council's performance. The resolution was reported to the Government Operations Committee—on which Jackson, not coincidentally, served—and over the next two years, a subcommittee chaired by Jackson conducted a wide-ranging investigation of Eisenhower's foreign policy that only tangentially related to the National Security Council. From a much different ideological perspective, Hubert Humphrey's Disarmament Subcommittee, an offshoot of the Foreign Relations Committee, looked to build a case for arms control initiatives. The hearings helped pave the way for the creation of the Arms Control and Disarmament Agency in 1961.

The decentralized committee structure gave senators interested in foreign policy questions an avenue for achieving direct influence—sometimes by facilitating informal ties with members of the national bureaucracy, sometimes through hearings that sought to influence political debate, sometimes by providing a vehicle for marshaling the appropriations power. Moreover, these three subcommittees starkly contrasted with the ineffective tactics associated with the "limited dissent," showing how members of Congress could—and did—influence national security policy even at the height of the Cold War. Until the early 1960s, the most effective congressional criticism came from the right. But that situation would soon change, since liberals would build upon the tactics pioneered by the likes of Jackson and Johnson to challenge the Cold War anticommunist consensus.

Subcommittee government also played a key role in bolstering congressional involvement in the foreign aid program. Moreover, because the Constitution required all revenue measures to originate in the House of Representatives, the lower chamber used foreign aid to enhance its foreign policy role. In another example of the power of foreign policy subcommittees, Otto Passman, the chair of the Foreign Operations Subcommittee, regularly used his position to reduce the total appropriations requested by Eisenhower, and later John Kennedy, by 20 or 25 percent—an effort that was aided by the program's consistent domestic unpopularity. Passman thoroughly enjoyed the effort: he informed one harried Eisenhower administration official that his sole pleasure in life was cutting the foreign aid budget.

For the early postwar period, congressional conservatives, worried about the excessive cost and the support it provided to left-of-center regimes, provided the most vociferous criticism of foreign aid. As long as these conservatives remained the only opposition, a bipartisan coalition of northern Democrats and moderate Republicans provided the votes necessary for passage. But beginning in the early 1960s, the program started coming under attack from liberals, mostly in the Senate. Democratic senators such as George McGovern, Albert Gore, Frank Church, and Ernest Gruening contended that both the Eisenhower and Kennedy administrations had excessively employed foreign aid as a tool of the Cold War, showering dictatorial regimes with military assistance solely because of their anticommunist credentials. The senators began by offering amendments to deny foreign aid to governments that came to power through undemocratic means. They also gradually expanded their efforts to launch an attack on military aid that began to veer toward repudiating Cold War liberalism itself.

This new base of opposition developed at a critical moment, for in the early 1960s foreign aid assumed a new importance in containment policy. Kennedy's counterinsurgency theories dictated a considerable expansion in military aid expenditures. And the administration's boldest new international initiative, the Alliance for Progress, promised a multiyear U.S. commitment of economic and military assistance to Latin America. Unfortunately for John F. Kennedy, in 1963 Passman's conservatives and the Senate liberals joined forces in an awkward ideological alliance that inflicted a serious setback to the administration. In the aftermath, foreign aid bills became a favorite vehicle for policy riders on issues as diverse as human rights, expropriation of U.S.-owned property, and the foreign policies of recipient regimes. The pattern of congressional deference had started to break down well before the surge of congressional activity in the late 1960s and early 1970s.

THE VIETNAM WAR

The Americanization of the Vietnam War thus arrived at a time when Congress as an institution was looking for new avenues to shape U.S. foreign policy. Until 1964, Congress had played a fairly minor role on Southeast Asian matters. In 1954, Eisenhower had invited legislative leaders to comment on whether the United States should use its military to rescue beleaguered French forces at Dien Bien Phu. But the president had little desire to send troops and almost certainly engaged in the charade so he would have an excuse to explain his lack of action to the French. The Kennedy years featured a more consistent level of congressional comment. Many of the same critics of foreign aid—Gruening, Gore, Church—also questioned the military and economic assistance program toward the dictatorial government of Ngo Dinh Diem and called for Congress to more aggressively counter administration policy. But at no point did a sustained legislative effort on Vietnam policy emerge.

That condition changed after Lyndon Johnson assumed the presidency in November 1963 and military conditions in Vietnam began to deteriorate. With only one exception, Johnson accomplished his goal of keeping public attention off Vietnam until after the 1964 elections. But that exception resulted in one of the most famous pieces of legislation in the postwar Congress. In

August 1964, after North Vietnamese vessels reportedly attacked U.S. forces in the Tonkin Gulf, the administration introduced a resolution granting the president authority to take all necessary measures to repel the attack. The open-ended wording disturbed some senators, but the chair of the Senate Foreign Relations Committee, J. William Fulbright, assured his colleagues that Johnson would never utilize the full breadth of the authority the Tonkin Gulf Resolution granted him. Although in retrospect Fulbright's words ring hollow, at the time his assertions seemed perfectly reasonable. Eisenhower and Kennedy had introduced similar offerings to deal with specific crises, and these had not resulted in a massive commitment of U.S. troops overseas.

By mid-1965, however, the increasing numbers of U.S. troops in Vietnam prompted a more active congressional response. For the rest of Johnson's term and most of Richard Nixon's, an increasingly powerful group of Senate liberals tried to end the war through congressional action. Perhaps their most important initiative came in 1966, when Fulbright convened public hearings on Vietnam policy that attracted a national television audience to witness divisions among the foreign policy elite regarding the administration's approach to matters in Southeast Asia. Indeed, although members of Congress failed to prevent the Americanization of the Vietnam conflict, their activities did help turn U.S. opinion against the war. In the process, Fulbright became the most powerful Foreign Relations Committee chair—and, perhaps, the most important congressional player on foreign policy matters—since William Borah in the 1920s.

Beyond the antiwar activities of Senate liberals were two other substantial areas of congressional involvement in 1960s foreign policy. The first centered on the wartime actions of congressional Republicans and prowar Democrats, such as Senators John Stennis (Democrat) and John Tower (Republican) and Representative Gerald Ford (Republican). Stennis and Tower were particularly significant because their extensive contacts made them the Capitol Hill voices for the military at a time when the Pentagon was often articulating its own perspective on international affairs. Second, quite apart from Vietnam, Senate liberals challenged Cold War principles elsewhere in the world. Because their dissent did not fully blossom until the United States already had tens of thousands of troops on the ground in Vietnam, Senate liberals always acted under some constraint. The full force of their perspective emerged only in their positions on newer issues—such as Greece, where they demanded a cutoff of U.S. aid after the military coup of 1967, and Thailand, where their anti-interventionism offered a clear sense of their desired role for the United States in Southeast Asia.

CONGRESSIONAL DISSENT BEYOND VIETNAM

For several years in the late 1960s and early 1970s, the most prominent of these Senate dissenters was Missouri's Stuart Symington, formerly a Cold Warrior and Harry Truman's secretary of the Air Force. Symington's break with the past symbolized the altered world of Congress in the early 1970s. The Missouri senator chaired one of the most important foreign policy subcommittees in U.S. history, one that launched inquiries of U.S. commitments in Thailand, Spain, and Laos and helped produce the 1971 National Commitments Resolution. In 1967 hearings looking into U.S. foreign arms sales, Symington offered a concrete demonstration of the link between military aid and foreign policy. In the 1968–1969 battle against the antiballistic missile (ABM), the first full-fledged congressional challenge to a Cold War weapons system, he showed that dissenters, who traditionally shied away from slots on the Armed Services Committee, needed detailed technical knowledge of military matters if they hoped to prevail in debates on national security policy. In his inquiry into U.S. agreements with Spain over military bases on the Iberian Peninsula, he uncovered how overseas bases, frequently obtained without congressional sanction, brought with them broader diplomatic requirements. And in the Laotian hearings, he offered a glimpse at how secrecy could obscure not only national security material but also secret wars that were occurring without legislative sanction.

In the broadest sense of the term, Symington himself was a transitional figure. His own transformation from a hard-line anticommunist to a skeptic of Cold War foreign policy helped him lead the Senate's transition into a more aggressive body on foreign policy matters. But his most significant achievement came in pioneering tactics that other liberals would use even as he himself faded from the ranks of active dissenters. Indeed, some of the highest-profile executive-legislative battles during the later Richard Nixon and early Gerald Ford administrations featured fresh-

man liberals employing devices prominently used by Symington, such as the efforts of Iowa senators Harold Hughes and John Culver in the early 1970s. Both Hughes and Culver elected to join the Armed Services Committee rather than the Foreign Relations Committee; both cultivated allies in the military; and both used the information gleaned from those allies to undercut their opponents' credibility. Behind all of these efforts stood perhaps the most important transition point of the post-Vietnam era: the willingness of Congress to challenge executive supremacy on Department of Defense matters—on policy, on specific weapons systems, and in roll-call votes.

Members of Congress were prepared to use these revived powers. Liberals in the Senate, often using foreign aid riders, expanded on the ideological alternative they first had outlined in the foreign aid revolt. First, they charged that policymakers from the Johnson and Nixon administrations had subordinated traditional American ideals—such as support for democracy, human rights, and self-determination—to the anticommunist dictates of the Cold War. Second, they charged that the national security apparatus associated with the Cold War had given the military an excessive role in the making of U.S. foreign policy. Finally, they contended that a democracy required a foreign policy of openness—and that a foreign policy of openness required a consistent congressional presence in international affairs.

This dissent produced attacks against U.S. policy toward Latin America, Asia, and Africa, regions in which, critics contended, a misapplication of containment principles had produced policies that contradicted the country's image as a champion of international reform, employed military solutions to political or social problems, and allied the United States with ideologically undesirable regimes. For example, after Augusto Pinochet's military government assumed power in Chile in 1973, Representative Donald Fraser and Senator Edward Kennedy opened hearings on Pinochet's human rights abuses. Congress then enacted a series of measures to gradually end U.S. assistance to the regime. The Turkish invasion of Cyprus in 1974 provided another opportunity to act, and Thomas Eagleton pushed through the Senate an amendment cutting off foreign aid to the Ankara government. Surveying the burst of activity, one European diplomat concluded, "It isn't just the State Department or the president anymore. It's Congress now."

But the most important of these congressional efforts concerned U.S. policy toward Angola, where a small Central Intelligence Agency covert operation mushroomed in mid-1975. The operation came to the attention of Iowa senator Dick Clark, who toured Africa in the summer of 1975 and returned home convinced that respecting Angolan self-determination would atone for earlier instances in which the anticommunist mindset of the Cold War had caused the United States to abandon its traditional anti-imperialist ideals. Concerned about the ramifications of the Ford administration's actions, he introduced an amendment to the 1976 foreign aid bill to cut off all covert assistance to Angola, thus forcing a public debate on the policy. In fact, he reasoned, publicity itself formed an appropriate method of oversight. A foreign aid amendment and the subsequent congressional debate provided the perfect vehicle. A few months later, the Senate passed an amendment to the Department of Defense appropriations bill introduced by John Tunney immediately terminating covert assistance to the Angolan anticommunists. The two amendments represented the high point of a congressional revolt against the anticommunist ethos of the Cold War and executive authority in foreign policy.

CONSERVATIVES AND CONGRESSIONAL POWER

That the amendments would not spawn ideological successors, however, was not apparent at the time. The congressional elections of 1972 and 1974 brought to Washington a sizable bloc of young Democrats for whom Vietnam rather than the postwar division of Europe provided their formative foreign policy experience. But while these Democrats shaped the congressional mentality of the era, the mid-1970s also witnessed a dramatic resurgence of the congressional right. Domestically, the social and cultural divisions of the 1960s—intensified by the antigovernment sentiments spawned by the Vietnam War and the Watergate scandal—produced a climate conducive to the rise of conservatism. Internationally, the conduct of the Soviet Union led a new group of intellectuals—dubbed the neoconservatives—to demand a more assertive U.S. foreign policy.

The sponsors of the Clark and Tunney amendments hardly expected that their passage would open up new avenues for congressional

conservatives to influence foreign policy. But over the next ten years, the amendments produced a host of unintended consequences. Their passage further eroded the Cold War institutional structure of Congress, in which the body had sacrificed potent foreign policy tools in deference to executive authority. But if this change represented a short-term victory for congressional liberals, subsequent developments defied expectations that empowering Congress would pave the way for an anti-interventionist, prohuman rights foreign policy. Instead, conservatives proved as successful as their ideological foes in utilizing the revitalized congressional power. Meanwhile, as Cuban-backed forces consolidated their position in Angola, the Clark amendment came under strong attack, beginning a process in which the amendment came to symbolize congressional recklessness and an overly idealistic foreign policy that failed to take into account national security needs.

Throughout much of the post–World War II period, most challenges to the legislature's institutional orthodoxy had come from liberals unhappy with the anticommunist foreign policies of the day. But the Tunney amendment also provided a precedent for members of Congress, regardless of their ideological persuasions, to use rejuvenated congressional power to challenge executive-branch foreign policy. President Jimmy Carter's international agenda suffered the consequences, coming under strong attack from senators who just a few years earlier had tried to block Tunney's initiative. In terms of immediately affecting policy, most of these conservative initiatives failed. But, as occurred with the liberal critics of containment a decade before, impassioned congressional debate framed the national discussion of foreign policy in a way that ultimately worked to the conservatives' advantage.

The newly strengthened conservatives had a more immediate impact on an area of traditional strength: national security policy. This effort culminated in the Senate battle against the SALT II treaty, which became the first arms-control agreement since the early 1950s that did not clear Congress. More important, the conservatives, led by Henry Jackson and Barry Goldwater, succeeded in beating back the Symington-led challenge to national security policy. By the late 1970s, in response to this conservative pressure, liberals such as John Culver, Carl Levin, and Patrick Leahy—the ideological heirs of the dissenters of the early 1960s—were on the defensive, attempting to show how their military philosophy would not undermine the U.S. position in the world. Conservatives again dominated debate over the armed services. The late 1970s and early 1980s thus joined the McCarranite era of the early 1950s as rare periods when the congressional right set the national agenda on foreign policy issues.

The growth of the congressional right also helped seal the fate of the foreign policy framework laws passed in the early 1970s, the most prominent of which was the War Powers Act of 1973. In contrast to domestic affairs, where the increasing tendency to handle through judicial or investigatory means disputes that previously would have been classified as political tended to increase congressional power, the last fifteen years of the Cold War featured the failure of the War Powers Act and other measures designed to restore the balance between the executive and Congress to work as their sponsors had desired. (The War Powers Act, for instance, required the president to obtain congressional approval within sixty days of initiating any overseas military authorization. But because the measure gave the president the authority to decide when to start the sixty-day clock, it has proven impossible to enforce.) In part, these initiatives did surprisingly little to alter the fundamental balance between the two branches because the legislation placed such a high priority on abstract constitutional concerns. By making their offerings such a frontal challenge to presidential authority, the sponsors of framework legislation almost always needed to gain a two-thirds majority in both chambers to overcome a presidential veto. But to achieve this goal, they needed to water down their proposals, as in the War Powers Act, when John Stennis insisted on a host of concessions that weakened the bill in exchange for his supporting the measure.

For example, the Cooper-Church Amendment, which cut off funds for Richard Nixon's secret incursion into Cambodia in 1970, was notable for the willingness of its sponsors to deny that its adoption would constrain the powers of the commander in chief, to decline to call for an instant cutoff of funding for the incursion, and to consent to a modifying amendment upholding the president's power to act in emergency situations to protect the lives of U.S. forces without consulting Congress. Similar developments frustrated congressional attempts to pass a restrictive war powers measure, where negotiations between the House and Senate produced a law limiting the amount of time in which the president could unilaterally send U.S. troops overseas (ninety days)

rather than limiting the justifications for such action. The bill also allowed the president to decide when troops were introduced into harm's way, thus triggering the start of the time limit, while a key strengthening amendment to include the CIA under the terms of the bill failed.

Many of the difficulties that had prevented Congress from assuming an active role using such formal assertions of its power persisted throughout the 1970s and 1980s. For instance, congressional investigations into the intelligence community produced less comprehensive reforms and more political problems for their champions than could have been anticipated when the hearings began in 1975. For example, Frank Church found that his chairing the Senate committee investigating CIA matters interfered with his pursuit of the 1976 Democratic nomination for president; his House counterpart, Otis Pike of New York, oversaw such an unruly inquiry that his report was repudiated by the House, and he retired from Congress two years later. And although both chambers ultimately established intelligence oversight committees, the CIA proved effective at using a variety of tactics to frustrate attempts at vigorous oversight, particularly during the tenure of Director William Casey, who served from 1981 until his death in 1987.

Casey's boss, President Ronald Reagan, received an overwhelming majority in 1980, carrying forty-four states and bringing with him a Republican-controlled Senate. Foreign policy played a key role in his campaign, as Reagan called for a massive arms buildup and a renewed ideological confrontation with the Soviets. In addition, the GOP nominee explicitly argued that Congress had grown too powerful and implicitly suggested that congressional actions (such as the Clark amendment) had harmed U.S. national security. Because Republicans controlled the Senate for most of his tenure, Reagan faced less effective opposition from the upper chamber than, arguably, any chief executive in the twentieth century. The House offered a different story: Democrats gained twenty-six seats in the 1982 election and had a comfortable working majority for the rest of the 1980s. Led by the partisan House Speaker Thomas P. "Tip" O'Neill, Jr., and Majority Leader Jim Wright, surviving Watergate-era Democrats such as Thomas J. Downey, Michael Barnes, and Mike Synar came into their own during Reagan's tenure. In the process they made the House as formidable a foreign policy force as at any point in American history.

The Reagan years yielded a mixed legacy regarding congressional power. As had been the case essentially since their passage, the War Powers Act and other framework legislation failed to bolster congressional power. Reagan undertook three provocative military operations during his presidency, sending armed forces to Lebanon and Grenada and launching air strikes against Libya. The Libyan and Grenadan operations ended quickly, but, particularly in the case of Grenada (where the United States sent troops to topple a Marxist government), there seemed to be no justification for not invoking the War Powers Act. The president called the marines sent to Lebanon "peacekeepers," but the peace they kept favored the Maronite Christian president in the country's long-running civil war. Facing congressional criticism, the administration negotiated a compromise in which it promised to seek legislative authorization if the intervention lasted longer than eighteen months. Even in this instance, Reagan maintained that the decision did not imply that he recognized the constitutionality of the War Powers Act, and, indeed, Congress's willingness to accept the plan essentially made the 1973 law a dead letter. In the end, the troops were withdrawn before the eighteen-month limit after the bombing of the marines stationed at the U.S. embassy in Beirut.

While the Reagan years shattered hopes that the framework legislation could succeed, the 1980s did show that—as Gouverneur Morris and James Madison long before had predicted—the power of the purse provided an important tool for Congress to influence foreign policy. Throughout Reagan's term, members of Congress used appropriations riders, hearings, and other unconventional methods to challenge the administration's foreign policy, especially toward the Third World. Few would have predicted this development in the late 1970s, when conservative critics targeted initiatives like the Clark amendment and other congressional expressions favoring human rights diplomacy. Theorists such as Jeane Kirkpatrick, Reagan's first ambassador to the United Nations, recommended distinguishing between totalitarian and authoritarian regimes, with the former worthy of support—despite human rights violations—because of the anticommunist nature of most totalitarian governments. This critique grew more powerful as anti-American regimes came to power in Iran and Nicaragua; and Reagan, after his election in 1980, adopted the Kirkpatrick philosophy as his own.

This deemphasis on idealism provided an opening for Reagan's congressional critics. Perhaps the most effective was Michael Barnes, a scholarly Democrat first elected in 1976 who took over as chair of the Inter-American Relations Subcommittee following the defeats of several more senior Democrats in the 1980 elections. Barnes, the first Watergate-era Democrat to chair a foreign policy subcommittee, made the most of his opportunity. Reagan's policy of aiding the contras (anticommunist guerrillas attempting to topple the Sandinista government in Nicaragua) dominated the debate regarding 1980s inter-American policy, but Barnes used his position to focus matters on human rights abuses by anticommunist governments in Chile, Uruguay, and Guatemala as well. Congressional criticism also helped cause a shift in U.S. policy toward Chile and the Philippines, where Reagan had come to office pledging to support the dictatorial regimes of Augusto Pinochet and Ferdinand Marcos. Examples of the pattern included senators with such diverse ideological viewpoints as Christopher Dodd, who led the Senate opposition to Reagan's policy in Central America, and Richard Lugar, who helped persuade the Reagan administration to end U.S. support for Marcos's regime in the Philippines. Moreover, a congressional willingness to use the appropriations power set the stage for the most important scandal of the Reagan years, the Iran-Contra affair, when the administration covertly funneled arms to anticommunist forces in Central America in direct contravention of the Boland Amendment. The revelation of the affair in late 1986 severely impaired Reagan's political standing and damaged his historical legacy.

CONGRESS AND THE END OF THE COLD WAR

The end of the Cold War broke down the established pattern of legislative-executive relations. The Cold War's conclusion accelerated the trend, which began with Vietnam and Watergate, of diminishing the federal government's role in the everyday lives of most Americans. The new international environment forced members of both branches to search for new ideological approaches to world affairs. And it coincided with—and perhaps contributed to—the most extended period of divided government (with one party controlling Congress and another the presidency) in American history.

Most academics and politicians had predicted that the end of the Cold War would establish a more consistent congressional presence in U.S. foreign policy because the threat of immediate nuclear attack had so dramatically receded. But the first post–Cold War president, George H. W. Bush, defied expectations, even though he faced a Congress controlled by Democrats for his entire term. Encouraged by his White House counsel, C. Boyden Gray, Bush proved extraordinarily aggressive at defending (and enlarging) executive prerogatives, using vetoes and especially presidential signing statements to outline a vision of presidential power whose scope would have stunned even a figure like Alexander Hamilton. A sign of his intentions came in his first year, when he sent marines to Panama in 1989—without congressional authorization—to remove from power and arrest Panamanian president Manuel Noriega, who was wanted in the United States on drug charges. Bush also rejected congressional attempts to influence policy toward the People's Republic of China, consistently vetoing bills to tighten sanctions on the Beijing regime after the Tiananmen Square crackdown against student dissidents.

Congressional Democrats, who generally outmaneuvered Bush on domestic issues, had more difficulty in adjusting to the post–Cold War environment. The new Senate majority leader, Maine senator George Mitchell, was a former judge and believed that framework legislation, if properly used, would allow Congress to play a greater foreign policy role. The run-up to the Gulf War of 1991 put this thesis to the test. After Saddam Hussein's Iraqi forces invaded Kuwait in August 1990, Bush, acting in concert with U.S. allies, eventually sent 250,000 troops to Saudi Arabia as part of Operation Desert Shield. But, citing the measure's unconstitutionality, Bush refused to invoke the War Powers Act. After the 1990 midterm elections, the administration moved another quarter million U.S. forces into the region, clearly anticipating the possibility of offensive action. Bush officials suggested that the president would go to war with Iraq without requesting a declaration of war from Congress, citing his power as commander in chief.

Led by Mike Synar, a group of House Democrats petitioned the Supreme Court for redress. But in line with precedent, the Court declined to involve itself in foreign policy battles between the executive and legislative branches. (Indeed, the few decisions the high court did render on international issues, such as the 1983 rul-

ing *Immigration and Naturalization Service* v. *Chadha,* which ruled the one-house legislative veto unconstitutional, tended to weaken congressional influence.) Although Synar's effort failed, political pressure eventually persuaded Bush to submit a bill authorizing him to use force. The president did so, however, only days short of an announced deadline to initiate offensive action and with more than 500,000 U.S. troops stationed along the Iraq–Saudi Arabia border. In such an environment it came as little surprise that Congress supported the war declaration; perhaps the real shock came in the forty-seven senators who opposed the resolution.

The record regarding congressional power after the Gulf War was somewhat mixed. Like his predecessor, William Jefferson Clinton struggled with the effects of divided government: a crushing defeat in the 1994 midterm elections brought Republicans to power in both the House and the Senate. Moreover, unlike the Mitchell-led congressional Democrats during the Bush administration, the new GOP majority was fairly united ideologically and was determined to use congressional power to implement its agenda. Clinton experienced difficulties with Congress almost from the start of his administration. Legislative pressure in part forced the administration to reverse itself on issues ranging from Clinton's commitment to end discrimination against gays in the military to the president's decision to continue an ill-conceived humanitarian intervention in Somalia. Even the passage of the North American Free Trade Agreement in 1993, Clinton's first legislative victory on a foreign policy matter (and, in many ways, the only significant one of his administration) came only after a bloody fight with Congress.

After 1994, a condition of almost permanent hostility between the president and Congress developed. Congressional Republicans offered a multifaceted program that coalesced into an unusually powerful—and effective—critique of the executive's approach to world affairs. Ideologically, the congressional Republicans had several basic viewpoints that reinforced each other. Some GOP legislators seemed eager to revive the Cold War, embracing a vehement anticommunism and supporting hard-line policies toward China, Cuba, and North Korea. Moreover, led by Senate Majority Leader Trent Lott, the congressional Republicans used Congress's power of the purse to prevent the scaling back of the Pentagon budget, partly for ideological reasons, partly due to a desire to funnel defense dollars to their home districts or states. From another angle, Republicans such as House Majority Leader Richard Armey of Texas boasted of their lack of overseas travel and espoused an anti-internationalism that targeted organizations like the United Nations. Most of the new wave of congressional Republicans also opposed overseas interventions—like Clinton's actions in Haiti and the Balkans—which they viewed as Wilsonian in theory.

Three other factors made the congressional power exercised by the 1990s GOP somewhat unusual. First, after their opposition to the Gulf War, congressional Democrats, for the previous forty years the more active of the two parties in seeking to utilize congressional power, all but ceased involvement on matters relating to foreign affairs. Second, after a series of weak leaders following the 1974 defeat of J. William Fulbright, the Foreign Relations Committee returned to a higher profile under the stewardship of the North Carolina senator Jesse Helms, whose aggressive posture made him a factor on virtually all international questions during the Clinton administration. Finally, the extreme distaste most congressional Republicans felt for Clinton gave party members a political incentive to oppose executive authority in foreign policy, as when Congress refused to renew Clinton's authority to "fast-track" trade agreements, a luxury enjoyed by every president since the passage of the Reciprocal Trade Agreements Act in 1934.

Still, the performance of the congressional GOP sometimes failed to live up to its rhetoric. For example, while Clinton's ability to negotiate tariff deals was impeded, he acted unilaterally and in opposition to the stated congressional position when he intervened to prop up the Mexican peso in 1995. Similarly, in the midst of the war in Kosovo, he initiated hostilities without formally consulting Congress and then ignored GOP-sponsored legislation that seemed to call for him to terminate the operation. Regardless of the precise balance between the two branches at the end of the twentieth century, however, older patterns in congressional power remained in place: the role of the appropriations process and other unconventional methods in measuring the congressional presence in conducting U.S. foreign policy; the importance of party divisions in shaping attitudes toward the congressional role in world affairs; and the tendency of Congress to offer more ideologically extreme viewpoints on international matters than did the executive.

BIBLIOGRAPHY

Accinelli, Robert. "Eisenhower, Congress, and the 1954–1955 Offshore Island Crisis." *Presidential Studies Quarterly* 20 (spring 1990): 329–344. A good study of the limits of congressional power during the Eisenhower years.

Ambrosius, Lloyd E. *Woodrow Wilson and the American Diplomatic Tradition.* Cambridge and New York, 1987. The best published study of the League of Nations battle in the Senate.

Arnson, Cynthia. *Crossroads: Congress, the Reagan Administration, and Central America.* New York, 1989.

Ashby, LeRoy. *The Spearless Leader: Senator Borah and the Progressive Movement in the 1920s.* Urbana, Ill., 1972. The best biography of the career of the 1920s Foreign Relations Committee chair.

Banks, William C., and Peter Raven-Hansen. *National Security Law and the Power of the Purse.* New York, 1994.

Bernstein, Barton, and Franklin Leib. "Progressive Republican Senators and American Imperialism: A Reappraisal." *Mid-America* 50 (1968): 163–205. An excellent study of the relationship between congressional power and liberal dissent before World War I.

Blechman, Barry M. *The Politics of National Security: Congress and U.S. Defense Policy.* New York, 1990. A nicely done study of how Congress has influenced national security matters since World War II.

Cole, Wayne S. *Roosevelt and the Isolationists, 1932–45.* Lincoln, Neb., 1983.

Franck, Thomas M., ed. *The Tethered Presidency: Congressional Restraints on Executive Power.* New York, 1981. A somewhat dated volume that remains valuable for the depth of its coverage.

Franck, Thomas M., and Edward Weisband. *Foreign Policy by Congress.* New York, 1979.

Gaskin, Thomas M. "Senator Lyndon B. Johnson, the Eisenhower Administration, and U.S. Foreign Policy, 1957–1960." *Presidential Studies Quarterly* 24 (spring 1994): 337–353.

Gibbons, William Conrad. *The U.S. Government and the Vietnam War: Executive and Legislative Roles and Relationships.* 4 vols. Princeton, N.J., 1986–1995. The standard account of Congress and the Vietnam War.

Gleijeses, Piero. "The Limits of Sympathy: The United States and the Independence of Spanish America." *Journal of Latin American Studies* 24 (1992): 481–505.

Griffith, Robert. *The Politics of Fear: Joseph R. McCarthy and the Senate.* Lexington, Ky., 1970.

Hietala, Thomas R. *Manifest Design: Anxious Aggrandizement in Late Jacksonian America.* Ithaca, N.Y., 1985. A good model of integrating congressional history with the broader study of U.S. foreign relations.

Hinckley, Barbara. *Less Than Meets the Eye: Foreign Policy Making and the Myth of the Assertive Congress.* Chicago, 1994.

Hoyt, Steven, and Steven Baker, eds. *Legislating Foreign Policy.* Boulder, Colo., 1984.

Johnson, Loch K. *A Season of Inquiry: Congress and Intelligence.* Chicago, 1988.

Lindsay, James M. *Congress and the Politics of U.S. Defense Policy.* Baltimore, 1994. Much broader than its title suggests, the best book to date on Congress and the Cold War.

Logevall, Fredrik. *Choosing War: The Lost Chance for Peace and the Escalation of War in Vietnam.* Berkeley, Calif., 1999. A remarkable example of how including the congressional perspective enriches the writing of international history.

Olmsted, Kathryn S. *Challenging the Secret Government: The Post-Watergate Investigations of the CIA and FBI.* Chapel Hill, N.C., 1996.

Pastor, Robert A. *Congress and the Politics of U.S. Foreign Economic Policy, 1929–1976.* Berkeley, Calif., 1980.

Paterson, Thomas G. "Presidential Foreign Policy, Public Opinion, and Congress: The Truman Years." *Diplomatic History* 3 (1979): 1–21.

Rakove, Jack N. "Solving a Constitutional Puzzle: The Treatymaking Clause as a Case Study." *Perspectives in American History,* n.s. 1 (1984): 207–248. The most thoroughly researched piece on congressional power in foreign affairs and the Constitutional Convention.

Reichard, Gary W. "Divisions and Dissent: Democrats and Foreign Policy, 1952–1956." *Political Science Quarterly* 93 (1978): 37–65. A solid study of the Democrats' "limited dissent."

Ripley, Randall B., and James M. Lindsay, eds. *Congress Resurgent: Foreign and Defense Policy on Capitol Hill.* Ann Arbor, Mich., 1993.

Schoultz, Lars. *Human Rights and United States Policy Toward Latin America.* Princeton, N.J., 1981.

Small, Melvin. *Democracy and Diplomacy: The Impact of Domestic Politics on U.S. Foreign Policy, 1789–1994.* Baltimore, 1996.

Smist, Frank. *Congress Oversees the Intelligence Community, 1947–1989.* Knoxville, Tenn., 1994.

Stone, Ralph. *The Irreconcilables: The Fight Against the League of Nations.* Lexington, Ky., 1970.

Widenor, William C. *Henry Cabot Lodge and the Search for an American Foreign Policy.* Berkeley, Calif., 1981. A model in congressional biography, of Wilson's leading foe in the League of Nations fight.

Woods, Randall Bennett. *Fulbright: A Biography.* New York, 1995. A much-needed study of arguably the most powerful Foreign Relations Committee chair in U.S. history.

See also AMBASSADORS, EXECUTIVE AGENTS, AND SPECIAL REPRESENTATIVES; BIPARTISANSHIP; THE CONSTITUTION; ELITISM; FOREIGN AID; PRESIDENTIAL POWER; PUBLIC OPINION; TREATIES.

CONSORTIA

Warren I. Cohen

As generally found in world affairs, consortia are multinational cooperative ventures designed to cope with some common problem, ostensibly apolitical. The best-known consortia, the so-called China consortiums, were banking syndicates—combinations of banking groups from several countries. Lacking adequate capital for export, the United States did not serve as a lender in international financial operations until the twentieth century. When it did begin to take part, American bankers proved to be imperfect instruments for national policy.

THE FIRST CHINA CONSORTIUM

In the early years of the twentieth century, a number of American financial institutions accumulated capital for which they sought foreign markets. J. P. Morgan and Company, Kuhn, Loeb and Company, and National City Bank of New York were prominent among firms interested in investing funds outside the United States. Opportunities for domestic investment were still plentiful: the United States remained a capital-importing nation, and Europe remained the world's banker until World War I. Opportunities for greater profit, however, were believed to exist abroad, and American bankers became deeply involved in the financial affairs of countries such as Mexico, Cuba, Haiti, the Dominican Republic, and Nicaragua. To a lesser extent, some bankers and industrialists were interested in East Asia, especially China. China was attempting to modernize, preferred U.S. capital to European or Japanese, and the Chinese government was a better credit risk than a number of U.S. state governments.

There were, however, other kinds of risks involved in investing in China. The Caribbean was an American lake, dominated by the growing power of the United States, and investors were confident that the U.S. government would protect their interests in Caribbean countries. But in China all of the great European powers and Japan struggled for advantage, sometimes political as well as economic. With rare exception, the U.S. government had shown itself disinclined to become involved in Chinese affairs, unwilling to give American businessmen support comparable to that which their European and Japanese competitors might reasonably expect from their own governments. As a result, little U.S. capital could be found in China in 1909, when William Howard Taft became president of the United States.

Taft was eager to expand American influence and power, and his administration was noted for its use of "dollar diplomacy" to achieve its ends. Taft not only continued Theodore Roosevelt's support of U.S. economic interests in Latin America, but also backed enterprises in places as remote as Turkey. The most striking contrast between the policies of Taft and Roosevelt could be found in East Asia, where Taft refused to acquiesce in Japanese expansion in Manchuria. He believed that Chinese and Americans shared a mutual interest in preventing Japanese hegemony over China's northeastern provinces and that the development of American economic interests in that region would serve the interests of both nations—perhaps all nations. Several schemes for forcing American capital into Manchuria, most notably the "neutralization" plan of Secretary of State Philander Knox, a scheme for internationalizing Chinese railways, failed; but in China proper the Taft offensive met with one apparent success: American bankers were awarded a share in a loan for the building of the Hankow-Canton or Hukuang Railway and allowed to join what became known as the consortium.

A group of American banking firms had come together in the last year of the Roosevelt administration to explore investment opportunities in East Asia, but had not acted in the absence of interest in the White House or on the part of the secretary of state. When Taft and Knox insisted, early in 1909, that the United States be allowed to participate in the financing of the Hukuang, the existing banking group was formally designated the American group and called upon to play the American role—if the British, French, and German groups, and their respective governments, as well as the Chinese government, would honor the American demand.

In June 1909, as a syndicate of British, French, and German bankers was about to conclude negotiations with the Chinese, Knox filed a formal protest, reminding the Chinese government of assurances it had given in 1904 that the United States would be able to share in any loan to build the Hukuang. Choosing to see the exclusion of the United States as an unfriendly act, Knox threatened to discontinue the remission of indemnity payments resulting from the Boxer Rebellion in 1900. Responding to American pressures, the Chinese urged the British, French, and German bankers to share their concession with the Americans. Almost a year of haggling over the terms of American participation followed, featuring the personal intercession of President Taft and the Department of State's refusal to permit the American group to accept anything less than a full quarter share of all components of the project. The American group, recognizing that its share of the bond issue that would ensue from the Hukuang loan would likely require listing in European exchanges, was willing to compromise with the European bankers in order to retain goodwill and preserve their own profits. The Department of State, however, was far more concerned with American prestige and influence, presumably contingent on the American group's participating on a basis of absolute equality. Finally, in May 1910, an agreement was signed between the three European banking groups and the American group that not only permitted the Americans to share in the Hukuang loan but brought them into the banking syndicate. As of the signing of the agreement, bankers of Great Britain, France, Germany, and the United States were united in a four-power consortium, committed to sharing equally all future business in China.

But the creation of the consortium did not lead to the immediate consummation of the Hukuang loan. To the consternation of the bankers, the Chinese government backed away, fearful that coming to terms with the consortium would exacerbate mounting unrest in China and lead to a revolution. Opposition to foreign control

of China's railways was growing among educated Chinese, and there was, in addition, a desire by provincial gentry to prevent central control of railways. The consortium bankers insisted that a preliminary agreement was binding upon the Chinese and asked for and received diplomatic support from their governments. The U.S. minister to China, William J. Calhoun, was greatly embarrassed by instructions that he demand that the Chinese conclude the loan negotiations. He argued that it was undignified, "unworthy of civilized powers," to force a loan on an unwilling government. But Calhoun's protests were brushed aside, and the U.S. government joined in the pressures to which the Chinese succumbed in May 1911. As the Peking government anticipated, conclusion of the £6 million loan led to increased violence in the provinces and ultimately to revolution.

Even Calhoun was willing to drop his opposition to the loan if the loan operations were essential to continued cooperation between the United States and its new European partners in China. In Washington, this cooperation was deemed vital to the furtherance of U.S. interests in China. Participation in the loan was a wedge for American investments, which would lead to expanded U.S. trade, greater public attention to East Asia, and a greater role for the United States in the political affairs of the region. By forcing the consortium to admit American bankers, the Taft administration assumed it had reserved a place at the table at which the future of China would be played out. As long as the game promised to be profitable, the bankers of the American group demonstrated a grudging willingness to play the pawn.

While negotiations over the American role in the Hukuang loan were under way, the American group responded favorably to a Chinese request for another large loan, partly for currency reform and partly for Manchurian development. The Chinese hoped that by turning to the American bankers they could obtain better terms than were available from European bankers—that they could play off the American bankers against the Europeans. To Knox, the Chinese proposal held the dual promise of American hegemony over Chinese finances and an opportunity to penetrate Manchuria in order to fulfill the goal of checking Japanese expansion there. The American banking group, however, brushed aside the visions of both the Chinese and the Department of State by insisting on offering the new loan to the European bankers. Again, the problem was the shortage of capital in the United States, which necessitated an international listing of the bond issue for the loan to be floated successfully. If the American group offered the currency loan to the European groups, the Europeans might prove less disagreeable about having been forced to offer the American group a share in the Hukuang loan and allow the American group to list the bonds of both its loans on European exchanges. Profits for the American bankers would thus be assured. The Chinese were indignant, but once Knox was converted, he bludgeoned them into permitting the currency loan to be taken over by the consortium. The currency loan was never issued, however, because the revolution began.

The creation of the four-power consortium worried the Japanese and Russian governments, especially when they learned that part of the currency loan was earmarked for use in Manchuria. The Russians attempted to block the loan, and, failing at that, they tried unsuccessfully to destroy the consortium by urging the French—to whom they were closely tied, politically and economically—to withdraw. Ultimately, the Russians accepted French assurances that their interests in Manchuria could best be served if they too joined the consortium. As early as November 1910, while the Russians were still being obstructive, the Japanese concluded that their interests could be protected most readily from within and expressed an interest in membership in the consortium.

Knox was willing to allow both the Russians and the Japanese to have a share in the loan business, but not in the management of the consortium. The bankers of the consortium were not eager to share their profits with new partners. Both the British and U.S. governments tried instead to reassure the Russians and Japanese by specifying the particular Manchurian enterprises for which the consortium would provide funds, trying to demonstrate the absence of any intention to threaten the existing interests of the two Manchurian overlords. But the Russians and Japanese continued to fear that the Chinese intended to allow the consortium a monopoly on development loans in Manchuria and were still opposed to the terms of the currency reform loan in October 1911 when the revolution began.

As Ch'ing rule of China disintegrated and warfare spread along the Yangtze River, the U.S. government surrendered its hope of using the consortium or other forms of dollar diplomacy against Japan and Russia in Manchuria. With China less able than ever to protect its own interests in the frontier regions of the empire, Knox

and his assistants concluded that American interests could be furthered only by cooperating with Japan and Russia, settling for an equal opportunity to trade in Chinese provinces under their control. The British Foreign Office reached similar conclusions, joining Knox in recommending that Japan and Russia be invited to join the consortium. Both France and Yüan Shih-k'ai, strong man and later president of the Chinese Republic, agreed; but the American bankers, reinforced by the Germans, both government and bankers, opposed Russian participation.

As Yüan's regime began to assert itself over the country, his prime minister, T'ang Shao-i, notified the consortium's representatives in Peking of his interest in a £60 million loan to enable the government to reorganize, pay off advances, and proceed with development projects. In return for an option on the reorganization loan, the consortium bankers agreed to an immediate advance on the currency loan. A few days later the consortium bankers learned that the Chinese had concluded another loan, with a Belgian syndicate that included the Russo-Asiatic Bank—the main instrument of the Russian equivalent of dollar diplomacy. To the Russian government and to bankers of England and France who were excluded from the consortium, the opportunity to disrupt the consortium's efforts to monopolize China's financial transactions proved irresistible. Similarly, the Chinese were delighted to find other bankers to play off against those who combined in order to dictate the terms under which China could obtain foreign capital. The consortium bankers were outraged and broke off negotiations with Yüan's government.

The few bankers involved in the consortium, of whatever nationality, wanted a monopoly over all Chinese loans. Their governments, especially the British and U.S. governments, were uneasy about the demands of their bankers and were more interested in establishing and preserving order in China and in using economic cooperation as a base upon which political cooperation in China could be built. The governments were more receptive to Chinese requests for a relaxation of the foreign controls that the consortium bankers demanded and were ready to admit Japan and Russia to the organization if that was necessary to facilitate operations in China proper. In addition, European political considerations made pacification of Russia imperative to France and Great Britain. Consequently, the French and British governments pressed for the admission of Japan and

Russia to the consortium, appeasing the consortium bankers by forcing British and French participants in the Belgian loan to withdraw, which led to cancellation of that transaction.

Although Japan and Russia were both interested in joining the consortium, they stipulated the exclusion of Manchuria and Mongolia from the scope of the organization's operations. The British and French governments were willing to accept the Russo-Japanese terms, and in May 1912, Knox assented, but it was June before a formula agreeable to all concerned could be discovered. In June 1912, the six-power consortium came into existence, and more money was advanced to Yüan's regime. Yüan used the money to consolidate his position against his enemies, especially against Sun Yat-sen's supporters in the south and in parliament.

As Yüan sought more money, the banking groups were caught up by the political machinations of their governments in the selection of foreign advisers to oversee the expenditure of the monies loaned. European politics prevailed as Britain, France, and Russia supported each other's proposals to the detriment of German suggestions. Yüan became increasingly irritated with the consortium, his political opponents anxiously opposed further loans, and the American bankers wearied of the entire process. The U.S. minister to China had never been comfortable with the loan operations, and by 1913, Sir John Jordan, the British minister, considered the consortium arrangements to be of benefit to the one British bank involved but detrimental to British interests generally. To the American bankers there appeared little prospect for reasonable profits. The U.S. government had abandoned hope of playing an important role in Manchuria. Only the principle of cooperation, to which the State Department had dedicated itself, remained. In 1913 the new U.S. president, Woodrow Wilson, did not consider cooperation with European or Japanese imperialists a virtue, and he refused the American group the support it no longer wanted. In April the American role in the consortium was terminated.

Wilson mistrusted the Wall Street bankers of the American group, and he mistrusted their foreign partners. He suspected the consortium of seeking to take advantage of China's weakness to infringe on Chinese sovereignty and to profit at the expense of the Chinese people. He wanted to help China but was determined to find another way. Yüan was pleased, hoping that an American loan on better terms would soon be available. But American money was not forthcoming, and Yüan, desperately in need of money, concluded the reorganization loan with the remaining five members of the consortium. His position thus strengthened, Yüan was able to crush a rebellion led by Sun's Kuomintang (Nationalist) Party.

By April 1915, with Europe embroiled in warfare, Wilson recognized Japan's intent to dominate China, as evidenced by the Twenty-one Demands (1915). To check Japanese imperialism and further American interests in China, he designed his own version of dollar diplomacy. Although hostile to the American group because of its monopolistic practices and attempts to infringe on Chinese sovereignty, Wilson was very much interested in the use of American capital to further the process of Chinese modernization. He failed, however, to elicit interest among other American bankers, and, in response to a request from the Chinese government in 1916, Wilson asked the American group to consider a loan to China.

The member banks wanted to disband the American group but were held together by their inability to rid themselves of their share of the Hukuang loan. They responded negatively to Wilson's proposition, refusing to compete with the consortium and willing to consider a loan outside the scope of the consortium only if the U.S. government would offer a guarantee that China would fulfill its obligations. The government would not offer a guarantee and appealed instead to the bankers' patriotism. But the bankers would lend to China only as a business proposition, and the matter was dropped.

When a U.S. bank outside the American group entered into a loan agreement with the Chinese in 1916, the other consortium banking groups protested angrily. Wilson rejected the protests, warning the British, French, Japanese, and Russian governments against excluding American bankers from participation in Chinese affairs. With most of these governments anxious to avoid conflict with the United States while involved in a life-and-death struggle with the Central Powers in Europe, their bankers could count on little support against an invasion of American capital. There was one hope: British, French, Russian, and Japanese bankers expressed a desire to see the United States rejoin the consortium, to co-opt the United States and contain the financial offensive the American bankers were now presumed capable of launching.

In March 1917 the American group notified the Department of State that it favored accepting the invitation to rejoin the consortium, contending that the time was ripe for advancing American commercial prestige. But Wilson was unyielding: loans should be made directly to China and not through the consortium. The president recognized the overtures from the consortium as an attempt to prevent independent American action.

THE SECOND CHINA CONSORTIUM

By June 1918 the Wilson administration was forced to concede failure in its efforts to find American capital for investment in China. Fearing that the Japanese, in the absence of American or European competition, would monopolize Chinese economic affairs, Wilson agreed to allow the American group to join its old associates in a new consortium. The American group was to become more inclusive, admitting to membership banking groups throughout the country, and it would pledge not to undermine Chinese sovereignty. In return, Wilson agreed to announce that the group was offering a loan to China at the suggestion of the government.

The Wilson administration had returned to the conception of an international banking consortium, because no other means could be found to move American capital into China. The American initiative for a new consortium was intended to serve the same purpose independent American loans would have served: the containment of Japanese economic expansion to preserve opportunity for U.S. expansion in China. Given Wilson's faith in the "liberal exceptionalism" of the United States, he readily assumed that U.S. expansion, unlike the Japanese variety, would be salutary for China—that Chinese and American interests were congruent.

For the American group, Thomas W. Lamont of J. P. Morgan and Company met with representatives of the British, French, and Japanese banking groups in May 1919, at the Paris Peace Conference. Lamont proposed and reached rapid agreement on the American plan for pooling all future business in China and for pooling all existing loan agreements and options involving public subscription except those relating to industrial undertakings upon which substantial progress had been made. The efficiency of cooperation and the expectation of the exclusive support of their governments were attractive to the bankers.

In June, however, the Japanese group reported that its government insisted on excluding from the consortium agreement all rights and options held by Japan in Manchuria and Mongolia, where Japan had "special interests." The Japanese expected the United States to consent to the exceptions on the basis of Secretary of State Robert Lansing's recognition of Japan's "special interests" in his 1917 agreement with Viscount Ishii Kikujiro. Once Japan's sphere in Manchuria and Inner Mongolia was thus protected, the Japanese government viewed the consortium with favor, as a means of improving relations with the United States and as an instrument for checking the anticipated torrent of American capital.

The purpose of the consortium, as understood in Washington and London, however, was to eliminate special claims to spheres of influence and to open all of China to cooperative international development. Not only the Wilsonians, but also Lord Curzon, Great Britain's secretary of state for foreign affairs, considered economic imperialism an anachronism in the face of the nationalist movement that was sweeping over China. When the French government expressed fear that refusal to grant the reservations Japan requested would result in the Japanese finding friends outside the circle of their wartime allies, Curzon insisted that the Japanese request was inadmissible and expressed confidence that they would back down in face of the unanimity of the British, French, and American groups supported by their governments.

Months passed as the Japanese and U.S. governments exchanged mutually unsatisfactory counterproposals. In February 1920 Lamont went to Tokyo in an attempt to break the deadlock. One area for possible compromise existed, and the State Department had focused on it in December 1919: Japan's existing economic interests ("vested" interests in Manchuria and Mongolia) could be conceded, excluded from the scope of the consortium. Both sides moved slowly toward this position. To prod the Japanese government, Wilson authorized a threat to reveal the secret protocol of the Lansing-Ishii Agreement, in which Ishii had committed Japan not to seek privileges in China at the expense of other powers.

As the negotiations proceeded, Lamont proposed an exchange of notes between the American and Japanese groups defining the attitudes of foreign bankers toward Japanese economic interests in Manchuria and Mongolia, specifying what would or would not come within the scope of consortium. Lamont's plan would allow for the acceptance of existing economic facts without giving official governmental recognition. Only the consortium would recognize Japan's economic interests. The American and British ambassadors to Japan liked Lamont's proposal, but the Department of State rejected it and suggested that Lamont reach an agreement on the basis of specific enterprises the Japanese wanted to exclude from the consortium's focus. The U.S. government would not accept a reference to the exclusion of any region of China. Lamont was angered by State Department scruples, but, insisting that Manchuria was in fact dominated by the Japanese and unattractive to nationals of the other banking groups, he was able to reach agreement with his Japanese counterpart on the department's terms. In April 1920 the Japanese government, in a last effort to strengthen the consensus within the leadership, bid once more for veto power over railway construction in Manchuria. If further concessions could be won from Japan's prospective partners, opposition to the agreement within Japan might be stilled. The effort alone might satisfy dissidents within the cabinet that the government had done all that was possible. But the U.S. and British governments held firm and the Japanese appeared to retreat.

In the following month, the Ministry of Foreign Affairs gave the U.S. ambassador, Roland Morris, a "draft reply" to the American rejection of Japan's last set of reservations, claiming that the earlier note had not been presented for the purpose of raising new conditions but simply to avoid future misunderstandings. The Japanese government would not insist on explicit American assurances but would accept the general assurances offered previously and refrain from insisting upon discussion of the veto power it sought initially. The Japanese were satisfied to make known to the U.S. government their interpretation of the questions at issue.

Lamont and the American ambassador were pleased, interpreting the Japanese position as complete acceptance of the position taken by the U.S. government and supported by the British and French governments. But J. V. A. MacMurray, chief of the State Department's Division of Far Eastern Affairs, argued that the Japanese had retracted nothing. MacMurray claimed that the Japanese note reemphasized Japan's claim to a veto on railway construction in Manchuria and had further placed on record their understanding that American assurances regarding Japan's right of self-preservation meant U.S. recognition of that veto power. But MacMurray was overruled; the

Department of State accepted the Japanese draft, and the consortium negotiations were concluded.

MacMurray was probably correct when he contended that the Japanese, in addition to receiving explicit acceptance of all of their existing and some of their projected economic interests in Manchuria and Mongolia, had established a strong basis for arguing that the United States had conceded to Japan veto power over railway construction in Manchuria. Certainly that was the view that prevailed in official Japanese circles. But MacMurray's superiors in the Department of State had concluded that the choice was between accepting the conditions obtained or surrendering the idea of the four-power consortium. To the U.S. government there appeared no alternative means of preserving American interests in China. After March 1920, when the Senate for the third time rejected U.S. membership in the League of Nations, the consortium offered the best, perhaps the only, basis for cooperation with the powers in China.

With the formation of the consortium in 1920 and the subsequent agreements reached at the Washington Conference (1921–1922), Great Britain, France, Japan, and the United States were committed to cooperation among themselves in assisting with the modernization of China. The consortium bankers were to provide the Chinese government with the funds it needed to build railroads and other major productive enterprises. But in the six years that followed the Washington Conference, China suffered from almost constant civil strife, and, despite prompting from the U.S. and British governments, the consortium did nothing to assist China's economic development: no loans were granted. The British frequently referred to the consortium as a financial "blockade," designed to prevent the Chinese government from obtaining funds it would presumably misuse.

Similarly, American businessmen anxious to develop or expand their interests in China failed to obtain needed capital. They did not lack support from the U.S. government, within which the Departments of Commerce and State competed to build up American economic interests in China. But American entrepreneurs in China, like the Chinese government, found the consortium an obstacle.

The core of the problem was the divergence between the interests of the Department of State and those of Lamont and his fellow bankers. The department wanted the consortium to provide capital for China's development—to help in the creation of a strong modern China in which American interests would thrive. For the bankers, the remote promise of China could not compete with the more immediate promise of Japan. In 1923 the House of Morgan floated a $150 million loan for the Japanese government, and other smaller loans followed in the mid-1920s. American capital that might have been available to China was lent instead to the Japanese, and some of it, by indirect means—by being "laundered" or simply by freeing other capital—facilitated the expansion of Japanese interests on the Asian mainland. Because the Japanese were competing with the Chinese for American capital, they could use their position in the consortium to discourage loans to China. The American group, led by Lamont, accepted this process. In short, one of the two competitors for capital worked in collusion with the potential lender to deny capital to the other. However permissible among businessmen pursuing profit, it was not consistent with the ends of public policy. Conditions in China, however, left the Department of State no means for changing the direction of the flow of capital. Lamont proved to be remarkably skillful in leading State Department officials to believe that he shared their views but was held back by partners less interested in helping China.

Twice during the early years of the consortium's existence the ability of Lamont and his colleagues to avoid lending money to the Chinese was tested. In both instances, in 1922 and in 1923, the U.S., British, French, and Japanese ministers to China and the Peking representatives of all four banking groups recommended that the loans be granted. In both instances the diplomats and group representatives argued that the consortium could not afford to reject Chinese overtures. But in neither instance could Lamont be moved, supporting or being supported by the head of the British group or the Japanese government in his opposition to taking up the Chinese business.

For the next two years, until the violence subsequent to the May Thirtieth Incident radically changed the context, Lamont and his British counterpart, with at least the public support of their governments, sang in praise of the success of the consortium's negative effort. They had stopped wasteful borrowing by the Chinese government, and their cooperation had a salutary effect on relations among the powers in China. Despite dissatisfaction with the inactivity of the consortium, the U.S. and British governments

were anxious to have it remain in existence. For the United States and Great Britain the consortium appeared to have assisted in checking the expansion of Japan's economic hold over China. For the British, continued Anglo-American cooperation in East Asia was itself a valuable end. And the Japanese indicated no dissatisfaction with the consortium, supporting a motion in 1924 to renew the agreement in perpetuity. France, the fourth party to the consortium agreement, appeared to its partners to be apathetic, unreliable, and forever bargaining for some trivial advantage, but supportive of the others when the agreement was renewed.

Although after 1923 there was never again serious consideration of a loan from the consortium to any Chinese regime, the organization continued to exist, at least in theory, until a decision in 1946 that the Japanese attack on U.S. and British forces in 1941 constituted abrogation of the agreement. The persistence of the consortium through the 1930s is remarkable because of the constant desire of the American group to withdraw and because of the determination of the British government to end the agreement in 1937. One stubborn man, Stanley K. Hornbeck of the Division of Far Eastern Affairs, Department of State, continually blocked dissolution, with an assist from the Japanese army in the summer of 1937.

The American group's desire to be rid of the consortium, voiced regularly by Lamont, reflected the leadership's conviction that there was no money to be made out of China and that continuation of the organization was not worth the bother or expense. From 1920 on, Lamont argued that there was no market for Chinese securities in the United States—that the American investor would not touch Chinese bonds until the Chinese demonstrated stability and paid off earlier loans, especially the Hukuang Railway loan, on all issues of which they had defaulted in 1925. After the Banking Act of 1933 prohibited banks of deposit from underwriting or offering securities, Lamont explained to the Department of State that his own firm and most members of the American group could no longer participate in loan operations even if they were to become feasible on a business basis. But for over a quarter of a century, Lamont deferred to the State Department's desire to maintain the consortium. It was not until January 1946 that he succeeded in getting the department to concede unequivocally that no useful purpose would be served by continuing the consortium, with or without the American group in it.

Despite their failure to get the consortium to lend money to China, officials of the Department of State fought to keep the organization in existence. Certainly it was not because American economic interests prospered. Lamont and his colleagues were concerned with their own profits and not with the expansion of the trade of their countrymen or with abstract conceptions of national interest. Sino-American trade remained static in the 1920s and rose slightly only in percentage terms for a few years in the early 1930s. The increase in American investments in China was not impressive. The American group hindered rather than helped the development of U.S. economic interests in China, as the Department of Commerce found when it tried to advance the prospects of American corporations.

Ultimately, men like MacMurray and Hornbeck fought to retain the consortium as a means of keeping the United States involved in East Asia, in the affairs of China. This had always been the fundamental purpose of a policy of cooperation with those powers earlier and more profoundly committed to activism in China. Without hitching a ride, the State Department's East Asian specialists, from John Hay's adviser, William W. Rockhill, through Hornbeck, feared not only that the United States would be deprived of an opportunity to expand its interests in their region, but also that interest in the area to which they were committed would cease to exist in the United States. The promise of U.S. expansion in China, however remote the reality, had become their raison d'être. The consortium, however inadequate, was the only vehicle they had for much of the interwar period.

THE INTERNATIONAL COMMITTEE OF BANKERS ON MEXICO

Formed in 1919, the International Committee of Bankers on Mexico (ICBM) provides an interesting comparison with the second China consortium. Once again Lamont was the central figure on the American side, and once again the bankers demonstrated that they would act independently of other business interests or the wishes of their government in pursuit of their ends. The ICBM, however, never loomed as large in the plans of the Department of State's Division of Mexican Affairs as the China consortium did in the visions of MacMurray and Hornbeck.

Claiming pressure from European bankers, Lamont solicited the approval of the Department of State for the organization of an international committee of bankers in 1918. In 1919 approval to bring together American, British, and French banking groups concerned with investments in Mexico was granted by the department, with the proviso that control of the committee's policy remain in American hands. Swiss, Dutch, and Belgian banking interests were subsequently given token representation on the committee.

The primary concern of the bankers was to protect the holders of Mexican securities, especially those of the Mexican government. Lamont and his colleagues were at best marginally concerned with the primary issue dividing the U.S. and Mexican governments in 1920: interpretations of Article 27 of the Mexican constitution and its effect on the claims of American oil companies. Fearing debt repudiation, the bankers were unsympathetic to Washington's tactic of withholding recognition from the Mexican government as a means of forcing it to respect the property rights and claims of the oil companies. Whereas the government of the United States wanted all American claims against Mexico to be settled simultaneously, the International Committee of Bankers on Mexico exhibited few inhibitions about negotiating a separate settlement of Mexico's foreign debt.

Restrained initially by the Department of State, Lamont obtained approval to begin negotiations with the administration of Alvaro Obregón in 1921. In June 1922 the Lamont–De la Huerta agreement was reached, recognizing $500 million of indebtedness and arranging for eventual payment. This arrangement paved the way for the Bucareli agreements between the Mexican and United States governments in 1923, ameliorating the differences between the two and leading to recognition of Obregón's regime.

In the years that followed, Mexico had difficulty meeting the schedule established in the Lamont–De la Huerta agreement, and in 1925 Lamont negotiated a new agreement. Payment remained irregular, however, and negotiations between the ICBM and the Mexican government continued throughout the 1920s and 1930s. In 1930 considerable friction arose between Lamont and the U.S. ambassador to Mexico, his former partner Dwight Morrow. Morrow and the Department of State insisted that a separate agreement between the bankers and the Mexican government was contrary to the interests of both the

United States and Mexico. Choosing on this occasion to understate the connection between the ICBM and the Department of State, Lamont insisted that he had reached a private arrangement with the Mexican minister of finance and was not asking for the department's consent. Unable to sway Lamont or the Mexican ambassador to the United States, Morrow warned the Mexican government that the United States did not see the agreement with Lamont as a constructive step toward financial stability. The Mexican government capitulated, assuring Morrow it would not submit the agreement to Congress except as a package comprising provisions for all of Mexico's debts. A final settlement between the ICBM and Mexico was not obtained until November 1942 in the Suarez-Lamont agreement ratified by the Mexican congress and the foreign bondholders. Legal problems kept the International Committee of Bankers on Mexico in existence until at least 1948, when its unrecorded demise appears to have occurred. It did not have any political significance after 1930, when it alienated the Department of State. The department was not kept informed of subsequent negotiations between Lamont and Mexican authorities.

The International Committee of Bankers on Mexico resembled the China consortium in that both consisted of groups of bankers from several nations, brought together with the approval of their governments, but ultimately indifferent to the interests of their governments or of other businessmen. The bankers of the ICBM were concerned with their own particularistic interests: any benefit derived from their activities by their governments or other peoples was incidental.

The ICBM differed strikingly from the China consortium in its relationship to the governments of the members' groups. The committee was formed at the initiative of the bankers, and only the government of the United States indicated a deep concern for its activities. There were no international political problems because none of the other countries that were represented had political interests in Mexico. All accepted American hegemony in Mexico, in contrast to the response to Japan's claims to hegemony over Manchuria. The government of the United States had other interests in Mexico and many other ways to exercise influence there. It never saw the committee as an important instrument of policy. After the friction between the Department of State and Lamont in 1930, only the bondholders cared about the future of the committee.

CONSORTIA SINCE WORLD WAR II

International banking consortia, involving in particular American banks based in New York, continued to be engaged in financing projects in developing countries, especially in Latin America, where they became dangerously overexposed in the 1970s and 1980s. After World War II, however, the U.S. government, specifically its Agency for International Development (AID), and international organizations, specifically the International Bank for Reconstruction and Development (World Bank), became major sources of loans. Both AID and the World Bank, in which U.S. influence has generally prevailed, have served American foreign policy interests far more effectively than did the private bankers of the prewar era.

BIBLIOGRAPHY

Borg, Dorothy. *The United States and the Far Eastern Crisis of 1933–1938: From the Manchurian Incident Through the Initial Stage of the Undeclared Sino-Japanese War.* Cambridge, Mass., 1964. Contains an account of Hornbeck's views and of the fate of the second consortium during the 1930s.

Cohen, Warren I. "America's New Order in East Asia: The Four Power Financial Consortium and China, 1919–1946." In Kwan Wai So and Warren I. Cohen, eds. *Essays in the History of China and Chinese-American Relations.* East Lansing, Mich., 1982. The most comprehensive account of the second consortium.

Curry, Roy W. *Woodrow Wilson and Far Eastern Policy, 1913–1921.* New York, 1957. Describes Wilson's initial attitude toward the American group and explains the Wilson administration's decision to create a new consortium.

Field, Frederick V. *American Participation in the China Consortiums.* Chicago, 1931. A clear and detailed description of both the old and new consortiums. The analysis of the problems of the old consortium is superior to the discussion of the new consortium; in the latter case, Field relied too heavily on Lamont for information.

Hoff, Joan. *American Business and Foreign Policy, 1920–1933.* Lexington, Ky., 1971. Provides a useful context for the workings of the second consortium and the ICBM, but Hoff did not have access to the Lamont papers.

Lamont, Thomas W. *Across World Frontiers.* New York, 1951. A charming but unreliable account.

Lewis, John P., and Richard Webb. *The World Bank: Its First Half Century.* Washington, D.C., 1997. The best starting point for examining the bank's work.

Porter, David. *U.S. Economic Foreign Aid: A Case Study of the United States Agency for International Development.* New York, 1990. Demonstrates how the agency functions.

Schmitt, Karl M. *Mexico and the United States, 1821–1973: Conflict and Coexistence.* New York, 1974. Includes reference to the International Committee of Bankers on Mexico in a chapter devoted to land and oil controversies.

Scholes, Walter V., and Marie V. Scholes. *The Foreign Policies of the Taft Administration.* Columbia, Mo., 1970. Contains an excellent discussion of the workings of the first consortium, based on multi-archival research. It is also important for the context of Taft's East Asian offensive.

Smith, Robert F. *The United States and Revolutionary Nationalism in Mexico, 1916–1932.* Chicago, 1972. Provides a thoughtful analysis of the problems of a less-developed country in a world in which international law is interpreted by advanced capitalist countries. Smith effectively uses the Lamont papers.

See also DOLLAR DIPLOMACY; ECONOMIC POLICY AND THEORY; WILSONIANISM.

THE CONSTITUTION

David Gray Adler

There is no comprehensive grant of a foreign affairs authority in the U.S. Constitution. Rather, the constitutional text carefully enumerates and allocates to the three branches of government a series of specific foreign relations powers, responsibilities, and duties. The relatively lean text, and the fact that it omits mention of particular powers, has no doubt contributed to the constitutional tension, controversy, and occasional crises that have marked American foreign affairs. Nevertheless the Constitution vests in Congress the bulk of the nation's foreign policy powers, a design which assigns to Congress senior status in a partnership with the president for the formulation, management, and conduct of U.S. foreign policy. The constitutional blueprint for foreign relations reflects the Constitutional Convention's conspicuous penchant for collective decision making and its fear of unilateral executive power.

This arrangement, however, has been overwhelmed in the post–Cold War era by sweeping assertions of unilateral presidential power that have laid the basis for a presidential monopoly over foreign affairs and advanced a conception of executive authority so capacious that it has produced a wide gulf between constitutional principle and governmental practice. To understand the constitutional allocation of foreign relations powers, it is necessary to examine the Constitution—the text, its design, the intentions of its Framers, and its history.

CONSTITUTIONAL TEXT

The preference for collective, rather than individual, decision making runs throughout the constitutional provisions that govern foreign policy. In addition to its exclusive jurisdiction over legislation and appropriation, Congress derives broad authority from Article 1, Section 8, to "provide for the Common Defence," to "regulate Commerce

with foreign Nations," "to define and punish Piracies and Felonies committed on the high seas . . . and offences against the Law of Nations," and make rules governing immigration and naturalization. Congress, alone, has the power to "declare War" and to "grant Letters of Marque and Reprisal" as well as to develop rules regarding "Captures on Land and Water." Congress also possesses the authority to raise, support, and maintain an army and navy, to "make Rules" for the regulation and government of the "land and naval Forces" and to call forth "the Militia to execute the Laws of the Union, suppress Insurrections and repel Invasions." It is also assigned the power and responsibility to organize, arm, discipline, and govern the militia.

As Article 2, Section 2, of the Constitution indicates, the president shares with the Senate the power to make treaties and appoint ambassadors. Specifically, the president is granted the authority, "by and with the Advice and Consent of the Senate, to make Treaties, provided two thirds of the Senators present concur." Another provision, known as the "supremacy clause," in Article 6, makes treaties, along with the Constitution and acts of Congress, the "supreme Law of the land." The constitutional grant of authority to the president to "appoint Ambassadors, other public Ministers and Consuls" is subject to the advice and consent of the Senate.

The Constitution assigns to the president only two exclusive roles in foreign affairs. He is "Commander in Chief of the Army and Navy of the United States, and of the Militia of the several states, when called into the actual Service of the United States," and he is enjoined by Article 2, Section 3, to perform two duties: "he shall receive Ambassadors, and other public Ministers," and "he shall take Care that the Laws be faithfully executed." This list exhausts the textual grant of authority to the president and Congress in foreign affairs. The president's constitutional powers are few and modest, and they pale in comparison with those vested in Congress.

The judiciary is assigned constitutional power that bears on the conduct of foreign policy. Article 3, Section 2, confers upon the Supreme Court original jurisdiction in "all Cases affecting Ambassadors, other public Ministers and Consuls," while it generally lodges in the federal courts jurisdiction in "controversies between a State, or the Citizens thereof, and foreign States, Citizens or Subjects."

The Constitution also imposes some significant and specific prohibitions, the effect of which is to ensure that control over foreign relations is vested in the national government. For purposes of foreign relations, federalism is virtually irrelevant. Bulked by the supremacy clause, federal acts are supreme and require the acquiescence of states. In *United States* v. *Belmont* (1937), the Supreme Court observed: "In respect of our foreign relations generally, state lines disappear. As to such purposes the State . . . does not exist." Thus, Article 1, Section 10, categorically forbids states from entering "into any Treaty, Alliance, or Confederation." Moreover, no state may, without the consent of Congress, "enter into any Agreement or Compact . . . with a foreign power, or engage in War, unless actually invaded," or in "imminent danger" of invasion. Other prohibitions touch upon the conduct of foreign affairs, although none of them in practice is very important. Thus, Article 1, Section 9, provides that no holder of any "Office of Profit or Trust" under the United States may "accept of any present, Emolument, Office, or Title, of any kind whatever, from any King, Prince, or foreign state," without the consent of Congress.

Some foreign affairs powers are not mentioned in the Constitution. For example, the Constitution is silent on the repository of authority to negotiate treaties, terminate treaties, recognize foreign governments and states, and make or declare peace. It may be plausibly argued that these powers are subsumed under enumerated grants of power or fairly inferred from the Framers' intentions or other constitutional provisions. This approach is faithful to the principle, articulated by the Court in *Reid* v. *Covert* (1957), that the government is "a creature of the Constitution. Its powers and authority have no other source." It has been asserted, however, that foreign relations constitute an exception to the principle that the federal government has only those powers expressly enumerated in the Constitution.

In the controversial decision of *United States* v. *Curtiss-Wright Export Corp.* (1936), the Court announced that the president's powers over foreign affairs are not derived from the Constitution but are a direct inheritance from the Crown of England. That case involved the constitutionality of an embargo that President Franklin D. Roosevelt had imposed upon the export of arms to Bolivia and Paraguay during the Chaco War. Roosevelt had issued the embargo on the basis of authority delegated to him in a joint resolution passed by Congress.

In a bizarre opinion, Justice George Sutherland argued that federal power in the field of foreign affairs differed radically from that with respect to internal matters. He observed that the internal federal power had been carved from "the general mass of legislative powers then possessed by the states," but that this was not at all true of the control of foreign policy, which had never been in the possession of the states. Instead, he maintained, before the Revolution general power over foreign affairs had been lodged in the British Crown. But with the Declaration of Independence, "the power of external sovereignty had passed . . . to the colonies in their collective and corporate capacity as the United States." The power over foreign affairs was "older than the Constitution" and had been inherited by the newly formed "Union" from the Confederation. It did not depend upon any direct grant of authority from the Constitution, for it is a necessary attribute of nationhood and sovereignty. Not only did the foreign affairs power inhere in the union, but it belonged to the president, who would exercise "plenary" power in his capacity as "sole organ" of American foreign policy, although the opinion did not explain how such authority came to belong to the executive.

Justice Sutherland's opinion has been roundly criticized. Scholars have criticized his reading of Anglo-American legal history by demonstrating that in 1776 states were sovereign entities. They point to Article 2 of the Articles of Confederation which stated: "Each State retains its sovereignty, freedom, and independence, and every power . . . which is not . . . expressly delegated to the United States, in Congress assembled." As sovereign entities, and jealous of their sovereignty, states only delegated powers to the Continental Congress. Through Article 9, for example, states delegated the war and treaty powers. That grant alone undermines Sutherland's premise that these powers were derived from a source other than the states. Moreover, even if it were assumed that the power of external sovereignty had been by some method transferred directly from the Crown to the union, it remains to be explained why that power would be vested in the president. Justice Felix Frankfurter noted in *Youngstown Sheet and Tube Company* v. *Sawyer* (1952) that "the fact that power exists in the Government does not vest it in the President." Indeed, the Supreme Court has ruled on several occasions that the sovereign power in foreign affairs is held by Congress. There is nothing in Sutherland's theory that would explain the location of this power in the presidency.

The contention, moreover, that the conduct of foreign policy is not restricted by the Constitution is at odds with Madison's statement in *Federalist* No. 45 that "the powers delegated by the proposed Constitution to the federal government are few and defined . . . [they] will be exercised principally on external objects, as war, peace, negotiation, and foreign commerce." Thus the foreign affairs powers are strictly constitutional. Since *Curtiss-Wright* the Court has taken the position that foreign affairs powers are tethered to the Constitution. In *Youngstown,* Justice Hugo Black, speaking for the Court, delivered a weighty rebuke to the claim of "extra-constitutional" power. In the same case, Justice Robert Jackson dismissed Sutherland's claim of an extra-constitutional presidential power as mere "dictum." The theory of extra-constitutional authority is irreconcilable with the central premise of American constitutionalism: All powers of the government—expressed and implied—have been delegated by the sovereign. As a consequence of this constitutional principle, all governmental acts—executive, legislative, and judicial—must be grounded within the four corners of the Constitution.

CONSTITUTIONAL CONVENTION

The Constitutional Convention was called for the purpose of correcting the deficiencies of the Articles of Confederation. Chief among the deficiencies were those that weakened the international position of the United States. Accordingly, few issues rivaled in importance the maintenance of national security and the conduct of foreign affairs, and thus the search for an efficient foreign policy design was a primary goal and an animating purpose of the convention.

There was broad agreement among American leaders that the foreign affairs flaws of the Articles of Confederation stemmed not from the absence of an independent executive but from the lack of authority granted to Congress. The Articles had created an ineffective national government that lacked coercive power over the states. Indeed, the outstanding characteristic of the Articles—state sovereignty—was reflected in theory by the fact that the governing document did not capitalize "united states," and in practice by the refusal of states to honor their federal obligations.

Contemporaries discussed three particular weaknesses. First, a depleted treasury undermined national defense and rendered the young Republic vulnerable to its enemies and adversaries. The Spanish in the South, British in the Northwest, and Indians throughout the land represented an ongoing threat. Second, without authority to regulate foreign commerce, Congress lacked bargaining power in its attempt to strike favorable trade agreements. Third, and most important, Congress had no power to prevent states from violating treaties negotiated in the name of the United States, which meant that individual states could undermine the reputation, integrity, and security of the nation. Indeed, the pervasive infidelity of the states to the international obligations and treaty agreements of the United States subverted the ability of the union to maintain its foreign credit and position as a sovereign nation. The frequent treaty violations, according to James Madison, justly known as the father of the Constitution for his role as its chief architect, constituted one of the principal "vices of the political system of the United States." They led Alexander Hamilton to lament in *Federalist* No. 22: "The faith, the reputation, the peace of the whole Union, are thus continually at the mercy of the prejudices, the passions, and the interests of every member of which it is composed. Is it possible that foreign nations can either respect or confide in such a government?"

The inadequacies of the Articles—mainly the debilitating weakness of the national government—supplied a critical focal point for the Framers' deliberations. The convention's decision to create the supremacy clause was a pivotal move, for the declaration in Article 6 that, "This Constitution, and the Laws of the United States and all Treaties, . . . shall be the Supreme Law of the land, . . . any Thing in the Constitution or Laws of any State to the Contrary notwithstanding," signified the end of "state sovereignty" and enabled the federal government to wrest control of foreign policy from the recalcitrant states.

While the supremacy clause certainly had profound implications for areas other than diplomacy, there is no exaggeration in the observation that it provided the sine qua non of a vital and vibrant national foreign policy.

The Articles of Confederation also supplied, in some key respects, a point of departure. The Articles had vested executive as well as legislative authority in Congress. Article 6 granted Congress control over the conduct of foreign policy, and Article 9 granted it "the sole and exclusive right and power of determining on peace and war." But the Philadelphia convention had embraced the principle of separation of powers, and now the delegates were forced to fashion a division of authority between the legislative and executive branches.

The Framers might have adopted the English model for reasons of familiarity, tradition, and simplicity; like other nations, Britain concentrated virtually unlimited authority over foreign policy in the hands of the executive. For the Framers were of course thoroughly familiar with the vast foreign affairs powers that inhered in the English Crown by virtue of the royal prerogative. Sir William Blackstone, the great eighteenth-century jurist, explained in his magisterial four-volume work *Commentaries on the Laws of England* (1765–1769) that the king exercised plenary authority over all matters relating to war and peace, diplomacy, treaties, and military command. Blackstone defined the king's prerogative as "those rights and capacities which the King enjoys alone." The monarch's prerogatives, "those which are 'rooted in and spring from the King's political person,'" include the authority to send and receive ambassadors and the power to make war or peace. The Crown, moreover, could negotiate "a treaty with a foreign state, which shall irrevocably bind the nation," and he could issue letters of marque and reprisal, which authorized private citizens to perform military actions on behalf of the nation. The king, according to Blackstone, was "the generalissimo, or the first in military command," and he possessed "the sole power of raising and regulating fleets and armies." In the exercise of this lawful prerogative, Blackstone explained, the king "is, and ought to be absolute; that is, so far absolute that there is no legal authority that can either delay or resist him" (vol. 2, pp. 238–250).

The Framers' rejection of the English model could not have been more emphatic. Their discussion of foreign affairs in Philadelphia began on 29 May 1787 with the introduction of the Virginia Plan, which provided for the creation of an executive that, in addition to "a general authority to execute the national laws . . . ought to enjoy the Executive rights vested in Congress by the Confederation." The apparent clarity of the proposal was illusory, however, since the Articles of Confederation had created only a single branch of government—Congress—and had not attempted to categorize powers as legislative, executive, or judicial. As a consequence the vague proposal allowed for the possibility that "Executive rights" might be interpreted to include the full panoply of foreign affairs and warmaking powers exercised by the English king—the authority to determine war and peace, and the powers of sending and receiving ambassadors and entering treaties and alliances, among others—all of which the Articles of Confederation had granted to Congress.

The prospect that the Virginia Plan might involve a transfer to the president of these broad powers provoked alarm in the convention barely a week into the proceedings, triggering a release of the Framers' deep-seated aversion to unilateral executive power in foreign affairs. In a critical debate on 1 June, Charles Pinckney of South Carolina stated that he favored a vigorous executive but feared that the Virginia Plan's proposal to place in a newly created executive the "Executive rights vested in Congress" might include its authority over decisions of war and peace, which, if delegated to a new executive, would make that office a "monarchy of the worst kind," an "elective one."

Pinckney's preference for congressional control over matters of war and peace was supported by his fellow South Carolinian John Rutledge, who argued against vesting such authority in the executive. James Wilson of Pennsylvania, second only to Madison as an architect of the Constitution and a future member of the U.S. Supreme Court, sought to assuage Pinckney's concerns by pointing out that "the prerogatives of the British Monarch" did not properly define the executive powers. Those prerogatives, he explained, included some powers that were of a legislative nature, among them war and peace. In fact, the only powers that Wilson considered to be "strictly executive" were enforcing the laws made by the legislature and the choice of officers not to be appointed by the legislature. Wilson agreed with Roger Sherman of Connecticut, who believed the executive was merely an agent of the legislature, which ought to retain authority over matters of war and peace. In the debate that day every speaker who addressed the issue shared that opinion, including Madison, who reminded the convention that as a matter of definition, executive powers did not include war and peace. Moreover, the delegates, filled with misgivings and apprehension, voted to delete the ambiguous proposal to vest in the president the "Executive rights vested in Congress by the Confederation." Later the Framers would embrace Madison's proposal to fix the extent of the executive powers through careful enumeration.

Wilson's reference to the "prerogatives of the British Monarch" captured the Framers' greatest fears about unilateral executive authority in foreign affairs. There was a deep worry in the convention's discussions about executive power, epitomized by Edmund Randolph's characterization of it as the "foetus of monarchy." The Framers' trepidations about executive power were greatly influenced by the constitutional crises and political convulsions of the seventeenth-century English Civil Wars. The absolutist claims of the Stuart Kings and the abuse of authority by manipulative ministers had hardened their view toward the executive. Their deep concern about executive abuse of power was not merely a reflection of their perceptive readings of history but also an outgrowth of their own experience, for the fear of power resonated from the colonial period. These pervasive fears, doubts, and concerns about executive power, which conduced to preclude, in the minds of the Framers, any unilateral presidential power over foreign affairs, were summed up by Hamilton in *Federalist* No. 75: "The history of human conduct does not warrant that exalted opinion of human virtue which would make it wise in a nation to commit interests of so delicate and momentous a kind, as those which concern its intercourse with the rest of the world, to the disposal of a magistrate created and circumstanced as would be a president of the United States."

Behind the Framers' emphatic rejection of the British model, rooted in a deep aversion to an unrestrained, unilateral executive power, lay an equally emphatic commitment to the republican principle of collective decision-making, grounded in the belief that the conjoined wisdom of the many is superior to that of one. The Framers perceived a broad equatorial divide between the hemispheres of monarchism and republicanism, between the values of the Old World and the those of the New World. The convention's deliberate fragmentation of powers relating to diplomacy, treaties, and war and peace, and the allocation of the various foreign affairs powers to different departments and agencies of government, reflected the Framers' determination to apply the doctrines of separation of powers and checks and balances, the principle of the rule of law, and the elements of constitutionalism to the realm of foreign relations as rigorously as they had been applied to the domestic domain.

This critical decision represented a bold departure from the prevailing wisdom of the day, which urged the unification and centralization of foreign relations powers in the executive and warned that the separation of those powers would invite chaos, disorder, and even disaster. But the Framers brought a fresh outlook, a new vision, to foreign policy, one that recognized that the conduct of foreign policy includes some elements that are primarily legislative in nature, others that are essentially executive, and still others characteristically judicial. In *Federalist* No. 47, Madison observed that "treaties with foreign sovereigns" assume, once they are made, "the force of legislative acts." The Constitution, moreover, characterizes the power to declare war as legislative, and the power to conduct it as executive. The supremacy clause imposes upon judges the duty to enforce treaties as the law of the land. The Constitutional Convention discarded the British model as obsolete and inapplicable to the republican manners of the United States.

The purpose of this new constitutional arrangement for foreign affairs, a distinctively American contribution to politics and political science, was to require and implement collective decision-making—joint participation, consultation, and concurrence—by the political branches in the formulation, conduct, and management of the nation's foreign policy. The Framers supposed that the infusion into the foreign policy process of checks and balances would maintain the constitutional allocation of powers and, therefore, prevent executive unilateralism, aggrandizement, and usurpation. They believed, moreover, that the structure of shared powers in the conduct of international affairs, bottomed on the premise and promise of legislative deliberation, would produce wise policies and, in the words of Wilson, "a security to the people," for it would afford in Congress an airing of the various political, economic, and military interests that were bound up in the nation's external relations.

But two centuries of history and practice have witnessed the virtual eclipse of the Framers' blueprint for foreign affairs. The premise of congressional primacy has given way to executive dominance, and the promise of joint participation has been subverted by presidential unilateralism. In the context of foreign affairs, the United States has been marching backward, for the president has largely secured the prerogatives of the English Crown that the Framers denied to him in the Constitutional Convention, and which the nation had roundly condemned since the writing of the Declaration of Independence. In truth, the rise of presidential hegemony, so ably captured by the title of Arthur Schlesinger Jr.'s influential book *The Imperial Presidency,* is the product of a regrettable mixture: one part usurpation and two parts acquiescence. Presidential aggrandizement of foreign affairs powers has been aided and abetted by a quiescent Congress, seemingly indifferent to the usurpation of its powers, and by a judiciary that has exhibited an attitude of deference to the executive, as reflected in its refusal to restrain presidential adventurism abroad.

The presidential monopoly of American foreign relations finds its justification not in constitutional norms but in the claims of necessity and national security, pleas that have flown high in the Cold War period and beyond, as the values of unity, speed, and dispatch have replaced the values of deliberation, concurrence, and consent. The growth of presidential power has been conspicuous in the aggrandizement of the war power and in the assumption of the authority to make international agreements, often in disregard of the principles and processes that govern the treaty power. It also has been reflected in the exercise of the president's duty to receive ambassadors, and in the executive's penchant for secrecy and the control of information.

THE WAR POWER

The Framers of the Constitution vested in Congress the sole and exclusive authority to initiate military hostilities, including full-blown, total war, as well as lesser acts of armed force, on behalf of the American people. The constitutional grant to Congress of the war power, which Justice William Paterson described in *United States* v. *Smith* (1806) as "the exclusive province of Congress to change a state of peace into a state of war," constituted a sharp break from the British model. The Framers were determined to deny to the president what Blackstone had assigned to the English King—"the sole prerogative of making war and peace." The president, in his role as commander in chief, was granted only the authority to repel invasions of the United States. But what the Framers sought to deny to the president has become a commonplace. Indeed, executive usurpation of the war power in the period since World War II has become a dominant characteristic of American foreign relations as presidents have routinely committed acts of war without congressional authorization.

The war clause of the Constitution provides: "The Congress shall have power . . . to declare War [and] grant Letters of Marque and Reprisal." On 29 May, in an early debate in the Constitutional Convention on the repository of the war power, a clear understanding developed among the delegates that the power of "war and peace"—the power to initiate war—did not belong to the executive but to the legislature. On 6 August the Committee of Detail circulated a draft constitution that granted Congress the power to "make" war. This bore sharp resemblance to the Articles of Confederation, which vested the "sole and exclusive right and power of determining on peace and war" to the Continental Congress. When the war clause was considered in debate on 17 August, the familiar voice from South Carolina, Charles Pinckney, was initially reluctant to place the power in the House of Representatives: "Its proceedings were too slow. . . . The Senate would be the best depository, being more acquainted with foreign affairs, and most capable of proper resolutions." Another South Carolinian, Pierce Butler, startled the convention when he announced that he "was for vesting the power in the President, who will have all the requisite qualities, and will not make war but when the nation will support it." Butler's opinion shocked Elbridge Gerry of Massachusetts, who declared that he "never expected to hear in a republic a motion to empower the Executive alone to declare war." Butler stood alone in the convention. There was no support for his opinion and no second to his motion.

The proposal of the Committee of Detail to vest Congress with the power to "make" war proved unsatisfactory to Madison and Gerry. In what must be regarded as one of the most famous joint resolutions in American history, Madison and Gerry moved to substitute "declare" for "make," and they explained that the purpose of the motion was to allow the president "to repel sudden attacks." The meaning of the motion was clear. The power to initiate war was granted to Congress, with the reservation that the president need not await authorization from Congress to repel a sudden attack on the United States. There was no quarrel whatever with respect to the sudden-attack provision, but there was some question as to whether the substitution of "declare" for "make" would effect the intention of Madison and Gerry. Roger Sherman of Connecticut thought the joint motion "stood very well." He believed that it permitted the executive "to repel and not commence war." Virginia's George Mason announced that he "was against giving the power of war to the Executive, because not safely to be trusted with it," then said he preferred "declare" to "make." The adoption of the Madison-Gerry proposal made it clear that Congress alone possessed the authority to initiate war. The warmaking power was specifically denied to the president; he was given only the authority to repel sudden attacks against the United States. No delegate to the Philadelphia convention and no member of any state ratifying convention contested this understanding. James Wilson, one of the most penetrating constitutional theorists of the founding generation, captured the precise intent of the convention: this system "will not hurry us into war; it is calculated to guard against it. It will not be in the power of a single man, or a single body of men, to involve us in such distress."

At the time of the convention, the phrase "declare war" enjoyed a settled understanding and an established usage. As early as 1552 the verb "declare" had become synonymous with the verb "commence"; they both implied the initiation of hostilities. This was the established usage in international law as well as in England, where the terms to "declare" war and to "make" war were used interchangeably. This practice was thoroughly familiar to the Framers. Given the equivalence of commence and declare, it is clear that a congressional declaration of war would institute military hostilities. According to international law commentators at the time of the founding, a declaration of war was desirable because it announced the institution of a state of war, and the legal consequences it entailed, to the adversary, to neutral nations, and to citizens of the sovereign initiating the war. Indeed, this is the essence of a declaration of war: notice by the proper authority of intent to convert a state of peace into a state of war. But all that is required under American law is a joint resolution or an explicit congressional authorization of the use of military force against a named adversary. This can come in the form of a "declaration pure and sim-

ple," or in a "conditional declaration of war." There are also two kinds of war, those that U.S. courts have termed "perfect," or general, and those labeled "imperfect," or limited, wars. In 1782, in *Miller* v. *The Ship Resolution,* the federal court of appeals, established by the Continental Congress, stated: "The writers upon the law of nations, speaking of different kinds of war, distinguish them into perfect and imperfect: A perfect war is that which destroys the national peace and tranquillity, and lays the foundation of every possible act of hostility. The imperfect war is that which does not entirely destroy the public tranquillity, but interrupts it only in some particulars, as in the case of reprisals."

It was decided at the dawn of the Republic that the power of determining perfect and imperfect war lay with Congress. In *Talbot* v. *Seeman* (1801), Chief Justice John Marshall wrote for the Court that the war power of Congress comprises the power "to declare a general war" and also to "wage a limited war." The power of Congress to authorize limited war is, of course, a necessary concomitant of its power to declare general war. If the president might authorize relatively minor acts of war or perhaps covert military operations in circumstances not demanding full-blown war, that power could be wielded in a way that would easily eviscerate the Constitution's placement of the war power in Congress. But the Framers withheld from the president the power to work such mischief. The Constitution granted the executive only the authority to respond defensively to the initiation of war through sudden attack upon the United States. In *United States* v. *Smith* (1806), Justice William Paterson of the Supreme Court, who had been a delegate to the Constitutional Convention from New Jersey, explained that, in the event of an invasion of the United States, it would be lawful for the president to resist such invasion for the "plain reason that a state of complete and absolute war exists between the two nations. In the case of invasive hostilities, there cannot be war on the one side and peace on the other. . . . There is a manifest distinction between our going to war with a nation at peace, and a war being made against us by an actual invasion, or a formal declaration. In the former case, it is the exclusive province of Congress to change a state of peace into a state of war." But the president's power of self-defense does not extend to foreign lands. The Framers did not give the president the authority to intervene in foreign wars, or to choose between war and peace, or to identify and commence hostilities against an enemy of the American people. Nor did they empower him to initiate force abroad on the basis of his own assessments of U.S. security interests. These circumstances involve choices that belong to Congress, under its exclusive province to change a state of peace into a state of war.

All of the offensive powers of the nation, then, were located in Congress. Consistent with this constitutional theory, the convention gave to Congress the power to issue "letters of marque and reprisal." Dating back to the Middle Ages when sovereigns employed private forces in retaliation for an injury caused by the sovereign of another state or his subjects, the practice of issuing reprisals gradually evolved into the use of public armies. By the time of the convention the Framers considered the power to issue letters of marque and reprisal sufficient to authorize a broad spectrum of armed hostilities short of declared war. In other words, it was regarded as a species of imperfect war.

THE COMMANDER IN CHIEF CLAUSE

While the Framers granted Congress the authority to decide for war, they provided in Article 2, Section 2, that: "The President shall be Commander in Chief of the Army and Navy of the United States, and of the Militia of the several states, when called into the actual Service of the United States." The Framers thus vested command of the military forces in the president, which meant that once Congress authorized military hostilities, the president as commander in chief would exercise authority to conduct and prosecute the war effort. As Hamilton explained in *Federalist* No. 74: "Of all the cares or concerns of government, the direction of war most peculiarly demands those qualities which distinguish the exercise of power by a single hand." But the designation of the president as commander in chief conferred no warmaking power whatever; it vested in the president, as Hamilton proposed to the convention, only the authority to repel sudden attacks on the United States and to direct war, "when authorized or begun." In this capacity, he would direct those forces placed at his command by an act of Congress.

The Framers adopted the title of commander in chief and its historical usage from England, where it was introduced in 1639 by King Charles I. The title was used as a generic term referring to the highest-ranking officer in a partic-

ular chain of command or theater of action. But the ranking commander in chief was always subordinate to a political superior, whether a king, Parliament, or, with the development of the cabinet system in England, a secretary of war. The practice of giving the officer at the apex of the military the title of commander in chief and of making him subject to instructions from a political superior was embraced by the Continental Congress and by most of the states in their early constitutions. When, on 15 June 1775, the Continental Congress unanimously decided to appoint George Washington as "General and Commander in Chief, of the Army of the United Colonies," it issued instructions that kept Washington on a short leash. He was ordered "punctually to observe and follow such orders and directions, from time to time, as you shall receive from this, or future Congress of these United Colonies, or Committee of Congress." Congress did not hesitate to instruct the commander in chief on military and policy matters. This usage had been established for a century and a half and was thoroughly familiar to the Framers when they met in Philadelphia. It is probable that this settled understanding and the consequent absence of concerns about the nature of the post accounts for the fact that there was no debate on the commander in chief clause at the convention. It is telling, moreover, that there was no effort at the convention or at any state ratifying convention to redefine the office of commander in chief.

Hamilton's speech on 18 June captured the essence of the president's power as commander in chief when he stated that the executive was "to have the direction of War when authorized or begun." There was no fear of the legal authority granted by the commander in chief clause, and there is no evidence that anyone believed that his office as commander in chief endowed the president with an independent source of warmaking authority. The narrow, military role of the executive was explained by Hamilton in *Federalist* No. 69, in which he said the president's power as commander in chief "would be nominally the same with that of the King of Great Britain, but in substance much inferior to it. It would amount to nothing more than the supreme command and direction of the military and naval forces . . . while that of the British king extends to the *declaring* of war and to the *raising* and *regulating* of fleets and armies,—all which, by the Constitution under consideration, would appertain to the legislature." The president as commander in chief was to be "first General and Admiral" in "the direction of war when authorized or begun." But all political authority remained in Congress, as it had under the Articles of Confederation. As Madison explained it in a letter to Thomas Jefferson in 1798: "The Constitution supposes, what the History of all Governments demonstrates, that the Executive is the branch of power most interested in war, and most prone to it. It has accordingly with studied care vested the question of war in the Legislature."

THE WAR POWER IN PRACTICE

The early practice and understanding of the government on the issue of warmaking closely conformed to the constitutional framework. There was, throughout the nineteenth century, no instance of a presidential assertion of a unilateral warmaking power. But there were disputes in the margins.

In 1793 war broke out between Great Britain and France. President George Washington declared that the Treaty of Alliance of 1778 did not obligate the United States to defend French territory in America, and he issued a proclamation of neutrality. Whether this power belonged to the president or Congress set off a remarkable debate between Hamilton and Madison. In a series of articles signed "Pacificus," Hamilton defended the substance of the policy as well as the president's unilateral authority to promulgate it. Hamilton acknowledged that "the legislature have the right to make war on the one hand," but it remained "the duty of the Executive to preserve peace till war is declared." In the fulfillment of that duty, Hamilton argued, the president "must necessarily possess a right of judging what is the nature of the obligations which the treaties of the country impose on the government." By this time, France was involved in several wars, and Hamilton's concerns about the force and nature of the treaties was evident: Did they obligate the United States to assist the French in their foreign adventures? He properly denied the existence of any such ironclad obligation, but his view that the president possessed discretionary authority, as part of his "duty" to preserve peace "till war is declared," triggered a response from Madison, who wrote under the pseudonym of "Helvidius" and asserted that if Washington's proclamation were valid, it meant that the president had usurped congressional power to decide between a state of peace or a state of war. Despite this difference, both agreed that the power to initiate war is vested in Congress. Madison wrote that the "executive has no right, in any case, to decide the question, whether there is or is not cause for declaring war; that the right of convening and informing Congress, whenever such a question seems to call for a decision, is all the right which the Constitution has deemed requisite or proper." It is to be emphasized that throughout their lives both Hamilton and Madison maintained the doctrine that it is for Congress alone to initiate hostilities. That agreement reflected the understanding of the war clause throughout the nineteenth century. In fact, presidents—Washington, Adams, and Jefferson among them—were particularly careful to avoid military actions that might encroach upon the congressional warpower.

In 1798 France repeatedly raided and seized American vessels. When asked whether a new law that increased the size of the navy authorized the president to initiate hostilities, Hamilton stated that he had not seen the law and that, if it did not grant the president any new authority but left him "at the foot of the Constitution," then the president had only the power to "employ the ships as convoys, with authority to *repel* force by *force* (but not to capture) and to repress hostilities within our waters, including a marine league from our coasts. Anything beyond this must fall under the idea of *reprisals,* and requires the sanctions of that department which is to declare *or make war.*"

Contrary to the claim that President John Adams engaged in an exercise of unilateral warmaking in the Quasi-War with France (1798–1800), the facts demonstrate that the war was clearly authorized by Congress, which debated the prospect of war and passed some twenty statutes permitting it to be waged. Moreover, Adams took absolutely no independent action. In *Bas v. Tingy* (1800), the Supreme Court held that the body of statutes enacted by Congress had authorized imperfect, or limited, war. In *Talbot v. Seeman* (1801), a case that arose from issues in the Quasi-War, Chief Justice John Marshall wrote for the Court, "The whole powers of war being, by the Constitution of the United States, vested in Congress, the acts of that body can alone be resorted to as our guides in this inquiry." In *Little v. Barreme* (1804), Marshall emphasized the control that Congress can wield over the president as commander in chief. One of the statutes passed by Congress during the Quasi-War with France authorized the president to seize vessels sailing to

THE RISE OF PRESIDENTIAL POWER

The rise of presidential hegemony over foreign affairs is perhaps the most outstanding, though lamentable, characteristic of a constitutional system that establishes congressional primacy. The emergence of what Arthur Schlesinger Jr. aptly described in the title of his splendid book *The Imperial Presidency*—the exaltation of presidential power in foreign affairs—is deeply in conflict with the constitutional blueprint for the formulation and conduct of American foreign policy. The Framers, who feared the exercise of unilateral presidential power in foreign affairs, rejected the conventional wisdom of their time—centralization of foreign affairs powers in the executive—and assigned to Congress senior status in a partnership with the president for the management of foreign relations.

That arrangement largely prevailed for most of the nation's first 150 years, but it succumbed to presidential domination in the post–World War II era. Thus constitutional governance of foreign affairs was a principal casualty of the Cold War, a chronic international crisis that afforded a pretext for the executive assumption of prerogative-like powers that the Framers had denied to the president.

In the context of the Cold War, Americans—members of Congress, judges, scholars, and reporters—exhibited fawning deference to the president in foreign affairs. Lacking confidence in its own information and judgment, the citizenry imbibed the rhetoric of presidential expertise, experience, and judgment; a literature of abnegation advised the nation of the virtues of unfettered executive control of foreign policy. The pervasive sentiment of the Cold War urged blind trust of the executive on the ground that he alone possessed the information, facts, and experience necessary to safeguard U.S. interests. And presidents acted the part. Executive usurpation of the war power became a commonplace; executive secrecy and control of information became the norm; and covert operations—military, political, and economic—avoided congressional radar and public perception. Congress was reduced to the role of spectator.

For many, presidential practice across two centuries confirms the wisdom of the original design, for the theory of executive unilateralism, as well as its traditional, underlying arguments, was exploded in the tragedy of the Vietnam War. Few doctrines have been so troubling, dangerous, and antidemocratic. It led not only to the Vietnam War and to the Iran-Contra affair but to the entrenchment of presidential supremacy in foreign relations, with its attendant military and policy failures from Cuba and Cambodia to Lebanon and Somalia.

Moreover, nothing in the broader historical record suggests that the conduct of foreign relations by executive elites has produced wholesome results. Indeed, the wreckage of empires on executive foreign policies provides ample evidence that, as the British jurist and diplomat Lord Bryce noted, the wisdom of "classes" is less than the "masses." The contention that the wisdom of one is superior to that of many is philosophically defective, historically untenable, and fundamentally undemocratic. Since Aristotle, we have known that information alone is not a guarantee of political success; what matters are the values of the system and ultimately those of its decision makers. There is "nothing more fallible," wrote James Iredell, a member of the first Supreme Court and a delegate to the North Carolina ratifying convention, than "human judgment," a fundamental philosophical insight reflected in the Framers' embrace of the doctrines of separation of powers and checks and balances, and their rejection of presidential unilateralism in foreign affairs.

French ports. President Adams issued an order directing American ships to capture vessels sailing to or from French ports, but in the opinion for the Court, Marshall held that Adams's order had exceeded his authority since congressional policy set forth in the statute was superior to presidential orders inconsistent with the statute. Subsequent judicial holdings have reiterated the fact that the commander in chief may be controlled by statute.

As president, Thomas Jefferson acknowledged that his powers of war were limited to defensive actions. In his first annual message to Congress in 1801 he reported the arrogant demands made by the pasha of Tripoli. Unless the United States paid tribute, the pasha threatened to seize American ships and citizens. Jefferson responded by sending a small squadron to the Mediterranean to protect against the threatened attack. He then asked Congress for further guidance, stating he was "unauthorized by the Constitution, without the sanction of Congress, to go beyond the line of defense." It was left to Congress to authorize "measures of offense also." Jefferson's understanding of the war clause underwent no revision. In 1805 he informed Congress of the dispute with Spain over the boundaries of Louisiana and Florida. Jefferson warned that Spain evidenced an "intention to advance on our possessions until they shall be repressed by an opposing force. Considering that Congress alone is constitutionally invested with the power of changing our condition from peace to war, I have thought it my duty to await their authority for using force."

Other early presidents, including Washington, Madison, James Monroe, and Andrew Jackson, also refused to exercise offensive military powers without authorization from Congress, which they understood to be the sole repository of the power to initiate war. There was no departure from this understanding of the war clause throughout the nineteenth century. In 1846 President James K. Polk ordered an army into a disputed border area between Texas and Mexico. One of its patrols was attacked by Mexican forces, which were defeated by the U.S. soldiers. In a message to Congress, Polk offered the rationale that Mexico had invaded the United States, which prompted Congress to declare war. If Polk's rationale was correct, then his action could not be challenged on constitutional grounds, for it was well established that the president had the authority to repel sudden attacks. If, however, he was disingenuous—if he had in fact initiated military hostilities—then he had clearly usurped the warmaking power of Congress. It is worth noticing that he made no claim to constitutional power to make war.

Although Congress declared war, the House of Representatives censured Polk for his actions because the war had been "unnecessarily and unconstitutionally begun by the President of the United States." It seemed evident that Polk had dispatched troops into the disputed area for the purpose of precipitating war by provoking a Mexican attack on American soldiers. His manipulative efforts were effective. Representative Abraham Lincoln voted with the majority against Polk. As president, Lincoln maintained that only Congress could authorize the initiation of hostilities. None of his actions in the Civil War, including the suspension of habeas corpus, the

appropriation of funds from the U.S. treasury, or his decision to call forth regiments from state militias, each of which was eventually retroactively authorized by Congress, constituted a precedent for presidential initiation of war. Moreover, in the Prize Cases (1863), the Supreme Court upheld Lincoln's blockade against the rebellious Confederacy as a constitutional response to a sudden invasion that began with the attack on Fort Sumter. The Court stated that the president, as commander in chief, "has no power to initiate or declare war either against a foreign nation or a domestic state." Nevertheless, in the event of invasion by a foreign nation or a state, the president was not only authorized "but bound to resist force by force. He does not initiate the war, but is bound to accept the challenge without waiting for any special legislative authority." According to the Court, the president had to meet the crisis in the shape it presented itself "without waiting for Congress to baptize it with a name; and no name given to it by him or them could change the fact."

THE CONTINUING WAR POWERS CONTROVERSY

Until 1950 it had long been established and well settled that the Constitution vests in Congress the sole and exclusive authority to initiate total as well as limited war. But at the midcentury mark, President Harry Truman asserted a unilateral executive warmaking power, and claimed authorization from the United Nations, to justify his decision to introduce U.S. troops into the Korean War without congressional authorization. Truman's decision in June 1950 to intervene in South Korea in order to counter the communist North Korean invasion commenced what was to become one of the bloodiest wars in America history. The president claimed that he acted in response to a UN Security Council call for military action. In fact, Truman had committed U.S. forces before the Security Council issued its request. Several senators and representatives attacked Truman's unilateral act on the floor of Congress as a violation of the Constitution. They point out that the UN Charter carried no specific obligation to go to war in support of its decisions any more than a treaty obligation alone could commit the United States to war without a decision to that end by both houses of Congress. Thus, Robert Taft of Ohio, in an embittered speech on the Senate floor, charged that President Truman had "usurped power and violated the Constitution" by his Korean intervention. Despite constitutional doubts expressed by Taft and several other senators, Congress regularly appropriated ample funds to support the war. In reality, it had little choice in the matter, unless it wished to see an American army far from home overwhelmed in the field.

In 1951, while the Korean War was still in progress, Truman announced that he was sending four army divisions to Germany in support of the new U.S. obligation to defend the Continent, in accordance with the North Atlantic Treaty and the Lisbon and Ottawa agreements. It was obvious that a large-scale American army on the Elbe River opposite Soviet-occupied East Germany constituted a heavy American commitment to go to war in the event of a Soviet invasion of western Europe, regardless of any constitutional limitation upon the war power. Indeed, the American divisions were commonly described as a "trip wire" for the very purpose of committing the United States to war should such an invasion occur.

Truman denied that he need congressional authorization before deploying the troops in Europe, and his decision triggered the so-called "great debate" on the constitutionality of his action. Several senators, among them Paul Douglas and Thomas Connelly, argued that the president has the power under the Constitution to move troops overseas, both in pursuance of treaty obligations and by virtue of his constitutional powers as commander in chief of the armed forces. In contrast, Taft and John Bricker criticized the president's action as grossly unconstitutional.

The outcome of the debate was a substantial victory for the president. The Senate adopted a weak resolution expressing its "approval" of the president's action, but declaring it to be "the sense of the Senate" that in the future the president ought to obtain the approval of Congress prior to the assignment of troops abroad, "in the interests of sound constitutional processes and of national unity." The acquiescence of Congress in the fact of Truman's usurpation of power inaugurated a new theme in matters of war and peace.

Since then a steady pattern of presidential warmaking has developed: Lyndon Johnson and Richard Nixon in Vietnam, Gerald Ford in Cambodia, Ronald Reagan in Lebanon, Grenada, and Libya, George H. W. Bush in Panama, and William Jefferson Clinton in Somalia, Iraq, Afghanistan, Sudan, and Bosnia, all without congressional authorization.

Following Iraq's invasion of Kuwait on 2 August 1990 under the leadership of Saddam Hussein, President George H. W. Bush began deploying U.S. troops to Saudi Arabia and other sites in the Middle East. By November, Bush had doubled the size of the deployment and established the capacity to wage war. Bush did not seek authorization from Congress, but persuaded the United Nations Security Council to authorize the use of military force, which it did on 29 November. Bush never sought authority (only support) from Congress, but on 12 January 1991 Congress authorized military action against Iraq. The approval, however, bore the appearance of a rubber stamp in the face of a presidential fait accompli, backed by a bloc of 439,000 U.S. troops that Bush had amassed in the region. There is surely nothing in the constitutional grant of authority to the president that justifies the deployment of troops, but in the postwar era, presidents frequently have deployed troops into hostilities or into situations in which hostilities were imminent, in numbers large and small and for durations long and short, a practice that has served to preempt the congressional power to decide on matters of war and peace.

Congressional acquiescence in the presidential usurpation of its authority to deploy troops has become a central factor in the demise of legislative control of the war power which, Madison stated, includes the power "to commence, continue and conclude war." President Bush's claim of UN authority—like Truman's in Korea or Clinton's invocation of authority from NATO to order air strikes against Yugoslavia on 24 March 1999—lacks credibility. These mutual security treaties provided that they would be carried out by the United States in accordance with its "constitutional processes," which vests in Congress the sole power to decide for war. The fact that treaties are the supreme law of the land does not imply that a mutual security treaty can amend the Constitution. In *Geofroy* v. *Riggs* (1890), the Court stated that the treaty-making power does not "authorize what the Constitution forbids, or [effect] a change in the character of government." Thus, the president and the Senate may not, through the exercise of the treaty power, deprive the House of Representative of its constitutional role as a joint partner in the warmaking power with the Senate.

Presidents have asserted a variety of arguments in defense of their unilateral military actions. Invocation of the commander in chief clause has become a commonplace. As Justice Robert H. Jackson observed in the Steel Seizure Case (1952), the clause has been adduced for the "power to do anything, anywhere, that can be done with an army or navy." Yet neither the history of the clause nor the debates in the Constitutional Convention afford any evidence to support this presidential claim. Moreover, no court has ever cited it as a source of independent warmaking authority for the president.

Twentieth-century presidents including Truman, Nixon, and Clinton also have advanced the executive power clause as authorization for presidential warmaking. Article 2, Section 1, of the Constitution provides: "The executive Power shall be vested in a President of the United States of America." As we have seen, the claim that the executive power clause includes authority to initiate hostilities was considered and rejected in the Constitutional Convention. For the Framers, the phrase "executive power" was limited, as James Wilson said, to "executing the laws, and appointing offices." No delegate to the convention sought to ascribe to the president a more capacious understanding of "executive power" than that articulated by Wilson.

Advocates of a unilateral executive warmaking power also have invoked the "Lockean prerogative," or the doctrine of necessity, as a source of inherent presidential power. Drawing on John Locke's defense of the right of an executive to act for the common good, even if it requires breaking the law, defenders have adduced a similar claim for the president. But there is no evidence whatever that the Framers intended to incorporate the Lockean prerogative in the Constitution. The lack of a textual statement to that effect renders such an intent indispensable to the presidential claim of a constitutional power. In fact, the evidence runs in the other direction. Fears of executive power led the Framers to enumerate the president's power and to "define and confine" the scope of his authority. An undefined reservoir of discretionary power in the form of Locke's prerogative would have unraveled the carefully crafted design of Article 2 and repudiated the Framers' stated aim of corralling executive power.

Presidents have also asserted a presidential warmaking authority on the basis of his role as the "sole organ" of American foreign policy. In *Curtiss-Wright,* Justice Sutherland stated that the authority in foreign affairs was essentially an executive power, which he explained "as the very delicate, plenary and exclusive power of the President as the sole organ of the federal government in the field of international relations—a power which does not require as a basis for its exercise, an act of Congress." Sutherland appropriated the term "sole organ" from a speech delivered by then Representative John Marshall in 1800 on the floor of the House of Representatives. Marshall noted: "The President is the sole organ of the nation in its external relations. . . . Of consequence, the demand of a foreign nation can only be made on him." At no point in his speech did Marshall argue that the president's exclusive authority to communicate with a foreign nation included a power to formulate or develop policy. All Marshall had in mind was the president's role as the sole organ of communication with other governments, a rather unremarkable point, at that, since officials had acknowledged since the founding that the president was the "sole" channel of communication with foreign nations. Thus it was Sutherland who infused a purely communicative role with a substantive policymaking function and thereby manufactured a great power out of the Marshallian "sole organ" doctrine. Of course, the sole organ doctrine completely undermines the Framers' design for cooperation in foreign affairs. And, given the allocation of foreign relations power to both Congress and the president, the claim is by definition indefensible.

Extollers of presidential control of the war power also have fashioned the argument that executive warmaking, if repeated often enough, acquires legal validity. This is the contention that history has legitimated the practice of presidential warmaking. The argument rests on the premise that the president frequently has exercised the war power without congressional authorization. The actual number of these episodes varies among the several compilations, but defenders usually list between one and two hundred unilateral acts, each of which constitutes a legitimizing precedent for future executive wars. In detail and in conception the argument is flawed. In the first place, the lists are inaccurately complied. An error common to the lists—the claim that President John Adams initiated unilateral executive warmaking in 1798 in an "undeclared war" with France—is altogether false. The fact is that Adams took absolutely no independent action. Congress passed some two dozen statutes that amounted, so the Supreme Court said, to a declaration of "imperfect war," and Adams complied with those statutes. Moreover, many of the episodes involved initiation of hostilities by a military commander, not by authorization from the president. If practice establishes law, then the inescapable conclusion is that every commander of every military unit has the power to initiate war. What is perhaps most revealing about presidential understanding of the constitutional locus of the war power is that in the one or two dozen instances in which presidents personally have made the decision unconstitutionally to initiate acts of war, they have not purported to rely on their authority as commander in chief or chief executive. Rather, in those cases the presidents have made false claims of authorization, either by statute or by treaty or by international law. It cannot be maintained that constitutional power, in this case the war power, can be acquired through practice. Writing for a unanimous Court in *Inland Waterway Corp.* v. *Young* (1940), Justice Frankfurter echoed a centuries-old principle of Anglo-American jurisprudence when he wrote: "Illegality cannot attain legitimacy through practice." If the president could acquire power through usurpation he might aggrandize all governmental power. Neither Congress nor the judiciary could lawfully restrain the exercise of the president's accumulated constitutional powers. This practice would scuttle U.S. constitutional jurisprudence. Thus, the most recent act of usurpation stands no better than the first.

In the post–World War II period presidential usurpation of the war power has been indulged by congressional acquiescence, for policy as well as political reasons. But it is unwarranted to conclude that presidential aggrandizement, indulged by congressional passivity, attains a legal status. Congress cannot divest itself of those powers conferred upon it by the Constitution, a necessary predicate of the separation of powers doctrine. Neither congressional abdication nor acquiescence can accomplish a transfer of power to the executive. As the Court held in *Federal Trade Commission* v. *Morton Salt Company* (1950), harking back to an old axiom of English law, once powers are "granted, they are not lost by being allowed to lie dormant, any more than non-existent powers can be prescripted by an unchallenged exercise."

In a somewhat anemic effort to reassert its control of the war power, Congress passed, within the context of the debate surrounding the Vietnam War, the War Powers Resolution of 1973, over President Nixon's veto. The statute sought to curb presidential warmaking and to require "the collective judgment" of the president and Congress before U.S. troops could be committed to hostili-

ties. In the absence of a declaration of war or authorization by statute, the statute required the president to consult Congress before introducing U.S. forces into hostilities "in every possible instance," to report to Congress when he has done so, and to terminate the involvement after sixty days unless Congress authorized an extension. The resolution was criticized as an ill-conceived and poorly drafted piece of legislation. Its chief defect from a constitutional standpoint lay in the fact that it represented an unconstitutional delegation of the war power. In its grant to the president of the authority to choose an "enemy" of the United States, and to initiate hostilities against the nation, it not only repudiated the statutory aim of ensuring "collective judgment" of both branches, but it also vested in the president power that is denied to him by the Constitution. Virtually every American president who took office after its passage found ways to circumvent the resolution. Unconstitutional, ill-conceived, and ineffective, the resolution amounted to what Arthur Schlesinger Jr. described as a "toy handcuff," and by the early twenty-first century there was wide agreement that it ought to be repealed.

THE TREATY POWER

Assumption of broad foreign relations powers by the executive, largely built atop the removal of specific checks by the Senate, has claimed the treaty power as one of its principal casualties. The diminution of the Senate's constitutional role as a treaty partner could not have been envisioned by the Constitutional Convention, which, with less than two weeks left in its proceedings, vested in the Senate alone the power to make treaties. As late as 6 September, the draft constitution of the Committee on Detail had given the Senate the exclusive authority to make treaties and appoint ambassadors. During the debate Madison pointed out that the "Senate represented the states alone," and, consequently, "the president should be an agent in Treaties." Madison, who hailed from Virginia, along with other delegates from large states, were concerned about Senate control of the treaty power. As a result of "the Great Compromise," which gave states equal representation in the Senate, large-state delegates were seeking means to control the Senate. They feared that the Senate would be convulsed by regional economic and state interests that would compromise the national interests in the pursuit of commercial treaties. A version of Madison's proposal eventually prevailed. Article 2 of the Constitution gives the president the "power, by and with the Advice and Consent of the Senate, to make Treaties, provided two thirds of the Senators present concur."

The convention's belated addition of the president to the treaty-making power reflected the Framers' desire to "check" the Senate in the formulation of foreign policy, an application to foreign relations of the doctrine of checks and balances and collective decision-making. There was nothing in the language of the provision, or in the records of the convention debates, to indicate that the president would assume the dominant role in foreign affairs. There was no hint that the president would enjoy any significant independent role in treaty-making. The requirement of a two-thirds majority acted to limit any independent power of the president in foreign relations. In fact, as Hamilton explained in *Federalist* No. 75, "the vast importance of the trust, and the operation of treaties as laws, plead strongly for the participation of the whole or a portion of the legislative body in the making of them. . . . It must indeed be clear to a demonstration that the joint possession of the power in question, by the president and Senate, would afford a greater prospect of security, than the separate possession of it by either of them." Hamilton's emphasis on the cooperative nature of treaty-making, from negotiation through ratification, is reflected in the further requirement of senatorial "advice and consent." The Framers borrowed the phrase from English parliamentary practice, which was descriptive of continuous participation in lawmaking. No bill could be enacted into law by the king without the advice and consent of both houses of Parliament. The employment of that phrase in the treaty clause was meant to convey Senate participation in all stages of treaty-making. It is not suggestive in any way of a treaty-making process that is divided into two distinct stages: negotiation by the president and approval by the Senate. But that phrase is otherwise employed in the appointment clause to indicate a process that does depend on exclusive and sequential steps: the president "shall nominate, and by and with the Advice and Consent of the Senate, shall appoint Ambassadors."

When President George Washington first communicated with the Senate regarding the appropriate procedure for treaties, he assumed the process of negotiating treaties was a matter of joint participation. He advised a Senate committee that oral communications "seem indispensably necessary; because in these a variety of matters are contained, all of which not only require consideration, but some of them may undergo much discussion; to do which by written communications would be tedious without being satisfactory." This approach indicates an active, continuous, consultative role for the Senate. Washington, moreover, repeatedly expressed his intention to send "propositions" to the Senate, a solicitation of Senate "advice" on of treaties.

In a well-known message to the Senate on 21 August 1789, Washington stated his intention to meet with senators in the Senate chamber "to advise with them on the terms of the treaty to be negotiated with the Southern Indians." Washington intended to seek the Senate's advice before, not after, the negotiation of a treaty. He met with senators the next day, put to them a series of questions, and sought their advice on the instructions that should be given to the commissioners selected to negotiate the treaty. Both sides were disappointed. Senators exhibited unease in relying solely on the information supplied by the secretary of war, who had accompanied Washington. The noise from carriages traveling past the chambers made it difficult to follow the discussion. When the senators announced that they would not commit themselves to any positions that day, Washington felt inconvenienced by the trip. He returned two days later and obtained the Senate's answers to his questions and its consent to the treaty, but he never again went to seek the Senate's advice on a treaty proposal.

It is a misreading of the incident to conclude that Washington had determined to exclude the Senate from any role in the negotiation process. Oral communications proved to be impracticable; but Washington continued to seek the Senate's advice through written communications rather than personal appearances. Senators were asked to approve the appointment of treaty negotiators and to advise on their negotiating instructions. Since the earliest day of the Republic, there have been many examples of executive-Senate discussions regarding treaty negotiations.

The twentieth century, however, witnessed the erosion of this joint effort and the assumption by presidents that negotiation was an exclusively executive concern. As an academic, Woodrow Wilson had argued, in *Congressional Government* (1885), that the president could treat the Senate with indifference. He encouraged the president to pursue negotiations independently, without consulting the Senate. He reasoned that after these unilateral actions, the Senate could be bullied into granting its "consent," if not its "advice," with the nation's honor at stake. This "mousetrap theory" had disastrous consequences for the nation in the aftermath of World War I. One of Wilson's gravest miscalculations was his decision to exclude prominent senators from the negotiation of the Versailles treaty. Efforts by the executive to present the Senate with a fait accompli can backfire; the Senate may retaliate by adding amendments, shelving treaties, or rejecting them outright.

While the Constitution requires joint action by the president and Senate in making treaties, it is silent on the repository of the authority to terminate treaties. The Framers certainly were aware of the fact that treaties, for a variety of reasons, might require termination, and international law provided rules and regulations to govern their repeal. Madison and Jay, among others, seemed to believe that treaties ought to be terminated by the president and the Senate, and, historically, some have. But the historical record also includes repeal by unilateral presidential action and by Congress as a whole. Since Article 6 vests treaties with the same domestic status as federal statutes, treaties may be terminated by subsequent acts of Congress through the regular legislative process. The fact that the House of Representatives, which is not a part of the treaty power, can play a role in terminating, if not making, treaties, may appear to be anomalous. The same may be said of the argument for a unilateral presidential termination power, which would negate the philosophy of the convention and the entire foreign policy apparatus, which is erected on the premise of collective decision-making. The issue of the authority to terminate treaties came to a head in 1979 with President Jimmy Carter's announcement that he intended to terminate the 1954 mutual defense treaty with Taiwan. The decision resulted in a lawsuit, *Goldwater v. Carter* (1979), in which the Supreme Court declined to reach the merits of the case and dismissed it as "nonjusticiable." The practical effect of the decision left President Carter's act of termination intact. While the question of treaty termination was pushed aside temporarily, it seemed likely to become prominent again.

The president and the Senate may clash over the continued meaning of a treaty. Once a treaty takes effect, the president is principally responsible for its interpretations and implementation. A treaty is a law, and under the Constitution the president is charged with its faithful execution. But a president may not "reinterpret," that is, ascribe to a treaty a meaning contrary to what the Senate understood it to mean at the time it granted its consent. Disagreements have arisen between the president and the Senate on interpretations of the 1972 Anti-Ballistic Missile (ABM) Treaty, on the question of the amenability of that treaty to the development of new weapons systems. As a result it is likely that the Senate will carefully examine future treaties and make publicly known in clear terms its understanding of particular treaty provisions.

EXECUTIVE AGREEMENTS

Reliance on the treaty power has declined since World War II, as presidents have increasingly turned to the use of executive agreements as a means of securing unilateral control of American foreign relations. When the president acts unilaterally, the agreement is referred to as a "sole executive agreement." When the president acts with the approval of a simple majority of both houses of Congress, the agreement is known as a "legislative-executive agreement." Presidents have "assumed" discretion to decide whether to pursue an international agreement as a treaty, a sole executive agreement, or in the form of a legislative-executive agreement. The president's decision typically hinges on political factors, including the likelihood of securing Senate approval. Presidents often have chosen to exclude the Senate in making some controversial and historic international pacts through the channel of executive agreements, among them, the destroyer-base deal with Great Britain in 1940, the Yalta and Potsdam agreements of 1945, the Vietnam peace agreement of 1973, and the Sinai agreements of 1975.

Controversy surrounds the legal authority of the president to make executive agreements. The practice of unilateral presidential accords with foreign nations conflicts with the constitutional emphasis on joint decision-making, and with the Framers' understanding of the reach and breadth of the treaty power, which Hamilton described in a letter under the pseudonym "Camillus" as "competent to all the stipulations which the exigencies of national affairs might require; competent to the making of treaties of alliance, treaties of commerce, treaties of peace, and every other species of convention usual among nations. . . . And it was emphatically for this reason that it was so carefully guarded; the cooperation of two-thirds of the Senate with the president, being required to make any treaty whatever." The text of the Constitution makes no mention of executive agreements. Moreover, there was no reference to them in the Constitutional Convention or in the state ratifying conventions. The *Federalist Papers* are silent on the subject as well. There is, then, no support in the architecture of the Constitution for the use of executive agreements. Yet their usage has flourished; presidents claim independent constitutional power to make them, and the judiciary has sustained such presidential claims of authority. The question of the constitutional authority that affords presidents a unilateral capacity to make executive agreements is to be distinguished from what would properly be characterized as legislative-executive agreements, which Congress has authorized the president to make and usually inspire little controversy, if only because they are more desirable than unilateral agreements from a constitutional perspective.

Presidents have advanced four sources of constitutional authority: (1) the president's duty as chief executive to represent the nation in foreign affairs; (2) the authority to receive ambassadors and other public ministers; (3) the authority as commander in chief; and (4) the duty to "take Care that the laws be faithfully executed." These claims are particularly open-ended, undoubtedly in conflict with congressional powers, and they strain the reach of credibility. It may well be the case that the president, in the context of military hostilities authorized by Congress, may, in his capacity as commander in chief, find it desirable to enter into a cease-fire agreement with an enemy, although this would be subject to congressional control. It may be necessary as well, in a military context, for the president to strike an agreement regarding protection of troops or deployment of troops. But it is difficult to justify unilateral executive agreements on the basis of these other claims.

Congressional efforts to rein in the practice of executive agreements and stem the tide of unilateralism have been largely unsuccessful. The first and most prominent effort occurred in 1951, when Senator John Bricker proposed a constitutional amendment to limit the use and effects of executive agreements and treaties within the United States. Supporters of the Bricker Amendment, including leaders of the American Bar Association, found virtue in the proposal for various reasons. Some "resented," as Alexander DeConde explained, "executive agreements such as those made at Yalta," and sought to curtail presidential unilateralism in foreign affairs. Others were fearful of the effect within the United States of such

treaties as the UN Charter, the Genocide Convention, and the UN's draft covenant on human rights. Still others supported it as a useful "isolationist" response to the "internationalism of Franklin Roosevelt and Harry Truman.

The Bricker Amendment, approved by the Senate Judiciary Committee in June 1953, reaffirmed the Constitution's supremacy over treaties; required implementing legislation "which would be valid in the absence of treaty" before a treaty could be effected within the United States; and granted Congress the authority to regulate all executive agreements.

President Dwight D. Eisenhower opposed the amendment on grounds that it would hamstring the presidency in the conduct of foreign policy. In a letter to his brother Edgar, an attorney who supported the resolution, Eisenhower declared that it wold "cripple the executive power to the point that we become helpless in world affairs." The Eisenhower administration was keenly aware that most Republicans embraced the proposal and thus its opposition was carefully measured. After failing in his efforts to seek compromise with the Bricker forces, Eisenhower sought assistance from Senate Democrats. Senator Walter George of Georgia introduced his own amendment, which reiterated the Constitution's supremacy over treaties and executive agreements. In a key passage that reflected the widespread opposition to the expansive use of unilateral executive agreements, the George proposal would have required implementing legislation for executive agreements (but not for treaties) to take effect within the United States. The Eisenhower administration lobbied intensively for the defeat of both the Bricker and George proposals, principally because advisers believed it would strip the president of important prerogatives and transfer authority over foreign affairs from the executive to the legislative branch. The Bricker Amendment was defeated in the Senate on 25 February 1954 by a vote of 50 to 42. But the George Amendment fared better; it fell just one vote short of the two-thirds required for approval.

Congress has attempted to curtail the practice of making secret executive agreements. A subcommittee of the Senate Foreign Relations Committee learned in 1969 and 1970 that U.S. presidents had negotiated significant covert agreements with South Korea, Laos, Thailand, Ethiopia, and Spain, as well as other nations. In response, Congress passed the Case Act of 1972, requiring the secretary of state to send to Congress within sixty days the text of "any international agreement, other than a treaty," to which the United States is a party. If the president decided that publication would compromise national security, he could transmit it to the Senate Foreign Relations Committee and the House Committee on Foreign Affairs under an injunction of secrecy removable only by the president. But presidents from Nixon to Clinton ignored or circumvented the statute, and congressional enforcement efforts have been largely ineffective.

RECEPTION OF AMBASSADORS

Presidential reception of ambassadors and other public ministers, understood by the Framers as a clerklike duty, a mere administrative function, was transformed by presidents in the twentieth century as a wellspring of discretionary authority to determine which nations the United States would have relations with and what the tone and temper of those relations would be.

The reception of an ambassador entails consequences under international law, chiefly the recognition of foreign governments and states. The Framers, operating against the backdrop of international law principles that held that the sovereign nations have a duty to receive ambassadors from other sovereign nations, determined, as Hamilton explained in *Federalist* No. 69, to impose this duty on the president as a matter of "convenience." Hamilton said that the authority "to receive ambassadors and other public ministers . . . is more a matter of dignity than authority. It is a circumstance which will be without consequence in the administration of government; and it was far more convenient that is should be arranged in this manner, than that there should be a necessity of convening the legislature, or one of its branches, upon every arrival of a foreign minister, though it were merely to take the place of a departed predecessor." Given Hamilton's explanation, there was no reason to view the "reception clause" as a source of discretionary policymaking authority for the president. In fact, Article 2, Section 3 of the Constitution emphatically declares, "He shall, [not 'may'] receive Ambassadors and other public Ministers," an injunction that stands in sharp contrast with the discretionary constitutional powers that the president may choose to exercise, such as the decision to "convene both

Houses" of Congress. Thus, the Framers, as James Madison wrote in 1793, gave the president no prerogative whatever to reject foreign ministers. Madison explained that "when a foreign minister presents himself, two questions immediately arise: Are his credentials from the existing and acting government of his country? Are they properly authenticated?" Those questions, Madison noted, "are merely questions of fact," and if answered affirmatively, the president was duty bound to receive the minister.

The Framers' emphasis on the mechanical nature of the reception function, reflected their acceptance of the doctrine of de facto recognition, which requires diplomatic relations with the government that actually exercises controlling power, as opposed to the principle of de jure recognition, which counsels a determination of the legitimacy or legality of a governing regime. In a letter written on 30 December 1792 to Charles Cotesworth Pinckney, the U.S. minister to London, for the purpose of clarifying U.S. policy toward the revolutionary French government, Secretary of State Thomas Jefferson explained the rationale behind the American doctrine of de facto recognition: "We certainly cannot deny to other nations that principle whereon our own government is founded, that every nation has a right to govern itself internally under what forms it pleases and to change those forms at its own will."

The transformation of a humble administrative duty into a broad discretionary power to conduct foreign policy began under Woodrow Wilson. From 1913 to 1921 President Wilson, adhering to a theory of democratic legitimacy with respect to Latin American countries, refused to grant recognition to governments in that region that had come to power through revolution or violence when lawful constitutional means of achieving change existed. Then in 1920, Wilson, through Secretary of State Bainbridge Colby, declared that the United States would not recognize the Soviet Union, on the ground that the USSR was dedicated to the revolutionary overthrow of other governments in the state system. During the next thirteen years successive presidents adhered to Wilson's unilateral decision to refuse recognition of the Soviet Union, a policy that went largely unchallenged by an isolationist Congress. Ironically, this process of turning the Framers' reception function into a broad-based presidential foreign policy tool reached its full development when, in 1933, President Franklin D. Roosevelt decided to reverse the policy and recognize the Soviet Union, under the same constitutional authority that Wilson had abused to refuse recognition. Roosevelt's act of recognition then broadened into a unilateral agreement called the "Litvinov Assignment"—an agreement on property claims between the two nations. In *United States* v. *Belmont* (1937), Justice Sutherland upheld the validity of the agreement and said the pact derived its force from both the president's status as the sole organ of American foreign policy and his power to recognize foreign governments. Justice Sutherland stated that Senate consultation was not required. The Court again considered the validity of the Litvinov Assignment five years later in *United States* v. *Pink* (1942). Once more, the Court upheld the agreement, and enthusiastically embraced the "sole organ" doctrine and a capacious view of executive power. These decisions represented an exercise in judicial activism, and inflated the reception function into a towering structure of executive power. Thus in later years President Harry S. Truman felt authorized in his decision not to recognize the People's Republic of China as well as several of the communist satellite states of Eastern Europe. Under changing circumstances in later years, President Richard M. Nixon felt similarly authorized to reverse that policy in 1972 to extend what amounted to diplomatic recognition to the People's Republic of China, an effort that was completed in 1978 when President Jimmy Carter fully "normalized" relations with China through a unilateral decision to recognize the regime of Beijing and de-recognize the competing government in Taiwan.

For many observers the extraordinary power exercised by the executive in the conduct of foreign policy is a principal element in Schlesinger's "imperial" presidency, and it constitutes a major threat to the democratic foundations of the American constitutional system. Yet the practice of executive usurpation, revelations of the activities of the Central Intelligence Agency abroad, the constitutional corruption inherent in the Iran-Contra affair, and the dangers posed by a pattern of unilateral presidential warmaking from Korea to Vietnam to Bosnia, have not moved Congress and the public to implement meaningful constitutional and political checks to halt presidential aggrandizement of power. Occasionally, individual members or even large blocs of members of Congress will challenge a unilateral presidential action. On 28 April 1999 the House of Representatives, by a tie vote, rejected a motion to authorize President Bill Clinton to conduct air and missile strikes against the former Yugoslavia. Clinton ignored the House vote and waged war on his own claim of authority. But the relatively infrequent and isolated criticisms that emerge from Capitol Hill have not risen to the level of an institutional challenge, in which Congress summons the will to defend its constitutional powers in foreign affairs. While defenders of the constitutional design for foreign policy might hope for a resurgent Congress, and even dare to dream of an ascendant Congress, there seems to be little political incentive for members to act because international issues rarely assume a significant role in election campaigns. There remains the possibility that some international issues, among them trade matters and environmental concerns, may assume greater importance among voters, which would transform those issues into constituent demands and thus stir Congress to assert its broad powers. However, George W. Bush declared early in his first term that he would halt U.S. participation in the Kyoto Accords, a worldwide effort to control global warming; announced that he would use military force to defend Taiwan against mainland China; and stated his intention to terminate the Antiballistic Missile Treaty of 1972, all unilateral executive actions that constitute a rank usurpation of congressional powers. Yet those declarations brought forth few protests from Congress in defense of its constitutional frontiers and provinces. Indeed, at century's turn, congressional acquiescence in the face of executive aggrandizement seemed as fully entrenched in the practice of American foreign policy as it did when the imperial presidency first took flight.

For others, however, the vast discretionary power exercised by the president is the price the nation pays to safeguard its national security interests abroad and its freedom at home. Executive domination of foreign policy, it has been asserted, is a reflection of the overweening realities of the international realm, which cannot be adequately addressed by a Constitution that is no longer relevant to international politics. Congressional primacy has become obsolete. There remains a debate, one initiated in the Constitutional Convention two centuries ago, on the question of whether unilateral executive control of foreign policy or legislatively inspired collective decision making is more suitable in a nation grounded on republican principles. It may well be the case that the values underlying the war clause and the other constitutional provisions that govern the conduct of American foreign policy are as compelling today as they were two hundred years ago.

BIBLIOGRAPHY

Berger, Raoul. *Executive Privilege: A Constitutional Myth.* Cambridge, 1974. Penetrating study that includes valuable chapters on presidential power in foreign affairs and warmaking.

Bestor, Arthur. "Separation of Powers in the Domain of Foreign Affairs: The Intent of the Constitution Historically Examined." *Seton Hall Law Review* 5 (1974). Powerful analysis of the legislative history behind the foreign affairs provisions of the Constitution.

Casper, Gerhard. "Constitutional Constraints on the Conduct of Foreign Policy: A Nonjudicial Model." *University of Chicago Law Review* 43 (1976). Influential study of foreign affairs from a legal and constitutional perspective.

Corwin, Edward S. *The President: Office and Powers, History and Analysis of Practice and Opinion, 1787–1984.* 5th rev. ed. New York, 1984. Very valuable on presidential powers in foreign policy.

DeConde, Alexander. *Presidential Machismo: Executive Authority, Military Intervention, and Foreign Relations.* Boston, 2000. Important account of the reasons why presidents engage in unilateral acts of warmaking.

Draper, Theodore. *A Very Thin Line: The Iran-Contra Affairs.* New York, 1991. Detailed and critical analysis of the political, legal, and policy issues.

Ely, John Hart. *War and Responsibility: Constitutional Lessons of Vietnam and Its Aftermath.* Princeton, N.J., 1993. Insightful critique of the constitutional debate and controversies surrounding the Vietnam War.

Fisher, Louis. "How Tightly Can Congress Draw the Purse Strings?" *American Journal of International Law* 83 (1989). An examination of the use of the power of the purse in foreign affairs.

———. *Presidential War Power.* Lawrence, Kans., 1995. Concise, penetrating analysis of the war power.

———. *Constitutional Conflicts Between Congress and the President.* 4th rev. ed. Lawrence, Kans., 1997. Excellent examination of the separation of powers issues.

Glennon, Michael J. *Constitutional Diplomacy.* Princeton, N.J., 1990. Highly useful study of the constitutional arrangement for the conduct of foreign policy.

Hayden, Ralston. *The Senate and Treaties: 1789–1817.* New York, 1920. Fine historical and analytical study of the Senate's role in treaty making.

Henkin, Louis. *Constitutionalism, Democracy, and Foreign Affairs.* New York, 1990. Fine analysis of theoretical and constitutional issues relevant to foreign policy.

———. *Foreign Affairs and the Constitution.* 2d ed. Oxford, 1996. Excellent, comprehensive analysis of the constitutional law of foreign policy, with good footnotes.

Johnson, Loch K. *The Making of International Agreements: Congress Confronts the Executive.* New York, 1984. Examination of the nature, uses, and impact of executive agreements.

Keynes, Edward. *Undeclared War: Twilight Zone of Constitutional Power.* University Park, Pa., 1982. Powerful, illuminating study of the legal issues surrounding the war powers debate.

Koh, Harold Hongju. "The Treaty Makers and the Law Makers: The Law of the Land and Foreign Relations." *University of Pennsylvania Law Review* 107 (1959). Useful on relationships between treaties and acts of Congress.

———. *The National Security Constitution: Sharing Power After the Iran-Contra Affair.* New Haven, 1990. Detailed examination of foreign relations law and the responsibilities of the three branches of government.

Lobel, Jules. "Covert War and Congressional Authority: Hidden War and Forgotten Power." *University of Pennsylvania Law Review* 134 (1986). Valuable examination of the legal and constitutional issues involved in limited war.

Lofgren, Charles A. "War-Making Under the Constitution: The Original Understanding." *Yale Law Journal* 81 (1972). Outstanding examination of the Constitutional Convention and constitutional governance of the war power.

Robinson, James A. *Congress and Foreign Policy Making: A Study in Legislative Influence and Initiative.* Homewood, Ill., 1962. Concise study of foreign policy as Congress influences it.

Schlesinger, Arthur M., Jr. *The Imperial Presidency.* Boston, 1973. Acclaimed study of the evolution of presidential powers in foreign policy and warmaking.

Scigliano, Robert. *The Supreme Court and the Presidency.* New York, 1971. Useful catalog and discussion of judicial rulings on presidential power.

Sofaer, Abraham D. *War, Foreign Affairs, and Constitutional Power: The Origins.* Cambridge,

Mass., 1976. Comprehensive analysis of the constitutional origins and early practice of foreign affairs powers.

Sutherland, George S. *Constitutional Power and World Affairs*. New York, 1919. Early publication of the future Supreme Court Justice's view on the constitutional law of foreign affairs.

Wormuth, Francis D. "The Nixon Theory of the War Power: A Critique." *University of California Law Review* 60 (1972). Outstanding analysis of the constitutional issues involving presidential warmaking.

Wormuth, Francis D., and Edwin B. Firmage. *To Chain the Dog of War: The War Power of Congress in History and Law*. Dallas, 1986. Nearly encyclopedic examination of war powers issues.

Wright, Quincy. *The Control of American Foreign Relations*. New York, 1922. Classic modern analysis of the subject.

See also CONGRESSIONAL POWER; JUDICIARY POWER AND PRACTICE; PRESIDENTIAL POWER.

CONTAINMENT

Barton J. Bernstein

The containment doctrine, with its ambiguities and imprecision, was a major strategy and the guiding conception in American foreign policy from shortly after World War II until the collapse of the Soviet Union in 1989–1991, and some might argue that containment remained a policy into the twenty-first century for the United States in dealing with communist regimes in Cuba, North Korea, and China. In its most general form, containment denotes the American effort, by military, political, and economic means, to resist communist expansion throughout the world. But precisely because of the looseness of the doctrine and the differing interpretations, including questions about the selective application of efforts to stop communism, the doctrine's author, George F. Kennan, an influential foreign service officer in 1947 and later a respected private scholar, often opposed important tactics that many American policymakers defined as the implementation of containment: the global rhetoric of the Truman Doctrine in 1947, establishment of the North Atlantic Treaty Organization (NATO) in 1949–1950, the heavy military emphasis of U.S. policy in the 1950s, the extension of alliances to Asia and the Middle East, and the prolonged military involvement in Vietnam in the 1960s and 1970s. As Kennan stated in 1967:

> If . . . I was the author in 1947 of a "doctrine" of containment, it was a doctrine that lost much of its rationale with the death of Stalin and with the development of the Soviet-Chinese conflict. I emphatically deny the paternity of any efforts to invoke that doctrine today in situations to which it has, and can have, no proper relevance.

While agreeing on the desirability of resisting communist expansion, Kennan and others disagreed on whether the doctrine remained relevant, and how and where to implement it. Their disputes have often rested on fundamental differences about the capacity of American power,

about the extent of American interests beyond western Europe, and especially about the nature of the communist threat. The last issue has raised many questions. Was the threat subversion, revolution, military aggression, economic encirclement, or some combination? With the exception of Yugoslavia, was world communism controlled by Joseph Stalin even after the successful Chinese revolution in 1949? After the death of Joseph Stalin in 1953 and after the obvious Sino-Soviet split in the early 1960s, did the nature of the communist threat sometimes change, even well before the collapse of the Soviet Union in 1989–1991? At times from the early 1960s, according to the proponents of containment, was the threat primarily China and wars of national liberation in the Third World, and not the Soviet Union mostly in the developed world? Was American policy in the 1990s and continuing into the twenty-first century in dealing with Cuba, North Korea, and the People's Republic of China often the policy of containment?

Beyond these important issues, scholars, as well as politicians and policymakers, have raised other questions: whether the doctrine in 1947 was new or necessary, whether it was ultimately self-defeating, whether it was active or passive, and whether it did or should have endured as American policy into the late 1980s and early 1990s and perhaps later. Many of the questions about containment, if it is interpreted as the general course of American foreign policy, become the basic questions about that policy itself, from Harry S. Truman's administration to the first years of President George H. W. Bush's and possibly beyond.

KENNAN'S PUBLIC STATEMENT OF CONTAINMENT

Writing mysteriously as "X" in 1947, George Kennan, then the head of the State Department Policy

Planning Staff, first publicly articulated the doctrine of containment in "The Sources of Soviet Conduct," in *Foreign Affairs* (July 1947), the influential journal of the Council on Foreign Relations. That mid-1947 statement, it might be said, became the near-canonical expression of containment, though Kennan himself, even in the 1940s when operating in the State Department, provided various formulations in speeches and reports that departed, sometimes, significantly from the 1947 essay.

When his identity quickly leaked out, his Mr. "X" analysis was interpreted as official policy, because of his position in the State Department and because the essay seemed to justify a recent bold departure in American foreign policy: Truman's call on 12 March 1947, in the so-called "Truman Doctrine" speech, for economic and military aid "to support free peoples who are resisting attempted subjugation by armed minorities or by outside pressures."

Kennan's essay offered both a diagnosis of and a prescription for treating the Soviet threat; actually, he frequently termed it "Russian" and thus often used that adjective and the noun "Russia" to mean "Soviet" and "Soviet Union." His prescription attracted the most attention: the need to confront "the Russians with unalterable counterforce at every point where [the Soviet Union] shows signs of encroaching upon the interests of a peaceful world." There would be perpetual crises, presumably frequent confrontations. Such a policy "must be . . . long-term, patient but firm and vigilant." Kennan predicted that it would increase enormously the strains in Soviet society, compel Soviet foreign policy to be cautious and circumspect, and produce the gradual mellowing or breakup of the Soviet system. Containment promised the liberation of Eastern Europe and an American victory in the long run, without preventive war. History was on the side of the West. His faith that the future belonged to democratic capitalism directly repudiated the Marxist faith that capitalism would crumble from its own contradictions.

Kennan's diagnosis of Soviet policy was central to his optimistic forecast and to much of his doctrine. Soviet policy was, he asserted, relentless but not adventurous—"a fluid stream which moves constantly wherever permitted to move toward a given goal." This patient but insatiable expansion, he explained, was the logical outgrowth of communist ideology. Soviet hostility to the West, in turn, was a result largely of the "neurotic world view" of Soviet leaders and of their need to create a foreign enemy to justify dictatorship at home. Their "world view" was both paranoid and functional; it misunderstood Western actions but also helped Soviet leaders to stay in power.

The Soviet policy, he stressed, could be altered only by Soviet authorities, not by any other national power. "Once a party line has been laid down," he asserted, "the whole Soviet governmental machine, including the mechanism of diplomacy, moves inexorably along the prescribed path, like a persistent toy automobile wound up and headed in a given direction, stopping only when it meets with some unanswerable force." In that view, Soviet officials at the middle levels were basically automatons, and there were presumably no important differences among top Soviet leaders.

Kennan's message was clear: Soviet hostility was not a reasonable response to America's wartime policy or to earlier American actions, nor could negotiations ease or end this hostility and produce a settlement of the Cold War. His analysis became the new orthodoxy: the Soviet Union was "committed fanatically to the belief that with the United States there can be no permanent *modus vivendi*, that it is desirable and necessary that the internal harmony of our society be disrupted, our traditional ways of life be destroyed, the international authority of our state be broken, if Soviet power is to be secure."

THE BACKGROUND OF THE MR. "X" ESSAY

Kennan, a member of the first generation of State Department specialists on the Soviet Union, was born in Milwaukee in 1904 to a well-to-do family, attended Princeton University in the early 1920s, and, perhaps because of his provincialism amid the glitter of the eastern elite, developed the sense of the outsider. A man of rarefied intelligence and strained sensibility, he was in many ways a latter-day Jamesian character. He was sensitive to the slightest rebuff, to minor breaches in etiquette, but, judging from his memoirs, when he returned to the United States from foreign service overseas in 1937, remained curiously untroubled by the economic depression, with its ravaging poverty, in his own nation.

In the diplomatic service, Kennan happily found what he termed "protective paternalism" and seemed to delight in the ordered tasks, the requirements of discipline, the acts of civic responsibility, the applications of intelligence, and the distance from the United States. When the United States opened diplomatic relations with the Soviet Union in 1933, Kennan became third secretary in Moscow. He later claimed that his four years in Moscow were "unavoidably a sort of liberal education in the horrors of Stalinism," and his hostility to Marxism and the Soviet system grew. They offended his taste, his sensibility, and his values.

During those early years in the Soviet Union, he had a zest to understand, to penetrate, and to participate in Russian society. He soon complained to Washington about repression in the Soviet Union, stressing, for example in 1937, that "the great majority of the Soviet citizens who have had . . . extensive social or official relations with diplomats during the past few years have now disappeared . . . they have been intimidated, arrested, exiled, or executed." Such politics, he told Washington in terms that could suggest personal grievance, had destroyed "any prestige and popularity which foreign envoys might otherwise enjoy in the eyes of the Soviet public."

Having become a fierce critic of the Soviet system, Kennan deplored America's welcoming the Soviet Union in 1941 as an "associate in defense of democracy," for this alliance, he complained, would identify the United States with Soviet oppression in Eastern Europe. By 1944, Kennan was already counseling that Soviet-American diplomatic collaboration was impossible. Fearing that the United States lacked "the political manliness" to stop the Soviets from carving out a sphere of influence in Eastern and Central Europe, he proposed, in despair, that the United States might as well divide Germany, partition Europe into spheres, and define "the line beyond which we cannot afford to permit the Russians to exercise unchallenged power or to take purely unilateral action." This was the containment doctrine in embryonic form.

In 1944 and 1945, Kennan's analysis was unacceptable to many policymakers, including his immediate superior, W. Averell Harriman, the American ambassador to the Soviet Union. Harriman and many American policymakers had often defined American interests in universalist terms to include Eastern Europe, but believed that Soviet-American cooperation was possible—that the Soviets would withdraw or reduce their influence and accede in this area to free elections. These policymakers concluded that American economic power and atomic prowess might compel the Soviets to accede to American wishes in this border area. Unlike Kennan, they believed

that Soviet policy was alterable, that accommodations could be reached—on American terms.

President Franklin D. Roosevelt, by some historical interpretations, had temporarily acceded to Soviet control in much of Eastern Europe, and confirmed that arrangement at the Yalta Conference of the "Big Three" (with Premier Joseph Stalin and British Prime Minister Winston Churchill) in February 1945. But Roosevelt had also hoped to bring the Soviets into a condominium of great powers, to involve the Soviets in the United Nations, and, through a combination of deftness and toughness, to push the Soviets to soften their policy in Eastern Europe.

In certain ways, Kennan's analysis of the Soviet Union seemed closer to that of former President Herbert Hoover. Most notably, Hoover, who had long chafed at the growth of Soviet power in Europe, had serious doubts about negotiating with the Soviets. In mid-1945, Hoover even recommended, about ten weeks before the August atomic bombings of Japan and Soviet entry into the Pacific war, his own policy of containment. Hoover wanted President Harry S. Truman, who had just succeeded Roosevelt, to greatly soften the surrender terms for Japan in order to end the war before Soviet entry into the conflict and in order to restrain Soviet influence in Asia. Hoover had even proposed letting Japan retain Formosa and Korea, among other generous terms, in order to end the war well before the Soviets could gain territorial advantages in Asia.

Hoover's counsel failed, largely because his proposal—very soft surrender terms for Japan—seemed politically unacceptable in America. But neither of the two high-level administration officials he approached—Secretary of War Henry L. Stimson and President Truman—seemed opposed, in principle, to Hoover's motivating desire to contain Soviet influence and power. These two American leaders, however, knew something important that was kept secret from Hoover and the American people—that President Roosevelt at Yalta, in return for Stalin's promise to enter the Pacific war within three months of Germany's surrender, had granted some important territorial concessions in Asia. State Department efforts to renege on those territorial terms failed in mid-1945, partly because Soviet armed intervention in the Pacific was still deemed necessary by American leaders in order to speed Japan's surrender and reduce U.S. casualties.

Practicing his own early form of containment in 1945, President Truman, disliking the fact that the Soviets had an occupation zone in Germany and thus a role in the postwar reconstruction of that nation, acted to bar the Soviets from any role in the postwar occupation and reconstruction of Japan. In mid-August 1945, when Japan surrendered, Stalin hoped speedily to land troops in northern Japan to establish a Soviet presence in Japan, but Truman insisted, successfully, that Stalin back down. The Soviets nevertheless stuck by their mid-August agreement with the United States on Korea. The Soviets occupied only the northern half of Korea, and southern Korea was unoccupied by Allied forces, until the American troops arrived in September 1945, a few weeks after the Soviets could have taken over the south.

In early 1946, when Stalin publicly warned of future capitalist wars, called for Soviet military strength, and refused to join the World Bank and the International Monetary Fund, the Department of State asked for an analysis of Soviet policy. That request evoked from Kennan his famous Long Telegram (about 5,500 words) of 22 February 1946, an early statement of his "X" essay. "The more I thought about this [opportunity]," he later wrote, "the more it seemed obvious that this was 'it.' For eighteen months I had done little else but pluck people's sleeves, trying to make them understand the nature of the phenomenon with which we in the Moscow embassy were daily confronted and which our government and people had to learn to understand if they were to have any chance of coping successfully with the problems of the world."

Kennan's telegram—explaining that the Soviet Union was expansionist, malevolent, warlike, and uncompromising—neatly expressed the emerging conclusions among policymakers in Washington. The response was, Kennan recalls, "nothing less than sensational." It lifted him from the relative obscurity of chargé d'affaires in Moscow, won the affection of Secretary of the Navy James Forrestal, brought Kennan a position at the newly created National War College, and gave him fame and popularity within the higher echelons of the Truman administration. Kennan had not offered new thoughts or insights, but rather, at a critical juncture, had phrased in telling words the emerging analysis within the administration.

According to some revisionist historians, his message arrived shortly after policymakers had moved away from "liberation" in Eastern Europe and the hopes of using "atomic diplomacy" to roll back Soviet influence there. The Soviets, while delaying elections in Bulgaria in August 1945,

had not yielded further to implied threats. The result was a virtual stalemate in this area. While pledged to universalism, and wanting democratic governments and an economic open door in Eastern Europe, the United States was not prepared to go to war to achieve its goals there.

Two weeks after the Long Telegram, on 5 March 1946, Winston Churchill, now former British prime minister, delivered his Iron Curtain address. The Soviet Union, he asserted, did not want war, only the "fruits of war and the indefinite expansion of [its] power and doctrines." The implication was that the Soviet Union was insatiably expansionist and would use subversion and aggression to take over Europe and Asia. Churchill's clarion call to the West had the endorsement of President Harry S. Truman, who had read the speech in advance and presumably welcomed it as part of the administration's strategy of reorienting the American public for a "get-tough" policy toward the Soviet Union.

That strategy included exploiting the dispute in Iran, where the Soviet Union had not yet withdrawn its troops from Azerbaijan, an oil-rich northwestern province once part of czarist Russia's sphere of influence. In early 1946, the United States pushed this issue into the United Nations forum and insisted upon keeping the matter there even after the Soviet Union promised in late March to remove its troops in a few weeks. American success in this venture established for many policymakers that firmness could compel the Soviets to withdraw from recently occupied areas beyond Eastern Europe and to accede to American demands.

In the summer of 1946, Truman requested an analysis of Soviet policy. Simplifying Kennan's analysis in the Long Telegram, the resulting study (put together by White House assistant George Elsey and endorsed by Truman's counsel Clark Clifford) stressed the influence of Marxist ideology on Soviet action. The Kremlin leaders, according to that report, "adhere to the Marxian theory of ultimate destruction [of capitalist states] by every means at their disposal." Efforts at accord or mutual understanding would be "highly dangerous" for the United States, because concessions would raise Soviet demands. Warning that the Soviet Union might start war to spread communism, the report called for "resisting [Soviet] efforts to expand into areas vital to American security." Among the potential "trouble spots" requiring American attention were three in the Far East—China, which needed a "unified and economically stable" system; Japan, which had to be reconstructed and made democratic; and Korea, which should be "united and independent."

"The language of military power is the only language which [the Soviet Union] understands," the Clifford-Elsey report asserted. Agreeing with the general tone and analysis of the report, which was still in draft form, Kennan urged the addition of a key paragraph, which with minor cosmetic changes ended up in the final report:

> Whether it would actually be in this country's interests to wage atomic and biological warfare against Russia in the event hostilities should develop is of course a question which would require careful consideration in the light of circumstances prevailing at the time. This decision might be influenced by a number of factors which can not now be estimated, but it is important that this country be prepared to use them if need be, for the mere fact of such preparedness may prove to be the only powerful deterrent to Russian aggressive action and in this sense the only sure guaranty of peace.

By late summer 1946, the Soviet Union's refusal to endorse the American plan for international control of atomic energy confirmed to policymakers that the Soviets were deceitful, suspicious, and uncompromising. How, Americans asked sincerely, could the Truman administration's offer, which they incorrectly deemed magnanimous, be rejected? Concessions were impossible. Compromise would not work. Kennan privately suggested that the United States use implicit "atomic diplomacy" to force the Soviets to accept the U.S. plan. He proposed, in the words of an associate, tactics "designed to convince the Russians of our serious intent and of the consequences if they chose to continue their present course." His proposal included the public announcement of "the construction of a new bomb-proof General Staff headquarters in a remote region"—a possible preliminary to war.

It is unclear whether or not Kennan in 1946 was mulling over the possibility of preventive war by the United States. He had given some thought to the prospects of actual war, and how it should be fought, if it occurred. Meeting during the summer with General Carl Spaatz, the chief of staff of the air force, Kennan said that the war, in the summary words of a minutes-taker's notes, should be "conducted by the U.S. [as] an air war in the strictest sense of the term." According to Kennan, there were only "about ten vital points" in the Soviet Union to be bombed in order to cripple the

Soviet Union and force its speedy defeat. They were not primarily cities but production areas and railroads. He saw no need to try to invade and occupy the USSR after such air attacks, and anticipated a revolution in which "the Bolshevik regime would crack."

In mid-1946, when Kennan met with Spaatz, the United States only possessed about five or eight A-bombs, though Kennan, like many American officials, was not allowed to know the top-secret number. Thus, his sketch of a bombing attack on the Soviet Union may have implied nuclear weapons or conventional weapons, or, most likely, a combination of both kinds of bombs. He may not have known that his thinking about virtually a push-button war was markedly at odds with the emerging secret American military planning at the time in which there was usually an assumption that war, if it came, would involve a long, costly conflict between armies on the European continent. According to those plans, the bomb could be helpful, but not decisive.

Amid the growing East-West tension, with his own expanding reputation as a prescient Soviet expert, Kennan found additional opportunities to refine and advance his views in Washington and in other influential quarters. In January 1947, Secretary Forrestal, Kennan's benefactor, asked him to comment on a manuscript on Soviet policy, and Kennan went beyond the assignment to present on 31 January his own lengthy interpretation. His paper for Forrestal—based on an early January speech before the Council on Foreign Relations in New York—became the "X" essay. It was speedily cleared by the State Department, because Kennan's thoughts were compatible with emerging American policy. Upon publication of the essay, he became the recognized philosopher-diplomat of containment. He had synthesized the emerging wisdom and dignified it within an acceptable intellectual framework.

THE TRUMAN DOCTRINE

Four months before publication of "The Sources of Soviet Conduct" and while it circulated within the administration, President Truman launched what became known as the Truman Doctrine. Speaking before Congress on 12 March 1947, he called for a global crusade against encroaching communism and requested $400 million in military and economic aid, as well as military and economic advisers, to halt what he described as communist aggression and subversion in Greece and communist threats to Turkey. The alternatives in beleaguered Greece, he contended, were totalitarianism or freedom. The world was at a critical turning point: the struggle was between the forces of light and darkness, of humanity and evil. America's commitment could turn back the hordes of oppression and guarantee freedom.

Although Truman never explicitly labeled the Soviet Union as the malefactor, his slightly veiled references left no room for doubt. Most policymakers then assumed that Stalin was supporting and planning the revolution in Greece, the intended recipient of most of the American aid. According to the later testimony of Milovan Djilas, a Yugoslavian revolutionary, Stalin opposed the revolution in Greece and tried to stop communist nations from supplying the Greek revolutionaries. Stalin was sometimes a counterrevolutionary, who believed, Djilas wrote, "that the creation of revolutionary centers outside Moscow could endanger its supremacy in world communism." American policymakers were apparently blinded by their own ideology, by their belief that the communist world was then monolithic, and by their conviction that Stalin was an ardent revolutionary and would extend communism whenever possible.

The Truman administration seized the opportunity to declare the Cold War in the Truman Doctrine speech. Until March 1947, partly because of some pro-Soviet attitudes in the United States and fears of a disastrous rift in the Democratic Party, policymakers had wavered publicly on whether the United States could reach an accommodation with the Soviet Union or whether the Russians were an implacable adversary. Resolving his earlier public ambivalence in March, Truman called for a global crusade against communism while limiting his specific legislative requests to Greece and Turkey.

Kennan, then in Washington at the National War College and active in the State Department's planning of the aid program, objected to the tone and ideological content of the message, and to some aspects of the program. Judging that the Turkish problem was one of morale that the Turks themselves could solve, he opposed military aid to Turkey. Truman's message, Kennan believed, went too far in its ideological analysis and in its global promises—the stark portrayal of two opposing ways of life and the open-ended commitment to aid free peoples everywhere. He feared that the Soviet Union might be provoked by the tone and crusading commitment to declare war.

Kennan's anxieties eased when the administration, in presenting its request to Congress, retreated from the promise of a global crusade and limited its commitment to Greece, Turkey, and western Europe. Like most policymakers, Kennan feared the results of a communist victory in Greece and linked that to what later became known as the domino theory: The triumph in Greece would destabilize the Middle East and weaken the morale of western Europe, so that the people there might "trim their sails and even abet" the victory of communism. For Kennan, the commitment to Greece was necessary, reasonable, and desirable; it was within American capabilities; it would halt "our political adversaries"; and its "favorable consequences will carry far beyond the limits of Greece itself." According to Kennan, other European nations, then beset by communist threats internally or near their borders, would gain hope and have confidence in the United States.

CRITIQUES OF MR. X'S DOCTRINE

Despite Kennan's doubts about some aspects of the Truman Doctrine, most commentators viewed Truman's speech and the "X" essay as parts of the same program—containment. Most unfriendly critics focused on the Truman Doctrine. They charged the United States with bailing out British imperialism in the Middle East, establishing American imperialism there, risking war against the Soviet Union, exaggerating the crisis, militarizing policy, abandoning negotiations, misinterpreting Soviet action, misunderstanding the civil war in Greece, supporting totalitarianism there, escalating the Cold War, and trying to scare the American people. Both right-wing critics like Senator Robert A. Taft, a leading Republican, and left-wing critics like Henry A. Wallace, who had recently left Truman's cabinet because of disagreements on foreign policy, agreed that the Soviet Union was not a military threat. A self-styled heir of Franklin D. Roosevelt's foreign policy, Wallace argued publicly for a settlement of the Cold War and the avoidance of the arms race.

Shortly after Kennan's essay appeared, Walter Lippmann, the respected columnist and sympathetic critic of American foreign policy, published in a series of columns a penetrating critique of the containment policy, later collected as *The Cold War: A Study of U.S. Foreign Policy* (1947). Interpreting the "X" essay as the intellectual rationale for the Truman Doctrine, Lippmann focused on the essay. It was, he contended, fundamentally wrong on two major grounds: it misunderstood the sources of Soviet behavior and offered recommendations for American policy that were a diplomatic and strategic "monstrosity."

Whereas Kennan had mostly stressed Marxist ideology as the major source of Soviet actions (belief in the "innate antagonism between capitalism and socialism"), Lippmann argued on the basis of Russian history that expansion—the quest for a sphere of influence in Eastern Europe and power in the Mediterranean—was an inherited czarist ambition, not a communist innovation. By emphasizing the continuity of Russian and Soviet history, Lippmann minimized the role of communist ideology. Yet, curiously, in explaining Soviet behavior, he did not stress the long history of Western hostility and American opposition to the Soviet system. Unlike later revisionist historians, Lippmann was not placing the burden for Soviet-American antagonism on American, or Western, actions.

Lippmann agreed with Kennan that Soviet power would expand unless confronted by American power, but he objected on pragmatic grounds to Kennan's plan for the next generation or beyond: resistance with "counterforce" wherever the Soviets threatened, until the pressure destroyed or mellowed the Soviet system. Lippmann argued that this plan was too optimistic: America did not have the patience, the economic power, or the armed forces to contain the Soviet Union wherever it showed signs of encroaching and until it collapsed. Kennan's doctrine was strategically dangerous to the United States; it gave the Soviet Union the initiative, allowed the Soviets to choose for confrontation the areas near their border where they were stronger, and would ultimately lead to excessive demands upon American forces. Lippmann warned that the United States, compensating for inadequate military strength, would recruit and organize a "heterogeneous array of satellites, clients, dependents, and puppets," who might plunge the United States into crises or compel it to abandon them and risk charges of appeasement and "sell out." Kennan's strategy required the United States to create "unassailable borders" near the Soviet Union, which would be an unnatural alliance for the West. For Lippmann, the doctrine of containment, as represented by the "X" essay, failed the test of realism. The essay did not recognize the limits of American power and thereby threatened to involve the United States in dangerous alliances, and ultimately to sap American will and morale when the policy of confrontation did not bring prompt victory.

Lippmann's alternative strategy—later known as "disengagement" when Kennan publicly advocated it a decade later—called for the withdrawal from Germany and eventually from continental Europe of the armies of the United States, the Soviet Union, and Great Britain. This policy, Lippmann argued, would be the "acid test" of Soviet intentions, and, if successful, would reduce tension, eliminate troubling issues, move the two great powers toward a modus vivendi, contribute to a better life for many Europeans, and conserve American resources.

More important than this specific proposal, Lippmann was counseling the continuation of negotiations, the use of diplomacy, in order to achieve at least a partial Soviet-American settlement. The Truman Doctrine and "X"'s diagnosis, the columnist asserted, erred because they rejected diplomacy. "The history of diplomacy," Lippmann wrote, "is the history of relations among rival powers, which did not enjoy political intimacy, and did not respond to appeals to common purposes. Nevertheless, there have been settlements. . . . For a diplomat to think that rival and unfriendly powers cannot be brought to a settlement is to forget what diplomacy is all about."

Drawing less attention in 1947 than Lippman's analysis but more concern in the early 1950s was the savage critique of Kennan's thinking from the right in America. Containment, to those critics, was appeasement, accepting Soviet domination of much of Eastern Europe. In their judgment, containment was timid, if not pusillanimous. A notable critic, the right-wing James Burnham, who had once been on the anti-Stalin American left, charged that containment was the "bureaucratic verbalization of a policy of drift [concealing] its inner law. . . . Let history do it." These critics wanted action—penetration of the "iron curtain," overthrow of communist regimes, liberation of the "captive peoples." At minimum, there should be, these critics contended, America-directed sabotage, clandestine activity, and paramilitary involvement against the Soviets and what was regarded as their "stooge" governments in Eastern Europe. None of those proposed aggressive tactics, according to the right-wing critics, was countenanced or encouraged by containment. Those critics were actually very wrong—but they could not know about the then-secret American tactics.

Significantly, Kennan had often used the terms "Russian" to denote "Soviet" and "Russia" to mean "Soviet Union," thus casually ignoring the fact that many Soviet citizens (about 25 to 30 percent or about 45 to 54 million of the USSR's population) were not ethnic Russians, and that Russian history, when Kennan discussed it, was not actually the history of many Soviet peoples. Kennan's prominent critics in the 1940s and 1950s usually neglected this important difference. But occasionally some hyphenated Americans, especially Ukrainians, did stress what was called the "nationalities problem" (the fact that the Soviet Union was composed of a number of different nationality groups) and argue that the Soviet Union might come apart, under American-directed pressure, and splinter into different nationality-based states.

REFLECTIONS ON KENNAN'S ORIGINAL MEANING

Twenty years after Kennan's "X" essay, when publishing his memoirs, Kennan lamented publicly for the first time that his "X" essay had been misunderstood and that he had been mistaken for the architect of those very features of the Truman Doctrine that he had opposed. He had not intended to offer a doctrine, he claimed, but wanted to show that war with the Soviet Union was neither inevitable nor necessary, that there was no need to conclude from the failure of American concessions to the Soviets that there must be an eventual war between the two great powers. Kennan regretted that he had not explained his meaning of "counterforce" and, thus, had seemed to endorse the militarization of American foreign policy. In 1967 he claimed that by counterforce he had meant "not the containment by military means of a military threat, but the political containment of a political threat."

Some scholars have regarded this belated explanation as disingenuous, as an effort to rewrite his past. Certainly, it is curious that, as a master stylist who presumably sought clarity, he chose a metaphor that was so clearly military to express what he claims was a nonmilitary meaning. Even some friendly critics suggest that Kennan's use of language revealed that he intended to propose more than just a political or economic response—also a military one.

Until 1955, despite Kennan's many speeches and articles, including the reprinting of the "X" essay in his *American Diplomacy* (1951), he never publicly clarified his 1947 meaning, never explained that his 1947 intentions had been grossly distorted. Even in 1967, he did not adequately explain his years of public silence before correcting the record. In his memoirs, however, he did provide a 1948 letter to Lippmann, which Kennan never sent, in which he clarified his understanding of the communist threat and of the American response. In that unsent letter Kennan wrote that he did not favor the stationing of military forces near the Soviet border to halt Soviet aggression, for the Soviets "don't want to invade anyone. . . . They don't want war of any kind. . . . They far prefer to do the job with stooge forces."

In clarifying his understanding of the Soviet threat, Kennan revealed in this letter that he considered the real communist threat internal but often military: "The violence is nominally domestic, not international, violence. It is, if you will, a police violence." The implication of this analysis, which he seemed to deny in 1967, was that small-scale American interventions might be necessary to deal with these "police" threats. For, presumably, Kennan did not think that the United States should rely in every case on words of support, friendly advice, and economic assistance, even if they were inadequate. In most cases, he assumed, they would be sufficient. But what if the "stooge forces" were not conquered so easily? Applying this logic in the 1960s, others could argue that the Truman Doctrine and the counsel of "X" shaped, if not dictated, the commitment of U.S. troops to Vietnam—a conclusion and policy that Kennan opposed by 1966.

In 1947 communism was, for Kennan, monolithic. It was in the service of Joseph Stalin. "Any success of a local Communist party," Kennan later explained, "any advance of Communist power anywhere [was] an extension . . . of the political orbit, or at least the dominant influence, of the Kremlin." Looking back on the 1940s, even in 1967, Kennan maintained that the Chinese Communist Party had been "an instrument of Soviet power"—a conclusion disputed by some experts who trace the Sino-Soviet rift back to this period and contend that Stalin opposed the revolution of Mao Zedong.

Yet, in the late 1940s, unlike in his "X" essay, Kennan actually started predicting that Chinese communism might become independent of the Soviet Union and even a threat to the Soviet state. "The men in the Kremlin," Kennan thought, might well "discover that this fluid and subtle oriental movement had quietly oozed away between their fingers and there was nothing left but a ceremonious Chinese bow and a polite inscrutable Chinese giggle."

Placing himself in 1967 closer to Lippmann's views than the text of his 1947 essay may have justified, Kennan emphasized that "X" did not mean to bar negotiations, only to postpone them until issues could be settled. Whereas in 1947 Kennan had seemed to locate that time in the distant future, in 1967 he implied that he had thought it was quite near when he wrote the essay. Nor, he claimed, did he want a permanent division of Europe, only a temporary division until the possibilities for negotiations developed.

Commenting in 1967 on "X"'s 1947 analysis of Soviet motivations, Kennan lamented, "much of it reads exactly like one of those primers put out by alarmed congressional committees or by the Daughters of the American Revolution, designed to arouse the citizenry to the dangers of the Communist conspiracy." This belated reassessment indicates how far in two decades Kennan and the American consensus had shifted. In 1947, however, his tough-minded, hostile analysis of Soviet policy won him respect within the administration and among scholars of the Soviet Union. Few then dissented or criticized him, even though he minimized Russian history and ignored Western hostility in explaining the sources of Soviet conduct.

THE SUPPLENESS OF CONTAINMENT

Although Kennan did not endorse the Truman Doctrine's global rhetoric, he, as well as many of its critics, applauded the Marshall Plan. Whereas the doctrine's military emphasis and ideological tone troubled many, the Marshall Plan with its promise of economic aid was attractive. To many Americans and Europeans, though not to Kennan or other policymakers, the plan seemed to offer a rapprochement to the Soviet Union, even an end to the division of Europe that the Truman Doctrine threatened. For Lippmann, the program of economic assistance was not a part of containment; but to Kennan and others in the administration it was simply another tactic in the implementation of containment.

Kennan, then head of the Policy Planning Staff of the State Department, had worked on the Marshall Plan in early 1947 and was among those who conceived of it as a way of shoring up west-ern Europe, improving its morale, halting communism there, prying the Eastern bloc out of the Soviet orbit, and weakening the Soviet Union. This American program of massive economic assistance promised to contain communism and Soviet expansion, maybe even to speed the liberation of Eastern Europe and hasten the destruction of the Soviet system—precisely the promise of the "X" essay. By Truman's own admission, the Marshall Plan and the Truman Doctrine were "two halves of the same walnut."

To the public, the Marshall Plan seemed generous and friendly, partly because the United States invited the Soviet Union, as well as the Eastern bloc nations, to participate in the program. Kennan and other policymakers knew that Soviet membership was unlikely, for they had devised the plan to be unacceptable to the Soviets. It required that European nations provide data on their economy, open their land freely to American agents, and move toward economic multilateralism. As policymakers knew, the Soviets would neither relax secrecy, upon which they believed their security partly rested, nor adopt multilateralism, which would have required them to reorganize their economy and abandon state trading. As Kennan later acknowledged, the Marshall Plan also anticipated that the Soviets would be a donor nation—an expectation that would make the plan even more unacceptable to Stalin.

By reintegrating Eastern European trade back into western European channels, the plan promised to weaken Soviet power in the Eastern bloc and reorient it to the West. How long—Vyacheslav Molotov, the Soviet foreign minister, had asked earlier—could, say, Romania or Bulgaria remain independent of the West after the introduction of American capital? Or, for that matter, how could the East industrialize, following Soviet plans, if it joined the Marshall Plan and once more played the role of supplier of raw materials and agricultural products to the West? To halt this "rollback" of its influence, the Soviet Union blocked East European nations from joining the American program.

The Marshall Plan, like the Truman Doctrine, contributed to the division of Europe and probably to the hardening of Soviet policies in its bloc. When the United States successfully helped drive communist parties out of Western coalition governments in 1947 and 1948, the price was increased Soviet suspicion and stepped-up suppression of dissent in Eastern Europe. As a result of the Marshall Plan, in "a defensive reaction," according to Kennan, the Soviet Union ended democracy in Czechoslovakia with a brutal coup in February 1948. That analysis by Kennan differed greatly from the American public analysis in 1948, which interpreted the Czech coup as virtually an act of unprovoked Soviet aggression.

Kennan did hope that war with the Soviet Union would be unnecessary, but he did not rule it out. He even, at least briefly, considered the possibility of preventive war. If Germany and the USSR ever combined, or if the Soviets' "total war-making potential [increased] at a rate considerably faster than that of ourselves," he told an Air War College audience in 1947, the United States might have to move to preventive war. Echoing much of his analysis presented in his mid-1946 meeting with General Spaatz, Kennan stated in 1947 "that with probably ten good hits with atomic bombs you could, without any great loss of life or loss of the prestige or reputation of the United States as a well-meaning and humane people, practically cripple Russia's war-making potential." At that time, the United States—unknown to Kennan—only had about ten to twelve A-bombs.

Kennan himself in the years after his "X" essay struggled to define America's vital interests, because he understood, in a way left unclear in his "X" essay but emphasized by Lippmann, that the United States lacked the resources to get involved substantially wherever in the world communism seemed to threaten. In August 1948, Kennan included among the key U.S. interests the Atlantic community ("Canada, Greenland and Iceland, Scandinavia, the British Isles, Western Europe, the Iberian Peninsula"), as well as Morocco and the upper part of the west coast of Africa, many of the countries of South America (in the area from bulge northward), the area of the Mediterranean, the Middle East, Japan, and the Philippines. That list, interestingly, excluded much of Africa and all of China, India, Korea, Indonesia, and Indochina.

Redefining his analysis in late 1948, he concluded that there were only five centers in the world of "industrial and military policy" of great value to the United States in terms of its "national security": the United States itself, Great Britain, Germany and nearby central Europe, the Soviet Union, and Japan. This was, in a sense, a sophisticated economic-industrial conception of American national security, stressing that these areas, based upon their resources and populations, could threaten the United States militarily and that the

American economic system also depended upon access to most of these areas. In the late 1940s, aside from the Soviet zone of Germany and the Soviet Union itself, the crucial areas, as defined by Kennan, were in the American orbit.

Emphasis on the importance of Germany and Japan, which before World War II were the key industrial powers in Europe and Asia, respectively, helped shape American postwar decisions to reconstruct these two nations economically and to anchor them in the American-directed international political-economic system. Partly under Kennan's aegis, the State Department urged the redevelopment of Germany in Europe to rebuild the western European economy, and of Japan in Asia so that the island nation could be the linchpin of American policy and of reconstructed international trade in that area.

Containment, as secretly conceived by Kennan and other policymakers, also involved various forms of covert action abroad. In early 1948 he secretly urged the government to create a permanent covert capability, including paramilitary activity and political and economic warfare. Under the then-secret National Security Council (NSC) paper 10/2, in June 1948, concealing his action, President Truman authorized the Central Intelligence Agency to handle such operations. They included both the blocking of left forces in the West (especially in Italy and France) in 1948, and clandestine assistance to anticommunist forces behind the "iron curtain." Put bluntly, covert activity could offer containment and, ultimately, liberation. Such efforts could speed the weakening of Soviet power, as forecast in Mr. "X"'s essay. Normally, as recommended by Kennan and approved by Truman, the covert action would be conducted in such a way as to maintain "plausible denial" that the American government was involved.

Whether or not covert activities, conducted without the knowledge of the American people, and generally without the knowledge or explicit approval of the Congress, lived up to the standards of traditional American value—democracy and public accountability—would be discussed only years later, when many of the CIA activities ultimately became known. Some critics, pointing to Mr. "X"'s own 1947 words ("To avoid destruction, the United States need only measure up to its own best traditions and prove itself worthy of preservation as a great nation"), would contend that clandestine CIA activities violated Kennan's publicly implied values.

Thus, the angry right-wing criticism of containment as being passive, charges that were never fully answered by the Truman-government practitioners of containment, had the unintended effect of helping to conceal from the American people that their government was sometimes following a secret policy of "liberation." Liberation seemed to men like Burnham and generally to the American public in the 1940s and early 1950s as the near-antithesis of containment. But liberation was either the close ally of containment or perhaps, as some would later cynically suggest, even the hidden other side of containment.

Containment, mixed with occasional hopes of liberation, continued as the policy of the Truman administration. It was, in short, a counterrevolutionary policy that tried to prevent revolutions of the left, block subversion, eliminate instability ("the breeding ground of communism") in the West, and stop Soviet expansion. Containment, like most other competing American doctrines then, interpreted revolutions as communist and Soviet inspired.

Analysts then and later questioned the mainsprings of this anticommunism. Why did policymakers conclude that American security was threatened by revolution abroad? Did they simply fear that the Soviet Union might benefit and hence that the United States would lose? No. Nor did they fear Soviet military aggression in the short run, for well into 1947 no policymaker expected the Soviet Union to expand militarily then or in the near future. In the long run, American leaders were less sanguine. Some revisionist historians have analyzed the fears of policymakers in a larger ideological context: American leaders believed that the removal of markets and resources from the world economy would disrupt international trade, impair production, and weaken the international economy and, in turn, the American economy, which depended upon the international capitalist system and expanding trade. In this view, for some analysts, policymakers believed that American freedoms depended upon prosperity at home, and that the spread of communism abroad, by threatening the American economy, also threatened the American political system and its traditional freedoms. These policymakers also preferred the creation of democratic governments abroad, and believed that they were useful, if not essential, to the flourishing of the American political economy at home.

The containment policy did prove sufficiently supple for the United States to give Josip

Broz Tito's Yugoslavian government economic aid in 1949, a year after he had broken with Stalin and the Cominform. The containment policy, despite its counterrevolutionary implications, also proved sufficiently flexible in practice that policymakers greatly modified, and practically abandoned, it in one notable case (China), where the cost of armed intervention, in American dollars and lives, would have been exorbitant to block the communist revolution. Earlier U.S. economic assistance and military advisers had not been able to check the erosion of Chinese Nationalist leader Chiang Kai-shek's political and military power. By early 1949, U.S. policymakers recognized that they could not halt the communist revolution in China unless they were willing to commit millions of American soldiers and billions of dollars. Whatever the sources of American anticommunism, whatever the reasons for trying to halt communism, policymakers were aware of the relationship of means and ends; they knew that some commitments to allies and some interventions were too costly. China was such a case.

The administration dramatically applied the doctrine of containment to Asia in 1950, when the United States stressed negotiations for a peace treaty with Japan and military bases there; provided economic aid in May to the French, who were trying to prevent a communist triumph in Indochina; and intervened in June in Korea, in the civil war between the communist north and the American "client state" in the south. That intervention, and the policies soon following it, ended for at least a few years the hopes of policymakers that the Soviet Union and China might split, that Chinese nationalism might overthrow Mao or make him another Tito.

DISPUTES OVER THE APPLICATION OF CONTAINMENT: NATO, THE H-BOMB, AND NSC 68

In 1949–1950, when western European governments feared armed insurrection, Soviet military expansion, and the power of a revived West Germany, the United States constructed the North Atlantic Treaty Organization to maintain stability, improve morale, block revolution, restrain Soviet pressure, and ease fears about the revival of West Germany. Kennan understood these purposes, but he still objected to the treaty, partly because he deemed it unnecessary. The United States would defend its vital interests (western Europe) without a treaty, he declared; there was no need to request from signatories a reciprocal pledge that they would go to the aid of the United States. A simple American pledge would suffice.

This attack on legalisms did not cut to the core of Kennan's objections. "The Russians had no idea," he later explained, "of using regular military strength against us. Why should we direct attention to an area where we were weak and they were strong?" He forecast correctly that the pact would mean "a general preoccupation with military affairs, to the detriment of economic recovery and of the necessity for seeking a peaceful solution to Europe's difficulties." In a lame effort to avoid what the Soviets might regard "as an aggressive encirclement of their country," Kennan proposed the exclusion of Greece and Turkey, and probably Italy, as outside the North Atlantic area. His criticisms found no favor with Dean Acheson, the new secretary of state.

Containment, as Kennan recognized, was taking on a life of its own. He was its uneasy sire, torn between pride and distress; he could not restrict it to the paths he wished to follow. Although popularly regarded as its preeminent philosopher and spokesman, he was being relegated within the councils of policy to the outer orbit reserved for critical scolds, for men whose judgment no longer commanded respect. Kennan and Acheson were differing on important issues involving the implementation of containment. Their differences, in important measure, were rooted in the very ambiguities of the "X" essay, especially its definition of "counterforce" and the nature of the communist threat. NATO was partly a military response to the potential insurrections that Kennan, in his unsent letter to Lippmann, had described as political, but which others labeled as military.

After the Soviet testing of their first atomic bomb in August 1949, the Truman government, which had been secretly but slowly pursuing development for some years of a thermonuclear (or hydrogen) bomb, confronted the problem of how the United States should respond to the Soviets ending the U.S. nuclear monopoly a few years before the West had predicted. Part of the Truman administration's answer was to accelerate the effort to develop the thermonuclear weapon, which could be a thousand times more powerful than the World War II A-bombs and thus could kill millions, not simply many thousands. Within the State Department, Kennan fruitlessly opposed development of this H-bomb. Reversing his 1947

positions, he pleaded, unsuccessfully, for an American doctrine of "no first use" of nuclear weapons, and decried the prospects of nuclear war. He likened nuclear war "to the concepts of warfare which were once familiar to the Asiatic hordes," and contended that use of nuclear weapons meant that "man not only can be but is his own worse and most terrible enemy."

Kennan believed that the military needs of containment could be met within the limits of the current defense budget (about $13.5 billion): the development of highly mobile, small, unified forces to deal with the likely military threats of localized, limited conflicts. In 1949–1950 his analysis conflicted sharply with that of Paul Nitze, whom Acheson would soon name as the new director of the Policy Planning Staff, for Nitze was concerned with the overall threat of Soviet arms and wanted a greatly expanded budget to provide both a limited-war capacity and, more importantly, overall strategic superiority against the Soviets.

Joined by Acheson, Nitze stressed "the Soviet purpose of world domination," and they disregarded Kennan's fears that policy should not be set down in a single document, that it would lead to distortion and a freezing of policy. In part, perhaps, Kennan had learned a lesson from the reception of the "X" essay and its hardening into dogma, albeit an ambiguous one. But more important, he believed that Nitze and Acheson were overmilitarizing American policy and misunderstanding Soviet aims. Acheson later characterized the Nitze-Kennan debate as "stultifying," for he concluded that the question of emphasis in Soviet aims—whether the Soviet Union placed world domination or survival of the regime first—made little practical difference. For Acheson, there was still a considerable "degree of risk of all-out war which the Soviet government would run in probing a weak spot for concessions."

Kennan, looking forward to the future, claimed that he was thinking of disengagement in Europe and stressed that there was no Soviet military threat to western Europe. Defeated by Acheson, Kennan watched unhappily as NSC 68, the security document embodying the Nitze-Acheson plan, moved to the president's desk. NSC 68 would cost between $38 and $50 billion, and promised, ironically, to provide the global capabilities that the Truman Doctrine had outlined, that the administration had retreated from in 1947, and that Lippmann had believed the "X" essay was promoting. NSC 68, when it was accepted after the outbreak of the Korean War, was a dramatic turning point, a bold new departure, in American foreign policy in terms of creating a larger capacity to extend and expand American commitments to stop communism.

THE KOREAN WAR: FROM CONTAINMENT TO LIBERATION TO CONTAINMENT

The Korean War led to the endorsement of NSC 68, vast expenditures for arms in Asia and in Europe, and the overextension of American power. American intervention in Korea was the most dramatic test to that date for containment. Although questions about the origins of the war linger, Truman and his advisers speedily concluded that North Korea had attacked South Korea, that Stalin had approved and planned the attack, and that the North Korean invasion was a Soviet test of American credibility and a possible preliminary to Soviet probes elsewhere—in Europe, perhaps in Germany. "This could be the Greece of the Far East," Truman declared to an associate.

Many later analysts would stress, in contrast to the dominant 1950s interpretation, that this shooting war had occurred in the context of an ongoing civil war since 1948 between the two parts of the then-recently divided Korea, and some historians would later argue that the Korean War was, in many ways, part of a revolution in Korea. According to such a view, the Korean War was primarily a war between Koreans, for the unification of Korea, and later evidence indicated that Stalin had even been reluctant to endorse the North's desire to attack. According to such evidence, Stalin had been wary and cautious, greatly fearing the commitment of Soviet power and prestige to the North's aim to unite Korea.

In late June 1950, over the course of just a few days, President Truman quickly expanded the American commitment and sent ground forces to assist the embattled South Koreans. At the time, his was a popular decision in the United States, even though he did not ask for a declaration of war. Kennan, among other advisers, agreed that "we would have to act with all necessary force to repel this attack." He had already urged that the United States should prepare for limited war, and Korea became the test case of his own counsel. The Kremlin, he concluded, had unleashed its puppets to try to block America's peace treaty with Japan and to exploit the opportunity in

Korea created by America's withdrawal of troops. A major concern of Soviet policy, he reaffirmed in 1951, was "to make sure that it filled every nook and cranny available. . . . There was no objective reason to assume that the Soviet leaders would leave the Korean nook unfilled if they thought they had a chance of filling it at relatively little risk to themselves and saw time running out." Containment, then, could mean "counterforce" by military means—precisely what Kennan claimed the "X" essay did not counsel; and the military test was in Asia, not Europe, which had been Kennan's preeminent concern.

Late in June 1950, after President Truman had committed the U.S. Air Force to the war in Korea but the day before the president committed ground troops there, Kennan assessed the likelihood of direct Soviet military involvement in the war. He thought that such intervention was unlikely, and that the possibility of the Soviets at that time attacking the United States was "remote." He did not believe, he explained, that the Soviets had the military capacity, but, according to the declassified minutes, he "thought if the Russians got into a world war now they would have stumbled in, and in the long run this might be the best situation for us."

In July 1950, Kennan agreed with others in the government that the air force should operate beyond the Thirty-eighth Parallel, but thought that American war aims should be sharply limited: restoration of the status quo ante. Unfortunately, the Truman administration wanted to achieve more and would not negotiate in July 1950, when the Chinese accepted an Indian proposal for a settlement of this nature. Casting aside Kennan's counsel, U.S. policymakers rejected India's proposal, partly because it "would leave South Korea defenseless [before] a renewed North Korean attack." Even before U.S. ground troops crossed the Thirty-eighth Parallel in October 1950 and moved toward the debacle near the Chinese border in late November, Kennan urged caution lest the United States overextend its lines and "frighten the Russians" into war. Unlike many policymakers then, he was content to limit the commitment of American power, not to try to "liberate" North Korea, but simply to stop what he later defined as a civil war ("'aggression' . . . was as misplaced here as it was to be later in . . . Vietnam"), and thereby to restrict containment. Kennan lost to Acheson and Truman, who wished to move beyond containment to "roll back" and "liberation." Korea, they then said, could not be "half slave and half free."

When in the fall and early winter of 1950–1951, the People's Republic of China sent in "volunteers," who pushed back U.S. troops and killed thousands of GI's, American policymakers promptly abandoned "liberation" and shifted back to containment. Some even denied that their war aims had ever included unification of the recently split nation and the vanquishing of communism there.

Relying on the strategy of containment, Truman and Acheson in early 1952, in opposition to their top-level military advisers, made decisions—involving mostly the insistence on voluntary repatriation of prisoners of war—that dragged out the armistice negotiations for more than fifteen months. That Truman-Acheson decision to insist on voluntary repatriation, instead of the standard procedure of automatic repatriation, was devised to give the United States a symbolic victory by establishing the unwillingness of many captured Chinese and Korean POWs to return to their communist homelands. According to Acheson, this new standard of voluntary repatriation might well stop communist nations in the future from going to war, lest their soldiers, when guaranteed voluntary repatriation, quickly surrender in order to flee communism.

LATER APPLICATIONS OF CONTAINMENT: EISENHOWER TO REAGAN

The stalemate in Korea led many frustrated Americans to question their nation's involvement in Korea, the tactics and purposes of limited war, and the policy of containment itself. John Foster Dulles, a Republican spokesman and State Department adviser who would become Dwight D. Eisenhower's secretary of state, issued the most forceful challenge. In "A Policy for Boldness," in *Life* (19 May 1952), Dulles castigated containment as negative and called for a new policy: one that would "liberate" the "captive peoples" of Eastern Europe and not shrink from the use of nuclear weapons in meeting communist military aggression. Sketching the strategy that would later be fleshed out and bear the name of "massive retaliation," Dulles proposed that the United States might retaliate anywhere ("where it hurts") "by means of our choosing." Such a strategy, he pledged, would deter communist aggression and eliminate limited war initiated by Soviet "stooges." His critiques and proposals, with some softening

and hedging, became the Republican Party's foreign policy plank in 1952: it promised victory in the Cold War and liberation of Eastern Europe.

Despite the bold rhetoric of massive retaliation and liberation, the Eisenhower administration generally subscribed in its actions to the containment doctrine, moving to "liberation" clandestinely to use the CIA to overthrow the nationalist government in Iran in 1953 and to overthrow in 1954 the elected leftist but not communist government in Guatemala. The administration avoided both nuclear war and significant limited war, and restricted liberation mostly to words of encouragement, when revolution erupted in Eastern Europe. In Korea, after bombing some irrigation dams and obliquely threatening nuclear escalation, the Eisenhower administration accepted the division of the country and the return to status quo ante—Truman's original war aims. Despite the much-heralded "unleashing" of Chiang Kai-shek in 1953, the Eisenhower administration soon "released" him and restricted his actions. Having learned lessons from Truman's involvements in Greece and Korea, Eisenhower would not commit troops to the war in Indochina but used other tactics to prevent a communist victory in his time—the establishment of a client state that received about $2 billion in military and economic aid. Expanding commitments in Asia and the Middle East, along the general lines of NATO, the administration created security pacts, which, critics charged, extended American alliances and power beyond their natural limits. Under Eisenhower, the government used subversion and sponsored revolutions and small armed military interventions to overthrow suspected communist governments and to maintain stability. Eisenhower's major failure, judged by the standards of containment, was the rise in Cuba of a communist government allied with the Soviet Union.

Kennan in the 1950s never discussed in public the use by the American government, under Truman and then Eisenhower, of covert activities to weaken communist regimes. Instead, he deplored the public pressures for liberation, but carefully implied that the only truly meaningful calls for liberation required American armed intervention against the Soviet Union or at least in the Iron Curtain area. Kennan's careful omission of covert activities had the effect, whether intended or not, of implying that there were no such American operations and thereby concealing an aspect of U.S. policy in dealing with communism abroad.

The most marked shift from the earlier policy of containment was Eisenhower's decision (endorsed by Kennan) that negotiations with the communists were desirable and that some important differences in Europe might be settled. In 1955, for the first time since Potsdam in 1945, a president of the United States met with a Soviet premier. Although Eisenhower, Soviet Premier Nikolai A. Bulganin, and Nikita S. Khrushchev, the head of the Soviet Union's Communist Party, did not resolve important issues, their summit meeting at Geneva did ease East-West tensions. Kennan, among others, wanted the two nations to go further. In late 1957, echoing Lippmann's plea in 1947, Kennan proposed disengagement—the creation of a unified, independent Germany, withdrawal of foreign troops from Germany and Eastern Europe, and the elimination of nuclear weapons in that area. The Soviet Union had changed under Khrushchev, Kennan declared. There were new "realities." The Eisenhower administration, while implicitly recognizing some of these "realities," would not endorse the plan and even considered giving nuclear weapons to West Germany. Former Secretary of State Dean Acheson, denying that the Soviet Union had changed and warning against Khrushchev's talk of peaceful coexistence, condemned Kennan for preaching a "new isolationism" and counseling a "futile and lethal attempt to crawl back into the cocoon of history."

Promising victory in the Cold War, John F. Kennedy's administration castigated Eisenhower for allowing communism in Cuba and for failing to provide a larger, more diversified arsenal that would give the United States "flexible options"— a capacity ranging from limited conventional war, through limited nuclear war, to holocaust. The Kennedy administration, while seeking to roll back communism in Cuba through CIA-directed assassination attempts on Castro (there is no clear but only suggestive evidence that President Kennedy knew or authorized these attempts) and the ill-fated Bay of Pigs invasion in April 1961, generally endorsed the containment doctrine and acted to enforce it by blocking communist expansion, including national liberation movements in Africa and Asia. The result was an escalated arms race and efforts to strengthen the faltering NATO alliance, but after the Cuban missile crisis, Kennedy achieved in 1963 a limited nuclear-test ban treaty and moved toward détente—a policy opposed by Kennan.

Perhaps the most dangerous application of the containment doctrine in the Cold War occurred in October 1962 in the Cuban missile crisis. The Soviets had clandestinely placed forty-two "offensive" missiles in Cuba, despite their private assurances to the contrary, and President Kennedy, in response, imposed a blockade (called a "quarantine" to avoid using the term "blockade," which in international law meant war) on all new arms shipments to Cuba to pressure the Soviet Union to withdraw its weapons. Privately, administration members believed the Soviets were testing America's (and Kennedy's) will and commitment, and probably hoping to use the missiles to buttress their policy to push the United States out of Berlin. Most likely, the Soviets were actually acting defensively: To protect the Cuban revolution, which seemed threatened by the United States, and to narrow the severely worsening missile gap, when the United States had about 175 intercontinental ballistic missiles and the Soviets had only between about 20 and 40 in the USSR. The overall U.S. strategic superiority, as measured in bombers and missiles, was estimated as better than ten to one. In October 1962 in the Cuban missile crisis, a shoot-out at sea was avoided, the Soviets began to back down, and a Kennedy-Khrushchev deal was arranged to have the Soviets withdraw their missiles from Cuba partly in return for a secret American promise to withdraw similar missiles from Turkey, where Kennedy had only recently installed them. Only twenty-five years later was that secret deal—long denied by Kennedy stalwarts—fully acknowledged.

Under Lyndon B. Johnson, national liberation movements in Asia became the focus of administration energies, as the United States abandoned the surreptitious warfare that Kennedy had initiated in Indochina and openly applied the policy of military containment in Vietnam—a policy that Kennan challenged in 1966. Containment, he suggested, could be extended from Europe in the Stalin years to China in recent years, but the doctrine was ill-suited for Indochina. The costs were too high, Kennan explained to a congressional committee in 1966: "If we had been able, without exorbitant cost in American manpower and resources . . . to do better in Vietnam I would have been delighted, and I would have thought that the effort was warranted." He also thought that Vietnam might well follow an independent, not a Russian- or Chinese-directed foreign policy. While warning against "a precipitate and disorderly withdrawal [which could be] a disservice to our own interests . . . and even to world peace," he recommended liquidation of American involvement "just as soon as this can be done without inordinate damage to our own prestige or to the stability of conditions in that area."

Undeterred by this unwelcome counsel, the Johnson administration publicly justified American intervention in Indochina as necessary to stave off communism, to defeat wars of national liberation, to establish the value of counterinsurgency, to affirm American credibility, to protect the security of the "free world," to halt the loss of dominoes, to maintain access to raw materials, to restore an important trading area for Japan, and, variously, to contain the Soviet Union or China, and sometimes both. The limited war proved to be one the United States could not win, as Kennan had lamented, and the cost in American lives and dollars, as well as the disruptions and protests at home, tore apart the nation. The war divided members of the elite, produced the defection of policymakers and old cold warriors, and ultimately compelled Presidents Richard Nixon and Gerald Ford to withdraw U.S. armed forces from much of Southeast Asia. Whether or not Nixon in the Paris agreement of January 1973 truly intended a permanent American pullout or only a temporary withdrawal, followed by a return as the southern government started to collapse, remains in some historical dispute. The decisions ultimately to withdraw and not return to Vietnam did not necessarily represent the abandonment of containment in principle, for that loose doctrine, at least since the fall of China in 1949, had always operated on the assumption that some interventions were too costly and too dangerous.

By the mid-1970s, with détente under Nixon and then Ford, scholars were unsure whether American policy still subscribed to containment. The détente with the Soviet Union, the recognition of communist polycentrism, the Sino-Soviet split, the erosion of Soviet influence in Eastern Europe, the uneasy settlement in Southeast Asia, the rapprochement with China, and the Soviet-American strategic arms limitation agreements—all marked the distance that American foreign policy had moved. Yet, American assistance under President Nixon and Secretary of State Henry Kissinger, despite public denials, led to the overthrow of Salvador Allende's elected communist government in Chile in 1973 and the establishment of the harshly repressive government of General Augusto Pinochet, who a quarter century later would be indicted for war crimes. Under Nixon and Ford, the continued fear of Soviet influence in the Middle East, the efforts to

maintain worldwide military alliances, and the desire to thwart national liberation movements all suggested that the policy of containment, modified at times, endured as a guiding principle in the conduct of American foreign policy through the end of the Ford administration in 1977.

Containment generally continued under President Jimmy Carter, and often it easily was mixed with his concern for human rights abroad. He initially seemed to want to work out better relations with the Soviet Union. He resisted getting tough when the Soviets and Cubans became involved in parts of Africa. But, in continuing and expanding the Nixon-Kissinger policy of playing off China and the Soviet Union, Carter's administration formalized relations with China in January 1979. In December 1979, when the Soviets moved troops into Afghanistan in a brutal war, Carter moved to a decidedly get-tough policy with the Soviet Union. The administration disregarded that Afghanistan had long been judged by some analysts as already within the Soviet sphere of interest. Carter contended, incorrectly, that the Soviets were aiming to move into the oil-rich Middle East. He proclaimed, in hyperbolic rhetoric, that the Soviet intervention in Afghanistan was the gravest threat to world peace since World War II. He announced a "Carter Doctrine" declaring that the United States would act, unilaterally if necessary, to protect American interests against Soviet encroachments in the Persian Gulf area. Through the CIA, Carter provided covert aid to anti-Soviet, rebel forces in Afghanistan, including apparently those of Osama bin Laden, and thereby unintentionally helped nurture military groups that would later turn against other governments, including the United States, and be termed "terrorists" in the 1990s and in the early twenty-first century. Having already recently expanded the military budget, the Carter administration, after the Soviet invasion of Afghanistan, again increased the U.S. military budget. In 1980, President Carter signed Presidential Directive (PD) 59 to provide a capacity to fight a prolonged, limited nuclear war.

President Ronald Reagan, building on the expanded defense spending of Carter's last two budgets, added significantly to American military spending. Reagan, moving beyond Carter's already heated rhetoric of 1979–1980, declared that the Soviet Union was a menace to world peace. Reagan called the USSR an "evil empire" in 1983, and yet, perhaps paradoxically, sought to work out some arms-limitation agreements on strategic weapons with the Soviets. In Latin America, frequently employing clandestine means, Reagan's government provided aid for overthrowing the left-wing Sandinista government in Nicaragua and sought to block efforts by the Sandinistas and left-wing rebels to overthrow the right-wing, U.S.-supported government in El Salvador. In 1985, in words that seemed to echo the ideology of the 1947 Truman Doctrine, Reagan announced the "Reagan Doctrine": "Our mission is to nourish and defend freedom and democracy [and to support those] on every continent from Afghanistan to Nicaragua . . . to defy Soviet-supported aggression and [to] secure rights which have been ours from birth. . . . Support for freedom fighters is self-defense." In his last years in office, however, Reagan softened his anti-Soviet words and policies and struggled, amid contentions that he knowingly violated congressional mandates, to escape from the political debacle at home emerging from his government's secret trading of arms for hostages and then arranging for the monies from some of the arms sales to be funneled clandestinely to the anti-Sandinista contras in Nicaragua.

The American military buildup under Reagan put more economic and military pressure on the Soviet Union. Already wracked by economic inefficiency, beset by lurking crises of legitimacy at home and in its satellite states, and suffering under heavy military budgets, the Soviet system was unable adequately to reform itself. Some analysts and politicians (most often Republicans) would later argue that the Reagan policy of increased American military spending had been devised to pressure the Soviets to increase military spending, further dislocate their economy, and add to their already severe problems at home. But other analysts pointed out that Reagan publicly, and apparently privately, had argued for larger American military budgets not to injure the Soviet economy but because he had sincerely—but incorrectly—believed that the Soviet military system was very powerful and threatening to the West. The Soviets were far weaker than he and many administration advisers had recognized. In a sense, Kennan's 1947 Mr. "X" forecast of Soviet self-destruction would prove prescient in 1988–1989.

THE WANING RELEVANCE OF CONTAINMENT AND NEW CHALLENGES

In 1989, Soviet Premier Mikhail Gorbachev, still struggling to reform the Soviet system after allowing in March the first free elections in the Soviet Union in seventy-two years, generally acceded to the defection of the Soviet satellites. Most dramatically, in November 1989, East Germany opened its border, and its citizens enthusiastically helped tear down the hated Berlin Wall, which had been erected in 1961 to halt the flow of East Germans to the West. In December 1989, Gorbachev declared that the Cold War was over. In early 1990, Kennan, now eighty-five and worried by Gorbachev's troubles in the Soviet Union, pleaded unsuccessfully for a more generous American policy toward the Soviets. Thus, as his 1947 prophecy of Soviet disintegration seemed close to coming true nearly a decade before the twentieth century ended, Kennan sought to devise ways of stopping that process because of the dangerous instability that might result. In early 1990 he also feared the de facto unification of Germany before other Europeans were prepared for that development, and urged in congressional testimony that "this dangerous situation which is developing has to be stopped in some way or other." The administration of George H. W. Bush, wary of taking the lead or significantly intervening in events, chose more cautious policies than Kennan had proposed. But in 1991, as the Soviet Union faced disintegration, President Bush, fearing the disorder there, actually counseled Ukraine (some 52 million people) not to leave the Soviet Union. But his words failed to halt the dissolution of the USSR. The Soviet Union formally dissolved in December 1991.

Containment—if understood primarily as an anti-Soviet policy—was clearly no longer relevant with the disintegration of the Soviet Union and the establishment of a number of states, and preeminently Russia, in place of the USSR. But among the challenges to Bush in his remaining thirteen months in office, to President Bill Clinton in his succeeding eight years (1993–2001), and to George W. Bush in his first year (2001) was to determine how much of the intrinsic anticommunism in the containment policy, as it had evolved between 1947 and 1991, was relevant in dealing with the very different communist regimes in Cuba, North Korea, and China. Up through 2001, all three U.S. administrations remained hostile to Cuba, and unwilling to open relations with Fidel Castro's government. All three American presidents continued to worry about North Korea, and instability on the Korean peninsula. For George H. W. Bush in 1989–1993 and Bill Clinton in 1993–2001, as well as the new George W. Bush presidency in 2001, generally the lure of trade with China, and frequently the belief that soft words were better than hard words in improving human rights policies, would guide the uneasy but often shifting American policy toward China.

At the same time, international "terrorism"—sometimes conducted by foreign groups nurtured initially by earlier American covert aid, under Presidents Carter and Reagan, when those secretly funded military groups were opposing Soviet policies—periodically plagued the Clinton administration and George W. Bush's early administration, too. Such challenges occurred in a rather new world. It was one in which the containment of communism was no longer generally a major issue and the quest for world order would often be defined broadly to mean capitalism, and sometimes democracy and human rights, in an international system in which there was only one superpower, the United States. In that post–Cold War world, terrorism was generally viewed as anathema to America and its values. But some critics, usually analysts on the left, suggested, sometimes uneasily, that terrorism unfortunately was rather similar, not infrequently, to the hidden side—the "liberation" side—that earlier containment policy, in various American administrations, had applied to help weaken communism abroad. Such an unsettling argument, suggesting similarities between some post–Cold War terrorism and some secret Cold War "liberation" policies under the CIA, departed greatly from dominant American, and Western, thinking. The dominant view denied that there were any meaningful similarities. That dominant view was perhaps best expressed by President George W. Bush and Secretary of State Colin Powell, as well as former Secretary of State Henry Kissinger, in September and October 2001, when they, among many outraged Americans, sharply condemned the terrorist attacks on the World Trade Center buildings in New York City and the Pentagon outside Washington, D.C., as assaults on the good by the forces of evil.

BIBLIOGRAPHY

Acheson, Dean. *Present at the Creation: My Years in the State Department.* New York, 1969. Disputes Kennan on NATO and the Korean War.

Ambrose, Stephen E. *Eisenhower.* Vol. 2. *The President.* New York, 1984.

Arnson, Cynthia. *Crossroads: Congress, the President, and Central America, 1976–1993.* 2d ed. University Park, Pa., 1993.

Bell, Coral. *The Diplomacy of Detente: The Kissinger Era.* London, 1977.

Berman, Larry. *No Peace, No Honor: Nixon, Kissinger, and Betrayal in Vietnam.* New York, 2001.

Bernstein, Barton J. "The H-Bomb Decisions: Were They Inevitable?" In Bernard Brodie et al., eds. *National Security and International Stability.* Cambridge, Mass., 1983.

Bernstein, Barton J., ed. *The Politics and Policies of the Truman Administration.* Chicago, 1970. Relevant revisionist volume on the Cold War.

———. *The Atomic Bomb: The Critical Issues.* Boston, 1976. The issue of postwar "atomic diplomacy" is disputed in this work.

Beschloss, Michael R. *The Crisis Years: Kennedy and Khrushchev, 1960–1963.* New York, 1991.

Brands, H. W. *The Wages of Globalism: Lyndon Johnson and the Limits of American Power.* New York, 1995.

Bundy, McGeorge. *Danger and Survival: Choices About the Bomb in the First Fifty Years.* New York, 1988.

Burnham, James. *Containment or Liberation? An Inquiry into the Aims of United States Foreign Policy.* New York, 1953.

Campbell, Colin, and Bert A. Rockman, eds. *The Clinton Presidency: First Appraisals.* Chatham, N.Y., 1996.

Chang, Gordon H. *Friends and Enemies: The United States, China, and the Soviet Union, 1948–1972.* Stanford, Calif., 1990.

Chomsky, Noam. *World Orders, Old and New.* New York, 1994.

Costigliola, Frank. "'Unceasing Pressure for Penetration': Gender, Pathology, and Emotion in George Kennan's Formation of the Cold War." *Journal of American History* 83 (March 1997).

Cumings, Bruce. *The Origins of the Cold War: Liberation and the Emergence of Separate Regimes.* Princeton, N.J., 1981.

———. *The Origins of the Cold War: The Roaring of the Cataract, 1947–1950.* Princeton, N.J., 1990.

Dallek, Robert. *Flawed Giant: Lyndon Johnson and His Times, 1961–1973.* New York, 1998.

Divine, Robert A. *Eisenhower and the Cold War.* New York, 1981.

Draper, Theodore. *A Very Thin Line: The Iran-Contra Affairs.* New York, 1991.

Foot, Rosemary. *The Wrong War: American Policy and the Dimensions of the Korean Conflict, 1950–1953.* Ithaca, N.Y., 1985.

———. *The Practice of Power: U.S. Relations with China Since 1949.* New York, 1995.

Freedman, Lawrence. *Kennedy's Wars: Berlin, Cuba, Laos, and Vietnam.* New York, 2000.

Fursenko, Aleksandr, and Timothy Naftali. *"One Hell of a Gamble": Khrushchev, Castro, and Kennedy, 1958–1964.* New York, 1997.

Gaddis, John Lewis. *Strategies of Containment: A Critical Appraisal of Postwar American National Security Policy.* New York, 1982.

———. *The Long Peace: Inquiries into the History of the Cold War.* New York, 1987.

———. *The United States and the End of the Cold War: Implications, Reconsiderations, Provocations.* New York, 1992.

———. *We Now Know: Rethinking Cold War History.* New York, 1997.

Gardner, Lloyd C. *Approaching Vietnam: From World War II Through Dienbienphu, 1941–1954.* New York, 1988.

———. *Pay Any Price: Lyndon Johnson and the Wars for Vietnam.* Chicago, 1995.

Garthoff, Raymond L. *Detente and Confrontation: American-Soviet Relations from Nixon to Reagan.* Rev. ed. Washington, D.C., 1994.

———. *The Great Transition: American-Soviet Relations and the End of the Cold War.* Washington, D.C., 1994.

Gati, Charles, ed. *Caging the Bear: Containment and the Cold War.* Indianapolis, 1974.

Gellman, Barton. *Contending with Kennan: Toward a Philosophy of American Power.* New York, 1984.

Grose, Peter. *Operation Rollback: America's Secret War Behind the Iron Curtain.* Boston, 2000.

Hixson, George L. *George F. Kennan: Cold War Iconoclast.* New York, 1989.

Hoff-Wilson, Joan. *Nixon Reconsidered.* New York, 1994.

Hogan, Michael J. *The Marshall Plan: America, Britain, and the Reconstruction of Western Europe, 1947–1952.* New York, 1987.

Hogan, Michael J., ed. *The End of the Cold War: Its Meaning and Implications.* New York and Cambridge, 1992.

Hyland, William. *Mortal Rivals: Superpower Relations from Nixon to Reagan.* New York, 1987.

Immerman, Richard H., ed. *John Foster Dulles and the Diplomacy of the Cold War.* Princeton, N.J., 1990.

Jackson, Henry. *From the Congo to Soweto: U.S. Foreign Policy Toward Africa Since 1960.* New York, 1982.

Karabell, Zachary. *Architects of Intervention: The United States, the Third World, and the Cold War, 1946–1962.* Baton Rouge, La., 1999.

Kaufman, Burton Ira. *The Presidency of James Earl Carter, Jr.* Lawrence, Kans., 1993.

Kennan, George F. *Realities of American Foreign Policy.* Princeton, N.J., 1954.

———. *Russia, the Atom, and the West* New York, 1958.

———. *Memoirs, 1925–1950.* Boston, 1967.

———. *Memoirs, 1950–1963.* Boston, 1972.

———. *American Diplomacy, 1900–1950.* Expanded ed. Chicago, 1984.

Kimball, Jeffrey. *Nixon's Vietnam War.* Lawrence, Kans., 1998.

Kolko, Gabriel. *The Politics of War: The World and United States Foreign Policy, 1943–1945.* New York, 1968. Relevant revisionist volume on the Cold War.

———. *Anatomy of a War: Vietnam, the United States, and the Modern Historical Experience.* New York, 1985.

———. *Confronting the Third World: United States Foreign Policy, 1945-1980.* New York, 1988.

Kolko, Gabriel, and Joyce Kolko. *The Limits of Power: The World and United States Foreign Policy, 1945–1954.* New York, 1972. Relevant revisionist volume on the Cold War.

Kuniholm, Bruce. *The Origins of the Cold War in the Near East: Great Power Conflict and Diplomacy in Iran, Turkey, and Greece.* Princeton, N.J., 1980.

Lacey, Michael, ed. *The Truman Presidency.* New York, 1989.

LaFeber, Walter. *America, Russia, and the Cold War, 1945–1975.* New York, 1976. Has a substantial bibliography.

———. *Inevitable Revolutions: The United States in Central America.* Rev. ed. New York, 1984.

———. *The Clash: A History of U.S.-Japanese Relations.* New York, 1997.

Larson, Deborah Welch. *Origins of Containment: A Psychological Explanation.* Princeton, N.J., 1985.

Leffler, Melvyn. *A Preponderance of Power: National Security, the Truman Administration, and the Cold War.* Stanford, Calif., 1992.

LeoGrande, William M. *Our Own Backyard: The United States in Central America, 1977–1992.* Chapel Hill, N.C., 1998.

Lippmann, Walter. *The Cold War: A Study in U.S. Foreign Policy.* New York, 1947.

Litwak, Robert. *Detente and the Nixon Doctrine: American Foreign Policy and the Pursuit of Stability, 1969–1976.* New York, 1984.

Logevall, Frederik. *Choosing War: The Lost Chance for Peace and the Escalation of War in Vietnam.* Berkeley, Calif., 1999.

Mastny, Vojtech. *The Cold War and Soviet Insecurity: The Stalin Years.* New York, 1996.

May, Ernest, ed. *American Cold War Strategy: Interpreting NSC 68.* Boston, 1993.

May, Ernest R., and Philip D. Zelikow, eds. *The Kennedy Tapes: Inside the White House During the Cuban Missile Crisis.* Cambridge, Mass., 1997.

Mayers, David. *George Kennan and the Dilemmas of U.S. Foreign Policy.* New York, 1988.

Miscamble, Wilson. *George F. Kennan and the Making of American Foreign Policy, 1947–1950.* Princeton, N.J., 1992.

Nathan, James A., ed. *The Cuban Missile Crisis Revisited.* New York, 1992.

Paterson, Thomas G. *Contesting Castro: The United States and the Triumph of the Cuban Revolution.* New York, 1994.

Paterson, Thomas G., ed. *Containment and the Cold War: American Foreign Policy Since 1945.* Reading, Mass., 1972.

———. *Kennedy's Quest for Victory: American Foreign Policy, 1961–1963.* New York, 1989.

Prados, John. *Presidents' Secret Wars: CIA and Pentagon Covert Operations from World War II Through the Persian Gulf.* New York, 1996.

Schmertz, Eric J., Natalie Datlof, and Alexej Ugrinsky, eds. *President Reagan and the World.* Westport, Conn., 1997.

Schulzinger, Robert D. *Henry Kissinger: Doctor of Diplomacy.* New York, 1989.

Sigal, Leon V. *Disarming Strangers: Nuclear Diplomacy with North Korea.* Princeton, N.J., 1998.

Smith, Gaddis. *Reason and Power: American Diplomacy in the Carter Years.* New York, 1986.

Smith, Michael Joseph. *Realist Thought from Weber to Kissinger.* Baton Rouge, La., 1986.

Stephanson, Anders. *Kennan and the Art of Foreign Policy.* Cambridge, Mass., 1989.

Stueck, William. *The Korean War: An International History.* New York, 1985.

Trachtenberg, Marc. *A Constructed Peace: The Making of the European Settlement, 1945–1963.* Princeton, N.J., 1999.

Ulam, Adam. *The Communists: The Story of Power and Lost Illusions, 1948–1991.* New York, 1992.

Williams, William A. *The Tragedy of American Diplomacy.* 2d rev. ed. Cleveland, 1972. Relevant revisionist volume on the Cold War.

Wittner, Lawrence. *America's Intervention in Greece.* New York, 1982.

Wright, C. Ben. "Mr. 'X' and Containment." *Slavic Review* 35 (1976).

Young, Marilyn. *The Vietnam Wars, 1945–1990.* New York, 1991.

Zubok, Vladislav, and Constantine Pleshakov. *Inside the Kremlin's Cold War: From Stalin to Khrushchev.* Cambridge, Mass., 1996.

See also COLD WAR EVOLUTION AND INTERPRETATIONS; COLD WAR ORIGINS; COLD WAR TERMINATION; COVERT OPERATIONS; DOCTRINES; DOMINO THEORY; INTERVENTION AND NONINTERVENTION; NUCLEAR STRATEGY AND DIPLOMACY.

CONTINENTAL EXPANSION

David M. Pletcher

A special providence, some believe, has looked after the affairs of the United States through its history. If this is so, part of the concern has been geographical, for Americans have taken over more than one-third of North America, including much of its best land—a broad swath stretching from sea to sea across almost twenty degrees of latitude.

Before the United States came into being, the three most powerful nations of the world in turn occupied most of this territory but had to give way eventually to the irresistible American advance. Some Americans were quite aware of what they called their destiny; at their independence, for example, Gouverneur Morris (as he later remembered) thought "that all North America must at length be annexed to us—happy, indeed, if the lust of dominion stop there." Fortunately, Morris's vision proved an exaggeration.

As the American nation grew, it worked out a flexible combination of expedience, usually legal or moral. To overcome each obstacle and obtain for it the land it wanted, the most direct method was negotiation followed by a treaty of some sort, providing for a land cession and certain benefits or safeguards for its inhabitants. On two occasions the negotiation followed a victorious war, once with Great Britain and once with Mexico. In the first the enemy grew tired of fighting and sued for peace; in the second, however, the Americans had to occupy the enemy's capital city and much of its country. On a third occasion, again involving Britain, the outcome was a draw and brought only minor boundary adjustments. On the fourth and last occasion, the United States resorted to purchase—this was the vast territory of Alaska.

The reasoning of Americans in acquiring their territory differed with the occasion. The first acquisition, specified in the Treaty of Paris of 1783 ending the revolutionary war, came with independence itself. For the other acquisitions the Americans worked out a flexible combination of expedients, usually legal or moral, to overcome

each obstacle; they thereby obtained the land they wanted. The most direct was negotiation followed by a treaty of some sort, providing for a cession and certain benefits or safeguards for its inhabitants. Another expedient of territorial expansion was purchase, again involving a treaty that usually contained other provisions and sometimes followed hostilities. There also was a lot of sheer luck—being at the right place at the right time. Behind the formalities of land transfer were such pressures as migration and trade that could bend or destroy boundary lines traced out on a map. The notorious mobility of Americans and their acquisitive instincts might thus defeat the plans of faraway Europeans. As Americans moved west across the continent these instincts were whetted by cultural contacts and reciprocal brutality between American settlers and their Native American neighbors and by prejudices against Spanish and French remembered from life in Europe and eventually against the mother country as well. As this developing American nationalism overcame the rivalry of individual colonies enough for cooperation during the Revolution and after, it inspired propaganda to reinforce expansionist instincts. While these factors encouraged expansionism in the New World, the international rivalries of the Old World claimed the attention and exhausted the resources of European rulers who would have liked to thwart the ambitious Yankees across the ocean if they could.

THE AMERICAN REVOLUTION AND ITS AFTERMATH

The Americans acquired their territory in four great expansions. The first of these resulted from the negotiation of peace following the revolutionary war. After the British surrender at Yorktown on 19 October 1781, talk of peace spread in Paris and London and informal exchanges began between representatives of both sides. (The Continental Congress in Philadelphia had been considering peace terms since 1779.) Talks stipulated the unqualified declaration of American independence as the first prerequisite and laid out extensive boundaries. While some members wanted to ask for all of Canada, the negotiating terms mentioned only the Ontario peninsula to the north, between Lakes Huron, Erie, and Ontario (the "Nipissing line") and territory around the Great Lakes as far west as the source of the Mississippi River. To the south, they optimistically included the eastern half of the Mississippi Valley down to 31 degrees, the northern limit of Spanish Florida and Louisiana. Cession of this lower valley was certain to be unacceptable to the ministers of France and especially Spain, who wanted to protect their nations' territory by shutting up the Americans east of the Appalachians. Agents of the two countries put pressure on Congress over the next two years with the result that by the Battle of Yorktown, instructions of June 1781 from Congress required the American peace commissioners to consult the French foreign minister, the Comte de Vergennes, on all matters except independence.

The Continental Congress named five commissioners to start negotiations, but only three played any active roles: Benjamin Franklin, John Adams, and John Jay, who were already in Europe seeking loans and other aid. They had good reason to suspect the motives of their European allies, especially Jay and Adams. They were also aware of more conciliatory feeling in some British circles, especially one minister who was rising to a leading position in the government. This was Lord Shelburne, who saw a chance to attract the Americans away from Vergennes, renew the formerly prosperous Anglo-American trade relations, and perhaps eventually restore some sort of imperial political connection.

The first half of 1782 was a time of rumor and confusion in both London and Paris. Shelburne became prime minister, but the British and French continued naval warfare in the Caribbean, and King George kept up his stubborn refusal to recognize the colonies' independence. The American commissioners concluded that it would be more rewarding to negotiate separately with Britain and avoid Vergennes's interference, although the alliance treaty specified a joint settlement. A breakthrough came when John Jay received what he thought was evidence that France and Spain intended to make a private

agreement on boundaries in the Ohio Valley to restrain the Americans. Without informing Franklin, the most pro-French of the trio, Jay sent an agent to Shelburne to argue for a Mississippi River boundary and indicate that he and his colleagues would negotiate separately for preliminary terms. Franklin approved Jay's action, and so did Adams, who arrived in Paris several weeks later from his own mission in the Netherlands.

Negotiation of a preliminary treaty took place during October and November 1782. Jay wrote the basic draft, but Adams, Franklin, and the British negotiators made so many changes and argued so heatedly that each major historian has assigned a different set of credits for individual sections. Recognition of American independence caused little trouble, but Franklin, who had always wanted to annex as much of Canada as possible, had to give up the Ontario peninsula. In its place he accepted an irregular boundary along the midpoints of four Great Lakes and a series of rivers and lakes west to the source of the Mississippi River. Unfortunately, this line missed the river, creating a gap that was not closed until 1818. In the interim, the British retained theoretically the right to navigate the river. The boundary then ran down the Mississippi to 31 degrees and eastward along that line and a nearby parallel to the St. Marys River and the Atlantic Ocean. The Americans' greatest territorial gain was the eastern half of the Mississippi Valley, a true seat of empire. However, a secret article (largely written by Jay) offered Britain another line north of 31 degrees as an inducement to retain the Florida coast and peninsula instead of turning it over to Spain. With Canada still a British colony, this would have put America's Atlantic trade in a pincer and kept Florida indefinitely out of its hands. (Fortunately, Spain, failing to recover Gibraltar in Europe, demanded Florida in its place.)

The preliminary articles disposed of the most important boundary questions, so the remaining discussions dealt with other matters. The most important of these were the colonial debts owed to British creditors, the treatment of loyalists living in America or owning property there, and the New England fisheries, concerning which Adams played the dominant role. Since nearly all of western Europe had been involved in the war, the British had accounts to settle elsewhere. This sometimes worked to the advantage of the Americans by distracting the British from North American affairs or placing an extra premium on American friendship. The American commissioners were shrewd men of the world who took advantage of every opening offered them. (Adams and Jay were lawyers, Franklin a businessman and bureaucrat.)

During the two decades after the revolutionary war the major problems affecting U.S. foreign relations were commerce and western settlements. The British had recognized the irregular line along the Great Lakes as the northern boundary. However, even as the king signed the treaty, providing that the chain of border forts on American territory from Ogdensburg west to Mackinac should be evacuated "with all convenient speed," his home secretary was issuing an order saying in effect, "take your time." The cabinet in London was concerned about the future of the international fur trade and peaceful relations with the Indians north of the border, and it anticipated that the Americans would commit other treaty violations and thereby justify the retention of the forts. Not surprisingly, however, the suspicious Americans assumed that the British were trying to hold onto the West. In the early 1790s, when the British resumed fighting with the French, their violations of American neutrality reinforced the complaints of western settlers about British soldiers in the border forts and brought on a major crisis. In 1794, John Jay negotiated a treaty that averted a probably disastrous war by bringing about the evacuation of the forts and securing a few commercial concessions. For other reasons, Jay's treaty was highly unpopular and cost him his reputation, but it confirmed Americans' occupation of their northern frontier, especially since a victory over the Indians in northwest Ohio at the same time discredited the traditional allies of the British.

Just as important to the growth of the American West was its boundary on the lower Mississippi, into which all the valley's rivers drained, so that the entire trade of the area was funneled through New Orleans. When the Spanish took over control of the Gulf of Mexico coast from the British under the 1783 treaty, they tried to anticipate the flow of American settlers over the Appalachian Mountains by a number of defensive strategies. First, they encouraged the Indian nations of Georgia, Alabama, and Mississippi to form a buffer, but the development of trade with the Americans and the lack of Indian cohesiveness frustrated this effort. In the late 1780s they sent an emissary to persuade the American government to give up its efforts to open the lower Mississippi to trade in return for concessions to

Americans trading across the Atlantic. However, the southern states (which had no large seaports but many western connections) formed a solid bloc in opposition. Finally, the Spanish government intrigued western leaders to secede and become a Spanish protectorate. A few, such as James Wilkinson, nibbled at the bait, but by this time the Constitutional Convention of 1787 foreshadowed a new government, strong enough to defend American interests in the West, and the Spanish efforts died out.

Although the Spanish could not prevent the migration of American settlers into the eastern Mississippi Valley, they denied them the right to ship their goods downriver to New Orleans and built several forts on the east bank, which they claimed as far north as the junction with the Ohio. The Americans, who held title to the east bank only from the British, had to wait and watch while Spanish politics moved languidly to and fro according to the progress of the French Revolution, then in its radical phase. From 1793 to 1795, Spain was actually an ally of its old enemy Britain against the Jacobins. In 1795 the Spanish withdrew from the war and indicated that they were ready to negotiate with the Americans—perhaps because they were nervous about the significance of the recent American Jay's Treaty with the British or because they had abandoned hope of stopping their westward migration. (Historians are still unsure.) The result was Pinckney's Treaty (1795), which was so popular that the Senate approved it unanimously. In it Spain recognized the 31-degree boundary and agreed to evacuate its forts (although this took two years). It also granted the Americans the right to navigate the lower Mississippi and warehouse their goods on shore while awaiting ocean shipment (the "right of deposit").

Like Jay's Treaty, Pinckney's Treaty confirmed an earlier expansion by giving the United States control over its borders. As Americans poured into the new states of Kentucky, Tennessee, and Ohio, they shipped their products down the Mississippi to New Orleans and out into the Gulf of Mexico and the ocean to the east coast and Europe. American attention turned again to the Atlantic world, and the United States fought a brief naval war with France over neutral rights, which formally ended the alliance between the two countries but did no serious damage to either one. A new leader in France, Napoleon Bonaparte, won victories over most of western Europe and signed a temporary truce with Britain.

LOUISIANA

The short-lived stability in Europe was the background for the second great continental expansion gained by the American Republic. Napoleon, seeking new worlds to conquer, looked to North America and considered an economic empire on the British model, based on trade: Caribbean sugar to Europe, French manufactured goods to French settlers in temperate Louisiana, and temperate climate foodstuffs to the Caribbean to feed the slave labor there. It was at best a risky scheme, for a slave revolt had been raging in Santo Domingo, the principal French sugar island; Americans were pressing across the eastern Mississippi Valley; and French factories were not yet prepared to supply colonial demands. Most important, the French navy was too weak to defend this ambitious trade against the jealous British. Nevertheless, Napoleon persuaded Spain to exchange Louisiana for the Italian province of Tuscany (intended for the king of Spain's brother-in-law) and prepared an army for Santo Domingo.

When the new American president, Thomas Jefferson, learned about the secret retrocession of Louisiana, he instructed the U.S. minister to France, Robert Livingston, that he must bring Napoleon to sell the city of New Orleans to the United States. "[From] the day that France takes possession of New Orleans," Jefferson declared, "we must marry ourselves to the British fleet and nation." Livingston spent most of 1802 trying to convince Napoleon of the worthlessness of Louisiana without the Florida coast (which Spain refused to give up) and the near-certainty of friction with the United States. After several months of this deadlock, the Spanish government, which, with characteristic delay, had not yet carried out the retrocession, withdrew the right of deposit in New Orleans—for reasons about which historians are still uncertain. The American westerners, seeing their flourishing New Orleans trade thus abruptly cut off, flared up in protest, calling for action, and the Federalist Party, now out of power, began to demand a renewal of the war with France and the seizure of New Orleans. To gain time, Jefferson sent James Monroe, a well-known Virginian who was popular both in the west and in France, to join Livingston. During the three months between Monroe's appointment and his arrival in Paris, Napoleon impulsively decided to sell to the Americans not only New Orleans but the entire province of Louisiana, comprising the western half of the Mississippi Valley. As recon-

structed by historians, the reasons for this momentous decision constitute one of the classic historic cases of multiple causation. In the first place, Napoleon's plan for an economic-based empire was falling apart. The conquest of Santo Domingo, the hub of the project, was going badly; yellow fever had decimated the French troops, and in November General Leclerc died of the disease. Napoleon had to send his successor troops that he had intended for the takeover of Louisiana from the Spanish. Those that remained were held in a Dutch port by an unusually hard winter. From his minister in the United States, Napoleon was learning of the American upheaval over the right of deposit, more serous than he had first thought. Finally, and perhaps decisive, tension in Britain and on the Continent suggested that the stalled war was about to break out again. Napoleon was beginning to turn his attention to possible hostilities in Europe, for which he would need funds.

Monroe and Livingston negotiated the terms of the purchase together, although each later tried to claim principal credit for the deal. The French asked 100 million francs at first but settled for 60 million ($11,350,000). The Americans, not having cash, arranged to pay in bonds at 6 percent. In addition, the United States assumed $3,750,000 of French citizens' claims, making the total purchase price about $15 million. The negotiations were hurried through in less than a month to forestall the outbreak of war or any interruption by Britain or Spain. The boundary of Louisiana was loosely drawn, but it clearly did not include East or West Florida or Texas, as some Americans later argued. Jefferson welcomed the news (which he had partly anticipated), although he was embarrassed by the doubtful constitutionality of the act. At first, he thought a constitutional amendment would be required, but he quickly dropped this scruple for fear that the providential deal might fall through at the last minute. Most of the Federalists held their peace too after a little grumbling.

The aftermath of the Louisiana Purchase was an anticlimax that took some of the bloom off Jefferson's successful first administration. After the negotiations were over, both Livingston and Monroe decided that the Louisiana Purchase included East and West Florida (that is, the peninsula and the Gulf coast to the Mississippi). On Jefferson's instructions, they put pressure on both Napoleon and the Spanish government with no success. Unwilling to go to war, Jefferson reconciled himself to a waiting game and got Congress to set up Mobile Bay as a customs district and later to appropriate $2 million to have on hand in case of an unexpected opportunity. The sorriest development of the whole period was the Burr Conspiracy (1804–1806), in which Aaron Burr, an outcast after his duel with Alexander Hamilton, exploited western unrest to concoct what was either a secessionist intrigue or a filibuster plot aimed at Texas and Mexico.

Madison, less patient than Jefferson, resorted to covert force and guile. When the inhabitants of the Baton Rouge area grew restive under Spanish rule, he sent an agent to tell them that the United States would welcome a revolution and warned off the British, whereupon the inhabitants seized the feeble Spanish fort. The rest of West Florida and part of East Florida fell to George Mathews, a revolutionary war veteran who led a force of "patriots" across the border. When Madison's opponents attacked the illegality of the act, he repudiated his agent, much to Mathews's disgust.

Following the War of 1812, the Monroe administration reverted to diplomacy to complete the acquisition of Florida. But force and the threat of force were not wholly absent from the process. After peace returned, General Andrew Jackson, commander of the military district on the southern border, broadly interpreted his vague orders and led troops into East Florida to fight Indians and protect border settlers. In the process, he captured several Spanish forts and executed two British army officers who, he said, were inciting the Indians against the Americans. Spain protested but realized that it might lose Florida anyway without action and agreed to treaty negotiations, especially after Secretary of State John Quincy Adams answered the protest with an aggressive reply, "a great gun from Washington to Madrid," as Adams's nephew pronounced it. (The British also protested but then dropped the matter.) The treaty was mainly devoted to the west boundary of the Louisiana Purchase, which was drawn on a zigzag line from the Sabine River on the modern Louisiana-Texas border to the modern north border of California (42 degrees). Many nationalists, especially southerners, resented the relinquishment of the slight American claim to Texas, but thereby the United States gained the equally weak Spanish claim to the Pacific coast, which helped to redirect American political power toward the West.

The War of 1812 gained no new territory for the United States, but it was important for avoid-ing the loss of land to the north and northwest. The United States went to war proclaiming, "On to Canada!" and hoping to acquire the Ontario peninsula at last. The British, for their part, hoped to set up an Indian protectorate between the Great Lakes and the Ohio River, both to halt the American westward movement and to create trade. They also planned sizable boundary adjustments in New England, New York, and the Northwest. By 1814 the ambitions had shrunk so far that the negotiations produced a status quo ante peace. This was quite enough for the Americans, who received it with relief as a renewed guaranty of their independence.

Two postwar agreements, each having the effect of a treaty, refined and strengthened the original treaty of 1783 fixing the northern boundary of the United States. The Rush-Bagot Agreement of 1817 limited naval armament on the Great Lakes. The Convention of 1818 drew the northern boundary along the parallel of 49 degrees from the Lake of the Woods to the "stony mountains" and provided that the territory from the mountains to the Pacific coast should be occupied by British and Americans without injury to claims of either country (generally called "joint occupation"). The convention was to last ten years, renewable until denounced. It also ended two vestiges of the past, the "boundary gap" of 1783 and the much-argued British right of navigation on the Mississippi.

A large boundary gap had existed since 1783 at the eastern end of the north border, from the point where the forty-fifth parallel crosses the St. Lawrence River to that where the St. Croix River enters the Bay of Fundy (comprising the modern north borders of New York, Vermont, New Hampshire, and Maine). Local inhabitants disagreed as to which of several rivers was "the true St. Croix." Afterward, a trail of boundary commissions, documents, and maps led from the Peace of Paris to the Treaty of Ghent without any definition of "the North West Angle of Nova Scotia," the "northwestern-most head" of the Connecticut River, and other place names on the outdated Mitchell map of 1755. The War of 1812 gave new importance to the boundary controversy, for it convinced the British that they needed a military road between Quebec and Halifax.

The admission to the union of the state of Maine in 1820 also complicated the question, because Massachusetts still had land claims in the disputed area, so now there were two sets of governors, legislatures, newspapers, and citizenry squabbling over geographical details, to say nothing of the federal government in the national system. Two efforts after 1815 to settle the question added further problems, because a boundary commission discovered that an expensive American fort at Rouse's Point had been built on Canadian soil through a surveying error. Also, a boundary line drawn by an arbiter, the king of the Netherlands, did not satisfy many Americans, who accused him of pro-British bias. The nationalist Andrew Jackson, however, thought the dispute had gone on long enough and tried in vain to get the king's award accepted.

It took a major Anglo-American crisis to bring about a solution to the Maine boundary problem. In 1837 a double revolution for self-government in Ontario and Quebec drew in hot-headed sympathizers and covetous expansionists from upper New York State, eager to strike a blow for freedom and mount a filibuster at the same time. A land war broke out in northern Maine when frontiersmen from both sides of the line discovered the Aroostook Valley, a pocket of fertile land, and started to fight over it. The commanding general of the American army, Winfield Scott, was sent to intervene and restore peace, and Britain appointed a diplomat, Lord Ashburton, to negotiate a settlement. He and Secretary of State Daniel Webster (who happened to be his personal friend) managed to draw a compromise line with information from sixty-year-old maps. By a curious anomaly, each side possessed information supporting the other side's case. Webster showed his maps to the Maine politicians to silence their objections; whether he also used money supplied by Ashburton has fascinated and baffled everyone who has written on the subject. In any case, it seems likely that Webster's attentions made a peaceful outcome possible but lost the United States about five thousand square miles of Maine woods and swamps. Smaller adjustments were made to the west in New Hampshire and Vermont, and the United States gained a sliver of land in New York, including "Fort Blunder" on Rouse's Point. More important was a cession of about six thousand square miles in Minnesota that proved later to contain some of that state's invaluable iron ore deposits.

The Monroe Doctrine, enunciated in the president's annual message of December 1823, did not contribute directly to continental expansion, for much of it applied to Central and South America. However, one part of it, the noncolonization principle, foreshadowed the annexation of Alaska forty-four years later. In 1821 the czar of Russia, seeking to expand his control over his faraway colony, issued a ukase claiming its boundary to 51 degrees north latitude and forbidding non-Russian ships to come within one hundred miles of this coast. When a burst of protest from New England farming and fishing interests followed, Secretary of State John Quincy Adams, their perennial champion, got Monroe to announce in his message that the Western Hemisphere was no longer open to European colonization. By implication Adams intended his warning for Britain as well as Russia. It had no basis for legality in international law, but the czar never enforced his ukase. In a treaty of 1824 Russia fixed the southern boundary of its colony at 54 degrees, 40 minutes—the "fifty-four forty" of a later American political slogan.

TEXAS AND THE MEXICAN WAR

The next great continental expansion of the United States comprised the entire western third of the lower forty-eight states, from the west boundary of the Louisiana Purchase to the Pacific Ocean. It was accomplished in only five years, from 1843 to 1848, but it was foreshadowed and prepared for by several migrations of American people, the spontaneous formation of governments on the American model, and the spread of an infectious propaganda resting on the brash assumption that American absorption of the desired territory was inevitable—that the Almighty had destined the territory for His "chosen people" as a kind of divine favoritism. This idea, like so many others in American colonialism, was inherited from the mother country. In the sixteenth century, the writings of Richard Hakluyt and others set forth the idea that, like the earlier Romans, Englishmen were preordained to take over, colonize, and develop the New World; no other people were capable of such a gigantic task. Destiny could be used just as easily to support American independence as to rationalize British imperial expansion, and revolutionary thought in the colonies was filled with echoes of the "city on a hill" and the "American Israel" blessed by Providence. Thomas Paine's statement in *Common Sense* that the Americans were fighting "the cause of all mankind" was only the most famous of many such declarations.

This potent propaganda, together with migration, American-style government, and an overall sense of an inevitability went to work in Texas during the 1820s. Texas had been a province on the north border of New Spain. When Mexico took over in 1821, its leaders thought to replicate the prosperous growth of the United States by encouraging the migration of American settlers as models into sparsely populated Texas, despite the warnings of a few prescient critics that this would amount to "settling the Goths at the gates of Rome." Americans, mostly Protestants speaking only English, gladly settled on the fertile cotton bottoms of east Texas and brought their slaves with them. (Mexico was officially Roman Catholic and Spanish speaking, and its constitution declared all men equal.) The new American population established commercial ties with New Orleans, since the nearest Mexican centers lay far to the south, and the people of central Mexico had little interest in Texan affairs, being much involved in their own political struggles. Frictions led to quarrels, and despite the efforts of a few Texan leaders to patch up disputes, the province revolted for independence in 1836. The Mexican president, Antonio López de Santa Anna led an army north to crush the rebels into submission, only to blunder into defeat at the Battle of San Jacinto in east Texas. Santa Anna was captured and forced to sign a treaty recognizing Texan independence.

Evidence of overt U.S. participation in the Texan revolution is slim. President Andrew Jackson's public behavior was correct, but the Texan general, Sam Houston, was his friend, and he followed the military action with keen interest. The American people, especially in the lower Mississippi Valley, were very sympathetic and contributed money and supplies freely; frontiersmen flocked into the Texan forces. An American general, Edmund P. Gaines, led a few troops fifty miles across the border but contributed nothing to Texan success. Not surprisingly, some Mexican nationalists have always believed that U.S. intervention gave the Texans their victory, and a small plot thesis has grown up among American historians, but their evidence is shallow.

Most of the victorious Texans hoped for prompt incorporation into the American Union, but this proved impossible because the United States was then implacably divided over the question of adding slave territory. In Europe, Britain and France opposed letting the United States strengthen itself through annexation. The British wanted an assured supply of cotton for their mills, and some inconsistently supported Texan abolitionism, as well. These contrary forces produced nine years (1836–1845) of frustrating diplomacy, while the ramshackle republic of Texas maintained a precarious existence, its government housed in log cabins on the western frontier, and a weak American president, John Tyler, tried to put together an annexation coalition to ensure his reelection.

In 1844, Tyler managed to sign an annexation treaty with Texas, only to see it defeated in the American Senate, partly because it came to a vote in the midst of a hard-fought presidential election campaign. The victor was an expansionist Democrat, James K. Polk. He favored annexing Texas, but Tyler tried to anticipate him during the three months he had left in office. In his hurry, he used an untried method, a joint resolution in both houses of Congress. At the same time, a diehard British agent in Mexico made a last-minute effort to secure that country's recognition of Texan independence. His failure and the Texan acceptance of terms offered by the joint resolution brought the annexation question to a dramatic conclusion.

On the Pacific coast the process of annexing California and Oregon was going on while that in Texas was drawing to a close. After Mexico won its independence it neglected its distant border provinces, and in the early 1830s American merchants established trading posts along the coast at Monterey, California, and a few other small ports, which became centers of American influence. At Monterey, Thomas O. Larkin, the most important merchant, became a U.S. consul and an important source of information about conditions in California. By the 1840s these merchants were joined by American explorers, hunters, and trappers crossing the mountains. They soon developed another center of American influence at a backwoods fort near modern Sacramento built by John A. Sutter, a German Swiss, who obtained a Mexican land grant in 1840 and founded a polyglot settlement. The Hudson's Bay Company, moving southward from western Canada, formed the third corner of the triangle competing for influence in California. The Mexican government maintained loose control over these disparate elements with little or no supervision from Mexico City. Americans on the East Coast exaggerated the European, especially the British, threat to California, and even Anglophile Daniel Webster tried to include in his negotiations with Ashburton some provision for the transfer of the San Francisco Bay area to no avail. The degree of American nervousness about California was shown by Thomas Catesby Jones, commanding the U.S. Pacific Squadron. In 1842, hearing a false rumor of an Anglo-American war, he took it upon himself to seize the port of Monterey, only to have to back out in an atmosphere of general embarrassment.

To the north of California, Americans were also much interested in the vaguely defined Oregon Territory, which the United States had occupied jointly with Britain since the northern boundary settlement at 49 degrees (1818). The British, who had explored and mapped the area as far as the Alaska border, had a better claim to it, but an American ship captain had discovered the mouth of the Columbia River, and the Lewis and Clark expedition (1804–1806) had explored the Columbia and Snake River valleys. Five years later, John Jacob Astor established a fur trading post and fort at Astoria, near the mouth of the Columbia, and in the Florida treaty of 1819 the United States acquired the Spanish claim south of the river. After that time, the Oregon question largely revolved around the triangle of land north of the Columbia River (modern Washington State), especially the coasts of Puget Sound, with their excellent harbors.

For the time being the British established monopoly control over the Columbia Valley through their fur trade and agriculture, and they even furnished food for the Russian settlements in Alaska. Meanwhile, the Americans, led by westerners in the House of Representatives, tried to alert their countrymen to the danger that Britain might forestall them in Oregon. In 1827 the two nations reviewed the whole question. The United States offered to extend the 49-degree line (established in 1818) and cede all of Vancouver Island to Britain (the eventual settlement); Britain offered only several ports on the Olympic peninsula, which its navy could easily take over in wartime. The joint occupation continued, and the Hudson's Bay Company remained the de facto ruling power in Oregon. To the disappointment of both governments, Webster and Ashburton decided not to included Oregon in their negotiations.

At this point the tide began to turn. A new British treaty with China raised trade possibilities in Asia, and British colonies in New Zealand and elsewhere began to compete for settlers with Puget Sound; also, the Hudson's Bay Company's interest in the lower Columbia valley began to cool. At the same time American concern over Oregon increased, and a new burst of speeches and memorials forced the issue on the public. Missionaries were sent out to work among the Oregon Indians, and their enthusiastic reports on the beauties of

the country stimulated the migration of families and sometimes whole communities to Oregon. A trail of sorts had existed as early as the War of 1812, and by the 1830s it was an institution—up the Platte River, across the prairies and mountains, through South Pass, down the Snake River, and finally to the Columbia. (At Fort Hall an alternate route led into California.) Many travelers went as far as a tributary of the Columbia, the Willamette, whose banks resembled parts of the Middle West so much that it became a common goal. The climax of the migration came in 1843 as returning prosperity made possible improvements in equipment and supplies. To many observers it seemed that time was working for the Americans, and a group of Southern Democrats led by John C. Calhoun spoke out for "a wise and masterly inactivity." At that point Calhoun became Tyler's secretary of state. Since Britain had about concluded that the 49-degree line was the best it could obtain at that time, preliminary negotiations began between Calhoun and the British minister, but these became hung up on details, and soon the presidential election of 1844 intervened. In the campaign, western activists kept alive their demand for all of Oregon up to the boundary of Russian Alaska—a grant of land altogether unjustified by circumstances and likely to cause war with Britain.

The new president, Polk, brought about a wholly unnecessary crisis with Britain as he maneuvered to keep together the two factions of his party, the activists (western) and the pacifists (southern, led by Calhoun). First he took advantage of a British misstep to close off Tyler's negotiations, in which he thought the American position was too weak. Then he referred the whole question to Congress, so the western fulminations could alarm the British. It was at this point, and not earlier, that the slogan "Fifty-four forty or fight" spread across the country. After a heated debate, Congress voted to send Britain a mild, unthreatening notice abrogating the joint occupation. The British took the initiative, as Polk had intended, and the diplomats quickly settled on the forty-ninth parallel, awarding all of Vancouver Island to Britain. The British gave up the right to navigate the lower Columbia, avoiding possible commercial friction in the future. Thus, Polk carried off his policy through rigid party discipline but he risked a costly war for purely partisan gains.

American migration into California during the early 1840s, though smaller than that into

Oregon, continued to tip California toward the United States, thanks especially to the publicity given to the Sacramento–San Joaquin area by the well-known explorer John Charles Frémont, whose report on his two expeditions was a best-seller. In September 1844 a group of native Californians with some Americans overturned the local Mexican governor and set up their own virtually autonomous government. When Polk took office in March 1848, he intended to negotiate for California, and the War Department sent Frémont back into the province. The British also dispatched a warship to visit the north Pacific and be on hand in case of a local revolt. For its part, the Mexican government gathered several hundred soldiers as reinforcements for California, but on their way to the West Coast they encountered a local uprising and joined it, bag and baggage.

As the Texas question wound down in 1845, Polk set his Mexican policy in motion. It was both aggressive and defensive at the same time—to mount a strong front, assume the benefit of every doubt, and challenge every assumption of his opponent, while avoiding any overt act that might commit him beyond recall—a policy of bluff, indeed, but bluff with an avenue of retreat. Since Mexico had broken relations with the United States over the annexation of Texas, Polk sent an envoy to start negotiations, although by usual practice Mexico should have acted first. The envoy, John Slidell, was chosen largely for his fluency in Spanish. Polk instructed him to offer $5 million for the cession of Texas to the Rio Grande and New Mexico and $25 million for California, including San Francisco and Monterey. The president indicated later that Slidell might bargain beyond the figure for California but he made no mention of an explanation or indemnity for the already completed annexation of Texas. Even before Polk drew up these instructions for Slidell, he took care that his envoy should negotiate from a position of strength by stationing troops under General Zachary Taylor at Corpus Christi in southeast Texas.

In early October news arrived from Polk's agent in California, the merchant Thomas O. Larkin, that forced Polk to hurry his plans. Larkin described British and Mexican activities that seemed to point to a British seizure of the province. It is now known that Larkin's information, five months old, was based on rumor and entirely false, but it must have deeply shocked Polk and his cabinet. He sent off new instructions to Taylor, Larkin, and the commander of the

Pacific Squadron, John D. Sloat. Taylor was to advance to the Rio Grande (the farthest line claimed by Texas). Sloat was to conciliate the Californians, keep his ships ready for further orders, and, if war broke out, seize the principal California ports; he was also reinforced. Larkin became confidential agent to report on developments and defeat any foreign efforts to control California. Separate orders were sent to Frémont in California. No one has discovered what these orders were or in particular how much freedom they gave to a notoriously flighty man of action.

Having set out his lines, Polk now had to wait to see their effect, while Congress plunged into debate over Oregon. Slidell arrived in Mexico at the beginning of December to find that the president, who favored negotiating but was only clinging to power, would not receive him. A new regime, more nationalistic and stubborn, soon took power, and Slidell resigned himself to waiting outside Mexico City and reporting on the situation. Meanwhile, General Taylor and his troops were marching to the Rio Grande, which they reached in March. They built a temporary fort across the river from the Mexican town of Matamoros (modern Brownsville, Texas). The Mexicans responded by sending a reconnaissance party across the river. On 25 April this force clashed with an American scouting party, took some prisoners, and shed the first blood of the war. At the same time, Polk recalled Slidell and he and news of hostilities on the Rio Grande arrived in Washington at the same time. On a Sunday morning, Polk, glad to have some justification for acting, called his cabinet together and drew up a war message. In this he branded the Mexicans as the aggressors and the conflict as a defensive one, "war by the act of Mexico." Polk's enemies in Congress, the Whigs and Calhoun, would not accept this, but Polk's Democrats introduced appropriation bills and other measures to support the troops, and presently patriotism blurred the distinctions, and a formal declaration of defensive war crept through. (Mexico too declared a defensive war.)

When the American cabinet discussed the goals of the war, the cautious James Buchanan (secretary of state) proposed a circular letter disavowing any territorial ambitions beyond the Rio Grande boundary for fear of a British or French intervention. Polk firmly vetoed such a statement. By the end of May he had decided on the annexation of all Upper California, New Mexico, and perhaps other parts of northern Mexico. As soon as

Congress passed the war bill, Polk ordered a blockade of the California coast and sent General Stephen W. Kearny, then in Missouri, to lead troops westward—eventually to occupy California. Taylor's initial victories over Mexico (Palo Alto and Resaca de la Palma), as well as the settlement of the Oregon question, reduced the danger of British intervention in California. During June, before the news of war reached the west coast, Frémont touched off a revolt against the local authorities and captured the town of Sonoma—whether on instructions from Washington, no one knows for certain. Commodore Sloat after some hesitation proclaimed American rule. (Actual conquest, however, would await the arrival of General Kearny and his regular troops.) Events in the principal theater of war had less connection with continental expansion. Taylor pressed southward through Matamoros, Camargo, Monterrey, and Saltillo, but a fierce battle at Buena Vista in February 1847 convinced Polk that the army had reached a dead end. He created a second army, commanded by Winfield Scott, which landed at and captured Veracruz, then pushed into the interior of the country toward Mexico City. Reaching the central valley of Mexico, Scott finally occupied the capital in September 1847.

Polk had not originally intended to go so far. He expected a short war, having no idea of the Mexican sense of honor or stubbornness. So the war became a series of advances followed by pauses in which action was stopped to see if the Mexicans would yield. During one of these pauses, after Scott had occupied Veracruz, Polk appointed Nicholas Trist to join Scott as a commissioner and be ready to act as soon as the Mexican showed any interest in negotiating. (Trist was a minor official in the State Department. Polk did not care to send the elderly Buchanan so far away.) After the American capture of Mexico City, the Mexican government, by now controlled by moderates, retreated to an interior town. An important force working for peace was the British legation, because after the fall of Veracruz, the British government had resigned itself to an American victory and was now anxious to end the war as quickly and cheaply as possible. Trist, Scott, and Mexican representatives with British advisers discussed terms in Mexico City, and a man on horseback carried these to the Mexican government a hundred miles away for further discussion. Polk played no active role in the negotiation of terms, and, indeed, was so disgusted with the proceedings that at one point he ordered Trist to stop negotiating and come home. Fortunately, Trist disobeyed; for this, the vindictive president stopped his pay (Congress made an appropriation twenty-two years later.)

The treaty so torturously produced kept surprisingly close to Polk's early idea of the war's goals. It ceded to the United States all of Upper California and New Mexico and drew the U.S.–Mexico boundary at the Rio Grande and Gila Rivers. In return the United States was to pay $15 million and assume $3.25 million of American claims against Mexico. The cessions did not include Lower California or the Isthmus of Tehuantepec, which had been mentioned as a transit route for a railroad or canal, but the United States had not occupied these territories, and annexing them at that time would have presented serious problems. Considering the sectional rivalries the country faced, it had taken perhaps too much as it was. During the last months of the war, a movement grew in the United States to annex all of Mexico as the only way to reimburse the nation for the expense of the war. In addition, among the divided Mexican parties one left-wing group favored an American protectorate as the only way of pushing through changes such as clerical reform, which Mexico badly needed but could not manage by itself.

When Polk saw the treaty signed by his disobedient agent, he was furiously disgusted, but he swallowed his rage and transmitted the document to the Senate with minor changes. A coalition of extremists who wanted to annex more of Mexico and who wanted a peace without annexations threatened to defeat the treaty and throw the negotiations open again. Proceedings were delayed by the sudden death of John Quincy Adams in the House chamber and this may have provided time for common sense to prevail. Eventually, moderates gathered themselves together and approved the Treaty of Guadalupe Hidalgo with Polk's amendments by a vote of 38 to 14.

THE GADSDEN PURCHASE

But the treaty did not complete American border expansion to the southwest. In the first place, the Treaty of Guadalupe Hidalgo, like the one after the American Revolution, was based on an inaccurate prewar map, so a boundary commission had to run the whole line on the ground, a process causing new quarrels with Mexican state and federal governments. Second, Mexicans complained that Indians north of the new border were increasing their raids into Mexico. They demanded that the United States carry out Article 11 of the peace treaty, requiring it to restrain the border Indians from raiding—an impossibility with the available infantry troops. Third, American filibusters crossed the border almost at will, seeking to detach Mexican states and complete the absorption process begun by the war. Fourth, American railroad interests discovered belatedly that the best route for a southern transcontinental railroad lay south of the Gila River in Mexican territory. Finally the question of rail transit across the Isthmus of Tehuantepec, omitted from the peace treaty, was taken up by the commercially minded Taylor-Filmore administration, as Americans acquired interests in transit concessions.

All of these considerations figured in the effort of the Franklin Pierce administration to acquire more land from Mexico. Pierce appointed the railroad owner James Gadsden minister to Mexico and gave him a list of desired territories and corresponding prices to be offered. The maximum price was for Lower California and a good part of northern Mexico, the minimum for a strip of territory south of the Gila River big enough for the contemplated transcontinental railroad.

In Mexico, Gadsden's negotiating partner was Antonio López de Santa Anna, the opponent of the Americans through the Texas question and the Mexican War. Santa Anna was as eager as ever for money but wary of nationalist opposition to more land grants. Gadsden was a bumbling diplomat given to grandiloquent and imprecise language. Other complications were efforts by another agent from Pierce to insert the Tehuantepec question and a filibuster expedition to Lower California by the notorious guerrilla leader William Walker. Santa Anna, now desperate, put out feelers for British or French aid to no avail. In the end, he gave up a thin triangle of land south of the Gila large enough for a railroad and released the United States from Article 11 of the peace treaty. For this minimal grant, the United States agreed to pay $15 million plus $5 million for private American claims. The Senate was in the midst of a furious debate over the Kansas-Nebraska Act but took up the Gadsden treaty, too. It lowered the purchase price to $10 million and somewhat increased the land area acquired. Outside the continent, it opened the Isthmus of Tehuantepec to American transit, but it did not give the United States access to the Gulf of California, as some had hoped.

ALASKA

The fourth and final great continental expansion that produced the present-day continental proportions of the United States was the purchase of Alaska from Russia in 1867. From the late eighteenth century, both Russia and America had sought out the northwest coast of North America for furs, mostly of sea otters and seals; Americans also pushed the whaling industry into the north Pacific. After the United States acquired California in 1848, San Francisco became the center of trading companies and other enterprises extending their activities northward. The most striking of these expansionist ventures was Perry Macdonough Collins's project to extend a telegraph line across western Canada, Alaska, and the Bering Strait to Siberia, where it would connect with Russian and other European lines. (Unfortunately, it could not compete with Cyrus Field's transatlantic cable for investment funds.)

American public interest in acquiring Alaska had already been rumored occasionally. At the time of the Crimean War, some Americans were considering taking over Russian holdings in the Alaska panhandle to keep them out of British hands, but the British avoided this action by agreeing to neutralize Russian property there. Even before then, a few American expansionists, especially William H. Seward, a Whig senator from New York, were attracted to Alaska. Seward regarded it as the key to an expanded Pacific commercialism pointed toward the Far East, especially China, which had long been a magnet for expansionist American businesspeople. At this time, Russia was losing interest in its remote, unprofitable colony. Fearful that the United States or Britain would take it over without paying for it, the czar and his government decided on the sale to the Americans. As secretary of state, Seward eagerly received the Russian overtures, and he and the Russian minister to the United States drew up a treaty literally overnight. The American public and press were taken by surprise and Seward and his fellow expansionists had to put together an intensive lobbying campaign to sell the treaty to Congress. The United States paid $7.2 million to Russia, and historians feel that perhaps $200,000 of that went to congressmen in one way or another to buy their votes for the bill appropriating the purchase price. (Perhaps many would have voted for it anyway.) Not for the first time in American history, expansionism was temporarily discredited, and later efforts to purchase the Danish West

Indies and the Dominican Republic were voted down amid accusations of scandal. Nevertheless, the United States promptly set up a government in Alaska, and American business promoters started to take over Russian enterprises.

After the Civil War, the United States was unable to extend is borders northward into Canada. During the late 1860s, annexationism raised its head in British Columbia and Manitoba and then fell back. In the first case, Seward tried to encourage the discontented British Columbians, and in the second case, a group of New York and Minnesota railroadmen and other business interests tried to exploit a local rebellion early in the administration of Ulysses S. Grant. At an earlier date either case might have led to further continental expansion, but at this time, all the Americans could achieve was an arbitral award of the San Juan Islands by the German emperor in 1871. (These islands, left in dispute by a vague passage in the Oregon Treaty of 1846, were strategically located in the channel just off Vancouver Island.)

CONCLUSION

Why did American continental expansion come to such an abrupt halt after the Alaska purchase? Perhaps the unsavory rumors of corruption were responsible but bickering and carping had not lessened American ardor for long after the Louisiana Purchase or the Mexican War. More likely, the formerly irresistible American expansionist impulse encountered a powerful counterforce, for in 1867, only three months after the annexation of Alaska, the Canadians formed a self-governing dominion, and soon afterward, the regime of the first prime minister, Sir John Macdonald, began construction of a transcontinental railroad that would bind the dissident provinces such as British Columbia and Manitoba to the nation. Probably also American businessmen came to realize that economic ties could be as valuable to them as political control over a people who, like the Americans themselves, wanted to be independent.

BIBLIOGRAPHY

Bemis, Samuel Flagg. *The Diplomacy of the American Revolution.* New York, 1935. Old but especially good for boundary settlement.
———. *John Quincy Adams and the Foundations of American Foreign Policy.* New York, 1949. Solid accounts of several episodes from 1815 to 1830.
DeConde, Alexander. *This Affair of Louisiana.* Baton Rouge, La., 1976. One of several good accounts.
Garber, Paul Neff. *The Gadsden Treaty.* Philadelphia, 1923. An old work but still useful.
Jensen, Ronald J. *The Alaska Purchase and Russian-American Relations.* Seattle, Wash., 1975. More detail on the treaty negotiations.
Jones, Howard. *To the Webster-Ashburton Treaty.* Chapel Hill, N.C., 1977.
Merk, Frederick. *Manifest Destiny and Mission in American History: A Reinterpretation.* New York, 1963. A minority view of manifest destiny and events of the 1840s. Should be compared to Weinberg.
Morris, Richard B. *The Peacemakers: The Great Powers and American Independence.* New York, 1965. More detailed scholarship.
Pletcher, David M. *The Diplomacy of Annexation: Texas, Oregon, and the Mexican War.* Columbia, Mo., 1973.
Saul, Norman E. *Distant Friends: The United States and Russia, 1763–1967.* Lawrence, Kans., 1991. Cross-archival study of a complex relationship.
Stuart, Reginald C. *United States Expansionism and British North America, 1775–1871.* Chapel Hill, N.C., 1988. Covers the whole span of continental expansion.
Weinberg, Albert K. *Manifest Destiny: A Study of Nationalist Expansion in American History.* Chicago, 1935. Still the standard work on the subject.

See also COLONIALISM AND NEOCOLONIALISM; IMPERIALISM; NATIONALISM.

THE CONTINENTAL SYSTEM

Marvin R. Zahniser

The continental system was the name given to those measures of Napoleon Bonaparte taken between 1806 and 1812 that were designed to disrupt the export trade of Great Britain and ultimately to bring that country financial ruin and social breakdown. This term likewise refers to Bonaparte's plan to develop the economy of continental Europe, with France to be the main beneficiary.

Although the continental system was formally inaugurated with publication of Napoleon's Berlin Decree in November 1806, its historical antecedents can be traced as far back as the Anglo-French commercial wars that began late in the seventeenth century. The maxims of mercantilist thought nourished the propensity of France and Britain to inaugurate blockades and carry on commercial war. A common argument of the mercantilists stated that trade, shipping, industry, and the world's bullion resources were fixed quantities that could not be significantly increased or decreased by human effort. This concept led inexorably to the conclusion that nations could increase their wealth and power only by depriving other nations of their sources of wealth, such as trade. Commercial wars, therefore, if successfully prosecuted, promised a meaningful augmentation to a nation's wealth and diminution of an enemy's.

Profit was generated, in part, by increasing the volume and value of a nation's exports and in compelling competitors to purchase one's exports on disadvantageous terms while purchasing the least possible amount of the competitor's goods. A favorable balance of trade indicated that a nation's profits and wealth were increasing; this could be gauged by the flow of bullion into the country.

With every nation perceiving that its own advancement could be made only at the expense of others, each country began to pursue trade and tariff policies that differed little in war or peace. War simply stimulated nations such as France and Britain to accept even fewer goods from the enemy while pressing their own exports upon the other by every conceivable device. In addition, it was presumed sound economic policy both in war and peace to protect native industries by appropriately stringent tariff legislation.

A new intensity in these policies shortly followed negotiation of the Anglo-French Commercial Treaty of 1786 (Eden's Treaty). Britain was largely satisfied with the treaty, but it provoked bitter criticism in France. Revolutionary France soon began to drift back to the pre-1786 commercial policies. In 1791 the Constituent Assembly adopted a tariff with rates high enough to indicate the new trend. France finally denounced Eden's Treaty early in 1793, an indication of the growing strain in French-British relations and of French determination to protect their industries against British competition. With the execution of Louis XVI in mid-January and the outbreak of war on 1 February 1793, Britain and France resumed their long-standing attempts to strangle each other economically.

Rigid exclusionist policies of early revolutionary France were slightly eased during the ascendancy of Robespierre; they were, however, adopted and strengthened by the government of the Directory (1795–1799). The notorious decree of 18 January 1798 (29 Nivose, Year VI) laid down the principle that the cargo of a ship would determine its nationality; thus, any vessel carrying goods from Britain or its possessions became subject to confiscation, both ship and cargo. Ships stopping at British ports could not enter French ports. The severity of this measure produced a virtual French self-blockade. Likewise, the Directory supported the Navigation Act, passed by the Convention on 21 September 1793. This act prohibited foreign vessels from importing into France products other than those of their own nation or engaging in the French coastal trade. It is clear that these laws of the revolutionary regimes had essentially the same purpose as their predecessors of the past two hundred years—to damage Britain by excluding British goods and ships and to foster French industry, agriculture, and the merchant marine by protecting them from British, and other, competition.

The harshness of French measures, prompted in part by the disturbing reality that British sea power was annihilating the French merchant marine, was bottling up the French fighting navy, taking possession of French colonies one by one, building an enormous carrying trade, and threatening to control neutral trade to its own advantage. Before 1789 there had been 2,000 French merchantmen; by January 1799 the Directory admitted that not a single merchant ship on the high seas flew the French flag. On the other hand, Britain's merchant marine prospered handsomely during these war years. Between 1793 and 1800 the number of ships under British registry rose from 15,000 to nearly 18,000.

British naval power appeared much less decisive than British mercantile superiority, overmatching the French fighting navy by only a two-to-one ratio. France believed it possible to reduce Britain's naval superiority by rapid shipbuilding and under Bonaparte launched major attempts to do so. French naval expenditures between 1803 and 1806 leaped from a projected triennium total of 240 million francs to more than 400 million francs.

NAPOLEON AND BRITAIN INAUGURATE WARTIME MEASURES

Coming to power through the coup d'état of 18 Brumaire, Year VIII (9 November 1799), First Consul Bonaparte, himself a mercantilist, became heir to French commercial traditions and current practices. He also inherited an unpalatable oceanic situation in which the French merchant marine had been driven from the high seas and the fighting navy had been destroyed or remained in port, fearful of the British navy. Bonaparte soon turned his enormous energies toward remedying these situations, but he wished for a period of internal consolidation before proceeding with his larger plans. Fortunately for him, the Second Coalition of 1799 soon dissolved. Russia, coming to fear British power in the eastern Mediterranean more than French ambitions, in effect withdrew from the coalition. When Austria was forced to sign the Peace of Lunéville in 1801, the Second Coalition disappeared. In March 1802, peace was concluded with Great Britain at Amiens. For the

first time since 1792 no great European power warred with another.

Peace proved to be only an interlude. Britain viewed with great anxiety Napoleon's activities during the months of peace: reorganizing the Cisalpine Republic with himself named president and reorganizing the Helvetic Republic as the Confederation of Switzerland with himself as mediator. Bonaparte also supervised the reorganization of Germany, resulting in consolidated and enlarged German states that now relied on Bonaparte to maintain their position. Britain proved unwilling to countenance this continuing expansion of French influence. Picking a fight over Malta, Britain declared war in May 1803 and began the search for coalition partners. After Austria signed an alliance with Britain in 1805, Alexander I brought Russia into the alliance, completing the Third Coalition.

Britain did not wait for the Third Coalition to coalesce before inaugurating its own measures in response to Napoleon's. In June and July of 1803, Britain declared that the mouths of the Elbe and Weser rivers were under blockade, thus cutting off the entire trade of Hamburg and Bremen. On 9 August 1804 Britain also declared all French ports on the English Channel and the North Sea under blockade. In the spring of 1805 Britain placed major restrictions on the carrying trade of the United States (in the *Essex* decision), a response to increasing American attempts to trade directly between the Continent and the enemy's colonies. In June 1805 and July 1806, Britain also took additional measures that underlined its determination to see American trade with enemy colonies carried on only in ways supportive of British interests.

Between 1803 and 1805 Napoleon expended enormous energy in planning means to gain temporary naval superiority in the English Channel and thus be able to ferry a formidable army to the British Isles. Warships and troop-carrying barges were certainly being built in numbers sufficient to alarm Britain. After two years of frustration and lost hopes, Napoleon temporarily abandoned his invasion plans in August 1805 in order to meet the continental challenge of the Third Coalition. As part of his strategy, he ordered the Cádiz squadron to attack Naples. Admiral Pierre de Villeneuve, under a cloud and fearful that he was going to be recalled in disgrace, put to sea on 19 October with a combined Franco-Spanish fleet of thirty-three vessels. Two days later the blockading force of twenty-seven British ships, commanded by Horatio Nelson, engaged the French fleet off Cape Trafalgar. When the battle of Trafalgar had ended, only one third of the Franco-Spanish squadron regained harbor whereas Britain did not lose a single ship. Any lingering hopes of Napoleon that England could be invaded and subdued by land armies had now to be abandoned. More indirect, subtle methods had to be devised to erode and eventually to destroy British power.

As Napoleon analyzed England, he perceived certain weaknesses that, if shrewdly exploited, could serve to disrupt its economy, provoke social unrest, and bring England to the conference table in a compliant mood. Napoleon believed the British economy vulnerable because he thought its prosperity was founded primarily on trade, rather than on its productive agriculture and industry. He also believed that by disrupting British export trade to the Continent and by forcing England into trade channels on disadvantageous terms, there would be a drain on Britain's bullion reserves. Dislocation of industry, banking, and the mercantile communities must occur as well as destruction of its overextended credit system. Strikes and other forms of social unrest must surely follow, placing the British government in a significantly weakened position. Since his own measures could be framed in such a way that French industry and agriculture would be protected, Napoleon felt certain of domestic support in pursuing a regulated blockade. Napoleon gradually persuaded himself that only a coordinated, Continent-wide refusal to accept British goods could produce the intended effects.

Napoleon was also propelled toward a trade war by Britain's blockading measures and by a series of his own military victories. While the British actions infuriated and challenged him, victories at Ulm and Austerlitz (October and December 1805) and the crushing defeat of Prussia at Jena (October 1806) led him to believe that he could compel, if not persuade, other continental nations to support him in enforcing anti-British trade measures. Napoleon himself later pointed to Jena as the antecedent to inauguration of the continental system, for that battle placed him in control of the Weser, Elbe, Trave, and Oder Rivers, and the northern coastline as far as the Vistula.

On 21 November 1806, some three weeks after his triumphal entry into Berlin, Napoleon issued his Berlin Decree. Announcing the decree as a measure of retaliation against Great Britain's blockade declaration of 16 May (Fox's blockade), Napoleon proclaimed the British Isles to be blockaded and all trade or communication with them prohibited. He likewise declared war on all British goods, prohibiting trade in British goods and all goods coming from Britain or its colonies. Further, every port on the Continent had orders to refuse entrance to every vessel sailing directly from any port of Britain or its colonies. A peculiarly brutal provision declared all British citizens in territory occupied by France to be prisoners of war and their property to be confiscated.

Contemporaries and some historians questioned the effectiveness of the Berlin Decree because Napoleon had no ships to blockade the British Isles or Britain's colonies. Ineffective (paper) blockades were declared by both powers, of course, but Napoleon believed France would stand on firmer legal ground in dealing harshly with foreign merchantmen, both neutrals and allies, if he could demonstrate they had violated his duly proclaimed blockade.

Others, following the arguments of the naval historian Alfred T. Mahan, have expressed surprise that the Berlin Decree, and subsequent decrees designed to strengthen the system, fell so harshly upon neutrals like the United States. Since France and its colonies were dependent on the merchant carriers of neutral nations to supply their needs, Napoleon, some claimed, should have wooed neutral trade rather than have treated it in a preemptive, cynical fashion. Such an argument does not properly weigh several factors in Napoleon's thinking. He reasoned that since Britain's navy controlled the high seas, neutral commerce could only come to the Continent on its terms. As Napoleon saw it, neutral trade was therefore ultimately British trade. Also, Napoleon was anxious to encourage hostility between Britain and the neutrals, hoping that the neutrals would, as his foreign minister said in 1810, "cause their rights to be respected." Neutrals who refused to trade with Britain must inevitably become part of France's continental system. Last, Napoleon believed the continental economy much more self-sufficient than Britain's. While the Continent might suffer some losses through denying itself neutral or British goods, the vulnerable British economy must experience catastrophe and ruin. If the French colonies suffered because of neutral trade denied them, one must remember that they survived only through British tolerance.

Napoleon's Berlin Decree gave Britain the excuse it needed to strengthen those measures designed to force neutral, that is, primarily American, trade into British ports. England had already blockaded all French ports on the English Channel and the North Sea. By a series of orders in council in 1807, the most significant being that of 11 November, England prohibited intercourse between enemy colonies and the northern countries. Further, England forbade direct trade between enemy ports and other ports except when those "other ports" were either European British ports (such as Malta) or ports of the vessel's own nation. Thus, trade was prohibited between enemy and neutral ports other than in the ports native to the neutral ships. Britain planned to enforce these regulations by compelling neutral vessels into British ports for inspection, by demanding payment of customs duties, and by issuing licenses authorizing the vessel's journey. Finally, mere possession of the required French "certificate of origin," showing that the vessel's goods were of non-British origin, brought British confiscation of ship and cargo.

Napoleon retaliated in his two Milan decrees (23 November and 17 December 1807) by announcing that vessels submitting to any of the three basic British regulations (examination of cargo and papers, call at a British port, or payment of duty on the cargo) was thereby denationalized, becoming a proper lawful prize. French privateers became the chief enforcers of these decrees. Napoleon again demonstrated his cavalier attitude toward neutral trade some four months later when in the Bayonne Decree (17 April 1808) he ordered confiscation of all ships flying the American flag and entering the ports of France, Holland, Italy, and the Hanse towns. Since the United States had declared an embargo, Napoleon reasoned, ships flying the American flag must be British vessels in disguise. Under the Rambouillet Decree of March 1810, he seized scores of American ships and imprisoned hundreds of the captured crewmen.

THE UNITED STATES CONFRONTS ECONOMIC WARFARE

The Rambouillet Decree underscored the cruel position in which the wars of the French Revolution and the continental system placed the United States. Articulation of the continental system, however, merely sharpened a major question confronting the United States since 1793: Would Britain or France become the primary benefactor of American trade? Federalist administrations essentially had answered that question through

negotiating Jay's Treaty (1794) with Britain, but American ratification of this treaty contributed to the Quasi-War with France between 1798 and 1800. The war led to internal unrest, the eclipse of the Federalist Party, a widespread assault upon the civil liberties of dissenters, and a national hope that such a war would not again be necessary.

During the four years prior to enunciation of the continental system, and the responsive British measures, American commerce prospered remarkably. British, continental, West Indian, and South American markets all contributed their share to this era of great commercial prosperity. It was President Thomas Jefferson's and Secretary of State James Madison's mistake to believe that this lucrative interlude could and should continue. Nor did many American merchants seem to grasp fully that the continuing flow of trade and relatively open markets remained entirely at the discretion of the belligerents. When the belligerents began to announce their regulations concerning neutral trade, many Americans reacted with shock, indignation, and a determination that the measures be repealed or modified.

Jefferson and Madison's perspective on how to resist the continental system and related British measures is complex and interesting. Both were sympathetic to the larger purposes of the French Revolution yet distressed by the rise of Napoleon Bonaparte and his bold aggressions against those nations resisting his program of conquest. However, both wished to keep their indignation within bounds, partly because they fervently hoped to persuade Bonaparte to help the United States deprive Spain of the Floridas at some opportune moment. Also, they struggled to keep some perspective on Napoleon; in essence, they viewed him as scum temporarily floating on the beneficial and permanent wave of the French Revolution. They believed that such a person should not be allowed to disrupt permanently the spirit of American and French comradeship arising out of their revolutions, so close in time and in their larger purposes.

In addition, Jefferson and Madison shared with Bonaparte the view that Britain was the greatest enemy of their respective nations. After all, they reasoned, Britain seized American sailors and forced them into naval service (impressment), in effect denying many Americans their right to life and liberty. Quite clearly, Britain remained the major culprit on the maritime trade issues, because it exercised effective naval power in regulating American trade while Bonaparte had

WAR IN DISGUISE

James Stephen (1758–1832), a crusty and argumentative British Admiralty lawyer, felt anger for years when he considered how the Americans were injuring Britain with their commercial carrying trade. Ever since 1800, those crafty Americans had been engaged in an enormous trade with the Continent because the British had allowed Americans to "neutralize" their cargoes from the French Caribbean by first landing them in America and paying a small duty. Even those minor British requirements were massively evaded by Americans; too few cargoes were landed and even small duties were quickly refunded by port authorities. From London, it appeared that Americans were growing rich while the British struggled to contain Napoleon, would-be dictator of the Western world. Ungrateful Americans, supposed lovers of liberty, assisted Napoleon and counted their coins while Britain defended America from Napoleonic incursions into the New World with great sacrifice.

Stephen, who hated Napoleon and Jefferson in equal measure, decided to urge his fellow citizens to crack down on the Americans. In October 1805 he published *War in Disguise; or, The Frauds of the Neutral Flags,* a pamphlet that appeared on the same day Admiral Nelson smashed the combined French and Spanish fleets at Trafalgar. Do not, Stephen warned, allow American neutral ships to continue trading freely with France; such trade "sustains the ambitions of France and prolongs the miseries of Europe." Since Britain ruled the oceans, why concede extensive rights to greedy neutrals, as Britain had in 1800? Why should Americans be allowed to prosper while Britain bled for freedom and the precious right of self-governance? When news of the Trafalgar triumph reached London, Stephen's arguments seemed even more convincing; Britain controlled the high seas and could enforce its will without contradiction. His powerful pamphlet became a best-seller in England for several months. Even those who favored leniency toward the American trade found his arguments difficult to refute.

British orders in council regulating American shipping soon followed. To a striking degree, they enacted policies suggested by Stephen. No longer could Americans neutralize their cargoes by landing them in an American port and paying a small duty. Britain was thus preparing in 1805 to reinforce Napoleon's coming continental system in making life miserable for the heretofore prosperous American commercial carriers.

power only to harass the trade lanes with commerce destroyers or to close continental ports to American trade. Finally, Britain continued to demonstrate contempt for the U.S. government by its ongoing intrigue with Native Americans in the Northwest Territory.

The historian Paul Varg has emphasized Jefferson and Madison's conviction that their infant nation should do its best to establish the rights of small naval powers. Since 1776, in fact, Americans had worked to expand the rights of neutral powers. Terms of the model treaty of 1776, the Treaty of Amity and Commerce with France in 1778, a commercial treaty with the Netherlands in 1780, Jay's Treaty in 1794, Pinckney's Treaty of 1795, and the Convention of 1800 with France all reflected America's intense concern to defend or expand neutral rights. Although Napoleon's trade restrictions were painful, the most bitter disappointments in defending neutral rights had occurred

with the British, particularly with Jay's Treaty. A certain principled rigidity therefore operated in American-British diplomacy that was not active in defining the American-French relationship.

As they contemplated measures to counter the economic systems established by France's continental system and a series of British orders in council, Jefferson and Madison, his successor, were confronted by a puzzling domestic situation. Jefferson in particular was regarded by fanatical New England Federalists as a devotee of everything French and a tool of Napoleon. Federalist merchants presumed his persistent hostility to Britain and to the advancement of American trade, though on the latter point they were very mistaken. The belief that Jefferson and Madison acted from partisan motives when dealing with both Britain and France became especially troubling when such views were held precisely by those who would be severely affected if the

United States pursued a course of economic retaliation. Another complicating factor arose because these same Federalist merchants expressed willingness to endure most maritime hardships imposed by Britain, including a system of licensed trade, mainly because such conformance guaranteed the continuance of their trade and profits. They also shared Britain's horror of Napoleon and the French Revolution that had spawned him. The fact that these merchant-Federalists were largely located in New England also raised Jeffersonian anxiety that coercive commercial measures might be interpreted as politically inspired punishment for the one geographical section having continuing Federalist strength.

Thus, whatever policy or series of policies Jefferson and Congress adopted in reaction to the continental system or to British measures, certain difficulties lay ahead. Submission to foreign commercial regulations would disturb militant patriots and those who believed neutral rights should be defended on principle; resistance promised to alienate both merchants and agriculturalists with a vested economic or political interest in continued trade. It is therefore interesting to note how decisively Jefferson eventually pressed for an embargo, a measure certain to have profound internal consequences. Jefferson and Madison, however, were intellectual cousins to Bonaparte and to British statesmen in believing that severe economic measures were likely to bring offending nations to reason. In this sense the continental system, the British orders in council, and the embargo (with subsequent American commercial laws) were all grounded in common postulates about the persuasive power of protective economic measures. As events turned out, only the American economic measures had their desired impact, but even repeal of the offending British orders in council came too late to prevent war between the United States and Britain in 1812.

Neither Britain nor France fully grasped Republican anger concerning their economic measures because they did not fully understand the principled, lengthy stand of Republicans for unfettered free trade. As Drew R. McCoy has shown, Republicans committed early to expanding America's commerce as a means to develop a citizenry that would be industriously and usefully employed. In such conditions, a virtuous citizenry would develop, equipped to support the ideals of republican government. At the same time, free markets must contribute to happiness and prosperity abroad and thus lead to a more humane and peaceful world. Clearly, when France and Britain destroyed the free exchange of trade, causing unemployment and disruption, they were attacking not only America's direct economic interests but sabotaging one basis of building a sound republic and an enlightened world.

Jefferson's embargo policy provoked consternation in Britain and New England, primarily because of the hardships it imposed on Anglo-American trade. But it also aroused deep anger because it appeared intended to complement Napoleon's continental system. Since the United States was not free to trade with France, given British control of the high seas, an American self-blockade seemed obviously designed to injure Britain. Jefferson's immediate objective, however, was not to aid Napoleon but through withdrawal of American trade to avoid war and to persuade Britain to modify its offensive trade regulations. If the chief culprit, Britain, modified its regulations, Jefferson and Madison felt confident that Napoleon would likewise be forced to ameliorate the continental system. Such a modification must in turn attract American trade to the Continent and to French colonies in the Caribbean. Jefferson, not a pacifist, continued to consider the possibility of war, though he met resistance to that idea within his own cabinet and circle of supporters.

American domestic pressures against the embargo eventually became so severe that Congress moved toward repeal in the last days of Jefferson's presidency. Pressures came from many directions, some anticipated and some not. Jefferson's support began to erode within his own party; this circumstance reflected the difficulties of enforcing embargo measures at the state level, even where the governors were Republicans and supporters of the administration. Madison's succeeding administration, together with a wavering and troubled Congress, never subsequently crafted a series of measures to persuade France and Britain to ameliorate significantly their virtual warfare on neutral trade. The Non-Intercourse Act (1809), which became effective three days before Madison entered office, proved to be an embargo measure with a difference: commerce was restored with every nation except France and Britain, but provision was made that trade with those nations would be resumed as soon as they repealed their noxious decrees and orders.

When this measure proved unavailing, Macon's Bill Number 2 was enacted in May 1810. This mischievous law reopened trade with France and Britain but provided that should either nation repeal its restrictive commercial measures, trade with the other power would be interdicted. Napoleon, who had learned about repeal of the embargo, saw an opportunity to stop American trade with Britain once again. He therefore informed Madison that as of 1 November 1810, he was conditionally revoking his Berlin and Milan decrees pertinent to American trade and called upon the United States to invoke nonintercourse against Britain. Madison understood Napoleon's action to be conditional upon Britain's revocation of certain orders in council.

With his eyes open, Madison decided to take the biggest gamble of his political life and presume that Napoleon intended to revoke his decrees before his precondition had been met. With questionable haste, Madison issued a proclamation in November stopping trade with Britain within three months if it had not canceled its orders in council. Britain refused to do so pending evidence that Napoleon had repealed his decrees. Since Madison could not prove Napoleon had acted, Britain refused to alter its measures. Bitter and embarrassed, Madison nevertheless encouraged Congress to renew nonintercourse against Britain, which Congress voted to do in March 1811.

Through Napoleon's shrewd diplomatic tactic and through Madison's untimely willingness to gamble, the United States once again became a reluctant partner in strengthening the continental system. The results of this episode, and the bitterness engendered by it, helped to pave the way for the War of 1812, for many Americans believed Britain had been inflexible and petty when there had been a chance to be constructive and conciliatory. Britain, angry because the United States seemed willing to help an aggressive conqueror such as Napoleon, found American actions to assist Napoleon further evidence of the Madison administration's fundamental ill will toward Britain.

It seems fair to say that the continental system, as manipulated by Bonaparte, played a crucial role in bringing about the War of 1812. The acts committed by Napoleon under the mantle of the continental system were serious enough to have provoked war with the United States; indeed, between 1806 and 1812, France and its allies had seized over four hundred American ships. But after considerable reflection, Madison and the Congress backed away from declaring war on France, believing Britain to be enemy enough.

The whole complex of maritime belligerent measures, of which the continental system was the centerpiece, had significant consequences for the United States other than the War of 1812. Because of trade interruptions of varying length, the enormous American carrying trade was hurt, as were American hopes to nourish a promising trade with Latin America and possibly East Asia. Also, domestic objections to Jefferson and Madison's seemingly pro-French policies were sizable and significant enough to provoke New England's Hartford Convention of 1814–1815, though reforms requested by the twenty-six delegates were moderate in tone. Aggressive federal enforcement of trade measures in the ports and states raised questions about the Republican Party's commitment to the primacy of local governance. On the positive side, some argue that American exclusion from continental markets proved to be a healthy stimulus to American invention and to manufacturing enterprises even though other sectors of the economy suffered unduly.

America's struggle with both French and British economic measures had a decided effect upon Republican concepts of political economy. The older ideals of full employment producing an industrious and virtuous citizenry could not be guaranteed by increasing foreign markets; other powers had the ability and will to close markets or restrict the American carrying trade. Gradually, Republicans became better disposed toward major manufacturing enterprise as a way to produce full employment and a balanced economy. Also, developing the American market itself became an attractive alternative to relying upon overseas markets controlled by Europeans. With the vast Louisiana Purchase territory waiting to be settled, Americans turned away from Europe and focused on other endeavors, an option not available to them since 1775.

Imposition of the continental system demonstrated the cruel situation in which small, neutral powers are placed when great belligerent powers determine to direct neutral resources to their enemies only upon disadvantageous terms or not at all. Jefferson and Madison's unsuccessful attempts to bluff or to pressure France and Britain underlined that truism of statecraft. Also, the experiences with Napoleon and the continental system reinforced the American belief that Europe remained the home of politically and morally corrupt politicians. George Washington's farewell advice on avoiding unnecessary entanglements with foreign powers received added emphasis through American experiences with Napoleon's economic system and Britain's cynical manipulation of American trade.

THE CONTINENTAL SYSTEM UNDERMINED

While Napoleon had substantial success in disrupting American-British trade, he found it difficult to achieve the larger objective: excluding British and British-controlled neutral trade from the Continent except on terms disadvantageous to Britain. The continental system continued to spring leaks. Portugal and Spain—particularly following the insurrection in Spain in 1808—served as ports of entry for goods from Britain and its colonies. In addition, Britain used depots along the coast of Europe as smuggling centers. British merchants crowded into these centers in great numbers in order to conduct business. From Helgoland in the North Sea, smuggled British and neutral goods made their way to Leipzig, Basel, Strasbourg, and Frankfurt. In the Baltic, Göteborg became the center for goods forwarded to Prussia, Poland, and Russia. Gibraltar, Sardinia, Sicily, the Dalmatian and Ionian Islands, and Malta most of all served as the depots for British goods in the Mediterranean. After Britain gained a foothold in Turkey in 1809, Belgrade and Hungary received British goods forwarded from Salonika and Constantinople. As late as 1810, Britain bought over 80 percent of its wheat from France or its allies.

Napoleon's need for money likewise undermined the continental system. Growth of an enormous smuggling trade deprived Napoleon's empire of desperately needed tax revenues. Searching for monies to pursue his campaign against Austria in 1809, Napoleon recognized the necessity to stem this tax loss and accordingly established a system of licensed trade in 1809 and 1810. For a time, Napoleon directly supervised granting these licenses. At first a secret operation, the license system was formalized through the Decree of St. Cloud on 5 July 1810. Licenses were sold for substantial, varying fees but often costing £14. In providing trading licenses, Napoleon virtually negated the rationale of his system. He angered his continental allies and associates by granting licenses in such a way that French economic needs and promotion of the French merchant marine were given first consideration. Needed British goods now flowed freely and legally into French ports. Coupled with the license system came the Trianon Decree of 5 August 1810, which raised tariffs on colonial goods to an exorbitant degree, so high in fact that smugglers saw nothing but good in the measure. Napoleon's need to build his war chest thus led him to abandon the continental self-blockade, but he did so in such a way that he made it appear the French empire had no higher purpose than the enhancement of French interests. He also confused both allies and enemies, for while the license system seemed designed to negate the smuggling trade, the new tariff rates furnished considerable incentive for the smuggling to continue.

Napoleon never formally ended the continental system, but inauguration of the license system in 1809 and adoption of the Trianon tariff rates in 1810 marked its virtual abandonment. The defection of Russia in 1810 proved the single greatest blow to the continental system, one that made further enforcement efforts ludicrous. Following Napoleon's downfall, the restored Bourbon regime quickly swept away the various edicts of the continental system. All that remained were the milder enactments of the commercial legislation passed between 1791 and 1793 and the continuing firm conviction that French trade and industry must be sheltered from foreign competition.

The continental system revealed the scope and some of the limitations of Napoleon's thinking and planning. It was Eurocentric in its focus, was dependent upon the Grand Army for its success, was nationalistic and traditional in its emphasis upon the promotion of French interests, and was parochial in assessing how far sea power could assist England in escaping Napoleon's net. He pursued his plan with method and a certain cunning but had to modify it drastically when resistance grew too great. Unfortunately for Napoleon the continental system proved politically counterproductive in that it fostered increasing hostility to French hegemony within Europe. Napoleon even had to dismiss his own brother, Louis, as king of Holland when he refused to prevent Dutch smuggling with England. Russia's failure to enforce the system after 1810 played a part in turning Napoleon toward his fateful venture to conquer Russia.

In terms of its primary goal, the continental system proved a failure. Britain suffered severely but devised a successful smuggling system to satisfy continental markets, developed new markets in Latin America and East Asia, and traded freely with the colonies of France. The war that Napoleon helped to provoke between Britain and the United States played no part in determining his larger destinies.

BIBLIOGRAPHY

Bonnel, Ulane. *La France, les États-Unis, et la guerre de course, 1797–1815*. Paris, 1961. Describes in lucid fashion the effects of the continental system upon the United States.

Clauder, Anna C. *American Commerce as Affected by the Wars of the French Revolution and Napoleon, 1793–1812*. Philadelphia, 1932. An old but useful analysis of trade statistics and maritime regulations.

Crosby, Alfred W. *America, Russia, Hemp, and Napoleon: American Trade with Russia and the Baltics, 1783–1812*. Columbus, Ohio, 1965. An important study for understanding why the continental system never effectively excluded neutral and British commerce from Europe.

Heckscher, Eli F. *The Continental System: An Economic Interpretation*. Oxford and New York, 1922. Especially useful in understanding the historical background to the continental system and provides a detailed analysis of the continental response to the blockade.

Hickey, Donald R. *The War of 1812: A Forgotten Conflict*. Urbana and Chicago, 1990. The account of the Hartford Convention of 1814–1815 emphasizes that the twenty-six New England delegates, led by Harrison Gray Otis, were never secession-minded.

McCoy, Drew R. *The Elusive Republic: Political Economy in Jeffersonian America*. Chapel Hill, N.C., 1980. Places Republican foreign policy within the goals they sought for establishing a domestic society, emphasizing land and trade expansion, creation of virtuous individual citizens, and a better, more humane world.

Mahan, Alfred Thayer. *The Influence of Sea Power upon the French Revolution and Empire, 1793–1812*. 2 vols. London, 1892. Demonstrates the difficulties Napoleon experienced in effectively countering the naval power of Britain.

Perkins, Bradford. *Prologue to War: England and the United States, 1805–1812*. Berkeley; Calif., 1961. Critical of Jeffersonian policies, the book is especially strong on the domestic political factors both in America and England that shaped policies leading to war.

Schon, Alan. *Napoleon Bonaparte*. New York, 1997. This single-volume biography, covering all of Napoleon's major activities, places his economic policies in the context of his larger ambitions.

Sears, Louis Martin. *Jefferson and the Embargo*. Durham, N.C., 1927. Supports Jefferson's positions on several disputed issues.

Spivak, Burton. *Jefferson's English Crisis: Commerce, Embargo, and the Republican Revolution*. Charlottesville, Va., 1979. Tells how English countermeasures to French policies brought both political and ideological crises upon Jefferson.

Tucker, Robert W., and David C. Hendrickson. *Empire of Liberty: The Statecraft of Thomas Jefferson*. New York, 1990. The authors are critical of Jefferson's failure to understand that America's future, and the creation of a better world, remained closely tied to the survival of England. They believe Jefferson virtually sided with Napoleon and the continental system.

Varg, Paul A. *Foreign Policies of the Founding Fathers*. East Lansing, Mich., 1963. Provides an astute analysis of the practical and ideological components in the thinking of Jefferson and Madison concerning foreign affairs.

See also BLOCKADES; ECONOMIC POLICY AND THEORY; NAVAL DIPLOMACY; NEUTRALITY.

COVERT OPERATIONS

John Prados

Unlike many concepts in foreign affairs, the secret, sub rosa practice of covert operations has a formal definition officially approved by the president of the United States and embodied in a National Security Council (NSC) directive. According to NSC Directive 10/2, approved on 18 June 1948, a covert operation is an activity sponsored by the United States government against foreign states or groups that is so planned and executed that U.S. responsibility for it is not evident to an unauthorized person and that, if uncovered, the government can plausibly deny responsibility for the action. The operation could be unilateral, in support of a foreign state or group, and have a state or nonstate target—the key aspect is that the activity remain secret. Although not provided for in Directive 10/2, covert operations also can be conducted unilaterally or in conjunction with other friendly, or even adversary, intelligence services in pursuit of common objectives and goals.

Beneath the formal definition, the kinds of activity involved in covert operations fall into a number of broad categories. Chief among these are political action, paramilitary activity, psychological warfare, and economic warfare. The evolution of technology suggests strongly that operational incentives in intelligence work will shortly add a new broad category of cyberaction or computer warfare to the traditional covert action menu. A large-scale covert operation usually has components that involve many or all of these categories.

In political action the object is to influence the internal situation in a foreign country by manipulating local political conditions. Intervention in an election is at the high end of the scale in political action, and might involve financial support for candidates, media advice, technical support for public relations, get-out-the-vote or political organizing efforts, legal expertise, advertising campaigns, assistance with poll-watching, and other means of direct action. More subtly, local situations could be influenced by agents, such as officials of the country targeted for action making decisions in their official capacities that are in the interest of the political action. Mechanisms for creating and deepening opinions are of key importance in covert political action, which often therefore involves propaganda. Some of the earliest Central Intelligence Agency (CIA) covert operations were political actions to influence elections. At the beginning of the twenty-first century, global and domestic interests in democracy and democratic values were such that intelligence agency political actions might be able to benefit from cooperation with or cover from private groups seeking to foment these kinds of institutions and values.

Political action may have objectives short of a change of government. This is particularly true given the perspective since the end of the Cold War, with nonstate actors increasingly dominating the attention of intelligence services. A hypothetical political action, one not known to be in progress but which very likely may be, would be an operation designed to worsen local conditions that permit drug cartels and international criminal enterprises to flourish.

In paramilitary operations the intelligence service (or military force) conducts activities similar to those of constituted military units. Again the target may be a nation or a nonstate actor, but the currency of influence will be force. An operation may involve unconventional warfare, such as commando raids, training, advice, equipment, or command of irregular forces; it may also include support of guerrilla activities, creation of secret networks to oppose an adversary even if a country falls, the active propagation of a coup d'état, collaboration with or reinforcement of local security forces (such as the creation of a security detachment to protect a foreign head of state), and other functions. A number of U.S. paramilitary initiatives during the Cold War period involved cooperation with third country intelligence or military services.

In psychological warfare the object is to mold opinion in the service of other activities, such as diplomacy, political action, paramilitary operations, or open warfare. Activities in psychological warfare run the gamut of the ways in which people absorb information. Traditionally, this has meant leaflets, newspapers, magazines, books, radio, and television, all of which have to be harnessed to convey the propaganda message appropriate to the operation. In the twenty-first century, techniques will expand to cover electronic communication by computer and the Internet as well, and intelligence services can create leaflets, finance books, journals, or television/radio programs. They may employ officers to work as journalists, recruit agents of influence, operate media outlets, plant certain stories or information in places it may come to public attention, or seek to deny and/or discredit information that is public knowledge. A distinction is made in psychological warfare regarding whether the target audience is permitted to be aware of the originator of the material they are receiving. In all such propaganda efforts, "black" operations denote those in which the audience is to be kept ignorant of the source; "white" efforts are those in which the originator openly acknowledges himself; and "gray" operations are those in which the source is partly but not fully acknowledged. In psychological warfare theory the attribution of a claim or piece of information included in a psychological warfare campaign has a bearing on the receptiveness of the audience, so that planners consider questions of black versus white carefully.

Economic warfare is aimed at the adversary's production capability and scientific-technological (research and development) base. Often used as part of paramilitary operations or psychological warfare, this technique reduces the target's actual output, retards innovation, or lends weight to claims being made in propaganda. A campaign of this kind may involve paramilitary-style commando raids to sabotage or demolish targets, or on-site actions by agents or sympathizers with identical aims. This variety of covert action can also involve semiopen measures such as preclusively or preemptively purchasing items on global markets to keep them out of the hands of the adversary, or diplomatic actions intended to reduce or eliminate international markets for the adversary's products. In fact, varieties of possible action are limited only by the imagination of practitioners.

EVOLUTION OF COVERT OPERATIONS

Under the general label of "subversion," covert operations in fact have a lengthy history in warfare. Fomentation of rebellions by agents of another power has occurred many times in history; examples are British plots with royalist agents against Napoleon (1800–1804), French schemes to overthrow the government of Mexico (1861–1867), German plots in Mexico, Persia, and Turkey (1912–1916), and various governments' machinations during the Spanish Civil War (1936–1939). Recruitment and employment of mercenaries, which can be categorized as a paramilitary activity, dates to at least the eleventh century, and accounts for a substantial fraction of forces in the field during periods of the Middle Ages. A major covert paramilitary operation, which eventually ended in full-scale military intervention, was France's provision of experts and equipment to rebels during the American Revolution (1777–1778). Spanish guerrillas fighting the French Empire (1807–1814) made a major contribution to the downfall of Napoleon I, while Boer commandos raiding into British South Africa (1895–1899) set the stage for the Second Boer War. An example of a political action would be the efforts of Sir William Stephenson and the unit he led, British Security Coordination, to encourage U.S. entry into World War II during 1940–1941.

While states and actors in international relations have always made efforts to convince audiences that their course is the righteous one, the targets of these information campaigns have shifted gradually over time. Propagandists in the American Revolution (1775–1783) sought to convince other Americans to support the rebellion and not the British Crown. In the French Revolution and the succeeding Napoleonic wars (1789–1815) the objects were similarly to justify actions by one's own side and denigrate the enemy. By the time of the Franco-Prussian War (1870–1871), when the Paris Commune printed leaflets it distributed to German soldiers in an effort to dissuade them from continuing the fight, the target of propaganda began shifting to the adversary side.

During World War I (1914–1918) the whole idea of propaganda was taken to a new level. Possibly because the question of who was responsible for that conflict was deemed so controversial, and possibly due to its intensity as modern "total" war, World War I brought a focused practice of propaganda. As the war continued, with frustrations mounting at the inability to achieve progress on the battlefront, and mutinies of soldiers in the French and Russian armies and sailors in the German navy, ideas for propaganda seemed more and more to have practical application. Propaganda coupled with political action figured in the German decision to provide a train and free passage home for Russian revolutionaries exiled in Switzerland, persons who eventually played key roles in the overthrow of the Russian monarchy. British propaganda in the United States plus astute leaks of intelligence (a telegram from the German foreign minister indicating an intention to conduct subversive activities in the Americas) had an important effect on the U.S. decision to enter the war.

There were more developments during the period 1919–1939. Nazi Germany for the first time created a cabinet-level government department named the Ministry of Propaganda. Since that time the propaganda and public relations roles of officials working in the information ministries of many nations have come to overshadow their role of providing knowledge to citizens. The Germans also created templates for effective propaganda techniques and built theories around them. Although the term "psychological warfare" is best credited to World War II, the main techniques and tenets of the theory existed by the 1930s and were tested by Germany, Italy, and Russia in their interventions in the Spanish Civil War. The Spanish war also proved important to the evolution of paramilitary operations, with the phrase "fifth column" used to denote a (subversive) force that attacks the adversary from within at the orders of an external foe, originating in that civil war.

World War II (1939–1945) featured the use of covert operations by all sides and the introduction of almost all the techniques utilized in modern times. The style of political manipulation used by Germany in Norway, Hungary, Romania, by Japan in India, Burma, French Indochina, by Great Britain in the Middle East, and by the United States in French North Africa all carried traditional propaganda activities to a new level and essentially created modern political action. The rise of popular resistance movements, to Germany in Europe—and to Japan in the Philippines, Burma, and China—brought demands for external assistance and led to the creation of organizations specialized in working with guerrilla movements, such as Great Britain's Special Opera-

tions Executive (SOE). The ability of the resistance movements to conduct systematic activities behind enemy lines, including both simple espionage and more forceful sabotage and ambush, affirmed the notion that a "fifth column" could function, leading to the postwar creation of "stay-behind networks" intended to replicate the functions of the World War II resistance. At the same time, the notion of supplementing resistance activities with teams of specialists from the outside, and reinforcing their actions with carefully targeted commando raids, added depth and comprehensiveness to the entire endeavor. This carried paramilitary operations to a new level as well.

One resistance function added sabotage to older forms of subversion. Sabotage was used against enemy transportation systems, communications networks, and war production. These tactics could be useful in specific situations, such as the work of the French resistance in hampering German transport, and thus the response to the 1944 invasion of Normandy. The technique could also work generally, reducing war production or inflicting delays on critical shipments. In the sense of World War II as a "total" war, the subversive effort against the enemy war economy could be fitted together with regular military operations, such as the bombing of factories, and with import-export controls, preclusive buying of raw materials, and other measures to affect the adversary's economy. The experience brought a realization that a nation could wage economic warfare. Ultimately this added a new category to the varieties of covert operations.

Psychological warfare also attained new levels during World War II. The growth of electronic means of communication started before the war, and by 1939 had reached the point that broadcast radio was widely distributed among populations in every nation. This created a new field for the dissemination of propaganda, and every belligerent was careful to put its message on the airwaves. By the same token, one could mimic and masquerade as the enemy's radio broadcasters, gaining credibility for a propaganda message that might otherwise be rejected. This in turn opened a field in "black" and "gray" media operations, which pretended to various degrees to be those of the adversary.

In leaflets and newspapers and other older techniques, World War II brought a more systematic approach to psychological warfare. Scientific research became a major contributor, with theories of how people absorb information, how they build belief systems, and why people change their minds. Psychological warfare planners began to make decisions on complete campaigns, with comprehensive activities in many media, consistent themes across the different forms, messages evolving over time (and modified to take into account actual developments on the war fronts), and specific goals and objectives. Opinion research and prisoner interrogation became an important guide for ways to frame the psychological warfare themes.

A further major development of World War II would be that belligerents realized that these distinct elements of covert operations could be combined into coherent efforts with multiple facets. In addition, one could build a "strategy," specific plans using numerous tactics to gain particular objectives. It is instructive that in at least three of the crucial war theaters of 1939–1945—western Europe, the Middle East, and Southeast/East Asia—the Anglo-American alliance created specialized headquarters to control all covert operations.

One more innovation of the 1939–1945 period was the creation of national-level organizations to carry out these activities. On the American side, for example, it is of interest that the initial entity in this field was formed to manage propaganda activity. This unit, the Office of the Coordinator of Information, soon metamorphosed into the Office of Strategic Services (OSS), a national intelligence organization headed by the same individual (William J. Donovan). The propaganda function continued to be consolidated, but under a second entity, the Office of War Information. Over a very short time the OSS became a full-service intelligence organization. Its branches for intelligence reporting (Research and Analysis), counterespionage (called X-2), and spying (Special Intelligence) were under a deputy director for intelligence and are not of concern here. But the OSS had a separate directorate for operations and that included branches for special operations (which worked with resistance networks), morale operations (for psychological warfare of the "black" and "gray" varieties), a set of operations groups (middle-size commando units tasked with specific targets), a maritime unit (for naval covert operations where necessary, but mainly to transport OSS officers and supply shipments to points behind enemy lines), and a special projects office (a parallel activity for highly sensitive operations, especially ones related to then-exotic weapons, such as atomic bombs or biological

weaponry). At its late-1944 peak the OSS employed almost 13,000 men and women, about 7,500 of them overseas, with a fiscal year 1945 budget (in then-year dollars) of $43 million.

At the field level, OSS operations were carried out by "detachments." For example, OSS Detachment 101 served in Burma and mobilized an army of Kachin tribesmen against the Japanese. Detachment 202 worked in China, training nationalist Chinese, carrying out some sabotage missions, and having some contacts with the Chinese communists. In Europe, OSS detachments worked in the Mediterranean, where they assisted resistance forces in Greece, Albania, Yugoslavia, and later in northern Italy. These operations succeeded an initial OSS penetration into French North Africa, from which later activities were controlled. Western European activities were controlled from London and included paramilitary actions in France, Norway, Germany, and Austria. In every one of these areas the OSS maintained a delicate relationship with allies, including secret services of Great Britain, France, and China. The covert operators of the OSS simultaneously learned from their allies and cooperated with them, but the nations frequently had cross-cutting purposes in local situations.

With the end of the war, President Harry S. Truman reorganized U.S. intelligence. Believing the existing OSS to have become superfluous, Truman dissolved it on 20 September 1945. The organization's analytical arm was folded into the Department of State as the Office of Research and Intelligence. The OSS espionage elements were attached to the Department of War as the Strategic Services Unit (SSU). Field detachments were broken up, with some personnel continuing on with the SSU, some going to related groups like the army's Counterintelligence Corps, and others demobilized. Psychological warfare capability at a reduced level continued within the army, and its ranger battalions contained whatever commando and unconventional warfare capability remained. The capacity for conducting paramilitary operations was entirely eliminated.

Two factors combined to change the system introduced in the immediate postwar period. One was President Truman's continuing dissatisfaction with the organizational structure of U.S. intelligence. In January 1946, Truman introduced an executive oversight body he called the National Intelligence Authority to supervise the work of a new director of central intelligence (DCI) who would run a central intelligence group. The new arrangement continued to be unsatisfactory and in 1947, when Truman designated omnibus legislation to deal with universal military training, create a national military establishment and secretary of defense, as well as the National Security Council, the president included provisions for the new Central Intelligence Agency (CIA).

Signed into law on 26 July 1947, the National Security Act of 1947 continues to this day as the statutory authority underlying the CIA. Apart from laws that govern restricted aspects of intelligence work, such as retirement policy, the DCI's responsibility to safeguard sources and methods, the public identification of undercover intelligence officers, and the like, the 1947 act is the only charter the agency has. This is significant for covert operations because the 1947 act says nothing about them. Instead, all covert operations (and many other CIA activities as well) have been based on a single clause of the law, which states that the CIA can "perform such other functions and duties related to intelligence affecting the national security as the National Security Council may from time to time direct." The mandate was simultaneously incredibly broad, very thin, and ambiguous, so much so that on at least four occasions (1947, 1962, 1969, and 1974) lawyers in the office of the CIA's general counsel warned that the statutory authorization was insufficient to cover covert operations.

The second factor that transformed intelligence roles and missions was the growth of hostility between the United States and Russia, which gave rise to the Cold War. This ideological conflict pitted democratic ideals against the authoritarian communist politics of Russia (then called the Union of Soviet Socialist Republics). The Cold War struggle seemed to call for the kind of all-out commitment, including covert operations, that had characterized World War II. Thus the NSC directive on covert operations made explicit reference to communism and Russia in establishing provisions for covert action.

In response to demands for action the U.S. intelligence community and the executive branch quickly devised new entities for covert operations. The CIA, Department of State, and military pooled personnel and resources to form the Office of Policy Coordination (OPC), which assumed the mantle of authority. The NSC 10/2 directive had specifically ordered the CIA to create the Office of Special Projects, much like the OSS did, for this purpose, and this unit, renamed OPC, also absorbed the Special Procedures Group the CIA had formed to carry out psychological warfare in December 1947. By 1949, OPC had 302 personnel, seven overseas stations, and a budget of $4.7 million. By 1952 personnel had risen to 2,812 plus 3,142 contract employees, who were spending $82 million and working from forty-seven overseas stations.

One of the first major U.S. covert operations was intervention in Italian politics in 1947–1948 to prevent an electoral victory by the Italian communist party. This political action started a lengthy involvement in Italy, which continued through at least the 1970s; it also set the standard for CIA political action programs. A similar intervention in France was designed to weaken the French communist party, while actions on the propaganda/psychological warfare front included funding journals and newspapers (the CIA would have a controlling interest in the *Rome Daily American,* for example), the Congress for Cultural Freedom, the World Assembly of Youth, the "gray" broadcast station Radio Free Europe, and the "black" (at least initially) station Radio Liberty. Both the CIA and OPC began programs to furnish financial support to publications and books deemed suitable for advancing the anticommunist cause, and money was laundered through the Marshall Plan and the Ford Foundation among others. Much of this knowledge emerged in a spate of revelations in 1967, forcing President Lyndon B. Johnson to appoint a special commission under deputy attorney general Nicolas deB. Katzenbach to investigate these political actions. One lesson that would be repeatedly relearned is that covert operations are fraught with political consequence for the initiator as well as the target.

Paramilitary operations got under way in collaboration with the British Secret Intelligence Service (SIS). The Americans made a start in 1950–1952 by joining in an attempt to overthrow the communist government of Albania. The OPC, by this time, had lost its institutional independence and become part of the Directorate of Plans (DDP) within the CIA (in another 1952 reorganization the OPC and the directorate's other major unit, the espionage-centered Office of Special Operations, would be entirely merged) so that the actor on the American side of these operations was officially CIA. The CIA and SIS were allied in paramilitary operations into Russia (now Ukraine and Belarus), Estonia, Latvia, and Lithuania. Much of the burden in those operations was carried by the SIS, but in Poland, where there would be another combined paramilitary-political action, the CIA carried the burden. Every one of these operations was known to the adversary and had been penetrated by means of the Russians placing spies of their own within the CIA–SIS apparatus. All the operations failed by 1953. (However, it should be noted that anticommunist Russians continued efforts to make some kind of inroad into the USSR until at least the late 1950s.) The CIA moved on to greener pastures. The lesson here would be that covert operations against the communist enemy—the mandated target when the CIA created its covert operations program—were too difficult to carry out.

In general, operations proved most successful where the CIA had freedom of movement and good access, which in this period meant western Europe. A particular concern was the creation of stay-behind networks that would function just like the World War II resistance had in the event the Russians overran western Europe in a future war. Such nets were successfully created in virtually every western European country from Italy to Norway, including neutrals such as Sweden and even nations under military occupation like Austria. In some countries the secret networks were tied in to North Atlantic Treaty Organization (NATO) defense planning. In all of them the conservative political bent of adherents to the groups gave the CIA certain political contacts. Secrecy lasted for several decades, until a rash of detailed revelations during the early 1980s led to controversy, with parliamentary inquiries in more than one European country and attendant embarrassment for the United States. The lesson here contradicts an aphorism often heard from intelligence officers, that successes remain secret while only failures become known to the public. More accurately, every covert operation above a certain size will ultimately become known.

It would be during the early 1950s that the CIA's Directorate of Plans achieved its classic covert victories. One came in Iran in 1953 in conjunction with SIS, where the Americans and British induced an unusual coup in which a constitutional monarch overthrew the government of his own country. Here the shah of Iran, relying upon popular support of the CIA, had mobilized and ousted a left-wing populist cabinet to create a virtual military dictatorship. In another victory in 1954, the CIA overthrew the elected Labor Party (socialist to communist ideologically) government of Guatemala, through a combination of psychological warfare, paramilitary action by a

small force, and diplomatic pressure. Again the successor government was a military dictatorship.

The shah of Iran managed to hold on to power through the late 1970s by a combination of economic modernization and political repression, but the suppression of moderate political forces in his country forced opposition to align with a fundamentalist religious movement that ultimately toppled the shah in a 1979 revolution. At that time the U.S. embassy would be taken over, and American diplomats (and the officers of the CIA station) held hostage for 444 days, with the United States painted as the "Great Satan" to the Iranian public. In the years since the Iranian revolution, the United States was unable to restore a balanced relationship with Iran. Worse, the Iranians supported terrorist groups in the Middle East through the 1980s, which significantly harmed American interests and took lives, hostages, and made other depredations in a succession of incidents.

In Guatemala the military government installed by the covert operation replaced a democratic tradition and handed power to other military regimes or authoritarian oligarchies that maintained authority by high security. Beginning in 1968 the military inaugurated a war against the peasantry that endured into the late 1990s, leaving more than half the population of the country displaced internally and with a death toll in excess of 60,000.

A lesson here is that covert operations successes do not always lead to achievements to be proud of, possibly due to the moral, political, and empirical compromises necessary in pursuit of the short-term action. In addition, long-term effects can be more detrimental to U.S. interests than the improvements gained by the original success.

A further characteristic of these covert operations is that they were aimed not at Russia or its Soviet bloc but at Third World countries. The Dwight D. Eisenhower administration in the end would be very active in covert operations, all of them against putative communist foes, and almost all in the Third World. Among these were projects carried out in Vietnam (1954–1956 paramilitary efforts), Eastern Europe (1953–1956 psychological warfare), Indonesia (1958 paramilitary), Laos (1958 political action; 1959–on paramilitary), Tibet (1959–on paramilitary), Cuba (1960–on paramilitary and economic warfare), and Congo (1960–on). Eisenhower bequeathed to John F. Kennedy a number of these ongoing activities. President Kennedy actually assumed the entire blame for the dismal CIA failure at the Bay of Pigs in Cuba, an operation whose dimensions had been set by his predecessor.

Aside from its effects on world opinion of the United States and consequences in Latin American diplomacy, the Bay of Pigs failure had a major impact on U.S. national security policy overall. President Kennedy and his advisers were induced to review ways of making policy, approving covert operations, and U.S. capabilities for covert and unconventional warfare. Kennedy determined to make the U.S. military, not the CIA, responsible for all paramilitary activity that met certain criteria. Kennedy also credited the CIA failure with instilling in him a new attitude of skepticism regarding advice from government bureaucrats. Finally, at the most fundamental level, Kennedy intimates report that in the wake of the Bay of Pigs failure, the president actually considered breaking up the CIA.

While President Kennedy changed the way he did business, he did not reduce reliance on CIA covert operations. Kennedy continued all the covert actions that had been in progress when he came to office. Far from giving up on the Cuba action after the Bay of Pigs disaster, he ordered a renewed project called Mongoose. Kennedy added major covert operations in Vietnam. In fact, where the Eisenhower administration had approved 104 covert operations in eight years, Kennedy's approved 163 in slightly more than three years. From political action in British Guiana to reorganized activity in Africa, the CIA's work was global during this period. Part of the rise in numbers of approvals can be accounted for by more stringent rules on what kinds of covert operations required National Security Council subcommittee approval—one post–Bay of Pigs reform—but reliance on the method nevertheless remained strong.

Kennedy's rules on approvals began an evolution of procedures, each time more explicit, that endured at least through the 1980s and that came to involve Congress as well as the executive branch. Even under the Kennedy-Johnson rules, most covert actions never rose to the NSC level. The Richard M. Nixon administration added a requirement that its NSC monitoring unit, called the 40 Committee, review annually the covert operations that were in progress. In 1974 reporting requirements expanded into Congress, with the CIA required to report to eight different committees under the Hughes-Ryan Amendment. The agency chafed under this restriction and later won

a reduction in the reporting requirements to where notifications must go to the Select Intelligence Committee in the Senate and the Permanent Select Committee on Intelligence in the House of Representatives. A "presidential finding" that a given operation is in the national security interests of the United States is the required notification. These findings, in turn, came into question during the Iran-Contra affair of the late 1980s, which raised questions as to whether findings could be retroactive, unwritten ("mental" in the phrase of Attorney General Edwin Meese), furnished after the activities in question had been carried out, and so on. Reforms that followed clarified the presidential finding system such that the documents are provided in advance, kept current, that covert operations are of a certain size, and provide other important details.

For a brief period during the Gerald R. Ford administration (1976–1977) the executive branch maintained its own Intelligence Oversight Board to monitor the appropriateness and implementation of covert operations. Otherwise this has been among many functions of the President's Foreign Intelligence Advisory Board (PFIAB), except during the James Earl Carter administration (1977–1981) when that entity was temporarily abolished. Subject to presidential goals, style, and whims, such executive monitoring has been of limited utility; for example, it did not protect President Ronald Reagan (1981–1989) from the excesses of Iran-Contra or other difficulties attributable to high-handed actions by his director of central intelligence, William J. Casey. Meanwhile, the NSC group approving covert operations has gone through a series of identity changes: 303 Committee (Johnson administration), 40 Committee (Nixon/Ford administrations), NSC Special Coordinating Committee (Carter administration), National Security Planning Group (Reagan administration), NSC Deputies Committee (George H. W. Bush, William Jefferson Clinton, and George W. Bush administrations); but the unit has retained essentially the same membership in terms of the offices held by participants.

The Johnson administration ended the covert operation against Cuba and phased out CIA action in the Congo. However, it encouraged a coup in Ghana and brought major intelligence resources to bear in Bolivia against Che Guevara, a hero of the Cuban revolution. In Chile the Johnson administration carried out a political action during the 1964 elections to prevent any victory by Chilean socialists. In Asia, the Johnson-era

CIA terminated the Tibetan paramilitary operation, attempted a political action in Indonesia (1965–1966), and carried out full-scale secret wars in Laos and South Vietnam. Johnson also continued CIA funding for Radio Free Europe and Radio Liberty's "gray" psychological warfare campaign.

In 1971, during the Nixon administration, funding for the radios stopped, no longer supported by Congress. This administration continued the secret wars in South Vietnam and Laos and escalated the latter by bringing into it whole battalions and artillery units of third-country nationals (in this case, Thais). The CIA's Directorate of Plans was retitled the Directorate of Operations. To benefit Israel, the administration carried out a mid-intensity paramilitary campaign in Iraq, arming Kurdish tribesmen to fight the national government. Nixon's best-known covert operation would be a large-scale political action in Chile aimed at preventing the emergence of socialist government and, when that failed, at creating such economic and social dislocation in Chile that the government of President Salvador Allende would topple. That occurred in 1973, giving way to a military dictatorship that held sway until the early 1990s. At the close of the century, General Augusto Pinochet, leader of the Chilean military junta, was defending himself from an array of foreign and Chilean criminal indictments flowing from his takeover and governance. The shift in international legal norms toward greater attention to human rights issues, termination of sovereign immunity in mass murder cases, and the absence of a statute of limitations for war crimes complicated recruitment for covert operations in the twenty-first century.

The end of America's Vietnam War (1961–1975), in which U.S. combat operations terminated in early 1973, brought a reduction in CIA covert operations capabilities as experts retired, their contracts were not renewed, and CIA proprietaries such as Air America were liquidated. One consequence would be fewer covert operations through the 1970s. The Ford administration initiated one significant paramilitary campaign in Angola, against a socialist majority party backed by Cubans and Russians. Halted by a Senate amendment prohibiting expenditure of funds, the Angola action attained the distinction of being the only covert operation formally ended by a congressional vote. The Carter administration worried about Angola but focused its covert efforts in west Africa and particularly Afghanistan, after the Rus-

sian intervention there at the end of 1979. The latter would be a fresh CIA multilateral initiative, with Egypt, Saudi Arabia, Pakistan, and China enlisted to assist a paramilitary effort.

William J. Casey ran the CIA for the Reagan administration between 1981 and 1987. This period was more active for covert operations than any time since the Eisenhower years. Under Casey the CIA resumed covert assistance in Angola and conducted additional paramilitary campaigns in Mozambique, Chad/Libya, Ethiopia, Cambodia, Iran, and Nicaragua. It was reported in 1984 that fifty major covert operations were in progress at that time as compared to ten during the final year of the Carter administration.

An operation the CIA conducted at a low level in Cambodia had the United States in support of a communist faction that had murdered more than a million people when it was in power. In both Cambodia and Afghanistan, the United States was allied with erstwhile enemy the People's Republic of China. Afghanistan would be the closest the CIA came to a classic covert victory in the 1980s. Fundamentalist Muslim groups—armed by the CIA and trained by the United States—and Pakistan fought the Russians to a standstill and forced them to withdraw in 1989. But neither the CIA nor the Russians stopped aid to their respective factions in Afghanistan until 1992; a decade later fighting was still disrupting that country and had brought to power a faction that shielded terrorists whom the United States considered a major threat to its national security. Worse still, the terrorists benefited from CIA training—Arabs actually have a term, "American Afghan," for Muslim fundamentalist fighters who got their start in the CIA war of 1980–1989—and the sophisticated weapons the agency provided. In the wake of the 11 September 2001 terrorist strikes on New York City and Washington, D.C., one irony would be the fact that this action could lead the United States into an alliance with Russia in a further covert operation in Afghanistan.

In Latin America a CIA covert operation of the Reagan years led to a constitutional crisis in the United States. This was the paramilitary effort against the communist Sandinista government in Nicaragua. Standard paramilitary tactics proved ineffective enough that the CIA resorted to third-country nationals and a CIA-directed ("unilateral" is the term) mining campaign against Nicaraguan ports. The CIA then misled Congress about these actions, resulting in a suspension of funds to the agency campaign. The zealous CIA director Casey combined with White House NSC staff aides to run the covert operation outside the system, using money derived from the sale of weapons to Iran. This involved President Reagan in several violations of U.S. law and called his leadership into question. The formal CIA program eventually resumed, and a negotiated end to Central American fighting ended the bloodshed, but in the United States a special prosecutor appointed by the court continued investigations and prosecutions of officials involved in these events until well into the administration of President George H. W. Bush.

Covert actions did not end with Reagan. In the Bush administration there were CIA paramilitary efforts in Iraq after the Gulf War of 1991 and in Panama (1989). The CIA would also become quite involved in political action in Somalia in conjunction with the U.S. humanitarian intervention there (1992–1993). For the most part, however, the time is too recent to report very much regarding covert operations during either the administrations of George H. W. Bush, Bill Clinton, and George W. Bush. Judging from the policy statements, however, a high proportion of these can be expected to have been against such "nonstate actors" as drug cartels and terrorist groups. Prime examples are the actions initiated globally by the United States following the terrorist attacks on 11 September 2001.

PROBLEMS OF COVERT OPERATIONS

It is significant that capabilities which the United States created to wage an ideological war against Russian communism have found their primary use against small nations in the Third World. In the aftermath of the Cold War, when American democratic ideals were extolled, the fact that covert operations posed an implicit political, paramilitary, and psychological warfare challenge to national self-determination in the Third World detracted from the luster of the United States. Suspicion of U.S. motives will also follow from public knowledge of the existence and practice of covert operations techniques.

It is problematic that more than fifty years after the creation of the Central Intelligence Agency no fundamental law existed that defined in detail the authority and responsibilities of U.S. intelligence. It remained questionable whether the legal authority to conduct covert operations

exists in U.S. law. Part of the recurring struggle over the approval and authorization for covert operations arose precisely because the charter for the mission remained ambiguous. If the public adopted a different understanding of "intelligence matters" or rejected an expansive definition of "national security," the limited legal framework provided by the National Security Act of 1947 would disappear instantly.

Covert operations also takes the CIA, and U.S. intelligence more broadly, out of its ideal role of informing statecraft. In a covert operation the CIA is an action agency, with practical policy interests and a need to advocate them. This puts the agency into the ranks of the rest of the government, arguing options and furnishing a rationale to slant the intelligence analysis, the objectivity of which is crucial to policymakers.

From the standpoint of control and management, there is little evidence that the CIA and other agencies, including military agencies, are out-of-control, "rogue elephants" in the idiom of the 1970s. The danger is more one of overzealousness in the implementation of presidential directives, as demonstrated in the Iran-Contra affair. A process of continual review is necessary to supervise covert operations.

From the standpoint of diplomacy, covert operations are a complicating factor. The degree of covert activism contributes to a global image of the United States, and established images would be difficult to change even if the United States were to cease the practice of covert operations. Moreover, actions taken in the past can influence present events, even the far distant past and the modernist present as in the case of Iran. Covert operations also have unanticipated consequences both foreign and domestic, especially where overzealous operators exceed instructions.

Unfortunately, presidents almost always have a full plate of vital issues of the day. They rarely have the opportunity for the detailed examination and management of covert operations, as Kennedy learned painfully from the Bay of Pigs. The formula of using an NSC subcommittee for control has limitations of its own, and congressional oversight has been a two-edged sword. In short, problems of management have persisted and are likely to do so. On the other hand, covert operations have been seductive, promising action on intractable international situations seemingly outside the awkward framework of war powers, nonintervention in the internal affairs of foreign nations, and coping for ways to get at nonstate actors. Some, especially former practitioners, hold up covert operations as a "third option" between doing nothing and going to war. The likelihood is that post–Cold War covert operations will be frequent, and that existing difficulties with the technique will endure.

BIBLIOGRAPHY

Higgins, Trumbull. *The Perfect Failure: Kennedy, Eisenhower, and the CIA at the Bay of Pigs.* New York, 1987. Presents a detailed analysis of one of the most spectacular covert operations failures.

Johnson, Loch K. *Secret Agencies: U.S. Intelligence in a Hostile World.* New Haven, Conn., 1996. An overview of intelligence with insightful comments on covert operations.

Kwitney, Jonathon. *Endless Enemies: The Making of an Unfriendly World.* New York, 1984. Shows several examples of a process by which covert operations rebound to the detriment of the United States.

Moser, Charles, ed. *Combat on Communist Territory.* Washington, D.C., 1985. Essays that examine progress in various countries at the high point of Reagan-era covert operations.

Prados, John. *Presidents' Secret Wars: CIA and Pentagon Covert Operations from World War II Through the Persian Gulf.* An in-depth survey of covert operations in which the author demonstrates common features and problems of use of these techniques. Rev. ed. Chicago, 1996.

Shackley, Theodore. *The Third Option: An American View of Counterinsurgency Operations.* New York, 1981. Argues for covert operations as a cost-effective alternative to military action.

Treverton, Gregory F. *Covert Action: The Limits of Intervention in the Postwar World.* New York, 1987. An investigator for the Church Committee warns of the inadequacies of covert action.

See also CONGRESSIONAL POWER; INTELLIGENCE AND COUNTERINTELLIGENCE; INTERVENTION AND NONINTERVENTION; NATIONAL SECURITY COUNCIL; PRESIDENTIAL POWER.

CULTURAL IMPERIALISM

Jessica C. E. Gienow-Hecht

Jamie Uys's humorous yet moving film *The Gods Must Be Crazy* narrates the story of what happens when a pilot flying across the Kalahari Desert of Botswana drops a Coca-Cola bottle into the midst of a tribal group. The confused aboriginals explain the object as a gift from the gods. But the bottle challenges and destroys the traditions and social mores of their world. To defy the object's destructive influence, the tribe sends out one of its members to toss the evil thing over the edge of the earth, a distance the clan believes is some twenty days' walk away. Uys's movie was so popular on the international market that its producers created a sequel. *The Gods Must Be Crazy* offered a conspicuous sample of American consumer imperialism and its victimization of the Third World. Released in 1981, the film struck a vital chord in the middle of what has come to be known as "The Grand Debate": Have Americans become cultural imperialists? Do manufacturers, policymakers, and other interest groups attempt to conquer and corrupt the rest of the world by flooding it with consumer products made in the United States of America?

Since 1945, the study of cultural transfer has formed a powerful tool for the analysis of America's interaction with other nations. But in contrast to other approaches, neither historians nor their peers in neighboring fields have ever devised a clear-cut terminology. Indeed, they have not even employed a single line of argument. Originating in political think tanks after World War II, the investigation of cultural transfer has made its way through academic institutes the world over, until it finally arrived in the public sphere in the 1980s. By far the most popular—or notorious—approach has been termed "cultural imperialism," a notion and an ideology that appealed to a long list of supporters in the 1960s and after, and that—because of its persistence and influence—deserves the attention of all scholars interested in the study of culture and foreign rela-

tions. However, sociologists, historians, anthropologists, and others have suggested that the notion of "cultural imperialism" should be replaced with a more fluid term that avoids what they regard as the naive active-passive dominator-victim dualism. Alternative terms include, for example, "cultural transmission" and "transcultural interaction." Students of culture and foreign relations should therefore use these terms with great caution and realize that they are based on specific arguments and interpretations.

THREE TRENDS OF CULTURAL TRANSFER

Cultural transfer does not represent a single, static trend or a set of criteria. Most historians of cultural transfer probably would deny that they all belong to one school. The specific meaning of the term is neither timeless nor free of ideological underpinnings. Instead, each meaning is generated out of its various discourses, its use. Since World War II, the study of cultural transfer has developed in cycles. Hence, its significance must be interpreted through historical lenses. First, the cold warriors deplored the absence of an active and forceful cultural diplomacy among U.S. officials. In contrast, their descendants, the critics of cultural imperialism, described the export of American culture as thinly veiled global capitalist exploitation. Finally, a third group of countercritics challenged the concept of cultural imperialism with a variety of different arguments. At the turn of the twenty-first century, a rather heterogeneous group of scholars argued that local resistance either modified or completely stymied imports as part of a global process. Begun as a purely political debate, the discussion has expanded into an increasingly academic dispute over culture as an instrument of power that either "functioned" or "did not function."

Scholars of U.S. cultural transfer are primarily concerned about U.S. cultural influence in the world but also deal with foreign influences in the United States. In contrast to their peers working in the field of political history, they look beyond the level of decision-making processes to figure out how culture, especially the export and osmosis of culture, can be explained as an instrument of political or economic power, a tool of international communication, and a dynamic force on its own. In particular, they seek to find out how governmental and nongovernmental actors exerted power abroad by importing and exporting material goods and ideas as well as by creating international networks and organizations. In this context, culture, and American culture in particular, does not connote a specific meaning but rather a conglomeration of aspirations, emotions, and identities shared by human beings living within a geographically and politically defined area. "Culture," contemplates Akira Iriye (1997), "determines what the ends of a nation are; power proves the means for obtaining them."

Cultural imperialism is based on the assumption that one nation tries to force its culture, ideology, goods, and way of life on another country. In the United States, critics of cultural imperialism as an instrument of diplomacy study the extent to which American culture reached and influenced foreign shores under governmental and private auspices. On one end of the spectrum, historians interested in cultural imperialism argue that postwar U.S. policymakers made a conscious effort to export American culture abroad in order to gain access to raw materials, cheap labor, and new markets for U.S. consumer products. On the other end of the spectrum, scholars have proposed to supplant the notion of cultural imperialism with cultural transmission, which seeks to deemphasize the question of agency and, instead, admits a more fluid concept of interaction.

In the past the idea and study of cultural transfer has appealed to many audiences outside of the academic world. It is this appeal to both scholars and the broader public that distinguishes the significance of cultural imperialism and cultural transmission from most other theoretical concepts discussed among diplomatic historians. Whether they liked it or not, since at least the early days of the Cold War, journalists, politicians, and intellectuals have fretted over the power and meaning of American culture abroad.

Since at least the 1960s, cultural imperialism has proven to be a tremendously popular and enduring concept. It has introduced culture as a variable into the study of foreign relations and thereby has significantly broadened the field. It has built the foundation upon which more than two generations of historians have based their research strategies and arguments. It has penetrated many academic disciplines, including musicology, sports, sociology, and political science. And it has left a long-lasting mark in the public arena; politicians the world over, for example, lament the manipulative influx of U.S. movies. Tiny nations, remote people, and unknown tribes find their way into the headlines of international journals through their outspoken protests against Western cultural imperialism. From Iceland to Latin America, Central Africa to the Philippines, local spokesmen presumably mourn the decease of their indigenous mores and traditions that is coupled with the rise of Anglo-American television and culture.

In harmony with the public debate, several generations of academics have struggled with questions of cultural transfer. Despite the scholars' intergenerational hostility and despite historians' increasing urge to defy old approaches for new configurations, students who desire to labor in the vineyard of cultural transfer need to know these interpretations. Each of the three principal trends still finds its way into early-twenty-first-century historiographical debates—and rightfully so. For despite all the ideological baggage, each trend offers viable methodological insights for research related to the meaning of American culture in the international arena.

In the years following World War II, policymakers and intellectuals began to believe that cultural diplomacy and cultural images made a difference in global politics. This assumption seemed radical if not revolutionary for most observers at the time. In 1938, when the State Department established the Division for Cultural Relations, many U.S. officials still criticized the use of culture as a diplomatic tool. Their reluctance reflected a consensus that culture belonged to the realm of creativity, public taste, and free enterprise. How and why should one win diplomatic negotiations by invoking art, music, books, and theater performances? On a more basic level, cultural programs were costly and there were no voters abroad to legitimize such investments.

After 1945 the situation changed as both U.S. diplomats and intellectuals began arguing that the United States needed to sell the American way of life abroad. Public figures as well as policymakers, such as the State Department consultant Arthur W. MacMahon, media czar Henry Luce, and Senator William Fulbright, encouraged governmental authorities to make more of an effort to influence foreign nations through culture around the world. In the early Cold War years, consequently, the American government created a number of organizations and programs, such as the United States Information Agency and the Fulbright exchange program, that sought to sell American culture—including literature, music, and art—abroad. The USIA was founded with the specific purpose of developing a cultural propaganda program for audiences abroad and to develop them with a full and fair picture of American life, society, and culture. The Fulbright program was created right after World War II to enable foreign students (notably German students) to study in the United States and become acquainted with the American way of life. Likewise, the program sent (and still sends) U.S. academics abroad to learn about cultural differences but also to act as informal ambassadors of the United States.

Designed in 1950, the "Campaign of Truth" was supposed to represent a psychological counterattack against Soviet indoctrination. Employing books, brochures, exhibitions, and lectures, the campaign was aimed at public opinion leaders and other "multipliers."

One might wonder why policymakers grew so interested in the American way of life. Why did they suddenly seek to impart American culture to others? First, on the ideological level, American culture was dizzily democratic; anything was allowed. American culture also seemed essentially resistant to autocracies on the left or the right, as reflected in the postwar consensus on liberalism manifest in the writings of intellectuals like Arthur M. Schlesinger, Jr., Daniel Boorstin, and Louis Hartz. Consequently, U.S. policymakers and scholars were convinced that the promotion abroad of an enterprise-based culture would help to spread democracy around the world and contain fascism, communism, and other repellent foreign ideologies.

Second, and on a more practical level, communist regimes, above all in the German Democratic Republic (GDR), made *Bildung* (knowledge, education) and *Kultur* (high culture) pivotal points of their own propaganda. The GDR government claimed to be a democratic institution and it attacked American culture as a manifestation of a degenerate democracy. Communist offi-

cials knew that Europeans identified strongly with their high culture. Public opinion polls taken between 1945 and 1950 revealed that many Germans dreaded the adaptation of democratic values at the expense of their cultural heritage. Communist propagandists had convinced German audiences that they could be communists and, simultaneously, admirers of high culture, such as the romantic music of the nineteenth-century composer Pyotr Tchaikovsky. According to their propaganda, democratic audiences in the Western world, in contrast, supposedly "drugged" their minds with jazz.

Third, in the decade after World War II many Americans felt a deep apprehension over what they saw as their worsening reputation in a world of cultural diversity abroad—new cultures, new nations, and new arms. Shortly after the Soviets launched the satellite *Sputnik,* Franz M. Joseph and Raymond Aron edited a collection of articles under the telling title *As Others See Us* (1959). In this book, some twenty representatives from all over the world portrayed their countries' impression of American society. The French, Aron asserted, detested America's "big industry, mass production, the lowering of standards in favor of the masses," as well as its race problems, superficiality, "industrial barbarism," and "the intellectual fodder offered to the American masses, from scandal magazines to digests of books." In the end, the book represented a most depressing analysis of America's image abroad. Most people believed that "Americans had done remarkable things in production and they had technical 'know-how,' but America itself was . . . [a] giant with the head of a lout."

Academic and journalistic investigations of American cultural transfer abroad in the late 1950s and 1960s underlined the prevalent belief that American information and exchange efforts represented a timid reaction to the Soviets' dynamic propaganda. "America is the greatest advertising country in the world," the journalist Peter Grothe complained in 1958. "Yet when it comes to the most important advertising campaign of all—that of advertising ourselves and the democratic way of life—we run a poor second to the Communists." Grothe reproached U.S. policymakers for not having made the most of cultural relations programs after World War II, blaming the small-mindedness and indifference of the president, Congress, and the American public. And sociologists like Princeton University's W. Phillips Davison demanded more effective programs with clear-cut values, detailed purposes, and a rigid selection and training of personnel. They urged policymakers to employ American books, films, and information programs as instruments to acquaint people the world over with U.S. history, politics, and culture. All people, in short, needed more American culture, and it was the government's task to export it abroad.

The men and women who took part in this debate, it should be added, employed a rather unspecific idea of American culture. Historians investigating the United States Information Agency—designed in 1953 to convince people abroad that U.S. goals were in harmony with their hopes for freedom, progress, and peace—have underlined the uncertainty to define the core and the ins and outs of American culture. As Laura Belmonte and others have shown, USIA's programs focused on areas that were regarded as representative of American culture and society, including consumer products, high living standards, and the advantages of a free-market economy. But throughout the 1950s the agency was hampered by conflicts over the content of its agenda and its mission. Michael Krenn has shown that at the World's Fair of 1958, endless debates over how to deal with the United States's "Achilles' heel" of race relations inhibited the entire organization of the U.S. exhibit.

In sum, until the 1960s the debate over the export of American culture remained primarily a political one. Its participants were civil servants, writers, and journalists who viewed the government's developing cultural programs abroad as worthy although insufficient weapons to contain totalitarianism in the world. These men and women did not ask whether foreign audiences would welcome such messages.

THE EMERGENCE OF A CULTURAL IMPERIALISM CRITIQUE

But in the late 1950s and early 1960s concern over the implications of American culture bounced back to Europe, where it inspired a debate that would dominate academia for the next thirty years. Indeed, academics everywhere increasingly internalized the debate on U.S. culture abroad but they also dramatically revised previous assessments. A blooming leftist movement associated capitalism with a host of things characteristic of twentieth-century society, including consumerism, modernity, bureaucratic "soulless" organization, and the

conflict between society and the individual. Their findings would lay the groundwork for the study of U.S. cultural imperialism.

Again, the theme—a critical interpretation of American culture in the world—was not entirely new. Since the early 1900s, if not before, European conservatives such as D. H. Lawrence and Adolf Halfeld had criticized American civilization for its lack of soul and education. Americans, these writers argued, scoffed at high culture. Americans' essential national identity and values, such as productivity, efficiency, and rationality, stood in contrast to the most fundamental characteristics of Kultur, including quality work, contemplation, and the creative use of leisure. Many observers, that is, interpreted American civilization not just as plainly different from but as a treacherous threat to European culture.

The critics of the early 1900s found a faithful audience among post–World War II intellectuals. In the 1940s and 1950s, European leftists also began worrying about American influences, such as McCarthyism and consumerism. Horror-stricken at the term "mass," the Frankfurt School, a group of philosophers, sociologists, and historians, viewed the United States as a mass society with a mass culture that annihilated liberty, democracy, and individualism. The sociologist Herbert Marcuse stated that Americans represented a prime example of how human existence in advanced industrial societies remained passive, acquiescent, and unaware of its own alienation. In his writings, Marcuse developed the image of the "one-dimensional man" (the title of one of his books), an individual incapable of thinking dialectically and of questioning his society. Instead, humans had willfully subordinated themselves to the domination of technology and the principles of efficiency, productivity, and conformity.

The Frankfurt School was particularly worried about the demise of Kultur. Intellectual leaders such as Max Horkheimer, Theodor W. Adorno, and Leo Lowenthal devised a theory based on Marxism that stressed the subliminal totalitarianism of news agencies, television, and broadcasting. Fostered by the media, American capitalism had turned into an economically and culturally repressive force. High culture no longer represented a foreign, opposing, and transcendental sphere that contrasted with reality. Instead, in the struggle between East and West, Kultur (that is, the individual philosopher, the preservation of theory, art, and high culture) had mutated into a propaganda tool and, thus, to a consumer good.

By materializing and mass-producing aspects of high culture, modern humankind had mutilated its original meaning.

The Frankfurt School influenced more than a generation of American thinkers. Disillusionment originating from the Vietnam War and domestic urban and student revolts captivated a culturally influential segment of Americans who came to condemn both the free-market economy and the U.S. government. The promotion of democracy by the United States seemed hypocritical and meaningless in the age of napalm bombs and the Watts riots. Journalists and scholars such as David Riesman, C. Wright Mills, Vance Packard, and William H. Whyte studied the subject of the mass media in the 1940s and 1950s. They believed that the United States was the dominant promoter of capitalism around the globe and concluded from their study of the mass media that it represented a tool of U.S. capitalist ideology, perpetuating U.S. capitalism at home and abroad. To criticize the United States for its military involvement in the Third World, notably Vietnam, implied automatically a critique of American capitalism proper. Capitalism was bad because it threatened human wholeness, true individuality, the sense of community, social bonds, self-realization, and authentic values.

This critical interpretation of the nature of American capitalism profoundly influenced the writing on U.S. foreign relations. Discontent with the "realist" approach of historians such as George Kennan, Hans Morgenthau, and others, a new generation of "revisionists" shifted the study of the international system to the impact of domestic ideology as well as economic and social forces on U.S. diplomacy. And as American society grew wealthier, critics turned their attention away from the American working class to suppressed domestic minorities and the Third World, where they found that American capitalism, in search of new markets, raw materials, and cheap labor, acted as a victimizer, brutalizer, and exploiter. The making of American diplomacy had to be seen as part of America's capitalist political economy, argued New Left historians such as William Appleman Williams, because the health and persistence of the domestic economy depended on ever-expanding markets abroad. Williams, Gabriel Kolko, and others stressed the economic motivations of U.S. diplomacy and, thus, turned the investigation of the East-West conflict into a struggle between capitalism and socialism. U.S. policymakers constituted the foremost guilty party in this scheme because their actions were motivated solely by their greed, their quest for new markets that the Soviet Union did not even want.

The historiography of U.S. economic and political imperialism formed the foundation for the study of cultural imperialism. Although the term "cultural imperialism" had appeared in scholarly analyses before, it was only in the 1960s that this critique came to be a catchword as well as a coherent argument. The 1977 edition of the *Harper Dictionary of Modern Thought* defines cultural imperialism as "the use of political and economic power to exalt and spread the values and habits of a foreign culture at the expense of a native culture." Critics of cultural imperialism were united in their portrayal of Western culture as an expansive, predatory force. They cast their critique in a structuralist framework that associates political ideas with an underlying discourse that, in turn, shapes the entire culture in the context of which such ideas are expressed. Unlike the discussants of the 1950s, who had called for more American culture abroad, the critics of cultural imperialism reproached the U.S. government and the business community for spreading that culture beyond U.S. borders.

FOUR DISCOURSES ON CULTURAL IMPERIALISM

John Tomlinson developed a most insightful critique, on the basis of which we can identify at least four different discourses of cultural imperialism. His categories are the media, national domination, the global dominance of capitalism, and the critique of modernity. Media imperialism is the oldest and by far most widely debated category. Most importantly, it relates to current political issues. The study of media imperialism originated in Latin America among students of communication research. In the 1950s and 1960s, Latin American economists interpreted their countries' economic relations to Europe and the United States by developing a theory of dependency. Chilean communication scholars quickly appropriated that concept when, at the time of the 1970 election that brought Salvador Allende to power, they began to admonish the United States for its involvement in Latin American affairs. One of the most dramatic and widely read essays written by these scholars came from Armand Mattelart, a professor of mass communications and ideology at the University of Chile, and Ariel Dorfman, a literary critic and novelist. In *Para leer al pato Donald* ("How to Read Donald Duck," 1971), they held that in an effort to protect U.S. economic interests in Chile, the Central Intelligence Agency financed and fostered an arsenal of psychological warfare devices to indoctrinate the minds of the Chilean people, including Disney cartoons and other consumer products. They denounced Hollywood's distorted version of reality and cautioned Latin Americans against U.S. propaganda. The danger of Walt Disney, Mattelart and Dorfman believed, consisted of the manner in which the United States "forces us Latin Americans to see ourselves as they see us." The authors stated that the Chilean people would eventually free their own culture and kick out the Disney duck: "Feathers plucked and well-roasted. . . . Donald, Go Home!" Published shortly before the Chilean revolution, this essay appealed to readers far beyond the borders of Chile; *Para leer al pato Donald* went through more than fifteen editions and was translated into several languages.

American scholars quickly borrowed the concept of media imperialism. The Watergate scandal propelled suspicions of a conspiracy between the government and the media and of abuses of executive power. In a variety of studies, the communication scientist Herbert I. Schiller retraced a powerful connection between the domestic business, military, and governmental power structure on the one hand and, on the other, the "mind managers"—that is, the leaders of the U.S. communications industry—who in his view had conspired to manipulate minds at home and abroad. As Schiller saw it, nineteenth-century Anglo-American geopolitical imperialism had been replaced in the twentieth century by an aggressive industrial-electronics complex "working to extend the American socioeconomic system spatially and ideologically" across the globe. "What does it matter," Schiller asked in 1976, "if a national movement has struggled for years to achieve liberation if that condition . . . is undercut by values and aspirations derived from the apparently vanquished dominator?"

A second group of critics understood cultural imperialism as the domination of one country by another. To no small degree, this discourse grew out of the growing concern of the United Nations Economic, Social, and Cultural Organization (UNESCO) with the protection of national cultures, as well as the rising interest in the study of nationalism in the 1970s and 1980s, as repre-

sented by Benedict Anderson and others. In this interpretation, "culture" suggests a natural and static heritage of traditions that are akin to a certain country. It also serves as a tool of social control as important as controlling material resources. Hence, cultural imperialism implies the efforts of one country to undermine another country's cultural heritage by imposing its own. Frank Ninkovich's analysis of the State Department's efforts to establish an art program between 1938 and 1947 showed that during World War II, policymakers attempted to use artifacts of American culture, notably paintings, to promote "a sense of common values among nations of varied traditions." Just as free trade would have a liberalizing effect by contributing to other nations' economic well-being, art would create a common sense of culture. Simply put, if everyone agreed that American culture qualified artistically and aesthetically and also politically as a universal way of life and taste, it would indeed increase foreign acceptance of American values and American politics.

A third group of scholars interpreted cultural imperialism as the expansion and sometimes global dominance of U.S. consumer capitalism. Historians like Ralph Willet identified imperialist motivations within the American business community and government. Carrying this argument even further, others, such as Emily S. Rosenberg, claimed that in the twentieth century U.S. foreign policymakers had purposely begun to spread American culture, information, and the concept of a free and open economy in order to expand the national market abroad. Here, culture identifies capitalism in its most materialist form, encompassing goods and ideas associated with such goods, both of which foster homogenization. Culture is thus turned into an instrument to fuse different societies into one international economic system. E. Richard Brown (1982) denounced U.S. medical and health education programs sponsored by the Rockefeller Foundation in pre-1949 China. They were a "Trojan horse," guided "in their conception and development by imperialist objectives." These programs, Brown held, "were more concerned with building an elite professional stratum to carry out cultural and technological transformation than with meeting the health needs of each country." The programs facilitated American control of foreign markets and raw materials.

The most persisting and intellectually challenging criticism of U.S. cultural imperialism, however, originated among a fourth group of scholars who redefined the debate into a critique of modernity. The arguments of Jürgen Habermas, Marshall Berman, and others followed the outline of the Frankfurt School, which had originally launched the postwar investigation of cultural imperialism. Building on the writings of Marcuse and others, they depicted cultural imperialism as the imposition of modernity. They studied how the primary agents of modernity, such as the media, bureaucracy, science, and other social and economic institutions of the West, transferred the "lived culture" of capitalism to non-Western cultures. These scholars admitted that members of a recipient society had choices but that these choices were conditioned and manipulated by the modern capitalist environment in which these societies existed. Culture and modernity thus became a global prison.

In the eyes of Habermas and others, "modernity" represents the "main cultural direction of global development." Culture entails capitalism but also mass culture, urbanism, a "technical-scientific-rationalist dominant ideology," nation-states and a certain one-dimensional self-consciousness. The domination of these all contribute to the core meaning of Western "imperialism."

The critics of modernity were the first group that focused their analyses not on the question of agency but on the process of manipulation itself. They expanded the study from "American" to "Western" cultural imperialism that left out no field, no people, and no culture. While this perspective retained the term "imperialism," it also served as a forerunner for later trends in the debate over cultural transfer by moving the emphasis from the question of guilt to the actual process of cultural imposition. Because of its innovative approach, much of the critique of modernity has remained fashionable after most other critiques of cultural imperialism have ceased to influence the debate.

CRITICS OF CULTURAL IMPERIALISM THEORY

Students who are interested in the concept of cultural imperialism should be aware of the unresolved theoretical and methodological problems within the debate. A number of scholars have claimed that the cultural imperialists "have shown remarkable provincialism, forgetting the existence of empires before that of the United States." Since

the sixteenth century, European governments have developed a variety of cultural exchange programs, although they may not always have hoped to expand their empire by exporting their culture. The British in India and the Middle East, the Germans in Africa, and the French in Indochina all imposed their own culture abroad as a powerful tool to strengthen trade, commerce, and political influence and recruit intellectual elites for their own purposes. The historian Lewis Pyenson has shown that between 1900 and 1930, "technological imperialism"—the attempt on the part of state officials to employ scientific learning to form an international network of communication and prestige abroad—skillfully complemented German expansion in China, Argentina, and the South Pacific. In addition, new studies on U.S. policies in Asia and Europe have demonstrated that American policymakers did not hesitate to sacrifice economic (and ideological) objectives in order to realize geopolitical interests.

Individual case studies on private interest groups, such as philanthropic foundations, the American Library Association, and the press corps, show that often neither policymakers nor businessmen, but rather nongovernmental American organizations, were among the most active advocates of American culture and values abroad. The State Department as well as Congress were often reluctant to develop a full-fledged policy of cultural diplomacy. Often, these institutions were omitted from the process altogether.

Yet by far the most emphatic attacks against the critics of cultural imperialism came from Tomlinson, Frederick Buell, and others, who reproached authors such as Schiller for falling into the very trap they originally wished to avoid. Tomlinson stated that their rhetoric "repeats the gendering of imperialist rhetoric by continuing to style the First World as male and aggressive and the Third as female and submissive." In doing so, Schiller and others had assumed an imperialist perspective that viewed the Third World as made up of fragile and helpless cultures while at the same time serving the interests of Western modernity. It was said that the critics of cultural imperialism employed a theory suffering from a vague language of domination, colonialism, coercion, and imposition. Thus, ironically, the critics of cultural imperialism were made to seem the worst cultural imperialists.

Cultural imperialism, according to John Tomlinson, consists of the spread of modernity. It is a process of cultural loss and not of cultural expansion. There never were groups of conspirators who attempted to spread any particular culture. Instead, global technological and economic progress and integration reduced the importance of national culture. Therefore, it is misleading to put the blame for a global development on any one culture. The notion of imperialism—that is, purposeful cultural conquest—is irrelevant; instead, all countries, regardless of whether they are located in the northern or southern hemisphere, are victims of a worldwide cultural change.

Since the mid-1980s, scholars have paid closer attention to both global and local aspects of the American and Western cultural transfer. Sociologists, anthropologists, and historians have stressed the peculiarity of individual cultures in the context of a nonbipolar world. Under the influence of resurfacing nationalism the world over, one group of scholars has studied the periphery in greater detail, producing analyses of individual communities that came in contact with American (or Western) culture after World War II. Inspired by the growing debate on globalization, a second group has opted for precisely the opposite approach. Instead of unilateral imperialism, it has developed a concept of global modernization.

Scholars of local responses to American culture have investigated individual case studies, weighing resistance against acceptance. Borrowed from both psychology and literary criticism, response theory addresses the preconceptions influencing the reactions of human beings exposed to an external impression such as a text, a sound, or a visual perception. Response theory moves the focus of research from the question of agency to the question of audience and reaction. Instead of looking at broadcasters and producers, these scholars investigate, for example, the audience of television shows like *Dynasty*.

Inspired by the public debate abroad over the impact of U.S. cultural imperialism, since about the mid-1980s response theory has affected nearly all studies of cultural transfer in history, sociology, and cultural studies. For example, *Culture and International Relations* (1990), edited by Jongsuk Chay, studies particular aspects of culture such as literature, music, religion, or television programs to calibrate the effects of American culture abroad. The authors' findings vary in their assessment of the impact of American culture, but they agree that indigenous people never simply accepted consumer goods from the United States.

Reinhold Wagnleitner, for example, argued that Austrian youth revised the original meanings of jeans, Coca-Cola, and rock and roll into something new that accorded with their own needs; those consumer products offered not only comfort but also freedom from social constraints as well.

A number of scholars delineated a profound appeal of Western culture to non-Western countries, but challenged the assumption that U.S. policymakers and businessmen sought to manipulate certain target groups. Other studies focusing on the effects of cultural imperialism underlined the difference between foreign people and foreign governments. James Ettema, D. Charles Whitney, and others suggested in their studies of the media that audiences make conscious choices concerning what they listen to, read, and watch. Studies of underground movements in China and Eastern Europe in 1989 also demonstrate that in many cases, Western television programs inspired audiences to start a revolution against their own political leaders.

Another group of scholars concluded that audiences not only simply accepted the fruits of Western cultural imperialism but developed a strong resistance to American products and culture. Scholars of Islamic societies have consistently emphasized the stark opposition of orthodox Muslims to Western influences. Individual studies in cinematography, drama, literature, and cultural studies in Latin America, Asia, and Africa demonstrate that, notwithstanding the influence of Western goods, since the mid-1970s local audiences began to reject individual aspects of Western culture.

In many cases, a more detailed analysis of the origins of local resistance shows that peculiar local conditions informed it more than an outright condemnation of American culture. Under the intriguing title *Seducing the French* (1993), Richard F. Kuisel investigated economic missions, foreign investment, and U.S. consumer products in postwar France. He emphasizes that French opposition to U.S. culture "was (and is) about both America and France," because it intensified French fears of losing their cultural identity. Kuisel concedes that the French underwent a process of Americanization. But at the same time, they succeeded in defending their "Frenchness." French consumers found some American products appealing but they also continued to cherish and idealize French national identity, notably the idea of a superior French high culture.

Likewise, the average German citizen traditionally tended (and tends) to adhere to a more exclusive image of culture than his or her American counterpart. German *Kultur* traditionally stressed high culture and was closely linked to the enhancement of *Bildung*. It was ethnically bound, deeply rooted in German history, and—particularly in the case of the arts, music, and performance—dependent on state funding. After World War II, West Germans did not view the intrusion of American popular culture as cultural imperialism. To them, American culture remained always incompatible with *Kultur*. In other words, adoption of cultural artifacts does not necessarily translate into cultural and political adaptation.

The response theorists concluded that the model of a unilateral attempt to force consumer products and ideas on foreign nations is fundamentally flawed: resistance and cultural identity played a powerful role in the perception of American culture abroad. U.S. officials, in turn, were uncertain of the scope and nature of cultural exports. Their actions, furthermore, were quite comparable to the efforts of cultural diplomats of other countries. As Will Hermes concluded in the periodical *Utne Reader*, "American pop culture isn't conquering the world." Perhaps, he wondered, American cultural imperialism is "just part of the mix."

Informed by the poststructuralist approach, scholars from a variety of disciplines suggested in the late twentieth century that the term "cultural imperialism" be replaced with another term that seeks to circumvent the simplistic active-passive, dominator-victim dualism. For example, musicologists and anthropologists developed a variety of concepts seeking to broaden our understanding of global music interaction. Their suggestions, including "artistic sharing" and "transculturation," could easily be translated into other fields as well.

"Cultural transmission," for example, became one of the most appealing "post-imperialist" interpretations. The notion stemmed from the vocabulary of psychology, where it alluded to the interaction between cultural and genetic influences on human behavior. One of the most important historical accounts is a collection of essays, *Cultural Transmissions and Receptions: American Mass Culture in Europe* (1993). The contributors addressed diverse issues such as rock music in Italy and the reception of Disneyland in France. *Cultural Transmissions* describes the various avenues of acceptance, rejection, and alteration that audiences may choose when confronted with American culture.

Spurred by the vision of a "global village," another group of scholars has advanced a theory of "globalization." That term alludes to the compression of the world as well as to humans' increasing perception of the earth as an organic whole. Many understand this phenomenon simply as an economic development. Yet globalization is multidisciplinary in its causes and its effects. Its vague meaning allows researchers to interpret the term broadly; thus, it includes many features of modernization, including the spread of Western capitalism, technology, and scientific rationality.

Once again, the theme—globalization—was not at all new. Modern ideas on the interconnectedness of the world could be found as early as the writings of turn-of-the-twentieth-century German sociologists. Max Weber, for example, offered various conceptual frameworks of universalism beyond political borders. In "Soziologie des Raumes" (The sociology of space, 1903), philosopher-sociologist Georg Simmel argued that a national border is not a geographical fact with sociological consequences but a sociological fact that then takes a geographical shape.

This theme received renewed attention in the late 1980s when sociologists came to believe that socioeconomic relations everywhere were undergoing a profound change that resembled the Industrial Revolution in scope. No longer could cultures and societies be analyzed in the framework of the nation-state, these scholars believed. They argued that, first, any society is in a constant exchange with other societies; that, second, most countries consist of a multitude of cultures; and that, third, cultures do not necessarily reflect the borders of a nation-state. Sociologist Roland Robertson, one of the most prominent advocates of a global theory, proposed that a new concept replace the prevalent social scientific system of mapping the globe into three different worlds after the end of colonialism in the 1960s. Instead of a tripartite worldview, he outlined a vision of the globe as a more organic, interconnected, single network.

Inspired by this argument, students of cultural transfer moved their research away from its anti-American focus and toward a more global level, with no one identifiable enemy. Scholars replaced the concept of U.S. cultural domination with the study of Western cultural influence, but they disagreed over the relationship between manipulation and globalization. A few, like Orlando Patterson, still maintained that the modern process of worldwide cultural interaction could be interpreted as a clandestine American push for global uniformity. Others, however, like Peter Beyer, believed that globalization comes "quite as much at the 'expense' of" Western as of non-Western cultures, since both are part of a dramatic change.

Scholars such as Karen Fog Olwig employed the global approach to reflect on the tension between local and supranational cultural and political developments. Some of these analyses presented a despairingly bleak picture of the future cultural world order. Samuel Huntington, for example, invoked the specter of a "clash of civilizations," a World War III, where Western and Eastern societies would battle not for political and ideological reasons but as a consequence of cultural conflicts. Huntington argued that in the future people would identify themselves by reference to their faith, food, and local traditions instead of ideas and national political systems.

Charles Bright and Michael Geyer's 1987 account painted a more optimistic picture. They interpret the shift from Westernization to globalization as the fusion of tradition and modernity: "This is not Spengler's Decline of the West, but the beginning of a global reordering in which the West seeks its place in a world order it must now share with radically different societies. It is the beginning of a truly global politics." John Urry and Scott Lasch (1987) even theorized that the globalization of economic, political, and social relationships indicates the "end of organized capitalism." In a completely interconnected global economy, no one country will be able to control the market. Frederick Buell claimed in his book *National Culture and the New Global System* (1994) that for almost every academic discipline the "world of hybrid cultural production" was becoming the rule.

Interestingly, major critics of U.S. cultural imperialism, too, revised their earlier reproaches along these lines. Herbert I. Schiller, for example, reframed his argument in terms of world-systems theory. In an article published in 1991, he portrayed an expansive, transnational corporate authority that has replaced an autonomous United States in influencing all economic and cultural activity. Literary critic Edward Said, who analyzed the image of Orientalism in Western society, argued in *Orientalism* (1978) that the West culturally dominated the Orient by creating an artificial cultural vision of the latter "as its contrasting image, idea, personality, experience." His

later study, *Culture and Imperialism* (1993), detailed how Western authors and audiences developed a literary perspective on imperial geography distinguishing between "us" (the West) and "them" (the Third World). "Western imperialism and Third World nationalism feed off each other," Said summed up, "but even at their worst they are neither monolithic nor deterministic."

It would be misleading to abandon the notion of cultural imperialism and replace it with another, equally exclusive term. Scholars who are interested in the study of cultural transfer need to understand that culture, just like power, may be used to attain any number of objectives and to pursue any number of policies. Therefore, cultural imperialism is as suitable or unsuitable a designation as any other one. In the end, each term provides only one perspective on the chaos of cultural interaction. To understand and partake in the research in this field is to realize that there is no central paradigm. Instead, scholars must borrow insights from all three discourses retraced above. Originally begun as an almost public debate among politicians, journalists, and scholars, the discussion focused on the political advantage of cultural diplomacy and called for the dissemination abroad of more information on the United States and on American cultural artifacts. In the 1960s and 1970s, the topic became part of the nascent discussion of U.S. imperialism, which stressed the economic and psychological implications of culture; there was too much American culture abroad, scholars implied. But under the impact of worldwide resistance against American cultural imperialism and the influence of poststructuralism in the late 1980s, leading scholars in the field reconsidered their findings or developed new approaches. As the twentieth century ended, many no longer viewed the spread of American and Western culture exclusively as unilateral "imperialism" but as an ongoing process of negotiation among regional, ethnic, and national groups.

THE FUTURE OF CULTURAL TRANSFER STUDIES

At least four points of the debate on American cultural transfer abroad and on the question of where students of cultural transfer should turn next merit scholarly attention. First, the Internet revolution represents one of many events pointing to both globalization and multiculturalism, implying that Americans may no longer be able to agree on the substance and meaning of their culture, let alone agree sufficiently to export the idea of an American culture. In a way, this discord echoes the original conviction that Americans have no culture worthy to export.

Second, at the same time, the American public has once again begun to fret over the portrayal of American culture abroad, thus reinventing the discussion of the 1950s. On 8 June 1997, the *New York Times Magazine* published a special issue titled "How the World Sees Us." International observers reluctantly admitted the preponderance of American power and culture. But they also stressed their respective countries' resistance. "American movies have achieved the impossible," exclaimed playwright Edvard Radzinsky in one article. "Russians are so sick of them that they have started watching films from the days of Socialist Realism." And American commentators concurred. "Some of America's cultural exports are so awful that you begin to suspect that we're using the rest of the world as a vast toxic waste dump," editor Michiko Kakutani said.

Third, the center of the debate is changing rapidly. Until recently, the discussion centered on the nation-state, with a few significant exceptions. After the end of the Cold War, however, scholars paid more attention to the individual entrepreneur. The debate, that is, shifted from a nation-centered critique to the study of the impact of private business. This change of argument not only obliterated national boundaries but, equally important, transferred the object under investigation from politics to capitalism.

Fourth, until the late twentieth century the debate in the United States centered almost exclusively on that century. With only a few exceptions, discussants seemed to agree that the transfer of American culture had no history before the formal establishment of a program and then an agency that was in charge of projecting U.S. culture abroad. Yet sociologists tell us that bureaucratic formations follow rather than outline the way of a political trend or need. By shifting the notion of cultural transfer from formal government programs to nongovernmental encounters, scholars have increasingly realized that cultural transmission has existed everywhere and much earlier in time. Indeed, cultural transmission often preceded formal diplomatic ties. Although their findings were for many years ignored in the debates over cultural transfer, students of American history have for decades been investigating nineteenth-century ambassadors of American culture abroad. They have looked at missionaries in China, soldiers in Cuba, and the encounter between American settlers and Indian nations. They have investigated actors, as in the examination of the exodus and exchange of private groups including political émigrés, businessmen, and artists. They have also studied ideas and products as transmitted, for example, by scientists, poets, tourists, and museum curators. Their findings underline the general point that there was quite a lot of cultural transfer prior to World War I.

BIBLIOGRAPHY

Belmonte, Laura. "Defending a Way of Life: American Propaganda and the Cold War, 1945–1949." Ph.D. diss. University of Virginia, 1996. An excellent analysis of American cultural programs abroad.

Beyer, Peter. *Religion and Globalization.* London, 1994. Globalization theory is a staple of this sociologist.

Bright, Charles, and Michael Geyer. "For a Unified History of the World in the Twentieth Century." *Radical History Review* 39 (fall 1987): 69–91.

Brown, E. Richard. "Rockefeller Medicine in China: Professionalism and Imperialism." In Robert F. Amove, ed. *Philanthropy and Cultural Imperialism: The Foundations at Home and Abroad.* Bloomington, Ind., 1982.

Chaplin, Joyce E. *Subject Matters: Technology, the Body, and Science on the Anglo-American Frontier, 1500–1676.* Cambridge, Mass., and London, 2001. Suggests possible future research topics.

Dorfman, Ariel, and Armand Mattelart. *How to Read Donald Duck: Imperialist Ideology in the Disney Comic.* Translated by David Kunzle. New York, 1975.

Gienow-Hecht, Jessica C. E. *Transmission Impossible: American Journalism as Cultural Diplomacy in Postwar Germany, 1945–1955.* Baton Rouge La., 1999. Accentuates the independent role of mediators in the process of cultural transmitters.

Grothe, Peter. *To Win the Minds of Men: The Story of Communist Propaganda in East Germany.* Palo Alto, Calif., 1958. An introduction to the postwar consensus on the export of American culture.

Hermes, Will. "Imperialism: Just Part of the Mix?" *Utne Reader* 66 (November–December 1994): 19–20.

Hollander, Paul. *Anti-Americanism: Critiques at Home and Abroad, 1965–1900.* New York, 1992. Describes the rise of an international critique of American consumer culture.

"How the World Sees Us." *New York Times Magazine* (8 June 1997).

Iriye, Akira. *Cultural Internationalism and World Order.* Baltimore, 1997.

———. *Global Community: The Role of International Organizations in the Making of the Contemporary World.* Berkeley, Calif., 2002.

Joseph, Franz M., and Raymond Aron, eds. *As Others See Us: The United States Through Foreign Eyes.* Princeton, N.J., 1959. Provides summaries of early postwar assessments of America's image abroad.

Kuisel, Richard F. *Seducing the French: The Dilemma of Americanization.* Berkeley and Los Angeles, Calif., 1993. An endorsement of response theory.

Neils, Patricia, ed. *United States Attitudes and Policies Toward China: The Impact of American Missionaries.* Armonk, N.Y., 1990.

Patterson, Orlando. "Ecumenical America: Global Culture and the American Cosmos." *World Policy Journal* 11 (summer 1994): 103–117.

Pells, Richard. *Not Like You: How Europeans Have Loved, Hated, and Transformed American Culture Since World War II.* New York, 1997.

Pyenson, Lewis. *Cultural Imperialism and Exact Sciences: German Expansion Overseas, 1900–1930.* New York, 1985. Points to forerunners of U.S. exports in other countries.

Robertson, Roland. "Mapping the Global Condition: Globalization as the Central Concept." *Theory, Culture & Society* 7 (June 1990): 15–30.

Rosenberg, Emily S. *Spreading the American Dream: American Economic and Cultural Expansion, 1890–1945.* New York, 1982.

Schiller, Herbert I. *Mass Communication and American Empire.* New York, 1969.

Siracusa, Joseph M. *New Left Diplomatic Histories and Historians: The American Revisionists.* Port Washington, N.Y., 1973.

Smith, Anthony D. "Towards a Global Culture." *Theory, Culture & Society* 7 (June 1990): 171–191.

Tomlinson, John. *Cultural Imperialism: A Critical Introduction.* Baltimore, 1991. A concise critique of the critiques of cultural imperialism.

Urry, John, and Scott Lasch. *The End of Organized Capitalism.* Cambridge, 1987.

Wagnleitner, Reinhold. *Coca-Colonization and the Cold War: The Cultural Mission of the United States in Austria after the Second World War.* Chapel Hill, N.C., 1994.

Whitton, John Boardman, ed. *Propaganda and the Cold War: A Princeton University Symposium.* Washington, D.C., 1963.

Willett, Ralph. *The Americanization of Germany, 1945–1949.* London and New York, 1989.

See also CULTURAL RELATIONS AND POLICIES; GLOBALIZATION; IMPERIALISM; THE PRESS; PROPAGANDA; TELEVISION.

CULTURAL RELATIONS AND POLICIES

Akira Iriye

Cultural relations may be defined as interactions, both direct and indirect, among two or more cultures. Direct interactions include physical encounters with people and objects of another culture. Indirect relations are more subtle, involving such things as a person's ideas and prejudices about another people, or cross-national influences in philosophy, literature, music, art, and fashion. When cultural interactions deal with such matters as officially sponsored exchange programs or dissemination of books and movies, they may be called cultural policies. But not all cultural relations are cultural policies; there are vast areas of cultural interactions that have nothing or little to do with governmental initiatives. This essay, therefore, will deal primarily with broad themes in the history of American cultural relations, mentioning cultural policies only when they play a significant role in determining the nature of the overall cultural relationship with other countries.

The basic assumption here, of course, is that the United States is definable as a culture, as are all other nations in the world. In other words, each country has its own cultural identity in that it is defined by people who share certain traditions, memories, and ways of life. In this sense, all international relations are intercultural relations. The United States's dealings and contacts with, and the American people's attitudes and policies toward, any foreign country are conditioned by the historical and cultural outlooks of the two countries. Insofar as no two nations are completely identical, any discussion of foreign affairs must start with the assumption that we are analyzing two societies of different traditions as well as two entities embodying distinct sets of interests.

This is a different approach to the study of foreign affairs from the usual interpretations that stress military, security, trade, and other issues that affect a country's "interests." In terms of such factors, nations are more or less interchangeable.

Balance-of-power considerations, for instance, have a logic of their own irrespective of the cultural identity of a given actor, as do commercial interests or national security arrangements. In a "realist" perspective, international affairs are comprehended in the framework of the interplay of national interests, and while each nation determines its own interests, all countries are similar in that they are all said to be driven by, or to pursue, considerations of their interests.

Cultural relations, in contrast, are both narrower and broader than the interaction of national interests. Instead of power, security, or economic considerations, cultural affairs are products of intangible factors such as a nation's ideas, opinions, moods, and tastes. Symbols, words, and gestures that reflect its people's thought and behavior patterns comprise their cultural vocabulary in terms of which they relate themselves to other peoples. Not so much a realistic ("rational") appraisal of national interests as a "symbolic" definition of a people's identity determines how they may respond to the rest of the world. In this regard, there are as many cultural relations as there are national cultures, and nothing as vague as "national interests" suffices to account for them. At the same time, cultural relations are also broader than the interplay of national interests in that they include cross-national interactions such as emigration and immigration, tourism, educational exchange, missionary and philanthropic activities, and various movements to promote human rights or the protection of the natural environment. These are cultural phenomena in that they cannot be reduced to security or economic considerations and deal with the interrelationships of individuals and groups across national boundaries.

A history of U.S. cultural relations, then, must deal with all those themes that together define a different world from the one consisting of sovereign rights and interests of nations. The bulk of work in international relations still focuses on the latter phenomenon, and historians have only begun to take the former themes seriously as objects of study.

THE EARLY REPUBLIC TO THE CIVIL WAR: DEFINING AN "AMERICAN" CULTURE

From the beginning, Americans were interested in cultural themes in their foreign affairs. For one thing, at the time of the American Revolution the political and intellectual leaders were fond of stressing the multiethnic nature of the new republic. In most instances, to be sure, multiethnicity consisted of diverse European nationalities rather than distinctive racial groups. Compared with western European countries, the United States seemed unique in that no nationality constituted a majority of the nation, even though those of English stock represented nearly half the population. There were Welsh, Irish, Germans, French, Scandinavians, and others whose admixture with, and adoption of the language of, the English-speaking Americans impressed European visitors for decades after the Revolution. This was as much a cultural as a political undertaking; to establish a republic made up of people from many countries who imagined themselves to belong to the same community required some shared memory, a sense of Americanness, to distinguish the new nation from all others. How such a republic could survive in a world consisting of sovereign states, on one hand, and of large empires, on the other, was the key question.

One way for the American people to assure themselves that this could be done was through developing a fairly precise image of themselves. The idea of the "city on a hill," and the idealized self-perception that the Americans had struggled for the "rights of man," not simply the rights of Englishmen, implied the coming into existence of a new kind of nation and assumed that others, too, would look to the United States as a land of freedom and opportunity. Conversely, Americans would carry out their mission to spread the blessings of civilization and liberty to the less fortunate in distant countries. If, as so many writers asserted, America was the most progressive land in the world, it was because it was a country without archaic encumbrances, where men and women from many countries would come and work together to build a new, ideal community.

Anybody, theoretically, could join the undertaking. By the same token, what happened here would be of universal applicability. If various races and groups could join together in the United States to realize an earthly paradise, there was no reason why they could not do so elsewhere in the world. It was in this sense that America was called humankind's best hope.

Such universalism implied a view of other peoples that was monolithic and an idea of history that was unilinear. Just as divergent groups who came to the United States would create one unified people, so the rest of the world would ultimately tend to that goal. The American dream would be realized globally, and the American experience would become a world experience. America would cease to be unique only when its ideals and institutions were firmly implanted in all parts of the globe. The entire world would become one great America.

This type of teleological idealism was quite obviously a cultural product and provided one basic framework in which Americans developed their cultural relations with other countries. Throughout most of the nineteenth century, this, the cultural framework, was probably the only way the majority of Americans knew how to relate themselves to others. Cultural relations in that sense were thus a vital aspect of national self-definition.

This can be seen in the ways in which Americans viewed non-European people. Europeans, of course, comprised the bulk of the population of the United States, and cultural ties across the Atlantic were quite important. At the same time, however, it was when Americans dealt, either directly or indirectly, with people outside Western civilization that their cultural self-awareness became most clearly articulated. For instance, they viewed Arabs, Hindus, or Chinese in the framework of their own self-definition. These people, in other words, would be judged in terms of their distance from the American ideals and of their capacity to approximate them—if not immediately, then in the future. It is not surprising that observers of non-European societies frequently argued about whether these societies would ever transform themselves and become more like America. The basic assumption was, of course, that at the moment they lacked most of the ingredients that made the United States so progressive. Native populations in the Middle East, South Asia, or East Asia were almost invariably described as ignorant, indolent, and oppressed by arbitrary despots. They were the exact opposite of the Americans. Joel Barlow, poet and diplomat, described Hassan Pasha, dey of Algiers, as "a man of a most ungovernable temper; passionate, changeable, and unjust to such a degree that there is no calculating his policy from one moment to the next." William Eaton, appointed consul at Tunis by President John Adams, wrote of the "continual altercations, contentions and delays among the Arabs." "Poverty makes them thieves," he reported, "and practice renders them adroit in stealing." Similar expressions can be found at random in American writings on Turks, Chinese, Japanese, and other non-European nationalities throughout the nineteenth century.

A key question, given such an image of non-Europeans, was whether they had some redeeming qualities. On this point American universalism decreed that no people was so inherently depraved as to be totally incapable of attaining a higher level of civilization. The basic credo of American democracy was that any individual had certain abilities that could be developed to their potential if artificial restrictions were removed. Even those suffering under poverty and despotism were not entirely hopeless creatures. Given external stimuli to make them aware of alternative possibilities, and under favorable institutional conditions, they were certain to transform themselves. For, as the *Democratic Review* put it in 1839, "The same nature is common to all men . . . they have equal and sacred claims . . . they have high and holy faculties." It followed that Americans, having developed these faculties and made good their claims to progress, had a unique obligation to the rest of humankind. It was up to them, declared the *Knickerbocker* in 1840, "whether our fellow men shall reach the elevation whereof they are capable, and . . . whether or not [we shall] confer on them the most inestimable of all earthly boons, the boon of civilization."

It might be thought that in such a situation, there could be no genuine, equal cultural relations, especially with non-Europeans; Americans would interact with other societies and cultures through the cultural vocabulary of their own. Other peoples would merely be at the receiving end of American civilization without anything to give in return. Such, however, was not always the case. Even in the first half of the nineteenth century, when optimism regarding American values was most notable, appreciation of different cultural standards and achievements was not lacking. One has only to recall the great interest in

porcelain, silks, paintings, and other objects brought back from China. Curiosity about other societies coexisted with a disdain for despotic institutions or alien religions. Samuel Goodrich's *A History of All Nations,* a popular textbook published in 1851, explained that while Asians on the whole were "slavish . . . superstitious . . . [and] treacherous," their arts compared favorably with those of Europe. "All the efforts of European art and capital," Goodrich wrote, "have been unequal fully to imitate the carpets of Persia, the muslins of India, the porcelain of China, and the lacquered ware of Japan." When the first Japanese embassy arrived at San Francisco in 1860, a correspondent for the *New York Times* recorded, "It makes a white man blush to see how much more simple, tasteful and sensible they were in their uniforms than our grandees were in theirs."

Such observations revealed a fascination with the strange and the exotic that appeared lacking in Western civilization. Some went a step further and found positive significance in things Oriental. No group was more interested in them than the Transcendentalists. As they grew dissatisfied with the Christian religion as it was practiced in the 1830s and the 1840s, they turned to Hinduism and Buddhism with a sense of fresh discovery. Their understanding of these Asian religions may have been superficial, but they were the first group of Americans who seriously viewed the non-West not as an object of their mission but as a good in itself, as something that might be relevant to their own life. Ralph Waldo Emerson, for instance, was struck by the pantheism of the Hindu religion, which perceived godliness in all beings and all things. The pervading sense of serenity and the absence of a rigid demarcation between self and nature appealed to one who found modern life increasingly distasteful. As he remarked in his celebrated Harvard Divinity School address of 1838, "moral sentiment" had "dwelled always deepest in the minds of men in the devout and contemplative East . . . Europe has always owed to oriental genius its divine impulses."

Only a handful of Americans went as far as the Transcendentalists in embracing the spirit of another civilization, but the appreciation of distinctive values and ways of life sustaining the Orient seems to have produced in many observers an awareness of cultural pluralism in the world. The East was much more than the negation of the West, an object of the latter's contempt or pity, something whose only hope lay in wholesale transformation. For example, in 1854 the *New York Quarterly* reported the longing of a traveler for the life, manners, and climate of the Orient, which "all our comfort and all our facilities for travelling by steamers and railroads cannot satisfy or dispel." Three years later, dissatisfaction with the "matter-of-fact, work-a-day age" prompted James P. Walker to publish the *Oriental Annual,* an anthology of Eastern folklore and poetry.

Such expressions approach cultural relativism, the feeling that each culture has its own autonomous tradition and inherent characteristics that cannot be artificially changed by external stimuli. In nineteenth-century America, thoroughgoing cultural relativism was a rare phenomenon; but to the extent that some thought about the question, it became inexorably linked with the idea of human progress. If a distinct cultural tradition was a product of centuries of history, could it ever be significantly altered from without? Would it ever be possible to change peoples' ways of life? If they lived in abject poverty and suffered from despotic rule, was it not because they were so conditioned by tradition, and by their collective traits? In short, were they not living as they were simply because they were made to be that way?

These questions were of particular interest to Americans because they had obvious implications for the slavery dispute. Just as they debated among themselves whether black men and women were capable of education and progress, and if they would be better off in an industrial than in a plantation economy, Americans discussed colors other than white and black. According to a popular view, humankind was divided into white, black, yellow, brown, and red races, each with distinctive traits that were often considered immutable. Almost invariably, the black people were placed at the bottom of the hierarchy of races. Samuel Morton's *Crania Americana* (1839) asserted that the Caucasian race was characterized by "the highest intellectual endowments" and that the Mongolian race was "ingenious, imitative, and highly susceptible of cultivation," whereas the "Ethiopian" was "joyous, flexible, and indolent—the lowest grade of humanity." The bulk of humanity, being neither white nor black, thus belonged to the gray area between the highest and the lowest categories. It is not surprising that there were considerable ambiguities in American attitudes toward them. They had unique features, some of which could be readily appreciated by Americans, but this did not mean that they were the equal of Westerners.

United States cultural relations before the Civil War, then, were of particular significance when Americans dealt with cultures and societies outside Western civilization. Their responses combined the prevailing sense of Western superiority with some appreciation of the strange. Confidence in the universality of certain values was coupled with more rigid racialist thinking. The overwhelmingly European-centered cultural framework was undermined by some individuals who looked to the East as a fascinating alternative. On the whole, however, it would seem that non-Western cultures and peoples had not yet made a strong impact on American society. If there were intercultural relations between them, they were not equal but basically unidirectional.

EXPANSION AND THE AGE OF IMPERIALISM

The situation did not change drastically after the Civil War, but there was a greater awareness of different civilizations than there had been earlier. Fundamentally this reflected the technological development of the last decades of the nineteenth century, when steam and electricity, as observers were fond of pointing out, narrowed distances between various parts of the world. One could travel far more easily and speedily than before, and news in one corner of the globe could be transmitted almost overnight to most other regions. Great migrations of people started from Asia to the American continent, and from Europe to Africa and South America. One saw more foreigners in one's lifetime than earlier. The opening of more and more Asian ports to Western trade served to introduce commodities from distant lands into the daily life of average Asians and Westerners. In many areas of the non-Western world, the process of reform and transformation began to remake traditional societies in the image of the modern West. But the very experience of modernization caused some hard rethinking about cultural values. Westernization meant a loss of innocence to many a non-Westerner, while the global character of the modern transformation often suggested to Westerners the dilution of their own identity.

These were extremely interesting phenomena, and most of the crucial questions raised then have persisted to this day. It may be said that toward the end of the nineteenth century, world history entered an age of globalization that had cultural, as well as political and economic, implications. Economically, the phenomenon has been referred to as modernization, a neutral term suggesting that any society with certain endowments may opt for change. Modernized nations would establish global networks of capital, goods, and technology, which in turn would help further modernize their economies and ways of life. Such globalization had obvious implications for international cultural relations. Not only did the more advanced nations become more than ever interdependent economically, but they also came to share a great deal of information and technology. For Americans, this meant a more cosmopolitan outlook, a renewed awareness that they had a great deal in common with Europeans, Canadians, and other "civilized" people. It is not surprising that they took advantage of the new means of transportation and communication to travel, live, and even work in Europe, while the latter also sent its scholars, artists, and musicians to the United States. There was a great deal of cultural exchange across the Atlantic. Against this sort of cosmopolitanism, there were, to be sure, nationalists who insisted on the uniqueness of the American historical experience and worried that modern civilization was making all nations interchangeable. Some even argued that conflict of interest and even war, rather than shared outlooks and ways of life, would preserve the vitality of the nation. This, too, it must be noted, was a cultural question. The often heated debate at the end of the nineteenth century on the character and future direction of the American nation was thus a response to globalization. Cultural relations across the Atlantic were becoming ever closer, as Americans and Europeans came to view themselves as members of the same intellectual, artistic, and technological universe.

In the meantime, Americans joined Europeans in linking other parts of the globe closer together. They were, at one level, helping modernize those regions. Since the capital and technology necessary for modernization were in short supply in almost every non-Western country, Western capital had to be introduced; and this inevitably involved the coming of European and American financiers, engineers, and manufacturers who would employ native labor and middlemen to establish their economic institutions. Americans, even though in the aggregate their country was still a net importer of capital from Europe, were already active. They were instrumental, for instance, in the construction of the

first railroad in China, in the 1870s. They invested in coastal shipping in China and Japan, established syndicates for obtaining railway concessions in Asia and the Middle East, and participated in the development of mines in all these regions. This was intercultural relations in a broad sense. Americans were relating themselves to other peoples through the medium of capitalist enterprises.

Although the profit motive was uppermost, an influx of foreign capital and technology invariably had noneconomic as well as economic effects on the targets of Western expansion. Americans in China, for instance, were never in a sufficient number to involve themselves at all levels of mercantile and industrial activities. They needed local personnel as interpreters, clerks, messengers, business assistants, and even associates, and as "compradors" who acted as liaisons between foreigners and officials. Such diverse contacts were bound to affect Chinese manners and ideas. In fact, among the most "Americanized" Chinese were those who lived in the treaty ports and learned modern capitalist practices. Associations such as local chambers of commerce provided a setting where Americans and Chinese met and conducted social affairs as well as business matters.

Politically, the process of globalization was synonymous with what was then called, and has since been called, imperialism. The world was divided into those who established control over distant territories and those who became objects of such control. A handful of imperialist nations appropriated among themselves the vast lands of Africa, the Middle East, Asia, and the Pacific Ocean as colonies, semi-colonies, or spheres of influence. This was a military-political process, since control necessitated that a power structure be imposed upon alien peoples. Without such a regime, it was feared that local instability would create a chaotic condition and threaten the interests of a particular imperialist nation or invite the extension of power by its rivals. It seemed impossible and unwise to leave things as they were. Americans, no less than citizens of other advanced countries, were exhorted to reach out to far corners of the globe to join the forces of imperialist expansion.

Imperialism even in such a narrow sense was an important chapter in intercultural relations, for the assertion of power over another people entailed both physical and mental contact. The Spanish-American War, for instance, called forth a fierce debate within the United States on the wisdom of acquiring tropical colonies. Americans had never established territorial control over lands in the tropics, and they had to think hard about the implications of the new action. Since they had not given much thought to Filipinos or Puerto Ricans, they turned to what few books were available on these peoples. They read Andrew Clarke and John Foreman, among others—English authorities on the tropical islands. English colonialism provided an intellectual framework within which Americans discussed the new empire. They turned to Charles Dilke, Joseph Chamberlain, Henry Norman, George Curzon, and others to learn how colonies should be governed. Colonial administration seemed a very different matter from the governing of new territories in the continental United States or of the American Indians. The country would have to establish a new colonial service and train men and women fit for work in the tropics. The numerous magazine articles on these subjects during and immediately after the Spanish-American War attest to the impact of the war upon America's intercultural relations. The American people had to learn from scratch what it meant to be masters over an alien race.

This learning took various forms. At the popular level, war stories and novels were written to familiarize the general reader with conditions in the tropics, and children's adventure books sought to impart a sense of patriotic destiny to the younger generation. Quick reference volumes with revealing titles were also published, such as Thomas C. Copeland's *The American Colonial Handbook: A Ready Reference of Facts and Figures, Historical, Geographical, and Commercial, About Cuba, Puerto Rico, the Philippines, Hawaii, and Guam* (1899). Adult education programs such as the Chautauqua Society conducted seminars on the history of the Philippines. As a matter of course the academic community was selected to provide the intellectual leadership needed to deal with imperial problems, and it readily obliged. Universities established courses in colonial administration, imperialism, and tropical geography; and professional organizations such as the American Historical Association and the American Economic Association were engaged in turning out data and ideas that would be useful to the government in administering the new empire. The acquisition of overseas territories broadened the horizon for historians, economists, political scientists, sociologists, and anthropologists, who would have to redefine the scope of their respective disciplines to take advantage of the new opportunities. For example, the *American Anthropologist* noted in December 1898 that students of folklore would find "a rich field awaiting them in our territory." Anthropological studies of the Filipinos provided an intellectual underpinning for the establishment of a colonial regime over the islands.

In all this literature there was a feeling of excitement. Imperialism compelled Americans to encounter, mentally if not physically, a host of alien peoples, whereas earlier their experience had been limited to dealing with Indians and blacks. The result was to reaffirm the sense of America's cultural superiority, which was now much more openly linked to Britain than it had been earlier in the century. It was as if imperialism made the United States akin to Great Britain. The two branches of the Anglo-Saxon race, it appeared, rediscovered their common heritage and vocabulary. They were both expansionists, many writers pointed out, better fitted than any other nation in the world for the administration of less-developed countries. They were to cooperate so that their respective empires would come to stand for enlightenment and efficiency. Elbridge S. Brooks was echoing a widespread sentiment when he told his young readers in *Lawton and Roberts: A Boy's Adventure in the Philippines and the Transvaal* (1900) that "the Stars and Stripes in the Philippines, and the Union Jack in South Africa, are advancing the interests of humanity and civilization. . . . [Untrammeled] liberty to the barbarian is as disastrous a gift as are unquestioning concessions to a republic which has been a republic only in name."

The last sentence reflected self-defensiveness about empire that was just beneath the surface optimism characteristic of the age of imperialism. In extending their control over alien races, Americans could look to the British for experience and guidance; but both of them had to confront the fact that as they advanced to far reaches of the globe, they were causing drastic changes in other societies. The non-Western parts of the world that earlier had been seen as decadent, static, or backward now seemed to be undergoing a period of profound crisis and instability as a result of the impact of Western technology, ideas, and institutions. If the expansionist thrust of the West was an inevitable development of history, then the consequent turmoil, confusion, and even anarchy in many regions of the world would have to be coped with. There were even more serious problems. If non-Western peoples should discard traditional values for new ones, what would happen to their indigenous cultures? Would they ever become thoroughly "Westernized"? What if they were transformed only superficially and remained basically uncivilized even though the superstructures of their societies were modernized? Would they become pro-Western or anti-Western?

These were some of the most interesting questions in America's intercultural relations during the age of imperialism. That was why so much was written toward the end of the nineteenth century about the nature of Western relations with other cultures. The future destiny of American civilization seemed bound up with the larger question of the evolving relationship between West and non-West. For example, in June 1897, Benjamin Ide Wheeler, who was soon to become president of the University of California at Berkeley, declared in an article in the *Atlantic Monthly* entitled "Greece and the Eastern Question" that the real question in the Middle East was "who is to lead, who is to champion, who is to represent Occidentalism in its antithesis between Occidentalism and Orientalism," an idea expressed in earlier decades but that now seemed an urgent question because of the resurgence of the East. Similarly, the naval strategist and historian Alfred Thayer Mahan discussed the "stirring of the East" and posed the question of "whether Eastern or Western civilization is to dominate throughout the earth and to control its physical terms." Observers like Wheeler and Mahan agreed that the West's hope lay in its spiritual superiority to the East; even if the latter should catch up technologically and economically, and even though non-Westerners vastly outnumbered Westerners, the future of Western civilization was bright because of its unique heritage. Nevertheless, the fear was always present that the East might prove to be a formidable threat precisely because it lacked the West's refinement, humanity, and self-restraint. A modern Orient without the Occident's values might prove to be totally unmanageable. The West should therefore brace itself for what was termed by many "the coming conflict of civilizations" in the twentieth century.

The cultural monism of the earlier decades was thus giving way to self-consciousness and defensiveness in the age of imperialism. Such apprehension, to be sure, was limited to a minority of writers. Most Americans would have agreed with the historian John Fiske's optimism, as he expressed it in an article on the new "manifest des-

tiny" in 1885, that "within another century . . . all the elements of military predominance on the earth, including that of simple numerical superiority, will have been gathered into the hands not merely of Europeans generally, but more specifically into the hands of the offspring of the Teutonic tribes who conquered Britain in the fifth century." Yet this type of complacency, reflecting a unilinear view of human (Western) progress, could not entirely accommodate some concurrent developments that had enormous implications for intercultural relations. Most notable among them were the growing fascination with non-Western civilizations and the influx of Asian immigrants.

LATE NINETEENTH-CENTURY ENCOUNTERS: ART, RELIGION, AND EVERYDAY LIFE

Americans had always been curious about other peoples and had cherished imports from distant lands. But in the age of globalization there arose serious interest not only in curios and exotica of strange peoples but also in the fine arts, religions, philosophies, and ways of life of other countries, especially in the East. During the 1880s, the United States legation in Constantinople was headed by General Lew Wallace and by Samuel S. Cox, both noted for their favorable views of Oriental cultures. Wallace, the author of the popular novel *Ben Hur,* wrote of the "bloodthirsty and treacherous, recklessly brave and exceedingly beautiful" cavalry of the Ottoman Empire. "Even among the meanest of them," he wrote, "you will see noble, well-set heads of the finest mould, testifying to unmixed blood of the most perfect of living races." Cox recounted his experiences in the East in *Orient Sunbeams.* The message he sought to convey to his readers was that they should remove their prejudice toward people of different religions. He wrote of Islam: "Whatever we may think of its founder, however unacceptable may be some of his doctrines . . . yet as a scheme of religion influencing as many, if not more millions of people than Christianity, is it not worthy of being considered by other peoples?"

This sort of serious interest in what would later be called cultural anthropology was quite visible at the end of the century. The World's Columbian Exposition of 1893, held at Chicago to commemorate the four hundredth anniversary of Christopher Columbus's voyage, provides a good case in point. Close to 30 million people visited the fair, which was spread over 686 acres of land in south Chicago. Most countries of the world participated, including Japan, which spent millions of dollars to construct buildings specifically for the fair and to present an exhibition of all aspects of traditional and contemporary life. Although this was not the first time that Americans had had an opportunity to examine Japanese artifacts closely—Japan had participated in the 1876 Centennial Exposition at Philadelphia—their observations led to awareness that Japanese culture was much more than a phenomenon to be appreciated in isolation from the rest of that people's life. If the Japanese craftsmen at the Columbian Exposition seemed polite, industrious, and capable of producing refined objects, this had to be related to the totality of Japanese history and values. Japanese civilization could not be understood only within the framework of Western moral standards. Indeed, it might be comparable on equal terms with American civilization; and it might be foolish to judge other peoples from the viewpoint of a self-centered value system. "I just made up my mind," says the hero of Carl Western's novel *Adventures of Reuben and Cynthy at the World's Fair* about the exposition, "that if they [the Japanese] were heathens, there were lots of things we could learn from them."

The Japanese were not the only heathens at Chicago. The Columbian Exposition coincided with the World Parliament of Religions, to which many non-Christian leaders were invited. From India came several prominent figures, including Swami Vivekananda, a Hindu leader noted for his belief that all religions contain truth. His arrival aroused much excitement among Americans. He not only attended the parliament but also traveled extensively in the United States. Americans were fascinated by his stress on religious toleration: "I preach nothing against the Great One of Galilee. I only ask the Christians to take in the Great Ones of India along with the Lord Jesus." To groups of ladies in Salem, Massachusetts, or Streator, Illinois, where he gave talks, it must have seemed quite a revelation that a Hindu monk should have so much to offer to contemporary society. Many were rude; in Chicago, Vivekananda recorded in his diary, "A man from behind pulled at my turban. I looked back and saw that he was a very gentlemanly looking man, neatly dressed. I spoke to him, and when he found that I knew English he became very much abashed." But the *Chicago Herald* probably expressed the predominant sentiment of those who heard Vivekananda's lectures

when it wrote, "Vivekananda is undoubtedly the greatest figure in the Parliament of Religions. After hearing him, we feel how foolish it is to send missionaries to this learned nation." Far more than an object of curiosity, Indian civilization could be considered an important entity, even an alternative to the modern ways of life.

Perhaps the most logical embodiment of the emerging attitude was that of Ernest Fenollosa, a philosopher and art critic from Salem, Massachusetts. As a lecturer at Tokyo University in the 1890s, he was instrumental both in transmitting Western thought to the Japanese and in discovering the aesthetic value of Japanese art for Westerners. He taught the philosophy of Friedrich Hegel to students in Tokyo while establishing a collection of Japanese prints for a museum in Boston. The two activities were, from his point of view, of equal importance. Whereas earlier Americans had assumed their superiority and gone to non-Western parts of the world as missionaries and educators, he was convinced that West and non-West had a great deal to learn from one another. The two civilizations were of equal significance. Each had its distinctive cultural tradition, and together East and West constituted complementary halves of the harmonious whole that was mankind. The two were like the Chinese dichotomy of yin and yang, standing for contrasting pairs such as darkness and light, moon and sun, or female and male. The West, as Fenollosa saw it, represented masculinity, strength, and vigor; but it was never whole in itself. Only through a harmonizing relationship with the East, standing for femininity and refinement, could it sustain its existence. No wonder that Fenollosa's favorite analogy was to marriage. As he said in the preface to *East and West* (1893): "The synthesis of two continental civilizations, matured apart through fifteen hundred years, will mark this close of our century as an unique dramatic epoch in human affairs. At the end of a great cycle the two halves of the world come together for the final creation of man."

Not all writers were as sanguine as Fenollosa about the peaceful relationship between East and West. It was at the end of the century that Rudyard Kipling's phrase "East is East, and West is West" became popular. Lafcadio Hearn, a Greek-born American novelist who had long resided in Japan, published his *Kokoro,* a study of the Japanese mentality, in 1896, and stressed that a Westerner could never hope to comprehend the depth of the Japanese mind. In his words, "The more complex feelings of the Oriental have been composed by combinations of experiences, ancestral and individual, which have had no really precise correspondence in Western life, and which we can therefore not fully know. For converse reasons, the Japanese cannot, even though they would, give Europeans their best sympathy." The overwhelming majority of Americans would probably have agreed more with Hearn than with Fenollosa. The popularity of David Belasco's play *Madame Butterfly* (1900) showed, if nothing else, that there was still a very widespread view that West and non-West might meet on a transient basis, but that their encounter produced tragic consequences because of their inability to understand one another fully.

One additional factor in the development of intercultural relations was the coming of Asians to the United States toward the end of the nineteenth century. Chinese laborers had arrived on the West Coast during the 1840s, but it was after the Civil War that their immigration and residence began to create serious social and political problems. And just when, in the 1880s, their influx was checked through treaty arrangements and congressional enactments, the Japanese began to arrive, first in Hawaii and, after the islands' annexation by the United States, in the western states. The bulk of these people were not exactly embodiments of Chinese or Japanese civilization. They were overwhelmingly poor, illiterate or undereducated, and without more than rudimentary skills. Still, they represented the societies from which they came, and to that extent their experiences in the United States constituted part of America's intercultural relations.

This is best seen in the rhetoric of the Oriental exclusionist movement. The exclusionists on the West Coast and their supporters elsewhere frequently resorted to the argument that the very fabric of American civilization was at stake. Should Asians be allowed to inundate the country, they said, not only would they compete with native labor because of their low wages, but they would also undermine the American way of life. Unlike European immigrants, they brought alien customs and modes of living and, unless checked, would most certainly Orientalize American society. The key to the Chinese immigration dispute, a writer pointed out in 1876, was that the Chinese "never adopts an iota of our civilization. . . . His civilization *displaces* exactly so much of our own; it substitutes Mongolianism." Similar expressions would be heard for many decades. The fundamental issue

appeared to be the inevitable conflict of civilizations. Americans were called upon to consider whether their country was to remain Occidental or to become Oriental, under Asiatic influence. To those deeply concerned with the problem, it must have seemed axiomatic that East and West could never live together in peace and harmony. Such particularism was a reflection of the growing proximity, physical as well as geographical, of West and non-West in the age of globalization. At this level, then, America's intercultural relations exhibited narrowness and racial prejudice as defensive measures to preserve what were considered unique features of Western civilization.

Not all non-Westerners who came to the United States, however, were poor and illiterate laborers. A small minority of scholars, officials, businessmen, and other members of the elite visited the country, some to stay for a long time. They contributed to America's intercultural relations by associating with their counterparts in the United States and by articulating their views to Americans and to people at home. Some of them came with good classical educations, attracted to an America that was envisioned as a land of the free. For those who were highly educated and politically conscious, but who felt themselves alienated from their own lands for political or cultural reasons, the United States beckoned as a land of freedom, opportunity, and humanism. The image of America as the place to go for education was established in China and Japan by the end of the nineteenth century, as was the image that in the United States one could find a refuge from oppression and persecution in one's own country. Baba Tatsui, a young activist, left Japan for America to pursue his struggle for political rights, and many of his compatriots with socialistic views followed him. Sun Yat-sen engaged in revolutionary activities among Chinese in Hawaii and the United States. Some of China's constitutionalists also visited America, where they founded newspapers and conducted fund-raising campaigns.

What the United States meant to these visiting non-Westerners must be considered an important aspect of the country's intercultural relations. To many of them, this was "the sacred land of liberty," as the Japanese said. But there were others who were shocked by the contrast between that image and the reality. Uchimura Kanzō, the Japanese Christian leader, was repelled by materialistic excesses. Some returned to their homelands to spread certain images of the United States. It can be said that at this time there were non-American as well as American agents of intercultural relations. The United States exerted subtle influences upon other countries not only through its own merchants, travelers, or missionaries but also through foreigners visiting the country. Often it was through America that the latter first encountered Western civilization, and the importance of this is hard to exaggerate. For better or worse, what they saw in the United States epitomized for them the essence of capitalism, constitutionalism, and Christianity. The experiences of a man like Uchimura, who had been introduced to Christianity through American missionaries in Japan but who came to the United States and discovered the gap between what he called Bible Christianity and American Christianity, are fascinating examples of cross-cultural interactions. It was as if America taught him what Christianity was not.

TWENTIETH CENTURY THROUGH WORLD WAR II: AMERICANIZATION AND REACTION

By 1900, then, there were already complex layers of intercultural relations, some subtle new forces and others that were crude echoes of the past, but all constituting parts of the developing trends toward globalization. These layers continued to evolve after the turn of the century. The history of intercultural relations in the twentieth century is extremely difficult to characterize, since it is an ongoing process. It is possible, however, to examine the period before the outbreak of World War II in terms of two contradictory currents: universalistic and particularistic tendencies. On the one hand, there was every indication that American influence was spreading to other lands; at the same time, there grew self-conscious opposition to American and Western cultural predominance in the world.

By the time of World War I, the United States had established its position as the leading Western power, not only in industrial production, trade, and foreign loans and investments but also in armaments and political influence. While this was not the same thing as cultural hegemony, there is little doubt that the United States came to stand and speak for Western civilization at a time when the European countries were engaged in fratricidal conflicts and disputes. One reason why President Woodrow Wilson wanted to postpone American entry into the war was his fear for the survival of Western civilization. He came to see

his country as a guardian of that precious tradition, a sentiment shared by an increasing number of British. But similar views had also been expressed by Presidents Theodore Roosevelt and William Howard Taft, who had come to take for granted the spread of benign American influence to the rest of the world. Civilization, as Taft never tired of saying, was based on an unlimited interchange of goods and capital, which in turn contributed to international peace, harmony, and understanding. Americans would carry their wares throughout the world and promote economic modernization and political awakening. Because of their superiority in technology, organization, and business practices, Americans were bound to emerge as the most influential group in the new world of enlightened international relations. They would be among the foremost agents of change in the twentieth century. Wilson fully accepted such ideas and elevated them to a vision of internationalism in which American values would reign—valid not as American but as universal values. No wonder that he was eager to promote missionary activities and was captivated by the idea of establishing American mandates in various parts of the world.

Because the European countries lost population, productive capacity, morale, and prestige as a result of the war, the United States was able to replace European power and influence in international affairs. American technology, epitomized by the automobile, dominated the postwar world, as did popular American culture such as jazz, radio, and motion pictures. In Europe one talked of the "decline of the West" after Oswald Spengler's book of that title was published in 1918, but somehow the West that was declining did not seem to include the United States. Observers such as the sociologists Thorstein Veblen and Pitirim Sorokin discussed the ramifications of the emerging mass society; but they implied that this was the way of the future, that developments in the United States portended what was to take place elsewhere. To understand modern society one looked at the United States. Whether one liked it or not, it seemed that Americanization was an inevitable phenomenon of the postwar world.

This was also the way American influence was perceived in non-Western countries. In Turkey, India, China, Japan, and elsewhere, the war had caused European prestige to suffer; but the United States appeared more vigorous and resilient than its European cousins. American trade was the most extensive in history, and a growing bulk of it was conducted with non-European countries. Americans appeared in areas where earlier one had seen only Europeans, investing in oil fields and establishing manufacturing plants. John Dewey's instrumentalism became the most popular philosophy in universities throughout Asia, and women in distant societies turned to American women not only for fashions but also for political ideals and social visions, such as women's suffrage and population control. Jazz, baseball, and Charlie Chaplin became just as popular in Japan as in America. "Modern times" was synonymous with American culture for people of the 1920s. Even in the 1930s, it is possible to argue, American influence did not abate; the process of cultural Americanization proceeded unchecked until well into the decade. Visits by American baseball teams were always important news to the Japanese, often overshadowing any feeling of crisis as a result of the latter nation's imperialistic activities on the Asian continent. Charles Lindbergh was as well known across the Pacific as across the Atlantic, and even Japanese martial music had definite traces of American influence. Children and women shed their traditional costumes and started wearing Westernized clothes, and bars and cabarets mushroomed. In many ways Japan on the eve of Pearl Harbor was a society more Americanized than ever before.

While the interwar era, then, was a period of rapid Americanization, it is also true that the 1920s and the 1930s saw self-conscious opposition to, and even rejection of, the West by some non-Western countries. They began to assert their identity, no longer content to remain objects of Western expansion and receptacles of Western influence. This second trend, toward particularism, was already visible at the beginning of the century, when people everywhere noted signs that seemed to indicate the non-West's rise against the West. The Russo-Japanese War, which the Japanese took pains to characterize not as a racial conflict but as one between civilization and barbarism, nevertheless was cheered by non-Westerners from Egypt to China as a victory of a colored nation over a white nation. In the Near East and North Africa, Islam was becoming self-conscious and militant; Islamic spokesmen talked of an Arab renaissance and the coming jihad against the Christian West. Mosques began to be built in American cities.

The Young Turks, the Persian nationalists, and the Armenian revolutionaries felt betrayed by the peace settlements after World War I. Asians became disillusioned by the alleged universalism of Wilsonian internationalism when the Western powers failed to adopt a racial equality clause as part of the League of Nations Covenant. The Chinese were bitter toward the United States and Great Britain for their alleged failure to stop Japanese encroachment on Shantung. The Turks viewed the postwar settlement as an imposition by the Western nations at the expense of the Ottoman Empire. For these varied reasons, the international order after 1919 appeared to be an "Anglo-American peace," as Prince Konoye Fumimaro of Japan said.

Nationalism, which had been inspired by the modern Western example, became a force against the West in many non-Western countries during the interwar years. It took on a culturally particularistic meaning as Chinese, Arabs, Indians, and others asserted their distinctive identity as separate from European or American civilization. In China, for instance, nationalism was not only aimed at recovering rights lost to the imperialists; it also revealed itself in a movement to develop native Christian churches and to replace Westerners in administrative posts at colleges and universities. The fascination the Chinese felt for Marxism and Leninism was in part due to the anti-Western messages, explicit or implicit, that they found in these ideologies. Marxist-Leninist thought gave the Chinese a conceptual tool with which to attack Western capitalism as well as Western civilization. The wholesale transformation of the country after the pattern of the West was no longer seriously advocated. Now there were other models and other choices; some sought a Soviet-type revolution, while others visualized a combination of Chinese tradition with modern technology as the best way to save China.

More or less the same phenomenon of self-conscious reassessment of Western values could be observed in Turkey, India, Japan, and other countries. The trend was no doubt encouraged by the literature of pessimism that Europeans were producing in the decade after the war. Many of these writers expressed doubt that Western civilization could survive, and some turned to the East as a source of salvation. As an article in a February 1925 issue of the *Europaische Staats und Wirtschafts Zeitung* put it, "Our Western world is weary; not weary of life, but of strife and hatred. Indeed, our peculiar society and civilization have been found wanting. . . . Men are looking to the East unconsciously, and therefore sincerely. . . . The world of Asia draws us with its promise of something new and something that will liberate." Eastern philosophers like Rabindranath Tagore and Vasudeo Metta were eager to oblige and to offer this "something" for which Westerners seemed to be looking. Unfortunately, very often their thoughts were utilized in Asia for nationalistic upheavals against pervasive Western influence.

The world crisis of the 1930s that culminated in World War II definitely had a cultural dimension; it may be argued that the major difference between the two world wars was the addition of the cultural factor in the second. World War I was mainly a civil war among Western countries, whereas World War II involved peoples of diverse cultural traditions and ideologies. It was in essence intercultural warfare. This was particularly true of the United States and its relations in Asia and the Pacific. Throughout the 1930s, Japan pursued an aggressive foreign policy and gave it an ideological sanction of pan-Asianism. The concept was transparently anti-Western. Asia, according to this view, was to reassert itself against the imperialistic exploitation by the West, which had cultural as well as political and economic aspects. For too long, Japanese nationalists declared, the West had permeated Asian life, subverting traditional values and destroying age-old social customs. Asians had ceased to be Asian; they had either become Westernized or objects of Western influence. They had lost their identities and their souls. If they were to regain these things, they must stand together as Asians and develop a regional system of cultural and economic autonomy. The ideology of Japanese militarism stressed the eradication of Western values from education, mass media, and daily living, and the need to return to the essence of national culture. Apologists for Japanese aggression also viewed pan-Asian regionalism as a viable alternative to both imperialism and particularistic nationalism, two vices that they attributed to the modern West. If Asia were to reject imperialism and yet to avoid repeating the experience of the modern nation-states constantly struggling against one another, it was imperative that Asian countries organize themselves into a regional system.

For the bulk of Americans, these events in distant Asia were of far less importance than their individual struggles for economic survival at home. But there was a genuine cultural dimension in the economic crisis, in that the values of bourgeois mass society seemed less and less relevant to the unemployed, the handicapped, and the racially segregated. Western civilization

appeared to be seriously threatened from within, as evidenced by the growth of Italian fascism, German nazism, and Soviet communism. Americans, no longer sure of the eternal validity of middle-class precepts and symbols, often turned to Benito Mussolini or Adolf Hitler or Joseph Stalin as possible saviors of civilization. At the same time, many of them embraced isolationism, in the belief that by staying out of war in Europe or Asia, the United States would be able to preserve what was left of civilization and help reconstruct Europe after it had been devastated by war. For a man like Charles Lindbergh, it was nothing short of a crime against Western civilization to enter the fray on the side of either Britain or Germany. Only the uncivilized in other lands would benefit from such fratricide.

In such a context, the war between the United States and Japan could be seen in a cultural context. The irony was that the combatants fought with modern weapons, utilizing all the techniques of scientific warfare. As noted earlier, despite its profession of indigenous values and pan-Asianism, Japan in 1941 was more Westernized than ever before. The decision to establish control in the areas of Asia that were rich in natural resources could also be seen as a device to proceed with further industrialization and economic strengthening. The Japanese dream of an autonomous empire was little different from a Western conception. Cultural particularism did not cloak these ambitions.

The United States, on the other hand, regained the sense of cultural identity and confidence when war came. The self-doubt and crisis-consciousness of the 1930s were replaced by a renewed faith in the essential soundness and goodness of Western values. The faith was expressed in the universalistic rhetoric of the Atlantic Charter, the Declaration of the United Nations, and the communiqués issued by the Big Three at the end of their meetings at Teheran (1943) and Yalta (1945). The language reaffirmed the principles of peace, justice, and human rights, which were seen to be as relevant as ever because the Axis powers were pictured as the would-be architects of a world based on diametrically opposed values. It is true that many Americans saw the Pacific war in more parochial ways, stressing the racial aspect. To cite one extreme example from within the government, Captain Harry L. Pence of the U.S. Navy reiterated, at meetings of the State Department Advisory Committee on Postwar Foreign Policy, that the war involved the question of "which race was to survive." He favored "the almost total elimination of the Japanese as a race," saying, "Japan should be bombed so that there was little left of its civilization." Moreover, the Japanese "should not be dealt with as civilized human beings. . . . We should kill them before they kill us." Although representative of a current of opinion in wartime America, such views were not part of postwar planning. On the contrary, officials and opinion leaders continued to stress universalistic principles and to search for a new world order in which Japan, no less than other countries, would participate. Japan's surrender thus implied, at the level of cultural affairs, the recognition that particularism had failed and the acceptance by Japan of American ideas as more applicable to its needs.

GLOBALIZATION AND THE COLD WAR

Intercultural relations after World War II were far more extensive and diverse than earlier. The United States became the virtual inheritor of European civilization, emerging as the strongest and richest country in the world, capable of supporting the arts and financing scholarly and artistic undertakings. European refugees enriched America's cultural life. For the first time it could be said that American art was in the vanguard of modern art, not a pale reflection of European works. The same was true of literature and music. Unlike the period after World War I, however, there was much less self-consciousness about American culture. It was assumed as a matter of course, rather than asserted as a matter of principle, that American artists, novelists, and musicians were engaged in creative work that had relevance to the contemporary world as a whole. Europeans looked to the United States to discern artistic and literary trends. Moreover, American troops stationed in most parts of Europe transmitted American popular culture and lifestyles to the Old World. It became important for European intellectuals to study in the United States if they wished to keep abreast of developments in scholarship.

The impact on the non-Western world was no less great. American influence was transmitted through soldiers, officials, and businessmen who were scattered throughout Africa, the Middle East, and Asia. Consciously or unconsciously, they contributed to a deeper cultural involvement of America in other lands. America came to stand for what was fashionable and up-to-date. At the same time, Americans abroad collectively and individually increased their nation's awareness of other cultures and contributed to a greater appreciation of non-Western traditions. Many who were trained during the war as language specialists and intelligence officers retained their interest in foreign countries, and some of them became leaders in the postwar development of "area studies." American colleges began seriously teaching courses in non-Western civilizations and founded institutes to further research in these areas. There was also a flood of non-Europeans to the United States as war brides, students, and visitors. Through them Americans came into contact with non-Western ways of life.

This flowering of cultural relations after World War II was in many ways a culmination of the globalizing trend that had begun in the nineteenth century. Globalization had connected different parts of the world closer together; it had also manifested itself in imperialism. It had often provoked fierce opposition on the part of nations and individuals that wished to preserve their traditional loyalties and ways of life. In many ways the atomic bombs that brought World War II to conclusion also ended such opposition in the sense that war from now on came to be seen as truly global, something that was to be avoided at all cost if civilization were to survive. This meant that military conflict and confrontation would come to constitute a lesser part of international relations than earlier. To be sure, the estrangement among the victorious powers after 1945, known as the Cold War, did become a pervasive phenomenon and defined one facet of world affairs for nearly half a century. But it would be misleading to subordinate all other phenomena to the geopolitical confrontation. For the Cold War failed to prevent another, even more substantive development, globalization, from gaining momentum after World War II. And globalization was fundamentally a nongeopolitical phenomenon. U.S. cultural relations in the second half of the twentieth century may be understood in such a context.

It would appear that the old opposition between globalization, on one hand, and local identities, on the other, gave way to the virtually universal forces of global interdependence and interpenetration after World War II. These forces were economic, social, and cultural. Modernization provided one easily recognizable framework to comprehend this phenomenon. In the wake of a war that had divided the globe, there resurfaced the idea that all the countries in the world were tending toward a more modern phase. Economic development, political democracy, and social justice appeared to be essential ingredients of modernity; and intellectuals discussed how such an outlook could be encouraged in a traditional society. Appreciation of non-Western civilizations often took the form of discovering elements in them that were potentially "modern." In this process, there grew some tolerance for cultural pluralism: not just greater appreciation for Japanese architecture, Chinese food, or Indian philosophy but economic, political, and social changes in those countries. The hope was that through such changes, coupled with the new outlook in postwar America, foreigners and Americans would come to a better understanding of one another. They would develop a common vocabulary of mutual respect as they cooperated to bring about a more modern world. The pace of globalization was being accelerated in a changing world. U.S. cultural relations contributed to globalization and at the same time to an appreciation of diversity. This was a far more significant story than the vicissitudes of the Cold War, for ultimately it was the globalizing world that put an end to the Cold War, not the other way round.

It might be objected that the Cold War did have a globalizing aspect. Not only did it provoke fears of a nuclear conflagration that would annihilate the whole world, but the vocabulary of the geopolitical confrontation often had global connotations. The Soviet Union and its allies spoke of a worldwide people's struggle against the evils of capitalism and imperialism, while the United States and its partners accused the opponents of infringing upon such universal values as freedom and democracy. Moreover, both sides frequently used cultural means to wage Cold War: propaganda, student exchanges, conferences of intellectuals, and the like. Even in the United States, where traditionally cultural pursuits had been considered to belong exclusively to the private sphere, the government did not hesitate to sponsor art exhibits, publications of journals, or meetings of labor leaders abroad in order to try to influence other countries' opinions. A cultural Cold War did exist, as did official cultural policies. But if such policies resulted in a growing interdependence among different parts of the world, it was more by accident than by design. What brought about the dissipation and, ultimately, the end of the Cold War were not these policies but the growing global consciousness, a

product of cultural interpenetration, not of the geopolitical confrontation whose fundamental orientation was to divide the globe, not to unite it.

INTERCULTURAL RELATIONS SINCE THE 1970S

That international cultural relations became an increasingly crucial factor in defining the world may be seen in certain remarkable developments during the 1970s. It was then that such broadly cultural agendas as the protection of the natural environment and the promotion of human rights came to be considered vital aspects of international affairs. The United Nations conference on the environment that was held in Stockholm in 1972, for instance, was a landmark in that the protection of the physical universe from pollution, or of wild animals from excessive killing, came to be viewed as a matter of concern to the entire international community so that nations and peoples would have to join forces to achieve these objectives. Likewise, the promotion of human rights, whether of "prisoners of conscience," ethnic minorities, women, the handicapped, or other groups subject to discrimination, was seen as something that required international cooperation to undertake. World conferences began to be held, with or without the sponsorship of the United Nations, that addressed the rights of these diverse groups. Under the circumstances, United States foreign affairs, too, were becoming broader; not just the protection of security and national interests as traditionally understood, but the realization of a more livable world, both for humans and for the ecological system, would become an objective of foreign policy. President Jimmy Carter sensed these changing circumstances when he launched an initiative to seek alternative, cleaner sources of energy and to ensure the protection of human rights worldwide, even in countries that were allied to the United States in the Cold War. Cultural questions, broadly defined, were increasingly attracting the attention of Washington and other capitals.

The 1970s were also a remarkable decade in that it was the time when cultural diversity became a matter of serious concern in international affairs and, at the same time, when the number of nongovernmental organizations mushroomed, to supplement and in some instances even to supplant the work traditionally carried out by states. The two phenomena were interrelated in that both reflected the growth of civil society and, by the same token, the decline of state authority. This was a circumstance that could be observed in the United States as well as in Soviet-bloc nations, among the rich as well as developing countries. The rise of Islamic fundamentalism and its challenge to the power of both the United States (as in Iran) and the Soviet Union (as in Afghanistan) is but one extreme example of the emergence of religious and cultural diversity as a factor in international relations. And the fact that neither superpower was able to dislodge the religious fundamentalists by force indicated the growing importance of culture as a determinant of foreign affairs. Since the traditional state apparatus was not well equipped or prepared to cope with the crisis, it is not surprising that a host of nongovernmental organizations emerged to respond to the situation. Many of them were engaged in humanitarian activities to alleviate the suffering of people caught in religious strife, while others sought to promote dialogue among different religious and ethnic groups. With respect to environmentalism and human rights, too, nongovernmental organizations grew in number and influence. One cannot discuss U.S. foreign affairs during the 1970s without taking these developments into consideration.

What such developments suggested was the possible emergence of a global civil society, a world defined by cultural forces, groups, and agendas, as opposed to the traditional world consisting of sovereign states. The latter world, of course, still existed and behaved very much as sovereign states had always done, seeking to protect and promote their national interests. But national interests were now more broadly construed than earlier, and soon many in the United States and other countries began speaking of "human security" as a shared agenda for all nations. Not separate national securities and interests, but common interests defined by shared values were coming to be seen as a desirable goal for all nations. But this was not all. Even outside the framework of sovereign entities, the key framework for international affairs as traditionally understood, many nonstate actors, including multinational enterprises and nongovernmental organizations, were coming to play more and more active roles throughout the world. Theirs was an arena for an interplay of economic, technological, and cultural forces that were not necessarily bound by national units or considerations. That arena came to be called an international civil society by students of international relations dur-

ing the 1970s and the subsequent decades who saw in its formation a fundamental challenge to the traditional state system.

How the challenge would be met, and whether the international civil society would some day come to establish a more viable world order than sovereign states, were questions that fascinated statesmen and citizens alike as the twentieth century drew to a close. During the 1980s and the 1990s, there was much debate in the United States as well as elsewhere about the changing nature of international relations. Did the end of the Cold War presage the coming of an indefinite period of U.S. supremacy in world affairs? Or, on the contrary, were all great powers, even including the United States, destined eventually to decline? Which power would take its place if the United States ever did lose its hegemonic position? Such geopolitically oriented questions, however, were missing the point. They ignored the fact that international relations were increasingly being defined by nongeopolitical forces and by nonstate actors. Many of these forces and actors were cultural, broadly speaking. The globalization of cultural activities, ranging from information technology to the spread of fast food, was continuing with its own momentum, promoted by multinational enterprises, international organizations, and many other nongovernmental entities. Sometimes globalization provoked opposition on the part of forces exemplifying cultural diversity, but this was a dualism that had always existed, as we have seen. What was remarkable as the century gave way to the new millennium was that the dualism was coming more and more to determine the shape of international political and economic, as well as cultural, affairs. Cultural relations were no longer marginal pursuits, if they ever were. For the United States as well as for others, culture was coming to claim center stage as they conducted their foreign affairs.

BIBLIOGRAPHY

Chisolm, Lawrence W. *Fenollosa: The Far East and American Culture.* New Haven, Conn., 1963. Biography that illuminates intellectual interchanges between Americans and Asians.

Cohen, Warren I. *East Asian Art and American Culture: A Study in International Relations.* New York, 1992. Analysis of the American reception of Asian art.

Costigliola, Frank. *Awkward Dominion: American Political, Economic, and Cultural Relations with Europe, 1919–1933.* Ithaca, N.Y., 1984. A close examination of transatlantic cultural influences during the interwar years, going in both directions.

Diggins, John P. *Mussolini and Fascism: The View from America.* Princeton, N.J., 1972. A detailed study of what Mussolini meant to various segments of the U.S. population.

Field, James A., Jr. *America and the Mediterranean World, 1776–1882.* Princeton, N.J., 1969. The best historical treatment of American cultural relations with Middle Eastern countries.

Gienow-Hecht, Jessica C. E. *Transmission Impossible: American Journalism as Cultural Diplomacy in Postwar Germany, 1945–1955.* Baton Rouge, La., 1999. A fascinating study of an attempt to reshape German culture after World War II.

Hay, Stephen N. *Asian Ideas of East and West: Tagore and His Critics in Japan, China, and India.* Cambridge, Mass., 1970. Another biography that casts light on the discourse on East-West relations.

Hixson, Walter L. *Parting the Curtain: Propaganda, Culture, and the Cold War, 1945–1961.* New York, 1997. A good study of U.S. cultural policy during the Cold War.

Iriye, Akira. *Mutual Images: Essays in American-Japanese Relations.* Cambridge, Mass., 1975. Includes several monographs on American-Japanese cultural relations.

———. "Culture and International History." In Michael J. Hogan and Thomas G. Paterson, eds. *Explaining the History of American Foreign Relations.* New York and Cambridge, 1991. An essay that notes some of the landmark studies of the history of intercultural, as distinct from intra-cultural, relations.

———. *Across the Pacific: An Inner History of American-East Asian Relations.* Rev. ed. Chicago, 1992. A multicultural treatment of American–East Asian relations.

———. *Cultural Internationalism and World Order.* Baltimore, 1997. Puts international cultural relations in the framework of the development of internationalism in modern history.

Isaacs, Harold R. *Scratches on Our Minds: American Images of China and India.* New York, 1958. American attitudes toward China and India.

Kloppenberg, James T. *Uncertain Victory: Social Democracy and Progressivism in European and American Thought, 1870–1920.* New York, 1986. Analyzes transatlantic intellectual and political movements at the turn of the century, comprehending developments within the United States as an integral part of the story of the Western world's coming to terms with the realities of modernization.

Koppes, Clayton R., and Gregory D. Black. *Hollywood Goes to War: How Politics, Profits and Propaganda Shaped World War II Movies.* New York, 1987. Study of wartime culture that focuses on use of the movies as a tool for indoctrination at home and propaganda abroad.

Kuklick, Bruce. *Puritans in Babylon: The Ancient Near East and American Intellectual Life, 1880–1931.* Princeton, N.J., 1996. Studies American fascination with and archaeological activities in the Ottoman Empire and Near East.

Lancaster, Clay. *The Japanese Influence in America.* New York, 1963. Impact on American philosophy and literature.

Ninkovich, Frank A. *The Diplomacy of Ideas: U.S. Foreign Policy and Cultural Relations, 1938–1950.* Cambridge and New York, 1981. Treats the origins and development of official U.S. cultural relations.

Northrop, F. S. C., and Helen H. Livingston, eds. *Cross-Cultural Understanding: Epistemology in Anthropology.* New York, 1964. Contains essays dealing with the problem of cross-cultural understanding.

Nye, Joseph S., Jr. *Bound to Lead: The Changing Nature of American Power.* New York, 1990. One of the most penetrating analyses of the relationship between the cultural and other aspects of U.S. foreign affairs.

Park, Robert E. *Race and Culture.* Glencoe, Ill., 1950. Contains some of the earliest and most penetrating observations on the global "melting pot."

Pells, Richard. *Not Like Us: How Europeans Have Loved, Hated, and Transformed American Culture Since World War II.* New York, 1997. One of the few systematic studies of transatlantic cultural relations.

Reynolds, David. *Rich Relations: The American Occupation of Britain, 1942–1945.* New York, 1995. Study of American culture during the war that explicitly treats international affairs.

Rodgers, Daniel T. *Atlantic Crossings: Social Politics in a Progressive Age.* Cambridge, Mass., 1998. Analyzes transatlantic intellectual and political movements at the turn of the century, comprehending developments within the United States as an integral part of the story of the Western world's coming to terms with the realities of modernization.

Rosenberg, Emily S. *Spreading the American Dream: American Economic and Cultural Expansion, 1890–1945*. Rev. ed. New York, 1982. Argues that officials in Washington often informally cooperated with private businessmen, religious organizations, and philanthropic as well as other associations to spread the American way of life to other lands.

———. "Cultural Interaction." In Stanley I. Kutler, ed. *Encyclopedia of the United States in the Twentieth Century*. Vol. 2. New York, 1996. Incorporates the vocabulary of cultural hegemony into a discussion of U.S. foreign relations.

Sumner, William Graham. *Folkways: A Study of Sociological Importance of Usages, Manners, Customs, Mores, and Morals*. Boston, 1913. An American anthropologist who not only described but also raised methodological questions about the study of other cultures.

See also COLONIALISM AND NEOCOLONIALISM; GLOBALIZATION; HUMAN RIGHTS; IMPERIALISM; RACE AND ETHNICITY.

DECISION MAKING

Valerie M. Hudson

American foreign policy may be studied from a variety of perspectives. Historical narrative, institutional analysis, issue area examination, rational choice theory, study of ideational and legal evolution, gendered perspectives, and Realpolitik accounts are all valid and useful approaches to understanding not only American foreign policy but the foreign policy of any nation.

DECISION MAKING AND FOREIGN POLICY ANALYSIS

Decision-making approaches and theories fall within the subfield of foreign policy analysis, within the larger field of internation relations. Foreign policy analysis (known as FPA) is distinguished from other theoretical approaches in international relations by its insistence that the explanatory focal point must be the foreign policy decision makers themselves and not larger structural or systemic phenomena. Explanatory variables from all levels of analysis, from the most micro to the most macro, are of interest to the analyst to the extent that they affect the decision-making process. Thus, of all subfields in international relations, FPA is the most radically integrative theoretical enterprise. Investigations into the roles that personality variables, perception and construction of meaning, group dynamics, organizational process, bureaucratic politics, domestic politics, culture, and system structure play in foreign policy decision making are the core research agenda of FPA. But as Richard Snyder, one of the founders of FPA, and his colleagues Henry Bruck and Burton Sapin noted in 1954, these are only important as they have an impact on the only true agents in international affairs—human decision makers:

> In a sense, then, in the age-old philosophy of social science debate concerning whether agents

or structures are the primary determinants of behavior in the social world, FPA comes down squarely on the side of agents. FPA is the agent-centered theory of international relations. Foreign policy analysts argue that without an account of human agency in international relations theory, one cannot develop a satisfactory account of change over time in international affairs. Furthermore, given the immense destructive power inherent in internation relations, explanations that omit an examination of the role and efficacy of human agency in using and containing that power do less than they ought.

Here, then, is yet another difference between FPA approaches and other accepted approaches to understanding international relations. Not only does FPA give an account of agency, but it gives a specific, rather than a general, account of agency. In such approaches as game theory and rational choice explanations of foreign policy, the actor is conceptualized as a generic, rational, utility-maximizing decision maker. In contrast, theories of FPA unpack that generic "black-boxed" actor and discover that the idiosyncrasies of the actor do affect foreign policy choice. To use terms coined by Alexander George, FPA is more interested in "actor-specific" theory than "actor-general" theory.

In sum, then, FPA produces radically integrative, agent-oriented, and actor-specific theory. In these three ways, it remains a unique and easily distinguishable subfield of international relations.

A Word About the Explanandum   What is it that foreign policy analysts seek to explain? To use a common phrase, what is the dependent variable in FPA?

Despite attempts to formulate "foreign policy" in terms of consistently operationalized variables, it must be admitted that what is to be explained may vary across research programs within FPA. Some programs focus on foreign policy as an *output* of decision making; others focus on the decision-making *process* in foreign policy. For example, the use of events data (discussed below) as one's dependent variable is an example of conceptualizing foreign policy as an output. In this tradition, foreign policy "events" gleaned from news media can be coded for some set of variables, such as the level of commitment implied by the event on the part of the acting nation. Standardized coding then allows for direct comparison of the outputs of various nation-state actors, as well as permitting a longitudinal analysis of the foreign policy behavior of one nation.

It is also possible to take a more process-oriented approach to what is meant by foreign policy. For example, one could use the policy positions of various actors as the dependent variable, tracing how a particular position becomes dominant within a decision-making group over time. One could walk the cat back yet another step and examine how such policy stances crystallize in the first place from basic cognitive processes such as perception, problem representation, and construction of meaning. Another step back would be to ask how the decision-making group comes to be in the first place, how structures and processes of groups are created and changed over time within a society. Role conceptions concerning the nation-state, and concerning various institutions and groups within the nation-state, could also be the focus of inquiry.

Both approaches to the explanandum in FPA have been fruitfully used, and insights from each type of research informs the other. It is true that choice of explanandum affects choice of methodology: aggregate statistical testing may be useful in events data studies, whereas process-tracing and interpretivist analysis might be more helpful with process-oriented conceptualizations of foreign policy.

SURVEY OF FPA THEORETICAL APPROACHES

Individual Psychology and Cognition   Characteristics of the individual decision maker may be very important in understanding the decisions ultimately made. Harold and Margaret Sprout, in their pioneering work *Man-Milieu Relationship Hypotheses in the Context of International Politics* (1956), believe that analysis of this "psycho-milieu" is crucial to understanding nation-state foreign policy. Margaret G. Hermann argues that certain conditions increase the probability that

the personal characteristics of leaders will affect foreign policy: when the decision maker has wide decision latitude within the governmental system, when the situation is nonroutine, ambiguous, or carries with it very high stakes, or when the policy under discussion is a long-term policy or strategy. In addition to these situational variables, the personality of a leader may also be more influential, according to Hermann, when the leader does not have formal diplomatic training or when the leader is not especially attentive or sensitive to changes in external circumstances.

Furthermore, the analyst must remain aware of the limitations and vulnerabilities of human beings, both in a physical sense and a cognitive sense. Physically, human decision making can be affected by stress levels, lack of sleep, acute or chronic illness, mental pathologies, medications being used, age, and so forth. For example, psychologists have found that decision making tends to be of higher quality when moderate levels of stress are present. Too low a stress level or too high a stress level can be counterproductive. But there are also cognitive limitations inherent in being human. The human brain is so complex that human beings often rely on reasoning shortcuts or heuristics to make decisions. Errors of representation, the "gambler's fallacy" (where the gambler believes that an outcome is more likely to occur if it has not occurred lately), and many other biases may affect choice. Furthermore, a person's ability to handle complexity has an upper limit: psychologists tell us that even the most conceptually complex human reasoner can only hold seven things in mind simultaneously. Robert Jervis explores these factors in depth in *Perception and Misperception in International Politics* (1976).

Humans are also a diverse lot in terms of their personal belief systems. At birth, each human begins to develop beliefs about how the world works and what is to be valued. In FPA, several scholars have created theoretical frameworks to typologize such belief systems. Margaret Hermann created a set of "foreign policy orientations" based on elements such as nationalism, belief in ability to control events, distrust of others, and task-affect orientation, among others. Alexander George promulgated the tool of "operational code analysis," wherein the analyst determines a leader's beliefs with reference to how best to accomplish goals. David Winter has sought to typologize the motivating forces for individual leaders. Such frameworks of analysis often rely on the methodology of content analysis, where a leader's speeches and writings are analyzed thematically or quantitatively to provide insight into the specifics of his or her belief system. Learning and change in knowledge systems has been a focus of inquiry for Jack Levy, and Matthew Bonham's methodology of cognitive mapping of content-analyzed material can be used to trace changes in knowledge structures over time.

Small-Group Dynamics and Problem Representation

It is arguably within the context of small-group deliberations that most foreign policy decisions are made. Thus, the study of group decision making becomes a very important element of FPA. As noted, FPA owes a great debt to Richard Snyder and his colleagues Henry Bruck and Burton Sapin for insisting that researchers look below the nation-state level of analysis to the actual decision-making groups involved.

With regard to small groups in particular, as opposed to larger collectivities such as organizations and bureaucracies, the seminal work is undoubtedly Irving Janis's classic *Groupthink* (1972). Using examples taken from the annals of American foreign policy, such as the Bay of Pigs invasion, Janis was able to show how the desire to maintain group consensus and subjective feelings of personal acceptance by the group can cause deterioration of decision-making quality. Such groups wind up being "soft-headed" but "hard-hearted" as outgroups are dehumanized and ingroup decision processes become sloppier. A hallmark of groupthink is the risky shift, where the group is prepared to make riskier decisions than any individual member of the group would be prepared to make on his own. A sense of group invulnerability and omniscience creates psychological disincentives to rethinking the group's initially preferred policy or even to constructing contingency plans in the event of failure of that policy. A later generation of scholars advanced Janis's work and explored the scope conditions under which groupthink is more or less likely.

The study of how a group comes to an initial representation of the problem at hand, and how, then, the group members aggregate their differing preferences, is another research agenda at this level of analysis. One way of analyzing group problem representation is to view group discussions as the attempt to jointly author a "story" that makes the problem intelligible. Donald A. Sylvan and Deborah Haddad, in the volume *Problem Representation in Foreign Policy Decision Making* (1998), suggest that such coauthorship allows for the action decision to be made collectively. When rival story lines are offered and collide, the group as a whole must work its way back to a consistent story line through persuasion and analysis. Yuen Foon Khong's important book *Analogies at War* (1992) demonstrates how the use of the conflicting analogies to frame the problem of Vietnam led to conceptual difficulties in reasoning about policy options. The "Korea" analogy gained ascendance, according to Khong, without sufficient attention paid to the incongruities between the two sets of circumstances. Thus, the debate over metaphors and analogies used to understand a new situation may predispose a group's policy response, possibly with tragic consequences.

How the structure and the process of a group affect decision outcomes, making some outcomes more or less likely, is also an interesting question. The role played by the members—as representatives of a larger group, or as autonomous actors—coupled with the size of the group and the leadership style used, may make deadlock more probable than agreement. These structural variables may in turn be influenced by rules for resolving conflict within the group, such as majority voting, two-thirds voting, or unanimity. Theory on coalition-building and bargaining may be invaluable in understanding how a particular decision is ultimately selected. Furthermore, certain types of leaders prefer certain types of group structures and processes. Theoretical leverage on the most likely outcome for various types of groups may be gained by these types of analysis.

Organizational Process and Bureaucratic Politics

Although actual foreign policy decisions may be made primarily in small groups, the policy positions of group members and the subsequent implementation of decisions made by small groups are only well understood when the analyst includes insights at the organizational and bureaucratic levels of analysis. American foreign policy is dominated by several large organizations, such as the Defense Department and the State Department, and the resulting web of organizations—the bureaucracy—may have a political dynamic all its own. Indeed, to see this bureaucracy as merely the executive arm of foreign policy is to underestimate the powerful political forces that drive organizations. These powerful motivations—the desire for expanded "turf," expanded budget, expanded influence vis-à-vis other organizations, as well as the desire to maintain organizational "essence," "morale," and "culture"—may result in a radical undermining of the supposedly rational decision-making process in foreign policy. Morton Halperin's *Bureaucratic Politics and Foreign Policy* (1974) gives unforgettable examples of this unhappy dynamic with reference to the era of the Vietnam War.

Graham Allison's 1971 *Essence of Decision* (and its 1999 update) examines not only the subversion of rationality at the decision-making stage but also the subversion of rationality at the implementation end. Large organizations typically develop standard operating procedures (SOPs) that allow for quicker, more efficient responses than would otherwise be possible with collectivities numbering in the thousands or even millions of persons. Unfortunately, these SOPs are fairly insensitive to the nuances of external circumstances as well as to efforts by national leaders to adapt or modify them. Indeed, national leaders may not even comprehend that when they give an executive order it is first translated into a series of sequential SOP steps. This translation may leave much to be desired in terms of flexibility, creativity, and appropriateness. For example, Allison found that the Soviet Strategic Rocket Forces, given the order in 1962 to construct ballistic missile sites in Cuba, used the same SOP they had developed for doing so in the Soviet Union. This SOP did not include a provision for camouflaging the construction sites. Thus, American U-2s were able to photograph the sites, and American analysts were immediately able to identify what they were, giving President John F. Kennedy and his advisers a crucial window of time in which to compel the Soviets to abandon their intentions.

Domestic Politics Surely there is no better case than that of American foreign policy with which to demonstrate the influence of domestic political considerations on policymaking. The chief executive must stand for election every four years and as a result may be constrained in his ability to act as he otherwise would absent such electoral considerations. The Congress and the judiciary also have unique roles to play in American foreign policy, and players there may also be facing political imperatives. The two-party system of American politics also plays havoc with the rationality of decision making, as actors must not only think of their own well-being but the relative standing of their party vis-à-vis the other. Furthermore, the variety of vocal special interest

and lobbying groups, not only national but also transnational in nature, is positively dizzying.

Robert Putnam suggests that we understand foreign policy as a "two-level game" being played by the leadership of the nation. At one level, the leadership is trying to retain its domestic political standing and enhance its electoral prospects and the electoral prospects of its allies. At another level, the leadership is trying to negotiate with foreign powers to achieve foreign policy objectives. A bad move at either level can imperil one's prospects at the other level. The astute leader attempts to create opportunities whereby moves at one level directly translate into advantage at the other. Interestingly, one counterintuitive finding is that the more constrained the leader can claim to be in the domestic arena, the more insistent he can be in the foreign arena. Thus, the threat that the U.S. Congress would never ratify a particular treaty can be used by administration officials to successfully maneuver other foreign actors to move closer to their own preferred bargaining position.

Of course, the reverse is also a recognizable phenomenon in international relations. Sometimes international situations or policies are used by the government to deflect domestic criticism and bolster support among its citizenry. The oft-noted "rally 'round the flag" effect, wherein an international crisis involving confrontation with a hostile power increases the approval rating of a president, is one that sometimes is purposefully used by an embattled regime. Both Argentina and Great Britain arguably used the Falklands controversy of 1982 for this purpose.

Joe D. Hagan has attempted to create a cross-national database of the fragmentation and vulnerability of political regimes, with special reference to executive and legislative structures. His data set includes ninety-four regimes for thirty-eight nations over a ten-year period. He was able to assess whether foreign policy behavior, such as level of commitment in policy, is affected by political opposition. He discovered, among many other findings, that military or party opposition to the regime does indeed constrain possible foreign policy action.

In addition to more formal political group influence, there has been a robust research agenda tracing the relationship between U.S. public opinion and U.S. foreign policy. After World War II but before the Vietnam War era, it was an American truism that public opinion did not drive foreign policy, as "politics stopped at the water's edge." The Vietnam trauma undermined that consensus, and this was accelerated by the end of the Cold War and the rise of the global economy. Now Americans could see plainly that what happened in Thailand, for instance, might affect their pensions. International arrangements such as the North American Free Trade Agreement and the World Trade Organization could be seen to have local effects. The responsiveness of the national leadership to public opinion can be seen most plainly in the swift retreat of U.S. forces in Somalia following the downing of two American helicopters in Mogadishu, with television footage of a paratrooper's body being dragged through the streets by an angry mob. Truly, as many have said, there is now a tangible "CNN effect" that must be taken into account when studying American foreign policy.

Culture and Ideational Social Construction

Those FPA scholars who study the effects of culture and ideational social construction on foreign policy justifiably assert that what large collectivities believe to be true and believe to be good affects what those collectivities then do. The world is not only material—it is ideational—and often the ideational can be a more powerful force than the material.

One way to examine this issue is to investigate the effects of differences in culture on resultant foreign policy. Each national culture constructs a unique web of beliefs, meanings, values, and capabilities based on their idiosyncratic historical experiences. The "heroic history" of a nation is replete with lessons in what is precious and how one best protects those values. Such differences may aggravate internation hostilities, sometimes even unintentionally. For example, on the eve of serious negotiations, American negotiators are likely to state what they think an acceptable compromise would be and view their task as persuading the other party of the correctness of this view. Chinese negotiators, on the other hand, are likely to denounce their negotiating partner on the eve of serious negotiations, suggesting there can be no compromise at all. Unless each party understands the cultural proclivities of the other, fundamental misunderstanding and heightened hostilities may result.

Value differences may lead to misunderstanding as well. For example, Americans proudly proclaim that they would never negotiate with terrorists or give in to their demands. The Japanese, on the other hand, see no shame at all in negotiating with terrorists. When faced with a threat by another nation, the American response is to isolate and threaten that nation. However, in a 1999 study, Valerie A. Hudson found the Russian response was to befriend and trade with that nation so that the threat might be erased in a peaceful manner.

How do these differences in culture arise in the first place? They arise through a shared national experience that is interpreted by human agents who then undertake the task of persuading their compatriots that this interpretation is a good and appropriate one. Scholarly work has been done on each of these elements.

Helen Purkitt has used the methodology of "think-aloud protocol" to study how it is that an individual comes to an interpretation of a situation. Experimental subjects, including policymakers, were asked by Purkitt to verbalize their thought processes as they deliberated on policy issues. Purkitt thus was able to "see" which aspects of a situation were salient for which persons, how they synthesized uncertainty with analogy in their interpretations, and how soon it took for a particular interpretation to become accepted and treated as a natural interpretation for a situation. G. R. Boynton used textual exegesis of congressional hearings to investigate crystallization of understanding among committee members, finding that members would attempt to narrate a version of the events under question to each other and build a coherent narrative of the whole through smaller pieces upon which all could agree. Only when testimony had been translated into recognizable elements from this jointly constructed narrative were committee members able to fully understand the events.

In addition to the construction of meaning for individuals and small groups of decision makers, meanings may be constructed and shared among larger groups as well. National identity is continually evolving. Although the roots of national identity may lie in the history of the nation, it is current interpretation of that identity that may be more useful to the analyst. One important theoretical framework in this area of inquiry is the national-role-conception approach first developed by Kal Holsti in 1970. He argues that any social system, including a social system made up of nation-states, creates a set of differentiable roles that include both privileges and responsibilities. A variety of factors, including domestic conditions, distribution of power within the system of states, history, legal precedent, and others, help determine which nations gravitate

DECISION MAKING AND CUBA

It is interesting to note that several of the most important works in foreign policy analysis use the same case study involving U.S. foreign policy toward Cuba during the Kennedy administration. Specifically, the Bay of Pigs invasion of 1961 and the Cuban missile crisis of 1962 have received more attention by foreign policy analysts than any other cases. The two crises provide a neat set of intellectual bookends: How could the same president, surrounded by approximately the same advisers, mess up so royally in April 1961 and yet acquit himself so heroically and save the world from nuclear holocaust sixteen months later? Two of the most important works in the foreign policy analysis tradition, Graham Allison's *Essence of Decision* and Irving Janis's *Groupthink,* use these cases to demonstrate the crucial role of decision making in international affairs.

Although one might think that such scholarly attention would eventually wane as the crises recede historically, events have sparked renewed interest. For example, the release in 1997 of tapes made by Kennedy

during ExCom (Executive Committee) deliberations prompted a whole new wave of theoretical analysis of the Cuban missile crisis. In the spring of 2001, the main participants in the Bay of Pigs, including Fidel Castro, rebel commanders, and Central Intelligence Agency handlers, convened for a first-ever conference in Havana, and information heretofore secret, such as transcripts of Castro's radio communications from the field, were made public at that time.

One of the best ways to view the immense reconceptualization of these cases that all of this new information has brought about is to read Graham Allison's original *Essence of Decision* (1971) side by side with the latest version of the book by Allison and Philip Zelikow (1999). An important lesson to be gleaned is that our understanding of decision making rests in large part upon our understanding of the empirical historical realities of decision making. When you change the latter, you inevitably change the former.

toward which roles. A nation-state then develops a distinctive national role conception, which renders that nation-state's behavior more intelligible and predictable to the analyst. So, for example, though the United States may see itself in the role of a "bloc leader" (leader of the Western bloc), France views itself as a "regional leader" in Europe. Such self-conceptions may clash, as they often do in the case of France and the United States. National-role-conception analysis may uncover differences that might otherwise go unnoticed; for example Marijke Breuning points out that although Americans might lump Belgium and the Netherlands together as nations with very similar attributes, the Dutch tend to see themselves playing a proactive role in encouraging development in less developed countries due to their heroic history of involvement in exploration and colonization. Belgium, on the other hand, a creation of the major European powers, never took such an initiative and became a particularly indifferent former colonial power.

National identity or national role conceptions do change over time. Tracking that change

involves detailed analysis of speeches and texts by those who help form opinion within society. Ideas are very useful to policy entrepreneurs, and identifying who is pushing what idea for what reason may help the analyst keep his or her finger on the course of identity evolution within a nation-state. Often ideas must be couched in the language of historical national identity to find favor with larger national audiences. For example, Hellmut Lotz noted in 1997 that on the eve of the Al Gore–Ross Perot debate over NAFTA, a sizable percentage of Americans were undecided over whether the agreement to include Mexico in a free trade agreement with the United States and Canada was a good thing or not. During the course of the televised debate, both men made reference to key themes of American national identity: the American Dream, American exceptionalism, American strength, American vulnerability, American isolationism, and so forth. Lotz found that the audience of undecideds resonated overwhelmingly with the Gore portrayal of America as strong and fearless rather than with the Perot portrayal of America as weak and needing to protect itself from foreigners. Thus, despite the fact that both men were speaking in the context of shared meaning concerning America, Gore was the more successful policy entrepreneur, for he was able to sway voters to his position by means of his selective emphasis on strategically chosen aspects of American identity. In a similar vein, in a 1993 article Jeffrey Checkel was able to reconstruct the trail of policy-entrepreneur intervention in the development of Mikhail Gorbachev's *perestroika* policies. To trace the positions and the network contacts of persons holding particular ideas is a formidable task for the analyst, but one which is very rewarding if the focus is on possible change in, rather than continuity of, foreign policy direction.

STRUCTURAL AND SYSTEMIC FACTORS

Although foreign policy analysis places its focus on decision makers and decision making, government officials are not ignorant of salient features of the international system. Characteristics of the international system may constrain what policymakers feel they can do, but simultaneously may provide opportunities to advance their nation-states' purposes. Furthermore, nation-states can attempt to reflexively shape the system in such a way that their nation-state is more secure.

Two broad approaches to this topic may be differentiated. One approach is to examine the national attributes of nations, including a comparison of such attributes. Nation-state behavior and internation interaction may then be explained by reference to these attributes. Second, one could look at the system in a more abstract manner, by investigating non-unit-specific factors such as anarchy within a system, the existence of international regimes on particular issues, evolving conceptualizations of legitimate and illegitimate behavior within the system, and so forth.

Regarding the first, attribute-centered approach, one of the classic works of foreign policy analysis is the "pre-theory" framework of James Rosenau. In a seminal 1966 article, Rosenau suggests that the key to understanding a nation-state's behavior is to uncover its "genotype." That is, every nation has particular attributes that may make certain factors more determinant of its foreign policy than others. Using three dichotomous variables (size: small/large; wealth: developed/underdeveloped; accountability: open/closed), Rosenau posited

eight genotypes: small/developed/open; large/ underdeveloped/closed, and so on. Depending on the genotype of the nation under scrutiny, Rosenau then posits that certain factors would be more important for the analyst to investigate. So, for example, in a large/developed/open nation-state, Rosenau asserts that role variables (akin to national role conception) would be the most important factor, with systemic and idiosyncratic (for example, personal characteristics of leaders) being least important. On the other hand, in a small/underdeveloped/closed nation-state, idiosyncratic and systemic factors would be precisely those of greatest significance.

A more modern variant of this attributional approach is the theory of the democratic peace, which highlights the empirical fact that democracies virtually never go to war with one another. Although some have debated the definition of democracy (is Yugoslavia a democracy?), and others have suggested that democracy here is serving as a stand-in for a more fundamental factor such as cultural similarity, the behavior of nation-states is again being explained in terms of their attributes. Indeed, one might claim this approach can also subsume Marxist-Leninist explanations of war, which focus on the profit imperatives of imperialist states to explain the bellicosity of the European powers.

The second approach—more oriented to the structure of the system itself as opposed to the attributes of its members—is a well-established research tradition in international relations. Here, no matter what the attributes of states, the system itself may express properties that can be determinant of state behavior. So, for example, in the work of Kenneth Waltz, the primary factor affecting state behavior is the anarchy of the international system. In the absence of a world government, benign or tyrannical, able to enforce a code of behavior, states must help themselves, for they cannot trust other states in the system not to deflect from pledges of cooperation that they may have made. An emphasis on deterrence, a search for primacy and power, and a notable lack of cooperation even on important issues are all hallmarks of anarchy. Even states that actively desire to behave otherwise may be constrained by the straitjacket of system structure in this theory.

There may be other elements of the system that fine-tune the effects of anarchy. For example, the existence or nonexistence of intergovernmental organizations, the strength of international legal precedent, the number of poles of power in the system (bipolar, tripolar, multipolar), the degree of globalization of interaction (including trade and communication), patterns of internation dependency, relevant technology (such as the development of weapons of mass destruction and the ballistic missiles to hurl them half a world away), may all play a role in modifying the effects of anarchy. Some theorists assert that anarchy can be overcome among states dealing with particular issues, and real sacrifice and cooperation can then be expressed by the nation-state. Agreements on ozone depletion, destruction of chemical and biological weapons, renunciation of land mines, and so forth can be seen as examples of this interpretation.

Other scholars would go even farther and claim that nation-states can proactively shape and mold the international system. As one such theorist, Alexander Wendt, put it in 1992, "anarchy is what states make of it." Drawing upon the more ideational literature mentioned, Wendt and others believe that shared meanings develop between governments in the system and that such shared meanings can transform what happens in the world system. For example, norms against genocide, assassination, rape in war, torture, slavery, use of land mines, and so forth have arisen within the international system and are becoming a robust basis for international action. Before the 1990s it would have been inconceivable for the former president of Chile, Augusto Pinochet, to have been held for an extradition hearing in Britain on the order of a Spanish judge. Yet by the turn of the twenty-first century Americans were wondering whether their own leaders might be tried for war crimes in a new international criminal court. These evolving norms did not arise from material conditions but from the formation of an ideational consensus or near-consensus.

In sum, then, the international systemic context of decision making must be factored into the theories of leader personality, small group dynamics, and bureaucratic and domestic politics that we have already examined.

Events Data   No discussion of foreign policy analysis or decision-making theories would be complete without at least a cursory mention of events data. In most of the theories pitched at the subnational level of analysis mentioned, data indicative of the process of decision making hold center stage. Thus, content analysis of speeches and texts, analysis of tapes or records of group discussions, simulations and experiments, and

process-tracing and other methodologies that lay bare the actual mechanics of decisions and their antecedents and consequences typically predominate the empirics of these theoretical efforts. We have previously mentioned that one could also focus on the outcomes of decision-making processes. The events data movement was designed to do just that.

Conceived when the social sciences were enamored of aggregate statistical testing of generalized hypotheses, the foreign policy "event" was to be the intellectual counterpart of the "vote" in the study of American politics. Votes could be tabulated, and a variety of statistical tests could be performed, to determine whether voting correlated with possible explanatory factors such as race, gender, ethnicity, socioeconomic status, and so forth. The foreign policy event was to have the same utility for international relations.

One could imagine tabulating every action every nation took every day, whether those actions be of a more diplomatic or rhetorical nature or something more concrete, such as the use of military force. A number of variables would naturally be coded, such as the identity of the acting nation, the identity of the recipients of the action, the date, and some scaling or categorization of the action itself. These events would be gleaned from open source material, such as newspapers and wire services. Once thousands of events had been collected, aggregate statistical testing for robust correlations, longitudinal tracking of the evolving relationships between any given nations, patterns preceding the outbreak of violence in the system, and a host of other potentially interesting questions could then be addressed.

Even the U.S. government was sufficiently interested in the potential of this data collection effort to fund various projects to the tune of several million dollars in the 1960s and 1970s. Some of these event data sets continued to be updated into the twenty-first century, some by computer programs. The more famous events data sets include WEIS (World Event/Interaction Survey), COPDAB (Conflict and Peace Data Bank), CREON (Comparative Research on the Events of Nations), and KEDS (Kansas Events Data Set).

Events data began to lose its appeal to the wider subfield as it became understood that much of the richness and complexity of decision making was simply missing in an events data format. Thus foreign policy analysis largely returned to the study of process variables more conducive to a focus on decision making.

Integrative Efforts   We have spoken of foreign policy analysis as a radically integrative intellectual exercise that requires the analyst to know quite a bit about phenomena at a variety of levels of analysis, from leader personality to system characteristics. All of this information must then be filtered through one's model of the decision makers and the decision-making process in order to gauge what policy choices are most likely in a given situation. This is a fairly tall order, and yet the foreign policy and national security establishment of the U.S. government must make these types of analyses every day.

It would be desirable for the foreign policy analysis scholarly community to offer some advice on how this is to be done in a theoretical sense. How does one actually accomplish such integration? What are the possible outputs of such an integrative exercise? Perhaps not surprisingly, FPA scholars struggle to provide such advice. When Rosenau wrote his "pre-theory" article in the 1960s, with its goal of tracing the influence of factors across several levels of analysis, the most he could offer was a ranking of the importance of each level of analysis based on the genotype of the nation under study. Frankly, FPA has not progressed much past Rosenau's offering; almost forty years later very little self-consciously integrative theoretical work existed in FPA. The CREON II project (1971–1993) developed a creative theoretical framework for integration. Three fundamental components comprised the model. In the first, called Situational Imperative, the details of the situation at hand, including the type of problem, the relationships between the nation-states involved in the problem, the power distribution across the involved nations, and other variables would provide a macro-level "cut" at what the probable foreign policy choice would be. A second component, called Societal Structure and Status, would offer information from the levels of domestic politics and culture. The third and central component was termed the Ultimate Decision Unit. Into this component, representing the actual decision makers in their decision-making setting, information from the first two components of the model would be introduced.

Three types of ultimate decision units were envisioned. Each type of unit came with its own set of most important decision-making variables. For example, in a predominant leader decision unit, variables relating to the head of state and his or her interaction with advisers and style of processing information about the situation at hand would be most important. In the second type of unit, the single group decision unit, theoretical literature about small-group structures and processes, groupthink, and coalition building become crucial. In the third type of unit, the multiple autonomous actor decision unit, literature about bargaining and conflict resolution would be most salient. In another innovative move, country experts would be asked to provide the majority of the inputs for the models. Several empirical cases analyzed by the decision units model were presented in a special issue of the journal *Political Psychology* in 2001.

The Question of Evaluation   Before concluding this survey of foreign policy analysis literature, it must be noted that although the contemporary focus is on explanation of foreign policy, the subfield began with the aspiration that the insights of FPA could be used to evaluate and improve the quality of foreign policy decision making. Many early FPA scholars, such as Irving Janis and Morton Halperin, understood that the price of low-quality foreign policy decisions was death for innocent persons, both combatants and noncombatants. Indeed, in an era of nuclear weapons, the scale of such tragic deaths could be massive. If no other subfield of international relations attempts it, at least FPA should shoulder the responsibility of revealing the true and large extent to which human agency shapes international affairs. By such revelation, useful lessons and insights for the policymakers of today and tomorrow might be drawn.

Although much of scholarly FPA has turned from that task, at the turn of the twenty-first century there were still scholars dedicated to its fulfillment. Alexander George, in particular, through such works as *Bridging the Gap* (1993), has done much to keep this normative agenda alive. Works in this vein, such as *Good Judgment in Foreign Policy* (2001), edited by Stanley Renshon and Deborah Welch Larsen, continued to appear. It is hoped that a fuller engagement of agential questions will arise again within the subfield of FPA. From such an engagement, greater policy relevance will be achieved, which would be a positive step forward.

CONCLUSION

The decision-making approaches and theories associated with the subfield of foreign policy analysis are unique in international relations for their attention to the specific human agents behind every foreign policy choice. Rather than agent-general deductive systems, such as found in game theory, a more detailed and particularistic account of human agency is sought. In addition to this agential focus, a decision-making approach mandates that information from multiple levels of analysis be collected and synthesized in a parallel fashion as the actual decision makers collect and synthesize such information. FPA thus becomes a profoundly integrative theoretical enterprise as well.

This type of approach is noteworthy for its potential not only to integrate disparate variables from distinct levels of analysis but also to integrate currently disconnected domains of human knowledge and activity concerning international affairs. Two notable examples are the disconnect between international relations and comparative politics within the discipline of political science, and the disconnect between international relations and comparative politics as found in the academy on the one hand and the foreign policymaking establishment of the government on the other.

Decision-making approaches and foreign policy analysis can provide some needed connections here. By integrating variables at the supernational and national levels of analysis (the traditional purview of international relations) with variables at subnational levels of analysis (the traditional realm of comparative politics), FPA provides theoretical and empirical linkages that demonstrate how each subfield could usefully inform the other. By emphasizing the decision maker and the decision-making process, by exploring the agency inherent in foreign policy making, by pointing out useful lessons from the study of past foreign policy decision making's successes and failures, FPA has the potential to render the knowledge of the academy useful to real practitioners. Given the immense destructive power that can be unleashed at the international level, it is surely incumbent upon the academy to "bridge the gap" and offer its best insights as a contribution to the peace and safety of the world.

BIBLIOGRAPHY

Allison, Graham T. *Essence of Decision: Explaining the Cuban Missile Crisis.* Boston, 1971. One of the best works of foreign policy analysis.

Allison, Graham T., and Philip Zelikow. *Essence of Decision: Explaining the Cuban Missile Crisis.* New York, 1999. An update of an important work using material declassified in the 1990s.

Bonham, G. Matthew, Victor M. Sergeev, and Pavel B. Parhin. "The Limited Test-Ban Agreement: Emergence of New Knowledge Structures in International Negotiations." *International Studies Quarterly* 41 (1997): 215–240.

Boynton, G. R. "The Expertise of the Senate Foreign Relations Committee." In Valerie M. Hudson, ed. *Artificial Intelligence and International Politics.* Boulder, Colo., 1991.

Breuning, Marijke. "Culture, History, and Role: Belgian and Dutch Axioms and Foreign Assistance Policy." In Valerie M. Hudson, ed. *Culture and Foreign Policy.* Boulder, Colo., 1997.

Callahan, Patrick, Linda Brady, and Margaret G. Hermann, eds. *Describing Foreign Policy Behavior.* Beverly Hills, Calif., 1982.

Checkel, Jeffrey T. "Ideas, Institutions, and the Gorbachev Foreign Policy Revolution." *World Politics* 45 (1993): 271–300.

East, Maurice A., Stephen A. Salmore, and Charles F. Hermann, eds. *Why Nations Act: Theoretical Perspectives for Comparative Foreign Studies.* Beverly Hills, Calif., 1978.

George, Alexander L. "The 'Operational Code': A Neglected Approach to the Study of Political Leaders and Decision-making." *International Studies Quarterly* 13 (1969): 190–222. Another seminal article for those interested in cognitive approaches.

———. *Bridging the Gap: Theory and Practice in Foreign Policy.* Washington, D.C., 1993. An impassioned call for the academy to inform foreign policy decision making.

Hagan, Joe D. "Regimes, Political Oppositions, and the Comparative Analysis of Foreign Policy." In Charles F. Hermann, Charles W. Kegley, Jr., and James N. Rosenau, eds. *New Directions in the Study of Foreign Policy.* Boston, 1986.

Halperin, Morton. *Bureaucratic Politics and Foreign Policy.* Washington, DC, 1974. A classic on the subject.

Hermann, Charles F. "Decision Structure and Process." In Maurice East et al. *Why Nations Act.* Beverly Hills, Calif., 1978.

Hermann, Margaret G. "Personality and Foreign Policy Decision Making: A Study of 53

Heads of Government." In Donald A. Sylvan and Steve Chan, eds. *Foreign Policy Decision Making: Perception, Cognition, and Artificial Intelligence.* New York, 1984.

Holsti, Kal J. "National Role Conceptions in the Study of Foreign Policy." *International Studies Quarterly* 14 (1970): 233–309. The seminal article on national role conception that started a new research agenda that continues to this day.

Hudson, Valerie M. "Cultural Expectations of One's Own and Other Nations' Foreign Policy Action Templates." *Political Psychology* 20 (1999): 767–802.

Hudson, Valerie M., with Christopher A. Vore. "Foreign Policy Analysis Yesterday, Today, and Tomorrow." *Mershon International Studies Review* 39 (1995): 209–238. A good and fairly comprehensive overview of the subfield of foreign policy analysis.

Janis, Irving. *Groupthink: Psychological Studies of Policy Decisions and Fiascoes.* 2d ed. Boston, 1982. A classic that is well known in social science circles.

Jervis, Robert. *Perception and Misperception in International Politics.* Princeton, N.J., 1976. Another classic work on perception.

Khong, Yuen Foong. *Analogies at War: Korea, Munich, Dien Bien Phu, and the Vietnam Decisions of 1965.* Princeton, N.J., 1992.

Levy, Jack. "Learning and Foreign Policy: Sweeping a Conceptual Minefield." *International Organization* 48 (1994): 279–312.

Lotz, Hellmut. "Myth and NAFTA: The Use of Core Values in U.S. Politics." In Valerie M. Hudson, ed. *Culture and Foreign Policy.* Boulder, Colo., 1997.

"Political Psychology." Special issue on the Decision Units model of *International Studies Review,* 2002.

Purkitt, Helen E. "Problem Representations and Political Expertise: Evidence from 'Think Aloud' Protocols of South African Elite." In Donald A. Sylvan and James F. Voss, eds. *Problem Representation in Foreign Policy Decision Making.* Cambridge and New York, 1998.

Putnam, Robert. "Diplomacy and Domestic Politics: The Logic of Two-Level Games." *International Organization* 42 (1998): 427–486. A foundational article that should be read by those seeking to link foreign and domestic politics.

Renshon, Stanley A., and Deborah Welch Larsen, eds. *Good Judgment in Foreign Policy.* New York, 2001.

Rosenau, James N. "Pre-Theories and Theories of Foreign Policy." In R. Barry Farrell, ed. *Approaches in Comparative and International Politics.* Evanston, Ill., 1966.

Schrodt, Philip A. "Event Data in Foreign Policy Analysis." In Laura Neack, Jeanne Hey, and Patrick J. Haney, eds. *Foreign Policy Analysis: Continuity and Change in Its Second Generation.* Englewood Cliffs, N.J., 1995.

Snyder, Richard C., H. W. Bruck, and Burton Sapin. *Foreign Policy Decision-Making: An Approach to the Study of International Politics.* Glencoe, Ill., 1962. Arguably the work that began the decision-making theoretical enterprise in foreign policy.

Sprout, Harold, and Margaret Sprout. *Man-Milieu Relationship Hypotheses in the Context of International Politics.* Princeton, N.J., 1956. Another classic, emphasizing the need to integrate models of human decision making with models of the context in which those decisions are being made.

Sylvan, Donald A., and James F. Voss, eds. *Problem Representation in Foreign Policy Decision Making.* Cambridge and New York, 1998.

'T Hart, Paul, Eric K. Stern, and Bengt Sundelius, eds. *Beyond Groupthink: Political Group Dynamics and Foreign Policy-Making.* Ann Arbor, Mich., 1997.

Waltz, Kenneth N. *Theory of International Politics.* Reading, Mass., 1979. A classic of more mainstream international relations.

Wendt, Alexander. "Anarchy Is What States Make of It: The Social Construction of Power Politics." *International Organization* 46 (1992): 391–425. A good introduction to the constructivist turn in international relations theory.

Winter, David G. *The Power Motive.* New York, 1973.

See also THE BEHAVIORAL APPROACH TO DIPLOMATIC HISTORY; PUBLIC OPINION.

DEPARTMENT OF DEFENSE

Steven L. Rearden

A major change in the conduct of American foreign policy after World War II was the growing involvement of the military, represented by the Department of Defense. The explanation stems in part from the heightened concern for national security during the postwar period when much of the U.S. government became transfixed with waging the Cold War. During these years, as foreign affairs eclipsed domestic policy as the government's top concern, discussion of foreign policy options often dwelt on military courses of action, thereby assuring the secretary of defense, the Joint Chiefs of Staff (JCS), and the military services numerous opportunities to contribute views. Indeed, some secretaries of defense, like James Forrestal, Robert S. McNamara, Caspar Weinberger, and William Perry, played such a conspicuous role in foreign affairs that they seemed at times to rival the secretary of state. The result was a foreign policy that increasingly reflected the priorities and concerns of the Pentagon.

Even without the Cold War, however, a case can be made that the Defense Department's role and influence in policy circles would have grown appreciably anyway as the logical outcome of American experiences in World War II and its immediate aftermath. As the war ended, the security problems that preoccupied Washington policymakers were not just those associated with deteriorating Soviet-American relations, but also the obligations the United States was apt to acquire as a member of the recently created United Nations, the threats posed by atomic weapons and other new technologies, and the lingering memories of recent military setbacks like Pearl Harbor. The upshot was a growing acceptance that the country would have to have a larger, better-trained, and better-equipped peacetime military force than it had known in the past.

Created in 1949, the Department of Defense was an outgrowth of the National Security Act of 1947, which unified the armed services under a civilian secretary of defense. The debate in Congress leading up to passage of the 1947 legislation had its origins in the experiences of World War II, which, despite the overall success, revealed numerous flaws and shortcomings in command relationships and the allocation of resources among the military services. Aiming to avoid such problems in the future, President Harry S. Truman endorsed a War Department plan calling for a highly centralized and closely unified postwar military structure. The navy, fearing that such a setup would threaten the future of naval aviation and the independence of the Marine Corps, championed a competing plan that rejected outright unification in favor of closer coordination. The resulting compromise, enshrined in the National Security Act, borrowed from both sides but leaned more toward the navy plan, in the interest of avoiding what many in Congress worried might become "a Prussian-style general staff" at the Pentagon.

The responsibilities of the secretary of defense, as head of the new organization, cut across traditional lines. His main job was to provide "general direction, authority, and control" over the military departments, made up of the army, the navy, and a newly independent air force, which were now grouped together under a hybrid organization known as the National Military Establishment. But the secretary was also "the principal assistant to the President in all matters relating to the national security." Exactly where the latter language came from or how it was meant to be applied are unclear. The most likely explanation is that it reflected the philosophy and influence of James Forrestal, secretary of the navy during the unification debate, who believed that the secretary of defense should be primarily a coordinator rather than an executive administrator. Truman never liked this loose description of the secretary's duties, and when the opportunity presented itself in 1949 to amend the National Security Act (at which time Congress converted the National Military Establishment into the present-day Department of Defense and strengthened the secretary's authority), he insisted that the wording of the secretary's mission be changed to "principal assistant to the President in all matters relating to the Department of Defense."

In addition to providing a framework for unification, the 1947 National Security Act created new machinery to promote closer coordination within the policy process. In practice this meant balancing competing claims of authority, influence, and resources among rival departments and agencies. In an effort to impose order on this situation, Congress created new mechanisms to help the president: the National Security Council to advise him on the formulation of overall policy; the National Security Resources Board to oversee future mobilization planning; and the Central Intelligence Agency to coordinate the gathering and analysis of intelligence. Although it was generally assumed that the military would be represented on each of these bodies, the only stipulation in the law was that the secretary of defense and the service secretaries would sit on the National Security Council.

EARLY EXPERIENCES

As a result of the National Security Act, the military establishment stood to gain considerably in its exercise of influence over peacetime foreign and defense policy. Forrestal, as one of the principal architects of the law, hoped that it would lead to closer politico-military collaboration, an area he thought had been slighted during World War II by what he saw as President Franklin D. Roosevelt's casual management style and haphazard approach to postwar planning. After the war, as relations with the Soviet Union deteriorated, Forrestal thought it all the more imperative that military planning and foreign policy be brought into closer harmony. As the first secretary of defense (1947–1949), he looked initially to the Joint Chiefs of Staff to be his principal politico-military advisers and adopted the practice of consulting with them on nearly every foreign policy matter that crossed his desk. In view of the proliferating number of foreign crises—in Greece, Italy, Palestine, Berlin, China, and elsewhere—the Joint Chiefs had numerous occasions to express their views and to exert their influence. Yet rarely did they make as much of these opportunities as they might have. Divided among themselves over

budgetary issues, the allocation of resources, and the assignment of service roles and missions, they seldom presented a united front. Where the use of force might be involved, their recommendations tended to be so unrealistic that they scarcely received serious consideration outside the Pentagon. A case in point was their finding in the spring of 1948 that 100,000 U.S. troops would be needed for peacekeeping duties in Palestine, an estimate built on worst-case scenarios that officials in the Office of the Secretary of Defense (OSD) and at the White House dismissed as overblown for budgetary purposes.

As it became clear that the Joint Chiefs were a less reliable source of advice than Forrestal had expected, he found himself turning to members of his immediate staff to deal with politico-military affairs. This was not something Forrestal had anticipated, nor did it fit easily into the organization he had planned for his office. During the unification debate, he had told Congress that in the interests of preserving service autonomy it would be counterproductive for the new secretary of defense to surround himself with too many aides and assistants who might interfere in the services' business. A small staff, he contended, would be more than adequate. Politico-military affairs became the responsibility of John H. Ohly, one of the secretary's three statutory special assistants, who oversaw a mixed staff of civil servants and uniformed officers borrowed from the military departments. Although Ohly usually stayed in the background, operating more as an administrator than as an adviser, his role was such that he could, and did, freely offer suggestions when it seemed appropriate.

Under Forrestal's successor, Louis A. Johnson (1949–1950), politico-military affairs acquired a more formal and centralized structure, in line with Johnson's philosophy (as well as the increased authority he wielded as a result of the 1949 amendments to the National Security Act), that the secretary of defense should exercise closer control over departmental policy. The impetus for the changes Johnson made in handling foreign affairs came initially from the State Department, which wanted a single point of contact with the Pentagon instead of having to deal separately with the OSD, the JCS, and the military services. One proposal up for consideration at the time Johnson took office in March 1949 was to vest primary responsibility for politico-military affairs in the JCS. Johnson, however, vetoed the idea in favor of keeping control in his immediate office, thereby setting a precedent that would guide all future secretaries of defense. Over the next several months he moved policy responsibility for occupied areas from the army to OSD, ordered his immediate staff to monitor all correspondence between the military services and the State Department, and set up the State Liaison Section to serve as the central point of contact for all communications with the State Department other than sensitive intelligence matters.

An isolationist at heart, Johnson faced the somewhat personally awkward task of having to help implement two major foreign policy initiatives: the defense of Europe as part of America's obligations as a member of the North Atlantic Treaty Organization (NATO), created in April 1949; and arming the allies under a companion measure, the Mutual Defense Assistance Program, enacted that autumn. Less than enthusiastic about either, Johnson turned coordination of these matters over to an assistant, James H. Burns, a retired army officer whose heart ailment allowed him to work only part-time. Fortunately, Burns had two exceptionally able deputies: Major General Lyman L. Lemnitzer, who handled military assistance; and Najeeb E. Halaby, who specialized in foreign military affairs, including NATO. Meanwhile, Johnson became involved in a running feud with Secretary of State Dean Acheson, which put a serious strain on State-Defense relations. Business between the two still managed to get done, but at a reduced pace with limited contacts and cooperation all around.

The low point came with the drafting of NSC 68 in the spring of 1950, when the State Department team, led by Paul H. Nitze, director of the Policy Planning Staff, effectively usurped leadership of what was supposed to have been a joint State-Defense endeavor. The product of the exercise was a paper tailored to Acheson's specifications, warning of great dangers ahead unless the United States abandoned the strict economy measures Johnson had imposed and stepped up the level of its military preparedness. From this point on, Johnson's credibility at the White House steadily diminished, until reverses at the outset of the Korean War that summer cast doubt on his continuing ability to manage the Pentagon and provided Truman with an excuse to fire him.

THE MARSHALL-LOVETT ERA

To replace Johnson, Truman turned in September 1950 to General George C. Marshall, army chief

of staff in World War II and secretary of state from 1947 to 1949, who brought with him his former undersecretary of state, Robert A. Lovett, to be his number two (and successor, beginning in 1951) at the Pentagon. Truman held Marshall in the highest regard, and it is not surprising that, with Marshall's return to government, Acheson found his authority and influence somewhat eclipsed. Meanwhile, Truman also decided to upgrade the National Security Council, thereby imposing greater discipline and efficiency on the policy process and opening avenues for shaping high-level policy that had not existed for either Forrestal or Johnson. With the additional impetus of the Korean War generating a growing list of U.S. politico-military commitments around the globe, the Defense Department became immersed in foreign affairs to an unprecedented degree. Not until the Kennedy and Johnson administrations of the 1960s would a secretary of defense exert as much influence over foreign policy as did Marshall and Lovett.

In sharp contrast to the confrontational tone of Johnson's tenure, Marshall and Lovett both promoted cordial working relations between the State and Defense departments. Truman was disgusted with the constant bickering between Acheson and Johnson, and he looked to his new team at the Pentagon to put politico-military collaboration on a more sound and professional basis. The goal, as Lovett later described it while testifying before Congress, was "constant, close, and sympathetic cooperation" between the two departments. This included not only increased contacts at the uppermost levels of policymaking, but also direct consultations on a regular basis involving the State Department's regional assistant secretaries, the Policy Planning Staff, and the Joint Chiefs, something that Johnson had sharply curtailed.

Despite an atmosphere of improved cooperation, Marshall and Lovett continued the practice begun by Johnson of exercising close administrative control of foreign affairs through OSD, under what became in November 1951 the Office of International Security Affairs, headed by Frank C. Nash, one of the many Forrestal protégés still around the Pentagon. Nash had a broad charter that gave him the authority to coordinate "all activities" within the Department of Defense relating to international security affairs. Nash himself was intimately involved in practically every detail of the office's operations, serving as principal liaison with the National Security Council and as a key aide to Marshall and Lovett. It was one of the Pentagon's most high profile jobs, requiring a judicious mix of administrative and diplomatic skills that continuously underscored the increasingly close relationship between military affairs and foreign policy.

FOREIGN AFFAIRS DURING THE EISENHOWER YEARS

During Dwight D. Eisenhower's presidency (1953–1961), the Defense Department's involvement in foreign affairs continued to expand as military responses increasingly became a part of the U.S. strategy for containing communist expansion. Ironically, however, the secretary of defense himself was a relatively minor figure in shaping foreign policy decisions during most of this period. Stressing the need for sound management, Eisenhower selected former business executives as his first two secretaries of defense —Charles E. Wilson (1953–1957), who had headed General Motors, and Neil H. McElroy (1957–1959), former president of Procter and Gamble. Hired for their ability to run large enterprises, they operated on the philosophy that, above all, the secretary of defense should concern himself with the managerial side of the department and leave policy and strategy decisions to be hammered out in the National Security Council by the president, the Joint Chiefs, and Eisenhower's number one foreign affairs adviser, Secretary of State John Foster Dulles.

Despite the limited role that Wilson and McElroy embraced for themselves, Defense Department involvement abroad continued to grow. Often the responsibilities were routine and dealt with administrative chores requiring prior defense arrangements with U.S. allies, such as those in NATO and the Southeast Asia Treaty Organization (SEATO), access to overseas bases, and the buildup, equipping, and training of allied forces under U.S. military aid programs. Accordingly, provisions had to be made to handle the influx of U.S. military personnel into foreign countries, arrange for the administration and allocation of assistance, define the duties and responsibilities of U.S. advisers, and negotiate agreements governing the status of forces, usually with the International Security Affairs office providing the initial liaison and coordination on the Washington end.

At the same time the department also faced a wholly new set of security problems arising from advances in military technology and correspond-

ing decisions by the president and the National Security Council on how these advances would be exploited. The advent of thermonuclear and tactical nuclear weapons and of ballistic missile technology, coupled with Eisenhower's decision to "conventionalize" the atomic arsenal, raised problems of unprecedented political complexity and diplomatic sensitivity. Never before had any country possessed such enormous power with so few guiding precedents on how to manage it. As it turned out, some of these new weapons would be deployed abroad and shared with America's allies. How much control, if any, the host country would have over the storage, movement, and use of these weapons invariably invited prolonged discussion, both within the U.S. government and between Washington and foreign capitals.

The inherent importance of being able to deal effectively with these problems was manifest when in February 1953 Wilson promoted the International Security Affairs assistant to the rank of assistant secretary of defense for international security affairs. The decision to elevate the job (a move Lovett was on the verge of making when he left office) was long overdue, but as a practical matter its only real significance was to reaffirm the office's already well established place among the Pentagon's elite. In 1956, Wilson tried to upgrade the office to the rank of undersecretary, to place it on a par with the service secretaries. However, legislation that would have effected the change died in the House Armed Services Committee.

In fact, the mandate of the International Security Affairs office was never so clear as to give it undisputed control of politico-military affairs. Each of the services continued to maintain its own politico-military and international affairs section, which could be used to circumvent the secretary of defense and his deputies. Best organized for this purpose was the navy, which maintained regular informal communications with the State Department through its Politico-Military Policy Division. In addition, the chief of naval operations had his own "back channel" contacts abroad, which infuriated Secretary of Defense Wilson when he learned of them. And while International Security Affairs was supposed to be responsible for policies governing the programming of foreign military aid, it often encountered resistance from the Joint Chiefs and the military departments when it attempted to probe the details of their recommendations concerning program development and implementation practices. Had Wilson and McElroy taken a greater personal interest in foreign affairs, many of these problems might have been avoided. But with secretaries of defense whose interests lay elsewhere, the assistant secretaries for International Security Affairs knew that they could count on little support and generally felt constrained from pressing their authority too far.

The situation started to change with the appointment in December 1959 of Thomas S. Gates, a Philadelphia banker, as Eisenhower's third secretary of defense. Although his tenure was short (1959–1961), it reestablished the secretary of defense as a major figure in foreign policy decision making. Occasionally criticized for trying to usurp the secretary of state's functions, Gates pursued a State-Defense partnership that would yield more truly integrated policies with less interdepartmental friction and parochialism. As a first step, Gates abandoned the practice of trying to control the flow of State-Defense business through his immediate office. Indicative of the results he hoped to achieve, he initiated regular one-on-one meetings with Secretary of State Christian A. Herter and encouraged subordinates to do the same with their State Department counterparts in an effort to improve interagency cooperation and coordination.

Gates was also highly instrumental in shaping Defense Department responses in the increasingly important area of arms control and disarmament, where prior to Gates the Pentagon's support and endorsement of such measures had been lukewarm. Although Wilson and McElroy had spent considerable time and energy studying arms control proposals passing across their desks, they were forever confronted by the unremitting skepticism and apprehension of the Joint Chiefs, whose opinions on such matters carried considerable weight both inside the Pentagon and on Capitol Hill. Since the chiefs knew that it was impossible for political reasons to keep arms control off the national agenda, they focused their objections instead on technical matters—the lack of adequate and effective verification measures, for example, or the debilitating consequences for research and development programs. As delaying tactics, these arguments worked well against such proposals as an atmospheric test ban and a cutoff of nuclear production. But they were also the kinds of arguments that wore thin after awhile and gave the Defense Department a reputation for contentiousness.

Gates was decidedly more inclined than his two immediate predecessors to bring arms control and disarmament into the mainstream of American defense policy. While he readily acknowledged to the press that there was a "negative attitude" in the Pentagon toward arms control, he was prepared to entertain any and all suggestions and told Eisenhower that he was thinking of appointing a special assistant on disarmament matters. Still, about the only arms control measures Gates was seriously willing to consider (without, as he put it, "a complete review of our force structure") were those that promised to result in some sort of U.S. advantage over the Soviets. Personally, Gates favored a cutoff of nuclear production, preferably sooner rather than later, not so much for disarmament purposes but to preserve what he estimated as a two-to-one American advantage over the Soviets in nuclear bombs and warheads. Moreover, he fully agreed with the Joint Chiefs that arms control for the sake of arms control was inherently dangerous, and that the administration should not allow itself to be stampeded into reaching agreements merely because of public opinion.

Whether Gates could or should have been tougher with the military on accepting the need for arms control falls into the realm of conjecture. Gates himself, although more open-minded toward such matters than Wilson and McElroy had been, was still very much committed to the concept of foreign and defense policies resting on ready military power rather than the negotiation of agreements with one's potential adversaries. Like Forrestal and Lovett, he was part of a generation whose view of international politics derived from memories and experiences of the 1930s, when military weakness and appeasement had seemed to invite oppression and aggression. International communism, to Gates's way of thinking, was basically no different from the Axis alliance that had bound Nazi Germany, Fascist Italy, and imperial Japan in World War II. Despite rumors and diplomatic reports of a growing Sino-Soviet rift, Gates remained convinced that there were no fundamental ideological differences between Moscow and Beijing, and that American foreign policy should treat such stories with utmost caution. It was, perhaps, a quintessential Cold War viewpoint, but not one that was uncommon or out of place for its times.

THE MCNAMARA ERA

If there was one individual who had more impact than anyone else on the Defense Department's role in foreign affairs, it was Robert S. McNamara. Appointed by President John F. Kennedy in 1961, McNamara served as secretary of defense until 1968, when the stalemated war in Vietnam prompted his resignation. Throughout most of his tenure, McNamara was an ardent advocate of American involvement in Southeast Asia and a key figure in planning and prosecuting the war. Indeed, in a very real sense, foreign policy toward Southeast Asia during these years was a product of the Pentagon, which was largely responsible for orchestrating the war. Victory, however, proved elusive, and as time passed McNamara saw his self-confidence and credibility steadily erode. Disillusioned and frustrated, he left office counseling withdrawal and stepped-up efforts at a negotiated settlement.

Yet the frustrations of Vietnam and their ripple effects were only part of the McNamara story. Indeed, without Vietnam, McNamara's tenure would probably be remembered as a period of extraordinarily positive accomplishments, from improved management of the Pentagon to reduced reliance on nuclear weapons and the initiation of the first serious efforts at strategic arms control. Outwardly, McNamara was an unlikely candidate to play such a major part in foreign affairs. A former president of Ford Motor Company, he seemed destined at the outset of his tenure to follow in the footsteps of Wilson and McElroy and become a business manager of the Pentagon. That he emerged instead as a pivotal figure in foreign policy was as much a product of his approach to the job of secretary of defense as it was the unique circumstances in which he found himself. The result was a far more active and involved Defense Department at all levels of the policy process, including especially high-level decision making.

Much of the power and authority that the Pentagon wielded under McNamara accrued by default rather than by design. President Kennedy had little use for the elaborate National Security Council system developed under Truman and Eisenhower, and in its place he substituted a slimmed-down version with limited capabilities for independent policy analysis. Further, he discontinued the practice of conducting elaborate annual national security reviews and expected the State Department to exercise primary responsibility for developing and coordinating policy. The weak link in this system proved to be Dean Rusk, Kennedy's choice as secretary of state. Although affable and intelligent, it soon became apparent

that Rusk lacked the temperament and drive to carry out the job entrusted to him. Eventually it fell to McNamara to fill the void.

For the record, McNamara accepted the conventional wisdom that defense policy derived from foreign policy and that the Pentagon's function was to serve and assist the State Department. But in day-to-day practice, McNamara, with Kennedy's blessing, generally followed his own lead. The approach McNamara adopted was to supply his own foreign policy guidance, which he included with each budget submission to the president and in his annual reports (termed "posture statements" to give them more prestige) to Congress. Going beyond a purely military rationale, McNamara's posture statements offered broad justification for new and ongoing defense programs based on the manner in which they would contribute to furthering U.S. foreign policy objectives. "It was essential," McNamara recalled in an interview, "to begin with a discussion of foreign policy because that had to be the foundation of security policy." Although the State Department routinely submitted advice and comments, its views often arrived too late in the budget process to be reflected in the final documents forwarded to the White House and Capitol Hill.

For support, McNamara assembled a highly skilled and talented staff, dubbed the "whiz kids," who implemented a host of far-reaching administrative and managerial reforms. Some of the changes they and McNamara made, including the extensive use of computer-driven "systems analysis" models and mission-oriented budgeting techniques, proved controversial and hard for the military services to swallow. But there is no doubt that they gave the secretary a stronger and firmer hand, both in running the department and in projecting his influence into foreign policy. Moreover, they liberated the secretary from having to draw as often on the Joint Chiefs of Staff and the military services for advice and analysis of politico-military problems. By the middle of the decade, McNamara had at his fingertips the most sophisticated and effective organization for analyzing and managing politico-military affairs that Washington had yet seen. Whether, as some critics charged, McNamara's reforms invited the further "militarization" of American foreign policy is debatable. Within the Pentagon, McNamara exercised an unprecedented degree of civilian control over the military and routinely used civilians in International Security Affairs and in other key positions to perform chores previously reserved for the services or the JCS. If this was militarization, it was most definitely of the civilian-shaded variety.

All the same, the tendency to apply military solutions to serious problems abroad grew steadily during the 1960s. This was true not only in Southeast Asia but also in dealing with incidents in Cuba, Berlin, the Dominican Republic, and other Cold War flashpoints. During the late 1940s and 1950s, U.S. military power had relied in the first instance on the presumed deterrent effects of nuclear retaliation to cope with the threat of communist aggression. But by the 1960s, with the United States and the Soviet Union approaching effective parity in strategic nuclear power, it was no longer realistic to threaten wholesale nuclear destruction. Seeking a more credible posture, McNamara seized on the doctrine of flexible response as a means of providing the president with a wider range of options for dealing with critical international problems.

The essence of flexible response was a varied mixture of forces allowing a greater choice in military actions, with emphasis on containing any conflict below the level of a nuclear exchange. Developed initially with Europe in mind, McNamara hoped that flexible response would provide an alternative to the all-or-nothing mentality that then dominated NATO strategic planning. To achieve the desired posture, he urged stepped-up procurement of conventional forces and changes in the programmed use of nuclear weapons to allow for a "pause" or "firebreak" between conventional conflict and a larger war. European critics countered that such a strategy would be prohibitively expensive and that it would undermine nuclear deterrence and increase the risk of a conventional conflict. But with patience and perseverance, McNamara gradually brought the Europeans around. Adopted by NATO in 1967, flexible response was, on paper at least, a major break with the past, although in practice its effects were somewhat negated by the reluctance of the European allies to commit themselves to a sustained conventional buildup. Even so, flexible response remained NATO's governing strategic doctrine for the duration of the Cold War and into the early 1990s.

Another of McNamara's contributions was to help institutionalize a more serious attitude within the Defense Department toward strategic arms control and disarmament. What prompted McNamara's involvement was mounting evidence by the mid-1960s that the Soviet Union had embarked upon the deployment of two prototype antiballistic missile (ABM) systems, thus putting pressure on the United States to respond in kind. Dubious of the technologies involved, McNamara sought to avoid a costly and perhaps futile ABM competition by proposing negotiations with the Soviets to curb both offensive and defensive strategic weapons. Although the Joint Chiefs remained skeptical about whether such talks would amount to much, they agreed with McNamara's basic premise that the strategic arms competition was getting out of hand and that restraint on both sides could serve a useful purpose. This was a dramatic turnaround from military thinking in the 1950s, and it went far toward paving the way for the Anti-Ballistic Missile Treaty and other arms control accords growing out of the Strategic Arms Limitation Talks (SALT) between Washington and Moscow in the 1970s.

Outside Europe, flexible response played a less conspicuous role in shaping American foreign policy. The escalating conflict in Southeast Asia defied the conceptual models that McNamara was so fond of applying, and by 1966 the United States found itself engaged in a war of attrition with North Vietnam. Nevertheless, McNamara approached the war as he generally approached other problems, seeking to reduce it to quantifiable proportions. Knowing McNamara's preferences, subordinates tailored programs and recommendations accordingly, stressing systems analysis techniques over less quantifiable means of assessing the war's progress and possible outcome. The use of statistical models, whether involving kill ratios, construction rates, frequency of incidents, or other indicators, gave a distorted picture of the war, often because the U.S. command in Saigon and the South Vietnamese government, knowingly or otherwise, provided erroneous data. By the time McNamara realized what was happening, the United States was so committed to prosecuting the war that there was no turning back without doing what he and President Lyndon B. Johnson considered serious damage to U.S. prestige and credibility.

McNamara's tenure at the Defense Department thus left a mixed legacy. While there was progress in curbing the menace of nuclear war, the United States found itself plunging ever more deeply into an ill-advised and ill-conceived conflict in Southeast Asia. McNamara demonstrated that a strong-minded and strong-willed secretary of defense could exercise enormous influence on American foreign policy. However, his immediate successors were leery of following suit.

POST-VIETNAM CHANGES

After Vietnam the role of military power in American foreign policy became less pronounced than it had been previously, a clear sign of popular misgivings over the war and of diminished confidence in military solutions to problems abroad. Indicative of the trend was the decision by Secretary of Defense Melvin Laird (1969–1973) in 1970 to cease prefacing his annual reports to Congress with foreign policy reviews, as had been the custom during McNamara's tenure. Nevertheless, the Defense Department continued to figure prominently in the foreign policy process through its representation on interagency committees and the secretary's membership on the National Security Council. As a rule, the Defense Department supplied two representatives—one from the Office of the Secretary of Defense, another from the Joint Chiefs of Staff—to each interagency forum while providing many of the action officers who made up the National Security Council staff. Although it was entirely conceivable that the president and his staff could have curtailed their contacts with the military, relying more on civilians from the State Department or elsewhere for advice, it was practically impossible to do so. The resulting policies may have been less overtly military in character, but they were still subject to military involvement in their development and execution.

One reason why the Pentagon acquired a lower foreign policy profile after Vietnam was that defense-related security problems in the 1970s gave way in importance to political and economic problems. The major exceptions were the SALT negotiations with the Soviet Union, which required military participation on technical as well as policy grounds, and ongoing U.S. involvement in NATO and foreign military assistance programs to American client states like Israel, Iran, Saudi Arabia, South Korea, and the Philippines. But otherwise attention focused on such matters as inflation, energy shortages, and other disruptions to the global political economy that were not normally high on the Pentagon's agenda. At the same time, a general improvement in relations between Washington and Moscow, known as détente, lessened the more overt dangers of an East-West confrontation.

The growing range and complexity of problems abroad invited the Defense Department to acquire more sophisticated means for approaching and handling foreign affairs. This included the staffing of a net assessment office in 1973, which operated under a broad charter to initiate studies of current and projected U.S. and foreign military capabilities; and the appointment in 1977 of an undersecretary of defense for policy, to oversee politico-military affairs, arms control, and the integration of defense plans and policies with basic national security policy. At the command and staff colleges run by the armed services and at the National Defense University in Washington, D.C., lectures and courses on national security affairs became more commonplace alongside traditional studies in military science. Language training likewise received closer attention at service schools.

The net effect was to generate a far greater appreciation within the military for the complexities of foreign affairs than at any time in the past. Many junior officers who had served in Vietnam were highly critical of what they found to be their superiors' simplistic and naive views on foreign policy; as these younger officers rose to prominence in the late 1970s and 1980s they brought with them a keen interest in developing U.S. policies less wedded to Cold War stereotypes. A case in point was the Pentagon's more flexible attitude toward the communist regime on mainland China during the 1970s and early 1980s and its ready acquiescence in dropping support for Taiwan, once a bulwark against communism and a stalwart American ally.

FROM COLD WAR TO POST–COLD WAR

By the late 1970s the pendulum was beginning to swing back toward more active military participation in foreign affairs. The faltering of détente, an across-the-board Warsaw Pact buildup in Europe, and the Soviet Union's 1979 invasion of Afghanistan all suggested that the Cold War was far from over and that U.S. foreign policy still needed the support of a strong U.S. military establishment. The response was a U.S. peacetime military buildup of unprecedented proportions. Begun toward the end of Carter's presidency, it gathered momentum under President Ronald Reagan in the 1980s to become the largest such effort in American history. Among the programs that Reagan initiated were the creation of a 600-ship navy to give the United States a more effective global power-projection capability, offensive strategic forces that would be more survivable in a general nuclear war, and the Strategic Defense Initiative ("Star Wars" to its critics) to explore the

CASPAR WEINBERGER ON MILITARY POWER

"I believe the postwar period has taught us several lessons, and from them I have developed six major tests to be applied when we are weighing the use of U.S. combat forces abroad. . . .

"First, the United States should not commit forces to combat overseas unless the particular engagement or occasion is deemed vital to our national interest or that of our allies. . . .

"Second, if we decide it is necessary to put combat troops into a given situation, we should do so whole-heartedly, and with the clear intention of winning. . . .

"Third, if we do decide to commit forces to combat overseas, we should have clearly defined political and military objectives. And we should know precisely how our forces can accomplish those clearly defined objectives. . . .

"Fourth, the relationship between our objectives and the forces we have committed—their size, composi-tion, and disposition—must be continually reassessed and adjusted if necessary. . . .

"Fifth, before the U.S. commits combat forces abroad, there must be some reasonable assurance we will have the support of the American people and their elected representatives in Congress. . . . We cannot fight a battle with the Congress at home while asking our troops to win a war overseas. . . .

"Finally, the commitment of U.S. forces to combat should be a last resort."

— Excerpts from "Uses of Military Power," address by Secretary of Defense Caspar Weinberger at the National Press Club, 28 November 1984 —

feasibility of rendering intercontinental ballistic missiles "impotent and obsolete."

Whereas Carter sent U.S. forces into harm's way only once, during the Iran hostage crisis in 1980, and even then with great reluctance, Reagan did so time and again with rarely a second thought. His operating premise was that a successful and effective foreign policy and readiness to use military power went hand in hand. Insisting that military involvement overseas was unavoidable, he often turned to the Defense Department to conduct operations in direct furtherance of American policy. This included providing a buffer between the warring factions in Lebanon, escorting neutral tanker traffic in the Persian Gulf, punitive raids against Libyan dictator Muammar Qaddafi, counterinsurgency operations in Central America, and the rescue of American civilians following a Marxist coup on Grenada in 1983.

Reagan also drew heavily on the military and Pentagon professionals to help staff his administration. His first secretary of state, Alexander M. Haig, Jr., was a retired four-star army general who had recently served as NATO Supreme Commander. Haig first came to prominence during the Nixon administration as Henry Kissinger's deputy at the National Security Council. During his year and a half as secretary of state under Reagan, Haig was often in the forefront of suggesting military pressure when diplomacy appeared to falter, especially in trying to counter Soviet and Cuban adventurism in the Caribbean, Central America, and Africa. Of the six national security advisers that Reagan had, two—Vice Admiral John M. Poindexter and Lieutenant General Colin L. Powell—were active-duty military officers. A third, Frank C. Carlucci, was a former deputy secretary of defense. Meanwhile, military officers "on loan" from the Pentagon continued to occupy key positions on the National Security Council staff; and after a succession of civilian heads, Reagan in 1987 named retired army Major General William Burns to direct the Arms Control and Disarmament Agency.

Not surprisingly, Defense Department influence rose appreciably during the Reagan years, though not always in ways that yielded predictable outcomes. Indeed, in certain respects, the department found itself ill-prepared for the more demanding role that Reagan thrust upon it. The unpopularity of the military after Vietnam and years of flat defense spending had left what many at the Pentagon considered a hollow force by the beginning of the 1980s. Although the Joint Chiefs of Staff planning mechanism was now capable of generating an enormous array of military options from which the president could choose, the effective implementation of these plans was often hampered by the lack of trained personnel, reliable equipment and spare parts, interservice friction, and limited access to foreign bases. For these reasons, Secretary of Defense Caspar Weinberger (1981–1987) and the Joint Chiefs were often averse to taking risks abroad, at least until the Reagan buildup had gathered its full momentum.

A further concern within the Pentagon was that stepped-up military involvement overseas would draw hostile reactions from Congress and the American public. Fearing another Vietnam, the Joint Chiefs cautioned against committing U.S. combat troops in Central America and insisted upon limiting U.S. military participation to a relatively small-scale assistance program, occasional exercises, and support of CIA-directed covert operations. The Joint Chiefs were likewise leery of becoming drawn into Lebanon, and when a terrorist bombing incident in October 1983 killed 241 U.S. servicemen, they believed their worst fears were confirmed. U.S. troops withdrew shortly thereafter. In a well-publicized speech of November 1984, entitled "Uses of Military Power," Secretary Weinberger laid down specific criteria that he thought should govern U.S. military commitments abroad. At the minimum, Weinberger argued, the armed forces should have a firm declaration of support at home, a clear-cut mission, and an agreed exit strategy from any operation in which they might become involved.

With so much at stake, Weinberger took a proactive stance toward foreign affairs that frequently led to friction with the State Department and the National Security Council. Like many of his predecessors, Weinberger required that State-Defense contacts have his prior approval. Adopting a broad view of his responsibilities, he insisted that the Defense Department should have a voice in practically every major foreign policy decision, not just those that might involve the use of military forces. As a direct consequence, he and Haig quarreled often and openly, so much so that the policy process seemed at times to grind to a halt. Weinberger's relations with Haig's successor, George C. Shultz, were only slightly better. In interdepartmental deliberations Weinberger fought hard for his views, often with success.

Weinberger was especially active in shaping the administration's stand on arms control and related issues. While framing an intermediate-range ballistic missile negotiating policy in 1981, he convinced President Reagan, over the objections of the State Department, the Joint Chiefs, and the Arms Control and Disarmament Agency, to hold out for a total global ban on theater-range ballistic missiles, a goal eventually realized in 1987. Weinberger also encouraged Reagan to persevere with the Strategic Defense Initiative, which critics dismissed as unworkable, but which Weinberger regarded as an exceedingly valuable military asset. Unlike Shultz and others in the administration, Weinberger was highly averse to seeing it bargained away. Although not as hostile to arms control as some of his critics maintained, Weinberger believed in negotiating from a position of strength and was dubious of being able to reach fair and reasonable agreements with the Soviets until the United States had improved its strategic posture.

While Weinberger sought to clarify the ground rules for the military's role in foreign policy, others sought to make it more responsive to such problems. Defense reform had been in the air since the debacle in Vietnam, and by the 1980s it took the form of a concerted effort in Congress to improve the performance of the Joint Chiefs of Staff and the joint command structure, under which the worldwide deployment of U.S. forces operated. Long criticized as unreliable and ineffectual, the JCS was a prime candidate for legislative reform. Even many senior military officers agreed that the system was inefficient and sorely in need of an overhaul. In the Goldwater-Nichols Act of 1986, Congress attempted to address these concerns by providing for a stronger and more active JCS chairman, with full control over the Joint Staff. The joint commands received added authority to participate in the budget, procurement, and planning process, and there was to be increased training and emphasis on "jointness" throughout the armed forces.

The intent of the Goldwater-Nichols reforms was to create a more unified and responsive defense establishment, although it was not until the Gulf War of 1990–1991 that the new machinery received its first major test. The war confirmed that in planning and executing such operations, the Department of Defense was probably better prepared and better organized than at any time since its creation. With the resources accumulated during the Reagan buildup, it was all the easier to prevail. Simply having a large, well-equipped defense establishment may not have made a military response to Iraq's seizure of Kuwait any more likely than the use of other options. But it certainly proved to be an asset that President George H. W. Bush and his advisers fell back on when the time came to take action. Knowing that they had such assets readily available undoubtedly increased their sense of confidence and resolve to see the crisis through.

The Gulf War was the last hurrah for the large military establishment built up over the Cold War. The collapse of communism across Eastern Europe, starting with the fall of the Berlin Wall in 1989 and culminating with the dissolution of the Soviet Union late in 1991, signaled a fundamental geopolitical change. Henceforth regional security problems began to replace the threat of global war as the focus of American military planning. The principal architect of this shift in U.S. strategy was the Joint Chiefs of Staff chairman from 1989 to 1993, General Colin Powell, whose concept of a smaller, more mobile "base force" helped guide the Defense Department through its post–Cold War downsizing. Subsequently, the department came to operate under what Secretary of Defense William J. Perry (1994–1997) described as a policy of "preventive defense." In practice, this meant trying to head off problems before they arose through Defense support of such measures as dismantling the former Soviet Union's nuclear arsenal, curbing the spread of weapons of mass destruction, and NATO's Partnership for Peace program with the former Soviet satellite states.

By far the most demanding post–Cold War foreign policy tasks that the department encountered were those associated with peacekeeping and humanitarian missions. Little anticipated when the Cold War ended, they proliferated rapidly in the 1990s and ranged from the policing of Iraqi air space (a carryover from the Gulf War) to refugee and famine relief in Africa and power-brokering in Haiti and the Balkans. For the Defense Department these were somewhat new or unique responsibilities that required a delicate weighing of diplomacy and military power, often under the aegis of a multinational or United Nations command. One such mission was the protection of UN famine relief workers in Somalia, which led to a bloody firefight in October 1993 between U.S. special forces and troops loyal to Somali strongman Mohamed Farah Aideed. Thereafter, the Joint Chiefs urged using technology in place of manpower in similar operations to reduce the risk to U.S. forces, advice the Clinton administration readily accepted. When called upon to help evict Serb troops from Kosovo in 1999, it insisted upon doing so at a distance, with a NATO-directed air campaign to apply the necessary pressure.

The beginning of the twenty-first century saw an emerging debate over the military's future role in American foreign policy. Many military planners and analysts still believed that the proper primary function of the armed forces was to guarantee the national security with ready warfighting capabilities, and that doctrine, training, and procurement should be tailored accordingly. An opposing group, citing the growing U.S. involvement in peace enforcement, drug interdiction, and other low-intensity types of conflicts, argued for a more flexible force, with lighter, less sophisticated weapons, more mobility, and closer coordination with international organizations. The debate is ongoing and how it will play out remains to be seen. Either way, however, it seems clear that, as long as the United States is involved in the world arena, military and foreign policy will remain inextricably linked and that the Defense Department will continue to be a major factor in both the policy process and the conduct of American affairs abroad.

BIBLIOGRAPHY

Betts, Richard K. *Soldiers, Statesmen, and Cold War Crises.* Cambridge, Mass., 1977. Crisis-oriented study of the military's role in policy.

Goldberg, Alfred, ed. *History of the Office of the Secretary of Defense.* Vols. 1, 2, and 4. Washington, D.C., 1984–1997.

Historical Division, Joint Chiefs of Staff. *History of the Joint Chiefs of Staff: The Joint Chiefs of Staff and National Policy.* 7 vols. Washington, D.C., 1986–2000.

Hoopes, Townsend, and Douglas Brinkley. *Driven Patriot: The Life and Times of James Forrestal.* New York, 1992. Most complete biography of the first secretary of defense.

Kinnard, Douglas. *The Secretary of Defense.* Lexington, Ky., 1980. Biographical profiles of key secretaries of defense.

Lederman, Gordon Nathaniel. *Reorganizing the Joint Chiefs of Staff: The Goldwater-Nichols Act of 1986.* Westport, Conn., 1999.

McNamara, Robert S. *In Retrospect: The Tragedy and Lessons of Vietnam.* New York, 1995.

McNamara's reflections on Vietnam and what went wrong.

Shapley, Deborah. *Promise and Power: The Life and Times of Robert McNamara.* Boston, 1993. Perceptive account of McNamara's successes and failures.

Trask, Roger R., and Alfred Goldberg. *The Department of Defense, 1947–1997: Organization and Leaders.* Washington, D.C., 1997.

Weinberger, Caspar W. *Fighting for Peace: Seven Critical Years in the Pentagon.* New York, 1990. A quasi-memoir dealing with selected issues.

Yarmolinsky, Adam. *The Military Establishment: Its Impacts on American Society.* New York, 1971. A dated but still insightful examination of the military's role.

See also DEPARTMENT OF STATE; PRESIDENTIAL ADVISERS.

DEPARTMENT OF STATE

Jerry Israel and David L. Anderson

Upon his resignation in 1792, Henry Remsen, the first chief clerk of the Department of State, left the following instructions:

> Such of the Foreign Letters as are not filed away in the cases, are for the present put on my desk in two pigeon holes at the right hand side. The Consular returns are at the bottom of said desk right hand side . . . the drafts of foreign proceedings . . . are filed in said desk left hand pigeon hole. The letters from our ministers and *charge des affaires* now in commission Mr. Jefferson keeps. . . . A little attention will be necessary in separating the foreign from the domestic letters, as they are sent to the Office by Mr. Jefferson to be filed. My rule in making the separation was by reading them. The domestic letters to be filed in the Office down stairs, the foreign letters in the Office up stairs.

Nearly two centuries later, commenting on the move from "Old State" to headquarters in "New State" (1947) and finally, "New, New State" (1961), the diplomat Henry Serrano Villard wrote:

> Even this fantastically outside complex is inadequate. Spilling over into nine rented buildings, using nearly 1.5 million square feet of space, the State Department premises are already too small; if AID [Agency for International Development], ACDA [Arms Control and Disarmament Agency] and USIA [United States Information Agency] are added, the total is twenty buildings with 2,547,377 square feet. Offices are overcrowded, tenants must double up, conference rooms must be lopped off, new outlets sought.

The irony of these comparisons of simple and complex styles is that Villard's larger department was if anything less rather than more involved in the making of American foreign policy, the State Department's primary responsibility. Along these lines, in modern times, especially since World War II, one notes the competitive foreign policies of departments such as Commerce, Agriculture, Defense, Labor, Treasury, Interior, and

Health and Human Services, plus the role of the Central Intelligence Agency and Federal Reserve Bank, not to mention semiofficial business, scientific, cultural, and journalistic groups. By the mid-1960s, only one-fourth of federal personnel in U.S. embassies were employees of the State Department. In addition, there is the superior and sometimes competitive power of the president and groups or individuals on the White House staff and otherwise outside the State Department that the president may especially empower.

Henry A. Kissinger noted the paradox of an increasingly specialized, bureaucratized society having negative consequences for American policy and policymakers. Calling for a return to the individual and intellectual approach to problems and policy, not uncharacteristic of the formative age of Jefferson and Remsen, Kissinger writes of policy "fragmented into a series of ad hoc decisions which make it difficult to achieve a sense of direction or even to profit from experience. Substantive problems are transformed into administrative ones. Innovation is subjected to 'objective' tests which deprive it of spontaneity. 'Policy planning' becomes the projection of familiar problems into the future. Momentum is confused with purpose. There is greater concern with how things are than with which things matter." As Richard Nixon's national security adviser and then as secretary of state, Kissinger waged his own assault against the inertia of bureaucratized foreign policy.

Borrowing from the example of Remsen and the explanation of Kissinger, it is possible to observe—at least until the mid-twentieth century—that amidst efforts to institutionalize the apparatus of the State Department, what machinery there was rested on a precious few long-lived cogwheels. Working backward not quite all the way from Kissinger to Remsen, one traces a remarkable continuity within the careers of just three men: Wilbur J. Carr, with forty-five years of service (1892–1937); Alvey A. Adee, with forty-six years in Washington (1878–1924) and seven before that for the Department of State in Madrid; and William Hunter, with fifty-seven years (1829–1886) as chief of bureau, chief clerk, and second assistant secretary (the latter two being key administrative posts held also by Carr and Adee).

As late as 1929, the Department of State was small and its central leadership even more scant. When Henry L. Stimson took office as Herbert C. Hoover's secretary of state, there were—including everybody from the secretary to chauffeurs, clerks, stenographers, and janitors—six hundred people. Yet Stimson, not unusually for the department, surrounded himself with an able, tight-knit group of assistants including Carr, Joseph Cotton, Francis White, and Nelson T. Johnson. Like Cotton, some assistants were new to foreign policy; others, like Carr and Johnson, had seen extended service in the consular and diplomatic corps. They blended together, however, to advise the secretary and the president on critical policy matters in Latin America, Europe, and Asia.

The history of the State Department until the mid-twentieth century was tied, it appears, to the history of the few men who had served as secretary of state or to their staffs. The role of the individual has since, however, become increasingly institutionalized, and with that change has come a State Department larger and yet often less effective than it was in its humbler days.

THE CALIBER OF LEADERSHIP

It is tempting to start at the very beginning with Jefferson, James Madison, James Monroe, and the Virginia dynasty. Indeed, it must be noted that these Founders and "systems builders" used the State Department's highest official, not the vice president, as counselor and successor. Yet it remained for one of the second generation of American revolutionaries, John Quincy Adams, to achieve the golden age of American diplomacy and thereby establish the model, perhaps yet unequaled, of a great secretary of state. Adams dominated events in which the United States signed the Treaty of Ghent (1814), which concluded the War of 1812; issued the Monroe Doctrine; and strengthened American maritime power by agreeing with England to clear the Great Lakes of warships and by obtaining rights to fish off Labrador and Newfoundland. Under Adams's leadership at State, the United States extended its landed empire by annexing Florida, removing

Russia from the west coast of North America, settling the Canadian boundary from the Great Lakes to the Rockies, and claiming, for the first time, the Pacific coast. Even amidst Adams's successes, however, the State Department and its secretary retained the highly personal and political character developed under the Virginia dynasty.

Adams himself dangled the post of secretary of state in front of Henry Clay in 1824 in what their political rivals, the Jacksonians, called a "corrupt bargain." While personally worlds apart, Adams and Clay were closer together in support of an "American system" of economic regulation and internal improvements than has been generally noted. Nonetheless, a pattern of granting political favors or rewarding factions with high office in the State Department was well established and would continue into the twentieth century with the appointments of William Jennings Bryan (by Woodrow Wilson in 1913) and Cordell Hull (by Franklin Roosevelt in 1933). Perhaps no period was more replete with political partisanship in the State Department than the years between Adams and the Civil War. First used by the followers of Andrew Jackson as patronage rewards, or the spoils of victory, the department's leadership positions were given—especially in the administrations of James K. Polk, Franklin Pierce, and James Buchanan—to proponents of southern slave expansion who styled themselves "Young Americans."

By 1860, and certainly after the Civil War, the rapid advance of the industrial economy of the United States and the transfer of power from planters to industrialists and financiers was closely mirrored in the composition of State Department leadership. In fact, resisting the divisive trends of the Young Americans, some department leaders such as Daniel Webster and William Learned Marcy had begun in the 1840s to develop interest in a new wave of expansionism directed toward California, Hawaii, and Asia. Foremost among postwar figures was William Henry Seward, next to Adams the greatest secretary of state of the nineteenth century.

Seward, like John Quincy Adams, was also an intellectual. He had read widely and well in the classics and contemporary works. His ties to Adams were as strong a link as was the more mundane relationship between Hunter and Adee, whose careers overlapped those of their more famous superiors. After Adams's death in 1848, Seward mourned, "I have lost a patron, a guide, a counsellor, and a friend—one whom I loved scarcely less than the dearest relations, and venerated above all that was mortal among men."

Seward's State Department years saw the outline developed for a vast, coordinated American worldwide empire with its great continental base producing goods for the consumers of Latin America, Africa, and Asia. While Seward's master plan was not fulfilled during his tenure in office, it was followed carefully by such capable, if less visible, successors as William M. Evarts and Hamilton Fish.

With Evarts, in particular, the State Department began to take on its modern cast as an organization intent, in its own way, on "the fostering, the developing, and the directing of . . . commerce by the government." In October 1880, under Evarts's supervision, the State Department received congressional approval and appropriations for the publication of monthly consular reports, a step urged by local chambers of commerce throughout the country. Also characteristic of the years ahead, Evarts was a lawyer. Indeed, like many future secretaries of state, he was a dominant figure in the American bar at the time—a profession gaining increased significance in modern American business and government.

THE LEGAL MIND

A list of the secretaries and undersecretaries of state of the twentieth century reads like a hall of fame of attorneys: Elihu Root, Philander C. Knox, Robert Lansing, Charles Evans Hughes, Henry L. Stimson, Edward R. Stettinius, Dean Acheson, John Foster Dulles, William P. Rogers, Cyrus R. Vance, George P. Shultz, James A. Baker III, and Warren M. Christopher, not to mention Huntington Wilson, William Phillips, Joseph C. Grew, Nicholas deBelleville Katzenbach, and Elliot L. Richardson. Indeed, a number of these men served both at the State and the Justice departments, and the number of secretaries of state who have also been attorney general is significant. The modern business flavor; cross-examining perception; studied, organized knowledge; attention to detail; and developed cynicism of the legal mind—as found, for example, in a Root or a Stimson—are important to note as traits common to the personnel of the Department of State. More precisely, those in leadership positions at State have often been Ivy League–trained, Wall Street lawyers whose careers have paralleled the growth of the American industrial system and policy. Such lawyers have been uniquely prepared to deal on a large scale with the

organization of railroads, banks, and other developing enterprises at home and abroad.

Dulles's law firm, Sullivan and Cromwell, was involved in the making of American foreign policy as early as the Panamanian revolution of 1903, in part engineered in a New York City hotel room by Phillip Cromwell. Stimson's clients included the Continental Rubber Company, the United States Printing Company, the National Sugar Refining Company, the Bank of North America, the Mutual Life Insurance Company, and the Astoria Power and Light Company. In such representations, Stimson, like his colleagues, was accustomed to high finance. In foreign policy matters, once in the service of State, a Stimson, Root, Dulles, or Christopher would easily fall into the conditions and attitudes emerging from a successful legal practice. Such men could easily talk as though they had the will and power to arrange a set of conditions for society. They were concerned, as always, with the important things: money, boundaries, goods, and, perhaps for the first time, guns.

Corporation lawyers derived their power from their relationship to the developing corporate economy they helped to construct. They had the power of expertise in legal matters. They also had the power of individuals who had a broader perspective of the total system and could thereby give advice to those functioning in narrower channels. By controlling various scientific, educational, and cultural projects through foundations and associations, they also could dramatically influence opinion and events in noneconomic aspects of American life. They served, in particular, as key people in educating persons who were going to be decision makers in foreign policy matters, which were less directly tied than domestic concerns to political and congressional sanctions. By taking the leadership at State and other departments (for example, Treasury), corporation lawyers came to dominate American foreign policy by the beginning of the twentieth century. They moved comfortably within expansionist objectives outlined by Seward. The primary concern of State Department officials became the articulation of a managed, professional structure by which to achieve this well-defined strategy.

MANAGEMENT EFFICIENCY

Developed—like all cabinet-level executive departments of the federal government—along the lines of precedent and personality rather than constitutional or legislative sanction, the State Department until the twentieth century had little organizational rhyme or reason. From Jefferson and Remsen through to Evarts and Adee, the department functioned by tradition, and often did so rather poorly. For example, in 1906 an inspector of American consulates in Asia found two consuls who were decrepit; two otherwise unfit for duty; one morally suspect; one charged with coercing a sultan into paying a debt for which he, the consul, was collector; one charged with drunkenness and the issuance of fraudulent papers; and one, "a coarse and brutal type," against whom eighty-two complaints were registered. Pressure to restructure the consular service, the branch of the department charged directly with the responsibility of looking after American citizens and business interests abroad, came, in great part, from those business interests themselves. Nearly a decade of lobbying went into the executive order of November 1905 and the passage in April 1906 of a consular reorganization bill. The purpose of the pressure and the proposals produced by it was the same, "in a word, to put the entire diplomatic system on a business basis, and to manage it in the future in accordance with the principles of sound common sense." Such principles included more effective training programs. Selective language training in the foreign service began in 1895 through the assignment of officers as "student interpreters" to the American legations in Persia, Korea, and Siam. In 1902 ten student interpreter posts were created at Peking (Beijing) for Chinese language training.

Training in consular responsibilities dates from 1907, when seven new consuls were given thirty-day courses of instruction. The purpose was "to give novitiates in the consular service some practical training in the running of a consular office before sending them off to their posts." In 1924 additional training for diplomatic and consular officers began with the establishment of a foreign service school, which sent new officers to divisions of the department for several months before their assignment abroad. In the 1930s the renamed Foreign Service Officers' Training School provided junior officers with training in consular and commercial work after their two-year probationary tour abroad.

Increasingly, some officers were also sent to universities for graduate study. While all training was suspended during World War II, it was resumed after the war with the establishment of the Foreign Service Institute. In theory, the intention was to copy a business model by creating the most efficient system with the most efficient people. Such changes included revised entrance examinations and consular associations, in addition to the foreign service schools.

The reforms were perhaps best represented in the internal system of ratings and inspections used to rule on promotions. Forms, which eventually swelled to some 212 questions by the 1920s, and departmental retention and promotion rating codes were used to provide uniform standards for personnel decisions. The most significant concern expressed by the forms and rating codes was to be a measuring device of the "efficiency of the individual." It was hoped that such evaluations would purge the "decrepit, unfit, morally suspect, drunken and coarse and brutal types, etc." from the consular service.

Deeply felt personal, status, and career differences separated the department's consular service from the diplomatic, which officially represented the government of the United States in international relations. Diplomats often considered themselves professional policymakers and were more bound to State Department traditions. Managers and planners, usually emerging, like Carr, from the consular side, were held in low esteem. One diplomat observed those "administrative types who inflate themselves with all sorts of rich and resonant titles like Career Evaluators, and General Services Specialists, and even Ministers of Embassy for Administrative Affairs. These glorified janitors, supply clerks, and pants-pressers yearn to get their fingers in the foreign affairs pie, and when they do, the diplomatic furniture often gets marked with gummy thumbprints."

It must be noted, however, that truly significant organizational reform in the Department of State did not stop at the consular-diplomatic demarcation. Diplomats such as Phillips and Grew remarked at how much of their work concerned the same business interests and pressures directed at the consuls. New departures were taken with a view to improving the efficiency of the State Department, not just one part of it.

Of most direct contact with the business-consular developments of the early twentieth century were modifications in the preparations of commercial reports. The Bureau of Statistics, a province of influential geopoliticians such as O. P. Austin, was renamed the Bureau of Foreign and Domestic Commerce. Although control of it was shifted to the Commerce and Labor Department in 1903, a corollary agency, the Bureau of Trade

Relations, was immediately established. The State Department advanced this effort to collect and analyze business data with the creation of the Office of the Economic Adviser in 1921. This position came to be held by important advisers such as Herbert Feis.

The State Department's approach to filing and record keeping, somewhat more detailed than in Remsen's day, was reworked several times in the twentieth century to provide greater systemization. Thus were created in turn the Numerical Files of 1906–1910 and the more comprehensive and efficient Decimal Files in 1910. In the 1960s began a subject-numeric system, and in the 1970s the department's central file was computerized. The Division of Information, created in 1909, took responsibility for preserving the department's data and publishing selected annual excerpts in the already established House of Representatives publication series, Foreign Relations of the United States (FRUS). This series entered what has been called its "modern era" in 1921, under the supervision of Gaillard Hunt and another agency he headed called the Division of Publications. During and after World War II, tremendous growth in the number of pages of files and the widespread practice of stamping documents with secret classifications slowed release of FRUS volumes. In 1989 more than thirty years separated the publication of official correspondence from its original date, and Congress set a statutory goal of a thirty-year maximum elapsed time for issuing the volumes.

Of greatest precedence on the diplomatic side was the creation in March 1908 of the Division of Far Eastern Affairs and the structuring of the whole State Department into a number of similar geographically grouped "divisions" in the years that followed. Before World War II, when the Department of State still numbered well below one thousand employees in all, these regional divisions were small, usually manned by only a few "desk officers" dealing with American embassies and legations overseas. Their purpose was to provide better machinery for the coordination of policy at all levels. In time, the five regional divisions (Europe, East Asia, Near East and South Asia, Inter-American, African) and a sixth desk, the Bureau of International Organization Affairs (responsible for relations with the American mission to the United Nations), grew dramatically in size and complexity. An assistant secretary headed each bureau and supervised the close contact with American embassies in the respective areas of

responsibility. Below the assistant secretary were office directors, each responsible for a small group of countries. The country desk officer was the "low man on the totem pole," concerned with policy toward a single foreign nation.

The culmination of all these administrative changes came in two efforts to make the various components of the State Department into "interchangeable" parts. First was the Rogers (Foreign Service) Act of 1924 and second was the movement known as "Wristonization" in the 1950s. The pressures and reasoning producing the Rogers Act, which merged the consular and diplomatic services into a single foreign service, were similar to those that resulted in the previously mentioned separate and more piecemeal reforms on both sides of the department. As Representative John Rogers remarked, business forces were united and once again exerting influence. He noted that "practically every chamber of commerce and trade organization in the United States and many of the American chambers and trade organizations functioning in other parts of the world have gone on record as favoring this particular reorganization of our foreign service." Rather than a radical departure, the Rogers Act was a culmination of the well-defined premises of efficient control and a transition to still further forms of administrative systemization. In place of the separation and distinction between the broadly separated categories of political interest in the diplomatic service and commercial interest in the consular service, there would be one unified Department of State.

With the increased size of the department, a movement had developed by the 1950s to merge still further the civil service staff of the State Department with the foreign service. With a shortage of personnel for positions, especially within the training programs, and a distrust between the "line" desk officers and the "staff" administrators, a committee was charged by Dulles with the task of additional State Department reorganization. The chairman of the committee was Henry M. Wriston, president of Brown University, and hence the merger of the two staffs became known as Wristonization.

This reform was not only another in a series; it also gave the first real evidence that the similar ones that had preceded it might not, after all, have been effective. Throughout the century, optimism had prevailed. Thus, Huntington Wilson had boasted in 1908, "I am happy to tell you that one of my pet hobbies, the politico-geographical divi-

A TALE OF TWO SPEECHES

In early 1950, two speeches, one by Secretary of State Dean Acheson and the other by Senator Joseph McCarthy, illustrated the tension between pragmatism and politics in the modern State Department. Acheson's 12 January address to the National Press Club, "Crisis in Asia," was a model of pragmatic policy analysis. Also known as the "defense perimeter speech," because it placed Korea beyond America's line of defense in the Pacific, this talk was quite perceptive. Noting "bewilderment" in the American reaction to the communist victory in China in 1949, Acheson detected "a failure to understand [the] basic revolutionary force which is loose in Asia" and explained that "the communists did not create this but they were shrewd and cunning enough to . . . ride this thing into victory and power." Such sophisticated, accurate, and timely analysis was precisely what State Department bureaucrats needed to provide to policymakers.

McCarthy's 9 February speech to the Republican Women's Club of Wheeling, West Virginia, advanced a strikingly different interpretation of what he labeled the "impotency" of U.S. policy. He charged that the United States had failed to prevent communist successes "because of the traitorous actions of those who have been treated so well by this Nation. . . . This is glaringly true in the State Department. There the bright young men who are born with silver spoons in their mouths are the ones who have been most traitorous." In the senator's inflammatory rhetoric, the department's elitist past remained to haunt it in the frightening uncertainty of the early Cold War.

The staff analysis that went into the Press Club speech demonstrated State's bureaucratic expertise. Contrary to partisan complaints based upon distorted or nonexistent evidence, the level of patriotism, competence, and strategic toughness within the department was high, as exemplified by its shaping of NSC 68, the April 1950 program for militarized containment of global communism. State remained at the center of foreign policymaking in the 1950s, but damage to the department's credibility from McCarthy's excesses revealed the vulnerability of its expertise to political and ideological challenges.

---

sion, has at last received final recognition by the creation of the Division of Far Eastern Affairs . . . so I now have much better machinery for my direction of the Far Eastern business." Or after the Rogers Act, Grew felt the State Department had "a new order . . . established, a new machine developed." But the Wriston committee described well the catalog of State Department problems after a half century of such administrative reforms. In sum, there was a marked decline in public confidence in the State Department; a similar decline in morale in the diplomatic ranks; and failure to carry through on various legislative mandates such as the Foreign Service Act of 1946, which provided for inducting officers into all levels of the foreign service so as to make it more flexible and successful.

Although Wristonization itself was another management panacea, it drew attention to the fact that the State Department's "management of human resources has been irresolute and unimaginative." Even though the question of personnel management had been under repeated study,

"substantially nothing has been accomplished." The committee remarked that "all modern personnel management organizations utilize machines to facilitate the mechanical tasks of keeping personnel records; the Department however has not effectively utilized such a system." In particular, Wriston's committee criticized the "occasional tinkering" and "token" programs of recruitment and training. Congress had intended the Foreign Service Institute to be "for the State Department, what the Naval War College, the Army War College, and the National War College are for the Armed Services—an advanced training ground for officers destined for high command." But since the institute had been given little attention by the department, it did not provide the kind of educational leadership and scholarship that had been intended. Such was characteristic of the State Department's general lack of a clear concept of training requirements, career planning, and development.

The Wriston committee missed the perhaps larger significance of the protracted failure of management reforms and put all its faith in a still bigger and, it hoped, better structure. While many civil servants had been seriously involved in foreign affairs and thus would benefit themselves and the State Department by merger with the foreign service officers, a larger number of straight administrative employees (office personnel, for example) were trapped by the move into being diplomatic officers, for which they had neither ambition nor preparation.

The career uncertainty that these bureaucratic reforms injected into the department coincided with the chilling effect on creativity and responsiveness caused by McCarthyism's assault on the foreign service. Unfounded allegations of communist sympathies cost many veteran diplomats their jobs in the 1950s. McCarthyism was a grotesque extreme of a problem that had plagued State in the past and would burden it in the future, namely the tension between careerists and politicians. Foreign service officers were trained to suppress their personal views, but political appointees to posts in the department or partisan leaders outside often put pressure on careerists for political or ideological loyalty. Caution and conformity became the order of the day in the diplomatic service, with a resultant weakening of State's leadership role in foreign policy.

Forgetting, or perhaps choosing not to remember, that organizational reform enthusiasm similar to Wristonization had failed to deter and might be blamed for the bad situation now at hand, the brightest people in and out of the Department of State continued to talk of what could be done to increase management efficiency and policy effectiveness. Thus, one had come almost full circle from Remsen to Kissinger. The larger and more complex the State Department and the world became, the less important was the role of the department in making foreign policy. Instead of individual advice, the department became expert in institutional adjustments and its influence shrunk proportionally. A Rand Corporation think-tank study, *United States Policy and the Third World* (1967), never once mentioned the State Department.

As State's structure grew and its power vanished in the mid-twentieth century, its once high and mighty place became almost laughable. Thus, satires of departmental memoranda about such things as waste-power removal were not uncommon, nor were genuine titles such as chief of the administrative management and personnel division of the Bureau of Educational and Cultural Affairs. While some flirted with participative management and Dean Rusk instituted a department suggestion box, few shared the Kissinger or Villard view that perhaps the goal might once again be "top-notch organization in which the human equation is not sacrificed to the Moloch of bureaucracy."

LEADERSHIP OR MANAGEMENT?

In the 1780s, Benjamin Franklin's diplomatic dispatches from France sometimes took months to cross the Atlantic. Two centuries later, flash cables or secure e-mail messages could be in the hands of the secretary of state within moments. Can, in short, the modern secretary of state, however talented and qualified, break free as Kissinger suggested from the management ethos?

The obstacles to such freedom were rather clear in duties and responsibilities of the secretary of state at the beginning of the twenty-first century. The secretary was a senior personal adviser to the president and the only cabinet officer primarily charged with looking at the nation as a whole in its relations with the outside world. The secretary of state was also the ranking diplomat in dealing with foreign governments at the same time that he served as an administration spokesman on American foreign policy to Congress, the country, and abroad. As chief of the State Department, the secretary was responsible to the president and accountable to Congress. Finally, the secretary was also in direct line to presidential succession. The modern secretary of state was thus adviser, negotiator, reporter of trouble, spokesperson, manager, and coordinator. One thinks of days filled with calls, conferences, talks with senators, ambassadors, delegations of private citizens, journalists, and bankers, not to mention the increasingly frequent global troubleshooting, all the time while running a department.

Secretary Stimson's biographer reports on one day, even in the more serene pre–World War II world, as follows:

A conference at ten o'clock with Silas Strawn, the United States delegate to a conference at Peking on Chinese tariffs. At 10:30 a press conference followed at 10:45 by an appointment with Dr. McClaren of the Williamstown Institute. Between 11:00 and 12:00 receiving the Spanish Ambassador and a representative from the Bolivian delegation. They were followed by Senator Howell at 12:00, Congressman Keyes at 12:40

and General Allen at 12:55. After lunch at 2:30 he began to sign the official mail, a task he had finished by 3:30 when Congressmen Robinson, Thatcher, Walker, Newhill, Kendall and Blackburn called upon him and talked for an hour. Elihu Root, Jr., appeared at 4:30 and remained until 5:00. Just before going home the Secretary called James M. Beck, then a congressman, in New York. That evening he attended a dinner given by the Chilean Ambassador in honor of the Chilean Minister of Finance.

How against these activities does one formulate the basic strategies and plans of action required? Even if time and attention are found, more myriad problems await in terms of the delegation of authority to bureaus that distrust each other's prerogatives or to individuals anxious for good assignments and promotions. Each bureau, each office within a bureau, each officer, is improvising from day-to-day, unaware, unprepared, or uninspired in the work of partners, neighbors, and colleagues.

Against this setting, some post–World War II secretaries of state have stood out in the effort to orchestrate the department's activities. Most notably mentioned by those in the State Department, George C. Marshall, accustomed to command, and Dean Acheson, experienced on the Hoover Commission for government reorganization, brought about a sense of planning amidst the chaos. Most secretaries of state since World War II, however, have been less engaged with the department itself and more in touch with the White House. Some, such as Dulles, Kissinger, and Christopher, were out of town a lot. Baker was George H. W. Bush's closest personal friend. Shultz stayed in the post for seven years in part because he was a better organization man than most, but he often clashed with Ronald Reagan's conservative loyalists, who thought Shultz was too close to foreign service liberals.

The task for secretaries of state has been difficult because the role of the State Department is, in the last analysis, so weak. Primacy in coordinating foreign policy itself, the lifeblood of the State Department's leadership in the days of Adams and Seward, has been challenged and the counterattack has had few bases for claims to legitimacy. The Constitution says nothing of the State Department and refers only to "executive" and "presidential" responsibilities. Congress has never helped. The original legislation setting up the State Department also recognized the president as supreme. Even when granting power to

the secretary of state, it has always been understood that he or she "shall act under the direction of the President." Such direction has wandered from giving State considerable room to those who have wanted State out of foreign affairs.

Some analysts of American diplomacy go even further to suggest that the State Department, while it never had a constitutional or legislative claim to primacy, did, at one time in the nineteenth century, come to hold such a position by tradition and that the department itself gradually allowed such power to erode. One of the first four departments to be established (along with War, Treasury, and Justice), the State Department came to view itself as the first among equals. This, in turn, led to an attitude of general superiority in the federal establishment—an attitude that, regardless of ability, the State Department had a special dispensation to control foreign policy. If other valid interests arose in other departments, the State Department worked for too long not to foster them but to cut them off. Thus began a movement to place control of foreign policy in more reasonable and responsive hands. Also, the "legal mind" and "administrative efficiency" movement made State more introspective and took it further from the center of integrated policy.

As the State Department failed to keep abreast and federal agencies multiplied, new voices emerged to decide, negotiate, and implement foreign policy. When the State Department cried "foul" but showed little aptitude, foreign policymaking moved elsewhere. The emergency experience of World War II, in particular, put personal presidential policy in the forefront. Self-defensively, the State Department took to eulogizing its establishment, and the American people had to be reminded frequently after the war that "the Department of State, under the direction of the President, in cooperation with Congress is responsible for the advancement of our foreign policy objectives."

In reality, however, such leadership moved most directly to the National Security Council. Created by the National Security Act of 1947 (the same statute that established the Central Intelligence Agency), the National Security Council was, in fact, charged with the responsibility of "effectively coordinating the policies and functions of the departments and agencies of the Government relating to the national security." It was provided with a staff and set about operating, close to the White House, as an interdepartmental committee with functions most immediately related to questions of foreign policy. Thus was created what the State Department had once been, a coordinating, orchestrating mechanism for the various elements of policy at the highest level. The State Department, at least in the contemporary United States, was not a part of the primary machinery by which the nation would set about to meet the demands of increased world leadership.

In the competitive world of Washington's bureaucratic politics, the State Department is one of the smallest players. Its annual budget and number of employees are dwarfed by such behemoths as Defense and Health and Human Services. Although the total amount is secret, the annual funds for the CIA far exceed those of State. With a lack of resources and an increasing centralization of foreign policymaking in the White House, it is not surprising that other departments and agencies in Washington often have more influence in shaping U.S. foreign policy than does the State Department.

Despite these challenges, the State Department has made various efforts to revitalize its headquarters' operations in the somewhat aptly named Foggy Bottom section of Washington. The program Diplomacy for the 1970s, embarked on by Secretary of State William P. Rogers and his chief assistant, Elliot L. Richardson, was one of the most publicized and professional. Yet it must be noted that when one scratches underneath the rhetoric of the program, it was, in short, still another management reform package, not unlike in design, if not in definition, the earlier programs that had failed and, in part, led to disaster for the department.

The Rogers-Richardson proposals at least incorporated the knowledge, which had begun with Wristonization, that structural reforms were not universally productive. Indeed, they noted, "substance can suffer at the hands of technique; spirit can be alienated from operation." The lessons of the participative managers, more serious than the mere superficiality of a suggestion box, were also deeply ingrained. A prime focus of Diplomacy for the 1970s was a new era in management-employee relations. Openness and creativity were encouraged. There was even concern, for the first time, for ensuring equal employment opportunities and new openings for women. The role of the foreign service wife was redefined, giving her more training and staff support for her unique position as an unofficial representative of the United States.

Still, characteristically, the new proposals clung to the same brass rings. First was the commitment to a belief that this was the only real, significant reform where all the acknowledged previous attempts were specious and superficial. All previous reformers of management guidelines had believed similarly about their proposals, from Huntington Wilson's geopolitical divisions through Wriston's merger. Second was a still-unshattered faith in techniques, no matter what the preamble, to solve problems. Demonstrating this faith was a program called Policy Analysis and Resource Allocation (PARA), under the aegis of the secretary's Planning and Coordination Staff (S/PC). One of the tasks of the program was to provide a structural way back into the top echelons of decision making for the department by writing annual reviews designed to serve as common denominators for discussion in the department, the Inter-Agency Group of the National Security Council, and the White House. In turn, Policy Analysis and Resource Allocation was to feed into an even more centralized executive council known as the Secretariat. The authors of Diplomacy for the 1970s proudly acclaimed this Secretariat, at the "heartbeat" of department operations, as "thoroughly modernized" and ready with "up-to-date techniques and equipment for high-speed telecommunications and automated information handling." Thus, Secretary Rogers urged development of a new operations center and improved information management known as Secretariat Automated Data Indexing System (SADI).

Into this nerve center of the Department of State in 1973 moved Kissinger, who had challenged the hegemony of efficiency while an outsider. It is difficult to perceive how a Kissinger or certainly a Remsen, Adams, Seward, Adee, or Evarts could function in the kingdom of PARA and SADI, that is, an environment where "substantive problems are transformed into administrative ones." What was the remaining role of leadership and policy in a department that could issue forth Airgram 5399, concerning the use of the title "Ms."? The message read in part: "The Department has added 'Ms.' to the personnel title codes . . . maintained in the automated master personnel file. All documents which access these codes and which are printed by the computer may now employ this form of address."

The "Ms." example reveals not only a preoccupation with management details but also a diversity problem in State. For the department specifically charged with representing the United States to the various peoples of the world, the career officers in State had always been remarkably homogeneous. In the 1970s the department made great strides to catch up with other government offices in the area of diversity. The number of new female foreign service officers doubled during the decade, and by the end of the decade the department was actively recruiting African-American candidates. As a result, by the end of the century the number of female and African-American ambassadors had noticeably increased even before the nation had its first woman as secretary of state with Madeleine Albright and its first African-American secretary of state with Colin Powell.

During the last quarter of the twentieth century, the State Department continued its parade of re-reorganizations that had begun with creation of the first geographic division in 1908 and the professionalization of the foreign service with the Rogers Act of 1924. The Foreign Service Officers Act of 1980 aimed to make career officers more effective through reform of the promotion and recognition system. The bureaucratic pyramid of functional and geographic divisions was continually readjusted, but the process of getting a policy recommendation through this maze of specialists remained time-consuming and an obstacle to policy innovation. During the Clinton administration a new undersecretary of state for global issues was added to make the department more responsive to contemporary world problems, such as the environment and population growth. One of the most significant changes of the 1990s was to bring the previously independent U.S. Information Agency and the Arms Control and Disarmament Agency into the department to save costs and enhance management efficiency.

The explanation of the shifting power of the secretary of state and the department itself since World War II was not in internal organization, or in major historical events like the Vietnam War and the end of the Cold War, or in scandals like Iran-Contra. The key was in the growth of power and complexity of the modern presidency, beginning with Franklin D. Roosevelt and continuing thereafter. Much public discussion focused on the relative balance of power between the National Security Council after its creation in 1947 and the State Department. During the Johnson years, Secretary of Defense Robert McNamara and national security advisers McGeorge Bundy and Walt Rostow were seen as overshadowing Dean Rusk. Under Nixon, Kissinger dominated the policy process through his NSC staff and his direct access to the president within the White House. Reagan claimed that George Shultz would restore

the primacy of the State Department, but Shultz was often in conflict with Secretary of Defense Caspar Weinberger and later the NSC staff over dealings with Iran and Central America. With the end of the Cold War, Bill Clinton elevated another player in the policy game, the secretary of commerce, as he gave priority to economic competitiveness. The determining consideration in all of these cases was how the president chose to exercise his executive prerogatives.

Despite efforts to improve its own organization, the State Department was unable to reclaim the leadership and coordination of foreign policy of which it had once been able to boast. The centralization of policymaking in the White House that had begun during World War II and increased during the Cold War remained. The National Security Council staff had the advantages of greater access to the president, more rapid response to changing situations, and more domestic political awareness than State. Indeed, bureaucratic battles between the department and the NSC staff at times—such as in the Iran-Contra scandal of the 1980s—wrecked the policy process. No national security adviser after Kissinger ever equaled his level of control over decisions, but policy unity was always difficult. The Defense Department, CIA, NSC, and other departments often had as much or more input into foreign policy than did the State Department.

The juxtaposition of Airgram 5399 about the use of "Ms." and Remsen's original instructions put one in mind of a debate between two diplomatic historians about the utility of speedy publication of foreign policy files by the Department of State. While both scholars supported such a policy, their reasons differed dramatically. The first argued the administratively defensible position that quick access to such documents and the resulting historical monographs, sure to follow, would teach contemporary diplomats how to do a better job. More reflectively, the second historian suggested that while scholarship and research demanded quick access, better policy would emerge not from monographs, but from "wisdom."

Leadership, the quality of greatness inherent in the work of an Adams or a Seward, is still possible. The Department of State is not beyond its grasp. Yet one must conclude that its achievement slips further and further out of reach in the wake of those variables the department has come to identify as progress since the mid-twentieth century: complexity, bigness, and accelerated change.

BIBLIOGRAPHY

Bemis, Samuel Flagg. *John Quincy Adams and the Foundations of American Foreign Policy.* 2 vols. New York, 1949. A good biography of a great secretary of state.

Bemis, Samuel Flagg, ed. *American Secretaries of State and Their Diplomacy.* Vols. 1–10. New York, 1928–1958. Good, short sketches.

Bemis, Samuel Flagg, and Robert Ferrell, eds. *American Secretaries of State and Their Diplomacy.* New series. Vols. 11–19. New York, 1963–1980. Continues the older Bemis series with the same title.

Crane, Katherine E. *Mr. Carr of State.* New York, 1960. Gives a favorable view of a key middle manager.

DeConde, Alexander. *The American Secretary of State.* New York, 1962. Contains useful analyses.

Elder, Robert E. *The Policy Machine: The Department of State and American Foreign Policy.* Syracuse, N.Y., 1960. A landmark political science study.

Graebner, Norman A., ed. *An Uncertain Tradition: American Secretaries of State in the Twentieth Century.* New York, 1961. One of the most used sources for general, interpretive information.

Hartmann, Frederick H., and Robert L. Wendzel. *America's Foreign Policy in a Changing World.* New York, 1994. Describes how policy is made in Washington, D.C.

Heinrichs, Waldo. *American Ambassador: Joseph C. Grew and the Development of the United States Diplomatic Tradition.* Boston, 1966. Besides being a biography of an important man, it traces the evolution of foreign policy implementation.

Ilchman, Frederick. *Professional Diplomacy in the United States, 1779–1939.* Chicago, 1961. A careful and documented study.

Kegley, Charles W., and Eugene R. Wittkopf. *American Foreign Policy: Pattern and Process.* 3d ed. New York, 1987. Discusses State's relationship to other departments.

McCamy, James. *Conduct of the New Diplomacy.* New York, 1964. A revision of the author's previous volume, *The Administration of American Foreign Affairs* (New York, 1950), based on the intervening decade.

Morison, Elting E. *Turmoil and Tradition: A Study of the Life and Times of Henry L. Stimson.* Boston, 1960.

Plischke, Elmer. *Conduct of American Diplomacy.* Princeton, N.J., 1950. A standard work.

Rubin, Barry M. *Secrets of State: The State Department and the Struggle over U.S. Foreign Policy.* New York, 1985. Analyzes the decline of State with regard to the National Security Council.

Schulzinger, Robert D. *Henry Kissinger: Doctor of Diplomacy.* New York, 1989. Examines Kissinger's significant role in shaping the policy process.

Stuart, Graham H. *The Department of State: A History of Its Organization, Procedure, and Personnel.* New York, 1949. An older source of itemized changes.

Villard, Henry S. *Affairs at State.* New York, 1965.

White, Leonard. *The Federalists: A Study in Administrative History.* New York, 1948.

See also DECISION MAKING; DEPARTMENT OF DEFENSE; DOCTRINES; NATIONAL SECURITY COUNCIL; PRESIDENTIAL ADVISERS; PRESIDENTIAL POWER.

DETERRENCE

David Coleman

In one form or another, deterrence is a motivational force in many everyday relationships: a child learns not to misbehave for fear of being scolded by its parents; a potential criminal might decide against committing a crime for fear of being caught and punished; a nation may choose one foreign policy course over another out of fear of military or economic retaliation; or an international alliance may threaten war if any one of its members is attacked. In each case, one party has influenced the choice of another by threatening consequences that outweigh gains.

In the field of foreign policy, the threat and fear of retaliation has been a powerful force. Imperial powers have found that making an example of an enemy or lawbreaker ultimately provided a cheaper and easier method of controlling peoples than maintaining a large standing police or armed forces, conforming to the common adage that prevention is usually better than cure. To that end, Roman legions deliberately cultivated a reputation for ruthlessness to promote stability, and European imperial powers did everything they could to impress their technological and military prowess upon the peoples they commanded. But it is in the nuclear age that deterrence assumed a special significance and was refined from a mostly instinctive practice to a deliberate, if still inexact, science. Throughout the nuclear age, deterrence has been a dynamic concept propelled by technological and historical developments. In turn, the concept of deterrence came to influence those technological and historical developments.

THE THEORY OF DETERRENCE

In its most basic theoretical form, deterrence is an equation involving two parties, where one party weighs the gain it may make by pursuing a course of action against the price it may pay by the retaliation of the other party. By way of illustration, it is useful to consider two nations, Nation A and Nation B, whose interests collide on a particular issue. If Nation A is known to be considering a course of action contrary to the interests of Nation B, Nation B may signal its intent to retaliate if Nation A does indeed choose that course of action. This leaves Nation A with a decision. First, it must decide whether Nation B has the capability to carry out its threat, and, second, it must decide whether Nation B has the will to carry out its threat. And the deciding factor in both of these judgments is the credibility of Nation B's capability and will to carry out the threat. If, as a result of this cost-benefit calculation, Nation A decides not to go ahead with the course of action, then deterrence has been successful; but if Nation A decides that the gains outweigh the risk or price, and goes ahead regardless of the threat, then deterrence has failed. This example, though, provides only the barest outline sketch of how deterrence operates in the foreign policy arena.

The simplicity of the theoretical formula belies the complexity of international diplomacy in practice and critics of deterrence have focused on the relative rigidity of the formula compared to the fluidity and unpredictability of international diplomacy. Furthermore, deterrence rests heavily on certain assumptions about the parties involved and the way they will react. First, deterrence rests heavily on the belief that rationality will prevail throughout the process. Not only do the various parties have to behave in fundamentally rational ways, but each party must perceive the other as behaving in a fundamentally rational way. In practice, this leads to a complicated process of perception and counterperception as policymakers and intelligence bodies from each nation estimate and try to influence what the other is thinking.

Critics of deterrence rightly point out that the decisions of political leaders often do not fall into neatly explainable categories and that how-ever carefully the deterrence situation may be con-trolled, ultimately the decision is a subjective one. In foreign affairs as in everyday life, behavior in deterrence situations is based on instinct as well as reason and this instinctive element can never be confidently discounted. Moreover, the way both parties view the situation can be influenced quali-tatively by any number of factors, including irra-tionality, misperception, poor judgment, or even just wishful thinking. In short, what may seem an unacceptable price to one person or under some circumstances could well be judged by another under different circumstances to be acceptable. Moreover, since history is filled with events that were quite simply unpredictable, it is clearly diffi-cult to account with any certainty for the myriad of accidents, mistakes, and emotions that may play a part in a decision. At best, employing deterrence is an approximation, but in the thermonuclear age, with weapons capable of global annihilation, the stakes are higher than ever before.

Because deterrence is very much in the eye of the beholder, and actual intentions and capabilities are less important than the other side's estimate of those intentions and capabilities, the process of communicating and interpreting information is crucial. Known as signaling, this two-way dis-course is open to a wide range of possible scenar-ios. One involves explicit communications, including public speeches and classified diplomatic correspondence. Another is implicit measures such as partial mobilization or the placing of forces on alert or more subtle measures designed to be detected by foreign intelligence bodies. Ideally, each method is designed to exploit the complex interplay of perceptions and counterperceptions.

Sometimes deterrence fails. Often in the his-tory of international affairs the cost-benefit calcu-lation has led to an unexpected result. In 1904 Russia ignored Japanese warnings that its policies would lead to retaliation, resulting ultimately in the Russo-Japanese War. In 1914 the Central Powers recognized that their policies risked draw-ing the Entente into war in Europe, but continued regardless. During World War II, Nazi Germany persisted with U-boat attacks on American transatlantic merchant shipping despite President Franklin D. Roosevelt's explicit warnings that it would likely provoke U.S. retaliation. In Decem-ber 1941, despite U.S. military strength, Japan calculated that its interests were best served by a surprise attack on the U.S. fleet at Pearl Harbor. In mid-1962 Soviet premier Nikita Khrushchev

installed nuclear missiles in Cuba despite Presi-dent John F. Kennedy's explicit warnings that doing so would provoke U.S. retaliation. And in 1991 the Middle East erupted in violence as Sad-dam Hussein ignored the threat of U.S. interven-tion should Iraq invade Kuwait.

STRATEGIC BOMBING

In diplomacy, threats that act as a deterrent have most often come in military form and have there-fore implied the capability to project military power. Possessing a powerful navy gave Britain such a capability, but for much of its early history, the United States was not able to project military power and therefore made threats rarely and with questionable success. One notable deterrent effort was President James Monroe's unilateral declara-tion on 2 December 1823 of the independence of the Western Hemisphere, issued in order to deter Spanish intervention in Latin America and Rus-sian expansion on to the American continent. Monroe's threat was twofold. First, he implied local military resistance if Spain tried to reestab-lish its colonies in Latin America or Russia expanded onto the American Northwest Coast. Second, he implied that if the European powers chose to interfere in the affairs of the Western Hemisphere then the United States would be forced to revoke its longstanding tradition of non-interference in European affairs. Ultimately, Spain did not try to reestablish its colonies, although this probably had less to do with Monroe's threats than it did with similar threats issued by Britain.

The advent of strategic bombing in the early twentieth century vastly increased the ability to project military force, and consequently led to the transformation of deterrence into its modern form. The twin technological developments of high explosives and aircraft that could deliver them to their targets made strategic bombing a decisive factor in modern warfare. It was first used in limited form in World War I in Germany's zeppelin (airship) attacks against Britain. German scientists had not only developed a way to incor-porate poison gas into a bomb, thereby creating the first type of the weapons now classed as weapons of mass destruction, but had also devel-oped a way to float zeppelins over enemy lines and drop their payloads on British cities. Although not widely recognized at the time, this ability to move beyond the confines of the battle-field and to attack an enemy's cities directly revolutionized modern warfare as offensive strategic bombing threatened to break the defensive deadlock that had evolved from tanks, machine guns, and trench warfare.

At the same time it introduced a new factor that, although intangible, was no less powerful. Like the German V-1 and V-2 rocket strikes during World War II, the German zeppelin of World War I resulted in few deaths, but the potential that the technology seemed to hold for extending the battlefront from the trenches to civilian homes captured the British public's imagination to an extent that far outweighed objective casualty counts. For the first time a military weapon was used not only for the tactical calculations of policymakers, but also to strike terror into the home front, which had become an increasingly vital component of modern warfare. The fluid variable of civilian morale suddenly became as important as military morale as the civilian population reacted to the new threat to their homes and lives. Moreover, during World War II, as strategic bombing became vastly more effective (and deadly), the industrial and economic hearts of an enemy became additional viable targets. Allied long-range bombers all but destroyed the German industrial city of Dresden, while the American firebombing of Tokyo started fires that raged out of control for days at a time. With the development of the atomic bomb, a weapon blatantly unable to discriminate between military and civilian targets, strategic bombing was taken to its extreme.

The development of the atomic bomb was the culmination of the top secret Manhattan Project, an extraordinary collaboration of international scientists headed by J. Robert Oppenheimer that was backed by vast resources provided by the U.S. government. Stringent security precluded public debate about what role the new weapon would have, but among those few who had information about the project's overall objective and progress, there was growing awareness that the new weapon would be unlike anything that had come before; it would perhaps even create "a new relationship of man to the universe," as a committee chaired by Secretary of War Henry L. Stimson put it. Such an unconventional weapon clearly required unconventional thinking. As Oppenheimer recognized, the elements of surprise and terror were as intrinsic to it as fissionable nuclei. In a top-secret report submitted to the War Department on 11 June 1945, a small committee chaired by physicist James Franck suggested that the psychological impact of the explosion might

be more valuable to U.S. military objectives than the immediate physical destruction. In the hope that a demonstration of the destructive potential of the atomic bomb might be enough to compel the Japanese to surrender, the Franck Committee proposed a public demonstration in an uninhabited region.

After considering the various proposals, President Harry S. Truman concluded that a demonstration in an uninhabited region would likely be ineffective, and therefore ordered that the bomb be used against Japanese cities, a decision that has been passionately debated ever since. Some have argued that Truman's motivation was less the war in the Pacific than the impending contest with the Soviet Union and that as such it represented the opening gambit of so-called "atomic diplomacy," while others argue that the decision was not only militarily sound but necessary, and that it ultimately saved hundreds of thousands of American and Japanese lives. But whatever Truman's motives, at 8:15 A.M. on 6 August 1945, an American B-29 Superfortress long-range bomber named the *Enola Gay* delivered its single atomic bomb to the target of Hiroshima, the second most important military-industrial center in Japan. Upward of seventy thousand people were killed instantly in the blast. Three days later another bomb was dropped on Nagasaki, killing at least twenty thousand. In the following weeks the death counts in both cities rose as the populations succumbed to radiation-related illnesses.

As the wire services flashed the story around the globe, journalists who had witnessed the Trinity test blast at Alamogordo, New Mexico, three weeks earlier on 16 July, were now free to write about what they had seen and help a startled world comprehend what had happened. The American public's reaction was a mixture of relief that the end of the war was in sight, satisfaction that revenge had been exacted upon the perpetrators of the Pearl Harbor attack, and a sober recognition of the responsibility the new weapon carried with it. In strategic terms, there was not yet such a thing as a U.S. atomic stockpile, despite President Truman's implication in his press statement announcing the Hiroshima bombing that atomic bombs were rolling off the production line. Had the first two atomic bombs failed to bring a Japanese surrender, some time would have passed before more were ready. Within days of the Nagasaki bombing, however, the Japanese leaders finally succumbed to the inevitable and formally surrendered to General Douglas MacArthur's forces on 2 September 1945. From that moment, the priority for U.S. military forces was not building more bombs, but going home.

As the United States demobilized in the postwar period, relations with the Soviet Union deteriorated. The coincidence of the beginning of the Cold War and the dawn of the nuclear age ensured that the history of the two would become inextricably entwined. During the early Cold War, the primary strategic contest was for Europe, and Germany in particular, but throughout the continent evidence mounted of a clash of interests and ideology. Within a few short years of the end of World War II, the U.S. government had publicly identified the Soviet Union as its primary strategic threat. And if war did break out in Europe, the Soviets had vastly more conventional forces and the geographical advantage as well. The challenge for U.S. defense planners, therefore, was to find a way to project the U.S. atomic force. Nevertheless, the planners moved slowly to devise a coherent nuclear strategy to serve foreign policy interests. Although fully recognizing that the Soviets would sooner or later develop the atomic bomb, American policymakers struggled to find a way to take advantage of the atomic monopoly. However, the American population was still weary from World War II and constrained military budgets were shrinking, so atomic development was a low priority. It was not until Dwight D. Eisenhower became president that a coherent deterrent role was found for the U.S. nuclear arsenal. But by the end of the Truman administration, defense budgets were growing rapidly, and that administration made some effort to bring military policy into the atomic age. Having recently witnessed how much sacrifice Soviet leader Joseph Stalin was willing to impose on his countrymen in the defense of the USSR, it was clear to U.S. policymakers that if war should break out between the two superpowers, the small stockpile of American atomic bombs that had been built up since Nagasaki would not guarantee victory.

In use, the atomic bomb was an offensive weapon. For the American atomic monopoly to be cast in a defensive role, that role had to be to prevent war altogether through the very threat of retaliation. Bernard Brodie, one of the first defense intellectuals to engage publicly the implications of the atomic bomb, succinctly summarized the momentous shift in military affairs that the bomb had sparked. "Thus far the chief purpose of our military establishment has been to win wars," Brodie commented in *The Absolute Weapon* (1946). "From now on its chief purpose must be to avert them." To that end, and recognizing that atomic weapons did not fall easily under the existing military force structure, the Truman administration in March 1946 created the Strategic Air Command (SAC) headed by General George Kenny. Adopting the motto "Peace is our profession," SAC's mission was to give the United States a long-term capability to project U.S. nuclear force anywhere on the globe. SAC's existence exemplified the paradox of deterrence strategies as summarized in the Latin adage *Qui desiderat pacem, praeparet bellum* (Let him who desires peace, prepare for war). Unlike the case with conventional military forces, for the remainder of its existence SAC's success would be measured not by its performance in battle, but by its never having actually to engage in combat.

The Cold War contest was ultimately a strategic one, but it was more often manifested in a series of short-term political contests. Committed to a policy of containing communist expansion, the Truman administration found itself having to rethink its assumption that atomic weapons would deter simply because they existed. By the end of 1948 there was mounting evidence that the American atomic monopoly was having little success in deterring communist political expansion through Europe; the threat of communist subversion in Greece and Turkey in 1947, the communist coup in Czechoslovakia in February 1948, and the strong communist presence during the Italian election of April 1948 all seemed to provide evidence to that effect. And in the first truly nuclear crisis of the Cold War, the Berlin blockade of 1948–1949, the Truman administration could manage only a half-hearted atomic threat that, if Stalin had pushed the matter, would likely have been revealed as a bluff. In a move with the twin objectives of temporarily bolstering the flagging British strategic bombing force and sending an atomic threat to Stalin, American B-29s were deployed in Britain at the height of the Berlin blockade crisis. But this early attempt at nuclear coercion was unconvincing. The B-29s initially sent were not modified to carry atomic bombs; furthermore, it was public knowledge that there was no procedure in place to store atomic warheads overseas. By mid-1948 even Secretary of Defense James Forrestal had to admit that American military planning, including its nuclear strategy, was "patchwork" at best. If America's national security was to realize the full

THE WORSE THE BETTER

On 1 March 1955, Prime Minister Winston Churchill spoke to the House of Commons:

"There is an immense gulf between the atomic and hydrogen bomb. The atomic bomb, with all its terrors, did not carry us outside the scope of human control or manageable events in thought or action, in peace or war. But when Mr. Sterling Cole, the Chairman of the United States Congressional Committee, gave out a year ago—17th February, 1954—the first comprehensive review of the hydrogen bomb, the entire foundation of human affairs was revolutionised, and mankind placed in a situation both measureless and laden with doom. . . .

"I shall content myself with saying about the power of this weapon, the hydrogen bomb, that apart from all the statements about blast and heat effects over increasingly wide areas there are now to be considered the consequences of 'fall out,' as it is called, of wind-borne radio-active particles. There is both an immediate direct effect on human beings who are in the path of such a cloud and an indirect effect through animals, grass and vegetables, which pass on these contagions to human beings through food.

"This would confront many who escaped the direct effects of the explosion with poisoning, or starvation, or both. Imagination stands appalled. There are, of course, the palliatives and precautions of a courageous Civil Defense . . . but our best protection lies, as I am sure the House will be convinced, in successful deterrents operating from a foundation of sober, calm and tireless vigilance.

"Moreover, a curious paradox has emerged. Let me put it simply. After a certain point has been passed it may be said, 'The worse things get the better.' The broad effect of the latest developments is to spread almost indefinitely and at least to a vast extent the area of mortal danger. This should certainly increase the deterrent upon Soviet Russia by putting her enormous spaces and scattered population on an equality or near-equality of vulnerability with our small densely populated island and with Western Europe. . . .

"Then it may well be that we shall by a process of sublime irony have reached a stage in this story where safety will be the sturdy child of terror, and survival the twin brother of annihilation."

---

potential of the atomic bomb for deterrence, a thorough rethinking would be needed.

One solution preferred by many was for the United States to exploit the window of opportunity by launching a preemptive strike against the Soviet Union. Former British prime minister Winston Churchill suggested sending Stalin an ultimatum stating that if he did not desist from his expansionist policies, U.S. planes would use atomic bombs against Soviet cities. The U.S. commander in Germany, General Lucius Clay, agreed. Other military voices in Washington lamented the wasting of an opportunity. The calls became more urgent as that window of opportunity seemed to be closing. When the Soviet Union detonated its first atomic device in August 1949, it caught the West by surprise. The mastering of the atomic process by Soviet scientists was not unexpected in a general sense, but beyond the inner sanctum of intelligence officials and defense planners, the Soviet achievement was never seriously anticipated beyond the vaguest of timetables. To make matters

more alarming, two months later, in October 1949, Mao Zedong's Communist Party emerged victorious in China's civil war, a development seen in Washington as proof that Moscow's ambitions were not confined to Europe but were global.

THE THERMONUCLEAR REVOLUTION

The twin developments of thermonuclear weapons and long-range missiles ushered in a new phase of nuclear deterrence. Now, thermonuclear warheads hundreds or even thousands of times more powerful than atomic bombs could be attached to missiles capable of reaching other continents and destroying cities in minutes. In these circumstances, deterrence became not just a policy imperative but a necessity for the survival of the human race. It was clear that a new stage had been reached not only in the history of international affairs, but also in the history of humankind. J. Robert Oppenheimer famously likened the situation to "two scorpions in a bottle, each capable of killing the other, but only at the risk of his own life." In delivering a comprehensive evaluation of British and NATO nuclear forces to the British House of Commons in March 1955, Prime Minister Winston Churchill observed that a paradox was likely to define international affairs in the future: "After a certain point has been passed it may be said, 'The worse things get the better.' . . . Then it may well be that we shall by a process of sublime irony have reached a stage in this story where safety will be the sturdy child of terror, and survival the twin brother of annihilation." Begun by technological innovation, the thermonuclear revolution aroused the most basic human fears and instincts.

In view of the apparently intensifying communist threat, and particularly in light of the recent development of Soviet atomic power, Truman in late January 1950 ordered a reexamination of U.S. strategic policy. Secretary of State Dean Acheson delegated the task to the new director of the State Department's Policy Planning Staff, Paul Nitze. The result, a document known as NSC 68, was a lengthy and dramatic call to arms. Before long, the report concluded, the Soviet Union would have the capability to launch a surprise atomic attack on the United States. To deter such an attack, NSC 68 recommended a massive buildup in conventional and atomic forces and that, moreover, the United States should commit resources to developing a new type of weapon, a "super" bomb harnessing the power generated by fusing hydrogen atoms rather than splitting them. Preliminary research into such a weapon had been undertaken within the Manhattan Project by a team of scientists headed by physicist Edward Teller. But with no hope of immediate success and with military budgets shrinking in the postwar economic environment, the research was halted. Based on theoretical data, Teller predicted that a hydrogen bomb would be several hundred times more powerful than the Hiroshima bomb and capable of devastating an area hundreds of square miles, with radiation traveling much farther. NSC 68 now proposed to resume H-bomb research at a greatly accelerated rate. After heated debate over the feasibility and morality of such a weapon, Truman ordered the project to proceed.

At the height of the debate about whether to proceed with the H-bomb project, communist North Korea launched an attack on pro-Western South Korea on 25 June 1950. Truman reacted by committing U.S. troops under the auspices of the United Nations. Since the deterrent had clearly lapsed or failed, General Douglas MacArthur, commander of UN forces in the theater, and General Curtis Le May, head of SAC, both recommended revitalizing it by using atomic weapons against Communist China. Truman, however, refused to expand the war and committed the United States to a limited conflict with limited objectives, a novel mission for American military forces.

For both political parties, Korea confirmed beyond a doubt that communist forces were on the offensive and that existing U.S. strategy was inadequate to stop them. The Democratic administration reacted by embracing NSC 68 and the massive military buildup it entailed, including the development of the H-bomb. For Republicans, Korea seemed to provide ample evidence for their charge that the Truman administration's approach to national security policy was based too heavily on reaction rather than prevention and therefore was putting the United States on track for financial bankruptcy. They argued that the primary failure lay not in the logistical difficulties of projecting U.S. military force to the distant shores of the Korean Peninsula, but in the administration's failure to prevent the war in the first place. The debate reached a crescendo in the presidential election campaign of 1952, as General Dwight D. Eisenhower, the Republican candidate, and his foreign policy adviser, John Foster Dulles, launched a sustained political attack on the Truman administration's foreign policy record.

Eisenhower and Dulles promised to take a new look at American national security policy and formulate a better plan for what was clearly going to be a long struggle with the Soviet Union. Dulles declared that the United States could not afford to keep fighting expensive "brushfire" wars like Korea and that what was required instead was an economically sustainable military posture designed to deter communist aggression over the long term. Since the United States could not in all likelihood compete with the Soviet Union in amassing conventional forces, Eisenhower and Dulles contended that the best use of American resources would be to invest in the next generation of nuclear weaponry and declare the intention to react to communist aggression "where it hurts, by means of our choosing." To illustrate Eisenhower's proposed deterrent strategy to the voters, Dulles called on the analogy of municipal police forces: "We do not station armed guards at every house to stop aggressors—that would be economic suicide—but we deter potential aggressors

DETERRENCE REDUCES COSTS

Secretary of State John Foster Dulles's comments on massive retaliation were published in the Department of State *Bulletin* on 25 January 1954:

"In the face of this strategy [of Soviet expansion], measures cannot be judged adequate merely because they ward off an immediate danger. It is essential to do this, but it is also essential to do so without exhausting ourselves.

"When the Eisenhower administration applied this test, we felt that some transformations were needed.

"It is not sound military strategy permanently to commit U.S. land forces to Asia to a degree that leaves us no strategic reserves.

"It is not sound economics, or good foreign policy, to support permanently other countries; for in the long run, that creates as much ill will as good will.

"Also, it is not sound to become permanently committed to military expenditures so vast that they lead to 'practical bankruptcy.' . . .

"We need allies and collective security. Our purpose is to make these relations more effective, less costly. This can be done by placing more reliance on deterrent power and less dependence on local defensive power.

"This is accepted practice so far as local communities are concerned. We keep locks on our doors, but we do not have an armed guard in every home. We rely principally on a community security system so well equipped to punish any who break in and steal that, in fact, would-be aggressors are generally deterred. That is the modern way of getting maximum protection at a bearable cost.

"What the Eisenhower administration seeks is a similar international security system. We want, for ourselves and the other free nations, a maximum deterrent at bearable cost. . . .

"The way to deter aggression is for the free community to be willing and able to respond vigorously at places and with means of its own choosing."

blunt choice: either to desist, or to persist with the risk of nuclear annihilation. The primary challenge for U.S. policymakers, therefore, was to make the other side believe that aggression carried a high risk of nuclear retaliation. To that end, Dulles declared that the administration would be prepared to engage in diplomatic "brinkmanship," a diplomatic policy some observers likened to the youthful, and often deadly, test of nerves known as "chicken." Eisenhower and Dulles argued that only by being ready to push the crisis to a point where the opponent backed down first would the United States be able to protect its interests. And in order to give communist leaders reason to pause, Eisenhower employed calculated ambiguity in responding to the question of whether a nuclear response would be automatic.

Once in office, Eisenhower and Dulles were confronted with the challenge of implementing the results of their promised New Look. Some of it was clearly impractical, even dangerous. Campaign promises of the political "liberation" of Eastern Europe were quickly abandoned after the June 1953 uprisings in East Germany. The deterrence strategy proved somewhat easier, although perhaps even more dangerous. Increasing the relative emphasis on nuclear technology as opposed to maintaining large standing conventional forces allowed the administration to cut defense expenditures by about 25 percent compared to the late Truman years, leading Secretary of Defense Charles Wilson to declare proudly that the Pentagon now had "more bang for the buck."

Having adopted massive retaliation as a long-term Cold War strategy, Eisenhower and Dulles found that strategy tested in the short term by a series of crises. Nevertheless, Eisenhower threatened massive retaliation in times of crisis sparingly and deliberately. In a series of confrontations with Communist China ranging from bringing an end to the Korean War in 1953 to the Taiwan Straits crisis of 1958, Eisenhower several times threatened nuclear attack. The primary focus of U.S. foreign policy, however, remained Europe. The struggle for Germany continued to manifest itself in crises over Berlin, which in turn presented U.S. deterrence strategies with perhaps their most serious test. Given the superior strength of Soviet conventional forces in Europe and the location of West Berlin deep inside communist territory, that city was militarily indefensible. The situation was, as Senate Foreign Relations Committee chairman J. William Fulbright put it, "a strategic nightmare." The only

by making it probable that if they aggress, they will lose in punishment more than they can gain by aggression." Massive retaliation, as Eisenhower's deterrent strategy came to be called, was designed to impose upon would-be aggressors a viable option available to the United States short of thermonuclear war was to deter the Soviets from moving against the city.

Simultaneous to these crises, the strategic balance was in a state of flux, which in turn affected thinking about deterrence. Although the Soviets had successfully tested their first atomic device as early as 1949, thoughtful observers recognized that one successful test did not make a deployable arsenal. By 1955, however, Soviet scientists had largely overcome the initial four-year lag and, particularly in the field of thermonuclear weapons, was on a par with the West. The Soviets still lagged far behind the United States both in quantity and quality of nuclear weapons, but the former's strategic arsenal was more than adequate to inflict considerable damage on the West and to play its own deterrent role. Furthermore, the accelerating arms race made it clear that the gap was narrowing. On 3 October 1952, Great Britain detonated its first atomic device on islands off the coast of Australia. Only weeks later, on 31 October, the United States detonated its first thermonuclear weapon. Less than a year after that, on 12 August 1953, the Soviet Union completed its first successful detonation of a thermonuclear device. In 1956 the first American tactical nuclear weapons were deployed in Europe. These new weapons, designed for battlefield use in localized action, came in the form of army artillery shells, each with explosive power roughly equivalent to the Hiroshima bomb.

This rapidly accelerating arms race confronted defense planners with a new question: How much was enough to deter? During the Eisenhower administration two main schools of thought defined the debate. The first held that the U.S. stockpile should consist of just enough weapons to play a deterrent role, a concept that became known as minimum deterrence. The opposing school of thought held that the United States should maintain a large and constantly growing nuclear arsenal in order to be able to engage in redundant targeting, or allocating several weapons to each target. Known as "overkill," it was this approach of building up an overwhelming nuclear force that prevailed, largely as a result of unchecked bureaucratic politics. As a result, for the remainder of the decade, the Eisenhower administration invested deeply in building up the U.S. nuclear stockpile.

On 3 August 1957 the successful Soviet test of a new type of missile, with the potential capability of reaching the continental United States

from a launch-point in the USSR, augured in a new phase of deterrence. This was dramatically confirmed two months later, on 4 October 1957, when Soviet Strategic Rocket Forces used the same type of intercontinental ballistic missile (ICBM) to propel the world's first artificial satellite into space. That satellite, known as *Sputnik,* was in itself harmless, being little more than a nitrogen-filled aluminum sphere fitted with a rudimentary transmitter that emitted a distinctive "beep" every few seconds, but it would nevertheless have profound ramifications. For the world public, it offered a dramatic demonstration that suggested Soviet missile technology was ahead of the West's, especially when contrasted with a spate of well-publicized American test failures. The American public's fears were manifested in accusations that the Eisenhower administration had allowed first a "bomber gap" and then a "missile gap" to develop. In reality, neither gap existed, but the administration's critics made considerable political mileage of the issue. For deterrence theorists and practitioners, *Sputnik* also demonstrated that the mainland United States was for the first time vulnerable to direct missile attack, potentially opening a window of vulnerability that introduced new challenges to the viability of massive retaliation as a deterrent strategy. In response to *Sputnik,* the American government put new emphasis on missile technology and the space race. By the late 1950s U.S. intermediate-range ballistic missiles (IRBMs) and medium-range ballistic missiles (MRBMs) were based in Turkey and Italy, aimed at targets in the Soviet Union. In 1959 the first generation of American ICBMs, Atlas D missiles with a range of 7,500 miles, were deployed in California. The following year the Polaris submarine-launched ballistic missiles (SLBMs), the final leg of what became known as the U.S. nuclear triad, were added to the U.S. arsenal to complement the strategic bomber and missile forces. By the early 1960s the Corona intelligence satellite program was sending back its first photographs of Soviet military installations, promising a quantum leap in the collection of military intelligence. Meanwhile, development continued of the massive Saturn V rockets that, by the end of the 1960s, would finally shatter any concept of safety in geography by propelling Americans to the moon.

Once again, technological developments introduced new challenges for deterrence strategy. Since missiles reduced to minutes the time available to respond to a nuclear strike, then conceivably the side that struck first would have an advantage if it could neutralize the enemy's retaliatory capability in that strike. Accordingly, the Eisenhower administration implemented new procedures to protect its retaliatory capability. Beginning in 1952, SAC's primary strike forces were on twenty-four-hour alert to guard against surprise attack and so-called fail-safe procedures had been implemented. In highly classified Chrome Dome missions, B-52 Stratofortress bombers flew to within striking distance of enemy targets and waited for a signal to proceed. If no signal came, the planes returned to base. The procedures were designed partly to improve the response time of the nuclear strike force, but more importantly to ensure that the strike force could not be destroyed in Soviet first-strike attacks on airfields. Scattered and airborne, the strike force was less vulnerable. The same principle was also applied to command and control procedures. To reduce the risk that a Soviet first strike on a few central underground command centers might disable the entire U.S. nuclear strike force—possibly an incentive for a Soviet preemptive first strike—a fleet of air force planes were specially outfitted with command and communications equipment to be able to take control of the American nuclear arsenal in the event the central underground command center was destroyed or disabled. From 3 February 1961 through 24 July 1990, a Looking Glass plane was in the air at all times. Protected by mobility, these Looking Glass missions, along with the Chrome Dome missions, became key elements of the U.S. deterrent in the missile age by protecting America's second-strike capability.

MASSIVE RETALIATION QUESTIONED

From the mid-1950s, criticism of massive retaliation became increasingly vocal. As Eisenhower well knew, the most challenging aspect of implementing massive retaliation was that it required a leap of faith on the part of the adversary that the United States would respond to localized and small-scale aggression by launching a nuclear strike, a reaction that was increasingly akin to suicide because of the rapid advances the Soviets were making in nuclear technology. As a consequence, there were a growing number of calls for the United States and NATO to bridge that leap of faith by modifying the strategy of massive retaliation to what retired British Rear Admiral Sir

Anthony W. Buzzard called "graduated deterrence." Only by being capable of responding in proportion to the threat, critics of massive retaliation argued, would nuclear threats become credible. Implicit here was a distinction between the tactical and strategic use of nuclear weapons, a distinction that massive retaliation explicitly disavowed. In 1957 Harvard professor Henry Kissinger elaborated on this argument by calling for increased investment in tactical nuclear weapons and acceptance of the possibility of limited nuclear war.

The observations of Buzzard and Kissinger were part of a trend toward public debate over nuclear policy. The increasing frequency of nuclear crises in the late 1950s and early 1960s and the growing absurdity of both superpowers' nuclear postures led to increased public concern with nuclear policy. For the first decade of the nuclear age, the American public had for the most part treated nuclear policy as "something best left to the experts," but by the end of the 1950s nuclear strategy had become a topic of public debate led by a cadre of increasingly visible professional strategists. Often civilians associated with think tanks such as the RAND Corporation, these professional strategists began to assume a new place in the U.S. military hierarchy and, in turn, in the public imagination. Scientists like Robert Oppenheimer, Edward Teller, and Werner von Braun had all become national figures through their contributions to the technology of the nuclear age, and by the late 1950s civilian professional strategists like Bernard Brodie, Henry Kissinger, Albert Wohlstetter, and Herman Kahn were becoming just as famous for their theorizing about how to use that technology. Although their fame most often came in the form of notoriety for their ability to discuss the absurdity of nuclear war in cold, calculating terms, they were nevertheless crucial for fueling the public debate. In the absence of hard evidence concerning Soviet decision making, these strategists were forced to form judgments about nuclear war without having any experience to draw on; thus, they substituted deductive hypotheses derived from the fields of political science, psychology, and economics for inductive historical experience. In a series of books, the most well-known of which is *On Thermonuclear War* (1960), Kahn challenged policymakers and the general public to get beyond what he called "ostrichlike behavior" and to "think the unthinkable." His central point, as he put it in *Thinking the Unthinkable* (1962), was that "thermonuclear war may seem unthinkable, impossible, insane, hideous, or highly unlikely, but it is not impossible."

The presidential election of 1960 further propelled the public debate on deterrence. Since Buzzard's call for "graduated deterrence" in 1956, Eisenhower's political opponents had adopted the strategy under a revised name: flexible response. Maxwell Taylor, the army chief of staff in the Eisenhower administration, had for some time been a voice of dissent on massive retaliation and had expressed his concerns in his book *The Uncertain Trumpet* (1960), in which he called for a reprioritizing of U.S. defense spending to place more emphasis on the ability to control the escalation of crises. When John F. Kennedy was nominated as the Democratic Party's presidential nominee, he quickly adopted flexible response as the basis of his military program.

The Kennedy administration thus came to office basing much of its military program on a political refutation of the Eisenhower administration's strategy of massive retaliation. Despite campaign promises to institute ways to control escalation and thereby make crises "safer," the Kennedy administration quickly assumed an aura of being in perpetual emergency. From the failed invasion of Cuba in April 1961, the renewed Berlin crisis just months later, and the civil rights crisis at the University of Mississippi in the fall of 1962, it appeared to many that the administration was careening from crisis to crisis. The first practical test of flexible response came in the summer of 1961, when Soviet premier Nikita Khrushchev revived his ultimatum to end Western rights in West Berlin and thereby once again provided U.S. deterrence strategy with perhaps its most difficult challenge. With the crisis brewing, and concerned that he had undermined his own credibility through the Bay of Pigs imbroglio a few months earlier, Kennedy responded with a massive buildup of conventional forces in Europe in order, in his words, "to have a wider choice than humiliation or all-out nuclear action." At the same time, he reaffirmed NATO's nuclear guarantee to the city. In turn, Khrushchev quietly lifted his deadline, as he had two years earlier.

Of all the crises confronted during Kennedy's short presidency, the Cuban missile crisis proved the most dangerous, with the United States and the Soviet Union coming closer to the brink of nuclear war than ever before or since. When Khrushchev decided to deploy Soviet MRBMs, IRBMs, tactical nuclear weapons, and nuclear-

capable medium-range bombers secretly in Cuba, where they would be positioned to strike most of the continental United States within minutes, his reasoning was to bolster the Soviet deterrent. Whether he wanted to use this deterrent in an offensive or defensive role has been debated by historians ever since. Once the deployments were discovered, Kennedy responded to the challenge by implementing a naval blockade of the island and threatening military action if the missiles and bombers were not removed. After a weeklong standoff, during which SAC's forces went on airborne alert, Khrushchev agreed to remove the missiles and a month later agreed to remove the bombers.

The crisis was resolved peacefully, but those who had witnessed the secret negotiations and the classified near misses had seen all too clearly how command and control might break down under crisis conditions. On the one hand, the resolution of the Cuban missile crisis without global destruction seemed to enhance the credibility of the deterrent on both sides. On the other hand, the missile crisis demonstrated that brinkmanship and ambiguity were simply too dangerous. Consequently, the crisis accelerated the momentum toward East-West détente. Formal negotiations to limit nuclear testing, which had been under way since 1958, finally bore fruit on 5 August 1963 in the form of the Limited Test Ban Treaty that effectively imposed mutual restraint on large-scale, above-ground nuclear weapons tests. And to reduce the risk of miscalculation and misinterpretation in a crisis, a communications hotline was established between the White House and the Kremlin.

MUTUAL ASSURED DESTRUCTION (MAD)

Paradoxically, however, one interpretation of the missile crisis held that the decisive factor in its resolution had been America's nuclear superiority—that if the American nuclear arsenal had not been more powerful than the Soviet arsenal, the crisis might have turned out differently. Both sides subscribed to this interpretation at least in part, which led to a new round in the arms race just as both sides were moving closer to agreements on nuclear testing. During the mid- and late 1960s, the Soviet Union expanded its military expenditures so that by the end of the decade, Soviet Strategic Rocket Forces had a new generation of even more powerful ICBMs at their disposal. At the same time, the administration of President Lyndon B. Johnson abandoned the idea of seeking an overwhelming nuclear superiority and settled upon a new measure of nuclear striking power called "sufficiency." As defined by the administration it meant having the ability to survive a Soviet first strike with enough forces intact to retaliate with a devastating second strike. To do so, the emphasis would be placed on a better balanced triad structure of U.S. nuclear forces, consisting of missile, air, and naval strategic forces, together leading to the power to "assure destruction" to an adversary without engaging in a destabilizing arms race. Secretary of Defense Robert S. McNamara argued that such a structure was both cost effective and stable, and it was retained as the structure of the U.S. nuclear force until the end of the Cold War.

By the beginning of the 1970s, the nuclear forces of the Soviet Union and the United States were at relative parity. In terms of sheer explosive power the USSR had surpassed the United States and was in the process of developing weapons with even larger payloads and greater accuracy, but the United States retained the technological lead. With this parity came new challenges to deterrence theory. No longer did one side have a preponderance of strategic power, and it appeared doubtful that even a preemptive first strike would hold the advantage, since it was increasingly clear that neither side would survive a nuclear exchange without casualties measured in the millions. American policymakers quickly found, however, that the promise of mutual destruction in the bipolar contest with the Soviet Union was frustratingly ineffective in conflicts such as Vietnam, which fell outside of the strictly defined U.S.–USSR relationship.

Mutual assured destruction (MAD) lay at the heart of the Strategic Arms Limitation Talks (SALT) that began in Helsinki, Finland, in November 1969. The objective of the talks was not to reduce the arsenals of either side but rather to negotiate limits on future growth of those arsenals precisely to preserve mutual vulnerability. Two technological developments of the late 1960s threatened to destabilize the nuclear status quo: antiballistic missile (ABM) systems and the development of multiple, independently targetable, reentry vehicles (MIRVs) technology. ABM systems, as they were conceived at the time, were designed to protect cities from incoming missiles. Both the United States and the Soviet Union had developed first-generation ABM systems that could

in theory, if not yet in practice, offer protection against first strikes. Partly to overcome such an advantage, both sides had invested considerable resources in developing the technology of MIRVs, a system whereby one missile could deliver several warheads to independent targets. Although these new technologies were designed to cancel each other out, in truth they threatened to destabilize the mutual destruction deterrent and spark off a new arms race, a race that would not only be dangerous, but expensive. The SALT process, therefore, was designed to limit these technologies and keep each side vulnerable to attack by the other.

With strategic nuclear war finally recognized as unwinnable, President Richard M. Nixon ordered Secretary of Defense James Schlesinger to review the military posture of the United States in light of recent technology. The result, known as the Schlesinger Doctrine, was essentially a refinement of flexible response, designed to balance Soviet bloc capabilities by threatening retaliation commensurate with the threat. Specifically, it enhanced the role of tactical nuclear weapons in a three-layered defense structure: conventional forces for conventional threats; tactical nuclear forces to counter tactical nuclear threats; and strategic nuclear forces to counter strategic threats. In essence, the Schlesinger Doctrine embraced what Henry Kissinger had proposed in the late 1950s: that a limited nuclear war was possible and was a desirable capability to have.

Despite President Jimmy Carter's efforts to further détente and continue the focus on nuclear sufficiency rather than superiority, the international and domestic political environments of the late 1970s actually pressured the administration to increase military spending drastically. During the presidential election campaign of 1980, the Republican candidate Ronald Reagan seized upon accusations made by prominent groups such as the Committee on the Present Danger, headed by Eugene Rostow and Paul Nitze, to accuse the Carter administration of allowing a window of vulnerability to open, claiming that détente had allowed the Soviets to gain a dangerous lead in the arms race to the point that even the hardened-silo Minuteman forces, the mainstay of the U.S. strategic missile force, were vulnerable to high-yield Soviet missiles. Reagan promised not only to neutralize that gap, but also to restore American military superiority and, to that end, deliberately strove to upset the balance of terror by focusing on defense rather than deterrence. The shift had important ramifications for the Cold War. Reagan reauthorized the development of the B-1 bomber and the next generation of highly accurate and MIRV-equipped Peacekeeper missiles to replace the aging Minuteman forces. He also authorized development of a controversial radiation-enhanced weapon, the neutron bomb, which killed living matter but left nonliving matter relatively unscathed. At the same time, Reagan endorsed the recommendations of a high-level commission chaired by Brent Scowcroft calling for an evolution toward small, single-warhead ICBMs backed up by Peacekeeper missiles.

In 1983 President Reagan ordered a large-scale scientific and military project to examine the feasibility of a new generation of ABM defenses. Officially labeled the Strategic Defense Initiative (SDI), but more commonly known as Star Wars after the popular science-fiction movie, the objective was to develop a multilayered shield capable of stopping thousands of incoming ballistic missiles. In theory, lasers mounted on satellites, electromagnetic guns, and charged particle beam weapons would be used to shoot down incoming ballistic missiles anywhere from boost phase (soon after launch) to reentry (final descent to target). In championing the project, Edward Teller, the reputed "father of the H-bomb," made a dramatic and controversial return to the public debate of deterrence. Not only was the technology unproven, but it quickly became apparent that the price tag of such a system was almost impossible to predict and entirely impossible to pay. Not surprisingly, the Soviet Union reacted angrily to what seemed a blatant disavowal of the 1972 SALT Treaty. Nevertheless, Reagan ordered the project to proceed. For the remainder of the 1980s, the Reagan administration struggled to find a way to make SDI a reality while at the same time continuing to pursue meaningful arms reduction.

AFTER THE COLD WAR

With the end of the Cold War and the disintegration of the USSR from 1989 to 1991, the bipolar balance of terror suddenly collapsed, and it became clear that the Soviet nuclear strength had been disguising severe internal weakness. Almost overnight, it seemed, the international environment had changed almost beyond recognition. But the U.S. and NATO defense postures, built up so carefully and at such expense over the previous half century, could not change so quickly; U.S.

foreign and military policies relied heavily on deterrence and they would need time to adjust. For deterrence, this had profound and often unforeseen challenges.

As it happened, cutting forces was relatively straightforward; the more difficult stage of adapting military strategy to the post–Cold War situation was that of reducing reliance on nuclear weapons. The problem was approached in two steps. First, the progress made over the previous decade in arms reduction was to be consolidated and advanced. The United States and Russia were committed to deep cuts in their strategic arsenals; under the terms of the START (Strategic Arms Reduction Talks) II treaty, those arsenals would be reduced to approximately one-third their size at the height of the Cold War, and both sides would eliminate the most destabilizing of the first-strike weapons, the MIRVed ICBMs. NATO, still formally committed to the defense posture of flexible response, concluded that it had to move away from a forward defense posture and that, accordingly, in the post–Warsaw Pact strategic landscape, substrategic, short-range nuclear weapons—that is, tactical IRBMs and MRBMs—no longer had a viable deterrent role. Consequently, at the NATO heads of state meeting in London on 5–6 July 1990, NATO committed itself to eliminating all nuclear artillery shells in Europe. At the same time NATO declared that it now regarded nuclear forces as "truly weapons of last resort." Simultaneously, negotiations were under way for what became the Conventional Forces in Europe (CFE) Treaty, which provided for drastic cuts in both NATO and Warsaw Pact conventional forces stationed in Central Europe. In September 1991, President George H. W. Bush declared that the forward deployment of tactical nuclear forces was no longer a useful part of the U.S. deterrent and that he was therefore ordering the removal of all tactical nuclear weapons from the U.S. Navy. Never fully abandoning Reagan's dream of an impenetrable shield against incoming missiles, the Bush administration quietly proceeded with a scaled-down version of SDI.

If the end of the Cold War drastically reduced the likelihood of strategic nuclear war, it nevertheless increased the risk of a small-scale nuclear exchange, mainly because of the growing problem of nuclear proliferation. In an effort to bring nuclear policy up to date and to confront head-on the problem that nuclear proliferation and the equalization of power that it created might one day work against the United States, the Clinton administration in late

1993 announced that it planned to redefine "deterrence." No longer would the emphasis be on preventing the use of weapons of mass destruction, since that risk had declined markedly; instead, the focus would be on preventing the acquisition of those weapons. The announcement was followed up in September of the following year with a formal replacement of the MAD doctrine with "mutual assured safety" (MAS), a long-term program designed primarily to make Russia's military reductions irreversible by reducing not only the number of weapons themselves but also reducing the technological and industrial infrastructures needed for nuclear weapons development. Through economic incentives and technological aid, steps were taken to dismantle what Soviet leader Mikhail Gorbachev called the "infrastructure of fear." By November 1997, in the first formal presidential directive on the actual employment of nuclear weapons since the Carter administration, President Clinton formally abandoned the Cold War tenet that the U.S. military forces must be prepared to fight a protracted nuclear war. Nuclear weapons would still play an important deterrent role, but the emphasis on them would be reduced in keeping with the changing nature of the threats in the post–Cold War international environment.

While the role of nuclear weapons in the U.S. military posture was reducing, the role of conventional weapons was increasing. Confronting crises in the Balkans and the Middle East, the United States and its allies demonstrated that they could now project conventional military force with great effectiveness. Exploiting the so-called "revolution in military affairs" of superior intelligence information coupled with technologically advanced conventional weapons, the United States and NATO were able to strike with overwhelming conventional military force in a precise and controlled manner, leading to successful combat in both regions while suffering few casualties. Such capability, demonstrated convincingly and publicly, became an important part of U.S. efforts to confront and deter what the defense community called "asymmetrical threats," or threats from rogue nations or terrorist organizations.

The role played by nuclear weapons and the deterrence strategies they bred since 1945 is a controversial issue. Many historians have argued that the very existence of nuclear weapons deterred the outbreak of another global war and kept what the historian John Lewis Gaddis called "the long peace" since 1945, while others have argued that other factors rendered major wars obsolete and that nuclear weapons were a largely irrelevant factor. Many others have argued that the sometimes absurd military postures that the existence of nuclear weapons encouraged greatly and needlessly increased the risk of global destruction and that the peace was maintained despite the existence of nuclear weapons. But whether a positive, negative, or irrelevant force, deterrence has made indelible impressions on the practice of foreign policy and the public imagination.

BIBLIOGRAPHY

Alperovitz, Gar. *Atomic Diplomacy: Hiroshima and Potsdam, The Use of the Atomic Bomb and the American Confrontation with Soviet Power.* 2d ed. New York, 1985. Makes a controversial argument that impending confrontation with the Soviet Union influenced Truman's decision to use the bomb against Japan.

Brodie, Bernard, ed. *The Absolute Weapon: Atomic Power and the World Order.* New York, 1946. Various authors contribute to one of the earliest efforts to assess the implications of the atomic bomb for international affairs.

Bundy, McGeorge. *Danger and Survival: Choices about the Bomb in the First Fifty Years.* New York, 1988. A first-rate historical study of the impact of the bomb on U.S. foreign policy during the Cold War.

Buzzard, Anthony W. "Massive Retaliation and Graduated Deterrence." *World Politics* 8, no. 2 (January 1956): 228–237.

Dockrill, Saki. *Eisenhower's New-Look National Security Policy, 1953–61.* London, 1996.

Gaddis, John Lewis. *Strategies of Containment: A Critical Appraisal of Postwar American National Security Policy.* Oxford, 1982.

Gaddis, John Lewis, et. al., eds. *Cold War Statesmen Confront the Bomb: Nuclear Diplomacy Since 1945.* Oxford, 1999.

Garthoff, Raymond L. *Soviet Strategy in the Nuclear Age.* Rev. ed. New York, 1962.

George, Alexander L., and Richard Smoke. *Deterrence in American Foreign Policy: Theory and Practice.* New York, 1974. A groundbreaking work in the field of political science that uses historical case studies of ten nuclear crises that took place between 1948 and 1962 to examine how deterrence has been employed in times of crisis.

Gowing, Margaret. *Independence and Deterrence: Britain and Atomic Energy, 1945–1952*. New York, 1974. A thorough study of the early British nuclear program.

Herken, Gregg. *The Winning Weapon: The Atomic Bomb in the Cold War, 1945–1950*. New York, 1980.

Holloway, David. *Stalin and the Bomb*. New York, 1994. Uses formerly closed archives to examine the early Soviet nuclear program.

Kahn, Herman. *On Thermonuclear War*. Princeton, N.J., 1960. The most widely read of several important books by this influential nuclear strategist. Challenges policymakers and the public to "think the unthinkable" and anticipate a post–nuclear war world.

Kaplan, Fred M. *The Wizards of Armageddon*. New York, 1983. An excellent study of professional nuclear strategists.

Kaufman, William W., et al., eds. *Military Policy and National Security*. Princeton, N.J., 1956. One of the earliest rebuttals of the massive retaliation doctrine.

Kissinger, Henry A. *Nuclear Weapons and Foreign Policy*. New York, 1957. An influential rebuttal of massive retaliation that advocates the development of tactical nuclear weapons to make limited nuclear war viable.

Leffler, Melvyn P. *A Preponderance of Power: National Security, the Truman Administration, and the Cold War*. Stanford, Calif., 1992. A meticulously researched account of the national security policy of the Truman administration.

Mandelbaum, Michael. *The Nuclear Question: The United States and Nuclear Weapons, 1946–1976*. Cambridge, 1979.

Mueller, John. "The Essential Irrelevance of Nuclear Weapons." *International Security* 13, no. 2 (fall 1988): 55–79. Makes a controversial argument that nuclear weapons were largely irrelevant to keeping the peace during the Cold War.

Osgood, Robert E. *Limited War Revisited*. Boulder, Colo., 1979. A concise reevaluation of the notion of limited war.

Quester, George H. *Deterrence Before Hiroshima: The Airpower Background of Modern Strategy*. New York, 1966. The development of strategic bombing, with particular emphasis on the years from World War I to the end of World War II.

Rosenberg, David A. "The Origins of Overkill: Nuclear Weapons and American Strategy, 1945–1960." *International Security* 7 (spring 1983): 3–71. A meticulously researched account of American nuclear programs during the Truman and Eisenhower administrations.

Sagan, Scott D. *The Limits of Safety: Organizations, Accidents, and Nuclear Weapons*. Princeton, N.J., 1993. Examines several of the Cold War's "near misses" and the chances of accidental nuclear war.

Schelling, Thomas C. *Choice and Consequence*. Cambridge, Mass., 1984. Applies economic principles and game theory to deterrence.

Stromseth, Jane E. *The Origins of Flexible Response: NATO's Debate over Strategy in the 1960s*. Houndmills, U.K., 1987.

Taylor, Maxwell. *The Uncertain Trumpet*. New York, 1960. A rebuttal of massive retaliation that became extremely influential in the formulation of the Kennedy administration's defense program.

Trachtenberg, Marc. *History and Strategy*. Princeton, N.J., 1991. Important essays on various aspects of nuclear policy.

———. *A Constructed Peace: The Making of a European Settlement, 1945–53*. Princeton, N.J., 1999. Argues that nuclear weapons were a decisive factor in the peaceful division of Europe.

Williamson, Samuel R., Jr., and Stephen L. Reardon. *The Origins of U.S. Nuclear Strategy, 1945–1953*. New York, 1993.

Wohlstetter, Albert J. "The Delicate Balance of Terror." *Foreign Affairs* 37, no. 1 (1959): 211–234. Argues that technological advances will ultimately destabilize deterrence.

See also ARMS CONTROL AND DISARMAMENT; BALANCE OF POWER; COLD WAR EVOLUTION AND INTERPRETATIONS; COLD WAR ORIGINS; COLD WAR TERMINATION; DOCTRINES; NUCLEAR STRATEGY AND DIPLOMACY; POST–COLD WAR POLICY; PRESIDENTIAL POWER; SUPERPOWER DIPLOMACY.

DEVELOPMENT DOCTRINE AND MODERNIZATION THEORY

Nick Cullather

Modernization theory, sometimes called development doctrine, supplied the working concepts through which the United States understood its obligations to unindustrialized, newly independent nations in the last half of the twentieth century. Described as both an ideology and a discourse, modernization comprised a changeable set of ideas and strategies that guided policies toward foreign aid, trade, nationalism, and counterinsurgency. Among its core precepts was the idea that the state of economic and political advancement enjoyed by the United States and the industrialized West was normative, and that it was in the U.S. national interest, as well as the general interest of all people, that steps be taken to bring the other two-thirds of humanity up to a comparable level. Social science theories explained the causes of Asian, Latin American, and African backwardness and suggested appropriate remedies.

Historians have traced modernization theory's intellectual lineage back to Aristotle, who first suggested that states followed a natural pattern of growth, like plants. But while linear progress is a recurrent theme in Western thought, it existed alongside Christian doubts about man's fallen state. Americans in the early Republic believed (as did Aristotle) that if societies grow naturally, they also decay. The idea that the process of human progress could be understood and controlled dates to the early nineteenth century, when France and Britain were struggling to reestablish their mercantile empires on a secular, commercial basis, and just before technology and scientific racism ushered in an era of guiltless imperialism. Since then it has tended to recur at times and places where systems of dominance required justification and explanation.

PROGRESS BECOMES MODERNIZATION

European liberals reconciled universalism and imperialism by arguing that although all men were not yet equal, they were ruled by universal economic laws and followed a common historical path. The philosophers Jean-Baptiste Say, John Stuart Mill, and Auguste Comte each contended that societies passed through successive stages from savagery through barbarism to finally reach a developed state that resembled industrial Europe. "Whoever knows the political economy of England, or even of Yorkshire," Mill claimed, "knows that of all nations, actual or possible." Comte called the science of human evolution "sociology" and proposed that the highest stage would be a "positive" society governed by science. American scientists similarly concluded that their own society was advanced relative to the surrounding peoples, who might with help "catch up." Lewis H. Morgan, a founder of American anthropology, speculated in 1877 that "American Indian tribes represent, more or less nearly, the history and experience of our own remote ancestors."

From this perspective the United States, as well as Germany—among the youngest of countries—could be seen as the oldest of societies, advanced beyond India or China in the arts of civilization. Seniority implied a duty to instruct and uplift, and a concept of trusteeship was integral to liberal developmentalism. In the latter part of the nineteenth century, German social theorists—George Friedrich List, Karl Marx, and Max Weber—debated the obligations and causes of economic progress. List asserted that the state held the primary developmental role; its true mission was to "furnish the economical education of the nation." Marx authored one of the boldest theoretical statements of the developmental vision, describing the "iron necessity" of historical laws that required the successive destruction of feudalism and bourgeois capitalism to make way for communism. He attacked the liberal developmentalists' assumption of trusteeship, which subordinated colonial subjects and domestic labor and furnished a disguise for exploitation. Marx's and later Lenin's critiques of imperial trusteeship were so appealing to anticolonial insurgents that Cold War–era modernization theorists would conceive their project as an attempt to devise an alternative to communist developmentalism.

Nationalists in the subject states constructed their own visions of modernity, and by the 1920s development was the subject of a global debate among disparate factions of anticolonial modernizers, primitivists, jingoes, and reformers. Two members of the Indian National Congress, Dadabhai Naoroji and Romesh C. Dutt, wielding British statistics and a historical perspective, demolished claims that the Raj acted for India's economic welfare. Dutt (using what would later be called a structuralist or dependency approach) showed that imperial taxes and terms of trade systematically milked India for England's benefit. "When I read Mr. Dutt's economic history of India," Mohandas Gandhi wrote, "I wept. . . . It is machinery that has impoverished India." Indian nationalists drew different conclusions as to the proper response. For Gandhi, development was the antithesis of community, and he urged a restoration of a preindustrial village economy. But Jawaharlal Nehru, insisting there was "only one-way traffic in Time," ruled out a return to communalism or Islamic theocracy. He represented a majority of Congress Party members who wanted to build an industrial India by wresting development planning from British control. In China, too, development became a principal rationale for the nationalist struggle. Sun Yat-sen authored an elaborate scheme that promised to cure China's backwardness as well as the global crisis of overproduction by using Western technology to dam rivers, build cities, and overlay China with a modern transport grid.

In the United States, "development" came into official use at the beginning of the twentieth century to distinguish the American civilizing mission from European colonial policy, which it resembled. "The Philippines are not ours to exploit," President William McKinley asserted, "but to develop, to civilize, to educate." Woodrow Wilson attested that the Allies were "fighting for the liberty, the self-government, and the undictated development of all peoples." In practice, the line between exploitation and development was porous. Gifts of science and technology facilitated economic and imperial penetration. Commodore Matthew C. Perry had presented the Japanese shogun with machinery and seeds, and by 1900, American agricultural missions, mining surveys, and sanitation experts made frequent stops in Japan and China. Professor Edwin W. Kemmerer circulated through South America in the 1920s modernizing currency and banking systems while opening new ground for U.S. investment. Educational and medical establishments, including the early work of the Rockefeller Foundation, were an extension of Christian evangelical missions.

An evangelical sensibility distinguished the American approach to development from the high-modernist ambitions of European colonizers and Asian nationalists. Early technical missions found their work "was not merely a matter of transferring scientific principles and factual data," Merle Curti observed, "it was more largely a problem of developing attitudes." Rockefeller initiatives in China in the 1920s and 1930s emphasized the transplantation of institutions and ways of thinking. American social science supported a perception of modernity as a kind of conversion experience. John Dewey, who defined American pragmatism in the 1920s and 1930s, conceived of freedom as development, as the realization of latent potential. The anthropologist Robert Redfield, writing in 1930, was the first to use the term "modernization" to describe linked processes of urbanization, literacy, secularization, and familial dismemberment. Although these were all concomitants of economic disruption, Redfield noted that modernization was fundamentally a cognitive, even spiritual event: A peasant, encountering a city for the first time, "develops a correspondingly new organ, a new mind." From the start, American modernization initiatives would measure achievement not by kilowatts or gross national product but by hearts and minds.

A TOOL FOR MANAGING DECOLONIZATION

New techniques devised during the 1930s and 1940s gave the sociology of modernization a harder, scientific edge. Demographers discovered the "demographic transition," a sudden drop in birthrate that served as a statistical marker of the arrival of modernity. National incomes accounting, invented by economists during World War II, measured the economic efficiency of nations relative to one another and across time. Talcott Parsons, a Harvard sociologist, served as advocate and symbol of the statistical, comparative turn in the social sciences, sometimes called the "Parsonian revolution." To Parsons, societies and nations were integrated systems that could be disassembled and compared. The results of empirical observations, fed into theoretical models, would allow social scientists to predict the trajectory of a society, and to plot alternate outcomes given the introduction of variables like industry, mass communications, the cash nexus, or Western contact.

Thinking in Washington moved along a parallel track. The experiences of the New Deal and World War II, particularly the Tennessee Valley Authority (TVA) and the Manhattan Project, reinforced confidence in the ability of science and planning to transform whole societies. Many in the Roosevelt administration believed such work would be essential to achieving a stable peace. David Lilienthal, co-director of the TVA, noted "a definite sequence in history from primitive or non-industrial conditions to more highly developed modern industrial conditions." American assistance could help societies avoid "wasted steps" in the transition. By the end of World War II, a number of suppositions about the nature of modernization were widely shared in academic and philanthropic communities and were gaining attention in government, although they had yet to be codified as theory or policy. Among these were the following precepts:

1. Development begins from a stable, uniform state of tradition. Since, as Redfield observed, peasants in Tepoztlan, Mexico, Melanesian islanders, and "the southern negro" are fundamentally identical in outlook and relationship to modernity, their developmental problems (and the solutions) would also be the same, regardless of geographic or historic differences.

2. All societies follow a common, linear path to modernity, passing through recognizable stages along the way. The final destination (known to development economists as "convergence") is a high plateau of industrialism and consumerism enjoyed by the urban societies of North America and Europe. Regardless of their point of origin, all cultures have the same trajectory. Nations with tragic histories could be assured they would not have a tragic destiny.

3. The journey can be accelerated in a number of ways but chiefly by contact with developed societies and through state interventions. Centralized planning was the

essential feature of development work.

4. The most difficult part of the transition is psychological. Once the comforts of custom and old patterns of thought are rejected progress would follow its natural course. Development is thus not a process of accumulation but of release, the freeing of restrained energies and resources.

5. Development is above politics but has the capacity to create political gains and risks. Since states, regardless of political form or ideology, share an impulse to modernize, there would be a chance for the United States, as well as for rival powers, to take the lead in the global movement.

These ideas served as a template for the management of the decolonizing world. The sudden collapse of the European and Japanese empires following the Allied victory confronted the United States with the immense problem of redirecting the political and economic alignment of two-thirds of the world's population. The Soviet military triumph displayed the fruits of Stalin's industrialization drives, and newly independent regimes looked to the USSR as a model of rapid modernization. New international organizations—the United Nations and the World Bank—lent expertise and institutional backing to the development of postcolonial areas. Nonetheless, the United States faced its greatest problems in Europe and Japan, where reconstruction took first priority. Although the Marshall Plan was often mentioned as the inspiration for later modernization schemes, no attempts were made to duplicate its formula elsewhere. American officials felt its reliance on heavy industry, labor unions, and the welfare state could not be adapted to Asia or Latin America, where more fundamental issues—education, health, low productivity—had to be dealt with. These issues became more imperative as the Cold War intensified. Nationalist China's sudden collapse, despite a hastily arranged aid package, revealed the dangers of failing to address the poverty and corruption that seemed to accelerate the communist advance.

President Harry Truman's dramatic announcement in January 1949 of Point Four, a "bold new program . . . for the improvement of underdeveloped areas," placed development at the top of the national agenda and simultaneously galvanized a worldwide movement. Like McKinley, Truman contrasted development against "the old imperialism," but he was the first world leader to apply the term "underdeveloped" to the subjects of the modernization process. The confrontation between colonizer and colonized, rich and poor, was, with one rhetorical gesture, replaced by a world order in which all nations were either developed or becoming so. Point Four affirmed the fundamental equality of nations recognized by the United Nations Charter while at the same time licensing interventions on an unprecedented scale.

Truman explicitly linked Point Four to American strategic and economic objectives. Poverty was a threat not just to the poor but to their richer neighbors, he argued, and alleviating misery would assure a general prosperity, lessening the chances of war. Moreover, the "triumphant action" of development superseded the merely ideological conflict of the Cold War. Communism and democracy were different routes to the same destination. Development in this sense was a hegemonic idea, presented not as the best but as the only possible course of action. (David Riesman observed in 1958 that alternatives to the Western and Soviet paths were simply unimaginable.) The response was startling. Truman "hit the jackpot of the world's political emotions," *Fortune* magazine noted. National delegations lined up to receive planning and assistance that a few years earlier might have been seen as a colonial intrusion.

The assignment of a World Bank technical assistance mission to Colombia in November 1949 reveals how this paradigm shift enabled an entirely new approach to managing the internal affairs of another country. Fifty years earlier it would have required gunboats for European and American creditors to seize Colombia's customhouses, but this delegation of European and American economists took charge of much more—foreign exchange, finance, banking, agriculture, transport, health, education, social welfare, and oil exploration—all at the invitation of the Colombian government, which assured implementation of the delegation's detailed plans. Development justified interventions on a grand scale and made accepting the instructions of foreign advisers the duty of every responsible government.

Point Four officials expected sudden, dramatic results from the introduction of American advice and technology. Norris Dodd, a Point Four agriculture adviser who later headed the UN Food and Agriculture Organization, described the sensation he created in northern Thailand by dispensing a few commonsense suggestions. "If I had been able to stay in that village another few hours," he believed, "we might have changed the fundamental agricultural methods for hundreds of miles around." Truman claimed there were "untold resources" in the underdeveloped regions needing only "somebody who knows the technical approach." He emphasized technology because of its mystique and the absence of alternatives. High rates of return on domestic investment and the chronic imbalance of payments known as the "dollar gap" made it nearly impossible to mobilize private capital for development, but engineering talent could easily be dispatched abroad. Point Four began by sending American engineering firms to Iran, Indonesia, Taiwan, and Korea, where they acted as purchasing agents, identifying applications for American technology and designing industrial, hydroelectric, and chemical plants and public works.

IMPORT SUBSTITUTION

In these early, untheorized foreign aid projects, American advisers worked out an impromptu strategy that came to be called import substitution industrialization (ISI). Engineers in Taiwan, noting that fertilizer imports consumed a large share of the island's scarce foreign exchange, imported equipment to manufacture artificial fertilizers domestically. They constructed hydroelectric dams to fuel the plants, and one by one they substituted domestically made articles for imported ones, freeing more capital for industrial expansion. In the Philippines and Turkey, U.S. financial missions imposed tax and exchange laws that accomplished the same result by placing barriers on the importation of products that could be made domestically. Import substitution policies shifted imports toward capital goods, equipment, and technologies and away from consumer goods and commodities, and in the process they enlarged state control over the economy. The success of such strategies often depended on the state's ability to administer controls effectively and without corruption.

Import substitution suited many new nations' vision of a gleaming industrial future. Nehru famously remarked in 1954 that dams were the temples of modern India and industry its religion. Surveying the immense Bhakra-Nangal canal, he observed that "when we see big works our stature grows with them, and our minds open out a little." Modernity was the goal and justification for many independence movements, and the erection of a new steelworks or railway span hailed the arrival of full nationhood. The Olympian planning commissions that met at the Yojana Bhavan in New Delhi or at the Central Bank in Manila exercised an authority over the national economy that few colonial viceroys could equal. Import substitution policies also partially counteracted international trade patterns that kept newly independent states in the subordinate role of exporting raw materials to the industrial nations and importing finished goods.

In the early 1950s, structuralist theories located the causes of underdevelopment in lingering colonial trade patterns and recommended import substitution as a solution. Raul Prebisch, secretary-general of the UN Economic Commission for Latin America (ECLA), pointed to the deterioration of the terms of trade between the industrial and nonindustrial areas. Beginning in the 1930s, the value of commodity and raw materials exports declined steadily relative to the value of manufactured imports. Left unchecked, the "Prebisch effect" would widen the gap between rich and poor nations. Gunnar Myrdal, a Swedish economist who had worked with the Rockefeller Foundation, delivered a series of lectures in 1955 at the Egyptian Central Bank in Cairo in which he explained that market expansion would cause inequality to increase, both internationally and within nations, unless counteracted by comprehensive planning and European-style state welfare programs. In Truman's usage, "underdevelopment" was a noun describing an age-old condition to be remedied with modern technology. Structuralists changed it into a transitive verb. Underdevelopment was a process; it was what the rich nations were doing to the poor nations.

Although the structuralist formula originated abroad, the United States endorsed the import substitution approach until the late 1950s. The State Department sympathized with nationalist ambitions short of expropriation or discrimination against U.S. investment, and preferred Prebisch's doctrine to the "extreme" economic nationalism of Argentine president Juan Perón. American support for import substitution stemmed from concern about the overdevelopment of U.S. heavy industry as a result of wartime mobilization. Capital goods purchases by industrializing nations provided a badly needed outlet for American production and a stimulus to European recovery. Import substitution aroused considerable opposition within the United States

from congressional conservatives, adversely affected industries, and the *Wall Street Journal,* but the economic and strategic benefits outweighed the political costs, at least until 1958. When criticism prevented the Eisenhower administration from participating directly in drafting economic plans, private companies and foundations stepped in. A U.S. engineering firm drafted Taiwan's first four-year plan, and the Ford Foundation dispatched a team of economists to advise India's planning commission. As the United States turned against import substitution, structuralism survived as a critique of American development policies that ignored the built-in inequities of the world system.

DEVELOPMENT AND THE SOCIAL SCIENCES

In few places did Truman's bold new program generate as much excitement as in American universities, and by the end of the 1950s an enormous body of homegrown theory was poised to replace Point Four's ad hoc strategy. For social scientists in the 1950s, the economist John Kenneth Galbraith remembers, "no economic subject more quickly captured the attention of so many as the rescue of the people of the poor countries from their poverty." The federal government's growing defense and intelligence establishments opened a new sphere of activity for researchers skilled in statistical and comparative methods. As prominent practitioners rotated between federal appointments, foundation boards, and faculty positions, professional codes adapted. Government collaboration, and even direction, aroused few concerns about objectivity. Faculties adopted the Area Studies organizational scheme devised by the wartime Office of Strategic Studies and took on an agenda of applied research useful to government. Much of this work focused on the "Third World," a term coined to describe a new academic division of labor that segregated work on industrialized democracies (First World), problems of communism (Second), and the underdeveloped (Third) world.

Political as well as professional motives drew academics to the Point Four mission. The social sciences came under particularly heavy attack from McCarthyite inquisitions, as did their institutional sponsors, such as the newly capitalized Ford Foundation. A 1954 congressional investigation accused the Ford Foundation of financing "the promotion of Socialism and collective ideas" in the United States. Development provided a safe outlet for social engineers whose New Dealism had become suspect. Sanctioned by development's anticommunist agenda, economists, planners, and researchers could apply abroad practices they were afraid to advance at home. The United States, in effect, exported its liberalism in the form of the energy and ideas of its best social thinkers and the funds of its largest philanthropies.

Within the national security establishment social scientists enjoyed prestige of a kind accorded in a later era only to software designers. Military and intelligence officials expected modeling techniques to be able to forecast the intentions and capabilities of foreign actors with increasing reliability. Psychology offered a particularly useful set of conceptual tools for engineering bloodless revolutions. Nuclear deadlock guaranteed that the Cold War would be fought largely in the Third World through techniques of subversion, propaganda, and attraction. In this atmosphere of expectancy and risk, government agencies and private foundations enlisted researchers to learn the secrets of modernization.

Foundations, government agencies, and universities jointly created institutional arrangements for generating theories of modernization. In 1953, with Ford Foundation assistance, the Social Science Research Council created a Committee on Comparative Politics among whose members Gabriel Almond, Lucian Pye, and George Kahin would make significant contributions to the modernization canon through the publication of the "Studies in Political Development" series. At the Massachusetts Institute of Technology, a State Department–sponsored research program on psychological warfare, Project Troy, evolved into the Center for International Studies (CENIS) in 1951. Its founder was Max Millikan, an economist in the new field of national incomes accounting who had just returned to the Massachusetts Institute of Technology after a year as assistant director of the Central Intelligence Agency. Millikan recruited an interdisciplinary team that featured Paul Rosenstein-Rodan and Walt W. Rostow (economics), Edward Shils (sociology), Daniel Lerner (communications), Clifford Geertz (anthropology), and Lucian Pye and Ithiel Pool (political science). Millikan also designed a budget formula that channeled State Department money funneled through the CIA into studies on the Second World, while research on the Third World was financed by the Ford and Rockefeller foundations.

CENIS mimicked the institutional style and "problem-oriented" work habits of the Manhattan Project in its development of the atomic bomb, breaking into teams to devise specific solutions that would then be subject to general discussion and criticism by the whole group. Millikan put an emphasis on finding answers to the practical problems of policymakers, and CENIS's work product typically appeared first as classified memoranda distributed to federal agencies and later as book-length monographs. Benjamin Higgins described it as "a community of scholars arriving at the same broad analytical framework." Its principal achievements were the creation of a rationale for an enlarged foreign aid effort, along with a set of concepts—"technology transfer," "takeoff," the "expectation gap," "self-help"—that informed aid policy and scholarship for the next two decades.

THE ROSTOVIAN REVOLUTION

If Millikan was CENIS's organizer, Rostow was its inspiration, its "shining light," according to Higgins. The son of Jewish immigrants from Russia, Rostow went to Yale at age sixteen, finished in three years, and went to Oxford on a Rhodes scholarship. While still in his teens he decided with characteristic prepossession to devote his life to "two large ideas: one is the application of modern economic theory and statistical analysis to economic history; and the other is the relationship between economic factors and society as a whole." The force of his ideas was magnified by his gusto for expressing them. "Walt can write faster than I can read," President John Kennedy quipped.

As an army captain in World War II, Rostow had participated in an operation that foreshadowed his later work in development. Along with Charles P. Kindleberger and Carl Kaysen, both of whom would also be leading figures in postwar economics, he served as a bombing targeter in the Economic Warfare Division of the London embassy. There the young economists debated how best to dismantle the German economy from the air, whether the whole system had to be taken down together or if there might be specific points—a ball bearing factory or a refinery—that could be removed, bringing the entire war machine to a halt. "We sought target systems where the destruction of the minimum number of targets would have the greatest, most prompt, and most long-lasting direct military effect," Rostow later remembered. In the run-up to the Normandy invasion, the targeters oscillated—just as development theorists later would—between a "systems" approach and a "bottleneck" approach, with Rostow on the systems side arguing for a comprehensive attack on German oil refineries and bridges. He lost the argument when General Dwight D. Eisenhower opted to hit the railroad marshaling yards in northern France. CENIS gave him a chance to prove his original judgment. Development was simply the opposite of bombardment, involving dropping in ingredients that would produce the quickest and longest-lasting economic (and political) gains.

Through CENIS, Rostow forged a consensus behind a developmental strategy known as the Big Push, "a development effort on all fronts," according to Higgins, "on a scale large enough to bring increases in productivity that would outrun population growth and promote structural change." Instead of targeting the industrial sector as import substitution did, large amounts of aid should go into "social overhead capital" such as education, administration, transport, and law. Properly timed, aid could generate a systemwide disruption that would shake a society from its traditional torpor and lift it into the modern age. The Big Push, sometimes called "balanced" development, was also a critique of President Eisenhower's aid programs, which were regarded as piecemeal efforts aimed at frontline states and with political strings attached. Development had to be an unconditional, massive, sustained effort, conveying the message, Rostow argued, "that we are in Asia to stay, not merely in a military sense, but politically and economically as well."

In memoranda and articles during the 1950s and in two seminal books, *The Process of Economic Growth* (1952) and *The Stages of Economic Growth* (1960), Rostow elaborated a vision of development rooted in American history and national interest. Updating Comte's formula, he observed that each society passes through five identifiable stages. In the opening phase, tradition, society's tranquil rhythms are regulated by the harvest and disturbed only by natural calamity. As pre-Newtonian attitudes give way to a scientific understanding of the natural world, societies enter a stage of accumulation. The fund of social overhead capital grows unevenly. Social investments are "lumpy," he argued, and private investors are unwilling to tolerate the high initial costs, long gestation periods, and indirect returns. The state, therefore, has the primary role in nurturing social capital, as state and local governments did in the United States between 1815 and 1840.

As obstacles to growth are cleared and modern habits and attitudes gain momentum, the society reaches a stage Rostow memorably named "takeoff." "During the takeoff," he wrote in *Stages,* "new industries expand rapidly, yielding profits a large proportion of which are reinvested in new plant. . . . The new class of entrepreneurs expands; and it directs the enlarging flows of investment." Modernization planes along the lumpy surface of social overhead capital, bearing itself aloft on the force of its own acceleration. Rostow's aeronautical image highlighted not only his sense of the sharpness of the transition, a change in both the kind and direction of growth, but the dangers of this stage, for it is at the moment of takeoff that crosswinds, mechanical flaws, or pilot error are most likely to prove fatal. Takeoff, for Rostow, was a period of cultural, technological, and political upheaval, and its forward trajectory could either continue toward maturity (the fourth stage) or suffer a violent interruption or diversion onto a dysfunctional nationalist or communist route to modernity.

By measuring the ratio of investment to national income, Rostow could calculate when a nation would reach takeoff and how much aid it could usefully absorb. Within a few years the National Security Council used "absorptive capacity" as its principle criterion for aid. The United States passed into takeoff just prior to the Civil War, and it appeared to Rostow in the 1950s that both India and the People's Republic of China were entering this stage. He anticipated that the contest between the two nations, "the one under Communism, the one under democratic rule—would constitute a kind of pure ideological test of great significance" for the United States and the world. Rostow's theory redefined the Cold War as a contest fought on the terrain of development, and he advanced a number of arguments for a stronger American effort. By easing the transition to modernity, he told CIA director Allen Dulles, the United States could steal a march on history by creating an "environment in which societies which directly or indirectly menace ours will not evolve." Failing to do so would concede "to Moscow and Peking the dangerous mystique that only Communism can transform underdeveloped societies." The cost would also be limited. By targeting nations just reaching takeoff, the United States could exercise a decisive influence without incurring an indefinite obligation.

The United States own level of development provided another imperative for action. Rostow concluded that the United States had reached the terminal stage of the modernization process, the stage of high mass consumption, but its position there was insecure. High population growth, a deficit of social overhead capital, and the cost of the arms race created drags that might cause it to lose altitude. A steady flow of raw materials was essential. Preserving the U.S. fragile forward momentum required expanding world trade and energizing external markets for U.S. products. Rostow warned policymakers not to draw a false dichotomy between humanitarianism and selfishness. In development, the national interest and the interest of mankind were inseparable.

Rostow assigned an important role to soldiers during the transitional period. Assembling the preconditions for takeoff, he believed, required the efforts of an elite coalition of landowners, merchants, and politicians who favored centralization and were "prepared to deal with the enemies of this objective." Military men were the natural leaders of this movement, and throughout his career Rostow argued that military regimes could supply the stability and administrative competence needed for development. The Mann Doctrine of 1964, which made stability rather than democracy the prime goal of U.S. policy in Latin America during the Johnson administration, would later echo Rostow's reasoning.

Extending the stages-of-growth framework to the Soviet Union, Rostow refuted assumptions that Soviet development presented an alternative to the model of the capitalist West. By his reckoning, Stalin's forced modernization resembled the path taken by the United States some thirty years earlier; the principal difference was in its "abnormal" emphasis on the military and industrial sectors. To Rostow, communism was not the agent of modernization but a side effect of it. It was a "disease of the transitional process" likely to spread in any nation during the early, difficult stages of development. Instead of accelerating growth, it disfigured it, producing an unbalanced and dysfunctional modernity. Rostow's avowed aim was to supplant Marx as the inspiration for revolutionary intellectuals (the subtitle of *Stages* is *A Non-Communist Manifesto*), and he presented his doctrine as a universal theory of history.

Rostow's syntheses standardized the vocabulary used by the CENIS and Social Science Research Council groups, and the theories they produced are appropriately referred to as "Rostov-ian," although other members contributed significant innovations. Lucian Pye placed newly independent regimes on the psychoanalyst's couch and interpreted Southeast Asian communism in light of Erik Erikson's concept of "identity crisis." Both nationalist leaders and their constituents suffered from incoherent, immature identities that made them resentful of their modernized elders. Because "individuals can become reasonably acculturated far faster than societies can be reconstructed," modernizing societies underwent a "revolution of rising expectations," allowing communists to recruit impatient young men. The psychoanalytic perspective, Nils Gilman has pointed out, "positioned the social scientist as a dispassionate physician, lording his wisdom over a postcolonial nation bereft of legitimate subjectivity." CENIS and Social Science Research Council studies borrowed across disciplinary lines in ways that disregarded the objectivity standards of any single discipline. The medley of terminologies threw a protective screen around political or cultural presuppositions and tendentious reasoning.

The format of CENIS dialogue encouraged participants to theorize from an interlocking set of reified concepts. Much like the Marxist doctrine it responded to, Rostovian theory achieved its plausibility and explanatory power from the tight fit between its conceptual parts, rather than from the correspondence between any of the parts and the actual conditions they were meant to describe. David Lerner's pithy *Passing of Traditional Society* reveals the appeal and versatility of the CENIS schema. Lerner framed his study in a parable of modernization in the Turkish village of Balgat, where in 1950 a U.S. Information Agency interviewer recorded the opinions of several hundred villagers. Of these, three stood out: the village chief, a grocer, and a shepherd. The very act of soliciting opinions disturbed the chief and the shepherd, who balked at stating their views of distant leaders and nations. The grocer, on the other hand, was brimming with opinions, particularly regarding other people's business. Moreover, the interviewer learned that villagers sought out the grocer's opinions on such issues as what movies to watch when they visited Ankara. The chief and the shepherd, at opposite ends of the social spectrum, were pious, contented, and cautious; the grocer, a marginal figure, was skeptical, self-conscious, and with an eye for the main chance.

Lerner's theme is the psychology of the "transitional personality," the grocers whose restlessness would unsettle established orders and lifeways, hastening the advent of modernity. When Lerner first visited Balgat in 1954 he found the village transformed. A new road and bus line, as well as municipal water and electricity, made it a suburb of the capital. The shepherd and his sheep had moved on, the chief's sons were now grocers, and the original grocer was dead but remembered as a prophet. For Lerner, the human instrument of modernization was the "mobile personality," the individual with a capacity to envision himself in another's place, a place better than his own. "Empathy," as Lerner called this quality, stirred people from traditional apathy, leading them to question old ways and hierarchies and making them full participants in the economic and political life of the new nation. Lerner's theory later provided a conceptual foundation for the strategic hamlet program and the forced depopulation of the Vietnamese countryside as a counterinsurgency measure. Pacification specialists expected relocation to generate mobile personalities among the refugees, stimulating them to discard village loyalties in favor of participation in national life.

With interviews and charts, Lerner established a relationship between the spread of mass media and the proliferation of the mobile psyche, but his empirical observations actually contradicted the implied link between psychology and material improvement. Lerner noted that neither the grocer nor anyone in Balgat had a hand in decisions about the bus service, water lines, or electricity. Balgatis ratified the changes by voting for the new ruling party and by preserving social hierarchies within the village and between the village and the center of power. Modernization came without help or hindrance from mobile personalities. Such discrepancies, however, did not disturb the model or its conclusions, which concern correlations among abstract variables (mass media, participation, satisfaction). The Rostovian approach answered structuralism by making structural inequities into one variable among many and eliding questions of causation and proportion. The result was a uniquely resilient theory, capable of absorbing and explaining away nearly any failure or challenge. Even nation building in Vietnam, Rostow later wrote, was a developmental triumph marred by "a difficult war."

Rostovian doctrine drew fire within social science disciplines (Stages got hammered by reviewers in economics journals) and from some generalists and policymakers who saw political agendas beneath the elaborate taxonomies.

Ambassador to India John Kenneth Galbraith noted that claims of aid's ability to induce takeoff were "convenient" considering that "once we admit that it is not the case, we become trapped in a series of previously complex problems." Louis Halle, a former State Department planner, found Stages to be "one long boast" about an idealized America leading the world into the future. It also evoked a suspiciously tidy vision of history: "this great, multifarious, fluid, and largely unknown world of ours is conceived as a child's plaything made up of a very few building blocks, all square and solid."

The CENIS framework gained the status of an orthodoxy almost overnight, an achievement that can be attributed to factors other than its strengths as theory. First, it furnished academic analysts and policymakers with a common language and a set of criteria for evaluating foreign aid as something other than a bribe offered in exchange for cooperation with U.S. policies. Second, it was a culmination of the social scientific enterprise initiated by Mill and Comte. While academics were eager to point out its imperfections, they were reluctant to question its perfectibility, because to do so was to challenge fundamental parts of the social scientific method (the comparability of societies, the application of reason to social change, the nature of progress). Finally, Rostovian theory resonated with American myths of national mission. It gave the United States the power and privilege of stepping in at the decisive moment in each nation's history to dispense the vital ingredients of progress. By touching societies that mirrored its own past, the United States could rescue itself from the decay and boredom of mass-consumption society. Two slogans Rostow contributed to the Kennedy campaign—the New Frontier and Let's Get America Moving Again—carried this message of regeneration. Development, in this formulation, was able for the first time to capture the popular imagination.

THE DEVELOPMENT DECADE

The new science of modernization arrived in Washington's hour of need. Following Stalin's death in 1953, Soviet leaders eagerly pursued diplomatic overtures toward uncommitted nations. Premier Nikita Khrushchev theorized a division of the world between a "zone of war," comprising the industrialized states, and a "zone of peace," the principle arena of Cold War competition. In December 1955 he captured the international spotlight with a bold tour of Afghanistan, India, and Burma, the first visit by a Soviet leader outside of the communist bloc. In Calcutta the Soviets were greeted by a throng of more than two million. Along the way he offered trade and aid, and India accepted Soviet assistance in the construction of the Bhilai steel works, its flagship development project. The Soviet move stunned the Eisenhower administration, which concluded that Soviet aid would create bandwagon effects that would draw the rest of Eurasia into the communist orbit. Having made "neutralism" a dirty word, John Foster Dulles was chagrined at the resistance in Congress to any American-aid counteroffensive directed at nonaligned nations. To its growing alarm, the administration found itself faced with a new danger against which it was powerless to act.

The deadlock was broken in 1958 with the appearance of *The Ugly American,* a book that has been described as the *Uncle Tom's Cabin* of the Cold War. It was the work of William Lederer, a publicist working for the U.S. Navy and the CIA, and Eugene Burdick, a University of California political scientist. At Lederer's home in Honolulu in 1957, the two men decided that a novel was the best device for warning the American people that the Soviets were gaining an upper hand in the poor countries of Asia. The narrative is a collection of vignettes set in a fictional Southeast Asian nation where communist economic and political offensives are winning the allegiance of a disgruntled peasantry. Sophisticated Americans, diplomats with Boston accents and courtly manners, are pouring U.S. aid into dams, roads, and colossal engineering projects that alienate the local populace. Meanwhile, the ugly American, Homer Atkins, an agricultural adviser and the hero of the story, is making a genuine connection. The simple presence of Homer and his wife, two mobile psyches, in an Asian village creates a productive stir. Women come to marvel at the tidy home kept by Mrs. Atkins, and men watch as Homer applies his instrumental view of nature to ancient problems. Homer soon finds a counterpart, Jeepo, an empathetic, mechanically minded native, and the pair harness a bicycle to a pump, creating an irrigation-driven economic takeoff. Atkins offered readers a counterpoint to Pyle, the guileless title character of Graham Greene's *The Quiet American,* who was "like a dumb leper who has lost his bell, wandering the world, meaning no harm." Lederer and Burdick reassured readers that "average Ameri-

cans, in their natural state . . . are the best ambassadors a country can have." *The Ugly American* bitingly attacked the administration's inaction and import substitution–style development aid, but its real achievement was to enfold Rostovian theory in myths of national identity and innocence.

Defying expectations that it would drop into an ocean of public indifference, *The Ugly American* remained on the *New York Times* best-seller list for seventy-eight weeks, sold an astonishing four million copies, and was made into a blockbuster movie starring Marlon Brando. The ensuing media frenzy put development on a par with the space race and created a new strand of populist internationalism that Senator John F. Kennedy seized to boost his presidential bid. Kennedy sponsored legislation to increase aid to India and announced the existence of an "economic gap" in Asia that was being filled by Soviet aid. In February 1958, Kennedy first met Rostow, and the modernization theorist moved into Kennedy's inner circle of advisers. Kennedy was drawn to the diagnostic precision of the CENIS model, and he adopted its language in his own critiques of foreign aid. The alliance of Rostovian theory and Kennedy-Johnson foreign policy ushered in the golden age of modernization theory in the 1960s. George Ball, undersecretary of state from 1961 to 1966, recalled in his memoirs the vogue for development economics in 1961 and "the professors swarming into Washington" who "talked tendentiously of 'self-sustaining growth,' 'social development,' the 'search for nationhood,' 'self-help,' and 'nation building.'"

In the first year of his presidency, Kennedy launched the Alliance for Progress, the Peace Corps, Food for Peace, and the Agency for International Development (AID). He declared the 1960s the "Development Decade" and substantially increased the budget for foreign assistance. Modernization theory supplied the design, rationale, and justification for these programs. *Stages* had called for an expanded foreign aid effort organized exclusively around the development mission. Rostow implied and Kennedy had declared during the campaign that State Department bureaucrats used aid for short-run diplomatic advantage, making the separation of the Agency for International Development from State an essential first step. Likewise, Food for Peace took established agricultural surplus disposal programs and organized them around a developmental mission. Rather than dumping the excess produced by federal price supports (or using the surplus to alleviate famine), the program's primary purpose was the generation of "counterpart" funds that could be steered into social overhead investment. At the administration's urging, the United Nations put food assistance on the same basis in its World Food Programme.

The Peace Corps institutionalized a belief (traceable through *The Ugly American* to Lerner and Redfield) that exposure to modern personalities could induce change. Kennedy announced the Peace Corps during the campaign and asked Rostow and Millikan to draft the proposal. Volunteers were expected to create a catalytic effect by introducing ideas from a higher point on the developmental arc. The Peace Corps sought not specialists but "representative Americans" who could transmit values by example. Theory informed expectations of what volunteers should achieve. Performing their assigned jobs as teachers or agronomists was considered secondary to the task of catalyzing community involvement in a spontaneous project. Many volunteers experienced at first hand the chasm between the theory and reality of development.

The most ambitious of Kennedy's development schemes, the Alliance for Progress, was planned along rigidly Rostovian lines. In anticipation of imminent takeoff in the Latin American countries, the Alliance for Progress called for a Big Push to raise investment rates, foster social capital, and induce thorough reforms in institutions, land tenure, and distribution of income. Once plans and institutions were in place, the alliance would ride a wave of rising expectations into the next stage of growth in which the Americas would be safe from the temptations of the Cuban model. Rostow predicted a transition to self-sustaining growth within the decade, allowing the administration to keep the problem of underdevelopment "off our necks as we try to clean up the spots of bad trouble." The anticipated follow-on effects, however, failed to materialize, and $20 billion in aid disappeared into the continent without leaving a noticeable accumulation of social capital. After the first year, growth rates were far below the ambitious target figures, and the press and Congress grew impatient with the alliance. As Michael Latham points out, Rostovian theory was never held to account for the alliance's failures. Instead, setbacks only reinforced the validity of concepts that provided explanations and remedies for failure. Theorists chalked up the alliance's problems to bureaucratic ineptitude, personnel problems, and stubbornly

antimodern Latin leaders who refused to carry forward the reforms. Since the theory was rooted in the historical experience of the industrial core, it could not be invalidated by contradictory experience in periphery nations. Modernization funneled dissent into its own framework, where it could challenge the execution but not the conception of the plan.

Throughout the 1950s and 1960s, academic theorists continued to dispute within the overall consensus a number of issues that affected policy design. The balanced or Big Push approach saddled government with an almost unreachable standard for effective policy and encouraged a revived effort to identify "bottlenecks" that could be removed to stimulate disproportionate returns. Albert O. Hirschman reconfigured this debate with a theory that gained popularity after 1964 as the Johnson administration faced tighter budgets. In *The Strategy of Economic Development* (1958), Hirschman explained that small inputs, "inducement mechanisms," could push one sector into the lead, forcing others to catch up. Rather than using aid to advance an economy to a new equilibrium, as in classic Rostovian theory, aid programs should try to create disequilibria that, like loose electrons in an atomic pile, would trigger chain reactions. The difference between the two approaches can be seen in the Ford Foundation's efforts to reform agriculture in India. In the 1950s and early 1960s, the foundation sponsored a "package program" to improve conditions in fifteen rural districts on a broad front, including advances in education, health, farm equipment, irrigation, and crop diversification. Disappointed with the results, the foundation shifted in the mid-1960s to a strategy built around development and dissemination of dwarf wheat and rice varieties (the inducement mechanism). Since the new plant strains required chemical fertilizer, irrigation, and modern transport and distribution networks, other sectors would be pulled along by success, stimulating a "green revolution."

Another controversy concerned whether there was a single route to modernity and whether the experiences of Europe and the United States, the "first movers," represented the best model. Alexander Gerschenkron, William Lockwood, Clark Kerr, and others argued that the requirements of "late" developers differed and that cultural proclivities, particularly an authoritarian tradition, might dictate alternative paths. At the height of his influence, Rostow felt he was fighting a rearguard battle against those who esteemed

China's Great Leap Forward. But the "developmental state" school, while persistent, lacked policy clout until the 1980s, when the manifest success of Japan, South Korea, and Taiwan (and the clear disparity between their strategies and development orthodoxy) led the World Bank to endorse an alternate "export-led" growth model.

Population was a third contested area. In both classical and Keynesian theory, a growing population accelerates economic development. Adam Smith noted that it was the industrious poor who "generally bring up the most numerous families, and who principally supply the demand for useful labor," and John Maynard Keynes attributed the Great Depression of the 1930s partly to a catastrophic decline in births. This view prevailed among economists through the 1950s in no small part because of the coincidence of the baby boom and high growth rates in the United States. But a dissenting view articulated by John D. Rockefeller III and the Population Council gained influence toward the end of the decade. In 1958 a presidential review of foreign aid led by Theodore Draper concluded that rapid population growth threatened to cancel the effects of any aid infusions. Rostow argued in *Stages* that population posed a serious but not insurmountable obstacle to takeoff. Kennedy made population control part of the Agency for International Development's mission, and Lyndon Johnson intensified the emphasis, eventually making aid contingent on action to reduce fertility. In the 1970s both theory and policy swung back from that extreme position as a number of studies connected population increases with expansions in consumption and accumulation of social capital. By the 1980s, economic opinion was mixed, and the Reagan administration had repositioned population control as a moral issue.

THE DECLINE OF MODERNIZATION THEORY

The Vietnam War afforded rich opportunities for the application of theory, and association with the pacification effort accelerated the splintering of the Rostovian consensus. Pacification proceeded under a succession of modernization buzzwords—"rural construction," "revolutionary development," "civic action," "three-machine revolution," "Operation Takeoff"—and repeated failures sapped the enthusiasm of the modernizers. After Saigon and the modernizing regime of

the shah of Iran fell in rapid succession, policymakers ceased to regard development as a counterinsurgency weapon. It had once been believed, according to Henry Kissinger, "that there was a sort of automatic stabilizing factor in economic development. That has turned out to be clearly wrong." But events in the industrialized world had already undermined the modernization paradigm. The rising tempo of urban riots following the Watts uprising in Los Angeles in the summer of 1965 disturbed the idealized image of the United States as the end point in the developmental process. In 1967 ghettoes in forty cities erupted. The Eighty-second Airborne had to be diverted from deployment to Vietnam to quell violence in Detroit. As the riots called American economic and political maturity into question, the belt of smog settling over the eastern seaboard and Los Angeles aroused fears that the United States had become dangerously overdeveloped. A growing environmental movement questioned the desirability of economic growth. Meanwhile, the student movement opened an attack on the "action intellectuals" whose theories sustained the Vietnam War.

Rostovian theory also came under intellectual attack from abroad. In 1968 the French sociologist Claude Lévi-Strauss was in *Vogue,* as well as on the pages of the *New Yorker* and *New York Times,* proclaiming that there were no superior and no inferior societies, and that supposedly apathetic primitives "possess a genius for invention or action that leaves the achievements of civilized people far behind." In an NBC television interview, the newscaster Edwin Newman pressed J. George Harrar, president of the Rockefeller Foundation, on whether "the Western nations, the richer nations" should impose their standards on the poorer countries if "we are simply presenting them with a different set of problems." Harrar replied that he could offer no justification for modernization "in terms of what we have done to ourselves" but that he was "afraid" that there was no turning back. This standoff characterizes discussions of modernization in the post-Rostovian age. In the early 1970s, social scientists on the left and the right toppled premises and tautologies at the heart of the theory, leaving an unsupported shell of prescriptions that policymakers continued to use. The academic study of development migrated outward from the pure social science disciplines to schools and institutes of applied policy studies. Policymaking bodies no longer relied on universities but on in-house experts and think tanks to supply justifications and strategies for the use of aid.

The trauma of the 1960s split the discourse of modernization into two conversations, one academic, the other oriented toward policy. Occasionally, sounds from one conversation reached the other, but so indistinctly as to distort their meaning. "Civil society" became a fashionable term in both academic and policy circles in the 1990s, but while social scientists described it as a set of rituals for identifying and mobilizing the public, policymakers referred to support for nongovernmental organizations (NGOs) and religious and private institutions. More often, the two conversations were simply separate. Within the university, Rostovian theory was replaced by a new structuralism in the form of dependency theory. In the 1960s, Latin American scholars had deepened and widened Prebisch's critique of the "unequal exchange" between North and South. Whereas Prebisch, Myrdal, and other early structuralists saw meliorist solutions within capitalism (redistribution, planning, and import substitution), *dependentistas* identified the instigators of those solutions, the state and the national bourgeoisie, as the core of the problem. Drawing on the Marxist tradition in Latin American thought, they argued that economic dependency created class alliances between elites at the center and the periphery, reproducing culture, social relations, and systems of exchange under the guise of development. The only way out of dependency was a mass movement of "popular forces" that would rupture connections to multinational corporations and international exchange and organize a socialist future.

Dependency theory reversed the optics of Rostovian theory, viewing development inward from the periphery rather than outward from the core. It adopted, with modifications, the reified concepts used by Marx and development economics, but it focused on the processes of underdevelopment rather than the dynamics of development. It recognized, as Rostovian theory did not, that local conditions are influenced primarily by a nation's subordinate position in the global economic hierarchy. To American scholars it offered the familiar typologies and analytic power of Rostovian theory but with a very different set of values. American consumers of dependency enlisted on the side of the Latin American popular forces. The principal texts, Andre Gunder Frank's *Capitalism and Underdevelopment in Latin America* (1967) and Fernando Cardoso and Enzo

Faletto's *Dependencia y Desarrollo en América Latina* (1969), dominated the teaching and study of underdevelopment (especially of Latin America) at American universities in the 1970s and 1980s. Its influence extended to the history of U.S. foreign relations, both in its original form and as world systems theory, which has been described as dependency without the nation.

As an orthodoxy, dependency theory was open to attack, and in the 1980s and early 1990s scholars took it to task for reproducing many of the illusions of development theory. Socialist regimes displayed many of the patterns of cultural reproduction, class relations, and distorted development that *dependentistas* ascribed to capitalist nations. The hope that isolation and socialism would open a "way out" of dependency (the Myanmar model?) dimmed as scholars recognized the irresistible spread of global networks of culture and influence. The apparent movement of Japan, Taiwan, and South Korea from semiperiphery to core within a capitalist framework forced modifications in dependency theory, while some of the leading theorists (Cardoso became president of Brazil on a neo-liberal platform) abandoned the approach altogether. Finally, new approaches—postcolonial and subaltern studies and postmodernism—moved the study of power relations in Asia, Africa, and Latin America toward issues of culture and knowledge-creation and away from economic development. The newer approaches appealed to a narrower, almost exclusively academic audience. By the 1990s, social scientists had completed their withdrawal from the heights of influence over policy and public opinion they had occupied in the early 1960s.

Within the Agency for International Development, the World Bank, and UN agencies, development doctrine continued to evolve in response to institutional constraints and political currents in the developed world. In 1968, under a new president, former Secretary of Defense Robert S. McNamara, the World Bank "discovered" poverty much as the Johnson administration had four years earlier. Declaring poverty a security threat to the rich nations, McNamara targeted enlarged aid funds at poverty within countries, encouraging programs that ignored issues of national investment and growth. Breaking the customary link between development and the nation that had prevailed since List, he freed the World Bank of concerns about absorptive capacity and state planning and enlarged its mandate. It invested heavily in the green revolution, already under way in South and Southeast Asia, which promised (convincingly at the time) to eliminate hunger and alleviate rural poverty.

Development agencies were increasingly sensitive to concerns raised by the new environmental movement. Rachel Carson's *Silent Spring* (1962), Paul Ehrlich's *The Population Bomb* (1968), and Donella Meadows's *The Limits to Growth* (1972) grimly predicted that slow poisoning lay along the path of accelerating industrial growth and the chemical-dependent agriculture of the green revolution. E. F. Schumacher, a British economist and author of *Small Is Beautiful* (1973), another bible of the ecology movement, encouraged an "economics of permanence" that recognized that "there cannot be unlimited, generalized growth" on a planet with limited capacity. By questioning the very possibility of progress, environmentalism undercut the rationale and methods of development. In 1983 the United Nations assigned a commission on environment and development under Norwegian Prime Minister Gro Harlem Brundtland to reconcile the objectives of environmental health and economic growth. The Brundtland Report, issued in April 1987, popularized the term "sustainable development" to describe a strategy based on careful husbanding of resources, population control, and reduction of toxic wastes. Sustainable development (ecotourism, microenterprise, rain-fed agriculture) opened space for the collaboration of environmentalists and development experts. With some effort, dissent was once again funneled into the framework.

At the policy level, development doctrine continued to accept an idealized vision of the North Atlantic nations as normative, allowing theory to adapt to the political and economic sea change of the 1970s and 1980s. Reagan administration reforms supplanted the New Deal model, and when the collapse of the Soviet bloc opened a vast new field for development experts, they applied a set of prescriptions almost the reverse of the Rostovian formula. "Structural adjustment" called for the withdrawal of the state from the economy: privatization, the lifting of import and exchange controls, the "importation" of legal codes and standards, and the subjection of all sectors to "market discipline." Jeffrey Sachs of Harvard's Kennedy School of Government urged the Russian government to step aside and allow universal rules of the market to surface. Boris Yeltsin's administration in Russia issued vouchers giving the public a share in worthless state enterprises, while profitable natural resource monopolies were quietly grabbed up by party officials. With a seat in the legislature an "entrepreneur" could amass a fortune in windfalls from privatization and development aid. When the market failed to impose discipline, the Yeltsin administration followed a U.S.-prescribed course of "shock therapy," putting the ruble into free fall against the dollar and wiping out the savings of millions. As evidenced by poverty and suicide rates, Russia's barter economy ("Zaire with permafrost," according to one journalist) was in worse shape ten years after the Soviet breakup than it was under communism.

As ever, development doctrine dispensed advice but not apologies. Sachs admitted that he felt like a surgeon who had cut open a patient to find that nothing was where it was supposed to be, but apparently this was the patient's fault. Development experts accused a lingering "peasant" mentality and Russia's stubborn bureaucracy of undermining a theoretically sound plan. Structural adjustment schemes supported by the Clinton administration opened stock markets in Southeast Asian economies that until the early 1990s were clocking respectable growth figures. Portfolio investments poured in, inflating bubble economies in real estate and construction, then poured out, leaving a sticky residue of debt and unemployment. In a number of nations—Indonesia, Democratic Republic of Congo (Zaire), Sierra Leone, Mexico—the decline of state control, followed by collapse of the market, created criminalized or "narco-economies." In 2001, President George W. Bush added minor modifications to the structural adjustment formula, advocating more grants for education and health initiatives to allow poor nations to increase productivity and pull themselves out of debt. This was thought to represent a small step forward even if the links between education and productivity, and productivity and debt reduction, remained unproven.

Historians are of two minds on the legacy of modernization theory. On the one hand, it has mobilized humanitarianism on a global scale and given the poor an entitlement to progress. On the other, it has licensed self-interested and sometimes brutal forms of intervention while peddling illusions as scientific certainties. Development aid has become a fixture in international relations. Nations and international agencies will continue to use it and to need principles and standards to guide its use and measure its effectiveness. A careful study of past theories and the practices they inspired may enable them to approach these problems with self-awareness and a healthy skepticism.

BIBLIOGRAPHY

Cooper, Frederick, and Randall Packard. *International Development and the Social Sciences: Essays on the History and Politics of Knowledge.* Berkeley, Calif., 1997. A collection of essays that provides a good introduction to the field of development.

Cowen, M. P., and R. W. Shenton. *Doctrines of Development.* London, 1996. Traces the development ideas from origins in the European Enlightenment.

Curti, Merle, and Kendall Birr. *Prelude to Point Four.* Madison, Wis., 1954. An early study of development in American foreign relations prior to Truman.

Gilman, Nils. "Paving the World with Good Intentions: The Genesis of Modernization Theory, 1945–1965." Ph.D. dissertation. University of California. Berkeley, Calif., 2001. Links Rostovian theory to the Parsonian revolution in social science.

Latham, Michael E. *Modernization as Ideology: American Social Science and "Nation Building" in the Kennedy Era.* Chapel Hill, N.C., 2000. An outstanding study of modernization's place in the Kennedy administration's Cold War strategy.

Lerner, Daniel. *The Passing of Traditional Society: Modernizing the Middle East.* New York, 1958. A seminal modernization study and one of the best examples of the discourse at the height of its influence.

Maxfield, Sylvia, and James H. Nolt. "Protectionism and the Internationalization of Capital: U.S. Sponsorship of Import Substitution Industrialization in the Philippines, Turkey, and Argentina." *International Studies Quarterly* 34 (1990): 49–81. Reveals that the United States systematically encouraged the strategy of import substitution.

Packenham, Robert A. *The Dependency Movement.* Cambridge, Mass., 1992. Follows the rise and decline of dependency theory in Latin America and the United States.

Pletsch, Carl E. "The Three Worlds, or the Division of Social Scientific Labor, circa 1950–1975." *Comparative Studies in Society and History* 23, no. 3 (1981): 565–590. Describes how academic politics and federal funding led American scholars to create the Third World.

Rostow, Walt W. *The Stages of Economic Growth.* Cambridge, 1960. The classic statement of Rostovian theory.

Simpson, Christopher, ed. *Universities and Empire: Money and Politics in the Social Sciences During the Cold War.* New York, 1998. Explores how modernization theory emerged from a collaboration between academe and the security establishment.

See also ECONOMIC POLICY AND THEORY; FOREIGN AID; HUMANITARIAN INTERVENTION AND RELIEF; IMPERIALISM; INTERNATIONAL MONETARY FUND AND WORLD BANK; THE NATIONAL INTEREST; PHILANTHROPY.

DICTATORSHIPS

David F. Schmitz

One of the most persistent and difficult problems that has faced the makers of American foreign policy, particularly in the twentieth century, has been the conflict between the desire to encourage democracy abroad and the need to protect perceived American interests around the world. Since its founding, the United States has been philosophically dedicated to supporting democracies and human rights abroad. This commitment is found in the most important documents and treaties of the nation, including the Declaration of Independence, the Constitution, and the United Nations Universal Declaration of Human Rights, and has been proclaimed by presidents and secretaries of state since George Washington and Thomas Jefferson. In addition, from its inception, the United States has been an expansive nation territorially, economically, and culturally. As a result, the American desire to promote democracy abroad has often conflicted with the support of dictatorships that promised stability, protected American trade and investments, and aligned themselves with Washington against enemies of the United States. American foreign policymakers have often supported right-wing dictatorships in their efforts to protect what they see as the national interest while opposing communist regimes and left-wing dictators. Dictatorships on the left have been seen as opposing both American political ideals and material interests. They have been, therefore, consistently criticized and opposed by the United States.

THE NINETEENTH CENTURY

In order to understand American attitudes toward dictatorships, it is essential to survey the development of the ideology of American foreign policy during the nineteenth century. The desire for land and greater economic opportunity, combined with the commonly held view that the nation and its

people were on a special mission, fueled the expansion of the United States. Territorial expansion was rapid, with the country growing from thirteen states on the Atlantic coast in 1789 to control over transcontinental North America by the end of the 1840s. The key was that this conquest was all done in the name of expanding liberty, as part of the mission of the United States to provide a moral example and guidance to the world. Expansion, therefore, was part of American political ideology from the outset. When establishing the Republic and the Constitution, one of the central questions the Founders grappled with was whether a vast territory could be compatible with a virtuous republic. Rome served as the most often-used historical precedent, and its lesson was that a republic could not expand and avoid the corruption and dictatorial power that emerged under Julius Caesar. It was generally believed that republics could only function and survive if they were the size of Greek city-states or Geneva. James Madison addressed this problem in *Federalist* No. 10 and provided an alternative view that solved the dilemma between expansion and a republic for the Federalists. Madison argued that expansion was a positive good for the nation and the ideology of republican values. With the proper constitution and checks on power, a large republic was not merely possible; it was necessary to maintain freedom. An expanding nation provided insurance against any faction, cabal, or region dominating national politics and seizing power. Institutional checks and balances were, therefore, aided by size. A large republic would guard against tyranny by making it impossible for a coherent majority or sizable minority to form and gain control.

The belief in an Empire of Liberty and vision of national greatness was captured well on the Great Seal of the United States with the inscription *annuit coeptis; novus ordo seclorum* (God has blessed this undertaking; a new order of the ages).

493

Throughout the nineteenth century this continued to inspire and guide Americans' actions and helped fuel the rapid expansion across the continent that John O'Sullivan termed "manifest destiny" in 1845. The notion of manifest destiny rested on the view that Anglo-Saxons had a right to land because they, according to Senator Thomas Hart Benton of Missouri, one of the most articulate exponents of manifest destiny, used it according to the intentions of the creator. By this reasoning, the material gains of the United States were not selfish acts, but benevolent undertakings in line with the principles of the nation. Manifest destiny became the ideological shield used to justify Indian removal and the taking of land from Mexico in the name of liberty and freedom. Nineteenth-century Americans did not see their actions as doing violence to their own moral instincts, religion, or republican and democratic values. With the belief that God willed that the United States control the continent, these actions could be carried forward without creating an ideological crisis.

The full expression of the compatibility of expansion and liberty came in Frederick Jackson Turner's 1893 "frontier thesis." Turner, speaking at the Columbian Exposition in Chicago, set out to provide an understanding of American history and development in the first century since the adoption of the Constitution. Central to Turner's thesis was the idea that westward expansion and the frontier experience were the key influences on American life and the development of American democracy, and it was this that made U.S. history and the American people unique. The United States was seen as an exceptional nation, free from the vices of Europe and its corrupt institutions. He argued, "Up to our own day, American history has been in a large degree the history of the colonization of the Great West. The existence of an area of free land, its continuous recession, and the advance of American settlement westward, explain American development." The frontier created and recreated an independent people and formed and regenerated American democratic government and values.

Yet, from the outset, challenges would appear in the world that created a paradox around the expansion of liberty and the support of democracy and human rights. The first of these was the French Revolution in 1789. Initially, it was welcomed by most Americans as a repeat of the American Revolution. The French appeared to be following the American example and the overthrow of their monarchy was seen as a harbinger of change from autocratic rule to a republican and a democratic future guided by the same enlightenment values that inspired the Declaration of Independence and the U.S. Constitution. As the events in Paris took a more radical course and the impact of the revolution brought international conflict, however, the Washington administration became divided over whether to support France or not. The ensuing disorder and wars in Europe harmed American trade and raised questions about the proper extent of change and democratic rule for other people. The question of supporting and promoting change and democratic values had quickly proven to be a complex and difficult proposition.

The revolutions that swept South America and then Central America in the first decades of the nineteenth century further complicated the question of how to respond to the collapse of colonial empire and the rule of monarchs. As with France, most Americans initially welcomed the fall of Spanish rule to the south, but concerns were quickly raised about the stability of the new nations and the danger of other European powers taking advantage of the upheaval to impose their own rule in the former Spanish empire. The United States responded to these threats with the Monroe Doctrine that declared that Spain could not reimpose its rule on the already independent states of the Western Hemisphere and that the United States would not permit any new colonization or military intervention by any European power. In turn, the United States promised not to meddle in European politics. Thus, the United States asserted its authority to determine the political future and course of events for the rest of the nations of the Americas. These developments prompted Secretary of State John Quincy Adams to issue a warning to his fellow citizens concerning the dangers of foreign intervention and the tension between expansion and democratic rule. Adams argued that the United States should not go abroad in search of monsters to destroy. Rather, the nation was better served in international affairs by upholding its own values and leading by example. It could seek to impose its will on other areas of the world, but in the process it would damage its own institutions and succumb to corruption.

By the middle of the century, a clear policy had emerged in Washington that the United States would recognize any government that could maintain itself in power and meet the minimum obliga-

494

tions of government. In 1848, Secretary of State James Buchanan, summarizing this policy, stated: "We do not go behind the existing government to involve ourselves in the question of legitimacy. It is sufficient for us to know that a government exists, capable of maintaining itself; and then its recognition on our part inevitably follows."

Simultaneously, however, Americans developed other positions that would come to shape the nation's attitudes toward dictatorships in the twentieth century. Central to these were the notions of the racial inferiority of other peoples, the desire for stability and order in the world as necessary for the promotion and protection of American economic interests, and a growing fear of revolution. The concept of race has been an all-pervasive one in American history from the first contact with Native Americans and the importation of Africans as slaves. By the nineteenth century, an essentialist outlook dominated white Americans' thinking on race. Different people were placed in categories based on what were believed to be their inherent traits as peoples, groups, and nations. Anglo-Saxons were considered the most advanced race, carrying civilization wherever they went.

Groups were ranked in descending order of civilization and ability to govern and maintain stability. Other western Europeans were seen as near equals to Anglo-Saxons. The rest of the peoples of the world were categorized as either inherently dangerous or unfit for self-rule, and usually both. Latin Europeans and Slavs were seen as fundamentally undemocratic as people, and all non-Europeans were seen as inferior and in need of guidance and direction from "their betters." These views were buttressed by the development of the "scientific" idea of social Darwinism that held that the domination of western Europe and the United States over world affairs as well as their greater wealth were merely the working out of natural selection and the survival of the fittest.

These ideas were consolidated at the beginning of the twentieth century in the Roosevelt Corollary to the Monroe Doctrine. In the wake of the Spanish-American War and the acquisition of the Panama Canal zone, the maintenance of order in the Caribbean and Central America was becoming an ever-growing concern to the United States. President Theodore Roosevelt worried about the negative impact of unrest to the south on American trade and investments, and sought various means to preserve order through the assertion of police power over the other nations in the hemisphere. Roosevelt believed that the increasing interdependence and complexity of international political and economic relations made it incumbent on what he saw as the civilized powers to insist on the proper behavior of other nations. In 1904, Roosevelt provided his rationale for why revolutions were dangerous and justification for American intervention in Latin America in what became the Roosevelt Corollary:

> If a nation shows that it knows how to act with reasonable efficiency and decency in social and political matters, if it keeps order and pays its obligations, it need fear no interference from the United States. Chronic wrongdoing, or an impotence which results in a general loosening of the ties of civilized society, may in America, as elsewhere, ultimately require intervention by some civilized nation, and in the Western Hemisphere the adherence of the United States to the Monroe Doctrine may force the United States, however reluctantly, in flagrant cases of such wrongdoing or impotency, to the exercise of an international policy power.

Soon after, U.S. troops were dispatched to Cuba, Nicaragua, Haiti, the Dominican Republic, and Honduras to maintain order.

THE GREAT WAR AND THE BOLSHEVIK REVOLUTION

Prior to World War I, therefore, the problems of unrest and disorder were seen as the manifestations of politically immature people, irresponsible individuals, or bandits. The postwar threats of nationalism and communism, unlike these previous disruptions, served to threaten the whole international system that the western nations operated within and forced American leaders to develop new approaches to these questions. In response to the broad revolutionary challenges of the 1910s, particularly the Bolshevik Revolution in Russia, a persistent concern with order and stability emerged among American officials. The revolutions in Mexico, China, and Russia could easily spread given the economic and political dislocation that had occurred during the previous decade. President Woodrow Wilson initially responded to these challenges with a policy that sought to promote self-determination and political democracy internationally as the best means to secure American interests and prevent the further spread of revolution. In 1917, he led the nation into World War I to destroy autocratic rule and militarism in Europe. Wilson hoped that by promoting liberal, democratic forces and states in Europe through his Fourteen Points he could solve the dual problem of war and revolution. The president placed his faith in the League of Nations as the mechanism that would allow peaceful, nonrevolutionary change to occur in Europe and guarantee collective security to prevent another war and concomitant revolution. The Bolshevik Revolution, however, shifted the president's attention from his battle with autocratic rule to the concern with revolution and containing communism.

President Wilson saw Bolshevism as a mistake that had to be resisted and corrected. He believed that the revolution in Russia was worse than anything represented by the kaiser, and that the Bolsheviks were a "group of men more cruel than the czar himself." A communist regime meant, according to Wilson, "government by terror, government by force, not government by vote." Furthermore, it ruled by the "poison of disorder, the poison of revolt, the poison of chaos." It was, the president believed, the "negation of everything that is American" and "had to be opposed." Secretary of State Bainbridge Colby reiterated Wilson's points when he set out the official United States policy of not recognizing the communist government in Moscow in August 1920. Colby wrote that U.S. policy was based on the premise that the "present rulers of Russia do not rule by the will or the consent of any considerable portion of the Russian people." The Bolsheviks had forcefully seized power and were using the "machinery of government . . . with savage oppression to maintain themselves in power." Moreover, the "existing regime in Russia is based upon the negation of every principle of honor and good faith, and every usage and convention underlying the whole structure of international law." It was, therefore, "not possible for the government of the United States to recognize the present rulers of Russia."

The policy of nonrecognition was based on the claim that a regime was illegitimate due to how it came to power and because it was a dictatorship that ruled by force against the will and interest of the people. Such nations were, therefore, a threat to American values and interests in the world. This policy would become a standard American diplomatic weapon for demonstrating its opposition to left-wing dictatorships and was used, most notably against China in 1949 after Mao Zedong's successful establishment of the People's Republic of China, Fidel Castro's regime in Cuba in 1961, and Vietnam in 1975 after the defeat of South Vietnam, to deny legitimacy, trade, and international aid to these governments and force political change.

The upheavals of World War I also led to a reevaluation of American views on right-wing dictatorships after the war. Republican policymakers rejected Wilson's criticism of autocracy and sought to back any individual or group they thought could ensure order and stability while opposing communism and protecting U.S. trade, investments, and interests. Beginning in the 1920s, American policymakers developed and institutionalized the logic, rationale, and ideological justifications for U.S. support of right-wing dictatorships that has influenced American policy ever since.

American officials first articulated their emerging rationale for supporting right-wing dictatorships in response to the post–World War I events in Italy. The United States came to support the fascist regime of Benito Mussolini based on a view that there was a Bolshevik threat in Italy and that the Italian people were not prepared for democratic rule. This unpreparedness and inability at self-government, American policymakers believed, created the instability that bred Bolshevism. These beliefs served to legitimize U.S. support of Mussolini in the name of defending liberalism. America's paternalistic racism combined with anticommunism to lead American officials to welcome the coming to power of fascism in Italy. The fascists, they believed, would bring the stability that would prevent Bolshevism and that was a precondition for economic recovery and increased trade.

This logic and rationale was quickly extended to other right-wing dictatorships, often after the overthrow of democratic governments, that were perceived to meet all of the qualifications for U.S. support: promise of political stability, anti-Bolshevism, and increased trade with the United States. The quest for order in a framework acceptable to Washington led the United States to support Anastasio Somoza Garcia in Nicaragua, General Maximiliano Hernández Martínez in El Salvador, Fulgencio Batista in Cuba, and Francisco Franco in Spain, and the Fourth of August regime in Greece during the interwar years. Similar to the situation in Italy, the specter of communism and the argument that the people of these nations were not yet ready for democracy underlay the United States support for these dictators. Moreover, in Latin America this policy had another benefit to U.S. officials. It allowed the United States to find a new means to establish order in the region without direct military intervention. American forces had intervened no fewer than twelve times in different nations in the Caribbean basin. These actions, however, failed to provide long-term stability. Rather, as Henry L. Stimson, secretary of state from 1929 to 1933, noted, disorder continued to grow. Yet, if the United States tried to take the lead in the area, Latin Americans complained of American domination and imperialism. Right-wing dictators provided the desired solution by providing both imposed order while ending the cry against American imperialism.

U.S. support for right-wing dictatorships after World War I, therefore, represented a new development and departure from both the policy of promoting self-determination and political democracy internationally, and earlier tolerance of military and authoritarian regimes, particularly in Latin America. American leaders grew preoccupied by international order in the wake of the disruption of World War I, the rise of radical nationalism combined with a decline of Western power, a questioning of traditional authority in nations, and greater demands for self-determination. This emphasis on order came to permeate policymaking in Washington, and the United States found strong-arm rule, the maintenance of stability, anticommunism, and protection of investments sufficient reasons to support nondemocratic rulers on the right. The often-quoted apocryphal statement by Franklin D. Roosevelt concerning Somoza of Nicaragua, "he may be a son-of-a-bitch, but he is our son-of-a-bitch," captures the American attitudes and policy toward right-wing dictatorships. While left-wing dictatorships would be opposed, those on the right found support in Washington. This "lesser-of-two-evils" approach to foreign policy, influenced by racism and at times irrational fears of communism, created blindness to the shortcomings of right-wing dictators, and led the United States to support and align itself with many of the most brutal regimes in the world.

WORLD WAR II AND THE COLD WAR

This view, however, did not remain static. Pendulum swings in the policy appeared after times of crisis and failure. Most notably, the rise of Adolf Hitler and World War II provided a fundamental challenge to the idea that supporting right-wing dictators enhanced American interests and

brought the debate over support of authoritarian governments to the fore within the Franklin D. Roosevelt and Harry S. Truman administrations. Roosevelt confronted the problem of Nazi Germany at first by efforts to appease Hitler, a strategy he abandoned when it became clear that Germany was intent upon war. The wartime opposition to fascism and the triumph of the Allies made the promotion of democracy and change paramount concerns, and the opposition to authoritarian governments, such as Juan Perón's in Argentina and Francisco Franco's in Spain, became U.S. policy.

The Allied victory in World War II appeared to mark more than the defeat of Germany, Japan, and Italy. It was to be, for many, the beginning of a new epoch. Central to that vision was the defeat of fascism and the triumph of democratic ideals and values over dictatorship and authoritarian rule. The world's nations had not only joined together in an antifascist coalition on the battlefield; they also produced documents such as the Atlantic Charter and the Charter of the United Nations that extolled human rights, self-determination, and freedom. At home, Roosevelt spoke the lofty language of the Four Freedoms, criticized tyranny and colonialism, and talked of the expansion of American institutions and values to other parts of the world. For Americans, the postwar period promised the vindication of their nation's values and institutions. From these ideas emerged the remarkable achievements in postwar West Germany, Japan, and Italy of establishing democratic governments and the rebuilding of the economies of western Europe and Japan.

In other areas of the world, events looked equally promising as independence movements were on the march in Asia and Africa, and dictatorships were under attack and apparently destined to be a thing of the past. The fledgling United Nations refused to admit Spain, and most nations agreed with its request that they withdraw their ambassadors from Madrid in protest of Franco's rule, while Argentina's strongman Juan Perón found himself under attack for his refusal to break relations with Germany until the spring of 1945. Outside of the Soviet Union and the areas controlled by the Red Army, it seemed that democracy was the force of the future. Even postwar disputes with the Soviet Union and the emerging Cold War seemed to demand, in the name of consistency with American criticisms of the governments being established in Eastern Europe, that the United States oppose dictatorships and support the establishment of free governments. In 1946 the Truman administration adopted an official policy of opposition to all right-wing dictatorships.

Yet the question was not so clear-cut as American efforts at appeasement of Nazi Germany indicated. Franklin Roosevelt had still distinguished between a regime such as Hitler's that threatened peace and those, such as Somoza's, that apparently did not. Roosevelt and others often adopted a pragmatic rationale for defending dictatorships they favored, and moral judgments were only invoked when the government opposed a regime rather than provide a consistent principle on which to base decisions. Ultimately, the logic and policy developed during the interwar years would be carried into the post–World War II period. The success of establishing democratic governments in Germany and Japan notwithstanding, with the emerging Cold War with the Soviet Union, the policy pendulum swung back to the right. By 1947 the United States came again to prefer "stable" right-wing regimes in the Third World over indigenous radicalism and what it saw as dangerously unstable democratic governments. The pronouncement of the Truman Doctrine and the adoption of containment as the global policy of the United States brought about the change. Truman announced in March 1947 that the United States now faced a global contest between two competing and incompatible ways of life: democracy and totalitarian communism. Democracy represented government "based upon the will of the majority" expressed through "free institutions, representative government, free elections, guarantees of individual liberty, freedom of speech and religion, and freedom from political oppression." Communism meant the "will of a minority forcibly imposed upon the majority. It relies on terror and oppression, a controlled press and radio, fixed elections, and the suppression of personal freedoms." It was now a bipolar world. It did not matter that many of the governments the United States came to support more resembled Truman's description of communism than democracy. If it was now a contest between only two ways of life, governments had to fit into one side of the divide or the other. Right-wing regimes became part of the free world no matter what the composition of their governments.

Truman had introduced important new variables into the basic assumptions of American foreign policy that were picked up by others. A distinction was now drawn between authoritarian dictators on the right and totalitarian dictators on the left. Autocratic regimes were seen as traditional and natural dictatorships for their societies while totalitarian regimes were classified as autocratic rule plus state control over the economy. The wartime view of fascism as the enemy had yielded to the danger of Soviet expansion. In this new understanding of the world, there was little room for moral arguments against right-wing dictators. They would be wedged into the free world, no matter what their record of abuses, as nations capable of being set on the course to democracy. No such hope was held out for communist nations. Authoritarian regimes now provided more than stability and the protection of American interests. They were a part of the "free world" and its struggle against communism.

In an analysis that became central to the Cold War justifications for supporting right-wing dictators, the Department of State argued that it was important to determine if a dictatorial regime was of the traditional Latin-American type, or if it was a communist or other police-state type. This distinction was crucial. The former were acceptable, but the latter had to be opposed. Further, it was necessary to distinguish between dictatorial governments who attempted to extend their influence beyond their own borders and those whose actions were not a threat to international peace and security. Communist states fell into the first category while authoritarian regimes did not. It was only totalitarian regimes that had to be opposed. Dictators such as Somoza in Nicaragua were mere authoritarians and deserved support. The Truman administration concluded that wherever dictatorships were overturned, the resulting governments were weak and unstable, making those nations susceptible to communist subversion. This idea was continued into the Dwight D. Eisenhower administration, which believed that when a dictator was replaced, the communists gained. The United States, therefore, had to "back strong men" and dictators. The conclusion was clear. Right-wing dictatorships were historically part of the Third World, unavoidable, and deserving of American support. So-called totalitarian regimes, however, still had to be opposed in the name of freedom. The Truman and Eisenhower administrations, therefore, chose to work with authoritarian rulers or the local military, in nations such as Greece, Spain, Iran, and Guatemala rather than nationalist leaders or democratic forces that appeared vulnerable to communist takeovers.

In addition, American policymakers found new positive reasons to support right-wing dictators. Although the policy of supporting autocratic regimes violated the stated ideals of postwar American policy, officials believed it would serve the national interest of the United States and promote development in other nations. Based upon a paternalistic racism that continued to categorize non–western European peoples as inferior, vulnerable to radical ideas and solutions, and, therefore, in need of a firm government to maintain order, authoritarian regimes were viewed as the only way Third World nations could undergo economic improvements that would allow the development of more "mature" populations without succumbing to communism or radical nationalism. While this attitude undermined the avowed rectitude of American leaders, democracy was not seen as a viable option for newly independent nations or many countries in Latin America. Strong dictators, therefore, were believed to be necessary antidotes for the ills of political and social disorder and conduits for modernization. Hence, policymakers believed that support for authoritarian regimes protected liberalism internationally by preventing unstable areas from falling prey to Bolshevism while allowing time for nations to develop a middle class and democratic political institutions. Expediency overcame a commitment to the ideology of democracy because the policy appeared to provide immediate benefits. The United States gained friendly—if brutal and corrupt—allies who provided stability, support for U.S. policies, and a favorable atmosphere for American business.

Moreover, authoritarian regimes now provided more than stability and the protection of American interests. Through nation building they would be the instruments to the creation of strong and free societies. These views were supported by social scientists in the postwar years. Proponents of nation building and the moving of Third World nations through the proper "stages of economic growth" argued that stability and strong rule were a necessary stage in the development and maturation of these societies. The guiding premise of the Eisenhower administration was that "political and economic authoritarianism prevails throughout the underdeveloped world in general and represents the predominant environment in which the U.S. must associate its interests with those of the emergent and developing societies." In 1959 the Department of State concluded that right-wing regimes would be the conduits to modernization

and provide a necessary stage in the development of Third World nations. Reflecting the influence and jargon of modernization theory, the Department of State noted that "our experience with the more highly developed Latin American states indicates that authoritarianism is required to lead backward societies through their socioeconomic revolutions." Moreover, if the "breakthrough occurs under noncommunist authoritarianism, trends toward democratic values emerge with the development of a literate middle class." Right-wing dictators would "remain the norm . . . for a long period. The trend toward military authoritarianism will accelerate as developmental problems become more acute and the facades of democracy left by the colonial powers prove inadequate to immediate tasks."

"It is of course essential in the Cold War," the State Department report continued, "to seek to promote stability in the under-developed countries . . . where instability may invite communism. A new, authoritarian regime, though less 'democratic' than its predecessor, may possess much more stability and may well lay the ground for ultimate return to a more firmly based 'democracy.'" The department found these to be "compelling reasons for maintaining relations" with authoritarian regimes in power. "In the bipolar world of the Cold War, our refusal to deal with a military or authoritarian regime" could lead to the establishment of regimes friendly with the Soviet Union. It was the task of the United States to discover "techniques whereby Western values can be grafted on modernizing indigenous developmental systems."

In the wake of the 1959 Cuban revolution and Fidel Castro's coming to power, the John F. Kennedy administration reevaluated U.S. policy toward Latin America and support for such regimes as Batista's. It decided to distance itself from authoritarian regimes and promote reform. Kennedy and his advisers worried that right-wing dictators were proving to be ineffective and even dangerous bulwarks against communism. They upset political stability as much as they protected it by frustrating desires for change and democracy, and they nurtured support for left-wing and communist opposition to their rule. The 1961 Alliance for Progress was the centerpiece of this vision, and the overthrow of Rafael Trujillo in the Dominican Republic a signal of change. This shift was not, however, primarily motivated by an ideological commitment to support constitutional governments at all times. Rather, it was seen as a better way to combat communism, and the administration's actions never matched the bold rhetoric of the policy. The problem was how to break the dependence on right-wing dictators for order and promote change without unleashing revolutionary movements. Kennedy provided an excellent example of his concern about this dilemma in 1961 when discussing the Dominican Republic. "There are three possibilities," he said, "in descending order of preference: a decent democratic regime, a continuation of the Trujillo regime, or a Castro regime. We ought to aim at the first, but we really can't renounce the second until we are sure that we can avoid the third."

Kennedy's policy quickly came into conflict with other American interests and the growing conflict in Vietnam, and his administration backed away from its policy of opposition to right-wing dictators in 1962. In the face of the continuing challenges of revolutionary nationalism and the choice between order and social change, the Kennedy and Lyndon B. Johnson administrations opted to again support military dictators over democratic governments they feared were slipping toward communism. The swing of the political pendulum back to supporting right-wing dictators took on the now-familiar ring of the need for stability in nations that were too politically immature to defend themselves against communism. With the overthrow of Ngo Dinh Diem in South Vietnam in November 1963, the crisis in Vietnam came to dominate the making of American foreign policy. Unrest and potentially unreliable governments were seen as dangerous invitations to Soviet advances.

The repositioning of the political pendulum on the right was completed in the first months of the Johnson administration. Following the assassination of Kennedy, Johnson backed away from the idealistic rhetoric of the Alliance for Progress. Facing continual unrest in Latin America and a rapidly deteriorating military and political situation in Vietnam, Johnson sought to impose order. The Johnson administration supported the military overthrow of the João Goulart government in Brazil in 1964 as security and stability again took precedence over supporting social change and democratic rule. In 1965, when authoritarian rulers failed to provide the stability and bulwarks against communism that Washington demanded, Johnson decided that the United States had to impose order through military intervention in the Dominican Republic and Vietnam. The Johnson administration's determination to establish stability and order acceptable to Washington, which had provided the basis for working with repressive dictators, forced the president to pursue the policy to its logical conclusion of a U.S. intervention to salvage the discredited regimes.

THE IMPACT OF THE VIETNAM WAR

After 1965, American policy toward right-wing dictators became a contested issue. The Vietnam War served to undercut much of the logic and rationale used to justify American support of authoritarian regimes. Critics charged that in addition to the questionable morality of supporting right-wing dictators, the policy, while providing short-term benefits, usually led to larger problems for the United States in the long run, mainly long-term instability. Many supporters of the policy realized this danger, yet saw no other way to protect more pressing U.S. interests. Dictatorships created political polarization, blocked any effective means for reforms, destroyed the center, and created a backlash of anti-American sentiment that opened the door to radical nationalist movements that brought to power the exact type of governments the United States most opposed and originally sought to prevent. From Cuba to Iran to Nicaragua, and most tragically in Vietnam, the limits of this policy were discovered.

Support of authoritarian regimes was not completely abandoned by any means, as Richard Nixon's policy in Chile of supporting General Augusto Pinochet's overthrow of the government of Salvador Allende and the continued good relations with leaders such as the shah of Iran demonstrate. But the political climate had changed and policymakers were now forced to defend their position in public and take into account sustained criticisms of American support of dictatorships. For many, the Vietnam War and the postwar revelations of American covert actions in the Third World provided convincing evidence that the old policy of support for dictators was flawed and, more importantly, damaging to American interests and doomed to fail. Critics called for the United States to reorient its moral compass and to find methods other than covert activity and support of brutal dictators to advance American interests in the world. Although no complete swing of the policy pendulum took place, new views were heard and different approaches would be implemented, most notably President James Earl Carter's emphasis on human rights.

The establishment of the Senate Select Committee on Intelligence (Church Committee) provided a central focus for investigations into American covert actions and support of right-wing dictators. The committee chair, Senator Frank Church of Idaho, summarized the position of many critics when he argued during the bicentennial year of 1976 that it was time to return to the objective of the nation's founders and place the United States at the helm of moral leadership in the world. Yet, as his committee revealed, that notion had fallen by the wayside, replaced by the support of brutal dictators, Central Intelligence Agency–orchestrated coups in democratic nations, and assassination plots against foreign leaders. For all of its efforts, the nation found itself involved in a divisive, immoral war in Vietnam and allied to countries that mocked the professed ideals of the United States. Church concluded that American foreign policy had to conform once more to the country's historic ideals and the fundamental belief in freedom and popular government.

President Carter echoed Church's views in his inaugural address when he called upon the American people to "take on those moral duties which, when assumed, seem inevitably to be in our own best interests" and to let the "recent mistakes bring a resurgent commitment to the basic principles of our nation." Carter adopted a new policy of human rights. He declared that the United States should have "a foreign policy that is democratic, that is based on fundamental values, and that uses power and influence . . . for humane purposes." The president was convinced that democracy was the wave of the future and the continued support of repressive dictatorships was not only against American ideals but also against the nation's self-interest. "Democracy's great successes—in India, Portugal, Spain, Greece—show that our confidence in this system is not misplaced." Moreover, Carter asserted that the nation was "now free of that inordinate fear of communism which once led us to embrace any dictator who joined us in that fear."

Carter succinctly summarized the criticisms of supporting right-wing dictators. "For too many years," the president announced, "we've been willing to adopt the flawed and erroneous principles and tactics of our adversaries, sometimes abandoning our own values for theirs. We've fought fire with fire, never thinking that fire is better quenched with water. This approach," he noted, "failed, with Vietnam the best example of

its intellectual and moral poverty." Carter, therefore, called for a policy based on a commitment to "human rights as a fundamental tenet of our foreign policy." The nation's policy must be guided by "a belief in human freedom." The old policy was, according to Carter, based on an inaccurate reading of history and the development of democracy. Strength and stability were not the prerequisites of freedom: "The great democracies are not free because we are strong and prosperous." Rather, Carter concluded, "we are strong and influential and prosperous because we are free."

Carter was aware of the limits of moral suasion, and did not believe that change would or should come overnight. Moreover, he realized that he would have to continue to support certain allies despite their record on human rights. As Carter noted, he was "determined to combine support for our more authoritarian allies and friends with the effective promotion of human rights with their countries." He hoped for reform to prevent revolution. "By inducing them to change their repressive policies," the president believed, "we would be enhancing freedom and democracy, and helping to remove the reasons for revolution that often erupt among those who suffer from persecution."

Advocates of the old policy of supporting right-wing dictators blamed Carter, rather than the widespread popular discontent in their two nations, for the overthrow of two dictators in 1979 who were among America's staunchest allies, Somoza in Nicaragua and the shah of Iran. The most vocal critic was the future Ronald Reagan administration ambassador to the United Nations, Jeane Kirkpatrick. She captured attention in 1979 and again in 1981 with her blistering critiques of Carter's human-rights policy and public defense of supporting authoritarian regimes. Kirkpatrick contended that the United States need not apologize for its support of "moderate autocrats." Such a policy was in the national interest and not incompatible with the defense of freedom. Using Nicaragua and Iran as her examples, Kirkpatrick argued that autocratic governments were to be expected in these nations and the rule of Somoza and the shah of Iran was not as negative as their opponents claimed. In discussing the Somoza dynasty, Kirkpatrick claimed that that government "was moderately competent in encouraging economic development, moderately oppressive, and moderately corrupt." In addition, it was a bulwark against communism and a loyal ally of the United States. Little more could be expected, she believed, given the development of Nicaragua.

Central to Kirkpatrick's argument was the concept of the fundamental difference between right-wing and communist dictatorships, what she called authoritarian and totalitarian regimes. The crucial distinction, according to Kirkpatrick, was that "traditional autocrats leave in place existing allocations of wealth, power, status, and other resources," and "they do not disturb the habitual patterns of family and personal relations. Because the miseries of traditional life are familiar, they are bearable to ordinary people who . . . acquire the skills and attitudes necessary for survival in the miserable roles they are destined to fill." The almost exact opposite was true, she claimed, for life under communist rule. Left-wing regimes established totalitarian states that create the type of "social inequities, brutality, and poverty" that traditional autocrats merely "tolerate."

The key to Kirkpatrick's argument lay in her claim that because right-wing dictators left traditional societies in place, "given time, propitious economic, social, and political circumstances, talented leaders, and a strong indigenous demand for representative government," their nations could evolve from autocratic states into democracies. Totalitarian communist states, she flatly asserted, could not. Indeed, by their very nature, communist nations shut off any of these avenues toward development and, therefore, democratic change. Hence, right-wing dictatorships were an inevitable and necessary stage of government for Third World nations. Support by Washington was not only in the national interest but was helping to provide the necessary conditions for modernization and the development of democracy.

When Ronald Reagan became president in 1981, he adopted Kirkpatrick's ideas as the basis for American policy and returned to supporting right-wing dictators while continuing American opposition to communism and heightening the Cold War. There was, of course, little that was new in Kirkpatrick's analysis or Reagan's policy. She had only publicly stated the rationale and arguments that were initially formed in the 1920s and further developed after World War II. It was rare, however, to have such a bold statement of the ideas and assumptions behind American policy toward dictatorships—on the right and the left—that were usually only discussed in such terms in policy memorandums and private meetings. It laid bare the contradiction between the U.S. claims that opposition to the Soviet Union and commu-

nist regimes was based on their denial of political rights to their citizens, while Washington supported governments that were equally as guilty of human-rights abuses and the denial of basic civil liberties to their populations. Moreover, the collapse of communism in Eastern Europe in 1989, the reunification of Germany in 1990, and the breakup of the Soviet Union in 1991 demonstrated the fallacy of these arguments as democracy took hold in many nations formerly considered totalitarian and incapable of political change.

The end of the Cold War challenged many of the ideas previously used to justify American support of right-wing dictators and opposition to left-wing regimes. Anticommunism no longer provided a unifying theme for American policy, and no other single policy replaced it. Still, the conflict between the American efforts to promote democracy in other nations and the need to protect other interests remains. While the 1990s provided examples of Washington's support for the democratic process from the Balkans to Southeast Asia, the United States has also continued to support many dictators in the name of stability and economic development. Moreover, as the only superpower, the United States has found itself drawn into conflicts around the world. Some of these interventions have led it to back local efforts at democracy and self-determination, while others have seen it support the status quo. Without a full commitment to make the promotion of democracy and human rights as the top priority over other interests and claims, the only thing certain is that the dilemma of what attitudes to take toward dictators will remain.

BIBLIOGRAPHY

Adler, Les, and Thomas Paterson. "Red Fascism: The Merger of Nazi Germany and Soviet Russia in the American Image of Totalitarianism, 1930s–1950s." *American Historical Review* 74 (April 1970): 1046–1064.

Filene, Peter G., ed. *American Views of Soviet Russia, 1917–1965.* Homewood, Ill., 1968.

Gardner, Lloyd C. *Wilson and Revolutions, 1913–1921.* Washington, D.C., 1982.

Garfinkle, Adam, et. al. *The Devil and Uncle Sam: A User's Guide to the Friendly Tyrants Dilemma.* New Brunswick, N.J., 1992.

Horsman, Reginald. *Race and Manifest Destiny: The Origins of American Racial Anglo-Saxonism.* Cambridge, Mass., 1981.

Hunt, Michael H. *Ideology and U.S. Foreign Policy.* New Haven, Conn., 1987.

Johnson, Loch K. *A Season of Inquiry: The Senate Intelligence Investigation.* Lexington, Ky., 1985.

Kirkpatrick, Jeane. "Dictatorships and Double Standards." *Commentary* (November 1979): 34–45.

———. "U.S. Security and Latin America." *Commentary* (January 1981): 29–40.

Latham, Michael E. *Modernization as Ideology: American Social Science and "Nation Building" in the Kennedy Era.* Chapel Hill, N.C., 2000.

Maddox, Thomas R. "Red Fascism, Brown Bolshevism: The American Image of Totalitarianism in the 1930s." *Historian* 40 (November 1977): 85–103.

Park, James William. *Latin American Underdevelopment: A History of Perspectives in the United States, 1870–1965.* Baton Rouge, La., 1995.

Pipes, Daniel, and Adam Garfinkle, eds. *Friendly Tyrants: An American Dilemma.* New York, 1991.

Ridge, Martin, ed. *Frederick Jackson Turner: Wisconsin's Historian of the Frontier.* Madison, Wis., 1986.

Rostow, W. W. *The Stages of Economic Growth: A Non-Communist Manifesto.* 3d ed., New York, 1990.

Schlesinger, Arthur M., Jr. *A Thousand Days: John F. Kennedy in the White House.* Boston, 1965.

Schmitz, David F. *Thank God They're On Our Side: The United States and Right-Wing Dictatorships, 1921–1965.* Chapel Hill, N.C., 1999.

Skotheim, Robert A. *Totalitarianism and American Social Thought.* New York, 1971.

Smith, Daniel M. "Authoritarianism and American Policy Makers in Two World Wars." *Pacific Historical Review* 43 (August 1974): 303–323.

Smith, Tony. *America's Mission: The United States and the Worldwide Struggle for Democracy in the Twentieth Century.* Princeton, N.J., 1994.

Stephanson, Anders. *Manifest Destiny: American Expansionism and the Empire of Right.* New York, 1995.

See also CONTAINMENT; DEVELOPMENT DOCTRINE AND MODERNIZATION THEORY; HUMAN RIGHTS; RACE AND ETHNICITY; RECOGNITION; SELF-DETERMINATION.

DISSENT IN WARS

Russell F. Weigley and David S. Patterson

"These men are not being supported as we were supported in World War I." So the Vietnam War appeared in contrast to the crusade of 1917–1918 to a speaker addressing a reunion of the First Infantry Division in 1969 and reported by the military journalist Ward Just. American military men who fought in Vietnam widely believed that wartime dissent of unprecedented intensity uniquely denied them the support of their compatriots at home. Wartime dissent might never have become a lengthy subject had not the Vietnam War raised the issue to unaccustomed prominence and created a wider debate, ranging well beyond disgruntled military men, over the extent to which the threat of dissent against subsequent use of force might cripple American foreign policy. General Maxwell D. Taylor, former chairman of the Joint Chiefs of Staff and ambassador to South Vietnam, wrote in *Swords and Plowshares* (1972): "As I see the lesson, it is that our leaders of the future are faced with a dilemma which raises questions as to the continued feasibility of a limited war option for future presidents faced with a compelling need to use military force in support of a national interest."

Yet the intensity of dissent during the Vietnam War was not so unprecedented as many critics of homefront attitudes thought. An exceptionally perspicacious military man of an earlier generation, General George C. Marshall, the army chief of staff during World War II, said that the strategic planning for that supposedly popular war had to seek success in short order, because "a democracy cannot fight a Seven Years' War." More than those who saw uniqueness in the dissent that marked the Vietnam War, Marshall probably approached the heart of the issue of dissent in any democratic, and particularly American, war: because democratic public opinion is impatient, popular support of a war depends on the war not dragging on indefinitely. If not simply a short war, to minimize dissent a war should be distinguished by continuous visible progress toward achieving popularly understood and approved goals.

In a 1973 study of dissent during the Korean and Vietnam wars, as reflected in public opinion polls, John E. Mueller similarly concluded in more precise fashion that dissent against war tends to increase with the duration of the war, or more specifically, that it can be expressed by the logarithm of the duration of the war and the casualties of the war. Thus, Mueller found that despite the apparent evidence afforded by the uncommon noisiness of dissent against the Vietnam War, the Korean War received less public support than the Vietnam War—until the latter conflict surpassed it both in duration and in its toll of American casualties.

To be sure, Mueller did not have available to him public opinion polls concerning earlier prolonged wars, and both the Korean and the Vietnam wars differed from many earlier American wars in that they failed to produce results generally recognizable as victory for the American armed forces and the defeat of the enemy. The historian may suspect that if polls such as those cited by Mueller had been taken during the American Civil War, they would show that the war was more popular in the North in November 1864, at the time of Abraham Lincoln's second election to the presidency, than earlier in the same year, in May 1864, when Lieutenant General Ulysses S. Grant was just beginning his slugging campaign in the Wilderness and at Spotsylvania—despite the accumulation of weary months and horrifying casualties in the interval. The intervening months brought morale-building military victories, and especially the triumphs of Mobile Bay, Atlanta, and Cedar Creek not long before the presidential election. Korea and Vietnam never afforded any such satisfying battlefield successes. The historian therefore would suggest that the effects of time and casualties on the popularity of a war might be at least partially offset by military victories, and especially by military progress toward some readily comprehended goal—for example, the destruction of the enemy armed forces pursued by Grant and his lieutenants in 1864.

Still, while in the end dissent in the North during the American Civil War was largely drowned out by a tide of military victories, until nearly the end the prosecution of the Civil War was nevertheless plagued by more internal opposition than was the later waging of World War II. It was easier to rally public support for retaliation against the Japanese after the attack on Pearl Harbor and for suppression of Adolf Hitler than to bind domestic political dissidents to the Union with the bayonet. The roots of opposition to a war can be found in the duration of the war, its casualties, and its measure of military success. But one cannot ignore the commonsense view that the war's political aims and circumstances have much to do with its popularity. Of course, the generation and expression of dissent even in wars of politically controversial origin are handicapped, because wars tend to appear as national crises so dramatically overpowering that they inherently require the whole nation to rally around the national standard.

Nevertheless, Mueller's analyses of recent wars and national emergencies tend to indicate—and the longer historical view would seem to confirm—that such a rally-round-the-flag phenomenon is fleeting. Even in the midst of wars, "politics as usual" soon tends to resume. The resumption of habitual political battles can then readily fuel dissent, especially because in the development of American partisan politics it has required a considerable accumulation of experience, and a considerable sophistication for partisan rivals of wartime administrations and congresses to learn to disentangle opposition to the incumbent political party from opposition to the war, and the process of disentanglement has never been complete. And as common sense would have it, the more politically controversial the origins of the war, the greater is likely to be the intensity of wartime dissent, especially if the political controversy involves conscientious opposition to the morality of the war, as in the Mexican and Vietnam wars.

Moreover, once initial patriotic enthusiasm subsides, the dissent fueled by partisan rivalries and the circumstances of the origins of a war can draw upon a still more fundamental source of restiveness, the traditional American hostility toward the armed forces and a traditional ambivalence, at the least, toward the very institution of war.

Once these persistent sources of dissent against war interact in wartime with the hardships, inconveniences, and simple nuisances inevitably attendant upon any war, and with the more or less severe political controversies of any war, the rise and expression of dissent become so likely, and in most wars have become troublesome enough, that wartime administrations have been perennially tempted to suppress dissent by the use of law and armed force, diluting the constitutional guarantees of free expression of dissent on the plea that the national crisis demands it. Supporters of wars have also been tempted to use informal extralegal means to eliminate dissent. Thus the record of such temptation and of consequent actions against dissent forms part of the history of dissent in American wars, although on the whole the ability of administrations and populace to resist these temptations is fairly heartening to believers in the American constitutional system.

THE REVOLUTIONARY WAR

Despite the quotation from General Marshall, the United States did manage to fight and survive a "Seven Years' War" at the very outset of national existence, the revolutionary war. It is possible that the revolutionary war was exceptional because it was so directly and unequivocally a war for national survival, with independence itself at stake. Modern nationalism is such a strong force that its survival may transcend ordinary rules concerning the depth of democratic support for war. It is at least as likely, however, that the safe emergence of the United States from the Revolution was largely a matter of fortunate historical accident.

Among British and Loyalist leaders there had developed a widespread impression by 1780, which lasted until October 1781, that for them the War of the American Revolution was almost won. In the southern colonies, 1780 witnessed the virtual completion of the reconquest of Georgia and South Carolina, and the following year Lieutenant General Charles Cornwallis pursued the remnant of the revolutionary forces in the area all the way northward across North Carolina and planted the royal standard in that province. The remaining resistance south of Virginia, although highly and perplexingly troublesome, was mainly of the irregular sort that later generations would call guerrilla warfare. Farther north, at British headquarters in New York, General Henry Clinton received consistently optimistic reports from his agents throughout the Middle Colonies. Typical was the conclusion of the prominent New Yorker William Smith that "the Rebels were a minority who governed by the army and that this [the revolutionary army] reduced, the Loyalists would overturn the usurpation." If it was the sole remaining prop supporting rebellion, the rebel army itself appeared well on the way to collapse. There had been a mutiny in the Massachusetts line as early as the beginning of 1780; in the Connecticut line in May 1780; in the large and critical Pennsylvania line at the beginning of 1781; and in the New Jersey line in response to the Pennsylvania mutiny. During this period General George Washington, the commander of the Continental army, repeatedly warned Congress that his army was on the verge of dissolution—from loss of supplies, pay, popular support, and internal morale. If Washington felt obliged to put on a show of pessimism in order to try to wring maximum assistance from a frugal Congress, accounts from other sources inside his army agreed with those of Clinton's informers that his exaggerations were small and that his army might collapse under the slightest British pressure, or simply expire. "Why need I run into the detail," Washington wrote John Laurens on 9 April 1781, "when it may be declared in a word that we are at the end of our tether, and that now or never our deliverance must come."

Deliverance, of course, came. Clinton did not muster the energy or the self-confidence to pursue his opportunities with even the slightest vigor; he was thinking instead of how to woo back to British allegiance the faltering revolutionaries without in the process antagonizing Loyalists who were crying for condign punishment of the rebels as a reward for their own loyalty—that is, the very flagging of the Revolution paradoxically contributed to Clinton's perplexities and thus to his irresolution. Meanwhile, Lord Cornwallis, the other principal British military commander in America and Clinton's nominal subordinate in the South, lapsed into the opposite kind of bad generalship—recklessness. Cornwallis presented the revolutionary army with the opportunity to join forces with the French navy in a manner that entrapped him at Yorktown in October 1781. Although Cornwallis's blunders were egregious, Washington and his French allies were able to capitalize upon them on account of a

most remarkable run of good fortune in weather and timing, to say nothing of what was to prove the only major French naval success against a British fleet in the whole second Hundred Years' War. The surrender of Cornwallis has no suggestion of inevitability about it but appears rather as historical accident. The United Kingdom in 1781 was no democracy, but the British government was far enough from a despotism and representative enough that it was having its own troubles in sustaining the war. The setback at Yorktown proved sufficient to push Britain into the hands of the peacemakers. Until Yorktown the American revolutionary cause had been in a much more perilous condition than the British cause, and except for the supreme good fortune of Yorktown it was the American cause that had been more likely to founder.

Dissent in the revolutionary war is otherwise difficult to measure on any scale similar to those applicable to later wars, when there was an established American government from which to dissent and more or less established channels of dissent. During the Revolution the prosecutors of the war on the side of the United States were themselves the dissenters from the accustomed American order of politics. The war was more confusedly an American civil war than the later war of 1861–1865, in which the antagonists were more clearly marked off from each other by geographical lines. Just as the revolutionary war was both a war for independence from Great Britain and a revolution seeking social change at home, so both thrusts of the war provoked their own sets of dissenters, with some who otherwise supported independence, for example, dropping out when the struggle set a course toward social revolution. In Pennsylvania, where the revolutionary movement most drastically changed the previous political order with the radically democratic Constitution of 1776, the sense of the revolutionaries that they must use the force of their new system of laws to compel the laggard to fall into their procession became most desperate, and it precipitated the most troublesome controversy in any province over test oaths of loyalty to the new regime. But everywhere, the revolutionary governments felt obliged to curb dissent with legal penalties of confiscation of property and political ostracism. Furthermore, the patterns of dissent were not easily predictable; loyalty oaths excited most controversy in Pennsylvania, where the Revolution became most radical, but dissent against the Revolution took its most ambitious military form—and apart from the incursions of the British army required the nearest approximation of full-blown military campaigns to repress it—in the Carolinas, where the movement toward independence changed little in the previous social and political order. The sources of dissent and its manifestations were at least as varied as the motives that separately guided each colony into statehood.

THE QUASI-WAR AND THE WAR OF 1812

After the American Revolution, dissent in the next war presents a special case; the war did not last long enough, or amount to enough as a military operation accompanied by casualties, for the effects of duration to have much play, but in its origins the war was perhaps the most politically controversial in the history of the country. It was the Quasi-War with France of 1797–1800. With the American political system still in process of formation, and partisan political opposition still widely regarded as illegitimate, it was hardly more a war against France, however, than a war conducted by the Federalists, who controlled the executive branch and Congress, against the Jeffersonian Republican opposition. French depredations against American maritime commerce and the XYZ Affair precipitated naval conflict with the French. Yet the causes of the war never ran deep enough to generate even a brief initial enthusiasm—despite the XYZ Affair—in more than a few localities. Moreover, the Federalists used the war to push through Congress authorizations of substantial increases in the army, although President John Adams remarked that as for an enemy army for this force to fight, "At present there is no more prospect of seeing a French army here than there is in Heaven." Stephen G. Kurtz's conclusion is that the new army, whose officers were carefully screened to assure their Federalist partisanship, was to be the tangible instrument for suppressing Jeffersonianism—a political army to cow the opposition. Against this threat to the antimilitary tradition and against the Quasi-War that nourished the threat, dissent became so sharp that Kurtz also concludes that fear and resentment of the political army ranked with the notorious Alien and Sedition Acts as a cause of disaffection from the Federalists and thus of the Republican "revolution" in the election of 1800.

Historians can perceive a deeper stream of causation leading to the War of 1812 than to the Quasi-War. In 1812 there was a fuller, more widespread patriotic spirit generated by the conviction that longstanding British refusal to grant the United States the rights of independent nationhood at sea represented a threat to the very independence of the Republic. Nevertheless, to the Federalists, now reduced to the role of opposition, the War of 1812 appeared as much a partisan war conceived for the political benefit of the rival party and for the ruination of themselves as the Quasi-War had seemed to the Republicans. By 1812 the Federalist Party had become a sectional party; except for enclaves of strength in the Carolinas, Philadelphia, and New York City, it was a New England party, and its interests and those of New England had come to seem indistinguishable. For commercial New England, the War of 1812 was the hideous culmination of a perverse Republican policy of countering British and French depredations against maritime commerce by terminating American overseas commerce altogether. For New England, no cause of the old revolution had loomed larger than the Boston Port Act; now the Republican strangulation, not just of Boston's but of all New England's commerce, naturally suggested a Boston Port Act much magnified. Thus, if the Boston Port Act had offered just cause for withdrawing from the British Empire despite all the benefits and ties of loyalty that the empire represented, then some New England Federalists saw Republican restrictions upon commerce as cause for seceding from the American Union. Republican trade restrictions and the ensuing war seemed all the more perverse to the Federalists because unlike the Republicans, the Federalists saw Great Britain as the defender of all people's rights against a revolutionary France whose excesses had descended into Napoleonic tyranny, while the Republicans responded to both French and British maritime depredations with an increasingly anti-British policy leading at last to a war whose only beneficiary was likely to be Napoleon.

The vote of the New England members of the House of Representatives, except for frontier Vermont, on the war resolution of 4 June 1812, was nineteen against war, nine for, and three not voting—surely a clear alignment against the war, although not nearly so one-sided as some accounts might suggest. Connecticut and Massachusetts soon rejected federal calls for their militia, and Rhode Island and New Hampshire supplied only a handful of militiamen for federal service in 1812. Federalist Governor Caleb Strong of Massachusetts proclaimed a fast day to mourn a war "against the nation from which we are descended," and New England Federalist leaders generally made no secret of their displeasure with the war. Nevertheless, New England's passive dissent threatened to turn into active resistance to the Republican administration only when the badly conceived war proved to be badly fought as well. Then twenty-six New England Federalists met in late 1814 at the Hartford Convention, "to protest," in the words of James M. Banner, Jr., "against the inept Republican management of the war with Great Britain and the whole system of Republican administration since Jefferson's election . . . to force the federal government to provide defensive help."

Early in the conflict, New England profited from it. Hoping to encourage New England's disaffection, Great Britain at first did not apply its naval blockade of the United States to New England. In the spring of 1814, however, with Napoleon defeated and Great Britain free to devote major military attentions to the American war, the British decided that making New England bear some of the brunt of the conflict would be a more productive encouragement to dissent. On 31 May 1814 the blockade was extended to the whole United States coast. Worse, British invasion of New England followed. In July an expedition from Halifax, Nova Scotia, took Eastport in the District of Maine; by early September, Lieutenant General John Sherbrooke had entered the Penobscot, taken possession of the whole Maine coast east of that river, and claimed the coast as far as New Brunswick. Towns around Cape Cod were raided, and under British guns Nantucket declared its neutrality. What brought the Hartford Convention movement to a head, according to established scholarship, was the inability of the government in Washington to provide respectable defense against these British attacks. The Federalist state governments and the Republican federal government still quarreled over who was to control the militia, the New England states insisting that in the crisis they must retain command of their militia for their own defense but that the federal government should pay the costs of defense. When early in 1815 Congress authorized compensation of state forces by the federal government, it met what Banner calls the Federalists' "central demand"; Harrison Gray Otis, perhaps the most influential Massachusetts Federalist, thought that passage of such an act earlier would have forestalled the Hartford Convention altogether.

This issue of defense was certainly more central to the Hartford Convention than the plots of secession that have sometimes been charged against the convention. The convention was engineered by the moderate leadership of the New England Federalist Party, of whom Otis was one example and George Cabot, the president of the convention, another, in order to press for effective action for defense and against Republican mismanagement. At the same time New England Federalists kept the political initiative in their section in their own hands—those of pragmatic politicians—and out of the hands of moralists, often led by the clergy, who increasingly couched their opposition to the Republicans in absolutist moral terms and were in fact likely to move toward extreme action, even including disruption of the Union. A convention of party leaders was an affair the pragmatists could control, and they did, confining the Hartford Convention to resolutions on behalf of federal support for state self-defense and proposals for constitutional amendments to pare the power of the Republican dynasty in Washington. This outcome fulfilled George Cabot's prediction that he could tell exactly what the convention would produce, namely, "a great pamphlet."

A delegation including Otis carried the Hartford resolutions to Washington, leaving Boston just after they learned of Andrew Jackson's victory at the Battle of New Orleans and arriving in the capital just in time for the celebrations of the Treaty of Ghent that ended the war in February 1815. Holding the convention and passing its resolutions were probably necessary to divert the New England extremists and maintain, for the time being, a viable Federalist Party in New England. But enough secessionist overtones were imputed to the Hartford Convention that Federalism was forever damned elsewhere for disloyalty in time of war.

THE MEXICAN WAR

The conventional wisdom surrounding what happened at the Hartford Convention consequently came to be that failure to support a war effort is likely to mean the death of a political party. Thus, in 1846–1848, when the Whig Party found itself opposed to the Mexican War, the party pragmatists argued that although they might challenge the policy of going to war, they must not fail to vote for funds and supplies to support the army that was fighting it. A rival faction of Conscience

Whigs nevertheless took the logical and principled position that if the war was wrong, supporting the fighting of it was also wrong, and that therefore opposition must be thoroughgoing at whatever risk to party fortunes. The resulting divisions within the Whig Party very nearly produced the fatal effect that the pragmatists hoped to avoid.

During the Mexican War the sources of Whig dissent were partially the same as those of Federalist dissent during the War of 1812. In both instances, New England was the stronghold of dissent, although opposition spread more widely from 1846 to 1848. In both instances, the grievances of New England against the administration in Washington included the administration's policies of westward territorial expansion, which implied a permanent diminution of New England's political power. In the Mexican War, of course, westward territorial expansion was immediately at issue. In both instances, fear of the diminution of New England's power sprang not only from direct political interests but from distaste for the whole southern and western economic and cultural system that the dissidents saw represented in the administration in Washington and in the administration's war. During the Mexican War such distaste for southern and western values was reinforced by the rise to prominence of the slavery issue, which had been merely a cloud on the horizon—although already perceptible—during the War of 1812. In August 1846 the Wilmot Proviso tied the slavery issue inextricably to the issues of the Mexican War by proposing to forbid slavery in any territory to be acquired from Mexico. In both instances, opposition to the war could draw upon and be reinforced by the self-conscious Christianity of New England tradition. New England dissent from the War of 1812 had in fact led to the founding of peace societies, which later helped mobilize opposition to the Mexican War.

In the 1840s the Christian antiwar tradition was readily mobilized against a conflict even more iniquitous than the War of 1812, in that the Mexican War could well be regarded—and is still regarded by some historians—as an act of aggression by the strong United States against weak Mexico. The mobilization of this Christian antiwar tradition in its New England centers, at a time when New England happened also to be experiencing its first great literary renaissance, gave an unprecedented literary aspect to dissent against the Mexican War, as illustrated by James Russell Lowell's *The Bigelow Papers* (1848) and Henry David Thoreau's essay "Civil Disobedience" (1849).

For all that, organized dissent against the Mexican War never attained a climax as notable, albeit ambiguous, as the Hartford Convention. The military campaigns of the war proved to be short and unvaryingly successful, which in turn proved an insurmountable handicap to effective dissent. Military success in fact diverted the pragmatic, political Whigs from the issue of whether to vote supplies to the more expedient issue of how to capitalize on the military fame of the victorious generals, Zachary Taylor and Winfield Scott, who chanced also to be Whigs.

Nevertheless, opposition to the Mexican War tended to grow more intense the longer the war lasted. When the conflict began in May 1846, only two members of the Senate and fourteen members of the House of Representatives voted against the bill, declaring that war existed "by the act of the Republic of Mexico." Congress authorized the president to call volunteers and appropriated $10 million for the conduct of the war. By the time the Thirtieth Congress assembled for its first session in December 1847, however, to be greeted by President James K. Polk's message that no peace had yet been obtained and there was no immediate prospect of one, Congress appeared much less ready to vote for more men and money, and certainly the Whigs were more determined to pin upon Polk and the Democrats responsibility for a war begun, as they interpreted it, not by Mexico but by American aggression. Furthermore, the Whigs had captured at least nominal control of the House, although their own divisions made their election of Robert C. Winthrop of Massachusetts as Speaker a very near thing, because the most dedicated Conscience Whigs refused to support Winthrop as too willing to sustain the war. The House then defeated a resolution declaring the war just and necessary. Opposition to slavery inevitably still influenced much of the opposition to the war, but even a southern Whig, Alexander H. Stephens of Georgia, could say, "The principle of waging war against a neighboring people to compel them to sell their country is not only dishonorable, but disgraceful and infamous." Playing upon the fact that hostilities had begun when Mexican troops attacked Taylor's forces after they had crossed south of the Nueces River, which Mexico claimed as the southern boundary of Texas, Representative Abraham Lincoln of Illinois introduced his "spot" resolutions calling on the president to say candidly whether the spot where the war began was Mexican or American soil.

Some powerful Democrats, too, had grown outspokenly critical—the elderly Albert Gallatin, who called it a war of subjugation; Thomas Hart Benton; even John C. Calhoun, who feared the war was becoming one for the conquest of central Mexico, which would bring into the Union a racially inferior people incapable of free government. Fortunately for the president, in the midst of congressional debate there arrived the Treaty of Guadalupe Hidalgo (1848), negotiated in Mexico by Nicholas P. Trist, which ended the war with the annexation of Texas confirmed and California and New Mexico added to the United States, in exchange for a payment of $15 million and the assumption by the United States of American claims against Mexico. Although Polk had earlier repudiated Trist as his negotiator, and although some Democrats thought Trist's terms too generous toward Mexico, Polk submitted the treaty for ratification lest the increasingly noisy dissent prove able to paralyze him and make a good treaty henceforth impossible. Under public pressure to end the war as swiftly as could be done, the Senate ratified the treaty.

The opposition Whigs became the immediate political beneficiaries of discontent with the war. Some Conscience Whigs split off from the party to join with various northern Democratic factions disgruntled over the pro-Southern tendencies of all Polk's policies and to form the Free-Soil Party for the election of 1848; but this third party hurt the Democrats more than the Whigs. Choosing Zachary Taylor as their presidential nominee, the Whigs carried the White House. The expedient course of the party pragmatists in supporting war measures if not the war itself apparently had accomplished far more than merely warding off the fate of the Federalists. But the Whig success of 1848 was deceptive. Wartime strains upon the relations between Conscience Whigs and pragmatists had so weakened the party that it could not survive another bout with the slavery issue. The slavery crisis of 1850 broke open the cracks imposed on the party structure by the war and destroyed the party.

THE CIVIL WAR

The foregoing events obviously threw into question the conventional wisdom derived from the War of 1812 about what opposition to both war measures and war alike would do to an opposition party. Discarding the expediential course of the Whigs in the Mexican War, then, most of the Democratic Party leadership in the role of opposition to the new Republican Party during the Civil War chose to revert to a relatively uncomplicated kind of dissent. In general, its opposition to the Republican administration of Lincoln and to the Republican Congress in their conduct of the war was not disentangled from opposition to the war itself.

Democratic policy might have been different if the great Democratic paladin of the Middle West, Stephen A. Douglas, had not died almost at the outset, on 3 June 1861. Douglas had said that "The shortest way to peace is the most stupendous and unanimous preparation for war." But it would have been difficult for Douglas to hold his party to such a policy. The style of American politics at mid-nineteenth century was one of rough-and-tumble conflict, with the business of the opposition regarded as straightforward opposition to virtually everything the party in power stood for. In this context the maneuverings of the Whigs during the Mexican War could more readily be perceived as having been too subtle and devious by far. Furthermore, the war at hand was a civil war, and the Democratic Party and politicians of the North had long been the comrades and allies of the leaders of the Confederacy, against which the federal government was now contending. It was too much to expect a prompt, wholehearted embrace of old political enemies in common cause against old friends. This matter was especially crucial; historical studies of the Copperhead dissent that was to develop have attempted to tie it to various economic and social interests—assuming, for example, that poor agriculturalists might have objected to the business alliances of the Republicans. But the one consistent gauge of any district's tendency toward Copperheadism seems to have been the Southern ties of segments of its population.

Aggravating the latter dissent, and displeasing others who initially supported the war, as hostilities continued Republican policy came to include emancipation of the slaves. Therefore the issues of race and slavery again became intermingled with dissent in war, and the Democrats became the voice for all of white America's deep fears of racial equality, toward which Republican war policies could be interpreted as tending.

Finally, American parties, although diverse coalitions, were by no means without ideology. The ideology of the Democratic Party was well summed up in its favorite wartime watchword, "The Union as it was, the Constitution as it is."

This maxim rightly implied that the methods taken by the Lincoln administration to prosecute the war—centralizing methods threatening to transform the old loose federation of states into a consolidated nation—seemed to many Democrats so subversive of a proper Union and the true Constitution that a victory for Lincoln's Union would be scarcely more appetizing than the independence of the Confederacy.

The Democratic position was so close to a plague-on-both-your-houses attitude that it is not surprising that under the tensions of civil war, Republicans were likely to suspect nearly the whole Democratic leadership of Copperheadism. Furthermore, after Douglas's death the core of the Democratic membership in the House, thirty-six Representatives, subscribed to a pact of party unity conceived and drawn by Representative Clement L. Vallandigham of Ohio, who was candidly an obstructionist. After the summer of 1861, the Democratic congressional delegations offered much more nagging of the administration and parliamentary foot-dragging than willingness to sustain the war. Most Democratic leaders would have protested sincerely that they were not disloyal to the Union—the old Union. Much recent scholarship has been at pains to deny that even the leaders of the Copperhead faction among the Democrats were disloyal to the Union. But the insistence of these Peace Democrats that the only Union worth preserving was the old noncentralized Union makes this a distinction of limited practical application.

By the fall elections of 1862, the prolonged war and the disappointingly few victories—none in the crucial eastern theater—were reflected in the Democratic gains in the congressional and state elections. By that time too, the Emancipation Proclamation added abolition to the Union war aims and aggravated discontent with Lincoln's leadership. In the State of New York the Democrats elected Horatio Seymour to the governorship. During his campaign Seymour had called emancipation "a proposal for the butchery of women and children, scenes of lust and rapine, and of arson and murder." As governor he employed a states' rights rhetoric reminiscent of Jefferson Davis, and his scornful opposition to conscription contributed to the New York City draft riots of July 1863. In the Midwest the Republican governors of Indiana and Illinois believed that the newly elected Democratic majorities in their legislatures were in league with an empire of secret societies planning a coup d'état

to ensure the victory of the Confederacy. The governors collected evidence that Indiana alone had 125,000 members enrolled in antiwar secret societies and that in Illinois 300 secret lodges met every Tuesday night. The Confederate government believed these and similar reports and sent agents to cooperate with the secret societies. Thus can a fratricidal war generate hysteria, because the threat of the secret societies was a chimera. No substantial danger ever emerged from their alleged plotting. The Confederate agents who made contact with them found the Copperhead malcontents unwilling to take risks or action, and no coup d'état ever had a chance of success because the overwhelming bulk of Northern sentiment—including that of the rank-and-file Democrats who continued to serve in or send their sons and brothers into the Union armies—remained determined to restore the Union by war, war-weariness notwithstanding.

This fact proved fatal to the Democratic Party's immediate antiwar policies and highly injurious to the party for many years to come. By the presidential election of 1864, the Democratic Party formed its ranks for the campaign around the principles that while the Union ought to be restored, Lincoln's centralizing war was the wrong way to restore it, and that in addition to being wrong the war was a practical failure. The Democratic platform of 1864 called for a cessation of hostilities "to the end that at the earliest possible moment peace may be restored on the basis of the Federal Union of the States." The assumption that peace could come first and be followed by restoration of the Union was one that was not supported in any of the attitudes of the Confederate leaders. Furthermore, to adopt the assumption would imply that all the sacrifices accepted thus far to seek reunion through war had been needless. Northern voters were not willing to concede that they had sustained so large an error so long, and at so high a price. In late August, Lincoln himself believed that war-weariness would defeat his bid for reelection, but the best remedy for war-weariness, a succession of military victories, intervened. On 5 November the electorate chose Lincoln for a second term by a margin of 55 percent, a respectable victory by the standards of American politics.

The Confederacy had its own problems of war-weariness and dissent. There were many contributing factors, but above all, Southern support for the war and for the Confederacy crumbled away as the South lost the battles. In contrast,

Northern support for the war solidified itself as the North at last won battle after battle. For partisan politics the consequence of this latter fact was that on 25 February 1865 *Harper's Weekly* could without much exaggeration proclaim: "We are at the end of parties." The Democratic Party had so identified itself with the idea of the war as a failure as well as a wrong that the Union victory left the party appearing impossibly myopic. So much had the Democratic leadership identified itself with opposition to the Civil War that during the war large numbers of War Democrats had felt obliged to join the Republican Party. So much had the Republican Party identified itself with the Union and the war that victory in the war represented such a complete vindication of the party that the memory of the war would go far to assure Republican supremacy in Northern politics for a generation. Heeding the implied warning, in no subsequent war has a major party been willing to risk joining its fortunes with those of dissent.

THE SPANISH-AMERICAN WAR AND THE FILIPINO INSURRECTION

In the small wars between 1865 and 1917, dissent would not have been likely to assume proportions highly troublesome for the administrations waging the wars even without such an object lesson. The wars with the Indians had become too remote from the interests of most voters, especially because they could be fought by a small professional army with a large enrollment of immigrants. Any given uprising and campaign was too brief to allow dissent to accumulate, with intervals of peace allaying such public concern as it developed. An Indian rights movement did generate growing support among eastern philanthropists, intellectuals, and some religious denominations, but never on a scale to seriously slow down the military conquest of the Plains tribes. The constraints both upon the army and upon the government's Indian policy, causing occasional spasms of congressional or executive peacemaking efforts, were more largely those of fiscal economy than of philanthropic concern.

Similarly, the war with Spain was brief enough and inexpensive enough in casualties that it was over before the customary initial patriotic enthusiasm had dissipated. Criticisms of the war effort came afterward and concerned the conduct of the war more than the war itself. The Filipino insurrection, the name most often applied to the Filipino-American War (1899–1902), which followed from the consequences of the Spanish-American War, was more unpleasant in every sense. It raised up anew the moral outcry against American expansionism at the expense of weaker peoples, which had agitated the opponents of the Mexican War. Suppressing the insurrection was a process prolonged enough (two and one-half years for the main insurrection on Luzon alone) and costly enough in casualties that it gave play to two of the principal wellsprings of dissent in war. Furthermore, the fighting involved guerrilla warfare in a difficult tropical climate, a type of combat that the European-style American army, attuned to European-style regularized war, has consistently found distasteful since its first major exposure to it in the Seminole Wars of 1816–1818 and 1835–1842. This distaste has also been shared by the society that supports the army. The strains imposed upon the army's patience by such irregular warfare in turn provoked acts of terrorism and atrocities against the Filipinos that still further exacerbated the moral dissent at home.

Nevertheless, dissent against the suppression of the Filipino insurrection never became a major political force. The outcry against this war, like the more general anti-imperialist movement of which it was a part, was the Indian rights movement writ somewhat larger. It was a movement centering in the eastern, or at least urban, aristocratic, and upper-middle-class intellectual and literary communities, with only occasional outposts in larger constituencies, such as Samuel Gompers in the labor movement; but it had no mass support. The inclusion of distinguished literary and academic figures gave it a high visibility, disproportionate to its strength. In the later era of public opinion polls, the evidence was to suggest—and more impressionistic evidence suggests it was already true—that except during a large-scale war touching numerous lives, foreign policy tends to be too remote from the concerns of most citizens and voters (again resembling the later Indian wars) for the "foreign policy public" to be very large. The opponents of imperialism and of the war in the Philippines were in this light the representatives of a schism within the elite segment of the population concerned with foreign policy that had propelled the nation into the Spanish-American War and overseas expansionism in the first place. The misgivings within that elite were severe enough to bring American territorial expansion overseas to an abrupt halt, with the elite foreign policy public in general soon reverting to its more traditional opposition to that kind of expansionism. Meanwhile, although the opposition party (still the Democrats) flirted with anti-imperialism, the party pursued at most an ambivalent course and after its Civil War experience did not again embrace outright dissent against the war. Dissent remained anything but a mass movement. Although it seemed prolonged at the time, the suppression of the major part of the Filipino insurrection within three years made the affair brief by contrast with the later Vietnam War, with the forces involved and the American casualties also much smaller.

THE WORLD WARS

The unhappy experience of the Democratic Party during the Civil War was surely not the only cause of the reluctance of major parties to embrace dissent in subsequent wars. The discipline and cohesion that modern industrial societies impose upon their populations, in contrast to less-centralized and more loosely organized agricultural societies, had already helped maintain the united front of the North during the Civil War, and that discipline of industrialism had grown immensely stronger by the time of the great world wars of the twentieth century. In World War I, the unity of the populace of every major power in support of nationalist war and patient endurance of the populace through prolonged war confounded the expectations of numerous prophets who had forecast that modern wars would be so costly that they could last only a few months. By World War II the public discipline of the great powers had become even more impressive. Democratic America certainly was no exception to this pattern; if anything, it was the democracies that displayed the greatest social cohesion. In both world wars, dissent in the United States was confined to minuscule fringe groups, mainly of socialists, radical leftists, and pacifists, and conscription focused far more attention upon the conscientious objector than it had done in the Civil War. This change occurred not only because the government and the public demonstrated increasing sensitivity to the demands of the pacifist conscience, but also because the conscientious objector was much more nearly alone as a dissenter than he had been in 1861–1865.

Before the entrance of the United States into World War I on 6 April 1917, it is true, there had been significant dissent over the course in foreign policy that proved to be leading to war, most conspicuous among the protesters being the Progressive elements of President Woodrow Wilson's own governing coalition. Although after the war the intractable realities of international politics were to cause among this coalition a speedy disillusionment with support for the war, nevertheless from Wilson's war message onward throughout the war itself, all but a small fraction of this group were enthralled by the president's promise that the fight was for a reformation of the whole world, and they joined ranks behind the war effort. Not surprisingly, however, the considerable dissent that had surrounded Wilson's foreign policy before the war contributed to an expectation that there would be more dissent during the war than actually materialized. This expectation in turn contributed to passage of stringent espionage and sedition acts seeking among other things to suppress any utterances that might discourage recruiting or the united prosecution of the war. These acts were enforced not only by an enlarged body of federal investigative agents but also by the federally sponsored American Protective League of private citizens. Abetted thus by what amounted to vigilantes, attacks upon civil liberties and particularly upon free speech became absurdly disproportionate to a mere trickle of dissent. No cases involving wartime suppression of dissent reached the Supreme Court until after the war. Then Justice Oliver Wendell Holmes's characterization of *Abrams* v. *United States* (1919) as involving merely a silly leaflet by an unknown man came close to what is likely to be the historian's view of all the targets of the espionage laws; but in *Abrams*, Holmes spoke for the minority of the court, and he himself had seen "a clear and present danger" in the earlier and not much different *Schenck* case (1919).

A greater sophistication and tolerance marked the government's attitude toward dissent in World War II—always excepting the relocation of more than 100,000 Japanese from the Pacific Coast. Tolerance could well be afforded. Although American entry into World War II was also preceded by much debate over the nation's course in foreign policy, the Japanese attack on Pearl Harbor assured that from the beginning of direct American participation there would be still less dissent than there had been in 1917–1918. Although such a leading Republican spokesman as Senator Robert A. Taft of Ohio suspected Franklin D. Roosevelt of exploiting the war emer-

514

gency to fix the changes of the New Deal permanently upon American institutions, he and most other Republicans permitted themselves only the most cautious criticism of the conduct of the war, which they carefully distinguished from criticism of the war itself. "Every problem," said Taft, "must be approached in a different spirit from that existing in time of peace, and Congress cannot assume to run the war"—a far cry from the attitudes even of members of Congress of Lincoln's own party during the Civil War, let alone the opposition. In World War II as in World War I, a certain amount of trouble did develop between the government and the labor movement, over labor's threats to strike to ensure itself a due share of war prosperity; but this friction can hardly be said to have involved dissent over the war. In World War II, national unity survived even though the American participation lasted nearly four years and was by American standards costly in casualties, unlike the American participation in World War I. The most evident explanation for this national unity was the nature of the enemy and of the circumstances with which the war began. But the historian seeking the sources of unity should also keep in mind that once the initial defeats were overcome, it would be hard to find a long war marked by so consistent a record of military success as favored America and surely helped sustain American morale in World War II.

THE KOREAN AND VIETNAM WARS

One of the meanings of the worldwide restlessness that marked the 1960s may well be that the notable social discipline characteristic of the populations of industrialized countries in the first century of the Industrial Age was breaking down. If so, a fundamental shift in social organization may underlie the contrast between the unity with which the United States fought the two world wars and the reversion to major dissent and internal conflict in the Korean and Vietnam wars. But more immediate explanations for the contrast readily present themselves. The most frequently voiced explanation is that the world wars fitted much better than the more recent wars the traditional American image of the nature of war. From the colonists' first struggles with the Indians, in which each side fought for the very survival of its culture, this argument goes, Americans came to regard wars as total struggles for absolute victory or defeat. The very aversion to war and the military that was so much a part of American tradition implied that when the nation went to war, it must be under the most extraordinary circumstances, and that so immoral an instrument must be employed only against such moral enormities as demanded absolute destruction. The American Civil War reinforced these preconceptions as the North fought for and achieved complete victory over the Confederacy. The argument concludes that after such a history, Americans could well sustain their unity against the Axis Powers during World War II, but they could not readily accept a limited war such as the Korean War, in which negotiations with the enemy to bargain for objectives far short of his destruction accompanied the very fighting of the war.

Allowing for some oversimplification—not every American war had been fought for the enemy's destruction, as witness the conflicts of 1846–1848 and 1898—such an explanation captures much of the American attitude toward war and goes far to account for the frustrations of the Korean War. Dissent against the Korean War also was much encouraged by a peculiarly uneasy political atmosphere troubling the United States in 1950 even before the war began. World War II had produced not a satisfactory peace but a Cold War with communism and the Soviet Union, in which the United States government held out the prospect of no more triumphant an outcome than containment. So low an expectation was itself a drastic departure from popular expectations of what America might accomplish in the world. Moreover, from 1945 to 1950 the containment policy did not even produce a satisfactory restriction of communism. China, with all its historic attractions to the American imagination, fell to the communists. Then there broke out the prolonged, costly, and militarily stalemated war in remote Korea, a war which itself could be perceived as springing from the mistakes of Harry S. Truman, whose Democratic administration had allowed China to be "lost" and had then supposedly invited communist attack on South Korea by excluding that country from America's publicly proclaimed Pacific defense perimeter.

During the Korean War the opposition party, the Republicans, did not revert to the risks of outright partisan opposition, although they came close to that in such statements as Senator Taft's denunciation of the war as "an unnecessary war . . . begun by President Truman without the slightest authority from Congress or the people." Here Taft touched also on another source of public dissatisfaction in the post-1945 limited wars, the unwillingness of presidents for various reasons to ask Congress to declare war. In such puzzling circumstances of undeclared war for limited but not clearly defined objects, it was not surprising that Republican objections came to focus on the theme that the war should either be fought to win or be terminated. This theme linked the Republicans with General Douglas MacArthur, the Far East commander whom President Truman felt obliged to relieve because of his insubordinate public calls for extension of the war in pursuit of "War's very object . . . victory."

The upshot of MacArthur's activities was the dramatic Truman-MacArthur crisis; but given the anomalies of the Korean War in terms of the American tradition of war, Korea would have provoked much the same partisan and popular discontent even if there had been nothing like that particular eruption. The concept of limited war was difficult for the sponsoring administration itself to master. The theorizing that was to make limited war a familiar conception at least to foreign policy and strategy intellectuals during the next decade still lay in the future. The Truman administration kept the Korean War limited not out of a sophisticated understanding of the conception but largely because of a misapprehension, namely that the war was a communist feint to divert American attention in preparation for a major Soviet offensive in Europe, and that, accordingly, American military resources must remain as much as possible concentrated in Europe and the United States. After China entered the war and destroyed the possibility of using the war to reunite all of Korea, the Truman administration lost its own enthusiasm for prosecuting the war, such as it had been able to summon up, and the administration became so eager for peace that it spared the enemy most military pressure as soon as it announced a disposition to negotiate. In these circumstances the negotiations dragged on inconclusively until the inauguration of a new government in Washington. With the very sponsors of the war so vague about its nature and objectives, so unskillful in its management, and so lacking in conviction that it was worth fighting, it is little wonder that public discontent with the prolonged bloodletting and the absence of clear military success made the Democrats extremely vulnerable in the elections of 1952. The electorate responded to Republican criticism of every aspect of the conduct of the war, and especially to the Republican candidate General

Dwight D. Eisenhower's promise that somehow he would end it. With the help of the East-West thaw that followed the fortuitous death of Soviet Premier Josef Stalin, President Eisenhower did end the war.

Dissent in the Vietnam War seemed to be still deeper and more widespread. Dissent certainly became a more conspicuous feature of the public scene, expressing itself in mass protest marches, demonstrations, and displays of civil disobedience. Public opinion polls indicate, however, that opposition to the Vietnam War grew stronger than opposition to the Korean War only after the Vietnam War had surpassed the Korean War in duration and in American casualties. The conspicuous public displays of dissent reflected not so much a greater opposition to the war in Vietnam than the war in Korea, but rather a shift in liberal opinion. Except for the extreme left wing, liberals had usually supported the Korean War as part of the staunch anticommunism that tended to mark their reaction to Stalinist Russia. By the 1960s, a less intransigent Soviet Union, the disruption of virtually all appearances of a monolithic international communism, and a rethinking of Cold War postulates in a more relaxed international atmosphere than that of the Truman years made liberals much less willing to support another war against a small Asian communist state than they had been in 1950–1953, especially when the Asian regime being supported by the United States was a distasteful blend of dictatorship and chaos. The conspicuousness of dissent against the Vietnam War was largely a product of the defection of many of the liberals from the foreign policy coalition of the establishment, because this group was an especially articulate one, in direct line of descent from the literary and academic dissenters against suppression of the Filipino insurrection. The conspicuousness of dissent against the Vietnam War was also much enhanced by employment of the methods of dramatizing dissent that liberals had learned from association with the civil rights movement of the late 1950s and early 1960s. Measured against the apparent volume and the new tactics of dissent, the tolerance of the government for controversy displayed an advance over World War I, despite conspiracy trials directed against dissenters and the illegal methods of attempting to discredit Daniel Ellsberg, who leaked the so-called Pentagon Papers to the press.

The liberal defection during the Vietnam War from the coalition that had supported the

Truman administration during the Korean War also reinforced the moralistic quality that dissent from the Vietnam War shared with dissent during the Mexican War and the Filipino insurrection. The liberal protest against the Vietnam War was another moral protest against an allegedly aggressive onslaught by the great and powerful United States against a weak and ill-armed adversary that was said to be seeking only the self-determination that America's own Declaration of Independence championed. Like dissenters during the Mexican War and the Filipino insurrection, liberal protesters against the Vietnam War charged that the war was betraying the highest ideals of the United States itself. Some of the more horrifying military expressions of modern technology, such as defoliation techniques and napalm, combined with an indiscriminate use of aerial and artillery bombardment by the American forces in Vietnam, gave special intensity to this moral protest.

Yet public dissent against the Vietnam War was not primarily moralistic. The conspicuous character of left-wing protest demonstrations against the war gave a misleading impression of the degree and the nature of the unpopularity of the war as compared with the Korean War. The left-wing protesters, especially the young among them, through the very tactics that made their protests conspicuous, antagonized moderate and conservative citizens. At any rate, the larger public discontent—including that discontent that most directly contributed to the electoral defeat of the original Democratic sponsors of the war and the triumph of their Republican opponents in 1968, much on the model of 1952—was not a moralistic dissent. It was again an expediential discontent that the issues of the war were puzzling in contrast to the great crusades of the world wars and that the Vietnam War was not being won.

THE GULF WAR AND AFTER

A major consequence of the U.S. military failure in the Indochina wars was the Vietnam syndrome—the anti-interventionist consensus in Congress and among the American public against sustained U.S. troop commitments in foreign crises. Unpleasant memories of the Vietnam debacle seemed to constrain American political leaders in the final quarter of the twentieth century from embarking on wars far away that might result in large numbers of U.S. casualties and still not bring quick victory.

The first two U.S. military undertakings in this period were short and occurred closer to the continental United States. Combined U.S.–Caribbean military forces landed on the island of Grenada in late October 1983 to protect lives and end the political chaos following a violent leftist takeover of the country. The "rescue mission," as President Ronald Reagan called it, quickly restored order and had mostly withdrawn by the end of the year. In December 1989 the U.S. Army decisively intervened in Panama to oust a dictator, curtail the drug traffic, and restore stability. Because both military actions were brief and successful, dissent was minimal.

Then dramatic political changes in the Soviet Union (including the collapse of the Soviet Union itself in 1991) and its European satellite states brought the end of the Cold War. The anticommunist rationale that had helped to justify U.S. military involvement in Korea, Vietnam, and elsewhere disappeared. Conflict nonetheless persisted in the international system, and the United States, now the lone superpower, found itself confronted in the last decade of the twentieth century with a series of regional, religious, and ethnic controversies abroad. Although seemingly remote from immediate U.S. interests, America's leaders felt strong responsibility to play a prominent role in these conflicts, including the prospect of military intervention.

Of the several U.S. military interventions in the 1990s, dissent against U.S. involvement in the Gulf War was the strongest. Following the invasion and takeover of neighboring Kuwait by the Iraqi dictator Saddam Hussein and his forces in the summer of 1990, George H. W. Bush's administration and the United Nations condemned the annexation and imposed economic sanctions on Iraq. When the strategy of economic strangulation failed to dislodge Hussein from Kuwait, the Bush administration mobilized a broad multinational coalition in the United Nations, which authorized military action to expel Iraq from Kuwait if its forces had not withdrawn from that country by mid-January 1991. The well-orchestrated gradual escalation of diplomatic and economic pressure on Hussein allowed time for extensive debate in the United States over the merits of prospective military involvement.

Public divisions on the Gulf War were mainly ideological, with opponents, many of whom were already committed to liberal and antiwar causes, forming coalitions composed mainly of student, religious, labor, African-American, and human rights groups. On college campuses, for example, students claimed that young people were being asked to risk their lives in a crisis for which there were no vital U.S. interests, and the war could result in the reimposition of the military draft. Referring to the U.S. interest in regaining ready access to the rich Kuwaiti oil fields, a popular slogan, especially among more radical opponents, was "No blood for oil." A smaller, but articulate opposition from the conservative right argued that the Gulf War did not directly involve U.S. interests and, objecting to the international coalition, believed the United States should pursue its national objectives unilaterally. Proponents of U.S. action meanwhile emphasized Hussein's naked aggression in Kuwait and stories of Iraqi atrocities to counter antiwar advocates' moral protest.

Following President Bush's request in early January 1991 for congressional authorization to use U.S. armed forces to force Iraqi withdrawal from Kuwait, Congress openly debated and then approved resolutions endorsing U.S. military action against Iraq. The votes were fairly close, 52–47 in the Senate and 250–183 in the House, with divisions along party, ideological, and regional lines. Even without a decisive mandate for military action, however, the war effort, once begun, received strong popular American support, ranging between 70 and 80 percent in various polls, even after the allies began heavy bombardments of Iraqi military targets, which resulted in many civilian casualties. Opinion polls also indicated that U.S. women on the whole were inclined to have somewhat stronger reservations than men about the need for bombing and a military solution. When the air strikes failed to dislodge Hussein from Kuwaiti territory, a U.S.-led coalition of ground forces launched a military assault, which took only four days to drive the disorganized and demoralized Iraqi forces from Kuwait and obtain Iraq's surrender.

The swiftness of the U.S. military successes along with the often lighter-than-anticipated U.S. casualties sustained American public support for the Gulf War. Subsequent U.S. military operations abroad—in Somalia (1992–1994), Haiti (1994–1995), Bosnia (1995), and Kosovo (1999)—were likewise short-lived and without heavy casualties. The political anarchy and famine in Somalia prompted UN intervention, including thousands of U.S. forces, to bring humanitarian aid, peacemaking, peacekeeping, and nation-building to the African state. Poorly conceived and executed, the

UN effort failed to restore political order, and ambushes and raids on the occupying contingents by Somali warlords resulted in the deaths of many American troops. U.S. public opinion, previously apathetic, directed its anger at the disastrous UN policies. President William Jefferson Clinton decided to cut the nation's losses, and dissent dissipated with the withdrawal of U.S. and UN forces from Somalia by early 1994.

In Haiti, an army junta's overthrow of a constitutionally elected government headed by Jean Baptiste Aristide in 1991 resulted three years later in a UN Security Council resolution authorizing a U.S.-led multinational force to invade and restore Aristide to power. Drawing on the War Powers Act of 1973, the U.S. Senate passed a nonbinding resolution requiring congressional approval before invading Haiti, but Clinton, like previous recent presidents, denied the right of Congress to restrict the commander in chief. The intervention quickly achieved its short-term political objective of restoring Aristide and political order, although a U.S.–UN peacekeeping presence continued in Haiti until 1997.

After UN forces and the major European nations failed to bring peace and stability to the ongoing political turmoil and fighting in the former Yugoslavia, President Clinton began to assume leadership of a U.S.–European coalition in response to the escalating conflict in Bosnia. Beginning in 1994, NATO planes made sporadic air strikes on the Bosnian Serbs who had violated no-fly zones and attacked "safe-haven" cities and towns for UN forces and Muslim civilians. Further reports of ethnic cleansing by Serbs and their intransigence resulted in more intensive NATO air assaults on Serb positions, and Clinton officials urged Congress to approve the deployment of several thousand U.S. troops to the beleaguered region. Polls suggested an almost even split in American opinion on military intervention in Bosnia. The House of Representatives first narrowly rejected the proposal. Following the Dayton Peace Accords in November 1995, which offered a framework for peacekeeping in Bosnia, Congress approved the deployment of 60,000 U.S. troops to implement the accords, although only by a very narrow margin in the House. Because large proportions of the American public and Congress were ignorant of or confused by the complex ethnic rivalries and conflicts in the Balkans, they wavered during the 1994–1995 crisis. While they seemed opposed to foreign military intervention, they also wanted the president to respond to Serbian atrocities. Dissenters did not question the humanitarian needs to relieve the suffering in Bosnia, but argued that the nation's interests were not involved. In the end, the allied forces implementing the Dayton Accords in Bosnia had no U.S. combat casualties, and Clinton ultimately succeeded in announcing that U.S. troops would remain there indefinitely.

The public's deep ambivalence about involvement in the Balkans reemerged following Serbian forces' massacres of ethnic Albanians in Kosovo (1999). Although many Republicans and Democrats in Congress held principled positions in supporting or opposing Clinton's authorization of U.S. and NATO bombing of Yugoslav positions, the partisan bitterness resulting from the recent impeachment and trial of President Clinton made more Democrats inclined to back the president. The Republicans by contrast were more unified in opposition. The failure of an antiwar House resolution as well as another one, by a tie vote, endorsing the air war suggested the hesitation. Meanwhile, the Senate approved the air strikes but rejected consideration of sending ground troops to Kosovo. Finally, after repeated NATO air strikes, Yugoslav President Slobodan Milosevic capitulated and withdrew Serbian forces from Kosovo, and Congress agreed to fund NATO troops to maintain peace and order in the area. Because the air war lasted only seventy-nine days and occurred without a single U.S. casualty, dissent in the war never escalated.

In summary, dissent in war is not a new phenomenon in American history, born during the Vietnam War. All American wars have provoked dissent. Dissent is implicit in historic American attitudes toward war itself and is nourished when war becomes prolonged, costly in casualties, and indecisive. Because the American electorate has always shown only a limited patience for war, those troubled by dissent are mistaken when they interpret it as a new constraint upon the use of military force in American foreign policy. The constraint has been present from the beginning of American history.

BIBLIOGRAPHY

Alexander, Thomas B., and Richard E. Baringer. *The Anatomy of the Confederate Congress: A Study of the Influences of Member Characteristics on Legislative Voting Behavior, 1861–1865.* Nashville, 1972. Approaches the subject indirectly but provides as satisfactory an index to dissent in the Confederacy as can be found.

Banner, James M., Jr. *To the Hartford Convention: The Federalists and the Origins of Party Politics in Massachusetts, 1789–1815.* New York, 1970. Despite its very local emphasis, the best study of New England dissent in the War of 1812.

Bauer, K. Jack. *The Mexican War, 1846–1848.* New York, 1974. This full-scale study of the Mexican War is based on primary sources, and includes a good brief treatment of partisanship and dissent.

Bennis, Phyllis, and Michel Moushabeck, eds. *Beyond the Storm: A Gulf Crisis Reader.* Brooklyn, N.Y., 1991. A collection of articles by area specialists and journalists on the Gulf War, several of which are critical of and document opposition to U.S. policies in the region.

Blum, John Morton. *V Was for Victory: Politics and American Culture During World War II.* New York, 1976. The best survey of the American home front in World War II.

Brune, Lester H. *America and the Iraqi Crisis, 1990–1992: Origins and Aftermath.* Claremont, Calif., 1993.

———. *The United States and Post-Cold War Interventions: Bush and Clinton in Somalia, Haiti and Bosnia, 1992–1998.* Claremont, Calif., 1998. Both this and the previous entry provide useful surveys and contemporary analyses of U.S. foreign policy crises in the 1990s. They also contain extensive bibliographies of the monographs, articles, and memoirs dealing with these foreign policy issues of that decade.

Buzzanco, Robert. *Masters of War: Military Dissent and Politics in the Vietnam Era.* New York, 1996. A comprehensive work on opposition to American involvement in the Vietnam War.

Calhoon, Robert McCluer. *The Loyalists in Revolutionary America, 1760–1781.* New York, 1973. Examines the Loyalists less in isolation and more in the whole context of the Revolution than do other works, therefore comes closest to treating the problem of Loyalism as a problem of dissent in war.

Curry, Richard O. "The Union As It Was: A Critique of Recent Interpretations of the 'Copperheads.'" *Civil War History* 13 (1967). An introduction to Civil War dissent by way of a survey of the relevant literature.

DeBenedetti, Charles, and Charles Chatfield. *An American Ordeal: The Anti-War Movement of the Vietnam Era.* Syracuse, N.Y., 1990. A comprehensive work on opposition to American involvement in the Vietnam War.

DeConde, Alexander. *The Quasi-War: The Politics and Diplomacy of the Undeclared War With France, 1797–1801.* New York, 1966. Concerns a small war, but a formative one in shaping the limits and acceptability of dissent.

Jensen, Joan M. *The Price of Vigilance.* Chicago, 1968. A history of the American Protective League of World War I.

Just, Ward. *Military Men.* New York, 1970. Includes profiles of American soldiers during the Vietnam War and is useful for its portrayal of how the military perceived dissent.

Kurtz, Stephen G. *The Presidency of John Adams: The Collapse of Federalism, 1795–1800.* Philadelphia, 1957. Another study of the Quasi-War, with grim implications that the legitimacy of dissent in war might have failed to become an American tradition.

Kurtz, Stephen G., and James H. Hutson, eds. *Essays on the American Revolution.* Chapel Hill, N.C., 1973. Includes a number of the essays that touch on dissent. (John Shy's essay on the conflict as a "revolutionary war" especially has pertinent passages.)

Morison, Samuel Eliot, Frederick Merk, and Frank Freidel. *Dissent in Three American Wars.* Cambridge, Mass., 1970. In the perspective of the Vietnam War, Morison examines the War of 1812, Merk the Mexican War, and Freidel the Spanish-American War and imperialism.

Mueller, John E. *War, Presidents and Public Opinion.* New York, 1973. The most valuable effort to use public opinion polls to analyze the extent and nature of dissent in the Korean and Vietnam wars.

Peterson, H. C., and Gilbert C. Fite. *Opponents of War, 1917–1918.* Madison, Wis., 1957. A standard work.

Polenberg, Richard. *War and Society: The United States, 1941–1945.* Philadelphia, 1972. Offers a good introduction to issues of dissent and personal liberty.

Rees, David. *Korea: The Limited War.* New York, 1964. Written from the perspective of a British journalist applied to dissent in what Americans saw as a new kind of war.

Schirmer, Daniel B. *Republic or Empire: American Resistance to the Philippine War.* Cambridge, 1972. The fullest study of dissent during the Filipino insurrection, despite a perhaps inordinate focus on Massachusetts.

Schroeder, John H. *Mr. Polk's War: American Opposition and Dissent, 1846–1848.* Madison, Wisc., 1973. Offers the most comprehensive study of Mexican War dissent.

Small, Melvin, and William D. Hoover, eds. *Give Peace a Chance: Exploring the Vietnam Antiwar Movement. Essays from the Charles DeBenedetti Memorial Conference.* Syracuse, N.Y., 1992. A comprehensive work on opposition to American involvement in the Vietnam War.

See also ANTI-IMPERIALISM; BIPARTISANSHIP; CONGRESSIONAL POWER; ELITISM; IMPERIALISM; ISOLATIONISM; JUDICIARY POWER AND PRACTICE; PACIFISM; PEACE MOVEMENTS; PRESIDENTIAL POWER; PUBLIC OPINION; THE VIETNAM WAR.

DOCTRINES

Marc Jay Selverstone

Since virtually the earliest days of its existence, the United States has seen fit to announce in grandiose fashion its intentions and purposes to the world at large. The Declaration of Independence, for instance, the grandest statement of all, took aim at a foreign audience more than a domestic one. Subsequent declarations, often imbued with a millennial vision and a sense of exceptionalism, continued to broadcast the nation's principles far and wide. The emergence of the United States as a global power endowed those statements with increasing authority, for Americans as well as for those abroad. In time they came to take on the status of "doctrine," establishing the precepts of U.S. foreign policy.

For the most part, these doctrines sought to address immediate crises. Each involved diplomatic statements of intent; several of them spelled out specific actions in support of those intentions. For the most part, they sought to ground themselves in the traditions and lore of the American past. In an effort to establish that continuity, presidents have frequently referred to previous statements of policy, offering their own approaches as contemporary applications of enduring principles. Most of these declarations have carried weighty ideological content, venerating "free peoples" and the virtues of liberty. Yet they have been equally grounded in the language of national security, promoting the survival and safety of the American way. As a whole, they offer a thumbnail sketch of the history of American diplomacy.

THE MONROE DOCTRINE

In many ways, the "doctrines" of American foreign policy take their cue from the Monroe Doctrine, the seminal statement of national purpose. Articulated in 1823, this doctrine reflects the concerns and aspirations of a young country, bold enough to assert its power on the world stage. In dictating that Europe maintain a "hands-off" policy toward the Americas, it established the United States as a global power, albeit one with limited, hemispheric ambitions. Those ambitions would expand, however, and in future decades the Monroe Doctrine would prove useful for interventionists and isolationists alike. As the most recognizable and perhaps most venerated of diplomatic principles, its hold on the popular imagination has been so strong that it has defined the limits of acceptable policy options, shaping the range of choices open to presidents for the better part of two centuries.

Any appreciation of the Monroe Doctrine must take into account the domestic conditions of a young America and the international dynamics of the European great power system. The United States had only recently withstood the economic and military challenges posed by France and Britain during the Napoleonic wars. The conclusion of hostilities in 1815 seemed to release a host of energies that Americans harnessed and then directed inward. Numerous projects dedicated to fostering a more robust national system—such as the building of roads and canals—expressed the desire of many to subdue the land. It was a project that Americans carried out with missionary zeal, believing it their destiny to inhabit and control vast reaches of space from the Atlantic to the Pacific.

Extending the empire of liberty across the continent demanded that the United States shore up its diplomatic position, for that project of territorial expansion sought to absorb lands still coveted by several European states. One of those states was the empire of Spain, a world power from a previous era suffering the death throes of imperial overstretch. From Argentina to its holdings in North America, Spain's colonies in the New World were declaring their independence, a process that accelerated during the early years of the nineteenth century. Developments in connection with one of those holdings—West Florida—led Congress to establish a policy of "no transfer," which forbade the transfer of Spain's former colonies to any other European power. Interest in wrenching Florida free from Spanish control continued throughout the 1810s; by 1819 the United States was able to capitalize on Spanish weakness and secure title to Florida as well as to regions in the Far West. It was thus well on the way to enlarging the domains under democratic rule.

Support for political liberty was not wholesale, however. While Americans considered a more democratic world to be a more peaceful world—and more conducive to American interests—they questioned the ability of one and all to participate in the democratic experiment. Several members of the Monroe administration, including President James Monroe and Secretary of State John Quincy Adams, regarded Latin Americans as poorly equipped for democratic government. Spanish misrule, Catholic hierarchies, and Old World cultures weighed heavily on those peoples, making U.S. officials leery of supporting revolutions that might ultimately fail—especially if Spain were to mount an effort to retake those lands. Concerns such as these led officials in the Monroe administration to curb their republican passions and withhold recognition. By the early 1820s, however, several of those nations had stabilized, warranting a more formal American commitment to their viability. That pledge would come via President Monroe's December 1823 address to Congress. Not only would the United States recognize those new nations; it would seek to prevent their recolonization by any European power.

While expectations of conflict with Spain created the general context for the Monroe Doctrine, the president's declaration stemmed from a more tangible and immediate dispute with Imperial Russia. The czar had long been interested in the Pacific Northwest, coveting the waters off the American coast as a valuable spot for commercial fishing. In 1821, Alexander I declared the waters above 51 degrees north latitude the exclusive province of the Russian American Company and sought to maintain ports as far south as San Francisco.

American officials were not the only ones eager to create a barrier between Europe and the Americas. British statesmen were similarly anxious about the signals coming out of continental Europe, particularly regarding the fate of imperial Spain. The breakdown of Spain's New World empire was accompanied by political disturbances at home; in the end, however, revolution abroad would not be accompanied by revolution at home as France invaded Spain in 1823, restoring monarchical control to the country. Fears that France, along with Prussia and Austria—the two other members of the Holy Alliance—were interested in regaining for Spain its American colonies unnerved the British. Such a reversal could threaten British holdings in the Atlantic as well as the balance of power in Europe.

These concerns led Britain to approach the United States in the hope of making a joint statement regarding the Western Hemisphere. The intended effect of that declaration would be to ward off Spanish efforts either to recolonize its lost domains or to transfer control of those nations to other European powers. In weighing the British proposal, Monroe sought the help of Thomas Jefferson and James Madison. Friends and political allies, both Jefferson and Madison leaned toward accepting the British proposal, an inclination Monroe shared. Secretary of State Adams, however, disagreed with both their appraisal of the situation and their recommended course of action. First, he pointed out, Spain was ill-prepared to reclaim its colonies, a condition that called into question the very basis of the British proposal. Moreover, even if the European monarchies were prepared to help Spain retake its lost domains, it would be foolish for the United States to throw in its lot with Great Britain. "It would be more candid," Adams argued, "as well as more dignified, to avow our principles explicitly to Russia and France than to come as a cockboat in the wake of a British man-of-war." The United States, Adams was saying, should go it alone. It would brook no "interposition" by a European power in the affairs of the Americas, nor would it look kindly on efforts to subjugate newly independent states. For its part, America would refrain from inserting itself into the troubles of Europe, thereby consigning Europe and the United States to their respective and distinct spheres of influence. Those three principles—no interposition, noncolonization, and no interference—would become wedded to the fabric of American foreign policy, attaining the status of dogma for much of the nation's history.

While those principles have been considered sacrosanct by generations of Americans, government officials have taken great liberties with the Monroe Doctrine, invoking or discarding its precepts at will. The frequency with which politicians, scholars, and citizens have appealed to the doctrine, as well as the malleability it affords, has generated a fascination with this seminal statement of American policy, turning the study of it into a veritable cottage industry. Interpretations of the Monroe Doctrine have been changing since the middle of the nineteenth century, the time when scholars began to treat it with much gravitas.

One of those areas of debate concerns the very authorship of the doctrine. Historians have pointed to either John Quincy Adams or President James Monroe—with help from Jefferson and Madison—as the man more responsible for the doctrine's final form. Both Monroe and Adams sought to wall off Europe from the affairs of the Americas, and both men—though perhaps Adams more so than Monroe—were disposed to keeping America out of European affairs. Nevertheless, it was Adams who prevailed upon Monroe to make his statement a unilateral one, rejecting the idea that Britain and the United States establish their positions jointly. The most persuasive accounts have accorded Monroe and Adams equal responsibility, with Monroe supplying the document's idealism and Adams its geopolitical realism. Yet it was Adams's insistence that America make that statement alone, without the backing of Great Britain, that elevated the doctrine to its place in American lore. His ability to persuade Monroe on this score—arguably the most important aspect of the president's message—has even led one historian to cite the doctrine as America's declaration of diplomatic independence.

An ancillary debate has grown up around the issue of why the doctrine even appeared in the first place. Scholarship has revealed that fears of a Spanish intervention to reclaim its lost colonies—the context for the principle of nonintervention—were essentially groundless. By the time that Monroe made his statement in December 1823, the Holy Alliance had given up its plans, if any existed in the first place, for helping to reestablish Spanish colonial rule. The seeming irrelevance, then, of the Monroe Doctrine to the actions it sought to prevent has led historians to attribute more personal and political motives to its enunciation. In this account the presidential election of 1824 looms large, as Adams sought to outmaneuver potential rivals, some of whom were associates in Monroe's cabinet. Although an intriguing argument can be made for the relevance of these dynamics to the policy process, the weight of evidence seems to run against the argument that the Monroe Doctrine was more the product of political machinations than the principled stand of disinterested public servants.

Further scholarship has delved into the purpose of the Monroe Doctrine, leaving historians to divide over its relative leanings toward interventionism and isolationism. These debates have often reflected concerns specific to the eras in which they took place. Reference to the doctrine, for instance, first appeared during the annexationist debates of the late 1840s. President James Polk would refer to it explicitly as justification for his policies of continental expansion. In that climate the Monroe Doctrine, with its apparent sanction of American privilege in the Western Hemisphere, captured the upsurge of nationalist feeling as the nation moved westward; indeed, historians have commented on the symbiotic relationship between the Monroe Doctrine and the spirit of "manifest destiny," regarding those ideas as being—in the minds of nineteenth-century Americans—mutually reinforcing, if not identical.

Government officials and diplomatic historians would continually refer to the Monroe Doctrine throughout the nineteenth and twentieth centuries, interpreting its rhetoric as support for their own isolationist or interventionist policy preferences. The doctrine would again assume an activist slant in the 1890s as Secretary of State Richard Olney invoked it with respect to the border dispute between Venezuela and British Guiana. According to Olney, British intervention in the quarrel would violate the time-honored principle of noncolonization; though sharp words were exchanged, tensions between the United States and Britain dissipated, inaugurating a period of much smoother relations.

Subsequent events would give the doctrine an increasingly interventionist spin. Fallout from the War of 1898 left the United States with a preponderance of power in the Caribbean, a power it codified with the Platt Amendment of 1901. Reserving for itself the right to intervene in Cuba's affairs, the administration of President Theodore Roosevelt began to mark out an entire policy toward the region that would expand upon Monroe's original dictum. What concerned Roosevelt was the ability of Latin American nations to pay their debts to European creditors. Fearing that a string of defaults might lead Europe to meddle in hemispheric affairs, Roosevelt chose to intervene in the economic and political lives of those nations, establishing the Roosevelt Corollary to the Monroe Doctrine. Episodes such as these have led historians to marvel at the doctrine's flexibility. As a statement of national interest, the Monroe Doctrine has appeared to sanction economic imperialism in the Western Hemisphere as well as the missionary impulse to bring good government to the region. Whatever the case, scholars have offered ample evidence for the argument that such interventionism, whether in the service of cynical or noble motives, was absent from the doctrine's original formulation.

It has questionable relevance to American foreign policy in the twenty-first century. The self-imposed injunction against intervening in European affairs—broken on account of World Wars I and II—was altogether abandoned during the Cold War as U.S. troop commitments and armaments cemented the NATO coalition of west European states. American leadership during the air war against Serbian targets during the 1998–1999 Kosovo crisis invalidated whatever was left of that portion of Monroe's injunction. Likewise, U.S. administrations have alternately supported and condemned foreign involvement in hemispheric affairs. While the Reagan administration supported Britain's war against Argentina over sovereignty of the Falkland Islands in 1982, it clearly demanded that the Soviet Union follow a "hands-off" policy in connection with insurrectionary movements in Central America, as had the Nixon administration before it. Such actions suggest that if presidents are to invoke the Monroe Doctrine in the future, they will likely do so selectively, according to their assessment of prevailing geopolitical winds.

THE HOOVER-STIMSON DOCTRINE

While the framers of the Monroe Doctrine and its corollary limited their horizons to the Western Hemisphere, a later statement of national purpose would extend that horizon halfway around the globe. The Hoover-Stimson Doctrine, named for President Herbert Hoover and Secretary of State Henry L. Stimson, actually reiterated earlier pledges regarding American interests in the Far East. In doing so, it sent a mixed message: that while the United States would not recognize territorial changes realized by force of arms, it had no interest in coming to the defense of that principle.

The events precipitating the doctrine's articulation took place in northern China in September 1931, along a section of track on the South Manchurian Railway, which had been administered by Japan since the first decade of the century. An explosion near the railway, subsequently attributed to the Japanese military, was blamed by Japan on Chinese rebels. Japan used the occasion—thereafter known as the Mukden Incident—as a pretext to pacify ever-larger regions of Manchuria. Continued Japanese conquest alarmed the international community, prompting the League of Nations to condemn such aggrandizement. In an effort to underscore its concern, the league sought to enlist on its behalf support from the United States and the administration of President Herbert Hoover. On 7 January 1932, Secretary of State Stimson delivered notes to both Japan and China stating U.S. opposition to the course of events in Manchuria. Stimson's announcement was twofold: first, that the United States would not recognize any treaty that compromised the sovereignty or integrity of China; and second, that it would not recognize any territorial changes achieved through force of arms. It was a statement of pure principle, made even purer by the disinterest and inability of the United States to back up those words with deeds. Given the economic, military, and diplomatic constraints ensuing from the Great Depression, violations of the Hoover-Stimson Doctrine would bring public rebuke by the United States but little else.

Although the Hoover-Stimson Doctrine is often derided as a manifestation of pie-in-the-sky American idealism, its articulation made great sense to a great many at the time. Reflecting widespread revulsion at what the Great War had wrought—the enormous loss of life, manifold disruptions of European societies, and an overwhelming reluctance to repeat the mistakes of the past—the doctrine sought to marshal world opinion in the service of peace. Its appeal to universal standards of conduct reflected the emergence of a new mind-set in world affairs—that there was, in fact, such a thing as an international community and that certain norms governed its behavior. No statement was more emblematic of that consciousness than the Kellogg-Briand Pact of 1928, an agreement signed by thirty-three nations outlawing the use of force as an instrument of national policy.

The doctrine was also rooted in the history of the region. Western interest in China stretched back hundreds of years, but the ability to exercise decisive influence on that country was a more recent phenomenon. Britain's 1842 victory over China in the first of the Opium Wars established a pattern whereby several countries, including the United States, were able to demand most-favored-nation trading status from the Chinese authorities. By the late nineteenth century, the imperial powers were carving up China into separate spheres of influence. As China lay prostrate, U.S. Secretary of State John M. Hay proposed that those nations adopt an Open Door policy for China, an arrangement that would preserve China's territorial and administrative integrity while maintaining equal trading rights for all. It was Japan, however, that would mount the greatest challenge to the Open Door. Having gained a foothold in Manchuria following the Russo-Japanese War of 1904–1905, Japan applied increasing pressure on China, resulting in its Twenty-One Demands of 1915. American remonstrations to Japan indicated that the United States would not recognize any agreements in violation of the Open Door, a position it reaffirmed in 1917 and then again in 1922. The Mukden Incident of September 1931 represented the clearest challenge to date of that long-stated U.S. position.

The Hoover-Stimson Doctrine also was part of the history of U.S. recognition policy. This policy dated to the early national period when Democratic-Republicans and Federalists, arguing bitterly over a proper response to the French Revolution, questioned whether the United States was obligated to carry out agreements signed with the ancien regime, and vice versa. The issue of diplomatic recognition would reemerge following the War of 1812, as a more assertive United States questioned the wisdom of establishing formal relations with a coterie of weak, newly independent Latin American nations; it was this debate, in fact, that was the backdrop for the Monroe Doctrine. The matter would demand executive attention once again during the administration of President Woodrow Wilson. A series of regime changes in Mexico—some of them bloody—led Wilson to withhold recognition of General Victoriano Huerta, reversing the general principle of conferring legitimacy on whoever could demonstrate de facto territorial control. The Mukden Incident would reopen the issue of whether, and on what grounds, the United States would recognize the sovereignty of a new controlling authority.

Despite America's absence from the League of Nations, U.S. officials hoped that body would act swiftly to resolve the crisis. To prod it into action, the United States sent an observer to attend its deliberations. This led to the formation of a commission of inquiry to investigate the dispute and report back to the league assembly. When in 1932 the commission announced its findings, which blamed Japan for the crisis, the Japanese delegation walked out of the League of Nations. In the interim, a new Japanese government had assumed power and embarked on the further conquest of Manchuria. It was this action, undertaken by Japan in the fall of 1931, that prompted Stimson to issue his policy of nonrecognition—a policy suggested, in fact, by Hoover himself.

Although Stimson had hoped his approach would garner European support, formal endorsements were not in the offing. Britain, reversing the role it had played earlier regarding the Monroe Doctrine, let America wave the banner of nonrecognition, hoping to benefit from that policy without having to tie itself too closely to the American kite. Ultimately, the League of Nations endorsed Stimson's pledge, although over the next several years a number of its members would recognize Japanese suzerainty over Manchuria.

By most any measure, the Hoover-Stimson Doctrine failed its first test. Only three weeks after the secretary of state delivered his diplomatic notes, Japan attacked the port city of Shanghai, extending its sphere of influence into central China. The United States refused to take action; Stimson wanted to impose sanctions on Japan, but Hoover was reluctant to engage the United States in measures he deemed tantamount to war. Moreover, given the domestic pressures Hoover was facing—including staggering unemployment figures, numerous bank failures, and a massive drop in consumer spending—it was all but impossible to send ill-prepared military forces around the world. The president hoped that China's size and culture would help it absorb the Japanese incursion, and that a dose of moral suasion would help convince the Tokyo leadership to cease and desist. Neither of these developments came to pass.

Insofar as Hoover dictated the nature of America's response during the Manchurian crisis, it seems wrong to castigate Stimson exclusively for policies that came to be associated with his name. Stimson envisioned a series of measures, increasing in severity, which he hoped would compel a Japanese change in behavior; the president, on the other hand, took the more isolationist position. Hoover, in fact, sought to wrestle authorship of the doctrine away from his secretary of state, a curious move given the manifest impotence of the measures it advocated. Yet grasping for evidence of leadership during the 1932 presidential campaign, Hoover wanted Stimson to consign its provenance over to the president. Eventually, Stimson did bestow that honor upon Hoover. Nevertheless, its principles continue to be associated with Stimson, and any mention of a doctrine continues to bear his name.

The Hoover-Stimson Doctrine would continue to amass a sorry record during the 1930s as the new political orders in Austria, Czechoslovakia, Albania, and Ethiopia—the fruits of German and Italian aggression and intimidation—received widespread international recognition. Fascism's ascendance, observers would argue, took its cue from Japan's earlier behavior in the Far East; reluctance to confront Japan emboldened Hitler and Mussolini, creating conditions for the greater horror to come. In this sense, the promulgation of both the Hoover-Stimson Doctrine and the League of Nations judgment might have done more damage to international peace than the withholding of such statements. The failure of both the United States and the international community to back up their words with effective retributive actions thus allowed the Japanese, and perhaps the Germans and Italians, to call the world's collective bluff, plunging hundreds of millions into global war.

Scholars have regularly disparaged the Hoover-Stimson Doctrine on those grounds, describing it as both toothless and dangerous. Some historians, in fact, have argued that Stimson's approach was even weaker than that of the League of Nations, for it offered no procedure for mediating the Manchurian dispute. Others have decried its reliance on "legalism"—the reliance on vague notions of universal norms to influence international behavior—at the expense of more "hard-headed" approaches to geopolitics. On the other hand, legal theorists have responded to the doctrine with guarded acclaim, pointing out that its injection of morality into global politics would help to shape an international consensus in the postwar era.

THE TRUMAN DOCTRINE

While the Hoover-Stimson Doctrine sought to constrain Japanese militarism, the Truman Doctrine addressed a new and more global threat—that of international communism. The purveyor of that creed, the Soviet Union, had enjoyed a rocky relationship with the United States; since October 1917, Americans had looked upon the Soviets as outcasts and irritants. Then, during World War II, they became allies. With the emergence of the Cold War their status changed again, with Moscow now taking on the attributes of an

implacable foe. President Harry S. Truman would help sear that image into the minds of Americans, most spectacularly when, on 12 March 1947, in a message before a joint session of Congress, he laid down a set of principles that would govern U.S.–Soviet relations for decades to come. "At the present moment in world history," Truman proclaimed, "nearly every nation must choose between alternative ways of life." Too often that choice was not a free one. It would therefore be the policy of the United States "to support free peoples who are resisting attempted subjugation by armed minorities or by outside pressures." Although Truman chose not to identify those minorities or groups by name, their identity as communists was hardly in doubt. To help those free peoples—in this case, Greeks and Turks—withstand communist pressure, Truman would ask Congress to provide them with $400 million in economic and military aid. Yet far more than just Greece and Turkey was at stake, Truman proclaimed. The United States was caught in a global struggle between two opposing ways of life. Consequently, Truman deemed all of "the free peoples of the world" equally worthy of American assistance. By implication, then, the president's proposal was no mere stop-gap measure. As many in the press and government realized, it aspired to nothing less than the preservation of Western civilization.

Fears of postwar Soviet expansion had ebbed and flowed during 1946. The presence of Red Army troops in northern Iran well past the date established for their departure raised Western concerns about the nature of Moscow's intentions. Remonstrations by U.S. officials, however, led to a Kremlin withdrawal by late spring. Tensions would heat up later that summer as the Soviets pressured Turkey into revising the Montreux Convention—the protocol governing access to the Dardanelles—to allow for a joint administration of the Turkish straits with an eye toward the eventual establishment of Soviet bases in Turkey. Reports of Soviet troops massing along the Turkish border led the Truman administration to conclude that invasion might well be imminent. Turkish and American resistance led Moscow to drop its request, but Soviet behavior continued to worry U.S. officials.

Greece appeared to be the next target of the Soviet pressure campaign. Civil war between communists and monarchists had been raging in that country since the Nazi retreat of 1944, and neither the British, who stepped in as the occupying power, nor the Americans, who sent millions in aid, were able to quell the strife. Support for the communists came from the Yugoslav leader, Josip Broz Tito, although U.S. officials feared—erroneously, as it turned out—that Moscow was the controlling force.

America's rise to power in the Mediterranean is also the story of Britain's fall from power. Previously, Britain had assumed the role of protector of the states in that area. With its economy in tatters following World War I, however, Britain found it could no longer play that role, and thus feared a Russian surge into the power vacuum it created. On 21 February the British embassy in Washington informed the State Department that Britain would soon be cutting off economic and military assistance to Greece and Turkey.

Committing the nation's resources and prestige to the security and survival of Europe during an era of nominal peace was a radical departure for American policymakers. It certainly stood in stark contrast to Monroe's pledge not to intervene in European affairs. As a result, administration officials thought it necessary to portray the situation in the most dramatic of terms. The president's address to the nation therefore employed rhetoric bordering on the apocalyptic, casting the struggle with Moscow in a highly dualistic light. The choice facing America, Truman argued, was between two opposing and irreconcilable ways of life: between the virtues of democracy and the horrors of totalitarianism. Although the East-West conflict had become more ideologically polarized during the preceding twelve months, the administration had yet to frame it—at least publicly—in such a dichotomous fashion.

In doing so, the Truman Doctrine wove together several themes running through the national dialogue on the Soviet Union and thrust them out into the public realm with substantial force. One of them involved the image of "Red fascism." Although parallels between fascism and communism had been popular for years, the Truman Doctrine helped to work that image into the public consciousness, locking in the notion that Soviet Russia posed an equal if not greater threat to world peace than had Nazi Germany. The Truman Doctrine also contributed to the emergence of an equally powerful representation of the enemy: the "Communist monolith." Belief in the "monolith" presupposed that Greek communists, like all communists, were tools of the Kremlin. This was a viewpoint shared widely—and not

without reason—by administration personnel and media figures alike. By minimizing the differences between any and all totalitarians, the Truman Doctrine reinforced that interpretation of communist behavior.

Not everyone in the administration embraced the overtly ideological cant of the president's speech. Officials such as policy planning director George Kennan, State Department counselor Charles Bohlen, and Secretary of State George Marshall thought Truman's comments either too dramatic, too overwrought, or too open-ended. Similarly, Walter Lippmann, the nation's leading journalist, likened the doctrine to "a vague global policy" devoid of any limits, and described it as "the tocsin of an ideological crusade." Indeed, fallout from the speech suggested that the public was—from the administration's point of view—focusing too narrowly on its military and ideological aspects and ignoring its economic dimension. The administration was thus caught in a public relations paradox. On the one hand, it sought to brief the country on what was transpiring in Europe; only by "shocking" the nation, it believed, could the American people grasp the issues at stake. Yet the resultant upsurge in anticommunist sentiment threatened to overwhelm the administration's capacity to manage it. Hoping to get the word out in a more sober fashion, a speech by Undersecretary of State Dean Acheson reframed the debate around the administration's preferred theme of economic reconstruction. Marshall would return to that theme in early June, laying the groundwork for the recovery plan that bore his name.

In the interim, Congress debated the terms of the Greek and Turkish aid bills. Their passage was by no means assured, for Republican victories in the 1946 election ushered in a Congress that was not in Democratic control for the first time since 1932. Many of those who now sat in the majority had won their seats on pledges of fiscal restraint and tax reduction. Lawmakers thus sought to limit the scope of Truman's policy, a restriction that Acheson refused to accept; future requests for aid, he stated, would receive consideration on a case-by-case basis. Congress raised additional concerns over whether the recipients of foreign aid could be considered democratic. Acknowledging that neither the Turkish government nor the Greek forces were paragons of liberal virtue, administration officials urged Congress to fund both groups nevertheless. Otherwise, they argued, both Turkey and Greece would lose the ability to govern themselves and lay vulnerable to forces aided and abetted by the Soviet Union. Time was of the essence, Acheson declared; he and his associates urged quick action on the Greek and Turkish aid bills, arguing that the United States, and not the United Nations—with its clumsy machinery—was the proper engine for the aid program. Congress passed the aid measures and on 22 May Truman signed the bills. The Truman Doctrine was now the operative principle of U.S. foreign policy.

If the Monroe Doctrine established the general principles for subsequent declarations of American foreign policy, the Truman Doctrine established the more particular guidelines for the duration of the Cold War. It was the most dramatic statement issued by the administration since the emergence of conflict with the Soviets. It established a precedent of sweeping appeals to aid democratic forces, leaving to subsequent administrations the privilege of deciding precisely what constituted democratic behavior. Perhaps the greatest testament to its impact is the legislation and diplomacy that followed, more or less logically, from the premises it established. Within three years, the administration would usher through Congress bills establishing aid programs and treaties such as the European Recovery Program (the Marshall Plan) and the North Atlantic Treaty Alliance, committing the United States both economically and militarily to the defense of Europe. NSC 68, a 1950 National Security Council report to the president, and the attendant legislation that tripled the defense budget, likewise were expressions of the themes and arguments contained in Truman's speech. Indeed, for the next several decades, much of the nation's international behavior—from its involvement in Korea and Vietnam to its support of Afghani and Nicaraguan rebels—grew out of the postulates laid down in the Truman Doctrine.

Historians have long debated the merits and demerits of the Truman Doctrine. Some have described it as an inherently self-serving policy. For these scholars, the Truman Doctrine was the opening gambit in America's quest for global economic hegemony; the plan, they charge, was to make the world safe for American capitalism. To be sure, U.S. policymakers were acutely aware of economic concerns as they mapped out American strategy in the postwar era. Fears of a "dollar gap" in Europe mounted when American leaders considered the domestic implications of the continent's misfortune; the inability of Europeans to

purchase U.S. goods threatened to slow down the American economic recovery, leading to renewed concern about recession and even depression. The Marshall Plan, as the argument goes, thus primed the American pump, allowing European consumers to maintain levels of spending adequate for U.S. economic vitality.

It is not entirely clear, however, whether American policymakers focused on those issues with such single-minded zeal. Administration officials certainly understood the reciprocal features of an economically vital Europe and United States and were no doubt interested in maintaining growth in the home market. But they also recognized the dynamic between the economic vitality of Europe and the political health of Europe; it was their contention that a vibrant economy, both home and abroad, was the best protection against communist gains. It was most likely this larger picture, involving a wider matrix of forces, that they had in mind as they contemplated their response to the British withdrawal notes of February 1947.

Scholars have also questioned the wisdom of Truman's rhetoric. Some have argued that his use of Manichean imagery locked the nation into a rigid, inflexible policy toward the Soviet Union. Diplomacy—the art of compromise—was all but impossible when one's counterparts were regarded as evil. Likewise, historians have argued, the persistence of that Manichean and monolithic framework prevented policymakers from recognizing difference and division within the communist world. An earlier appreciation of fragmentation in the Soviet bloc—and of downright hostility between some of its members—might have prevented America from pursuing some disastrous policy options, such as those involving the war in Vietnam.

These arguments need to be qualified, especially in light of evidence emerging from the former Eastern bloc. While the Truman Doctrine certainly did its part in establishing a powerful vocabulary for the Cold War, it seems as though the language it used reflected some fundamental truths about international communism. Stalinist Europe was very much a closed system, with the Soviet Union controlling much of what went on there. True, Tito's Yugoslavia was able to assert its independence from the Soviet grip, but that was the exception; the regionwide purge resulting from the Tito split only reinforced the tendency for the other Eastern European nations to do Moscow's bidding. Chinese Communists were no more willing than their European counterparts to contravene Soviet wishes. Although tensions often resulted from tactical differences between Moscow and Beijing, on the larger questions the two stood side by side. As a result, American officials had little chance to court the Chinese Communists either before or after the death of Soviet leader Joseph Stalin. Things would change during the late 1950s and the 1960s, but so, too, would U.S. policy; the consensus established by Truman during the late 1940s would come unraveled as the nation plunged further into the jungles of Southeast Asia, leading another generation of policymakers to recast some of the early Cold War premises.

THE EISENHOWER DOCTRINE

By the mid-1950s the Cold War had undergone a transformation. Stalin's death in March 1953 ushered in a period of transition for the Soviet Union, prompting the Kremlin's new leadership to stabilize its own power as well as Moscow's position with regard to the NATO alliance. Yet changes in the international arena would encourage those men, as well as their counterparts in the West, to view the developing world as a new site for East-West competition. President Dwight D. Eisenhower would engage the Soviets in that global battle for hearts and minds, a conflict that threatened to become particularly fierce in a region vital to U.S. national security: the Middle East. Eisenhower's January 1957 pledge to defend that region from "any country controlled by international communism" recalled his predecessor's commitment to "support free peoples" resisting foreign aggression. Eisenhower's willingness to commit American troops to that project went beyond what Truman had offered in March 1947; still, both statements were cut from the same cloth. Working from the premises of the Truman Doctrine while extending its range of policy options, Eisenhower added his name to a growing list of policymakers whose statements had risen to the level of American political doctrine.

Like the Monroe and Truman Doctrines, the Eisenhower Doctrine grew out of a specific set of historical circumstances. Since 1946 the United States had sought to counter Soviet encroachment in the Mediterranean and the Persian Gulf; its program of assistance to Greece and Turkey, as well as its rhetorical defense of Iran, served to keep those nations within the Western orbit.

Efforts to strengthen anticommunist forces in the region fell through, however, as Arab support for a Middle Eastern defense organization foundered over U.S. aid to Israel. Failure to erect a security structure for the Middle East in general—and for Western oil interests in particular—loomed large as the tide of anticolonialism grew in that part of the world.

Egyptian leader Gamal Abdel Nasser would rise to power on the force of anticolonialism, and the attraction of Nasser's equally potent message of pan-Arabism would pose further challenges to Western interests. The Eisenhower administration equated Nasser's radicalism and anti-imperialism with communism and hoped to contain the spread of those forces, a project of equal interest to Britain. In an effort to foster pro-Western sentiment, Britain tied itself to Iraq, Iran, Turkey, and Pakistan—each a nation bordering the Soviet Union—in a mutual defense organization known as the Baghdad Pact. Tensions in the region continued to ratchet upward as Nasser received arms from Czechoslovakia and, more dramatically, nationalized the Suez Canal in 1956. The ensuing crisis over Suez damaged British and French prestige, embarrassed the United States, and resulted in a propaganda windfall for Egypt and the Soviet Union. Political power in the region thus seemed to be swinging away from the West and toward the communist world.

Eisenhower attempted to reverse that trend in early 1957. Addressing a joint session of Congress on 5 January, the president outlined what came to be known as the Eisenhower Doctrine, a plan of action for combating communism in the Middle East. A resolution designed to implement the doctrine authorized the president to provide economic and military cooperation and assistance to "any nation or group of nations in the general area of the Middle East" fighting to maintain their independence. Money for that initiative, amounting to $200 million, would come from funds previously earmarked for the Military Security Act of 1954. Aside from providing economic aid, the resolution granted the president the option of using armed force "to assist any such nation or group of nations requesting assistance against armed aggression from any country controlled by international communism." After months of sometimes pointed debate—with lawmakers questioning both the imminence of communist aggression and the wisdom of granting the president a blank check for engaging U.S. forces—Congress passed the resolution, providing the

DOCTRINES ABROAD

During the Cold War, America's allies and enemies also resorted to doctrinal statements of policy. Here are two of the more noteworthy declarations.

The Hallstein Doctrine This doctrine was enunciated by the West German foreign minister Walter Hallstein in the context of the struggle to codify the postwar fate of the two Germanys and the shape of Eastern Europe. The Soviets had proposed that the two sides end their wrangling over Berlin and ratify the boundaries of the two German states. West German Chancellor Konrad Adenauer, who continued to endorse the Bonn government as the true government of Germany, resisted this plan and countered with his own statement of intentions. The Hallstein Doctrine declared that West Germany would have no relations with any country that recognized the existence ("entered into diplomatic relations") with the German Democratic Republic. The Bonn government followed through on its pledge, breaking off relations with Yugoslavia in 1957. Moscow's inability to settle the German question led Soviet premier Nikita Khrushchev, in 1958, to issue an ultimatum to the United States on the fate of Berlin, demanding the full incorporation of that city into East Germany. Failure to achieve that settle-ment heightened tensions over Berlin and contributed to Khrushchev's placement of missiles in Cuba in 1962. Cuba, in fact, became the second nation to run afoul of the Hallstein Doctrine, leading Bonn to break relations with Havana in 1960.

The Brezhnev Doctrine During the spring and summer of 1968, reformers in the Czechoslovak Communist Party, led by Alexander Dubcek, sought to create a new brand of socialism with a human face. Those moves, and the Czech leadership's resistance to Moscow's disapproval, occasioned the Soviet invasion of Czechoslovakia in August 1968. Defending his policy of force, Soviet premier Leonid I. Brezhnev maintained that "when internal and external forces that are hostile to socialism seek to reverse the development of any socialist country in the direction of restoring the capitalist system, when a threat to the cause of socialism in that country appears, and a threat to the security of the socialist community as a whole, that is no longer only a problem for the people of that country, but also a common problem, a matter of concern for all socialist countries." President Ronald Reagan would cite the Brezhnev Doctrine in his own doctrinal statement of principles.

commander in chief with the tools needed to carry out the nation's foreign policy.

The administration would invoke the Eisenhower Doctrine a number of times over the course of the following two years. A political crisis in Jordan, which involved King Hussein's ouster of pro-Soviet members from his cabinet in April 1957, provided the first opportunity for doing so. Claiming that Jordan's independence was vital to the United States, Eisenhower ordered the Sixth Fleet into the eastern Mediterranean. When stability returned to Jordanian politics, Eisenhower attributed that relative tranquility to the American show of force. The administration would deploy naval and air units to the region for a second time in 1957, as Syria's acquisition of Soviet arms generated concern for the future independence of Turkey and Lebanon. Once again the conflict receded, and once again Eisenhower ascribed that development to American resolve.

Tensions in the region remained high nevertheless, with Nasserism adding a potent ingredient to the East-West conflict. Lebanon would bear the brunt of that mix when an internal political struggle mushroomed into an international one. President Camille Chamoun initiated that conflict in 1958, when he tried to circumvent the Lebanese constitution and extend his hold on power. Fearing a loss of control, Chamoun appealed to the United States for support under the Eisenhower Doctrine, citing Syrian meddling in Lebanese affairs as a pretext for his request. For six weeks the United States did not oblige him. It was not until 14 July, when a coup in Iraq installed a Nasserite and pro-Soviet regime in Baghdad, that the administration acted. Responding to Chamoun's renewed calls for support, and coming on the heels of British aid to Jordan, the

United States inserted fifteen thousand troops into Lebanon, the clearest application of the Eisenhower Doctrine to date.

Some have argued that Eisenhower's Euro-centrism and unfamiliarity with regional concerns blinded him to Middle Eastern realities, making him too willing to interpret the region's nationalist movements as hostile to U.S. interests. Much of this stemmed from Eisenhower's equating of Nasserism with communism. The president, in fact, attributed the Lebanese turbulence to the work of communist elements, a development that, he believed, threatened to engulf the entire region. His fear was that a single communist success might precipitate a domino-like chain reaction in which the governments of Lebanon, Jordan, and Saudi Arabia would each fall to the forces of Nasserism. Invoking the Munich analogy as well as the domino metaphor, Eisenhower declared Lebanon to be the victim of "indirect aggression from without," aggression that spelled trouble for pro-Western forces from Europe to Asia. His decision to send in the marines, therefore, stemmed largely from those broader concerns.

It is far from clear whether the destabilization of Lebanon would have resulted in the domino-like scenario Eisenhower envisioned. Nor is it clear whether anti-Western or pro-Soviet elements in the region would have been as hostile to America as Eisenhower imagined. Scholars have pointed to Iraqi general Karim Kassem as a case in point. Although Kassem would sign a defense treaty with Egypt and take his country out of the Baghdad Pact, Iraq emerged from the crisis as less ensconced in the Soviet camp than first believed. Neither of those measures—neither the arms deal nor the abrogation of the defense treaty—indicated complete subservience to the Kremlin. Moreover, while Kassem did increase his ties with Moscow, he also increased the flow of Iraqi oil to the West, hardly the response of an out-and-out Soviet lackey.

Historians have likewise questioned the wisdom of dispatching the U.S. Sixth Fleet to the eastern Mediterranean. While that show of force was supposed to deter Syria from meddling in Jordanian, Lebanese, and Iraqi politics, the move backfired, according to some historians, encouraging greater Arab unity in the face of Western intervention. Other scholars have claimed that the Eisenhower Doctrine sought to combat a threat that was largely imaginary. Nasser had no great affinity for the Soviet Union, and even less for Marxism. Rather, his anticolonialism was

directed largely at Britain and France—not at the United States—leading Eisenhower to squander whatever good will he might have had with the Egyptian leader. Still others have cited Eisenhower's own actions as testaments to his doctrine's futility. Six months after the marines landed in Lebanon, they point out, the administration was reevaluating its entire approach to the Middle East, choosing to work with, and not against, Arab nationalism. By 1958 the Eisenhower administration was funneling over $150 million in aid to Egypt, hardly the result one would have expected prior to the doctrine's enunciation.

THE NIXON DOCTRINE

Eisenhower's vice president, Richard M. Nixon, would challenge the premises and augment the scope of Cold War presidential doctrines. One of Nixon's goals, in fact, was to limit the type of intervention that Eisenhower had joined in Lebanon, where the commander in chief responded to an international crisis by "sending in the marines." He would introduce his new approach on 25 July 1969, the very day that America began its lengthy retreat from the jungles and marshes of Vietnam. Speaking to reporters on the island of Guam, Nixon described the U.S. troop withdrawal in terms that endowed it with a broader, strategic rationale. Retrenchment, according to Nixon, would subordinate the nation's commitments to its interests, reversing the recent trend of American policy. Nixon's policy would likewise encourage friends and allies to marshal greater resources in their own defense, even as the United States continued to meet its treaty obligations. Finally, it would grant the United States greater flexibility to respond to new diplomatic realities.

Nixon derived these principles from his appraisal of the postwar international environment, the features of which, he argued, had undergone a recent and dramatic transformation. As Nixon explained, the United States was the only major country to escape the social and economic destruction of World War II. Consequently, in those first years after the war, friends and former enemies depended on the United States for aid in rebuilding their economies and resisting communist penetration. By the late 1960s, however, that first postwar era had given way to a new international configuration. Former recipients of U.S.

economic and military assistance were now capable of contributing more to their own defense; developing nations, at one time easy marks for communist agitators, now required less American help and protection. Of perhaps greater importance were the events taking place within the Eastern bloc. Soviet crackdowns on East Germany, Hungary, and Czechoslovakia, as well as border clashes with China, were easing earlier fears of a monolithic communist movement. Those incidents, according to Nixon, testified to the "emerging polycentrism of the communist world," an altered landscape that presented the United States with "different challenges and new opportunities."

The Western alliance had also undergone something of a transformation. France withdrew from NATO's military command in 1966, challenging U.S. leadership of a united Western front. Britain, America's foremost partner in Europe, continued its fall from imperial glory, retreating from positions east of Suez in 1968. Economic troubles in both Europe and the United States would further tax the alliance, straining America's ability to "pay any price" for the survival of liberty. And the war in Vietnam continued to straitjacket America's flexibility and drain its resources.

Those realities led Nixon to reshape the rhetoric and practice of U.S. foreign policy. Although he accepted the premise that the United States remained "indispensable" to world peace and stability, Nixon also recognized the limits of American power. Other nations, he maintained, "should assume greater responsibilities, for their sake as well as ours," a clear admission that the United States could not go it alone. America would, therefore, seek to balance the "ends" it desired in its foreign policy with the "means" available for doing so.

Nixon's Guam statement was the first indication that the president would be adopting a new strategic posture, prompting reporters to label its particulars the Guam Doctrine. Nixon and his national security adviser Henry Kissinger resisted that appellation and sought to change it, believing that a statement of such importance should commemorate its originator rather than its place of origin. Yet the newly coined Nixon Doctrine was vague enough to require repeated and lengthy explanation. The president sought to clarify his intent in an address to the nation on 3 November 1969. First, he noted, the United States would "keep all of its treaty commitments." Second, it would "provide a shield" should a nuclear power threaten either the freedom of a nation allied with

the United States or the existence of a country deemed vital to U.S. security. Finally, and perhaps most significantly, Nixon vowed to maintain the outward flow of economic and military assistance in accordance with U.S. treaty commitments. "But," he added, "we shall look to the nation directly threatened to assume the primary responsibility of providing the manpower for its defense."

Southeast Asia would be the setting for the most visible application of the Nixon Doctrine. In an attempt to extricate the United States from the war in Indochina, Nixon sought to "Vietnamize" the conflict by having indigenous troops supplant American forces. It was a program that took four years to complete, with the last U.S. troops leaving Saigon in 1973. That policy, part of a broader effort to reduce American commitments abroad, would also find a home in the Middle East, where Nixon tried to build his new security structure upon the "twin pillars" of Iran and Saudi Arabia. The shah of Iran, Mohammad Reza Pahlavi, would benefit greatly from America's reliance on proxies, receiving a virtual blank check from Nixon and Kissinger to purchase enormous sums of American military hardware. It was a shopping spree that would boomerang on the shah—and on the United States—before the decade was out.

These manifestations of retrenchment were themselves part of a broader plan to alter relations with the Soviet Union and China. As he laid out in his Guam remarks, Nixon sought to capitalize on the "polycentrism" of the communist world. His visit to China in 1972 opened a new chapter in the Cold War; America would now practice "triangular diplomacy" and engage both the Chinese and the Soviets, creating new opportunities for U.S. foreign policy. One of those was in the field of arms control, where U.S. and Soviet officials sought to rein in a costly and dangerous arms race. Agreements regarding strategic weapons and antiballistic missile systems signaled a new spirit of cooperation between the superpowers, a relaxation of tensions that came to be known as détente. Given the overlap between those developments and his strategic vision, Nixon would ascribe his Soviet initiatives, as well as the commercial, cultural, and diplomatic ventures begun with the People's Republic of China, to the Nixon Doctrine as well.

Supporters hailed the Nixon Doctrine and the diplomacy of the Nixon-Kissinger team as a new, remarkable, and genuine alternative to the bitter contentions of the first postwar years. The domestic and international circumstances of the late 1960s and early 1970s, they observed, simply would not allow for massive interventions along the lines of Korea and Vietnam. Instead, the United States would "balance" the distribution of power in the international arena rather than pursue preponderant advantage. Many commentators found this a welcome change, even a sign of political maturity. For the first time in the postwar era, the United States was to a great degree experiencing and acclimatizing itself to the limits of American power.

Critics of the doctrine divided over its novelty, meaning, and effect. Some regarded Nixon's policies in Southeast Asia—widening the war to Cambodia and dragging out American involvement for another four years—as fully consistent with the tactics of his predecessors. Others have charged that Vietnamization, a policy supposedly born out of a new strategic calculus, was less an inspired idea than an acceptance of, and rationalization for, failure. In fact, Nixon's use of proxies seemed to inaugurate a new phase of the Cold War; his successors would build upon that policy, supporting "freedom fighters" throughout the developing world. Far from signaling a lessening of tensions or an American retreat from the Cold War, the Nixon Doctrine simply shifted the responsibility for fighting it. Now others would bear America's burden.

Still other scholars have questioned Nixon's use of proxy forces to safeguard American interests. Iran provides the most glaring example of that policy gone awry. In opening America's military coffers to the shah, Nixon fed the appetite of a ruler increasingly out of touch with his own people, accelerating tensions in a country deemed vital to the U.S. national interests. While that unrest derived most of its energy from internal factors, initiatives associated with the Nixon Doctrine contributed to such instability, paving the way for the Iranian revolution in 1979.

Detractors have also faulted the Nixon Doctrine for actually expanding the ranks of nuclear-capable nations. According to this critique, pledges to take friends and allies under the American shield left countries to wonder whether, and under what circumstances, they qualified for such protection. Nixon's failure to identify potential beneficiaries led nations such as Israel, India, Pakistan, and Brazil to join the nuclear club, preferring their own nuclear shields to the ambiguities inherent in an American one.

Finally, scholars have pointed out inconsistencies in the Nixon Doctrine. If its goal was to bring America's commitments in line with its resources, then pledges to aid countries threatened by communist subversion threatened to widen those commitments immeasurably. Application of the doctrine to the communist world seemed equally muddled. Although Nixon professed a recognition that international communism was polycentric rather than monolithic, he continued to oppose communist forces as though a victory for any of them was a victory for all of them, and especially for Moscow.

In the end, the Nixon Doctrine suffered from an inherent ambiguity. In trying to fashion a broad strategic posture for the United States, it became too diffuse, being associated with everything from détente to Realpolitik, to triangular diplomacy, to arms control, and to the use of proxy forces. In sum, it became the Nixon foreign policy agenda writ large. As such, it lacked a single, unifying principle tying administration initiatives together, even promoting one set of policies at the expense of another.

THE CARTER DOCTRINE

The era of détente would prove to be short-lived. Challenges to the Nixon administration emerged from both the right and left of the American political spectrum, questioning the moral basis as well as the geopolitical rationale of engaging the Soviets as equal partners. President James Earl Carter was no more adept at salvaging the spirit of cooperation than was President Gerald Ford before him. Carter's focus on human rights alarmed Soviet leaders, who were accustomed to Nixon's disregard for such issues. From Carter's perspective, a series of events, including conflict in the Horn of Africa and the discovery of Soviet troops in Cuba, led Carter to adopt a more hawkish position toward the USSR. Moscow's invasion of neighboring Afghanistan would bring him more firmly into the cold warrior camp. The Kremlin's December 1979 push south of its border jolted the administration, leading Carter to take several measures that, collectively, marked the clearest indication that relations between the United States and the Soviet Union were in a free fall.

The president clarified the new situation one month later in his State of the Union Address of 23 January 1980. Referring specifically to the Soviet invasion, Carter declared that "an attempt by any outside force to gain control of the Persian Gulf region will be regarded as an assault on the vital interests of the United States of America, and such an assault will be repelled by any means necessary, including military force." By the following morning, the *New York Times* had given that policy a name: the Carter Doctrine.

Although the Soviet invasion was the proximate trigger for the Carter Doctrine, momentum for the president's policy shift had been building over the previous two years. Much of that energy flowed from concern over the fate of Iran. One of the "two pillars" undergirding America's security structure in the Middle East, Iran had been supporting U.S. interests for close to twenty-five years. Its position was so vital that the administration rarely, if ever, questioned Iran's ability to play that role; Carter himself labeled Iran "an island of stability" as late as January 1978. Yet in just over a year, the shah would be deposed, Ayatollah Ruhollah Khomeini would return from France and transform the country into an Islamic republic, and fifty Americans would be taken hostage by Iranian students and militants. With the Nixon Doctrine in tatters, U.S. policymakers sought to fashion a new strategy for the region.

Fears of regional instability were only partly responsible for Carter's movement toward a new strategic posture. According to the president, an amalgam of three distinct forces had combined to prompt his declaration of U.S. policy: "the steady growth and increased projection of Soviet military power beyond its own borders; the overwhelming dependence of the Western democracies on oil supplies from the Middle East; and the press of social and religious and economic and political change in the many nations of the developing world, exemplified by the revolution in Iran." In all, a host of events had led the administration to conclude that American interests in the Persian Gulf were under grave threat. Only a more forceful statement of purpose could begin the process of redressing the regional and—in the administration's calculation—global balance of power.

The doctrine also emerged out of a long-running debate within the administration over its policy toward the Soviet Union. Carter's principal foreign policy aides, Secretary of State Cyrus Vance and national security adviser Zbigniew Brzezinski, differed over the degree to which Washington should confront the Soviets. It was Brzezinski's contention that Moscow had never stopped probing for weak spots around the globe; for him, instability in both Central America and Africa testified to the Kremlin's continuing desire for ideological competition, especially in the developing world. Détente, he surmised, had

merely allowed the Soviets to continue their expansionist thrust there under the cover of superpower cooperation. In contrast to Vance's preference for conciliation, Brzezinski had been lobbying for a more aggressive stance toward Moscow since the earliest days of the administration. A series of developments, including the discovery of Soviet soldiers in Cuba and the Soviet invasion of Afghanistan, provided further support for Brzezinski's arguments. By the time that Carter delivered his State of the Union Address in January 1980, the Brzezinski approach had won out.

A host of measures associated with the Carter Doctrine followed quickly on the heels of its enunciation, signaling a new phase in Carter's approach to the Soviet Union and to his overall practice of foreign policy. Within a month of his address, Carter sanctioned the creation of a Rapid Deployment Force, a contingent of as many as 200,000 troops, designed to expedite the projection of American military power around the globe, and especially in the Middle East. He would take additional steps to improve America's combat readiness, preparing the groundwork for a reimposition of the military draft and asking Congress for a sharp increase in defense spending. Other policies would impinge on U.S.–Soviet relations as Carter enacted a partial grain embargo and boycotted the Moscow Olympics. Still further actions, whereby Carter withdrew a second Strategic Arms Limitation Treaty from senatorial consideration and extended the number of Soviet sites targeted by U.S. missiles, recast the nuclear dimension of the two countries' relationship. On top of those actions, Carter embraced Pakistani ruler Mohammad Zia-ul-Haq, indicating his willingness to subordinate human rights concerns to the struggle against Soviet aggression. By and large, those measures appealed to a Congress eager for action after the previous year's indignities.

They also struck a chord with the American public. Opinion polls revealed general support for the president's statement, suggesting that Carter had correctly gauged the popular mood. Responding to criticism that Carter had engaged in pandering and political grandstanding, Brzezinski defended his president, explaining that the administration needed to make such a proclamation if only to steel the public for the demands ahead. Journalists, however, while hardly indulgent of Soviet behavior, interpreted Carter's speech as a fundamentally political move, designed to reshape the president's image at the outset of an election year. Scholars, too, have subjected the doctrine to withering critiques. Some have described it as little more than empty posturing, crafted more to improve Carter's political fortune than to alter Soviet behavior. Still others maintain that Carter acted rashly, drawing conclusions about Soviet motives based on very little evidence—motives he himself would qualify throughout the remainder of his presidency. Still others have faulted the Carter Doctrine for its ambiguity, noting that it failed to define, with any sense of precision, the nature of aggression, the characteristics of an outside force, or even the boundaries of the Persian Gulf itself.

Moreover, scholars have argued, the Carter Doctrine and policies associated with it offered little in the way of tangible benefits. None of the measures aimed at the Kremlin—not the grain embargo, nor the Olympic boycott, nor the curtailment of additional trade—forced the Soviets out of Afghanistan. Nor did the president's unilateralism sit well with his European allies; only British Prime Minister Margaret Thatcher supported Carter's approach. At the same time, however, European business capitalized on the chillier relationship as several firms concluded lucrative deals at America's expense.

While the Carter Doctrine secured few if any tangible gains—even its progenitor lost at the ballot box that November—it would continue to shape U.S. policy during the Cold War, largely because subsequent administrations bought into its premises. President Ronald Reagan and his advisers regarded the Soviet Union as an aggressive, expansionist power; if anything, they, and the Bush administration that was to follow, were even more willing to protect U.S. interests in the Persian Gulf from Soviet predations and political instability.

The Carter Doctrine also hastened the buildup of American arms, a process that was already under way by January 1980, and for which some historians give him high marks. It would be the Reagan administration, however, that would capitalize on the perceived need for military expenditures, expanding the size and cost, and revamping the shape, of America's military forces.

In relation to other Cold War presidential statements, the Carter Doctrine fit squarely within their rhetorical barriers. It maintained Truman and Eisenhower's focus on the Mediterranean and Middle East, a region that had become increasingly vital to U.S. officials in the aftermath of the October 1973 Yom Kippur War and the ensuing Arab oil boycott. Indeed, it echoed the excited language of both the Truman and Eisenhower Doc-

trines, offering to assist those nations threatened by totalitarian aggression. And in associating himself with those two statements of national policy, Carter distanced himself from the previous two administrations. His willingness to intercede unilaterally in Middle Eastern affairs testified to the poverty of the Nixon Doctrine's "twin pillar policy," the very structure of which was now obsolete. Nevertheless, U.S. support for the Afghani resistance to the Soviet Union suggests that elements of Nixon's approach remained intact; the United States would continue to assist proxy forces resisting Soviet advances when such a policy proved fruitful, and would seek to impose its own forces when the situation demanded it.

THE REAGAN DOCTRINE

For the most part, the doctrines of American foreign policy have sprung largely from a sense of crisis in the world at large. From the early nineteenth until the late twentieth century, whenever presidents saw fit to articulate certain principles of American foreign policy, they did so in an environment of either apparent danger or impending opportunity. The Reagan Doctrine was no different. Presupposing a world of good and evil, it operated on the assumption that evil, in the form of the USSR, was gaining the upper hand. To Reagan and his advisers, examples of Soviet perfidy, including support for Marxist movements around the globe, were numerous; moreover, Soviet adventurism, from the Horn of Africa in the 1970s to Central America in the 1980s, showed no signs of abating. Reagan was intent on arresting that trend—a trend, he believed, that Carter had done little to reverse. Therefore, he adopted the rhetoric of the early Cold War, advocating policies equally assertive and bold in scope.

Reagan laid out that vision in his State of the Union Address of 6 February 1985. "We must not break faith," he declared, "with those who are risking their lives—on every continent from Afghanistan to Nicaragua—to defy Soviet-supported aggression and secure rights which have been ours from birth." The president went on to equate anticommunist forces with American colonists who had fought the revolutionary war, describing those latter-day patriots as "freedom fighters" for democracy. Providing aid to those groups was not only morally just but geopolitically sound. "Support for freedom fighters," Reagan avowed, "is self-defense." It would be months before those declarations would take shape as a fixed statement of policy. In the interim, a further pledge to support "freedom fighters," made on 22 February by Secretary of State George Shultz to the Commonwealth Club in San Francisco, lent added heft to Reagan's message. But it was neither Reagan nor his advisers who put the president's name to the set of policies he was announcing. Rather, it was Charles Krauthammer, a commentator on foreign affairs, who coined the term "Reagan Doctrine" in a *Time* magazine column of April 1985. Reagan's practice of waging Cold War through proxy forces had a long doctrinal pedigree, one that dated back to the early years of the Cold War. Presidents from Truman through Carter had all sought to aid governments or movements battling communism, but it was Reagan who, arguably, endowed that policy with its greatest energy. The belief that Moscow was supporting leftist movements in the Third World was one of the doctrine's guiding principles. As Reagan commented during the 1980 presidential campaign, "the Soviet Union underlies all the unrest that is going on. If they weren't engaged in this game of dominoes, there wouldn't be any hot spots in the world." Reagan himself chose to play that game early in his administration, authorizing the Central Intelligence Agency in 1981 to begin financing the "contra" forces battling the pro-Soviet Sandinista movement for control of Nicaragua. Funding for such anticommunist units suggests that the Reagan Doctrine appeared in practice long before it became enshrined as such.

Aside from injecting an explicitly moral component into the nation's conduct of foreign affairs, the Reagan Doctrine augmented the geopolitical rationale of earlier efforts. It was the administration's position that the Truman Doctrine's version of containment, which had been designed originally to thwart Stalin's aims in Europe, was obsolete. Since the 1950s the Kremlin had achieved considerable influence in the Third World, indicating that Moscow's ambitions were more global than originally imagined. This new reality, according to the administration, called for a revision of those basic postulates first laid down by Policy Planning Staff director George Kennan during the early years of the Cold War. With the Reagan team prepared to challenge the Soviets all over the globe, administration spokespersons began to call their approach "containment plus."

Reagan officials would add an offensive component to containment that was at least as explicit—and more wide-ranging—than anything that policy had sanctioned during the early Cold War. Secretary of State George Shultz, like Secretary John Foster Dulles before him, spoke of "rolling back" Soviet gains, recapturing nations and peoples for democracy. Yet Shultz pledged to do so in a new environment, where Moscow was a global power committed to the safeguarding of communist regimes. That Soviet conceit, known as the Brezhnev Doctrine—a 1968 statement by Premier Leonid Brezhnev declaring the irreversibility of socialist gains—was anathema to Reagan, "an arrogant pretension," as he termed it, "that we must face up to."

The administration's reluctance to cede virtually any ground to communism revealed another shift in America's Cold War policy and led Reagan to contravene a principle established in the Nixon-Ford years during the 1970s. That principle, known as the Sonnenfeldt Doctrine—after State Department counselor Helmut Sonnenfeldt—upheld the Nixon-Kissinger strategy of according greater legitimacy to Soviet security concerns. Speaking to a gathering of U.S. ambassadors in December 1975, Sonnenfeldt urged the Soviets and the Eastern Europeans to seek a more "organic" relationship, downplaying the oppressiveness of that relationship while at the same time advocating a "more autonomous existence" for Eastern Europe "within the context of a strong Soviet geopolitical influence." Displeasure with that position, on both moral and geopolitical grounds, led the Reagan administration to adopt a more aggressive, global policy that challenged the legitimacy of Soviet power.

Although Reagan was unquestionably supportive of the doctrine that bore his name, his role in formulating it seems to have been quite limited. His distance from that project accords with the operating style of a president whose involvement in the day-to-day tasks of policymaking was minimal at best. Clearly, however, Reagan was in tune with the doctrine's precepts—ideas that sprang from key advisers such as CIA director William Casey, UN ambassador Jeane Kirkpatrick, Defense Secretary Caspar Weinberger, and Attorney General Edwin Meese. Speechwriters and publicists such as Anthony Dolan, Peggy Noonan, and Patrick Buchanan were equally important in shaping the message for public consumption. In the end, however, it was Reagan, through his mastery of public speaking, who sold it to the nation.

Reagan would implement his doctrine in a variety of locales around the world, from Asia to Africa to Central America. In Afghanistan, the president sought to aid forces working to topple the pro-Soviet government in Kabul. Using means reminiscent of the Nixon Doctrine, Reagan provided the guerrillas with substantial amounts of military assistance in their battle against the invading Soviets. The administration offered similar support to Nicaraguan contras battling communist-dominated Sandinistas who had overthrown longtime dictator Anastasio Somoza Debayle. Likewise, Reagan offered aid to anticommunists in Angola competing with the Soviet-backed government for control of that newly independent country. And in Cambodia the administration propped up a coalition of forces working to unseat a government installed by the Soviet-sponsored Vietnamese after Hanoi's invasion of 1979.

The track record of the Reagan Doctrine is mixed. The administration got what it wanted in Afghanistan: strong resistance to Soviet armed forces and an eventual troop pullout by Mikhail Gorbachev. To the extent that it accelerated popular distrust of the Communist Party and the Soviet government, the war in Afghanistan—and the Reagan administration's contribution to it—helped bring down the Soviet empire and the USSR itself. Yet those immediate gains were offset in later years as Afghani forces turned on their former patrons, targeting U.S. interests around the world.

The Reagan Doctrine also gave a boost to the CIA, an institution that had come under fire during the 1970s as its abuses of power, investigated by Congress, came to light. Under the guidance of William J. Casey, the CIA resuscitated its operations division, carrying out policies largely shielded from public view. That emphasis on clandestine activity, however, would backfire during the second Reagan administration. Fears that "rogue" elements within the government were running U.S. foreign policy were borne out with the unfolding of the Iran-Contra affair, a political scandal that revealed how elements of the National Security Council undermined congressional legislation in an effort to aid the Nicaraguan rebels.

Scholars have questioned the distinctiveness of the Reagan Doctrine. The containment plus designation applied by its supporters suggested that the Reagan Doctrine added the element of "rollback" to the decades-old policy of restricting Soviet encroachment. In doing so, however, the administration exaggerated the novelty of its approach; though George Kennan might have called for engaging the Soviets on a more limited geographic basis in the late 1940s, by the time

that Paul Nitze had replaced Kennan as head of the Policy Planning Staff in 1950—and certainly by the time that Truman had made way for Eisenhower—the United States was challenging communist and leftist movements far afield from the Soviet periphery. Similarly, Reagan's use of proxy forces echoed tactics used by every administration from Truman forward; indeed, the speech that launched the Reagan Doctrine included verbatim numerous paragraphs from Truman's 1947 speech. From Greek guerrillas to Guatemalan generals to anti-Castro Cubans to conservative Chileans, indigenous forces with anticommunist pedigrees had long fought America's Cold War battles on many a distant shore.

Others have criticized the administration for applying the Reagan Doctrine selectively. According to these observers, recipients of American aid were often lacking in liberal virtues; the Afghani guerrillas, for instance, hardly merited support on democratic grounds. Use of such proxies led commentators to label the Reagan approach as Realpolitik masquerading as morality, the very criticism Reaganites themselves had leveled at Nixon and Kissinger. It also led critics to charge Reagan with pandering to public opinion, since administration references to "freedom fighters" seemed more reflective of the president's domestic political needs than of the makeup of those forces receiving American assistance.

Aside from the more cosmetic aspects of the Reagan Doctrine, it is far from clear whether it succeeded in rolling back communist gains. Critics have charged that administration policies, such as those pursued in Nicaragua, actually retarded the emergence of stability and the growth of a more pro-American sentiment. Although the Sandinistas did lose at the ballot box in 1990, scholars have described similarly favorable outcomes in locales such as Cambodia and Angola as owing more to changes in the international arena than to Reagan's policies themselves. The breakup of Moscow's Eastern European empire in 1989 and the fall of the Soviet Union in 1991 altered the geopolitical environment, undercutting support for pro-Soviet or Marxist regimes. Settlement of those regional conflicts, in ways largely favorable to Western interests, thus became easier to achieve.

Indeed, it is far from clear whether the allegedly greatest achievement of the Reagan Doctrine—the fall of communism itself—is attributable to Reagan at all. Historians have argued repeatedly that a host of troubles internal to the

Soviet Union—from a stagnant economy to a crisis of political legitimacy to the intractable nationalities question—were far more consequential to the undoing of the Soviet system than any challenge mounted by Reagan. Nevertheless, other scholars point out that Reagan gave the final push to the Soviet house of cards. It was his pursuit of the Strategic Defense Initiative, the argument runs, that bankrupted the Kremlin leadership, prompting a liberalization of the Soviet political economy that, in turn, loosed the forces that brought down the entire system. Likewise, it was Reagan's rhetoric that emboldened Eastern Europeans to become more assertive, leading to the events of 1989 and the fall of the Berlin Wall. Judgment on these matters still awaits a more thorough historical treatment.

Clearly, though, the last presidential doctrine of the Cold War was every bit as hawkish as the first. It sought to reinject a moral component to America's foreign policy, hearkening back to the language of the Truman years. In doing so, the Reagan team—rhetorically, at least—abandoned the amoral practice of Nixon-Kissinger Realpolitik, launching an all-out offensive against the "evil empire." Reagan's appraisal of the Soviets would undergo a shift, however, leading to a more productive relationship with Moscow, especially after the emergence of Mikhail Gorbachev. Still, the administration remained hawkish in its approach to what it perceived as pro-Soviet forces. Working from a Manichean view of the world, the Reagan administration regarded all leftist regimes as tools of the Kremlin, a position that added greater force to its public rhetoric while possibly reducing the efficacy of its foreign policies.

CONCLUSION

At the most basic level, one can understand the doctrines of American foreign policy as statements of principle, designed to forestall crises or to meet them head on. The Monroe, Truman, Eisenhower, Carter, and Reagan Doctrines all sought to preempt actions deemed hostile to the United States by warning potential aggressors of American intent. They also pledged, save for the Monroe Doctrine, to support allied forces in their campaigns against predatory forces. To some extent, then, most of these doctrines carried deterrent qualities. The Hoover-Stimson Doctrine and the Nixon Doctrine stand out as exceptions: the former because it sought to compel the undoing of past actions as

much as to deter future behavior, and the latter because it sought to do so many things, especially on the strategic level, with none of them targeting any specific threat.

In other ways, the story of America's foreign policy doctrines, at least during the Cold War, is the story of the United States supplanting Britain as a world power. Britain's inability to prop up pro-Western forces in Greece and Turkey precipitated Truman's request of $400 million in assistance for those two nations and a global commitment to aid others similarly imperiled. Eisenhower's pledge to aid Middle Eastern nations threatened by international communism came as a direct response to British, along with French, stumblings during the Suez crisis of 1956. Nixon's reliance on a "twin pillar" policy, while a recognition of America's limited resources, was itself brought on by Britain's withdrawal from territories east of the Suez.

And yet each of those statements exist as quintessentially, if not exclusively, American. Their content reflects the values of a nation imbued with a sense of mission to carry democratic principles around the world. Again, that sense of transcendent purpose shows up most clearly during the Cold War, yet previous statements contain elements of that creed. Nevertheless, the doctrines of American foreign policy are also clearly designed to promote the national interest. Whether they involved the creation of an Atlantic buffer between Europe and the Americas, or the defense of freedom—and free enterprise—in Europe itself, those doctrines have sought to protect American interests, be they material or nonmaterial, so that U.S. citizens could enjoy the blessings of liberty.

Those doctrines, in fact, reveal a close relationship between the missionary ideal of a more democratic world and the security ideal of a resilient America. For the most part, each presumes that the proliferation of democratic government would result in a more peaceful world and a more secure United States. Grounded in the belief that the peoples of the world are more desirous of peace than war, they posit that a government responsive to the will of the people would likewise seek pacific relations. These ideas are embedded in U.S. foreign policy doctrines from Monroe to Reagan. From the protection of democratic regimes in the Western Hemisphere, to the nonrecognition of military conquest in East Asia, to support for "freedom fighters" in the Middle East and around the world, those doctrines operated on the assumption that a more democratic world would be a safer world—and a more secure world for the United States.

At the same time, one might wonder why all presidents, especially from the middle of the twentieth century onward, did not have a doctrine of their own. Surely in an age of increasing American power, Franklin D. Roosevelt might have tapped into a legacy of past presidents and associated himself with a particular statement of purpose. Recent experience with such declarations, however, suggests at least one reason why a Roosevelt Doctrine failed to materialize. While the Monroe Doctrine and the Roosevelt Corollary of Theodore Roosevelt were familiar concepts to Americans, the Stimson Doctrine—the latest in a growing line of policy proclamations—was hardly worthy of emulation. Moreover, previous statements of American purpose were made unilaterally; Franklin Roosevelt's grand declarations—most notably, the Atlantic Charter—were declarations of multilateral intent. Of Roosevelt's many pronouncements, therefore, the statement most likely to have merited doctrinal status might have been his 1937 pledge to "quarantine" aggressor states. Offered in response to Japanese depredations in China, Roosevelt's call for a moral embargo on predatory regimes was so vague, however, and supported with such little force, that a doctrinal statement of principle would likely have gone the way of Stimson's pledge.

The absence of a Kennedy Doctrine is also curious, though perhaps less so than at first thought. President John F. Kennedy devoted much of his energy to the Caribbean. After the Bay of Pigs debacle, however, Kennedy was loathe to commit himself publicly to the removal of the Castro regime, especially given the negative press the effort had received. Certainly it was an outcome Kennedy greatly desired, and he devoted considerable resources to its realization Yet it might have proved difficult to make so bold a statement on Cuba following his April failure. Indeed, it probably would have been ludicrous for him to have proffered a doctrine designed to rescue him from his earlier defeat. Moreover, having been roughed up by Nikita Khrushchev at the Vienna summit, Kennedy was in no position to be establishing rigid guidelines governing American policy. Aside from those considerations, Kennedy, his associates, and lawmakers in Congress had all spoken of the Monroe Doctrine both before and during the Cuban missile crisis in 1962, so that a Kennedy Corollary to the Monroe Doctrine would have seemed superfluous.

Kennedy's successor, Lyndon B. Johnson, has received scholarly credit for various statements of principle; scattered references to a Johnson Doctrine do exist in the literature. In fact, scholars have identified two such doctrines: one relating to American policy in Southeast Asia, the other relating to U.S. policy in the Caribbean. The first Johnson Doctrine invoked several principles of recent American policy, including the Munich Analogy and the Truman Doctrine. He meant it to apply, however, specifically to Indochina. As he declared on 4 August 1964, the United States would "take all necessary measures in support of freedom and in defense of peace in Southeast Asia." This first Johnson Doctrine, then, was synonymous with the ensuing Tonkin Gulf Resolution; in fact, they were one and the same. Scholars nevertheless usually invoke the resolution rather than the president in their treatments of the episode.

Johnson's second statement, concerning communism in the Caribbean, mirrors the one Eisenhower made regarding the Middle East. Delivered on 2 May 1965, following the insertion of U.S. troops into the Dominican Republic, this first Johnson Doctrine pledged "the American nations" to prevent the establishment "of another communist government in the Western Hemisphere." Its wording indicated the frustration policymakers felt at having to live with one communist regime only ninety miles from the United States. While Johnson's actions in the Dominican Republic receive wide treatment in the literature, few scholars make reference to a "Johnson Doctrine" as such. Perhaps this is because of the "credibility gap" that opened up in the wake of the action. Claims that Dominican leftists were brutalizing the local populace and shooting at the U.S. embassy turned out to be false, prompting Americans to question the veracity of their president. Although the negative press Johnson received might have doomed his efforts to elevate the stature of his policy, equally rough treatment failed to prevent other grand statements, such as the one Stimson made, from rising to the level of doctrine.

In the post–Cold War era, the search for a guiding policy has proved frustrating and elusive, primarily because no international reality, such as that which followed World War II, has congealed. Nor were policymakers able to talk one into existence. President George H. W. Bush's "new world order" failed to materialize, although during the winter of 1990–1991 he was able to array a constellation of powers, the likes of which had never been seen, to resist the Iraqi invasion of Kuwait. Bush's successor, President William

Jefferson Clinton, was no more successful in attaching his name to any grand declaration of policy. While Clinton often spoke out in support of human rights, the tardiness with which the United States and the international community addressed the horrors in Rwanda and the Balkans indicates, perhaps, a problem with making sweeping statements about such issues. Establishing a doctrinal position on the evils of ethnic cleansing, for example, a position that might commit the United States to eradicating those practices, would likely compel a president to make good on that—a position that future presidents would likely resist.

Perhaps another reason for the absence of doctrinal statements lies with the nature of the international environment near the close of the twentieth century. The end of the Cold War brought with it a diminution of public concern over a host of high profile issues, including the possibility of superpower war. Matters of "high politics," then, such as those involving the United States and Russia over the proliferation or reduction of nuclear arms, seemed less important than matters of "low politics," such as global trade and economics. While the Balkan conflict carried the seeds of a much wider war—indeed, that was part of the administration's reasoning for entering it in the first place—it never threatened the United States in ways that touched on the nation's very existence, in contrast to the superpower rivalry of the Cold War.

Still, during the presidency of William Jefferson Clinton, commentators attempted to affix doctrines to his name. None, however, seemed to have any staying power. Critics likened the Clinton Doctrine to a form of "social engineering," focusing on the president's attempts at nation building in Somalia or Haiti. Others have used the term when discussing Clinton's interest in "cooperative security" and his efforts to create an intricate web of economic interdependence. Again, only time will tell if these "doctrines" seep into the public consciousness.

Perhaps the most that can be said about the future of these grand statements of principle is that presidents will likely treat them as they have always treated them—with great amounts of discretion and latitude. Policymakers have routinely opted for liberal interpretations of these doctrines—the Monroe Doctrine being a case in point—invoking, discarding, or fudging their precepts at will. Nothing in the past offers any evidence for believing that future administrations will do otherwise.

BIBLIOGRAPHY

Ammon, T. Harry. "The Monroe Doctrine: Domestic Politics or National Decision." *Diplomatic History* 5, no. 1 (winter 1981): 53–70. This and the response from Ernest R. May in the same issue provide a snapshot of the debate surrounding the circumstances of the doctrine's enunciation.

Arnson, Cynthia J. *Crossroads: Congress, the Reagan Administration, and Central America.* New York, 1989.

Berman, Larry, ed. *Looking Back on the Reagan Presidency.* Baltimore, 1990.

Combs, Jerold A. "The Origins of the Monroe Doctrine: A Survey of Interpretations by United States Historians." *Australian Journal of Politics and History* 27, no. 2 (1981).

Crabb, Cecil V., Jr. *The Doctrines of American Foreign Policy: Their Meaning, Role, and Future.* Baton Rouge, La., 1982. The best monograph available on the origins, implications, and legacies of America's foreign policy doctrines, from the Monroe through Carter.

Daalder, Ivo. "And Now, a Clinton Doctrine?" *Haagsche Courant* (10 July 1999).

DeMuth, Christopher C., et al. *The Reagan Doctrine and Beyond.* Washington, D.C., 1988.

Ferrell, Robert. *American Diplomacy in the Great Depression: Hoover-Stimson Foreign Policy, 1929–1933.* New Haven, Conn., 1957.

Fischer, Beth A. *The Reagan Reversal: Foreign Policy and the End of the Cold War.* Columbia, Mo., 1997.

Freeland, Richard M. *The Truman Doctrine and the Origins of McCarthyism: Foreign Policy, Domestic Politics, and Internal Security, 1946–1948.* New York, 1972. Links the Truman speech with a corresponding loyalty-security program for containing communism at home.

Gaddis, John Lewis. "Reconsiderations: Was the Truman Doctrine a Real Turning Point?" *Foreign Affairs* 52, no. 2 (1974): 386–402.

Gardner, Lloyd C. *Architects of Illusion: Men and Ideas in American Foreign Policy, 1941–1949.* Chicago, 1970. Includes a chapter on Dean Acheson's role in formulating the Truman Doctrine.

Garthoff, Raymond L. *Détente and Confrontation: American-Soviet Relations from Nixon to Reagan.* Washington, D.C., 1985.

———. "Détente and Deterrence in the Cold War." *Diplomatic History* 22, no. 1 (winter 1998): 145–148. On the Nixon Doctrine.

Gendzier, Irene. *Notes from the Minefield: United States Intervention in Lebanon and the Middle East, 1945–1958*. New York, 1997. Covers the Eisenhower Doctrine.

Hyland, William G., ed. *The Reagan Foreign Policy*. New York, 1987.

Ivie, Robert L. "Fire, Flood, and Red Fever: Motivating Metaphors of Global Emergency in the Truman Doctrine Speech." *Presidential Studies Quarterly* 29, no. 3 (1999): 570–591.

Johnson, Robert H. "Misguided Morality: Ethics and the Reagan Doctrine." *Political Science Quarterly* 103, no. 3 (autumn 1988): 509–529.

Jones, Joseph M. *The Fifteen Weeks (February 21–June 5, 1947)*. New York, 1955. Offers the perspective of a State Department official and speechwriter who authored the 12 March address; a classic account of the Truman Doctrine and the Marshall Plan.

Kaplan, Lawrence S. "NATO and the Nixon Doctrine: Ten Years Later." *Orbis* 24, no. 1 (1980): 149–164.

———. "The Monroe Doctrine and the Truman Doctrine: The Case of Greece." *Journal of the Early Republic* 13, no. 1 (1993):1–21.

Kaufman, Burton I. *The Presidency of James Earl Carter, Jr.* Lawrence, Kans., 1993.

Kuniholm, Bruce. "The Carter Doctrine, the Reagan Corollary, and Prospects for United States Policy in Southwest Asia." *International Journal* (Toronto) 41, no. 2 (1986): 342–361.

Lagon, Mark P. *The Reagan Doctrine: Sources of American Conduct in the Cold War's Last Chapter.* Westport, Conn., 1994.

Leffler, Melvyn P. "From the Truman Doctrine to the Carter Doctrine: Lessons and Dilemmas of the Cold War." *Diplomatic History* 7, no. 4 (fall 1983): 245–266.

Lesch, David W. *Syria and the United States: Eisenhower's Cold War in the Middle East.* Boulder, Colo., 1992.

Little, Douglas. "His Finest Hour?: Eisenhower, Lebanon, and the 1958 Middle East Crisis." *Diplomatic History* 20 (winter 1996): 27–54.

Litwak, Robert S. *Détente and the Nixon Doctrine: American Foreign Policy and the Pursuit of Stability, 1969–1976.* New York, 1984.

Manning, Robert, and Patrick Clawson. "The Clinton Doctrine." *Wall Street Journal* (29 December 1997).

May, Ernest R. *The Making of the Monroe Doctrine.* Cambridge, Mass., 1975.

McFaul, Michael. "Rethinking the Reagan Doctrine in Angola." *International Security* 14, no. 3 (winter 1989–1990): 99–135.

Pach, Chester J., and Elmo Richardson. *The Presidency of Dwight D. Eisenhower.* Lawrence, Kans., 1993.

Perkins, Dexter. *A History of the Monroe Doctrine.* Rev. ed. Boston, 1955. The classic, and still the most persuasive, account of the doctrine.

Rabe, Steven. "The Johnson (Eisenhower) Doctrine for Latin America." *Diplomatic History* 9, no. 1 (1985).

Schmertz, Eric J., et. al., eds. *President Reagan and the World.* Westport, Conn., 1997.

Schweizer, Peter, ed. *The Fall of the Berlin Wall : Reassessing the Causes and Consequences of the End of the Cold War.* Stanford, Calif., 2000.

Smith, Gaddis. *Morality, Reason, and Power: American Diplomacy in the Carter Years.* New York, 1986.

———. *The Last Years of the Monroe Doctrine, 1945–1993.* New York, 1994.

Takeyh, Ray. *The Origins of the Eisenhower Doctrine: The U.S., Britain, and Nasser's Egypt, 1953–57.* New York, 2000.

Teicher, Howard, and Gayle Radley Teicher. *Twin Pillars to Desert Storm: America's Flawed Vision in the Middle East from Nixon to Bush.* New York, 1993.

Telhami, Shibley. "Raise Stakes via a Clinton Doctrine." *Los Angeles Times* (3 November 1999).

Tucker, Robert W., ed. *Intervention and the Reagan Doctrine.* New York, 1985.

Wittner, Lawrence S. "The Truman Doctrine and the Defense of Freedom." *Diplomatic History* 4, no. 2 (spring 1980): 161–187.

Xydis, Stephen G. *Greece and the Great Powers, 1944–1947: Prelude to the Truman Doctrine.* Thessalonika, Greece, 1963. Provides solid background on the situation in Greece.

Zakaria, Fareed. "The Reagan Strategy of Containment." *Political Science Quarterly* 105, no. 3 (autumn 1990): 373–395.

See also COLONIALISM AND NEOCOLONIALISM; CONTAINMENT; CONTINENTAL EXPANSION; INTERVENTION AND NONINTERVENTION; ISOLATIONISM; THE MUNICH ANALOGY; THE NATIONAL INTEREST; RECOGNITION.

DOLLAR DIPLOMACY

Eugene P. Trani

In his final message to Congress on 3 December 1912, President William Howard Taft looked back at the foreign policy followed by the United States during his administration and noted: "The diplomacy of the present administration has sought to respond to modern ideas of commercial intercourse. This policy has been characterized as substituting dollars for bullets. It is one that appeals alike to idealistic humanitarian sentiments, to the dictates of sound policy and strategy, and to legitimate commercial aims."

Taft's remarks gave formal definition to the term "dollar diplomacy," a phrase synonymous with the diplomacy his administration pursued between 1909 and 1913. During those years the goal of diplomacy was to make the United States a commercial and financial world power. It was a narrowly constructed view of foreign relations, arising in great part out of the natural alliances between the corporate lawyers who came to people Taft's administration and the bankers and businesses that were their clients. Thus, the Taft administration concentrated on assisting American businessmen in the protection and expansion of investment and trade, especially in Latin America and the Far East.

The idea of protecting American commercial interests around the world was not new and had been part of the diplomacy of the United States since its earliest days. Efforts to trade with British and Spanish colonies in the Western Hemisphere, defense of the rights of neutrals to trade in wartime, and support of the most-favored-nation concept were all predecessors of dollar diplomacy. Yet dollar diplomacy was the subject of much controversy during the Taft administration and in the years that followed.

Much of the contemporary controversy over dollar diplomacy stemmed from the fact that Taft, the handpicked successor of Theodore Roosevelt, had embarked on a policy that differed from the one Roosevelt had followed. Roosevelt was an expansionist and had supported the American move into world affairs. For a variety of reasons, Roosevelt believed expansion necessary for the United States, with benefits for the rest of the world. He viewed foreign affairs in strategic terms, with Europe as the center of world power. He felt an affinity for Britain and based much of his diplomacy on cooperation between Washington and London. To be sure, Roosevelt supported the expansion of American business throughout the world, but he was much more concerned with the balance of power and improving the Anglo-American relationship. As a result, Roosevelt mediated the Russo-Japanese War (1904–1905) and the conflict between France and Germany over Morocco in 1906.

Taft came to office with a different view. Ever the lawyer, he viewed foreign policy in terms of legal institutions. He thus came to support arbitration treaties. He had differences with Roosevelt over Europe, feeling that the United States had little or no interest in events there. Taft kept the United States out of the second Moroccan crisis in 1911, and, while supporting mediation, he was not willing to mediate the Italo-Turkish War (1911) nor the first Balkan War the following year. Taft believed that the most important relations with Europe occurred in developing nations where the United States and Europe shared interests.

Taft's view of the role of American business in foreign policy also differed from Roosevelt's. Taft long had been concerned with foreign trade. He recognized that by 1909 the United States was producing more goods than Americans could consume and therefore had to increase exports. It was perhaps symbolic that during the Taft administration, in 1910 to be exact, that the United States began to export more manufactured goods than raw materials, changing the focus of trade from industrial nations in need of raw materials to lesser developed countries that required finished products. In this regard the developing areas of Latin America and East Asia seemed particularly important. A concentration on economic opportunities in Latin America and East Asia, especially China, would have many benefits. Such a policy would help the American economy by solving the problem of overproduction. It would benefit recipient nations, bringing economic progress, which in turn would mean political stability; and stability would guarantee American strategic interests in underdeveloped areas. It was not surprising that in Taft's first annual message (7 December 1909) he stated: "To-day, more than ever before, American capital is seeking investment in foreign countries, and American products are more and more generally seeking foreign markets."

While Taft had ideas as to the diplomacy the United States should follow, he had no interest in serving as his own secretary of state, further distinguishing his administration from Roosevelt's. The man whom Taft chose to carry out his foreign policy, after refusals by Elihu Root and Henry Cabot Lodge, was Philander C. Knox, a wealthy conservative Pennsylvania lawyer then in the Senate. Knox had been attorney general between 1901 and 1904; and this fact, in the president's view, more than made up for his lack of experience in foreign affairs, since Taft wanted lawyers in his cabinet. Knox had been what is now known as a corporation lawyer, the Carnegie Steel Corporation being one of his clients. He was thus sympathetic to big business.

Knox shared Taft's views concerning the goal of American diplomacy—protection and expansion of economic interests. A State Department memorandum of 6 October 1909 pointed out that all developed countries were seeking trade and noted that trade was essential to American prosperity. There could be no more important task than expanded investment and trade. Diplomacy had to support American financiers and businessmen by finding opportunities abroad. The State Department appeared to anticipate the activities of the Bureau of Foreign and Domestic Commerce in the 1920s, when Herbert Hoover was secretary of commerce, although Hoover strenuously objected to the concept of dollar diplomacy, making it a priority following his election to the presidency to eliminate its effects, particularly in Latin America. But locating commercial opportunities abroad was not enough for Knox and Taft. As the 1909 memorandum indicated, the United States would insist that Americans compete with Europeans in the developing countries by buying bonds, floating loans, building railroads, and establishing banks.

So it was that the State Department during the Taft years turned to dollar diplomacy. The policy gained support throughout the diplomatic corps, a fact that was especially important as Knox concentrated on policy and allowed subordinates to run day-to-day operations. Francis M. Huntington Wilson, first assistant secretary of state, presided over the daily activities of the State Department and carried out a reorganization of the department into geographical bureaus. Huntington Wilson, Willard D. Straight, and Thomas C. Dawson, the latter two the initial heads of the Division of Far Eastern Affairs and the newly created Latin American Division, respectively, all shared the views of Taft and Knox on trade and investment.

When the administration talked about dollar diplomacy in Latin America, it was almost always referring to the Caribbean, which had strategic implications because of the soon-to-be-completed Panama Canal. Concerned over the general instability of the Central American governments, Taft and Knox set a goal of stable governments and prevention of financial collapse. Fiscal intervention would make military intervention unnecessary. As Knox told an audience at the University of Pennsylvania on 15 June 1910: "True stability is best established not by military, but by economic and social forces. . . . The problem of good government is inextricably interwoven with that of economic prosperity and sound finance; financial stability contributes perhaps more than any other one factor to political stability."

Such statements did not mean that Taft and Knox were unwilling to use military power in the Caribbean. They did use it. They thought that fiscal control would lessen the need for intervention. They believed that the United States and nations of the Caribbean would both benefit. For the United States, an increase in trade, more profitable investments, and a secure Panama Canal would result. For the local inhabitants, the benefits would be peace, prosperity, and improved social conditions.

Taft and Knox believed that the way to control the finances of the Caribbean countries was to take over customhouses, following the example of the Roosevelt administration in the Dominican Republic. According to the Taft-Knox doctrine, it was important to get the Caribbean nations to repay European debts by means of loans from American businessmen or at least from multinational groups in which Americans participated. In Nicaragua, Honduras, Guatemala, and

Haiti, the United States pushed refunding schemes. The State Department believed that these sorts of reforms would end political instability in the Caribbean.

Nicaragua proved the classic case of dollar diplomacy in the Caribbean. While the American economic interest in Nicaragua was small, the country had been an alternate route for the trans-Isthmian canal. The United States was sensitive to activities in Nicaragua. The longtime dictator José Santos Zelaya had never been popular in Washington and was seen as the cause of much instability in Central America, the result of his efforts to dominate the area. When Knox took control of the Department of State, he ordered withdrawal of the chargé d'affaires from Nicaragua, began to press private business claims against the Zelaya government, and sought, albeit unsuccessfully, to discourage a Franco-British consortium from making a loan. In cooperation with Mexico, the United States also sent warships to stop Zelaya from filibustering in Central America.

In October 1909 the situation became complex with the outbreak of civil war in Nicaragua. Insurgency centered on the eastern coast in Bluefields, a city dominated by foreign businessmen and planters. These foreigners and conservative politicians in Nicaragua followed the lead of General Juan J. Estrada. Foreign money, some of it American, bankrolled the revolutionaries. While declaring itself neutral, there was little question as to which side the U.S. government supported. Formal neutrality disappeared when Zelaya executed two Americans captured while fighting with the rebels. The United States broke off relations, asserting that the revolutionaries represented "the ideals and the will of a majority of the Nicaraguan people more faithfully than does the Government of President Zelaya."

Washington made known that Zelaya's resignation in late 1909 was not enough. Huntington Wilson pushed for expulsion of the liberal party from power, hoping the rebels would take control. U.S. forces landed at Bluefields to make sure fighting did not damage American interests. Successes followed for the insurgents, and by the end of August 1910 they had taken the capital, Managua. The United States expected fiscal reform in Nicaragua, and refused to recognize the new government until it had agreed to American control of the customhouses and to the refunding of the debt owed to British bankers by means of a loan from American financiers. Dawson went to Nicaragua to negotiate the terms of recognition.

This did not end the difficulties, for the American demands were unpopular. The United States went ahead with its financial program, even though the Senate delayed action on the treaty (known as the Knox-Castrillo Convention) worked out between Washington and Managua in June 1911, which called for refunding of Nicaragua's internal and external debts and administration of the customs by a collector approved by American officials. While the Senate debated, bankers went ahead with the rehabilitation of Nicaraguan finances, making a loan with the national railroad and the national bank as collateral. American citizens also began to collect Nicaraguan customs and to serve on a mixed claims commission, all in anticipation of Senate action. Much to the distress of Taft and Knox, the treaty died in a Senate committee in May 1912, along with a similar treaty with Honduras.

Another revolution broke out in Nicaragua in July 1912, and this also brought American intervention. Approximately 2,700 marines landed to protect U.S. citizens and property and to suppress the revolution, which was over by early October. Although the majority of the marines was soon withdrawn, a legation guard remained as a symbol of intervention until 1925. The Taft administration went out of office in March 1913, convinced that the policy it had followed in Nicaragua was correct. Intervention had proved necessary, the administration admitted, but it was only for a short time and continued fiscal intervention would make further military intervention unlikely.

The Taft-Knox policy toward Nicaragua, and for that matter toward the rest of Central America, was unquestionably offensive to Latin Americans. Even a goodwill visit through the Caribbean by Knox could not overcome suspicions. Knox said the United States did not covet an inch of Latin territory, but such utterances were not accepted south of the Rio Grande.

In the years after 1912, political leaders in both Latin America and the United States attacked Taft's policy toward Central America. Elihu Root believed that dollar diplomacy rekindled Latin fears and suspicions of the United States that he had worked so hard to overcome while secretary of state from 1905 to 1909. In 1913, President Woodrow Wilson made clear that he would not support special interests trying to gain advantages in Latin America. The Bryan-Chamorro Treaty, finally approved in 1916, contained provisions similar to the second treaty

Knox had worked out with President Adolfo Díaz of Nicaragua in early 1913. Even so, Wilson and Secretary of State William Jennings Bryan were much less interested in protecting U.S. businesses in Latin America than Taft and Knox. Dollar diplomacy as a policy was at an end in Latin America. Criticism of the policy continued. Like President Hoover, President Franklin D. Roosevelt renounced dollar diplomacy. Both presidents attempted to construct what became known as the Good Neighbor Policy in dealing with Latin America, and the concept of the Taft-Knox doctrine was all but dead by the time of the Hoover administration. In the long run, of course, American businessmen did increase trade and investment in Latin America, but it was World War I, not dollar diplomacy, that decreased European economic interests in that part of the world.

If the results of dollar diplomacy were meager in Latin America, where the United States was the dominant power, they were a disaster in China, the target for the Taft-Knox policy in East Asia. Of course, the situation in the Far East was difficult. In the late nineteenth century and the first decade of the twentieth century much change had taken place. With victories over China in 1895 and Russia in 1905, Japan had become the major power in the Far East. Theodore Roosevelt had supported Japan's new prominence in East Asia. He decided that Japan did not threaten American interests there. He saw the Japanese as a barrier to Russian expansion; a preserver of the balance of power in East Asia; protector of the Open Door; and stabilizer of China, a nation for which he had little respect. Roosevelt had backed Japan in its war with Russia and in 1905 had mediated the peace.

Roosevelt had hoped to arrange a balance of power between Russia and Japan after the war, but the Japanese victory was so decisive and other events in Japanese-American relations so important that he gave up on the Open Door in China, especially in Manchuria, which the Japanese began to close after 1905. Because of the need to protect the Philippines, which Roosevelt believed was the "heel of Achilles" of the United States, and the war scare that resulted from the Japanese immigration crisis, Roosevelt accepted Japanese expansion on the mainland of Asia. He came to feel that the Open Door was not worth war with Japan. The United States should do what it could to preserve interests in China, but should recognize Japan as the dominant power on the Asian mainland. In short, he gave a green light to Japan-

ese expansion. One of the best expressions of this belief appeared in a letter to Knox on 8 February 1909, shortly before Roosevelt left office. He noted that Japanese-American relations were of "great and permanent importance." While immigration to the United States had to stop, the United States should "show all possible courtesy and consideration." The Taft administration had to understand that "Japan is vitally interested in China and on the Asiatic mainland." Since the Pacific coast of the United States was defenseless and "we have no army to hold or reconquer the Philippines and Hawaii," the country had to avoid war. Roosevelt felt that American interests in China were insignificant in American Far Eastern policy.

Even as his administration came to an end, forces were at work that would change Roosevelt's policy in East Asia. In 1908 Root had established the State Department's first geographic unit, the Division of Far Eastern Affairs. Headed by Willard Straight, the division opposed Japanese expansion in China, and this opposition was to dominate the division in the years between 1909 and 1941.

Roosevelt's East Asian policy thus was reversed. With urging from the State Department and because of a combination of motives—economic expansion, suspicion of Japan, faith in the future of China—the Taft administration decided to challenge Japan in China. During the Taft years, the Open Door Notes, which had frequently changed in meaning after 1900, assumed new importance in the Far Eastern policy of the United States.

In Far Eastern policy, department officials now proved important. Taft and Knox did not need convincing. Both believed China was the country of the future in the Far East and that if the United States desired influence with that emerging nation it had to increase its financial interests there. If the president and secretary of state had any doubts about such policy, they were overcome by State Department advice. Huntington Wilson, who had served in Tokyo, and Straight, who had been consul in Mukden, Manchuria, were both hostile to Japanese ambitions in China. They had tried unsuccessfully in the last days of the Roosevelt administration to enlarge the Open Door to include investment and trade. With Taft and Knox they had more success.

The Taft administration came to see investment in railway development and loans to the Chinese government as the means to increase influence in China. Knox demanded that American financiers be given the opportunity to join the

British, French, and German consortium in lending money to China to finance railroad construction in the Yangtze Valley, the so-called Hukuang Railway loan. When the demand met with European hostility, Taft appealed to the Chinese head of state: "I have an intense personal interest in making the use of American capital in the development of China an instrument for the promotion of the welfare of China, and an increase in her material prosperity without entanglements or creating embarrassments affecting the growth of her independent political power and the preservation of her territorial integrity." The State Department persuaded a group of investors to assume part of the loan. Knox grudgingly got his way, but only at the price of irritation in Britain, France, and Germany. In the long run, this project was a failure.

From the Hukuang loan the State Department turned to Manchuria. The result was the Knox neutralization policy, which more than any other proposal epitomized dollar diplomacy in China. In the fall of 1909, Knox proposed that American, Japanese, and European bankers lend China enough money to repurchase the Chinese Eastern Railroad, held by Russia, and the South Manchurian Railroad, in the possession of Japan. Manchuria would be neutralized and open to all commercial activities. Washington feared that southern Manchuria was being closed to non-Japanese influences. Knox realized that the Japanese would be difficult, but he thought the proposal would be supported in Europe. Britain, France, and Germany eventually decided to defer to the wishes of Japan and Russia, and in January 1910 the latter two nations rejected the plan. Only the Chinese showed interest, but that soon turned to concern when Russia and Japan agreed in July to cooperate in guaranteeing the status quo in Manchuria. Knox had only succeeded in driving the former enemies into a virtual alliance to prevent American interference in Manchuria. A companion proposal by Straight, who had left the State Department to head the American consortium planning a railroad that ran parallel to portions of the South Manchuria line, met a similar fate.

By the fall of 1910, Knox recognized defeat in his railroad plans for Manchuria. Throughout the rest of his term as secretary of state, he continued to work for increased American involvement in China, but through plans that did not contest the Japanese and Russians in Manchuria. He became involved in plans for a multinational currency reform loan, but the Chinese revolution that began in 1911 put an end to that scheme. The

government that overthrew the Manchu then negotiated with a six-power consortium for a reorganization loan. Negotiations dragged on until the Taft administration left office.

Dollar diplomacy in China stimulated international controversy. The Taft-Knox policy succeeded in causing distress, irritation, and even anger in London, Paris, Berlin, St. Petersburg, and Tokyo. Knox's clumsy attempts to help China only weakened the empire, since Japan and Russia agreed on a policy. The policy aroused controversy in the United States, where bankers were reluctant to participate. Roosevelt opposed the policy, writing to Taft in late 1910 that the Open Door in China could only be maintained by general diplomatic agreement. He noted that "as has been proved by the whole history of Manchuria, alike under Russia and under Japan, the 'Open Door' policy, as a matter of fact, completely disappears as soon as a powerful nation determines to disregard it, and is willing to run the risk of war." Roosevelt was convinced that Japan was one such nation, and that the United States ought not to try to bluff the Japanese on the mainland of Asia, especially since Americans would never agree to fight a war there.

Wilson later withdrew government support from American investors planning the reorganization loan, charging that the loan violated Chinese sovereignty and threatened China with intervention. The American investors backed out of the loan, and the last of the dollar diplomacy schemes came to an end. In the long run, Wilson reversed his position, approving participation in a consortium in 1918. But Japan remained the dominant power in China until World War II, and Roosevelt's policy seemed valid in retrospect. Taft and Knox failed in their goal—to dislodge Japan from the Asian mainland.

There were other areas to which the Taft administration tried to apply dollar diplomacy, such as in Turkey. Breaking sharply with the traditional American policy toward the Ottoman Empire, which centered on protecting the rights of American citizens, the Taft administration attempted to share in the mining, irrigation, and railroad concessions then being negotiated by the Turkish government. Taft hoped that the United States would obtain a larger share of the commerce of the Near East. He was to be disappointed. The United States found the European powers too entrenched, and dollar diplomacy failed in Turkey. But Central America and China were the most spectacular examples of the doctrine.

The controversy over dollar diplomacy lasted well after 1913. Generally recognized by students of international relations as a failure, dollar diplomacy has engendered controversy concerning its motives and the people responsible for carrying it out. Some writers have argued that the policy was primarily economic, while others have contended that it was dominated by strategy, especially in Latin America. Others have defended the desire of the Taft administration to "do good" in Latin America and Asia, in some cases noting that its failure was probably owing more to diplomatic bumbling than imperialistic urges. The most recent writings of scholars have additionally argued that the logic of imperialism undermined the logic of "dollars for bullets," which ended up relying on military intervention to protect the interests of businesses and individual investors. In effect, dollar diplomacy created, rather than mitigated against, havoc. The most balanced account of dollar diplomacy, that of the historians Walter and Marie Scholes, has combined these motives and also noted that Taft's diplomacy anticipated U.S. foreign policy after World War II. Taft and Knox chose private capital as their instrument, whereas President Harry S. Truman used public capital. In both instances, the most important consideration was preservation of vital American interests abroad by helping underdeveloped countries establish viable governments and integrating them into the twentieth century.

Debate as to responsibility for the policy has taken two directions. Historians have argued over the roles of Taft, Knox, the State Department, and American businessmen. Straight has especially been the subject of debate. One account has convincingly argued that Straight's role in the Far East has been exaggerated. The most reasonable conclusion would seem that there was a common purpose among the advocates of dollar diplomacy.

Another direction of the debate over dollar diplomacy has been whether it was only one aspect of a continuous policy followed in the twentieth century by the United States—to expand American economic opportunities abroad. It is clear that Taft's predecessor, Theodore Roosevelt, and his successor, Woodrow Wilson, as well as the rest of the American leaders in the twentieth century, supported the expansion of American business, up to and including the Clinton administration's crafting of the NAFTA agreement and approaching foreign relations with China on economic, rather than human rights,

terms, to the dismay of many Americans and their congressional representatives. Indeed, the term "dollar diplomacy" was revived by the media to describe the thrust of U.S. foreign relations during the 1990s. There has, however, been no extensive scholarly investigation into the validity of using the policy of the Taft administration to define the economic foreign policy being carried out by the United States at the beginning of the twenty-first century. No president, other than Taft, has made such a policy the principal goal of diplomacy. As a result, the term "dollar diplomacy" remains synonymous with the diplomacy of 1909 to 1913.

BIBLIOGRAPHY

Bemis, Samuel Flagg. *The Latin American Policy of the United States.* New York, 1943. Although dated, the work is still valuable.

Cohen, Naomi W. "Ambassador Straus in Turkey, 1909–1910: A Note on Dollar Diplomacy." *Mississippi Valley Historical Review* 45 (1959).

Coletta, Paolo E. *The Presidency of William Howard Taft.* Lawrence, Kans., 1973. Gives a comprehensive study of Taft's administration.

Collin, Richard H. "Symbiosis vs. Hegemony: New Directions in the Foreign Relations Historiography of Theodore Roosevelt and William Howard Taft." *Diplomatic History* 9, no. 3 (summer 1995), 473–497. An excellent historiographic article.

Drake, Paul W., ed. *Money Doctors, Foreign Debts, and Economic Reforms in Latin America from the 1890s to the Present.* Wilmington, Del., 1994.

Esthus, Raymond A. "The Changing Concept of the Open Door, 1899–1910." *Mississippi Valley Historical Review* 46 (1959). Important to see how the Taft administration tried to change the meaning of the Open Door policy.

Gardner, Lloyd C. "American Foreign Policy 1900–1921: A Second Look at the Realist Critique of American Diplomacy." In Barton J. Bernstein, ed. *Towards a New Past: Dissenting Essays in American History.* New York, 1968. Argues the importance of economic motives.

Hunt, Michael H. *Frontier Defense and the Open Door: Manchuria in Chinese-American Relations, 1895–1911.* New Haven, Conn., 1973. Disputes Straight's importance in the formulation of America's East Asian policy.

Israel, Jerry. *Progressivism and the Open Door: America and China, 1905–1921.* Pittsburgh, 1971. Stresses continuity in America's Far Eastern policy.

Kahn, Helen Dodson. "Willard D. Straight and the Great Game of Empire." In Frank J. Merli and Theodore A. Wilson, eds. *Makers of American Diplomacy: From Theodore Roosevelt to Henry Kissinger.* New York, 1974. Portrays Straight as architect of dollar diplomacy in East Asia.

Minger, Ralph E. *William Howard Taft and United States Foreign Policy: The Apprenticeship Years, 1900–1908.* Urbana, Ill., 1975. Gives extensive treatment to Taft's involvement in foreign affairs before he became president.

Mulhollan, Page Elliott. *Philander C. Knox and Dollar Diplomacy, 1909–1913.* Austin, Tex., 1966.

Munro, Dana G. *Intervention and Dollar Diplomacy in the Caribbean, 1900–1921.* Princeton, N.J., 1964. Cites the importance of strategy as the motivation of dollar diplomacy in the Caribbean, and is very comprehensive.

Nearing, Scott, and Joseph Freeman. *Dollar Diplomacy: A Study in American Imperialism.* New York, 1966. A socialist view in an update of a 1926 work.

Rosenberg, Emily S. *Financial Missionaries to the World: The Politics and Culture of Dollar Diplomacy, 1900–1930.* Cambridge, Mass., 1999. Goes beyond the defined period of 1909–1913.

Scholes, Walter V., and Marie V. Scholes. *The Foreign Policies of the Taft Administration.* Columbia, Mo., 1970. The best study of the diplomacy followed by Taft.

Smith, Robert. "Cuba: Laboratory for Dollar Diplomacy, 1898–1917." *Historian* 28 (1966). A revisionist account of relations with Cuba.

Varg, Paul A. *The Making of a Myth: The United States and China, 1897–1912.* East Lansing, Mich., 1968.

Vevier, Charles. *The United States and China, 1906–1913: A Study of Finance and Diplomacy.* New Brunswick, N.J., 1955. A generally balanced treatment.

See also CONSORTIA; ECONOMIC POLICY AND THEORY; INTERVENTION AND NONINTERVENTION; OPEN DOOR POLICY.

THE DOMINO THEORY

Edwin E. Moïse

Vietnamese communist leaders founded the Democratic Republic of Vietnam in 1945, but it took them until 1975 to achieve control of the whole country. For most of that thirty-year period, there were people who argued that communist control of Vietnam must be blocked, not just for the sake of Vietnam itself, but to prevent communism from spreading through Vietnam to other countries.

Historically, the spread of communism had usually involved proximity; of all the countries that were communist during the Vietnam War, only the Soviet Union and Cuba had become so without bordering on lands already under communist control. It was easy enough, therefore, to argue that if Vietnam were to become communist, this would increase the threat to neighboring countries. Some people did make the argument in this reasonable and realistic form. Others, however, found it inadequate. The only country bordering on Vietnam that did not already have a communist neighbor was Cambodia, a country of which few Americans had much awareness. To say that if Vietnam fell, Cambodia would be endangered, might not stir drastic action. To inspire a massive effort to save Vietnam, it was necessary to predict that a massive disaster would result if Vietnam were allowed to fall—great danger or even certain doom for a whole string of countries, most of which did not border on Vietnam. This prediction was given the name "domino theory" after President Dwight D. Eisenhower's classic statement of it at a press conference on 7 April 1954:

> Finally, you have broader considerations that might follow what you would call the "falling domino" principle. You have a row of dominoes set up, you knock over the first one, and what will happen to the last one is the certainty that it will go over very quickly. . . . When we come to the possible sequence of events, the loss of Indochina, of Burma, of Thailand, of the [Malay] Peninsula, and Indonesia . . .

Eisenhower's language was contradictory; first he referred to the "certainty" that the last domino in the string would fall if the first one did, but then he referred to the "possible" sequence of events. Eisenhower seems not in fact to have believed that the fall of Indochina would be certain to trigger the fall of a whole string of other countries; he only thought the danger was very great. Others committed themselves more firmly to a prediction of doom. A few months before Eisenhower's press conference, Donald R. Heath—the U.S. ambassador to the Associated States of Indochina (Vietnam, Laos, and Cambodia)—had written that if the French abandoned their effort to save Indochina, "Only the blind could doubt the immediate Communist engulfment of Southeast Asia."

Some versions of the theory envisioned a longer row of dominoes than others. Eisenhower's classic statement had predicted the fall of everything down to Indonesia, but not of the Philippines or countries beyond. That was about average. Modest versions of the theory reached only as far as the fall of Thailand. The most extreme ones reached very far indeed. Thus, Walt W. Rostow, formerly Lyndon Johnson's national security adviser, said in 1969, the year the withdrawal of U.S. troops from Vietnam began, "There's nobody in Asia who doesn't understand that if we pull out of Vietnam, we'd have to pull out of all of Asia, the place would fall."

Even in its weaker form, with the fall of the dominoes treated only as a danger, not a certainty, the theory was a strange one. There was no previous country the fall of which to communism had triggered the rapid fall of a whole string of other countries. Why should it have been thought probable, or even possible, that the consequences following from the fall of Vietnam would be so much greater than those that had followed from the fall of China?

ORIGINS OF THE THEORY

To the extent that there was a historical foundation for the theory, it lay in the origins of World War II. Late in 1938 at the Munich Conference, Britain and France had allowed Adolf Hitler to take the Sudetenland from Czechoslovakia. Many people believed in retrospect that Hitler would have been relatively easy to stop at that time, if the democracies had stood firm in defense of Czechoslovakia. There is no way to tell whether this belief was correct, but at least it was not obviously foolish. However, the opportunity to try to stop Hitler before he became too strong was not taken. Within less than two years after Munich, Hitler partitioned what had remained of Czechoslovakia; invaded and partitioned Poland; overran Denmark, Norway, Luxembourg, the Netherlands, Belgium, and France; and started the Battle of Britain.

The end of World War II eliminated Hitler and his government, but Joseph Stalin remained. Stalin was a ruthless and extraordinarily brutal dictator, a mass murderer on a huge scale. He had emerged from World War II controlling not only the Soviet Union but also much of East-Central Europe. Stalin seemed obviously similar to Hitler, and some of the differences between the two—that Stalin ruled a larger area with a larger population and more industry than had Hitler, and that control of the international communist movement gave Stalin a worldwide influence—made Stalin seem a greater menace than Hitler had been. In 1949 Stalin got the atomic bomb, and the conclusion of the Chinese civil war brought the largest country in the world under communist rule, which many in the United States assumed to mean Stalin's rule.

Even before 1949 some people had begun to worry that any further territorial gains by Stalin or communism—little distinction was made between the two—could trigger a cascade effect, like the rapid sequence of Nazi conquests in the two years after Munich. Dean Acheson described in his memoirs the arguments he had used in February 1947 to persuade U.S. congressional leaders that they must support measures to prevent a Communist victory in Greece:

> I knew we were met at Armageddon. . . . Like apples in a barrel infected by one rotten one, the corruption of Greece would infect Iran and all to the east. It would also carry infection to Africa through Asia Minor and Egypt, and to Europe through Italy and France, already threatened by the strongest domestic communist parties in Western Europe.

The geographic logic was rather peculiar. For Greece to have gone communist would not have opened up a single new country to communist contagion, assuming that communism spread by contagion like rot from one apple to another in a barrel, because the only non-communist country bordering on Greece was Turkey, and Turkey already bordered directly on the Soviet Union. The congressional leaders, however, seem to have found Acheson's case persuasive. It was also suggested that if West Berlin (a small and strategically valueless enclave in the middle of Soviet-controlled East Germany) were to be lost, then Western Europe as a whole would crumble and fall under Soviet domination.

THE THEORY EXTENDS TO ASIA

The pattern of thinking soon extended to Asia, where communist parties were engaged in armed struggles in several areas. The Chinese civil war was clearly tending toward a communist victory by the end of 1948. The First Indochina War, in which the Vietminh—a Vietnamese nationalist group under communist leadership—fought the French, was stalemated until 1950, when the balance tipped toward the Vietminh. Guerrilla struggles on a much smaller scale were occurring in Malaya and the Philippines, and there was a brief communist rebellion in Indonesia in 1948.

In November 1948 Madame Chiang Kai-shek, wife of the president of the Republic of China and quite popular in the United States, told the American people that "if China falls, all of Asia goes." This statement was given considerable publicity in the American press. In December the government of the Republic of China declared in a message to the U.S. Congress that "if China should unfortunately be conquered, the Far East will be sovietized and so would Asia and Europe." Several prominent Americans said much the same, but the theory that the fall of China would trigger a widespread disaster did not take hold at the top levels in Washington.

It was French government officials who originated the idea that the loss to communism of Indochina, or even a part of Indochina, would lead to the loss of a huge area. In January 1949 French president Vincent Auriol commented upon a proposal that France attempt to negotiate peace with

Ho Chi Minh. He rejected this idea, arguing that to negotiate with Ho, an "agent of Moscow," would lead to the loss not only of Indochina but of the rest of Southeast Asia. Southeast Asia under Soviet control would constitute a barrier between the United States and Europe; the result would be to "hand over Europe to Russia." The later spread of the theory in the United States, however, was more a matter of independent invention than French influence, although the French did make an effort to spread it.

One might have thought that when the fall of China, the world's most populous country, to communism in 1949 failed to trigger the rapid loss of a string of other countries, Americans would have come to doubt that the loss of smaller and less important countries could trigger the disaster. Instead, the idea that the fall of Indochina, or just Tonkin in the northeastern corner of Indochina, could trigger a cascade of other losses, took hold within the U.S. government only after China had fallen without causing such a result.

In the last years of the Truman administration, the National Security Council staff tried to maintain some restraint about statements concerning the dire consequences of Indochina's fall. The State Department went a little further, and the Joint Chiefs of Staff were the most extreme, saying for example in April 1950: "The fall of Indochina would undoubtedly lead to the fall of the other mainland states of Southeast Asia. Their fall would . . . bring about almost immediately a dangerous condition with respect to the internal security of the Philippines, Malaya, and Indonesia, and would contribute to their probable eventual fall to the Communists."

THE EISENHOWER ADMINISTRATION

When Dwight Eisenhower became president at the beginning of 1953, he appointed John Foster Dulles as secretary of state. Dulles pushed a very radical version of the domino theory, more extreme than had ever before been advocated by anyone so high in the U.S. government. At a meeting of the National Security Council on 31 March 1953, Dulles listed the vital strong points around the periphery of the communist bloc—Japan, Indochina, India, Pakistan, Iran, and NATO—and then, according to the record, "warned that the loss of any one of such positions would produce a chain reaction which would cost us the remainder."

In August 1953 President Eisenhower defined the threat in terms almost as extravagant: "If Indochina goes, several things happen right away. The Malayan peninsula, the last little bit of the end hanging on down there, would be scarcely defensible . . . all India would be outflanked. Burma would certainly, in its weakened condition, be no defense." Eisenhower acknowledged that it would be possible to stop this chain of events by major intervention even after Indochina fell, but he said that halting the process at any later point would be more expensive than stopping it in Indochina.

In early 1954, as it began to appear that a French defeat in Indochina might be imminent, Admiral Arthur Radford, chairman of the Joint Chiefs of Staff, was urging that the United States commit combat forces to Indochina, and he used the domino theory as a major argument. He said that if the communists gained control of the Red River delta, in northern Vietnam, they would win Indochina as a whole, and if they won Indochina they would then win the rest of Southeast Asia. The eventual fall of Japan would be probable. Sometimes he simply said each stage would trigger the next. At times he acknowledged that strong U.S. intervention might be able to prevent the fall of Indochina from causing the fall of the rest of Southeast Asia, but like Eisenhower the previous year, he said that intervention on a much larger scale would then be needed.

The press tended to endorse the domino theory, though not in its most extreme forms. Press versions of the theory typically suggested the fall at most of Southeast Asia, sometimes just the mainland of Southeast Asia, and indicated that this was likely to happen if Indochina fell, rather than saying it would definitely happen.

When the National Security Council met on 6 April 1954 to consider among other things whether the United States should intervene militarily in Indochina, President Eisenhower "expressed his hostility to the notion that because we might lose Indochina we would necessarily have to lose all the rest of Southeast Asia." But when Secretary of the Treasury George Humphrey asked whether the United States should really be committing itself to oppose communism everywhere in the world, Eisenhower came close to endorsing the view that a few minutes earlier he had rejected. The record of the meeting first summarizes Eisenhower as having said: "Indochina was the first in a row of dominoes. If it fell its neighbors would shortly thereafter fall with it, and where did the process end? If he was correct, said the President, it would end with the United States directly behind the 8-ball." The record then goes on to quote Eisenhower as having said that "in certain areas at least we cannot afford to let Moscow gain another bit of territory. Dien Bien Phu itself may be just such a critical point." The very next day, Eisenhower made in a press conference the famous statement of the domino theory that has already been quoted.

The oddity of the logic comes into clearer focus if one considers Burma. Eisenhower mentioned Burma specifically; Radford included it implicitly when he said that if the Red River delta fell to communism then the rest of Southeast Asia would also fall. China had become communist in 1949. Burma shared a long border with China, essentially undefended. A very large area along this border had been in dispute between China and Burma even before the communists came to power in China. Anticommunist forces were mounting armed raids into China from Burmese territory, which would have provided the Chinese with ample excuse for taking action against Burma if they wished to do so. Roads capable of carrying military supplies from China into Burma (the Burma Road and Ledo Road of World War II fame) existed, although they were probably in poor repair. Despite all of these factors, the Burmese government did not seem about to be overthrown by either Chinese or Burmese communists. Yet communist rule in Indochina, which had a land area about 8 percent of China's and a population 5 percent as large, barely bordering on Burma at all and having no military roads leading into Burma, was expected to cause the fall of that nation. While some of Eisenhower's remarks show at least a little caution, the part of them in which the domino metaphor occurs suggests not only that Burma would fall if Indochina fell, but that it would fall quickly. According to Radford, the fall of just the Red River delta (not bordering on Burma, with a population less than half that of Burma and less than 2 percent as large as that of China) would make the fall of Burma inevitable, when the fall of China had not made the fall of Burma inevitable. None of the proponents of the domino theory ever attempted to explain this oddity, to describe some way in which the international context had changed to make Southeast Asia more vulnerable to a chain reaction than it had been in 1949 when China fell.

The mechanism of the predicted disaster was not traced to concrete issues of strength. The domino theorists said that the fall of Southeast Asia as a whole would give the communists resources and population that would add dangerously to their strength, but they did not try to argue that the reason the fall of Tonkin, Vietnam, or Indochina would lead to the fall of the rest of Southeast Asia was that the population or resources of Tonkin, Vietnam, or Indochina would add decisively to communist strength.

The theory appears, instead, to have been based primarily on issues of symbolism and perception. If the United States allowed Tonkin, Vietnam, or Indochina to fall to communism, this would indicate to the world that the United States did not have the will to oppose communism. The communists would be encouraged to launch assaults on other countries, and the noncommunist countries, no longer trusting the United States to defend them, would be demoralized and would not resist the assaults. In effect, proponents of the theory appear to have been presuming that the United States could not adopt a policy of defending some areas but not others, because neither the enemies nor the friends of the United States would be capable of understanding such a policy.

Statements of the theory were often vague about the identity of the communists whose victory was feared, and never acknowledged that the takeover of a small country by domestic communists might have different implications than conquest by some larger communist country. When discussing the struggle in Vietnam in the early 1950s, American officials sometimes suggested that the country was in danger of being taken over by the Chinese, sometimes by the Soviets (note Eisenhower's comment, quoted above, that "Moscow" might be about to take Dien Bien Phu). Sometimes the likelihood of a takeover by Vietnamese communists was acknowledged, but in carefully restricted language; they were "Vietminh," or occasionally "Reds," but never "Vietnamese communists." The word "Vietnamese" had in fact dropped completely out of the vocabulary with which the U.S. government discussed the Vietminh in the late 1940s; calling Ho Chi Minh or his men "Vietnamese" would have granted them too much legitimacy. Very often it was simply "communists" of unspecified nationality who were said to be trying to take over Vietnam. The theory was similarly vague about which communists would take over the other countries of Southeast Asia should Vietnam fall. Occasionally it was predicted to be the Soviets, more often the Chinese, most often just "communists" of unspecified nationality.

One reason the domino theory was so poorly thought out was that for many of its proponents, it was not so much a theory as a call to action. Whenever any country seemed about to fall to communism, anticommunists tried to persuade the American government and people to take action to prevent this from happening. In an effort to generate enthusiasm for the project, some of them always argued that the United States must hold the line against communism in whatever country was currently under threat, because that was where the chances of holding the line would be best; an effort to fall back and defend in some other country would be utterly hopeless, or would at least involve a much more difficult and dangerous effort than defending the country currently threatened. Also, since the country currently endangered was always a country where the communists were strong, the domino theorists were each time in the position of arguing that it would be easier to stop the communists in that country, where they were strong, than in some other country where they were much weaker.

The fact that the theory was basically a call to action helps to explain why so few people in the U.S. government chose to apply it to China in the late 1940s. China was very large, and an American commitment to prevent communist victory there seemed likely to be very expensive in money and lives. Few officials had much enthusiasm for a theory that might have obligated them to make such a commitment. Indochina was much smaller, and the prospects for blocking communist victory at reasonable cost seemed much better than in China. American officials therefore were more inclined to endorse a theory obligating them to defend Indochina.

It does not seem likely that Eisenhower tried to make a rational calculation of the effects that would follow from a Vietminh victory in Indochina, and concluded that the communist conquest of Indochina would have a tremendously greater effect on the Asian balance of power than had the communist conquest of China. For one thing, a rational calculation of effects should have produced a theory that was a bit more specific on things like the identity of the communists whose victory was feared. For another, if Eisenhower really believed that the collapse of the French position in Indochina would have so disastrous a result, it seems likely that he would have tried considerably harder than he did to prevent that collapse.

On the other hand, it is not likely that Eisenhower was deliberately and consciously lying when he propounded the domino theory. Five factors are all probably relevant to Eisenhower's statements, and those of most other proponents of the domino theory, including even Radford. First, what they really meant by their statements was that communism was expanding, and that this was very dangerous and should be stopped. Second, they genuinely believed this to be true. Third, they had not bothered to think much about whether the words they had used to express that belief were true if taken literally. For that matter, they tended to think about communist expansion in very vague terms; to them communism was something that "expanded," and they did not always ask themselves exactly how it expanded when they were thinking about this problem. Fourth, belief in the danger of communist expansionism was universal in the circles in which they moved, and maintaining that belief was considered morally obligatory. This stance deterred them from questioning the literal truth of any particular words chosen to describe the danger. Fifth, they were convinced that the communists had the same ambitions for conquest as Hitler. This implied that the communists were likely to embark on a massive campaign of overt international aggression—with Chinese armies pouring south through Laos and Thailand into the Malay Peninsula—as soon as they felt strong enough.

The legacy of the 1938 Munich Conference hung heavily over Americans of Eisenhower's generation. The lesson of Munich, as it was understood in the United States in the 1950s, was that aggression will go on until it is stopped, and that stopping it becomes more difficult the longer one waits to do so. The combined armies of the communist powers were by the 1950s larger than the Nazis had ever had, far larger than would have been necessary to initiate the feared wave of aggression had the communist leaders really been a unified group, with ambitions and daring that approximated Hitler's. American policymakers, seeing that the disaster had not yet happened, did not ask whether they really faced a Hitlerian menace. Instead they worried that even the smallest addition to the total of communist strength would finally trigger the deluge.

When France lost the battle of Dien Bien Phu and it became apparent that the first domino in the row was actually likely to fall, President Eisenhower did not descend into the despair that some of his previous statements would leave one to expect. When asked about this at a press conference on 12 May 1954, he simply explained that he was working to ensure that the fall of the first domino would not knock down the rest of the row. Secretary of State Dulles had said the day before that the domino theory had been based on the assumption that the endangered countries would be facing the threat singly; he said that if they were bound together in an alliance, the theory need not apply.

The habit of American policymakers of saying, at any given time, that the country currently under threat was the final barrier, after the loss of which the forces of communist aggression would be so strong that there would be no stopping them at any acceptable price, is easier to understand if one bears in mind the alternatives. They could not say that the communists were not bent on world conquest; their peers would have called them dupes of the communists and their careers would have been destroyed. For the same reason, they could not say that the communists were weak enough so that even the addition of another country would not strengthen their expansionist drive to a dangerous extent. It was marginally acceptable to say that the communists were already so strong that they could be stopped only by a big expensive war, but this was an uncomfortable position to take, since the United States did not want a big expensive war. The only really acceptable thing to say was that the communists were still weak enough to be stopped cheaply if they were stopped immediately, but only if they were stopped immediately.

American policymakers faced a fundamental problem when they tried to win public support for programs designed to oppose communism in distant parts of the globe. Vietnam was a country of moderate importance. President Eisenhower wanted to make a moderate effort to save it from communism, not involving a degree of cost or risk grossly out of proportion to its real significance. If he had described the situation to the public in these terms, however, he would have been attacked from two directions: first, a large portion of the public, which did not even know where Vietnam was, would not have approved any risk or any expenditure had they been told that it was not a matter of high importance, and second, with the "Who Lost China?" debate still going on, it would have been extremely dangerous for any American political figure to have described the defense of Vietnam or any other country as a matter of less than the highest importance. Had Eisenhower said that the relatively modest efforts he was making were all Vietnam was really worth, he would have been accused of abetting communist aggression.

Eisenhower endorsed the domino theory rhetorically, and so strongly that he gave the theory its name, but he did not commit more resources to Indochina than the real importance of the area could justify. This worked for him in 1954, but he was storing up trouble in the long run. The domino theory slid out of view for several years, but it was waiting to reassert itself whenever some country in Asia seemed in danger of falling to communism. One of Eisenhower's last actions as president, on 19 January 1961, was to tell John F. Kennedy and the top foreign policy officials of the incoming Kennedy administration that if Laos were to fall to communism, it would be "just a question of time" before South Vietnam, Cambodia, Thailand, and Burma did the same.

THE 1960S: HIGH TIDE OF THE DOMINO THEORY

The period from the early to the mid-1960s represented the high point of American belief in the theory. The proportion of top officials who endorsed it was higher than it had been in 1953 and 1954 under Eisenhower. Some of the 1960s officials—most conspicuously Secretary of Defense Robert McNamara—decided years later that the theory had been mistaken, but they confirmed that they really had believed it in the 1960s; their assertions of it had not been mere rhetoric.

Some authors have commented on the rise in the 1960s of the "psychological domino theory," a belief that the danger of allowing South Vietnam or Laos to go communist lay in what this would do to American "credibility." One country after another would decide that they could not depend on American assistance, and that it therefore was not worth trying to resist communism. They might submit without any massive invasion by foreign communist armed forces. At the same time, communist countries, no longer fearing the United States, would become more aggressive. Such ideas became more common in the 1960s, but this did not represent a total change in thinking. The phrase "psychological domino theory" is associated with that decade, but there had been an important psychological component to the domino theory ever since the late 1940s.

FUTURE PRESIDENTS SPEAK

"The battle against Communism must be joined in Southeast Asia with strength and determination to achieve success there—or the United States, inevitably, must surrender the Pacific and take up our defenses on our own shores. Asian communism is compromised and contained by the maintenance of free nations on the subcontinent. Without this inhibitory influence, the island outposts—Philippines, Japan, Taiwan—have no security and the vast Pacific becomes a Red Sea. . . .

"Vietnam and Thailand are the immediate—and most important—trouble spots, critical to the U.S. . . . We must decide whether to help these countries to the best of our ability or throw in the towel in the area and pull back our defenses to San Francisco and a 'Fortress America' concept."

— *Then-vice president Lyndon Johnson
to President John F. Kennedy, 1961* —

"If South Vietnam falls, through U.S. withdrawal, political settlement, or neutralization (which is surrender on the installment plan), there is no doubt that Cambodia (already on the brink) will go; that Laos, practically gone now because of our gullibility, will go; that Thailand (which wants to be on our side but has held her independence by being on the winning side) will go; . . . and that Indonesia will go. . . .

"In three or four years, then, we would have the necessity of saving the Philippines. Could we avoid a major war to save the Philippines? . . .

"If southeast Asia goes Communist, Japan will eventually be pulled irresistibly into the Red orbit.

"If the United States gives up on Vietnam, Asia will give up on the United States and the Pacific will become a Red sea."

— *Richard M. Nixon, 1965* —

In 1961 the Departments of State and Defense sent President Kennedy a joint memorandum, the product of prolonged deliberation at the highest level. William Bundy had written the first draft; U. Alexis Johnson and Robert McNamara, among others, had revised it. It stated: "The loss of South Viet-Nam would make pointless any further discussion about the importance of Southeast Asia to the free world; we would have to face the near certainty that the remainder of Southeast Asia and Indonesia would move to a complete accommodation with Communism, if not formal incorporation within the Communist bloc." The theory had sometimes been put in terms this strong or stronger under Eisenhower, but that usually happened when an individual was speaking without a prepared text. Strong statements of the theory had not appeared in formal documents coming from a wide group.

Policymakers were still vague about the identity of the communists to whom Southeast Asia would fall and about the mechanism of the fall. The most common scenario, when a scenario of some sort was presented, was that the nations of Southeast Asia would submit to unspecified Chinese pressures. Shortly before his death in 1963, when Kennedy was asked about the domino the-

ory in a televised interview, he replied, "I believe it. I believe it . . . China is so large, looms so high just beyond the frontiers, that if South Viet-Nam went, it would not only give them an improved geographic position for a guerrilla assault on Malaya, but would also give the impression that the wave of the future in southeast Asia was China and the Communists. So I believe it."

The domino theorists' frequent vagueness about the national identity of the communists whose conquests they feared reflects a generally low evaluation of the strength of nationalism in Asia. They do not seem to have felt it mattered whether an Asian country was taken over by native communists or conquered by some larger communist power. They knew that the Chinese Revolution had not brought the Soviet army to the borders of Southeast Asia, and indeed that the Soviet military forces that Chiang Kai-shek had permitted at Port Arthur in the late 1940s had been withdrawn in the 1950s. They were aware that when North Vietnam came under communist rule in 1954, the Chinese army had not moved down to the seventeenth parallel, the border between North and South Vietnam. But they did not treat these facts as relevant to the question of whether the fall of South Vietnam to communism would lead other Southeast Asian nations to fall under Chinese or Soviet domination.

The domino theorists also did not feel that the leaders of the non-communist nations of Southeast Asia could be trusted to care very much about preserving their independence. Even those nations that did not harbor strong domestic communist parties might easily be stampeded into accepting, without a fight, Chinese or Soviet domination. An exception, however, was made for South Vietnam. The domino theory was basically a call for the United States to pick South Vietnam as the place to take a stand against communism. Its proponents often exaggerated the strength of anticommunist nationalism in South Vietnam, trying to make it seem more attractive than it was, and more attractive than possible alternatives such as Thailand, as a place to make a stand.

As vice president, Lyndon B. Johnson in 1961 endorsed the domino theory without hesitation; he told President Kennedy that the United States must either hold the line in Vietnam and Thailand or pull its defenses back to San Francisco. In 1964 as president, however, he did ask questions. Johnson was trying to shift the priorities of the national budget away from military spending and toward his Great Society programs. He was, therefore, horrified by the prospect of making the major commitment of U.S. forces that seemed the only way to save South Vietnam from falling to communism. When he asked whether the domino theory was valid, the question was probably not purely rhetorical. Some mid-level officials, notably the intelligence analysts at the CIA's Board of National Estimates, said that the theory was not valid. But all the top national security officials—Secretary of State Dean Rusk, Secretary of Defense McNamara, Director of Central Intelligence John McCone, and the Joint Chiefs of Staff—ringingly affirmed the theory.

The Joint Chiefs were the firmest. When Assistant Secretary of State for Far Eastern Affairs William Bundy, one of the second-level officials who doubted the theory, asked the Joint Chiefs whether it might not be possible to establish another defensive line and save the other dominoes, the Joint Chiefs strongly rejected this notion. "We have no further fall-back position in Southeast Asia. . . . Strengthening other areas of Asia, in the context of our having been pushed out of SVN [South Vietnam], would be a thoroughly non-productive effort militarily, and politically it seems dubious we'd even be offered the opportunity to

attempt it." Thailand would fall "almost automatically"; Burma would probably fall.

Belief in the theory was also widespread outside the administration. Influential members of both houses of Congress made very strong statements about it. Richard Nixon, the future president, said in January 1965 that "if Vietnam is lost, all of Southeast Asia is lost." If the people of Southeast Asia decided, because of events in Vietnam, that the wave of the future was communism, "they are going to go Communist before the wave engulfs them." In a February 1965 Harris poll, an overwhelming majority (78 percent to 10 percent) said they believed that if the United States withdrew from South Vietnam, "the Communists would take over all of Southeast Asia."

The domino theory had always been a call to action. Lyndon Johnson felt in 1965 that he had no choice but to make an actual commitment of large-scale combat forces to Vietnam, and the fact that the domino theory said this commitment was necessary was an important part of his motive. But as the scale of the war expanded during the following years, belief in the theory faded. People endorsed the theory only if they were willing to endorse the commitment of enough resources to save South Vietnam, and as the definition of "enough" expanded to 500,000 men and beyond, the number of people willing to endorse the commitment shrank dramatically. There were still believers in the domino theory in 1968, but far fewer than there had been in the early 1960s. Also, the theory was openly derided by many, unlike several years before.

THE 1970S AND AFTER

Once the theory had become a bone of contention, some defenders of the war began to moderate the theory so as to make it more reasonable; then, opponents of the war would not be able to ridicule it and say that its absurdity symbolized the absurdity of the war. When Richard Nixon defended the domino theory in 1970, he did not say (as he had five years earlier) that other nations would promptly fall to communism if South Vietnam fell; he said only that such an event would be "immensely discouraging" to the non-communist nations of Asia, and "ominously encouraging" to China and the Soviet Union.

The fall of South Vietnam in 1975 did not trigger the fall of the rest of Southeast Asia or of any long string of dominoes. Cambodia had already fallen before South Vietnam did. The fall of Laos was in a sense triggered by the fall of South Vietnam, but only because the Vietnamese communist leaders in Hanoi, who could have completed the communist victory in Laos long before, had been holding back because they feared a premature victory in Laos might complicate the struggle for South Vietnam. The United States did not have to fight a war on some line farther back to prevent the further spread of communism. Indochina under communist rule did not become a conduit for the application of Chinese pressure against Thailand. Instead, in the 1980s Thailand and China were allied against the communist governments in Indochina.

These events have not ended the arguments about the validity of the domino theory. Opponents of the theory say that it was proven false when South Vietnam fell without triggering the fall of most of Southeast Asia, and without the United States even having had to make any major effort to prevent the fall of the rest of Southeast Asia. Supporters of the theory say that it had been a correct description of the situation of the early 1960s. They say that the American defense of South Vietnam had provided a shield during the years when Thailand, Malaysia, and Indonesia had been vulnerable and China very aggressive. By the time this shield was removed in the 1970s, the Southeast Asian nations were stronger and China much mellowed. The most detailed form of the argument states that it was the firm American stand in Vietnam that gave anticommunist military officers the confidence to defeat the communists in Indonesia in 1965. The evidence for this argument, however, is very thin.

A cascade effect very much like that predicted by the domino theory swept communist regimes out, rather than into, power at the very end of the Cold War. In 1989 it became apparent that the Soviet Union under Mikhail Gorbachev would no longer intervene to preserve communist governments in Eastern Europe. This emboldened anticommunist forces and so discouraged the communist leaders that in one country after another they allowed communist rule to be overturned without a serious fight. Communism collapsed in most of Eastern Europe and in the Soviet Union itself between 1989 and 1991.

BIBLIOGRAPHY

Jervis, Robert, and Jack Snyder, eds. *Dominoes and Bandwagons: Strategic Beliefs and Great Power Competition in the Eurasian Rimland.* New York, 1991. A collection of essays.

Khong, Yuen Foong. *Analogies at War: Korea, Munich, Dien Bien Phu, and the Vietnam Decisions of 1965.* Princeton, N.J., 1992.

McMahon, Robert. "What Difference Did It Make? Assessing the Vietnam War's Impact on Southeast Asia." In Lloyd C. Gardner and Ted Gittinger, eds. *International Perspectives on Vietnam.* College Station, Tex., 2000.

Ninkovich, Frank. *Modernity and Power: A History of the Domino Theory in the Twentieth Century.* Chicago, 1994. Traces American statesmen's fears about international security, fears that eventually evolved into the domino theory, back as far as Woodrow Wilson and even Theodore Roosevelt.

U.S. Congress. *Congressional Record.* Vols. 100, 107–121. Washington, D.C., 1954, 1961–1975.

U.S. Department of Defense. *United States–Vietnam Relations 1945–1967.* 12 vols. Washington, D.C., 1971. Better known as the Pentagon Papers.

U.S. Department of State. *Foreign Relations of the United States.* Washington, D.C. See volumes from 1952–1954, 1961, 1982, 1984, and 1988.

U.S. General Services Administration. *Public Papers of the Presidents of the United States.* 33 vols. Washington, D.C., 1961–1974. Contains virtually everything Presidents Truman through Nixon said in public about the domino theory.

See also CONTAINMENT; THE VIETNAM WAR AND ITS IMPACT.